DISCARD

Religion in America

RELIGION

IN

AMERICA

A COMPREHENSIVE GUIDE TO FAITH, HISTORY, AND TRADITION

EDITED BY

HAROLD RABINOWITZ AND **GREG TOBIN**

Foreword by
Jane I. Smith

STERLING
New York

STERLING
New York

An Imprint of Sterling Publishing
387 Park Avenue South
New York, NY 10016

Please note that although the publisher has attempted to confirm that all contact information and web sites are valid at the time of inclusion, such physical and digital addresses are always subject to change.

ISBN 978-1-4027-4301-6 (hardcover)
ISBN 978-1-4027-8320-3 (ebook)

Library of Congress Cataloging-in-Publication Data

Religion in America : a comprehensive guide to faith, history, and tradition / edited by Harold Rabinowitz and Greg Tobin ; foreword by Jane I. Smith.
    p. cm.
  ISBN 978-1-4027-4301-6
  1. United States—Religion. I. Rabinowitz, Harold, 1948- II. Tobin, Greg.
  BL2525.R4642 2011
  200.973—dc23

2011021211

Distributed in Canada by Sterling Publishing
c/o Canadian Manda Group, 165 Dufferin Street
Toronto, Ontario, Canada M6K 3H6
Distributed in the United Kingdom by GMC Distribution Services
Castle Place, 166 High Street, Lewes, East Sussex, England BN7 1XU
Distributed in Australia by Capricorn Link (Australia) Pty. Ltd.
P.O. Box 704, Windsor, NSW 2756, Australia

For information about custom editions, special sales, and premium and corporate purchases, please contact Sterling Special Sales at 800-805-5489 or specialsales@sterlingpublishing.com.

Manufactured in the United States of America

2 4 6 8 10 9 7 5 3 1

Produced by

The Reference Works, Inc.

Harold Rabinowitz, Editorial Director
Megan Stearns, Jane Kim — Managing Editors
Adam Alexander, Helen W. Clarke, Emily Feldman, Rebecca B. Fineman,
Jonathan Heilig, Elizabeth O'Sullivan, Jessica Sirkin, and Catherine Stolfi — Section Editors
Photo Research — Edward Robinson

Writers		Copy Editor	Editorial Assistants
Jess Austen Michalik	Briana Lugo	Bonnie Smolen	Jonathan Londino
Cynthia Hamilton	Michele Rosenberg		Qing Li
Jonathan Heilig	Jessica Sirkin	**Indexer**	
Laura Hoffman	Sara Werden	Jay Kreider	

DESIGNED BY OXYGEN GRAPHICS, INC. AND THE REFERENCE WORKS, INC.

Dedications

To the memory of Irving and Bertha Rabinowitz,
who named me, loved me, and taught me that
"The righteous shall live by his faith."
(Habakkuk 2:4)

HR

To my fellow American citizens
who believe and practice their faiths,
and with a special prayer for those who do not believe,
that all of us may be appreciative
and tolerant of one another.

GT

Motto

"Throughout this endeavor, I have tried to be
fair and respectful. In the end, I can only hope
—and this is my solemn prayer—that my pen
did not get the better of me."

Sherman A. Jackson

CONTENTS

FOREWORD

By Jane I. Smith
Harvard Divinity School

RELIGION IS A REMARKABLY FLEXIBLE PHENOMENON in the history of human experience. It displays a great many faces and features, and involves numerous practices and perspectives. It can also hide with great skill when anti-religious pressures become too strong, as people in many places and ages can testify. But it then has an amazing ability to resurface when the coast is clear and take up residence again in living communities as well as in individual hearts.

The twentieth century gave us numerous examples of the resilience of organized religion. Kemal Attaturk wielded the sword of secularism with great precision in Turkey after World War II, but he failed to remove religion from the private realm and now it is reappearing there publicly. Similar stories can be told of the Soviet Union, China, and many other places where the ashes of destroyed religion turn out to be embers ready to take flame when times are more propitious. Some sociologists have claimed that contemporary Europe may be the exception to the rule that religion dies hard, with Christianity seeming to fade from the consciousness of most of its citizens. But the jury is still out on the future of religion in the European Union, as Muslim countries (of all people) seeking membership encourage Europeans to recall their Christian heritage. There is no question, however, of the presence, visibility, and power of religion in America, as this volume eloquently testifies.

Anyone who wishes to understand what is going on in today's world obviously needs to have some knowledge of the historical, political, sociological, economic, and other conditioning factors that make people and communities act as they do. They also must have some sense of the role that religion continues to play in the lives of most of the world's people. Western societies are now faced with the reality of religious pluralism within their own borders in ways that raise new questions about toleration and openness. Does the guarantee of the separation of religion and state in the U.S. Constitution protect all forms of religious belief and practice? Should religious groups be allowed to proclaim their faith in public ways or does freedom for one become imposition for another? Americans find themselves obliged to pay attention to the importance of religion, as well as the range of religions represented in the United States, as their country struggles to remain a major player on the world stage.

Sadly, many of the armed conflicts around the globe today are framed (and flamed) by the rhetoric of religion. Hindus are fighting Buddhists in Sri Lanka; Shi'ites struggle against Sunnis in Iraq; Jews, Muslims, and a few remaining Christians continue to bomb each other in the Middle East. To understand the extent to which such conflicts can accurately be called religious wars, one must know, along with the political histories of the groups involved, something about the religions that are implicated and what expectations are placed on their followers. The religions of America are often directly affected by events overseas, as those events themselves are often directly affected by American foreign policies.

The need for basic information is the most obvious reason why a volume like this is so useful. It provides sharply focused images of the major religions of the world themselves, as well as the divisions and groupings within Christianity in the United States. Religions that were once thought of as "over there" are now part of Western culture, claiming a home in both East and West. Others have grown and been nourished in the West, and are now themselves having to respond to the rapidly growing pluralism of multireligious western cultures. The second part of the volume addresses the kinds of questions that this pluralism raises, taking the reader into a challenging study of the issues facing communities of worship as well as secular citizens today.

If gaining essential information about a range of religious traditions in order to better understand what is going on in the world is one benefit of this volume, another equally important benefit is the possibility that engagement with the material might affect the reader in some quite personal ways. It has become axiomatic in the circles of those who engage in interfaith conversation to say that learning about another person's religion through dialogue and discussion often serves to make one a "better Christian" or a "better Jew"—a more informed, more persuaded member of one's own religious tradition. The interaction itself, the argument goes, makes participants more cognizant of and responsive to the dictates of their own religion. This indeed seems to be one of the very predictable results of serious interfaith engagement. Learning about another religion gives perspective not only on the religion under consideration, but often serves to ground practitioners in their own particular faith.

Participation in interreligious engagement can also serve another purpose. Dialogue, of course, means not only conversation between people, or sets of people, who come together to learn from each other. It also can refer to the conversations one has with oneself after encountering some new, engaging and seriously challenging concept. Entering into a dialogue with new information about these religions can provide the means for making one more open, more flexible, more positioned to learn and be challenged by worldviews and ethical imperatives that may be quite different from those that have shaped one's own religious identity.

A Harvard professor, grounded in both Christi-anity and Hinduism, once commented in a class that the study of other religions is a very dangerous business. At first his students were confused about where the danger lay. Then they began to recognize that one who takes seriously the beliefs of others runs the risk of having his or her own preconceptions challenged. To really think about the different worldviews presented in this volume means "trying them on," seeing how it feels to assume different views of God, of humans and their responsibility, and of time and eternity. The risk is not that one will rush to change religious identities, but rather that one's own understanding will be stretched, enhanced, and possibly even changed. (Risky business indeed!)

Perhaps the most serious challenge the professor was setting down is a wake-up call to break down the barriers of self-satisfaction and exclusion. If religion defines others as wrong or misguided it can be a dangerous force. But when those walls of exclusion are lowered, and believers of any tradition can look past and contemplate the possibility of truth experienced more expansively, the process of learning and of mutual engagement has endless possibilities. None of that can happen without information, knowledge, and careful reflection.

The study of religion is unquestionably exciting. This book provides an entrée into that venture, whether one reads consecutively or randomly. If taken seriously, and discussed with serious colleagues, it offers the possibility of at least three significant learning opportunities: to be informed about ways in which religion shapes lives and decisions; to be a better citizen of one's own inherited or adopted religious tradition; and to risk the challenge of becoming open to the possibility of truth wearing many different kinds of garb. The book will not make all these things happen simply by its reading. But its great array of information and interpretation provides essential tools to help in understanding the world's faith traditions, in engaging with and reflecting personally on the material, and in preparing to better understand the diversity and richness of the religious cultures that now inhabit America. ∞

PREFACE

SEVERAL YEARS AGO, THE HARRIED BAND WHO produced this volume worked on a popular encyclopedia of health for a prestigious medical school. In the interest of creating that work quickly (so that it would be timely when published), we agreed that our authors would produce the entries, and the physician advisers, all heads of departments in the medical school and in its celebrated teaching hospital, would review the material. And review it they did, since their photos and bios were prominently displayed in the frontmatter of the work. A problem arose, however, with regard to those subjects that could be considered part of several disciplines. Who, for example, should review the article on Alzheimer's Disease—the head of gerontology, the head of neurology, or the head of psychiatry? Since a reader might conclude the article fell under the purview of any one of those specialists, it was decided that they would *all* review the article, and all entries like it; thus, all such cross-disciplinary entries would have to be acceptable to all of them.

There then ensued a series of meetings in the conference room outside the Dean's office in which physicians, all eminent practitioners widely respected the world over, argued over detail after detail, while we editors watched the seconds (and calendar pages) pass by. It often seemed that the issues under dispute were so fundamental, that we could not help but ask the physicians with some exasperation, "Haven't you people worked all this out yet?"

It was then that the Dean (who presided Solomonically over these disputes) shared an important insight with us that we have never forgotten: We erroneously believe that medicine, as a science, does not admit of any dispute, opinion or judgment except at the frontier. Whatever is true, we think, is agreed to by all men and women of science, just as

Newton's laws or the principles of chemistry are the same everywhere and to everyone. When we are urged to seek second opinions in health matters, it isn't always a strategy for finding *the* right answer and prescription. It's often a way of finding other perspectives and views where subtle differences can mean the difference between a successful outcome and an unsuccessful one (and we all know what *that* means). In fact, the Dean explained further, medicine in his medical school is not the same as medicine in any other one—not the same as medicine in the equally prestigious medical college across town or anywhere else.

After that experience, we approached this work with some apprehension. If such differences of opinion and perspective were true of medical science, what, we wondered, were we going to find in producing a popular reference work on the full range of religion in America? We anticipated hour-long Disputations that would turn into month-long Conferences that stretch into years-long Councils, during which details of theological doctrine and practice would be argued and refined, only to be re-argued and re-refined *ad infinitum*. Every religious tradition has myriad sects, schools, approaches, doctrines, texts, versions of texts, etc., and we frankly dreaded the prospect of having to provide explanations that would be acceptable to all of them.

But here is what we *did* find. We found a sense of commonality and camaraderie—one might call it a sense of community. There was an awareness on the part of thinkers and scholars, on the part of clerics and theologians in very diverse religious traditions, that they—that we—were all trying to deal with the mysteries and grand issues of existence: material existence, emotional existence, political existence, and spiritual existence. We recognized a profound sense of humility and respect by men and women of diverse and far-separated areas on the religious spectrum from their counterparts "on the other side," an awareness that they were all grappling with many of the same enduring problems, paradoxes, and puzzles of life, and intense interest in what others had found, what conclusions they had arrived at.

We found there was no certainty or unanimity about what ought to be done or how one ought to live, and no contentiousness or fanaticism. We found a deliberative assuredness that the endeavor was a collective one: that it was going to somehow require the talents, insights, experience, and special innate abilities to which we all owe our individual histories and heritage if we are going to come to an understanding of what is our place in the world and in the universe, and how we can ensure a blessed life for our children and our children's children.

In other words, we are going to have to figure it all out—together. And to do that, we are going to have to first learn *about* each other, and learn to talk *to* one another. To deprive ourselves of what these traditions have to teach us would be like studying the universe using only a narrow band of the spectrum or believing we have an understanding of nature by studying only land animals in one particular corner of the world.

A half-century ago, Leo Rosten first published a groundbreaking nonfiction survey of religious life in the United States. *Religions of America*, as it was originally called, lifted the veil on a hitherto unexplored "world within a world," i.e., the beliefs and practices of the American people in their private, religious lives and how religious life in the U.S. was conducted and organized (by denonimation, tradition, etc.)—all in a single, comprehensive volume.

Prior to that 1955 publication in book form, many of the articles by well-known experts in their respective fields had been published in *Look* magazine, the nationally circulated picture magazine that was a rival to Time Inc.'s formidable *Life*. Does anyone today remember *Look* magazine? Well, we do.

Along with *Life, Time, Holiday, The Saturday Evening Post*, and others of that era, such magazines served the same purpose as many current television programs and websites do: providing timely news and information in an easily digestible format.

This book begins with over thirty chapters on the various faiths practiced in the United States; it then presents over a dozen essays by eminent scholars and religious leaders on some issues of wide concern in religious communities across the land; and then it presents figures, maps, and survey results that give a picture of how religion is practiced, where it is practiced, and how it is applied to the concerns we face day in and day out, as measured by several capable and dedicated polling and survey organizations.

Now, we hear many of you asking, all of this is on the Internet, isn't it? Perhaps much of it is—and perhaps much else may be found on the Internet that is incorrect. But one thing we believe the reader of this book (Forget about *Look* magazine—does everybody remember *books*!?) will find on virtually every page here that will *not* be found in abundance on the Internet: the sense of conviction that the process of learning how our fellow human beings have devoted themselves and their lives to understanding faith and unpacking spirituality is *itself* a devotional act, and is in some sense a step in that journey that *something* beckons each of us to undertake.

Amazingly, Alexis de Tocqueville, the nineteenth-century French politician who observed life in a young Jacksonian-era United States, got it right. He saw clearly, a century and a half ago, that Americans tend to be attracted to voluntary associations: political, financial, social, and religious. We are a gregarious people who love to share our thoughts and opinions, sometimes to fight about them, to gather around us others of like mind who may be questing for the same thing—a better, more just society or eternal happiness—and stick closely together to achieve a common end. Those qualities are what gives American religion its unique and special character, and it is the endlessly fascinating subject to which we have tried to do justice in this volume. ∞

Pub. as the Act Directs March 2 1819.

Camp Meeting of the Methodists in N. America

PART ONE

The Religions

Introduction

I. Christianity: Catholicism and Orthodoxy

II. Christianity: Protestantism

III. Islam

IV. Judaism

V. Eastern Faiths

VI. Other Religious Groups

INTRODUCTION

FAITH AND INTERFAITH IN THE NEW AMERICA

BY DIANA L. ECK

HARVARD UNIVERSITY PLURALISM PROJECT

IN THE SIXTY YEARS SINCE WORLD WAR II, FAITH CAME to America—not as a vision or in the person of a savior or a redeemer, but in the person of millions of immigrants, who brought with them not only the meager possessions they could rescue as they fled war, depredation, and persecution, but also centuries of rich traditions and fervent beliefs. The headline of the story of religion in America in our time is: "Religion Emigrates to America."

The Immigration and Nationalities Act of 1965, passed in tandem with another important legislative landmark, the 1964 Civil Rights Act, has had a profound impact on the development of religion in American life. In speaking for this new immigration legislation, Attorney General Robert F. Kennedy said that we as a nation could not be struggling to remove the legal vestiges of racism from America's school system and voting rights, and yet maintain race discrimination as the cornerstone of our immigration policy, giving preference to ethnic and national groups already here in America. So the 1965 Act was passed, and people of every race and national origin have come to the United States. They have changed the "we" of "We the people of the United States of America" in remarkable ways. They have enlarged the global scope of the American project—the creation of a nation of belonging based on the free exercise of religion, the sanctity of conscience, and the nonestablishment of religion in the public square. Today the American project is more challenging and much more significant to multireligious democracies all over the world struggling with these issues.

Today, with the "new immigration," more than 10 percent of us are foreign born. That is the highest percentage since the great waves of immigration at the beginning of this century. Most of the new immigrants are Latinos and Asians. A city such as Los Angeles, which foreshadows America's future, leans toward the Pacific and sprawls toward Mexico. In 1960 it was 80 percent white, 10 percent Latino, 8 percent black, and 2 percent Asian. In 2000, forty years later, it was 32 percent white, 46 percent Latino, 9 percent black, and 13 percent Asian.

Race and religion have both undergone a sea-change in complexity in this new America. In the 1950s, at the end of *Notes of a Native Son,* James Baldwin wrote, "The world is white no longer and will never be white again." Now we can survey almost any city in the country and observe that America is white no longer, nor even black and white any longer, but multiracial, in countless shades and hues. On the religious scene we can say American normatively is neither Christian nor Judeo-Christian any longer, but multireligious in countless ways.

Of course, "we" are still numerically 80 percent Christian, but our national "we" is much more complex. The new immigrants who have come to America have brought not only their economic ambition and their dreams of freedom, but their Bhagavad-Gitas and their Qur'ans, their Buddhas and Bodhisattvas, their images of the Goddess Durga and the Virgin of Guadalupe. They have built mosques and Islamic centers; Hindu, Jain, and Buddhist temples; Sikh gurdwaras; Hispanic and Vietnamese churches all over this land, in cities large and small. Some of these new immigrants have had quite enough of the dominance and oppression of religion in the countries of their birth and have chosen not to be religious at all. The freedom that they cherished is the freedom to forego religion altogether in this land of the free exercise of conscience.

The Washington, D.C., metropolitan area, for example, is fringed with Hindu temples, from the Siva-Vishnu Temple and the Murugan Temple in Lanham, Maryland, over to the Durga Temple and the Rajdhani Mandir in Virginia, and the Mangal Mandir in Silver Spring, Maryland. Driving out that famous spoke of the wheel, New Hampshire Avenue, into Silver Spring, one comes to the Cambodian Buddhist temple and monastery, right next door to the Ukrainian Orthodox Church, right next door to the Islamic Center, right next door to the Disciples of Christ Church and the Chinmaya Mission, and on out to the Mangal Mandir of Gujarati origin. The Islamic Center on Massachusetts Avenue is now but one of dozens of mosques in the greater Washington area. When President Eisenhower attended the dedication in 1950, the mosque was understood to be a link between America and the nations of the Islamic world and their diplomatic missions. Now, fifty years later, America is itself part of that Islamic world; the Islamic world is no longer confined to some other corner of the globe. The many mosques in cities like Chicago, Washington, D.C., New York, Kansas City, Houston, and Seattle have made America part of the Islamic world. And American Muslims, whether from West Africa or the West Bank, come to that mosque on Massachusetts Avenue in Washington for prayers—or to receive President Bush when he came to express solidarity with America's Muslims there shortly after September 11, 2001.

Looking back over the years since 1965, so much has changed in American life. Racially and religiously we have become even more complex, and the issues of difference are ever more with us. From now on, we will need to be more conscious and intentional as we grapple with the ever-changing mosaic of America's many religious and cultural traditions. We will need, in fact, to recognize that our religious traditions are not like the well-defined little squares, or even like patterns of squares in a mosaic. Our religious traditions are dynamic—more like rivers and rushing streams that meander and merge. Like rivers, religious traditions must change with each continent and land into which they move, or they dry up and die. Despite the language of "eternity" and "firm foundations" that is ubiquitous in religious discourse, it is simply a fact of history that religious traditions are always in motion, and we can see that movement all too clearly in the landscape of America today if we are at all attentive.

Immigration instigates change. Leaving one place and moving to another is about change, with cultural and religious implications. Immigrant communities are challenged to express themselves and discover their identities in a new context. But immigration instigates change not only for those who arrive to live among us, but for everyone else as well. We are about the business of expressing ourselves and discovering our identities in a new and more complex context as we come into contact with each other. People begin to think and act differently as they build face-to-face relations with next-door neighbors of a different faith. It stretches our self-understanding, both as people of faith and as citizens of a secular society.

We also need to recognize that the little mosaic squares of America's religions are not homogeneous, not all red or green or any one thing. Within each of our seemingly unified religious communities, there are virulent arguments going on. The Episcopal Church has its arguments; the Methodist Church (of which I am a part) has its own arguments. There is diversity, difference, and internal discussion and disputation among Muslims and Jews, no less than among Hindus, Buddhists, and Sikhs. So it is with every one of the pieces of the mosaic.

For new immigrants in every wave of immigration, religious communities are important sites for affirming and reformulating identities in a new context. At least at the outset, immigrants seek out people of their own ethnic, cultural, or religious background. Even people who had scant involvement with their own communities in the land of their origin might well find their temple, mosque, or church to be more important to them here than it was back home. Just as my own great-grandparents sought out Swedish Lutheran churches when they arrived from Sweden nearly one hundred years ago, so today a Tamil-speaking immigrant from India might seek out Tamil friends here and might participate in the activities of a Hindu temple with Tamil-speaking priests, even though they were never involved in a temple at home. In the early years of the new immigration, some even became the planners and fundraisers of new Hindu temples, involved in ways that they would never have imagined had they remained in Madras. Some held their first elective office as one of the temple trustees or as a member of the governing body commission. As in earlier periods of immigration, involvement in voluntary associations and especially religious institutions has been a training-ground for involvement in civic and governmental institutions. This is one of the "styles" that newcomers observe, appreciate, and adopt: they acquire a taste for participant engagement in the life of a democratic society.

Religion in the United States is voluntary, and religious institutions that want to engage in tax-exempt fund-raising must do this as incorporated nonprofit groups. Nobody is going to support one's religious community unless its adherents do. And as de Tocqueville observed a century ago, despite the uncoupling of religious institutions from government support, religious institutions seem to flourish all the more because they must engage people's pocketbooks as well as their faith. Muslim, Sikh, and Buddhist immigrants discover the energy and leverage of religion in this voluntaristic society. Here freedom of religion is constitutionally protected, and as an ironic result, "religious identity" claims a power and priority far greater than those of one's ethnic or homeland identities. Some might argue that it is easier to be influential as a Muslim American than as a Pakistani or Bengali American. There is power in religious identification and in the lobbying efforts of religious groups in the United States. In the wider context of American voluntary organizations, the gradual development of local, state, and national Muslim or Sikh organizations is a natural development. There are advocacy groups such as the Muslim Public Affairs Council, watch-dog groups such as the Council on American Islamic Relations (CAIR) or the Sikh Coalition. These are easily recognizable American advocacy groups with a structure parallel to that of many Christian and Jewish organizations.

As the past four decades have passed, all of these religious communities have become more visible as they have built what are, by now, new landmark institutions—the great mosque outside Toledo; the Hindu temple in the western suburbs of Nashville; the Sikh gurdwara in El Sobrante, California; the great Jade Buddhist Temple in Houston. These are but four of literally hundreds of such institutions across the United States where we see the visible expression of something new. These communities are also more visible in the ceremonial and performative life of the American public square. An imam from New York opened a session of the U.S. Congress with the invocation of the day in 1992. A Hindu priest from Cleveland opened a joint session of Congress with an invocation in 2000. State legislative prayers and city council prayers have gradually included a roster of Buddhist, Muslim, Hindu, Jain, Sikh, and Native American contributions to the civil religion of the public square. Shortly after September 11, 2001, a group of Jain nuns offered the opening invocation in the State Legislature in Ohio. The gathering roster of proclamations has also grown more representative of the complexity of America's "we." The governor of the state of Kansas issued a public proclamation for the month of Ramadan. The governor of Arizona took ceremonial note of the Buddha's birthday. The State Legislature of Michigan passed a congratulatory resolution on the Sikh's celebration of their sacred scripture. In the 1990s especially, during the Clinton administration, America's religious diversity was recognized in Washington, D.C., in a variety of ways: the first-ever ceremonial recognition of Ramadan at the White House; the first-ever iftar to break the fast at the end of a day of Ramadan fasting, hosted by Secretary of State Madeleine Albright at the State Department; the first-ever iftar at the White House, hosted by President George W. Bush in the fall of 2001. It is now clear that America's "pluribus" has within it distinctive religious components, and we have gradually begun to recognize this in the patchwork of ceremonial expressions that form our "civil religion." President Clinton's November 1998 greeting to the Sikh community on the occasion of the birthday of Guru Nanak acknowledged this new era when he said, "We are grateful for the teachings of Guru Nanak, which celebrate the equality of all in the eyes of God. This is a message that strengthens our efforts to build one America. Religious pluralism in our nation is bringing us together in new and powerful ways."

But there are some for whom religious pluralism is not a vision that brings us together, but one that threatens to tear us apart, and that is a question that needs be considered as one enters into this tome on the many religions practiced across this land.

For we must recognize that the rising visibility of minority religious communities in the United States has also meant their rising vulnerability at the hands of people who may not include Muslims or Sikhs or Buddhists in their view and vision of who we are as Americans. Just as the media often tend to illustrate difference by resorting to visual reference points of religious meaning, so do these visual reference points become the flash points for xenophobia. A Hindu woman with a dot on her forehead, a Sikh man wearing a turban, a Muslim woman wearing hijab—all bear markers of difference that appear threatening in the eyes of some people. So it is that people who appear with a visible difference have become the targets of the new bigotry. The fear of difference, which we know so well from our racial struggles, is now taking aim at religious minorities in some extremist quarters of American life.

By now, the post-1965 immigrants have had first-hand experience of both the opportunities of America and the discrimination and prejudice that can be rooted in difference. There have been outbursts of xenophobia, and while they do not represent the major thrust of American life, they are virulent and persistent. Even in the first decade of the twenty-first century, one hears echoes of the mobs that attacked the homes of Sikh lumber workers in Bellingham, Washington, in 1907, crying "'Hindoos Go Home!" In 1907, the Bellingham Herald editorial pronounced, "The Hindu is not a good citizen; it would require centuries to assimilate him, and this country need not take the trouble. Our racial burdens are already heavy enough to bear, our cloak of brotherly love is not large enough to include him as a member of the body politic." If we fast-forward a century, South Asian immigrants still experience episodes of graffiti and violence directed at them. In Pittsburgh, a Hindu temple was desecrated and the word "Leave!" painted on the altar. In New Jersey, a gang, the Dotbusters created a climate of harassment that turned to violence when an Indian immigrant, a Parsi, was beaten to death by a gang, who all the while chanted, "Hindu, Hindu, Hindu." Race, religion, and sheer difference have merged into a cry of hatred.

American Muslims, as we have seen, are targeted for being South Asian—or for being Arab, African, African American, even Latino. And they are also targeted simply for being Muslim. Within six months in 2004, mosques were the focus of vandalism and arson in College Park, Maryland, where a cross was set ablaze on the lawn; in East Tempe, Arizona, where swastikas were painted on the doors, and in Lubbock, Texas, where windows were shattered, computers smashed, and hate graffiti scrawled on the walls. Muslims have worked hard to displace the stereotypes that have portrayed them with the one broad-stroke image of violence. Yet we know that that image was put into play almost immediately after the Oklahoma City bombing in 1995. In the days following the tragedy, the Council on American-Islamic Relations (CAIR), which came to prominence at that time, reported in detail more than two hundred incidents of anti-Muslim threats, harassment, property damage, and so on. CAIR now publishes annual reports that document this anti-Muslim violence and discrimination. Its 2003 report documented a 43 percent rise in these incidents during 2002. The executive summary put it this way: "These incidents included termination or denial of employment because of religious appearance; the refusal to accommodate religious practice in the workplace, school, or prison; the singling out of individuals at airports because of their distinctive names, appearances, and travel destinations; the detention or interrogation of Muslims by federal and local authorities based on profiling criteria; and the denial of services or access to public accommodation facilities because of religious or ethnic identity." All of these experiences, the report concludes, "have common elements of setting apart religious and ethnic features of Muslim life or Muslim religious and political views from what is considered normal and acceptable." The report also estimates that Muslims are more apprehensive than ever about discrimination and intolerance, and that the U.S. government's actions alone after September 11, 2001, have impacted more than 60,000 individuals. Each year, the number of incidents reported has risen.

In the immediate aftermath of September 11, incidents of harassment and violence were legion.

(The Pluralism Project—at www.pluralism.org—has meticulously recorded and reported these all-too-many incidents). In Sterling, Virginia, for example, Muslims gathered at the mosque to take a chartered bus to a blood drive and found a message inscribed on the building in big black letters: "Die, pigs. Muslims, burn forever." In Toledo, Ohio, a rifle was fired through the stained-glass dome of a mosque. In Denton, Texas, a mosque was firebombed. In Alexandria, Virginia, someone hurled bricks wrapped with hate messages through the windows of an Islamic bookstore. As the year 2001 ended, vandals attacked the mosque on Broad Street in Columbus, Ohio, pulled the water pipes from the walls, and tore up copies of the Qur'an. The range of incidents recorded spread beyond the Muslim and Arab American communities to the whole spectrum of people perceived as "different" or "threatening." A Gujarati convenience store owned by a Hindu was firebombed in Somerset, Massachusetts. A Hindu pizza deliveryman was brutally beaten in New Bedford, Massachusetts. An Egyptian Coptic Christian was murdered in California. South Asians, Arabs, Muslims, Hindus, and Sikhs were all enmeshed in a web of fear and difference.

Sikh Americans were especially affected by the aftermath of 9/11. Their beards and turbans marked them in the eyes of the uninformed as followers of Osama Bin Laden. The Sikh Coalition tracked more than two hundred attacks in a matter of a few weeks. A Sikh was attacked with a baseball bat in Queens, another beaten unconscious in Seattle, and a third assaulted at a stoplight in San Diego. One of the first incidents involved a Sikh who was pulled off an Amtrak train in Providence, Rhode Island, for nothing other than the suspicion aroused by his turban and his voluntary disclosure that he was carrying his ceremonial knife (a *kirpan*). Only weeks later, after a deluge of letters to the governor of Rhode Island and the mayor of Providence, were the charges against him dropped. The most tragic incident, however, was the murder of Balbir Singh Sodhi, the Arizona Sikh who was killed by a would-be patriot while he was planting flowers around his Chevron station.

The documentation of these acts of violence is far easier to assemble than the documentation of the *response* to these acts of violence. These outbreaks of violence were often followed by a powerful wave of restorative community response that sought healing, embraced the victims, and rejected bigotry. Our challenge is to determine whether the forces tearing our social fabric apart are stronger than those bringing us together. The FBI has documented a discouraging rise in hate crimes; but there has also been a heartening conciliatory response. The Pluralism Project has also documented the interfaith responses to violence over the years. While one self-proclaimed patriot shot and killed Balbir Singh Sodhi, thousands of people stopped at his gas station to leave candles and flowers and to write messages of condolence, and thousands of people who did not know him and had most likely never met a Sikh in person nonetheless attended his memorial service at the civic auditorium. In Denton, Texas, after a mosque was fire-bombed, there was an immediate response by an interfaith circle of clergy, who gathered at the mosque in a show of support. The Virginia bookstore owner whose windows were shattered by bricks of hatred met hundreds of people he had not previously known who stopped by with flowers and messages expressing sorrow at what had happened. In Toledo, where the rifle shot pierced the dome of the mosque, 2,000 people, mostly Christians, showed up to hold hands and ring the mosque in a circle of support. The vandalism and arson at the mosque in Lubbock, Texas, elicited an outpouring of community support and the strengthening of interfaith connection and solidarity. For all this, the interfaith movement in Lubbock, Texas, has become much stronger than it was before.

In the first decade of the new century in the U.S., there are many examples of the ways in which Americans have grappled with what seems to be a more threatening world of religious difference by building bridges of communication and relationship.

First, we must take note of the emerging role of the interfaith movement. Interreligious councils and initiatives are rapidly producing new instruments of relationship that are prognostic of a hopeful future. There are older interfaith organizations, such as the Interfaith Conference of Metropolitan Washington, that already had a network of working relationships that enabled it to spring into action immediately in the period following September 11. Across the country, countless new local interfaith organizations have been formed where none had existed before. In Portland, Oregon, an "Abrahamic coalition" has come into being, and Corvallis, Oregon, has developed the Community Interfaith Conference. In my hometown, Bozeman, Montana, a Christian clergy association has expanded to become an interfaith organization, including Baha'i, Muslims, and Buddhists. In Syracuse, New York, InterFaith Works brings religious people together to address social issues, and Women Transcending Boundaries draws women together for discussion and action across the lines of religious difference. In Memphis, Tennessee, which had never had an active interreligious organization, a new initiative began. On August 16, 2003, the following story appeared in the local Memphis newspaper, the *Commercial Appeal*, telling of the evolution and self-understanding of the Memphis initiative:

> They started talking a few weeks after September 11, 2001—Memphis Christians and Jews, Muslims and Hindus, Buddhists and Baha'is. Their first gathering was on neutral ground at a local public high school. Hundreds of people came from many religious traditions. They started talking about what they had in common, they prayed for peace, they called it an interfaith prayer service. The focus was on unity and diversity.
>
> Afterward they decided to keep on talking, but instead of looking for safe ground they began to go into one another's territory. They got together

once a month through 2002 at churches, synagogues, mosques, temples. Instead of talking about what they had in common, they listened to each other talk about their own beliefs and practices. The more they talked and listened, the more they began to understand and appreciate the value of each other's tradition.

"This is the only forum in Memphis," said Rabbi Micah Greenstein, "where you can experience the great religions of the world through the eyes of the people of faith; learning about other faiths has strengthened my own." And he said, "The emphasis now is not on unity and difference; it's on understanding, not unanimity; on appreciation, not assimilation. The focus is on strength in diversity."

Beyond explicitly interfaith groups and initiatives, city governments have played a significant role in setting a new climate of expectations for the diversity of cities and towns. In September 2003, for example, the mayor of Worcester, Massachusetts, called citizens together for an interfaith prayer breakfast, attended by 250 citizens representing ten faiths. It was no ordinary or ceremonial mayor's prayer breakfast, however, but the culmination of several years' work by the Worcester chapter of the National Conference for Community and Justice. The group carefully drafted a statement of shared values, in which they affirmed, "With religious faith as our common ground and sustained by prayer and meditation…we discovered that the spiritual values that unite us are more significant and empowering and enduring than the differences that divide us."

Impromptu initiatives of various kinds bring people together in civic life and service—and there are hundreds of these across the country. In April 2004, in Plano, Texas, Jewish, Christian, and Muslim communities came together to hold a blood drive. *The Dallas Morning News* set up the story:

Privacy fences. Big houses. Corporate campuses. That's what you see when you drive across Plano, one of Texas' wealthiest and most influential suburbs. You might not think the cause of social justice has much traction there or, for that matter, in any suburb. The common image of the Planos, the Greenwich and the Orange counties, is that they're filled with families who have fled bad urban schools, want to wall themselves off from poverty and work at a fancy Fortune 500 headquarters. And that this is Christian right territory, complete with mega churches. But there's a surprising phenomenon unfolding in Plano. Some residents are hungering to connect with others.

The *Collin County News* in Plano displayed the headline: "Faiths Unite for Blood Drive, Work to Build Understanding." The blood drive was held in a climate that had been filled with suspicion and mistrust, spoken and unspoken. "There was so much hoopla surrounding 'The Passion of the Christ,'" said a Ms. Rosenquist about the Mel Gibson movie, "I wanted to prove the misconception wrong by bringing different faiths together for a common good." One of the Muslim participants explained, "The important thing for husbands and wives and children of different faiths is to do things together. We felt this was an excellent way to start." Another of the Jewish participants, Rabbi Jordan Parr, said, "In our tradition—and it's echoed in the Muslim tradition and others—whoever saves a life is saving the world." He went on, "We're not going to solve the problems of the world standing out here in the parking lot in Plano, but we can handle Plano if we work together."

This seems to be the testimony of the multiple forms of interfaith activity that have grown across the United States: We may not be able to solve global problems, but we can handle Plano if we work together—wherever Plano happens to be.

This volume claims to be a successor to the classic work edited by Leo Rosten a generation ago. In that work, many religions were presented with an almost homespun charm; some religions that were going to become important to us all were hardly mentioned. The book's question-and-answer format seemed to some to have a voyeuristic undertone, as if the body language or facial expression of the questioner was adding to the plain text, "Why in the world would you do *that*?" This work attempts to present the history, organization, and tenets of these faiths with (at least) the same thoroughness, but it hopes to accomplish much more. It hopes to drive home the importance of diversity as a value in American culture, especially in the religious sphere, just as diversity has been a source of strength and resourcefulness in the arts, science, technology, and, well, virtually every area of human endeavor.

Now, diversity can be seen as merely the multiplicity of views, but it is hoped that this book will promote the next step—what is to be *done* with the diversity that has been created and fostered. This is what is meant by the term "pluralism," and I would like to take this opportunity to summarize three elements of pluralism in religious life that tries to utilize the positive elements of a diverse spiritual landscape. What, to put it simply, does pluralism mean for us?

To answer simply and in outline, I see three basic elements to pluralism: First, pluralism is *engagement*. Diversity alone can and has led to the creation of religious ghettos without very much traffic between or among them. Pluralism means contact, discussion, exchange, explanation, and mutual appreciation of what lies at the heart of belief and practice, sometimes beyond the understanding even of practitioners.

Second, pluralism isn't just tolerance, but it is the *active seeking of insight* and understanding. Tolerance doesn't remove our ignorance of one another; it lets lie the half-baked truths and stereotypes we hold in our minds about who Muslims or Sikhs are, or notions that Sikhs and Muslims might have about who Christians and Jews are. More than ever, in the world in which we live today, ignorance is the scourge, and our ignorance of one another has and will become increasingly costly.

Finally, pluralism is not compromise; quite the opposite of leaving our identities and commitments behind, it presses us to *encounter* those commitments and examine them. It means holding our differences—and that includes our deepest differences, our religious differences as well—not in isolation but in relationship. The language of pluralism is that of dialogue, of encounter, of criticism, and also of self-criticism. In the world in which we live today, that language of dialogue is one we simply have to learn.

Writing in the mid-1950s, James Baldwin wondered whether perhaps the experience of black and white relations in America, for all its tragedies, might still be of value in the world we face today. He said, "For all the divisiveness and shamefulness of the color line, the one achievement is that both black and white Americans live in a society peopled with each other and have been deeply involved with one another. They have not been isolated by seas and continents." This observation is apt in a profoundly different way today, at the outset of the twenty-first century, in an America where native people, people of European descent, and people of Asian, Latino, and African descent live not isolated by seas and continents, but in proximity and in palpable contact with one another. It is also true for our religious life, that we have in the United States the opportunity to make good on the promise of human dignity and equality for people of every race and religion, and on the promise of free and unfettered exercise of religion.

In a world of increasing fragmentation, we have an unparalleled opportunity to build, intentionally and actively, a culture of pluralism among people of many races, cultures, and faiths. We may not succeed; we may indeed find ourselves fragmented and divided by religious lines and by color lines, with too much *pluribus*—more, perhaps, than we can handle—and not enough *unum*. But if we manage to succeed, this, I think, is the greatest lesson and most enduring form of leadership that America and its people can offer the world.

I. CHRISTIANITY

Catholicism and Orthodoxy

I Christianity: Catholicism and Orthodoxy

Historical Introduction

The Life of Jesus

CHRISTIANITY, THE WORLD'S LARGEST UMBRELLA religion with nearly 2.1 billion adherents worldwide, stems from the life and work of just one man: Jesus of Nazareth.

According to the biblical Gospels of Matthew, Mark, Luke, and John, Jesus was immaculately conceived by Mary, wife of Joseph, and humbly born in a barn in Bethlehem, Judea. That Jesus was considered from birth a man of special purpose is indicated by the journey of "wise men from the east to Jerusalem (Matthew 2:1)," who worshipped the young child as Christ—the Messiah, or expected deliverer.

Biblical records of Jesus's youth and adolescence are strikingly brief. Luke 2:40 states that, "the child grew, and waxed strong in spirit, filled with wisdom: and the grace of God was upon him." Seven verses later, an incident is described in which Jesus—discovered by his parents as missing after attendance at the feast of Passover—is found conversing with learned theologians in a temple, and "all that heard him were astonished at his understanding and answers."

Jesus's public ministry began in 27 CE upon his baptism by John the Baptist, a known prophet, who recognized Jesus as "the Son of God." Following his baptism, Jesus journeyed to the desert to embark on

The main sanctuary at Saint Patrick's Cathedral in New York City seats more than 2,000 people.

This ca. 1442 painting by the Italian artist Fra Angelico, a Dominican friar, depicts Jesus's final meal with the twelve apostles on the eve of his death. According to the book of Matthew (26:26–29), during the meal Jesus broke bread and then asked his disciples to "Take, eat; this is my body." He next passed a cup of wine, stating, "This is my blood of the new testament." Jesus then implored them to partake of the bread and wine in remembrance of his ministry.

a fast for forty days and forty nights, after which—in his weakened state—he was purportedly tempted by the devil three times. Jesus successfully rejected each temptation, and upon his return to civilization, began calling his first disciples.

The Gospels next illustrate Jesus's exalted life of impeccable morality, spiritual understanding, leadership, and humble submission to God's will as natural law. His comprehension of human existence in accord with "God's kingdom" (God's law of the universe) allowed him to free humanity from the constraints of sin, sickness, and death. According to the Gospels, he also demonstrated power over material phenomena: when aboard a ship one stormy night, he saved fellow shipmates from destruction by calming a life-threatening tempest—and then walked upon the stilled sea. The Scriptures also include instances in which he caused a fruitless fig tree to shrivel and die, and turned water into wine at a wedding in Cana.

Jesus's compassion made no distinction between class, race, profession, or gender. He dined with known sinners, and when criticized for it, explained in his usual style of metaphor that the sick are in greater need of a physician than the healthy. He sought to exemplify this principle of unconditional forgiveness in an incident involving a woman accused of adultery: the latter was brought before Jesus by a throng of angry men who quoted Mosaic Law (the law as laid out by the prophet Moses) as justification for stoning her to death. Jesus's reply was, "He that is without sin among you, let him first cast a stone at her." As the book of John relates, each accuser was then "convicted by [his] own conscience," and left, until none remained standing in offense. Jesus then turned to the woman and asked, "Woman, where are those thine accusers? Hath no man condemned thee?" The woman answered, "No man, Lord." Jesus replied, "Neither do I condemn thee: go, and sin no more."

Jesus's teachings and actions did not go unnoticed. Those who had experienced healing and uplift at his message revered him as a savior, or "the Son of God." But many were greatly offended at such claims made by the populace, calling them heretical. Roman authorities at last decided that Jesus was too great a threat to their power, and brought a charge of sedition against him for claiming to be King of the Jews.

Jesus foresaw the nature of his fate, and in the hours before his arrest, prayed vigilantly in the Garden of Gethsemane. Here he endured a great emotional struggle between fear of what was to come and reliance on God for ultimate delivery from evil. As Jesus waited in great angst, he was further unsettled by the fact that his disciples slept through his time of need, offering him no solace. At last, Roman soldiers arrived on the scene and Judas Iscariot—one of Jesus's supposedly loyal disciples—knowingly betrayed Jesus to the soldiers by identifying him with a kiss. Jesus was seized and delivered to Pontius Pilate, the Roman Prefect.

As the Gospels relate, Pilate did not himself believe Jesus guilty of the alleged crime, and—as was the custom of the day—offered the militant crowd who attended Jesus's trial a choice: he would free either Jesus, or Barabbas (another criminal under persecution). The crowd requested that Barabbas be freed and Jesus executed. Pilate, personally mourning their decision, washed his hands to symbolize removal of responsibility from the impending crucifixion. He then ordered Jesus to crucifixion, declaring that his charge should be displayed on a sign affixed atop the cross he was nailed to, and should read, "Jesus of Nazareth, King of the Jews."

The man some called Christ was therefore left to die on a knoll called Golgotha on the outskirts of Jerusalem. According to all four Gospels, he passed away before late afternoon. Some time later, Joseph of Arimathea—a disciple of Jesus—begged Pilate for possession of Jesus's body. Pilate consented, at which point Joseph prepared the body for burial by wrapping it in linen and spices. Jesus was then placed in a tomb hewn of rock, and a large rock was rolled before the tomb's entrance. The Gospels state that three days later, a mourner by the name of Mary Magdalene (among others) visited Jesus's tomb to find the large rock rolled away from the entrance, and Jesus's body missing. Mary turned to see Jesus standing behind her, alive and well. Thus, Christians believe that Jesus overcame death, and call this event the Resurrection. The Gospels of Mark, Luke, and John relate that forty days following the Resurrection, Jesus disappeared from human sight in the presence of his disciples. This phenomenon is called the Ascension; the book of Mark explains that Jesus was "received up into heaven."

Following Jesus's time on earth, the Christian movement was split into many different factions,

This ca. 1526 painting by the German artist Albrecht Altdorfer—who was also the architect of the city of Regensburg, Germany—depicts Jesus on the center cross, between two criminals who were crucified with him. This was seen as a fulfillment of the biblical prophecy, "He was numbered with the transgressors" (Isaiah 53:12).

each practicing its own belief system. The original three main sects were Gnostic Christianity, Jewish Christianity, and Pauline Christianity. The movement known as the Catholic Church must have appeared on the scene as early as 107 CE, for in that year Ignatius of Antioch wrote in a letter, "Where the bishop appears, there let the people be, just as where Jesus Christ is, there is the Catholic Church." By the middle of the second century, Roman Catholicism was well under way with an organized church authority centered at Rome. However, Christianity was not legalized until 313, when Constantine I issued the Edict of Milan, a letter that proclaimed religious toleration in the Roman Empire. By 380, Christianity had been declared the Roman state religion.

Catholicism traces its roots back to Jesus and the twelve apostles. One of the apostles—originally named Simon but given the name Peter by Jesus—is considered by Catholics the first pope, because in

Matthew 16:18 Jesus calls Peter the "rock" upon which he will build his church. The apostles ordained bishops, who in turn ordained the next generation of bishops, and so on. This continuous line of ordination is known as "apostolic succession" and is a doctrinal foundation of the Catholic Church, which holds that apostolic succession is inherent to the legitimacy of a bishop's actions.

Pope Siricius, who ruled from 385–399, was the first bishop given the title of pope. However, he was not granted authority to speak for the church as a whole; popes would not receive this authority until centuries later. In the meantime, church decisions (procedural and doctrinal) were made by the entire body of bishops in ecumenical meetings such as the Council of Nicaea in 325 CE, which resulted in the Nicene Creed—official Catholic doctrine still in use by both sects of Catholicism today.

The Great Schism

SINCE THE FOURTH CENTURY CE, INTERNAL ISSUES festered within the eastern and western sections of the Christian Church, threatening its unity. Originally, the church was organized into patriarchates, with three bishops—called patriarchs—presiding over them as evangelical authorities: the bishop of Rome (in the West), the bishop of Alexandria, and the bishop of Antioch (the latter two in the East). In 330, the small fishing village of Byzantium was christened "Constantinople" and transformed into the capital of the Roman Empire, an important new center of Christianity. In 451, the Council of Chalcedon added the bishops of Constantinople and Jerusalem to the eastern roster. Among the patriarchs, the bishops of Rome and Constantinople were allotted precedence—Rome, because it was the seat of Saint Peter and held imperial status; and Constantinople because it was considered the "New Rome."

In 395, Theodosius, the last emperor of the united Roman Empire, died. His territory was divided in half and an emperor was installed over each half. This greatly heightened the vulnerability of the Empire's political unity—and indeed, when barbarians devastated the western half, while the eastern (known as the Byzantine Empire) continued to flourish, the empire ceased to function as a whole. Linguistic differences further contributed to the disbandment in progress. Latin was predominantly spoken in the West, and Greek in the East. The ruin of the western Roman Empire resulted in a paucity of individuals fluent in both languages; thus, cultural

Saint Peter's Basilica, located in Vatican City, is, according to Catholic tradition, the burial site of Saint Peter the apostle. Its historical, religious, and cultural significance mark it as a place of pilgrimage. Primarily associated with the papacy (though the basilica of Saint John Lateran is the pope's official seat), Saint Peter's is regarded by some as the greatest of all churches of Christendom. The Italian architect Donato Bramante supplied the original design for the edifice, and the cornerstone was laid in 1506. With contributions from Michelangelo and other prominent Renaissance architects during construction, the basilica was finally completed in 1590.

Hagia Sophia in Istanbul, Turkey, is considered the most breathtaking example of Byzantine architecture. Constructed by Emperor Justinian I from 532 to 537, it was the largest cathedral in the world for a thousand years, with the largest unsupported dome, reaching an elevation of 182 feet. The cathedral originally served as the basilica of the patriarch of Constantinople (the former name of Istanbul) and was the focal point of the Eastern Orthodox Church. It was converted into a mosque in 1453, and into a museum in 1935.

unity also suffered a blow. Doctrinal differences comprised the remaining factor inherent to the impending split. The division of the empire in 395 occurred according to preexisting ritual and liturgical disparities; it only required a deepening of such differences—allowed by the developing political and cultural separateness—to initiate a formal split.

Leading up to 1054, political partnership between Pope Leo IX and a Byzantine administrator named Argyrus facilitated loyalty between the papacy and the Byzantine court, and therein functioned as a unifier of West and East. However, Norman invasions caused a rift when papal forces were defeated at the Battle of Civitate and the pope imprisoned—an outcome that may have been avoided had Argyrus arrived on the scene of battle as planned. The invading Normans took it upon themselves to impose Latin customs—such as the use of unleavened bread in Communion—with the approval of the imprisoned pope. This enraged the patriarch of Constantinople, Cerularius, who ordered the churches of his patriarchate to maintain eastern

usages. When they failed to comply, he promptly shut them down. The angered patriarch then drafted a letter to all Western bishops—the pope included—in which he condemned their "Judaistic" practices. Pope Leo's response was to write his own letter in which he replied to each charge and reminded Cerularius of papal supremacy. The points of disagreement were thus sent in writing to the imperial capital for sorting out, but this action—aimed at reconciliation—had just the opposite effect. The pope's legates were not received respectfully, and they delivered the letter to Cerularius in a huff before storming from the palace. The patriarch, in the meantime, discovered that the legates had tampered with the letter—had, in fact, published their own version in Greek that bore a far less civil tone. Cerularius refused to acknowledge the communication, thereby indirectly ignoring the pope's call for obedience, and the issues were left unaddressed.

On July 16, the three legates returned to Constantinople and, during a Saturday afternoon mass, placed a bull of excommunication on the altar.

In a fury, the people of the patriarchate anathematized the legates, arrested Argyrus (still considered a papal ally) and his family, and burned the bull. As Pope Leo IX had since died, his emissary, Cardinal Humbert, took the action of excommunicating Cerularius, who in turn excommunicated the cardinal. The Great Schism had commenced.

The church remains split along fundamental lines of doctrine, theology, linguistics, politics, and geography to this day. Attempts at reconciliation have occurred, but have failed, overall. Some progress was made when in 1965 Pope Paul VI and ecumenical patriarch Athenogoras I abolished the mutual excommunication of 1054. However, the two resulting sects of Eastern Orthodoxy and Roman Catholicism each consider themselves the "One Holy Catholic and Apostolic Church," intimating that the practices observed by the opposite sect remove it from the true church. The Eastern Church refuses to acknowledge several issues promulgated by the Western Church, such as the infallibility of the pope of Rome regarding church doctrine, the doctrine of Purgatory, the immaculate conception of the Virgin Mary, and the use of unleavened bread in Eucharist. A major point of doctrinal contention that arose long before the Great Schism is the addition of the filioque clause in the Nicene Creed. In 864, Patriarch Photius I declared the insertion of "and from the Son" (in Latin, *filioque*) after the words "who proceeds from the Father" to the Nicene Creed heretical. Such a clause implies that the Holy Ghost proceeds from both God and from Jesus—a claim the Eastern Church refuses to accept.

Belief concerning the primacy of the pope was arguably the most central issue around which each church's identity ultimately solidified. The pope claimed he held authority over the eastern patriarchs, while Eastern Orthodoxy grants him only honorary primacy (the right to call and preside over meetings, or operate as a spokesman) at most. The West came to identify itself under the authority of the pope—a divinely instituted office established by

Christ—as the Roman Church, hence, Roman Catholicism. After the eleventh century, Eastern Christians felt united by heritage and the doctrine established by the first seven ecumenical councils (only), but no longer aligned themselves with the Roman Church. They became instead the Byzantine, or later, Eastern Orthodox, Church.

One Shepherd, Two Flocks

In 381, at the Council of Constantinople, the assembled bishops added the Four Marks of the Church to the Nicene Creed (set forth at the Council of Nicaea fifty-six years earlier), encompassed in the sentence, "[We believe] In one holy catholic and apostolic Church." Thus, the Four Marks, or adjectives that constitute the "True Church," are one (unified), holy (sanctified), catholic (universal), and apostolic (originating with the apostles). The need for unity arises from the idea that a church divided from within cannot be unified with Christ. Jesus said, "I have other sheep that do not belong to this fold. These also I must lead, and they will hear my voice, and there will be one flock, one shepherd" (John 10:16). Sanctity is considered inherent to the church, as it is believed "built by Christ." A universal church is one that is open to and accepting of all races, sexes, and nationalities—as Jesus's ministry was. Catholicity also implies the omnipresence of the church and universal consistency of its rituals and beliefs. Finally, this catholic church is believed "built upon the foundation of the apostles and prophets, with Christ Jesus himself as the capstone" (Ephesians 2:19–20). Its legitimacy lies in its heritage.

Certainly "Christ's Church" was founded upon principles of sufficient substantiality to promote longevity and a Christ-like approach to the implementation of Jesus's message; however, one cannot help but recognize the irony of a schism within a church founded upon unity and catholicity. While each sect believes itself the "one holy catholic and apostolic church" and relegates the other to false-hood, the original Universal Church intended to emulate Christ's direction will remain two flocks, though both under the guidance of one shepherd.

— Megan Stearns
Section Editor

༄

Timeline of the Catholic Church

4 BCE Jesus of Nazareth is born in the town of Bethlehem. Church doctrine says Jesus was the son of the Virgin Mary and that his father was the Holy Spirit, thus making Jesus the Son of God.

Although calculations of Dionysius Exiguus put the birth of Jesus in the year that in consequence is called AD 1, history places his birth more likely some time between 6 and 4 BCE.

30 CE Major preachings of Jesus—Sermon on the Mount. The teachings of Jesus later spread by several apostles, and form much of the content of the Gospels.

33 CE Jesus of Nazareth crucified by authorities of Roman Empire after Jewish leaders in Jerusalem accuse Jesus of blasphemy. Christians believe he was raised from the dead by God three days later, and instructed his followers to baptize and form disciples who would constitute his Church, with Saint Peter as its leader, a position that passed to the bishop of Rome, known as the pope.

110 CE Ignatius of Antioch uses term "Catholic Church" in a letter to the church at Smyrna (date disputed—some insist it is a forgery written in 250 or later; others that he merely

meant catholic, as in "universal"). Also believed first to advocate rejection of the Sabbath.

150 First known versions of the *Vetus Latina* circulated among Christian communities: Latin translations of Koine Greek and Hebrew scriptures will become the foundation for later formation of the Bible.

155 The teachings of Marcion, the gnostic Valentinus, and the pentecostal Montanists cause disruptions in the Roman community. Persecution of Christians.

180 Irenaeus' Adversus Haereses brings the concept of "heresy" to the fore, excluding all nonconforming Christians and establishing "fourfold" canon of gospels.

195 Pope Victor I, first Latin pope, excommunicated the Quartodecimans in a growing Easter controversy.

200 Tertullian, first great Latin Christian writer, invents terms *Trinitas, tres Personae, una Substantia, Vetus Testamentum, Novum Testamentum.*

Jan. 20, 250 Emperor Decius begins widespread persecution of Christians in Rome. Pope Fabian is martyred during this purge; afterward the Donatist controversy over readmitting lapsed Christians disaffects many in North Africa.

250 Pope Fabian sends out seven bishops from Rome to Gaul to preach the Gospel: Gatien to Tours, Trophimus to Arles, Paul to Narbonne, Saturnin to Toulouse, Denis to Paris, Austromoine to Clermont, and Martial to Limoges.

Oct. 28, 312 Emperor Constantine leads forces of the Roman Empire to victory at the Battle of

Milvian Bridge. According to Church tradition, Constantine has vision the night before the battle that he will be victorious if he fights under the Symbol of Christ. After winning the battle, Constantine converts to Christianity (though he will not be baptized till just before death).

CHURCH OF THE ROMAN EMPIRE (313–476)

313 The Edict of Milan declares the Roman Empire neutral toward religious views, in effect ending the persecution of Christians.

321 Granting the Church the right to hold property, Constantine donates the palace of the Laterani to Bishop Miltiades, with its Basilica of San Giovanni for his Episcopal seat.

325 The Arian controversy erupts in Alexandria, causing widespread violence and disruptions among Christians. Constantine calls the First Council of Nicaea, which establishes the Nicene Creed, declaring the belief of orthodox Trinitarian Christians in the Holy Trinity. The form of the Nicene Creed has undergone controversy over the Filioque clause but is still used by the Catholic Church to this day.

Nov. 24, 380 Emperor Theodosius I is baptized a Christian and declares Christianity the state religion of the Roman Empire.

382 The Council of Rome under Pope Damascus I sets the Canon of the Bible, listing the accepted books of the Old Testament and the New Testament. No others are to be considered Scripture.

391 The Theodosian decrees outlaw most pagan rituals still practiced in Rome, thereby encouraging much of the population to convert to Christianity.

400 Jerome's Vulgate Latin Bible translation is published. This is a highly influential compilation of Old Testament and New Testament books that has become the basis for the Bible that is known today.

431 The Council of Ephesus declares that Jesus existed both as Man and God simultaneously, clarifying his status in the Holy Trinity. The Nicene Creed is also declared a permanent holy text of the early church.

Sept. 4, 476 Emperor Romulus Augustus is deposed in Rome, marked by many as the fall of the Western Roman Empire. Focus of the early Church turns to expanding in the Eastern Roman Empire, also known as the Byzantine Empire, with its capitol at Constantinople. In the 11th century, the Church splits into Orthodox Christianity and Catholicism.

CHURCH OF THE EARLY MIDDLE AGES (476–800)

480 Saint Benedict begins his Monastic Rule, setting out regulations for the establishment of monasteries.

496 Clovis I pagan, king of the Franks, converts to the Catholic faith.

502 Pope Symmachus rules that laymen should no longer vote for the popes and that only higher clergy should be considered eligible.

590 Pope Gregory the Great reforms Church structure and administration. Establishes Gregorian Chant.

596 Saint Augustine of Canterbury is sent by Pope Gregory to evangelize pagan English.

638 Christian Jerusalem and Syria are conquered by Muslim armies.

642 Egypt falls to the Muslims, followed by the rest of North Africa.

664 The Synod of Whitby unites the Celtic Church in England with the Catholic Church.

718 St. Boniface, an Englishman, is given a commission by Pope Gregory II to evangelize the Germans.

726 Iconoclasm begins in the eastern Empire. The destruction of images persists until 843.

756 Popes are granted independent rule of Rome by Frankish King Pepin the Short.

793 Sacking of the monastery of Lindisfarne marks the beginning of Viking raids on Christian Europe.

CHURCH OF THE HIGH MIDDLE AGES
(800–1499)

800 King Charlemagne of the Franks is crowned Holy Roman Emperor in the West by Pope Leo III.

829 Ansgar begins missionary work in Sweden near Stockholm.

863 Saint Cyril and Saint Methodius sent by the patriarch of Constantinople to evangelize the Slavic peoples. They translate the Bible into Slavonic.

910 Great Benedictine monastery of Cluny rejuvenates western monasticism. Monasteries spread throughout the isolated regions of Western Europe.

1003 Pope John XVII dies five months after installation, making this year one of the few when three legitimate popes reigned.

1012 Burchard of Worms completes twenty-volume Decretum of Canon Law.

1054 Liturgical and other divisions cause a permanent split between the Eastern and Western Churches—the Great Schism. But parting of the ways between East and West began much earlier—1054 is often viewed as the official date for the separation between Western Christians (Roman Catholics) and Eastern Christians (Eastern Orthodox).

1095 Pope Urban II urges Crusade at Council of Clermont to defend the Eastern Christians, and pilgrims to Holy Land.

1098 Foundation of the reforming monastery of Citeaux; growth of Cistercian order.

1099 Recapture of Jerusalem by First Crusade.

1144 The Saint Denis Basilica of Abbot Suger is the first major building in the style of Gothic architecture.

1150 Publication of *Decretum Gratiani.*

1205 Saint Francis of Assisi becomes hermit, founding the Franciscan order of friars.

1229 Inquisition founded in response to the dangerous Cathar Heresy, at the Council of Toulouse.

1231 Charter of the University of Paris granted by Pope Gregory IX.

1305 French influence causes the pope to move from Rome to Avignon.

1370 Saint Catherine of Siena calls on the pope to return to Rome.

1378 Western Schism. Opposing popes elected in Avignon and Rome.

Church of the Renaissance (1500–1629)

1517 Martin Luther posts his Ninety-five Theses, protesting the sale of indulgences.

1521 Baptism of the first Catholics in Philippines, first in Asia—commemorated with the feast of the Sto. Niño.

1531 Our Lady of Guadalupe is believed to have appeared to Juan Diego in Mexico—second largest Catholic population.

1534 Saint Ignatius of Loyola and Francis Xavier and five others meet in Montmartre to found the Jesuit Order.

1536–1540 Dissolution of the monasteries in England, Wales, and Ireland.

1540 Pope Paul III confirms the order of the Society of Jesus.

1545–1563 Council of Trent convened to prepare Catholic response to Protestant Reformation. It sets tone of Catholic society for next three centuries.

1568 Saints John Chrysostom, Basil, Gregory Nazianzus, Athanasius, and Thomas Aquinas are all made Doctors of the Church.

1577 Teresa of Avila writes *The Interior Castle,* classic work of Catholic mysticism.

1582 Beginning of the Gregorian Calendar; adopted by Italy, Spain, and Portugal.

1593 Robert Bellarmine finishes his *Disputationes de controversiis christianae fidei.*

1598 Papal role in the Peace of Vervins.

Church in the Age of Reason (1630–1799)

1638 Shimabara Rebellion leads to a repression of Catholics, Christians in Japan.

1685 Louis XIV revokes the Edict of Nantes in hopes of currying Papal favor.

1691 Pope Innocent XII declares against nepotism and simony.

1713 Encyclical Unigenitus condemns Jansenism.

1715 Clement XI rules against the Jesuits in the Chinese Rites controversy.

1721 Kangxi emperor bans Christian missions in China.

1738 Grey Nuns founded.

1769 Passionist order granted full rights by Clement XIV.

1793 French Republican anticlerical measures.

Nineteenth-century Catholic Church (1800–1899)

1847 The Latin patriarch of Jerusalem resumes residence in Jerusalem.

1850 The Archdiocese of Westminster and twelve others are erected, reestablishing a hierarchy in the United Kingdom.

1870 First Vatican Council issues the dogma of papal infallibility before the fall of Rome in the

Franco-Prussian War, causing it to end prematurely, and brings an end to the Papal States. Controversy leads to formation of the Old Catholic Church.

TWENTIETH-CENTURY CATHOLIC CHURCH (1901–2000)

1929 The Lateran treaties establish an independent Vatican City, resolving the dispute with Italy since the seizure of the Papal States in 1870.

1939 World War II begins in Europe. The Vatican declares neutrality to avoid being drawn into the conflict and also to avoid occupation by the Italian military.

1944 German Army occupies Rome. Hitler proclaims he will respect Vatican neutrality; however, several incidents, such as giving aid to downed Allied airmen, nearly cause Nazi Germany to invade the Vatican. The Allies liberate Rome after only a few weeks of occupation.

1950 Assumption of Mary defined as dogma.

1962–1965 Second Vatican Council, the 21st ecumenical council of the Catholic Church makes many changes, and increased emphasis on ecumenism; fewer rules on penances, fasting and other devotional practices; and initiating revision of the services, making them slightly simplified and more accessible through the use of native languages instead of Latin. Opposition to changes inspired by the Council give rise to Traditionalist Catholic movement who reject changing old forms of worship.

1970 Novus Ordo Mass in vernacular languages introduced, replaces the Tridentine Mass that was principally in Latin.

1978 Pope John Paul II becomes the first non-Italian pope in 450 years.

1992 A Catechism of the Catholic Church is first printed in French.

THE CATHOLIC CHURCH IN THE TWENTY-FIRST CENTURY

Jan. 1, 2001 The church solemnizes the start of the third Christian millennium by extending into part of the year 2001 the jubilee year that it observes at twenty-five-year intervals and that, in the case of the year 2000, is called the Great Jubilee.

Jan. 18, 2002 Former priest John Geoghan is convicted of child molestation and sentenced to ten years in prison. The Geoghan case one of the worst scandals of the Catholic Church in modern times.

Apr. 2, 2005 Pope John Paul II dies at the age of 84. Funeral is broadcast worldwide. Millions of Catholic pilgrims journey to Rome, Italy, to pay final respects.

Apr. 19, 2005 German-born Cardinal Joseph Ratzinger elected Pope by College of Cardinals. Benedict XVI, becoming first pope elected in third millennium.

July 7, 2007 Pope Benedict XVI issues the Summorom Pontificum, which heals schisms with the Eastern Orthodox church and traditionalist Catholic groups, but raises concerns with Jewish, Muslim, Protestant, and Eastern religious groups.

1 Roman Catholicism

I. Roots and History

A. Introduction

FOR CATHOLICS, CATHOLICISM MEANS LIFE IN Christ—that is, an encounter with Christ in the sacraments and through the teachings of the church. It implies a living relationship with Christ through a life of prayer and service. Such a living Catholicism has personal, social, historical, and even political implications, as demonstrated by the lives of the prominent people who have contributed to and continue to take part in the realization of Catholicism as the world's largest single religious body.

As the world's largest Christian Church, the Catholic Church currently claims near one-sixth of the world's population—or over one billion people—as adherents. Since its debut as a major religious presence in the fourth century, Catholicism has profoundly influenced the history of Western civilization. The church's mission of ecumenism, or the achievement of worldwide spiritual unity, is largely responsible for the fact that its practitioners have touched nearly every corner of the globe. According to church tradition, by the year 100, the earliest apostles had established forty Christian communities in northern Africa,

Asia Minor, Arabia, Greece, and Rome. After Christianity's legalization in 313, Catholicism established major power centers throughout the Byzantine Empire, and in the sixth century, missionaries spread from thence into northern Europe, working among the Germanic, Irish, and Slavic peoples, and eventually reaching the Vikings and other Scandinavians in later centuries.

The High Middle Ages were marked by contention and warfare as the Christian Church irreparably split in 1054 into Eastern and Western factions over matters of jurisdiction and doctrine, and the Holy Crusades were launched against the Turks. Missionaries resumed their work throughout

The Bible is sacred to all Christian denominations. The crucifix is a common devotional object in Eastern Orthodox, Catholic, and Episcopalian churches (most Protestant denominations use the cross, without Christ's body). The rosary is a traditional form of devotion among Catholics, who use rosary beads like the ones shown here to keep track of their prayers.

the late fifteenth and early sixteenth centuries, spreading Catholicism to the Americas, Asia, Africa, and Oceania. Martin Luther's Ninety-Five Theses of 1517, attacking major doctrinal points of Catholicism, led to the Protestant Reformation, which in turn sparked wars in Germany and France, and resulted in the dissolution of monasteries and the confiscation of Catholic churches throughout England, Wales, and Ireland. However, the church would recover from the blow with their Counter-Reformation of the mid-1500s, which reaffirmed many basic Catholic doctrines, improved the education of clergy, consolidated the central jurisdiction of the Roman Curia, and initiated the development of new religious orders, some of which would become highly influential themselves—such as the Jesuits. In fact, Jesuit missionary Francis Xavier was responsible for the introduction of Christianity to Japan; by the end of the sixteenth century, tens of thousands of Japanese followed Roman Catholicism.

In the seventeenth and eighteenth centuries, the church focused mainly upon the New World, where Jesuit and Franciscan missionaries were hard at work converting Native Americans. Though Junipero Serra did succeed in establishing missions along the California coast, the introduction of Western civilization to the area on account of these missions resulted in the annihilation of nearly a third of the native population, primarily through disease. New technologies and weaponry developed in the nineteenth century allowed European powers to gain control of most of the African interior. Catholic missionaries were close on the heels of the newly installed colonial governments, building schools, monasteries, and churches.

The twentieth century saw comprehensive doctrinal reforms within the Catholic Church, especially after the Second Vatican Council from 1962–1965, which, in an attempt to modernize the traditional teachings of Catholicism, made changes to old rites and ceremonies. The public responded in a variety of ways, from ceasing to attend church to gracefully embracing the changes. Some congregations dis-

sented, forming today's Traditionalist and Liberal Catholic groups. The twenty-first century brought church scandal to the attention of the public sphere when several major lawsuits were brought against priests in 2001 for sexual abuse of minors. The United States Conference of Catholic Bishops commissioned a nationwide study that found that 4 percent of all priests who served in the United States from 1950 to 2002 faced some sort of sexual accusations. Further criticism of the church ensued when it was discovered that some bishops knew about allegations and, rather than removing the accused, reassigned them. Pope John Paul II responded with the statement, "there is no place in the priesthood and religious life for those who would harm the young." In an effort to curb further instances of abuse, the church now requires background checks for church employees and disallows ordination of men with "deep-seated homosexual tendencies." The church asserted its concern in 2008 with acknowledgement that the scandal was a very serious problem.

Despite setbacks encountered through the ages, the Catholic Church remains a staunch force in the religious arena, with representatives in almost every country and niche of society. In light of its successful growth and development into the dominating Christian denomination, achievement of its goal of ecumenism, instilled at a time when the Christian minority was persecuted as heathens, must be considered an overall success.

B. The Religion in America

The history of Catholicism in America precedes British colonization; in fact, the first American Catholics were Native American and black slave converts—the products of Franciscan and Jesuit missionary work. Throughout the sixteenth century, French and Spanish missionaries—hailing in ancestry from the Church of Rome—served as the two primary forces of Catholic evangelism in the uncharted territory of the New World. Spanish explorers devoted their colonizing endeavors to the southern and western regions of present-day America, establishing settlements in what are now the states of Florida, Texas, New Mexico, and California. Such settlements became centers of an intense (and often oppressive) effort to Christianize and "domesticate" the indigenous population inhabiting the land. While a minority of Native Americans did come to adopt a more European way of life—living in towns and taking on work as herdsmen, carpenters, blacksmiths, or masons—they did so at the cost of their freedom, for attempts to leave the mission were met with severe corporal punishment. Concurrent with Spanish colonization, French missionaries were making similar efforts with Native Americans living along the banks of the St. Lawrence River in areas that are now Maine and northern New York, and around the Great Lakes and in the Mississippi River valley. Such work at the hands of the French took a great toll on all parties involved, as priests of differing orders often pitted tribes against each other, resulting in large-scale massacres and "martyrdom."

In 1634, an unusual band of English immigrants landed in Maryland. The members of this group were, for the most part, wealthy upper-class Catholics led by the Calvert family, who sought to build a refuge for Catholics fleeing persecution and handicaps in England. Aided by Jesuit missionaries, the Calvert's small Maryland Catholic population kept its faith alive, but lost effective political and social control of the colony to Protestant settlers by the end of the seventeenth century. To protect itself from the visceral anti-Catholicism of English Protestant settlers, the Catholic minority espoused the principle of religious toleration. Though the plurality of Protestantism inhibited the movement from gaining total control on a united front, and the American Revolution encouraged religious freedom, Catholicism continued

The Most Reverend John Carroll (1735–1815) is depicted in this 1811 portrait painted by the American artist Rembrandt Peale. Carroll, a founder of Georgetown University, was America's first Roman Catholic bishop and archbishop.

to face limitations throughout the American colonial period—and even into the early nineteenth century, in some cases—as American colonial and state governments enacted laws denying Catholics political and property rights. A few Catholic families in Maryland managed to transcend such strictures through their personal wealth, social connections, and contributions to the American Revolutionary cause, but most Catholics entered the nineteenth century highly conscious of their status outside of the main currents of American religious and social development.

AUTHORITY IN AMERICA

In 1789, the year of George Washington's inauguration as the first president of the United States, American Catholics—disillusioned by a growing number of rebellious trustees and disobedient priests—increasingly felt the need for an authority figure on home soil. Recognizing the need for such appointment, Pope Pius VI erected an American bishopric at Baltimore to oversee American Catholic growth and, in 1790, consecrated John Carroll as the first American Bishop. Carroll brought family prestige and political acumen to the church, which helped dilute anti-Catholic prejudices and allowed the movement in America to lay a strong ecclesiastical foundation in the nineteenth century. Carroll believed that Catholics had little to fear from the dominant American society and culture, and he encouraged his coreligionists to adapt to local conditions.

Carroll's policies guided the church in its formative years. He felt strongly that Catholicism's New World counterpart needed to adopt several different strategies to better integrate with American society. Among them, Carroll advocated the separation of church and state and a democratic church organization. He prompted Catholics, as a minority in America, to espouse patriotism, to be especially cooperative with their non-Catholic fellows, and to go out of their way in demonstrating model citizenship. He emphasized the importance of disseminating their religion by way of reason and logic, rather than merely parroting the teachings of the pope. And he described Catholic education for children from elementary school onwards as key to the strength of the church. Despite Carroll's efforts, by 1800, territorial acquisitions, westward expansion, and significant foreign immigration functioned as a countercurrent to Carroll's vision of American Catholicism, and he turned his gaze somewhat from the model of the new republic, back to Europe. He abandoned the democratic electoral process by which he had come into authority, and himself recommended new bishops to Rome.

By 1808, the American church was growing rapidly, so much so that Carroll asked for a division of his diocese. It was in that year that four new suffragan dioceses (Boston, New York, Philadelphia, and Bardstown, Kentucky) were formed, and Baltimore became the first archdiocese. In 1808, Rome raised Baltimore to the rank of a metropolitan see and created several suffragan sees in the United States. However, no greater problem nagged the church than a shortage of priests. In hopes of relieving the shortage, bishops established colleges and seminaries to nurture and train a native clergy, and attempted to attract religious communities into their dioceses. This effort was so successful that by 1908, Rome removed the United States from the jurisdiction of the Roman Congregation for the Propagation of the Faith and transferred it to the authority of the Roman Curia. No longer a missionary area, the American church relied more on its native sons to staff the priesthood.

BIRTH OF AMERICAN CATHOLICISM

At the time of Carroll's death in 1815, American Catholicism was divided between two schools. One remained faithful to the notion of a uniquely indigenous church, representative of American values. The other followed Carroll's later inclination to pattern the church after Europe's example. Hence, many of the millions of immigrants from Europe, Canada, and Mexico who flooded America beginning around 1830 found themselves faced with a decision: adhere to European religious roots, or embrace assimilation. This created a multifaceted face of Catholicism—one in which ethnic parishes worshipped in foreign languages right next door to territorial parishes. No matter the number of Catholics who clung to the old European ways, Catholicism in America could not help but reflect the nature of the land it was nurtured upon. It also grew to reflect robustness. As a minority population in 1820 of about 195,000 adherents, Catholics became the largest Christian population in American by 1850, numbering near one and a half million. Thanks to the multitude of immigrants from Europe, that number would double by 1860.

In June 1887, 75,000 people marched in protest over the removal of Father Edward McGlynn from the pastorate of Saint Stephen's Church in New York City. The controversy began in 1886, with Father McGlynn's public support for mayoral candidate Henry George, an economist who advocated the "Single Tax," or land value tax. Father McGlynn deeply lamented the problem of unemployment in America, and advocated the Single Tax doctrine as the universal remedy for poverty. To some Catholics, this sounded like an attack on private property. Cardinal Simeoni, prefect of the Congregation of the Propaganda, had long ago ordered McGlynn to retract his support of the land tax, and after McGlynn's removal, summoned him to Rome. McGlynn did not comply, instead asking his canonical advocate, the Reverend Dr. Richard Lalor Burtsell, to send a letter in defense of his position. The letter never reached Roman authorities, and Pope Leo XIII finally ordered McGlynn to proceed to Rome within forty days under penalty of excommunication. Allegedly not realizing that his letter had never been received by the pope, and claiming ill health, McGlynn failed to appear in Rome. He was excommunicated in 1887, but was readmitted to the church in 1892. Upon recovering his priestly duties, McGlynn visited the pope and defended his support of the land tax. The pope was satisfied with his explanation and decided it did not contradict the ethical teachings of the church. McGlynn continued to speak at Single Tax meetings from there on out, staunchly declaring that the church had not forced him to retract his views.

Catholicism's American branch tested Roman authority in many other ways in the nineteenth century, partially on account of its secular nature, and partially due to its oft-times unwieldy physical growth. Pope Leo XIII was uneasy about the separation of church and state and the independence of some of the church's American leaders. The pope sought to salvage his eroding authority through a series of encyclicals in which he decried secularization and stated that the church would be more fruitful with government support of its institutions. Also threatening to church authority was the phenomenon of lay trusteeism in the early nineteenth century. Like their Protestant counterparts, Catholic laymen, through their elected trustees, held title to and administered parochial property. Eventually, a dearth of priests forced lay leaders to assume religious duties, including the teaching of catechism and reading of prayers. When laymen attempted to extend this authority to ecclesiastical affairs, claiming the right to appoint and remove pastors, bishops guarded their church-vested right jealously. The disputes festered for years and led to interdicts, excommunications, and schism. The trustees' charges of church autocracy also provided ammunition for nativist arguments about the Catholic danger to American congregational and democratic practices. By mid-century, the bishops quelled the rebellions, and when church councils called for uniform church practices and obedience, they asserted their control over the ecclesiastical communities.

A resurgence of lay activity occurred in the 1880s and 1890s, but was largely confined to a few Catholic intellectuals critical of the American church's submission to Irish Catholic religious and social norms. Vatican II, which invited self-criticism and openness in the church, altered church discipline, promoted a vigorous devotional life, and bred a more demanding and critical laity in the American church. In the 1960s and 1970s, increased lay initiatives and independence from clerical control resurfaced, as evident in burgeoning lay organizations. In some instances, lay leaders even clashed with church policy, as in questions of unions and race.

Throughout the church's expansion and growing pains, the Catholic press has been an important instrument of religious and moral instruction, and of building Catholic consensus. In 1822, Bishop John England of Charleston founded America's first Catholic weekly, the *United States Catholic Miscellany*. Under England's vigorous editorship, the *Miscellany* assailed nativism, advocated obedience to church doctrines, and offered Catholic positions on a host of public policy issues, including slavery. By 1900, most dioceses had their own papers, and many Catholic organizations also sponsored papers and journals. Catholic publishing houses produced mountains of catechisms, devotionals, prayer books, and religious books that preached a common Catholic faith and discipline.

In the twentieth century, Catholic efforts to win converts scored modest success at best, with conversion rates per thousand between 3.5 in 1930 and 4.8 in 1960. Interestingly, the conversion rates are highest in the dioceses where Catholic population is the smallest. In areas of high Catholic concentration, approximately three-quarters of the converts enter the church because of marriage to Catholics.

Since World War II, the church has recorded a steady erosion of Catholic identity and observance of religious duties, although Vatican II showed signs of arresting this trend.

C. Important Dates and Landmarks

1511 Puerto Rico established (now the oldest diocese in United States territory).

1564 Fort Caroline established in present-day Jacksonville, Florida, by French Huguenots.

1565 Fort Caroline overrun by Spanish explorers, accompanied by priests who established parishes by which they might convert Native Americans to Catholicism.

1634 The first Roman Catholics land in America, aboard the *Ark* and the *Dove*.

1769 Junípero Serra establishes Mission San Diego de Alcala, first of nine Spanish missions he will establish in California.

1789 Pope Pius VI (1775–1799) ratifies changes in *Ex hac Apostolicae* that make the Catholic Church in America a formal ecclesiastical entity. Baltimore becomes the first diocese, and John Carroll is appointed its bishop one year later. Also in this year, Georgetown is founded as America's first Catholic university.

1830 The First Plenary Council of Baltimore is held in the United States. Also, the first wave of European immigrants arrives in the United States.

1882 Father Michael McGivney founds the Knights of Columbus in fulfillment of the desire of Catholic men to have their own lodge.

1887 United States bishops found The Catholic University of America in Washington, D.C. Father McGlynn removed from pastorate because of his outspoken support of Henry George's "Single Tax" doctrine.

1892 Pope Leo VIII first sends an apostolic delegate to the United States.

1899 In *Testem Benevolentiae*, Pope Leo VIII warns American Catholics against "[those] among you who conceive of and desire a church in America different from that which is in the rest of the world."

1908 Pope Pius X signs *Sapienti Consilio*, an apostolic constitution that frees America from consideration as a missionary church.

1910 Pope Pius X requires clerics to take an oath against modernism, which he considers a heresy.

1911 Maryknoll Catholic Foreign Mission Society of America, Inc., the brainchild of American bishops, is established.

1919 American bishops gain their first official organization with the establishment of the National Catholic Welfare Council.

1931–1939 Father Charles Coughlin uses radio to reach millions regarding Catholic concerns and social issues. Criticized for his pro-Nazi and anti-Semitic remarks; taken off the air in 1939.

1933 Dorothy Day and Peter Maurin found the Catholic Worker Movement, which encourages Catholics to embrace poverty voluntarily as a means of fighting involuntary poverty.

1960 John F. Kennedy, member of a prominent Irish Catholic family, elected first Catholic president of the United States.

1965 Pope Paul VI visits New York in the hopes of urging the United Nations to put end to war.

Pope John Paul II greets crowds at Shea Stadium in Queens, New York, during his visit to the United States in October of 1979.

1965 A second wave of immigrants enters the United States from Latin American and Southeast Asia.

1968 Pope Paul VI issues *Humanae Vitae*, in which he prohibits the use of birth control by Catholics. Eighty-seven Catholics, including prominent theologians, publicly voice their dissension from such teachings in a statement published by the *New York Times*.

1973 The United States Supreme Court rules that abortion is legal in Roe vs. Wade. Ruling criticized by church leaders.

1979 Pope John Paul II first visits the United States; tours Boston, New York (*see* photo above), Philadelphia, Chicago, and Washington.

1984 President Ronald Reagan and Pope John Paul II agree that America should have an ambassador of representation to Rome, establishing official diplomatic relations between those two countries.

1987 Pope John Paul II makes his second visit to the United States, appearing in Miami, South Carolina, New Orleans, New Mexico, Arizona, Los Angeles, San Antonio, San Francisco, and Detroit.

1992 Catechism of the Catholic Church—the first universal catechism released in 400 years—is approved as a compendium of the teachings of the church.

1995 Pope John Paul II makes his third visit to the United States, appearing in New Jersey, New York, and Baltimore.

1998 While visiting Cuba, Pope John Paul II decries U.S. embargo policy against Cuba.

2000 Cardinal John O'Connor dies on May 3 in New York City.

2003 Catholic archbishop Oscar Lipscomb of the Mobile, Alabama, archdiocese admits he allowed Rev. J. Alexander Sherlock to remain in the pulpit after he admitted in 1998 to sexual abuse of teenage boys in the 1970s.

2004 Bishop Thomas O'Brien, former head of Arizona's largest Roman Catholic diocese, becomes the first American Catholic bishop to be convicted of a felony—in this case, a hit and run.

2004 CNN survey reports children made over 11,000 allegations of sexual abuse by Catholic priests. The 4,450 priests involved are about 4 percent of the 110,000 priests who served during the fifty-two years covered by the study.

2006 Eight Roman Catholic women are ordained as priests in Pittsburgh, PA, by three consecrated female bishops.

Nov. 30, 2006 Pope Benedict XVII and Patriarch Bartholomew hold prayer service at Church of St. George in Istanbul, seat of the Eastern Orthodox Patriarchate, committing to quest for reunification of Roman and Orthodox Catholic Churches.

2008 Pope Benedict XVI makes his first visit to United States, visiting New York City and Washington, D.C.

D. Important Figures

Saint Peter

Saint Peter, also known as Simon or Simon Peter, is recognized by the Roman Catholic Church as the first leader of the church in Rome. Catholics see him as first among the twelve apostles of Jesus and he has subsequently been called the "Rock upon which the Church was built" due to his role both during and after the life of Jesus. Subsequently, all popes since the creation of the church have been considered the successors of Peter, and as such, the voice of God on earth.

Saint Peter is also known for his role in the Passion Story as the denier of his relationship with Jesus. In all four Gospels it is noted that Peter denied Christ three times during the apprehension and trials of Jesus; however, in the last chapter of the Gospel of John, Peter repudiated his denial by declaring his love for Christ three times during one of the resurrection appearances of Jesus. As a result, Jesus reconfirmed Peter's place as leader and first among the apostles.

Junipero Serra (1713–1784)

Junipero Serra was born Miguel Jose Serra on the Spanish Island of Mallorca, Spain. Serra began his Catholic service (and took his new name) at the age of sixteen, when he entered the Order of Saint Francis of Assisi in Palma. Serra would later earn a doctorate in philosophy at the University of Luliana, also in Palma.

At the age of thirty-six, Serra sailed for Vera Cruz, Mexico to serve the Franciscan missionaries who

hoped to Christianize the indigenous of the New World. He dedicated the next seventeen years to missionary service in the area that is now Sierra Gordo, Mexico. In 1767, Spain asked the Franciscans to assume responsibility for the territory in present-day Baja, California that had been under the jurisdiction of the Jesuits. Serra found himself at the head of this new operation, and set off in 1769 on an expedition with Gaspar de Portola to found missions at San Diego and Monterey. At fifty-six, he founded his first mission in San Diego; he would found nine more during his lifetime. Though Father Serra primarily resided in Alta, California, he traveled over 24,000 miles along the coast of that state for the sake of his work. Father Serra died at the age of seventy at Mission San Carlos Borromeo, where he is now buried under the sanctuary floor.

Dorothy Day (1897–1980)

Born in Brooklyn, New York, but raised in Chicago, Dorothy dropped out of the University of Illinois at Urbana-Champaign two years before graduating to return to her native New York, where she took up a bohemian life in Greenwich Village. After two common law marriages and one abortion, she gave birth to a daughter, Tamar, which experience inspired a spiritual awakening. In 1927, she joined the Catholic Church with a baptism at Our Lady Help of Christians parish on Staten Island.

Six years later, Day founded the Catholic Worker Movement with Peter Maurin. The organization began with the *Catholic Worker* newspaper, which urged Americans to adopt a position of neutrality and pacifism toward the issues that had sparked World War I. Eventually, the movement's espousal of nonviolence expanded to encompass charitableness toward the impoverished, and a "house of hospitality" was established in New York's slums, as well as communal farms in outlying communities. By 1941, the movement had spread beyond New York to the establishment of similar communes throughout the United States and in Canada and the United Kingdom; today, more than one hundred such affiliated communities exist throughout the world.

Though Day had adopted a very orthodox approach toward Catholic ethics, morality, and piety, she publicly espoused a liberal stance on women's rights, birth control, economics, and social policy. Day was also a member of the Industrial Workers of the World, and in 1971, was bestowed with the Pacem in Terris (Latin for "Peace on Earth") Award from the Catholic Church.

Father Charles Coughlin (1891–1979)

A Canadian-born Roman Catholic priest at Royal Oak, Michigan's National Shrine of the Little Flower Church, Father Coughlin was one of the first political leaders to use radio to reach a mass audience during the 1930s. The son of Irish Catholic parents, Coughlin was born in Hamilton, Ontario and ordained in Toronto at the age of twenty-five. He taught classes at Ontario's Assumption College for seven years before relocating to the United States, where he started his radio career.

Coughlin's first broadcasts involved weekly sermons for Detroit's station WJR. When the CBS radio network dropped free sponsorship of the program in 1931, Coughlin managed to fund his own national network and his commentary shifted focus from matters of religion to economic and political concerns. Coughlin was an early and enthusiastic supporter of 1932 Presidential candidate Franklin D. Roosevelt and his New Deal agenda, and he famously coined the phrases "Roosevelt or ruin" and "The New Deal is Christ's Deal." However, as the Great Depression deepened during the 1930s, Coughlin's message changed. He called the Depression a "cash famine," and decried the influence of international business and Wall Street on America's depleted monetary flow. Coughlin proposed that the Federal Reserve be done away with, and he attacked Roosevelt and the New Deal.

Father Charles Coughlin appears in this portrait taken around 1933 in Detroit, Michigan.

By 1934, Coughlin's radio audience numbered in the millions, making him the most prominent Roman Catholic spokesman on economic and political issues. When Coughlin began to denounce capitalists and "Jewish conspirators," and accused Roosevelt of "leaning toward international socialism or sovietism on the Spanish question," Roosevelt took action. In 1936, he sent prominent Irish Catholics Joseph P. Kennedy and Frank Murphy to curb Coughlin's rhetoric. When the two men failed, Kennedy cooperated with Bishop Francis Spellman and Eugenio Cardinal Pacelli (the future Pope Pius XII) in an attempt to get the Vatican to shut Coughlin down. Though the Roman Catholic Church did not approve of Coughlin, they had no canonical authority to silence him. Only Coughlin's superior, Detroit Bishop Michael Gallagher, had the means of curbing him, and Gallagher pledged support to the "Radio Priest." Facing Gallagher's support and Catholic fear that the Coughlin issues might lead to a schism, Roman Catholic leadership did nothing.

In the mid-1930s, Coughlin's ideology grew ever more anti-Semitic. He founded the newspaper *Social Justice* and used it to publish anti-Jewish polemics, such as claiming that Marxist atheism in Europe was a Jewish plot. He made such statements as: "Jewish persecution only followed after Christians first were persecuted" following Germany's 1938 Kristallnacht; and at a subsequent rally, Coughlin gave the Nazi salute before proclaiming, "When we get through with the Jews in America, they'll think the treatment they received in Germany was nothing."

At its height in the early 1930s, Coughlin's program attained an estimated listenership of up to one-third of all Americans, and his office received up to 80,000 (mostly supportive) letters per week.

Coughlin's downfall in public popularity began with his professed association with the Christian Front, an organization that was discovered by the FBI to be arming for a planned murderous attack against Jews, communists, and "a dozen U.S. Congressmen." When Coughlin continued to maintain his loyalty to the Christian Front even after J. Edgar Hoover exposed the organization's fascist designs, the public abandoned its support. The Roosevelt administration continued placing new regulations and restrictions on radio broadcasting, reaching the conclusion that the radio spectrum was a "limited national resource" and regulated as a publicly-owned commons, so that the First Amendment did not necessarily apply to that field.

Many stations dropped Coughlin, and when radio broadcasters were newly required to obtain permits to operate, Coughlin's permit application was denied. Coughlin sought to work around the restrictions by purchasing airtime and playing recorded speeches, but this drained his resources and limited his influence. As a last resort, he turned to *Social Justice* as a means of continuing his campaigns, but the government revoked his mailing privileges, granting him the right to publish, but not the right to use the U.S. Post Office Department to deliver his materials.

Finally, Detroit received a successor to Bishop Gallagher—a new bishop not sympathetic to Coughlin. In 1942, the one authority figure with the power to stop Coughlin's controversial political activities did so, and ordered Coughlin to confine himself to his duties as a parish priest. Coughlin complied, retaining his pastorship of the Shrine of the Little Flower until retiring in 1966, though he continued to write anti-Communist pamphlets until his death at the age of eighty-eight.

Mario Cuomo (1932–)

Mario Cuomo, a Queens, New York, native, was born to Italian Catholic parents. After earning his bachelor's and law degrees at St. John's University, he played minor league baseball for the Pittsburgh Pirates until receiving a head injury.

Cuomo's career in politics began in 1974 when he ran for lieutenant governor of New York. Though defeated, he was appointed secretary of state in New York in 1975 by Governor Hugh Carey. Cuomo was defeated in his bid for the mayoralty of New York City in 1977 by Ed Koch. He was elected lieutenant governor one year later on Carey's ticket. In 1982, Cuomo was elected governor of New York, defeating Democratic candidate Koch and Republican Lewis Lehrman in the general election. He retained this office for three consecutive terms, serving until 1995. Cuomo's political views were notably liberal, reflected especially in his opposition to the death penalty. Cuomo was politically pro-choice on the abortion question, though he pointed out that, as a Catholic, he was personally opposed to abortion.

After Cuomo gave the keynote speech at the Democratic National Convention in 1984, media reports suggested that a run for President of the United States was in his future. He considered entering the New Hampshire primary in 1992, but did not; he also declined nomination to the United States Supreme Court during the Clinton administration. Cuomo left the gubernatorial office in 1994 after his defeat by Republican (and also a Roman Catholic) George Pataki. Cuomo's son, Andrew Cuomo (1957–), also a Roman Catholic, was elected govenor of New York in 2010.

John F. Kennedy (1917–1963)

John Fitzgerald Kennedy, popularly known as "JFK," is the only practicing Roman Catholic to have served as President of the United States. Kennedy was born in Massachusetts, but, after his family left Massachusetts in 1927 for the Bronx and then Bronxville, New York, Kennedy spent his childhood from the age of ten in several private Catholic boarding schools and his family's multiple vacation homes. After dropping out of the London School of Economics and Princeton University due to illnesses, Kennedy enrolled at Harvard College in 1936 and graduated cum laude with a degree in international relations.

On July 2, 1963—just days after his coronation—Pope Paul VI met with U.S. president John F. Kennedy at the Vatican. Kennedy shook the pope's hand, but (pointedly) did not kiss his ring. The pontiff praised Kennedy for his "untiring" efforts to achieve world peace.

A year before graduating, in 1939, Kennedy spent eight months touring Europe, the Soviet Union, the Balkans, and the Middle East as part of his research on British participation in the Munich Agreement for his Harvard senior honors thesis. Kennedy completed the thesis, entitled "Appeasement in Munich" in 1940, and his father convinced him to publish it as a book. He did so in July of that year, and the result, entitled *While England Slept,* became a bestseller.

Kennedy enrolled in the Navy in September 1941. He earned the rank of lieutenant and was aboard patrol torpedo (PT) boat 109 when, during a nighttime patrol, the vessel was rammed by the Japanese destroyer Amagiri. Though Kennedy's back was hurt, he swam, first to one island, then another, towing an injured man, before his crew was rescued. He received the Navy and Marine Corps Medal for his bravery and endurance. Kennedy also received the Purple Heart, Asiatic-Pacific Campaign Medal and the World War II Victory Medal during his service in World War II. He was honorably discharged in 1945.

Following his military service, Kennedy debated between a career in journalism or politics. His family had pinned their political hopes on his older brother Joseph, but the torch was passed to John when Joseph was killed in World War II. In 1946, Kennedy ran for United States representative and won, serving as a congressman for six years. In 1952, he defeated incumbent Republican Henry Cabot Lodge, Jr. for the U.S. Senate. Four years later, Kennedy won the Pulitzer Prize for his work *Profiles in Courage.*

Kennedy declared his intent to run for president of the United States in 1960, and the Democratic convention nominated Kennedy as its candidate in July of that year. Kennedy's Catholicism was one of the major issues surrounding his campaign. In answer to fears that his religious views would influence his decision-making, Kennedy famously told the Greater Houston Ministerial Association, "I am not the Catholic candidate for President. I am the Democratic Party's candidate for President who also happens to be a Catholic. I do not speak for my Church on public matters—and the Church does not speak for me."

In the first televised Presidential debate in American history, Kennedy debated Republican candidate Richard Nixon. Nixon, refusing make-up, sporting a "five-o'clock shadow," and nursing an injured leg, fared poorly with television audiences compared to relaxed, fresh-faced and healthy-looking Kennedy (though radio listeners polled indicated Nixon had won the debate). The event became a landmark as the first instance in which television strongly impacted a national political campaign. On November 8, 1960, Kennedy defeated Nixon to become (at age forty-three) the youngest President elected to office in one of the closest presidential elections of the twentieth century. At his inaugural address of January 20, 1961, Kennedy famously said, "Ask not what your country can do for you; ask what you can do for your country."

Events during the new President's administration included the Bay of Pigs invasion, the Cuban missile crisis, the building of the Berlin Wall, the space race, the African American civil rights movement, and early stages of the Vietnam War. Kennedy was assassinated on November 22, 1963, in Dallas, Texas, presumably by Lee Harvey Oswald. The circumstances of Kennedy's murder are still hotly debated. Kennedy continues to be one of the most favorably remembered United States Presidents.

The Kennedy family has been an important source of support, influence, and pride for the American Roman Catholic community for the past century. Robert F. Kennedy (1925–1968), JFK's younger brother, served as attorney general and in the U.S. Senate, and was assassinated during a promising run for the presidency in 1968. Edward M. ("Ted") Kennedy (1932–2009) served in the U.S. Senate from 1962 until his death in 2009, and was a staunch advocate of liberal social causes.

‹‹›

II. Tenets and Beliefs

A. Articles of Faith

In 325, Emperor Constantine convened the Council of Nicaea, the first ecumenical council of the Christian Church, bringing together the bishops of Christian communities around the world. The assembly converged in modern-day Iznik, Turkey, to craft a definition of Christianity and secure the unity of the church. A creed was then created that introduced the concept of the Holy Trinity, which belief affirms that there is one God who exists in the form of three persons: Father, Son and Holy Spirit; and that Jesus, as born of the Holy Spirit, is divine. This resulting Nicene Creed summarizes the basic beliefs of Christianity and the Roman Catholic Church:

We believe in one God, the Father, the Almighty, maker of heaven and earth, of all that is seen and unseen.

We believe in one Lord, Jesus Christ, the only son of God, eternally begotten of the Father, God from God, Light from Light, true God from true God, begotten, not made, one in Being with the Father. Through him

all things were made. For us men and our salvation he came down from heaven: by the power of the Holy Spirit he was born of the Virgin Mary, and became a man. For our sake he was crucified under Pontius Pilate; he suffered, died, and was buried. On the third day he rose again in fulfillment of the Scriptures; he ascended into heaven and is seated at the right hand of the Father. He will come again in glory to judge the living and the dead, and his kingdom will have no end.

We believe in the Holy Spirit, the Lord, the giver of life, who proceeds from the Father and the Son. With the Father and the Son he is worshipped and glorified. He has spoken through the Prophets.

We believe in one holy catholic and apostolic Church. We acknowledge one baptism for the forgiveness of sins. We look for the resurrection of the dead, and the life of the world to come. Amen.

Over the centuries, important points arose that distinguished Roman Catholicism doctrinally from other Christian faiths. Many of these concepts dated back to the first century, but most of them were not fully actualized by the time of the Council of Nicaea. The most important of these include the following:

The Mass

The Mass is also referred to as the Eucharist, Celebration of the Liturgy, or Lord's Supper. This is the central ritual of the Catholic Church. The exact form of the Mass has mutated considerably over the years, but its centerpiece is the re-enactment of the Last Supper of Christ, in which Jesus, according to Catholic belief, transformed bread and wine into his body and blood, which he then fed to his apostles. The Council of Trent reaffirmed the traditional teaching that the Mass is the unbloody renewal, or rather representation, of the Sacrifice of Calvary upon the altar—not that Christ is sacrificed again at each Mass, but that Christ's sacrifice on the cross is made present at every Mass.

The Papacy

The pope, also referred to as the Vicar of Christ and Bishop of Rome, is the leader of the Catholic

Church. The position traces its lineage in an unbroken succession (called the "apostolic succession") from St. Peter, who is believed to have been the first bishop of Rome. Catholics view the teachings of the pope to be infallible. According to the First Vatican Council (1870–1871) and as reaffirmed at Vatican II (1963–1965), the pope's teachings are infallible when speaking *ex cathedra* on issues of faith and morals. The Latin phrase *ex cathedra*, meaning "from the chair," refers to an authoritative teaching issued by the pope in his official capacity.

The Sacraments

Derived from the Latin word sacramentum ("a sign of the sacred"), the seven sacraments Catholics receive are ceremonies that point to what is sacred, significant, and important to believers. There are three categories of sacraments: those of **initiation** (Baptism, Confirmation, and the Eucharist), those of **healing** (Reconciliation and Anointing of the Sick), and those at the service of the **community** (Holy Orders and Matrimony). Traditional Catholic theology holds that sacraments are commanded by God and are channels of God's Grace to the recipient/believer.

Essential to the validity of the sacraments are:

(1) The right **matter** (bread and wine for the Eucharist, water for Baptism, etc.);

(2) The right **form** (words or signs which are necessary to confect the sacrament, for example, "this is my body" at the Eucharist or "I baptize thee in the name of the Father and of the Son and of the Holy Spirit" at Baptism); and

(3) The right **intention** (that the priest or minister must have the intention to do what the church does and adults must have willful intention).

Catholics receive **seven sacraments:**

1. Sacrament of Reconciliation, also referred to as **Confession** or the **Sacrament of Penance.** According to Catholic doctrine, priests are permitted to forgive the sins of Catholics who go to a priest and confess their sins with genuine repentance in order to restore their relationship to God and to receive the

In this photograph, taken on February 2, 2003, chaplain Bill Devine gives U.S. Marine corporal Joseph Duarte a communion wafer during Catholic Mass at the Camp Coyote Chapel in Kuwait. According to Paul's account of the Last Supper (I Corinthians 11:23–25), Jesus distributed bread (unleavened, for it was Passover) and wine to his disciples. Thus, eating the wafer of communion and drinking the wine allows Catholics to palpably participate in the Last Supper. Traditionally, the communion wafer should be deposited by the priest on the tongue of the one receiving it, but health concerns have allowed placement of the wafer on the outstretched palms of the worshipper (as above). For the same reason, some Catholics allow the wine to be replaced with mustum, a minimally fermented grape juice.

fullness of God's grace and salvation. Catholics believe that no priest, as an individual man, has power to forgive sins. This power belongs to God alone; however, God can and does exercise it through the Catholic priesthood. As such the priest is acting *in persona Christi*, or in the person of Christ. Although presumably based on a line from the New Testament attributed to Jesus, the practice of individual confession as it is understood in the modern world appears to be much more recent, perhaps originating in the seventh or eighth century and formally codified in the fifteenth century at the Council of Trent.

2–4. Initiation, which consists of three sacraments:

(i) Baptism. The first and basic sacrament of Christian initiation. It is administered by immersing the recipient in water or by pouring (not just sprinkling) water on the person's head "in the name of the Father and of the Son and of the Holy Spirit" (Matthew 28:19).

(ii) Eucharist. The second sacrament of Christian initiation by which Catholics partake of the body and blood of Jesus Christ. The first of these two aspects of the sacrament is called Holy Communion. Participation in the Eucharistic celebration is considered so important that it's viewed as obligatory on every Sunday and holy day of obligation, and is recommended on other days. Catholics believe that during this reenactment, a Catholic priest literally transforms bread and wine into the body and blood of Christ, a process referred to as "transubstantiation." Through transubstantiation, the wheaten (meaning, glutenated) bread and wine are in reality, not merely symbolically, converted into Christ's body and blood, so that his body and blood, together with his soul and divinity, and, therefore, the whole Christ, is truly and substantially contained in the sacrament of the Eucharist.

(iii) Confirmation. The third sacrament of Christian initiation. Like baptism, confirmation may be received only once, and the recipient must be in a state of grace (meaning free from any known unconfessed mortal sin) in order to receive its effects. Through the sacrament the grace given in baptism is "strengthened and deepened." The sacrament is customarily conferred only to persons old enough to understand its significance, and the originating minister is a bishop.

5. Anointing of the Sick. Administered only by a priest (bishop or presbyter), this sacrament is given to a person who is in "danger by reason of illness or old age" (Canon 1004, Code of Canon Law). This sacrament may be performed more than once if a new illness or a renewal or worsening of an original illness makes such action necessary. The rite consists of a priest anointing the ill person's forehead and hands with oil, which is intended to give grace, spiritual aid, and strength.

6. Holy Orders. Considered among three sacraments that make an indelible mark (a sacramental character) on the recipient's soul (the other two are baptism and confirmation), ordination is the sacramental act of integrating a man into the order of deacons, presbyters (priests), or bishops. It is typically in the last year of seminary training that a man will be ordained to the diaconate. Deacons are licensed to

preach sermons, to perform baptisms, and to witness marriages, but to perform no other sacraments. They may assist at the Eucharist or the Mass, but are not the ministers of the Eucharist. After six months or more as a transitional deacon a man will be ordained to the priesthood. Priests are able to preach and perform baptisms, witness marriages, hear confessions and give absolutions, anoint the sick, and celebrate the Eucharist or the Mass. The Catholic Church, in accordance with theological tradition, and the explicit clarification of the issue found in the encyclical letter *Ordinatio Sacerdotalis* (1994) written by Pope John Paul II, teaches that it has no authority to ordain women, and thus female priests are not possible.

7. Marriage. This sacrament creates a vinculum, an indissoluble union, between the two participants, created by human contract and ratified by divine grace. Therefore, divorce is not possible. This bond can only be broken on various specific grounds that it never happened in the first place, i.e., by annulment. The nature of the covenant requires that each member of the couple be free to marry, that they willingly and knowingly enter into a valid marriage contract, and that they validly execute the performance of the contract. Catholic theology holds that a valid marriage contract can only be formed between one man and one woman.

B. Basic Beliefs of Roman Catholicism

The beliefs of the Roman Catholic Church are contained in a document known as the *Catechism of the Catholic Church*, first published in its entirety in 1992, and appearing in English (as a *Compendium of the Catechism of the Catholic Church*) first in 2006—though individual beliefs, principles, and teachings have been discussed and analyzed for many centuries.

Following are some of the elements of the *Catechism of the Catholic Church* with comments regarding their meaning and place in the structure of

Roman Catholic Theology. The full English text of the *Catechism of the Catholic Church* is available (downloadable) online at:

www.usccb.org/catechism/text/index.htm.

THE TEN COMMANDMENTS

1. I am the Lord your God; you shall not have strange gods before me.
2. You shall not take the name of the Lord your God in vain.
3. Remember to keep holy the Lord's Day.
4. Honor your father and your mother.
5. You shall not kill.
6. You shall not commit adultery.
7. You shall not steal.
8. You shall not bear false witness against your neighbor.
9. You shall not covet your neighbor's wife.
10. You shall not covet your neighbor's goods.

Some elements of the Old Testament (The Hebrew Scriptures) continue to have authority for Christians, such as the Ten Commandments (given by Moses to the Israelites, as described in Exodus 20 and Deuteronomy 5). In Matthew 19, Jesus (speaking to the Rich Young Man) exhorts the keeping of the Ten Commandments and sums them up by saying that "Love thy neighbor as thyself" is the essence of the Ten Commandments (Mt 19:16–19).

THE GREAT COMMANDMENTS

- You shall love the Lord your God with your whole heart, and with your whole soul, and with your whole mind.
- You shall love your neighbor as yourself.

Jesus urged his followers to go beyond the letter of the commandments to achieve a higher form of devotion, both toward God and toward one's fellow human beings. In Matthew 22 (35–40), above, the Two Great Commandments are summarized.

THE TRINITY

By the Blessed Trinity we mean one and the same God in three distinct Divine persons: the Father, the Son, and the Holy Spirit.

The doctrine of the Trinity has probably been one of the most difficult doctrines to explain and decipher in the Catechism; it is also the most central. In essence, it states that God, who is one and eternal, existed in three "persons"—the Father, the Son (incarnate as Jesus), and the Holy Spirit (Matthew 28:19). In some verses, the different aspects of the Trinity seem distinct (Luke 3:22–"And the Holy Ghost descended in a bodily shape as a dove, upon him."), and elsewhere unified (John 10:30–"I and the Father are one.") Above is the Catechism's statement of this tenet.

THE CARDINAL VIRTUES

Prudence, Fortitude, Temperance, and Justice.

The Church Fathers were very influenced by the Greek ideals of virtue and character, so there are several lists in Scripture of the "Cardinal Virtues," meaning those from which all others derive. Thomas Aquinas defines "prudence" as "right reason in action"; Paul tells the Philippians to do "all that is true, honorable, just, pure, lovely and gracious." (Phil 4:8). St. Gregory of Nyssa teaches that "the goal of a virtuous life is to become like God."

THE THEOLOGICAL VIRTUES

Faith, Hope, and Charity

The Theological Virtues are those directed to God and that emanate from God. Faith means "blind faith" ("Blessed are they who have not seen and yet have believed."–John 20:29). And of the three, "...the greatest of these is charity." (Corinthians 13:1–2). The four Cardinal Virtues can be developed by training and will; the Theological Virtues are gifts from God.

THE SEVEN CARDINAL SINS

Pride – Unrestrained appreciation of one's worth.
Greed – Immoderate desire for earthly goods.

Lust – Longing for impure pleasures.

Anger – Inordinate desire for revenge.

Gluttony – Unrestrained use of food and drink.

Envy – Sorrow over another's good fortune.

Sloth – Laxity in keeping the Faith and the practice of virtue, due to the effort involved.

Also called "Mortal," "Capital," and "Deadly" sins, these are the character flaws that lead to other sins. These are distinguished from "venal" sins, which can be forgiven through confession. Because intention plays so large a role in Catholic moral theory, the presence of these attitudes can render otherwise minor acts into great transgressions. These sins also prevent a person from performing acts of charity, and are thus contrary to the highest virtue espoused by the Gospels.

THE SEVEN GIFTS OF THE HOLY SPIRIT

Wisdom, Understanding, Counsel, Fortitude, Knowledge, Piety, Fear of the Lord.

The "gifts" are the seven human qualities that are bestowed by God on the righteous-blessed (Galatians 5:22–23). These qualities had already been enumerated by Isaiah and were seen as the tools the righteous individual needs in order to know what is the right and charitable thing to do.

THE FRUITS OF THE HOLY SPIRIT

Charity, Joy, Peace, Patience, Kindness, Goodness, Long-suffering, Humility, Fidelity, Modesty, Continence, and Chastity.

The book of Galatians, chapter 5, distinguishes between the "gifts" and the "fruits" that derive from the Holy Spirit: the former (see above) are tools of the righteous, but these qualities are in the nature of rewards—admirable character traits that come from a life of service, charity, and devotion. Both show a profound influence of the "architecture of human character" developed by Plato and the Hellenistic philosophers.

THE SEVEN SPIRITUAL WORKS OF MERCY

1. To counsel the doubtful.
2. To instruct the ignorant.
3. To admonish the sinner.
4. To comfort the sorrowful.
5. To forgive all injuries.
6. To bear wrongs patiently.
7. To pray for the living and the dead.

THE SEVEN CORPORAL WORKS OF MERCY

1. To feed the hungry.
2. To give drink to the thirsty.
3. To clothe the naked.
4. To shelter the homeless.
5. To visit the sick.
6. To visit the imprisoned.
7. To bury the dead.

The structure of moral righteousness continues in Matthew, directing all matters of virtue away from ritual and Temple and toward the care and welfare of one's fellow human beings. The exact number and content of the lists may vary slightly in Scripture; the reports in Matthew 5–7 and Luke 6 are of sermons delivered by Jesus and the list may well have been tailored for the specific occasion of the sermon.

THE LAST THINGS

Death, Judgment, Heaven, Hell

The resurrection of Jesus places him at the eternal meeting place of life and death, able to reach into both realms. His testimony of the eternal existence of the soul, its certain judgment and its eventual reward according to its actions in life—these are the blessed tidings of Jesus's resurrection.

THE EIGHT BEATITUDES

1. Blessed are the poor in spirit, for theirs is the kingdom of heaven.
2. Blessed are they who mourn, for they will be comforted.
3. Blessed are the meek, for they will inherit the land.
4. Blessed are they who hunger and thirst for justice, for they will be satisfied.

5. Blessed are the merciful, for they will be shown mercy.
6. Blessed are the clean of heart, for they will see God.
7. Blessed are the peacemakers, for they will be called children of God.
8. Blessed are they who are persecuted for the sake of justice, for theirs is the kingdom of heaven.

The passage from Matthew (5:3–10) presents a vision of a world in which the standing of a person before God is determined, not by wealth or power, but by righteousness and acts of love. The balance of the world that is built into Creation by God assures that acts of virtue will not go unrewarded; undeserved pain and suffering will not go unhealed. The Beatitudes are among the most oft-quoted and beloved passages of the Gospels.

The Six Laws of the Church

1. To assist at Mass on all Sundays and holy days.
2. To fast and abstain on the days appointed.
3. To confess our sins at least once a year.
4. To receive Holy Communion during Easter.
5. To contribute to the support of the Church.
6. To observe the laws of the Church on marriage.

C. Scripture and Sacred Literature

The New Testament

Numerous sacred books began circulating in the early centuries after Christ as many religious thinkers sought to tell the story of Jesus with a slightly different slant or purpose. Eventually, so many versions of the Christ story had infiltrated the public venue that authorities of each religious community felt it was necessary to rule upon which version contained the most authentic message of Scripture.

For a considerable period of time, the canon was somewhat flexible, varying from group to group in the early Christian Church. Irenaeus of Lyons insisted that only Matthew, Mark, Luke, and John could be used. The Catholic Church in Syria happily used a compilation of the four. In Rome, Church leaders used the same four Gospels, but they also included favored writings such as the Wisdom of Solomon.

The Roman Catholic Church ultimately decided that only books that had connections to the apostles and conformed to the emerging faith of the Church could be used. By the end of the fourth century, only twenty-seven books met these criteria: the four Gospels, the Acts of the Apostles, the Book of Revelation, thirteen letters attributed to Paul, and eight other letters attributed to various writers of Christ's period. These books in compilation are now known as the New Testament.

The Old Testament

The earliest versions of the Old Testament were written in Hebrew. However, as many Jews spoke Greek and wished to read the Scriptures in their own language, the sacred scrolls of the centuries preceding Christ were translated into Greek. The early Christian Church used the same Greek-language Scriptures as the Jews of the time (some of whom spoke no Hebrew), called the Septuagint, which consisted of the books of what is now the Old Testament, and the deuterocanonical or apocryphal books—that is, those books not available in Hebrew or not considered canonical by the Jews. Significant separate manuscript traditions in the canonic Hebrew Bible are represented in the Septuagint translation's variants from the Masoretic text that was established through the Masoretes' scholarly collation of varying manuscripts, and in the independent manuscript traditions that are represented by the Dead Sea Scrolls. Additional, otherwise unrecorded texts for Genesis and the early chapters of Exodus lie behind the Book of Jubilees. These, and the Dead Sea Scrolls themselves, emphasize that even canonic Hebrew texts did not possess any single hard and fast authorized manuscript tradition in the first centuries BCE.

The Modern Bible

New Testament Greek and Latin texts presented enough significant differences that a manuscript tradition arose of presenting diglot texts, with Greek and Latin on facing pages. By about 90 CE, the Jewish Canon of Scripture had reached the last stages of finalization. Nevertheless, Greek-language scriptures, including all books of the Septuagint as well as all of the Greek New Testament, constituted "Holy Scripture" for early Christians.

In about the fourth century CE, as Greek was no longer used in the Western Empire, there was a need for translation of the Christian Scriptures into Latin, the tongue of the common people. The scholar Jerome undertook this task. Using the best texts he could find (including Hebrew when available), he produced the so-called Vulgate Bible. Jerome also consulted the deuterocanonical Old Testament.

Catholics and Protestants now accept the same twenty-seven inspired books as making up the New Testament. But significant differences emerge when we turn to the Old Testament. The exact number of books accepted as inspired Scripture for Catholics was not decided until the Council of Trent in 1546. The Council accepted forty-six Old Testament books. The leaders of the Protestant Reformation, on the other hand, rejected some books agreed upon at Trent. The seven disputed books are: Tobit, Judith, Wisdom, Sirach, Baruch, and 1 and 2 Maccabees. There are also some sections of Esther and Daniel not considered inspired Scriptures by Protestants. Protestants and Catholics call these disputed books "Apocryphal." The Douay-Rheims English translation of the books was approved in 1635, and used by Catholics until the mid-twentieth century.

D. Secondary Sources

Theologians, Artists, and Writers

St. Thomas Aquinas (1225–1274)

Recognized as one of the greatest thinkers of the Catholic Church, as well as one of its thirty-three Doctors, Aquinas was an Italian Catholic philosopher and theologian in the scholastic tradition. He is the most famous classical proponent of natural theology. He gave birth to the Thomistic school of philosophy, which was long adopted as the primary philosophical approach of the Catholic Church.

The thirteenth century was a critical period in Christian thought, torn between the claims of the Averroists and Augustinians. Saint Thomas opposed both schools—the Averroists, led by Siger de Brabant, who would separate faith and truth absolutely; and the Augustinians, who would make truth a matter of faith. He held that reason and faith constitute two harmonious realms in which the truths of faith complement those of reason; both are gifts of God, but reason has autonomy of its own. Thus, he vindicated Aristotle against those who saw him as the inspiration of Averroës and heresy.

Central to Saint Thomas's philosophy is the idea of God as creator *ex nihilo* (out of nothing). Within Aquinas's framework, God is the cause of there being anything apart from himself. Aquinas's conviction that the existence of God can be discovered by reason is shown by his proofs of the existence of God. His metaphysics relies on the Aristotelian concepts of potency and action, matter and form, being and essence.

The *Summa Theologica,* a scientifically arranged exposition of theology and a summary of Christian philosophy, is Aquinas's most notable work. Aquinas opens his masterwork with five arguments for the existence of God. These Five Ways, or *Quinque Viae,* are considered some of the best known and most influential theistic proofs formulated.

St. Augustine of Hippo (354–430)

Considered by theologians to be one of the founders of Western theology, Augustine has had highly significant influence on Christian thought. His early discovery of Cicero's Hortensius inspired his lifelong love of philosophy. He later became familiar with Plato's thought through reading the works of Plotinus. Influenced by Plato, he adopted a philosophy that saw absolute good as the center of reality, transcending thought and the material world. After traveling to Rome and then Milan, where he gained a teaching position in the university and fell under the influence of Bishop Ambrose, he underwent a conversion experience and was baptized in 387. He returned to his birthplace in Africa and in 396 was consecrated bishop of Hippo. As bishop, Augustine championed Catholic doctrine, opposing the Donatists, a sect that was in schism from the main body of the church, and the followers of Pelaginism, whom Augustine considered heretics.

A prolific writer (five million words of his books, letters and sermons survive to this day), Augustine was a deft promoter of his church in difficult political times. As Christianity spread and its critics began to emerge, Augustine was prompted to write *The City of God*. Both a philosophy of history and a critique of Greco-Roman culture, *The City of God* deals with Christianity's relationship with competing religions and philosophies, and to the Roman government with which it was increasingly intertwined. The book presents human history as conflicted between what Augustine calls the City of God and the City of Man (a conflict that is destined to end in victory for the former). The two cities were not intended to represent any actual places, though Augustine clearly thought that the Christian Church was at the heart of the City of God.

He later wrote what is considered to be his definitive work, the devotional *Confessions*. Considered a classic of Western and Christian autobiography, it recounts (in thirteen volumes) Augustine's painful spiritual journey and gives thanks to the God who he believed redeemed him: "You made us for yourself and our hearts find no peace until they rest in you." While neither an autobiography nor a confession in a modern sense, it does contain elements of both. The conversion scenes offer a complex exposition of the forms of the spiritual and intellectual redemption that Augustine had experienced. In the end, for Augustine, there is only one story in the world (creation, fall, redemption) and only two players (God and human-

ity). He recounts the deeds of his youth in order to relate a moral tale of a fall into sin and rise to salvation.

For Augustine, God is invisible but ubiquitous; he allows humankind to stray and is inexorable in exacting justice but also boundless in mercy. Augustine's biblical commentaries and sermons pursue these themes in various ways. The most austere of his later years address what would later emerge as the Calvinist doctrines of double predestination (i.e., God elects those who will be saved and selects at the same time those who will be damned). But Augustine was not the most severe of moral judges. His Christianity has space for those who struggle imperfectly to better themselves, who rise and fall again. He opposed Donatism and Pelaginism for forwarding philosophies that held a perfectionist view of human life.

Flannery O'Connor (1925–1964)

Flannery O'Connor is considered one of America's greatest writers of fiction and one of the strongest apologists for Roman Catholicism in the twentieth century. O'Connor's work combined a disarming Catholic orthodoxy with a Hawthorne-like knowledge of the effect of sin on human relationships—both situated within the fundamentalist South. Few postmodern writers have written with as clear a vision of their audience as O'Connor did. For "the hard of hearing you shout, and for the almost-blind you draw large and startling figures," she said, alluding to the grotesque imagery she employed to communicate her Christian orthodoxy to readers no longer conversant with common Christian symbols.

Her work centers on the theme of redemption— the struggle for salvation through faith or grace. For O'Connor, grace is the fundamental core of Catholicism, involving God's efforts to awaken each human individual to an understanding of his or her fundamental condition.

William F. Buckley Jr. (1925–2008)

William Frank Buckley, Jr. has been called "the most important public intellectual in the United

States in the past half century. For an entire generation he was the preeminent voice of American conservatism and its first great ecumenical figure."

In 1955, Buckley founded the bi-weekly magazine *National Review,* a forum for conservative (generally Republican) news and commentary. From 1966–1999, he hosted 1,492 episodes of the television program, *Firing Line,* an American public affairs show in which Buckley interviewed a (usually) liberal political guest. Buckley was also a nationally syndicated newspaper columnist, and was known for his wit and erudition. His writings include the 1951 book *God and Man at Yale,* as well as fifty other books on current affairs, speaking, history, politics,

and sailing. Buckley's views most notably reflected a fusion of traditional American conservatism with economic libertarianism and anticommunism, an ideology that founded the platforms of Presidential candidate Barry Goldwater and President Ronald Reagan. Buckley was a practicing Catholic and frequently spoke and wrote about Roman Catholic issues.

In 1973, William F. Buckley, Jr., became a delegate to the United Nations General Assembly. This photograph of Buckley was taken in 1976.

Daniel Berrigan (1921–   )

Daniel Berrigan was born in Virginia, Minnesota, the son of a second-generation Irish-Catholic father. As a youth, Berrigan was highly attracted to the Catholic religion. Upon graduating high school in 1939, he joined the Jesuits, and in 1952 he was ordained to the priesthood. Berrigan served as the assistant director of Cornell United Religious Work (CURW) from 1966 to 1970, during which time he played an instrumental role in the national peace movement.

Berrigan is widely known for his radical protests of various United States government causes, such as

the Vietnam War, nuclear warfare, American intervention in Central America, the 1991 Gulf War, the Kosovo War, the United States invasion of Afghanistan, and the 2003 invasion of Iraq. In 1968, Berrigan manufactured homemade napalm and—with the help of eight other Catholics (the group became known as the Catonsville Nine)—used it to destroy 378 draft files in the parking lot of the Catonsville, Maryland draft board. Berrigan was arrested and sentenced to three years in prison, though he managed to avoid serving his sentence for a time by going into hiding. After the FBI finally apprehended him, Berrigan went to prison until 1972.

Berrigan's outlaw activities also include involvement with an organization known as the Plowshares Eight. In 1980, the group broke into the General Electric Nuclear Missile Facility in King of Prussia, Pennsylvania, where they damaged nuclear warhead nose cones and poured blood onto documents and files. Berrigan served another ten years in prison before he was released on probation in 1990.

Berrigan has authored several volumes of poetry as well as a play entitled *The Trial of the Catonsville Nine,* which, after a brief run on Broadway, was made into a movie. His life has also been the inspiration for the creative works of other writers, filmmakers, and musicians. He appears in the documentaries *In the Year of the Pig,* and *The Holy Outlaw,* as well as the films *The Mission,* and *In The King of Prussia.* Aside from his role as poet in residence at New York City's Fordham University, where he currently teaches, Berrigan is also a contributing editor of *Sojourners* Magazine.

Fulton Sheen (1895—1979)

Sheen's role in the Catholic Church began as an altar boy in the early twentieth century and culminated with beatification and subsequent canonization by the church on April 15, 2008. His legacy as television's first notable religious broadcaster lives on with reruns of *The Fulton Sheen Program.*

Born in El Paso, Illinois, Sheen studied at Saint Viator College in Illinois (since closed), Saint Paul

This photograph of Fulton J. Sheen, who was appointed an archbishop in 1969, was taken in 1952.

Seminary in Minnesota, and The Catholic University of America in Washington, D.C. He received ordination in 1919, then traveled to the Catholic University of Leuven in Belgium. While a student there, Sheen became the first American to win the Cardinal Mercier award for a philosophical treatise. He graduated in 1923 with a doctorate in philosophy.

Sheen used his degrees to teach at both Saint Edmund's College in Ware, England and The Catholic University of America. Although he was a well-liked professor, Sheen's potential as a great theologian was best realized through broadcasting. In 1930, he began a weekly radio broadcast called *The Catholic Hour*, which ultimately gained an audience of four million. One decade into the show's run, he turned to television, conducting the first religious service ever televised.

In 1951, Sheen was ordained a bishop. In that same year, he more fully turned his focus to television, hosting a weekly show called *Life Is Worth Living*, in which he lectured to a live audience on matters such as Communism and Stalin's regime—which he forcefully denounced. Sheen was awarded an Emmy for the show after only one year, holding his own against such ratings giants as Milton Berle and Frank Sinatra. *Life Is Worth Living* ran for six years and drew an audience of thirty million. In 1961, Sheen embarked on a new television venture, hosting the nationally syndicated *The Fulton Sheen Program*, which utilized a similar format to the previous show.

Aside from his use of the radio and television for theological expression, Sheen authored seventy-three books, including *God and Intelligence in Modern Philosophy*, *The Seven Last Words*, *Way to Happiness*, *Way to Inner Peace*, *Life of Christ*, and *Treasure in Clay: The Autobiography of Fulton J. Sheen*.

Jack Kerouac (1922–1969)

Born Jean-Louis Lebris de Kerouac, in Lowell, Massachusetts, to French-Canadian parents, "Jack" Kerouac is now known as one of the most prominent writers (and friends) of the artists included among the Beat Generation. Kerouac notably influenced such writers as Tom Robbins, Lester Bangs, Richard Brautigan, Johnny Knoxville, and Ken Kesey, as well as writers of the New Journalism. Kerouac's impact is also evident in the music of the Beatles, Ben Gibbard, Bob Dylan, Tom Waits, Simon and Garfunkel, Ulf Lundell, and Jim Morrison. Kerouac's best-known books are *On the Road*, *The Dharma Bums*, *Big Sur*, and *Visions of Cody*.

His arguably most famous book, *On the Road*, details the road-trip adventures of Kerouac and friend Neal Cassady across the United States. Kerouac had a difficult time selling the original manuscript—which was more detailed and explicit than the published version—as it included graphic descriptions of drug use and homosexual activity considered shocking at that time. The book is written in a confessional style and was completed in an uninterrupted three-week session at the typewriter, fueled by coffee and Benzedrine. Kerouac claimed that the writing was spontaneous, though one of his former professors contended that much of the book had been previously outlined in Kerouac's journals.

Upon release of *On the Road*, a *New York Times* review hailed Kerouac as a major American writer and the voice of a new generation. This new generation would be called the "Beat Generation," and Kerouac's friendships with Allen Ginsberg, William S. Burroughs, and Gregory Corso, among others, become notorious representations of it. Kerouac himself was deemed "the king of the beat generation," though he would never feel comfortable with this newfound celebrity. He once protested, "I'm not a beatnik; I'm a Catholic."

Kerouac's lifetime of heavy drinking took its toll when he died at the age of forty-seven as a result of internal bleeding caused by cirrhosis of the liver.

AMERICAN CATHOLIC LITERARY FIGURES

William Peter Blatty (1928–   )

Author of bestseller *The Exorcist* and Oscar-winning screenplay. Though presenting an unflattering picture, it ultimately promoted interest in the church.

Haywood Broun (1888–1939)

Celebrated journalist, sportswriter; founder of the Newspaper Guild.

F. Scott Fitzgerald (1896–1940)

Iconic Jazz Age novelist, author of *The Great Gatsby*, though not a devout Catholic.

Andrew Greeley (1928–   )

Prolific and outspoken Roman Catholic priest. Writer of fiction and nonfiction of many genres.

Tony Hillerman (1925–2008)

Author of over twenty novels (mostly mystery) set in the American Southwest and featuring Navajo characters.

Joyce Kilmer (1886–1918)

Journalist and poet; he is famous for the poem "Trees," which ends:

Poems are made by fools like me,
But only God can make a tree.

Russell Kirk (1918–1994)

Prolific writer on economics, history, and fiction—seen as founder of neoconservativism.

Dean Koontz (1945–   )

Author of many best-selling suspense thrillers.

Elmore Leonard (1925–   )

Jesuit-trained, author of over forty acclaimed mystery novels. *Get Shorty* made into a successful film.

John Lukacs (1924–   )

Hungarian-born historian; prolific conservative author; and challenger of Holocaust deniers.

Thomas Merton

(See chapter on **Buddhism** for Biography.)

Walter M. Miller (1923–1996)

On-again, off-again Catholic; famous for the sci-fi apocalyptic book *A Canticle for Leibowitz.*

Michael Novak (1933–   )

Outspoken conservative commentator on economic, political, and religious issues.

Walker Percy (1916–1990)

Acclaimed author of fiction and nonfiction tinged with Catholic overtones. Also was a physician.

Katherine Ann Porter (1890–1980)

Pulitzer Prize-winning author of *Ship of Fools.*

George Santayana (1863–1952)

Spanish-born American philosopher. Author of the oft-quoted aphorism, "Those who cannot remember the past are condemned to repeat it."

The Supreme Court: Of late, six Roman Catholics have been appointed to the U.S. Supreme Court: Chief Justice John Roberts (2005) and Associate Justices: Antonin Scalia (1986); Anthony Kennedy (1988); Clarence Thomas (1991); Samuel Alito (2006); and Sonia Sotomayor (2009).

III. Rites and Rituals

A. The Calendar

JANUARY

Solemnity of Mary, Mother of God – January 1.

Holy Day of Obligation to honor Mary, the Mother of God.

The Feast of the Holy Name Jesus – January 3.

A day to celebrate Jesus's' name.

The Epiphany/Feast of the Three Kings – first Sunday in January.

Commemorates the visit of the Magi, the three kings of the East, to Jesus upon his birth.

FEBRUARY

Presentation of the Lord – February 2.

Commemorates the presentation of Christ by Mary and Joseph to the Temple.

Ash Wednesday – first day of the Lenten season.

Catholics attend Mass during which ashes are placed on each person's forehead. Ashes are used to remind Catholics that upon death their bodies will turn to dust as their souls are returned to God.

MARCH THROUGH APRIL

Solemnity of the Annunciation of the Lord – March 25.

Celebrates the Archangel Gabriel's request of Mary that she be the mother of Jesus Christ.

Palm Sunday – Sunday before Easter Sunday.

The start of Holy Week. Commemorates Jesus's entry into Jerusalem. Palms are blessed and distributed to congregants. The palms recall the palm branches that were spread under the feet of Jesus as he entered the city.

APRIL THROUGH MAY

Holy Thursday (or Maundy Thursday) – Thursday before Easter Sunday.

Commemorates the institution of the holy Eucharist by Christ during the Last Supper, which took place the night before he was crucified. Only one Mass is celebrated in each church on this day.

Good Friday – Friday before Easter Sunday.

Marks the crucifixion of Jesus. Day of fasting. A full Mass is not celebrated.

Holy Saturday – Saturday before Easter Sunday.

Day for mourning the death of Jesus, yet anticipating his resurrection.

Easter Sunday.

Commemorates Jesus's rising from the dead, on third day after his crucifixion. End of Lenten season.

MAY THROUGH JUNE

The Ascension – forty days after Easter.

Holy Day of Obligation. Commemorates the ascent of Jesus into heaven.

Pentecost – fifty days after Easter.

Commemorates the Holy Spirit's descent upon the apostles fifty days after the resurrection of Jesus Christ.

AUGUST

Feast of the Transfiguration – August 6.

Commemoration of the occasion upon which Jesus Christ took his disciples Peter, James, and John up to Mount Tabor, where Moses and Elijah appeared and Jesus was transfigured, his face and clothes becoming white and shining as light.

Feast of the Assumption of the Blessed Mary – August 15.

Celebrates Mary's ascent into heaven.

SEPTEMBER

The Nativity of the Blessed Virgin – September 8.

Celebrates the birth of Mary.

Triumph of the Cross – September 14.

Celebrates the recovery of the Holy Cross from the Persians by Emperor Heralius and its return to Jerusalem in 629.

Feast Day of Saints Michael, Gabriel, and Raphael, The Archangels – September 29.

Feast honoring the three Archangels.

NOVEMBER

All Saints' Day – November 1.

   Holy Day of Obligation for the purpose of honoring all saints, especially those that do not have a feast day during the year.

All Souls' Day – November 2.

   Commemorates and honors the deceased.

DECEMBER

The Immaculate Conception – December 8.

   Holy Day of Obligation—day the Blessed Mother Mary was conceived without original sin.

Feast of Christ the King – last Sunday of the liturgical year

   Commemorates Jesus as King and ruler of world.

Christmas Day – December 25.

   Celebrates the birth of Jesus Christ.

Feast of the Holy Family – Sunday after Christmas.

   Celebrates Jesus, Mary, and Joseph as a family.

Feast of the Holy Innocents – December 28.

   Commemorates the massacre of the children by the command of King Herod in his attempt to kill the infant Jesus.

B. Worship and Liturgy

The celebration of the Eucharist varies depending on the day of the Mass, the liturgical season, the specific occasion and the setting of the celebration. The order of the Mass illustrates the variables in the celebration of the Eucharist in the Catholic Church.

Outline of Opening Rites

• Procession (optional on weekdays; to be accompanied by music on Sundays and Solemnities)

• Penitential Rite (replaced by Sprinkling Rite during Easter)

• Gloria (sung on Sundays and Solemnities and during Easter; omitted during Lent and on weekdays)

• Opening Prayer (text varies for the occasion)

Outline of Liturgy of the Word

• First Reading (typically from the Old Testament, may be from the New Testament on certain Sundays and Solemnities)

• Psalm (text varies daily by season and occasion)

• Second Reading (Sundays and Solemnities only, typically from a New Testament letter)

• Gospel Acclamation (text includes the "Alleluia" antiphon, except during Lent. Typically sung, it may be recited on weekdays)

• Gospel Reading (text varies by day and season)

• Homily (may be omitted on weekdays)

• Profession of Faith (Nicene Creed is recited in unison by the congregation; Sundays and Solemnities only)

• General Intercessions (always)

Outline of Liturgy of the Eucharist

• Procession with the Gifts (may be omitted on weekdays)

• Preparation of the Gifts (always)

• Preface (text varies by day and season)

• Eucharistic Prayer (text has only minor additions for specific occasions such as weddings and funerals)

• Distribution of Communion (offered under one or both species—the body alone or the body and the precious blood, depending on country and occasion)

Outline of Closing and Sending Rites

• Prayer after Communion (text varies on the day and season)

• Final Blessing (simple on most Sundays and Weekdays, Solemn during Advent, Christmas, Lent, and Easter seasons and on certain Solemnities)

   Following are these rites in detail.

Opening Rites

After an entrance hymn or the recitation of an antiphon, Mass begins with all participants making the sign of the cross (the fingertips of the right hand touch in sequence the forehead, breast, left shoulder, and right shoulder), while the priest says the Trinitarian formula, "In the name of the Father, and of the Son, and of the Holy Spirit," to which the congregation responds, "Amen."

The priest then invites those present to take part in the Act of Penitence, of which the Missal proposes three forms, the first of which is the Confiteor. This is concluded with the priest's prayer of absolution. On Sundays, especially in the Season of Easter, in place of the customary Act of Penitence, the blessing and sprinkling of water may take place.

After the Act of Penitence, the Kyrie is always begun, unless it has already been included as part of the Act of Penitence. Since it is a chant by which the faithful acclaim the Lord and implore his mercy, it is ordinarily done by all; that is, by the people and with the choir or cantor having a part in it.

The Gloria in Excelsis Deo is sung or spoken on Sundays outside the seasons of Advent and Lent, and on solemnities and feasts. It is also omitted for ordinary feast days of saints, weekdays, and Votive Masses.

At this point, the priest invites the people to pray. All, in concert with the priest, observe a brief silence so that they may be conscious of the fact that they are in God's presence and may formulate their petitions mentally. Then the priest says the prayer that is customarily known as the Collect.

The Liturgy of the Word

On Sundays and solemnities, three Scripture readings are given. On other days, there are two. If there are three readings, the first is from the Old Testament and the second is from the New Testament, reserving for the final reading a passage from one of the Gospels (except during the Easter season). The lector who proclaims the one or two readings that precede the Gospel reading begins each with the phrase, "A reading from . . ." and concludes the reading with, "This is the Word of the Lord." The congregation responds, "Thanks be to God."

The first reading is followed by a Responsorial Psalm (which is the congregation's response, in word or song, to the reading), a complete Psalm or a sizeable portion of one. A cantor, a choir, or a lector leads, and the congregation sings or recites a refrain. Next, before the Gospel reading, the congregation rises and sings the Alleluia or, in Lent, a less joyful acclamation, and remains standing during the Gospel procession (if there is one) and the reading of the Gospel. A member of the clergy reads the Gospel—never a layperson. Then the priest gives the liturgical greeting, "The Lord be with you," to which the people respond, "And also with you." The Gospel reading is then preceded by the phrase, "A reading from the Holy Gospel according to (Matthew, Mark, Luke, or John)," to which the congregation responds, "Glory to you, Lord." At the same time, all trace a small cross on forehead, lips, and breast.

At the conclusion of the Gospel reading, the priest or deacon proclaims: "This is the Gospel of the Lord" and the congregation responds, "Praise to you, Lord Jesus Christ." The congregation is then seated. A bishop, priest, or deacon may then give a homily, a sermon that draws upon an aspect of the readings or the liturgy of the day. The homily is obligatory on Sundays and Holy Days of Obligation. On Sundays and Solemnities, the congregation then recites or sings a creed. Traditionally the Nicene Creed is used at Mass, but since the promulgation of the 2002 edition of the Roman Missal, the Apostles' Creed may be used instead.

The Liturgy of the Word concludes with the General Intercessions or "Prayers of the Faithful." The priest makes a general introduction, then a deacon or layperson presents some intentions for prayer, to which the congregation responds with a very short prayer, "Lord hear our prayer," and finally the priest says a concluding prayer.

The Liturgy of the Eucharist

The Eucharistic Liturgy begins when bread and wine are brought to the altar. The unleavened wheat bread is placed on a paten, and the grape wine is poured into a chalice. A linen corporal is spread over the center of the altar. The priest places the bread and the wine on the corporal and says a silent prayer over each individually. If this rite is unaccompanied by singing, he may say these two prayers aloud, in which case the congregation responds each time, "Blessed be God forever." Then the priest washes his hands, to signify the need for purity on the part of those approaching the central part of Mass.

The congregation, which has been seated during this preparatory rite, rises, and the priest gives an exhortation to pray: "Pray, brothers and sisters, that our sacrifice may be acceptable to God, the almighty Father." The congregation responds, "May the Lord accept the sacrifice at your hands, for the praise and glory of his name, for our good, and the good of all his Church."

The Eucharistic Prayer may now begin with a dialogue between priest and people. This dialogue opens with the normal liturgical greeting, but in view of the special solemnity of the rite now beginning, the priest then exhorts the people, "Lift up your hearts." The people respond with, "We lift them up to the Lord." The priest then introduces the great theme of the Eucharist, a word originating in the Greek word for giving thanks: "Let us give thanks to the Lord, our God," he says. The congregation joins in this sentiment, saying, "It is right to give him thanks and praise." The priest continues with one of many Eucharistic Prayer prefaces, followed first by the Sanctus acclamation, "Holy, Holy, Holy Lord . . . "sung or recited, and then by the part of the Eucharistic Prayer that contains, among other elements, the narration of the central event of Christ's Last Supper, of which the Mass is a reenactment in fulfillment of Jesus's instruction to "Do this in memory of me." Since, according to Catholic faith, at the Words of Institution the bread and wine become the body and blood of Christ, it is the universal rule that the congregation should kneel at this point. In some countries, including the United States, the kneeling begins immediately after the Sanctus.

When this most solemn point of the Mass, referred to as the Consecration, has been concluded, the priest invites the people to proclaim the mystery of faith and the congregation joins in reciting an acclamation known as the Memorial Acclamation, of which the Roman Missal gives four forms:

- Christ has died, Christ is risen, Christ will come again.
- Dying you destroyed our death, rising you restored our life. Lord Jesus, come in glory.
- When we eat this bread and drink this cup, we proclaim your death, Lord Jesus, until you come in glory.
- Lord, by your cross and resurrection, you have set us free. You are the Savior of the World.

The Eucharistic Prayer concludes with a doxology, with the priest holding up the paten with the host and the deacon (if there is one), holding the chalice, and the singing or recitation of the Amen by the people.

The Communion Rite

The congregation recites or sings the Lord's Prayer (also called the Our Father). The priest introduces it with a short phrase and follows it up with the prayer: "Deliver us, Lord, from every evil, and grant us peace in our day. In your mercy keep us free from sin and protect us from all anxiety as we wait in joyful hope for the coming of our Savior, Jesus Christ." The people then add: "For the kingdom, the power, and the glory are yours, now and forever."

Next comes the rite, or sign, of peace. After praying, "Lord Jesus Christ, you said to your apostles, 'I leave you peace, my peace I give you.' Look not on our sins, but on the faith of your Church, and grant us the peace and unity of your kingdom where you live for ever and ever," the priest wishes the people the peace of Christ: "The peace of the Lord be with you always." The priest may then invite those present to offer each other the sign of peace. The form of the sign of peace varies according to local custom. A handshake is common in many countries, including the United States.

While the "Lamb of God" litany is sung or recited, the priest breaks the host and places a piece in the main chalice. If extraordinary ministers of Holy Communion are required, they may come forward at this time, but they are not allowed to go to the altar itself until after the priest has received Communion. The priest then presents the transubstantiated elements to the congregation, saying, "This is the Lamb of God who takes away the sin of the world. Happy are those who are called to his supper." Then all recite: "Lord, I am not worthy to receive you, but only say the word and I shall be healed." The priest then receives Communion and, with the help, if necessary, of extraordinary ministers, distributes Communion to the people, who generally approach in procession. The distributing minister says, "The body of Christ" for the consecrated bread or, "The blood of Christ" for the consecrated wine. The communicant responds, "Amen." Catholic Eucharistic theology points out that, because Christ is not now divided, whoever receives only the bread that has become his body also receives his blood, together with his soul and divinity.

While Communion is distributed, an appropriate song is recommended. If that is not possible, a short antiphon is recited before the distribution begins.

After the deacon or the priest cleanses the sacred vessels (chalice, paten, etc.), the priest concludes the Liturgy of the Eucharist with the Prayer after Communion, for which the people are invited to stand.

Concluding Rite

After the Prayer after Communion, announcements concerning news or events at the parish may be made. The priest then gives the usual liturgical greeting and imparts his blessing. The liturgy concludes with a dialogue between the priest and congregation. The deacon or the priest then dismisses the people. The congregation responds, "Thanks be to God."

C. Daily Life: Precepts and Restrictions

Dietary Restrictions

Roman Catholics observe several feast and fast days during the year. Few foods are associated with these feasts internationally, though Catholics in each country observe many food traditions.

Fasting and/or abstinence (meat is prohibited, but eggs, dairy products, and condiments with animal fat are permitted) may be practiced during select feast days during the year. In the United States, there are only two obligatory days of fast: Ash Wednesday and Good Friday. The Fridays of Lent are days of abstinence: those observing the practice may not eat meat. Pastoral teachings since 1966 have urged voluntary fasting during Lent and voluntary abstinence on the other Fridays of the year. The regulations concerning such activities do not apply when the ability to work or the health of a person would be negatively affected. Prior to 1966 in the United States, abstaining from meat was required on every Friday. Today, Catholics must avoid meat only on the Fridays of Lent, although some Catholics still practice the pre-1966 Friday meat restriction.

In addition to the feast-day fasts, Catholics must also observe the Eucharistic Fast, which involves taking nothing but water and medicines into the body for a period of time before receiving the Eucharist during the Mass. The ancient practice was to fast from midnight until Mass that day, but as Masses in the afternoon and evening became common, this was soon modified to fasting for three hours. Current law requires one hour of Eucharistic fast.

Precepts

• Attending Mass on Sundays and holy days of obligation is required of Catholics, and to not do so (without valid reason) is considered a sin.

• A practicing Catholic should participate in the Sacrament of Reconciliation at least once a year.

• The Eucharist offers forgiveness of sins. Many practicing Catholics take the Eucharist weekly and some even daily. It is prescribed that one take the Eucharist at least once during the Easter season.

D. Life Cycle Events

Birth

Baptism is the Catholic Church's sacrament of initiation. It is also a rite of purification—cleansing, the person from original sin through baptismal waters. During the ceremony, water is poured over the head of the baptized. The oath, "I baptize you in the name of the Father, and of the Son, and of the Holy Spirit" accompanies this blessing.

Roman Catholics believe baptism leads to salvation and, ultimately, entry into heaven. Therefore, one who knowingly rejects baptism has no hope of salvation. Three forms of baptism are acknowledged by the church: baptism by water refers to the traditional baptism where the individual is immersed in water, baptism of blood refers to unbaptized individuals who are martyred for the Faith, while baptism of desire refers to catechumens who die before they can be baptized. Each candidate for baptism must be sponsored by one or more baptized persons. Sponsors of adults and older children present their candidates and thereby signify their endorsement of the candidates and their intention to support them by prayer and example in their Christian life. Sponsors of infants, called godparents, present their candidates, make promises in their own names, and also take vows on behalf of their candidates.

Confirmation

Confirmation is the third sacrament of Christian initiation. Like baptism, confirmation may be received only once, and the recipient must be in a state of grace (meaning free from any known unconfessed mortal sin) in order to receive its effects. Through the sacrament the grace given in baptism is "strengthened and deepened." The sacrament is customarily conferred only to persons old enough to understand its significance, and the originating minister is a bishop. It is conferred by anointing with

chrism, oil into which balm has been mixed, together with a special prayer that refers to a gift of the Holy Spirit that marks the recipient as with a seal.

Nuptials

In Roman Catholicism, one does not need to be Catholic to be married in the Catholic Church. If at least one's future spouse is Catholic, one may have a Catholic wedding. Couples who wish their marriage to be recognized by the Catholic Church must attend Pre-Cana classes on marriage. (The name is derived from John 2:1–12: during the wedding feast at Cana in Galilee, Jesus performed the miracle of turning water into wine.) In the Pre-Cana class, married Catholic couples give presentations on various topics to educate and support the marriage candidates. A priest might discuss the importance of the fact that in Catholicism, marriage is a sacrament, or an outward sign of Christ's love.

The wedding ceremony consists of at least three biblical readings, the exchange of vows, the exchange of rings, the Prayer of the Faithful, the nuptial blessing, prayers, and appropriate music. A Roman Catholic Wedding can only be performed within church buildings. Outdoor weddings are not permitted. There are two types of service for a Roman Catholic wedding: a wedding ceremony without a Mass or a wedding ceremony with a Mass. Many practicing Catholics choose a Mass with the wedding to give an extra blessing to their marriage. A wedding ceremony with a Mass is approximately one hour in duration; a ceremony without a mass lasts approximately twenty minutes. A wedding without a mass does feature readings and hymns, but not the celebration of the Eucharist.

Death and Burial

Friends and family of the deceased gather the evening before the main funeral liturgy to pray and to keep watch during a night vigil. Prayers are said for the deceased and those dealing with the loss. This prayer service may take place at the funeral home or at the church.

A celebration of the Eucharist with the body present is the general process for a funeral liturgy. During the service, the community gathers with the family and friends of the deceased to give praise and thanks to God for Christ's victory over death, and to commend the deceased to God's mercy. Funeral Masses are not permitted in funeral homes.

Burial of the body, or the Rite of Committal, normally takes place at the cemetery, although the committal can be done at the end of the Funeral Mass. Care is taken to prepare the body of the deceased for burial as a reflection of the Roman Catholic belief in eternal life and the resurrection of the body. The body should be treated with great respect. The prayers and gestures of the funeral rites also affirm the Church's reverence for the body as a temple of the Holy Spirit. The body is to be interred in a grave or tomb in memory of Jesus, whose own body was placed in a tomb.

Cremation

The Catholic Church accepts the practice of cremation. In most cases cremation should take place following the funeral liturgy, as this rite should take place with the body present. This allows for the body to be honored by the community, and the bereaved are allowed proper time to mourn. In particular circumstances, it may be necessary for cremation to take place prior to the funeral. This liturgy may then be celebrated with the ashes present. The ashes are viewed as the body of the deceased in a changed form. They must be buried or entombed in a place reserved for the burial of the dead as soon after cremation as possible. The Roman Catholic Church does not deem it acceptable to put off this burial, to scatter ashes, or to keep them in the home.

E. Family Life

Husband and Wife

In Roman Catholicism, marriage is one of the seven sacraments. According to the *Catechism of the Catholic Church*, "spouses as ministers of Christ's grace mutually confer upon each other the sacrament of Matrimony by expressing their consent before the Church." Marriage forms the foundation of the family, which is the fundamental unit of the referring community (ordinarily the parish). The Roman Catholic Church views the Holy Family (Mary, the mother of Jesus, and Saint Joseph, his father) as the ideal familial unit.

The primary purpose of marriage is to fulfill a vocation in the nature of man and woman, for the procreation and education of children, and to stand as a symbol of the union between Christ and his church. Fertility and procreation are viewed as a gift and the ultimate goal and purpose of marriage. By giving life, spouses participate in God's fatherhood. Carnal union is morally legitimate only when the bearing of children is the ultimate goal of this aspect of the marital relationship.

Traditionally, sexual intercourse was termed the marriage debt. This refers to the idea that marriage is a contract where each party assumes total control of the other's body. In modern times, it is understood that both spouses intend, by accepting the sacrament of marriage, to fulfill the reproductive moral mandate at some point in their marriage, but not on the demand or whim of one spouse.

Intermarriage

As for marriage between a Catholic and a non-Catholic, (called "disparity of cult"), the Roman Catholic Church does not view this union as a sacrament, since canon law expressly defines the marriage as a covenant between baptized spouses. Still, a marriage between nonbaptized spouses, or a baptized and an unbaptized person, is legitimate when validly celebrated, but it is not encouraged.

Divorce

For Roman Catholics, Holy Matrimony is a sacrament and a binding contract. The man and the woman marry each other with the "church" (bishop or priest) standing as a witness to it. Hence, divorce is not an accepted dissolution of a marriage. The Roman

Catholic Church looks to the exhortation of Jesus on the issue in the Gospel of Mark: "At the beginning of creation God made them male and female: for this reason a man shall leave his father and mother and the two shall become as one. They are no longer two but one flesh. Therefore let no man separate what God has joined." However, a couple may obtain a religious annulment after obtaining a civil divorce, so that either may remarry, within the church or elsewhere, and have the second union recognized by the church.

IV. Denominations and Demographics

Catholicism in the United States has flourished since the colonial era. The Catholic Church in the United States is the largest Christian denomination in the nation, with 76.9 million people professing the faith in 2003, making it the third-largest Catholic population in the world after Brazil and Mexico. Approximately 26 percent of the American population is Catholic, making it four times the size of the next-largest denomination, the Southern Baptist Convention.

With over 19,000 parishes exist in 195 dioceses or archdioceses. As a result, the Roman Catholic Church has the third highest total number of churches in the U.S., behind Southern Baptists and Methodists. However, because the average parish is significantly larger than the average church from those denominations, there are about 2.5 times as many Catholics as Southern Baptists and almost five times as many as Methodists.

There are approximately 60 to 70 million people in the United States who were baptized as Catholics, or 26 percent of the U.S. population. As of 2002, a Pew Research poll found that roughly 24 percent of the adult U.S. population self-identifies as Catholic. Other estimates from recent years generally range around 20 percent to 28 percent. Catholics in the U.S. are about 6 percent of the church's total worldwide membership.

States in which Roman Catholicism is the Largest Denomination*

RANK	STATE	CATHOLIC POPULATION (%)
1	Rhode Island	52
2	Massachusetts	47
3	New Mexico	41
4	New Jersey	39
4	Vermont	39
6	New York	38
7	New Hampshire	35
8	California	34
8	Connecticut	34
10	Arizona	31
11	Illinois	30
12	Texas	29
12	Wisconsin	29
14	Nebraska	28
15	Pennsylvania	27
16	Florida	26
17	Maine	25
17	Minnesota	25
20	Colorado	24
20	Hawaii	24
20	Montana	24
20	Nevada	24
24	Iowa	23
24	Maryland	23
24	Michigan	23

* American Religious Identity Survey (ARIS) conducted in 2001, with a sample size of 50,000 Americans

V. Organization and Infrastructure

A. Hierarchy and Education

HIERARCHY

The Council of Trent defined that, besides the priesthood, there are other orders in the church, both major and minor, including priests, deacons, subdeacons, acolytes, exorcists, readers, and doorkeepers. The priesthood thus includes bishops, for a total of seven orders (deemed the number of perfection). In 1972, seven years after the Second Vatican Council, the minor orders were suppressed for simplicity under Pope Paul VI. Today, most of the Latin rite retains only the major orders—priest, deacon, and bishop.

Every baptized male can validly receive ordination. Though in former times there were several semi-clerical ranks of women in the church, they were not admitted to orders properly, and had no spiritual power. The first requisite for lawful ordination is a divine vocation, or "calling": the belief that God selects certain persons to be His special ministers, endowing them with the spiritual, mental, moral, and physical qualities required for the fitting discharge of their order, and inspiring them with a sincere desire to enter the ecclesiastical state for God's honor and their own sanctification.

It is important to note that, as proclaimed by Vatican II, even the laity are assigned a divine vocation as Christians: to live according to the Christian spirit that moves one to sanctify one's daily work; to aspire to the fullness of Christ in demonstrating perfect love and holiness of manner (as exemplified by Jesus); to make spiritual sacrifices to God; and to proclaim God's virtues and express gratitude for His guidance out of spiritual darkness. Every member of the Catholic Church is called to "reverence Jesus in his heart and by the spirit of prophecy give testimony of Jesus," for each person who is consecrated by baptism makes a direct commitment to apostolate (Christian ministry). Wrote Saint Josemaría in 1932, "The prejudice that ordinary faithful can do no more than limit themselves to assisting the clergy in ecclesiastical apostolates must be rejected. There is no reason why the apostolate of the laity always has to be simply a participation in the apostolate of the hierarchy: they have the duty of doing apostolate. And this is not because they receive a canonical mission, but because they are part of the Church. They carry out . . . this mission through their profession, trade, family, relations with colleagues, and friendships."

Ceremonies of Ordination

From the beginning, the diaconate, priesthood, and episcopate were conferred with special rites and ceremonies. Though over the course of time there has been considerable development and diversity in different parts of the church, the imposition of hands and prayer were always and universally employed and date from Apostolic times (Acts 6:6; 13:3; 1 Timothy 4:14; 2 Timothy 1:6).

For Catholics, it is typically in the last year of seminary training that a man will be ordained to the diaconate, called by Catholics in recent times the "transitional diaconate" to distinguish men bound for priesthood from those who have entered the "permanent diaconate" and do not intend to seek further ordination. Deacons, whether transitional or permanent, are licensed to preach sermons (under certain circumstances a permanent deacon may not receive faculties to preach), to perform baptisms, and to witness marriages, but to perform no other sacraments. They may assist at the Eucharist or the Mass, but are not the ministers of the Eucharist. Orthodox seminarians are typically tonsured as readers before entering seminary, and may later be made subdeacons or deacons; customs vary between seminaries and between Orthodox jurisdictions. After six months or more as a transitional deacon, a man will be ordained to the priesthood. Priests are able to preach, perform baptisms, witness marriages, hear confessions and give absolutions, anoint the sick, and celebrate the Eucharist or the Mass.

All candidates should present themselves in the church in clerical dress (in earlier times, candidates would shave the tops of their heads, a practice known as tonsure), carrying the vestments of the order to which they are to be raised, as well as lighted candles. They are all summoned by name, each candidate answering "Present" (or "Adsum"). When a general ordination takes place, the tonsure is given after the Introit or Kyrie, the minor orders after the Gloria, the subdiaconate after the Collect, the diaconate after the Epistle, and the priesthood after Alleluia and Tract. After the Tract of the Mass the archdeacon summons all who are to receive the priesthood. The candidates, vested in amice, alb, stole, and maniple, with folded chasuble on left arm and a candle in their right hand, go forward and kneel around the bishop. The latter inquires of the archdeacon, who is here the representative of the Church, whether the candidates are worthy to be admitted to the priesthood. The archdeacon answers in the affirmative and his testimony represents the testimony of fitness given in ancient times by the clergy and people. The bishop, then charging the congregation and insisting upon the reasons why "the Fathers decreed that the people also should be consulted," asks that, if anyone has anything to say to the prejudice of the candidates, he should come forward and state it.

The bishop then instructs and admonishes the candidates as to the duties of their new office. He kneels down in front of the altar; the *ordinandi* lay themselves prostrate on the carpet, and the Litany of the Saints is chanted or recited. On the conclusion of the Litany, all rise, the candidates come forward and

Catholic priests usually wear a white clerical collar (now plastic, once made of linen) under a "collaret" to simulate the garb of a monk. The one shown above left is worn by the Jesuit father Richard Scannell, a chaplain at Alcatraz federal penitentiary who counseled prisoners during a 1953 visit, as documented in this photograph by Margaret Bourke-White. Seminarians or high church officials will also wear a cassock (or soutane). Above right, Catholic nuns wear habits for modesty and to signify their consecration; each order has its distinctive design elements. This 1954 photograph shows a nun of the Order of the Daughters of the Most Holy Savior at Holy Redeemer College.

kneel in pairs before the bishop while he lays both hands on the head of each candidate in silence. The same is done by all priests who are present. While bishop and priests keep their right hands extended, the former alone recites a prayer, inviting all to pray to God for a blessing on the candidates. After this follows the Collect and then the bishop says the Preface, toward the end of which occurs the prayer, "Grant, we beseech Thee, etc." The bishop then with appropriate formulæ crosses the stole over the breast of each one and vests him with the chasuble. This is arranged to hang down in front but is folded behind. Afterward the bishop recites a prayer calling down God's blessing on the newly ordained. He then intones the Veni Creator, and while it is being sung by the choir he anoints the hands of each with the oil of catechumens.

Celibacy

The practice of clerical celibacy is theologically based. The church desires to imitate the life of Jesus with regard to chastity and the sacrifice of married life for the "sake of the Kingdom" and to follow the example of Jesus in being "married" to the church. Also important are the teachings of Saint Paul that chastity is a superior state of life, and his desire expressed in I Corinthians 7:7–8, "I would that all men were even as myself [celibate]—but every one has his proper gift from God; one after this manner, and another after that. But I say to the unmarried and the widows. It is good for them if they so continue, even as I."

The first pope, Saint Peter, as well as many subsequent popes, priests, and clergymen during the church's first three hundred years were in fact married men, and often fathers. The practice of married clergy fell out of favor around the time of the Council of Elvira and clerical celibacy was made law in the 800s.

Marriage

Married men may be ordained deacons, but may not be ordained priests or bishops, nor may one marry after ordination. Since the Second Vatican Council, exceptions may be allowed for married Protestant priests or ministers who convert to Catholicism and wish to become priests in the Catholic Church, provided their wives consent. In select instances, laicized Catholic priests are allowed to marry by special dispensation. Additionally, dispensations can be granted for deacons whose wives have died to marry a second time.

Monks

A monk is a member of a religious order who leads a life of prayerful contemplation within the cloistered confines of a monastery, abbey, or priory. Western monasticism was founded by Saint Benedict of Nursia, who established the first monastic community according to what is now called the "Rule of Saint Benedict": the community's members must take vows of obedience, conversion of life, and stability. These observances developed into today's solemn vows of obedience, poverty, and chastity. Taking such vows implies that a monk will practice obedience to the Catholic Church, possess only those items allowed him by his superior, and sanctify the love between man and woman by abstaining from marriage and sex.

A man who wishes to become a monk will first test this desire through a probationary period, during which time he resides at a monastery as a postulant. Postulants are not bound by vows, and may leave the monastery at any time. If the postulant feels called to become a monk and the monastic community agrees, he will become a novice for a period of six months to one year, during which time he may take temporary solemn vows which may be annually renewed. Upon a final decision to commit to monkhood, a novice will take permanent vows.

Most religious orders of monks follow a day-to-day routine that involves prayerful recitation of the Liturgy of the Hours (or the Divine Office), a celebration of Conventual Mass, divine reading and manual labor. Monks cultivate and prepare their own food, dine communally in a refectory, live in austere

rooms known as cells, wear a simple uniform of habit, cloak, and shoes, and refrain from unnecessary talking—often observing periods of silence or even extensive vows of silence.

Some monks are ordained into Holy Orders as priests or deacons. These are known as choir monks, and must daily recite the entire Liturgy of Hours in choir. Monks who are not ordained are known as lay brothers. Historically, lay brothers were those monks who could not read Latin, and therefore could not learn the Liturgy of Hours. Lay brothers of old were restricted to manual labor and recitation of shorter, easily memorizable prayers, such as the Our Father or Hail Mary. Such prayers might be repeated by lay brothers as frequently as 150 times a day. Since the Second Vatican Council, the Liturgy of the Hours has been printed and repeated in vernacular languages; therefore, the role of lay brothers is no longer especially distinct from that of choir monks.

The several orders of monks include all Benedictines as well as the Order of Saint Benedict and its later reforms (the Cistercians and the Trappists). The Carthusians are also a monastic order, though they do not follow the Rule of Saint Benedict.

Friars

Rather than live in cloistered seclusion like monks, friars lead a life in service to others. Because they are not part of a self-sufficient community, they must depend upon charitable donations to live. All orders of friars must gain papal approval to follow a mendicant lifestyle as recognized by the church.

There are four major orders of friars and several lesser orders. The four major orders are:

The **Carmelites** were founded ca. 1155 CE. Also known as the White Friars because of the white cloak worn over their brown habit, they began as contemplative monks, becoming mendicants in 1245.

In 1209, the **Franciscan** order was founded by Saint Francis of Assisi, and came to be known as the Grey Friars or Friars Minor.

The **Dominicans**, also called the Friar Preachers or Black Friars, because of their black mantles, were founded by Saint Dominic under the Rule of Saint Augustine. This order became mendicant in 1223.

The **Augustinians**, also known as the Hermits of St. Augustine or the Austin Friars base their rule upon the writing of Augustine of Hippo. The original Augustines were congregated from groups of hermits by Pope Alexander VI.

Lesser orders include:

- the Minims, established in 1474
- the Conventual Franciscans, established in 1517
- the Third Order Regular of St. Francis, established in 1521
- the Capuchins, established in 1525
- the Discalced Carmelites, established in 1568
- the Discalced Trinitarians, established in 1599
- the Order of Penance, established in 1781

Religious Sisters; Nuns

In Roman Catholicism, Religious Sister and "nun" are terms for an enclosed female monastic regular, equivalent in many ways to that of a male monk. In common parlance, the terms are often used interchangeably, but in the Roman Catholic Church, "nun" and "religious sister" have distinct meanings. Women belonging to orders like the Sisters of Charity or third order Franciscans or Dominicans are religious sisters, not nuns. Nuns and sisters are distinguished by the type of vows they take (solemn vow versus simple vow), and the focus of their good works. The religious community of a nun is referred to as a "religious order" while the religious community of a sister is referred to as an "institute" or "congregation."

In the Roman Catholic tradition, there are a number of different orders of religious sisters, each with its own charism, or special devotion. In general, when a person enters a convent, she has a trial period (Novitiate) that lasts a number of years. Upon completion of this period she may take her vows. In the various branches of the Benedictine tradition (Benedictines, Cistercians, and Trappists) sisters usually take formal vows of stability (that is, to remain a member of a single monastic community), obedience (to an abbess or prioress), and "conversion of life" (which includes poverty and chastity) while in other groups like the "Poor Clares" (a Franciscan order) and Dominicans, the three-fold vows of chastity, poverty, and obedience are professed.

Religious sisters observe "papal enclosure" rules and their monasteries typically have walls and grilles separating them from the outside world. The sisters rarely leave, though they may have visitors in specially-built parlors that allow them to meet with outsiders. They are usually self-sufficient, earning money by selling jams or candies or baked goods by mail order, or by making liturgical items (vestments, candles, bread for Holy Communion).

Historically, nuns wore the black religious habit and wide white collar often stereotyped in popular culture, with a wimple covering the head. Today's nuns usually wear contemporary clothing, though of subdued color and simple design. The wimple is still retained by some modern nuns.

They sometimes undertake contemplative ministries—that is, a monastery of nuns is often associated with prayer for some particular good: supporting the missions of another order by prayer (the Maryknoll order has both missionary sisters and cloistered nuns; and the sisters of Daughters of Saint Paul are supported in their media ministry by the nuns of Daughters of Divine Wisdom), prayer for a diocese, etc.

A religious sister who is elected to head her monastery is termed an abbess if the monastery is an abbey, a prioress if it is a priory, or more generically may be referred to as the mother superior. The distinction between abbey and priory has to do with the terms used by a particular order or by the level of independence of the monastery.

SEMINARIES

There are many Catholic seminaries in America. They are listed by state—further information can best be obtained on the websites listed:

California

Saint Anthony's Seminary, Santa Barbara (closed)
www.sasarchive.org

Saint John's Seminary, Camarillo
www.stjohnsem.edu

Saint Patrick Seminary & University, Menlo Park
www.stpatricksseminary.org

Colorado

Saint John Vianney College Seminary, Denver
www.vianney.net

Connecticut

Holy Apostles College and Seminary, Cronwell
www.holyapostles.edu

Saint John Fisher Seminary, Stamford
www.saintjohnfisher.org

District of Columbia

Dominican House of Studies
www.dhs.edu

National Seminary of the Catholic
University of America
www.theologicalcollege.org

Washington Theological Union
www.wtu.edu

Florida

Our Lady of Perpetual Help Retreat
and Spirituality Center, Venice
www.olph-retreat.org

Saint John Vianney College Seminary, Miami
www.sjvcs.edu

Saint Vincent de Paul Regional Seminary,
Boynton Beach
www.svdp.edu

Illinois

Archbishop Quigley Preparatory
Seminary, Chicago (closed)
www.quigley.org

Catholic Theological Union, Chicago
www.ctu.edu

Immaculate Heart of Mary Novitiate,

Missionary Oblates of Mary Immaculate, Godfrey
www.omiusa.org

Mundelein Seminary in University of
Saint Mary of the Lake, Chicago
www.usml.edu

Saint Joseph College Seminary, Chicago
www.stjoseph.luc.edu

Indiana

Moreau Seminary, University of Notre Dame
www.nd.edu

Saint Meinrad Archabbey and Seminary, St. Meinrad
www.saintmeinrad.edu

Iowa

Divine Word College Seminary, Epworth
www.dwci.edu

Louisiana

Josephite House of Studies, New Orleans
www.josephite.com

Maryland

Mount Saint Mary's College and Seminary,
Emmitsburg
www.msmary.edu

Saint Mary's Seminary and University, Baltimore
www.stmarys.edu

Massachusetts

Blessed John XXIII National Seminary, Weston
www.blessedjohnxxiii.edu

Saint John Seminary, Brighton
www.sjs.edu

Michigan

Sacred Heart Major Seminary, Detroit
www.aodonline.org/SHMS

Minnesota

Immaculate Heart of Mary Seminary, Winona
www.ihmseminary.org

Saint John Vianney College Seminary, Saint Paul
www.sjvcs.edu

Saint John's School of Theology and
Seminary, Collegeville
www.csbsju.edu/sot

Saint Paul Seminary/School of Divinity
at the University of St. Thomas, St. Paul
www.stthomas.edu/spssod/

Missouri

Conception Seminary College, Conception
www.conception.edu

Kenrick-Glennon Seminary, Archdiocese
of Saint Louis
www.kenrick.edu

Saint Dominic Priory, Order of Preachers,
Saint Louis (Aquinas Institute of Theology)
www.ai.edu

Nebraska

Saint Gregory the Great Seminary, Seward
www.stgregoryseminary.org

New Jersey

Immaculate Conception Seminary, School of
Theology, Seton Hall University, South Orange
www.shu.edu/academics/theology/

Saint Michael House of Formation, Ramsey
www.adornofathers.org/mission.htm

New York

Seminary of the Immaculate Conception,
Huntington
www.icseminary.edu

Wadhams Hall, Ogdensburg
www.wadhams.edu

North Dakota

Cardinal Muench Seminary, Fargo (closed)
www.cardinalmuench.org

Ohio

Pontifical College Josephinum, Columbus
www.pcj.edu

Saint Mary Seminary and Graduate School
of Theology, Cleveland
www.stmarysem.edu

Pennsylvania

Saint Charles Borromeo Seminary, Wynnewood
www.scs.edu

Texas

Moreau House, The Congregation of Holy Cross,
Austin
www.stedwards.edu/holycrosslegacy

Oblates School of Theology, San Antonio
www.ost.edu

The 1964 mural entitled The Word of Life *by the artist Millard Sheets, on the front of the Hesburgh Library at the University of Notre Dame in South Bend, Indiana, is popularly known as the Touchdown Jesus. It is clearly visible looming over the end zone of the school's football stadium.*

Saint Mary's Seminary at the University of Saint
Thomas, Houston
www.smseminary.com

Washington

Bishop White Seminary, Spokane
www.bishopwhiteseminary.com

Wisconsin

Sacred Heart School of Theology, Hales Corner
   www.shst.edu
Saint Francis Seminary, Saint Francis
   www.sfs.edu
Saint Lawrence Seminary, Mount Calvary
   www.stlawrence.edu

CATHOLIC COLLEGES AND UNIVERSITIES

The following is a sampling of the prominent Catholic undergraduate colleges and universities in America (with their website addresses). A complete listing and/or additional contact information may be found at www.catholiccollegesonline.org.

Boston College, Chestnut Hill, MA
   www.bc.edu
Catholic University of America, Washington, D.C.
   www.cua.edu
College of the Holy Cross, Worcester, MA
   www.holycross.edu
DePaul University, Chicago, IL
   www.depaul.edu
Duquesne University, Pittsburgh, PA
   www.duq.edu
Fordham University, Bronx, NY
   www.fordham.edu
Loyola College in Maryland, Baltimore, MA
   www.loyola.edu
Marymount University, Arlington, VA
   www.marymount.edu
Providence College, Providence, RI
   www.providence.edu
Sacred Heart University, Fairfield, CT
   www.sacredheart.edu
Seton Hall University, South Orange, NJ
   www.shu.edu
University of Notre Dame, Notre Dame, IN
   www.nd.edu
Villanova University, Villanova, PA
   www.villanova.edu

B. Shrines and Houses of Worship

The following are major churces of the Catholic faith.

Saint Patrick's Cathedral
460 Madison Avenue
New York, NY 10022
212-753-2261
www.saintpatrickscathedral.org

Visited by over 3 million people annually, Saint Patrick's Cathedral is the largest decorated Gothic-style Catholic cathedral in the United States and the seat of the Archbishop of New York.

Saint Patrick's Cathedral in New York City, designed by architect James Renwick, opened its doors in 1879.

Basilica of the National Shrine of the Immaculate Conception
400 Michigan Avenue NE
Washington, D.C. 20017-1566
202-526-8300   Fax: 202-526-8313
info@nationalshrine.com

The Basilica of the National Shrine of the Immaculate Conception is a prominent minor basilica in Washington, D.C., dedicated to the Blessed Virgin Mary. It is the largest church in the Western Hemisphere. The basilica is located on Michigan Avenue in the northeast quadrant of Washington on land donated by The Catholic University of America. The church opened in 1959, after thirty-nine years of construction. It is designated as a National Historic Landmark on the National Register of Historic Places.

Basilica of the National Shrine of the Assumption of the Virgin Mary

(The Baltimore Basilica)
409 Cathedral Street
Baltimore, MD 21201
410-727-3565   Fax: 410-539-0407

This photograph of the Basilica of the National Shrine of the Assumption of the Virgin Mary was taken in 2006, after an extensive renovation.

Also known as the Baltimore Basilica or Baltimore Cathedral, was the first Roman Catholic cathedral built in the United States, and the first metropolitan cathedral constructed in America after the adoption of the Constitution. It was constructed from 1806–1821 according to a design of America's first professionally trained architect and Thomas Jefferson's architect of the U.S. Capitol, Benjamin Henry Latrobe, and under the guidance of America's first bishop, John Carroll. Situated on a hill above Baltimore Harbor, this basilica is the location of the country's first archdiocese, from which two-thirds of United States catholic dioceses can trace their heritage. In 2006, the basilica emerged newly restored from a thirty-two-month, $34 million restoration project. The project included a total incorporation of modern systems throughout the building, while also restoring the interior to Latrobe's original design.

C. Governance and Authority

Derived from the Latin *jus canonicum*, canon law is the ecclesiastical law of the Roman Catholic Church. Catholic ecclesiastical law is a fully developed legal system, with all the necessary elements: courts, lawyers, judges, precedent, a fully articulated legal code, and principles of legal interpretation. The canon law concerns the constitution of the church, the relations between the church and other bodies, and matters of internal discipline.

The Decretum served as the definitive collection of canon law for several centuries. New compilations of papal laws and decisions were continually added to it. In 1500, the collection known as the *Corpus Juris Canonici* ("Corpus of Canon Law") was published in Paris. In 1917, a commission of cardinals officially promulgated the *Codex Juris Canonici*. In 1983 a revised Codex was issued to reflect the changes of the Second Vatican Council (1962–1965).

The degrees of education in canon law are the JCB (Juris Canonici Baccalaureatus, Bachelor of Canon Law, normally taken as a graduate degree), the JCL (Juris Canonici Licentiatus, Licentiate of Canon Law), and the JCD (Juris Canonici Doctor, Doctor of Canon Law). Because of its specialized nature, advanced degrees in civil law or theology are normal prerequisites for the study of canon law.

Courts in the Catholic Church tend to follow the Roman Law style of the continent of Europe, featuring collegiate panels of judges, a somewhat neutral presumption before verdict, and an investigative form of proceeding, called "inquisitorial," from the Latin *inquirere*, "to inquire." This is in contrast to the adversarial form of law found in the Common Law jurisdictions of British and American law.

D. Social Service Organizations

Catholic Charities USA
1731 King Street
Alexandria, VA 22314
703-549-1390   Fax: 703-549-1656
www.catholiccharitiesinfo.org
Founded in 1727 in New Orleans by the French Ursuline Sisters as an orphanage, Catholic Charities is now one of America's largest voluntary social service networks. Comprised of numerous independent, local Catholic Charities agencies and institutions across the nation, serving more than 7 million people annually, their community-based programs and services provide assistance regardless of religious, social, or economic background. Catholic Charities agencies provide a wide range of immediate services, including disaster relief and soup kitchens, as well as long-term services, such as family counseling.

Catholic Relief Services
209 West Fayette Street
Baltimore, MD 21201
410-625-2220   Fax: 410-685-1635
www.catholicreliefservices.org
The official international relief and development agency of the American Catholic community, Catholic Relief Services was founded in 1943 by the United States bishops. The agency provides assistance to 64 million people in ninety-nine countries and territories. Overseas work is done in partnership with local church agencies, non-governmental organizations and local governments.

Catholic Legal Immigration Network, Inc. (CLINIC)
415 Michigan Avenue, NE
Suite 150
Washington, D.C. 20017
202-635-2556   Fax: 202-635-2649
national@cliniclegal.org
www.cliniclegal.org
Established in 1988 by the U.S. Conference of Catholic Bishops, CLINIC provides a range of legal and nonlegal support services to indigent and low-income immigrants, principally through diocesan immigration programs. The network employs approximately 1,200 attorneys and paralegals that serve 400,000 low-income immigrants each year. CLINIC and its member agencies represent low-income immigrants without reference to their race, religion, or nationality.

Knights of Columbus
1 Columbus Plaza
New Haven, CT 06510
203-752-4270
www.kofc.org
Founded in 1882, the Knights of Columbus is the world's largest Catholic fraternal service organization. It is named in honor of Christopher Columbus and dedicated to the principles of Charity, Unity, Fraternity, and Patriotism. There are more than 1.7 million members in 14,000 councils, including nearly 200 on college campuses. Membership is limited to men over the age of eighteen who are "practical Catholics" (defined as one who is in "union with the Holy See and who practices the precepts of the Catholic Church").

Society of Saint Vincent de Paul
58 Progress Parkway
St. Louis, MO 63043
314-576-3993 Fax: 314-576-6755
usacouncil@svdpusa.org
www.svdpusa.org

Founded in France by Frédéric Ozanam in 1833, and established in the United States in 1845, the Society of Saint Vincent de Paul is a volunteer organization comprised of lay men and women, known as Vincentians, who offer person-to-person service to individuals in need. The society's purpose is to provide direct aid to those who suffer and to help individuals reduce and even eliminate the causes of their suffering. Society members use their own resources, not only sharing possessions but also visiting those in need directly. Members operate through grassroots-level organizations called "conferences." A conference may be based out of a church, community center, school, hospital, etc., and is composed of Catholic volunteers who dedicate their time and resources to help those in need in their community.

E. Media and Communication

America
106 West 56th Street
New York, NY 10019
212-581-4640   Fax: 212-399-3596
america@americamagazine.org
www.americamagazine.org

Founded in 1909, *America* is the only national Catholic weekly magazine in the United States. Published by the Society of Jesus, also known as the Jesuits, the magazine provides editorials and news on the Roman Catholic Church and moral and social issues, along with book and movie reviews. Because of its Jesuit origins, the perspective of *America* encompasses a moderate to liberal view on Catholicism.

Commonweal
475 Riverside Drive, Room 405
New York, NY 10115
212-662-4200   Fax: 212-662-4183
editors@commonwealmagazine.org
www.commonwealmagazine.org

Commonweal is America's oldest independent journal of opinion edited and managed by lay Catholics. Founded in 1924, it publishes editorials, essays, and reviews of media and books. While focusing on religious and ethical issues relevant to Catholics, the journal also includes significant discussion of political issues. Although *Commonweal* does not adhere to a strict ideology, its general point of view is liberal, reformist Roman Catholic.

Eternal Word Television Network (EWTN)
5817 Old Leeds Road
Irondale, AL 35210
205-271-2900
viewer@ewtn.com   www.ewtn.com

Eternal Word Television Network (EWTN) broadcasts Catholic religious programming via satellite radio, television, shortwave radio, and the Internet. Founded in 1981 by Mother Angelica and broadcasting from a monastery in Irondale, Alabama, EWTN transmits 24-hour programming to 118 million homes in 127 countries and 16 territories. Programming includes a talk show, a daily mass, youth programming and live coverage of Catholic world events. Programming is from a more traditional Roman Catholic perspective. EWTN is the largest religious media network in the world.

Ignatius Press
2515 McAllister Street
San Francisco, CA 94118
415-387-2324   Fax: 415-387-0896
info@ignatius.com
www.ignatius.com

Founded in 1978, Ignatius Press is among the largest publishers and distributor of Catholic books, magazines, videos, and music in the United States. As the primary publisher in the United States of Pope Benedict XVI, this house publishes material from an orthodox Catholic perspective, emphasizing the traditional tenets of the Catholic faith. Ignatius publishes the monthly magazine *Catholic World Report* and the journal *Homiletic & Pastoral Review*.

The National Catholic Register
432 Washington Avenue
North Haven, CT 06473
203-230-3800   Fax: 203-230-3838
editor@circlemedia.com
www.ncregister.com
Founded in 1927, *The National Catholic Register* is the oldest English-language Catholic newspaper in the United States and features news, editorials and popular culture reviews. Owned by the Legion of Christ, a Catholic religious congregation established in 1941 by Father Marcial Maciel; emphasizes a traditional Roman Catholic ideology.

National Catholic Reporter
The National Catholic Reporter Publishing Co.
115 East Armour Boulevard
Kansas City, MO 64111
816-531-0538   Fax: 816-968-2292
Founded in 1964, *National Catholic Reporter* is an independent weekly newspaper published by laymen and women, nuns and priests. NCR is considered one of the more progressive Roman Catholic periodicals in America, offering news and editorials on a variety of issues relevant to Catholic readers from a liberal Roman Catholic perspective.

FURTHER READING

One Faith, One Lord: A Study of Basic Catholic Belief
Barry, Rev. Msgr. John F.
Ticknor & Fields: 1994

A Concise History of the Catholic Church
Bokenkotter, Thomas
Doubleday: 2004

Roman Catholicism in America
Gillis, Chester
Columbia University Press: 1999

Mission to Paradise: The Story of Junipero Serra and the Missions of California
King, Kenneth
Society of California Pioneers: 1975

Catholic Christianity
Kreeft, Peter
Ignatius Press: 2001

The Catholic Tradition
Langan, Thomas
University of Missouri Press: 1988

The Roman Catholic Church (A History)
Norman, Edward
University of California Press: 2007

A People Adrift: The Crisis of the Roman Catholic Church in America
Steinfels, Peter
Simon & Schuster: 2003

Saints and Sinners: The American Catholic Experience Through Stories, Memoirs, Essays and Commentary
Tobin, Greg, ed.
Doubleday: 1999

How the Catholic Church Built Western Civilization
Woods Jr., Thomas
Regnery Publishing: 2005

FDR, The Vatican and the Roman Catholic Church in America, 1933–1945
Woolner, David
Macmillan: 2003

2 Eastern Orthodoxy

I. Roots and Early History

A. Introduction

CHRISTIANITY EMERGED ONTO THE HISTORICAL stage during the first century of the common era, mainly in the eastern portion of the Roman Empire, then under the influence of Hellenism and Greek culture. Christians were viewed by the Roman authorities of the day as a Jewish sect, though authorities noted that other Jewish-like groups, unlike this one, showed little inclination toward proselytization. Paul and the other disciples preached to a largely pagan population with varying degrees of success, but ultimately established centers in Jerusalem, Alexandria, Antioch, and eventually in the political centers of Rome and Constantinople.

The Christians remained a minority and were periodically persecuted until 313 CE, when Emperor Constantine the Great issued the Edict of Milan in the form of a letter to the Governor of Bithynia, in which Christians were not only offered religious toleration, but official protection, paving the way for Christianity's adoption as the Empire's official religion. From that time forward, the Byzantine emperor exerted continued influence (by deed or threat) over the church by, for example, convening ecumenical councils to resolve disputes involving doctrine or administration, and to develop statements of church dogma that would become official church doctrine. If necessary, emperors deposed patriarchs and even sided with the iconoclasts of the eighth and ninth centuries.

The period of the late Byzantine Empire represents the golden age of the Orthodox Christian culture. It continued to flourish even after the fall of Constantinople in 1453, first in Russia and later in Eastern Europe, the Slavic areas, the Balkans, and the Near East.

The word Pantocrator *can be translated from the Greek as "Ruler of All" or "Almighty," and icons with this name are common in Eastern Orthodox churches. This one, by an artist from Cefalù, Sicily, dates from 1150.*

The First and Second Councils of Nicaea (325 and 787, respectively) and several other ecumenical councils convened in this period and established definitive doctrine of the church, though not without dissension and division. Following the Council of Chalcedon (451), the Church in Egypt (the Patriarchate of which was in Alexandria) was divided over the issue of the divine and human natures of Jesus. Each group soon established its own patriarch (pope). Those that agreed with the Council's conclusions (known as Melkites, or the emperor's men, because Constantinople was the capital city of the emperors) are today known as the Greek Orthodox Patriarchate of Alexandria, led by Pope Theodoros II. Those who disagreed with the Council are today known as the Coptic Orthodox Patriarchate of Alexandria, led by Pope Shenouda III.

The Syrian church experienced a similar schism in the fourth century. The "Oriental Orthodox" refused to accept the decisions of the Council of Chalcedon, and are thus known as non-Chalcedonians" or anti-Chalcedonians. Oriental Orthodox were also referred to as "monophysites," though they prefer the term "miaphysite," which indicates their belief in the "joined" nature of Jesus. The Eastern Orthodox and Oriental Orthodox churches both believe they are the legitimate "communion" (community) and continuation of the church and that the other churches are founded on heretical beliefs. In recent decades, however, there has been some progress in effecting a reconciliation of the two bodies.

The Eastern Orthodox Church recognizes only seven of the many ecumenical councils convened:

• The First Council of Nicaea, convoked by the Roman Emperor Constantine in 325, rejected and condemned the view of Arius—that Jesus, the Son, is a created being inferior to God, the Father.

• The Second Ecumenical Council, held at Constantinople in 381, ratified the Nicene Creed and defended the equality of the Holy Spirit against those asserting him unequal to the other persons of the Trinity.

• The Third Ecumenical Council of Ephesus in 431, affirmed that Mary is the true "birthgiver" or "mother" of God—in support of Theotokos and contrary to the teachings of Nestorius.

• The Fourth Ecumenical Council of Chalcedon in 451, affirmed that Jesus is truly God and truly man, one person in two natures, without mixture or confusion of the two natures—contrary to Monophysite teaching.

• The Fifth Ecumenical Council, the second of Constantinople, in 553, interpreted the decrees of the Council of Chalcedon and elaborated on the relationship of the two natures of Jesus. The council also condemned the teachings of Origen on the pre-existence of the soul. (Orthodoxy has had conflicting views on whether the Fourth and Fifth Councils were binding, or, as most believe, merely advisory.)

• The Sixth Ecumenical Council, the third of Constantinople, in 680–681, declared that Christ has two wills, derived from his two natures, human and divine, contrary to the teachings of the Monothelites.

• The Seventh Ecumenical Council, called under the Empress Regent Irene in 787, is also known as the Second Council of Nicaea. It permitted the making and veneration of icons, but forbade the worship of icons and the making of three-dimensional statuary. It rejected the earlier council that had called itself the Seventh Ecumenical Council and nullified its authority. (That earlier council had been held under the iconoclast Emperor Constantine V in Constantinople and Hieria in 754, declaring the making of icons of Jesus or of the saints an error.)

Eastern Orthodoxy—today the second largest Christian community in the world—arose as a distinct branch of Christianity as a result of the "Great Schism" between the Greek Eastern Church and the Latin Western Church that occurred in the eleventh century. The split was not totally unexpected. For centuries, the two branches realized they had significant theological, liturgical, cultural, and political differences. Religiously, they differed widely on such issues as the use of images (icons); on the nature and origin of the Holy Spirit; and, in a more practical vein, the date on which Easter should be celebrated.

Doctrinal issues—like the filioque ("and from the Son") clause added to the Creed of 381, and the nature of the authority of the pope—were only exacerbated by the many cultural and linguistic differences that had evolved between the Latins and Greeks.

The final breach came in 1204, with the Latin conquest of Constantinople by the Fourth Crusade. The Eastern Church still views with rancor the sacking of the Church of Holy Wisdom. The Byzantines would recover Constantinople in 1261, and the empire would continue until its final conquest by the Ottomans in 1453.

While Egypt had been under Muslim control for some seven centuries, Orthodoxy had become very strong in the interim in Russia, acquiring an autocephalous status. ("Autocephalous" means self-governing, indicating an autonomy that still places the church within a church hierarchy, further explained below.) Moscow called itself the Third Rome and considered itself the cultural heir of Constantinople. While the Greek Orthodox Church was an oppressed minority under Ottoman rule, the church retained substantial autonomy. The ecumenical patriarch was considered the religious and administrative ruler of the entire "Greek Orthodox nation" under the Ottoman "Millet" system, which divided the non-Muslim religions into four governing sects.

Since virtually its beginnings, Greek Orthodoxy tended toward the philosophical, abstract, and mystical in its thinking, whereas the Latin West was more inclined toward the pragmatic and legalistic. (An old saying had it that "while the Greeks build metaphysical systems, the Romans build roads.")

Of course, the political source of the split dates back to the Emperor Constantine, who moved the capital of the Roman Empire from Rome to Constantinople. Upon his death, the empire would be divided between his two sons, one of whom ruled the western half of the empire from Rome, while the other ruled the eastern empire from Constantinople.

The tension between the two churches finally erupted in 1054, when Pope Leo IX excommunicated the patriarch of Constantinople, the leader of the Eastern Church. The patriarch responded by "anathematizing" (condemning) the pope—inalterably dividing the Christian church into West (Roman Catholic) and East (Greek Orthodox). When the West came to the aid of the East against the Turks at the onset of the Crusades later that century, some hoped for a reconciliation. But such hopes were dashed when Western crusaders sacked Constantinople during the Fourth Crusade (1200–1204), resulting in deeper hostility between the two.

The late twentieth century has seen several attempts at reconciliation. In 1964, the Second Vatican Council issued the following statement praising its Eastern Catholic counterparts:

"The Catholic Church values highly the institutions of the Eastern Churches, their liturgical rites, ecclesiastical traditions, and their ordering of Christian life. For in those churches, which are distinguished by their venerable antiquity, there is clearly evident the tradition which has come from the Apostles through the Fathers and which is part of the divinely revealed, undivided heritage of the Universal Church."

After nearly a thousand years, on December 7, 1965, Pope Paul VI and Patriarch Athenagoras officially removed the mutual excommunication of 1054. In 2004, Pope John Paul II extended a formal apology for the crusader sacking of Constantinople eight hundred years earlier, which Patriarch Bartholomew of Constantinople formally accepted.

B. Orthodoxy Comes to America

Though the first formal Orthodox Christian mission to the United States arrived in the late eighteenth century, seeds of Orthodox Christianity can be found earlier than that. Russian traders who settled in Alaska during the 1700s brought their religious beliefs with them; in 1740, a Divine Liturgy was celebrated on board a Russian ship off the

Alaskan coast. Greek laborers, imported to Florida in the mid-1700s by a British entrepreneur, formed what is today New Smyrna, Florida, in 1754. But the first formal Orthodox Christian Mission to America arrived on September 24, 1794, in Kodiak, Alaska. The mission—eight monks, two novices, and ten Alaskan natives who had been taken to Russia by Gregory Shelikov in 1786—discovered hundreds of natives on Kodiak Island who had been taught the rudiments of the Orthodox faith and had been baptized by laymen. Shelikov, a founder of what was later to be known as the Russian-American Company, had himself baptized about two hundred Aleuts on Kodiak Island. The 1794 mission was instrumental in converting many natives to Orthodox Christianity. A diocese was established with Saint Innocent of Alaska as the first bishop. The headquarters of this North American Diocese of the Russian Orthodox Church would be moved from Alaska to California in the late nineteenth century.

In 1798, Archimandrite Joasaph returned to Irkutsk, Siberia, and was consecrated as bishop of Kodiak, the first bishop for America on April 10, 1799. On his voyage back to the New World, however, he and his entourage, including Hieromonk Makary and Hierodeacon Stephan, both members of the original mission, died in a shipwreck somewhere between Unalaska and Kodiak Island. The mission, however, continued its work in North America in spite of this setback.

The Alaska Purchase

Alaska was sold by Russia to the American government in 1867, and though the Russian government continued to send aid to the territory, the seat of the diocese now became San Francisco, and an English-language mission was undertaken by the church. This mission encountered many obstacles, not the least of which was that it was operating in an English-speaking area that already had other established Christian churches.

In the late nineteenth century, the headquarters of the Orthodox Church in the United States moved again, this time to New York City. An important reason for this move was the sudden influx of many "Uniates"—Christians seeking a union between the Orthodox and Roman churches—to the Orthodox Church in the eastern United States. This movement was the result of a conflict between the politically powerful Roman Catholic archbishop of St. Paul, Minnesota, John Ireland, and Alexis Toth, an influential Ruthenian Catholic priest. Upon Archbishop Ireland's refusal to accept Father Toth's credentials as a priest, Father Toth returned to the Orthodox Church of his ancestors, bringing with him tens of thousands of other Uniate Catholics in North America to the Orthodox Church. Ireland is therefore sometimes referred to ironically as the "father of the Orthodox Church in America."

These Uniates joined large numbers of Greeks and other Orthodox Christians then immigrating to America into the existing North American diocese of the Russian Orthodox Church, placing all Orthodox Christians in North America under the "omophorion" (church authority and protection) of the patriarch of Moscow, through the Russian Church's North American diocese. The unity was more than just theoretical; in the absence of any other diocese on the continent, it was a firm reality. At the turn of the century, the diocese was headed by Bishop (and future Moscow patriarch) Tikhon, and Orthodox Christians of different ethnic backgrounds were ministered to by both Russian and non-Russian clergy. A Syro-Arab mission was established under the episcopal leadership of Saint Raphael of Brooklyn, the first Orthodox bishop consecrated in America.

The Russian Revolution

The Russian Revolution of 1917 meant the end of the Russian Orthodox mission and that Moscow could no longer be looked to for support or guidance. The effect was to splinter American Orthodoxy into many groups, all left to fend for themselves spiritually.

One effect of the Bolshevik Revolution was a flood of refugees from Russia to the United States,

Canada, and Europe. Among this throng were Orthodox lay people, deacons, priests, and bishops. In 1920, Patriarch Tikhon issued an emergency ukase (decree) that dioceses of the Church of Russia that had been cut off from contact with the Russian patriarchate should continue independently until a seat of church authority could be reestablished. The North American diocese of the Russian Orthodox Church (known as the Metropolia) thus continued to function autonomously.

The administrative chaos that resulted from the Russian Revolution forced many Orthodox churches in North America to turn to the churches in their respective homelands for pastoral service and church governance. In the period between the World Wars, the Metropolia worked closely alongside of an independent European synod later known as the Russian Orthodox Church Outside Russia (ROCOR), sometimes called the Russian Orthodox Church Abroad. The ROCOR moved its headquarters to North America after the Second World War and claimed jurisdiction over all parishes of Russian origin in North America. Eventually, however, their authority was not recognized and the two groups went their separate ways. The Metropolia, as a former diocese of the Russian Church, continued to look to Moscow as its highest church authority, though conditions in the communist regime in Russia made that very difficult. When communication with Moscow in the early 1960s resumed, and autocephaly was granted in 1970, the Metropolia became known as the Orthodox Church in America (OCA). However, not all Orthodox churches recognize this autocephalous status; for example, the ecumenical patriarch (under whom is the Greek Orthodox Archdiocese of America) and some other Orthodox churches have not officially accepted it. Yet the ecumenical patriarch and the other jurisdictions continue to work in communion with the OCA.

C. Important Dates and Landmarks

1741 Explorers Vitus Bering and Alexei Chirikov, who formally claimed Alaska and the Aleutian Islands, lead a group of missionaries to North America. This marks the first attempt to bring the Orthodox Faith to the Aleuts, the Athabascan Indians, the Tlingits, and the Eskimos—the natives of that region.

1768 Greek colony established in New Smyrna (near St. Augustine), Florida.

1794 A small Apostolic mission group comprised of eight monks, two novices, and ten Alaskan natives lands on Kodiak Island, Alaska, to find hundreds of baptized natives who were already well-versed in the rudiments of Orthodoxy. Archimandrite Joasaph Bolotov, as leader of the American Mission, would overcome great difficulties to establish the Orthodox Church in Kodiak, the Aleutian Islands, and mainland Alaska. Within three years of Joasaph's arrival, nearly all of the remaining natives who had yet to be baptized are converted.

1798 Archimandrite Joasaph Bolotov returns to Irkutsk in Siberia.

1799 Bolotov and his entourage drown on their return to Kodiak Island in 1799, when their ship, the *Phoenix*, is lost at sea. Tragedy reduces the American mission by half, but surviving members continue their work.

1812 Russian-American Company establishes Fort Ross in northern California.

July 29, 1824 John Veniaminov arrives on Unalaska Island, Alaska. He is ordained as Innocent Veniaminov, first Orthodox bishop in the New World, Dec. 15, 1840.

1828 Iakov Netsvetov ordained as first Native American Orthodox priest.

late 1830s At this point, Unalaska contains five active priests and five religious centers with more than 10,000 Orthodox Christians and eight schools.

Dec. 13, 1837 Death of Saint Herman of Alaska.

1863 Serbian, Bulgarian, Romanian, Greek, Russian, Syrian, and Albanian Orthodox immigrants arrive in America in greater numbers. Orthodox mission extended to Canada; missionary school founded in Minneapolis, Minnesota.

1864 First U.S. Orthodox parish formed in New Orleans.

1867 Alaska Purchase by U.S. (from Russia).

1891 Father Alexis Toth founds Saint Mary's parish in Minneapolis. Parishes formed in New York and Chicago following year.

1890s The first attempts to develop English liturgical text to be used in the church.

1898 Bishop Tikhon Bellavin begins his nine-year rule over the church in America, bringing mission work to a new stage of maturity. The American Mission becomes a full diocese for the first time, its presiding bishop wholly responsible for a church on continental North America.

1899 Bolotov consecrated bishop of Kodiak, making him the first American bishop. Many today consider him a saint.

1904 Raphael Hawaweeny is first Orthodox bishop ordained in America.

1905 Saint Nicholas Cathedral in New York becomes the center of the church, and the newly elevated Archbishop Tikhon is given two auxiliary bishops to help with his administration of the quickly expanding church in America.

Oct. 1917 Communist Revolution in Russia. Russian Archdiocese declares itself "temporarily self-governing" six years later.

1921 Archbishop Meletios Metaxakis (later patriarch) creates Greek Orthodox Archdiocese (Metropolia) of North and South America.

1924 National Origins Quota Act greatly increases Orthodox immigration.

1930 Athenagoras Spirou becomes Greek Orthodox archbishop of America.

1936 Metropolitan Antony Bashir becomes head of Antiochan Orthodox Archdiocese.

1944 Federated Orthodox Greek Catholic Primary Jurisdictions is formed.

1948 Archbishop Athenagoras becomes patriarch of Constantinople.

March 15, 1960 Standing Conference of Canonical Orthodox Bishops in the Americas (SCOBA) is organized.

1970 Father Herman is canonized as the first saint of the American Orthodox Church.

1970 The oldest of these missionary dioceses is granted ecclesiastical independence from her mother church, thereby becoming one of the fifteen autocephalous churches of the world, taking the name of the Orthodox Church in America (OCA).

1992 International Orthodox Christian Charities (IOCC) founded.

1999 Archbishop Demetrios Trakatellis becomes head of Greek Orthodox Archdiocese, replacing Archbishop Spyridon.

2003 Patriarch of Antioch grants self-rule to Antiochan Orthodox Archdiocese.

2006 Pope Benedict XVI and Patriarch Bartholomew meet in Contantinople and vow to work toward unification of the Eastern Orthodox and Roman Catholic Churches.

~

II. Tenets and Beliefs

A. Doctrines of Jesus and Mary

JESUS CHRIST

As is the case in all of Christianity, Jesus of Nazareth is the central figure of the faith. Much significant information regarding Jesus's life as a first-century teacher and prophet is derived from the Gospels of Matthew, Mark, Luke, and John in the Bible. Orthodox theology (as with other denominations of Christianity) focuses on specific aspects of the life story of Jesus and emphasizes specific elements of that ministry, without dismissing or belittling any other aspects of Jesus's career.

Orthodox Christians believe that Jesus Christ is God incarnate, being one of the three divine persons—Father, Son, and Holy Spirit—who make up the single substance of God. This tripartite view of God is called the Holy Trinity. In this respect, Jesus is both distinct and yet of the same being as God the Father and God the Holy Spirit. They believe Jesus is the Son of God, and also the Messiah ("the anointed one").

The Gospels provide details of Jesus's life: He was miraculously conceived, the son of Joseph's wife, Mary, and born in the Judean town of Bethlehem. The Gospel of Luke recounts how the angel Gabriel visited Mary and told her that, because she had been born without original sin, she was chosen to bear the Son of God.

Upon his baptism by John the Baptist, Jesus began his public ministry as a preacher, teacher, and healer. Following his baptism, according to the Gospel of Matthew, Jesus fasted in the desert for forty days and forty nights while Satan tempted him. In all, Jesus was tempted three times, and after rejecting each temptation, Jesus called his first disciples.

During his lifetime on this earth, the Gospels relate, Jesus performed various miracles, including healings, exorcisms, walking on water, turning water into wine at the wedding feast at Cana, and raising several people (such as Lazarus) from the dead.

Jesus showed a great interest in and often met with the outcasts of society and those the established religious (Pharisaic) elements of Judea considered sinners. When the Pharisees criticized Jesus for attending to sinners rather than to the righteous, Jesus replied, according to the Gospel of Matthew, that it was the sick who were in need of a physician, not the healthy.

Jesus's activities and teachings continued to evoke skepticism and hostility as he ministered to the people of Judea, particularly in the northern areas of Galilee. When Jesus and his followers came to Jerusalem for Passover, he was, according to the Gospel of Luke, greeted by the populace enthusiastically. Because he was a threat to the Romans, Roman soldiers arrested him while he was praying at the Garden of Gethsemane. According to Luke, Judas Iscariot, one of Jesus's apostles, identified Jesus to the guards by kissing him.

Jesus was tried by the Roman prefect Pontius Pilate on a charge of sedition for claiming to be

"King of the Jews." According to the Gospels, Pilate offered the crowd a choice of freeing either Jesus of Nazareth or a criminal named Barabbas. The crowd chose to have Barabbas freed and Jesus crucified. According to the Gospel of Matthew, Pilate then washed his hands to indicate that he himself was innocent of the decision. All four Gospels relate how Pilate then ordered Jesus to be crucified with a plaque placed atop the cross that read "Jesus of Nazareth, King of the Jews."

The four Gospels relate that Jesus died before late afternoon. According to Mark and Luke, Joseph of Arimathea took possession of Jesus's body and placed it in a tomb. Christians believe that Jesus rose from the dead three days after his crucifixion and that it is his resurrection that makes human salvation possible.

THEOTOKOS

The Virgin Mary, the mother of Jesus Christ, is the Theotokos (meaning "God-bearer" or "birth-giver to God"). She conceived by the power of the Holy Spirit, and was cared for by her earthly husband, Joseph, who took the child and his mother into his home as his own. One very strong tradition in the Orthodox Church holds that the birth of Jesus was also miraculous and left Mary's virginity intact as a sign; it is also the tradition of the church that Joseph and Mary did not have relations after the birth of Jesus. Mary is also called Panagia, the "All-Holy," an indication of her closeness to God by virtue of her obedience.

The title of Theotokos for the Virgin Mary was recognized by the Eastern Orthodox Church at the Third Ecumenical Council held at Ephesus in 431, though it had been in use for some time in the devotional and liturgical life of the church. The title's theological significance is to emphasize that as Mary's son, Jesus is fully God as well as fully human, and that Jesus's two natures (divine and human) were united in a single person of the Trinity. Another view presented at the council by Nestorius, then patriarch of Constantinople, was that Mary should be called Christotokos instead, meaning "birth-giver to Christ." The intent was to limit her role to being only the mother of the human part of Jesus's nature and not also of his divine nature.

Nestorius's view was rejected as heresy by the Council; it was seen as dividing Jesus into two distinct persons: one who was the son of Mary, and another, the divine nature, who was not. The Council affirmed that although Jesus has two natures, human and divine, these are eternally united in one personhood. And since Mary is the mother of God the Son, she is therefore duly entitled to be called Theotokos.

The Eastern Orthodox Church teaches that Mary is Aeiparthenos—"ever-virgin," that is, that she remained a virgin before, during, and eternally after the birth of Jesus Christ. This view that Mary is ever-virgin is meant as an affirmation of who Jesus is, and is a firm tradition of the Orthodox Christian Church found in much of its liturgy. One can also find references to and discussions of the ever-virginity of Mary in the writings of Peter of Alexandria, Epiphanius, Athanasius, Cyril of Alexandria, Leo, and John of Damascus, among others. Saint Ambrose of Milan (fourth century) writes: "The virgin did not seek the consolation of bearing another child." Another example is found in the Capitula II of the Second Council of Constantinople:

"If anyone shall not confess that the Word of God has two nativities, the one from all eternity of the Father, without time and without body; the other in these last days, coming down from heaven and being made flesh of the holy and glorious Mary, Mother of God and always a virgin, and born of her: let him be anathema."

B. Articles of Faith

The Trinity

God the Father. The root of the Holy Trinity. According to Orthodox belief, the Scriptures reveal the one God is three persons: Father, Son, and Holy

Spirit. From the Father, the Son is begotten, and it is from the Father that the Holy Spirit eternally proceeds.

Jesus Christ. The second person of the Holy Trinity is born of God the Father. He became man, and thus he is at once fully God and fully man. The prophets foretold his coming to Earth in the Old Testament.

Orthodox Christians regularly affirm their historic faith concerning Jesus by reciting the Nicene Creed, which in part says: "I believe . . . in one Lord Jesus Christ, the Son of God, the only begotten, begotten of the Father before all ages, Light of Light, true God of true God; begotten, not made; of one essence with the Father; by whom all things were made; who for us men and for our salvation came down from heaven, and was incarnate of the Holy Spirit and the Virgin Mary, and was made man; and was crucified also for us under Pontius Pilate, and suffered and was buried; and the third day he rose again according to the Scriptures; and ascended into heaven, and sits at the right hand of the Father; and he shall come again with glory to judge the living and the dead; whose kingdom shall have no end."

The Holy Spirit. The final person of the Holy Trinity is the Holy Spirit, which is one with God the Father. Orthodox Christians repeatedly confess, "And I believe in the Holy Spirit, the Lord, the Giver of life, who proceeds from the Father, who together with the Father and the Son is worshipped and glorified . . ." Eastern Orthodox Christians believe the biblical promise that the Holy Spirit is given through chrismation (anointing) at baptism.

Incarnation

Incarnation refers to Jesus Christ coming "in the flesh," as he assumed a complete human form and nature from the Virgin Mary. It is through his incarnation, and crucifixion, the Eastern Orthodox Church believes, that Jesus redeemed human nature.

The Eucharist

The Eucharist is the center of worship in the Orthodox Church. In the Eucharist, Eastern Orthodox adherents believe that they are partaking of Christ's body and blood, in an effort to attain Theosis—mystical union with God. (See page 92, under "Worship and Liturgy.")

Communion of Saints

According to Eastern Orthodoxy, when one dies, one remains a vital part of the church and the body of Christ, and thus communes with other saints. The deceased—this communion of saints—are viewed as a "great cloud of witnesses," that surrounds the living (after Hebrews 12:1). To reject or deny this communion of saints is to heretically reject the basic belief that those who have died in Christ are still part of his holy church.

Mary or Theotokos

Mary is called Theotokos in the Eastern Orthodox, meaning "God-bearer" or "mother of God," because, according to Christian theology, she bore the Son of God in her womb. The Eastern Orthodox Church honors Mary as the model of holiness and the first of the redeemed.

Apostolic Succession

This has been a critical issue since the second century. The early church insisted there was an authoritative apostolic succession passed down from generation to generation. They recorded that actual lineage, showing how clergy were ordained by those chosen by the successors of the apostles, who were chosen by Christ himself. Apostolic succession is viewed as an indispensable factor in preserving church unity and that those who are in the succession are accountable to it, and are responsible to ensure all teaching and practice in the Church.

Creeds

Creeds are statements that were approved by the various church councils, usually to give a concise and precise statement of the tenets of belief in the face of the corrupting influence of confusion or heresy. The most important creed in Christianity is the Nicene Creed, the product of two ecumenical councils in the fourth century. It contains the essence of New Testament teaching about the Holy Trinity. Called the Symbol of Faith and confessed in many of the services of the church, the Nicene Creed constantly reminds the Orthodox Christian of what one personally believes.

Second Coming

Orthodox Christians believe that Jesus Christ "will come again to judge the living and the dead," and that subsequent to his arrival, his "kingdom will have no end."

Creation

Orthodox Christians believe that God is the creator of Heaven and Earth (Nicene Creed) and do not believe the Bible to be a textbook on creation. They believe scientific investigation can actually serve as an encouragement to faith.

The Nicene Creed

The creed as defined at the First Council of Nicaea and the First Council of Constantinople declared that the Holy Spirit "proceeds from the Father." It did not state that the Holy Spirit also proceeds from the Son.

In the ninth century, however, churches in France and Spain began to add the words "and from the Son" to the article of faith about the procession of the Holy Spirit. In 1014, the Roman Catholic pope, Benedict VIII, added the phrase "and the Son" to the creed as it was recited in the Western Church. In Latin, the phrase "from the Son" is *filioque*, which is how church historians refer to the phrase.

The Eastern Orthodox Church does not include the filioque in their recitation of the creed. They insist the Gospels contradict it and therefore consider it a heresy. The text of the Nicene Creed reads:

We believe in one God, the Father, the Almighty, maker of heaven and earth, and of all that is seen and unseen. We believe in one Lord, Jesus Christ, the only Son of God, eternally begotten of the Father, God from God, Light from Light, true God from true God, begotten, not made, one in being with the Father. Through Him all things were made. For us and for our salvation he came down from heaven. By the power of the Holy Spirit he was born of the Virgin Mary, and became man. For our sake he was crucified under Pontius Pilate; he suffered, died, and was buried. On the third day he rose again in fulfillment of the scriptures; he ascended into heaven and is seated at the right hand of the Father. He will come again in glory to judge the living and the dead, and his kingdom will have no end.
We believe in the Holy Spirit, the Lord, the giver of life, who proceeds from the Father. With the Father and the Son he is worshipped and glorified. He has spoken through the prophets.
We believe in one Holy Catholic and Apostolic Church. We acknowledge one baptism for the forgiveness of sins. We look for the resurrection of the dead, and the life of the world to come. Amen.

C. Scripture and Sacred Literature

HOLY BIBLE

The Bible is customarily divided into two books: The Old Testament and the New Testament.

The Old Testament

The scriptures are divided into three parts: The Law (consisting of the first five books), the Prophets (the Former Prophets: Joshua, Judges, First and Second Samuel, and First and Second Kings; the Latter Prophets: Isaiah, Jeremiah, Ezekiel, and the Twelve "Minor" Prophets), and the Writings (the remaining books of the Old Testament). Just before the New Testament era, around 325 BCE, the Hebrew scriptures were translated into Greek at Alexandria, Egypt (the so-called Septuagint, which means "translation of the 70," and is thus signified by "LXX," Roman for 70). It is this later Greek (LXX) scripture that is considered the official text for the Orthodox Churches.

The Orthodox Bible contains some material (including whole books) not normally found in the Hebrew Bible or in most English-language Bibles. These works are often referred to as the Apocrypha, but because the word "apochryphal" commonly means of dubious authenticity, the church prefers using such terms as Deuterocanonical, which means "canonized later" (meaning later than those canonized earlier) or the "protocanonical" works.

Both the Orthodox and Roman Catholics accept the Apocrypha as authentic parts of the biblical canon, whereas, since the Reformation, most Protestants have rejected them, regarding them as spurious. The Orthodox Church accepts these books as Holy Writ, treasures them, and uses them liturgically, but it does not use them as primary sources in defining or elucidating church doctrine.

The Greek additions to the Old Testament accepted by the Orthodox Churches are as follows:

- First Esdras
- Second Esdras (The Greek Orthodox Church accepts First Esdras, but not Second Esdras, believing Second Esdras to be the protocanonical Ezra-Nehemiah. The Russian Church accepts both, but calls them Second and Third Esdras, First Esdras, again, being the protocanonical Ezra-Nehemiah.)
- Tobit
- Judith
- Additions to Esther
- The Wisdom of Solomon
- Ecclesiasticus, or the Wisdom of Jesus the Son of Sirach
- Baruch
- The Letter of Jeremiah
- Additions to Daniel
- Song of the Three Youths
- Susanna
- Daniel, Bel and the Dragon

- The Prayer of Manasseh
- First Maccabees
- Second Maccabees
- Third Maccabees
- Fourth Maccabees (Fourth Maccabees is not accepted by the Russian Church and is placed in an appendix by the Greek Church.)

The New Testament

The twenty-seven books of the New Testament fall into four categories: (1) Gospels from Evangelion or Good News, which tell the "Good News" of Jesus Christ and Saints Matthew, Mark, Luke, and John; (2) church history in The Acts of the Apostles; (3) Epistles (or Letters), of which there are twenty-one, written by Saints Paul, James, Peter, John, and Jude; and (4) the Apocalypse, that is, a Revelation or disclosure of God's will for the future, hence the title: The Revelation to St. John. All of these books were written in the widely-used Greek of the time, which was in common use throughout the Roman Empire at the beginning of the Christian era.

LITURGICAL BOOKS

The liturgical books used in Orthodox worship fall into three main groups. The first group of these are three books containing readings from Holy Scripture. These are the Book of Gospels, the Book of Epistles (Apostol), and the Book of Psalms (Psalter).

Book of the Gospels. This book contains the text of the four Gospels (Matthew, Mark, Luke, and John) arranged in sections called *pericopes* (or *zachalo* in Russian). In the Orthodox Church, this book normally rests on the Holy Table, and is customarily treated in the same way as the Holy Icons. The book itself is regarded as an "Icon of the Savior" in his teaching ministry.

Book of Epistles (Apostol). This contains the readings from the Acts of the Apostles and the Epistles for the whole year, covering the entire New Testament except for the Gospels and the Apocalypse (Revelation) of Saint John. It is also divided into pericopes and includes the Prokeimena and Alleluia verses, which precede and follow the Epistle readings.

Book of Psalms (Psalter). The Psalter contains the traditional 150 Psalms of David, divided into twenty *kathismas* (sections), as well as the text of the nine biblical canticles sung at matins.

The second group of liturgical books are those that pertain to fixed parts of the services, and thus do not usually change according to any season or saint. Among these are the Euchologion and the Book of Hours.

Euchologion. The Euchologion (or Book of Prayers) is for the use of the priest and deacon and contain the sacraments and other services, as well as many special prayers and blessings. The Euchologion is usually divided into several books:

a. The Great Euchologion contains the fixed parts of vespers, matins, and the liturgy (primarily the priest's parts), the six remaining sacraments (baptism, chrismation, holy orders, confession, marriage, anointing of the sick), and other services (monastic profession, consecration of a church, blessing of waters, etc.)

b. The Priest's Service Book (Greek: *Ieratikon*; Russian: *Sluzhebnik*). An altar book containing primarily the priest's recitations at vespers, matins, and the Divine Liturgy.

c. The Book of Needs (Russian: *Trebnik*). This book contains five of the sacraments (with the divine liturgy and holy orders omitted), the funeral service, and other services commonly used.

d. Pontifical Service Book (Greek: *Archieratikon*; Russian: *Chinovnik*). This is a special book of prayers and blessings used specifically by the bishop.

The Great Book of Hours (Greek: *Horologion*) is a choir book for the use of the reader and singers. It contains the fixed portions of the daily offices (vespers, matins, etc.) with most of the priest's and deacon's parts omitted. It also contains a list of feasts and saint's days throughout the year as well as appropriate troparia and kontakia for each. In addition, there is a section containing *troparia* and *kontakia* for Sundays and movable feasts of the period of the Triodion and Pentecostarion, as well as Theotokia for the whole year. There are also contained in this book various canons and other services in frequent use. In the Russian Church, there is an abbreviated form of the Great Book of Hours, called simply the Book of Hours (Russian: *Chasoslov*).

The third group of texts are used for the "movable parts" of the services (i.e., those that change day to day), there are four volumes that cover the three main cycles of the church year:

1. the weekly cycle: Octoechos;
2 and 3. the annual cycle of movable Feasts: Triodion and Pentecostarion; and
4. the annual cycle of feasts: the Menaia.

The **Octoechos** (or Book of the Eight Tones) contains the movable parts of the daily offices sung throughout the week. Eight series of offices, one for each of the eight tones, are provided, within which are seven sets of services, one for each day of the week. The first tone begins on St. Thomas Sunday and proceeds in sequence each week until tone eight is completed, at which time the whole cycle is repeated. The texts of the Octoechos are combined, more or less, with fixed feasts from the Menaia, and on Saturdays and Sundays during Great Lent (except from Lazarus Saturday to the Sunday of All Saints).

The **Triodion** is characterized by its extensive use of three-ode canons (along with some four-ode canons), generally termed the Lenten Triodion, within which are found the services of Great Lent.

The **Pentecostarion** is a companion to the Lenten Triodion (often called the Flowery Triodion), which contains the texts from Pascha to the Sunday of All Saints (the first after Pentecost).

The **Menaia** is divided into twelve volumes (corresponding to the twelve months) and contains the texts for the fixed feasts of each day of the year. In addition, there are two companion volumes that contain certain texts from the major fixed feasts (the Festal Menaion) or general offices for certain classes of saints (the General Menaion).

In addition to these three main groups of liturgical books, there are two further books, the Irmologion and the Typikon.

The **Irmologion** contains the texts of all of the *irmosi* (theme songs) sung at the beginning of the various canticles of the canon. (Some editions of service books, such as the Menaia and Triodion, only give the opening words of the irmos, making it necessary to use the Irmologion, which provides the full texts.)

The **Typikon** contains the rules governing every aspect of the church services and their celebration throughout the year. According to church tradition, the Typikon was drawn up by Saint Sabbas of Jerusalem (flourished 532) and later revised by Saint Sophronius, patriarch of Jerusalem (638). A further revision was made by Saint John of Damascus (749), a monk at Saint Sabbas' Monastery, hence it is also known as the Jerusalem Typikon of Saint Sabbas' Monastery.

In 1888, a new edition of the Typikon was prepared at Constantinople, and it is this work that, in modern times, is used primarily by the Greek-speaking churches. The Church of Russia and much of the Orthodox Church in America still use the Jerusalem Typikon, as do the older Greek monasteries, such as those of Mount Athos, Saint Sabbas at Jerusalem, and Saint John on Patmos.

The Three Holy Hierarchs of the Eastern Orthodox Church— Basil the Great, Gregory the Theologian, and John Chrysostom—are depicted in this sixteenth-century Russian icon.

D. Theologians and Thinkers

The Three Holy Hierarchs

During the reign of the Emperor Alexius Comnenus (1081–1118), a controversy arose in Constantinople among learned men regarding who was to be considered the greatest of the three holy hierarchs and fathers of the Church: Basil the Great, Gregory the Theologian, or John Chrysostom, archbishop of Constantinople. Some argued it was Saint Basil because, according to his supporters, he was able to explain the mysteries of the faith. He was superior to Saint Chrysostom because Chrysostom was by

nature more easily inclined to absolve sinners, they contended.

The partisans of Saint Chrysostom argued that the archbishop of Constantinople had been no less zealous than Saint Basil in combating vices, and he had displayed superior oratorical eloquence and exemplary piety in his daily life.

According to a third group, Saint Gregory the Theologian was to be preferred to the others by reason of his linguistic gifts. Possessing a mastery of the wisdom of ancient Greece, his supporters argued, he had attained the ability to express the dogma of the Holy Trinity as well as one possibly could. What was at stake in this debate was the question of who would prevail in the event they differed on any point of church law or theology.

Then one night during this debate—the night of October 5 according to Eastern Orthodoxy—the three holy hierarchs appeared in a dream to Saint John Mauropus, the metropolitan of Euchaïta, separately at first, then together. In this dream, the group expressed to Saint John that there were no divisions among them, and asked the leader to counsel the factions not to create divisions in the Church because of them. At the end of this plea, they were "taken up into heaven in a boundless light while conversing with one another."

Saint John immediately assembled the people and informed them of this revelation. As he was well respected, the three parties made peace and every one urged him to lose no time in composing the "service of the joint feast."

Leo the Great (?–461)

Pope Leo I, or Saint Leo the Great, was an aristocrat and theologian who sat as pope of Rome from 440 to 461. Because he is the first widely known pope, he is often referred to as the "first pope," though others occupied the office before him. He is credited with halting the invasion of Italy by Attila the Hun in 452.

He actively promoted the convening of the Fourth Ecumenical Council at Chalcedon in 451 to condemn the heresy of the Monophysites (who held that that Christ has only one nature). At the Council of Chalcedon, a letter by Leo to the deceased Saint Flavian, patriarch of Constantinople, was read in which the Orthodox teaching about the two natures of Christ (divine and human) was set forth. The bishops present at the council accepted the contents of the letter, and excommunicated Eutyches and Dioscorus for their heresy.

Augustine of Hippo (354–430)

Augustine of Hippo is considered one of the preeminent theologians of the fourth century and a central figure in the history of Western thought. Influenced by Platonism and the neo-Platonism of Plotinus, Augustine was important for his analysis of Greek thought and for introducing it into the Western Christian intellectual tradition.

The Fifth Ecumenical Council, held in Constantinople in 553, listed Augustine among the fathers of the church (though without offering an unqualified endorsement of his theology):

"We further declare that we hold fast to the decrees of the four councils, and in every way follow the holy fathers, Athanasius, Hilary, Basil, Gregory the Theologian, Gregory of Nyssa, Ambrose, Theophilus, John of Constantinople, Cyril, Augustine, Proclus, Leo, and their writings on the true faith."

In the Comnenian Council of Constantinople in 1166, he is referred to as "Saint Augustine."

Despite these laudits, most of his works were not translated into Greek until 1360, by Demetrios Cydones, and some Orthodox Christians believe there are errors to be found in his theology—especially those in his Triadology, which gave rise to the filioque addition to the Nicene-Constantinopolitan Creed—and they regard him as one of the major instigators of the Great Schism between the Church in the East and in the West. Thus, there are some Orthodox thinkers who see Augustine as a heretic, though there has never been any conciliar condemnation of either him or his writings.

At best, one can claim that Augustine, though perhaps not a saint nor a church father, because he made many mistakes in his theology, is yet a theologian who warrants the word "blessed" (and not "saint") before his name. (In the Orthodox Church, it should be noted, a distinction is rarely made between "blessed" or "saint.")

Seraphim Rose (1934–1982)

Seraphim Rose was a hieromonk of the Russian Orthodox Church Outside Russia in the United States, whose writings helped spread Orthodox Christianity throughout modern America and the West. Although not formally glorified (canonized), he is celebrated by many Orthodox Christians as a saint in iconography, liturgy, and prayer.

He began as a convert and eventually rose to the position of hieromonk in the Russian Church Abroad. In his book, *Orthodoxy and the Religion of the Future,* he pointed out what he saw as dangerous trends in both the secular and ecclesiastical worlds— mainly modernism and ecumenism.

One major issue of contention between Father Seraphim and the Holy Transfiguration Monastery was the ecclesiastical standing ("the presence of grace") within what many felt was the Soviet-compromised hierarchy of the Moscow Patriarchate. Father Seraphim argued that Moscow, though ailing, still had grace. Throughout his life, Father Seraphim stressed an "Orthodoxy of the heart," which he felt was absent in much of American ecclesiastical life.

One of his more controversial books is *The Soul After Death,* which includes the so-called Aerial Toll-Houses doctrine regarding the soul's journey after its departure from the body. In some Eastern Orthodox tradition about the afterlife, the aerial tollhouses are stations through which the recently departed soul must pass in order to approach the throne of God. Many in the Orthodox Church have criticized this work and teaching as gnostic.

III. Rites and Rituals

A. The Calendar

THE EASTERN ORTHODOX LITURGICAL CALENDAR dictates the rhythm of the life of the Eastern Orthodox Church. Associated with each date are passages of Holy Scripture, saints and events for commemoration, and special rules for fasting or feasting that correspond to days of the week or times of year in relationship to the major feast days.

The ecclesiastical year begins on September 1 and is divided into "immovable" holy days and "movable" holy days. The cycle of the movable feast days is built around Pascha, or Easter, which is determined by a formula established by the Council of Nicaea in 325. Fixed dates generally follow the Western (Gregorian) calendar, though Christmas and Theophany or Epiphany may be celebrated later than in Western churches. Movable dates in some Orthodox churches may follow the practices of Western churches, but most Orthodox churches determine the date according to the Julian calendar.

Days of Regular Observance

September 8: Nativity of the Theotokos ("God-bearer"), that is, of the Virgin Mary, Mother of the Son of God; first day of the liturgical calendar.

September 14: Elevation of the Cross.

November 21: Presentation of the Theotokos (Virgin Mary) in the temple.

December 25: Nativity of Christ (Christmas— may be celebrated on January 7 by churches using the Gregorian calendar).

January 6: Theophany (the day of the baptism and manifestation of Jesus Christ as the Son of God);

Epiphany (commemorating the presentation of the baby Jesus to the Magi): may be celebrated on January 19 by churches using the Gregorian calendar.

February 2: Presentation of Christ in the Temple.

March 25: Annunciation (commemorating Archangel Gabriel announcing to Mary that she will be Mother of the Son of God).

Palm Sunday (entrance of Jesus Christ into Jerusalem; beginning of Holy Week): date varies according to formula for date of Easter.

Pascha (Holy [Good] Friday to Easter)—crucifixion, death and resurrection of Jesus Christ: **date varies** according to formula for determining date of Easter; calculations using the Gregorian calendar yield a different date from that determined using the Julian calendar.

August 6: Transfiguration of the Lord (Jesus Christ's transfiguration into his heavenly form before the apostles Peter, James, and John on Mount Tabor, revealing his divinity).

Ascension of our Lord (ascension of Jesus Christ into heaven): **forty days after Pascha.**

Pentecost (Holy Spirit's descent upon the apostles): **fifty days after Pascha.**

August 15: Dormition (falling asleep) of the Theotokos (assumption of Mary into heaven).

The Paschal Cycle

The Paschal Cycle is comprised of approximately ten weeks before and seven weeks after Pascha. The ten weeks before Pascha are sometimes called the period of the Triodion. This period includes the three weeks preceding Great Lent (the "pre-Lenten period"), the forty days of Lent, and Holy Week. The fifty days following Pascha are called the Pentacostarion. Each week begins with a commemoration on Sunday, followed by special commemorations on the other days of the week as well.

Pre-Lent

The Publican and the Pharisee: tenth Sunday or 70 days before Pascha.

The Prodigal Son: ninth Sunday or 63 days before Pascha.

The Last Judgment: also known as Meat-Fare Sunday (the last day meat is to be eaten); eighth Sunday or 56 days before Pascha.

Sunday of Forgiveness: also known as Cheese-Fare Sunday (the last day dairy products, fish, wine, and olive oil may be consumed); seventh Sunday or 49 days before Pascha.

Great Lent

Clean Monday: the actual beginning of Great Lent; 48 days before Pascha.

Triumph of Orthodoxy: commemoration of the restoration of icons after the defeat of the iconoclast heresy in 843; sixth Sunday or 42 days before Pascha and first Sunday of Lent.

Saint Gregory Palamas: fifth Sunday or 35 days before Pascha and second Sunday of Lent.

Adoration of the Cross: fourth Sunday or 28 days before Pascha and third Sunday of Lent.

Saint John of the Ladder: third Sunday or 21 days before Pascha and fourth Sunday of Lent.

Saint Mary of Egypt: second Sunday or 14 days before Pascha and fifth Sunday of Lent.

Holy Week

Lazarus Saturday: the beginning of Holy Week; 8 days before Pascha

Palm Sunday: the entry of Christ into Jerusalem; last Sunday or 7 days before Pascha.

Great and Holy Monday: Joseph the stepfather of Jesus, and the withering of the fig tree; 6 days before Pascha.

Great and Holy Tuesday: parable of the Ten Virgins; 5 days before Pascha.

Great and Holy Wednesday: Anointing of Jesus with myrrh by the woman in the house of Simon the Leper in Bethany; also, the Holy Unction; 4 days before Pascha.

Great and Holy Thursday: the washing of the disciples' feet, the institution of the Holy Eucharist, the "Marvelous Prayer," and the betrayal by Judas Iscariot; 3 days before Pascha.

Great and Holy Friday: the holy, saving, and life-giving Passion of Christ.

Feast of Joseph of Arimathea: 2 days before Pascha.

Great and Holy Saturday: The sepulcher of Christ, his descent into Hades to raise up mankind and defeat the powers of death; last day before Pascha.

Great and Holy Pascha

The Resurrection of Jesus Christ: very late Saturday night (usually midnight).

Agape Vespers: proclamation of the Gospel to the four corners of the world, symbolized by the reading of the Gospel in various languages from the four corners of the church: Sunday afternoon.

Pentecostarion (Paschaltide)

Bright Week: week following Pascha.

Saint Thomas: first Sunday or 7 days after Pascha.

The Holy Myrrhbearers: second Sunday or 14 days after Pascha.

The Paralytic: third Sunday or 21 days after Pascha.

The Samaritan Woman (Photini): fourth Sunday or 28 days after Pascha.

The Blind Man: fifth Sunday or 35 days after Pascha.

The Ascension of Jesus Christ: 39 days after Pascha.

The Fathers of the First Ecumenical Council: sixth Sunday or 42 days after Pascha.

Pentecost: when the Holy Spirit descended on the apostles, and the Christian Church began; seventh Sunday or 49 days after Pascha.

All Saints: eighth Sunday or 56 days after Pascha.

B. Worship and Liturgy

Mysteria/Sacraments

Today the Eastern Orthodox Church recognizes seven Mysteria, or sacraments: Baptism and Confirmation ("Chrismation"); Communion; holy orders; penance; anointing of the sick; and marriage. However, no council recognized by the Eastern Orthodox Church ever determined the precise number of sacraments; it is only through the "Orthodox confessions" of the seventeenth century directed against the Reformation that the number seven has come to be generally accepted.

Baptism and Confirmation. Baptism is normally performed by a triple immersion in water as a sign of the death and Resurrection of Christ. It is immediately followed by confirmation, performed by the priest, who anoints the newly baptized Christian with oil from the Holy Chrism, which has been blessed by the bishop. Children who have been baptized and confirmed are admitted to Holy Communion.

Communion. Both canons presently in use (that of Saint Basil and Saint John Chrysostom) include the words of "institution" ("This is my Body..."

"This is my Blood..."), which are traditionally considered in the West necessary for the sacrament to be valid. In the East, however, the climactic point of the prayer is not in the remembrance of Christ's act but in the invocation of the Holy Spirit, which immediately follows: "Send down thy Holy Spirit upon us and upon the gifts here spread forth, and make this bread to be the precious body of thy Christ..." Thus, the central mystery of Christianity for the Orthodox Church is seen as being performed by the prayer of the church and through an invocation of the Spirit. The nature of the mystery that occurs in the bread and wine is signified by the term "metabole" (meaning, "sacramental change"). After the seventeenth century, the Western term "transubstantiation" occurs in some confessions of faith.

Holy Orders. The Orthodox Church recognizes three major orders—the diaconate; the priesthood; and the episcopate (bishop)—as well as the minor orders of the lectorate and the subdiaconate. All the ordinations are performed by a bishop and, normally, during the Eucharistic liturgy. The consecration of a bishop requires the participation of at least two or three bishops, as well as an election by a canonical synod.

Penance. In the Eastern Orthodox Church today, there is variety to be found in both the practice and the rite of penance. General or "group" confession is also occasionally practiced. The rite of confession in the Euchologion retains the form of a prayer, or invocation, recited by the priest for the remission of the penitent's sins. Confession, in Orthodox practice, is generally viewed as a form of spiritual healing.

Anointing of the Sick. Anointing of the sick is a form of healing by prayer. In the Greek Church, it is performed in church each year for the entire congregation, and takes place on the evening of Holy Wednesday.

Marriage. Marriage is celebrated through the rite of "crowning," performed with great solemnity and signifying an eternal union of husband and wife with each other and with God (*see* page 96).

The Orthodox Service

On entering a church, the central icon in the narthex is acknowledged with three prostrations. This is done by making the sign of the cross twice with a bow (bending and touching the ground with the right hand) or, if one wishes, a prostration (falling to the knees and bending the head almost to the ground). Then the icon is kissed (preferably on the saint's right hand, if the saint is blessing or holding a cross) and one crosses oneself a third time, making a final bow or prostration.

Eastern Orthodox churches always have candles available at the back of the church. A candle is lit and placed before an icon as one enters the church.

Having reverenced the icon in the center of the church and lit a candle, men arrange themselves on the right side of the church (facing the altar), women on the left. A traditional church will have no pews, but only several benches (*stasidia*, in Greek) around the periphery of the church, for the infirm or aged. Worshippers stand through most of the services.

As one stands, the hands should be at one's sides; placing hands behind the back or in pockets is considered improper and disrespectful. While standing in worship, the sign of the cross should normally be made at the end of each petition chanted by the deacon or priest, accompanied by a slight bow.

One makes the sign of the cross:
- when the name of God, Christ, or the Trinity is mentioned;
- when the Theotokos (Virgin Mary) or any saint's name is mentioned;
- when the Trisagion ("Holy God, Holy Mighty, Holy Immortal, have mercy on us"), "Glory to the Father and to the Son and to the Holy Spirit, both now and ever, and unto the ages of ages," the Lord's Prayer ("Our Father"), and any other similar prayers are recited;
- at the end of each petition in a litany;
- whenever the deacon or priest says, "Let us beseech the Lord;" and
- whenever the altar curtain is opened or closed.

There are also circumstances when the sign of the cross is not made. Two such instances are:
- when a priest or bishop blesses with his hand (one bows slightly during this blessing);
- during the reading of the Six Psalms during matins—the late night service (*orthros* in Greek).

There are also times during the services when the faithful bow (bowing slightly or touching the ground with the right hand) or perform a prostration (*metanoia* in Greek, or *poklon* in Russian).

One bows:
- when the icon is venerated;
- at the beginning of any service and each time that the reader says, "O come, let us worship..."
- when the priest or bishop makes an entrance into the altar during vespers (evening services) or liturgy;
- when the deacon, priest, or bishop censes in the direction of the congregation;
- toward the bishop, if present in the church, when he is commemorated during the petitions.

Prostrations are made when entering the church and venerating the central Icon, as long as it is outside Paschaltide and it is not a Sunday.

Bowing is also proper when anyone enters the altar outside Paschaltide and on days other than Sunday. After prostrating or bowing, a bishop, priest, or deacon kisses the holy table.

At the end of any service, the priest emerges, faces the congregation, and recites a list of saints. As each name is mentioned, each person crosses himself.

The **weekend cycle** of Divine Services begins with attendance at vespers (or the vespers–matins vigil), on Saturday afternoon or evening, or on the afternoon or evening before a feast day. The second service in the cycle of Orthodox worship is matins, which is celebrated Sunday morning before the Divine Liturgy. In the Slavic churches, vespers and matins are often combined into one service called the "all–night vigil." If attending a vigil, the end of vespers is immediately followed by the Six Psalms. These Six Psalms constitute the most solemn set of prayers read in any service, for they are believed to be the prayers that will be heard at the beginning of the Dread Judgment, when Christ will appear at the end of the world. If matins is performed separately, then some opening prayers and Psalms and a short litany are read before beginning the Six Psalms.

The Divine Liturgy

Afterward, the priest will bring out the Holy Gospel (an ornate book containing the Gospel readings for the church year) for veneration. First, one bows toward the icon in the center of the church. Then proceeding to the priest, two bows are made, the Gospel is kissed, and then a third bow is made.

After vespers and matins, the Divine Liturgy is attended. Orthodox Christians fast starting at midnight the night before this service. If the Divine Liturgy is being held at midnight, then one would fast six to eight hours before the start of the liturgy. This is a strict fast that excludes all food and liquids.

If one is participating in Communion, then Wednesday and Friday fasts are to be kept at a minimum. One should also fast from meat on Saturday. From midday on Saturday one should maintain a Wednesday or Friday fast. Married couples should abstain from sexual activity before Communion.

After the matins service or the reading of the hours, the Divine Liturgy begins. During the most solemn parts of this service, Orthodox Christians are called upon to participate in the following ways:

• At the time of the great entrance, one bows slightly as the gifts are brought out from the altar and stands upright just before the priest enters the Gates.

• When the priest says, "Take, eat . . . ," one bows and then stands upright.

• When the priest says, "Take, drink . . . ," one makes a slight bow again and then stands upright.

• When the priest says, "Thine own of thine own . . . ," one bows and remains bowed down (or prostrate) until the priest says: "Especially for our most holy . . ." It is during this time that the priest reads the prayers of "consecration" inside the altar.

• After the "Our Father . . . ," when the priest exclaims, "Holy things are for the holy," one bows and then remains bowed down (or prostrate) until the choir finishes "One is holy . . ."

• When the deacon or priest presents the chalice and chants, "With fear of God . . . ," one either bows or makes a quick prostration, and then stands upright again.

To commune, one goes to the central icon in the church and venerates it as was practiced when entering the church. Then a line is formed to the right of the ambon. The arms are crossed over the chest with the right arm over the left.

Arms remain folded on the chest when receiving the mysteries. With the Communion cloth carefully held under the chin, the mouth should be opened in advance so that the priest can place the spoon in it easily. The lips are then closed on the spoon as the priest communes the worshipper; he is then allowed to draw the spoon out, past closed lips, so that the spoon is wiped clean. Then one moves over to take some "antidoron" (noneucharistic bread, made from the loaves from which the Eucharist is made), dipping a piece lightly in the wine provided.

After the final blessing, the Communion Prayers of Thanksgiving are read quietly by the worshipper. After these prayers are completed, the icons are venerated as they had been upon entering the church, and the worshipper then leaves quietly.

C. Daily Life

Fasting

Members of the Eastern Orthodox Church fast every Wednesday and Friday during the year, except during specified weeks which are fast-free: the weeks following Christmas, the Sunday of the Publican and Pharisee, Pascha, and Pentecost. The Wednesday fast recalls Judas Iscariot's betrayal of Christ and the Friday fast commemorates Jesus's crucifixion.

The Orthodox Church also has four fasting periods established many centuries ago designed to allow Orthodox Christians to prepare themselves for feasts in the church's liturgical cycle.

Unless otherwise noted, animal products are not permitted on a fast day, including any part of any mammal (beef, lamb, pork, etc.), bird (chicken, turkey, duck, etc.), or fish (tuna, cod, sardine, etc.). This prohibition includes byproducts of these animals (milk, cheese, or eggs). Olive oil is also restricted on fast days.

Hard liquor (i.e., any beverage stronger than wine) may be consumed only when meat or dairy products are permitted. Wine is allowed on specific fast days when the saint of the day is commemorated with a musical doxology (a hymn or verse praising God) or when a Polyeleos is appointed. Olive oil is also allowed on these days. Such days are commonly referred to as "wine and oil days." Beer may be consumed at any time since it is not considered an alcoholic beverage.

Shellfish (shrimp, clam, lobster, etc.), reptiles (alligator, turtle, etc.), and amphibians (frog legs) are all permitted on any fast day.

Married couples are to abstain from sexual relations on fast days and on nonfast days during which they are preparing for Holy Communion. This is referred to as "fasting from the flesh."

The four fasting periods are:

Great Lent. During the first week of Lent, a total fast is observed on Monday, Tuesday, and Wednesday. On Wednesday, the fast is kept until after the Liturgy of the Presanctified, celebrated on Wednesdays and Fridays during Lent and on the first three days of Holy Week. There is no prayer of consecration during this liturgy.

During the second through sixth weeks of Lent, meat, animal products (cheese, milk, butter, eggs, lard), fish with backbones, olive oil, wine, and all alcoholic drinks are prohibited during weekdays. Octopus, shellfish, and vegetable oil are allowed. On weekends, olive oil and wine are permitted; one meal a day is eaten on weekdays and two meals on weekends during Great Lent.

Fish, oil, and wine are allowed on the Feast of the Annunciation (March 25) and on Palm Sunday (one week before Easter). On other feast days, wine and oil are permitted.

Apostles' Fast. This fast begins on the Monday after the Sunday of All Saints' and ends on June 29. Consumption of fish is permitted on weekends and on several feast days during the fast. Wine and oil are allowed on Tuesdays and Thursdays. If the Feast of Saints Peter and Paul is on a Wednesday or Friday, fish, wine, and oil are permitted.

Dormition Fast. Beginning August 1 and ending August 15, the fast in honor of the Dormition (falling asleep) of the Theotokos (the Virgin Mary) is the shortest fasting period, lasting a period of two weeks. Fish is only allowed on the Feast of the Transfiguration (August 6). Weekends during this fast are wine and oil days. If the Dormition falls on a Wednesday or Friday, that day becomes a fish, wine, and oil day.

Nativity Fast. This fast starts forty days before the Feast of the Nativity (Christmas) on November 15. Until December 20, fish is allowed on weekends. After December 20, wine and oil are appointed for the weekends. Tuesdays and Thursdays are wine and oil days throughout this fast.

D. Life Cycle Events

Adult Baptism

The Baptism ceremony consists of three elements: exorcisms, baptism, and Chrismation.

During the **exorcisms**, the priest reads a series of prayers that ask God to expel every demonic influence or spirit that has a hold on the candidate for baptism. At one point, the priest breathes on the person saying, "Expel from him/her every evil and impure spirit which hideth and maketh its lair in his/her heart."

The exorcisms are immediately followed by a declaration of faith in Christ, after which the "catechumen" (the worshipper being baptized) recites the Symbol of Faith (also referred to as the Nicene Creed). Through this recitation, the catechumen is proclaiming his faith before God. After the exorcisms, the priest blesses the baptismal water in preparation for the baptism.

The Eastern Orthodox Church considers **baptism** to be an assault against demons, and, as such, the ceremony emphasizes the rejection of evil, in the form of Satan. The priest asks the catechumen three times: "Dost thou renounce Satan, and all his Angels, and all his works, and all his service, and all his pride?" And the catechumen must answer, "I do," each time.

The priest then blesses olive oil, part of which is then used to bless the water and part of which is used to anoint the person being baptized. After the anointing, the catechumen is fully immersed in the water three times. Catechumens are dressed, often in modest swimwear, for the immersion.

Immediately after the baptism, the person dons a white robe emblazoned with red crosses on the back and each breast (or, in the case of an infant, new white clothes). The following troparion is sung as this is done: "Vouchsafe unto me the robe of light, O thou who clothest thyself with light as with a garment, Christ our God, plenteous in mercy."

The priest then anoints the newly baptized person with "holy chrism" (a consecrated mixture of olive oil and balsam) in the **chrismation** ceremony.

The brow, eyes, nostrils, lips, ears, breast, both hands, both feet, and between the shoulders are anointed with the chrism. Every part of the body that interacts with the physical world is "sealed," as it were, rendering the individual immune to evil intent. A small amount of hair is also cut from the head of the newly baptized person to signify his new commitment.

Infant Baptism

Children who are to be baptized into the Eastern Orthodox faith are initiated after they are forty days old. The purpose of baptism is the renewal of the individual and to remove the stain of the ancestral (original) sin of Adam and Eve.

As a matter of course for an infant baptism, the church provides a sponsor, or a godparent, for the child who agrees to take responsibility for the child should anything happen to the parents. To sponsor a child at baptism means that, should the child be left an orphan, the sponsor would be expected to take the child into his home and raise him to adulthood. The godparent is also responsible for the child's spiritual development. As such, a godparent must be an Orthodox Christian.

Wedding

The marriage rite contains two parts: betrothal and crowning. Earlier in history, the common practice was to perform these two rites separately, with some time lapsing between them; the betrothal was the engagement service, and the crowning was the actual wedding. Today, these two rites are performed together as one unified rite of matrimony.

The **betrothal** begins outside the church doors, where the rings are blessed and exchanged. The bride and groom exchange rings three times, in honor of the Holy Trinity, and to symbolize that in marriage their gifts, talents, and bounties are shared between each other. In the Eastern Orthodox Church, rings are placed on the right hand, historically a symbol of strength and honor, and symbolic of the couple's willingness to share each other's strengths and talents, and of their becoming whole by virtue of their union. The couple are also given candles at the church doors, which they will hold throughout the service. The candles symbolize the light of hope and vigilance and represent the couple's constant readiness to accept Christ into their home and into their marital relationship.

The priest then leads the couple into the church and onto a white rug or cloth in the processional, on which the couple will stand throughout the rite of crowning. The white cloth represents the road of life, on which, from that day forward, the couple will walk as one.

The **crowning** is the central act of the Orthodox wedding service. Metal crowns or floral wreaths, sometimes attached with ribbon, are placed on the heads of the bride and groom to symbolize their roles as king and queen of their family—which is viewed in Orthodoxy as a "micro-kingdom" of God. They are expected to rule over their kingdom with wisdom, justice, integrity, and, above all, selfless love.

The couple drinks wine from a common cup to remind them that, from that day forward, they will share everything in life, both the bitter and the sweet. The right hands of the bridegroom and bride are then joined as an expression of the unity of the married couple, and the priest leads the couple in a procession around the table, on which are placed the Gospel (containing the word of God), and the cross (the symbol of redemption through Jesus Christ). The couple walks around the altar or table three times. In the eyes of the world, husband and wife are taking their first steps as a married couple, and the church, in the person of the priest, is leading them in the way they should walk. All their life will be seen as a journey in which Jesus Christ is at the center. Some also see this walk as a dance of joy for the union of man and woman in holy wedlock.

There are certain times during the year when the sacrament of Holy Matrimony (weddings) may not be celebrated:

• On the eves of Sundays, Wednesdays, and Fridays throughout the year.

• On the eves of the Twelve Great Feasts, patronal feasts of the parish or monastery, and other great feasts.

• During all of the fasts (Great Lent, Apostles' Fast, Dormition Fast, and Nativity Fast).

• From the Nativity of Christ (December 25) through the Synaxis of the Baptist (January 7).

• During the course of Cheesefare Week, the week before Great Lent (from the Sunday of Meatfare through the Sunday of Cheesefare).

• During the course of Bright Week.

• On the day and the eve of the Beheading of the Baptist (August 29) and the Elevation of the Cross (September 14).

Death and Burial

When a person has died, a priest should be called to read the prayers for the departure of the soul from the body. The body should not be embalmed, as it is preferred that the body be buried the day after death. Embalming is also disapproved of because it is viewed as an unnatural procedure that seeks to preserve the body after the soul has departed. Cremation is forbidden. In addition, the family should not allow an autopsy, unless it is legally required. The Eastern Orthodox Church holds that an autopsy is a violation of the sanctity of the body, which is viewed as a temple of the Holy Spirit.

As soon as possible after death, the body should be taken to the funeral home, washed, and dressed in simple clothes. If the deceased was an adult convert to Orthodoxy, he or she should be buried in his or her baptismal gown, which can be placed over other clothing, if desired. After the body is placed in a simple wooden casket, it should be covered by a *savanon*, or burial shroud, which has a depiction of the burial of Christ on it.

If possible, the body should then be taken immediately into the church, feet first, and placed in the center of the church with the deceased facing the altar. The Psalter should be read continuously over the body all night, until the time of the funeral. After the funeral, the body is taken out from the church, feet first, to the graveyard for burial.

Memorial services should be held on the third, ninth, and fortieth days after death, as well as on the anniversary of the person's death and on his Name Day (the feast day of the saint after whom one is named). Churches and monasteries are to be contacted to offer prayers for the deceased. The deceased's name should also be submitted for commemoration at a number of Divine Liturgies, as each commemoration is viewed as a blessing on the soul.

E. Family Life

Husband and Wife

In the Eastern Orthodox tradition, when a couple marries they are forming an agreement to submit their lives to God and to their spouses. This extends to personal possessions, so that all possessions become communal. Holy matrimony is deemed a Mystery of the Church, not a simple contract to be broken when it is no longer convenient.

An Orthodox Christian home is modeled on the relationship between Christ and the church. Each person has a specific function in the family unit, and these functions are seen as important for a stable family relationship.

If a man chooses to marry a woman in the Orthodox Church, he should do so with the full intention of taking the lead in the growth and development of the spiritual life of his family. He should volunteer to set up an icon corner in the home; to make the arrangements for keeping the vigil lamp lit; to organize and lead the family in prayer on a daily basis; to ensure that the family attends divine services regularly (which includes regular confession and reception of the Holy Mysteries); and to ensure that the children are properly instructed in the Eastern Orthodox faith. In Eastern Orthodoxy, a wife should follow her husband's lead in all things, in order to see that the family functions well.

Divorce

The Eastern Orthodox Church allows divorce and allows divorced people to remarry under specific circumstances (infidelity, apostasy, etc.) as judged by a Spiritual court or bishop. Yet, it is regarded as a great tragedy, and a second marriage normally requires special permission from a bishop. A second wedding ceremony always has an element of repentance on the part of the previously married party.

The church will permit up to, but not more than, three marriages for any Orthodox Christian. If both partners are entering a second or third marriage, another form of the marriage ceremony is conducted, much more subdued and even more penitential in character. Marriages end either through the death of one of the partners or through ecclesiastical recognition of divorce. The church grants "ecclesiastical divorces" on the basis of the exception given by Christ to his general prohibition of the practice.

Those Orthodox jurisdictions that issue ecclesiastical divorces require a thorough evaluation of the situation, and the appearance of the civilly divorced couple before a local ecclesiastical court, where another investigation is made. Only after the presiding bishop issues an ecclesiastical divorce can a couple apply for an ecclesiastical license to remarry.

IV. Denominations and Demographics

A. History

In 1054, as a service was about to begin in the Hagia Sophia Cathedral at Constantinople, Cardinal Humbert and two other legates of the pope entered the building and placed a bull of excommunication—a notice that the recipient has been excommunicated from the church—upon the altar. This incident marked the beginning of the Great Schism between the Eastern Orthodox Church and the Roman Catholic Church. But the exact date of the Great Schism cannot be determined with such precision; the schism was, in fact, many years in the making, the result of a long and complicated process.

Though the schism was spurred on by cultural, political, and economic factors, its fundamental cause was not secular but theological. In the final analysis, it was over issues of doctrine that the East and West quarreled.

From the end of the third century, the Roman Empire was seen as divided into an eastern and western kingdom, each with its own emperor. Constantine furthered this process of separation by founding a second imperial capital in the East, alongside Old Rome in Italy.

During the late sixth and the seventh centuries, East and West were further isolated from each other by the Avar and Slav invasions of the Balkan Peninsula. Illyricum, which had served as a bridge, now became a barrier between Byzantium and the Latin world. The separation was widened still further by the rise of Islam.

The iconoclast controversy (in which East and West debated the propriety of images of Jesus in the church—a debate that at times erupted in violence and caused great rifts between East and West over the course of the eighth and ninth centuries) contributed still further to the division between Byzantium and the West. The popes were firm supporters of the iconodule standpoint, and so for many decades they found themselves out of communion with the iconoclast emperor and patriarch at Constantinople. Cut off from Byzantium and in need of help, Pope Stephen turned northward and visited the Frankish ruler, Pepin, in 754.

On Christmas Day in the year 800, Pope Leo III crowned Charles the Great, king of the Franks, as emperor. Emperor Charlemagne (as he was then called) sought recognition from the ruler at Byzantium, but without success; for the Byzantines, still adhering to the principle of imperial unity, regarded Charlemagne as an intruder and the papal coronation as an act of schism within the empire. Instead of drawing closer together, the creation of a Holy Roman Empire in the West only served to alienate East and West more than ever.

Refused political recognition by the Byzantine emperor, Charlemagne charged the Byzantine Church with heresy. He denounced the Greeks for not using the filioque in the Creed and he rejected the decisions of the seventh ecumenical council.

There were two points of doctrine on which the two sides stood in direct and irreconcilable conflict: the papal claims and the filioque.

The pope claimed an absolute power only in the West, to which Byzantium raised no objections. The Byzantines did not want the papacy to interfere in the East. The pope, however, believed his power of jurisdiction to extend to the East as well as the West. The Greeks assigned a primacy of honor to the pope, but not the universal supremacy that he regarded as his due. The pope viewed infallibility as his own prerogative; the Greeks held that in matters of faith, final decisions rested not with the pope, but with a council representing all the bishops of the Church.

The second great difficulty was the filioque. The dispute involved the words about the Holy Spirit in the Nicene Constantinopolitan Creed. The original phrase: "I believe...in the Holy Spirit, the Lord, the Giver of Life, who proceeds from the Father, who with the Father and the Son together is worshipped and together glorified" is recited unchanged by the Eastern Orthodox Church to the present day. But the West inserted a phrase "and from the Son" (in Latin, *filioque*), so that the creed now reads, "who proceeds from the Father and from the Son..."

The Eastern Orthodoxy objected (and still objects) to this addition to the Creed, for two reasons. First, the Creed, in their view, is the possession of the whole church, and if any change is to be made, only the Ecumenical Council can do this. Second, the Eastern Orthodox Church believes the filioque to be theologically untrue. They hold that the Spirit proceeds from the Father alone, and consider it a heresy to say that he proceeds from the Son as well.

B. Comparisons in Tenets and Practices

Eastern Orthodoxy v. Roman Catholicism

Oneness

The Nicene Creed, adhered to by most Christians, contains the phrase, "One holy catholic and apostolic church." From a Catholic ecclesiological perspective, Orthodoxy is not "one" church, but an amalgamation of at least seventeen, each with separate governance. Catholics would respectfully reply that none of these "autocephalous" (meaning, independent) churches could speak with the doctrinal definitiveness that existed in the church before 1054.

The Papacy

Since the Eastern schism began, the Orthodox have generally claimed that the pope has only a "primacy of honor" among the bishops of the world, meaning the right to call and preside over meetings and councils, as well as the right to be the spokesman for the church. However, Eastern Orthodoxy does not recognize the pope's primacy of authority over all other bishops and regional churches. Catholics assert that Orthodoxy's rejection of the papacy is inconsistent with the nature of the church through the centuries. In Roman Catholicism, the papacy is a divinely instituted office, not a political and historical happenstance.

Ecumenical Councils

A more substantive disagreement between Catholics and the Eastern Orthodox concerns the role of the pope and the ecumenical councils in the church. Eastern Orthodoxy accepts the first seven ecumenical councils (up to the Second Council of Nicaea in 787), but no more. Both sides agree that ecumenical councils have the ability to infallibly define doctrines, but a question arises concerning which councils are ecumenical.

The Eastern Orthodox communion bases its teachings on Scripture and the "seven ecumenical councils"—I Nicaea (325), I Constantinople (381), Ephesus (431), Chalcedon (451), II Constantinople (553), III Constantinople (680), and II Nicaea (787). Catholics recognize these as the first seven ecumenical councils, but they are not the only seven, nor the only that are authoritative.

While Catholics recognize an ensuing series of ecumenical councils, leading up to Vatican II, which closed in 1965, the Eastern Orthodox believe there have been no authoritative ecumenical councils since 787, and hence no teaching of any council after II

Nicaea is accepted as having universal authority.

Contraception

Orthodoxy differs from Catholicism over the question of the issue of contraception. Catholics regard it as a mortal sin, whereas much of Orthodoxy (except some of the more conservative or traditional branches) does not even forbid it.

Divorce

Catholics believe that Jesus and the apostles, in keeping with an ancient Christian tradition, considered a valid sacramental marriage between two baptized Christians as indissoluble. Orthodoxy accepts divorce and second and third marriages with penitential sadness, viewing it as falling short of the Christian ideal. In Orthodoxy, divorce is viewed as a tragic social and pastoral necessity, indicative of the fallen human condition—but it is not forbidden.

C. Organization and Distribution

The Orthodox Church is a fellowship of independent churches. Each is said to be "autocephalous," that is, governed by its own head bishop. These autocephalous churches share a common faith, common principles of church policy and organization, and a common liturgical tradition. Only the languages used in worship and minor aspects of tradition differ from country to country. The head bishops of the autocephalous churches may be called patriarchs, metropolitans, or archbishops. These prelates are presidents of episcopal synods, which, in each church, constitute the highest canonical, doctrinal, and administrative authority. Among the various Orthodox churches there is an order of precedence, which is determined by history rather than by present-day numerical strength. The ecumenical patriarch of Constantinople holds titular or honorary primacy.

The number of autocephalous churches has varied in history. Today there are many: the Church of

Constantinople, the Church of Alexandria (Egypt), the Church of Antioch (with headquarters in Damascus, Syria), and the churches of Jerusalem, Russia, Ukraine, Georgia, Serbia, Romania, Bulgaria, Cyprus, Greece, Albania, Poland, the Czech Republic, the Slovak Republic, and America.

There are also "autonomous" churches, which retain a token canonical dependence upon a mother see, in Crete, Finland, and Japan. The first nine autocephalous churches are headed by "patriarchs," the others by archbishops or metropolitans. These titles are strictly honorary.

The order of precedence in which the autocephalous churches are listed does not reflect their actual influence or numerical importance. The patriarchates of Constantinople, Alexandria, and Antioch, for example, today present only shadows of their past glory. Yet there remains a consensus that Constantinople's primacy of honor, recognized by the ancient canons because it was the capital of the ancient empire, should remain as a symbol and tool of church unity and cooperation. The modern pan-Orthodox conferences were thus convoked by the ecumenical patriarch of Constantinople. Several of the autocephalous churches are de facto national churches, by far the largest being the Russian Church; however, it is not the criterion of nationality but rather the territorial principle that is the norm of organization in the Orthodox Church.

Since the Russian Revolution, there has been much turmoil and administrative conflict within the Orthodox Church. In Western Europe and in the Americas, in particular, overlapping jurisdictions have been established and resulting political passions have led to the formation of ecclesiastical organizations without clear canonical status. Though it has provoked controversy, the establishment in 1970 of the new autocephalous Orthodox Church in America by the patriarch of Moscow has as its goal the resumption of territorial unity in the Western Hemisphere.

V. Organization and Infrastructure

A. Education and Hierarchy of Clergy

WITHIN THE EASTERN ORTHODOX CHURCH, THE leaders of the church are known as *episkopoi* (over-seers—*episkopos* is the singular), which translates as "bishop" in English. The other ordained roles are *presbyter* (which became *prester*, and then "priest" in English), and *diakonos*, which became "deacon." There are numerous administrative positions in the clergy that carry additional titles. In the Greek tradition, bishops who occupy a historically ancient See are called "metropolitan," while the lead bishop in Greece is known as the archbishop. Priests can be archpriests, archimandrites, or protopresbyters. Deacons can be archdeacons or protodeacons. The position of deacon is often occupied for life and a deacon serves as a bishop's assistant.

The patriarch (and bishop) of Constantinople is considered a "first among equals" among the patriarchs of the Eastern Orthodox churches. He is the church's spiritual leader and has the power to extend autocephalous authority (that is, independent jurisdiction) to national churches such as the Bulgarian, Romanian, Serbian, Russian, and Ukrainian Orthodox Churches.

There are three major orders: bishop, priest, and deacon, and two minor orders: subdeacon and reader.

Bishop. Bishops form the leadership in the Eastern Orthodox Church. The traditional role of a bishop is as pastor of a diocese. A metropolitan bishop is an archbishop in charge of an ecclesiastical province, or group of dioceses, and exercises some oversight over the other dioceses. Sometimes, a metropolitan may also be the head of an autonomous church.

Priests. The most significant liturgical acts reserved for Eastern Orthodox priests are the administration of the sacraments, including the celebration of the Mass or Divine Liturgy, the Eucharist, and the

Orthodox Churches in the United States*

Jurisdiction	Number of Parishes	Membership: Full	Adherents (Est.)
1. Orthodox Church in America (OCA)	456	39,400	115,100
1a. Regular Territorial Diocese of OCA	368	29,600	76,000
1b. Albanian Diocese of OCA	12	1,500	6,500
1c. Bulgarian Diocese of OCA	19	1,500	8,800
1d. Romanian Episcopate of OCA	57	6,800	23,800
2. Greek Orthodox Archdiocese of America	525	N/D	440,000
3. Antiochian Orthodox Christian Archdiocese	206	41,840	83,700
4. Serbian Orthodox Church in the USA	78	N/D	57,500
5. Serbian Orthodox Church	40	N/D	N/D
6. Ukrainian Orthodox Church of the USA	106	9,200	30,000
7. American Carpatho-Russian Greek Cath. Diocese	76	11,753	20,000
8. Romanian Orthodox Archdiocese–US/Canada	14	N/D	6,200
9. Bulgarian Eastern Orthodox Diocese, USA	9	N/D	4,340
10. Albanian Orthodox Diocese in America	2	350	500
11. Patriarchal Parishes of Russian Orthodox Church	33	N/D	N/D
12. Russian Orthodox Church Outside of Russia	128	N/D	N/D
13. Parishes of Macedonian Orthodox Church, USA	16	N/A	14,500
14. Holy Orthodox Church in North America	25	N/A	1,900
15. Greek Orthodox Archdiocese of Vasiloupolis	39	5,000	28,500
16. Holy Apostolic Catholic Assyrian Church... East	8	N/A	36,016
17. Armenian Church of America	89	11,400	45,800
18. Armenian Apostolic Church of America	38	11,100	23,200
19. Archdiocese N.A. of Coptic Orthodox Church	116	N/A	N/D
20. Syrian Orthodox Church of Antioch	23	N/D	15,100
21. Malankara Archdiocese, Syrian Orthodox Church	22	N/A	4,340
22. American Diocese of Malankara Orthodox Syrian Church	59	N/A	13,300

* Religious Congregations Membership Study: 2000, Hartford Institute for Religion Research.
"N/A": not applicable; "N/D": no data available.

Full members are generally defined as the persons older than eighteen, who regularly pay annual church membership fees and are officially recorded as members by the church. These data were obtained from the headquarters of various Orthodox jurisdictions in America. Adherents are generally defined as all those baptized Orthodox, who are well known to the local parish and attend church services several times a year (at least on major celebrations such as Easter, etc.) and their children. These figures were obtained through analysis of various sources (number of full members, average attendance on regular Sunday versus major holidays, number of persons on mailing lists of each jurisdiction, the size of the circulation of the major church news, etc.). **Informal surveys indicate numbers may have increased significantly since 2000.**

Sacrament of Reconciliation, a rite of Repentance also called Confession. Holy Baptism is also normally administered by a priest, as is Chrismation, which corresponds to Confirmation in the West. Additionally, priests administer the other sacramental mysteries, including the anointing of the sick and marriage. The only sacrament that is always reserved to a bishop is that of ordination.

Deacon. In addition to reading the Gospel and assisting in the administration of the Eucharist, the deacon "censes" (perfumes with incense) the icons and people, calls the people to prayer, prays the litanies (series of petitions), and has a role in the dialogue of the Anaphora. In keeping with Eastern tradition, and contrary to Western practice, he may not be the imparter of the mysteries of crowning (marriage) or of baptism, which includes Eucharist and Chrismation (confirmation).

Deacons may not marry after being ordained, but a married man may be ordained a deacon regardless of whether he remains a deacon or is ultimately elevated to the priesthood.

The Orthodox Church has always allowed married priests and deacons, provided the marriage takes place *before* ordination. In general, married priests become parish priests because they can live in normal society (that is, "in the world" and not in a monastery) since Orthodoxy views marriage as a normal human state. Unmarried priests usually live in monasteries since there it is the unmarried state that is the norm. (Sometimes, however, an unmarried priest may be assigned to a parish.) Widowed priests and deacons may not remarry, and it is common for widower clergy to retire to a monastery. This is also true of widowed wives of clergy, who often do not remarry and may become nuns if their children are grown. Bishops are always celibate. Although the Eastern Orthodox Church considers men and women equal before God, only men who are qualified and have no canonical impediments may be ordained bishops, priests, or deacons.

In addition to the clergy mentioned above, there are both monks and nuns in Eastern Orthodoxy. The monastic men and women in Orthodoxy are usually restricted to monasteries and do not normally participate in the active ministry of the Church because the monastic vocation of contemplation and prayer is considered to be a unique calling different from that of being a pastor, teacher, or nurse. Normally the monastic vocation is a lay vocation with each monastery having just one or two priests to attend to the sacramental life of the community.

Becoming a Member of the Clergy

To become a priest, one must enter the seminary with a bachelor's degree. Upon entering the seminary, one undertakes a three-year program of theological study that would lead to a master of divinity degree. Graduation from a seminary does not necessarily guarantee ordination to the priesthood, however, as this is ultimately the decision of a bishop.

Ordination. Ordinations to the Major Orders always occur during the course of the Divine Liturgy, whereas those to the Minor Orders usually take place during the hours preceding the liturgy. Only the bishop has the power to ordain (although in cases of necessity an archimandrite or archpriest, as representative of the bishop, may be granted permission to ordain a reader). Because of the collegial nature of the episcopacy, a college of bishops (at least two or three) are necessary to consecrate another bishop. And since any ordination requires the consent of the whole people of God, at a particular point in the service, the assembled congregation proclaims, "*Axios!*" ("He is worthy!"), indicating their assent.

The rite of consecration to the episcopacy is very solemn and the bishop is ordained in the sanctuary, in the midst of the congregation, before the singing of the Trisagion (Holy God). Thus the reading of the Holy Gospel is done already with his blessing.

The priest is ordained after the singing of the Cherubic Hymn, but before the sanctification of the Holy Gifts. The rite of ordination to the deaconate is not as solemn and takes place before the singing of the Lord's Prayer, when the sanctification of the Holy Gifts has already taken place, since the deacon only assists at the performance of the sacraments and does not perform them. At the conclusion of the liturgy, the priest goes out to the people to read the prayer before the ambo and the deacon to say the final litany, these actions being the first external signs of their ministry.

Laying-on of Hands. In all cases of ordination to the Major Orders, there is a laying-on of hands on the head of the one being ordained and the grace of the Holy Spirit is invoked. Like ordination to the Major Orders, ordination to the Minor Orders also involves a laying-on of hands, but there is no invocation of the Holy Spirit in these ordinations.

Orthodox priests and deacons are divided into two distinct groups: the married ("white" or parochial) clergy and the monastic (or "black") clergy. The monastic clergy are by nature unmarried, but one seeking ordination to the ranks of the white clergy may now choose to be celibate (unmarried) or married, but must make the choice prior to ordination since, under Orthodox Canon Law, one may not marry after ordination. A celibate priest or deacon may not later marry and a married priest or deacon whose wife dies may not remarry. Also, one who has been divorced is not permitted to be ordained. Bishops are drawn exclusively from the ranks of the monastic clergy, although a celibate or widower may be consecrated a bishop after having taken monastic vows. In ancient times, married men were permitted to become bishops, but such has not been the case since at least the sixth century.

Monasticism. When a man enters a monastery, he normally passes through three steps or stages: (1) probationer (novice, including the *riasaphor*, or Rassophore, stage), (2) monk of the lesser schema (cross-bearer or *stavrophore*), and (3) monk of the great schema (Russian: *skhimnik*). The probationer who enters a monastery desires to do so to acquit himself worthily in the angelic state, so called because monks renounce all worldly things, do not marry, do not acquire and hold property, and live as do the angels in heaven, glorifying God night and day and striving to do God's will in all things.

For a period of at least three years, the novice must train himself under the guidance of one skilled in the monastic life and the direction of souls, by immersing himself in the life of the monastery, struggling to perform the obediences given to him, and preparing himself physically (through his labors, fasting, vigils, etc.) and spiritually (through his rule of prayer and obedience to an elder).

Traditionally, a novice, after spending a short time in lay clothing, is vested in part of the monastic habit, that is, the inner *riasa* and the *skouphos* (or monastic cap). The inner riasa is a narrow-sleeved robe reaching to the ankles (*podriznik* in Russian) and the skouphos is a cup-shaped cap. These garments are always black in color (as are all the monastic garments), signifying penitence and deadness to (and rejection of) the ways of the world.

Riasaphor. After one has been a novice for a while, he could take the next step, which is that of riasaphor monk, who, it must be noted, is still considered to be a novice, but in a special sense. He does not make solemn vows, as do the monks of the lesser and greater schemas, but he is still considered to be, although imperfect, a true monk. He cannot marry, or leave the monastery, and if he were to leave and marry, he would be subject to excommunication.

The Order of the Riasa is usually performed after one of the canonical hours. Standing before the abbot, the candidate is **tonsured** (hair cut in a crosswise form) in the name of the Father, and of the Son, and of the Holy Spirit, signifying that he casts from himself all idle thoughts and acts, and takes upon himself the yoke of the Lord. The abbot then vests him with the outer riasa (a wide-sleeved outer robe) and *kamilavka* (a flat-topped hat).

In ancient times, the riasa was worn on days of mourning and it signifies to the novice that he must grieve for his sins. The kamilavka (cap protecting from the heat) signifies to the novice that he must tame the heat of the passions. Henceforth, the novice is called riasaphor (wearer of the robe).

Once one has attained the status of riasaphor, he is under no obligation to advance further in the monastic grades.

Order of the Lesser Schema (Stavrophore). The main feature of the Order of the Lesser Schema is the tonsure and the making of solemn vows. The candidate stands unclothed in the narthex of the church as though about to be baptized by immersion. Vows are made similar to the baptismal vows of renunciation, faith, and obedience to the end of life, and these are given in response to specific questions. A new name is given, and the hair is shorn, just as at baptism. The new monastic is given a cross, just as a cross is placed around the neck of the newly baptized, and he is also given a lighted candle to hold.

As he is conducted to the abbot, the novice performs three prostrations on the way, and then stops before the holy doors where the abbot is waiting. Before him stands a lectern upon which are laid a cross and a testament.

The abbot then asks him what he seeks in coming here. The reply is given, "I seek a life of mortification." Then, in order to test his willingness, the abbot hands scissors three times to the novice, asking him each time to "take these scissors and give them to me." Each time the novice takes the scissors and hands them back to the abbot, kissing his hand. Then the abbot tonsures the novice's head in the form of a cross.

The Monastic Habit. At the completion of the tonsure, the new monk is now vested in the monastic habit. At the same time a cross is hung on his neck, signifying that he is to follow Christ.

The Order of the Great Schema. The highest level of Orthodox monasticism entails a more intense ceremony and is entered into by those with the highest level of monastic commitment.

B. The Hierarchy of the Eastern Orthodox Church in the U.S.

The Standing Conference of Canonical Orthodox Bishops in the Americas—or SCOBA—was established in 1960 for the purpose of bringing together the canonical hierarchs of the Orthodox jurisdictions of North America. With headquarters in New York City, SCOBA hierarchs meet twice annually to discuss matters of common interest. Several agencies have been established by SCOBA to carry out specific missions of the organization:

- The Orthodox Christian Education Commission (OCEC);
- International Orthodox Christian Charities (IOCC);
- The Orthodox Christian Mission Center (OCMC).

Other organizations are: the Eastern Orthodox Committee on Scouting, the Orthodox Christian Fellowship, and the Orthodox Christian Network.

Currently, SCOBA is chaired by Most Rev. Archbishop Demetrios, primate of the Greek Orthodox Church in America.

The vice-chair is Most Rev. Metropolitan Philip, Primate of the Antiochian Orthodox Christian Archdiocese of North America; the other officers are Most Rev. Metropolitan Christopher, primate of the Serbian Orthodox Church in the United States and Canada; and Most Rev. Metropolitan Nicholas of Amissos, primate of the American Carpatho-Russian Orthodox Diocese of the United States.

The remaining hierarchs of SCOBA are:

Rt. Rev. Bishop Ilia of Philomelion, Primate of the Albanian Orthodox Diocese of America; Most Rev. Metropolitan Joseph, Primate of the Bulgarian

Archbishop Beatitude Metropolitan Theodosius of the Orthodox Church in America, left; Archbishop Demetrios, chairman of the Greek Orthodox Archdiocese of America, center; and Archbishop Metropolitan Christopher of the Serbian Orthodox Church as they emerge from Saint Sophia Cathedral in Washington, D.C., on May 2, 2001, following an enclave and evening vespers at the cathedral.

Orthodox Church; Most Rev. Metropolitan Herman, primate of the Orthodox Church in America; Most Rev. Archbishop Nicolae, primate of the Romanian Orthodox Archdioces in America and Canada; and Most Rev. Metropolitan Constantine, primate of the Ukranian Orthodox Church of the United States.

∞

C. Seminaries in the United States

Saint Herman's Orthodox Seminary
414 Mission Road
Kodiak, AK 99615
907-486-3524   Fax: 907-486-5935
info@sthermanseminary.org
www.sthermanseminary.org

Established as a pastoral school in 1972, the seminary now provides a number of educational programs to prepare students for work in the Orthodox Church as readers, choir directors, church school-teachers, and clergy.

Saint Herman's is one of three seminaries (along with Saint Tikhon's and Saint Vladimir's) providing professional theological education for the Orthodox Church in America.

The Patriarch Athenagoras Orthodox Institute
2311 Hearst Avenue
Berkeley, CA 94709
510-649-3450   Fax: 510-841-6605
paoi@gtu.edu
www.orthodoxinstitute.org

The institute is an inter-Orthodox endeavor, representing the diversity of Orthodoxy in America: Albanian, Antiochian, Bulgarian, Carpatho-Russian, Greek, OCA, Romanian, Serbian, and Ukrainian.

The institute is a member of the Graduate Theological Union, an ecumenical and interfaith consortium of nine independent seminaries and ten affiliated centers based in Berkeley, California.

Hellenic College
Holy Cross Greek Orthodox School
     of Theology
50 Goddard Avenue
Brookline, MA 02445
617-731-3500
www.hchc.edu/holycross.html

The institution was originally founded as Holy Cross Theological School in 1937 in Pomfret, Connecticut. In 1946, the school was moved to Brookline, Massachusetts. In 1966, Holy Cross expanded its collegiate division with a full four-year liberal arts college called Hellenic College, a distinct undergraduate institution, and offers graduate programs leading to the degrees of Master of Divinity (MDiv), Master of Theological Studies (MTS), and Master of Theology (ThM).

Saint Sophia Ukrainian Orthodox Theological
     Seminary
PO Box 495
South Bound Brook, NJ 08880
 732-356-0090   Fax: 732-356-5556
www.uocofusa.org/seminary.html

Saint Vladimir's Orthodox Theological Seminary
575 Scarsdale Road
Crestwood, NY 10707-1699
 914-961-8313   Fax: 914-961-4507
www.svots.edu

This seminary is one of three institutions of professional theological education in the Orthodox Church. Along with priestly vocation, Saint Vladimir's also provides education for other church leaders, such as choir directors and religious educators. In addition to the Master of Divinity program (MDiv), the seminary offers the Master of Arts in Theology (MA), the Master of Theology (MTh), and the Doctorate of Ministry (DMin).

Holy Trinity Orthodox Seminary

Russian Orthodox Church Outside Russia
PO Box 36
Jordanville, NY 13361
315-858-0945
info@hts.edu
www.hts.edu

Under the jurisdiction of the Russian Orthodox Church Outside Russia (ROCOR), this seminary trains students in disciplines that are preparatory for active service to the church: clergy, monastics, choir directors and cantors, iconographers, and lay leaders. The seminary offers a five-year program of study leading to the degree of Bachelor of Theology (BTh).

Christ the Saviour Carpatho-Russian Seminary

American Carpatho-Russian Orthodox Diocese
225 Chandler Avenue
Johnstown, PA 15906
814-539-0116
csseminary@atlanticbb.net
www.acrod.org/seminary.html

This is the seminary for the American Carpatho-Russian Orthodox Diocese (ACROD), a self-governing diocese within the jurisdiction of the ecumenical patriarchate. The seminary provides training for men to become priests in the Orthodox Church.

Saint Tikhon's Orthodox Theological Seminary

The Orthodox Church in America
PO Box 130
South Canaan, PA 18459
570-937-4411   Fax: 570-937-3100
info@stots.edu
www.stots.edu

Saint Tikhon's is another of the three seminary institutions of professional theological education in the Orthodox Church in America. It is attached to Saint Tikhon's Orthodox Monastery.

Saint Nersess Armenian Seminary

150 Stratton Road
New Rochelle, NY 10804
914-636-2003
www.stnersess.edu

Two graduate-level programs are offered by this seminary: the Master of Divinity (MDiv) degree through a joint program with Saint Vladimir's Orthodox Theological Seminary, and the Master of Arts (MA) degree in Armenian Christian studies.

Pope Shenouda III Coptic Orthodox Theological Seminary

2 Woodstone Drive
PO Box 287
Cedar Grove, NJ 07009
714-775-7912
PO Box 9415
Fountain Valley, CA 92728-9415
562-596-1916
www.geocities.com/Athens/Aegean/9944

Established by Pope Shenouda III, pope and patriarch of Alexandria, in November 1989.

Saint Athanasius Theological Seminary

San Antonio, Texas; the Coptic Orthodox Diocese of the Southern United States
Father Jacob Billatos Nadian
1480 Falcon Lane
Hoffman Estates, IL 60192
fr_jacob@yahoo.com
www.suscopts.org/seminary

Degree programs offered: Bachelor of Divinity, Master of Divinity, Audit certificate.

D. Shrines and Houses of Worship

Organizations

The Eastern Orthodox Church is a communion comprising the collective body of fifteen separate autocephalous hierarchical churches that recognize each other as "canonical" Orthodox Christian churches.

Autocephaly is the status of a church within the Orthodox Church whose primatial bishop does not report to any higher-ranking bishop. An ecumenical council or a high-ranking bishop, such as a patriarch or other primate, grants autocephaly by releasing an ecclesiastical province from the authority of their bishop. The newly independent church, however, remains in full communion with its former hierarchy.

The highest-ranking bishop of the communion is the patriarch of Constantinople, who is also primate of one of the fourteen or fifteen churches. These organizations are in full communion with each other, so any priest of these churches may lawfully minister to members of other, and no member is excluded from worship in the other churches.

Autocephalous Churches

- Orthodox Church of Constantinople, under the ecumenical patriarch, in modern Turkey
- Orthodox Church of Alexandria, patriarch also styled pope, historically second patriarchate in rank
- Orthodox Church of Antioch, historically third patriarchate in rank
- Orthodox Church of Jerusalem, historically fourth patriarchate in rank
- Russian Orthodox Church, younger but linked to Imperial Russia's claim to succeed to Byzantium as the Third Rome
- Georgian Orthodox and Apostolic Church
- Serbian Orthodox Church
- Romanian Orthodox Church
- Bulgarian Orthodox Church
- Orthodox Church of Cyprus
- Church of Greece
- Polish Orthodox Church
- Albanian Orthodox Church
- Czech and Slovak Orthodox Church
- Orthodox Church in America (autocephaly not universally recognized)

Autonomous Churches

- The Church of Sinai (Patriarchate of Jerusalem)
- The Church of Finland (under the Patriarch of Constantinople)
- The Church of Ukraine (under the Patriarch of Moscow)
- The Church of Japan

Major Enclaves

Saint Nicholas Cathedral
3500 Massachusetts Avenue NW
Washington, D.C. 20007
202-333-5060
office@stnicholasdc.org
www.stnicholasdc.org

Founded in 1930 as the Russian Orthodox Church of Saint Nicholas, Saint Nicholas Cathedral is the primatial cathedral of His Beatitude Herman, archbishop of Washington and New York, metropolitan of all America and Canada of the Orthodox Church in America.

The cathedral architecture is based on the twelfth-century Saint Demetrius Cathedral of Vladimir, Russia. Beginning in 1991, dedicated iconographers from Moscow wrote icons throughout the nave in the traditional style.

Greek Orthodox Cathedral of the Holy Trinity
319-337 East 74th Street
New York, NY 10021
212-288-3215/6   Fax: 212-288-5876
cathedral@thecathedral.goarch.org
www.thecathedral.goarch.org

Chartered in 1892, the Holy Trinity Church has been serving the Greek Orthodox community of New York for over a century. The cornerstone for the present building was laid on September 14, 1931, in the presence of Eleanor Roosevelt, representing her husband, Governor Franklin D. Roosevelt. Holy Trinity Church was consecrated on October 22, 1933. It was designated the Archdiocesan Cathedral of the Greek Orthodox Archdiocese in 1962.

E. Governance and Authority

The holy canons (principles), which are the basis of the Eastern Orthodox Church's canonical tradition, stem from three main sources: Ecumenical Synods (representing the universal church), Local Synods (subsequently ratified by the ecumenical synods as representing the tradition of the universal Church), and the Fathers of the Church. All these canons—about a thousand—are contained in several collections. The one most widely used today in the Greek-speaking Orthodox churches is the *Pedalion* (the rudder), which takes its name from the metaphor of the church depicted as a ship.

The *Pedalion* is a collection of guiding canons composed by the apostles, local or regional and general or ecumenical councils, and used by the hierarchs to govern the church. This text has always been understood to be a guide and not a rulebook. Orthodox bishops have the ability to relax the strictness of the guide in special cases. This ability is called *economia* (leniency).

Since the Orthodox Church structure is based on the concept of spiritual guidance, it has always been understood that every situation is different and nothing can be treated in a legal way or automatically (*latae sententiae*). According to the canon law of the Orthodox Church, economia is the suspension of the absolute and strict applications of canon and church regulations in the governing and the life of the church. The application of economia only takes place through the official church authorities and is only applicable for a particular case.

Unlike the canon law of the Roman Catholic Church, the canon law of the Orthodox Church has not been codified. Neither is it prescriptive in character, anticipating a situation before it actually takes place; instead, it is corrective in nature, responding to a situation once it has occurred. Because of the absence of a universal codification binding upon all autocephalous, Orthodox Churches, great importance is attached to the local legislation of each of these churches.

The Saint Paul Armenian Church in Fresno, California, is one of hundreds of Orthodox Christian churches to be found across North America.

Local regulations are the means by which the church's universal canonical tradition adapts itself to changing circumstances. Although this is true, it must not be supposed that any local custom automatically establishes itself as part of the church's canonical tradition. Two conditions are necessary for acceptance of a custom as law: it must have enjoyed a long and steady practice, and the consensus of opinion must be that it has the force of law. In order for custom to be accepted as a source of the church's canonical tradition, it must be in full harmony with the holy tradition, scripture, and doctrine.

As a province of the Ecumenical Patriarchate, the first-ranking See among the autocephalous Orthodox Churches, the Greek Orthodox Archdiocese of America is an ecclesiastical body deriving its authority from a central source. The various components comprising its canonical structure are elements of the legal system of every local Orthodox church.

F. Social Service Organizations

International Orthodox Christian Charities
110 West Road, Suite 360
Baltimore, MD 21204
410-243-9820   Fax: 410-243-9824
relief@iocc.org   www.iocc.org

As the official humanitarian aid agency representing the member churches of the Standing Conference of Canonical Orthodox Bishops of the Americas (SCOBA), IOCC has delivered more than $140 million in humanitarian assistance to twenty-one countries since 1992.

Ladies Philoptochos Society
Greek Orthodox Archdiocese of America
345 East 74th Street
New York, NY 10021
212-774-4390   Fax: 212-861-1956
philosny@aol.com
www.philoptochos.com

This is the philanthropic heart of the Greek Orthodox Archdiocese of America. Established in 1931 by the late Ecumenical Patriarch Arthenagoras, it has for over seventy-five years overseen many philanthropic programs. Since 1987, the National Philoptochos has employed a professional social worker engaged in assisting the Greek Orthodox community. The Philoptochos raises money for several funds: Cancer Fund, Children's Cardiac Fund, Children's Medical Fund, Emergency and General Medical Fund.

Project Mexico
PO Box 120028
Chula Vista, CA 91912
619-426-4610   Fax: 619-426-4619
info@projectmexico.org
www.projectmexico.org

Project Mexico is an Orthodox Christian Charitable Mission founded in 1988 by Gregory Yova. It has built more than 130 houses for homeless families and started an orphanage for boys, the Saint Innocent Ranch, a half-acre ranch near Rosarito, Mexico. Volunteers from forty-three states and eleven foreign countries assist the project's ongoing work.

Tolstoy Foundation
104 Lake Road
Valley Cottage, NY 10989
845-268-6722   Fax: 845-268-6937
tfhq@aol.com

The Tolstoy Foundation, established in 1939 by Alexandra Tolstoy, youngest daughter of novelist Leo Tolstoy, is a nonprofit international philanthropic organization that focuses on orphaned and disadvantaged children in Russia, through education and vocational training programs at the center in Valley Cottage, New York. It also operates homes for the aged in the U.S., France, and Latin America.

G. Media and Communication

Newspapers and Periodicals

Orthodox Observer
Greek Orthodox Archdiocese of America
8 East 79th Street
New York, NY 10021
212-570-3555   Fax: 212-774-0239
observer@goarcdh.org
www.observer.goarch.org

The Church Messenger
Carpatho-Russian Metropolis
145 Broad Street
Perth Amboy, NJ 08861
732-826-4442   Fax: 732-826-5383
mrosco2@excite.com

The Word
Antiochian Archdiocese
358 Mountain Road
PO Box 5238
Englewood, NJ 07631
201-871-1355   Fax: 201-871-7954
archidiocese@antiochan.org

Credinta – The Faith Magazine
Romanian Orthodox Archdiocese, U.S. & Canada
5410 North Newland Avenue
Chicago, IL 60656
773-774-1677   Fax: 773-774-1805
romarch67@aol.org   www.romarch.org
44 Midland Street
Worcester, MA 01602
508-756-9866   Fax: 508-845-8850
nka@net1plus.com

Path of Orthodoxy
Serbian Orthodox Church
PO Box 883
Bridgeport, WV 26330
740-264-4809   Fax: 740-282-0313
radmerk@attbi.com   nedlunich@att.com

The Orthodox Church
PO Box 675
Syosset, NY 11791-0675
516-922-0550   Fax: 516-922-0954
 www.oca.org (click on "publications")
The Orthodox Church, the bi-monthly official publication of the Orthodox Church in America, published since 1965, is sent gratis to all members of parishes of the Orthodox Church in America.

Radio Broadcasting

Orthodox Christian Network
815 NE 15th Avenue
Ft. Lauderdale, FL 33305
1-877-2-RECEIVE
www.receive.org

The Orthodox Christian Network's flagship program, *Come Receive The Light* (CRTL), is a call-in radio ministry broadcasting via satellite across the United States and Canada. CRTL covers contemporary moral and religious issues with clergymen, lay theologians, and guests in specific areas of expertise.

Incarnation Broadcast Network
c/o Holy Assumption Church
2027 18th Street NE
Canton, OH 44641
staff@inbn.net   www.inbn.net
Incarnation Broadcast Network provides 24-hour-a-day Orthodox Christian Internet radio, news, teaching, and live programming, including live liturgical services, daily scriptural readings, Bible studies, and lectures by prominent Orthodox speakers.

INBN.net is a ministry of Holy Assumption Orthodox Church in Canton, Ohio—a parish of the Orthodox Church in America, Midwest Diocese.

TV Broadcasting

GOTelecom
Greek Orthodox Telecommunications
8 East 79th Street
New York, NY 10075
212-570-3588   Fax: 212-774-0223
gotel@goarch.org
GOTelecom serves as the television ministry of the Greek Orthodox Archdiocese of America. The mission is three fold: (1) to archive the activities of the entire Greek Orthodox Archdiocese of America; (2) to produce in-house programs that educate the faithful about the ministries of the archdiocese; and (3) to produce programs of quality that can be distributed nationally through the mediums of television and video.

FURTHER READING

Encountering the Mystery
Patriarch Bartholomew
2008: Doubleday

Orthodox Christians in America
John H. Erikson
2008: Oxford University Press

The Orthodox Church
Timothy Ware (Bishop Kallistos of Diokleia)
1997: Penguin

II. CHRISTIANITY

Protestantism

Historical Introduction
1. Baptist Church
2. Christian Science
3. Congregationalism
4. Disciples of Christ
5. Episcopal Church
6. Evangelical Denominations
7. Jehovah's Witnesses
8. The Church of Jesus Christ of Latter-day Saints (Mormonism)
9. Lutheran Church
10. Mennonites
11. Methodists
12. Presbyterianism
13. Quakers
14. Seventh-day Adventists
15. Unitarian Universalists

II Christianity: Protestantism

Historical Introduction

THE HISTORY OF PROTESTANTISM IN AMERICA IS inseparable from the history of America itself—America as an independent nation; America as a land of religious freedom and pluralism; America as a battle-scarred champion of civil rights and social reform. From its inception to the present, the Protestant movement has mirrored the specific qualities that have come to be considered essentially American: those of diversity, tenacity, evolution, adaptation, aspiration, and innovation. And its movers have come in every race, age, and gender. While it is difficult to pin exact numbers on Protestant demographics, largely because the movement is so internally diverse and not easily theologically categorized, a 2006 Baylor Institute study entitled "American Piety in the 21st Century" found that over 60 percent of Americans identify as Protestants (see Part III on page 829). The movement continues to be a strong force in America, emerging in offices of great authority and persuasion.

The Protestant Identity

Unfortunately for pollsters, there is no singularly identifiable profile of a Protestant. Fortunately for the American nation, the contentions spurred by such pluralism have frequently catalyzed necessary change, transforming benighted conditions of society and government in a wake of forward progression. The multifaceted movement is generally traced back to a common ancestor: Martin Luther, a Catholic monk whose protest of ninety-five points of Catholic Church doctrine and practice earned the movement its name. Ironically, Luther's rebellion arose from his overwhelming desire to comply. An overtly conscientious member of the German Roman Catholic religious community, Luther was incessantly harassed by the fear that his endless spiritual supplications for divine forgiveness were futile in the face of his inborn sin. Unable to garner satisfactory reassurance from church authorities, Luther turned to the Bible, and in his studies arrived at a new understanding of divine justice and redemption. Luther found the passage "the just will live by faith" (Romans 1:17) revelatory, intimating that man could gain salvation through faith alone, rather than through faith *and* works, as advocated by the Catholic Church. Luther's resulting Ninety-Five Theses, nailed to the door of the Castle Church in Wittenberg on October 31, 1517, posed suggested points of reform for the Catholic Church. But the church did not receive Luther's suggestions with grace. Rather, it took arms against what it viewed as gross audacity and ordered him to recant. Luther's reply to Holy Roman Emperor Charles V was, "Unless I am convinced by the testimony of the Scriptures or by clear reason (for I do not trust either in the pope or in councils alone, since it is well known that they have often erred and contradicted themselves), I am bound by the Scriptures I have quoted and my conscience is captive to the Word of God. I cannot and I will not retract anything, since it is neither safe nor right to go against conscience." Thus began the movement coined the "Protestant Reformation."

Luther's insights quickly caught on in Europe, consuming large swaths of dissatisfied Catholics in Germany, England, Scotland, the Netherlands, and Switzerland. Many citizens of these countries would take their new beliefs to the New World in search of more fertile ground for cultivation and growth. While the Reformation was almost immediately characterized by theological variety, five fundamental points founded the basis of most denominations. Known as the Five Solas (the Latin *sola* translated as "alone"), these phrases name the only elements requisite for Christian salvation, in contradistinction to Catholic teachings:

1. *Solus Christus* (Christ alone) – Christ is the only intermediary between God and man; clergy do not hold a special spiritual status.

2. *Sola scripture* (scripture alone) – The Bible should serve as the primary guide for spiritual understanding and religious life, and such interpretation is accessible to all—not only church authorities.

3. *Sola fide* (faith alone) – Man may achieve salvation, or redemption from sin, through faith alone. Works attest one's faith, but are not necessary for salvation.

4. *Sola gratia* (grace alone) – Christ's death and resurrection granted man the gift of God's salvation as an unmerited favor—not needing to be earned.

5. *Soli Deo gloria* (glory to God alone) – Human beings, even saints canonized by the Catholic Church, are not equal to the glory due God, who grants man salvation through His will alone.

Evangelicalism

Arguably, the most recognizable demarcation within Protestantism lies between evangelicals and mainline Protestants. Evangelicalism arose in the eighteenth century as a merging of two earlier colonial movements in America: Pietism and Puritanism. Pietism called for spiritual rebirth, demanded righteous living, emphasized the need for inner spiritual fervor, and warned against stagnation in the performance of religious duties. Puritans were

This painting of George Whitefield, by the British artist John Russell (d. 1806), captures Whitefield's strabismus, or crossed eyes—a condition that, according to contemporaneous accounts, had a profound effect on his listeners. Benjamin Franklin confirmed rumors that Whitefield's revival meetings attracted audiences in the thousands, after which he became Whitefield's publisher, though he never shared the preacher's views.

known for their rigorous moral standards and the demand for a conversion experience, as notably exemplified in Calvinism, an orthodox denomination preeminently founded on the teachings of French reformer John Calvin. Calvinists upheld the idea of original sin—that Adam's mistake in the second chapter of Genesis left an indelible mark of ignominy on humanity. Salvation could be achieved only by a predestined minority elect, they posited, and it could not be determined who this elect were except through the testimony of conversion experiences. The authenticity of such conversion narratives was judged by church elders, who subsequently granted church membership to those decided predestined for salvation. Church membership, in turn, offered colonists special privileges, such as the right to vote, in accord with the theocratic state of early American social organization.

Among Puritans and Pietists, some affiliations were members of the Reform movement in that they hoped to reform the Anglican Church from within

(Calvinists, for example). But other groups were Separatist in nature, or dissenters (often called Pilgrims), asserting the need for complete separation from the pope's affairs as well as worldly corruption. Groups falling under the Separatist category were Radical Spiritists (Anne Hutchinson was one notable member), who eschewed the conversion experience in lieu of the belief that one could determine the fate of one's own soul; Anabaptists, who upheld "believer's baptism," or the idea that comprehending adults should be baptized rather than ignorant infants; and Millenarians, who searched biblical prophecy (especially in the books of Daniel and Revelation) for some indication of the date of Christ's return to earth.

The Great Awakening

Evangelicalism as a distinct movement was born of the Great Awakening—a period of religious revivals that swept the nation in the mid-eighteenth century. Led predominantly by an Anglican actor-turned-preacher named George Whitefield, the revivals began in New England and raced south, ultimately transforming the mostly Anglican colonies of white planters, yeomen, and African slaves (the latter holding fast to indigenous beliefs) into the Bible Belt we know today. With a knack for galvanizing audiences, Whitefield largely changed the face of Protestant religion in America from outward, formal expressions of religiosity to an inward focus on personal, heartfelt spiritual fervor. His message was the "New Birth," or a demand for personal conversion and adherence to upright living. Whitefield's ardent urgings were clearly more Pietistic than Puritan in nature, yet elements of Calvinism remained in the advertising of man's inherent sinfulness and subsequent need to beg God for salvation.

Whitefield's 1740 tour through New England was a phenomenon of unprecedented religious practice and public reach in young American history. Preaching wherever he'd be heard to whoever was listening at whatever time of day, Whitefield managed to secure crowds of up to 8,000 listeners on a daily basis for month-long stretches. His form of public speaking was unusual for the topic: rather than sermonizing *at* the audience, he spoke *to* them, manipulating their emotions with dramatic perspicacity. The youthful preacher's work in the majority of colonies brought people together in the formation of many new churches: Baptist in the middle and southern colonies, Presbyterian in Virginia, Lutheran in Pennsylvania, and Methodist everywhere.

In New England, a young, pious man of the name Jonathan Edwards contributed to such unification in carrying out what he called "the surprising work of God." As the minister of a Congregationalist church in Northampton, Massachusetts, Edwards clung to orthodox Calvinistic beliefs, sermonizing on predestination and depraved humanity's helpless dependence on God. Edwards's method of effectively terrorizing his congregation into submission to God with impassioned "fire and brimstone"–style sermons won him an enormous following throughout the Connecticut River Valley. Edwards's most famous awakening sermon, "Sinners in the Hands of an Angry God," conveys with awful import the great burden of sin, the terrible wrath of God, and the unexpectedness of the moment when God will execute justice.

Edwards's work aside, the revivals had a very different effect in other areas of New England. Rather than unify the colonists and spark new organizations of worship, revivalism caused a splintering within churches and towns, best seen in the formation of the New Lights and the Old Lights. The New Lights were avid enthusiasts of the revivals; the Old Lights considered such emotionalism and fervor distasteful and untrustworthy. One highly illustrative case of the disunion may be found in New Haven, Connecticut, where two meeting houses sit side by side on the village green: one built by New Lights; the other by Old Lights.

Protestantism and Social Standing

The awakenings had an interesting ripple effect through America's social hierarchy. Samuel Davies was a Presbyterian preacher who aided in the southern revivals—most notably among black slaves. The slaves of William Byrd III's Virginia plantation were the first to establish their own formal fellowship for worship in 1758, but Savannah, Georgia, proved the main seat of black Christianity. George Leile was the slave of a Baptist deacon in Georgia who was freed upon his owner's death. Leile baptized Andrew Bryan, a fellow Georgian slave, who in turn was ordained as a Baptist preacher in 1788. Bryan organized what is now known as the First African Baptist Church, which, by 1812, claimed almost fifteen hundred members. Black churches offered

From a small drive-in church in Garden Grove, California—which the young Dutch Reformed minister Robert H. Schuller (b. 1926) rented for $500—came one of the most successful televangelical ministries of the last half-century. The Crystal Cathedral, the interior of which is seen in this 2005 photograph, was designed by architect Philip Johnson and constructed with more than ten thousand panes of glass. It seats nearly three thousand worshippers. Schuller's Hour of Power broadcasts blended a message of life-affirming "Possibility Thinking" with an engaging, homespun style ("Inch by inch, everything's a cinch") that also found expression in best-selling books.

slaves a measure of autonomy within the organizations that their socially oppressed lives otherwise lacked.

The large gatherings of blacks under their own jurisdiction made white coreligionists nervous at best and furious at worst. Indeed, Bryan was publicly whipped for his temerity. During the first Great Awakening, the Protestant belief in a "priesthood of believers"—or the idea that every member of the faithful is equal before God—drew thousands of African Americans to worship among whites. In fact, black ministers often shared the pulpit with white ministers, and white worshippers often praised the spiritual perceptiveness and power of black fellow congregants. Black women were often specially recognized for their ability to bring about conversions. But, as the years passed, the egalitarian nature of evangelical worship deteriorated. White men became increasingly intolerant of large African contingents in their congregations, and seating became segregated.

Women, too, first gained a measure of autonomy that they later lost. Evangelicalism offered them leadership opportunities and a venue for self-expression in the form of exhortation: during a revival, exhorters brought worshippers to an emotional state ideal for conversion. But again, white men became disturbed by the prominence of women in churches, and took the same segregation measures they had for blacks. Ironically, this action did not have the desired effect, as men consequently decided that sitting apart allowed women too much independence and implied their prioritizing of church over family. So, seating was again desegregated by gender, and family seating restored.

One last group gained a newfound equality in revivalism that proved more permanent than that of blacks or women. The revival tradition, still practiced by evangelicals today, is characterized by dynamic expressions of heartfelt emotion, usually expressed bodily through jumping up and down in exaltation, rolling on the floor, laughing and/or dancing. Such behavior thoroughly challenged the Puritan hallmarks of outward dignity, poise, and proper comportment practiced by white gentry. And therein, America's lower class "plain folk" defiantly embraced it. In large revival meetings, black and white, man and woman, rich and poor commingled in an emotionally charged atmosphere that facilitated the breakdown of social status and erased the traditional lines of authority.

It is easy to see how the spread of evangelicalism came to underlie many of the social movements that dominated early American history—from temperance to feminism to abolition. But, it was characteristic of nineteenth-century evangelicals to feel that they were operating from scriptural authority no matter which side of an issue they supported. This was especially evident concerning slavery. In the North and among slaves, abolitionists upheld the phrase in Romans, "there is neither bond nor free because you all are one in Christ Jesus." In the South, white planters and their wives looked to the story of Ham, who was punished and his descendants (Africans) cursed. Whites used this example to contend that the bondage of Africans was a fulfillment of biblical prophecy.

It may also be argued that the establishment of secularism in America is due to evangelical Protestants. While separation of church and state was desired long before the Revolution, it was the war that finally drove home to Americans the importance of the preservation of religious freedom—not just religious toleration. Evangelical groups pushed mightily for religious disestablishment following the war—especially the Baptists of Virginia. Due to strength of number and noteworthy devotion to the revolutionary cause, the Baptists held considerable political clout, and used it to combat a standing legal obligation to pay taxes to the Anglican Church. Baptists throughout Virginia elicited the signatures of thousands who opposed supporting the church, and used them to petition the state body in charge of matters of taxation—the Assembly. The Assembly responded by disestablishing the Anglican Church but insisting that all citizens must continue to pay taxes to a religious institute of their choosing. These terms did not satisfy voters, who persevered in

their battle until the instatement of the Virginia Statute for Religious Freedom, authored by Thomas Jefferson. Jefferson wrote that religion and state must remain separate not for the welfare of government, but for the protection of religion.

The Second Great Awakening

Antebellum America was perhaps understandably drawn to a theory of postmillennialism—the idea that Christ would reinstate his reign on earth after one thousand years of peace and righteousness named in the book of Revelations. Evangelicals approached this idea from a standpoint of optimism, confident that the millennium was already underway (despite the occurrence of the Revolutionary War), and could even be sped along if all contributed to the reformation of a more godly society.

Postmillennialism was not the only new theology on the market during this period. Charles Grandison Finney, a towering man with piercing blue eyes who hailed from New York City, became a Presbyterian minister at the age of twenty-nine after undergoing a powerful conversion experience. Finney was led to reject his old Calvinistic principles and embrace the ideas of Dutch theologian Jacobus Arminius. Arminianism taught that salvation was attainable to all who sought it. God was loving and willing to forgive the truly repentant. Americans quickly abandoned their Calvinistic leanings and accepted the new theology with open arms. Revivals took on new meaning, as worshippers no longer felt they had to wait on God's clemency, but could take matters into their own hands and choose to convert. Rather than hail down wrathful oaths upon their congregations, exhorters now cajoled worshippers to choose a life patterned after Christ Jesus. Finney's precedent informed the current look of revivalism today, especially that led by Billy Graham.

Finney's evangelizing took on new scope in his use of public media to spread his message. He called door-to-door, distributing leaflets, and advertised revival meetings in newspapers. Finney's goal was to "win" converts—and having once won them, to retain their allegiance by counseling them after the meeting. His efforts were highly successful. Critics of Finney adopted his methods when they witnessed the great number of conversions his tactics elicited.

The emerging movements of postmillennialism and Arminianism combined to bring about a frenzy of philanthropy throughout America. A plethora of new charities were developed, temperance was championed, orphanages were established, and education was offered to women. And finally, emancipation of the slaves was achieved. Biracial worship was still frowned upon in churches, however, and many offended blacks left white churches to form their own congregations.

This photograph of Billy Graham (b. 1918), a Southern Baptist who set the standards for American evangelism in the twentieth century, was taken in April of 1966.

Mainline Protestantism

A new form of Protestantism arrived on the religious landscape toward the end of the eighteenth century. It had persisted behind the scenes since the initial settling of America, but it gained preeminence with the great attention allotted to social reforms. Called the Social Gospel, this new tradition focused not only on the purification of the human soul, but the purification of human society as well, addressing such issues as child labor, corruption in politics, the increasing presence of slums, and squalid tenement housing. While Protestants who took a more liberal stance on theological points met these social challenges with vigor, Evangelicals became increasingly pessimistic, ultimately turning from postmillennialism to premillennialism—the idea that Jesus's return was imminent, at which point he'd wreak justice upon the sinful. In light of the feared repercussions of being found unfaithful, evangelicals abandoned attempts to remedy society and focused entirely on personal regeneration.

Science also contributed to the rise of mainline, or liberal Protestantism. Darwin's introduction of *Origin of the Species* in 1859 contradicted the evangelical understanding of evolution, which was based on literal interpretation of the book of Genesis. The controversy spawned by Darwin's theory would reach a head in 1925 at the "Scopes Monkey Trial," in which evangelicals brought charges against high school teacher John Scopes for using Darwinian principles to teach evolution. Because science versus religion had by that time become a hot-button issue (one that still circulates in the public atmosphere), the media treated the trial as a publicity stunt. Over two hundred reporters covered the proceedings, and newspapers gave the event front-page real estate for days at a time. Top lawyers Clarence Darrow and William Jennings Bryan represented the defense and the plaintiff, respectively, and when Bryan agreed to submit to Darrow's questioning on the scientific accountability of the Bible, the media made the most of the dramatic circumstances. Influential journalist H. L. Mencken did much to disservice evangelicalism, calling Bryan a "buffoon" who spouted "theological bilge." He also portrayed the townspeople of Dayton, Tennessee, as backwards "yokels." Darrow, on the other hand, was "magnificent." Mencken's accounts and others' subsequent dramatic portrayals of the trial (the play and film *Inherit the Wind*, for instance) brought much ridicule upon creationism, as well as Fundamentalism—a movement that asserted the fundamentals of evangelicalism, such as the inerrancy of Scripture and divinity of Jesus.

Liberal Protestants challenged evangelicals on many counts. In addition to questioning the authenticity of the Bible, they cast doubt on the verity of traditional church creeds, and wondered whether religion did not better serve as an ethical guidepost than a means of "salvation." What if Jesus were one wise teacher among many, rather than the sole Son of God? Many Americans in the twentieth century found these new thoughts appealing, and evangelicalism became increasingly marginalized, eventually relegating itself to the perimeter of society. From 1925–1950, Evangelicalism condemned worldliness to the point of turning its back on society, rather than reaching out as it had during the awakenings. During this time, mainline Protestantism, with its accommodation of science and advocacy of religious laxness—its attempt to find the happy medium between religiosity and pragmatism—shone regnant. But Billy Graham would tip the scale again. In 1950, the Southern Baptist evangelist embarked on a revival "crusade" through Portland, Oregon that made overtures to all who cared to listen. Fundamentalists frowned upon his reintroduction of evangelicalism into the public spotlight, but Graham pressed on, utilizing the television to reach even broader audiences. In 1976, America elected evangelical Jimmy Carter as president. As the movement regained footing in politics, it gradually dropped its bitterness toward "worldliness" and willingly rejoined the public arena.

Today, evangelicals are the majority among Protestants, with mainline Protestantism on the decline. Graham's revivals were a phenomenon of enormous proportion: it is estimated that he has preached to nearly 215 million people in total, in almost two hundred countries. Mainline Protestantism, on the other hand, continues to fragment, and church membership decline. One might argue that liberal Protestantism's trend toward "serving two masters" (science and religion) results in a failure to serve either one. While evangelicals, holding staunchly to their distinctly drawn theology despite the fact that science's explanation of existence is increasingly accepted as the norm, persist as a strong strain in American evolution.

— Megan Stearns
Section Editor

Important Dates in American Protestantism

Oct. 31, 1517 Martin Luther nails his Ninety-five Theses to the door of Wittenberg Cathedral—Protestant Reformation begins.

1607 Jamestown, Virginia settlers conduct Anglican service.

1611 King James Version of the Bible published in England.

1619 Slaves first brought to Virginia; some are instructed in Christianity.

1620 Pilgrims (separatist Puritans) arrive in America aboard the Mayflower.

1628 Dutch minister Jonas Michaëlius conducts first Protestant service in New Amsterdam (later called New York).

1630 English Puritans sail for Massachusetts Bay, led by John Winthrop. They found Plymouth Colony.

1662 Halfway Covenant—a form of partial church members—created.

1683 William Penn founds Pennsylvania Colony for Quakers—and other Protestants.

1730-1745 The Great Awakening. George Whitefield tours New England preaching to huge crowds in the Fall of 1740.

1754 Jonathan Edwards of Massachusetts publishes *The Freedom of the Will* in defense of Calvinism.

1770s First African-American churches founded in South Carolina.

1775–1782 American Revolutionary War. Most Protestant ministers support Independence, though many Anglicans remain loyal to England, and many Quakers, Mennonites, and others are pacifists.

1784–1789 Methodists, Episcopalians, and Presbyterians reorganize as American churches in the wake of Independence.

1791 U.S. Constitution ratified; includes First Amendment prohibiting the establishment of a national religion or government interference in religious practice.

1795–1835 Second Great Awakening.

Aug. 1801 Cane Ridge, Kentucky, camp meeting.

1810 American Board of Commissioners for Foreign Mission created to promote Protestantism to other lands.

1816 American Bible Society founded.

1835 Burning down of the Ursuline Roman Catholic Convent by mob of Boston Protestants.

A Methodist church in Williamstown, Vermont, is depicted in this watercolor by Richard C. Moore.

Oct. 22, 1844 Contrary to William Miller's prediction, Second Coming of Christ did not occur on this day.

1845 Baptist Church divides into North and South groups over slavery issue.

1852 *Uncle Tom's Cabin* by Harriet Beecher Stowe is published.

1859 Charles Darwin's *The Origin of Species* published in America. Pheobe Palmer publishes *The Promise of the Father* in defense of women preaching.

1861 Women's Union Missionary Society of America founded.

1867 National Campmeeting Association for the Promotion of Christian Holiness founded to unite diverse elements of the holiness movement.

1874 Francis Willard begins making Women's Christian Temperance Union into active and effective reform organization.

1880 Salvation Army, an English organization, begins activities in America.

Summer 1886 Student Volunteer Movement for Foreign Missions established at Mount Hermon, Massachusetts.

1896 Henry McNeal Turner, minister in the African Methodist Episcopal Church, asserts in article that "God is a Negro."

Jan. 1, 1901 Student at Bethel Bible College, Topeka, Kansas, speaks in tongues.

1906–1909 Azusa Street (Los Angeles) Revival at the Apostolic Faith Gospel Mission inspires formation of the Pentecostal movement.

1910–1915 *The Fundamentals* published.

1917 President Woodrow Wilson, a Presbyterian, leads the U.S. into WWI. Promotes cause of peace as Protestant value.

July 1925 Scopes "Monkey Trial" takes place in Dayton, Tennessee. John Scopes found guilty and ordered to pay small fine, but Clarence Darrow's defense (and cross-examination of William Jennings Bryan, arguing the prosecution), seen as victory for liberal principles.

1949 Billy Graham's Revival "Crusade," Los Angeles, catapults him to national fame.

Nov. 1949 National Council of Churches formed in Cleveland.

Dec. 1955 Martin Luther King Jr. leads Montgomery, Alabama, bus boycott.

Oct. 12, 1958 Eisenhower lays cornerstone of Interchurch Center in Manhattan.

1962–1965 Second Vatican Council. Relations between Catholics and Protestants improve.

Aug. 1963 March on Washington climaxed by Reverend King's "I have a dream" speech.

1968. In Dallas, the Methodist and the Evangelical United Brethren churches unify to form the United Methodist Church, creating the second largest Protestant denomination in the U.S.

1972 Reverend William Johnson becomes the first openly gay person ordained by any Christian organization (United Church of Christ) in the U.S.

1974 International Congress of World Evangelization in Lausanne, Switzerland, helps American denominations connect with coreligionists around the world.

Sept. 1976 The Episcopal Church approves ordination of women as priests and bishops.

Nov. 2, 1976 Jimmy Carter, an Evangelical Baptist, is elected president of the U.S.

1980 Carter defeated by Reagan in presidential election, thanks to the support of Reagan by the Religious Right, a coalition of conservative Evangelicals.

1987–1988 Three smaller Lutheran groups merge to form the Evangelical Lutheran Church in America (ELCA)—largest Lutheran denomination in the U.S.

1989 Christian Coalition founded by Pat Robertson and Ralph Reed to promote issues and candidates friendly to conservative evangelical agenda.

1995 Donald Argue, a Pentecostal minister of Assemblies of God, becomes head of the National Association of Evangelicals.

1998 United Methodist minister performs a marriage ceremony for two openly gay congregants.

1999 Evangelical Lutheran and Episcopal Churches agree to intercommunion.

Summer–Fall 2003 The Alabama Ten Commandments case occupies much of the religion headlines, ending with statue (and judge, Roy Moore) removed.

1 Baptist Church

I. Roots and History

A. Introduction

THE HISTORY OF THE BAPTIST CHURCH IS NOT ONLY complicated; it is hotly disputed. Some declare Baptist belief a "New Testament Faith," originating with biblical figures—even, according to a few, the original Adam. Others find it hard to ignore the fact that the first officially Baptist church was founded in the seventeenth century, emerging from the disputes of Puritans and Separatists with the Church of England. Ultimately, three distinct groups advancing three distinct interpretations of the history of the Baptist Church have arisen. They are the Landmarkists, the Separatists, and the Anabaptists.

The **Landmarkist** belief is founded on the opinion that Baptist churches and traditions have preceded the Catholic Church and have been in existence since the time of John the Baptist and Christ. This view is theologically based on Matthew 16:18: "And upon this rock I will build my church; and the gates of hell shall not prevail against it." According to Landmarkism, Baptist churches are unstained by and ultimately separate from what they see as the corruptions of Catholicism.

This viewpoint was common in the 1800s, but has since fallen into disfavor. Among modern Baptist churches, the American Baptist Association and the Baptist Missionary Association of America have origins in Landmark beliefs, but few churches within these organizations hold to the extreme viewpoints of the early twentieth century.

According to **Separatist** theorists, the Baptist faith emerged out of the teachings of seventeenth-century English Separatists who believed that the church should be made up of only a regenerate membership and that only adult baptism was valid according to Scripture. John Smyth and Thomas Helwys led a group of Puritan Separatists to the Netherlands and in 1609 organized the General Baptist Church, following Arminian theology.

Arminian theology was one of two Protestant creeds that were very important to the Baptist movement, the other being Calvinism. According to Arminian theology, all of humanity was saved by the Crucifixion, but people can still fall from grace by turning away from God. According to Calvinist doctrine, however, only a small portion of humanity— the Elect—were saved by the Crucifixion. Calvinists believed the Elect were pre-destined to be saved from the very beginning of Creation by an unfathomable (and undeserved) act of Divine Will.

When these separatists reached Amsterdam they were influenced by the Anabaptists, a group that had its own origins in the 1500s.

Anabaptists rejected the practice of infant baptism while favoring the "rebaptism" of adults. While Anabaptists shared many of the same beliefs as the early Baptists, the group differed in its views on other issues such as pacifism and the communal sharing of material goods. This group was probably influential in the development of many modern Baptist characteristics. The theory of Baptist origins that cites Anabaptist beginnings is improbable because of differences in theological positions held by each group.

John Smyth and Thomas Helwys's Separatist group incorporated many Anabaptist traditions into their own belief system. They believed that the Bible was the only guide in all matters of faith and practice, not church tradition or creeds. They also maintained that church membership should be made up of believers only, not people who were simply born into the local parish. In accordance with this belief, these Separatists decided that the church should be governed by those believers rather than by bishops.

In 1609, Smyth baptized himself and Hewlys, along with others of their congregation, because they followed the Anabaptist rejection of infant baptism. Smyth believed that his own baptism was false because it was performed by a false church and had occurred when he was an infant, a period in his life where he could not have been a believer. Thus began the first General Baptist church.

In 1612, Helwys returned to England and established the first Baptist church in England. That year he also published his book, *A Short Declaration of the Mystery of Iniquity,* which had a profound effect on the history and development of the Baptist faith. In this book, Helwys strongly rejected the authority of the king of England to govern the religion of the people and also explored several other themes which became important standards in the Baptist church.

Helwys stressed the importance of the freedom of the local congregation to govern itself, the freedom of individual interpretation of Scripture, the importance of "believer's baptism," freedom from coerced uniformity in worship practices, and the freedom of the church to acknowledge Christ as the true "king" of the church and not be bound by creed, clergy, or civil government. For the publication of the *Mystery of Iniquity,* Hewlys was imprisoned and later died while in jail.

In 1616, Henry Jacob headed a group of Puritans in England with a Calvinist theology to form the church that would eventually become the Particular Baptists. These Baptists believed that grace through Christ's death was only meant for the pre-destined or elect and that salvation was not possible for all people. This is referred to as "limited atonement" and is associated with Calvinistic teachings. In 1641, the Particular Baptists began to practice believer's baptism by immersion. This is a practice that is still employed by all Baptist churches today and is based on a close reading of the Scripture, especially Colossians 2:12 and Romans 6:4. Baptists believe that baptism should be conducted by dipping the whole body of the believer into water, signifying the death of the self and resurrection to the Christian life.

Both groups ultimately emigrated to America in search of religious freedom. Until the formation of the Baptist Union of Great Britain in the 1800s, the Particular and General Baptists disagreed over Arminianism and Calvinism. The Separatist view is the most common of those held by modern Baptists.

Since its origins, the Baptist faith has included a strong emphasis on missionary work. In England in 1792, Andrew Fuller, John Sutcliff, and William Carey organized the Particular Baptist Missionary Society for Propagating the Gospel among the Heathen, later known as the Baptist Missionary Society. William Carey traveled to India in 1793, and American Adoniram Judson established an outpost in Burma in 1813, beginning missionary work among American Baptists.

Missionary work was important even within America itself. Baptist missionaries from the North aided the rebuilding of churches in the South during the Reconstruction era following the Civil War. Missionaries from the North and the South contributed greatly to the spread of Baptist culture as the nation expanded westward, and later immigrants to America often found comfort in the Baptist missions that were in place all along the west coast.

In 1813, the Baptist Union of Great Britain was founded as a Particular Baptist organization of churches. It was restructured in 1833 to allow for the membership of General Baptists. The Baptist Union is the oldest and largest national association of Baptist churches in Great Britain today.

B. The Religion in America

The various Baptist denominations in America today trace their origins to the nineteenth century, when they were primarily divided by region, race, and ethnic identity. All contribute to the complex history of the Baptist church, but they do not follow a shared single theological or ecclesiastical tradition. Today, Baptists are the second largest Christian denomination in the United States, after Roman Catholics.

Baptists first appeared in America during the "great migration" of English Puritans fleeing religious persecution during the years between 1625 and 1649. Baptists distinguished themselves from other Protestant groups through their rejection of infant baptism and their insistence upon the baptism of adult believers as the necessary basis of church membership. Congregational in nature, Baptists depended upon the primacy of the local congregation in matters of faith and practice.

Although Baptists shared many common beliefs with other Protestant sects in colonial America, the early New England Baptists faced persecution and hatred from Massachusetts colonials. In 1635, a man named Roger Williams was banished from Massachusetts for advocating religious tolerance and secularism. He traveled to Rhode Island and organized the colony called Providence at the head of the Narragansett Bay. It was here that Williams founded the first Baptist church in America in either 1638 or 1639.

John Clarke arrived around the same time and helped to found a second Baptist church in Newport, Rhode Island. These two congregations often served as a refuge for other Christian dissenters from the Massachusetts and Connecticut Puritan establishments. In 1714, the first Baptist church was founded in the South. These first churches were all Arminian in theology.

Controversy over Calvinism and Arminianism followed the Baptist colonials from England. Jacobus Arminius, a Dutch Reformed minister, disagreed with the Calvinist position regarding predestination

Roger Williams (1603–1683), seen in this undated portrait, founded the first Baptist church in America, in Providence, Rhode Island.

and human freedom. According to John Calvin, Christ's atonement applied only to a select and pious few, and all people on earth are at the mercy of God. Those Baptists who adhered more closely to the teachings of John Calvin were referred to as Particular Baptists, while those who believed in the Arminian doctrine of universal, or general, atonement and salvation were called General Baptists.

For the most part, those Baptists who settled in New England and the South were General Baptists and those who settled in the middle colonies of New Jersey and Pennsylvania were Particular, or Regular, Baptists.

The Particular Baptists encountered little or no resistance in the middle colonies and were able to achieve stability and influence, which allowed for their churches to become the center of Baptist strength by the eighteenth century. The Philadelphia Association was founded in 1707, in Pennsylvania as an organization designed to advise, consult, and generally facilitate the interaction of local congregations. The organization was given no governing rights in accordance with the Baptist congregationalist tradition.

The Philadelphia Association allowed for the preparation of a confessional statement that unified all Regular Baptists. This confessional statement was based on the 1677 English Baptist Assembly, or Second London Confession, and was intended to unify Baptists as well as identify with other Puritan church traditions. There were four main objectives in establishing the Philadelphia Association: first, to promote fellowship among the churches; second, to affirm commonly held beliefs; third, to provide counsel and assistance to local churches; and fourth, to establish a structure through which the churches could cooperate within their broader ministries.

Another sect, known as the Separate Baptists, originated during the Great Awakening of the 1740s and 1750s. Members of this group were formerly Congregationalists who left the established order and declared themselves Baptists. During the time period of the Great Awakening, at least 130 Baptist churches were formed.

A famous Separate Baptist, Isaac Backus, once a New Light Congregational minister in Middleborough, Massachusetts, was among those harassed for challenging orthodox principles. He married a Baptist woman and was immersed according to Baptist ritual in 1749. By 1756, he founded a new Baptist church. Although Separate Baptists thrived throughout most of New England, the movement flourished most widely in the South, during the latter half of the eighteenth century.

American independence from England in the second half of the eighteenth century helped to emphasize certain Baptist beliefs and spread Baptist teachings throughout the newly formed U.S. During this time, Baptists became strong advocates for religious freedom and the separation of church and state.

The church expanded, and with the help of the Philadelphia Association, institutional stability was established. Additional regional associations were introduced at this time and various programs and institutions were also organized. In 1764, James Manning was commissioned by the Philadelphia Association to found Rhode Island College, which

Harry Emerson Fosdick (1878–1969) was an outstanding example of the oratorical tradition that has characterized the Baptist church. This photograph of Fosdick was taken in the Park Avenue Baptist Church in New York City (now the Central Presbyterian Church), where Fosdick was pastor from 1922 to 1929.

would later become Brown University. The college was intended to provide Baptists with a strong program of liberal arts education similar to that of other colleges that had already been established. It soon became a center of interaction between colonial and British and European Baptists.

Around this time, the Association also established a publishing facility and released church materials including a confession of faith, a catechism, and a hymnal, as well as various Baptist writings.

Missionary work among American Baptists began with the Philadelphia Association. Missionaries were sent to work with the Native American tribes as well as overseas. In 1814, as a result of the missionary work abroad of Adoniram and Ann Hasseltine Judson and Luther Rice, the Philadelphia Association created the General Missionary Convention of the Baptist Denomination in the United States for Foreign Missions, also known as the Triennial Convention. Later it was officially renamed the American Baptist Foreign Mission Society.

In 1832, John Mason Peck and Jonathan Going created the American Baptist Home Mission Society in New York City. This organization was created to facilitate missions in the American frontier colonies.

By the end of the nineteenth century, Separate and Regular Baptists had lost most of their distinguishing characteristics. In 1851, a quest for Baptist unity based on a common affirmation of faith was exemplified by the American Baptist Publication Society's publication of *The Baptist Catechism*. This was based on the New Hampshire Confession of 1833. The goal of the *Catechism* was to reaffirm the theological unity between all Baptist churches and to identify with other Protestant denominations.

Although the churches strived for unity, such cooperation went against the essential roots of the Baptist tradition. This, in addition to the common sentiment of emphasis on the unique, the distinctive, and the different that characterized this time period, ultimately led to the continued plurality of Baptists.

Landmarkism resurfaced as the need arose for a unique Baptist identity set apart from Christianity. Also during this time, the emergence of the Free Will Baptists in New England in 1780 signified the presence of General Baptists in America. Both Landmarkists and Free Will Baptists challenged the Calvinistic theology that was present in other Protestant faiths and preached free will and the acceptance of saving grace offered by God to all persons. Another extreme group that arose at this time was known as the Two-Seed-in-the-Spirit Predestination Baptists. These Baptists embraced an extreme interpretation of Calvinistic predestination, according to which there are two types of "seeds" within people: good and bad, each inherited according to the Will of God. They rejected organized missions because they believed conversions were an act of God.

Such antimission Baptist groups are still present today in the American South. The Seventh Day Baptist organization, which established its first church in 1671, in Newport, Rhode Island, maintained its Regular Baptist roots despite the Regular-Separate unity.

By the end of the eighteenth century, black Baptist churches began to emerge. Although slaves at some plantations were allowed to listen to white church preaching, many met secretly and mixed African religious expressions and evangelistic Christianity. Soon distinctively black congregations arose, aided by the policy of local congregationalism in the Baptist church. In 1821, Lott Cary and Collin Teague became the first American missionaries to Africa. They were members of the Richmond African Baptist Missionary Society, which was founded in 1815.

The Black American Baptist Missionary Convention was formed in 1840, in New England and the Middle States. The Colored Baptist Convention was organized during the 1850s in Illinois and Missouri. Some black Baptist preachers, such as Nat Turner, were known to lead slave rebellions in the South.

In 1845, the Civil War created a schism between Baptists of the North and South. Northern abolitionist sympathizers gained power in the church and attempted to prohibit slaveholders from becoming missionaries. This was rejected by Southern Baptist leaders and both sides agreed to separate. That year, delegates from southern churches met in Augusta, Georgia and created the Southern Baptist Convention (SBC). It was expressly stated that the split did not occur as the result of theological differences. The convention declared itself a permanent organization after the war in 1868.

The Civil War left the American South in ruins. After the war, the SBC was instrumental in reestablishing the cultural and religious identity of Southerners. By the end of the nineteenth century, the SBC was the largest Protestant denomination in the United States. As a result of the loss of northern influence in the South, northern Baptist societies once again returned their focus to foreign and national missions. It was at this time that the Women's Baptist Foreign Mission Society was created, along with several other female-orientated groups that focused on different forms of social outreach. These northern organizations openly participated in social projects with other Protestant denominations in America, and in 1907 the societies came together under one name, the Northern Baptist Convention.

Beginning in the middle of the nineteenth century, America experienced a population boom mostly due to the increase in immigration of peoples from all over Europe, and later China, Japan, Mexico, and Latin America. Baptists soon turned their attention to these new Americans and home missionary work took a new precedence.

The twentieth-century civil rights movement had a major effect on American Baptists, most notably those belonging to African-American congregations. Dr. Martin Luther King Jr. was a famous proponent of the civil rights movement during the 1950s and 1960s and also an ordained American Baptist Convention minister. King was arrested twenty-nine times during his crusade for social justice and was awarded the Nobel Peace Prize in 1964, but was tragically assassinated in Memphis, Tennessee, in 1968.

Although many of King's Baptist brethren did not agree with his efforts to rid the U.S. of racial segregation, King did bring the problem to the forefront and began the slow process of changing the conscience of the nation. King was not the first Baptist leader to fight for social justice; before him came Isaac Backus, Roger Williams, and John Clarke. At the turn of the twentieth century, Walter Rauschenbusch was also a strong advocate for social reform in regards to poverty and economic injustice. The Baptist World Alliance, founded in 1905, is devoted to the struggle for human rights around the world. Baptists around the world will be celebrating their 400th birthday in 2009.

C. Important Dates and Landmarks

1609 John Smyth and Thomas Helwys lead a Separatist group to the Netherlands and organize the first Baptist church.

1612 Helwys establishes the first Baptist church in England.

1612 Helwys publishes *A Short Declaration of the Mystery of Iniquity*.

1619 Henry Jacob forms the first Particular Baptist congregation in England.

1635 Roger Williams banished from Massachusetts.

1638 Roger Williams founds the first Baptist church in the American colonies in Providence, Rhode Island.

1639 John Clarke founds the second Baptist church in America in Newport, Rhode Island.

1641 Particular Baptists begin the practice of believer's baptism by immersion.

1707 Philadelphia Association founded in Pennsylvania.

1724 National Association of Free Will Baptists founded by Paul Palmer in North Carolina.

1740s–1750s The Great Awakening.

1764 James Manning commissioned by the Philadelphia Association to found and become the first president of Rhode Island College (later Brown University).

1791 Ratification of the First Amendment of the federal Constitution, establishing freedom of religion.

1792 William Carey, Andrew Fuller, and John Sutcliff establish the first missionary society in England, the Particular Baptist Missionary Society for Propagating the Gospel among the Heathen (later known as the Baptist Missionary Society).

1813 Organization of the Baptist Union of Great Britain.

1814 Formation of the General Missionary Convention of the Baptist Denomination in the United States for Foreign Missions (the Triennial Convention), later known as the American Baptist Foreign Mission Society.

1824 Baptist Tract Society, later known as the American Baptist Publication Society, formed.

1827 Organization of the Primitive (Old-School) Baptists.

1832 American Baptist Home Mission Society founded to facilitate the establishment of churches and schools among pioneer settlers.

1845 Southern Baptist Convention (SBC) formed in Augusta, Georgia.

1851 *The Baptist Catechism* printed by the American Baptist Publication Society.

1852 Baptist General Conference organized.

1859 Formation of the General Conference of Baptist Churches in America by German-American Baptists (renamed the North American Baptist Conference in 1982).

1864 Formation of the Danish-Norwegian Baptist Conference of the Northwest.

1865 North American Baptist Conference founded.

1870 General Association of General Baptist Churches founded.

1879 Organization of the Swedish General Conference (renamed the Baptist General Conference in 1945).

1895 Formation of the National Baptist Convention of America.

1905 Baptist World Alliance organized.

1907 Northern Baptist Convention (later the American Baptist Convention; then the American Baptist Churches in the USA) founded.

1907 National Primitive Baptist Convention established.

1915 National Baptist Convention of the USA organized.

1921 Spanish-American Baptist Seminary founded in Los Angeles, California.

1924 American Baptist Association organized.

1932 General Association of Regular Baptist Churches formed.

1935 National Association of Free Will Baptists organized.

1947 Conservative Baptist Association of America formed.

1954 Reformed Baptist Church established.

1961 Progressive National Baptist Convention formed due to a schism over leadership in the National Baptist Convention, USA.

1964 Martin Luther King Jr. awarded the Nobel Peace Prize.

1965 New Testament Association of Independent Baptist Churches organized.

1968 American Baptist Convention forms the Study Commission on Denominational Structure to reexamine and organize their ordered denomination life in keeping with their twentieth-century history.

1968 Martin Luther King Jr. assassinated in Memphis, Tennessee.

1972 American Baptist Convention changes its name to American Baptist Churches in the USA.

1988 National Missionary Baptist Convention organized by former members of the National Baptist Convention of America.

1991 Cooperative Baptist Fellowship organized.

2000 Baptist World Alliance achieves 100 million membership mark.

2009 World Baptist community celebrates 400th anniversary of Baptist church.

D. Important Figures

John Smyth (1570–1612): founder of the first Baptist church in Holland; introduced the practice of the believer's baptism.

Thomas Helwys (1550–1616): founder of the Baptist church in England; wrote *A Short Declaration of the Mystery of Iniquity* (1612).

Roger Williams (1603–1684): Banished from Massachusetts for advocating secularism and religious tolerance; founded the settlement of Providence, Rhode Island, in 1636; founded the first Baptist church in America in 1638.

John Clarke (1609–1676): Co-founder of the colony of Rhode Island; established the second Baptist church in America in 1641 in Newport, Rhode Island.

Hezekiah Smith (1816–1887): Separate Baptist leader, became pastor in Massachusetts during the Revolutionary War.

John Gano (1727–1804): Separate Baptist leader; became a pastor in New York (Revolutionary War).

James Manning (1738–1791): Commissioned by the Philadelphia Association to found and become the first President of Rhode Island College (Brown University) in 1738.

John Leland (1754–1841): Virginia Baptist minister instrumental in the passage of Jefferson's Statute for Religious Freedom in the Virginia Assembly (1785), which led to the disestablishment of the Anglican Church in 1786.

Isaac Backus (1724–1806): Massachusetts pastor appointed by the Warren Association as an evangelist-lobbyist to promote the cause at the Continental Congress; wrote *Government and Liberty Described and Ecclesiastical Tyranny Exposed* (1788), which was influential in the ratification of the First Amendment to the federal Constitution in 1791.

Benjamin Randall (1749–1808): leader of the Freewill Baptists.

William Carey (1761–1834): English Particular Baptist missionary; organized the first Baptist missionary society in England in 1792; sailed to India in 1793 to begin foreign missionary work.

Daniel Parker (1781–1844): Founded the Two-Seed-in-the-Spirit Predestinarian Baptists, 1826.

John Mason Peck (1789–1858): Baptist frontier missionary in St. Louis; organized the First Baptist Church of St. Louis and the first missionary society in the West, the United Society for the Spread of the Gospel, in 1818.

Helen Barrett Montgomery (1861–1934): Lay church leader, teacher, and preacher from Rochester, New York; feminist; first woman president of the Northern Baptist Convention (1921–1922); delegate to the Baptist World Alliance meeting in Stockholm (1923); president of the Woman's American Baptist Foreign Mission Society (1914–1924).

II.Tenets and Beliefs

A. Articles of Faith

Baptists do not have a central governing authority and do not believe the authority of historic confessional creeds, catechisms, or manuals of worship. Each church is autonomous and has the right to control its ideas on policy, polity, and doctrine. Although the churches differ in their opinions on many subjects, they all share the same fundamental belief in Scriptural authority.

The Baptist Faith and Message, prepared by Southern Baptists, is a statement of generally-held convictions that serves as a guide to understanding the beliefs of members of the Southern Baptist Convention (SBC). This document defines the SBC view on (among other issues) the Scriptures, God and the Holy Trinity, man's relation to God, salvation, grace, baptism and the Lord's Supper, education, family, and missions. This document was written for the purpose of providing a general understanding of the beliefs of Baptists in America.

The New Hampshire Confession of Faith, similar to *The Baptist Faith and Message*, is also used as an official doctrinal statement in the individual local Baptist church or as the starting point for an official statement. *The New Hampshire Confession* is more widely accepted in Northern and Western Baptist churches, while the *Baptist Faith and Message* is usually only accepted in southern churches.

"B.A.P.T.I.S.T." is an acronym used by some Baptist churches as a mnemonic summary of distinguishing Baptist beliefs:

    Biblical authority;
    Autonomy of the local church;
    Priesthood of all believers;
    Two ordinances (baptism and the Lord's Supper);
    Individual soul liberty;
    Separation of church and state;
    Two offices of the church (pastor and deacon).

B. Scripture

Baptists believe that the Bible is the only authoritative source of God's truth and each person is responsible before God for his or her own understanding of the Bible. The Scripture is inerrant and infallible and is the only reliable guide to Christian faith and behavior. Many Baptists believe that the Bible is also without error in regard to history, geography, and even science.

C. Important Writers and Theologians

Henry Dunster (1609–1659): the first president of Harvard; forced to resign in 1653 after twelve years of service because of his preaching against infant baptism.

George Whitefield (1714–1770): associate of John and Charles Wesley (Methodists); English preacher who toured America seven times encouraging a period of revivalism in the eighteenth century.

John Leadley Dagg (1794–1884): professor of theology at Mercer University; wrote *Manual of Theology* (1856), a standard text in the Southern Baptist Theological Seminary.

Francis Wayland (1796–1865): Baptist president and professor at Brown University; wrote *The Elements of Moral Science* (1835) and *The Elements of Political Economy* (1837).

Benoni Stenson (1798–1869): Arminian theologian; founded the Liberty Church in Evansville, Indiana; laid original foundation for the General Association of General Baptist Churches.

Walter Rauschenbusch (1861–1918): the father of the Social Gospel in America; advocated social reform of poverty and economic injustice in the beginning of the twentieth century.

Harry Emerson Fosdick (1878–1969): America's most widely heard liberal Protestant preacher; famous sermon "Shall the Fundamentalists Win?" (1922); professor at the Union Theological Seminary; minister of Park Avenue Baptist Church (renamed Riverside Church) of New York (1915–1946); gave many radio sermons. (Also considered in the Presbyterian denomination.)

Kenneth Scott Latourette (1884–1968): known as one of the great historians of modern times; Professor of Missions and Oriental History at Yale (1921–1953); published over one hundred books, including the seven volumes of *The History of the Expansion of Christianity*.

Martin Luther King, Jr. (1929–1968): Nobel Prize winner; black civil rights leader; ordained American Baptist minister; educated at Morehouse College, Crozer Seminary, and Boston University; his liberal theological appreciation and advocacy for nonviolent civil disobedience made him a central and controversial figure in the American Baptist Convention.

Jesse Jackson (1941–): American politician, civil rights activist and Baptist minister.

Billy Graham (1918–): prominent member of the Southern Baptist Convention, world-renowned American Protestant Christian evangelist.

Walter B. Shurden: Baptist historian; developed the "Four Freedoms" of Baptist tradition:
- Soul freedom—the soul is competent before God and capable of making decisions in matters of faith without coercion or compulsion by any larger religious or civil body;
- Church freedom—freedom of the local church from outside interference, whether government or civilian;
- Bible freedom—the individual is free to interpret the Bible for himself or herself, using the best tools of scholarship and biblical study available to the individual;
- Religious freedom—the individual is free to choose whether to practice their religion, another religion, or no religion.

III. Rites and Rituals

A. The Calendar

Baptists follow the conventional Christian calendar, focused primarily on the life and death of Jesus Christ. Many special organizational days are observed locally, nationally and worldwide.

B. Worship and Liturgy

Baptists recognize two ordinances, or sacraments, to be performed on a regular basis by churches: baptism and communion.

Baptism is referred to as "believer's baptism" and is performed only after a person professes Jesus Christ as Lord and Savior. Because Baptists do not believe that baptism plays any role in salvation, but rather should be performed after salvation has been achieved, baptism is not performed at infancy, but later in life. It is believed that an "age of accountability" must be achieved and a person must be able to make the decision of salvation before they can participate in baptism. This is not a specific age, but is based on the capability of the person to know the difference between right and wrong.

Baptism is viewed as an outward expression symbolic of the inward cleansing of sins that has already taken place. Baptism by full immersion, subsequent to salvation, is a criterion for membership in most Baptist churches.

Communion, often referred to as the Lord's Supper or Eucharist, is held either weekly, monthly, quarterly, or annually, depending on the policy of the individual church. Baptized participants communally eat the bread and drink of the wine that represents the body and blood of Jesus. The passage 1 Corinthians 11:23–34 is cited as instructional for the practice of this sacrament.

Foot-washing is practiced by some Baptist sects and is considered an obligation to be administered to all true believers. The ritual is intended to teach humility and remind participants of the necessity of a daily cleansing from sin. This sacrament is usually practiced after the Lord's Supper, as it is said was done after the Last Supper in Scripture when Jesus washed the feet of the disciples (John 13:14–15).

Traditional Baptist church architecture reflects the focus of the church service, which is to proclaim the word of God. The pulpit is the largest piece of furniture in the Baptist church and is centered on the platform, while the communion table is placed below it in a symbolically subservient position. The sermon is often surrounded by periods of musical worship usually led by a song leader, choir, or band.

Some fundamentalist Baptists will only sing traditional hymns that were written between the

Baptism—immersion in water—has been used by many religions throughout history, either as a symbol of initiation or as an act of renewal and spiritual rebirth. Baptists believe that baptism must be undergone by an adult (a "believer's baptism") who has been "born again." This river baptism, signifying entrance into the New Covenant and into the church, took place in 1935 near Mineola, Texas.

1700s and the 1950s and will oppose the use of some instruments that might associate the hymns with rock music.

Most Baptist congregations are small, consisting of about 200 members.

C. Life Cycle Events

Baptism is only conducted once a person is old enough to understand and profess their own faith and belief in Jesus Christ as their savior. This is in contrast to other Christian faiths where the sacrament of baptism is enacted soon after a child is born.

D. Family Life

In the Baptist tradition, God is considered to have established the family as the foundation of human society. Baptists frown upon divorce and same-sex marriage, reserving the right of marriage to a man and a woman, who are regarded as equal before God. Baptists consider the marriage relationship a model of the relationship between God and humankind. Furthermore, Baptists believe that life begins at conception and that children are to be considered a blessing from God.

IV. Denominations and Demographics

A. History

There are over 90 million Baptists worldwide with an estimated 47 million in the U.S. These numbers include only those members who have been baptized. If unbaptized congregants and children were to be included in these figures, the number would probably be over 100 million.

The oldest debate in the Baptist church occurred between Arminian and Calvinistic followers. There are specific theological points on which these two groups have always disagreed: election, atonement, grace, perseverance, and the inherent good of man.

According to Arminian beliefs, God elected those individuals whom He knew would believe in Christ and persevere in the faith, while Calvinism states that God has elected certain people for salvation only because of His sovereignty; it is not based on any foreseen virtue on the part of the individual. According to Calvin, Christ's death on the cross was only intended to save those elected by God, while those following Arminian teachings believe that Christ's death provided redemption for all humankind, but is only effective for those who believe.

Arminian Baptists believe in "prevenient" grace, meaning grace from the Holy Spirit enables a person to respond to the Gospel and cooperate with God in salvation. Calvinistic Baptists follow a belief in irresistible grace and believe that those whom God has chosen for eternal life will come to faith and thus to salvation, only because it is God's irresistible will.

Arminian theology follows a belief in conditional perseverance, meaning that believers have been empowered to live victoriously, but they are capable of turning from grace and losing salvation. Consistent with Calvinistic teaching, according to the belief in the perseverance of the saints, those who are genuine believers will endure in the faith to the end.

Finally, the good nature of man is believed to be nonexistent by Arminians; only the Holy Spirit can affect the new birth in baptism and humans cannot save themselves. Calvinism teaches that humans are not completely devoid of good impulses, but because every human is engulfed by sin, an individual can do nothing to earn merit before God.

Once the Baptist church was established, there arose two distinct sects within the larger denomination. The General Baptist and the Particular Baptists differ because of the adherence to either Arminian or Calvinistic theologies, respectively. Today, it is the General Baptist/Arminian view that is most commonly held by modern Baptists. The other sect follows the Landmarkist belief that Baptists were present before any other Christian faith, and were not involved in the General vs. Particular theological debate.

The Southern Baptist Convention (SBC) broke from the national Baptist organization in 1845 over several issues, especially slavery. Some southern congregations separated from the American Baptist Home Mission Board when the board refused to send slave owners into the missionary field. They believed that the board had no right to judge the moral character of slave owners and so decided to form the Southern Baptist Convention, which established its own boards for foreign and home missions.

Today the Southern Baptist Convention is the largest Baptist body as well as the largest Protestant denomination in the United States.

The American Baptist Churches in the USA (ABCUSA) descends from the Triennial Convention. It began as the Northern Baptist Convention in 1907 and then became known as the American Baptist Convention in 1950. Finally, in 1972, the name was changed to the American Baptist Churches in the USA, what it is known as today.

The National Baptist Convention has its roots in the Triennial Convention and resulted from the former segregation laws that regulated Southern Society until the mid-twentieth century. In 1880, the Foreign Mission Baptist Convention was created in Montgomery, Alabama. In 1886, the American National Baptist Convention was formed in St. Louis, Missouri. In 1893, the Baptist National Education Convention was formed in the District of Columbia. It was not until 1895 that these three conventions joined in Atlanta, Georgia, to create the National Baptist Convention of America.

At the end of the Civil War in 1865, black Baptists began to establish their own separate programs and agencies to help the newly emancipated slaves. In 1866, Baptists in North Carolina organized the first state convention, and by 1870, all of the southern states had formed similar conventions. In 1867, the Consolidated American Baptist Convention was organized, which continued until 1880.

In 1880, the Foreign Mission Baptist Convention of the U.S.A., made up of various southern Negro Baptist churches, associations, and state conventions, was formed. In 1886 the American National Baptist Convention was organized and in 1893, the Baptist National Educational Convention was established. In 1895, these three groups merged to form the National Baptist Convention, USA, Incorporated, and in doing so brought northern and southern black Baptist churches together.

Then, in 1915, a dispute arose over whether the National Baptist Publishing Board, the organization that provided all of the Sunday School and Christian Education materials, was part of the Convention or a separate entity. When it was finally decided to incorporate the Publishing Board, a split occurred, and the National Baptist Convention of America was formed. In 1961, several members withdrew from the National Baptist Convention, USA and formed the Progressive National Baptist Convention. These churches disagreed with the National Baptist Convention's nonviolence policies regarding the Civil Rights movement.

Finally, in 1988, many prominent members of the National Baptist Convention of America withdrew to join a new organization, the National Missionary Baptist Convention of America.

B. Comparison of Tenets and Practices

In general, Baptist churches all believe that the Bible is the divinely inspired Word of God and all practice baptism and the Lord's Supper. All Baptists believe in the autonomy of the local church and in the importance of missionary work, although the actual practice of these standards differs from convention to convention. There are, however, many differences between denominations.

The Southern Baptist Convention maintains a fundamentalist theological orientation. All churches associated with the SBC share a confession of faith based on the New Hampshire Confession, known as the *Baptist Faith and Message*. These churches also share a belief in the inerrancy of the Bible and practice the sacraments of baptism and the Lord's Supper. Members of the SBC believe that salvation is offered to all who accept the true faith and all believers will endure to the end and not fall away from their salvation. Because the SBC is the largest organization in the United States, these practices are common for most Baptists in this country.

The American Baptist Association (ABA), one of the smaller organizations, with 275,000 members spread out over 1,760 congregations, follows the distinctive Landmarkist theology. This organization stands against the convention system in general and specifically against the Southern Baptist Convention. Members of the ABA still believe in the inerrancy of the Bible and subscribe to similar beliefs in terms of God, Jesus, the Holy Spirit, and salvation. They also practice baptism and the Lord's Supper, both restricted to church members.

The Landmark sect believes that the church must always be a local, visible assembly of scripturally baptized believers who are in a covenant relationship with God to carry out the Great Commission. Members of the ABA also believe that missionary work should only be carried out on the level of the local church, not to be overseen by a convention board.

The American Baptist Churches in the USA (ABCUSA) is progressive in both theology and practice. As an organization, the ABCUSA promotes doctrinal diversity and is typically more liberal in its beliefs than the SBC. The ABCUSA rejects all creeds and statements of faith because they might hinder the ability and freedom of individual members to interpret the Bible. While members of the ABCUSA practice baptism and the Lord's Supper, they do not believe that they are required in order to achieve salvation.

Independent Baptist churches adhere to the same doctrines as other Baptists. but they stress the biblical principle of churches' individuality and so choose not to align themselves with any larger communities. Independent Baptists believe that work in the local ministry, as opposed to a national ministry, allows for more efficiency in the government and education of the congregation. Independent Baptists are usually fundamentalists and adhere to a strict literal interpretation of the Bible.

C. Membership and Distribution

There are approximately 47 million members of the Baptist church in America today. The five largest denominations are the Southern Baptist Convention with almost 16 million members, the National Baptist Convention, USA, Inc. with 7.5 million members, the National Baptist Convention of America, with 3.5 million members, the Progressive National Baptist Convention with 2.5 million members, and the American Baptist Churches in the USA with 1.5 million members.

The Southern Baptist Convention (SBC), concentrated in the southern states, is the largest and most political Protestant group in America. In 2005, the SBC recorded almost 300,000 baptisms, making it the fastest growing Baptist group. Some of the largest churches in the United States are Southern Baptist. Currently the SBC claims that there are more than 16.3 million members belonging to their organization.

At one time, all the churches affiliated with the SBC were located in the South, but today churches are in all fifty states, working through some 1,200 local associations and forty-one state conventions.

The National Baptist Convention, USA, Inc. is the largest African-American religious convention in the United States and has its center in Atlanta, Georgia. The National Baptist Convention of America (NBCA) was created after a large group of churches split from the National Baptist Convention, USA, Inc. in 1915. It is now the second largest African-American Baptist convention in America, with 3.5 million members contributing to 2,500 congregations, and has its headquarters in Shreveport, Louisiana.

The Progressive National Baptist Convention was also formed after a debate caused a schism within the National Baptist Convention, USA, Inc. in 1961. It is the fourth largest Baptist denomination, and the third largest African-American Baptist group in America, with 2.5 million members making up over 2,000 congregations.

The American Baptist Churches in the USA (ABCUSA), formerly the Northern Baptist Convention, consists of 5,800 congregations made up of 1.5 million people. Most of its congregations are located in the northern United States.

V. Organization and Infrastructure

A. Education and Hierarchy of Clergy

Baptists believe in the priesthood of all believers. They argue that the work of Christ belongs to all Christians, not merely clergy. Clergy are respected in the Baptist church, but they are not unique, because all members are considered ministers of the church.

Baptists recognize two clerical offices, those of pastor-teacher and deacon. The office of overseer or bishop is considered to be the same as that of pastor, although some Southern Baptist churches do ordain bishops to preside over small regional church groupings. Only men are allowed to hold clerical offices in the Baptist church.

The pastor delivers the weekly sermon to the assembled congregation, performs weddings, and officiates at funerals. Usually, a Baptist pastor is married and has children. A deacon serves to assist a pastor with members' needs and helps during the ordinance of the Lord's Supper. Deacons are usually members of the church who have demonstrated exceptional Christian piety; they are generally unpaid for their work.

SEMINARIES

Southern Baptist Convention Seminaries

Golden Gate Baptist Theological Seminary
201 Seminary Drive
Mill Valley, CA 94941
415-380-1300
www.ggbts.edu/

Midwestern Baptist Theological Seminary
5001 North Oak Trafficway
Kansas City, MO 64118
816-414-3700   800-944-MBTS
www.mbts.edu/index3.html

New Orleans Baptist Theological Seminary
3939 Gentilly Boulevard
New Orleans, LA 70126
504-282-4455   800-662-8701
www.nobts.edu

Southeastern Baptist Theological Seminary
PO Box 1889
Wake Forest, NC 27588
919-761-2100
120 South Wingate Street
Wake Forest, NC 27587
www.sebts.edu

Southern Baptist Theological Seminary
2825 Lexington Road
Louisville, KY 40280
800-626-5525
www.sbts.edu

Southwestern Baptist Theological Seminary
PO Box 22000
Fort Worth, TX 76122
817-923-1921
2001 W. Seminary Drive
Fort Worth, TX 76115
www.swbts.edu

Baptist Seminaries

Western Seminary
Portland Campus
5511 SE Hawthorne Boulevard
Portland, OR 97215
877-517-1800   503-517-1800
www.westernseminary.edu/Portland/index.htm
San Jose Campus
16330 Los Gatos Boulevard, Suite 100
Los Gatos, CA 95032
408-356-6889   877-900-6889
www.westernseminary.edu/SanJose/index.htm

Sacramento Campus
2924 Bacerra Way
Sacramento, CA 95821
916-488-3720   800-250-7030
www.westernseminary.edu/Sacramento/index.htm

McAfee School of Theology at Mercer University
1400 Coleman Avenue
Macon, GA 31207-0001
3001 Mercer University Drive,
Atlanta, GA 30341-4155
1-800-MERCER-U
www2.mercer.edu/theology

Baptist Theological Seminary
3400 Brook Road
Richmond, VA 23227
804-355-8135
www.btsr.edu

The Divinity School at Wake Forest
1834 Wake Forest Road
Winston-Salem, NC 27106
336-758-5121
divinity.wfu.edu

Duke Divinity School
PO Box 90968
Durham, NC 27708
919-660-3400
www.divinity.duke.edu

Truett Seminary at Baylor University
Waco, TX 76798
1-800-BAYLOR-U
www.baylor.edu/truett

Gardiner-Webb School of Divinity at Gardiner-Webb University
PO Box. 997
Boiling Springs, NC 28017
704-406-4000
www.gardner-webb.edu

Baptist Seminary of Kentucky
631 South Limestone Street
Lexington, KY 40508
859-455-8191   866-420-9297
www.bsky.org

Palmer Theological Seminary
6 East Lancaster Avenue
Wynnewood, PA 19096
610-896-5000   800-220-3287
www.palmerseminary.edu

Campbell University Divinity School
PO Box 567
Buies Creek, NC 27506
800-334-4111   910-893-1200

The Abyssinian Baptist Church in New York City has served Harlem since its founding in 1808 by Ethiopian merchants who joined forces with African-American Baptists who had resigned from the First Baptist Church of New York over its racial policies. A long line of distinguished and gifted preachers have led the church—a tradition continued by the Reverend Dr. Calvin O. Butts III, the current pastor.

The First Baptist Church of Providence, Rhode Island, celebrated its 370th anniversary in 2008, making it one of the oldest still-functioning religious institutions in the United States.

B. Shrines and Houses of Worship

Organization

Churches usually belong to a national organization, but all churches are self governed and answer to no higher power. All questions regarding faith, practice, and interpretation of Scripture are the responsibility of the individual church and its members.

The First Baptist Church in America
75 North Main Street
Providence, RI 02903
401-454-3418
www.fbcia.org

The First Baptist Church in America is the oldest Baptist church in the U.S. It was founded in 1638 by Roger Williams in Providence, Rhode Island. It is part of the Free Will Baptist group.

American Baptist Churches in the USA
PO Box 851
Valley Forge, PA 19482-0851
588 North Gulph Road
King of Prussia, PA 19406
610-768-2000   800-ABC-3USA

The American Baptist Churches Mission Center in Valley Forge, Pennsylvania, serves as a major site for the ongoing planning of domestic and overseas mission work.

C. Governance and Authority

There is no one body that officially establishes the rules governing the faith and practice of all members of the Baptist church. While there are major conventions and associations to which many churches belong, the individual church is autonomous in deciding laws of faith and practice. Administration, leadership, and doctrine are usually decided democratically by the lay members of each individual church.

D. Social Service Organizations

North American Mission Board, SBC
4200 North Point Parkway
Alpharetta, Georgia 30022-4176
770-410-6000   Fax: 770-410-6082
800-634-2462
webmaster@namb.net
www.namb.net

The North American Mission Board (NAMB) serves missionaries involved in evangelism and church planting in the United States and Canada, while the International Mission Board (IMB) sponsors missionaries internationally.

GuideStone Financial Resources
2401 Cedar Springs Road
Dallas, TX 75201-1498
888-98-GUIDE
www.guidestone.org

GuideStone Financial Resources provides insurance, retirement, and investment services to ministers and employees of Southern Baptist churches and agencies.

Women's Missionary Union (WMU)
100 Missionary Ridge
PO Box 830010
Birmingham, AL 35283-0010
205-991-8100
www.wmu.com

The **WMU** was founded in 1888 and acts as an auxiliary to the Southern Baptist Convention, helping to facilitate the annual Annie Armstrong Easter Offering and the Lottie Moon Christmas Offering.

E. Media and Communication

All Baptist groups have websites, some of which are listed at the end of this chapter. Most associations also release their own regular newsletters and other publications.

LifeWay Christian Resources was founded as the Baptist Sunday School Board in 1891, and is one of the largest Christian publishing houses in America. It currently operates the LifeWay Christian Store chain of bookstores, and may be found online at www.lifeway.com/lwc.

The Baptist Press, established by the SBC in 1946, is the largest Christian news service in the country. It may be found online at www.bpnews.net.

The NBCA news network, run by the National Baptist Convention of America, provides convention press releases, state conventions and associations in the news, and current and past issues of the *Lantern*, the convention's online newsletter.

FURTHER READING

Protestantism in America
  Randall Balmer and Lauren F. Winner
  2002: Columbia University Press

A Survey of Black Baptists in the United States
  William L. Banks
  1987: Continental

The Baptists
  William Brackney
  1988: Greenwood

Southern Cross: The Beginnings of the Bible Belt
  Christine Leigh Heyrman
  1997: Knopf

Baptists in America
  Bill J. Leonard
  2005: Columbia University Press

Baptist Ways: A History
  Bill J. Leonard
  2003: Judson

WEBSITES

American Baptist Association: www.abaptist.org
American Baptist Churches USA:
    www.abc-usa.org
Baptist General Conference: www.bgcworld.org
General Association of General Baptist Churches:
    www.generalbaptist.com
National Association of Free Will Baptists:
    www.nafwb.org
General Association of Regular Baptist Churches:
    www.garbc.org
National Baptist Convention of America:
    www.nbcamerica.net
National Baptist Convention, USA, Inc:
    www.nationalbaptist.net
National Primitive Baptist Convention:
    www.nationalprimbatconv.org
North American Baptist Conference:
    www.nabconference.org
Primitive Baptists: www.pb.org
Progressive National Baptist Convention:
    www.pnbc.org
Reformed Baptist Church: www.vor.org
Southern Baptist Convention: www.sbc.net

2 Christian Science

I. Origins and Early History

A. Introduction

IN 1821, AMERICA WAS IN THE MIDST OF THE Second Great Awakening, led by revivalist Charles Grandison Finney. "Old Divinity," characterized by Calvinistic notions of predestination, was challenged by Finney's new theology of elective salvation. Men and women throughout the country—especially in the South—embraced the freedom to choose redemption and were "saved" by the hundreds. But in the wilderness of New England, Calvinism proved tenacious. Founded on Puritan principles, this region of the country adhered to ideals of fixed fate and absolute foreknowledge. Though northern pioneers were forced to focus the majority of their energies on hewing a simple existence out of unforgiving terrain, much emphasis was placed on development of the intellect, which was recognized as a necessary supplement to religious understanding. The Bible was considered the ultimate source of truth, and many read it from a fundamentalist perspective, interpreting it literally.

Such were the conditions that Mary Baker was born into in Bow, New Hampshire. Her father a fervent Calvinist expounder, she was frequent audience to his heated debates with neighboring religionists, many of which consisted of stern condemnations of local "backsliders." Mark Baker assigned religion much prominence in the family lives of his six children, engaging them in daily Bible readings and prayer sessions. Though none of Mary's siblings, all

older, "took" to religion, Mary proved highly receptive to it, and was the only Baker child to join a church. But Mark Baker's Calvinist doctrines were troublesome for her. In nineteenth-century America, religion was an aspect of freedom enjoyed by American citizens who could choose their ideologies at will. But many churches, such as the Congregational Church Mary would join, examined their applicants before admitting them. In these cases, the clergy questioned the applicant on his status of salvation: had he experienced a conversion and renounced his sin? Most churches would only accept those who seemed appointed by God to receive spiritual awakening. Mary rejected the idea that some people—such as her siblings—might never receive salvation. In her autobiography, *Retrospection and Introspection,* Mary described her examination:

Mary Baker Eddy, the founder of the First Church of Christ, Scientist, was born in New Hampshire and lived there for many years. This room is from her home in Concord.

The minister then wished me to tell him when I had experienced a change of heart; but tearfully I had to respond that I could not designate any precise time. Nevertheless he persisted in the assertion that I had been truly regenerated, and asked me to say how I felt when the new light dawned within me. I replied that I could only answer him in the words of the Psalmist: "Search me, O God, and know my heart: try me, and know my thoughts: and see if there be any wicked way in me, and lead me in the way everlasting" (p. 14).

Mary was received into the church despite her asserted lack of a distinct conversion experience. She had not escaped her father's insistence on repentance, however, and he relentlessly threatened her with the dire consequences of rejecting the tenet of salvation. Her response was to fall sick with anxiety, and the doctor summoned to her case warned Mark Baker to cease worrying Mary with his theology.

Search for Health

Mary's illness was not merely a product of the religious emotionalism that swept the country hand-in-hand with the revivalism of that period. In fact, the first half of her life was dominated by ill health. What began as a fragile constitution in childhood worsened into semi-invalidism in middle age. Adulthood was punctuated by numerous hardships and tragedies, and these only contributed to the deterioration of her condition. Her first husband, George Glover, died suddenly after only six months of marriage, leaving her pregnant and penniless. The delivery of her son did not lessen her grief; a difficult childbirth rendered her physically unfit to care for the child. In later years, Mary entered a second marriage with dentist Daniel Patterson under the promise that it would provide a reunion with her son. Instead, in a supposed effort to alleviate the ailing mother, Mary's older sister arranged for young George Glover to move across the country with his guardian. The marriage was further unfortunate in

that it was characterized by financial insolvency and numerous infidelities on the part of Daniel Patterson. Through twenty years of persistent disappointment, Mary was not well, suffering mainly from spinal problems that often consigned her to bed.

Mary constantly sought some means of relief from her ailments. She experimented with traditional medicine, hydropathy, allopathy, mesmerism, and homeopathy—none of which produced the desired results. Her work with the latter first sparked the idea that illness had a mental basis. While in her early forties, she heard of Phineas Parkhurst Quimby, a magnetic doctor with widely heralded curative powers. Mary immediately settled on Quimby as the solution to her difficulties and went to great efforts to visit him in Portland, Maine, in1862. Quimby's technique involved physical manipulation (rubbing the heads of his patients and wetting the hair of female patients) and mesmeric suggestion, which he called the "talking cure." After her encounter with Quimby, Mary found herself instantaneously free of her physical constrictions, and, overjoyed, became a dedicated disciple of the "doctor." Her healing was not permanent, however, and over the next four years she frequently turned to Quimby for further aid. This did not halt her faith in him; rather she worked more assiduously to discover what she felt must be a science behind his method. Though Quimby did not base his skills on any sort of biblically based spiritual revelation, Mary felt his healing resembled the lost art of Jesus Christ, and studied the Bible thoroughly for answers.

Discovery

In 1866, when Mary was forty-five, devoid of financial support, and virtually homeless (she relied upon the charity of friends who took her in for brief periods), two events occurred that would prove epochal to the advent of Christian Science. First, Quimby died, leaving her to carry on his mysterious work by herself. Second, while traversing an icy road on her way to a temperance meeting, Mary suffered an accident that left her in critical condition. Whether or not her injury was deemed terminal by the doctor who attended her is debated; what is certain is that those familiar with her medical history doubted she would ever walk again. Finding herself again confined to bed, Mary turned desperately to her Bible. On the second day of bed rest, her attention turned to the story of the bedridden palsied man in the book of Matthew who experiences healing at Jesus's behest to rise. Suddenly gaining the sense that her physical state had no bearing on her spiritual identity, Mary found herself sufficiently relieved of her injury to rise, dress herself, and greet her astonished visitors downstairs.

Mary felt she had discovered some spiritual truth, though she could not yet explain how she had been healed. In *Retrospection and Introspection*, she wrote:

> Even to the homeopathic physician who attended me, and rejoiced in my recovery, I could not then explain the modus of my relief. I could only assure him that the divine Spirit had wrought the miracle—a miracle which later I found to be in perfect scientific accord with divine law (p. 24).

In a short time, Mary experienced complete and permanent healing—not only of the effects of the fall, but of other long-standing ailments. But it would take Mary three more years of intense, individual study of the Scriptures to decipher what she believed to be the science behind Jesus's healing work. In doing so, she would find that Quimby's practice had no spiritual basis, and develop a system entirely her own. As she gradually presented her discovery to the world in a manner that allowed its practical application, she restored the lost element of healing to Christianity. She believed that such a discovery was merely a fulfillment of Jesus's claim that, "He that believeth on me, the works that I do shall he do also; and greater works than these shall he do; because I go unto my Father" (John 14:12).

Mary eventually named her system Christian Science, stating that she "named it Christian, because it is compassionate, helpful, and spiritual." She included "Science" in the title because she found that any person's correct utilization of the system afforded demonstrable and repeatable results. Realizing that the veracity of Christian Science depended upon its ability to reap results, Mary dedicated much time to healing cases deemed incurable by the medical community. Word spread, and Mary took on informal students (mainly in the families she boarded with) before holding her first class in 1870. She taught these students with a manuscript entitled, "Questions and Answers in Moral Science":

Question: What is God?
Answer: A principle: Wisdom, Love, and Truth
Question: What is this Principle?
Answer: Life and intelligence...

Mary still made references to Quimby in her earliest teachings, but when questioned where Quimby's use of physical manipulation fit into a metaphysical system based on the unreality of matter, she realized that she must separate her findings entirely from his work, which was based on mesmerism.

Christian Science is founded on the belief that healing occurs through an understanding of God's omnipotence, omnipresence, and omni-goodness—and thus, the fundamental powerlessness of anything unlike God. Difficulties of any sort could be overcome through approximation of existence from a spiritual basis. In a message to her church written in 1902, Mary explained,

> When the human mind is advancing above itself toward the Divine, it is subjugating the body, subduing matter, taking steps outward and upwards. This upward tendency of humanity will finally... rise from sense to Soul, from earth to heaven.

"Sense" is personal sense—or an estimation of the human experience based on the testimony of the physical senses. Healing occurs when one replaces the physical perception of reality with the spiritual.

Widening Circles

Upon graduation, Mary's students would often establish their own healing practices or teach Christian Science to others. However, the teachings of students so new to science were, not surprisingly, often inaccurate. Mary realized the importance of providing a single authoritative source of information for all who sought it, and in 1872 began work on a textbook. She continued to take students while writing, but over the course of the next three years focused most of her attention on the new manuscript. In 1875, it was finally published as *Science and Health* and would go through many revisions over Mary's lifetime, and was ultimately renamed *Science and Health with Key to the Scriptures*.

Now that her teachings were firmly grounded in one authoritative source, Mary made efforts to widen the reach of Christian Science. As increasing numbers of her students established their own practices even as America moved toward restricting use of the word "doctor," Mary realized the need to legitimize her students' work in the eyes of the government. In 1881, she chartered the Massachusetts Metaphysical College, which conferred degrees in accord with the usual educational standards of accreditation. CSB was conferred as the equivalent of a bachelor's degree in Christian Science, and CSD a doctorate. Mary was performing her own healing work less and less, feeling that her purpose was better served as a teacher.

In 1877, Mary married one last time, to **Asa Gilbert Eddy**, a promising student and practitioner of Christian Science whom she came to rely on as a great source of strength and support. In the union, she gained the name she is now famously known by: Mary Baker Eddy. Mrs. Eddy described the marriage in a letter to one of her students as "a union of affection and of high purposes. It is not a sexual union[;] in this my husband coincides with me..." As Christian Science gained an ever-widening popularity in America, it suffered increasing attacks from clergy, defected students, and skeptical individuals. Gilbert Eddy dutifully stood by his wife through the

lawsuits, copyright infringement, and public defamation that beset her and her movement. But Eddy would die after only five years of marriage, leaving his widow temporarily overwhelmed with grief.

The Church

The founder of Christian Science had hoped that the Protestant churches of her day would embrace her cause. However, though many clergymen did end up in her classes, it quickly became evident that Christian Science would have to be introduced as a new denomination. For a long while, Mrs. Eddy was opposed to the idea of church, as the establishment of no such human institution was present in Jesus's ministry. In the first edition of *Science and Health* she wrote:

> We have no need of creeds and church organizations to sustain or explain a demonstrable platform, that defines itself in healing the sick, and casting out error.... The mistake the disciples of Jesus made to found religious organizations and church rites, if indeed they did this, was one the Master did not make.... No time was lost by our Master in organizations, rites, and ceremonies, or in proselyting for certain forms of belief...

However, church was such an integral part of life in nineteenth-century America that many of her students greatly desired it, and Eddy came to understand that Christian Science would be more widely appealing if advanced in the usual context of religion. So, in 1879, she and several of her followers obtained a charter for "The Church of Christ (Scientist)" from the Commonwealth of Massachusetts. Boston was decided on as the location.

Having become a very prominent figure in the newspapers of the day, Mrs. Eddy felt the need for her own organ in which she could control the information disseminated on Christian Science and address falsities released by other publications. In 1883, she fulfilled this need with *The Journal of Christian Science*, later known as *The Christian Science Journal*. Aside from the aforementioned functions, the *Journal* also allowed Mrs. Eddy a forum in which to answer questions from her students and the general public, and, most importantly, provided a record of healings. *The Journal* is still released as a monthly publication.

By 1891, the *Journal* listed nineteen formally organized Christian Science churches, seventy-five additional groups that held regular meetings, and nearly three hundred practitioners. The movement had spread not only across the country, but also across the Atlantic, making some appearances in the United Kingdom. However, Mrs. Eddy was not satisfied with the direction of the movement, and decided reformation was needed from within. She witnessed the competition among the various branches, and decided that those organizations were too grounded in human ambitions. And so, in 1889, she dissolved the church she had chartered ten years earlier and would rebuild it on a more spiritual basis.

Taking control of the church out the hands of its members, she appointed four directors (later numbering five) to serve as the authoritative basis for the new church. In 1892, she asked them to take out a new charter. She had already purchased land in the Back Bay area of Boston, and, now that she had a new organizational system, was eager to build an edifice. She deeded the land to the directors and their successors in perpetuity, and asked them to carry out construction of what would be called The Mother Church. She instructed them not to go into debt, and told them the project must be finished by the end of 1894. Though it seemed to be impossible, both instructions were accomplished, and the church held its first service on Sunday, January 1, 1895. But who led this service? While the new edifice was under construction Eddy gave great consideration to the fact that there were simply too few preachers whom she believed adequate to fulfill the need of every Christian Science church. She finally settled on the

Mary Baker Eddy (1821–1910), the founder of Christian Science, in this undated photograph.

solution of making the Bible and *Science and Health* universal "pastors," to be read from every week in lieu of a sermon. This decision is still in effect today. As further issues arose and decisions were made, Eddy drafted them as rules for the governance of church affairs, and compiled them in the *Manual of the Mother Church*. Her organizational work would culminate in 1898, though she continued to make revisions to the *Manual* until her death in 1910.

Final Details of Establishment

Eddy's last fifteen years were, perhaps, the busiest of her life, as she continued to fend off attacks and nurture the growth of her cause. In 1898, she established a Board of Lectureship to allow those she did feel were articulate in Christian Science to publicly express their thoughts and experiences. She inaugurated a weekly magazine to address world news, now called the *Christian Science Sentinel*. And she set up the Christian Science Publishing Society as a separate legal entity from the church, run by a Board of Trustees. In 1899, she formed the Committee on Publication to address fallacies published in the media. In that same year, Eddy founded the Board of Education (BOE) using the same charter obtained for the Massachusetts Metaphysical College, which she had closed in 1889. The BOE now provided official certification of new teachers of Christian Science. Finally, in 1910, she made the last revisions to *Science and Health with Key to the Scriptures*, which were implemented after her death.

The Christian Science Monitor

Eddy authored and founded numerous publications in her lifetime, but aside from *Science and Health with Key to the Scriptures*, her most well known contribution is *The Christian Science Monitor*. In fact, Eddy considered it her most important accomplishment after writing the textbook.

In 1908, Eddy realized that Christian Scientists must put their healing efforts to broader use. She wanted practitioners of the Science to look beyond personal affairs to world needs. Also, she lamented the sensationalism of the media, which fed on the misfortune of others—real or contrived. Eddy had long felt the need for a paper that offered news in an objective and balanced manner. In 1883, she wrote:

> Looking over the newspapers of the day, one naturally reflects that it is dangerous to live, so loaded with disease seems the very air. These descriptions carry fears to many minds, to be depicted in some future time upon the body. A periodical of our own will counteract to some extent this public nuisance; for through our paper we shall be able to reach many homes with healing, purifying thought.

Twenty-five years later, she was finally ready for such a venture. And, as was so often the case after settling on a decision, she asked that it be carried out immediately. It was. In three months' time, a structure for printing presses and the building to house them were constructed; more than one hundred employees were hired; and an editorial concept was developed. Mrs. Eddy had made her request of the directors on July 28, 1908. On November 25, 1908, she composed a brief editorial for the first edition, and in it expressed the paper's purpose: "to injure no man, but to bless all mankind."

Many involved in the *Monitor*'s development resisted the inclusion of "Christian Science" in the title, suspecting it would limit the paper's appeal to those sympathetic to the movement. But Eddy held fast to her original title, confident that the paper's excellence would prove the deciding factor in its acceptance. In his biographical novel *Years of Authority*, Robert Peel wrote, "the designated title was an identification of the paper with the promise that no human situation was beyond healing or rectification if approached with sufficient understanding of man's God-given potentialities. Nor did the 'good news' of Christianity involve the prettification of bad news, but rather, its confident confrontation."

The *Monitor* has since won many awards:
- 2007 Robert F. Kennedy Journalism Award for Editorial Cartoons;
- 2004 Military Reporters and Editors Award in Print Overseas Reporting;
- 2004 Eliav-Sartawi Award for Middle Eastern Journalism in the Western Press;
- Pulitzer Prize in Journalism in 2002 for Editorial Cartooning, and in Journalism in 1996 for International Reporting;
- Pulitzer Prizes in 1969, 1968, 1967, 1950.

B. Important Dates and Landmarks

1875 *Science and Health with Key to the Scriptures* first published.

1876 Eddy forms Christian Scientist Association.

1879 Founds Church of Christ, Scientist.

1881 Massachusetts Metaphysical College chartered.

1881 Eddy ordained as pastor for church.

1883 *The Christian Science Journal* founded.

1886 National Christian Scientist Association formed.

1889 Eddy dissolves church, college, and Christian Science Association.

1892 Church reorganized.

1892 *Journal* transferred to church.

1898 Christian Science Publishing Society formed.

1908 Eddy founds *Christian Science Monitor.*

1984 *Monitor* launches Monitor Radio.

1986 *Monitor* buys WQTV Boston.

1991 Start of national Monitor (cable) Channel.

1992 Sells WQTV to Boston University.

1992 Monitor Channel cable network closes.

1997 Monitor Radio service closes.

C. Important Figures

Judge Septimus J. Hanna (1845–1921)

A Civil War veteran and judge in the Old West, Septimus Hanna left his profession to join the Christian Science movement, ultimately filling more offices under Mrs. Eddy's direction than any other individual.

Hanna grew up in the rural town of Springs Mill, Pennsylvania. At the age of eighteen, he entered the Civil War, achieving the rank of Captain. After completing his service, the young man took up the study of law, and at the age of twenty-three, was appointed judge of the County Court in Council Bluffs, Iowa. Thereafter, he was always known as "Judge Hanna." Hanna married a woman named Camilla Turley and, in 1872, the pair relocated to Chicago, where he was offered a partnership. A bout with tuberculosis forced him to move to a drier climate, however. In 1879, the Hannas took up residence in Leadville, Colorado.

The couple first heard of Christian Science in 1885 through two of Camilla Hanna's friends, who had experienced healings. Camilla began a study of *Science of Health*, and therein was healed of chronic semi-invalidism. Her newfound understanding proved beneficial to her husband, as well, who received relief from various symptoms of illness. Hanna's curiosity piqued, he took up his own study, and was thoroughly healed of several longstanding ailments, including the aforementioned tuberculosis. Within four years, Hanna had decided to devote his life to the Christian Science movement.

In 1890, the Hannas attended a national association of Christian Scientists in New York City. At the meeting, they were asked to take charge of a society of Christian Scientists located in Scranton, Pennsylvania. They accepted, and continued this work until Mrs. Eddy asked them to come to Boston in 1892, for she desired that Hanna assume editorship of *The Christian Science Journal.* He complied, and his wife accepted the assistant editorship. In 1893, Mrs. Eddy asked that Hanna serve as pastor of The Mother Church. When she instated the Bible and *Science and Health* as impersonal pastors, Hanna was assigned the role of first reader. In 1898, Eddy inaugurated the *Christian Science Sentinel*, at which point Hanna was made editor of that publication as well.

In 1902, after ten years in his multifaceted role, Hanna resigned as Editor of the *Journal* and *Sentinel*, and as first reader. Mrs. Eddy had asked him to embark on a new venture: she appointed him to the Board of Lectureship. In 1908, Hanna took on his final role as a teacher of Normal classes, educating others to become teachers of Christian Science. He and his wife fully retired in 1911.

Edward A. Kimball

Edward Kimball left his successful career as a manufacturer in Chicago in 1888 after experiencing a dramatic healing through Christian Science. He took classes with Eddy that year and the next, and Eddy found him so perceptive of Science that she asked him to represent the religion at the World's Parliament of Religions in 1893.

In 1894, Kimball was elected first reader of First Church of Christ, Scientist, Chicago. In 1898, he received further instruction, enabling him to become a teacher of Christian Science in Chicago. Eddy later appointed him to the Board of Lectureship, and it is estimated that he gave over 1,000 lectures while in service. In 1889, Kimball became a teacher of teachers when Eddy included him among the first members of the Board of Education.

Kimball assisted Eddy with a major revision of *Science and Health* in 1901. One year later, he proposed that a $2 million extension be added to the edifice of The Mother Church to provide badly needed additional seating. That extension was completed in 1906.

Calvin A. Frye

Frye first had Primary class instruction with Eddy in 1881, a period of time when eight of her students defected from the movement. The desertion shook Eddy, but it merely strengthened Frye's resolve to further dedicate himself to the cause of Christian Science. In 1882, Eddy asked Frye to join her household as her personal secretary, and he remained in service to her until her death in 1910, never leaving her presence for longer than a day. He fulfilled the duties of bookkeeper, secretary, trustee of copyrights and property, and coachman. Frye went through two further classes with Eddy, attending her last class (a two-day gathering of those she considered her most advanced students) in 1898. After Eddy's death, Frye served as First Reader from 1912–1915 in Concord, New Hampshire. In 1916, he was elected president of The Mother Church.

II. Tenets and Beliefs

A. Articles of Faith

Christian Science is based on the life, teachings, and works of Jesus Christ. Christian Science does not have an organizational creed. However, the following are the tenets of the religion as outlined on page 497 in *Science and Health*:

As adherents of Truth, we take the inspired Word of the Bible as our sufficient guide to eternal Life.

We acknowledge and adore one supreme and infinite God. We acknowledge His Son, one Christ; the Holy Ghost or divine Comforter; and man in God's image and likeness.

We acknowledge God's forgiveness of sin in the destruction of sin and the spiritual understanding that casts out evil as unreal. But the belief in sin is punished so long as the belief lasts.

We acknowledge Jesus' atonement as the evidence of divine, efficacious Love, unfolding man's unity with God through Christ Jesus the Wayshower; and we acknowledge that man is saved through Christ, through Truth, Life, and Love as demonstrated by the Galilean Prophet in healing the sick and overcoming sin and death.

We acknowledge that the crucifixion of Jesus and his resurrection served to uplift faith to understand eternal Life, even the allness of Soul, Spirit, and the nothingness of matter.

And we solemnly promise to watch, and pray for that Mind to be in us which was also in Christ Jesus; to do unto others as we would have them do unto us; and to be merciful, just, and pure.

Christ Jesus

Christ Jesus is both "wayshower" and savior in Christian Science theology. Eddy distinguished between the corporeal Jesus, the human man in the flesh (the son of man), and the incorporeal Christ, "the divine manifestation of God, which comes to the flesh to destroy incarnate error" (*Science and Health*, p. 583). This incorporeal Christ is the "spiritual selfhood" (or spiritual identity) of Jesus (*Science and Health*, p. 38). In Eddy's "Message to The Mother Church for 1901," on page 8 in the section titled "Christ is One and Divine," she writes:

The Christ was Jesus's spiritual selfhood; therefore Christ existed prior to Jesus, who said, "Before Abraham was, I am." Jesus, the only immaculate, was born of a virgin mother, and

Christian Science explains that mystic saying of the Master as to his dual personality, or the spiritual and material Christ Jesus, called in Scripture the Son of God and the Son of man—explains it as referring to his eternal spiritual selfhood and his temporal manhood.

This accords with a basic plank in the platform of Christian Science:

"The invisible Christ was imperceptible to the so-called personal senses, whereas Jesus appeared as a bodily existence. This dual personality of the unseen and the seen, the spiritual and material, the eternal Christ and the corporeal Jesus manifest in flesh, continued until the Master's ascension, when the human, material concept, or Jesus, disappeared, while the spiritual self, or Christ, continues to exist in the eternal order of divine Science, taking away the sins of the world, as the Christ has always done, even before the human Jesus was incarnate to mortal eyes" (*Science and Health,* p. 334).

Christian Science teaches that Jesus's history is factual, including the virgin birth, the crucifixion, the resurrection, and the ascension. Because of his special status due to the virgin birth and his pure, selfless nature, Jesus voluntarily faced his struggle in Gethsemane, death, resurrection, and ascension to show humanity that no phase of mortal existence was beyond God's redeeming love. Eddy wrote:

Jesus could have withdrawn himself from his enemies. He had power to lay down a human sense of life for his spiritual identity in the likeness of the divine; but he allowed men to attempt the destruction of the mortal body in order that he might furnish the proof of immortal life. Nothing could kill this Life of man. Jesus could give his temporal life into his enemies' hands; but when his earth-mission was accomplished, his spiritual life, indestructible and eternal, was found forever the same (*Science and Health,* p. 51).

Christian Science also teaches that we are not Christians until we "go and do likewise," that is, until we in some degree "come in the unity of the faith, and of the knowledge of the Son of God, unto a perfect man, unto the measure of the stature of the fullness of Christ," as it says in the Scriptures (Ephesians 4:13). We never become Christ, but we are called upon to fully reflect Christ or be Christ-like, to emulate our Master's great words and works in some measure. Eddy stipulated, however, that one ought never make "careless comparison or irreverent reference to Christ Jesus." She also wrote that just as there is but one God, there is but one Christ Jesus.

The Trinity

Christian Scientists are Trinitarian, but in an unorthodox way:

Life, Truth, and Love constitute the triune Person called God, that is, the triply divine Principle, Love. They represent a trinity in unity, three in Divine one—the same in essence, though multi-form in office: God the Father-Mother; Christ the spiritual idea of sonship; divine Science or the Holy Comforter. These three express in divine Science the threefold, essential nature of the infinite. They also indicate the divine Principle of scientific being, the intelligent relation of God to man and the universe (*Science and Health,* p. 331).

Here, Eddy calls God "Father-Mother," signifying not an androgynous God but a God "without body, parts or passions," who nevertheless functions both to govern (as fundamental Truth) and comfort (as divine Love). Eddy stresses departure from the idea of an anthropomorphic God, basing her concept totally in principle. She calls the Holy Ghost "divine Science or the Holy Comforter," the spiritual law of God operating as the impartation of divine Mind to man.

Creation

In *Science and Health with Key to the Scriptures,* Eddy argues that given the absolute goodness and perfection of God, sin, disease, and death were not created by Him, and therefore cannot be truly real. She bases this reading on Genesis 1, deeming that chapter the true record of creation in contrast to Genesis 2, the false record of creation obscuring the true (symbolized by "a mist [that] went up from the face of the ground"). According to Eddy, this second chapter mirrors evil's role in obscuring good. Rather than being ontologically real in Christian Science, evil and its manifestations are merely the suppositional opposite of God and His creation. The demand for Christians, therefore, is to "unmask" such untruths through Christ, revealing the true and eternal perfection of God's creation. Eddy therefore termed evil "error," the opposite of truth, and felt it could be remedied through a better spiritual understanding of one's relationship to God. She contended that this understanding was what enabled the biblical Jesus to heal people, and accords with the Scripture: "We are of God: he that knoweth God heareth us; he that is not of God heareth not us. Hereby know we the spirit of truth, and the spirit of error" (I John 4:6).

This teaching is the foundation of the Christian Science principle that disease—and any other adversity—can be cured through turning to divine Mind to fully understand this spiritual relationship. It is encapsulated in *Science and Health* as "The Scientific Statement of Being," which is read aloud in churches and Sunday Schools at the end of every Sunday service, along with I John 3:1–3 and a biblical benediction:

"There is no life, truth, intelligence, nor substance in matter. All is infinite Mind and its infinite manifestation, for God is All-in-all. Spirit is immortal Truth; matter is mortal error. Spirit is the real and eternal; matter is the unreal and temporal. Spirit is God, and man is His image and likeness. Therefore man is not material; he is spiritual" (*Science and Health*, p. 468).

Alternatives to Medicine

This belief in the allness of God, Spirit, is the basis of Christian Scientists' characteristic reliance on prayer in place of traditional medical care, often with the aid of Christian Science practitioners.

Practitioners are students and teachers of Christian Science who devote their full time to a public practice of healing through Christian Science. Such treatment is requested by patients for health-related or personal problems, including relationship issues, employment or financial difficulties, and so on. Additionally, practitioners are available to simply answer questions regarding Christian Science.

B. Scripture

The Bible and *Science and Health with Key to the Scriptures* are the primary texts used for individual study and spiritual growth. Together they are the foundation for Christian Science teaching and practice, and are used during church services. Eddy ordained these books as a "dual and impersonal pastor" for these services. It was the specific mission of *Science and Health* to provide the world this key to the Scriptures—"to open up their treasures and enable everyone to use them."

C. Important Writers, Thinkers, and Theologians

Robert Peel (1909–1992)

Englishman Robert Peel is widely acclaimed as Mary Baker Eddy's most astute biographer. Himself a Christian Scientist and one-time counselor with his church's Committee on Publication, Peel authored a meticulous three-volume examination of the life and works of Mrs. Eddy, as well as the religio-historical context in which Christian Science developed. An alumnus of Harvard, Peel studied closely with Perry Miller, an authority on American Puritanism. Such scholarship no doubt informed his ability to objectively present in detail the varied cultural influences under which Mrs. Eddy's discovery was wrought out. Peel also contributed numerous articles to Christian

Science periodicals, and authored books on metaphysical healing in contrast to physical science.

Bliss Knapp (1877–1958)

Bliss Knapp was an early Christian Scientist and author of *Destiny of the Mother Church* (ca. 1891). Knapp was born in 1877 to Ira O. and Flavia S. Knapp, who were students of Mary Baker Eddy.

As a child, he studied the teachings of Eddy, completing a Primary class before his enrollment at Harvard in 1898, where, he helped organize informal services among Christian Scientists.

Knapp held that Eddy represented a personal fulfillment of biblical prophecy as the woman referred to in the twelfth chapter of the Book of Revelation. While Knapp's father, Ira Knapp, had subscribed to that belief himself, Ira later conceded that Eddy had never taught this interpretation herself. Others felt that Knapp meant that Eddy as a mortal could not physically embody the Woman; but as an idea of God, her spiritual purpose and life's work could represent the symbolic travails of the Woman. It was felt by supporters of Eddy as "the Woman" that any attempt to paint her in this light would meet with universal condemnation of her and her church for deifying her, and so this notion must never be put forth as an official view of the church.

While Eddy herself did not hesitate to identify with the impersonal spiritual type the woman represented and apparently tolerated early ambiguities on the subject, opponents of Knapp's view argued Eddy disavowed individual, personal interpretations specifically. She had written in her final edition of *Science and Health:* "The woman in the Apocalypse symbolizes generic man [her term for all mankind, understood spiritually], the spiritual idea of God; she illustrates the coincidence of God and man as the divine Principle and divine idea" (p. 561). In comments elsewhere she expanded the distinction, writing, "What St. John saw in prophetic vision and depicted as 'a woman clothed with the sun and the moon under her feet' prefigured no specialty or individuality. His vision foretold a type, and this type applied to man as well as to woman...." (Peel, *Years of Authority,* p. 165).

Stephen Gottschalk (1931–2005)

Historian, writer, and Christian Science scholar Stephen Gottschalk authored two books on Christian Science and its founder: *The Emergence of Christian Science in American Religious Life* (ca. 1971), and *Rolling Away the Stone: Mary Baker Eddy's Challenge to Materialism* 1890–1910 (ca. 2005). The first examines Christian Science in the context of American religion as a transformative influence on Christianity, while the latter focuses more upon the last twenty years of Eddy's life: her overseeing of the Mother Church's structural and governmental formation, her address of dissension within the movement and attack from without, her final revision of *Science and Health,* and her founding of *The Christian Science Monitor.*

Gottschalk taught college courses in the 1960s and 1970s on the American Revolution, American cultural history, poetry, political philosophy, and arts. In 1978, Gottschalk relocated his family from California to Boston, where he took a position with the Christian Science Church's Committee on Publication. Ultimately growing disillusioned with what he viewed as risky financial ventures within the Church's media campaign, and strongly opposing the Church's approval of Bliss Knapp's *Destiny of the Mother Church,* which he felt inaccurately portrayed Eddy as on par with Jesus Christ, Gottschalk resigned his position. During the 1990s, he was recognized as a vocal critic of the leadership of The Mother Church.

Gottschalk's second book, completed just before his death in 2005, was released to excellent reviews for its methodical, scholarly approach to the historical material made available in The Mother Church archives, and painstaking appraisal of its subject.

Gillian Gill

Gillian Gill is a non–Christian Scientist scholar who wrote *Mary Baker Eddy* (ca. 1998), a biography that examines Eddy's life from a largely feminist perspective. In her biography, Gill gives special emphasis to Eddy's display of revolutionary female leadership in the face of nineteenth-century society's constricting Victorian notions of femininity. While Gill apparently earned hitherto unparalleled access to documents held by The Mother Church, her exposition of New Thought contemporaries of Mrs. Eddy is criticized as inaccurate. However, her work overall is praised for its depth and academic acumen.

Mary Baker Eddy (1821–1910)

Apart from her leadership in forming the church (see above), Eddy's published writings, in addition to *Science and Health,* include:

- *Retrospection and Introspection*
- *Unity of Good*
- *Pulpit and Press*
- *Rudimental Divine Science*
- *No and Yes*
- *Christian Science versus Pantheism*
- *Message to The Mother Church, 1900*
- *Message to The Mother Church, 1901*
- *Message to The Mother Church, 1902*
- *Christian Healing*
- *The People's Idea of God*
- *The First Church of Christ, Scientist, and Miscellany*
- *Manual of The Mother Church*
- *Miscellaneous Writings*

III. Rites and Rituals

A. The Calendar

The Church of Christ, Scientist observes the usual Christian holidays, Thanksgiving (celebrated as a Christian holiday), Christmas, and Easter, though emphasis is placed on the spiritual aspects of these holidays. Twice a year, during Sunday services, the congregation is invited to kneel in silent commemoration of the morning meal beside the Lake of Galilee attended by the risen Jesus.

B. Worship and Liturgy

Churches hold a one-hour service each Sunday, consisting of hymns, prayer, and readings from the Bible and *Science and Health with Key to the Scriptures.* These readings comprise the weekly Lesson-Sermon, which is read aloud at all Sunday services in all Christian Science churches worldwide, and is studied at home throughout the preceding week. The Lesson, as it is informally called, is compiled by a Christian Science Publishing Society committee and consists of alternating (related) passages from the Bible and from *Science and Health.*

There are twenty-six set topics for the Lesson-Sermon found in the *Christian Science Quarterly,* selected by Eddy herself. The topics follow each other in an unchanging, predetermined order, and the progression starts over midyear so that every week in the year has a topic devoted to it.

The topics are:

1. God
2. Sacrament
3. Life
4. Truth
5. Love
6. Spirit
7. Soul
8. Mind
9. Christ Jesus
10. Man
11. Substance
12. Matter
13. Reality
14. Unreality
15. Are Sin, Disease and Death Real?
16. Doctrine of Atonement
17. Probation After Death
18. Everlasting Punishment
19. Adam and Fallen Man

20. Mortals and Immortals
21. Soul and Body
22. Ancient and Modern Necromancy
23. God the Only Cause and Creator
24. God the Preserver of Man
25. Is the Universe, Including Man, Evolved by Atomic Force?
26. Christian Science

In years in which there are fifty-three Sundays, the topic "Christ Jesus" occurs a third time, in December.

Because there are no clergy in the church, branch church Sunday services are conducted by two Readers elected by the congregation: the First Reader, who reads passages from *Science and Health,* and the Second Reader, who reads passages from the Bible. First Readers determine the beginning scriptural selection, hymns to be sung on Sundays, and the benediction. The vast majority of the service is the reading of the weekly Bible Lesson supplied by the Christian Science Publishing Society, and order of service set out by the *Manual.*

Churches also hold a one-hour Wednesday evening testimony meeting. At this service, the First Reader reads passages from the Bible and *Science and Health* on a topic of current concern, and members of the congregation can give first-hand accounts of healing through prayer, share inspiration or make general remarks on Christian Science.

Recently some branch churches started to hold a social fellowship meeting at the conclusion of Sunday services. Branch churches also sponsor annual public talks given by speakers selected annually by the Board of Lectureship in Boston. A Sunday School is typically provided for children up to the age of twenty.

C. Daily Life

Christian Science teaches how to rely progressively on prayer alone for physical cure. For those practicing it, such healing often affirms its primary mission—to heal "the sins of the world" through understanding the power of Christ, or divine Truth.

Christian Science practice teaches that in order to heal systematically and consistently, understanding the nature of God and His laws is necessary. It is praying with understanding and "bringing into captivity every thought to the obedience of Christ" (II Cor. 10: 5) that heals sin and sickness and adjusts human circumstances. The teachings of Jesus are central to Christian Science, and his healing work provides the foremost example of how his followers also can turn to God's omnipotent love for healing. Jesus's words, "And these signs shall follow them that believe" (Mark 16:17) precede a description of healing effects. Of course, true understanding of Christ's principles can only be reflected by an adherence to them in daily life. One must emulate the nature of Christ, the church teaches, to be successful in practice.

Verification of Healings

The church claims to have thousands of testimonies of healing through Christian Science treatment alone. While most of these testimonies represent ailments neither diagnosed nor treated by medical professionals, the church does require three other people to vouch for any testimony published in its official organ, the *Christian Science Journal.* However, some critics of the church complain that the verification guidelines are not strict enough, allowing verifiers who have not witnessed the claimed healing to "vouch for [the healings'] accuracy based on their knowledge of [the claimant]." (taken from the church's Testimony Guidelines.) The church also has a number of statements regarding diagnosed conditions accompanied by legal affidavits of authenticity signed by medical practitioners who witnessed a non-medical healing. A book entitled *Spiritual Healing in a Scientific Age* by Robert Peel chronicles many of these accounts and quotes from the affidavits. Peel is widely considered the most academic/scholarly writer of the church's published biographers of Mary Baker Eddy and metaphysical healing.

Christian Scientists normally choose prayer alone for healing for themselves and their children. However, individuals are always free to choose whatever form of treatment or care they feel will best answer their needs. Eddy stated that one might accept certain temporary aid from *materia medica* if a person is in such pain that he is unable to pray.

"If patients fail to experience the healing power of Christian Science, and think they can be benefited by certain ordinary physical methods of medical treatment, then the Mind-physician should give up such cases, and leave invalids free to resort to whatever other systems they fancy will afford relief" (*Science and Health,* p. 443).

While physical cure appears as a noticeable element of the outcome of prayer, it is important to recognize that Christian Scientists believe that character flaws as well as discord in relationships, school, career, marriage, mental health or any other aspect of life, can be healed through prayer. Christian Science teaches that spiritual healing is a natural result of following Jesus's teachings. Healing was a major part of Jesus's ministry, and Christian Scientists see no basis for excluding it from the practice of modern day Christians. They believe Jesus proved the veracity of his teachings by his healings.

Christian Science Practitioners

It is customary for Christian Scientists to pray for themselves for healing. For additional assistance through prayer, they can call Christian Science practitioners. Practitioners are men and women in the public healing ministry, helping those who wish to rely on spiritual treatment alone for healing. Practitioners claim no personal healing power, nor do they act as intercessors. They turn to God alone, who is the healing power in all cases. Christian Scientists believe that Jesus was speaking to all, for all time, when he said, "He that believeth on me, the works that I do shall he do also...." (John 14:12).

Christian Scientists who wish to become public practitioners of Christian Science—spiritual healers —complete an intensive two-week Primary class. A

teacher provides the instruction in this class.

The Mother Church certifies teachers of Christian Science every three years from the pool of active public practitioners. The church selects the candidates, who then take another class, designated Normal. Both classes are based on the Bible and the writings of Mary Baker Eddy. In particular, the Primary class focuses upon the chapter entitled "Recapitulation" in *Science and Health with Key to the Scriptures.* This chapter uses the Socratic method of teaching, posing questions on the nature of existence, man, and Christian Science. The Normal class focuses upon the chapter entitled "Science of Being."

Christian Scientists are sometimes criticized for denying the sick conventional medical care, particularly children. Such criticism is often lodged without due recognition of several facts:

(a) Christian Science does not prohibit the application of conventional medicine; in many instances, such care is sanctioned and even encouraged—it is simply not the only option.

(b) In forty-five states, statutes hold that the application of spiritual methods of treatment for illness (according to the tenets of a recognized religion) does not constitute neglect or abuse. (See *Wall Street Journal*, June 12, 2008.)

(c) Studies indicate that between one-quarter and three-quarters of a million deaths occur each year as a result of doctor, hospital, or treatment misapplication or error (JAMA, 284:4; 272:23)—in spite of the best of intentions of the conventional medical community.

D. Life Cycle Events

Christian Scientists acknowledge the sacraments of baptism and Eucharist in a manner entirely divorced from materialistic ritual. "Our baptism," wrote Eddy, "is purification from all error.... Our Eucharist is spiritual communion with the one God. Our bread, 'which cometh down from heaven,' is Truth. Our cup is the cross. Our wine the inspiration of Love, the draught the Master drank and commended to his followers" (*Science and Health,* p. 35).

Nuptials

Eddy wrote, "Marriage is the legal and moral provision for generation among human kind" (*Science and Health,* p. 56). Christian Science views marriage as a concession necessary for the maintenance of virtue, and requires a legal, religious marriage ceremony: "If a Christian Scientist is to be married, the ceremony shall be performed by a clergyman who is legally authorized" (*Manual,* p. 49).

Divorce

The church takes no official position on divorce or other aspects of the marital relationship.

IV. Denominations and Demographics

A. Schisms

Throughout the history of Christian Science there have been a small number of dissenting sects, unacknowledged by the Boston organization. Such dissenters often point to certain estoppel clauses of the last church *Manual* issued by Mary Baker Eddy before her death which, had they been interpreted literally, would have led to a radical decentralization of the Christian Science Church. The issue has involved the church in repeated litigation brought by dissenters, most prominently between 1919–22, when a group of Trustees of the Christian Science Publishing Society filed a suit against the Christian Science Board of Directors.

Additionally, Anne Bill led a breakaway sect called the Christian Science Parent Church after Eddy's death. This evolved into the Church of Integration, which disbanded in the 1950s.

There are currently no existing subsets or sects of The Church of Christ, Scientist operating within the United States.

B. Organization and Distribution

According to its governing by-laws, The Church of Christ, Scientist does not report for publication the number of its members, as it contends that popularity is no measure of spiritual vitality. It does report that there are readers of *Science and Health* in about 120 countries and over 2,000 congregations in over 70 countries worldwide.

A special U.S. Census in 1936 recorded 268,915 Christian Scientists in the U.S. In the Spring 1992 edition of the *Christian Research Journal,* William Alnor asserts that church membership had gone from 268,000 members in the 1930s to 150,000 members in 1992. As an indirect measure of the church's strength, that same article cites statistics showing that the circulation of the church's celebrated *Christian Science Monitor* decreased from 240,000 in the 1960s to 100,000 in 1992. Other estimates place membership in a wide range from 150,000 members to 400,000.

The church went through a period of rapid growth during the first half of the twentieth century. Membership leveled out by 1950 and has since gradually declined.

V. Organization and Infrastructure

A. Education of Clergy

There is no ordained clergy in the church. Lay readers are elected from the congregation normally every three years. They read the Lesson-Sermon from the Bible and *Science and Health,* and conduct services. As noted previously, these two books together are considered the pastor of the church by its members.

Schools

Acorn Pre-, Lower, Middle, and Upper Schools
www.acorn.org

The Principia
13201 Clayton Road
Saint Louis, MO 63131
314-434-2100

Principia College
Elsah, IL 62028
618-374-2131
www.prin.edu

B. Houses of Worship

The church has about 2,000 branch congregations in over seventy countries. There are about 1,600 congregations in the U.S.; about sixty in Canada. They operate Christian Science Reading Rooms where the public is invited to read the Bible and literature published by the church.

The church itself was built in 1894, and an annex was added in 1906. It boasts one of the world's largest pipe organs, built by the Aeolian-Skinner Company of Boston. The Mary Baker Eddy Library for the Betterment of Humanity is housed in a nineteen-story structure originally built for the Christian Science Publishing Society between 1932 and 1934, and the present plaza was constructed in the 1970s to include a large administration building, a colonnade, and a reflecting pool with fountain, designed by Araldo Cossutta of I. M. Pei and Partners.

The Mother Church is the church's world headquarters, and is located in Boston, Massachusetts (pictured at top).

Branch Christian Science churches and Christian Science Societies are subordinate to The Mother Church, but are self-governed in the sense that they have their own constitutions, bank accounts, and assets. In order to be recognized, they must abide by the practices that Mary Baker Eddy laid out in the *Manual of The Mother Church*. Church services, along with every other aspect of

The First Church of Christ, Scientist, in Boston, Massachusetts—also known as the Mother Church—was built in 1894 and serves as the administrative headquarters of the Christian Science Church.

church government, are regulated by the *Manual*, a constitution of sorts written by Eddy, and consisting of various regulations covering everything from the duties of officers, to discipline, to provisions for church meetings and publications. Branch churches of The Mother Church may take the title of First Church of Christ, Scientist; Second; but the article "The" must not be used.

The First Church of Christ, Scientist
210 Massachusetts Avenue
Boston, MA 02115
617-450-2000
info@churchofchristscientist.org
Media Inquiries: 617-450-1644
info@churchofchristscientist.org
infoline@csps.com
customerservice@spirituality.com
www.churchofchristscientist.org
www.spirituality.com
www.christianscience.com

C. Governance and Authority

The *Manual of The Mother Church* provides the by-laws that govern church activities, officers, and members. Originally published in 1895, the slim book was revised extensively during Eddy's lifetime.

Authority for conducting church business according to the *Manual* is vested in the church's Board of Directors, composed of five members who hold their positions for an undefined period and select their own successors. Local congregations (branches) are democratically self-governed.

The Christian Science Board of Directors is a five-person executive created by Mary Baker Eddy to administer the Christian Science Church under the terms defined in her church constitution (the *Manual*). Its operations are defined by various by-laws throughout the *Manual*.

The board functions in accordance with a Deed of Trust written by Eddy (one of several) under which it consisted of four persons, though she later expanded the board to five persons. This later bore on a dispute during the 1920s, known as the Great Litigation in Christian Science circles, regarding whether the Christian Science Board of Directors could remove trustees of the Christian Science Publishing Society or whether the CSPS trustees were established independently.

Another minority believed that Eddy intended various matters for her consent ("estoppels") to cause the church to dissolve on her passing (since they could no longer be followed). Ironically, a strong argument against this position came from a respected theologian, Clifford P. Smith, who claimed that Eddy had indicated that her lawyer had assured her that these consent clauses would not hinder normal operation after her death.

D. Social Service Organizations

Christian Science Reading Rooms

A ubiquitous feature of the American landscape, most branches of the Church of Christ, Scientist provide a Reading Room, open to the general public, usually located in storefronts of business districts, though they may also be found within a branch church. This space offers a quiet place for the study of Christian Science literature and for prayer, and offers Christian Science media—books, CDs, cassette tapes, magazines, etc.—for borrowing or purchase. An attendant of the Reading Room is always present to provide information or answer visitors' questions.

Reading Room Orders:
617-450-2790
sales@csps.com

E. Media and Communication

Newspaper

The Christian Science Monitor
210 Massachusetts Avenue
Boston, MA 02117-0098
617-450-7929
monitor@csps.com   www.csmonitor.com

The *Christian Science Monitor* is a highly regarded, Pulitzer Prize–winning daily newspaper that has been published in Boston since 1908. In March 2009, the paper began publishing weekly while maintaining daily on-line reporting.

Radio

The church has a short-wave network that broadcasts news, religious discussions, and services from The Mother Church in Boston.

Periodicals

The Christian Science Journal

210 Massachusetts Avenue
Boston, MA 02117-1291
617-450-7919
service@csps.com   www.csjournal.com

A monthly that is the church's official organ. It features reports of healing, "illustrates an understanding of the spiritual laws," and provides a comprehensive worldwide directory of Christian Science.

The periodicals below are all based at 210 Massachusetts Avenue in Boston:

Christian Science Sentinel (weekly)

Boston, MA 02117-0955
617-450-7919
service@csps.com   www.cssentinel.com

Christian Science Quarterly Bible Lessons

Boston, MA 02117-0568
617-450-7919
service@csps.com   www.csquarterly.com

The Herald of Christian Science

Boston, MA 02117
617-450-7919
service@csps.com   www.csherald.com
Published in 12 languages.

Science and Health with Key to the Scriptures

Orders: 617-450-2790
customerservice@spirituality.com
www.spirituality.com

The Mary Baker Eddy Library for the Betterment of Humanity

200 Massachusetts Avenue
Boston, MA 02115
617-450-7000
mail@marybakereddylibrary.org
www.marybakereddylibrary.org

FURTHER READING

Science and Health with Key to the Scriptures
Mary Baker Eddy
First Published 1875: Mary Baker Glover (*oft reprinted*)

Mary Baker Eddy
Gillian Gill
1998: Perseus Books

The Emergence of Christian Science in American Religious Life
Steven Gottschalk
1974: University of California Press

Rolling Away the Stone: Mary Baker Eddy's Challenge to Materialism
Steven Gottschalk
2005: Indiana University Press

Persistent Pilgrim
Richard A. Nenneman
1997: Nebbadoon Press

Mary Baker Eddy: The Life and Times (3 Volumes)
Robert Peel
1966; 1971; 1977: Holt, Rinehart and Winston

Spiritual Healing in a Scientific Age
Robert Peel
1987: Harper and Row

WEBSITES

www.spirituality.com
www.tfccs.com
www.christianscience.com

3 Congregationalism

I. Origins and Early History

A. Introduction

CONGREGATIONALISM IS A MOVEMENT IN protestant Christianity that belongs to the "Reformed" tradition founded by John Calvin and Ulrich Zwingli in the sixteenth century. Calvin's followers in England later became known as Puritans because they sought to reform or purify the established Church of England. In contrast to other Reformed churches, the distinguishing mark of Congregationalism was its fervent opposition to any hierarchy external to the gathered congregation.

Some early Congregationalists were called Separatists or Independents to distinguish themselves from other Puritans who believed the established church could be reformed from within. They argued for separation from the state church in congregations that were self-governing under a

The Mayflower Compact was the document that set forth the rules and regulations that the Mayflower's passengers agreed to live by. The original document has been lost; this is a page from William Bradford's Of Plimoth Plantation.

covenant binding their members together. Persecuted by the English government, which demanded conformity to the doctrine and ritual of the Church of England, the Separatists were driven underground and worshipped in private. Others found sanctuary in the Netherlands, where Dutch Protestants practiced a Reformed faith similar to their own.

In 1620, a community of Separatist exiles in Leyden, fearing assimilation into Dutch society, decided to risk a voyage across the Atlantic to establish a new way of life in North America. They were called Pilgrims. Their pastor, John Robinson, remained behind. On the eve of their departure on the *Mayflower*, Robinson preached a farewell sermon including his famous words, "I am very confident the Lord hath more truth and light yet to break forth out of His holy Word."

B. Congregationalism in America

The Mayflower reached New England after a two-month voyage. Anchored off the coast of Cape Cod, the Pilgrims concluded an agreement, "The Mayflower Compact," which set the pattern for later constitutional government in the colonies. In it, they pledged "mutually in the presence of God and one of another, [to] Covenant and Combine ourselves together into a Civil Body Politic...."

Nine years later, a second group of religious exiles arrived in Massachusetts. These were "nonseparatist" Puritans who, unlike the Pilgrims, still hoped for a reformed Church of England. Within a decade, the two groups were virtually indistinguishable. The goal of reforming the Church of England disappeared from view, and instead the Puritans established their own Congregational churches throughout New England.

The Puritan colonies were an early experiment in theocracy, an attempt to create a just and equitable society ordered by God. The first governor of the Massachusetts Bay colony, John Winthrop, described a society that was to be "knit together as one man." Such a society, living in justice, would be a symbol of hope to other nations, a "city upon a hill." But the theocratic ideal had a shadowy side, of course, which included the persecution of Baptist dissenters who founded the independent colony of Rhode Island in 1636.

Also in 1636, the Massachusetts Great and General Court allocated four hundred pounds sterling to establish the first English university in North America, Harvard College. In the following century, Congregationalists also founded Yale in Connecticut (1701) and Dartmouth in New Hampshire (1769).

Although Congregationalists rejected ecclesial hierarchy, they also stressed that congregations were bound to each other in "covenants" that assured some uniformity of practice and belief. The resulting tension between covenant and freedom continues to occupy the attention of virtually all of the churches that trace their history to the Congregational Churches of New England. One early attempt to create a sense of order among the self-governing congregations of New England was the Cambridge Platform (1648), which remains the great classic of Congregational polity. It describes the church as a "monarchy" subject to the authority of Christ, an "aristocracy" of pastors and elders who "feed and rule the church of God," and a "democracy" in which all baptized members participate in its government.

The theological consensus of the Cambridge Platform did not survive the seventeenth century. By the time of the American Revolution, competing theological visions began to divide the churches in New England. The rejection of hierarchy made it nearly impossible to impose theological conformity. In a sense, churches that in the seventeenth century had fostered an ideal of theocratic government became the incubators of liberal civil society and liberal religion. Congregationalists eagerly embraced the cause of independence from Great Britain, and Congregationalists, such as the cousins John and Samuel Adams, were among the most radical leaders in the American Revolution.

The most notable Congregationalist thinker of the mid-eighteenth century was Jonathan Edwards. His influence spread far beyond the boundaries of the Congregationalist tradition and endures today. A defender of orthodox Calvinism, Edwards polemicized against the Arminian theology of potential universal salvation that was then gaining ground in the English colonies. Edwards championed the idea of a personal relationship between God and the believer. Reason alone, he believed, cannot grasp the glory of God; only a "divine and supernatural light" can "convey the excellency in divine things." Edwards followed the latest discoveries of seventeenth-century scientists like Isaac Newton and saw no inherent conflict between science and religion. Instead, he believed, the discovery of the secrets of nature could only cast more light on God's loving care for the creation.

But Edwards was also a reformer. His preaching was an inspiration for the first "Great Awakening" in North America—a revival movement that profoundly changed the American religious and cultural landscape. The Great Awakening made religion intensely personal by fostering a deep sense of guilt resolved in an emotional experience of spiritual redemption. It helped convert African slaves to Christianity and challenged established authority. It also incited the opposition of traditionalists who believed in rational religion and orderly worship. With an influence far beyond the boundaries of the Congregational churches, it reshaped other Protestant traditions and set the stage for the modern evangelical movement in American Christianity.

The Awakening promoted a new, passionate and emotional style of preaching. For many caught up in the movement, the personal event of conversion displaced intellectual discourse as the center of religious experience. The movement encouraged Christians to study the Bible on their own, which effectively decentralized and individualized religious practice.

The individualization of religious experience was an understandable result of the decentralization of ecclesial power that had been inherent in the Congregationalist idea from the beginning.

By the nineteenth century, Congregationalism had become a pluralistic movement, and it became increasingly difficult to find common ground. The New England churches finally divided over the "Unitarian Controversy"—a fundamental debate over the nature of Christ. Unitarians argued on the basis of Scripture and reason for a radical unity of God. The doctrine of the Trinity, they believed, defied logic and the teaching of Scripture that God is "one." If God is a unitary being, then Christ could not be both human and divine.

At first, the Unitarian movement did not result in schism. But the move toward a separate denomination began with the election in 1803 of an openly Unitarian minister, Henry Ware, as professor of divinity at Harvard College. Trinitarians reacted by founding Andover Seminary in 1807, the first graduate school of theology in the United States. In 1825, the schism reached the point of no return when more than 100 congregations founded the American Unitarian Association, the predecessor of today's Unitarian Universalist Association. Most Congregational churches, however, did not join the new denomination and remained Trinitarian in their theology

The crisis in New England Congregationalism did not demoralize the church as it moved westward with the expanding frontier. Rather than compete, Congregationalist and Presbyterian missionaries decided to cooperate in a "Plan of Union" that united their frontier congregations and allowed each one to choose between the Presbyterian or Congregational form of church governance. But the loose ecclesial relationships inherent in Congregationalism meant that ties between the new congregations and the church's demographic center in New England were weak. Most of the frontier congregations even-

In 1620, the Pilgrims—Anglicans seeking religious freedom from the Church of England—disembarked from the Mayflower and came ashore in Massachusetts, beginning a new chapter in American history. This lithograph depicting the event was published by Currier & Ives around 1876.

tually gravitated toward the Presbyterian Church. The Plan of Union was finally dissolved in 1852.

In the years leading up to the Civil War, American Congregationalism was a bastion of resistance to the institution of slavery. As a Northern church with no congregations in the South, Congregationalism was not deeply divided over the issue as were the Methodist, Episcopal, and Presbyterian churches. In New England's Congregational churches, public opposition to slavery dated back to 1700, when the first antislavery pamphlet in North America, the "Selling of Joseph" by Judge Samuel Sewall, was published in 1700 in Boston. But the high-water mark for the abolitionist cause came in the first half of the nineteenth century. Some of the leading abolitionists of the period, including the brothers Arthur and Lewis Tappan, were Congregationalists.

The Tappan brothers were at the center of the movement to free fifty-three African captives who had seized control of the slave ship, *Amistad*, while sailing to sugar plantations in Cuba. Arrested by the U.S. Coast Guard off the coast of Long Island, the slaves were imprisoned while the ship's owners sued to have them returned as property. The case was a rallying cry for the abolitionist movement. Congregationalists and other northern Christians paid for the prisoners' legal expenses, and when the Supreme Court ruled in 1840 that they were not property, helped them return to their homeland.

In the years following the war, Congregationalists sent teachers and founded schools in the South to help educate former slaves. Many historically African-American schools founded after the war—including Fisk University in Nashville, Dillard University in New Orleans, Talladega College in Alabama, and Howard University in Washington, D.C.—were founded with the help of Congregationalist educators and missionaries. For the first time, Congregationalism began to spread in the South. At the same time, the Congregationalist churches began to recognize the need for denominational structure, although they still shunned hierarchy. The result was the founding of the National Council of the Congregational Churches of the United States in 1871.

In the late eighteenth and early twentieth centuries, Congregationalist ministers began to address issues of social justice and peace. In a sense, the dream of a just and equitable society which had inspired John Winthrop and the Puritans had never disappeared from the horizons of Congregationalism. The individualization of religious experience, a legacy of the Great Awakening, was still a strong motif in Congregationalist piety, but so was the "prophetic" dimension of the Bible that had inspired the movement to abolish slavery. Religion was therefore both private and public, personal and social. Although the early experiment in New England theocracy had not survived the seventeenth century, Congregationalists believed the United States might still become a "city upon a hill" through the gradual reform of society and its institutions.

One expression of this quest for human justice was the "Social Gospel Movement" in which Congregationalists, such as Washington Gladden (1836–1918), played a key role. The movement tried to apply biblical values to public life, and often found itself aligned with broad coalitions opposing war and advocating for civil and labor rights. Its influence continues to shape many churches in the Congregationalist tradition today.

In the twentieth century, Congregationalists began to explore, along with other Christian churches, the vision of a united church freed from its historical divisions. The move toward ecclesial reconciliation found its form in the modern "Ecumenical Movement" which sought the visible unity of the churches of Christ. The unions that brought Congregational churches into relationship with other denominations would change the institutional landscape of Congregationalism forever. In 1931, the National Council of Congregational Churches united with the General Convention of Christian Churches—a smaller church with roots in the early nineteenth century. The result was a new denomination called the Congregational Christian Churches.

Almost immediately, the Congregational Christian Church entered into negotiations with another united church, the Evangelical and Reformed Church, which had a similar theological heritage but with roots in the ethnic German immigrations to North America in the eighteenth and nineteenth centuries. This resulted in yet another union in 1957, forming the United Church of Christ (UCC). With 1.2 million members and 1,500 congregations, the UCC is today the largest church with roots in American Congregationalism.

Three smaller denominations also share the Congregationalist heritage. In 1955, a minority of "continuing Congregationalists" who refused to join the UCC organized their own denomination, the National Association of Congregational Christian Churches. It has approximately 67,000 members in more than 400 congregations.

The Conservative Congregational Christian Conference was organized in 1948 by conservative congregations who identified with the evangelical expression of Christianity. It now has about 40,000 members in more than 480 churches.

In 1961, the American Unitarian Association united with the Universalist Church of America to form the Unitarian Universalist Association of Congregations. It has an estimated 158,000 members in more than 1,000 congregations in the U.S. However, the UUA no longer considers itself a Christian church, and a recent survey suggested that 13 percent of UUA members identify as "Christian" while an equal percentage describe their beliefs as "pagan." Fifty-four percent identified as "humanist."

C. Important Dates and Landmarks

1582 Robert Browne publishes his "Treatise of Reformation Without Tarrying for Any." It argues that churches should be independent of state power, govern their own affairs, and cooperate with each other under a mutual covenant.

1620 Pilgrims arrive in Cape Cod, New England, aboard the *Mayflower*. Form the first political covenant in American history, the "Mayflower Compact."

1629–1630 Puritans settle the Massachusetts Bay Colony, including the town of Boston. Their governor, John Winthrop, describes the Puritan experiment as a "city upon a hill."

1636 The Massachusetts Great and General Court founds Harvard College, the first English institution of higher learning in North America.

1648 The Cambridge Platform creates a model for church governance that assures self-government of each congregation, but in a covenant that binds them to each other and provides for mutual consultation to settle disputes.

1730s–1740s Jonathan Edwards becomes key leader of the First Great Awakening, a revival that changes the landscape of American religion and culture.

1810 Congregationalists and members of other churches found the first mission agency in the United States, the American Board of Commissioners for Foreign Missions.

1825 A schism between Trinitarian and Unitarian Congregationalists is completed when the American Unitarian Association is founded by one hundred Congregational churches. Most congregations continue to affirm Trinitarian Christianity.

1839 African captives seize control of a slave ship, the *Amistad*, which is impounded by the U.S. Coast Guard. Congregational churches join with other Christians to organize legal defense. In 1840, the Supreme Court rules that the Africans are not property—and they return to their homeland.

1846 Congregationalists and other Christians organize the American Missionary Association—first antislavery organization in North America with integrated leadership. After the Civil War, the AMA founds a number of schools and colleges throughout the South to educate the newly liberated slaves.

1871 American Congregationalism creates a loose denominational structure in the National Council of the Congregational Churches of the United States.

1931 The General Convention of Christian Churches and the National Council of Congregational Churches unite to form a new, united denomination, the Congregational Christian Churches. It is the first union of separated churches in the United States.

1934 The Evangelical and Reformed Church is formed by the merger of the Evangelical Synod of North America and the Reformed Church in the United States. Both churches were founded by German immigrants in the eighteenth and nineteenth centuries.

1948 Evangelical congregations organize the Conservative Congregational Christian Conference.

1957 Congregational Christian Churches unite with Evangelical and Reformed Church to create the United Church of Christ.

D. Important Figures

Robert Browne (1540–1630)

Robert Browne was the first to secede from the Church of England; In 1582, he published the first theoretical exposition of Congregational principles; went on to found the first church based on Congregational principles in Norwich, England.

William Brewster (1567–1644)

William Brewster was a Pilgrim colonist leader who came to the New World on the *Mayflower* in 1620; was the senior elder of the colony; religious leader and adviser to Governor William Bradford.

John Robinson (1575–1625)

John Robinson was a follower of Robert Browne and one of the early leaders of the English Separatists; pastor of the "Pilgrim Fathers" before they left on the *Mayflower*. He is regarded as one of the founders of the Congregational Church.

William Ames (1576–1633)

William Ames was a Congregational theologian; influenced John Robinson in his conversion to Congregationalism.

John Cotton (above left) was a minister of the Massachusetts Bay Colony church. John Winthrop (above right), who arrived in America in 1630 aboard the Arabella, *belonged to Cotton's church. Although more than half the four hundred Pilgrims who arrived with Winthrop either died or returned to Europe, he managed to establish a solid community among those remaining.*

John Winthrop (1587–1649)

John Winthrop led a group of Puritans to the New World in 1629; was elected governor of the Massachusetts Bay Colony in 1630; and is famous for the "City on a Hill" sermon (real title was "A Model of Christian Charity"), in which he said that the pilgrims were part of a special pact with God to create a holy community.

John Cotton (1584–1652)

John Cotton was one of the leading ministers of the Massachusetts Bay Colony; drafted the "Cambridge Platform," the document that would serve as the basis for the polity and doctrine of Congregationalism until the nineteenth century.

Thomas Hooker (1586–1647)

Thomas Hooker was a founder of the Colony of Connecticut and settlement of Hartford in 1636; a creator of the "Fundamental Orders of Connecticut," world's first constitution, forerunner of the U.S. Constitution; was the first minister of the First Parish in Cambridge, still functioning.

William Bradford (1590–1657)

William Bradford was a Pilgrim leader who came over on the *Mayflower* in 1620; Governor of

Plymouth County; the second signer and primary architect of the Mayflower Compact.

Edward Winslow (1595–1655)

Edward Winslow was a Pilgrim leader who came over on the *Mayflower* in 1620; was the governor of Plymouth County in 1633, 1636, and 1644.

Richard Mather (1596–1669)

Richard Mather arrived in Boston in 1635 and was the pastor of the church in Dorchester, Massachusetts, until his death.

John Davenport (1597–1670)

John Davenport was a minister in New Haven, Connecticut; co-founder of the colony of New Haven in 1638; large proponent of education and co-founded the Hopkins School.

John Milton (1608–1674)

John Milton was a poet and one of the seminal literary figures in world literature. His most famous work was "Paradise Lost." Most of his prose was dedicated to the Puritan and Parliamentary cause; the Bible was a crucial influence on his work.

Isaac Watts (1674–1748)

Isaac Watts was a hymn writer and theologian, educationalist; recognized as the "Father of English Hymnody"; credited with penning over 750 hymns, many of which are still used today and have been translated into other languages.

William Ellery Channing (1780–1842)

William Ellery Channing was a Unitarian preacher; famous for his sermon, "Unitarian Christianity," which argued against the idea of the Trinity.

David Livingstone (1813–1873)

David Livingstone was a missionary and explorer; named Victoria Falls in Africa; subject of H. M. Stanley's 1872 search of Africa (during which he is supposed to have uttered the sentence, "Dr. Livingstone, I presume?".

Dwight Lyman Moody (1837–1899)

Dwight Lyman Moody was a nineteenth century evangelist and publisher; founder of the Northfield Schools, Moody Publishers, and the Moody Bible Institute of Chicago; president of the Young Men's Christian Association; president of Christian Endeavor.

Eric Liddell (1902–1945)

Eric Liddell was the son of missionaries from the London Missionary Society; Olympic runner and missionary; focus of the film, *Chariots of Fire*; worked as a missionary in North China after he competed in the 1924 Olympics.

Notable American Congregationalists

Abigail Adams (1744–1818; became Unitarian)
John Adams (1735–1826; became Unitarian)
John Quincy Adams (1767–1848)
Samuel Adams, early American statesman
Benjamin E. Bates, founder of Bates College
Henry Ward Beecher, clergyman, social reformer
Calvin Coolidge, 30th president of the United States; first honorary moderator of the Congregational Christian Churches
Walt Disney, animator and entertainment mogul
John Eliot, missionary to the Massachusett Indians
Hubert Humphrey, vice-president of the United States, 1963–1969

One of the world's most famous Congregationalists is Barack Obama, the forty-fourth president of the United States. President Obama's official portrait was taken in January of 2009.

Barack Obama, U.S. senator from Illinois; elected 44th President of the United States in November 2008 (previous page, bottom).

Laura Ingalls Wilder, Pioneer and author of *Little House on the Prairie*.

II. Tenets and Beliefs

Fundamental to Congregational churches is the revelation of God in Jesus Christ. By this fact Congregationalists declare themselves to be one in basic doctrine with other Christian communions. They make themselves different by emphasizing the importance of the congregation gathered for worship and ministry in the name of Christ. The relationship between God and God's people in a congregation is felt to be sacred, since all of the saving powers available in the church are focused there. Therefore, no outside ecclesiastical or political authority, whether bishop or presbyter, another congregation or magistrate, is allowed to intervene.

Congregationalists subscribe to the theory of the priesthood of all believers. There is only one spiritual status for any human being, that in which one receives God's grace and in the Holy Spirit shares it with his brothers. Because of this relationship with God, a believer does not need to await the authorization of any high church authority to unite with like-minded believers to form or maintain a congregation.

A. Articles of Faith

The denomination has announced its beliefs in a series of statements and confessions, beginning with the Cambridge Platform of 1648. Later came the Confession of Faith of 1680 (a redaction of the Westminster Confession of 1647, which was repeated in the Saybrook Platform of 1708), the Burial Hill Declaration of Faith of 1865, the Kansas City Statement of Faith of 1913, and the United Church of Christ statement of 1959. These statements have no binding authority over any church member, but have been used only to express the conviction of the majority and so provided a center of gravity for the whole denomination.

The 1959 statement adopted by the newly formed General Synod was designed specifically for its congregations to be used as a common affirmation of faith in worship. Since 1959, there have been two revisions to the original statement, one in 1976 and another in 1981. These revisions were done in order to make the statement's language more inclusive. Along with these statements, more traditional creeds are also utilized by the Congregational Church, including the Apostle's Creed, the Nicene Creed, the Heidelberg Catechism, the Evangelical Catechism, and the Augsburg Confession.

B. Scripture

The only Scripture Congregationalists subscribe to is the Holy Bible. They do not believe the Bible is inerrant or that human nature is depraved from birth (the doctrine of original sin), as their Calvinistic forefathers maintained, but declare that the chief end of man is to learn God's will and do it.

C. Theologians and Thinkers

John Wise (1652–1725)

John Wise was a Congregational minister of Ipswich, Massachusetts; wrote *A Vindication of the Government of New England Churches* in 1770, in which he singled out the democratic principles in Congregationalism and set them forth as standards for the state; came to be known as the Primer of the Revolution.

Jonathan Edwards (1703–1758)

Jonathan Edwards was a Congregationalist preacher who started the Great Awakening in New England in 1734; wrote *The Freedom of the Will*; known as one of the greatest and most profound American evangelical theologians and wrote and preached mostly in defense of Calvinist theology and the Puritan heritage; his most famous sermon was "Sinners in the Hands of an Angry God" in Enfield, Connecticut, in 1741, which is known as one of the greatest examples of the "fire and brimstone" style of preaching.

Horace Bushnell (1802–1876)

Horace Bushnell was pastor of the North Congregational Church in Hartford, Connecticut, from 1833 to 1859; wrote *Christian Nurture*, in which he opposed revivalism and turned the current of Christian thought to the young; led a revolt against the Calvinistic orthodoxy of his day and preached the idea that theology is based in the feelings and intuitions of humankind's spiritual nature, rather than intellectual.

The writer and abolitionist Harriet Beecher Stowe was the daughter of a Congregationalist preacher from Connecticut. This photograph of Stowe was taken some time in the 1870s.

Harriet Beecher Stowe (1811–1896)

Harriet Beecher Stowe the abolitionist, was the daughter of abolitionist Congregational preacher Lyman Beecher and author of the classic antislavery novel *Uncle Tom's Cabin*.

Washington Gladden (1836–1918)

Washington Gladden drew on British and Continental as well as incipient American social Christianity and stood strongly for political and industrial changes that would provide equal justice for all classes.

III. Rites and Rituals

A. Worship and Liturgy

Baptism and the Lord's Supper are sacraments practiced in all Congregational churches, although the method and frequency varies by denomination. Other rites such as marriage and confirmation are completely sacramental. Infant baptism is practiced, as well as adult baptism when necessary. The regular form of baptism is by sprinkling water, using the Trinitarian formula, "In the name of the Father, the Son, and the Holy Spirit."

The Congregational regular Sunday morning worship consists of a shared adoration of God, confession of sin, singing of God's praise, supplication for His mercies, reading of His Word and interpretation of it in preaching, and the blessing of all believers, and is relatively simple in form.

Previously hymns, responsive reading, and the Lord's Prayer were usually the only parts of worship inviting vocal congregational participation. Today, printed services with prayers and responses to be spoken in unison are utilized. Responses are almost never sung or chanted by the congregation. The *New Century Hymnal* is a comprehensive hymnal and worship book that was first published in 1995 for the United Church of Christ. It contains a wide variety of traditional Christian hymns and worship songs, many contemporary hymns and songs, a substantial selection of "world music," a full lectionary-based Psalter, service music selections, and a selection of liturgies from the United Church of Christ *Book of Worship*.

Once a year the Sunday morning service in many churches is conducted by laymen or young people trained for the occasion. In regular practice, laymen do not celebrate the Holy Communion except by special authority.

B. Family Life

The UCC sees the increasing diversity in family structure not as a crisis, but as a means to adapt. Diversity, they say, is the result of physical, social, and psychological changes that occur during the process of human growth and should be understood as an instance of God's constant re-creation. The exact structure of the family is not important; a family can be a two-parent household, single parent household, or a household headed by the grandparents or other family members. All families are considered important and are to be supported by the church according to Scripture and tradition. The church is viewed as a wider body that serves to support the individual family bodies that are contained within the church.

IV. Organization and Structure

A. Education of Clergy

Early New England Congregationalists founded some of the first colleges and universities in this country, including Harvard College, Yale College, Dartmouth College, Williams College, Bowdoin College, Middlebury College, and Amherst College. These schools were self-perpetuating institutions with their own boards of trustees, not directly sponsored by, nor responsible to, the church.

Several seminaries and colleges are closely related to Congregationalist denominations, mostly to the United Church of Christ. These include the oldest graduate school of theology in the U.S., **Andover Newton Theological School** in Newton Centre, Massachusetts. Also affiliated with the UCC are **Bangor Theological Seminary** in Bangor, Maine; **Chicago Theological Seminary** in Chicago, Illinois; **Eden Theological Seminary** in St. Louis, Missouri; **Lancaster Theological Seminary** in Lancaster, Pennsylvania; **Pacific School of Religion** in Berkeley,

California; and the **United Theological Seminary of the Twin Cities** in New Brighton, Minnesota.

Seminaries with historical ties to the United Church of Christ include **Harvard University Divinity School** in Cambridge, Massachusetts; **Howard University School of Divinity** in Washington, D.C.; **Interdenominational Theological Center** in Atlanta, Georgia; **Seminario Evangelico de Puerto Rico** in San Juan, Puerto Rico; **Union Theological Seminary** in New York, New York; **Vanderbilt University Divinity School** in Nashville, Tennessee; and **Yale University Divinity School** in New Haven, Connecticut.

For all ordained clergy, a bachelor's degree is a prerequisite for a Master of Divinity (MDiv). The MDiv must be obtained from an Association of Theological Schools (ATS) accredited seminary. The master's degree normally takes about three years to complete. Both men and women can be ordained.

B. Houses of Worship

Each local church is autonomous, owns its own property, and is free to act in accordance with the collective decision of its members. The associations of churches, conferences, general synods, and covenanted ministries also are free to act in their particular sphere of responsibility. While they may belong to a larger group, there is no overarching government controlling their actions and decisions. Each group is bound together with the other groups through shared faith, belief and mission.

C. Governance and Authority

Government is graduated from the local church through the communion as a whole by a system of representative assemblies. At the level of the county, or comparable geographical unit, the assembly is called an association; at the state level, a conference. At the national level the assembly is known as the General Synod.

Basic to the government of the denomination is the local church, with the protection of its autonomy, and basic to the local church is its covenant, whereby members bind themselves "in the presence of God to walk together in all His ways" (according to the Salem Covenant of 1629). Local church government resides in the adult members. These members choose their own officers, including the ranking lay authorities of the church—the deacons—that are responsible for its spiritual affairs, and trustees, to whom the care of the church's material properties is assigned. In consultation with denominational leadership in the state, the adult members also choose and "call" the minister who is to serve the church. Local government is adjusted depending on the needs of the particular parish, often through a council consisting of the heads of recognized groups within the church serving to correlate their work.

The special responsibility of the association is to sanction the standing of the churches and ministers within its boundaries on behalf of the communion. The association provides primary oversight and authorization of ordained and other authorized ministers. The association ordains new ministers, holds ministers' standing in covenant with local churches, and is responsible for disciplinary action. The official delegates of an association are comprised of all ordained clergy within the bounds of the association together with lay delegates sent from each local church.

The conference nurtures the churches under its care and serves as a liaison between them and the national synod and mission boards. A conference is made up of multiple associations. In the UCC there are a total of thirty-eight conferences. They provide the primary support for the search-and-call process by which churches select ordained leadership and often provide significant programming resources for their constituent churches. Conferences, like associations, are congregationally representative bodies, with each local church sending ordained and lay delegates.

The UCC's General Synod guides the work of the entire communion. The Synod meets every two

The First Congregational Church of Middletown, New York, appears in this 2007 photograph.

years and is comprised of delegates elected from the Conferences together with the boards of directors of each of the four covenanted ministries. The covenantal polity of the denomination means that the General Synod only speaks to the local churches, not for them.

The UCC also maintains national offices for its four covenanted ministries, which carry out the work of the General Synod and support the local churches, associations, and conferences. These ministries include the Office of General Ministries (OGM) responsible for administration, common services, covenantal relations, financial development, and proclamation, identity, and communication; Local Church Ministries (LCM), responsible for evangelism, stewardship and church finance, worship and education, Pilgrim Press and United Church Resources (the publishing house of the UCC), and parish life and leadership; Wider Church Ministries (WCM), responsible for partner relations, local church relations, global sharing of resources, health and wholeness ministry, and global education and advocacy; and the Justice and Witness Ministries (JWM), responsible for ministries related to economic justice, human rights, justice for women and transformation, public life and social policy, and racial justice.

The United Church of Christ employs a mixed congregational and presbyertal polity. Most issues are decided by the local church and churches are given the right to own property and call their own ministers. The national conference serves to provide nonbinding advice to all member churches.

D. Social Service Organizations

The Congregational Church has a tradition of missionary work beginning with Samuel J. Mills, who initiated the missionary groups that would bring Congregationalism to the new western frontier. While attending Williams College in Massachusetts, Mills was a leader of a prayer society that held one of the most important meetings in the history of Congregationalist social service while taking shelter in a haystack during a thunderstorm. This event came to be known as the Haystack Meeting, and is regarded as the beginning of the foreign mission movement in the United States. In 1810, the American Board of Commissioners for Foreign Missions came into being. This was the first foreign missionary group in North America. In 1826, the American Home Missionary Society was formed with the intention of spreading Congregationalism to the new American west. The American Missionary Association was established in 1846, and was primarily dedicated to missionary work among African Americans and Native Americans.

During the nineteenth century, Congregationalists contributed to the growing evangelical revival that was sweeping the nation. In Massachusetts, Mary Lyon started the first academy for women, which subsequently became Mount Holyoke College. Oberlin, in Ohio, was founded by Congregationalists, and became the first coeducational college in the United States. The American Missionary Association, by 1863, was the ranking organization for the betterment of freed slaves. The Association began as a society for the legal defense of the shipload of slaves who had seized their vessel in 1839 while en route from Africa to the United States. Eventually the Association was responsible for the founding of hundreds of schools and colleges that trained Negroes for leadership.

In 1934, the Center for Social Action was founded based on the ideas of Washington Gladden and other social activists who stood strongly for political and industrial changes in order to better provide justice for all classes.

The UCC's Justice and Witness Ministry is specifically designed to advocate and work toward economic justice, human rights, justice for women, fair social policy, and racial justice.

E. Media and Communication

The UCC offers an online catalog at www.unitedchurchpress.com, which offers books, other media, and supplies. *The United Church News* is the official publication of the denomination. It is published by the Office of Communication, United Church of Christ, which is related to the Proclamation, Identity and Communication Ministry of the United Church of Christ. Several regional editions are published by conferences as inserts to the nationally distributed edition. The newsletter can also be viewed at www.nes.uss.org.

The Pilgrim Press is the UCC publishing division. One of their books, *The Living Theological Heritage of the United Church of Christ,* is an 835-page, seven-volume set that includes materials that impacted the shaping of the UCC's theological identity. *New Conversations* is an annual magazine of the United Church of Christ's Board for Homeland Ministries and focuses on a variety of missionary issues. *Prism* is a theological journal that is published twice a year and is produced jointly by the seven seminaries of the UCC. It offers "serious theological reflection from a diversity of viewpoints on issues of faith, mission, and ministry."

"Troubled Waters"

In 2006, ABC television studios broadcast a documentary on the UCC entitled "Troubled Waters," starring the late actress Lynn Redgrave, a member of First Congregational UCC in Kent, Conn. The sixty-minute documentary was filmed in various locations around the world, including Porto Alegre, Brazil, where UCC justice advocates joined ecumenical partners in February to raise water-availability concerns at the World Council of Churches' Ninth International Assembly.

While there, global delegates affirmed that "access to freshwater supplies is becoming an urgent matter across the planet. . . . The survival of 1.2 billion people is currently in jeopardy due to lack of adequate water and sanitation," the WCC Assembly's resolution states. "Unequal access to water causes conflicts between and among people, communities, regions and nations."

UCC film crews also traveled to the Middle East; Bolivia; Waukesha, Wisconsin; Washington, D.C.; and Boston, Massachusetts, among other locations, to capture stories of water's evaporating availability. Even in Cleveland, Ohio, where the UCC's national offices are located, crews filmed a segment on Lake Erie, due to emerging fresh-water fights brewing along the Great Lakes.

FURTHER READING

The Shaping of the United Church of Christ: An Essay in the History of American Christianity
Luis H. Gunneman
1977: United Church Press

The Shaping of American Congregationalism
John Von Rohr
1992: Pilgrim Press

The Congregationalists
J. William T. Youngs
1990: Greenwood Press

V. The Conservative Congregational Christian Conference

The Conservative Congregational Christian Conference
8941 Highway 5
Lake Elmo, MN 55042
651-739-1474   Fax: 651-739-0750
www.ccccusa.com

There are over 40,000 members of the Conservative Congregational Christian Conference (CCCC), belonging to approximately 256 congregations. The headquarters for the CCCC is in St. Paul, Minnesota.

The Conservative Congregational Christian Conference was based on the fellowship created by the publication of the *Congregational Beacon* (1935) by Hilmer Sandine. The *Beacon* served as a platform for theologically conservative Congregationalists. The need for fellowship arose and in 1945 evangelicals within the Congregational Christian churches formed the Conservative Congregational Christian Fellowship. In 1948, the CCCC reorganized to become the association that it is today. The conference was established in order to facilitate cooperation in evangelism, education, edification, stewardship, missions, and youth activities, as well as to promote the autonomy of the local church and freedom of individual belief.

The CCCC maintains that the Bible is the inerrant Word of God; that God exists in the Holy Trinity; that the Holy Spirit guides believers in understanding God's Word; and that redemption is accessible only through faith in Christ. Baptism is performed on both children and adults and the Lord's Supper is also practiced. Within the Conservative Congregational Christian Conference, each local congregation decides the role of women in the church.

The CCCC publishes monthly *The Foresee Newsletter* (www.ccccusa.com/theforesee.html).

VI. The National Association of Congregational Christian Churches

NACCC Office
8473 South Howell Avenue
PO Box 288
Oak Creek, WI 53154
414-764-1620   Fax: 414-764-0319
www.naccc.org

There are currently over 65,000 members belonging to 432 congregations of the National Association of Congregational Christian Churches (NACCC). Its headquarters is in Oak Creek, Wisconsin.

The National Association of Congregational Christian Churches was founded in 1955 in reaction to the formation of the United Church of Christ. The merger caused concern because of the fear of a predominantly Presbyterian form of church government. The association still strongly emphasizes the autonomy of the local church; it has no binding ecclesiastical authority and advertises no creed to which its members must subscribe.

The NACCC operates the Congregational Foundation for Theological Studies (CFTS) with the intention of serving the requirements of the diverse Congregational Fellowship in which no single theological or social viewpoint can represent all the churches. The foundation, established in 1961, provides financial aid in the form of grants and scholarships to ministerial candidates. CFTS also provides a directed study in Congregational history and polity and annual seminars on topics related to ministry in the Congregational churches. Each student receiving aid from the CFTS is required to serve an internship in an approved NACCC teaching church. As with the UUC, women are ordained in the NACCC.

The Arabella Society, established in 2002 by the NACCC, acknowledges pastors ordained in another tradition that have decided to serve the Congregational Way. These ministerial candidates must attend and complete the CFTS-sponsored Congregational history and polity seminar and polity paper in order to officially obtain pastoral status within the NACCC. The Society was named in honor of the *Arabella*, the ship that carried the second wave of pilgrims to the New World, one of the passengers being the influential John Winthrop.

The NACCC publishes *The Congregationalist*, a magazine that is also available online at www.congregationalist.org. They also publish a monthly newsletter entitled *NA News* and a series of books entitled the Congregational Way Series. The communication services committee also releases a seasonal newsletter called *Congregational Communication*. For their youth population, the NACCC releases two newsletters, *Ananias*, for their college-aged HOPE (Heritage of Pilgrim Endeavor) group, and *Crossroads*, for their high school–aged NAPF (National Association Pilgrim Fellowship) group. The NACCC also offers streaming media of annual meetings on their website.

4 Disciples of Christ

I. Origins and Early History

A. The Religion in America

IN THE MIDST OF THE PERVASIVE RELIGIOUS FERVOR of the Second Great Awakening, three men privately harbored an increasing dissatisfaction with the practice of Christianity in America. One of them, **Barton W. Stone**, was himself an integral part of the Awakening. As a prominent Presbyterian minister in Kentucky in the nineteenth century, Stone shared the desire of other Southern and Western clergymen that the rugged frontier become more attuned to religion. Hearing of spiritual rebirth sweeping the more established eastern half of the country, Stone and other ministers watched and waited for an opportunity to invoke the same urgency in the West. That opportunity presented itself in 1801, with the conversion of just one woman in Logan County, Kentucky, brought about by the exhortations of preacher **James McGready**. News of the woman's joyful salvation spread quickly and inspired others to seek the same experience. When Stone scheduled a public Communion—a three-day service culminating in observance of the Eucharist—for August 1, the frontier was ripe for revival. Rather than the usual hundreds in attendance of such Communions, Stone's event drew 25,000. By the second day, conversion experiences dominated the masses, characterized by laughing, shrieking, weeping, rolling on the ground, singing, dancing, and even falling into comas. The service did not end until August 6. It came to be known as the Cane Ridge Revival.

Stone felt that the unity of Christians reflected in this event was not otherwise reflected in the divisive nature of denominational worship. He blamed what he felt were man-made creeds that discouraged worshippers from seeking their own paths to salvation through personal interpretation of the Bible. Soon after the Cane Ridge Revival, Stone and several other members of the Presbyterian Church in Cane Ridge formed their own Springfield Presbytery.

In 1806, Stone and a few others drafted the "Last Will and Testament of the Presbytery," in which they

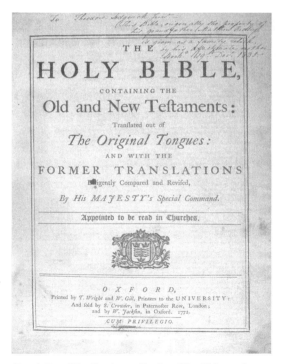

Translation of the King James Version of the Bible was begun in 1604 and completed in 1611. This title page is from an edition printed in 1772.

announced their desire that "this body [the Springfield Presbytery] die, be dissolved, and sink into union with the Body of Christ at large; for there is but one body, and one Spirit, even as we are called in one hope of our calling." Stone and his followers now denoted themselves merely as "Christians" in recognition of a universal church of Christ. The Christians called for congregational self-governance; that every person study the Bible alone to find rules for faith and practice; and that one's spiritual authority be determined solely by the degree to which Christ "speaks within him." It is estimated that by 1830, Stone's Christian Church numbered about 12,000.

Meanwhile, two other men in Pennsylvania were conducting their own breakaway from the Presbyterian Church. In 1807, Irishman **Thomas Campbell** arrived in America, joined a Presbyterian Church in Pennsylvania, and was promptly chastised for refusing to follow the Presbyterian creeds for communion. He responded by leaving the church and founding the Christian Association of Washington, Pennsylvania, in 1808. He and his supporters adopted the motto "Where the Scriptures speak, we speak; where the Scriptures are silent, we are silent." They did not wish to disband church organizations, but to restore them to their original, first-century forms. Their cause thus became known as the Restoration Movement. Campbell composed what is now recognized as the "Magna Carta" of his movement: *Declaration and Address*. In the Address, he urged that "we form ourselves into a religious association...for the sole purpose of promoting simple evangelical Christianity, free from all mixture of human opinions and inventions of men." Campbell did not originally intend to create a new church; but in 1811, the Association erected its own building in Brush Run, Pennsylvania, in which the members held congregationally governed worship services. The building was named Brush Run Church.

In 1809, Thomas Campbell's son, **Alexander Campbell**, left Ireland, joined his father in Pennsylvania, and assumed a leadership role in his movement. After thorough study of the Bible, the members of Brush Run Church began to practice full-immersion baptism, a rite also observed by the Baptists. Before long, the reform-minded Redstone Baptist Association invited Brush Run Church to worship with them. This union did not last, however, and Thomas Campbell relocated his movement in 1824 to Mahoning, Pennsylvania, where they joined the Mahoning Baptist Association.

A prolific writer, Alexander Campbell had, in 1823, founded a journal promoting reform—*The Christian Baptist*. In 1830, the Mahoning Association came under attack for its refusal to accept the Philadelphia Confession. It was forced to disband, and *The Christian Baptist* ceased publication. In 1831, Campbell inaugurated a new periodical called the *Millennial Harbinger*. Campbell's writing and public speaking skills had gained much attention for the Reformation Movement over the years, as did two great debates. In 1829, prominent social reformer Robert Owen challenged the younger Campbell to a widely-followed public debate. In 1837, Campbell famously debated the Roman Catholic archbishop of Cincinnati, John B. Purcell.

In 1832, the Stone and Campbell groups tied a denominational knot with a handshake in Lexington, Kentucky. The groups came together in what they initially called a "brotherhood," otherwise informally known as the "Stone-Campbell movement." There was much confusion about what to call the union. Stone insisted on "the Christians" to promote nonsectarianism; Thomas Campbell wanted "Disciples of Christ." Finally, both names were used, resulting in the church's current name: "Christian Church (Disciples of Christ)." It is also referred to as, "The Church of Christ."

Disunity

The unity of the movement was shaken by the formation of a missionary society in the late 1840s, and by the adoption soon afterward by some congregations of instrumental music, predominantly (at first) pianos and organs. After the American Civil War, the dispute became more strident, as many old regional animosities surfaced. By the 1870s and

1880s there were essentially two groups within the Restoration Movement. However, because the "brotherhood" of churches in the movement had no central organizations or assemblies in which a schism could be formalized, the break was not official until the congregations that rejected instrumental music and missionary societies asked to be listed separately as the Churches of Christ in the United States Religious Census of 1906.

Another group, perhaps as conservative as the Church of Christ (but favoring the use of musical instruments during worship), was disturbed by the liberalism that it perceived displayed at a church conference in Memphis, Tennessee, in 1926. In 1927, this group formed the North American Christian Convention.

Another faction within the Disciples sought greater unity and cooperation among the churches. In response to the ecumenical movement, some Disciples sought to create a structure by which leaders could be chosen to represent the full brotherhood of Christian churches in discussion with other Christian churches and denominations. In 1956, the United Christian Missionary Society and the Board of Higher Education of Disciples of Christ, two of the largest parachurch organizations in the brotherhood, created the Panel of Scholars to examine the issues facing the churches. The 1963 publication of *The Panel of Scholars Reports* contained a proposal for restructure of the Disciples of Christ. It called for the creation of regional and general "manifestations" of the church that would be recognized as ministries in their own right. This proposal was put before a convention of the Christian churches in 1968. The churches that endorsed the restructure became part of the Christian Church (Disciples of Christ), while the remainder became known as the Independent Christian Churches, or Churches of Christ.

At the time of the 1906 division, the Disciples of Christ were by far the larger of the two bodies; now it would seem possible that they might be the smallest of the three current major divisions of the Restoration Movement.

B. Important Dates and Landmarks

1807 Thomas Campbell arrives in America.

1809 Thomas Campbell publishes *Declaration and Address*.

1812 Alexander and Thomas Campbell adopt necessity of immersion as part of salvation.

1816 Alexander Campbell's "Sermon on the Law" at Redstone Baptist Association meeting.

1820 Campbell-Walker Debate (infant baptism).

1823 Campbell-McCalla Debate (infant baptism).

1823 *The Christian Baptist* begins publication (1823–1830).

1827 The Campbellite churches break with the Baptists.

1829 Campbell-Owen Debate (on evidences of Christianity).

1830 Campbell-Owen debate (natural religion and utopianism).

1830 Alexander Campbell publishes first issue of *Millennial Harbinger*.

Dec. 31, 1831 Handshake merger of Alexander and Thomas Campbell's Disciples and Barton Stone's Christians.

1832 Stone and Campbell unite.

1835 *The Gospel Advocate* begins publication; *Christianity Restored* published by Alexander Campbell.

1837 Campbell-Purcell Debate (on Roman Catholicism).

1846 Christian Tract Society founded.

1849 American Christian Missionary Society formed.

1856 The Annual Meeting of the American Christian Missionary Society becomes in effect a national convention of Christian Church and Churches of Christ. It will grow into the International Convention of Disciples of Christ.

1866 Alexander Campbell dies.

1893 The World Congress of the Disciples of Christ is held in connection with the General Missionary Convention.

1894 Disciple Divinity House opens as part of University of Chicago.

1906 Churches of Christ formally separate from the Disciples of Christ.

1968 At an assembly meeting in Kansas City, overwhelming approval of the Provisional Design for the Christian Church; The Disciples of Christ formally votes to become a full denomination, the Christian Church (Disciples of Christ).

1985 Disciples of Christ enter into an ecumenical partnership with the United Church of Christ.

2005 General Assembly votes nearly unanimously to elect Rev. Dr. Sharon Watkins as general minister and president of the Disciples. Reverend Watkins is the first woman to be elected as the presiding minister of a mainline Protestant denomination.

C. Important Figures

Barton W. Stone (1772–1844)

Presbyterian minister Barton W. Stone was born in Port Tobacco, Maryland, December 24, 1772. He died in Hannibal, Missouri, November 9, 1844. Stone was educated as a schoolteacher and entered the ministry through the Presbyterian Church. He served a church in Cane Ridge Kentucky, and after hosting the historic Cane Ridge Revival of 1801, he and several others formed the Springfield Presbytery denouncing all man-made creeds and appealing to the Bible as the only rule of faith and practice. They soon dissolved the Springfield Presbytery, and published *The Last Will and Testament of the Springfield Presbytery*, one of the documents the Christian Church (Disciples of Christ) considers key in its development. They dissolved their denominational ties to enter into unity with "the body of Christ at large." They called themselves, simply, Christians.

Thomas Campbell (1763–1854)

Thomas Campbell was born in County Down, Ireland, February 1, 1763. He died in Bethany, Virginia (now West Virginia) on January 4, 1854. He came to America from Scotland in 1807, and was chastised by Pennsylvania church authorities for refusing to use Presbyterian creeds as terms of communion. In 1808, he and others founded the Christian Association of Washington, Pennsylvania. That group adopted the motto, well known by Disciples, "Where the Scriptures speak, we speak; where the Scriptures are silent, we are silent."

Campbell and others were called Reformers, for their desire to restore the church's first-century roots. This way of life came to be known as the Restoration Movement. Near Washington, Pennsylvania, Campbell and his son, Alexander, and the Christian Association established the Brush Run Church, which, in 1815, became part of a nearby Baptist Association.

Reformers and the Baptists differed on key issues. By 1830, the Reformers cut their last ties with the Baptist Association and became known as

This ca. 1885 engraving—inscribed with the legend "Where the Scriptures speak, we speak; where the Scriptures are silent, we are silent"—features portraits of four of the early leaders of the Disciples of Christ. Clockwise from the top, they are: Thomas Campbell, Barton W. Stone, Alexander Campbell, and Walter Scott (1796–1861).

Disciples. Thomas Campbell's passion for Christian unity is summed up in his proclamation: "The church of Christ upon earth is essentially, intentionally, and constitutionally one." This statement is the first and key proposition of Thomas Campbell's *Declaration and Address*, a work called by some the Magna Carta of the movement that preceded the denomination known as the Christian Church (Disciples of Christ).

Alexander Campbell (1788–1866)

Alexander Campbell was born September 12, 1788 in the County of Antrim, Ireland. He was raised as a Presbyterian. He attended the University of Glasgow, Scotland.

In 1809, Campbell arrived in America from Scotland, and joined his father, Thomas, in western Pennsylvania. He carefully read and fully endorsed the principles of Thomas Campbell's *Declaration and Address*. Biographer Nathaniel Haynes states

that Thomas and Alexander Campbell were "one in their aims, spirit and work."

The younger Campbell was a prolific writer. In 1823, he founded the periodical *The Christian Baptist*. After the Reformers dissolved ties with the Baptists, Campbell founded a new publication called *The Millennial Harbinger*. He was a talented debater, and in 1829 drew attention to the Restoration Movement in a widely known debate with social reformer Robert Owen. In 1837, he engaged the Roman Catholic John B. Purcell, archbishop of Cincinnati, in a widely publicized eight-day debate on the traditions and beliefs of the Catholic Church.

II. Tenets and Beliefs

A. Articles of Faith

Following the precept "No Creed But Christ," the Disciples oppose the use of creeds as "tests of fellowship" in the body of Christ. They believe such language creates a barrier to those who wish to participate in Disciple churches. The recitation of such creeds was, in the view of Disciples, the major cause of division among Christians. Disciples hold one essential tenet: the belief in Jesus Christ as Lord and Savior. Disciples are encouraged to follow their consciences guided by the Bible, study, and prayer, and are expected to extend that freedom to others.

Although the Disciples do not have an official doctrinal statement that delineates what they believe, Disciples do point to the preamble to The Design of the Christian Church (Disciples of Christ) put forth in 1968 as a delineation of their faith. It is not viewed as a creed, nor is it meant to be a substitute for a creed. It reads:

As members of the Christian Church we confess that Jesus is the Christ, the Son of the living God, and proclaim him Lord and Savior of the world. In Christ's name and by his grace we accept our mission of witness and service to all people. We rejoice in God, maker of heaven and earth, and in God's covenant of love which binds us to God and one another. Through baptism into Christ we enter into newness of life and are made one with the whole people of God. In the communion of the Holy Spirit we are joined together in discipleship and in obedience to Christ. At the table of the Lord we celebrate with thanksgiving the saving acts and presence of Christ. Within the universal church we receive the gift of ministry and the light of scripture. In the bonds of the Christian faith we yield ourselves to God that we may serve the One whose kingdom has no end. Blessing, glory and honor be to God forever. Amen.

B. Scripture

While they hold both New and Old Testaments to be equally inspired, the New Testament, particularly the Book of Acts, is regarded as the model for ecclesiology and theology. The Disciples accept the Bible as an all-sufficient revelation of the Divine will.

C. Secondary Sources

David Lipscomb (1831–1917)

David Lipscomb was an important minister, editor, and educator in the American Restoration Movement. Under his leadership of the theologically conservative faction of that movement, the 1906 division between itself as the Church of Christ and the more liberal faction, which is now generally known as the Christian Church (Disciples of Christ) was formalized.

Lipscomb was greatly influenced by conservative Tennessee church leader Tolbert Fanning. Fanning was an enforcer of strict orthodoxy with regard to Restoration doctrines, seeing anything not specifically authorized by the New Testament as an unnecessary and hence sinful addition to the primitive Christianity of the first century, which the movement was by definition dedicated to restoring.

In 1855, Fanning and David's brother, William,

began publishing a magazine aimed at dissemination of this view throughout the Restoration Movement, the *Gospel Advocate*. Following the Civil War, David Lipscomb revived the *Gospel Advocate* in July 1866.

Lipscomb became engaged in an ongoing correspondence with Alexander Campbell. Lipscomb disagreed strongly with Campbell on the topic of the American Christian Missionary Society, a cooperative effort to fund and coordinate foreign missions among various congregations, but Lipscomb totally rejected it as a sinful, unscriptural innovation.

Lipscomb noted that most of the congregations that supported the Missionary Society were likewise those who were not opposed to the use of instrumental music. He began to attack both of these practices. The triumph of this line of thought within the conservative Restoration congregations was the impetus behind the 1906 decision to list the Church of Christ and the Christian Church as separate bodies, formalizing the schism between these factions.

J. W. McGarvey (1829–1911)

At the beginning of the twentieth century, J. W. McGarvey was one of the most influential scholars within the Disciples of Christ movement.

McGarvey began his career as a preacher in Missouri. Later, he preached for ten years for the Broadway Church in Lexington. He also served there as an elder until 1902. In 1865, he began teaching Bible survey at the College of the Bible in Lexington. Called by *The London Times* "... the ripest Bible scholar on earth," he taught there for forty years, served as president for sixteen years, and resigned as president at the age of 80.

During the early twentieth century, the Disciples were forced to grapple with modernist theology, which had gained a following in the Campbell Institute at the Disciples Divinity House at the University of Chicago. McGarvey launched a series of attacks on modernism, which culminated in a dispute with faculty at the College of the Bible in 1917.

A champion of the traditional doctrines and view of the Bible, he was an opponent of the musical instrument in worship. As a leader in the Restoration Movement, McGarvey took a strong stand on the issue, even refusing to hold membership where it was used. He favored cooperation among congregations and lent encouragement to the missionary society.

McGarvey was a prolific writer, contributing articles to the *Millennial Harbinger, American Christian Review*, and *Lard's Quarterly*. He produced commentaries on Matthew, Mark, Acts, the Gospels (in conjunction with P. Y. Pendleton), and six epistles.

W. K. Pendleton (1817–1899)

One of the most influential of pre–Civil War preachers and pioneer leaders, W. K. Pendleton was born into a wealthy Virginia family that became interested in the works of Alexander Campbell and was baptized into the Campbellite movement.

Pendleton left the University in the spring of 1840 and returned to his home in Louisa County. In June that year he listened to Campbell preach, and was baptized by Campbell near the Mount Gilboa Church. Later that year, Pendleton met and married Alexander Campbell's daughter, Lavina.

Although Pendleton studied law at the University of Virginia and had an interest in a career in politics, he became an instructor in physical sciences when Campbell opened Bethany College in 1841. Four years later, he was elected to the office of vice-president. Campbell was gone frequently and the need of someone to take his place in his absence was evident.

During the months of May to October 1847, Campbell was in England, and the editing of the *Harbinger* was left entirely to Pendleton. As Campbell's health began to deteriorate, Pendleton stepped into his place. In 1864, Campbell turned the *Harbinger* over to Pendleton, who continued its publication until 1870. After Campbell's death in 1866, the trustees elected Pendleton president of the college, a position he held until 1884.

III. Rites and Rituals

A. The Calendar

SUNDAY WORSHIP

For Disciples of Christ, the primary activity of the faith community is the weekly gathering "at the Lord's Table," at which members gather around the Table in local congregations to celebrate the Lord's Supper (Communion). During this period, they sing hymns and read the Bible aloud, particularly those portions in which Jesus extends an invitation to become his Disciple. Each congregation determines the nature of its worship, and in some congregations, worshippers are invited to acknowledge their faults and sins, to remember the death and resurrection of Jesus Christ, to remember their baptism, and to give thanks for God's redeeming love.

ADVENT

The liturgical period preceding Christmas, Advent is celebrated on the fourth Sunday before Christmas. Observed by Christians as a period of prayer and penitence, it is the beginning of the church year and serves as a dual reminder of the original waiting that was done by the Hebrews for the birth of their Messiah as well as the anticipation that Christians endure in awaiting the Second Coming of Jesus Christ.

CHRISTMAS DAY (DECEMBER 25)

Celebrates the birth of Jesus Christ.

EPIPHANY (JANUARY 6)

Commemorates the revelation of Jesus to humanity and the visit of the Magi, or the Three Wise Men, to Jesus.

LENT

The forty-day period from Ash Wednesday to Holy Saturday. Lent is a time of preparation for Holy Week. Holy Week recalls the events preceding and during the crucifixion of Jesus.

PALM SUNDAY

Observed on the Sunday before Easter, this feast day celebrates the entry of Jesus into Jerusalem in the days before his Crucifixion.

EASTER

The most important religious feast of the Christian liturgical year, it celebrates the resurrection of Jesus, which his followers believe occurred after his death by crucifixion.

PENTECOST SUNDAY

Commemorates the descent of the Holy Spirit upon the apostles, and the followers of Jesus fifty days after Easter.

B. Worship and Liturgy

Weekly worship, often led by both ministers and laypersons, involves prayer, singing and sermons, as well as Communion. The Lord's Supper, or Communion, is celebrated in weekly worship and is open to all who believe in Jesus Christ. Disciples consider Communion as a memorial feast, a commemoration of Jesus Christ's Last Supper with the apostles, and increasingly as a sacrament.

C. Life Cycle Events

Baptism by Immersion

Disciples of Christ practice baptism by full immersion, the mode presumed to have been used by John the Baptist. This consists of lowering the candidate in water while the baptizer (a pastor or any baptized believer) invokes the Trinitarian formula of Matthew 28:19 ("In the name of the Father, and of the Son, and of the Holy Ghost") or other words concerning a profession of faith.

In addition, Disciples see the use of the specific form of baptism, immersion, as symbolic of Jesus's own baptism; it symbolizes dying with Christ and emerging to new life. At the conclusion of a Disciples baptism, the congregation most often is asked to pledge support of the newly baptized person in her or his faith journey. Disciples typically are baptized when they can express as a personal choice their desire to become part of the Body of Christ, a practice known as a "believer's baptism."

Infant dedication is also a common Disciples tradition. A baby is brought into the church where parents and congregation pledge themselves to nurture the child in the faith of Christ. An infant so dedicated confirms that dedication with a faith-response usually during the early teenage years, about the same time when many Disciples are baptized. Most Disciples today recognize other forms of baptism as valid. A person baptized in another Christian tradition wishing to join a Disciples congregation is simply asked: "Do you believe that Jesus is the Christ, the Son of the living God, and proclaim him Lord and Savior of your life?" The person who answers, "I do," is warmly welcomed.

Death and Burial

Disciples of Christ observe standard Christian funeral and burial practices, as follows:

Funeral. A service officiated by clergy from the deceased's church. Usually held three to five days after the death of the deceased, a funeral may take place at either a funeral home or church.

Funeral services include prayers, readings from the Bible or other sacred texts, hymns, and words of comfort by the clergy. Frequently, a relative or close friend will be asked to give a eulogy, which details happy memories and accomplishments. In some instances, the clergy delivers the eulogy.

Tradition also allows the attendees of the memorial service to have one last opportunity to view the decedent's body and say good-bye. This opportunity can take place immediately before the service begins, or at the very end of the service.

Burial. The burial service will sometimes immediately follow the funeral, in which case, a funeral procession (the hearse, followed by the immediate family and then the other attendees) accompanies the deceased from the site of the memorial service to the burial site. At other times, the burial service takes place at a later time, when the final resting place is ready.

D. Family Life

Divorce

The autonomous nature of churches of Christ is evident when varying positions on marriage, divorce, and remarriage are considered. Some congregations do not approve of divorce for any reason; others are considerably more lenient in their views than the norm stated above. However, divorce is always considered a sin in the sense that it represents a failure to attain God's ideal for marriage, as sin is viewed as the failure to achieve God's ideal.

IV. Denominations and Demographics

A. History—Schisms

While charismatic leadership and religious journals held the first generation of Disciples together, organizational structure began to emerge in the 1830s with the formation of state associations for evangelism. By 1849, a national association, the American Christian Missionary Society, was formed to support home and foreign missions. Though Alexander Campbell was chosen president, the national association proved fractious. While most Disciples opposed slavery on moral or economic grounds, they professed to find biblical sanctions for the institution and rarely expressed sympathy for abolitionism. However, small groups of the abolitionists were determined to use the society as a platform. Though the denomination did not divide at this time, factions within the Disciples began to emerge.

A resolution adopted by the society in 1863 in the absence of representatives from the South endorsed the Union cause and alienated Southern Disciples, thereby laying the foundation for a denominational schism at the end of the century. The Churches of Christ, first enumerated separately from Disciples of Christ in the 1906 census, objected to the use of missionary societies and of instrumental music in worship on the grounds that these practices are not commanded in Scripture.

Twenty years later, in 1927, a second schism would shake the foundation of the Disciples of Christ. In the latter years of the nineteenth century, Disciples moved with the population to the South, West, and to the industrial centers of the Midwest. Some Disciples adapted to the more cosmopolitan and pluralistic character of urban American society while others held firmly to the ways of an older, simpler, more agrarian society. As many embraced the style and substance of America's metropolitan areas, conflicts arose among the Disciples over the use of instrumental music in worship and missionary societies in the work of the church. They also struggled to assess the significance of Darwinism and biblical criticism for religious life. To many Disciples it appeared that their traditional appeal for Christian unity through the restoration of primitive Christianity was no longer viable. While a few liberal Disciples were willing to move into the modern ecumenical movement, most Disciples sought a middle ground. Gradually liberalism and ecumenism triumphed among them, but few were willing to admit their virtual repudiation of the restoration platform prior to the middle of the twentieth century.

Another major division accompanied this admission as many conservative churches withdrew from fellowship and institutional cooperation. These "independents," who wanted to escape the growing centralization and liberalism of the movement, formed the North American Christian Convention. These churches maintain a strict congregational polity but meet for consultation and fellowship in the North American Christian Convention. Though this division was gradual after 1927, it was completed in the aftermath of Disciple denominational restructure in 1968. By 1971 they were listed in the *Yearbook of American Churches* as the Christian Churches and Churches of Christ.

B. Comparison of Tenets

The Churches of Christ

Those who self-identify as members of Churches of Christ generally emphasize their belief that the modern Churches of Christ represent the intent of the original, primitive Christian church established by Jesus Christ and the apostles.

The Churches of Christ are distinguished by their refusal to hold to any creeds other than the Bible itself; the practice of youth and adult baptism as a requirement for the remission of sins; autonomous nondenominational congregational church organization, with congregations overseen by a plurality of male-only elders; the weekly observance of The Lord's Supper; and the belief in a cappella congregational singing during worship.

It is the Churches' absence of instrumental music during services that is the major difference between the Churches of Christ and the Disciples of Christ. Most Churches of Christ practice a prohibition against instrumental music in services. As the Churches of Christ hold that there is no evidence indicating that the first-century church used instruments, most Churches of Christ today refrain from incorporating them into worship services. The primary argument against instrument use is the principle of silence. This argument states that since singing and making music with the heart is specified when the New Testament speaks of music in worship, instrumental music is thus unauthorized and excluded.

Christian Churches and Churches of Christ

The Christian Churches and Churches of Christ continue to embrace the tradition of Primitive Christianity. The Christian Churches view the Disciples of Christ as abandoning their Restorationist roots in favor of ecumenism with other Christian denominations, which also was a major commitment of Thomas Campbell. The Christian Churches view Campbell's goal as being "undenominational" rather than explicitly cooperative Christianity. The Churches of Christ are viewed as having become dogmatic on a number of issues, especially on the use of instrumental music in services of congregational worship. It should be noted that the Christian Churches and Churches of Christ fellowship hold much more in common with the Churches of Christ than with the Disciples of Christ.

Thus, the Christian Churches and Churches of Christ branch of the family is more conservative than liberal; it remains committed to the words of the Bible, bent on retaining local-church independence and rejects all "manmade creeds"; it is highly self-conscious about its particular nature and mission. At the same time, it repudiates legalism and has a generally open, cooperative, and respectful attitude toward other bodies of Christians.

V. Organization and Infrastructure

On the next page is a table that indicates the state-by-state distribution of members of Disciples of Christ.

A. Education and Hierarchy of Clergy

The congregation, instead of being assigned by a central organization, calls ministers to service. Disciples' ministers are ordained by their respective regional church, based on criteria established by the general church, and after an intensive in-care process with the region. They must have sponsor-

Disciples of Christ Members in the United States:

Alabama	8,496	Missouri	101,756
Alaska	247	Montana	3,222
Arizona	4,925	Nebraska	14,605
Arkansas	10,773	Nevada	651
California	39,654	New Jersey	1,968
Connecticut	683	New Mexico	4,224
Delaware	141	New York	12,389
Florida	23,725	North Carolina	50,460
Georgia	14,083	Ohio	66,665
Hawaii	305	Oklahoma	58,901
Idaho	4,328	Oregon	13,657
Illinois	65,546	Pennsylvania	17,619
Indiana	89,932	South Carolina	5,958
Iowa	50,77	South Dakota	544
Kansas	58,314	Tennessee	20,986
Kentucky	66,798	Texas	105,495
Louisiana	6,073	Utah	644
Maine	115	Virginia	42,038
Maryland	7,176	Washington	14,787
Massachusetts	154	Washington, D.C.	1,358
Michigan	9,170	West Virginia	13,351
Minnesota	2,282	Wisconsin	436
Mississippi	5,534	**TOTAL:**	**975,245**

- Christian Church (Disciples of Christ) Congregations: 3,792 congregations.
- Disciples in North America: 834,037 total members; 537,658 participating members.
- Disciples' Pastors: 7,007 pastors.

ship by at least one local congregation, and normally that congregation hosts the ordination service. An ordained Disciples minister normally holds a Master of Divinity degree from a theological seminary.

The Order of Ministry includes two offices: ordained minister and licensed minister. Qualifications and conditions for both offices are set by each of the thirty-five regions of the church, in cooperation with the congregations in that region.

Ordained ministers are authorized for ministry throughout the church. Candidates for ordination normally must possess a bachelor's degree and complete a program of theological education and profes-

sional study at a theological institution accredited by the Association of Theological Schools in the United States and Canada, usually leading to the Master of Divinity degree.

Licensed ministers are authorized for representative ministry in specific situations and with periodic review. Classifications of licensed ministers include commissioned church workers, licensed lay preachers, and licensed theological students. The educational experiences of licensed ministers may vary according to their life histories and the church's needs, but participation in a continuing process of education is expected.

Since ordination and licensing of ministers is the responsibility of the regions of the church, requirements for ordination vary somewhat from region to region. Laypersons often lead worship, and lay elders and deacons preside at Communion. Lay elders are chosen by the congregation to act as hosts of the Lord's Supper, as well as to provide pastoral care for congregation members; these are honored positions and are generally unpaid.

SEMINARIES

Brite Divinity School
2800 University Drive
TCU Box 298130
Fort Worth, TX 76129
817-257-7575
www.brite.tcu.edu

Brite Divinity School is located on the campus of Texas Christian University in Fort Worth. With an enrollment of approximately 250 students and a teaching faculty of twenty-three, Brite combines a small student-faculty ratio with a comprehensive array of academic programs.

Christian Theological Seminary
1000 West 42nd Street
Indianapolis, IN 46208
317-924-1331
Fax: 317-923-1961
www.cts.edu

Disciples Divinity House of the University of Chicago
1156 East 57th Street
Chicago, IL 60637
773-643-4411
ddh.uchicago.edu

The Disciples Divinity House of the University of Chicago is a center for graduate theological education for Disciples of Christ students. Disciples Divinity House is a unique institution that is neither a divinity school of a larger university nor a free-standing denominational seminary. Scholars earn their degrees—the MDiv, the AM, or the PhD—at the University of Chicago's Divinity School.

Disciples Divinity House at Vanderbilt University Divinity School
1917 Adelicia Avenue
Nashville, TN 37212
615-321-0380
www.vanderbilt.edu/divinity/disciples.html

Disciples Seminary Foundation
300 West Foothill Boulevard
Claremont, CA 91711-2709
909-624-0712
www.dsf.edu

The Disciples Seminary Foundation has as its primary purpose the support of Disciples MDiv, MA, and PhD students enrolled in any of the schools of the Claremont Theological Cluster or Graduate Theological Union in California:
Claremont School of Theology
Pacific School of Religion
San Francisco Theological Seminary
Graduate Theological Union
Claremont Graduate University

Lexington Theological Seminary
631 South Limestone Street
Lexington, KY 40508
859-252-0361
www.lextheo.edu

Phillips Theological Seminary
901 North Mingo Road
Tulsa, OK 74116
1-800-843-4675
www.ptstulsa.edu

B. Shrines and Houses of Worship

There are three "expressions" (manifestations) of church within the Disciples of Christ. The highest is the general church, which oversees all Disciples congregations in the United States and Canada. Next, the regional expression. Because the United States is a country of significant size, the Disciples divided the church into geographical regions. The last expression is the local church. These manifestations are held in covenant, which means that no manifestation can hand down edicts to another. Local congregations are still free to adopt specific worship practices, and elect ministers and other leadership without consulting the other expressions of the Disciples of Christ.

A number of institutions of higher learning are associated with the Disciples of Christ and have special programs for both professionals (ministers) and laity:

Barton College: Wilson, North Carolina
Bethany College: Bethany, West Virginia
Chapman University: Orange, California
Columbia College: Columbia, Missouri
Culver-Stockton College: Canton, Missouri
Drake University: Des Moines, Iowa
Drury University: Springfield, Missouri
Eureka College: Eureka, Illinois
Hiram College: Hiram, Ohio
Jarvis Christian College: Hawkins, Texas
Lynchburg College: Lynchburg, Virginia
Midway College: Midway, Kentucky
Northwest Christian College: Eugene, Oregon
Texas Christian University: Fort Worth, Texas
Tougaloo College: Tougaloo, Mississippi
Transylvania University: Lexington, Kentucky
William Woods University: Fulton, Missouri

C. Governance and Authority

Governed by The Design of the Christian Church, Disciples' churches practice Congregationalist church governance. Each church within the Disciples controls its own property and has the right to choose any minister. Decisions made by a local church cannot be appealed to the regional or general church, although regional ministers are often asked to intervene in disputes within a church. Management and doctrinal authority are centered in the local congregation.

The General Assembly of the Christian Church (Disciples of Christ), a biannual gathering of congregations, expresses only the views of that particular assembly and holds little power to bind the denomination as a whole, although decisions may be made that affect the general expression of the church.

At their General Assembly in 1968, a Provisional Design for the Christian Church (Disciples of Christ) was adopted, which provided a connectional polity by creating the offices of General Minister, President, and moderator, and establishing a biennial General Assembly of elected delegates, a general board, and an administrative committee. Requirements, such as seminary education, were implemented. Local governing boards are still held by the laity. The highest elected office of the Christian Church is the moderator of the general church, which can be held by either laity or clergy.

D. Social Service Organizations

National Benevolent Association
149 Weldon Parkway, Suite 115
Maryland Heights, MO 63043-3103
314-993-9000   Fax: 314-993-9018
nba@nbacares.org
Serving older adults, children, and families and persons with developmental disabilities.

Disciples and Home Missions (DHM)
130 East Washington Street
Indianapolis, IN 46204-3645
317-713-2679   Fax: 317-635-4426
Toll free: 888-346-2631
mail@dhm.disciples.org
DHM staff provides services to congregations, regions, and the general church.

A growing division within DHM is **North American Pacific/Asian Ministries**, which provides pastoral care and nurture to churches and ministers; consults on racial, ethnic, and multicultural (language-specific) ministries.

All Peoples Christian Center
Los Angeles, CA
Disciples Center in South Central Los Angeles offers a variety of ministries to people of all cultures.

Inman Christian Center
San Antonio, TX
Involved with Hispanic families in need.

Southwest Good Samaritan Ministries
Los Fresnos, TX
Works with refugees in building projects.

Yakama Christian Mission
White Swan, Wash.
Provides for Native-American and Hispanic communities on the Yakama Reservation.

PROMINENT MEMBERS OF THE CHURCH

Edgar Cayce, psychic and healer

J. William Fulbright, U.S. senator, Arkansas

James Garfield, 20th president of United States

David Lloyd George, British Prime Minister

Lyndon Baines Johnson, 36th president of the United States, whose family was staunchly Baptist; wife, Lady Bird Johnson, was a devout Episcopalian

Frances McDormand, Oscar-winning actress

James Clark McReynolds, U.S. Supreme Court justice (1914–1941)

Ronald Reagan, (*right*), 40th president of the U.S. (baptized into the Disciples as a youth and graduated from the Disciples' Eureka College; but was a member of Bel Air Presbyterian Church in his later years)

Ronald W. Reagan, America's fortieth president, was a member of the Disciples of Christ in his youth—his mother's denomination.

Colonel Harlan David Sanders, founder of Kentucky Fried Chicken

John Stamos, actor

Lew Wallace, author (*Ben-Hur*); Civil War general

E. Media and Communication

DisciplesWorld Magazine
6325 North Guilford Avenue, Suite 213
Indianapolis, IN 46220
317-375-8846   Fax: 317-375-8849
A journal of news, opinion, and mission for the Disciples of Christ.

Disciples News Service
Disciples Center
PO Box 1986
Indianapolis, IN 46206-1986
317-713-2492   Fax: 317-713-2489
pnews@cm.disciples.org
The official communications and media relations division of the Disciples of Christ.

FURTHER READING

A Social History of the Disciples of Christ 1865–1900 (2 Vols.)
    David Edwin, Jr.
    2003: University of Alabama Press

The Origins of the Restoration Movement
    Richard M. Tristano
    1988: Glenmary Research Center

WEBSITES
    www.disciples.org
    www.disciplesworld.org
    www.discipleshistory.org
    www.churchesofchrist.org

5 Episcopal Church

I. Origins and Early History

A. Introduction

THE EPISCOPAL CHURCH USA IS THE AMERICAN derivative of the Church of England, or Anglican Church. The word "Episcopal" comes from the Greek word *episkopos*, meaning "bishop" or "overseer," and is used in describing the American denomination because it is a church ruled by bishops in apostolic succession from the apostles of the early Christian church.

The Anglican Communion is a worldwide association of churches that are in full communion with the Church of England, which is often regarded as the "mother church," and specifically with its primate, the Archbishop of Canterbury. The Archbishop of Canterbury is the religious head of the Church of England, but has no formal authority outside that jurisdiction. Despite this, he is still recognized as the symbolic head of the worldwide communion. Since each national or regional church has full autonomy, there is no single "Anglican Church" possessing universal juridical authority.

The Anglican Communion considers itself to be part of the one holy, Catholic, and apostolic church (as declared in the Nicene Creed) and as being both Catholic and Reformed. The Communion is a theologically broad and often divergent affiliation of thirty-eight provinces that are in communion with the Archbishop of Canterbury. It is the third largest Christian denomination in the world, claiming approximately 73 million members.

The first recorded Christian martyr in Britain was Saint Alban during the early fourth century. It wasn't until the late sixth century that Saint Augustine of Canterbury, the first Archbishop of Canterbury, arrived in England.

The Reformation began in England—having gained ground in Europe since the time of Martin Luther earlier in the sixteenth century—when King Henry VIII sought a papal annulment of his marriage to Katherine of Aragon because she was unable to bear him a son to succeed him. When Pope Clement VII declined Henry's request in 1529, the monarch, who had once been an important apologist

Washington National Cathedral is an Episcopal church. Construction began in 1907 and the last finial was placed in 1990. The Ter Sanctus *reredos in the cathedral's East End features 110 carved figures surrounding Jesus.*

Samuel Seabury (1729–1796), portrayed in this undated engraving, was the first Episcopal bishop in the United States, having been consecrated bishop of Connecticut in 1784. His father, also Samuel Seabury, was a Congregationalist minister who had become an Episcopal priest in 1731. His grandson Samuel Seabury was an Episcopal priest; his great-great grandson Samuel Seabury was a prominent New York City judge.

for the Catholic Church and earned the title Defender of the Faith, initiated a series of acts that resulted in the establishment of the Church of England, independent of papal control. He also seized church properties throughout his realm, including monasteries and convents, and disenfranchised Catholic clergy wherever he could.

During the reign of Henry's son, Edward VI (1547–1553), who took the throne when he was nine years old, the Church of England became more Calvinistic and Protestant in nature. When Edward died, after ruling for only six years, his half-sister, Mary Tudor (1553–1558), took the throne. Mary was a staunch Catholic and returned the country to communion with the Church of Rome during her reign. The majority of English citizens were opposed to papal control; consequently, Mary ordered over three hundred dissenters to execution, from which came her nickname, Bloody Mary.

Upon Mary's death, her cousin Elizabeth I (1558–1603) assumed the throne at the age of twenty five. Elizabeth was a Protestant, but wanted national unity and an end to the religious factions. In 1559, she proposed a Religious Settlement that blended Catholic and Protestant elements and offered a compromise between the theological extremes.

Despite Elizabeth's strenuous efforts at reconciliation, the country continued to experience religious turmoil. High Church policies forced a number of Calvinists from office. In an attempt to regain unity,

subsequent rulers Charles II and James II both converted the country back to Roman Catholicism. During the Commonwealth period, Puritans ruled the church. But since the time of William and Mary (1689–1702) and Anne (1702–1714), all monarchs of England have been Anglican, assumed the position of head of the church, and retained the style of Defender of the Faith, as was Henry VIII.

The Church of England produced only one doctrinal statement: the Thirty-Nine Articles of Religion in 1571. The articles display the common Anglican fear that over-precision in doctrinal definition would only prove divisive. The articles have never been required of laity in England or the United States. The American *Book of Common Prayer* includes the articles in its contents, but only in the section entitled "Historical Documents of the Church," while the Apostles' and Nicene creeds are viewed as the church's principal doctrinal symbols.

Since the Elizabethan period, the Anglican Church has experienced internal debate over its loyalty to Catholicism, whether it is reformed enough for Protestantism, or whether a proper balance has been achieved. Because of these debates, three parties have been developed: the High Church party, the Low Church party, and the Broad Church party.

The High Church party places an emphasis on ministry and sacraments and maintains the apostolic succession, sacramental systems, and creeds of ancient and early medieval Christianity. Members of this party believe that Anglicanism is a true representative of Catholic Christianity.

The Low Church party takes a more stripped-down Protestant approach to the Church. This party stresses the primacy not only of Scripture over the Church, but also of the primitive over the medieval church. It also places a low value upon the episcopate, priesthood, and sacraments, and makes lesser use of symbolic acts in worship.

The Broad, or Central, Church party follows the tradition of the Elizabethan Settlements and strives to incorporate the best of both traditions. The majority of Anglicans fall into this category.

Although tensions between the parties persist, the Church claims to be a body that is both truly Catholic and fully Protestant, both loyal to the past in creed and polity, yet open to reform and change.

B. The Religion in America

Anglicanism first came to America in the seventeenth century with the English settlers who established colonies in Massachusetts and Virginia. Although the settlers in New England were quick to adopt a congregational form of government, those in Virginia continued to obey an Episcopal polity and follow the liturgical forms of Anglicanism. Virginia remained the center of Anglican strength throughout the colonial period. Anglicanism did spread throughout the thirteen colonies before the American Revolution. This was in part due to the founding of two missionary organizations in England, the Society for Promoting Christian Knowledge, in 1698, and the Society for the Propagation of the Gospel in Foreign Parts, in 1701.

The American Revolution fought against the English was certainly a trying time for Anglicanism in America. Most of the clergy, especially those in the northern colonies, were loyal to the English crown and preferred to close their church buildings rather than alter their services and pray for the American cause. In the southern colonies, however, most Anglicans were sympathetic to the rebellion. In fact, two-thirds of the signers of the Declaration of Independence were Anglican laymen.

After the Revolution, the concern of the new Episcopal Church was to create a denomination that was American and independent of the English king, who was the "supreme governor" of the Church of England. The most important facet that needed to be put in place for the church to succeed was the presence of an American bishop. The sacramental rites of ordination and confirmation could not be performed without a bishop. Because an American clergyman could not be ordained by the English Church,

Samuel Seabury went north to Scotland and in 1784, was the first American bishop to be consecrated.

A few years later, the British Parliament passed legislation allowing the consecration of clergymen who were not British subjects, and so the second and third American bishops were consecrated, William White of Pennsylvania, and Samuel Provost of New York.

During the nineteenth century, three separate church "parties" emerged, each with distinctive theological and liturgical views of the Christian life. The High Church party, later called Anglo-Catholicism, stressed the apostolic succession of bishops from the time of the apostles and the historic catholicity (i.e., universality) of the church. The Low Church, or Evangelical, party emphasized individual conversion and a disciplined moral life, a concept similar to other American Protestant groups. The third party, the Broad Church, or Liberal, party urged an openness to modern intellectual and social trends.

The only major schism in the Episcopal Church occurred in 1873, when the assistant bishop of Kentucky, George David Cummins, was censured by High Church Episcopalians for participating in a Protestant communion service. Cummins resigned and helped to organize the Reformed Episcopal Church (REC). Leaders of this new church adopted a prayer book and rules of order similar to those of the Episcopal Church, but involved a closer relationship with other Protestant groups.

Today, the Episcopal Church USA is in turmoil, with potential schism looming over theological and social issues. On the surface, the ordination of an openly gay man as a bishop has prompted scores of local parish churches and some dioceses within the United States to question or to challenge the authority of the national church in America. There are also (very broadly defined) liberal vs. conservative, or orthodox, theological teachings that have divided some congregations from their priests and some priests from their bishops—on core Christian doctrines such as the divinity of Jesus and the literal acceptance of his resurrection from the dead.

In 2006, the Episcopal Church USA elected Kathryn Jefferts Schori as presiding bishop, the first woman within the worldwide Anglican Communion to be elected as a national primate.

The Episcopal Church has been a leading denomination in dealing with issues of sexuality and gender. V. Gene Robinson (above left), photographed at Saint Paul's Episcopal Church in Concord, New Hampshire, in 2003, is the first openly gay non-celibate priest to be ordained a bishop in a major Christian denomination. Katharine Jefferts Schori (above right), photographed at the Church of the Holy Spirit in Bullhead City, Arizona, in 2006, is the first woman elected presiding bishop of the Episcopal Church in the United States of America.

C. Important Dates and Landmarks

Early 4th century Era of first recorded Christian martyr in Britain, Saint Alban.

Late 6th century Arrival of first archbishop of Canterbury, Saint Augustine of Canterbury, England.

664 Synod of Whitby established: held the church throughout Britain should conform to contemporary Roman customs introduced by Augustine and other missionaries to the Anglo-Saxons.

672-673 Synod of Hertford; English bishops for the first time able to act as one body under the leadership of the archbishop of Canterbury.

1529 King Henry VIII of England calls a Parliament that would last seven years (Reformation Parliament); passes many acts that cut political ties to Rome.

1531 Convocation of Canterbury grants assent to the King's Five Articles and Henry VIII recognized as the "sole protector and supreme head of the Anglican Church and clergy."

1533 "Statute in Restraint of Appeals" drafted by Thomas Cromwell on behalf of Henry VIII and approved by Parliament: forbids all appeals to the pope in Rome on religious or other matters and makes the King the final legal authority in all such matters in England, Wales, and other English possessions; enables Thomas Cranmer to grant Henry VIII a divorce from Catherine of Aragon so he can marry Anne Boleyn.

1533 Act in Restraint of Appeals instated by Henry VIII.

1534 First Act of Supremacy instated by Henry VIII: declares English crown is "the only supreme head of the Church of England, called Ecclesia Anglicana," and enjoys "all honors, dignities, preeminence, jurisdictions, privileges, authorities, immunities, profits, and commodities to the said dignity." Bishop of Rome given no "greater jurisdiction in England than any other foreign bishop."

1538 Introduction of the Great Bible, a vernacular translation of the Scripture.

1538-1541 Dissolution of the Monasteries brings huge amounts of land and property under the jurisdiction of the crown.

1549 First Act of Uniformity instated by Edward VI: first publication of *The Book of Common Prayer* (BCP)—first vernacular prayer book—established as sole legal form of worship; English as language of public worship.

1552 Second Act of Uniformity instated by Edward VI: a second edition of the prayer book published with a Protestant spin; anyone not attending a service where the BCP is used faces up to six months in prison for a first offense, one year for a second, and life sentence for a third.

1559 Third Act of Uniformity instated by Elizabeth I: authorizes a third edition of *The Book of Common Prayer*; combines elements of the Calvinistic book of 1552 with the traditional Catholic liturgy of Sarum, as transcribed in the 1549 version; states that every man must attend church once a week or be fined 12 pence. Second Act of Supremacy (reinstatement of the 1534 Act) instated by Elizabeth I: the Queen is named the Supreme Governor of the Church of England; anyone who takes public or church office is required to take the Oath of Supremacy.

1563 Thirty-Nine Articles established during Convocation of the Church under the direction of Archbishop Matthew Parker.

1571: Parliament makes adherence to the Thirty-Nine Articles legal.

1642–1651 English Civil War between Parliamentarians (Roundheads) and Royalists (Cavaliers).

First War (1642–1645) and Second War (1648–1649) Supporters of Charles I against supporters of the Long Parliament.

Third War (1649–1651) Supporters of Charles II against supporters of the Rump Parliament. Casualties include King Charles I and Archbishop of Canterbury William Laud; two factions established, the Puritans who seek more far-reaching reform, and the conservative churchmen who aim to keep closer to traditional beliefs and practices; failure of political and ecclesiastical authorities to submit to Puritan demands for more extensive reform is cause of open warfare.

September 3, 1651 The Battle of Worcester ends the war with a Parliamentary victory.

1649–1660 Protectorate of the Commonwealth of England; Anglicanism disestablished, Presbyterian ecclesiology introduced as an adjunct to the Episcopal system; the Articles replaced with the Westminster Confession; and the *The Book of Common Prayers* replaced by the *Directory of Public Worship*.

1660 Charles II restored as monarch after Cromwell's death.

1662 Fourth Act of Uniformity instated by Charles II: reintroduces Episcopal rule to the Church of England after the Puritans had abolished many features of the church during the civil war; requires the Episcopal ordination for all ministers which results in the Great Ejection when 2,000 clergymen leave the church; the Restoration—Anglicanism restored but ideal of encompassing all of the people of England in one religious organization is abandoned; the Anglican established church occupies the middle ground, and Roman Catholics and those Puritans who dissented from the establishment, too strong to be suppressed altogether, must continue their existence outside the national church rather than control it.

1784 Samuel Seabury, a Connecticut clergyman, consecrated as the first American bishop by three bishops of the Scottish Episcopal Church.

1789 William White of Pennsylvania and Samuel Provost of New York are the second and third American bishops to be consecrated.

1789 Official organization of the Episcopal Church in America; the first General Convention held, a constitution adopted, a set of church canons ratified, and a *The Book of Common Prayer* (BCP) authorized for use in worship services.

1873 George David Cummins resigns from his position as Bishop of Kentucky after being censured by High Church Episcopalians for participating in a Protestant Communion service.

1873 Cummins organizes the Reformed Episcopal Church (REC).

1870 Chicago-Lambeth Quadrilateral, a four-fold position document used in considering ecumenical relations, proposed by William Reed Huntington, accepted by the Episcopal bishops.

1892 Revisions made to the BCP.

1928 Another set of revisions made to BCP.

1977 Anglican Church in North America formed in response to the decisions made during the Congress of St. Louis.

1978 Anglican Church in North America split into three separate churches: the Anglican Catholic Church, the Anglican Province of Christ the King, and the Anglican Catholic Church of Canada.

1979 A new *Book of Common Prayer* is introduced, the most radical revision of the book since the introduction of an English-language prayer book in 1549; scholars insist that the new book best represents liturgical thinking of the day.

1984 Five diocese of the Church of India received by the Anglican Catholic Church and constituted as its Second Province.

1989 Barbara Harris becomes the first female bishop of the Anglican Communion; protest from theological conservatives.

1989 Bishop John Spong of the Diocese of Newark ordains an openly homosexual man to the Episcopal priesthood.

2004 E. Gene Robinson elected Bishop of New Hampshire and ordained, first openly homosexual man to be elevated to the episcopacy.

2006 Kathryn Jefferts Schori is the first woman elected as presiding bishop (or primate) by the American Episcopal Church.

D. Important Figures

Thomas Cromwell (1485–1540)

Cromwell was the First Earl of Essex and Chief Minister to Henry VIII. While serving under the latter, he drafted the Act in Restraint of Appeals and authorized the Dissolution of Monasteries.

King Henry VIII (1491–1547)

Henry VIII was the second monarch of the Tudor dynasty. Marrying six times in hopes of bearing a son, he began the English Reformation when he decided to replace papal supremacy with supremacy of the English crown.

King Edward VI (1537–1553)

Edward VI was the long-awaited son of Henry VIII. He became king when he was only nine years old; thus, his entire rule was mediated through a council of regency that was first led by his uncle, Edwards Seymour, and then by John Dudley. During his reign, Protestantism was first established.

Queen Mary I (1516–1558)

Mary was the daughter of Henry VIII. She returned Protestant England back to Roman

Catholicism, ordering three hundred religious dissenters executed in the process. For this reason, she is known as Bloody Mary. Queen Mary I reversed all Church of England reform during her reign and re-established papal supremacy.

Queen Elizabeth I (1533–1603)

Elizabeth, known as the Virgin Queen because of her staunchly declared intention to never marry, established the English church as a reformed Catholic church, incorporating elements of Protestant theology with the Religious Settlement of 1559.

Samuel Seabury (1729–1796)

Seabury was the first American Episcopal bishop. He was consecrated in 1784 as first bishop of Connecticut

John Henry Hobart (1775–1830)

Hobart was the third bishop of New York and representative of the High Church party. He founded the General Theological Seminary in New York City and Geneva College in the Finger Lakes area of upstate New York.

Alexander Viets Griswold (1841–1908)

Griswold served as bishop of the Eastern Diocese. He was also representative of the Low Church, or Evangelical, party.

Phillips Brooks (1835–1893)

Brooks was clergyman from Trinity Church in Boston, and one of the leading spokesmen for Broad Church Episcopalians.

George David Cummins (1822–1876)

Cummins resigned from his position as the assistant bishop of Kentucky in 1873 to help organize the Reformed Episcopal Church.

Barbara Clementine Harris (1930–   )

Harris, a member of the Union of Black Episcopalians, was ordained suffragan (assistant) bishop of Massachusetts in 1989, making her the first female bishop of the Anglican Communion.

John Shelby Spong (1931–   )

Spong is the Bishop of Newark. Most notably, he challenged the church's sexual mores by ordaining a homosexual to the priesthood in 1989.

Katharine Jefferts Schori (1954–   )

Schori was the first female to be elected presiding bishop of the Episcopal Church USA in 2006.

II. Tenets and Beliefs

A. Articles of Faith

The *Book of Common Prayer* is the church's official service book and was originally published in 1549. It has since been revised many times in both England and America. *The Book of Common Prayer* has served as a principal standard of doctrine for Anglicism. It witnesses to the Anglican belief that the highest privilege of the Christian is worship. The book includes the Thirty-Nine Articles of Religion, ancient creeds, prayers, liturgies, a church calendar, a catechism, and a lectionary.

The **Nicene Creed** is the main statement of faith for the Episcopal Church USA (ECUSA). The Nicene Creed is an epitome, but not a full definition, of what is required for orthodoxy. It is an implicit condemnation of specific errors. The creed was first adopted in 325 CE at the First Council of Nicaea, the first ecumenical council in history. In 381, a section was added, but only the Eastern Orthodox and Greek Catholic Churches use this amended version of the creed.

The **Apostles' Creed** is also used in ecumenical matters and as a baptismal covenant.

The Thirty-Nine Articles

The Thirty-Nine Articles, established by Convocation of the Church in 1563 under the direction of

Archbishop Matthew Parker, are the defining statements of Anglican doctrine. The Articles were intended as a statement of the position of the Church of England as it was against the Roman Catholic Church and dissident Protestants. While the ECUSA does not require its members to adhere to the Articles, the American Methodist Church uses a similar document as its official doctrine. John Wesley, founder of the Methodist Church, adapted the Thirty-Nine Articles during the eighteenth century, naming them the Articles of Religion.

B. Scripture

The Episcopal Church maintains that the Holy Scriptures, embodied in the Old and New Testaments, are the Word of God, containing all that is necessary for salvation. However, the church believes the Bible should not be interpreted apart from tradition and human reason. The collective wisdom, experience, and understanding of Christians over the past two thousand years, as well as personal experience, provide a basis for proper interpretation.

C. Theologians and Thinkers

Thomas Cranmer (1489–1575)

Cranmer served as the archbishop of Canterbury during the reign of Henry VIII and Edward VI. He was the principal author of the first two *Books of Common Prayer,* which works provided the foundation for Anglican liturgy for over 400 years. Cranmer's work was influenced by the ideas of reformers John Calvin and Martin Bucer, as well as the Roman Catholic theologian Desiderius Erasmus. Queen "Bloody Mary" had Cranmer executed for his religious position in 1556.

Matthew Parker (1504–1575)

Matthew Parker served as the archbishop of Canterbury beginning in 1559 under Queen

Elizabeth. He established the Thirty-Nine Articles at the 1563 Convocation of the Church, and, in an effort to return church values to those of tradition, paid for the publication of *A Testimonie of Antiquitie,* which conveyed "the ancient faith of the Church of England touching the Sacrament of the Body and Blood of the Lord . . . above 600 years ago."

Richard Hooker (1554–1600)

Hooker co-founded much of Anglican theological thought with Thomas Cranmer. He wrote *Of the Lawes of the Ecclesiastical Politie* (1597), in which he argued for a "via media" (middle way) between Catholics and Puritans. Hooker believed that both reason and tradition were important for interpreting the Bible because it was written in a specific historical context. He also believed that people should focus on what united them rather than on what divided them. His most important written work is *A Learned Discourse of Justification*, in which he argues for the Protestant idea of justification by faith, but agrees that anyone can be saved by God, including Catholics.

William White (1748–1836)

White was the second American bishop. He was consecrated in 1789, after the British Parliament passed legislation allowing the consecration of clergymen who were not British subjects. White was also the first and fourth presiding bishop of the Episcopal Church, USA, and the first bishop of the Diocese of Pennsylvania. In 1782, he wrote *The Case of the Episcopal Churches in the United States Considered,* which would become the theological basis of the Episcopal Church in America. In the work, White argues that the church was to be independent not only of foreign but also of American civil powers. He says that the church desires and acknowledges three historic orders in the ministry: deacons, priests, and bishops; but that the church was to be democratically operated, with not only clergy but also laity participating in all church councils.

John Stark Ravenscroft (1772–1830)

Ravenscroft was the first bishop of the Protestant Episcopal Church in North Carolina and a representative of the High Church Party. He publicly opposed the teachings of the American Bible Society and the theology of baptism promoted by Baptists.

William Reed Huntington (1838–1909)

Huntington devised the Chicago-Lambeth Quadrilateral, a four-fold position for the Episcopal bishops to consider when discussing ecumenical relations in 1886. The four points cited as articulations of Anglican identity are:

1. The Holy Scriptures, as containing all things necessary to salvation;

2. The Creeds (specifically, the Apostles' and Nicene Creeds), as the sufficient statement of Christian faith;

3. The Sacraments of Baptism and Holy Communion;

4. The historic episcopate, locally adapted.

James Pike (1913–1969)

Pike served as bishop of California and questioned how the Gospel related to the modern world. He denied the virgin birth of Jesus and questioned the relevance of the doctrine of the Trinity for his time. He also introduced the ordained ministry of women to the Episcopal Church, a living wage for workers in San Francisco, the acceptance of lesbian, gay, bisexual, and transgender lifestyles in the church, and civil rights. Pike marched with Martin Luther King Jr.

III. Rites and Rituals

A. The Calendar

The Episcopal Church follows a calendar similar to that of the Catholic Church. They observe many of the same feast days on the same calendar dates throughout the year.

On October 16, some Episcopal churches commemorate the deaths of the Oxford Martyrs: Archbishop Thomas Cranmer and Bishops Hugh Latimer and Nicholas Ridley.

B. Worship and Liturgy

There exist a variety of liturgical practices within the Episcopal Church, as well as a variety of worship styles. These include traditional hymns and anthems, praise and worship music, Anglican chant, liturgical dance, charismatic hand movements, vested clergy, and clergy in street clothing. However, there is one central binding aspect among all Episcopalians: *The Book of Common Prayer.*

The Book of Common Prayer contains most of the worship services, or liturgies, used in the Episcopal Church. It is both a reflection and source of theology for Episcopalians. The current edition dates from 1979, and is marked by an attempt to return to full lay participation in all services and the recovery of the Eucharist as the principal service of the church. This version also reduces the emphasis on personal sin.

Often a congregation or a particular service will be referred to as "Low Church" or "High Church." The High Church is considered to be "more Catholic," or "Anglo-Catholic," and is inclined toward embellishments such as incense, formal hymns, and a higher degree of ceremonial touches. Clergy of the High Church are usually vested in albs, stoles, and chasubles, and the lay assistants might also be vested in albs. The Low Church is simpler and may incorporate other elements such as informal praise and worship music. These congregations may tend toward a more "truly" Protestant or evangelical outlook. The Broad Church incorporates elements of both the Low and High Church.

Typical parish worship features Bible readings from the Old Testament as well as from both the Epistles and the Gospels of the New Testament. Every Eucharist or Holy Communion service must use real wine, not water or grape juice, in order for the sacrament to be valid. Only baptized members of the church are eligible to receive Communion.

Two major sacraments are considered by all Anglicans necessary for salvation: baptism and the holy Eucharist. The other five rites, confession and absolution, confirmation, holy matrimony, holy orders, and the anointing of the sick, are either considered as full sacraments or are simply regarded as "sacramental rites," depending on the liberal or conservative nature of the church. Three of the seven sacraments—baptism, confirmation, and ordination—may only be received once in a lifetime because they make an indelible sacramental character on the recipient's soul.

Baptism is the reception of the Holy Spirit and the initiation of individuals into the Christian faith. It is usually performed on infants, but can be performed on adults in the case of conversion.

The Eucharist, also known as Holy Communion or the Lord's Supper, is the means by which Christ becomes present to the Christian community gathered in his name. It is the central act of gathered worship, believed to be the renewing of the Body of Christ as the Church through the reception of the Body of Christ as the Blessed Sacrament, his spiritual body and blood. The matter of this sacrament is the bread and wine, and the form is the Eucharistic Prayer.

According to the Episcopal Church, confession and absolution is the sacrament by which an individual is restored to God when his or her relationship with God has been broken by sin. This sacrament is normally performed as a whole congregation. The congregation is invited to confess their sins during a moment of silent prayer, a spoken general confession is recited, and then the priest offers words of absolution. An individual can participate in aural confession and privately meet with a priest to confess his or her sins. A priest can provide counseling, urge reconciliation with parties that have been sinned against, and suggest certain spiritual disciplines, or penance. Anglican clergy do not require acts of penance as a precondition to receiving absolution; these acts are intended to be healing and preventative. The priest is

also bound by the seal of confession, which binds them to never speak of what he or she has heard in the confessional to anyone.

Confirmation involves the reaffirmation of faith through the strengthening and renewal of the baptismal vows. This is accomplished through prayer and the laying on of hands by a bishop.

Holy matrimony is the blessing of a union between a man and woman and acknowledging the presence and grace of God in the life of the couple. The couple seek God's blessing, a prayer that is answered through the mediation of the priest. The form of the sacrament is the vows.

Holy orders, the sacrament also known as ordination, is the setting aside of individuals to specific ministries in the Episcopal Church. Individuals are appointed as deacons, priests, or bishops. The matter and form of ordination are the laying on of hands by a bishop and prayers. Priests are essentially delegates of the bishop and minister to congregations in which the bishop cannot be physically present. Deacons are the "church in the world" and administer to the pastoral needs of the community and assist the priest in worship. The bishop is the chief pastor of the diocese. Consecration as an archbishop involves taking on more Episcopal responsibilities.

The anointing of the sick is an act of healing through prayer and sacrament and is performed on both the sick and the dying. The matter consists of laying on of hands or anointing with oil, and the form is prayer.

A rite that has the intended sacramental effect is known as a "valid" sacrament. Only a priest properly ordained by a bishop, or a bishop consecrated by other bishops, can perform such actions. The only exception is in the case of an emergency baptism, which can be performed by a layperson. In order to be validly ordered, all Anglican clergy must be ordained and consecrated by bishops whose own consecration can be traced to the apostles.

Sacraments have two elements, form and matter. A form is the verbal and physical liturgical action.

The matter refers to any material objects used when the sacrament is delivered. For example, in the case of baptism, water and chrism are considered to be the matter element of the sacrament.

C. Daily Life

Members of the Episcopal Church follow certain dietary restrictions on the fast days of Ash Wednesday and Good Friday. On these days a believer's diet may only consist of meatless foods and meals should not be lavish. Some Episcopalians refrain from eating meat on Fridays throughout the year in honor of the crucifixion of Christ, which is believed to have occurred on a Friday. There are no mandates in the church that require such dietary restrictions, but some members choose to adhere to the tradition for their own reasons.

D. Life Cycle Events

Birth

Baptism is the sacrament by which one is initiated into the Christian faith. It is the act of receiving an individual into the household of God, thus allowing them to receive the grace of the other sacraments. During the sacrament of baptism, an individual receives the grace of the Holy Spirit.

The matter of baptism is the water and chrism and the form is the words of the Trinitarian formula. Baptism is performed in order to renounce sin and all of that which is opposed to the will of God, state belief in God, Father, Son, and Holy Spirit, and to show a commitment to follow Christ as Lord and Savior.

Confirmation

Confirmation is the reaffirmation of faith through the strengthening and renewal of one's baptismal vows. This is accomplished through prayer and the laying on of hands by a bishop. Baptism and confirmation were once practiced as a unified rite, but now it is seen as an opportunity for those baptized as infants to make an adult profession of faith, and to affirm the vows made on their behalf. It was also once viewed as a precondition to participation in the Eucharist throughout the Communion.

Nuptials

Holy matrimony is deemed the blessing of a union between a man and a woman and acknowledging the presence and grace of God in the life of the couple. The sacrament must be celebrated under the presidency of a priest, who witnesses and mediates the prayers and vows of the couple.

Matrimony was actually the final sacrament added to the Anglican faith. It arose as a result of the civil necessity during the Middle Ages to regularize intimate relationships and legitimize children. In many parts of the Anglican Communion, there is provision to bless civil marriages and in some diocese there is also a provision for the blessing of same-sex unions.

Death and Burial

The anointing of the sick, also known as healing or unction, is an act of healing through prayer and sacrament. It is performed on both the sick and the dying. In the case of death, the sacrament is known as Extreme Unction. The priest acts as a mediator of Christ's grace and will frequently administer the consecrated bread as part of the sacramental action.

Family Life

If two divorced people would like to get married they must obtain permission from the bishop of the diocese in which they are to be married. There is usually no difficulty in obtaining permission as such, unless the bishop finds evidence that the two people should not be married.

IV. Denominations and Demographics

A. History

The Episcopal Church USA formed in Philadelphia in 1789 as a religious body autonomous from (though still retaining ties with) the Church of England.

The Reformed Episcopal Church in America emerged in 1873, as a result of increased frustration among Evangelicals in the denomination regarding its openness to the High Church group. The Evangelicals believed that the Protestant character of the Anglican Church was being compromised. Another cause for dissent was the church's unwillingness to interact and create fellowships with non-Episcopal churches.

When Reverend George Cummins was publicly criticized by fellow Episcopalian bishops for participating in an interdenominational Communion service sponsored by the Evangelical Alliance in New York City in 1873, he resigned his position and, along with several other like-minded individuals, organized the Reformed Episcopal Church. As their basis for the new denomination, they drew up The Declaration of Principles, a document based on the Thirty-Nine Articles of Religion.

The Episcopal Orthodox Christian Archdiocese of America was founded in 1963, based on the teachings of Reverend James Dees. Dees led a protest against the Episcopal Church for its failure to firmly proclaim biblical doctrine. He felt the church was more interested in the social gospel of helping the poor than in traditional Anglicanism. The denomination is grounded in the 1928 unrevised version of *The Book of Common Prayer* and the unrevised Thirty-Nine Articles of Religion.

The Congress of St. Louis was called in 1977 in response to decisions made by the Episcopal Church to approve the ordination of women and to issue a heavily revised *Book of Common Prayer*. A significant group was opposed to these changes and, as a result of the desire to maintain the apostolic tradition of male-only clergy and the exclusive use of the historical Anglican liturgical forms, the group founded the Anglican Church in North America.

In 1978, the Anglican Church split into three separate churches, the Anglican Catholic Church, the Anglican Province of Christ the King, and the Anglican Catholic Church of Canada.

In 1984, the five Anglican diocese of the Church of India were received by the Anglican Catholic Church and constituted as its Second Province. Since 1990, the Anglican Catholic Church has expanded to include bishoprics around the world and now has twelve dioceses in the Americas, the United Kingdom, and Australia. Also during this time period, a large number of parishes left the Anglican Catholic Church and merged with the American Episcopal Church to form the Anglican Church in America. Another thirty parishes left the Church and formed the Holy Catholic Church (Anglican Rite).

B. Comparison of Tenets and Practices

All Anglicans recognize two sacraments, baptism and the holy Eucharist, as having been ordained by Christ. As such, they are the only two sacraments considered by the Episcopal community necessary for salvation. There are five other acts that are regarded as full sacraments by Anglo-Catholic Anglicans or as "sacramental rites" by evangelical Anglicans. The other rites are confession and absolution, confirmation, holy matrimony, holy orders, and the anointing of the sick. Depending on the opinion of the individual church, different rites hold different value to Anglicans.

Members of today's Episcopal Church USA, Anglican Catholic Church, and Reformed Episcopal Church all believe that the Bible must not be interpreted apart from tradition and human reason because it is a document written within a specific historical context. While the Bible is authoritative, church tradition and human reason enables Episcopal Christians to sort out their own understanding of religious and moral issues as they relate to their own lives.

Members of the Reformed Episcopal Church reject the Episcopalian doctrine that Christ resides in the elements of the Eucharist, arguing instead that the Lord's Supper is symbolic of Christ. They also reject the Episcopalian doctrine that baptism is necessary for regeneration, arguing instead that baptism is an outward expression of salvation. In addition, Reformed believers argue that the word "priest" should not be used for only clergy, but is applicable to all Christians, as cited in the Bible (1 Peter 2:9).

The Anglican Catholic Church bases its worship in the liturgy contained in *The Book of Common Prayer*. The principle act of worship in each service is the celebration of the Eucharist, also known as Mass. A person becomes a member of the church after baptism and most people attend an instruction class before being baptized. The Anglican Catholic Church holds to all seven sacraments of grace: baptism, confirmation, holy Eucharist, holy matrimony, holy orders, penance, and unction of the sick, but the most important sacrament is the Eucharist. According to the Anglican Catholic Church, in the Eucharist, Christ in His body and blood is truly and really present to each church member. This sacrament should be celebrated every Sunday and holy day, if not daily.

In the Episcopal Orthodox Christian Archdiocese of America, believers subscribe to the Athanasian Creed, in addition to the Apostle's and Nicene creeds. These Orthodox Episcopalians also believe that the Bible contains all things necessary for salvation and whatever is not contained in the Bible is not required of any human being.

C. Organization and Distribution

The Episcopal Church in the United States of America (ECUSA) has a membership of 2.5 million people, 2.3 million of whom are formally Episcopalian and 200,000 more are counted as "other baptized."

The ECUSA has nine ecclesiastical provinces, each of which is subdivided into dioceses. The provinces are numbered and grouped as follows:

1. New England
2. New York, New Jersey, Haiti, United States Virgin Islands, and Convocation of American Churches in Europe
3. Delaware, District of Columbia, Maryland, Pennsylvania, Virginia, West Virginia
4. Alabama, Georgia, eastern Louisiana, Florida, Kentucky, Mississippi, North Carolina, South Carolina, Tennessee
5. Illinois, Indiana, Michigan, eastern Missouri, Ohio, Wisconsin
6. Colorado, Iowa, Minnesota, Montana, Nebraska, North Dakota, South Dakota, Wyoming
7. Arkansas, Kansas, western Louisiana, western Missouri, New Mexico, Oklahoma, Texas
8. Alaska, Arizona, California, Hawaii, Idaho, Oregon, Nevada, Utah, Taiwan, Washington
9. Colombia, Ecuador, Honduras, Puerto Rico, Dominican Republic, Venezuela

Each diocese consists of various congregations: cathedrals, parishes, missions, and chapels.

V. Organization and Infrastructure

A. Education and Hierarchy of Clergy

There are three specific ministries in the Anglican Church: deacon, priest, and bishop. Priests are considered to be the delegates of the bishop, ministering to congregations when a bishop cannot be physically present. The original orders were only deacons and bishops, but the expansion of the Church after the legitimization by Constantine the Great led to the development of the presbyterate. Deacons administer to the pastoral needs of the community and assist the priest in worship. The bishop is the chief pastor of a diocese.

The Anglican Communion does not require the celibacy of its clerics. Over the last thirty years, the ordination of women has become common in many parts of the Communion, even allowing for female bishops in some places.

SEMINARIES

Berkeley Divinity School at Yale
409 Prospect Street
New Haven, CT
203-432-9285
http://research.yale.edu/berkeleydivinity

Bexley Hall Episcopal Seminary
583 Sheridan Avenue
Columbus, OH 43209-2325
26 Broadway Street
Rochester, NY 14607
614-231-3095   Fax: 614-231-3236
www.bexley.edu
Columbus@bexley.edu

The Church Divinity School of the Pacific
2451 Ridge Road
Berkeley, CA 94709-1217
510-204-0700   Fax: 510-644-0712
800-353-CDSP
www.cdsp.edu
Info@CDSP.edu

Episcopal Divinity School
99 Brattle Street
Cambridge, MA 02138
617-497-0614

Episcopal Theological Seminary of the Southwest
606 Rathervue Place
PO Box 2247

Austin, TX 78768
512-472-4133
www.etss.edu/index.shtml

The General Theological Seminary
175 Ninth Avenue
New York, NY 10011
212-243-5150   Fax: 212-727-3907
www.gts.edu

Nashotah House Theological Seminary
2777 Mission Road
Nashotah, WI 53058
262-646-6500
www.nashotah.edu/contact_us.htm
nashotah@nashotah.edu

Seabury-Western Theological Seminary
2122 Sheridan Road
Evanston, IL 60201
800-275-8235   Fax: 847-328-9624
847-328-9300
seabury@seabury.edu
www.seabury.edu

School of Theology at The University of the South
735 University Avenue
Sewanee, TN 37383
931-598-1000
http://theology.sewanee.edu

Trinity Episcopal School for Ministry
311 Eleventh St.
Ambridge, PA 15003
724-266-3838   Fax: 724-266-4617
800-874-8754
www.tesm.edu/people

Virginia Theological Seminary
3737 Seminary Road
Alexandria, VA 22304
703-370-6600 / 800-941-0083

COLLEGES

A number of colleges have had a historical association with the Episcopal Church:

Bard College
Clarkson College
Hobart and William Smith Colleges
Kenyon College
Saint Augustine's College/No. Carolina
Saint Augustine College/Chicago
Saint Paul's College
The University of the South
Voorhees College

B. Shrines; Houses of Worship

Organizations

Each diocese is composed of congregations of various kinds: cathedrals, parishes, missions, and chapels. Cathedrals act as the mother church of a diocese. The cathedral is home of the cathedra, or the bishop's chair. Usually a cathedral is led by a priest, called a dean. A cathedral's lay governing body is known as a chapter, although some cathedrals have a vestry as well.

Parishes are self-sustaining congregations, meaning they are not financially supported by the diocese. Most congregations in the ECUSA are parishes. The ordained leader of a parish is a priest, also known as the rector. There are two lay leaders of each congregation, known as the wardens. In addition, there is the vestry, elected laypersons who support the mission and ministry of the congregation. The rector, wardens, and these laity compose what is known as the vestry. Missions are congregations that are partially supported by the diocese.

Missions are governed in a way similar to the parish, but are more directly responsible to the diocese in which they belong. A mission is led by a clergyperson, known as the vicar. The lay leadership of a mission is either called the mission committee or the bishop's committee, rather than a vestry. Chapels are often connected to another institution, such as a hospital, or may be congregations that are only active for part of the year. In charge of a chapel is a clergyperson known as the chaplain.

The Cathedral Church of Saint John the Divine
1047 Amsterdam Avenue
New York, NY 10025
General: 212-316-7490
Tours: 212-932-7347
info@stjohndivine.org

Episcopal churches are traditionally small buildings designed to seat only the members of their small congregations. However, the largest Episcopal church (and the largest Gothic church of its kind in the world) is the Cathedral of Saint John the Divine in New York City. It is the church of the diocese of New York and can seat 6,000 people. The well known National Cathedral in Washington, D.C., also has a large seating capacity.

At the Cathedral of Saint John the Divine in New York City, two golden menorahs—one of which appears in this 2003 photograph—stand on either side of the altar. They were donated to the church in 1930 by Adolph S. Ochs, then the publisher of The New York Times, *in recognition of the church's long-standing support of immigration rights and its outspoken defense of Jews and other persecuted minorities the world over.*

Trinity Church and St. Paul's Chapel
74 Trinity Place
New York, NY 10006
Trinity Church: 212-602-0800
St. Paul's Chapel: 212-233-4164

Trinity Church in New York City is the oldest Episcopal Church in the United States. It was built in 1697 and still stands in the same location in Manhattan's Wall Street district. On September 11, 2001, Trinity Church provided a refuge for people fleeing terrorist attacks on the World Trade Center.

C. Governance and Authority

The basic unit of governance in the ECUSA is the diocese. The ordained leader of the diocese is a bishop. Groups of dioceses constitute provinces, but unlike in other Anglican churches, the provinces of the Episcopal Church do not have an archbishop with jurisdiction over the other bishops in his or her province. Usually the diocese also owns the individual churches in its care. Other ordained leaders include priests and deacons.

The ECUSA has its national offices in New York City, but the cathedra of the presiding bishop is housed at Washington Nation Cathedral. The governing body is the General Convention, which convenes every three years. The General Convention is made up of the House of Bishops and the House of Deputies. The House of Bishops includes all the current bishops and its head is the presiding bishop of the Episcopal Church. The House of Deputies is made up of priests, deacons, and laypersons, all of whom are elected by each diocese.

D. Social Service Organizations

Ecclesia Ministries
67 Newbury Street
Boston, MA 02116
617-247-4927   Fax: 617-247-4927

info@ecclesia-ministries.org
www.ecclesia-ministries.org/index.html

Ecclesia Ministries and Common Cathedral is a daily street ministry dedicated to helping the homeless.

Episcopal Charities
1055 Taylor Street
San Francisco, CA 94108
415-673-5015 x 3330   Fax: 510-663-1421
scoates@Episcopalcharities.org
www.Episcopalcharities.org

Episcopal Charities provides services and support to congregations that wish to operate or sponsor programs serving people in their communities. Grant making and educational and fund developments are just some of the services provided.

Episcopal Community Services
Main Office at Old Saint Paul's
225 South Third Street
Philadelphia, PA 19106
215-351-1400   Fax: 215-351-1497
info@ecs1870.org
www.ecs1870.org

Episcopal Community Services California is dedicated to providing shelters, housing and vocational training to those in need.

Episcopal Relief and Development
815 Second Avenue
New York, NY 10017
800-334-7626, ext 5129 Fax: 212-687-5302
www.er-d.org

Episcopal Relief and Development (ERD) is a worldwide emergency assistance organization that provides relief to people in the wake of disaster and other times of need.

Episcopal Urban Caucus
Park West Station
PO Box 21182
New York, NY 10025

212-699-2998   Fax: 212-699-2998
www.Episcopalurbancaucus.org
Episcopal Urban Caucus (EUC) is devoted to articulating a vision of a church without racism.

Five Talents International
PO Box 331
Vienna, VA 22183
800-670-6355
www.fivetalents.org
Five Talents International combats poverty in the developing world by micro-enterprise development.

Habitat for Humanity International
1-800-422-4828 (1-800-HABITAT)
www.habitat.org/default.aspx
Habitat for Humanity International is an ecumenical Christian organization that is dedicated to eliminating substandard housing and homelessness.

Jubilee Ministry of the Episcopal Church
815 Second Avenue
New York, NY 10017
212-716-6000
episcopalchurh.org/109342_ENG_HTM.htm

The National Cathedral of Washington, D.C., formally known as the Cathedral Church of Saint Peter and Saint Paul, has served as a solemn setting for state functions, such as the 2004 funeral of president Ronald Reagan.

Jubilee Ministry is a network of congregations engaged in mission and ministry among and with the poor and oppressed.

United Thank Offering
815 Second Avenue
New York, NY 10017
212-922-5130
800-334-7626
www.Episcopalchurch.org/uto
United Thank Offering (UTO) was founded by Julia Emery and Ida Soule in 1889. UTO encourages daily prayers, offerings and awareness of the abundance of God's blessings. All offerings go towards funding a grant program that provides needed assistance all over the world.

E. Media and Communication

The ECUSA maintains a website at www.ecusa. anglican.org. Many of the diocese have their own newspapers available on the website.

Anglican Theological Review
600 Haven Street
Evanston, IL 60201
847-864-6024
http://anglicantheologicalreview.org
ATR is a quarterly journal of theological reflection.

Anglican Communion Office
Saint Andrew's House
16 Tavistock Crescent
London, W11 1AP   England
Telephone: + 44 (0) 20 7313 3900
Fax: +44 (0) 20 7313 3999
aco@anglicancommunion.org
www.anglicancommunion.org
Anglican/Episcopal World is the official magazine of the Anglican Communion and is published by the Anglican Communion Office.

The Episcopal Church Annual, also known as the Red Book, is a comprehensive, updated reference book on the Episcopal Church, with a wealth of information and current statistics. The Red Book is online at the website: www.theredbook.org.

Episcopal Life Online
815 Second Avenue
New York, NY 10017
212-716-6000 / 800-334-7626
www.Episcopal-life.org/Episcopal_life.htm
A national monthly publication of the ECUSA, providing broad coverage of the church.

Forward Movement
300 West Fourth Street
Cincinnati, OH 45202-2666 USA
513-721-6659   Fax: 513-721-0729
800-543-1813
Orders@forwarddaybyday.com
www.forwardmovement.org
Forward Day by Day provides daily inspirational reflection and mediation centered on a daily lectionary reading and using BCP-sanctioned lessons.

The Witness
The Episcopal Divinity School
99 Brattle Street
Cambridge, MA 02138
857-225-0433
editor@thewitness.org   www.thewitness.org
The Witness, a quarterly, is the voice of gospel witness in the Episcopal Church and Anglican Communion—an independent, unaffiliated operation, dedicated to progressive causes within the church.

Church Publishing Incorporated
445 Fifth Avenue
New York, NY 10016
www.theredbook.org/
Producer of prayer books, hymnals, and titles mandated by the General Convention through the Commission on Liturgy and Music.

Morehouse Publishing produces books on spirituality, liturgy and worship, prayer, the Bible, church history, theology, and Christian education.

St. Mark's Press
Good Shepherd Episcopal Church
8021 West 21st Street
Wichita, KS 67205
1-800-365-0439
goodshep2@sbcglobal.net
www.Episcopal-ks.org/shepherd/smpress.html
Produces the New Revised Standard and Revised Standard *Episcopal Eucharistic Lectionary.*

The Episcopal Cathedral Teleconferencing Network is a television/internet initiative of Trinity Episcopal Church in New York City. **The Episcopal Media Center** is an independent nonprofit facilty that develops mass media resources.

The Alliance for Christian Media
644 West Peachtree Street, Suite 300
Atlanta, GA 30308
1-800-229-3788   Fax: 404-815-0495
www.Grace.com
Part of the Grace Cathedral ministry, with programming on personal narrative, and spirituality.

FURTHER READING

A Brief History of the Episcopal Church
David L. Holmes
1993: Trinity Press International

A History of the Episcopal Church
Robert W. Pritchard
1991: Morehouse Publishing Co.

6 Evangelical Denominations

I. Origins and Early History

A. An American Christianity Is Born

THE CONTEMPORARY EVANGELICAL MOVEMENT WAS born of a wave of revivals that swept through America in the mid-eighteenth century. The First Great Awakening, sparked by charismatic preacher George Whitefield in 1740, made Americans receptive to the Second Great Awakening fifty years later, during which Charles Grandison Finney developed the style of revival meeting characteristic of evangelicalism today.

But such religious fervor was not isolated to America. At the same time Whitefield's captivating sermons were transforming the religious landscape of the New World, Anglican minister John Wesley was renewing British Christianity through the Methodist movement. Whitefield himself led the Evangelical Awakening in England, and revivalists throughout Europe (Germany, Scotland, the Netherlands, etc.) followed America's burgeoning evangelism even as America kept close watch on European developments. The transatlantic movement helped maintain ties between America and Europe—while simultaneously deepening American insistence on disestablishment of religion.

Indeed, the strains of evangelicalism were European in origin. A blending of Puritanism and Pietism, the main ideas espoused by evangelicals— personal conversion, piety, and sincere conviction of faith—were products of the German Reformed movement. Initiated by German Roman Catholic

Signs promoting revivals and tent meetings, such as this one for a revival in Yakima, Washington, were a common sight throughout the United States in the nineteenth and twentieth centuries.

monk Martin Luther in 1517, the Protestant Reformation commenced out of a desire by dissatisfied Catholics to break free of a church they believed had strayed from biblical precedent. Martin Luther's Ninety-five "protests" of Catholic Church doctrine and practices initiated a movement called Pietism, which sought to restore the life of the church through thorough study of Scripture, the belief in a "universal priesthood," practical demonstrations of Christianity in daily life, reaching out to unbelievers, and strong inner faith. In short, Pietism called Christians to a more genuinely pious life—one developed inwardly and expressed outwardly—and this was possible to anyone through study of the Bible alone. It moved away, then, from traditional church teachings and the church hierarchy, and the idea that good works alone could make a person more faithful.

Pietism arrived in America with the Pilgrims, and Puritanism was soon to follow. The Puritans desired a "pure" church, free of "popeish superstitions" and empty professions of holiness. While Puritans called for deeper reformation of the Church of England than had occurred, many Pilgrims, or "dissenters," were Separatists: they believed they must break from the Anglican Church altogether. Both groups placed much emphasis on the "conversion experience"—characterized by a sudden overwhelming desire to renounce sin and repent, newly taking on a life of righteousness—as integral to salvation.

Calvinism dominated the Protestant scene until the Second Great Awakening. Calvinism held that salvation (spiritual rebirth) was only possible for a predestined few, the "elect." All humans are born into sin, and remain so unless they undergo a conversion experience. The authenticity of such experiences was decided by church elders, who listened to conversion narratives and judged whether or not the narrators were members of the elect, and thus worthy of church membership.

George Whitefield had Calvinistic leanings himself, as did his contemporary, Jonathan Edwards. But these two men had a flair for the dramatic. Whitefield made his first appearance in the colonies in 1738, and by 1749 he was preaching throughout New England. A former actor, Whitefield utilized his personal charisma to engage large audiences—sometimes of up to eight thousand. Whitefield preached extemporaneously, though his sermons were well-prepared—meetings were held every day, and at any time. These gatherings would not be called "revivals" until fifty years later, but his method of preaching was revivalistic in nature in that he aimed to "revive" the dead husk of religion and instill people with spiritual yearning.

Edwards, occupying the pulpit at a Congregationalist church in Northampton, Massachusetts, delivered sermons full of fire and brimstone, bellowing warnings and stern demands for repentance. His most famous sermon, "Sinners in the Hands of Angry God," was typically of his style, which galvanized much of the Connecticut River Valley.

Revivalism spread from the North, down through the middle colonies, where Baptist, Methodist, Presbyterian, and Lutheran churches sprang up, and on to the South, where arose additional Methodist and Baptist organizations. The South witnessed perhaps the greatest transformation during the first awakening. Originally comprised of white settlers with lax ties to the Anglican Church, and African slaves of indigenous beliefs, both races were quickly caught up in the fever of salvation. The movement emphasized humanity's inherent equality in the eyes of God, and this appealed to both slaves and white women who must submit to a patriarchal society. Many blacks formed their own churches, where they found a measure of autonomy. Still others worshipped alongside their white masters—though seating was later segregated. Women were offered leadership roles in church services, functioning as exhorters, or those who inspired others to seek redemption. Evangelicalism reformed the South socially as well as religiously, and the subsequent loyalty it invoked is still evident in the phrase "Bible Belt" used to demarcate southern evangelicalism today.

More characteristic of modern evangelicalism is the theology and nature of the revivals led by Charles Grandison Finney. As a twenty-nine-year-old law student in Adams, New York, of no particular religious upbringing, Finney experienced a conversion that turned him from practicing law to pleading for Christ. Finney was ordained a Presbyterian minister five years later, but found himself at odds with his fellow clergymen. Having rejected the Calvinistic theory of predestination, Finney stressed that all men could be saved if only they chose to be. Just as the sinner chose to sin, Finney reasoned, the saved could choose to repent. God's love and forgiveness was available to all who were ready to accept it. In 1832, the tall, striking minister began to preach in New York City to thousands who embraced his message. Many chose to convert, and soon Finney began to consider such work "reaping converts." His desire to attain as many converts as possible led to notices of his revival meetings posted in newspapers, and door-to-door advertising. Finney's initiative is recognizable in the efforts of modern day evangelizer Billy Graham, who likewise used the media to reach broad audiences, and asked his listeners to "make a decision for Christ." Finney's era came to be known as the Second Great

Awakening, and persisted until the mid-nineteenth century. Many of his followers became ardent leaders of movements such as the abolition of slavery, prison reform, orphanage establishment, hospital building, and the founding of educational institutions.

In 1846, eight hundred Christians from ten countries met in London and set up the Evangelical Alliance. They saw this as "a new thing in church history, a definite organization for the expression of unity amongst Christian individuals belonging to different churches." However, the Alliance floundered on the issue of slavery. Despite this difficulty it provided a strong impetus for the establishment of national and regional evangelical fellowships.

William Booth, a Methodist minister, founded the Christian Mission in London, England, on July 5, 1865. This became the Salvation Army in 1878 as it took on a quasi-military style.

At the turn of the twentieth century, Modernist Christianity in the Protestant denominations was producing novel interpretations of the role of the Bible for a Christian, and the Bible's teachings. Their opponents saw these trends as a threat to Christian faith and the welfare of society, as accommodations to the Enlightenment and an abandonment of the principles of the Protestant Reformation.

The Niagara Creed

In the summer of 1878, evangelicals gathered in Clifton Springs, New York, for a one-week Bible conference. Known as the Believers' Meeting for Bible Study, participants continued to meet at Clifton Springs for two more years. The annual meetings moved to Niagara-on-the-Lake, Ontario, Canada, and became known as the Niagara Bible Conference. Some historians consider the Niagara Bible Conference, and the First and Second American Bible and Prophecy Conferences which it spawned, to be the primary sources from which the American fundamentalist and premillennial evangelical movements came.

As a basis for their meetings, leaders adopted a fourteen-point confession of faith, later known as the Niagara Creed:

1. All scripture is given by the inspiration of God.

2. The Godhead exists in the form of the Trinity, or three persons: Father, Son, and Holy Spirit, and that all three entities are similar in nature and attribute to God.

3. When Adam ate the forbidden fruit, he lost all spiritual life and subjected himself to the power of the devil.

4. This corruption of human nature was transmitted to the entire human race (excepting Jesus); therefore, every child is born essentially bad.

5. Therefore, no one can enter the kingdom of God unless born again—implanted with a new nature from the Holy Ghost.

6. Man is redeemed by the blood of Jesus Christ alone, who died for man's sinfulness in his stead.

7. Man may attain salvation through faith in Christ as savior alone.

8. Every man who accepts Jesus as his savior may himself be saved.

9. All scriptures should be read in relation to the ministry of Jesus Christ, and all serve as practical instruction.

10. The church is comprised of all who accept Christ; those baptized by the Holy Spirit are of one body, no matter race nor creed. Therefore, all should love one another.

11. The Holy Spirit is ever available to testify of Christ and serve as a divine Comforter.

12. Man must resist the temptations of the flesh, and live after the spirit.

13. The souls of believers are present with Christ after death; those of unbelievers are subject to eternal punishment.

14. Jesus will return after the millennium, and all should keep joyful watch for him.

The Fundamentals

In 1910, the General Assembly of the Presbyterian Church distilled Niagara's fourteen-point profession of faith into what later became known as the five fundamentals.

The Fundamentalist movement was a conservative Protestant response to liberal trends in their churches. The term "fundamentalist" derives from a series of twelve volumes entitled *The Fundamentals: A Testimony To The Truth*. The essays were written by sixty-four British and American conservative Protestant theologians between 1910 and 1915.

The movement sought to preserve what they saw as being a minimum orthodoxy, a fundamental Christianity, over against the liberals' abandonment of such basic features of a traditional understanding of the faith as the inerrancy of the Bible, the virgin birth of Christ, the bodily resurrection of Jesus, the authenticity of his miracles, and the belief that his death on the cross takes away sins. This defense of fundamental Christian tradition was called Fundamentalism, though in fact it was little more than orthodoxy as found in the official statements of faith of Protestant denominations.

Some Fundamentalists strongly advocated separation from those denominations and institutions in which modernism was dominant. Many of these identified the Fundamentalist cause with certain specific doctrines, approaches to culture, and styles of worship, preaching, or plans of church governance, which were not shared by their fellows—some of which, in fact, had only arisen in the previous century. Others strongly reacted against separatism and exclusiveness. They sought to distinguish their agenda to defend the fundamental orthodoxy familiar to their forebears, from the Fundamentalists who sought to establish a new orthodoxy. Some of the leaders of this broader party called themselves 'neo-"evangelicals."'

The Neo-Evangelical movement was a response among traditionally orthodox Protestants to fundamentalist Christianity's separatism, beginning in the 1920s and 1930s.

Neo-Evangelicals held the view that the modernist and liberal parties in the Protestant churches had surrendered their heritage as evangelicals by accommodating the views and values of the world. However they saw the Fundamentalists' separatism and rejection of the social gospel as an overreaction. They charged the modernists with having lost their identity as evangelicals, and attacked the Fundamentalists as having lost the Christ-like heart of Evangelicalism. They argued that the Gospel needed to be reasserted to distinguish it from the innovations of the liberals and the Fundamentalists.

Neo-Evangelicals sought to engage the modern world and the liberals in a positive way, remaining separate from worldliness but not from the world—a middle way, between modernism and the separating variety of Fundamentalism. They sought allies in denominational churches and liturgical traditions, among non-dispensationalists, and trinitarian varieties of Pentecostalism. They believed that in doing so, they were simply reacquainting Protestantism with its own recent tradition. The movement's aim at the outset was to reclaim the evangelical heritage in their respective churches, not to begin something new; and for this reason, following their separation from Fundamentalists, the same movement has been better known as merely evangelicalism. By the end of the twentieth century, this was the most influential development in American Protestant Christianity.

The term neo-evangelicalism no longer has any reliable meaning except for historical purposes. It is still self-descriptive of the movement to which it used to apply, to distinguish the parties in the developing fundamentalist split prior to the 1950s.

A lasting contribution of the Neo-Evangelical movement is the Fuller Theological Seminary of Pasadena, California. Founded in 1947, by famous radio evangelist Charles E. Fuller, Boston pastor Harold Ockenga, Carl F. H. Henry, Wilbur Moorehead Smith, and Harold Lindsell, it was established with the hopes of resurrecting fundamentalism from the depths of its anti-intellectual and socially isolationist stance. The seminary was founded with the intention of making it "the Caltech of Christian scholarship." Fuller's faculty and students represent a wide variety of Christian theological backgrounds, and vehement debates between students and professors on an array of issues are not uncommon in classrooms. Fuller is now the largest multidenominational seminary in the world.

Also opposed to evangelicalism's isolationism was Billy Graham, a Southern Baptist evangelist and spiritual adviser to multiple American Presidents. Graham suddenly came into national prominence in 1949, while holding an eight-week long series of revivals under circus tents in a Los Angeles parking lot. Graham's overt patriotism and appeals to youth (he himself was youthful) caught the interest of newspaper magnate William Randolph Heart, who ordered his editors to "puff Graham." Graham hosted a series of "crusades" throughout the United States and internationally, in countries such as England, Russia, and Australia. Graham's particular technique was to rent a large venue, preach the gospel, and then invite those who were inspired to learn more to come forward. The inspired, called "inquirers," were received by counselors, who spoke with them about evangelical theology, gave them instructional material, and prayed with them. The addition of counseling to the revival meeting was originated by Charles Grandison Finney. Also recalling Finney was Graham's desire to reach as many people as possible. A *Time* magazine article of 1993 claims that more than 2.5 million people have stepped forward at Billy's crusades to "accept Jesus Christ as their personal saviour."

B. Important Figures

John Wesley (1703–1791)

John Wesley was an eighteenth-century Anglican clergyman and Christian theologian who was an early leader in the Methodist movement.

In 1729, the famous "holy club" at Oxford University was formed by John's younger brother, Charles Wesley, and fellow students who called themselves Methodists because of their methodical habits.

In 1735, Wesley traveled to the Province of Georgia with his brother, Charles, to become a clergyman. He would remain in the colony for two years, returning to England in 1738. Upon his return to England, Wesley joined the Moravians, a Protestant denomination that he had encountered in Georgia.

He and other Methodists would firmly establish the religion in the 1740s through itinerant preaching and the subsequent founding of societies for believers.

Jonathan Edwards (1703–1758)

Jonathan Edwards was a colonial American Congregational preacher and theologian. His work is very broad in scope, but he is often associated with his defense of Calvinist theology and the Puritan heritage.

In 1734–1735, Edwards oversaw the initial stirrings of the First Great Awakening. He gained international fame as a revivalist and "theologian of the heart" after publishing *A Faithful Narrative of the Surprising Work of God* (1738), which described the awakening in his church and served as an empirical model for American and British revivalists alike.

During the widespread revivals of the 1730s and 1740s Edwards became very well known as a revivalist preacher who subscribed to an experiential interpretation of Reformed theology that emphasized the sovereignty of God, the depravity of humankind, the reality of hell, and the necessity of a "New Birth" conversion. While critics assailed the convictions of many supposed converts as illusory (and even the work of the devil), Edwards became a brilliant apologist for the revivals. In *The Distinguishing Marks of a Work of the Spirit of God* (1741), *Some Thoughts Concerning the Present Revival* (1742), *A Treatise Concerning Religious Affections* (1746), and *The Life of David Brainerd* (1749), he sought to isolate the signs of true sainthood from false belief. His intellectual framework for revivalism pioneered a new psychology of affections, later invoked by William James in his classic *Varieties of Religious Experience* (1902).

Jonathan Edwards (1703–1758) was a clergyman and theologian whose writings paved the way for the "Great Awakening" of religious fervor in mid-eighteenth-century America.

In 1750, Edwards's church dismissed him from Northampton after he attempted to impose stricter qualifications for admission to the sacraments upon his congregation. Concerned that the "open admission" policies instituted by Stoddard allowed too many hypocrites and unbelievers into church membership, he became embroiled in a bitter controversy with his congregation, area ministers, and political leaders.

From Northampton, Edwards went to the mission post of Stockbridge, on the western border of Massachusetts, where he served from 1751 to 1757. Here he led a small English congregation, was a missionary to 150 Mohican and Mohawk families, and wrote many of his major works, including those that addressed the "Arminian controversy."

Edwards rejected the Arminian modification of the Calvinist doctrines of predestination and that the divine grace and will of God alone will save humanity. In *A Careful and Strict Inquiry into the Modern Prevailing Notions of that Freedom of Will* (1754), he attempted to prove that the will was determined by the inclination of either sin or grace in the soul.

George Whitefield (1714–1770)

One of the greatest evangelists of all time, George Whitefield was ordained in the Church of England, with which he was constantly at odds. Whitefield became a sensation throughout England, preaching to huge audiences. In 1738, he made the first of seven visits to America. Whitefield's preaching tour of the colonies, from 1739 to 1741, was the high-water mark of the Great Awakening there. A sermon in Boston attracted as many as 30,000 people. Whitefield's success has been attributed to his resonant voice, theatrical presentation, emotional stimulation, message simplification, and clever exploitation of emerging advertising techniques.

The "new birth," prescribed by Christ for Nicodemus (John 3:1–8), was the term evangelicalism used for the conversion experience. For George Whitefield and other evangelical preachers the new birth was essential to Christian life, even though, as

Whitefield admitted, "how this glorious Change is wrought in the Soul cannot easily be explained."

Whitefield acquired many enemies, who assailed evangelicalism as a distortion of the Gospel and attacked him and his followers for alleged failings.

Charles Grandison Finney (1792–1875)

Primarily raised in the wilderness of western New York, Finney had very little exposure to religion as a child. His parents, simple farmers, were not well-versed in any creed, and the few sermons he heard were, in his opinion, so ignorant, that they often kept the townspeople laughing in derision for days afterwards.

At the age of twenty-four, Finney took up Freemasonry, a fraternal system of morality, and joined Sun Lodge No. 32 in Warren, New York. He advanced to Master Mason and held this title for eight years. Also, though Finney never attended college, he was able to study the law as a lawyer's apprentice. His tall stature, piercing blue eyes, and strong presence helped him progress toward positions of leadership in both ventures. According to Finney's memoirs, at the age of twenty-nine, he experienced a spiritual awakening, and was "saved." The very next day, Finney's client asked if he was prepared for the trial scheduled that afternoon. He replied, "I have a retainer from the Lord Jesus Christ to plead his cause, I cannot plead yours" (*Memoirs*, 24). Finney became a minister of the Presbyterian Church, and left the Freemasons in 1824. In 1832, he relocated to New York City, where he became pastor of the Free Presbyterian Chatham Street Chapel. He would later found and pastor the Broadway Tabernacle (today's Broadway United Church of Christ).

Finney's unique "revival" approach to the evangelicalism planted in America by the first Great Awakening would launch a second Great Awakening—and set the precedent for modern evangelists such as Billy Graham. Finney's most catching addition to established evangelism was the idea that salvation was dependent merely upon one's will to repent. Directly opposing Calvinism, which held that only a select few were predestined for salvation, Finney's theology made redemption available to all who desired it. He advertised his revival meetings in newspapers and pamphlets, drawing many who sought conversion experiences at the hands of the fiery preacher. Finney's popularity appealed especially to Methodists and Baptists, and soon many of his critics had adopted his "new measures." Finney's new revivalism occupied much of the American religious attention for fifty years, from 1790–1840.

II. Tenets and Beliefs

A. Articles of Faith

Evangelical Christians hold four concepts central to their ideology:

• Emphasis on the conversion experience, also called being saved, or new birth or born again after John 3:3. Thus Evangelicals often refer to themselves as born-again Christians. This experience is said to be received by "faith alone" and to be given by God as the result of "grace alone."

• The Protestant canon of the Bible as the primary, or only, source of religious authority, as God's revelation to humanity. Thus, the doctrine of Sola Scriptura is often affirmed and emphasized. Bible prophecy is also emphasized.

• Encouragement of evangelism (the act of sharing one's religious beliefs with others) in organized missionary work or by personal encounters and relationships with others.

• A central focus on Christ's redeeming work on the cross as the only means for salvation and the forgiveness of sins.

Evangelical Distinctives

Author Alistair McGrath expands upon these concepts and posits six "Evangelical Distinctives":

• The supreme authority of Scripture as a source of knowledge of God and a guide to Christian living.

• The majesty of Jesus Christ, both as incarnate God and Lord and as the Savior of sinful humanity.

• The lordship of the Holy Spirit.

• The need for personal conversion.

• The priority of evangelism for both individual Christians and the church as a whole.

• The importance of the Christian community for spiritual nourishment, fellowship, and growth.

B. Statements of Belief

There have been three international statements of beliefs that have been written by Evangelicals from many nations:

Lausanne Covenant (1974)

The Lausanne Committee for World Evangelization (LCWE) is an "international movement for the purpose of encouraging Christians and churches everywhere to pray, study, plan, and work together for the evangelization of the world." During 1974, Fundamentalist Christians and other evangelical Protestants from over 150 nations attended the International Congress on World Evangelization at Lausanne, Switzerland. British theologian Rev. John R. W. Stott of England, led the Drafting Committee for the Lausanne Covenant. He writes: "The reason the expression 'Lausanne Covenant' was chosen in preference to 'Lausanne Declaration' is that we wanted to do more than find an agreed formula of words. We were determined not just to declare something, but to do something, namely to commit ourselves to the task of world evangelization."

The Covenant discusses many evangelical beliefs, such as the inspiration and inerrancy of the Bible, the Trinity, the Second Coming, The Anti-christ, the Great Commission to witness to the entire world— particularly the two thirds of the world's population who have not been evangelized—the exclusivity of Christianity, and concern over Christian faith groups who have deviated from historical Christian teachings. They are committed to ending oppression based on race, religion, color, culture, class, gender, and age. The banning of discrimination on the basis of sexual orientation, and the nature and existence of Hell are not discussed.

The Amsterdam Affirmations (1983)

In 1983, attendees of the International Conference for Itinerant Evangelists in Amsterdam composed the Affirmations. The conference was organized by members of the Billy Graham Evangelistic Association (BGEA) and Campus Crusade for Christ. Attending "Amsterdam '83" were approximately 3,870 invited conservative Protestants from 133 nations.

A second, larger conference, sponsored by the BGEA and modeled on Amsterdam '83, was held in 1986 in Amsterdam. It was also called the International Conference for Itinerant Evangelists and is commonly called Amsterdam '86.

The Manila Manifesto (1989)

This document was prepared by evangelicals attending an international conference sponsored by the Lausanne Committee for World Evangelization (LCWE). It was held in Manila, the Philippines, and was attended by over 3,000 conservative Protestants.

The Manila Manifesto consisted of two parts: a section consisting of twenty-one affirmations and a larger document that elaborates on these affirmations. Although the Manila Manifesto of 1989 did not refer to biblical inerrancy, it confirmed the participants' commitment to the Lausanne Covenant.

C. Scripture and Sacred Literature

The Bible is accepted by evangelicals as reliable and the ultimate authority in matters of faith and practice. The Protestant Reformation doctrines of sola scriptura and sola fide are primary. The historical accuracy of the miracles of Jesus and the virgin birth, crucifixion, resurrection, and Second Coming are asserted, although there are a variety of under-standings of the end times and eschatology.

Evangelical churches, unlike Eastern and Roman churches, reject an infallible authoritative tradition that is on par with scripture. Some evangelicals hold that the Bible confirms its own authority, pointing out that Jesus frequently quotes scripture as his final "court of appeal" (see Matthew 4:4, 6, and 10; 21:13; Mark 9:12). Protestants continually ask if an aspect of belief and practice is true to the Bible, based on the reasoning that, if the Bible is inerrant and the only form of God's Word, then it must be fully reliable. Tradition, on the other hand, is subject to human memory, and may have many versions of the same events or truths, some contradictory.

A small group of Fundamentalists and theologians believe that God guided the translators of the King James Version, so that that version should be considered as authoritative. However, those who hold this opinion do not extend it to the King James translations of the Deuterocanonical books, which were produced along with the rest of the Authorized Version. Modern translations differ from the King James Version on numerous points, sometimes resulting from access to different early texts. Upholders of the KJV would nevertheless hold that the Protestant canon of KJV is itself an inspired text and therefore remains authoritative. The King James Only movement asserts that the KJV is the sole English translation free from error.

In regard to biblical inerrancy, a summit was convened in Chicago in 1978, sponsored by the International Council on Biblical Inerrancy. The result of this gathering of 300 evangelical scholars was a statement defending the position of biblical inerrancy against a perceived trend toward liberal conceptions of Scripture.

Leading inerrantists regard the Chicago Statement as a thorough statement of what they mean by inerrancy. The Statement established that inerrancy applies only to the original manuscripts (which no longer exist, but can be inferred on the basis of extant copies), not to the copies or translations themselves. Moreover, inerrancy does not mean blind literalism, but allows for figurative, poetic and phenomenological language, as long as it is accurate—according to a doctrine formulated in 1880.

D. Important Thinkers and Theologians

Reinhold Niebuhr (1892–1971)

Born in Wright City, Missouri, to parents heavily involved with German Evangelicalism (Niebuhr's father was an ordained minister, and his mother the daughter of a missionary), both Reinhold and his brother, Helmut Richard, would assume active leadership roles in theological thinking. Reinhold was very close to his father, and decided

Theologian Reinhold Niebuhr composed what is popularly called the Serenity Prayer in 1943.

to likewise join the ministry. From 1807 to 1810 he enrolled in the evangelical Elmhurst College, near Chicago. Upon graduation, he moved on to his father's alma mater, Eden Seminary at St. Louis, Missouri, then completed his studies at Yale Divinity School, earning a bachelor's degree in divinity. Finally, in 1915, he was ordained as a pastor.

That year, the German Evangelical missionary board appointed Niebuhr minister of Bethel Evangelical Church in Detroit. Situated in the heart of the booming automobile industry, Detroit afforded Niebuhr plenty of exposure to the working-class conditions tolerated by automobile industry laborers who flocked to the area in search of work. In fact, over the thirteen years Niebuhr served in Detroit, his congregation rose from 65 to 700 hundred—reflective of the nation's desperation for employment under any conditions. But Niebuhr would not remain silent on this point.

In 1929, Niebuhr published *Leaves from the Notebook of A Tamed Cynic,* in which he deplored the conditions suffered by laborers of the Henry Ford factory in Detroit. Niebuhr became an outspoken advocate of socialist principles in social and economic matters, even allowing union organizers to speak from his pulpit regarding workers' rights.

Niebuhr's opposition to a variety of social evils found a centralized target in his criticism of the Social Gospel of the early twentieth century. He lamented such theology as helpless in its eschewal of violence, which he considered essential to profound reformation. In the 1930s, he joined the militant faction of the Socialist Party of America, and in 1932 supported the socialist candidate for President. A decade later, he supported Roosevelt's New Deal mixed economics. He considered himself a "Christian realist," a phrase that caught on and evolved into an entire movement known as Christian Realism, captured in Niebuhr's work, *The Nature and Destiny of Man.* According to this philosophy, the kingdom of heaven cannot be realized in a world inherently corrupt, and so those on earth must compromise their ideals.

Niebuhr taught Applied Christianity (Ethics and Theology) at Union Theological Seminary in Manhattan, New York, from 1928 to 1960. He also used this time for activist work, supporting the U.S. involvement in World War II, anticommunism, and nuclear weaponry. He wrote *The Irony of American History* in 1952, an accounting of the various struggles on political, theological, and moral fronts he had weathered in the face of the nation's social ills. Niebuhr's writings and ideologies have influenced many prominent subsequent social leaders, such as Martin Luther King Jr., Kenneth Waltz, and Barack Obama.

In 1964, President Lyndon B. Johnson awarded Niebuhr the Presidential Medal of Freedom, and Union Theological Seminary named the section of West 120th Street between Broadway and Riverside Drive in New York City Reinhold Niebuhr Place.

Harold Ockenga (1905–1985)

Harold Ockenga was a leading figure of twentieth-century American evangelicalism, part of the reform movement known as Neo-Evangelicalism. He was a prolific author on biblical, theological, and devotional topics. Ockenga helped to found the Fuller Theological Seminary and Gordon-Conwell Theological Seminary, as well as the National Association of Evangelicals.

In addition to his pastoral career and writings, Ockenga became a significant leader in a mid-twentieth century reforming movement known as Neo-Evangelicalism or New Evangelicalism. The roots of this are found in the theological controversy between Protestant fundamentalists and Protestant liberals in the earlier part of the twentieth century. Much of this controversy centered on questions of the historicity of the Bible, biblical inerrancy, creationism, and evolution, and various doctrines such as the deity of Christ, the virgin birth of Christ, the bodily resurrection of Christ, and the second advent of Christ. The reaction of many fundamentalists to liberal Protestant theology and modern beliefs was a withdrawal from culture and higher education.

However, Ockenga, and other younger, emerging figures inside these churches, felt uncomfortable about the militant isolation from culture. These included figures such as Carl F. H. Henry, Harold Lindsell, Wilbur Smith, and Edward John Carnell.

In an effort to redress these concerns Ockenga and J. Elwin Wright of the New England Fellowship planned the establishing of a new organization known as the National Association of Evangelicals. Ockenga served as its founding president from 1942–1944. Those affiliated with the association were interested in maintaining many of the biblical concerns of militant Fundamentalists, but also sought to reform Fundamentalism from its anti-cultural and anti-intellectual tendencies.

III. Rites and Rituals

A. The Calendar

The vast majority of evangelicals disregard the conventional church calendar. Some holidays, however, are celebrated by many:

- **Advent Season** (Preparation for the Birth of Jesus)–The 4 Sundays before Christmas.
- **Christmas Season** (The birth of Jesus)–December 25 to January 5.
- **Epiphany Season**–January 6 through start of Lent.
- **Epiphany** (or manifestation) **of God**–January 6.
- **The Baptism of our Lord**–Sunday after Epiphany.
- **Transfiguration Sunday**–Last Sunday of Epiphany.
- **Ash Wednesday**–6 weeks before Easter.
- **Palm Sunday**–Sunday before Easter.
- **Holy Week**–Week before Easter (Events leading up to the death and resurrection of Jesus).
- **Maundy Thursday** (Commemorates the Last Supper)–Thursday of Holy Week.
- **Good Friday**–Friday of Holy Week.

Easter Season

- **Easter Day** (Celebrates the resurrection of Jesus)–First Sunday after the first Paschal full moon after the start of spring.
- **Pentecost** (Commemorates the Descent of the Holy Ghost upon the Apostles, 50 days after the Resurrection of Christ, on the ancient Jewish festival called the "feast of weeks" or Pentecost)–8 weeks after Easter.
- **Season of Pentecost**–Pentecost through the start of Advent.
- **Trinity Sunday**–Week after Pentecost.
- **Reformation Day** (Martin Luther nails his Ninety-five Theses to the door of the church of Wittenberg, Germany, on Oct 31, 1517)–October 31.

- **Reformation Sunday**–Last Sunday of October.
- **All Saints Day**–November 1.
- **All Saints Sunday**–First Sunday of November.
- **Christ the King Sunday**–Last Sunday of Pentecost (Sunday before Advent).

B. Worship and Liturgy

While the style of a liturgy can vary at the denominational subset and congregation levels, with elements added or modified, below is a general overview of an evangelical worship service:

- **Call to Worship**

The words of invitation with which a worship service begins (often a verse or two of Scripture).

- **Prayer of Confession**

A prayer spoken by the congregation in unison that confesses both one's individual sins and the congregation's collective sins.

- **Assurance of Pardon/singing of the Gloria Patri**

After the Prayer of Confession, the minister declares, "In Jesus Christ, we are forgiven." This is done to reaffirm the Scripture's teaching, "If we confess our sins, He who is faithful and just will forgive our sins and cleanse us from all unrighteousness." The congregation responds to this declaration by singing Gloria Patri, which is a song of praise to the Trinity (Father, Son and Holy Spirit).

- **Announcements,** read by the pastor
- **First Scripture lesson,** usually from the Old Testament (read by the pastor or a lay person).
- **Anthem:** Music sung by the choir or a soloist just before the sermon.
- **Second Scripture lesson**, usually New Testament (read by the pastor).
- **Sermon:** The interpretation or explanation of the Scripture lesson used during the worship service.

C. Life Cycle Events

Baptism

Many evangelical Christians hold that baptism is something of an "outward expression of an inward change." Baptism is done in obedience to Christ, showing others outwardly that they were changed inwardly when they committed their life to Christ and became a new creation.

The ecumenical paper Baptism, Eucharist and Ministry, prepared by representatives across a spectrum of Christian, Orthodox, Roman Catholic, and Protestant traditions of Christianity, attempts to express a common understanding of baptism, as it is derived from the New Testament:

. . . According to Acts 2:38, baptisms follow from Peter's preaching baptism in the name of Jesus and lead those baptized to the receiving of Christ's Spirit, the Holy Ghost, and life in the community: "They devoted themselves to the apostles' teaching and fellowship, to the breaking of bread and the prayers" (2:42) as well as to the distribution of goods to those in need (2:45). Those who heard, who were baptized and entered the community's life, were already made witnesses of and partakers in the promises of God for the last days: the forgiveness of sins through baptism in the name of Jesus and the outpouring of the Holy Ghost on all flesh (2:38). Similarly, in what may well be a baptismal pattern, 1 Peter testifies that proclamation of the resurrection of Jesus Christ and teaching about new life (1:3–21) lead to purification and new birth (1:22–23). This, in turn, is followed by eating and drinking God's food (2:2–3), by participation in the life of the community—the royal priesthood, the new temple, the people of God (2:4–10)—and by further moral formation (2:11 ff.). At the beginning of 1 Peter the writer sets this baptism in the context of obedience to Christ and sanctification by the Spirit (1:2). So baptism into Christ is seen as baptism into the Spirit (cf. 1 Cor. 12:13). In the fourth gospel Jesus' discourse with Nicodemus indicates that birth by water and Spirit becomes the gracious means of entry into the place where God rules (John 3:5).

The most commonly cited reference for the practice of baptism by Christians is the "Great Commission," found in Matthew 28: 18–20. It is typically viewed as the rite by which a person is joined to Jesus and his body, the Church, in connection with which the baptized person who has received the Holy Spirit is considered to be a Christian.

Those who reject infant baptism often substitute infant "dedication," pledging the church's support of the infant's family during the child's upbringing. They will defer actual baptism until the child reaches the age of moral apprehension. Prior to that age, the child is regarded as "innocent" of sin.

Since the first ecumenical Council of Nicaea in 325 CE, the common baptismal formula used in most churches has been based on the Trinitarian formula found in Matthew 28:19 where Jesus commanded his disciples to baptize in the name of the Father, Son and Holy Ghost. Generally, Evangelical Christians, including Pentecostals, practice this form of baptism. However, several subsets of the Evangelical Christian movement reject or modify this tradition.

Oneness Pentecostals, for example, reject the decision made in 325 CE and instead baptize by saying "in the name of Jesus Christ," "in the name of the Lord Jesus Christ," or "in the name of Jesus." Baptism "in the name of Jesus" (or any other synonymous Christological phrasing) is how they claim the primitive church baptized before the ecumenical council. They also believe water baptism by full immersion and receiving the baptism of the Holy Ghost with the immediate and outward evidence of speaking in other tongues is essential to their salvation.

Nuptials

Evangelical Christian denominations typically follow the traditional Christian wedding ceremony outlined below. Elements may be added or excluded according to the traditions or beliefs of a congregation or denominational subset:

Opening Remarks/"The Call to Worship." In a Christian wedding ceremony, the opening remarks, which traditionally begin with the phrase "Dearly Beloved," are an invitation to worship God. These opening remarks will invite guests present to participate with the couple in worship.

The Opening Prayer. As prayer is an essential ingredient to Christian worship the beginning prayer, also called an invocation, invites God's presence and blessing to be upon the wedding ceremony.

Giving Away of the Bride. A parent, usually the father, "gives" his daughter to the groom as a symbol of the parent's blessing of the marriage.

Worship Song or Hymn. The music for this portion of the ceremony is not only an expression of worship but is also a reflection of the couples emotional and spiritual bond. The piece performed can be a worship song sung by the congregation, a hymn, an instrumental, or a solo.

The Charge to Bride and Groom. The minister performing the wedding ceremony will direct the charge to the couple as a reminder of their individual duties and roles in the marriage and prepare them for the vows they are about to take.

The Pledge. During the pledge, the couple declares to the gathered guests and witnesses that they make this commitment of their own free will. This is distinct from the wedding vows, in which the couple declares their promises directly to each other.

Wedding Vows. The bride and Groom now face one another. Although every element of a Christian wedding is important, this is the central focus of the service. During the vows, the couple makes a promise to one another publicly, before God and the witnesses present, to do everything within their power to help each other grow in becoming what God has created them to be, despite all adversities, as long as they both live. It is a sacred vow, expressing the entrance into a covenant relationship.

Exchanging of the Rings. The exchanging of the rings expresses the couple's promise of faithfulness to each other. The ring is a concrete expression of the couple's bond.

Lighting of the Unity Candle. The lighting of the unity candle in a Christian wedding ceremony symbolizes the joining of two lives into one. Typically two taper candles are placed on either side of the larger pillar candle or unity candle. The taper candles represent the lives of the couple as individuals prior to marriage. The couple will pick up their individual candles and, in unison, will light the unity candle. Then they will blow out their own candles, symbolizing the end of their separate lives.

The Pronouncement. The pronouncement officially declares that the bride and groom are now husband and wife. The wedding guests are reminded that everyone should respect the union God has created and that no one should try to separate the couple.

Communion. Many times couples will incorporate Communion into the wedding ceremony, making C ommunion their very first act as a married couple.

The Closing Prayer. This benediction concludes the Christian wedding ceremony. It typically expresses the wishes of the congregation, through the minister, that God may bless the new couple with His presence.

D. Family Life

Husband and Wife

Evangelicals take a strict view of the nature of marriage. For Evangelicals, marriage is the only appropriate channel for sexual expression and divorce is permissible, if at all, only in very specific circumstances such as infidelity. Marriage is seen as a solemn covenant between the couple and God. The man is seen as the head of the household and his wife is expected to submit to him. However, there are two views within Evangelicalism of how this should work out in practice:

The traditionalist or complementarian view sees the husband as having loving authority over the wife as the servant-leader of the household in following Christ's example. The wife's role is to cheerfully sub-

mit to this authority where it does not conflict with her conscience or with biblical teaching.

The egalitarian view sees the husband's headship as meaning he is the source who works to ensure his wife's growth and development as a person. The wife's submission is seen in the context of Paul's injunction (Ephesians 5:21) for all Christians to submit to one another.

Proponents of both views emphasize that headship and submission are worked out in the context of a husband being expected to protect and care for his wife and put her needs before his own. These principles reflect the concept that Christ is the head of the church, or those who are his followers, and loves her even to the point of dying for her.

IV. Denominations and Demographics

A. History

There are three senses in which the term "evangelical" is used today as we enter the twenty-first-century. The first is to see as "evangelical" all Christians who affirm a few key doctrines and practical emphases. British historian David Bebbington approaches evangelicalism from this direction and notes four specific hallmarks of evangelical religion: conversionism, the belief that lives need to be changed; activism, the expression of the Gospel in effort; biblicism, a particular regard for the Bible; and crucicentrism, a stress on the sacrifice of Christ on the cross. A second sense is to look at evangelicalism as an organic group of movements and religious tradition. Within this context "evangelical" denotes a style as much as a set of beliefs. As a result, groups as disparate as black Baptists and Dutch Reformed Churches, Mennonites and Pentecostals, Catholic charismatics and Southern Baptists all come under the evangelical umbrella, demonstrating just how diverse the movement really is. A third sense of the term is as the self-ascribed label for a coalition that arose during the Second World War. This group came into being as a reaction against the perceived anti-intellectual, separatist, belligerent nature of the fundamentalist movement in the 1920s and 1930s.

Importantly, Evangelicalism's core personalities (like Harold John Ockenga and Billy Graham), institutions (for instance, Moody Bible Institute and Wheaton College), and organizations (such as the National Association of Evangelicals and Youth for Christ) have played pivotal roles in giving the wider movement a sense of cohesion that extends beyond these "card-carrying" evangelicals.

Fundamentalism

"Fundamentalist" is a term that is frequently bandied about in the news media these days. Unfortunately, this term has been used so casually in describing anyone who seems to hold some sort of traditional religious belief, be they a Bible Baptist TV preacher, a Hasidic rabbi, a Mormon housewife, or a soldier of the Islamic Jihad—the word has become nearly useless. When used within the North American historical context, however, there are precedents for the use of this term that restores a sense of descriptive cohesion. Fundamentalism was a movement that arose in the late-nineteenth and early-twentieth centuries within American Protestantism reacting against "modernist" theology and biblical criticism as well as changes in the nation's cultural and social scene. Taking its name from "The Fundamentals" (1910–1915), a twelve-volume set of essays combating Liberal theology, the movement grew by leaps and bounds after World War I.

During the 1920s, fundamentalists waged a war against modernism in three ways: by (unsuccessfully) attempting to regain control of Protestant denominations, mission boards, and seminaries; by supporting (with mixed success) Prohibition, Sunday "blue laws," and other measures defending traditional Protestant morality and sensibilities; and (fairly successfully) by attempting to stop the teaching of evolution in the public schools, a doctrine which they

saw as inextricably linked to the development of "German" higher criticism and the source of the Great War.

This last strategy resulted in the infamous Scopes Trial fiasco of 1925 (later fictionalized in the Hollywood-exaggerated play and film *Inherit the Wind*) in which a substitute biology teacher in Dayton, Tennessee was charged with illegally teaching evolution to his class. The circus atmosphere of the trial, pitting Presbyterian layman, former Secretary of State and three-time Democratic presidential candidate William Jennings Bryan for the prosecution against the famed Chicago criminal lawyer Clarence Darrow for the defense, discredited the movement in the eyes of the intellectual and media elites, resulting in fundamentalism's virtual disappearance from the nation's cultural stage.

Since the 1940s, the term "fundamentalist" has come to denote a particularly aggressive style related to the conviction that the separation from cultural decadence and apostate (read liberal) churches are telling marks of faithfulness to Christ. Most self-described fundamentalist churches today are conservative, separatist Baptist (though often calling themselves "Bible Baptist" or simply "Bible" churches) congregations such as the churches of the General Association of Regular Baptist Churches (GARBC), or the Independent Fundamental Churches of America (IFCA). Institutions associated with this movement would include Bob Jones University (Greenville, S.C.) and Tennessee Temple (Chattanooga, Tenn.); representative publications are *The Sword of the Lord* and *The Biblical Evangelist*.

The original twentieth-century Fundamentalist movement broke up along very definable lines within conservative Evangelical Protestantism as issues progressed. Many sects, large and small, were produced by this schism. Neo-Evangelicalism, Reformed and Lutheran Confessionalism, the Heritage movement, and Paleo-Orthodoxy have all developed distinct identities, but none of them acknowledge any more than a historical overlap with the Fundamentalist movement. They are fundamentalists in a sense, but there is a more precise definition for each and they do not refer to themselves as fundamentalist. In contrast, today's Fundamentalist movement looks to the Fundamentalist-Modernist Controversy for its identity and as its primary historical point of reference.

Thus, many Evangelical groups may be described as "fundamentalist" in the broad sense, who do not belong in the "Fundamentalist movement" in the narrow sense. Many Evangelicals believe in the doctrine of biblical inerrancy, a basic issue of difference in the Fundamentalist-Modernist Controversy a century ago. The Chicago Statement on Biblical Inerrancy, for instance, was signed in 1978 by nearly 300 conservative scholars, including James Boice, Norman Geisler, John Gerstner, Carl F. H. Henry (founder of *Christianity Today*), Kenneth Kantzer, Harold Lindsell, John Warwick Montgomery, Roger Nicole, J. I. Packer, Robert Preus, Earl Radmacher, Francis Schaeffer, R. C. Sproul, and John Wenham. Very few if any of these men fit the definition of or identify themselves with today's Fundamentalist Movement.

Pentecostalism and the Charismatic Movement

One of the fastest-growing segments of the wider evangelical movement has been its Pentecostal branch. Pentecostalism as a movement came into being in the early 1900s in a series of separate revivals. The new movement embodied an evolving body of teachings from itinerant evangelists and Bible teachers such as Charles Parham, William Seymour, and A. J. Tomlinson on the end-times, signs and wonders, and the gifts of the Holy Spirit. While the early revivals associated with these individuals occurred in (respectively) Kansas and Texas, California, and the mountains of Tennessee and North Carolina, the news of a "new" outpouring of God's Spirit spread quickly in North America and almost simultaneously spread, or was reported, overseas. Most distinctive about this movement was an exuberant worship style and the experience of glossolalia—speaking in tongues—which was seen as a return to the apostolic experience of the Book of Acts and the biblical baptism of the Holy Spirit.

While the Pentecostal movement was traditionally associated with the impoverished margins of American culture—particularly among southern whites and blacks—its influence began to spread during the 1950s through the visibility of healing evangelists like Oral Roberts, groups like the Full Gospel Business Men's Fellowship, and the migration of large numbers of Southern Protestants to the Midwest and Pacific Coast. By the 1960s, Pentecostal ideas and style began to surface in the "mainline" Protestant churches, "officially" beginning in 1960, when Dennis Bennett, an Episcopal priest in Van Nuys, California, announced to his congregation that he had spoken in tongues. The movement quickly spread to other mainline denominations and, by the mid-1960s, to the Roman Catholic and Orthodox Churches. The movement's visibility and networks were further strengthened by the success of the Pentecostal-leaning "Jesus People" movement among American youth in the late '60s and 1970s. In the 1980s, a vigorous, independent network of charismatic churches and organizations (at times described as the "Third Wave") emerged, including churches such as the Vineyard Christian Fellowship. In recent years, a wave of new revivals characterized by such manifestations as "holy laughter" and associated with the Toronto Airport Fellowship and Brownsville Assembly of God in Pensacola, Florida have been highly influential within Pentecostal and charismatic circles.

Most significant about the contemporary impact of these movements is the effect they have had overseas, leading many to tag Pentecostalism "world evangelicalism." In many parts of the Third World, Pentecostalism has made significant numbers of new converts. In fact, many analysts speculate that within the next decade Pentecostalism may even overtake the Roman Catholic Church as the largest Christian presence in Latin America.

B. Comparison of Tenets and Practices

Fundamentalism

Christian fundamentalists see their scripture, a combination of the Hebrew Bible and the New Testament, as both infallible and historically accurate. The New Testament represents a new covenant between God and human beings, which is held to fulfill the Old Testament, in regard to God's redemptive plan. On the basis of this confidence in Scripture, many fundamentalist Christians accept the account of scripture as being literally true.

It is important to distinguish between the "literalist" and Fundamentalist groups within the Christian community. Literalists, as the name indicates, hold that the Bible should be taken literally in every part. English-language Bibles are themselves usually translations and therefore not a literal word-forword rendering of the original texts; the King James Version is a notable exception, which, while poetic, uses arcane language. Literalism can also encompass believing that only one translation of the Bible (usually the KJV) is valid for use.

Many Christian Fundamentalists, on the other hand, are for the most part content to hold that the Bible should be taken literally only where there is no indication to the contrary.

The term "fundamentalist" has historically referred specifically to members of the various Protestant denominations who subscribed to the five "fundamentals" (inerrancy of the Scriptures, virgin birth and the deity of Jesus, doctrine of substitutionary atonement through God's grace and human faith, bodily resurrection of Jesus and the authenticity of Christ's miracles), rather than fundamentalists forming an independent denomination. Over time the term came to be associated with a particular segment of evangelical Protestantism, who distinguished themselves by their separatist approach toward modernity, toward aspects of the culture that they feel typify the modern world, and toward other Christians who did not similarly separate themselves.

Fundamentalists differ from Pentecostals in their strong insistence upon "correct" doctrine and often advocate separatism (which often also divides fundamentalists from each other) as opposed to the experiential emphasis of Pentecostals.

Fundamentalists also criticize evangelicals for a lack of concern for doctrinal purity and for a lack of discernment in ecumenical endeavors in working cooperatively with other Christians of differing doctrinal views

Pentecostals

One of the most prominent distinguishing characteristics of Pentecostalism from Evangelicalism is its emphasis on the work of the Holy Spirit. Pentecostals believe that everyone who is genuinely saved has the Holy Spirit with them. But unlike most other Christians they believe that there is a second work of the Holy Spirit called the baptism of the Holy Spirit in which the Holy Spirit is now in them, and which opens a believer up to a closer fellowship with the Holy Spirit and empowers them for Christian service. Speaking in tongues, also known as glossolalia, is the normative proof, but not the only proof, of the baptism with the Holy Spirit. Most major Pentecostal churches also accept the corollary that those who don't speak in tongues have not received the blessing that they call the Baptism of the Holy Spirit. This claim is uniquely Pentecostal and is one of the few consistent differences from Charismatic theology.

Most Pentecostal churches and denominations accept a Trinitarian Theology. The world's largest Pentecostal denomination, the Assemblies of God, holds to this belief, as does the Elim Pentecostal Church, the Apostolic Church, Church of God, the Church of God in Christ, and the Foursquare Church. Some Pentecostal churches however hold to Oneness theology, which decries the traditional doctrine of the Trinity as unbiblical. The largest Pentecostal Oneness denomination in the United States is the United Pentecostal Church. Oneness Pentecostals, are sometimes known as Jesus-Name, Apostolics, or by their detractors as Jesus-only Pentecostals. This is due to the belief that the original apostles baptized converts only in the name of Jesus. They also believe that God has revealed Himself in different roles rather than three distinct persons.

Charismatic

The Charismatic movement shares many similarities with Pentecostalism. The influence of Pentecostalism upon the charismatic movement cannot be denied. Both acknowledge the power of the Holy Spirit. Faith healing has major acceptance among adherents of both faiths, and both are known for their fiery services. Even still, many differences will allow a person to discern a Charismatic from a Pentecostal, though some consider themselves both.

Pentecostals developed their own denomination, but Charismatics tend to remain in their respective established churches or religious bodies. Charismatics have been susceptible to criticism that exceeds that of Pentecostalism, but criticism of both is widespread in comparison to other religious movements. Pentecostalism also developed significantly earlier than the Charismatic movement.

V. Population and Distribution

One of the most difficult things to establish about evangelicals is a precise estimate of just how many there are in the United States. With so many different evangelical denominations, evangelical constituencies of varying sizes within historically evangelical "mainline" and even nonevangelical denominations (thousands upon thousands of independent churches), there is no single entity that can possibly serve as a representative gatekeeper for the nation's evangelicals. For that reason, the best approach to an evangelical head count is a judicious triangulation of various scientific surveys. But even this is fraught with problems. As the discussion about the intricacies of definition would indicate, the

framing of the definition or wording of survey questions is important, since these are variables that can produce varying results. Estimates of the number of evangelicals in the United States, therefore, are just that: estimates.

Since 1976, the Gallup organization has been asking roughly 1,000 adults the question "Would you describe yourself as a 'born-again' or evangelical Christian?" In that first survey 34% of the people being surveyed responded "yes." Over the years, the number has fluctuated dramatically, reaching a low of 33% in 1987 and 1988 during the televangelist scandals, and a high of 47% in 1998.

In its most recent sampling in 2001, approximately 40% of survey participants described themselves as evangelicals, compared to 45% the previous year. Over the years the Gallup numbers have averaged fewer than 39% of the population as accepting identification as born-again/evangelical.

However, describing one's self as "born again" as the definitive label for evangelical believers—or even the term "evangelical" for that matter—is a questionable benchmark for tabulating the evangelical population (in one study, only 75% of Southern Baptists accepted either term). For a variety of reasons, some groups and individuals who one would describe as "in the team picture" simply do not use those words to describe themselves. For instance, several recent studies and surveys by sociologists and political scientists that utilize more complex definitional parameters have estimated the number of evangelicals in the U.S. at about 25–30% of the population, or 70 to 80 million people. It should be noted, however, that even these estimates tend to separate out nearly all of the nation's African-American Protestant population (8–9% of the U.S. population), which is overwhelmingly evangelical in theology and orientation (for example, 61% of blacks—the highest of any racial group, by far—described themselves as "born-again" in a 2001 Gallup poll). A general estimate of the nation's evangelical population could safely be said to average somewhere between 30–35% of the population, or about 100 million Americans.

Pentecostalism

Estimated numbers of Pentecostals vary widely. *Christianity Today* reported (in an article entitled "World Growth at 19 Million a Year") that historian Vinson Synan, dean of the Regent University School of Divinity in Virginia Beach, estimates that about 25% of the world's Christians are Pentecostal or Charismatic.

The largest Pentecostal denominations in the United States are the Assemblies of God, the Church of God in Christ, New Testament Church, Church of God (Cleveland), Pentecostal Assemblies of the World, Assemblies of the Lord Jesus Christ, and the United Pentecostal Church. According to a Spring 1998 article in *Christian History*, there are about 11,000 different Pentecostal or Charismatic denominations worldwide.

The size of Pentecostalism in the U.S. is estimated to be more than 20 million including approximately 918,000 (4%) of the Hispanic-American population, counting all unaffiliated congregations, although the numbers are uncertain, in part because some tenets of Pentecostalism are held by members of non-Pentecostal denominations in what has been called the charismatic movement.

Pentecostalism was estimated to number around 115 million followers worldwide in 2000; lower estimates place the figure nearer to 22 million (e.g., *Cambridge Encyclopedia*), while the highest estimates apparently place the figure between 400 and 600 million. The great majority of Pentecostals are to be found in Third World countries, although much of their international leadership is still North American. Pentecostalism is sometimes referred to as the "third force of Christianity." The largest Christian church in the world is the Yoido Full Gospel Church in South Korea, a Pentecostal church. Founded and led by David (Paul) Yonggi Cho since 1958, it had 780,000 members in 2003. The True Jesus Church is an indigenous church founded by Chinese believers on the mainland but whose headquarters is now in Taiwan. The Apostolic Church is, reportedly, the fastest growing church in the world.

According to *Christianity Today*, Pentecostalism is "a vibrant faith among the poor; it reaches into the daily lives of believers, offering not only hope but a new way of living." In addition, according to a 1999 U.N. report, "Pentecostal churches have been the most successful at recruiting its members from the poorest of the poor." Brazilian Pentecostals talk of Jesus as someone real and close to them and doing things for them, such as providing food and shelter.

VI. Organization and Infrastructure

A. Education and Hierarchy of Clergy

Clergy in Evangelical Christianity fill a wide variety of roles and functions. In many denominations, clergy are very similar to Roman Catholic or Anglican clergy, in that they hold an ordained pastoral or priestly office, administer the sacraments, proclaim the word, and lead a local church or parish.

Some denominations reject the idea that church leaders are a separate category of people. Some dislike the word clergy and do not use it of its own leaders. Often they refer to their leaders as pastors or ministers, titles that, if used, sometimes apply to the person only as long as he or she holds a particular office.

Several other varieties of ordination exist in Evangelical Christianity. Different churches and denominations specify various requirements for entering into office. While the process of ordination is given a ceremonial structure depending on the church, it is less magisterial than the sacramental versions used in the Episcopalian churches. Many Protestants still communicate authority and ordain to office by having the existing overseers physically lay hands on candidates for office and pray over them.

The Methodist model is loosely based upon the Anglican model and was first devised under the leadership of Thomas Coke and Francis Asbury in the late eighteenth century. In this scheme, an elder is ordained to word (preaching and teaching), sacrament (administering baptism and the Lord's Supper), and order (ordaining others), and a deacon is someone who is ordained to word and service.

Congregationalist churches implement different schemes, but the officers usually have less authority than in Presbyterian or Episcopalian forms. Some ordain only ministers and rotate members on an advisory board (called a board of elders or deacons). Because the positions are comparatively less powerful, there is less rigor in how officers are ordained.

Seminaries – United States

Asbury Theological Seminary (Kentucky)
Kentucky Campus:
204 N. Lexington Ave.
Wilmore, KY 40390
1-800-2ASBURY / 859-858-3581
Florida Campus:
8401 Valencia College Lane
Orlando, FL 32825
407-482-7500
Virtual Campus
204 North Lexington Avenue
Wilmore, KY 40390
859-858-3581
Admissions: 800-2-ASBURY / 859-858-2211
admissions_office@asburyseminary.edu

City Seminary of Sacramento
2020 16th Avenue
Sacramento, CA 95822
916-451-4168
information@cityseminary.org

Covenant Theological Seminary
12330 Conway Road
St. Louis, MO 63141
800-264-8064 / 314-434-4044
Admissions@covenantseminary.edu

Dallas Theological Seminary
3909 Swiss Avenue
Dallas, TX 75204
800-3-DALLAS /
214-841-3661 / 214-841-3664

Denver Seminary
6399 South Santa Fe Drive
Littleton, CO 80120
info@denverseminary.edu
803-761-2482 / 1-800-922-3040

Fuller Theological Seminary
135 North Oakland Avenue
Pasadena, CA 91182
626-584-5200 / 1-800-2FULLER (Admissions)

Gordon-Conwell Theological Seminary
South Hamilton, MA Campus:
130 Essex Street
South Hamilton, MA 01982
978-468-7111   Fax: 978-468–6691
800-428-7329 (Admissions)
info@gcts.edu; adminfo@gcts.edu (Admissions)
Charlotte, NC:
14542 Choate Circle
Charlotte, NC 28273
704-527-9909   Fax: 704-527-8577
charinfo@gcts.edu
Boston, MA (CUME) Campus:
The Center for Urban Ministerial Education (CUME)
90 Warren Street
Roxbury, MA 02119
617-427-7293   Fax: 617-541-3432
cumeinfo@gcts.edu
Jacksonville Extension Site:
Kent Gilbert, Assistant to the Dean
904-874-2556   jaxinfo@gcts.edu
Doctor of Ministry Program:
130 Essex Street
South Hamilton, MA 01982
978-646-4132   Fax: 978-468-6208

dmininfo@gcts.edu
Semlink: Distance Education:
130 Essex Street
South Hamilton, MA 01982
978-646–4144   Fax: 978-646-4565
semlink@gcts.edu

Midwestern Baptist Theological Seminary
5001 North Oak Trafficway
Kansas City, MO 64118
816-414-3700   Fax: 816-414-3799

Moody Bible Institute
820 North LaSalle Boulevard
Chicago, IL 60610
1-800-DLMOODY / 312-329-4000
pr@moody.edu

New Orleans Baptist Theological Seminary
3939 Gentilly Boulevard
New Orleans, LA 70126
800-662-8701 / 504-282-4455

Reformed Theological Seminary
Atlanta Campus:
3585 Northside Parkway NW
Atlanta, GA 30327-2309
404-995-8484   Fax: 404-995-8997
Boca Raton Campus:
2400 Yamato Road
Boca Raton, FL 33431
561-994-5000   Fax: 561-994-5005
Charlotte Campus:
2101 Carmel Road
Charlotte, NC 28226-6399
704-366-5066   Fax: 704-366-9295
rts.charlotte@rts.edu
Jackson Campus:
5422 Clinton Boulevard
Jackson, MS 39209-3099
601-923-1600   Fax: 601-923-1654
rts.jackson@rts.edu

Orlando Campus:
1231 Reformation Drive
Oviedo, FL 32765
407-366-9493   Fax: 407-366-9425
rts.orlando@rts.edu
Virtual Campus:
2101 Carmel Road
Charlotte, NC 28226
704-366-4853   Fax: 704-366-9295
Washington, D.C., Campus:
12500 Fair Lakes Circle, Suite 325
Fairfax, VA 22033
703-222-7871   Fax: 703-738-7389

Southeastern Baptist Theological Seminary
120 South Wingate Street
Wake Forest, NC 27587
919-761-2100

Southern Baptist Theological Seminary
The Billy Graham School
2825 Lexington Road
Louisville, KY 40280
800-626-5525 admissions@sbts.edu

Southwestern Baptist Theological Seminary
Havard School for Theological Studies
The College at Southwestern
2001 West Seminary Drive
Fort Worth, TX 76115
817-923-1921
http://college.swbts.edu/

Talbot Theological Seminary
13800 Biola Avenue
La Mirada, CA 90639
800-OK-BIOLA

Trinity Evangelical Divinity School
Deerfield Campus:
2065 Half Day Road
Deerfield, IL 60015
847-945-8800 / 1-800-445-8337

847-317-8000   Fax: 847-317-8097

tedsadm@tiu.edu

www.tiu.edu/divinity

South Chicago Regional Center:

14200 Dante Avenue

Dolton, IL 60419

312-952-0644

Chicago@trinet.tiu.edu

South Florida Regional Center:

111 NW 183d Street, Suite 500

Miami, FL 33169

305-770-5100   Fax: 305-770-5170

tedsmadm@tiu.edu

B. Megachurches

A megachurch is a large church, defined as having more than 2,000 worshippers; it is predominantly an evangelical and Pentecostal phenomenon. Globally, these large congregations are a significant development in Protestant Christianity, challenging the roles of denominations as the primary sources of ministry resources and ministerial training.

Denominational megachurches generally have more in common with other megachurches than they do with smaller churches within their own denomination. Megachurches affiliated with the seeker movement do not include their denomination in their name or otherwise publicize their affiliation, so as not to alienate potential visitors.

Much of the actual teaching work of a megachurch is handled by committees and smaller meetings outside the weekly services themselves, which are almost exclusively meant for collective (sometimes enthusiastic) but passive worship. Congregational oversight is generally limited to an annual meeting (where a budget and board of directors is approved); in some cases, the senior pastor has complete authority over all decisions.

The Hartford Seminary has an extensive database of all U.S. megachurches, available online at: http://hirr.hartsem.edu/megachurch/database.html.

C. Governance and Authority

Governance and church law within the evangelical denominations varies among denominations and churches. Generally, however, church law and authority are handled at the parish level. Two organizations —the National Association of Evangelicals and the Pentecostal World Conference—provide a framework and collective voice for the over sixty churches within their membership.

National Association of Evangelicals

The National Association of Evangelicals (NAE) is an agency dedicated to coordinating cooperative ministry for evangelical denominations of Protestant Christians in the United States.

The National Association of Evangelicals was formed by a group of 147 people who met in St. Louis, Missouri, on April 7–9, 1942. The fundamentalist/modernist controversy, and the related isolation of various fundamentalist and evangelical denominations and leaders, provided the impetus for developing such an organization. Early leaders in the movement were Ralph T. Davis, Will Houghton, Harold Ockenga, and J. Elwin Wright. Houghton called for a meeting in Chicago, Illinois, in 1941. A committee was formed with Wright as chairman, and a national conference for United Action among Evangelicals was called for April 1942. Ockenga was appointed the first president.

Carl McIntire and Harvey Springer led in organizing the American Council of Christian Churches (now with seven member bodies) in September 1941. It was a more militant and fundamentalist organization set up in opposition to the Federal Council of Churches (now National Council of Churches with thirty-six member bodies). McIntire invited the Evangelicals for United Action to join with them, but those who met in St. Louis declined the offer.

The tentative organization founded in 1942 was called the National Association of Evangelicals for United Action. In 1943, the proposed constitution was amended and adopted, and the name shortened to the National Association of Evangelicals. The National Religious Broadcasters was formed in 1944.

The National Association of Evangelicals currently has fifty-two member denominations and headquarters in Washington, D.C. There are twenty-seven regional affiliates of the NAE. See online: www.nae.net.

D. Denominations: U.S.

- Advent Christian General Conference
- Assemblies of God
- Association of Life-Giving Churches
- Association of Vineyard Churches-USA
- Baptist General Conference
- Bi-lingual Churches of America
- Brethren in Christ Church
- Christ Community Church
- Christian Church of North America
- Christian Reformed Church in North America
- Christian Union
- Church of God
- Church of God (Holiness)
- Church of God Mountain Assembly
- Church of the Nazarene
- Churches of Christ In Christian Union
- Congregational Holiness Church
- Congregational Methodist Church
- Conservative Baptist Association of America
- Conservative Congregational Christian Conference
- Conservative Lutheran Association
- Elim Fellowship
- Evangelical Assembly of Presbyterian Churches
- Evangelical Church of North America
- Evangelical Congregational Church
- Evangelical Free Church of America
- Evangelical Friends Church Eastern Region
- Evangelical Lutheran Conference
- Evangelical Methodist Church
- Evangelical Presbyterian Church
- Evangelistic Missionary Fellowship

- Fellowship of Evangelical Bible Churches
- Fellowship of Evangelical Churches
- Free Methodist Church of North America
- General Association of General Baptists
- General Council Christian Union
- Hispanic World Harvest Churches
- International Church of the Foursquare Gospel
- International Pentecostal Church of Christ
- International Pentecostal Holiness Church
- Midwest Congregational Christian Fellowship
- Missionary Church, Inc.
- Northern Pacific Latin American Assemblies of God
- Open Bible Churches
- Pentecostal Church of God
- Pentecostal Free Will Baptist Church Inc.
- Presbyterian Church in America
- Primitive Methodist Church USA
- Reformed Episcopal Church
- Reformed Presbyterian Church of North America
- Southern Pacific Latin American Churches
- The Brethren Church
- The Christian & Missionary Alliance
- The Salvation Army
- The Wesleyan Church Corporation
- Third Day Worship Centers
- United Brethren in Christ
- US Conf. of the Mennonite Brethren Churches
- Worldwide Church of God

Pentecostal World Conference/Pentecostal World Fellowship

The Pentecostal World Conference or Pentecostal World Fellowship is a fellowship of Pentecostal believers and denominations from across the world. The Fellowship is a cooperative body of Pentecostal churches and groups worldwide of approved standing. Any national council or fraternal organization, that (demonstrably) subscribes to the Fellowship's Statement of Faith is eligible to apply for membership. Since 1947, the Pentecostal World Conference meets every three years.

E. Social Service Organizations

Parachurch organizations—pioneered in the Second Great Awakening of the ninteenth century, but perfected in the second half of the twentieth century—are vehicles by which evangelical Christians work collaboratively both outside of and across their denominations to engage with the world in mission, social welfare and evangelism. Through many decentralized organizations, parachurch organizations function to bridge the gap between the church and culture. These are organizations "alongside" church structures, and often seek to be less institutional; however over time, with growth and success, and in response to environmental pressures, they can become more institutional.

These bodies can be businesses, nonprofit corporations, and private associations. They generally operate within the broad movement of evangelicalism without sponsorship of any particular church or association of churches, while attempting to avoid encroaching on roles traditionally belonging to churches alone. They offer centralized efficiency of mission and operation to accomplish specialized ministry tasks that independent churches without denominational or associational strength are not able to accomplish on a national or international scale.

Parachurch organizations generally require members or staff to agree to an evangelical Statement of Faith or creed used to define an organization's biblical and doctrinal beliefs, convictions, and mission distinctives. Some statements are deliberately general in nature to allow for maximum outreach to community or culture. Others are more specific and constraining, potentially excluding those who would disagree, but defining the organization more clearly.

Though evangelicals have generally sought to remain within their denominations, alternative church-like arrangements have been set up.

Evangelical house church projects have been established in some neighborhoods, which may even avoid using the word "church" to describe their meetings. Special meeting places, a professional clergy, even the sacraments might be set aside by an evangelical church, not because they reject these institutions , but in order to extend outreach beyond traditional bounds.

In Protestant and Catholic theology, parachurch organizations are termed "sodalities," as distinct from modality, which is the term for the structure and organization of the local or universal church.

Call to Renewal
3333 14th Street NW
Suite 200
Washington, D.C. 20010
202-328-8745   Fax: 202-328-6797
ctr@calltorenewal.org
Call to Renewal is a national network of churches, faith-based organizations, and individuals working to overcome poverty in America. Through local and national partnerships with groups from across the theological and political spectrum, they work with local and national agencies, while growing and developing a movement of Christians committed to overcoming poverty.

ProLiteracy Worldwide/ProLiteracy America
1320 Jamesville Avenue
Syracuse, NY 13210
315-422-9121   Fax: 315-422-6369
Toll Free: 888-528-2224
www.proliteracy.org
A nonprofit international literacy organization based in Syracuse, NY—the oldest and largest nongovernmental literacy organization in the world. It represents 1,200 community-based volunteer and basic education affiliates in all 50 states and in D.C.

Samaritan's Purse
PO Box 3000
Boone, NC 28607
828-262-1980   Fax: 828-266-1053
A nondenominational Evangelical Christian organization providing aid to disadvantaged people worldwide. Since 1970, Samaritan's Purse has helped

victims of war, poverty, natural disasters, disease, and famine. **Children's Heart Project,** identifies children with life-threatening heart disease in third-world countries and matches them with North American volunteer hospitals and surgeons; and **Prescription for Hope,** sponsors grassroots HIV/AIDS programs around the world.

F. Media and Communication

Christianity Today

Christianity Today International
465 Gundersen Drive,
Carol Stream, IL 60188
630-260-6200   Fax: 630-260-0114
www.ChristianityToday.com

Christianity Today is the flagship publication of Christianity Today International, with circulation of 150,000 and readership of 350,000.

Founded in 1956 by evangelist Billy Graham as an alternative to *The Christian Century* (the predominant independent periodical of mainline Protestantism) and as a way of unifying the evangelical Christian community. Its first editor was Carl F. H. Henry. Notable contributors in its first two decades included F.F. Bruce, Edward John Carnell, John Warwick Montgomery, and Harold Lindsell. Notable current writers include Philip Yancey, Richard Mouw, Yale law professor Stephen Carter, and Prison Fellowship's Charles W. Colson.

Sojourners

Sojourners/Call to Renewal
3333 14th Street NW, Suite 200
Washington D.C. 20010
202-328-8842   800-714-7474
Fax: 202-328-8757
sojourners@sojo.net   www.sojo.net

Sojourners as an organization was founded in 1971 in Washington, D.C. *Sojourners* emphasizes Christian teachings on issues of social justice, such as poverty and war, from an Evangelical Christian per-

spective. Although its slogan is "Not from the Left, not from the Right, but from the Spirit," the organization's opposition to conservative economic and foreign policy gives it a left-leaning flavor.

The Gideons

An Evangelical Christian organization dedicated to distributing the Bible in over 80 languages and more than 180 countries of the world. "Gideon Bibles" are a ubiquitous feature of American hotel and motel rooms. The organization was founded in 1899 in Boscobel, Wisconsin, and named after the biblical character of Judges 7. The Gideons also distribute Bibles to members of the military, to hospitals, nursing homes, prisons and college students.

FURTHER READING

Protestantism in America
Randall Balmer and Lauren F. Winner
2002: Columbia University Press

Fundamentalism and American Culture
George M. Marsden
1972: Oxford University Press

The Divine Dramatist: George Whitefield
Harry S. Stout
1991: Wm. B. Eerdmans

∽

7 Jehovah's Witnesses

I. Origins and Early History

A. Introduction

JEHOVAH'S WITNESSES CONSTITUTE ONE OF THE largest Christian religions to appear in late nineteenth-century America. Noted characteristics of the group include its focus on the present-day fulfillment of biblical prophecy, their nonparticipation in politics and war, and their rejection of practices and beliefs common to other Christian religions.

The Witnesses are known worldwide for their volunteer door-to-door ministry and distribution of religious literature, which in 2008 appeared in 448 languages. Their principal publication is *The Watchtower*. The thirty-two-page journal has an average printing of thirty-seven million in 167 languages and is read and distributed by Jehovah's Witnesses in 235 countries. *The Watchtower* carries definitive statements on Witness doctrine and practice; each issue is read by literally millions of people worldwide.

The religion, practiced by nearly 7 million active Witnesses, is supervised by the Governing Body of Jehovah's Witnesses, which provides spiritual direction and oversees the editorial and administrative functions of the organization.

The term Watch Tower Society (WTS) has often been used to designate the organization of Jehovah's Witnesses as a whole, but it specifically refers to the Watch Tower Bible and Tract Society of Pennsylvania, a legal corporate entity representing the Witness community.

B. The Religion in America

Founding and Mission

Jehovah's Witnesses largely reject church traditions and hierarchies, claiming to model their doctrine and mode of worship after the first-century Christians. The Witnesses trace their modern origins to a Bible study group started by businessman Charles Taze Russell in 1870 near Pittsburgh, Pennsylvania. Bible research and discussions with religious thinkers convinced Russell that the "harvest period" had begun and that Christ would soon gather his true followers. Russell (as he describes it) "at once resolved upon a vigorous campaign for the truth." Using his personal fortune, he wrote and published numerous

The Watchtower *was first published on July 1, 1879, and was titled* Zion's Watch Tower *and Herald of Christ's Presence. The name changed to* The Watch Tower *in 1908, shortly after the publication of this issue on October 1, 1907.*

works and, in July 1879, commenced publishing and editing *Zion's Watch Tower and Herald of Christ's Presence* (now *The Watchtower Announcing Jehovah's Kingdom*). In 1881, he founded Zion's Watch Tower Tract Society. Early Watch Tower (WT) literature explored such themes as the invisible return of Christ, redemption and salvation, and the pitfalls of "sectarianism."

Russell and his associates scrupulously resisted denominationalism, believing that churches had mixed Bible truths with human speculation. Their work, as they saw it, consisted of gathering "these long scattered fragments of truth" into a consistent whole, presenting them to fellow Christians (again, as he put it) "not as new, not as our own, but as the Lord's." The study group adopted a number of distinctive views, many of which Jehovah's Witnesses still hold today. Thus, the modern-day community of Jehovah's Witnesses began as a coalescing fellowship of *Watchtower* readers, who simply called themselves Bible Students.

Watchtower Readership

In 1879, *The Watchtower* had a circulation of 6,000 copies. By 1883, *The Watchtower*'s 10,000 subscribers included at least 800 ministers. By its fifth year, it had reached at least thirty-five of thirty-eight states then belonging to the Union. By 1889, readers corresponded from eleven countries (by contemporary borders) on four continents. In one four-month period in 1881, the WTS distributed 1.2 million copies of the book *Food for Thinking Christians*.

The editor and four assistants struggled to answer hundreds of letters arriving weekly. Many requested large quantities of literature to distribute, while others sought dialogue on biblical questions. Analysis of the admittedly selective collection of published letters indicates that early Bible Students were highly literate, whether formally educated or not, and remarkably conversant with biblical texts and current religious issues. A few had theological training or schooling in biblical languages. Most correspondents were active Protestants. Others had left their churches over doctrinal disagreements. Where the letter-writer's gender was indicated, approximately one-third of them were women.

Readers' socioeconomic and occupational status is less clear. Historians have commonly assumed that the Bible Students' millenarian message appealed primarily to the "disinherited;" that is, to the destitute and deprived who had hopes for the next world only because the present world offered none. Many Bible Students hardly fit this generalization. Without a formal fund-raising mechanism, WTS publishing relied on freewill donations by appreciative readers. Impoverished individuals could submit their names for the list of "the Lord's Poor" and receive *The Watchtower* free. No more than ten percent of readers signed up, some later asking to be taken off the list when their finances improved. Despite professing to be the "poor of this world," most readers had disposable income with which to give the suggested donation for literature; some contributed generously. For instance, three donors paid for WT tracts to be distributed throughout Pennsylvania, Maryland, and West Virginia.

Initially, Bible Students met in small, informal groups for reasoned discussion. WT literature contained complex exegetical discussions that presumed the Bible's internal logic and consistency. Articles featured numerous scriptural citations and references to lexicons and commentaries. The scholarly appeal of the Bible Students differed greatly from that of revivalists who drew enthusiastic crowds during the "Second Great Awakening" earlier in the nineteenth century.

Russell became a well-known and outspoken critic of Christian denominations, rejecting the doctrines of the Trinity, hellfire, and predestination. He encouraged readers to come out of worldly "nominal churches" and to form nondenominational Bible study groups with like-minded Christians. Ministers, deacons, and Sunday school leaders responded, recounting their confrontation with religious error. Some had resigned from their churches, others had preached their newfound beliefs and had been sub-

Charles Taze Russell (1852–1916), founder of the magazine now known as The Watchtower, *in an undated photograph.*

ject to heresy trials, and many were officially ostracized by their hierarchy.

Numerous lay members reported leaving the pews in favor of "Bible Student" gatherings, where no salaried minister presided and no collections were taken. The WTS sent itinerant "pilgrims" to visit study groups. Visitation schedules in *The Watchtower* bespoke the widening circle of Bible Students. Following Russell's lead, they stood outside church services to distribute "truth" as found in WT tracts and pamphlets. In 1910, to better attract religious seekers, Bible Student congregations were invited to advertise and conduct their meetings under the umbrella name International Bible Students Association (IBSA). Although a collective had been forming for some time, the term "Bible Student" only then became an official designation.

The Watchtower weighed in on hotly debated religious issues of the day, commenting on current events such as the secularizing influences of Darwinism and biblical criticism, spiritualism and atheism, and labor-movement struggles. The Bible Students observed the growth of nationalism, com-munism, and anarchism, scrutinizing world developments in the light of Bible prophecy. Their readings of "time prophecy" progressed over time, and a sense of urgency infused their literature.

Clerical Criticism and Public Reception

Their interest in world events notwithstanding, Bible Students believed they should be apolitical. They served as "watchmen" announcing God's impending judgment and denouncing religions involved in politics and war. Before World War I, Bible Students circulated tens of millions of tracts, pamphlets, books, and Bibles, which generated hostility among mainstream clergy and prompted a stream of anti-Russell works. Perhaps the clergy's predominant attitude is best exemplified by the article, "Millennial Dawn: A Counterfeit of Christianity," in the twelve-volume 1909 series, *The Fundamentals,* edited by evangelist R. A. Torrey, and sent free to hundreds of thousands of ministers worldwide. Though it mainly defended traditional Christian teaching in the face of "godless doctrine," *The Fundamentals* harshly criticized four religious groups, including what it called the "calamitous doctrines of Mr. Russell."

Nevertheless, the public welcomed Russell's writings and lectures. From 1886 to 1904, Russell authored six volumes of *Millennial Dawn,* which received favorable newspaper reviews. For example, in the *Atlanta Constitution*, a famous journalist of the pseudonym Bill Arp wrote effusively about Russell's repudiation of hellfire and his strong defense of God's love. *Millennial Dawn* reached a printing of over 10 million during its forty-year run. The press covered Russell's appearances before capacity crowds in venues such as London's Royal Albert Hall and the New York Hippodrome, dubbing him "the Spurgeon of America." At one time, 2,000 newspapers carried his weekly sermons, aimed at religiously disillusioned and secular readers, in what he called, "newspaper gospeling."

Several hundred full-time "colporteurs" spearheaded the distribution of WT literature, opening up new territories. In the late nineteenth and early twentieth centuries, unprecedented waves of immigrants to the U.S. and growing African-American churches provided further opportunities. Russell went on twelve evangelizing tours to Europe, Asia, the South Pacific, and the Caribbean. Bible Student missionaries went to Africa and South America, not just to achieve world conversion but to find "the Lord's consecrated." In January 1914, the IBSA launched an innovative motion-picture and slide presentation with synchronized sound, called *The Photo-Drama of Creation*. By year's end, nine million people in North America, Europe, and Australia had viewed the eight-hour epic. Bible Students preached their message in thirty countries with literature in thirty-five languages.

By 1916, some 500 Bible Student congregations had elected Russell as their pastor. He asked selected Christian women in these congregations to perform volunteer "pastoral work," organizing home visitation, introducing Bible literature, and inviting interested persons to religious meetings. The method reportedly proved successful, and men soon joined in the house-to-house activity that would eventually become characteristic of all Jehovah's Witnesses till today. Partial records estimate that in the mid-1910s, 21,000 attended 1,200 Bible Student meetings, and 5,700 participated in the preaching work.

Wartime Conduct

In October 1916, while on a speaking tour, C. T. Russell died at age sixty-four. By then, the U.S. had entered World War I. Long before, *The Watchtower* had decried the "bloodguilt" of warring "Christian" nations and the incompatibility of war with the Gospel of peace. An 1887 issue exhorted Christians to be "neutral" toward political disputes and in 1904, the journal first applied the term specifically to abstention from armed combat. *The Watchtower* did not then outline an explicit position toward military service, but a 1903 article stated that a genuine Christian would not kill his fellow man; even on the battlefield, he would be obliged to shoot into the ground or the air.

Most male Bible Students did not take up arms, some filling noncombatant positions and others refusing induction altogether. After Britain passed the Conscription Act in March 1916, hundreds of Bible Students were imprisoned for refusal to fight. Five British Bible Students received death sentences, later commuted to ten years' imprisonment. The U.S. passed the Selective Service Act in May 1917, which exempted religious objectors but required them to perform noncombatant service. Some Bible Students applied for exemption, which was often denied. Others rejected noncombatant service outright, viewing it as supporting the war effort.

The 1917 book *The Finished Mystery* condemned clergymen who acted as recruiting agents and war fomenters. It quoted pacifist Unitarian minister John Haynes Holmes as saying, "War is in open and utter violation of Christianity." Bible Students advertised the book with ten million copies of the stinging tract "Fall of Babylon: Why Christendom Must Now Suffer." Canada banned *The Finished Mystery* in February 1918. The U.S. followed suit that March. Local officials harassed and jailed Bible Students, refusing to intervene when they were beaten and mobbed.

Soon thereafter, the U.S. issued arrest warrants for WTS President J. F. Rutherford and seven associates, charging them with conspiring to violate the Espionage Act by publishing antiwar statements. Seven of eight men, including Rutherford, received four concurrent sentences of twenty years. While awaiting appeal, they were denied bail and spent nine months in the Atlanta Federal Penitentiary. A nationwide petition drive collected 700,000 signatures calling for their release. In May 1920, the government reversed the convictions and dropped the case. The Bible Students were certain that hostile clergy had maneuvered the government's actions, and *The Watchtower* stepped up its denunciation of "false religion."

Following the war, "Advertise the King and his Kingdom" became the Bible Students' motto. In 1931, they adopted the name Jehovah's Witnesses, based on Isaiah 43:10, emphasizing their public testimony about Jehovah and his Kingdom by Christ. The lecture series "Millions Now Living Will Never Die" reflected the Bible Students' conviction that besides those going to heaven, millions would live eternally on a paradise earth. The Bible Students had already believed this for some time, but they had felt no special responsibility to preach the Gospel to those destined to live forever on earth. The year 1935 brought a new emphasis on evangelizing these multitudes, and expanded worldwide outreach began. Convinced of the imminent end of corrupt politics and religion, the Witnesses urgently pursued their mission. They used creative strategies, such as vast radio networks, sound cars, poster-board processions, and doorstep sermons, maintaining high public visibility. From 1920 to 1935, they had spread from forty-six countries to 115, numbering over fifty-six active "publishers" of their message.

War Tensions Mount

With patriotic fervor rising in the mid-1930s, Jehovah's Witnesses faced renewed challenges to their apolitical stance. In Nazi, Fascist, and Communist countries, Witnesses endured intense state-sponsored oppression. German Witnesses refused to give the Hitler salute. About 13,400 Witness men, women, and children suffered brutal persecution and incarceration for refusing to conform. The Nazi military executed some 270 male Witness objectors. Nearly 2,000 Witnesses died during the Nazi reign of terror.

In the interwar period, American veterans organizations and school officials promoted patriotic ceremonies, including the Pledge of Allegiance, often with a stiff-arm salute. J. F. Rutherford, arguably thinking of the Nazi situation, compared saluting any national emblem or official to idol worship. Witness children began refusing to participate in flag rituals and school officials expelled hundreds of them, while penalizing parents for their children's "truancy." Witnesses set up temporary "Kingdom Schools" with the volunteer help of certified Witness and non-Witness teachers.

Meanwhile, Witnesses successfully challenged the expulsions in lower courts, but in 1940 the U.S. Supreme Court voted 8–1 in *Minersville School District v. Gobitis* to affirm the right of school officials to compel patriotic expressions. Jurists and editorialists criticized the Gobitis decision as a blow to freedom. Public opinion, however, branded the Witnesses as Communists or Nazis, sparking a wave of violence. In 1940 alone, the American Civil Liberties Union reported 335 mobbings in forty-four states, involving 1,488 Jehovah's Witnesses. Angry crowds assaulted Witnesses, demanding that they salute. Sheriffs often jailed victimized Witnesses, rather than their attackers, for disturbing the peace. Vandals ransacked homes and houses of worship. Witness employees were harassed or fired. As the violence escalated, First Lady Eleanor Roosevelt and U.S. Attorney General Francis Biddle called for calm.

The Supreme Court ruled eighteen more times against the Witnesses from 1940 to 1942. Then three high-court justices signaled their view that *Gobitis* had been wrongly decided, and the Witnesses returned to court with the case *West Virginia State Board of Education v. Barnette*. In a 6–3 vote announced on Flag Day, June 14, 1943, the court reversed *Gobitis*. Justice Robert Jackson's majority opinion defined the First Amendment with the classic language:

> If there is any fixed star in our constitutional constellation, it is that no official, high or petty, can prescribe what shall be orthodox in politics, nationalism, religion, or other matters of opinion or force citizens to confess by word or act their faith therein.

During World War II, Jehovah's Witnesses legally contested the draft classification of more than 3,400 Witnesses who went to U.S. prisons for refusing military service. Witnesses won the right to receive ministerial exemptions, whether or not they supported themselves with secular work in addition to serving as ministers. However, many American Witnesses still faced imprisonment for their conscientious stand during the Korean and Vietnam Wars.

Jehovah's Witnesses' Supreme Court cases have shaped jurisprudence regarding pamphleteering, a long time feature of American civic culture. *Lovell v. City of Griffin* (1938), *Cantwell v. Connecticut* (1940), and *Murdock v. Pennsylvania* (1943), as well as the recent *Watchtower Bible and Tract Society of New York v. Village of Stratton, Ohio* (2002), helped define and strengthen freedom of speech and press. Witnesses won a record fifty of sixty-two cases they argued before the Supreme Court. Notwithstanding official and public suspicion during the Cold War, American Witnesses endured fewer direct challenges to their civil rights. Witnesses elsewhere have faced legal challenges and official oppression, such as in Canada, East Germany, France, Spain, the Soviet Union and countries of the former Soviet Union, South Korea, Singapore, and newly independent African states.

Post-War Education and Expansion

Nathan H. Knorr, third WTS president, oversaw worldwide educational and evangelization programs and sweeping organizational restructuring to accommodate the expanding Witness ranks. In 1942, the WTS launched the Watchtower Bible College of Gilead to train missionaries for overseas assignments. Since then, 8,000 Gilead graduates have gone to more than 200 countries. The weekly Theocratic Ministry School trained all Witnesses in teaching and public speaking beginning in 1943. These programs set the stage for substantial post-war growth.

The increasing diversity of Jehovah's Witnesses is exemplified by their large annual conventions. In August 1950, an eight-day international gathering at New York City's Yankee Stadium drew 123,707 delegates from sixty-seven countries. The attendance doubled in 1958, with 253,922 delegates representing 123 countries at Yankee Stadium and the Polo Grounds, and a record 7,136 baptized, symbolizing their dedication to God and ordination as ministers.

The 1950s and 1960s wrought great social changes in the United States and elsewhere. Material prosperity, racial tensions, the civil rights movement,

the sexual revolution, the feminist movement, decolonization, independence movements, liberation theology, the culture of rebellion, and secularization shaped the post-war generation. The Witnesses ranks during this period saw exponential increases.

Synchronously with the civil rights movement, Jehovah's Witnesses in the southern United States integrated congregations that had been racially segregated during the Jim Crow years because of legal or ad hoc local ordinances. Where integrated crowds could assemble safely, Witnesses held mixed-race conventions. Contemporary *Watchtower* articles compared toleration of segregation to the early Christians' toleration of the evil of slavery. The Witnesses disagreed with the practice, but they would not agitate for change in society at large, since they saw political activism as outside the purview of Christian responsibility. Witnesses should instead expunge racism from their own minds and hearts. Sociological studies have shown that Witness congregations are among the most racially integrated social institutions in the country. Witnesses in South Africa, under apartheid, implemented integration along similar lines.

As Jehovah's Witnesses expanded outside the United States, Gilead School instructed Witness missionaries not to view themselves as agents of westernization. Yet, congregations should not allow practices that clearly violated Christian principles. For instance, those who practice polygamy or common-law marriage could not become Jehovah's Witnesses until they adjusted their marital status. Female genital mutilation, abortion, elaborate mourning and burial rituals, and gendered segregation during religious services have been highly discouraged or condemned outright.

Procedures for congregational discipline, as outlined in 1 Corinthians 5, were formalized in 1952. A baptized Witness unrepentantly guilty of serious sin can be "disfellowshipped," or expelled from the congregation, especially if the act is habitual. The congregation elders first meet with the individual to determine the circumstances of the alleged wrongdoing and his or her attitude toward it. Counseling is provided for repentant persons, but one who, by word or action, refuses to repudiate the wrong is no longer viewed as one of Jehovah's Witnesses. In essence, disfellowshipping occurs less because of the serious moral infraction itself than the person's attitude toward the act. Disfellowshipping is seen as protecting the congregation's moral condition and reputation and as a disciplinary measure to bring the wrongdoer to his or her senses.

Disfellowshipped persons may attend Witness religious services but are not permitted to participate in meetings, interact with attendees, or engage in the public ministry. Congregation members are urged to strictly limit social and spiritual contact with the willfully erring one, except for necessary family or business matters. Sexual misconduct and habitual substance abuse are common reasons for disfellowshipping. Financial misconduct, domestic abuse, or activist dissidence on major doctrines may also lead to congregation discipline. Disfellowshipped individuals may be reinstated in the congregation upon ceasing the wrongdoing and demonstrating repentance. A large percentage of disfellowshipped Witnesses eventually return to the congregation.

The Witnesses' emphasis on personal Bible study influences their view of education. In areas with low literacy rates, Witnesses have held reading classes for countless individuals to facilitate their full participation in congregational life and the public ministry. Where young children customarily quit school to work, Witnesses are reminded that responsible parenting includes an effort to ensure that their children diligently fulfill the requirements of compulsory schooling, despite any economic hardship on the family.

At the same time, Witnesses are cautioned to balance the value of secular education against potential spiritual dangers. Until the latter half of the twentieth century, university education in many countries was primarily the province of the wealthy elite. Many U.S. veterans of World War II under the GI bill became the first in their families to attend college. The "hippie culture," prevalent on college campuses in the 1960s and 1970s, was seen as featuring sexual and drug experimentation and rebellion against authority and social convention. *The Watchtower* then counseled families to consider the spiritual impact of campus life and of college curricula stressing human philosophies and materialistic goals when making educational choices. Though the decision is left to each Witness, similar caveats are still emphasized. Jehovah's Witnesses promote an ethic of self-sacrifice and urge their young people to make the public ministry their primary pursuit in life, putting career, education, childbearing, or financial prosperity in secondary place.

Medical advances have raised challenging ethical issues for Witnesses. They recognize the lack of explicit Scriptural comment on modern medical practices but endeavor to extrapolate divine views from general biblical principles. Their prohibition against abortion at any time after conception stems from Exodus 21 and Psalm 139. When doctors first performed experimental organ transplants, the Witnesses, like many other religions, registered serious reservations, some equating the procedure with cannibalism. However, the 1980 *Watchtower* explained that accepting transplants is a matter for individual conscientious decision.

Perhaps the Witnesses' most controversial doctrine is their view that ingestion of blood, either by mouth or intravenously, violates the injunction at Acts 15 to "abstain...from blood." The medical profession practiced bloodletting as standard therapy for centuries, but it honed the technique of blood transfusion on the battlefield during the world wars. Dangers of disease transmission and human error offset advances in blood-typing and storage. The Witnesses' rejection of blood transfusion even in apparently life-threatening situations, however, stems from religious rather than medical principles. The blood issue has been at the center of many court cases involving patients' rights and the medicolegal standing of minors.

The Witnesses' insistence on bloodless treatment converged with the AIDS crisis and chronic blood shortages in compelling researchers to develop safer blood-conservation technologies, which now benefit the public. *The Watchtower* states that adhering to biblical principles involves avoidance of whole blood or its four major components: red blood cells, white blood cells, plasma, and blood platelets. The acceptance of derivatives or fractions of these components is considered permissible as a personal decision. Blood-conservation techniques, such as cell salvage, are also viewed as a matter of personal choice.

Structural Developments

The transition from small, autonomous study groups before World War I to the coordinated network of large, unified congregations occurred over time. The Jehovah's Witness community today is a highly structured international organization focused on preaching about God's Kingdom. The Witnesses consider Jesus the leader of the Christian congregation. They address one another as "brother" and "sister" in accord with egalitarian Christian principles and do not use honorific titles. Nevertheless, the format of their religious meetings calls for knowledgeable persons to take the lead, even as in apostolic times.

Early Bible Student congregations chose elders democratically, which occasionally led to electioneering and dissension. Women held no leadership positions. A 1938 *Watchtower* introduced "theocratic [God-ruled] procedure" to appoint presiding elders, or overseers, following first-century precedents. The congregation recommended individuals to the Governing Body of Jehovah's Witnesses or its representatives, which in turn evaluated their qualifications, using the guidelines in 1 Timothy 3 and Titus 1. Congregation structure was revised in 1972 so that a collective body of elders, composed of an indeterminate number of qualified Witness males, served congregational needs.

Organization-wide structure changed along similar lines. The WTS president had historically held broad authority. In 1971, the WTS enlarged the Governing Body to include other members on the corporation's board of directors and instituted a rotating chairmanship. Until 2000, Governing Body members had always served as WTS directors. In that year, the directorship was turned over to others on the headquarters staff so that the Governing Body could fully attend to spiritual matters, including its supervision of the ministerial work of Jehovah's Witnesses. Some one hundred corporate entities and appointed branch committees worldwide care for the Witnesses' legal interests.

Spreading the Word

Recent developments have improved the Witnesses' ability to spread the good news and to care for fellow believers. To publish Bible literature in more languages, Witnesses invented the Multilanguage Electronic Phototypesetting System (MEPS). This and other innovations in printing and translation methods facilitated simultaneous printing of WT literature in more than 145 languages. Consequently, some 95 percent of Witnesses worldwide study the same material during the same week.

The coordinated structure of the organization has also enabled large-scale construction and relief efforts. Beginning in the 1980s, volunteer building crews were trained to erect "Kingdom Halls," Witness houses of worship, in a matter of days. The availability of volunteers with specialized skills has proven invaluable in times of natural disaster. Thousands of Witness volunteers and millions of dollars in donated funds have been devoted to massive reconstruction of hurricane-damaged homes and Kingdom Halls in the southern United States. Similar efforts have aided Witnesses and other victims of earthquakes, floods, and typhoons in the Caribbean, Central and South America, the South Pacific, and Asia. In Africa, drought, famine, and unrelenting war have necessitated large and hazardous humanitarian missions by French, Belgian, and Swiss Witnesses. European Witnesses risked their lives to bring relief supplies to the war-torn Balkans.

The Witnesses have repeated their pattern of defending their rights by legal means, as guaranteed by law. Their courtroom contests throughout the world have created precedents that strengthen liberties for all citizens. The European Court of Human Rights in Strasbourg, France, has handed the Witnesses major victories that compel emerging democracies to live up to their human rights commitments. The Witnesses are currently litigating about 400 religious-liberty cases worldwide.

From their modern beginning over 130 years ago until today, Jehovah's Witnesses have persistently preached about the imminent reign of God's Kingdom. Through periods of intense persecution, social and political unrest, public apathy, and growing secularization, the Witnesses have sustained a remarkable level of commitment and focus in their "campaign for the truth."

C. Important Dates & Landmarks

1870 Charles Taze Russell and acquaintances form a Bible study group in Allegheny (Pittsburgh), Pennsylvania.

1876–1879 Russell writes for various religious publications; he asserts that 1914 is a marked year in Bible chronology.

1879 First issue of *Zion's Watch Tower* released.

1881 Zion's Watch Tower Tract Society established; four-month pamphlet distribution surpassed by eight times the annual distribution by the American Tract Society.

1884 Zion's Watch Tower Tract Society legally chartered in Pennsylvania.

1900 First WTS branch office opens in London.

1909 WTS moves to Brooklyn, where it has remained—except for a brief return to Pittsburgh in 1918.

1910 International Bible Students Association established.

1914 "Photo-Drama of Creation" opens in New York in January.

1916 C. T. Russell, aged 64, dies.

1917 J. F. Rutherford becomes WTS president.

1918 Rutherford and seven associates convicted under the Espionage Act.

1919 Rutherford and associates released on bail and government prosecution withdrawn; WTS begins publishing *The Golden Age* (now published under the title *Awake!*).

1922 Bible Students begin radio broadcasting; a Cedar Point, Ohio, convention of the theme "Advertise the King and his kingdom" is held.

1931 Bible Students adopt the name "Jehovah's Witnesses" at their annual convention.

1933 Nazis ban Jehovah's Witnesses and in 1939 sentence Witness August Dickmann, the first conscientious objector of the war, to be condemned to death.

1935 Outreach held to a "great multitude," who will survive Armageddon and live on earth forever.

1938 Theocratic procedure replaces democratic procedure for selecting overseers.

1940 U.S. States Supreme Court rules 8–1 that officials can force students to salute flag.

1942 J. F. Rutherford dies; N. H. Knorr becomes WTS president.

1943 Watchtower Bible College of Gilead opens. Flag decision reversed.

1950 New World Translation of the Christian Greek Scriptures released.

1958 International convention at Yankee Stadium—with 253,922 in attendance.

1961 United States Witnesses reach concentration of 250,000; complete English New World Translation of the Holy Scriptures released.

1963 Density of Witnesses reaches 1 million residing in 198 countries.

1967 Waves of prolonged, savage persecution of Witnesses in Malawi (Africa).

1971 The Governing Body is enlarged and annual rotating chairmanship instituted.

1974 United States membership reaches 500,000; worldwide membership reaches two million in 207 countries.

1982 Witnesses develop Multilanguage Electronic Phototypesetting System.

1985 Density of Witnesses reaches over 3 million residing in 222 countries.

1986 Regional Building Committees organized for rapidly built Kingdom Halls.

1990 Witnesses win freedoms in Eastern Europe; four million Witnesses believed to exist worldwide.

1993 European Court of Human Rights rules that Greece violated the rights of Witness Minos Kokkinakis and that Jehovah's Witnesses are a "known religion"; 7,402 are baptized at a convention in Kiev, Ukraine—largest modern-day Witness gathering.

1994 About 400 Hutu and Tutsi Witnesses are killed during the Rwandan genocide; relief mission from France, Belgium, and Switzerland provides 35 tons of supplies.

1995 *The Watchtower* revises explanation of the "1914 generation;" 5 million Witnesses preach in 232 countries.

1998 Witnesses send volunteer medical teams and 400 tons of relief supplies to the Democratic Republic of Congo and the Republic of Congo.

2000 Active U.S. Witness membership reaches 1 million; 6 million worldwide.

2002 Supreme Court rules 8–1 in *Watchtower v. Village of Stratton* that a door-to-door permit ordinance is unconstitutional.

2005 Massive rebuilding effort organized in New Orleans after Hurricane Katrina.

2007 United States peak of 1,084,005 members in 12,494 congregations, and worldwide peak of 6,957,854 in 236 countries; the total attendance at an annual Memorial of Jesus's death is 17,672,443.

2008 European Court of Human Rights rules that Austria violated the Witnesses' religious freedom by denying them legal recognition as a religious society, leading to discrimination.

D. Important Figures

Charles Taze Russell (1852–1916)

Born in Allegheny, Pennsylvania, C. T. Russell grew up in a Presbyterian Scotch-Irish family. His mother, Ann Eliza, died when he was nine years old, and he and his father, Joseph, built a successful men's clothing business. In his autobiographical sketch, Russell describes his wide-ranging spiritual search as a teenager. The hellfire doctrine troubled him greatly. He briefly joined the Congregationalists, and later met Second Adventists, some of whom became his close associates. Russell initially avoided "time prophecies" because of failed Adventist expectations, but he reexamined the issue in discussions with religious thinkers, such as Jonas Wendell, George Storrs, George Stetson, and Nelson Barbour. In 1881, Russell founded the Watch Tower Tract Society.

As Russell's religious understandings solidified, several associates disagreed and broke with him over procedure or doctrine. Some critics had been *Watchtower* writers or lecturing "pilgrims." In 1894, Russell weathered an attempt to gain control of the society. Dissenters circulated surreptitious letters charging Russell with financial misconduct. Some Bible Students joined them, but an outpouring of support for Russell came from Bible Students in all quarters. Russell's wife, Maria, regularly contributed *Watchtower* articles, served as secretary-treasurer, and addressed groups of Bible Student women. However, in 1897, after eighteen years of marriage, she moved out of their home. Russell provided her with a separate home and financial support. In 1908, Maria obtained a legal separation from Russell for alleged "mental cruelty." Though she denied in court that Russell had been guilty of adultery, Russell's opponents seized on the proceedings to publicize unfounded rumors about his moral character.

Another scandal surrounded the sale of so-called Miracle Wheat. A 1907 Department of Agriculture report noted the discovery of a strain of high-yield wheat. The report received nationwide press coverage and piqued Russell's interest in a possible parallel with biblical prophecies. Two Bible Students grew thirty bushels of the wheat, offering the seeds at a discount to readers and donating the funds to the society. Total proceeds amounted to nearly $1,800. The *Brooklyn Daily Eagle*, a New York newspaper long critical of Russell, teamed up with religious critics, claiming that he profited personally, a difficult charge to sustain given Russell's extensive business interests and personal donations to the society's work. Nevertheless, historical accounts of Russell's life and reputation have often been molded by such polemical writings.

Ministers of mainstream churches evidently viewed Russell's popular ministry as a threat. Several ministers challenged Russell to a series of public debates. The Eaton-Russell debates of 1903 were held at Allegheny's Carnegie Hall before overflow crowds. According to press reports, Russell, a lone figure with Bible in hand, faced his Methodist-Episcopalian opponent, flanked by an ecumenical array of ministers occupying the stage in a show of support. Russell's syndicated weekly newspaper columns reached an estimated twelve million readers in 1911, nearly equivalent, he claimed, to the audience of all Protestant ministers in the country combined. In addition to lost members, one Baptist minister reportedly complained that the Bible Students' "no collections" policy had embarrassed New York ministers into ceasing use of collection plates, seriously impacting church coffers.

C. T. Russell died in 1916, leaving behind an international organization of volunteer evangelizers and an extensive body of theological writings.

Joseph Franklin Rutherford (1869–1942)

Born on a farm to a Baptist family in Morgan County, Missouri, Joseph Rutherford studied law, was a court reporter, and spent two years under the tutelage of Judge E. L. Edwards. Rutherford was admitted to the Missouri bar at age twenty-two and became a trial lawyer. He later served as a public prosecutor and then as "special judge," substituting for the Fourteenth Judicial District of Missouri. He subscribed to *The Watchtower* in 1894. Rutherford gave his first sermon, "Life, Death, and the Hereafter," to a small group of African-American farm workers near his home. He was baptized in 1906, and in 1907 became the WTS's legal counselor, overseeing the Society's move to Brooklyn, New York, in 1909.

Rutherford faced daunting challenges upon succeeding C. T. Russell to the presidency. Some Bible Students resented Rutherford's personality and leadership style, which differed from Russell's. Rutherford reprimanded Bible Students who seemed to create a personality cult around Russell, to the neglect of the Bible Students' mission. In July 1917, four WT directors sought administrative control over the society's affairs and the presidency, charging Rutherford with incompetence. After attempts at dialogue failed, Rutherford removed the four dissident directors, whose directorships, it turned out, had never legally been confirmed by corporation members. A war of words ensued, resulting in a number of schismatic groups. The reverberations of the succession controversy still echo in the historiography, which often depicts Rutherford as "authoritarian," in contrast with Russell. This perception is largely attributable to dissident Bible Student groups that have perpetuated the memory of these early disputes. Rutherford and the WTS survived the controversy and he assumed the role of inheritor of Russell's work.

On the heels of Rutherford's struggles over internal affairs came his conviction under the Espionage Act. While Rutherford and his seven associates were incarcerated, the Bible Students' activities flagged amid severe opposition. After the government released the eight men and dropped the charges, Rutherford launched new initiatives to revive the Bible Students' spirits and sense of mission. Like his predecessor, Rutherford authored numerous works and lectured widely, condemning the clergy, especially the Catholic hierarchy, at every opportunity. His direct, hands-on leadership set the tone for Jehovah's Witnesses as they entered the dif-

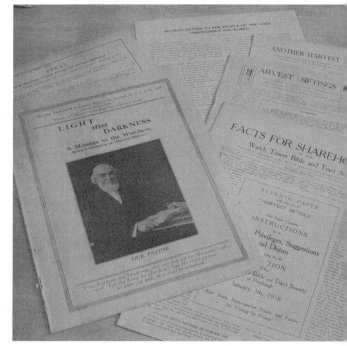

These 1917 pamphlets are just some of The Watchtower *publications issued during the schism between those who supported J. F. Rutherford and those who opposed him.*

ficult pre–World War II period. Their anticlerical message garnered attention disproportional to their modest numbers—only about 115,000 at the time of Rutherford's death. His efforts to centralize administration and standardize procedures can be seen as contributing greatly to the Witnesses' ability to withstand external challenges during the war.

Nathan Homer Knorr (1905–1977)

A native Pennsylvanian, Nathan Knorr was baptized and joined the WTS headquarters staff in 1923. Knorr became factory manager in 1932 and WTS president in 1942. He was known for his organizational abilities and his commitment to Bible education. Under his oversight, WTS headquarters and branch facilities expanded to accommodate escalating need. Knorr presided over a period of rapid growth, and in 1977, the year of his death, Witnesses numbered over 2.22 million.

Frederick W. Franz (1893–1992)

Since the Governing Body's restructuring in 1971, three presidents have held office. Frederick W. Franz became president in 1977. Serving at headquarters since 1920 and in the editorial department since 1926, Franz traveled extensively with N. H. Knorr, addressing audiences in several languages.

Milton G. Henschel (1921–2003)

Milton G. Henschel worked at WT headquarters for sixty years and became N. H. Knorr's secretary in 1939. Henschel visited over 150 countries, supporting missionaries and branch staff. He became president of the Watch Tower Society in 1992, and held that position for eight years.

Don A. Adams (1925–   )

Don A. Adams succeeded Henschel as president when the Governing Body changed the directorship of the WTS in 2000. The first non-Governing Body member to be president, and at headquarters for over sixty years, Adams has also traveled widely on behalf of Jehovah's Witnesses.

II. Tenets and Beliefs

A. Articles of Faith

Jehovah's Witnesses have no formal creed. They point to the teachings of Jesus Christ and the apostles, as outlined in the Christian Greek Scriptures, to support their key teachings. Principles from the Hebrew Scriptures also elucidate their doctrine. Witnesses believe in progressive revelation, expecting their doctrine to be refined over time. They acknowledge that although they attempt to discern the significance of prophecy, complete understanding of the fulfillment of prophecy often comes only after foretold events take place.

Jehovah, Jesus, and Holy Spirit

"Jehovah" is the personal name of Almighty God, Creator and Universal Sovereign. The name, based on the Hebrew tetragrammaton, occurs in Hebrew Bible manuscripts over seven thousand times. Only Jehovah should be worshiped and obeyed by Christians as absolute ruler. His cardinal qualities are love, wisdom, justice, and power. In accord with Jesus's model prayer, sanctifying God's name by word and deed is a Jehovah's Witness's primary focus.

According to Witness doctrine, Jesus is the only begotten Son of God, the firstborn of all creation—that is, the only creature directly created by Jehovah. Through the prehuman Jesus, Jehovah created all other spiritual and material creation. Witnesses believe that before coming to earth as a human, Jesus lived in heaven with Jehovah, along with other angels, or spirit sons. In his role as archangel, Jesus is called Michael. Jehovah appointed Jesus to come to earth to die a sacrificial death for sinful humans. Hence, the Witness definition of the term "Christ," or messiah: anointed by God to be humankind's savior. Witnesses offer all prayers to God in Jesus's name. They believe that after Jesus's death, God resurrected him as an immortal spirit and exalted him to a higher position than he had before. In time, Jesus became king of God's Kingdom, and according to Witness interpretation of biblical prophecy, he will lead angelic armies against the wicked at God's war of Armageddon. He will then rule the earth for one thousand years.

"Holy spirit" is defined by Jehovah's Witnesses as God's impersonal but powerful active force used to accomplish his will. By this force, they believe, Jehovah created the universe, guided Bible writers, empowered prophets to perform miracles, and answers prayers. Jehovah's Witnesses reject the Trinity doctrine as a fourth-century interpolation of Christian teaching. Consequently, many mainstream Christian churches do not consider the Witnesses to be Christian. Scholars admit, however, that neither the word nor the explicit concept of "Trinity" is found in Scripture.

Soul and Spirit

Humans and animals are considered souls, having no immaterial part that survives after death. "Spirit," as applied in scripture to humans, refers to their active life force, which ceases to function at death.

Life and Death

Jehovah's Witnesses literally interpret man's origins according to the second chapter of Genesis, in which Adam and Eve are said to have had perfect human life in the earthly Garden of Eden, where God intended them and their children to live forever. As the account relates, when Adam and Eve sinned, they rejected Jehovah's rulership, introducing sin and death to humanity. The word "sin" in the original languages means to "miss the mark" of perfection. Death is the "wages," or result, of sin and is a total cessation of life functions, compared in Scripture to sleep or unconsciousness (Ecclesiastes 9:15). The belief that life is sacred compels Jehovah's Witnesses to abstain from war. The Witnesses respect governmental authority to exact penalties, including capital punishment, but they recognize that human governments often abuse power and make misjudgments.

Salvation and Resurrection

Though Witnesses believe all sinful humans deserve death, they hold that Jehovah provided Jesus as a ransom to save humankind. Therefore, they maintain that those exercising faith in Jesus's ransom sacrifice receive the undeserved gift of eternal life. Life is not earned by righteous acts, but such acts demonstrate genuine faith and appreciation for the love of God and Christ. However, Witnesses warn that salvation is provisional and can be lost by unrepentant sinners. Those deemed unworthy of life undergo the punishment of eternal death. The Witnesses do not believe that God punishes the wicked in hellfire. The vast majority of the dead will be resurrected with perfect human bodies to help fulfill God's original purpose for a paradise on earth.

Heaven and God's Kingdom

Witnesses maintain that God and faithful spirit creatures dwell in the invisible heavens, to which a limited number of humans are resurrected as spirit creatures. These 144,000 male and female Christians from Christ's time down till now have been anointed with God's holy spirit. They constitute "the Israel of God" and will be kings and priests with Jesus (Galatians 6:16; Revelation 14:1). Witnesses believe that while on earth, anointed Christians constitute the "faithful and discreet slave" who supplies "spiritual food" to the "household of faith" (Matthew 24:45–47). All Witnesses view themselves as subjects of God's kingdom and maintain neutrality toward politics and military affairs. They seek to imitate Jesus and early Christians, who did not take up arms or political causes. Based on Daniel's prophecy of the "Gentile Times," the Witnesses maintain that God's kingdom was established in heaven in 1914, signaling the impending end of Satan's system.

Last Days and Armageddon

Bible chronology has long been a part of Witness doctrine. Passages in Daniel, 2 Timothy, and Revelation, and Jesus's "great prophecy" in the Gospels, underpin the Witnesses' belief that the present world system will soon end. Divine destruction first comes against "Babylon the Great," defined as worldwide false religion (Revelation 17). Armageddon follows, destroying the corrupt political and commercial system, along with those judged as wicked by God. Righteous survivors form the core of a new world society based on divine rule.

Although Jesus stated that no one knows in advance when the day will come, Bible Students and Jehovah's Witnesses have periodically attempted to calculate the likely timing of Jehovah's progressive purpose. Bible Students expected the earthly resurrection of ancient prophets in 1925. Many Witnesses considered 1975 significant, marking the end of 6,000 years of human history from the biblical creation of Adam. Although Witness literature did not state dogmatically that 1975 would bring

Armageddon, it later acknowledged that some published statements "were likely more definite than advisable." Following periods of disappointed expectations, Witness ranks saw slight, short-term decreases. Until 1995, the Witnesses had held that the literal generation of people alive when the "last days" began in 1914 would also see the wicked system end. The "generation" mentioned in Jesus's prophecy is now understood to mean the group of anointed Christian contemporaries who experience the "end," rather than a set span of years.

Jews and the Mosaic Law

In the book of Genesis, God promises Abraham that the entire human family will be blessed through his offspring. Furthermore, God makes a covenant with the nation of Israel to become King, Judge, and Lawgiver. They, in turn, become dedicated to God as his chosen people, through whom the Messiah, or Christ, would come. "The Mosaic Law"—rules of religious observance given to the Israelites through Moses—guided the nation and demonstrated the blessings that accrue to worshippers of Jehovah. Jesus, the apostles, and all the Bible writers were Jews. Jesus, the promised Messiah, fulfilled the Law Covenant and inaugurated a new covenant with his disciples who acknowledged him as God's anointed. After Jesus's death, all humans could enjoy a dedicated relationship with God based not on birth but on faith. Witnesses hold that Christians are not bound by the Mosaic Law, such as the Sabbath or dietary laws. The Bible Students once believed that the literal nation of Israel held special significance in prophecy, but that view changed in the late 1920s. The Witnesses do not teach that Jews as a people are responsible for Jesus's death; nor do they believe that Jews now hold a special place in God's purpose.

Gifts of the Spirit

Witnesses believe that God empowered Jesus's apostles to speak in tongues, heal, and prophesy to demonstrate God's favor on the newly established Christian congregation and to facilitate the preaching work. However, they also believe that these miraculous gifts of the spirit ceased at the death of the apostles and those to whom they passed these abilities.

Devil, Demons, and Spiritism

Witnesses say that a rebellious angel became God's chief adversary shortly after the creation of the first humans. He is called Satan, meaning "resister," and Devil, meaning "slanderer," because he lied to Eve and seeks to turn all intelligent creatures away from worshipping Jehovah. According to Witness doctrine, an unknown number of angels followed Satan and are called demons. These demons wield unseen but destructive influence on earth and will be defeated at Armageddon.

B. Scripture

Jehovah's Witnesses view the entire Bible, comprised of sixty-six books penned by approximately forty writers over 1,600 years ago, as God's inspired and infallible word, far superior to any human writing. The Witnesses believe that some Bible texts are to be taken literally and other passages are figurative. Scribal errors and interpolations in Bible manuscripts have been corrected through comparative reading. According to Witnesses, arguably the most serious violation of the sacred Scriptures has been the removal of God's name, Jehovah.

In 1950, Jehovah's Witnesses released the *New World Translation of the Christian Greek Scriptures*, based primarily on Westcott and Hort's 1881 master Greek text. The complete *New World Translation of the Hebrew Scriptures* was issued in 1960 and restored the divine name as in the original text. The translators relied on Kittel's *Biblia Hebraica*, 1951–1955 edition, as well as on available manuscripts of the Dead Sea Scrolls and other early manuscripts. Religious studies professor Jason BeDuhn evaluated the *New World Translation* as "one of the most accurate English translations of the New Testament currently available." The complete *New World Translation* is published in forty-three languages and the *New World Translation of the Christian Greek Scriptures* in twenty additional languages.

C. Secondary Sources

Bible Students and Jehovah's Witnesses have distributed vast amounts of literature containing biblical truth as they understand it. Since 1942, the editorial policy of the WTS has been to publish articles anonymously in order to place greater emphasis on the author of the Bible, Jehovah. The New World Bible Translation Committee also followed this policy. Writers of WT publications are Jehovah's Witnesses from diverse backgrounds and many countries.

In addition to WT publications, biographical accounts by longtime Witnesses, such as those by Alexander H. MacMillan, Marley Cole, and Victor Blackwell, provide further background on Jehovah's Witnesses and their organizational and congregational life. The courtroom triumphs of Witness attorneys, such as Hayden C. Covington and Canadian H. Glen How, have established a foundation of legal precedents upon which fundamental civil liberties have been built. Constitutional scholars frequently comment on the historical significance of the Witnesses' fifty Supreme Court victories. The 2006 film documentary *Knocking*, by non-Witness directors Joel P. Engardio and Tom Shepard, is the most recent work to acknowledge the Witnesses' contribution to religious freedom.

As with most social or religious groups, Jehovah's Witnesses have their critics. A small number are "apostates," former members who actively propagate their discontent. *The Watchtower* encourages Jehovah's Witnesses not to examine apostate writings, cautioning that such material is likely laced with false statements and slander. The Internet has facilitated the spread of critical views, helping to mold media and public opinion by reinforcing stereotypes common to minority religious groups. The religious mainstream and anticult groups have also targeted Jehovah's Witnesses, lumping them with groups they deem physically or psychologically dangerous. Jehovah's Witnesses have not entered into public dialogue with such critics, choosing to allow the public ministry of Jehovah's Witnesses to speak for itself.

III. Rites and Rituals

A. The Calendar

Jehovah's Witnesses refer to the Bible to set their religious calendar. The only annual celebration recorded in the Christian Greek scriptures is the Memorial of Jesus's death, instituted by Christ himself. After concluding the Jewish Passover with his apostles on the night before his death, Jesus gave them red wine and unleavened bread as symbols of his blood and body. Held on Nisan 14, according to the Bible calendar, the Memorial is viewed by Jehovah's Witnesses as the most sacred night of the year, during which all congregations gather to consider the significance of Jesus's ransom. Following the pattern Jesus set, red wine and unleavened bread are passed to all attendees, but only those who claim to have been anointed as members of the 144,000 actually partake of the emblems.

Since 1925, Witnesses avoid celebrating religious or political holidays, especially if their rituals mimic those of non-Christian religions or if they tend to unduly exalt a human. Birthday celebrations are said to include pagan rituals and are spoken of unfavorably in Scripture, whereas Witness couples often mark wedding anniversaries and other life events.

Aside from their weekly congregational meetings, Jehovah's Witnesses gather three times a year for larger assemblies and conventions, which include Bible talks, interviews, reenactments, and costume dramas. Large Witness conventions have traditionally provided international Christian fellowship and often feature the release of new publications.

B. Worship and Liturgy

The weekly meetings of Jehovah's Witnesses are free and open to the public. Their worship includes few formal rituals and their Kingdom Halls display no images or religious symbols. Their simple religious services, like the meetings of early Bible Students, emphasize group study and instruction. Congregations usually meet twice a week for a total of four hours, during which prescribed scriptures and supplementary literature are discussed, primarily by audience participation. The curriculum covered includes thematic scriptural talks, public speaking instruction, teaching models, and advice on Christian living. Meetings begin and end with song and prayer.

C. Daily Life

Jesus stated that the two greatest commandments for Christians are to "love Jehovah your God" and "to love your neighbor as yourself." Witnesses endeavor to focus their life goals and decisions around these principles. Love of neighbor is shown by treating others with respect and dignity, by performing good deeds, by not engaging in harmful or dangerous practices, and foremost by preaching about God's Kingdom.

Witnesses show love for God in daily life by adhering to the Bible's moral standards, despite liberalizing trends. They believe that God approves of sexual relations only between marriage partners, and therefore view premarital, extramarital, and homosexual sex as immoral. Witnesses are to harmonize their employment, recreation, and entertainment with their moral standards. Witnesses must "render Caesar's things to Caesar" by complying with the law, unless it requires violation of divine law as it would be applied to marriages, finances, taxes, and so forth.

With the exception of a prohibition on ingesting blood, the Witnesses have no dietary restrictions. Modest dress and grooming is stressed, since Wit-

nesses consider themselves ministers and representatives of Jehovah in the community.

D. Life Cycle Events

Witnesses have no prescribed birth rituals. Wedding ceremonies are a matter of individual choice, though moderation is encouraged. No set rituals or strictures govern burial or cremation.

The main rite of passage for Witnesses is baptism by full water immersion, publicly symbolizing their Christian dedication to God. Adults and mature children who demonstrate a sufficient scriptural knowledge, a life in compliance with Bible morality, and a desire to make a lifelong dedication to Jehovah are eligible for baptism.

E. Family Life

The family is highly esteemed as the basic unit of the congregation. Marriage of a man and a woman is viewed as a vow of fidelity for life. The man is considered the head of the household, and he is to treat his wife in the same considerate manner that Christ does the congregation. Children are a blessing from God, to be reared in the faith, but they are not considered full participating members of the Witness community until they personally decide on dedication and baptism. Contraception is a matter of personal choice except for types that induce abortions. Divorce and remarriage are permitted only on the grounds of adultery, although an innocent mate may choose to forgive the adulterer and remain in the marriage. If a Witness mate is disfellowshipped from the congregation for reasons other than adultery, the marriage is still binding. In cases of severe abuse or neglect, separation is permissible. Mixed-race marriages are common. Religiously mixed marriages between a Witness and a non-Witness are also common, especially when one mate becomes a Witness after the couple marries. Witnesses whose marriage partners have different religions or no religion are urged to treat their mates with respect and love, fully living up to their marriage vows.

IV. Denominations and Demographics

Scholar J. Gordon Melton's *Encyclopedia of American Religions* (2002) names twelve schismatic groups founded by former Bible Students or Jehovah's Witnesses. Some groups claim to faithfully represent C. T. Russell's theological views, while others broke over doctrine, policy, or personal disagreements. Information on group membership is difficult to obtain, as most have no figures or number adherents according to mailing lists. According to best estimates, the groups range in size from a few hundred to several thousand; all appear to rely on newsletters and periodicals to maintain cohesion.

Among larger groups, Melton names the Dawn Bible Students Association, which dates back to the late 1920s and currently has an estimated 3,000 U.S. adherents; 9,000 worldwide. "The Dawn," Melton states, "carries on the most extensive outreach ministry of any of the Bible Student groups other than the Jehovah's Witnesses."

The Laymen's Home Missionary Movement was founded by Paul S. L. Johnson, who broke with J. F. Rutherford in 1918. Melton calls the movement "one of the 'orthodox' Bible Student groups," which still relies on Russell's writings, and estimates their numbers at 10,000.

V. Organization and Infrastructure

A. Education and Leadership

Jehovah's Witnesses have no professional clergy; all baptized congregation members are considered ordained ministers. Witnesses perform pastoral duties or congregational functions according to their abilities and circumstances. After the apostolic pattern, qualified male elders teach, counsel, perform weddings and funerals, and assess the suitability of baptismal candidates and others who may assume congregation responsibilities. Ministerial servants handle operational matters, such as building maintenance, public address, and literature stock. They may assist in conducting meetings and leading groups in the public ministry, which trains them to be elders.

Witnesses attend training schools according to their ministerial responsibilities. Besides the weekly Theocratic Ministry School, the society sponsors schools for elders, ministerial servants, and pioneers (full-time evangelizers). Schools are tuition-free and are arranged locally by branch offices. Training schools for congregation elders, missionaries, traveling ministers, and branch and headquarters personnel are held at the Watchtower Educational Center in Patterson, New York.

All congregation members in good moral standing are expected to share regularly in preaching publicly. In 2007, Jehovah's Witnesses spent 1.4 billion hours doing that. Most Witnesses work secularly to support their families and are called "publishers," that is, they publicize their message, averaging ten hours a month. Roughly 10 percent of Witnesses enter the full-time ministry as "pioneers," spending about seventy hours each month in preaching work. Missionaries and special pioneers spend around 140 hours monthly, with time goals adjusted for age. They receive a small reimbursement to cover living expenses, with the local branch office generally caring for their health needs. Pioneer and missionary service are voluntary and may be discontinued at any time.

Congregations are organized into circuits, and circuits into districts. Traveling ministers known as circuit and district overseers are the modern counterparts of early Christian itinerants and Bible Student pilgrims. These overseers visit congregations and organize circuit assemblies, an arrangement to promote unity, peace, and enthusiasm for the ministry.

Traveling overseers and their wives receive a small stipend for living and travel expenses.

Witnesses support all congregational, ministerial, and publishing activities by means of voluntary donations. The Witnesses do not practice tithing or pass collection plates at their meetings. Every Kingdom Hall or assembly site has donations boxes, where attendees anonymously contribute funds to support local and worldwide activities. In their ministry, Witnesses sometimes meet non-Witnesses who wish to contribute toward the work of Jehovah's Witnesses. These donations are sent to the local branch office.

B. Houses of Worship

Since 1935, Jehovah's Witnesses have called their houses of worship "Kingdom Halls," reflecting the theme of their Bible message. Kingdom Halls are owned and maintained by local congregations. Larger assemblies and conventions are often held at rented facilities. However, in areas with large concentrations of Witnesses, assembly halls may be built and used by nearby circuits or districts. Kingdom Halls and Assembly Halls are usually simple structures with a lobby, main auditorium with a speaker's platform, and several smaller meeting rooms.

C. Governance and Authority

The Governing Body is made up of a varying number of anointed Christian men and supervises the worldwide work of Jehovah's Witnesses, providing theological and administrative direction. The Witnesses' international headquarters is in Brooklyn, New York, with additional facilities in upstate New York. The volunteer staff of about 20,000 work in 114 branches worldwide and live in self-sufficient facilities called Bethel, meaning "House of God" in Hebrew.

The Watch Tower Bible and Tract Society—one of a number of corporate entities established by Jehovah's Witnesses to support the operation of their cause—is supervised by the Governing Body. This particular corporation functions as the main legal entity for the religion.

In 2000, the Witnesses set up three additional nonprofit corporations in the United States to take over much of the business and administrative work of the movement, and free the Governing Body to devote more of their resources to spiritual matters.

These corporations are

- **Christian Congregation of Jehovah's Witnesses,** which deals with religious and educational issues;
- **Religious Order of Jehovah's Witnesses,** which deals with full-time workers;
- **Kingdom Support Services, Inc,** which deals with buildings and vehicles.

D. Social Service Organizations

Relief efforts for natural and manmade disasters are coordinated by the Governing Body through local branch offices. Close-knit congregations provide social support, such as hospital visitation, family and bereavement counseling, transportation assistance, and support for the elderly and infirm. Where individuals qualify for government assistance, congregation members may assist them to apply. Branch offices also assist Witnesses who are victims of religious discrimination to pursue their legal options. All such services are rendered without charge.

E. Media and Communication

Jehovah's Witnesses today still use the door-to-door ministry as their main means of communicating their faith. However, in addition to several basic text books on doctrine, a couple of widely circulated publications serve as additional disseminators of information.

The Watchtower

Founded by Charles Taze Russell as *Zion's Watch Tower and Herald of Christ's Presence* in 1879, *The Watchtower* is printed semimonthly in 167 languages with editions in 130 languages simultaneously. Each issue of the edition dated the first of each month includes the article series "Did You Know?", "Draw Close to God," and "Our Readers Ask," which present information on specific Bible passages and answers to common Bible questions. The series entitled "Keys to Family Happiness," "Imitate Their Faith," and "What We Learn From Jesus" appear every three months, and the series "Teach Your Children" and "For Our Young People" are published in alternate issues.

The Watchtower issues dated the fifteenth of each month feature four or five study articles based on scripture. Virtually all of the Jehovah's Witness communities worldwide discuss the same information each week at the Watchtower Study. A typical issue usually includes topics such as Bible prophecy, Christian conduct and morals, and the history of religion and the Bible.

A writing committee within the organization oversees the research, editing, and development of the articles. The articles are written by the editorial staff at headquarters and by writers at the branch offices worldwide. All copy is checked by a team of editors at headquarters, and then translated into the languages of publication by over 2,600 translators in 139 countries. All articles are produced under the direction of the Governing Body; therefore, the content is considered the official position of the organization.

Awake!

First published in 1919 by International Bible Students as *The Golden Age*, *Awake!* is a companion magazine to *The Watchtower*. *Awake!* publishes articles on science, nature, and geography, usually from a biblical perspective.

More information may be found at: www.watchtower.org.

FURTHER READING

Between Resistance and Martyrdom: Jehovah's Witnesses in the Third Reich
Detlef Garbe (Dagmar Grim, Translator)
2008: University of Wisconsin Press

Jehovah's Witnesses: Portrait of a Contemporary Religious Movement
Andrew Holden
2002: Taylor & Francis

8 The Church of Jesus Christ of Latter-day Saints (Mormonism)

I. Origins and Early History

A. Introduction

THE CHURCH OF JESUS CHRIST OF LATTER-DAY Saints, perhaps better known as Mormonism, is a faith that can be legitimately called a homegrown American brand of Christianity. The church's founder, Joseph Smith, was American born and hailed from Palmyra, New York, and the current Church is headquartered in Salt Lake City, Utah. It is from the United States that this religion has spread all over the world, for Mormonism now has attracted adherents in many other lands.

The Angel Moroni was said to have visited Joseph Smith Jr. on numerous occasions. This statue was sculpted by Karl Quilter and sits atop the Mormon temple in Bern, Switzerland.

Mormonism has also had its many critics and detractors since its inception. Some criticism has been brought on by what have been perceived as its breaks from mainstream Christianity, while at other times it was brought on by practices that have offended the sensibilities of fellow citizens. Time and again, Mormonism has tested the ideals of freedom of religion and the separation of church and state on which the United States was founded. The Mormon practice of polygamy was a contentious issue in the area of religious freedom, since the congressional ban against plural marriage seemed in direct conflict with Mormon religious practices—until the Church of Jesus Christ of Latter-day Saints itself officially banned polygamy among its members.

Then, when Utah was originally made a territory of the United States of America there were fears that it would become a theocracy, violating the boundary between church and state, and this led to U.S. military action (as we will see below).

More recently, however, Mormonism has entered the mainstream consciousness of American culture. The HBO television series *Big Love*, which portrays in a sympathetic light a fundamentalist sect of Mormonism that still practices polygamy, has become popular, bringing what was once a taboo subject into pop culture awareness. And what is perhaps the most significant measure of Mormonism's acceptance by mainstream America is the fact that a practicing Mormon, Mitt Romney, could be elected governor of a New England state and mount a serious campaign for the Republican nomination for president. For a religious movement that has, since its beginnings, been plagued by controversy, public ignorance, and prejudice, this represents a major step forward and makes the need to understand the beliefs and practices of the Church of Latter-day Saints all the more pressing.

B. The Religion in America

Quiet contentment among nineteenth-century Americans with traditional religious values, practices, and institutions was dealt a mighty blow by the Second Great Awakening, which swept through young America in 1800, leaving in its wake widespread regions of bustling religious pioneering. Palmyra, New York, was one such region. In 1820, a fourteen-year-old boy—one Joseph Smith—began to question the veracity of commonly practiced religions. According to Smith's writings, he received in response a revelation from God telling him that none of the established churches was the true church. The local Palmyra minister discounted Smith's vision, which brought about severe ostracism by the community.

This did not quiet Smith's inquiring mind, however, and, on September 22, 1823, an angel named Moroni allegedly visited Smith and led him to a treasure guarded by the angel: Smith dug up a 1,400-year-old book of golden plates, buried in a box on Cumorah Hill in Manchester, New York, on which the history of God and the ancient inhabitants of the New World was written. Smith was not allowed to remove the plates from their hiding place in the ground until four years later, when Moroni deemed him worthy of the gift. Smith and his wife, Emma, then quickly relocated to Pennsylvania, where they began to translate the plates with the help of Smith's scribe, Oliver Cowdery. Their translation later became the *Book of Mormon*. The book was published in March 1830, and on April 6 of that year, Joseph Smith organized the Church of Christ—now called the Church of Jesus Christ of Latter-day Saints—in Fayette, New York.

The fourteen years that followed were pivotal in Mormon history. Membership in the Church continued to rise and with it came persecution. Early in the history of the Church, the behavior of outsiders towards the Mormons was discriminatory and close-minded. This greatly influenced the history of the Church, and it is this history that it is essential to understand in order to comprehend the present state of the Church.

Soon after the Church's establishment, Joseph Smith sent missionaries to Missouri to preach the Gospel to Native Americans. During a stop in Kirtland, Ohio, the missionaries, led by Cowdery, found much success among residents. In the next few months, a hundred new members were baptized. Joseph Smith, allegedly guided by divine direction, moved himself and his followers to Ohio. During the seven years Smith spent in Ohio, three significant changes occurred: church membership grew to over 16,000; Smith recorded his own revelations; and the first temple was built in 1836. Church debts mounted and Smith, along with many of the other Mormons, became the target of persecution and violent threats, forcing many of them to leave their homes. Smith was directed to once again move his church westward—this time to Missouri.

Joseph Smith arrived in Independence, Missouri, in July of 1831. In 1838, he came to Far West, Missouri, which had been settled by members of the church who had been driven from their homes in

Joseph Smith (1805–1844) was the founder of the Mormon religion. His tenth "Article of Faith" was that Zion would be established on the American continent.

Brigham Young (1801–1877) was nicknamed the Mormon Moses as much for his appearance as for his actions.

Independence. Almost immediately, the Mormons suffered intense persecution. The violence continued to increase, fueled by Governor Lilburn W. Bogg's Extermination Order. This led to what was called the Mormon War, which left seventeen Mormons dead. With 2,000 soldiers surrounding their camp, 10,000 Church members fled Missouri in the 1830s for a new settlement in Commerce, Illinois (later named Nauvoo).

The most important aspect of Nauvoo ("beautiful" in Hebrew,) was that the state granted them their own community and rights to a fair court system and a militia. By 1841, the community was settled and preparations began to build what would later become an imposing 50,000-square-foot temple, a project that took five years to complete.

By 1844, anti-Mormon sentiments began to flare again because Nauvoo had become the biggest, most prosperous town in Illinois. This resentment was fueled by the publication of newspaper articles and pamphlets about Joseph Smith and the Mormon practice of plural marriage—a type of polygamy. Fearing for the safety of his followers, Smith surrendered to Governor Thomas Ford and agreed to be tried. Incarcerated in Carthage Jail on June 25, 1844, both Joseph Smith and his brother Hyrum were killed on June 27 by an angry and armed mob of approximately 200 people.

Since the plan of succession was unclear to many members of the church, internal power struggles ensued, splitting the church. However, within the next two years, with persecution intensifying against them, the majority of the Mormons left Illinois, heading west toward Utah. Their leader was Brigham Young, the president of the Quorum of the Twelve Apostles, who became the president of the church, and, according to the doctrine of the Church of Jesus Christ of the Latter-day Saints, the next prophet. Young was possessed of a great organizational capability, able to lead the church to a new home, westward across the Great Plains and Rocky Mountains to the Salt Lake Valley. This westward movement is known today as the "Pioneer Trek."

Despite physical hardships and multiple deaths, Brigham Young and the initial group of Mormon pioneers arrived in Salt Lake Valley on July 24, 1847. Almost immediately, a large number of converts began emigrating from abroad, and, in 1849, Young established the Perpetual Emigrating Fund, an interest-free loan provided to those who wanted to settle in Utah. (This program was disbanded in 1887 after the government froze the Church's financial assets due to their polygamous practices.)

Settling the Church's headquarters in Salt Lake City quickly became a priority, and when Utah became a territory, the governmental center was established there as well. Fearing competition for land and space, the Mormons founded more than 500 communities in an area stretching from the Midwest to California and from Canada to Mexico by the end of the nineteenth century.

Brigham Young was named Utah's governor when it became a territory in 1850. Immediately, two major issues began to concern the U.S. government: plural marriages and fear that Mormons were trying to create a theocracy. The U.S. government in 1857—in what came to be called the Utah War—sent troops to forcibly remove Young from his post as governor. Peace between the Mormons and the U.S. government came when the Mormons agreed to receive a new governor appointed by President Buchanan.

Subsequently, the Mormons lived in fear of an attack from the United States government. In September 1857, an emigrant train passed through Utah. A group of Mormons in southern Utah waged an attack on the emigrant passengers, causing the deaths of more than 120 civilians. This event is now known as the Mountain Meadows Massacre.

The Church of the Latter-day Saints officially banned the practice of polygamy in 1890 when the laws set up against this practice were found to be constitutional. Over the next few years, the church restored a positive image when its choir placed second at the Chicago World's Fair. Another factor was the completion of the Salt Lake Temple—forty years in the making—which demonstrated the Mormon's dedication to Utah. Despite its appeals to the public, people continued to criticize Mormons, especially as related to polygamy, even long after the ban had gone into effect. The Church's ongoing welfare program—founded during the depression—the missionary program, the genealogical resources and library, the humanitarian aid projects, and public relations efforts with the media, have helped improve the image of the Church. Although many of their efforts paid off, the Church still battles negative stereotypes today.

C. Important Dates and Landmarks

1805 Joseph Smith is born.

1820 Joseph Smith receives his first vision.

1827 Joseph Smith receives the golden plates at Hill Cumorah.

1830 The *Book of Mormon* is published. "Church of Christ" is organized in Fayette, New York.

1836 The first temple of the Church of Jesus Christ of the Latter-day Saints—the Kirtland Temple—is dedicated.

1842 The *Articles of Faith* is published. Female Relief Society of Nauvoo is formed.

1844 Joseph Smith and his brother, Hyrum, killed by mob while in Carthage, Illinois, jail.

1846 Brigham Young becomes Church's second president. Arrives in Salt Lake Valley.

1862 Congress passes legislation that defines polygamy as criminal bigamy.

1870 Women in Utah receive right to vote.

1877 Brigham Young dies at 76.

1880 *Pearl of Great Price* is canonized.

1890 The Church of Jesus Christ of the Latter-day Saints bans polygamy.

1893 Salt Lake Temple is dedicated.

1896 Utah becomes a state.

1929 Mormon Tabernacle Choir begins weekly network radio broadcasts.

1961 First non-English–speaking stake is organized in The Hague, Netherlands.

1970 Monday is named Family Home Evening.

1982 Subtitle *Another Testament of Jesus Christ* is added to the Book of Mormon's title. Membership hits the 5 million mark.

1978 Priesthood extended to all males deemed worthy.

1984 Personal Ancestral File software is released, providing a genealogical program for personal computers.

1991 *Encyclopedia of Mormonism* is published, prepared by Brigham Young University editors.

1995 "The Family: A Proclamation to the World" is issued.

1996 Church announces that a majority of its members live outside the U.S.

1999 FamilySearch Internet Genealogy Service is launched. Generates 3 billion hits in its first year.

2000 100 millionth copy of the *Book of Mormon* printed.

2000 Conference center with 21,000-seat capacity dedicated.

2002 Salt Lake City hosts the Winter Olympic Games.

2002 Rebuilt Nauvoo Temple dedicated on the anniversary of Joseph Smith's martyrdom.

2008 Gordon B. Hinckley, 15th president, dies at age 97.

2007-2008 Mitt Romney, former governor of Massachusetts and church member, mounts run for Republican presidential nomination.

2008 Thomas S. Monson is ordained the 16th Church president.

D. Important Figures

Joseph Smith (1805–1844)

Joseph Smith stands as the most significant figure in Mormon history. He is credited not only with founding the religion, but also with its initial expansion. His scribe, Oliver Cowdery (1806–1850) was also influential in the founding of Mormonism because he supported Smith, testified to the veracity of his claims, and served as a missionary in order to spread the newly acquired revelation.

Others key figures from this time period include Joseph Smith's brothers Hyrum (1800–1844) and Samuel (1808–1844), and his son Joseph Smith III (1832–1914); Sidney Rigdon (1793–1876), Smith's friend and counselor; and Brigham Young (1801–1877), the leader of the pioneer trek into Utah and the second president of the Church. Martin Harris (1783–1875) was an early convert to the Church and underwrote the *Book of Mormon*. John Taylor

(1808–1887), a member of the Quorum of Twelve, was wounded at Carthage jail and later served as the third Church president. Parley P. Pratt (1807–1857), another member of the Quorum of Twelve, was an influential writer, poet, and missionary within the Church of the Latter-day Saints. Wilford Woodruff (1807–1898) was also influential because as fourth president of the church, he signed the 1890 Manifesto that ended plural marriage. Joseph F. Smith (1838–1918), Hyrum's son, was an important voice in the church for many years, and as the sixth president of the church received an important revelation that is now included in church scripture. His son, Joseph Fielding Smith (1876–1972), served as the tenth president.

Reed Smoot (1862–1941)

Reed Smoot (right on *Time* cover) paved the way for Mormon participation in the American political system when he was elected to the Senate as the first native Utahan and Latter-day Saints member. Joseph Freeman (1952–present) was the first black member of the

Latter Day Saints church member Reed Smoot, a Republican, served the United States Senate for five terms, from 1902 to 1932.

Church of Latter-day Saints to be ordained into the priesthood and receive temple ordinances. He was able to join after a ban was lifted in 1978. Gordon B. Hinkley (1910–2008) is known for dedicating more temples than any other—more than half of the temples that exist today.

Other Celebrated Church Members

Other nationally and internationally famous members of the Church of Latter-day Saints are:

• **Stephen R. Covey**, the best-selling author of *The 7 Habits of Highly Effective People,* a self-help book tinged with Mormon gospel, which has sold over 15 million copies;

- **Orrin Hatch,** a prominent Republican senator from Utah since 1977;
- **Mitt Romney,** governor of Massachusetts in 2002, and a serious contender for the 2008 Republican nomination for president of the United States;
- **Gladys Knight,** Hall of Fame singer;
- **The Osmond family,** entertainers and TV stars;
- **Steve Young,** professional football star, Super Bowl champion—and Brigham Young descendant.

II. Tenets and Beliefs

A. Articles of Faith

While the Church of Jesus Christ of the Latter-day Saints has a group of distinctive doctrines and teachings, it does not have a formal creed system. The fundamental tenet of the religion is the belief that God gave revelations to Joseph Smith and that such direct communication continued—and still continues today—through successors, all of whom are considered prophets. The ability to receive revelation is not limited to church leaders, but is available to all Mormons. This principle of revelation therein forms the foundation of the Church of Jesus Christ of the Latter-day Saints.

The church leaders provide answers for the congregants to the large questions, such as "Why are we here?" and "Where are we going?" They do so through God's plan of salvation, which takes humans through four distinct stages of existence. The phases are: the premortal life, mortal probation or the "second estate," the spirit world, and the three degrees of glory.

Premortality

The notion of premortality is central to the Church of Jesus Christ of the Latter-day Saints. Joseph Smith taught that the essence of each individual human being, or "intelligence" in Church terms, was not created, but has always existed. He said that God, or the Heavenly Father, created the spirit bodies for the billions of intelligences with his eternal wife, the Heavenly Mother. These spirit children lived with their Heavenly Parents where they developed individual personalities and prepared to prove their faith to God through an earthly test.

A significant aspect of the transition from premortality to the second estate is that the spirits themselves choose to adopt physical bodies and undergo the test of mortality on earth. Through Scripture and statements from prophet leaders, some major events in the premortal world are understood, but events associated with individual lives are generally not known. However, through personal revelation or patriarchal blessing, a member may learn a limited amount of information about his or her premortal life, but must rely on faith concerning most aspects of it. But life on earth is not easy: there are constant temptations from devils, and God allows accidents and tragedies to occur in order to test his children. God does not interfere with human decisions, however; Mormons believe in the principle of personal choice. In addition to resisting temptation and living a faithful life on earth, humans must participate in specific rituals, or ordinances, that will allow them to live with God in the afterlife.

Mormons do not believe in the concept of original sin. They consider Eve's decision to eat the forbidden fruit a lesser of two evils and although they refer to it as the Fall, they do not regard it as a failure. Instead of viewing it as a mistake, they consider it a necessary decision—the product of free will. Adam and Eve shed their innocence when they ate the apple; this act allowed them not only to procreate and bring spirits out of the premortal stage, but also to progress along the plan of salvation.

According to the belief of the Mormons, when humans die, they retire their physical bodies and return to the spirit world; this world is also on earth but remains invisible to mortals. The spirit world is divided into a spirit paradise—for those who repented their sins and lived righteously on earth—and a spirit prison—for those who "died in their sins." One can eventually come forth from spirit prison by accepting the gospel.

God will, according to church doctrine, eventually resurrect everyone in the spirit world into perfect physical bodies and assigns them to one of three heavenly kingdoms, originally referred to as the three degrees of glory. One's assignment depends on the extent of their belief and on their earthly actions, emphasizing the importance of free will.

The telestial kingdom is where adulterers, rapists, and sinners who die without repenting go after suffering in spirit prison. Although some might consider it a marvelous world that experiences frequent visits from the Holy Ghost, those sent to the telestial kingdom live without family ties—a major punishment in the worldview of the Mormons.

The second degree of glory is the terrestrial kingdom and is for those who live good lives but were confused or waited too long to accept the gospel. The denizens of this kingdom may spend time in the presence of Jesus Christ, but are stripped of their family ties as well.

The final, and the greatest, of the three kingdoms is the celestial, which is reserved for those who received the proper ordinances and lived faithful lives. Importantly, this is also where those go who never had the chance to hear the gospel on earth, but embraced it in the spirit world after death. It is also the inheritance of children who died before age eight, the age of accountability. Here resurrected persons can become eternal parents, like God, and have unlimited access to him, Jesus Christ, and the Holy Ghost. In the celestial kingdom, family ties are retained.

There is also a version of eternal hell in this final stage of existence: the "outer darkness." This is reserved for those who knew the truth, according to the Church of Jesus Christ of the Latter-day Saints, by revelation, but rejected it as well as every chance for forgiveness and redemption.

The Mormon Idea of God

It is impossible to understand the faith of the Church of Jesus Christ of the Latter-day Saints without having some understanding of the nature of their beliefs regarding God. The central reason many do not consider the Church of Jesus Christ of the Latter-day Saints to be a Christian church is its rejection of the concept of the Trinity. Instead of thinking of God, Jesus Christ, and the Holy Ghost as a single entity, like most other Christians, the Mormons view them as three separate deities.

God is a physically resurrected man with a perfect physical body who endured the same earthly test as his spirit children. Mormons consider him to be an omniscient and omnipotent father who has a perfect love for all of his children. Because the elements have always existed, he is seen as an organizer with a detailed plan for the universe, rather than as one who created everything from nothing, as in most Christian denominations.

In Mormon theology, Jesus Christ was the firstborn and the most advanced of all God's spirit children. In the premortal world he was a leader named Jehovah who volunteered to come to earth as a savior to help humans recover from the sin they would experience on earth. Because he possesses both mortal and divine characteristics, Jesus could be resurrected, and eventually he paved the way so everyone could be resurrected. Mormons regard this as the propitiation for the sins of mankind, and refer to his resurrection as the Atonement. To them, Jesus' suffering in the Garden of Gethsemane (Luke 22:44) is as important as his death by crucifixion. Because Mormons emphasize the risen Christ rather than the dying Christ, they do not use the symbol of the cross.

During the days between Jesus's death and resurrection, he preached the gospel to the spirits of persons who had already lived on the earth. Mormons believe that during this time he also came to teach people living in the western hemisphere. Mormons anticipate a second coming of Christ, but maintain this cannot happen until the gospel is preached to every nation.

The third deity in the Mormon godhead is the Holy Spirit or Holy Ghost, the only one without a physical body. Mormons believe that the Holy Ghost

According to Mormon church history, Joseph Smith and Oliver Cowdery—who later became the Second Elder of the Latter Day Saints church—were endowed with the Aaronic priesthood by Saint John the Baptist on May 15, 1829. This illustration by an unknown artist depicts the event, after which the men said they baptized each other in the Susquehanna River.

can communicate with every human spirit, offering them guidance and support, and working quiet wonders in their lives. The Holy Ghost is not only a witness of Christ, but also a comforter and a sanctifier. Some of the specific gifts of the Holy Ghost include the gift of healing, the gift of prophecy, the gift of personal revelation, and the gift of the knowledge that the Gospel of Jesus Christ is true. After baptism, Church members receive this "constant gift" of the Spirit through a complete baptism, a process required to achieve full salvation.

B. Scripture

The Bible and the *Book of Mormon*

The Bible and the *Book of Mormon* are the two central texts that guide the Mormon belief system. Both are considered to be the word of God, and the Church encourages the frequent and in-depth study of both. Mormons view their church as the restoration of religion as described in the Old and New Testaments; the *Book of Mormon* is seen as an addi-

tional witness to the truths of the Bible. In addition to these two sacred works, Mormons also recognize two other books of Scripture: the *Doctrine and Covenants* (sometimes referred to as the D&C) and the *Pearl of Great Price*. Together, the four books are referred to by the Latter-day Saints Church as the "standard works" (or the "Quad").

Mormons use the King James Version of the Bible, the version that Joseph Smith used, as their official Bible, and publish their own copies filled with Mormon-specific notes and supplements. Although Mormons believe the Bible is the word of God, the religion is founded on the idea of continual revelation from God, and, therefore, additions to it must and will be written.

Mormons believe the Bible contains certain inaccuracies and omissions, but that these problems have been resolved not only by the addition of other scriptural sources, but also by a prophetically received new "translation" by Joseph Smith. Smith's version included quite a few significant changes and even some additional chapters. The Mormon Church has never published the "Joseph Smith translation," but has included pieces of it within other scriptural publications.

When Mormons say that they know the *Book of Mormon* is true, they are not only referring to its content but also to its origin—that it came into being miraculously, just as Joseph Smith claimed. In September 1823, a seventeen-year-old Smith received his second major spiritual vision from a resurrected man named Moroni. Moroni told the young prophet about a book he had buried 1,400 years earlier, and gave him directions to the site on Hill Cumorah, and instructions about how to translate it. Four years later, Joseph was permitted to take the golden plates from the hillside near his family's home.

After moving to Pennsylvania, Smith translated the 588-page book in about three months during the spring of 1829. According to some traditions, he had the help of a seer stone that caused each character to appear when he looked in his hat. Mormons believe that God gave him the translation through revelation. According to Smith's account, he returned the plates to Moroni soon after the translation was completed. The fact that there is no physical evidence of the original golden plates, save the word of Joseph Smith and that of the eleven others who claim to have seen the plates, has been a source of skepticism for some outside the church since the *Book of Mormon*'s publication in 1830.

World History in the *Book of Mormon*

The *Book of Mormon* is a religious account that also covers over 1,000 years of history, approximately from 600 BCE to 421 CE. It consists of teachings of Jesus Christ, and prophecies along with accounts of wars and migrations. It is divided into fifteen books that, like the Bible, are organized into chapters and verses. The book reads chronologically with the exception of the Book of Ether, which takes place well before any other book.

The majority of the *Book of Mormon* centers on the conflicts in the New World between the righteous Nephites and their rebellious brethren, the Lamanites. Despite a few brief truces, the two groups did not find peace until Christ visited them in the days after his resurrection and preached, healed, and appointed twelve apostles for the New World. They united under the same religion and lived together in peace. But after 200 years, problems of pride and greed arose once again and war broke out between the two groups. Envisioning the end, two Nephite prophets, Mormon and Moroni, engraved their history onto golden tablets and buried them, their whereabouts to be disclosed to Joseph Smith 1,400 years later.

Since its first publication in 1830, 116 million copies of the *Book of Mormon* have been printed in over 100 languages. It has proven a challenge for outsiders to understand the significance this book has for Mormons. First, it is a guide for life, teaching important lessons about avoiding the sin of pride, raising children, helping the poor, and repenting sins. But equally as significant, it is a testament to Jesus's atonement and demonstrates his power.

The Doctrine and Covenants

The third major book of Mormon Scripture, the *Doctrine and Covenants*, is a modern book of revelations for the guidance of the church, containing revelations from 1830 onward. Although it has undergone some title and organizational changes since its publication in the early 1830s, its current format assigns each revelation to a section, which is then divided into verses. Some of the key teachings include: the divine power of the priesthood and the divine nature of humanity, specific dietary laws, eternal marriage, living in the spirit world and the three degrees of glory, baptism by immersion, and tithing. In addition, there are two official declarations: the prohibition of polygamy (1890) and the extension of the priesthood to all races (1978).

There are also other revelations not included in the *Doctrine and Covenants* that give guidance to the members of the Church. In texts such as "The Family: A Proclamation to the World" and "The Living Christ: The Testimony of the Apostles" they cover other subjects. For instance, they include discussions of gender as an eternal characteristic, marriage as limited to a man and a woman, and gender specific roles of men and women.

The *Pearl of Great Price*

Lastly, the *Pearl of Great Price* is a sixty-page text that brings both ancient and modern Scripture together in a variety of writing styles. The book includes a Book of Moses, a Book of Abraham, and a "retranslation" of chapter twenty-four of the Gospel of Matthew. It also contains an autobiographical account of the first twenty-four years of Joseph Smith's life. Perhaps the most significant aspect of the *Pearl of Great Price* is Joseph Smith's list of the *Articles of Faith*, thirteen statements about the Mormon faith that he gave to a Chicago reporter when asked about its tenets. They are by no means comprehensive, and likely would not have existed had Smith not been asked. They are as follows:

1. We believe in God, the Eternal Father, and in His Son, Jesus Christ, and in the Holy Ghost.

2. We believe that men will be punished for their own sins, and not for Adam's transgression.

3. We believe that through the Atonement of Christ, all mankind may be saved, by obedience to the laws and ordinances of the Gospel.

4. We believe that the first principles and ordinances of the Gospel are: first, Faith in the Lord Jesus Christ; second, Repentance; third, Baptism by immersion for the remission of sins; fourth, laying on of hands for the gift of the Holy Ghost.

5. We believe that a man must be called of God, by prophecy, and by the laying on of hands by those who are in authority, to preach the Gospel and administer in the ordinances thereof.

6. We believe in the same organization that existed in the Primitive Church, namely, apostles, prophets, pastors, teachers, evangelists, and so forth.

7. We believe in the gift of tongues, prophecy, revelation, visions, healing, interpretation of tongues, and so forth.

8. We believe the Bible to be the word of God as far as it is translated correctly; we also believe the Book of Mormon to be the word of God.

9. We believe all that God has revealed, all that He does now reveal, and we believe that He will yet reveal many great and important things pertaining to the Kingdom of God.

10. We believe in the literal gathering of Israel and in the restoration of the Ten Tribes; that Zion (the New Jerusalem) will be built upon the American continent; that Christ will reign personally upon the earth; and, that the earth will be renewed and receive its paradisiacal glory.

11. We claim the privilege of worshipping Almighty God according to the dictates of our own conscience, and allow all men the same privilege, let them worship how, where, or what they may.

12. We believe in being subject to kings, presidents, rulers, and magistrates, in obeying, honoring, and sustaining the law.

13. We believe in being honest, true, chaste, benevolent, virtuous, and in doing good to all men; indeed, we may say that we follow the admonition of Paul: We believe all things, we hope all things, we have endured many things, and hope to be able to endure all things. If there is anything virtuous, lovely, or of good report or praiseworthy, we seek after these things.

C. Secondary Sources

From its inception, there has been a great deal of literature written on Mormonism, both in support of and against the religion. In fact, some of the early writings were in response to the public hostility that early Mormons felt. In order to increase morale among believers and to promote unity within the newly established church, leaders published journals and periodicals, encouraging tolerance despite the constant threat of violence. Mormon women, too, played a large role in early Mormon writing. Eliza R. Snow, Louisa Greene Richards, Emmeline B. Wells, and Lucinda Lee Dalton, as well as others, reasserted their strong feelings of faith through poetry, which was embraced by the church as having the ability to inspire truth.

The majority of secondary sources to have impacted Mormonism are those which are critical in nature. One of the most significant anti-Mormon work from this early period was published in 1834 by Eber D. Howe and is called *Mormonism Unvailed* [sic]. This work attempted to discredit Joseph Smith by including affidavits and letters that suggested he was irresponsible. Another, from 1842, was titled *History of the Saints* and was written by the former Latter-day Saints leader John Cook Bennett. It was meant as an exposé of Joseph Smith and developed accusations of adultery and prostitution. By the middle of the nineteenth century, the practice of polygamy was disclosed and created a new fury of criticism. Probably the most influential anti-Mormon publication of this period was Pomeroy Tucker's *Origin, Rise, and Progress of Mormonism* in 1867, which again attacked Joseph Smith's character.

III. Rites and Rituals

A. The Calendar

Mormons celebrate all local and national holidays along with the few additional days commemorating special historical events. Christmas is especially significant within the Mormon Church and is celebrated with the traditional tree, gifts, and Santa Claus. Similarly, Easter is a sacred Mormon holiday. Members make special efforts to remember Christ's atonement and resurrection, keeping him at the center of the holiday.

There are five additional days during the calendar year that are Mormon holidays; each celebrates the history of the church:

• **April 6** is not only when Mormons believe Jesus' birth actually occurred, but also the day that the Mormon Church was established in 1830.

• **May 15** commemorates the day in 1829 when John the Baptist appeared to Joseph Smith and Owen Cowdery, Smith's scribe.

• **June 27** is the day on which Joseph Smith and his brother Hyrum were martyred in 1844; it is a day that Mormons consider particularly important. In homage to this event, the reconstructed Nauvoo Temple was dedicated on this date in 2002.

• **July 24** Arguably, the most important Mormon holiday—known as **Pioneer Day,** it commemorates the 1847 arrival of Brigham Young and the Mormon pioneers to Salt Lake Valley. It is also a state holiday in Utah.

• **December 23** Lastly, Mormons remember December 23 annually as the anniversary of Joseph Smith's birth.

B. Worship and Liturgy

There are two specific locations where Mormons express their faith: First, there is the meetinghouse of the local "ward," or congregation, where sacrament meetings (Sunday services), baptisms, confirmations, baby blessings, and funerals are held. In addition to these daily worship activities, meetinghouses are used for recreational and educational activities. Second is the temple, which Mormons consider to be a literal house of God. In contrast to the meetinghouses, temples are large and ornate structures and used only by adults and strictly for worship and the performance of ordinances. To date, 130 temples exist globally, with just over half in the United States.

Unlike temples, meetinghouses are open to visitors on Sundays for the sacrament meeting. Meetings begin with announcements from the bishop, followed by the first of three or four hymns. Singing is an important part of Mormon worship and although many hymns in the Latter-day Saints' hymnbook are common in other religions, there are some songs that are unique to the church. The tone of Mormon hymns is usually serious and the tempo slower than hymns in other Christian denominations. Members do not stand to sing hymns, and instead sit down and focus on the music.

After the opening hymn, members bow their heads and fold their arms for the opening prayer. Someone from the ward goes to the pulpit to read the prayer, which always addresses God using the formal "thee" and "thou." Prayers end with some form of the phrase, "In the name of Jesus Christ, amen." This "amen" is the only time that members of the church speak out loud during the service.

Next in the order of events is ward business. The bishop conducting the meeting announces new callings, or the new work at the ward that will be offered to a member. Every member must volunteer in some capacity at the ward, viewing any call to work as a direct communication from God. After the announcement, congregants raise their right hands in support of the calling. If a baby's blessing or a baptism is scheduled, it will take place at this point in the meeting.

Participating in the sacrament—taking bread and water blessed by a member of the priesthood—is the main purpose of a Sunday service in the meetinghouse. Members sing a specific hymn prior to the administration of the sacrament by the priesthood, after which the sacrament is passed to the congregation. It is important to note that Mormons do not believe in the idea of transubstantiation—that the bread and water become the body of Christ; rather it is seen as a symbolic ritual performed to remind believers of his sacrifice and of their dedication to him.

The longest part of the meeting is the talks, when two to four laypeople deliver prepared sermons, ranging from Scripture to principles of the gospel. The talks are followed by a closing hymn and prayer, which mark the end of the service.

The first Sunday of every month offers a special sacrament meeting, called the fast and testimony meeting. This differs from the regular pattern in two ways: First, when members arrive, they have been fasting for twenty-four hours. Second, the fast and testimony meeting includes a public forum wherein any member can testify as to what they believe to be true about the Savior, the Gospel principles, the church, and the leaders of the church. It may also include personal stories of struggle or gratefulness relating to the truth of the gospel. This forum is distinct from the regular talks because members speak when and if the Spirit moves them, instead of delivering a prepared speech. Blessing of babies and confirmation of baptisms usually take place on Fast Sunday.

Rituals that occur within the temple are much more serious than those that take place in the meetinghouse. Temples are places where adults perform ordinances, also called "temple work," both for themselves and for people who have died. Three of the six essential ordinances are carried out in a temple: washing and anointing, endowment, and sealing. Baptism and confirmation, which occur in the meetinghouse, take place in the temple on behalf of the dead. Genealogical researchers sort through global death records and compile lists of people who have died without receiving the essential ordinances. Mormons who do temple work act as proxies on behalf of the dead; it is believed that the dead, in the spirit world, can choose to accept or reject the performed ordinances.

Children are only allowed in temples under certain circumstances and there are rules they must follow. The child must have been baptized for at least one year, he must attend a preparation class, pass a worthiness evaluation by a church leader, and wear special temple clothes—a basic white outfit—in order to be allowed inside the temple. Each qualified member will receive a "temple recommend," a special card that must be shown at the front desk of the temple in order to be admitted. However, regardless of whether or not they meet these qualifications, children are allowed in the temple to be "sealed" to parents and those over twelve years of age, regardless of when they were baptized, can enter the temple to be baptized for the dead.

C. Daily Life

The Mormon Church has a number of rules that affect the daily lives of its members. Living a disciplined lifestyle and sacrificing earthly things are the main ways that Mormons demonstrate their obedience to God. First and foremost, their beliefs regarding chastity forbid sexual relations between anyone not in a heterosexual marriage. This law not only prohibits, for example, pornography and masturbation, but it also emphasizes wearing modest clothing—clothing that covers temple garments, covers the torso and shoulders and reaches at least to the knee—and sets rules for dating. If a Mormon succumbs to sexual temptation, he or she must follow a strict guideline for repentance.

The Mormon Church also has a number of regulations with regard to diet. The basis for these rules lies in a revelation made to Joseph Smith as described in a section of the *Doctrine and Covenants* entitled "Word of Wisdom." Alcohol, tea, and coffee (both hot and iced) and tobacco are strictly forbidden. Members are encouraged to use their common sense to extrapolate what they should do—or not do—in regards to what the "Words of Wisdom" does not mention. Mormons believe that good health and physical purity are directly connected to good spiritual health and therefore take these restrictions seriously, but there are still some confusing questions. Heber J. Grant, seventh president of the church, taught this in regard to what is or is not permissible: "The Lord," he said, "does not want you to use any drug that creates an appetite for itself" (Conference Report, April 1922, 165).

One other dietary rule is the fasting requirement on the first Sunday of every month. For Mormons fasting offers the opportunity to test, cleanse, and master their bodies. It allows them to shift their focus of the day from eating and consuming to thinking more about God. Secondly, it forces them to think about the poor and to experience the pain of hunger, thus instilling a sense of compassion for those less fortunate. It also helps the poor in a concrete way, because members donate the amount of money they would have spent on the two meals to a church welfare fund. Lastly, they believe that fasting helps them not only grow closer to God, but also to one another. Fasting together on the same day each month builds a sense of communal effort. Furthermore, since prayer is central to Fast Sunday, Mormons say they are also fostering a stronger spiritual connection with God. The church does make an exception in regard to fasting for pregnant and nursing women, those "delicate in health," and children under eight.

A final significant requirement that affects the daily life of most Mormons is the responsibility of tithing. Mormons are required to contribute a full ten percent of their income to the church, thus forcing everyone to live in a financially responsible manner. Members are taught that tithing is essential for full salvation and exaltation and is a requirement for entering the temple. Unlike many Christian churches, Mormons tithe privately by handing the money directly to a bishop or by mailing it to him. Tithing money supports genealogy programs, meetinghouse and temple construction, salaries, publications, universities, and the global missionary program. Members are also encouraged to contribute to other funds.

D. Life Cycle Events

Birth

The Mormons make their religious practices an essential part of their way of life. There are daily and weekly rituals—called ordinances—but there are also a number of ordinances that take place at very specific points throughout a person's life. The first is a blessing that takes place a month or two after a baby is born, almost always on Fast Sunday. To begin the baby blessing, the father and other invited members of the priesthood stand in a circle. While the father holds the baby, who is dressed in white, the other men put their left hands on the shoulders of the men in front of them and their right hands under the baby. With someone holding a microphone, the father pronounces a blessing, and, saying the baby's full name, talks directly to him or her with advice and promises. Since women cannot be members of the Melchizedek Priesthood (see Education and Hierarchy of Clergy on page 266), the mother does not participate in the ceremony.

Baptism and Confirmation

Baptism is an important ordinance for the church because it is the moment when the person being baptized makes significant covenants with God and becomes a member of the church. The earliest age that one can be baptized is eight, an age considered by Mormons to be the age of accountability. Children are baptized by full immersion, which not only represents the washing away of sins, but the act of being buried and resurrected. More generally, baptism solidifies a covenant with God and qualifies a person to receive salvation by keeping this covenant.

In order to prepare for baptism, candidates must learn Gospel principles taught by family or church members, or with the help of missionaries. They must demonstrate their faith, repent of their sins, experience the Holy Ghost, and have an interview with a church leader. For eight-year-olds, group baptismal services takes place monthly at a stake center, a larger meetinghouse, while there are individual services for converts. Those being baptized wear white clothing and sit at the front. The service includes prayers, hymns, and talks on the significance of baptism and confirmation. Then the person performing the baptism raises his right arm, calls the candidate by his or her full name, says a prayer, and lowers him or her into the water, making sure every part goes under.

Confirmation can occur immediately after the baptism or during the following Sunday's sacrament meeting. Confirmation gives a baptized member the gift of constant companionship with the Holy Ghost. Confirmation is the second part of baptism, and is an essential ordinance for full salvation. The Mormons believe it to provide the confirmed with strength, protection, knowledge, and guidance. When a person is being confirmed, he or she sits in a chair while a member of the Melchizedek Priesthood (assisted by others) places both hands on his or her head. He says the person's full name, confirms his or her as a member of the church, and confers the gift of the Holy Ghost.

Nuptials

Most Mormon marriages occur in temples, but if a couple is not yet qualified to enter the temple, they can get married civilly and have their marriage "sealed" after a year. When a couple is married in a temple, this marriage is referred to as celestial or eternal marriage that continues after death, a necessary step in becoming more like God. Mormons believe that by performing this sealing, they also create an eternal bond with their children.

Sealing ceremonies are performed by temple officiators. The couple holds hands while kneeling on opposite sides of a cushioned altar. There is a brief ceremony followed by a kiss over the altar. Rings are exchanged informally after stepping away from the altar or at a later date. It is important to note that if a widow is getting remarried, she cannot be sealed to her second husband. However, if a widower remarries he can become sealed to his second wife—providing she had not been sealed in the past—while remaining sealed to his first wife.

Death and Burial

The final life cycle event that involves a specified ritual is death. Funerals are usually held in the person's local meetinghouse. Funerals for the aged tend to have a rather upbeat, celebratory tone. Although they are mourning the loss of a family member or friend, they are comforted that the person is one step closer to God. However, funerals for the young or those who die tragically are more solemn and emotional. The meeting involves hymn, prayer, and memorial talks. Adults who have been through the endowment ceremony (similar to confirmation) are buried in their temple clothes. Another short service—the dedication of the grave—takes place by the graveside, a place that is considered the temporary shelter before resurrection. After the burial, in many cases, women in the Relief Society serve lunch for the extended family. Cremation is strongly discouraged by the Mormon Church unless the laws of another country require it.

E. Family Life

Husband and Wife

Since the nuclear family is considered to be part of God's eternal plan, family life is one of the most important foundations for Mormons. Eternal marriage not only adds a deeper dimension to a husband and wife's relationship, but also to their roles as parents. In order to keep families strong, they must adhere to traditional gender roles. Men usually go out and work while women stay home with the children. While this is becoming somewhat less of the standard in the United States, it is still the traditional code among Mormons. Husbands are the heads of the household, but they are instructed to treat their wives as equals. Church leaders also encourage husbands and wives to continue courting each other throughout their marriage, setting aside at least one night a week to spend alone together.

Child-rearing

Mormons are well known for having large families and view parenting as one of the most important earthly experiences. Although there are many family-related activities at the church, Mormons families can strengthen their relationships in a number of other ways. Monday evenings are considered family home evenings, a night set aside for families to study the Gospel, discuss problems, or participate in activities together. This night is so special that church buildings are closed and it is not advisable to disturb another Mormon family. Other activities that are to be done as a family include prayer, meetings before major decisions, Scripture study, work, and leisure.

Extended Family

The extended family is also very important to Mormon believers. They enjoy organizing reunions and maintaining traditions with their many extended family members. Furthermore, due to the notion of eternal family, the LDS Church remains dedicated to researching genealogical records. It is so important that they have buried master copies of this record in a mountain vault. For Mormons, family history is essential to performing temple ordinances on behalf of the dead. Much energy is devoted to research, so that each person may be eternally sealed to his extended family. Records are gathered through voluntary submissions and through annual "extractions," during which teams of researchers travel all over the world to microfilm records.

Divorce

Because families are eternal and such a vital part of Mormon life here on earth, divorce is strongly discouraged. If a couple does divorce, the sealing remains valid for the woman until she desires to be sealed to another husband. At that point, she can apply for a cancellation of the sealing. A man, however, can be sealed to his new wife even if he is still sealed with his first wife. If parents become resealed to other spouses, their children remain sealed to them with the belief that any problems caused by the situation will be resolved in heaven. If a divorced couple passes away before they are sealed, their children are able to hold a proxy sealing so that they may become part of the eternal family.

IV. Denominations and Demographics

A. History: Schisms and Mergers

The early years were a very trying time for the Mormon Church, especially during the years following Joseph Smith's death. This event caused a rift among believers, and led to what is known as the Succession Crisis of 1844. After some debate, Brigham Young and the Quorum of the Twelve Apostles became the new leadership over the Church of the Latter-day Saints. With anti-Mormon sentiment still flaring, Young and the Twelve decided they could no longer stay settled in Nauvoo, Illinois, and began their journey to Utah.

The decision to migrate led to a number of schisms within the church. While the majority followed Young to Salt Lake Valley, some stayed in the Midwest and established their own factions of Joseph Smith's original Church of Christ. These followers believed that some of the practices Smith introduced in Nauvoo, such as polygamy and baptism for the dead, had strayed from God's original intentions for the church. Some of the new churches formed include The Church of Jesus Christ, referred to as the Rigdonite or the Bickertonite church because Sidney Rigdon and William Bickerton both lay claim to succession after Joseph Smith's death; the Strangite church that believes Smith had appointed James Strang to succeed him; and the Church of Christ

(Temple Lot) which owns part of the land Joseph Smith dedicated for a temple in Independence, Missouri, where they believe Christ's Second Coming will occur.

The largest division came in 1860 when Joseph Smith III, the founder's eldest son, received a revelation telling him to assume his role as the prophet of a new organization of the Church of Latter-day Saints. Joseph Smith III recruited members from the various groups and labeled the new church the Reorganized Church of Jesus Christ of Latter-day Saints, known since 2001 as the Community of Christ. Early members of the church included Joseph Smith Jr.'s widow, Emma Smith; and Joseph Smith III's mother, Lucy Mack Smith, and brother, William Smith. From its inception until 1996, all of the Reorganized Latter-day Saints' presidents were direct descendants of the original prophet.

Another significant offshoot of the Latter-day Saints Church is what is known as the Fundamentalist Church of Latter-day Saints. Its roots can be traced back to the late 1920s when many members of the Latter-day Saints Church were still practicing plural marriage. Despite the ban thirty years earlier, amnesty had been granted for those already in plural marriages so as to prevent the breaking up of families.

Members in the community of Short Creek (now known as Colorado City), Arizona, were excommunicated after refusing to sign an oath that they would stop practicing polygamy. Consequently, they started their own church focused on the preservation of the practice. The many disagreements within this fundamentalist branch during the early years led to the establishment of many different groups, the largest of which became the Fundamentalist Latter-day Saints. This denomination, which has no official connection to the Latter-day Saints Church, gained worldwide notoriety in 2007 due to the arrest of its leader, Warren Jeffs, on sex-crime charges. In 2008, the settlement was once again put in the international spotlight when Texas officials raided them and welfare workers removed their children.

B. Comparisons in Tenets and Practices

Like the Latter-day Saints Church, the Bickertonite Church of Jesus Christ relies on both the King James Version of the Bible and the *Book of Mormon* as its scriptural authority. It does not, however, accept the *Doctrine and Covenants* or the *Pearl of Great Price* as valid Scripture, claiming that they both contain false revelations. The church believes in continuing revelation from God, but only when supported by the Bible or the *Book of Mormon*. Other notable variations exist with regard to practice. For example, members of the Bickertonite Church consume bread and wine (not water) during the sacrament. Also, members of the Church of Jesus Christ perform foot washing (described in John 13:5) four times per year as a sign of humility and greet one another with a "holy kiss" on the cheek. It is important to note that this church has been a proponent of racial integration since its beginnings.

The Strangite Church, which had about 12,000 members during James Strang's life, differed from the Latter-day Saints Church in that they believed in a seventh-day Sabbath—observing Sabbath on Saturday, not Sunday. They were also known for believing in continuing revelation, and performing animal sacrifices similar to those described in the Old Testament. Some members, including Strang himself, practiced plural marriage. The group all but dissolved following Strang's murder in 1856, and only a couple hundred members, concentrated in Michigan and Wisconsin, survive today.

Although the Church of Christ, or Temple Lot, accepted the revelations of Joseph Smith in the beginning, they declared in 1920 that anything published after the *Book of Commandments* in 1833 did not come from divine inspiration. They claimed that the prophet had fallen from his calling by accepting plural marriage and developing a hierarchical system of authority. The Temple Lot therefore does not have a prophet or First Presidency; instead, a Quorum of Twelve Apostles heads the church.

The Community of Christ is dedicated to peace and reconciliation. It believes in the inherent worth of all humans and added a statement to the *Doctrine and Covenants* in 2007 that proclaimed that value. In keeping with its dedication to equality, the church began ordaining women to the priesthood in 1984 and made all offices of the organization available to them. In addition, the temple in Independence, Missouri is open to the public and offers communion to all, which is a major difference from the Latter-day Saints Church. Also unlike the Latter-day Saints Church, the Community of Christ accepts the concept of the Trinity and other elements of standard Christian doctrines.

Fundamentalist Church of Latter-day Saints

The Fundamentalist Church of Jesus Christ of Latter-day Saints is the faction that has strayed the most from original Latter-day Saints doctrine and beliefs. First of all, plural marriage is accepted and universally practiced within the church. This doctrine also teaches that women are subordinate to men. The Fundamentalist Latter-day Saints practice the law of placing, whereby women are assigned to marry men after a revelation is made to the church's leader. This church's members are also required to abide by a strict dress code of very modest and often homemade clothing. The church prohibits members from owning personal real estate or other property and requires that all children be home-schooled.

The media frequently confuses the Fundamentalist Church of Jesus Christ of the Latter-day Saints with the Church of Jesus Christ of the Latter-day Saints, leaving readers with the mistaken impression that the practices of the Fundamentalist Church are widespread throughout Mormonism. (As recently as July 27, 2008, the *New York Times Magazine* published a photo-essay entitled "Children of God," in which the sect was referred to as "FLDS," with no text to distinguish the group from the Mormon church, which is often referred to as "LDS" by the church and in the media.)

C. Organization and Distribution

The **Church of Jesus Christ of Latter-day Saints** (the Latter-day Saints Church) has by far the largest membership, with close to 13 million members worldwide and almost 6 million in the United States. Its headquarters is located in Salt Lake City, Utah. While nearly 2 million of the American members live in Utah and close to 70 percent of the state is Mormon, there is solid representation in all fifty states. An incredible amount of statistical information, including state-by-state numbers, can be found on an official Latter-day Saints website: http://newsroom.lds.org/facts-and-stats.

The **Community of Christ** is the largest splinter group from the Latter-day Saints church and also has its headquarters in Independence, Missouri, where it owns a temple. The church also owns the temple in Kirtland, Ohio. It sponsors Graceland University, which has a campus in Lamoni, Iowa, as well as in Independence. The Community of Christ also owns and operates various Latter-day Saints historic sites throughout the Midwest, where most of its members are located. It claims to have about 250,000 worldwide members in fifty different nations, and approximately 130,000 in the United States.

The **Bickertonite church** is the third largest to emerge from the Succession Crisis of 1844, and claims to have about 12,000 members worldwide. Its headquarters is located in Monongahela, Pennsylvania, and it has a total of almost eighty churches throughout the seven regions of the United States.

The **Church of Christ** headquarters is also located in Independence, Missouri, and has 2,000 to 3,000 members, most of whom are located close to Independence.

Lastly, the **Fundamentalist Latter-day Saints**, with reports of having as many as 10,000 members, is by far the largest Mormon fundamentalist denomination. The exact number is not known because the group is usually closed off from the outside world. Although the church has been historically centered in the bordering cities of Colorado City, Arizona, and Hildale, Utah, many members have left for Eldorado, Texas, where the church has established the Yearning for Zion Ranch. They also have an established colony in Bountiful, British Columbia, a town created especially for Fundamentalist Latter-day Saints members.

V. Organization and Infrastructure

A. Education and Hierarchy of Clergy

For Mormons, holding the priesthood means having the authority to act in God's name. The church is a lay church and ordains all "worthy and willing" males from the age of twelve. No special education or schooling is needed. Once a boy turns twelve, Church leaders will decide if he is worthy of the priesthood. There are two levels of the priesthood: the Aaronic, which serves as a preparatory priesthood for teens, and the Melchizedek, the higher priesthood, reserved for adults. In contrast to many other churches, no one in either priesthood receives compensation for their services.

Those ordained in the Aaronic Priesthood typically help perform ordinances having to do with repentance such as baptisms or administering the sacrament. There are three ranks of the Aaronic priesthood—deacon, teacher, and priest—which the boys normally advance through every two years. The primary job of the deacon is to pass out the sacramental bread and water during the sacrament meetings. Deacons also act as messengers for leaders and help take care of the meetinghouse. Furthermore, it is their duty to go to the homes of all members and collect a freewill offering, known as a fast offering, to aid the poor. The teacher's main job in the Aaronic priesthood is to fill the sacrament trays with bread and water. They can also go with leaders on home teaching visits, monthly visits to check up on members and teach a short Gospel lesson. At sixteen, boys

become priests and have all the rights and responsibilities of a deacon and teacher as well as the authority to bless the bread and water, perform baptisms, and ordain younger boys into the priesthood.

The Melchizedek Priesthood is the greater of the two. A man must be interviewed to qualify for this priesthood. The offices of the Melchizedek Priesthood are apostle, seventy, patriarch, high priest, and elder. The president of the church is the only man to hold all of the keys to the priesthood. Men in their twenties and thirties typically hold the office of elder. They have the job of teaching, bestowing the gift of the Holy Ghost, and doing missionary work, among other things. Although it includes some younger men who have been called to hold higher leadership positions, the office of high priest is usually reserved for middle-aged or retired men. The bishop, though technically part of the Aaronic Priesthood, because he oversees the boys in the priesthood, is a high priest and the leader of a ward. A bishop also oversees all of the volunteer work at his ward and spends a lot of individual time with members. They are able to receive revelation to guide their congregations and have the power to act as judges.

The office of patriarch is held by mature members of the Melchizedek Priesthood called and ordained to this office. Each stake within the church has one or two ordained patriarchs. It is the duty of the patriarch to give advice and blessing. There is also a small group of men who hold the "office of seventy" and "office of apostle." Unlike the others, they serve the Church full-time as the General Authorities that oversee and govern the church.

According to the guidelines of the church, the most important duty of a high priest or elder is to make sure that the home is all that was envisioned in the Scriptures and the counsel of the prophets. They are to take initiative in the home, along with their wives, to make sure it is a safe place and that the Gospel is lived there. Another duty of the members of the Melchizedek Priesthood is to perform ordinances. Some examples include: blessings of comfort in difficult times, confirmation, building or gravesite

The Mormon Tabernacle Choir, pictured above in front of the tabernacle's organ, performs live and in recorded broadcasts from the remarkable Salt Lake Tabernacle, the low structure alongside the cathedral-like Salt Lake Temple, left. The tabernacle was built in 1867; the temple was dedicated in 1893.

dedications, fathers' and husbands' blessings, healing the sick, and priesthood ordination.

It is important to note that under no circumstances are women admitted to the priesthood and therefore are unable to perform these ordinances. Although it has been met with a certain amount of criticism, the church is unapologetic about this rule. It does, however, expect that men respect their wives and other women as equal members of the church, reminding them that without women they themselves will not achieve exaltation. Furthermore, women can hold some positions of authority outside of the priesthood. Women run the Relief Society—the largest women's organization in the world—as well as societies for children and young adults. They also organize and conduct meetings and activities, counsel members of their organizations and call people to fulfill assignments and serve others at the general church level, the stake level, and the ward level.

Young men and women are expected to attend "seminary" in high school and "institutes of religion" as college students. These special schools, available throughout the world, are designed to supplement secular education with a Mormon view. Every Mormon teen is expected to attend seminary every morning before school throughout all four years of high school, with each year corresponding to one of the main books of Scripture. The college-level program, usually shortened to "institute," is more academically challenging and covers a wider variety of subjects. While the church has built many institutes near colleges around the United States, those without access to one can attend classes at a local meetinghouse or use home study courses available.

B. Historical Sites; Houses of Worship

It is doubtful that anyone can talk about the Latter-day Saints Church in the United States and not think about Utah. Since Brigham Young and the Mormon pioneers settled there over 160 years ago, they have consistently been establishing themselves further in Salt Lake City and the surrounding areas. Temple Square is one of the city's major attractions, and it is said that Young planned the city so that all roads led to the Salt Lake Temple. The square also houses a dome-shaped building, home to the Mormon Tabernacle Choir; an Assembly Hall, previously used for worship, but currently for concerts and meetings; and two visitor's centers.

Salt Lake City is also home to many other Mormon organizations and historical and cultural centers. They include the Joseph Smith Memorial Building (a former hotel used for weddings, office space, meetings, and film screenings), the Family History Library, the Museum of Church History and Art, the Beehive House (Brigham Young's nineteenth-century home), the Latter-day Saints Conference Center, and the Latter-day Saints Humanitarian Center. Nearby Provo, Utah, is about 95 percent Mormon, home to Brigham Young University, with an enrollment of nearly 30,000.

Other important buildings and temples are located in landmark sites of Mormon history. In Sharon, Vermont, one can visit Joseph Smith's birth site. In 2002, a temple was dedicated in Palmyra, New York, Joseph Smith's childhood home and near where the angel Moroni appeared to him. Visitors to Palmyra can visit the Smith family farm, a replica of their house, the Sacred Grove where Joseph prayed about his First Vision, and the Grandin Building where the first *Book of Mormon* was printed.

Kirtland, Ohio, is the location of the Mormons' first major settlements on their journey westward. There is a visitor's center and the Newel K. Whitney home and store, where Joseph Smith received some of his revelations. The Kirtland Temple, dedicated in 1836 by Smith, is now under the control of the Community of Christ and open to the public. Nauvoo and Carthage, Illinois, see a great deal of visitors, especially after the reconstructed Nauvoo Temple was dedicated in 2002. Nauvoo also has a number of restored homes, including Joseph and Emma Smith's, as well as shops and historical sights.

The Mormon temple on Broadway in New York City stands out dramatically across the street from Lincoln Center.

The Carthage Jail, where Joseph Smith and his brother were killed, is some twenty miles away.

Two other notable temples are: the Los Angeles Temple, a good example of a Latter-day Saints temples with a statue of the angel Moroni on top of the steeple, and the Washington, D.C., Temple, which is a more modern architectural rendition of the six-spire Salt Lake Temple. It is not only the tallest temple in the church, but also the third largest at 160,000 square feet. While older temples tended to be built to a large scale, most of the newer temples are much smaller. As of 2008, there are nearly sixty temples located in the United States with seventy more throughout the world. Contact information for all meetinghouses and temples may be found at http://www.lds.org.

Salt Lake Temple (Church Headquarters)
50 North West Temple Street
Salt Lake City, UT 84103
(801) 240-2640.

C. Governance and Authority

The Church of Jesus Christ of the Latter-day Saints is administered from its Salt Lake City, Utah, headquarters by high-level leaders and a couple of thousand supporting employees. The role of the president of the church is to, guided by revelation, guide the Church, explain Church doctrine, and to testify of Jesus Christ. Together with his counselors, the Quorum of Twelve Apostles and the other General Authorities, they direct the work of the church throughout the world and speak counsel to the members of the church at conferences. These men are known as the First Presidency. Most of these men, because of their seniority in the Church, are well past seventy years old. Others with governing authority in the church are the Presiding Bishopric, which is made up of a bishop and two counselors. Together, these men are known as the General Authorities or the Brethren. Like those in the priesthood, General Authorities do not receive salaries or special training. The General Authorities supervise nine women with leadership positions at the church headquarters. A president and two counselors lead each of the following groups: the Relief Society, a global women's organization; Young Women, for girls twelve to seventeen; and Primary, for girls and boys three to eleven years of age.

One of the prophet's most important roles is to interpret and explain church doctrine and policy. A revelation to Joseph Smith requires that all decisions made by the First Presidency and the Twelve Apostles be unanimous, and the church has been governed by that principle since the beginning. Yet because Mormons believe that all people have moral agency, no members are compelled in their behavior or beliefs. Still, the vast majority of participating Mormons, as they view their church president as a prophet and inspired by God, will try to live according to his council.

Prophets always serve the church until their death and because so many have lived well into their nineties, the Latter-day Saints Church has only seen the full terms of fifteen presidents. On January 27, 2008, Gordon B. Hinkley was, until his death at age ninety-seven, the oldest living. Thomas S. Monson succeeded him as the Church's sixteenth president a week later.

Twice each year, on the first weekends of April and October, the Mormon Church holds the General Conference. During the two-day event, with many members watching on televisions around the world, leaders make significant announcements, reaffirm teachings, and discuss successful missionary projects. Until recently, the General Conference was held in the Tabernacle building in Salt Lake City. However, because of the church's steady growth rate, they constructed a new building, the Conference Center, with a 21,000-seat capacity, opened in April 2000, for special events, concerts, and theater.

D. Social Service Organizations

A key teaching of Joseph Smith in the *Doctrine and Covenants* is that people should help the hungry and the afflicted, and Mormons are very committed to following this teaching by giving and (striving to be more Christlike) going out of their way to minister to the poor. The church sponsors three programs that fulfill these goals: the Welfare Program, the Perpetual Education Fund and the Latter-day Saints Humanitarian Relief program.

Mormon Church, Southern California

1581 East Temple Way
Los Angeles, CA 90024
1-800-533-2444

Their private welfare program was created in 1936 to help members become independent of government aid while providing them with basic necessities. In exchange, the members contribute time in the form of extra volunteer work for the church. It is funded mostly through Fast Sunday donations and has the three basic goals of providing for the needy, encouraging self-reliance, and teaching the value of service. It was one of the first work exchange programs in the country and today is the largest private welfare program in the world.

LDS Philanthropies

15 E. South Temple, 2nd Floor East
Salt Lake City, UT 84150
801-240-5567
http://www.ldsphilanthropies.org/

The Latter-day Saints Humanitarian Relief program began in 1985, after a special fast and donation was arranged to relieve a crisis in Ethiopia. After members donated $6 million in one day, the church decided to start an official relief program. Although the Latter-day Saints Church still contributes to other relief organizations like the Red Cross, this program provides international aid in cases of famine, natural disasters, and displacement.

E. Media and Communication

Mormons are urged to avoid pornography or movies with graphic sexuality or violence, or activities considered unbefitting for followers of Jesus Christ. In 1908, the Correlation Committee was formed in order to insure that all of the churches around the world had a uniform message and curriculum. Thus, wherever a Mormon goes in the world, they can find a church that teaches the same things according to the same principles as their home church.

Deseret Management Corporation
55 North 300 West, Suite 800
Salt Lake City, UT 84101
801-538-0651 Fax: 801-517-4600
www.deseretmanagement.com

The church owns a number of official media outlets. The largest and most influential is the Deseret Management Corporation, which not only publishes the Deseret *News*, the second largest newspaper in Utah behind the Salt Lake *Tribune*, but also owns Deseret Book Company, a publisher and chain of thirty Latter-day Saints bookstores, which operate independently, but under Church guidelines.

Dialogue Business Office
PO Box 58423
Salt Lake City, UT 84158
www.dialoguejournal.com

Sunstone Education Foundation
343 North Third West
Salt Lake City, UT 84103
801-355-5926   Fax 801-274-8210
www.sunstonemagazine.com/

There are also several journal publishers that, while not directly affiliated with the Church, cover the Church of Jesus Christ of Latter-day Saints: The Dialogue Foundation and the Sunstone Education Foundation are two such houses. *Dialogue* attempts to place Mormonism in a global context through scholarly articles and literature. *Sunstone* focuses on news analysis and public issues. Neither is an official Church publication, and so are not primary sources for the Church beliefs.

Religious Studies Center
167 Heber Grant Building
Brigham Young University
Provo, UT 84602
801-422-6975
http://rsc.byu.edu

Neal A. Maxwell Inst. for Religious Scholarship
Brigham Young University
Provo, UT 84602
801-422-9229
http://maxwellinstitute.byu.edu/

Other journals that promote academic inquiry, historical research, and women's issues include: the *Journal of Mormon History, BYU Studies,* and the *Exponent II.* Research institutes at Brigham Young University at the forefront of LDS scholarship are the Religious Studies Center and the Maxwell Institute for Religious Scholarship, both of which promote academic research and publish books and journals.

FURTHER READING

Latter Days: An Insider's Guide to Mormonism, The Church of Jesus Christ of Latter-day Saints
    Coke Newell
    2001: St. Martin's Griffin
Mormon America: The Power and the Promise
    Richard Ostling
    2000: HarperSanFrancisco
Mormonism
    Jan Shipps
    1987: University of Illinois Press
Sojourner in the Promised Land
    Jan Shipps
    2000: University of Illinois Press
Teachings of the Prophet Joseph Smith
    Joseph F. Smith (compiled by)
    1976: Deseret Book Company

9 Lutheran Church

I. Origins and Early History

A. Formation of Lutheranism

THE LUTHERAN CHURCH WAS FOUNDED IN THE SIX-teenth century and is based on the beliefs of Martin Luther, a German Augustinian monk and professor of theology at the University of Wittenberg in Saxony. On October 31, 1517, Luther posted his Ninety-five Theses on the church door of the castle of Wittenberg, challenging the Catholic Church's practices and sparking the beginnings of the Protestant Reformation. Following this act of defiance, Luther and his followers were excommunicated by the pope. As a result, Lutheranism developed in separate national and territorial churches in Switzerland, the Netherlands, Sweden, and Finland.

Luther began the Reformation by establishing certain demands for change within the Roman Catholic Church. He was disturbed by the corruption in the Catholic Church, especially with regard to the value of indulgences, or the practice of making donations to the church to reduce one's time in Purgatory. He believed that people are made right with God *sola gratia* and *sola fide,* only by the divine initiative of grace as received through God's gift of faith. Luther also believed in the exhortation *sola scriptura,* which means that the Bible alone should be the source of religious teachings.

In the 1500s, the Lutheran movement was able to gain popularity quickly in Germany because of a rising nationalism among the people who resented sending their wealth to Rome. Early Lutherans were based in universities and used their learning to spread the faith among an international community of scholars.

The term "Lutheran" was opposed by Luther himself and was at first used by opponents of his teaching during the Leipzig Disputation in 1519. Luther preferred the term "Evangelical," and today in the United States the usual title of the sect is the Evangelical Lutheran Church. In Germany the

Martin Luther's translation of the New Testament from Greek into German was first published in 1522. This title page is from a 1769 edition.

The German pastor and theologian Martin Luther (1483–1546) appears in this undated fifteenth-century portrait.

term "Lutheran" has been completely discarded and the state church is called Evangelical or Evangelical United.

From its earliest inception, Lutheranism has faced a multitude of doctrinal disputes. One such disagreement arose between Luther and Huldrych Zwingli, the leader of the Reformation movement in Switzerland. The hostility between Lutherans and the Zwinglians, or the Reformed, began in 1524 with the Sacramentarian controversy between Luther and Zwingli. Zwingli's followers numbered among the Sacramentarians, who denied both the Catholic creed of transubstantiation and the Lutheran sacramental union. In 1549, the strife was renewed when the Zwinglians accepted French theologian John Calvin's view of the Real Presence. German Protestant reformer Philipp Melanchthon, friend and associate of Luther, developed his own following after Luther's death, made up of Protestants who favored Calvin's doctrines and had been denounced by orthodox Lutherans.

On September 25, 1555, the Peace of Augsburg was signed by Charles V, Holy Roman Emperor, and the forces of the Schmalkaldic League. The Schmalkaldic League was founded in 1531 by Philipp I of Hesse and John Frederick, Elector of Saxony, to defend their territories against attacks of Charles V and promote the spread of Lutheranism. The Peace of Augsburg officially established Lutherans in the Holy Roman Empire according to *cuius regio, eius religio* ("whose territory, his religion"). This allowed rulers to choose between Lutheranism and Catholicism as the religion of their land. The Peace of Augsburg was

good for Lutherans, who were ruled by a Lutheran prince and ended violence between Catholics and Lutherans, but did not protect other Protestants, namely Calvinists. Because of this omission, intolerance toward Calvinists continued, eventually leading to the Thirty Years' War.

After Luther's death in 1546, new disagreements continued to arise between the followers of Melanchthon and strict Lutherans. Saxony was divided between these two groups, Electoral Saxony consisting mainly of Melanchthonians, while Lower Saxony and Württemberg remained strictly Lutheran. In 1576, a group of Lutheran theologians and churchmen met in the Saxon city of Torgau to organize a statement of faith, one that would settle the disputes between the two groups of Lutherans, at the request of Elector August of Saxony. Under this agreement, any union with the Reformed Church was made unattainable. In 1577, the Formula of Concord was completed and signed by three electors of the Holy Roman Empire, twenty dukes and princes, twenty-four counts, four barons, thirty-five free imperial cities, and over eight thousand pastors. The agreement upon and proliferation of this document played a major role in the unification and preservation of Lutheranism. The Formula of Concord later became a major statement of Lutheran faith and was included in the *Book of Concord,* the Lutheran Body of Doctrine, first published in 1580.

The Thirty Years' War (1618–1648) originated out of the religious discords between Protestants and Catholics. The Peace of Augsburg began to unravel during the second half of the sixteenth century as Calvinism began to spread throughout Germany and rulers in Spain and Eastern Europe sought to restore the power of Catholicism in the German region. Once again, Catholic, Lutheran, and Calvinist theologians made many attempts to unite the faiths, to no avail. The war ended with the Peace of Westphalia, which divided Germany among many territories, all of which had *de facto* sovereignty, decentralizing German power. This treaty established the idea of a need for the separation of church and state that later became a key political principle of the United States Constitution.

During the Thirty Years' War, a fanatical orthodoxy resulted from the use of the Scholastic method in German universities to resolve controversial issues. This new orthodoxy was primarily concerned with doctrine and believed that the Reformation was a conservative movement. These theologians focused on what Luther retained from the historic church and the preservation of pure doctrine.

As a reaction against the orthodoxy that arose during the Thirty Years' War, Pietism began with the teachings of Philip Jacob Spener who asserted the claims of spiritual holiness and believed in the freedom to change within the church. Pietism maintains that it is the task of the church to reform itself continually in order to fit the time and place in which it exists. According to Spener, the personal experience of the pious is the ground of certainty for theological knowledge. August Francke founded the University of Halle in 1694 as a stronghold of Pietism. Many of the founders of the American Lutheran Church were graduates of the University of Halle. The Lutheran Church-Missouri Synod (LCMS) has its origins in orthodoxy while the Evangelical Lutheran Church in America (ELCA) is based in Pietism.

Lutheranism is now the largest non-Roman Catholic body in the Western Christian Church, and is the third largest Protestant denomination in the United States. Although Protestants generally refer to Luther's teachings as the basis of their faith, some Lutherans consider their own faith to be outside the Protestant tradition.

(Detailed analysis of the texts involved in the Reformation may be found on the website www.bookofconcord.org.)

B. Important Dates in Lutheranism

October 31, 1517 Luther posts his ninety-five Theses on church door of the castle of Wittenberg.

1519 Leipzig Disputation; Luther joins debate.

1520 Pope Leo X excommunicates Martin Luther.

1521 Edict of Worms places ban on Lutherans; declares Luther a heretic.

1523 Luther returns to Wittenberg and publishes his German translation of the New Testament; beginning of Lutheran Reformation.

1523–1524 Luther's translation of the Old Testament is published in parts.

1525 Lutheran Reformation in the state of the Teutonic Order.

1525 German War of the Peasants; Nürnberg adopts Lutheran Reformation.

1529 Luther publishes his Great Catechism and Small Catechism.

1530 Augsburg Confession is written by Melanchthon.

1531 Schmalkaldic League is assembled.

1531 Apology of Augsburg Confession is written by Melanchthon.

1537 Articles of Schmalkald by Luther.

1546–1547 Opening of the Council of Trent.

1546 Luther dies.

1555 Peace of Augsburg treaty signed.

1577 Formula of Concord—prepared by theologians to resolve disputes among Lutherans—is signed by political leaders.

1631 Professor Pareus proposes plan to unite the Evangelical Churches.

1631 The Reformed Synod of Charenton votes to admit Lutheran sponsors in baptism.

1648 Peace of Westphalia ends Thirty Years' War.

1670 Philip Spener holds the first *collegia pietatis* (meetings to discuss the devotional passages of the Scriptures).

1694 August Francke founds the University of Halle (stronghold of Pietism).

1722 The United Brethren is founded by Count von Zinzendorf.

∞

C. The Religion in America

Lutherans from the Netherlands were among the first settlers of Manhattan Island in 1624. Swedish settlers established the first Lutheran congregation in 1639, at Fort Christina (now Wilmington), Delaware. Exiles from the Palatinate established German Lutheran churches in New York, Pennsylvania, Delaware, and Maryland, and in 1693 founded Germantown, now a part of Philadelphia. The Salzburger migration to Georgia in 1734 introduced Lutheranism to the Southern territories. Before the middle of the eighteenth century, approximately 30,000 German Lutherans had settled in Eastern Pennsylvania.

Synods

Heinrich Melchior Mühlenberg, known as the patriarch of American Lutheranism, began the organization of the churches by establishing the first synod in the American colonies, the Synod of Pennsylvania, in 1748. The Synod of New York and adjoining states

followed in 1786, and the Synod of North Carolina was created in 1803. Pioneers from Norway, Denmark, and Finland later formed many small synods while settling the western portion of the country.

By the turn of the nineteenth century, the Pietism of the founders of the American Churches, most of whom were educated at the University of Halle, was deteriorating and the churches increasingly lost their Lutheran identity. The Pennsylvania Ministerium eliminated all confessional texts in its constitution of 1792 and within the New York Ministerium the original Lutheran catechisms and hymnbooks were substituted with works that conformed to the prevailing theology. A transition began at this time from the use of German to English, which also caused a split in many congregations.

In 1820, the General Synod was organized at Hagerstown, Pennsylvania, with the intention of preventing the threatened disintegration of the Lutheran Synods of America. This new organization was regarded with suspicion by many of the smaller synods, and only three years later the Pennsylvania Synod withdrew from the general body. The General Synod wished to favor a doctrinal compromise with the Reformed Church, and in order to strengthen the conservative party, the Pennsylvania Synod rejoined the General Synod in 1853.

In 1805, traveling preachers from the Pennsylvania Ministerium founded a conference in connection with the General Synod. This conference was reorganized into a synod in 1818 and, in 1833, became known as the Joint Synod of Ohio.

Lutheran emigrants from Saxony, Prussia, Bavaria, and the Scandinavian countries formed several organizations in the western United States. One of these was the Missouri Synod, organized by Reverend Carl Walther in 1847. Walther also opened a theological seminary in St. Louis. In 1854, a party within the Missouri Synod seceded to form the Iowa Synod because they were displeased with what they believed to be extreme congregationalism and the denial of open question in theology within the Missouri Synod.

The American Civil War (1861–1865) ended any hopes of uniting all of the Lutheran organizations into one body. In 1863, five southern district synods withdrew from the General Synod to become the General Synod of the Confederate States.

The Pennsylvania Synod established a new seminary in Philadelphia in 1864 to reduce the attendance at the General Synod seminary in Gettysburg. This was a result of the disagreements between the liberal and conservative elements within the General Synod. At a convention in 1866, it was declared that the Pennsylvania Synod was no longer in practical union with the General Synod. In response, the Pennsylvania Synod sent an open invitation to all other American and Canadian synods to form a new general body. Later that year, a convention was assembled in Reading, Pennsylvania, and thirteen synods were organized into the General Council.

The controversy among the northern synods kept the southern Lutherans from rejoining them after the end of the Civil War. Instead, they reorganized and became the United Synod in the South in 1886. Their doctrinal position was essentially the same as the General Council.

The Synodical Conference was formed in 1872 and is still the strongest organization of all the Lutheran Churches of America. It is made up of the Missouri Synod and other western synods. The basis of the Synodical Conference is the Formula of Concord. The Ohio and Norwegian synods withdrew because of differences in interpretation of the doctrine of predestination in 1881 and 1884.

In 1918, many of the independent Lutheran bodies combined to become the United Lutheran Church in America. The Evangelical Lutheran Synodical Conference of North America was formed in 1872 but disbanded in 1960 when the Wisconsin Evangelical Lutheran Synod (WELS) withdrew. The American Lutheran Church (ALC), formed in 1961, and the Lutheran Church in America (LCA), formed in 1962, united in 1988 to become the Evangelical Lutheran Church in America (ELCA), and is now the largest Lutheran group, with 5.2 million members. In 1997, the ELCA agreed to share full communion with three other Protestant churches, the Presbyterian Church, the United Church of Christ, and the Reformed Church in America. This meant that the churches could exchange clergy and that members could worship and receive sacraments at other churches.

The Lutherans of the United States are divided into various conflicting bodies, and there are still many independent synods that are not affiliated with any of the general organizations. Among the main organizations, the majority of the membership is of German descent.

D. American Lutheran Timeline

1624 Settlers from Holland arrive in the Dutch colony of New Netherlands.

1639 The first Lutheran congregation of the New World is established at Fort Christina (now Wilmington), Delaware.

1664 New Amsterdam (later New York) is captured by the English and freedom of worship for its citizens is obtained.

1669 Dutch Lutherans in the New World organize in what will eventually become the two oldest Lutheran congregations (both of which still survive in Albany and Manhattan).

1693 German Lutherans arrive in the New World and found Germantown (now part of Philadelphia).

1734 Ebenzer, Georgia, founded by a colony of Lutherans from Salzburg, Germany.

1741 Count von Zinzendorf becomes pastor in Philadelphia.

1742 Reverend Henry Mühlenberg arrives in Philadelphia to succeed Zinzendorf as the pastorate.

1748 Mühlenberg founds the Synod of Pennsylvania.

1771 The Swedish Lutherans of Delaware and Pennsylvania dissolve their union with the Mother Church of Sweden.

1818 Pennsylvania Lutherans adopt new service-book.

1818 The Joint Synod of Ohio is formed by traveling preachers from the Pennsylvania Ministerium.

1820 The General Synod is organized at Hagerstown, Pennsylvania.

1823 The Pennsylvania Synod withdraws from the General Synod.

1825 The General Synod establishes the theological seminary at Gettysburg, Pennsylvania.

1841 Emigrants from Saxony found the Buffalo Synod.

1846 The Norwegian Hague Synod is formed by Scandinavian emigrants.

1846 The Swedish Lutherans of Delaware and Pennsylvania declare full communion with the Episcopalians.

1847 The Lutheran Church–Missouri Synod is founded by Reverend Carl Walther.

1850 The Wisconsin Evangelical Synod is organized in Milwaukee, Wisconsin.

1853 The Pennsylvania Synod returns to the General Synod.

1854 A party within the Missouri Synod secedes and forms the Iowa Synod.

1860 The Scandinavian Augustana Synod is created by Scandinavian emigrants.

1863 The Norwegian Synod is formed by emigrants from Scandinavia.

1863 Five southern district synods withdraw from the General Synod to become the General Synod of the Confederate States.

1864 The Ministerium of Pennsylvania establishes a new seminary in Philadelphia.

1866 The Pennsylvania Synod is declared to be no longer in practical union with the General Synod.

1866 General Council is formed, consisting of the Pennsylvania Ministerium and thirteen American and Canadian synods.

1872 The Synodical Conference is formed, comprising the Missouri and other Western synods.

1881 The Ohio Synod withdraws from the Synodical Conference.

1884 The Norwegian Synod withdraws from the Synodical Conference.

1886 The southern Lutherans reorganize their general body into the United Synod in the South.

1900 The Church of the Lutheran Brethren of America is founded by five independent Lutheran congregations in Milwaukee, Wisconsin.

1918 The Norwegian Synod of the American Evangelical Lutheran Church (later named the Evangelical Lutheran Synod) is formed by conservatives breaking away from the Norwegian Lutheran Church near Lake Mills, Iowa.

1962 Association of Free Lutheran Congregations founded by conservatives opposing the merger of the Lutheran Free Church with the American Lutheran Church.

1962 German, Danish, Slovak, Swedish, and Icelandic Lutheran congregations merge to form the Lutheran Church in America.

1963 German, Danish, and Norwegian Lutheran congregations merge to form the American Lutheran Church.

1976 Moderates from the Lutheran Church-Missouri Synod break away from the main body to form the Association of Evangelical Lutheran Churches.

1987 The American Association of Lutheran Churches is formed by conservative Lutherans in Bloomington, Minnesota.

1988 The Evangelical Lutheran Church in America is organized in Columbus, Ohio, when the Lutheran Church in America, the American Lutheran Church, and the Association of Evangelical Lutheran Churches merge into one body.

E. Important Figures

Martin Luther (1483–1546)

Began the Protestant Reformation and founder of the Lutheran Church.

Philipp Melanchthon (1497–1560)

German professor and theologian, friend and associate of Martin Luther; wrote many of the writings in the *Book of Concord.*

John Campanius (1601–1683)

First Lutheran pastor of the Swedish settlement in Delaware; consecrated the first Lutheran church in the New World on September 4, 1646; translated Luther's Shorter Catechism into the language of the Delaware Indians.

Philip Spener (1635–1705)

Began the Pietism movement, placing importance on inner spiritual phenomena and individual experiences of faith; wrote *Pia Desideria* (1675).

Christian Wolff (1679–1754)

Argued that faith must be based on reason and rational proofs. Began (with John Semler) theological rationalization movement in Germany.

Samuel Schmucker (1799–1873)

Helped organize the General Synod in 1820 and founded the Lutheran Theological Seminary at Gettysburg, Pennsylvania, in 1826; advocate for the adaptability of the Lutheran church in America.

Johann Semler (1725–1791)

Applied a historic critical method to the Bible in relation to human development.

Reverend Henry Muhlenberg (1711–1787)

The patriarch of American Lutheranism; organized the first synod in America, the Ministerium of Pennsylvania.

Philipp Melanchthon (1497–1560) was Luther's friend and collaborator, and was also coauthor of the Augsburg Confession, a seminal statement of Lutheran beliefs.

Reverend Carl Walther (1811–1887)

First president of the Lutheran Church-Missouri Synod.

COMPOSERS
George Frideric Handel (1685–1759);
Johann Sebastian Bach (1685–1750);
Dietrich Buxtehude (1637–1707); **Michael
Praetorius (1571–1621)**; and **Heinrich
Schütz (1585–1672)**—all of whom had a
profound influence on Lutheran worship.

PHILOSOPHERS
Immanuel Kant; **J.G. Fichte**; **G.W.F.
Hegel**; and **Soren Kierkegaard**

BIBLICAL SCHOLARS:
D.F. Strauss and **Albert Schweitzer**

THEOLOGIANS
Albrecht Ritschl; **Adolf von Harnack**;
Rudolf Otto; **Rudolf Bultmann**; and **Paul Tillich**.

The History of the Lutheran Church in America
is treated in detail on the websites:
- www.lifeoftheworld.com
- www.taalc.org (site of the American Association of Lutheran Churches)

II. Tenets and Beliefs

A. Articles of Faith

The *Book of Concord*, published on June 25, 1580, is the accepted companion to Lutheran teaching. The word "*Concordia*," as the book was originally titled, refers to the Latin word meaning "harmony." *The Book of Concord* was designed to establish and maintain doctrinal harmony among practicing Lutherans. It includes three confessional creeds, which originated in the ancient church: the Apostles' Creed,

the Nicene Creed, and the Athanasian Creed. It also contains the following Reformation writings: the *Augsburg Confession*, the *Apology of the Augsburg Confession*, and the treatise "On the Power and Primacy of the Pope," all of which were written by Philipp Melanchthon; the *Small Catechism* and the *Large Catechism* and the *Smalcald Articles* by Martin Luther; and the *Formula of Concord* written by Jacob Andreae, Martin Chemnitz, and Nickolaus Selnecker.

The three creeds included in the *Book of Concord* are considered to be universal. Lutherans believe these creeds should be accepted by Christians worldwide as proper representations of Christian beliefs. The Apostles' Creed is a confession of apostolic doctrine that is based on the creed used by the Romans. The Nicene Creed is spoken on communion Sundays and festive occasions. Its roots can be traced back to the Council of Constantinople, which took place in 381. The Athanasian Creed, with origins from the sixth century, is the longest of the three creeds and is used on Trinity Sunday, the first Sunday after Pentecost. This creed is named after the fourth-century champion of orthodoxy, Athanasius, who spoke out against heretics who denied the deity of Christ. The inclusion of the creeds in *The Book of Concord* shows that Lutherans embrace and confess the ancient and orthodox faith, rather than envision themselves as a sect.

The Lutheran Confessions contained in the *Book of Concord* comprise works written by both Martin Luther and his friend Philipp Melanchthon. In 1530, Melanchthon was required to present the confessions of the Lutheran faith to the emperor in Augsburg, Germany. The Augsburg Confession gives a clear but conciliatory summary of the teachings and practices of Lutheran congregations. The *Apology of the Augsburg Confession*, also by Melanchthon, was published one year later in 1531 and defends the confession against accusations of the Roman Catholic Confutation.

Luther wrote the *Smalcald Articles* in 1536 with the intention of presenting them during a council with the pope. Although they were never used for this purpose, they are included in the *Book of*

Concord as a list of non-negotiable doctrines or steadfast beliefs of the Lutheran faith.

The Formula of Concord was written in 1577, after Luther's death. Discord had arisen among theologians studying the *Augsburg Confessions* that threatened to tear the very foundations of Lutheranism apart. The *Formula* presented a sound biblical doctrine on the disputed issues and served as a unifying factor among those arguing the intentions of the original document. The first part of the Formula is called the "Epitome," containing eleven articles devoted to the assessment and decision of the disputed points of doctrine. The dispute is explained, and the orthodox view of the disputed points is summarized concisely in the "Affirmativa." The doctrine that stood against it is indicated in the "Negativa," or "Antithesis," according to its main points and immediately rejected and condemned. In the second part, known as the "Solid Declaration," the same articles are discussed in context.

The *Small Catechism* and the *Large Catechism* were two handbooks written in 1530 by Martin Luther to help pastors and heads of families teach the Lutheran faith. They were organized around six topics: the Ten Commandments; the Apostles' Creed; the Lord's Prayer; Holy Baptism; Confession; and the Sacrament of the Altar. Luther recognized the need for the unification of Lutheran teachings and sought to accomplish this by making the formulas of his faith easier to understand by his followers.

B. Scripture

The general basis for the Lutheran Confessions is the acceptance of the Bible as the actual word of God. "The Word of God is and should remain the sole rule and norm of all doctrine" (FC SD, Rule and Norm, 9). The confessions are the "basis, rule, and norm indicating how all doctrines should be judged in conformity with the word of God" (FC SD RN). The confessions serve as the standard to determine what is faithful in biblical teaching.

The teachings of Luther can be summarized in three short phrases: *sola gratia, sola fide, sola scriptora,* or "Grace alone, Faith alone, Scripture alone." "Grace alone" is the belief that God loves all people and that he sent his son to save everyone, including the ungodly. "Faith alone" means that if one adheres to the belief that Jesus died for the sins of all humanity, one is granted eternal life. "Scripture alone" refers to the belief that the Bible is God's "inerrant and infallible Word" and should be considered the "sole rule and norm" for Christian doctrine.

C. Sacred Literature

The books of the Apocrypha of the Old Testament are said to be inspired, but are not considered canonical. They should be used for Christian edification and have traditionally been included in vernacular versions of the Bible. These books are included in the Greek translation of the Bible, known as the *Septuagint.* The Apocryphal Books were first separated from the canonical in the earliest Protestant edition of the German Bible in 1530. With the Reformation, Luther reverted to the Hebrew Canon and placed these books apart under the title of *Apocrypha.* He also placed the books of Hebrews, James, Jude, and Revelation at the end of the New Testament and referred to them as books of "lesser value."

D. Secondary Sources

Luther's Other Work

Martin Luther also wrote hymns, the most popular of which is called "A Mighty Fortress Is Our God," which are still sung during Lutheran worship services today.

Luther's translation of the Bible into German not only contributed to the development and stabilization of literary German, but also began the era of the printing press and the mass distribution of printed works.

Important Composers and Artists

The musical compositions of George Frideric Handel and Johann Sebastian Bach had a profound influence in Lutheran worship and have become important in religious affirmation for Lutherans worldwide. Handel's oratorios, which include the immensely popular *Messiah*, are used in the Anglican and Protestant churches, but are still Lutheran in nature. The church music of Bach can "certainly be regarded as the principal single cultural monument of the Lutheran heritage" (J. Pelikan, *The Christian Tradition*, p. 427).

Bach wrote the *Orgelbuchlein* based on the Lutheran liturgical year, and composed a series of cantatas to be used on Sundays.

Paul Gerhardt is another author of hymns who gave voice to the Lutheran understanding of faith, hope, and charity during the Thirty Years' War.

III. Denominations and Demographics

A. History (Schisms, Mergers, etc.)

The first major dispute in the Lutheran church was centered on the orthodox Lutherans and the Pietists. Lutheran orthodoxy began around 1600 and originated out of the tradition of the confessional writings. The works produced during this period were based on the principle of *sola scriptura*. The adoption of Aristotelianism in German universities also highly influenced the development of orthodox teachings. The scholastic philosophy prompted a more pronounced scientific and metaphysical treatment of theological questions.

The orthodox movement stimulated the occurrence of the countermovement, Pietism. Philip Spener wrote the *Pia desideria* and called for a reform movement within Lutheranism. Spener believed that the personal experience of the individual is the ground of certainty for theological knowledge.

Christian Wolff and Johann Semler began the theological rationalization movement in Germany in the eighteenth century. These men argued that reason was the path to true faith and that learning should be based on distinct concepts.

When Frederick William III created the Prussian Union of 1817 with the purpose of uniting Lutherans and the Reformed into one congregation, he intended for a similar union throughout Prussia, but received few results. Instead, Prussia experienced a revival of Lutheran confessionalism in reaction to the increase in doctrinal indifference as well as an interest in biblical criticism that endangered the doctrinal basis of the church. It was at this time that many Lutherans immigrated to the United States.

The debate between Pietism and orthodoxy also made its way to the United States. In 1818, new hymnbooks were introduced in certain churches, and a transition from the use of German in church to English was suggested, causing a schism within the church. The German party began to relate more closely to the German-speaking Reformed and advocated an evangelical union such as what had occurred in Prussia.

Disputes such as these, between the conservative orthodox thinkers and the liberal Pietists, facilitated the formation of the General Synod, which even then was regarded with suspicion by many of the individual synods. The Pennsylvania Synod left three years after the formation of the General Synod and rejoined later. In 1866, the General Synod declared that the Pennsylvania Synod was no longer in union with the general body. The Pennsylvania Synod was forced to leave and then formed the General Council along with thirteen other American and Canadian synods.

Within the Missouri Synod, there was a debate regarding the extreme congregationalism and denial of open questions in theology, which caused dissatisfied members to create the Iowa Synod.

The American Civil War caused five southern district synods to secede from the General Synod and create the General Synod of the Confederate

States, later becoming the General Synod of the South.

The Lutheran Church-Missouri Synod (LCMS) and the Association of Evangelical Lutheran Churches (AELC) debated over the Bible being the actual Word of God. At the St. Louis seminary, students were being taught that the Bible only contains the Word of God, not that it is actually God's Word. Professors and students from the seminary left the Missouri Synod to form the Concordia Seminary in Exile (Seminex) in 1974. Later, supporters of Seminex and followers of this school of thought also left LCMS and formed the Association of Evangelical Lutheran Churches (AELC) in 1976. According to the AELC, the Confessions in the *Book of Concord* are simply documents that illustrated the past beliefs of the church, thus allowing for the inerrancy of the Bible to be challenged. The LCMS still maintains that the Lutheran Confessions do speak the truth and that Luther was a faithful confessor rather than simply a radical of the Reformation.

The AELC, the American Lutheran Church, and the Lutheran Church in America (once the General Synod) merged and formed the Evangelical Lutheran Church in America (ELCA) on January 1, 1988. As of August 1997, the ELCA is in a fellowship and full communion with the Presbyterian Church (USA), the Reformed Church in America, and the United Church of Christ, as well as with the Episcopalians and Moravians. The ELCA is still in talks with the Roman Catholic Church and the United Methodist Church to create an affiliation. Although this unity of churches is seen by many as a step forward, many traditional Lutherans believe that these fellowships compromise the true Lutheranism of the ELCA.

The most common cause of dissension among the Lutheran churches in America is the diversity of opinion regarding the importance or the interpretation of the official Confessions.

B. Comparison of Tenets and Practices

Lutherans believe in two sacraments, baptism and Holy Communion. All local Lutheran churches are autonomous and congregational in polity but as part of a larger synod receive advice and help from a larger church body. Conferences do not enact any laws or rules that the churches must follow.

In the Evangelical Lutheran Church in America (ELCA), Lutherans believe in a nonliteral interpretation of the Bible and that the Bible can be better interpreted through critical study. At ELCA seminaries, students are taught a historical-critical method of biblical analysis that allows students to understand the Scripture and the process of tenet construction with reference to historical and social context. Lutherans belonging to the ELCA also believe in the doctrine of Sacramental Union—that Christ is truly present (body and soul) in the Eucharist during Communion. The ELCA is the only Lutheran church that allows women to be ordained as clergy and practices open Communion, inviting all baptized persons to receive Communion.

Members of the Lutheran Church-Missouri Synod (LCMS) believe that the Bible is the only standard for Church teachings and that the Bible is inspired by God and thus without error. Lutherans in the LCMS maintain that Scripture is best explained and interpreted by the *Book of Concord*. The LCMS also follows the doctrine of the Sacramental Union, that the body and blood of Christ are present in the bread and wine of the Eucharist. The Missouri Synod practices closed Communion and shares Communion only with Christians with belief as set forth by the LCMS.

The Wisconsin Evangelical Lutheran Synod (WELS) and the Evangelical Lutheran Synod (ELS) both follow a similar scriptural interpretation as that of the LCMS and maintain that the Scripture is inerrant and is not open to different interpretations. The teachings of the WELS differ from the LCMS in regard to fellowship with other Christians because they believe that there are varying degrees of fellowship based on the extent of doctrinal disagreements. The WELS teaches that extramarital sex and homosexual relations are sins, while the ELCA has no official stand but has traditionally been open to different viewpoints concerning these matters. The ELCA believes that Christians do not have to agree on all doctrines of Scripture in order to enter into a fellowship, but the WELS does not agree. Women are not ordained in either the WELS or the ELS.

Members of the Association of Free Lutheran Congregations (AFLC) and the Church of the Lutheran Brethren of America (CLBA) maintain a conservative Lutheran view. They believe that the Bible is the inerrant Word of God, that the Holy Spirit serves as a guide for the Church and the individual, and that his ministries include the regeneration and sanctification of believers. These Lutherans believe that all human beings are fallen in sin because of the actions of Adam and Eve in the Garden of Eden and that salvation is found only through personal faith in Jesus Christ. Women are not ordained into ministry within either the AFLC or the CLBA. The Lord's Supper is performed monthly and is only for those who profess personal faith in Jesus as savior.

C. Organization and Distribution

The four major Lutheran denominations in the Unites States are the ELCA, LCMS, WELS, and the AFLC. The Evangelical Lutheran Church in America (ELCA) is the largest Lutheran denomination in the United States, with about 4.9 million members in its congregation. The Lutheran Church–Missouri Synod (LCMS) is the second largest Lutheran body in the United States, consisting of about 2.46 million baptized members. The Wisconsin Evangelical Lutheran Synod (WELS) has congregations in all fifty states and has a membership of over 400,000 people. The Association of Free Lutheran Congregations (AFLC) is made up of 145 congregations and has about 28,100 members.

Other Lutheran denominations in the United States include the Apostolic Lutheran Church in America, the Church of the Lutheran Brethren in America, the Church of the Lutheran Confession, the Concordia Lutheran Conference, the Conservative Lutheran Conference, the Estonian Evangelical Lutheran Church, the Evangelical Lutheran Federation, the Evangelical Lutheran Synod, the Fellowship of Lutheran Congregations, the International Lutheran Fellowship, the Latvian Evangelical Lutheran Church, the Lutheran Churches of the Reformation, and the Protestant Conference.

The Church of the Lutheran Brethren of America (CLBA) has about 9,000 members in 145 congregations; it dedicates some 40 percent of denominational funds to missions around the world. The Evangelical Lutheran Synod operates 139 congregations with about 17,000 members across the United States.

Evangelical Lutheran Church in America (ELCA)
8765 West Higgins Road
Chicago, IL 60631
773-380-2700   Fax: 773-380-1465
1-800-638-3522
www.elca.org

The Lutheran Church–Missouri Synod (LCMS)
1333 South Kirkwood Road
St. Louis, MO 63122
314-965-9000   Fax: 314-996-1016
888-THE-LCMS (843-5267)
www.lcms.org

Wisconsin Evangelical Lutheran Synod (WELS)
2929 North Mayfair Road
Milwaukee, WI 53222
414-256-3888
www.wels.net

Association of Free Lutheran Congregations (AFLC)
3110 East Medicine Lake Boulevard

Plymouth, MN 55441

763-545-5631   Fax: 763-545-0079

www.aflc.org

Church of the Lutheran Brethren of America
(CLBA)

1020 Alcott Avenue West

Fergus Falls, MN 56537

PO Box 655

Fergus Falls, MN 56538

218-739-3336   Fax: 218-739-5514

www.clba.org

Zion Lutheran Church in Chelsea, Michigan. Founded in 1842, the church began as a group of congregations served by a single minister until there were enough Lutherans to create their own church. The name and the Gothic style have become hallmarks of Lutheran churches across the U.S.

IV. Rites and Rituals

A. The Calendar

The Lutheran calendar is based on two major events, the life and death of Christ. Christmas, the celebration of the birth of Christ, is always on December 25. December 26 is Saint Stephanus Day, in remembrance of the first Christian martyr. The New Year, also referred to as the Namegiving of Christ, is always eight days after Christmas on the first of January. January 6 is the Epiphany to mark the day when the Three Holy Kings visited Jesus. This is no longer a holiday but serves as a marker for other holy days. Easter, the Resurrection of Christ, occurs on the first Sunday after the full moon after the vernal equinox. Lent occurs during the last forty days before Easter, to signify the fasting of Jesus in the desert for forty days. Good Friday is the last Friday before Easter Sunday and is in honor of the day Jesus was crucified on the cross. The Monday after Easter Sunday is called the Second Day of Easter and is also considered a holiday. In the early Lutheran Church, Whitsunday, or White Sunday, was on the seventh Sunday after Easter and was traditionally a festival in the Church to celebrate the descent of the Holy Spirit on the day of Pentecost. Trinity was on the Sunday after Whitsunday when a feast would be held in honor of the Holy Trinity. The Commemoration of the Reformation is held on October 31.

A popular way to remember important dates of Lutheran calendar is to become familiar with Johann Sebastian Bach's *Orgelbuchlein*, which was intended to follow the liturgical year.

B. Worship and Liturgy

The Bible is central to Lutheran worship and the two sacraments (baptism and Communion, or the Lord's Supper) are practiced because it is believed that Christ, according to the Bible, instituted them. Lutheran worship is based on the service-book originally published by Luther in 1523 and 1526, which eliminated the offertory, canon, and all forms of sacrifice from the Mass, and a common service based on the liturgies of the sixteenth century is used by almost all English-speaking Lutherans in the United States. Traditionally, worship in Lutheran churches is conducted in the language of the people, and congregational participation is encouraged, notably through the singing of liturgy and hymns. The Lord's Supper is administered only a few times a year and is preceded by a service of public confession and absolution. Other sacred rites include confirmation, ordination and confession, and ceremonies for marriage and burial.

The chorale is central to all Lutheran church services. This tradition extends from Luther's belief that hymns and music should play a central role in worship. The most widely used hymnals are *Christian Worship*, *The Lutheran Book of Worship*, *The Lutheran Hymnal*, and *Lutheran Worship*.

C. Daily Life

There are no restrictions on clothing or diet in Lutheranism. Lutherans are asked to live their daily lives in observance of a "priesthood for all believers." In the Lutheran church, all baptized members serve God in their chosen vocations. They are equally close to God, no less than ordained pastors.

D. Life Cycle Events

Baptism

Baptism is one of the two sacraments in the Lutheran tradition. Baptism is believed to be an act during which God imparts the blessings of forgiveness, life, and salvation to individuals, both children and adults.

Confirmation

Confirmation is a sacred rite in the Lutheran tradition; it is not considered a sacrament.

Nuptials

It is not necessary for a pastor to perform the marriage ceremony because it is not so written in either the scripture or the Confessions. The tradition of "Christian" marriages, those blessed by a pastor and congregation, is an ancient one. Most couples

desire such weddings so that they may be "strengthened and taught by the Word of Christ as they begin their new life together" (www.lcms.org). Pastors now work as servants of the state when performing marriages in that they must complete the proper paperwork and return it to a county office.

Death and Burial

Lutherans view death as the separation of the eternal soul from a mortal body, to await the "final day when soul and body shall be reunited." In death, the soul is in the presence of Christ.

E. Family Life

Husband and Wife

Luther rejected the practice of clerical celibacy, and with his own marriage, confirmed the importance of marriage and family life. Luther was the first in Christian history to encourage parish clergy to marry; clergy traditionally led monastic lives of lifelong virginity.

Lutherans believe that the role of a Lutheran wife is to be submissive to her husband, as the church is submissive to the teachings of Christ. Husbands are expected to respect their wives, while maintaining a leadership role within the household. This is stated in the *Book of Concord*:

Submit to one another out of reverence for Christ. Wives, submit to your husbands as to the Lord. For the husband is the head of the wife as Christ is the head of the church, his body, of which he is the Savior. Now as the church submits to Christ, so also wives should submit to their husbands in everything. Husbands, love your wives, just as Christ loved the church and gave Himself up for her to make her holy … In this same way, husbands ought to love their wives as their own bodies. He who loves his wife loves himself
— (Eph. 5:21–33).

Child-rearing

A Lutheran parent is to be a role model for his or her children. Parents should provide discipline to their children with love and compassion and always do what is best for their children. Families are expected to attend church every Sunday and receive the sacraments together. Luther's Small Catechism should be recited with children beginning at a very young age and parents should also teach them the Lord's Prayer, the Ten Commandments, and the Apostles' Creed. Faith and prayer should be experienced as a family and parents should model the Lutheran faith.

Divorce

Divorce, according to Scripture as interpreted by Lutherans, is a concession to the fact and reality of sin in a fallen world. Jesus explained divorce as resulting from the hardness of human hearts (Matthew 19:8; Mark 10:5); it is viewed as a consequence of human sinfulness. True Christian spouses will do everything in their power to restore their marriage and will, before they decide on divorce, evaluate all of the consequences of the termination of the marriage. Lutheran couples thinking about divorce seek the counsel of their pastor or other competent counsel. If after careful consideration, the continuation of the marriage has been deemed destructive, the decision for divorce may be accepted. The couple should seek God's grace in forgiveness of their sins.

The church deals with the problems of divorce and divorced persons in a nonlegalistic manner; they are fully included in the Lutheran Church.

V. Organization and Infrastructure

A. Education and Hierarchy of Clergy

Lutheran pastors must have bachelor's degrees as well as master's degrees in divinity from one of the many Lutheran seminaries located throughout the country. Each Lutheran denomination operates its own seminaries, and pastors must obtain their degrees from those specific schools to be ordained.

The ELCA has eight seminaries in the United States: the **Lutheran Theological Seminaries** at Gettysburg and Philadelphia, Pennsylvania; the **Lutheran Theological Southern Seminary** at Columbia, South Carolina; the **Lutheran School** at Chicago, Illinois; the **Trinity Lutheran Seminary** at Columbus, Ohio; the **Wartburg Theological Seminary** at Dubuque, Iowa; the **Luther Seminary** at St. Paul, Minnesota; and the **Pacific Lutheran Theological Seminary** at Berkeley, California. In the ELCA, pastors are ordained by bishops under episcopal terms, meaning the ELCA has adopted an apostolic succession in its ordained ministers. The ELCA also believes in the "priesthood of all believers" in accordance with traditional Lutheran doctrine, which means that all those baptized have equal access to God and are all called to serve Christ. Some, however, are called to "rostered ministry"—church leadership and service. A rostered minister must go through training and certification by the local synod. The four types of rostered ministry are pastor, deaconess, associate in ministry, and diaconal minister.

The LCMS operates two seminaries: the **Concordia Seminary** in St. Louis, Missouri, and the **Concordia Theological Seminary** in Fort Wayne, Indiana. The LCMS does not believe in apostolic succession in regard to ordination because it believes the office of the pastor is grounded in the word and sacrament ministry of the gospel.

The WELS has four schools of ministry education: **Michigan Lutheran Seminary** and **Luther Preparatory School**, both college preparatory schools; **Martin Luther College**, a preseminary and teacher training college; and **Wisconsin Lutheran Seminary**, a seminary for training pastors. The ELS operates the **Bethany Lutheran College** and the **Bethany Lutheran Theological Seminary**, both in Mankato, Minnesota.

B. Shrines and Houses of Worship

The ELCA sees itself as having three expressions: the national church, the local synods, and the local congregations. The ELCA is divided into sixty-five geographic regional synods in the United States and the Caribbean and operates over 10,000 local congregations. The LCMS is synodical in structure and is run by the congregations, rather than by bishops. The LCMS has thirty-five districts within the United States and maintains more than 6,000 congregations. Local congregations are autonomous and hold legal title to their church buildings and other property. The WELS has more than 1,200 congregations in all fifty states and the ELS has 142 congregations and twelve mission churches.

C. Governance and Authority

Lutherans do not associate church governance with doctrinal standards; different churches are allowed to govern as they see fit. American Lutheran churches are generally governed democratically. The individual congregations own their church building and property and are self-governing in local matters.

An elected presiding bishop heads the ELCA, while elected presidents lead the other Lutheran bodies. District leaders are also elected at conferences and serve for a set number of years and terms. For example, in the ELCA, a church-wide Assembly meets every two years and consists of elected lay and ordained voting members. Between these meetings, the Church Council governs the church. A bishop and council also head each synod within the ELCA.

D. Social Service Organizations

Most Lutheran organizations operate foreign missions in different countries around the world.

Lutheran Services in America
700 Light Street
Baltimore, MD 21230
800-664-3848   Fax: 410-230-2710
www.lutheranservices.org

Church of Lutheran Brethren of America
1020 Alcott Avenue West
PO Box 655
Fergus Falls, MN 56537
218-739-3336   Fax: 218-739-5514
www.clba.org

The Lutheran Services in America (LSA) consists of over 300 health and human service organizations operating within America and the Caribbean. About 40 percent of denominational funds of the Church of the Lutheran Brethren of America are dedicated to missions throughout the world.

E. Media and Communication

All of the major Lutheran groups maintain websites on the Internet, listed throughout this chapter.

Northwestern Publishing is the official publishing house for the WELS. The main WELS periodicals are *Forward in Christ,* the *Wisconsin Lutheran Quarterly*, and *The Lutheran Educator.* The LCMS operates Concordia Publishing House, and the Lutheran Hour Ministries conducts outreach ministries, including *The Lutheran Hour* radio program. *The Lutheran Annual* is published by Concordia.

FURTHER READING
Here I Stand: A Life of Martin Luther
   Roland H. Bainton
   1995: Penguin Group
Book of Concord
   Robert Kolb, et al, translators
   2000: Augsburg Fortress Press
Organization of the Congregation in the Early Lutheran Churches in America
   Beale M. Schmucker
   2007: Dodo Press

10 Mennonites

I. Origins and Early History

THE MENNONITE LANDSCAPE OF THE UNITED STATES is surprisingly diverse. Some Mennonites are rural separatists with conservative worldviews and lifestyles; others are cosmopolitan city-dwellers who actively participate in mainstream culture. Some Mennonites drive horse-drawn carriages, read by lantern light, and go to one-room schools, while others participate in public life as stockbrokers, physicians, politicians, college professors, and corporate executives.

Until the middle of the twentieth century, most Mennonites came from German, Swiss, Dutch, or Russian heritage. Worldwide, most of them lived in Europe, the United States, or Canada. Today there are thriving Mennonite communities around the world with a total membership of about 1.4 million.

Hay tedders were first used in the 1850s. They are still common among Amish and Mennonites. This recent photograph was taken in Lancaster County, Pennsylvania.

Mennonites live in Central and South America, Africa, and Asia, in addition to Europe and North America. Ethnic diversity has blossomed in Mennonite communities in the United States as well. Some Mennonite congregations are predominantly African American, Asian American, Latino American, and Native American. Across the United States, Mennonites worship in more than a dozen languages.

Members of these widely varying groups would happily debate the dozens of differences in belief and practice among themselves. Indeed, some of the groups will shun or excommunicate members of other groups over points of doctrine and practice. Nevertheless, these communities of faith claim a common heritage and a similar theological identity.

On the surface, Mennonites are characterized by social, cultural, and religious diversity. There are wide variances in lifestyle, but many core convictions remain similar across the Mennonite world. Mennonite communities aspire to embody the spirit of Jesus in daily life. In city and farm, in work and play, in school and family, they seek to practice peacemaking amid conflict; to build community among diversity; to live with integrity amid deceit; and to serve their neighbors in the name of Christ.

A. History

The Mennonite story began in 1525, in Switzerland when a group of young adults baptized one another in a private home. Such an event would hardly be newsworthy today, but in the early days of the Protestant Reformation, adult baptism was an outrageous act of defiance. Because they had already been baptized as infants, these young reformers came to be known as Anabaptists, meaning re-baptizers.

The Anabaptists believed that only adults—those who could voluntarily make a decision to follow the teachings of Jesus—should be baptized. Their adult re-baptisms provoked irritation and outrage because baptism in sixteenth-century Europe was not just a matter of personal religious conviction; it was a form of census-taking and political control. Baptism conferred membership into both Catholic and Protestant churches, but it also granted state citizenship, thereby giving authorities the power to tax and conscript church members. The Anabaptists' refusal to obey established traditions (along with their refusal to swear oaths of allegiance) outraged both political and religious authorities. The name Anabaptist became a negative word for a dangerous movement that threatened to overturn long-standing political and religious traditions.

Anabaptists were persecuted for their convictions, especially because those convictions toppled many of the pillars upon which European society had rested for generations. Leaders of this new movement were called heretics and were banned from many regions. Hundreds were brutally tortured and killed. They were often forced to flee for their lives, and members had to meet in secret for worship. *The Martyrs Mirror,* a book of nearly 1,200 pages that was published in 1660, chronicles the harsh persecution that many Anabaptists faced.

Although adult baptism became the public symbol of the Anabaptist movement, the deeper issue was one of authority. Could government officials prescribe religious practices such as infant baptism, or should the Bible be the ultimate authority for the church? The Anabaptists believed that Scripture and the Holy Spirit were the ultimate authorities in all areas of life and that the government should not have authority over the church. Anabaptists were among the first to call for a sharp separation between church and state.

The early Anabaptist movement attracted a young Dutch Catholic priest named Menno Simons who, while in his thirties, began to question some key Catholic beliefs, such as infant baptism and transubstantiation. After consulting the Bible, he decided that neither belief was validated by Scripture, and he gradually began to place the authority of Scripture above that of the Catholic Church.

In 1530, the state executed an Anabaptist man for "re-baptism" in the Dutch province where Menno lived. He heard about the execution and became intrigued by the idea of a second baptism. Again, he consulted the Bible. This time he became convinced of the scriptural integrity of adult baptism. By 1536, he had renounced Catholicism and converted to Anabaptism. He eventually became a gifted writer and powerful leader of the Anabaptist movement, but he was not its founder. Rather, he was an important leader who emerged ten years after its beginning, at a time when the movement was in danger of losing its identity to the influence of millennial and revolutionary leaders. During this volatile time in the Netherlands, Menno maintained the original, peaceful, and biblical Anabaptist principles. As early as 1545, some of Menno's followers were called Mennists. In regions beyond the Netherlands, Anabaptists became known as Mennists, Mennonists, and eventually Mennonites.

Once the enthusiasm of the first few decades of the movement cooled, the surviving Anabaptist communities settled into more stability. For the most part, Anabaptists affirmed the historic creeds of the Christian Church. Along with Protestant reformers, they emphasized the authority of scripture, salvation by grace through faith, and the priesthood of all believers. The Schleitheim Confession, written in 1527 in Switzerland, is the first known Anabaptist confession of faith. Within the great umbrella of Christianity, unique Anabaptist emphases include a believer's (adult) baptism, excommunication, the Lord's Supper, separation from the world, nonresistance, and the nonswearing of oaths.

The next official statement of Anabaptist belief, the Dordrecht Confession of Faith, appeared nearly a century later in the Netherlands. An elder of the Flemish Mennonite congregation in the city of Dordrecht wrote the confession in 1632, but it was not adopted in the United States until 1725. The more conservative Mennonite groups in the United States continue to use this document as their official articles of faith. The eighteen articles of the Dordrecht Confession teach the basic doctrines of the Christian faith, such as God as a trinity, the presence of original sin, and Jesus as Savior and Son of God. Like the Schleitheim Confession, these articles include the unique Anabaptist practices of believer's baptism, feetwashing, nonswearing of oaths, and peaceful nonresistance.

The prescriptions for excommunication and shunning are among the most interesting elements of the Dordrecht Confession. Article XVI counsels that a baptized member of the church should be excommunicated if she or he reverts to a life of sin. "Such a one, after the deed is manifest and sufficiently known to the church, may not remain in the congregation of the righteous, but as an open and offensive member, shall and must be separated..." from the community. Such a ban strives to keep the community pure and goad the sinner to repentance. Excommunicated apostates are also to be shunned or avoided, according to Article XVII. Church members are to cease social fellowship with the excommunicated member. The purpose of this shunning is to bring the admonished member to knowledge and sorrow for their sins "so they may become reconciled to God and consequently received again into the church." The most traditional Old Order Mennonites still practice shunning, but the overwhelming majority of Mennonites no longer follow this practice.

The Dordrecht Confession is written in simple and direct language with many Scripture quotations. Overall, the confession conforms to the pattern of evangelical Protestant thought. However, it stresses that obeying Christ in everyday life is more important to the Christian life than is correct belief.

B. The Religion in America

During the first century of the Anabaptist movement, persecution drove members into hiding and safe areas in many regions of Europe, from the Netherlands to Switzerland. After decades of persecution, Anabaptists were understandably attracted to William Penn's experiment of religious freedom in Pennsylvania. Soon religious minorities from across northern Europe began to flock to Penn's Woods. By 1685, 8,000 immigrants (mostly Mennonite and Quaker) had come to the American colonies through the port of Philadelphia.

Most Mennonites, however, arrived in the United States in two large waves of immigration. The first wave in the eighteenth century brought Mennonites of mostly Swiss and South German ancestry. These immigrants settled in the eastern states, and even today, Pennsylvania hosts the highest number of Mennonites in the United States. Mennonites of Dutch and Russian ancestry arrived in the second wave in the nineteenth century. Most of these later immigrants settled in the western prairie states and provinces of Canada.

About 53,000 Mennonites remain in Europe, but the vast majority of the worldwide Mennonite population resides in the United States and Canada (about 500,000), in Africa (about 530,000), and in some forty other countries combined (about 400,000).

C. Important Dates and Landmarks

1517 Martin Luther posts Ninety-five Theses citing abuses of Papal authority, to the Wittenberg church door on October 31.

1525 Conrad Grebel re-baptizes George Blaurock as the first convert to Anabaptism.

1527 Swiss leaders draw up the Schleitheim Confession, identifying seven distinctives of Anabaptist belief.

1528 Missionary Conference of Augsburg, organized by the Anabaptists, serves the first Protestant missionary conference.

1529 Melchior Hoffman joins Anabaptists, proclaims Strasbourg "New Jerusalem."

1535 A second "New Jerusalem"—Munster—fails miserably, sparking widespread persecution of Anabaptists.

1536 Menno Simons leaves the priesthood in the Catholic Church and becomes a prominent Anabaptist theologian.

1555 Peace of Augsburg, treaty signed between the Holy Roman Emperor and alliance of Lutheran princes, permits German nobility to determine religion of their district.

1632 The Dordrecht Confession unites Mennonites around eighteen articles of faith.

1660 Tieleman Jansz van Braght compiles the 1,200 page *Martyrs Mirror*—a book that recounts the persecution and martyrdom of Anabaptists.

1683 At William Penn's invitation, Mennonites and Quakers establish Germantown just north of Philadelphia.

1693 Jakob Ammann breaks fellowship with Swiss Anabaptists to form the Amish church.

1698 Mennonites appoint William Rittenhouse to pastor the first Anabaptist congregation in America.

1775 American Anabaptists meet with revolutionary authorities to offer humanitarian aid rather than fight the British.

1872–1901 Traditional leaning Mennonites reject progressive changes and form Old Order Mennonite groups.

1927 One group of Old Order Mennonites splits over the adoption of the automobile.

1946 Mennonite Mutual Aid is organized to help young men returning from Civilian Public Service camps.

D. Important Figures

Conrad Grebel (1484–1527)

Sometimes referred to as the Father of Anabaptists, Grebel was one of the founders and early leaders of the Anabaptist movement. Born into a wealthy Swiss family of high social status, Grebel studied at the University of Basel, the University of Vienna, and the University in Paris. Though Grebel dedicated six years to study at three universities, he did not receive a degree. In 1521, Grebel joined a group that studied with Ulrich Zwingli, Protestant pastor in Zurich. Zwingli was the leader of the Reformation movement in Switzerland. Born on New Year's Day, 1484, Zwingli studied at the University of Vienna, receiving his degree in 1506. Upon completing his studies, Zwingli became an ordained priest, beginning his career in Glarus, Switzerland, later moving to Einsiedlin near Zurich.

Under his tutelage, Grebel and other students, including Felix Manz, studied the Greek classics and the Bible. Through the preaching of Zwingli, Grebel changed from a loose-living university student to a devout Christian, and developed a close friendship with Zwingli.

A public disputation in Zurich, however, challenged Grebel's support of Zwingli in October of 1523. Grebel and Zwingli disagreed over abolishing the Mass. Zwingli argued before the city council for abolishing the Mass and removing images from the church. But when he saw that the council was not ready for such radical changes, he chose not to abide by the council's reasoning and continued to officiate at the Mass until it was abolished in May 1525. Grebel saw this as an issue of obeying God rather than men, and, with others, could not conscientiously continue to abide by Zwingli's teachings. Grebel and fellow reformer Felix Manz began meeting in their homes with other like-minded seekers in order to study the scriptures together.

The issue that completely separated the radicals and Zwingli was the question of infant baptism. A public debate was held on January 17, 1525. Zwingli argued against Grebel, Manz, and former priest George Blaurock. The city council decided in favor of Zwingli and infant baptism, ordered the Grebel group to cease their activities and that any unbaptized infants must be submitted for baptism within eight days. Failure to comply with the council's order would result in exile from the canton. During a meeting at the home of Felix Manz, Blaurock asked Grebel to baptize him upon a confession of faith. Afterward, Blaurock baptized the others who were present.

Grebel continued to preach to surrounding cities. During one such mission in October 1525, he was arrested and imprisoned. With the help of friends, he escaped in March 1526. He continued his ministry and ultimately found the means to have a pamphlet of his teachings printed. Grebel moved to the Maienfeld area in the Canton of Grisons. Shortly after his arrival in 1527, however, Grebel fell ill and died.

The early Anabaptist leaders in the Zurich area opposed infant baptism and refused to join Zwingli's state church. Zwingli thus persecuted them mercilessly with imprisonment, torture, and death; one of their leaders, Felix Manz, was drowned in 1527, two years after the first adult baptisms. The war against the Anabaptists was more serious for Zwingli than that against Rome.

Menno Simons (1496–1561)

Menno Simons was born in 1496 in Witmarsum, The Netherlands. At the age of 15, he entered a novitiate and five years later became a deacon in the Catholic Church.

Shortly after his assignment to the vicariate of Pingjum, Simons experienced doubts about his faith. However, it was the beheading of Sicke Snijder in 1531 by state officials for the crime of re-baptism that prompted Simons to reexamine the Bible. Though intrigued by the Anabaptist movement, he accepted a promotion as a priest in his home church at Witmarsum in 1531 and continued to carry out his duties for the next three years.

In 1535, Simons wrote his first surviving tract, a polemic against Jan of Leyden, in which he laid the foundation for a biblical analysis based on the teachings of Christ. In January of the following year, Menno Simons resigned his office and publicly aligned himself with the Anabaptist cause.

Shortly thereafter, Obbe Philips, a Dutch Anabaptist leader, ordained Simons as an Anabaptist pastor. Upon ordination, Menno Simons set about to rebuild the fractured Anabaptist movement. For the next three years, he traveled almost constantly—preaching, baptizing, evangelizing—while writing a number of treatises, including *The Spiritual Resurrection* (1536), *The New Birth* (1537), and *Foundation of the Christian Doctrine* (1539–1540). By 1542, Dutch authorities offered a reward of 500 guilders for Simons's capture. Traveling with his wife, Gertrude, and their three children, Menno Simons eluded capture for two decades.

Simons preached a gospel of the New Birth, giving prominent attention to Anabaptist teachings regarding adult baptism, pacifism, and a rejection of

Menno Simons (1495–1561), depicted in this ca. 1754 engraving, was the founder of the Mennonite faith. Initially ordained as a Roman Catholic, he joined the ranks of the Anabaptists in 1536.

the oath and magisterial offices. He died on January 31, 1561, at the age of sixty-five in Fresenberg, Germany.

II. Tenets and Beliefs

The different Mennonite groups in the United States in the twenty-first century may look different from one another and may act differently in society, but they do share some common convictions. These communities of faith claim a common religious heritage and hold relatively similar theological beliefs. Five distinctly Anabaptist themes continue to shape contemporary Mennonite faith and life.

A. Articles of Faith

New Testament Authority

Early Anabaptists believed that the authority of Scripture trumped state mandates and religious customs. They were often persecuted because they followed biblical instructions rather than the dictates of state rulers. Scripture was important to them, especially the Sermon on the Mount (Matthew 5–8), and they viewed Jesus as the key to interpreting the entire Bible. Jesus was the final norm of revelation, so they interpreted the Old Testament through the lens of Jesus and his teaching. Most contemporary Mennonites maintain this practice and view the New Testament, specifically the Gospels, as a higher authority than the Old Testament.

Mennonites continue to look to the teachings and life of Jesus for authority rather than to creeds or church doctrine. Many affirm various confessions of faith but grant them less authority than a creed. They often emphasize right living or obedient discipleship as followers of Jesus, over right belief.

Discipleship

What does it mean to follow Jesus in daily life? This question guides the actions and activities of many Mennonites. They seek to be obedient disciples of Jesus in concrete and practical ways. These actions include loving enemies, going the second mile, forgiving injustices, and serving the needy. Mennonites aim to adhere to Jesus's life example regardless of the social consequences. They focus on the fruits of righteousness, the practical expressions of faith in daily behavior, and social relationships.

Believer's Baptism

Along with scriptural authority, adult believer's baptism was one of the hallmarks of the Anabaptist movement. Three key Anabaptist beliefs undergirded their insistence on adult baptism: their confidence in New Testament authority; their understanding of the nature of the church; and their concept of discipleship. When Anabaptists read about baptism in the New Testament, they saw that it was always tied to repentance and faith. They contend that because only adults are capable of true faith and repentance, only adults should be baptized.

Secondly, Anabaptists understood the church to be a voluntary fellowship of believers who had experienced a conversion and were committed to remain separated from the world. Baptism is thus a distinguishing mark of commitment and separation, a commitment that only an adult can make.

Adult baptism is also grounded in the Anabaptist concept of discipleship. Once a person is baptized in the church of Christ, she or he is expected to become a radical disciple and follow the teachings of Jesus in everyday life. The decision for baptism requires a full awareness of the social consequences of being an obedient disciple of Jesus.

Adult baptism grants full participation in the life of the church. Most Mennonites today undergo baptism between the ages of twelve and sixteen, although the age is higher (sixteen to twenty-two) in the more traditional groups. Most Mennonite groups baptize by pouring. The baptismal candidate kneels before a minister, who pours water from his or her hands over the candidate's head. Other Mennonite groups baptize by immersion, either a single immersion backwards or a single or trine immersion forwards.

Peacemaking

Peacemaking was not characteristic of all Anabaptists in the first decade of the movement, but by 1540, nonresistant love became one of its distinguishing marks. Many, but not all, early Anabaptists rejected all force and violence in human relations. Menno Simons was particularly attracted to the nonresistant aspect of Anabaptism, and he helped to keep the movement from straying away from its peaceful convictions.

Most Mennonites take seriously Jesus's instructions to love enemies and not resist evildoers. For this reason, many Mennonites advocate Christian pacifism and refuse to perform military service. Their commitment to pacifism was tested by all of the major wars fought by the United States. When they refused to pay war taxes to support the Revolutionary War, some Mennonites were accused of being British loyalists. (Indeed, after the British were defeated, some Mennonites fled to Canada for protection by the crown.) During the Civil War, Mennonites in the South had an especially difficult time escaping military service because the Confederacy was in dire need of manpower.

World War I proved to be the greatest test of Mennonite pacifism. Many Mennonites immediately drew the suspicion of their neighbors because they spoke German, the enemy's language. Some Mennonites were drafted into the United States military. Of those drafted, some were granted farm deferments and others worked in some type of noncombatant service, but these men had no legal alternative to military service.

After the war ended, Mennonite leaders met with leaders from the Church of the Brethren and the Society of Friends (Quakers) to organize themselves so they could have a more proactive response to any future programs of national conscription. These leaders held a joint peace conference in Kansas in 1935, where they affirmed their peace stance. As a

result of this conference, the Brethren, Mennonites, and Quakers are still known today as the Historic Peace Churches. These churches have continued to collaborate in efforts to declare their opposition to war and maintain a legal alternative to military service for conscientious objectors.

The Historic Peace Churches worked to create service opportunities for their members that the United States and Canadian governments would accept in lieu of military service. During World War II, the Korean War, and the Vietnam War, Mennonites performed national service in areas such as fire fighting, road construction, agriculture experiments, health care (especially in mental hospitals), social welfare, and education as an alternative to military service.

Almost all Mennonites today affirm the importance of peacemaking, but its centrality to their faith varies widely. Some report that it is at the core of their faith; others say that it is only peripheral to their faith. Traditional and conservative Mennonite groups will excommunicate members who perform military service. More assimilated groups may discourage military service but do not discipline members who choose to participate. These groups usually leave such matters up to members' individual consciences despite the denomination's official peace position. Some of the more traditional Mennonite groups forbid litigation because they see it as a use of legal force or coercion.

For some Mennonites, the emphasis on nonresistance led to an ethic of separation and withdrawal from the larger society. However, involvement in the civil rights movement and the protests of the Vietnam War in the mid-twentieth century prodded a large number of more assimilated Mennonites toward more activist forms of peacemaking. In these groups, the historic commitment to nonresistance has been transformed into active programs of conflict mediation, social transformation, and social justice. For example, some Mennonite groups support Christian Peacemaker Teams, an organization that trains volunteers to intervene in volatile and violent situations of conflict around the world. These Mennonites also support Mennonite Conciliation Service, which offers training and expertise in mediation and conflict transformation. Mennonite Central Committee—a relief, development, and peace agency of the North American Mennonite churches—maintains many global and domestic service projects that focus on peace and justice.

Church as Community

Early Anabaptists believed that church membership should be voluntary, not compulsory. Therefore, they rejected the idea of a state church where every person was required to become a member through infant baptism. Instead, they sought to restore the model of the apostolic church. This view of church requires a voluntary fellowship of believers who commit themselves to discipleship and remain separated from the values and practices of the larger society.

Anabaptists gathered as a visible church for mutual edification, support, and accountability. They argued that Jesus had granted the church the authority to make and enforce decisions about moral order. They looked to scripture, specifically Matthew 18:15–20, for guidance in how to relate to one another as a church community. This scripture passage advises the followers of Jesus to excommunicate willfully sinful members, but only after they have been admonished by church members. Mennonites believe these guidelines should regulate accountability in the corporate life of the church. The underlying assumption to all of these beliefs is that the collective wisdom of the church supersedes the freedom and rights of the individual.

Most Mennonite communities continue to endorse this view, but embody it in many different ways. The more traditional groups emphasize cultural boundaries that separate them from the larger world and excommunicate members who step across them. The more progressive and assimilated churches tend to focus on the confessional core of faith rather than on the borders that separate them from the larger society. Many assimilated congregations rarely, if ever, excommunicate members.

Radical discipleship and a serious commitment to the church often produce a counter-cultural witness. Most Mennonites believe that the church should embody a distinct culture that reflects the Gospel and teachings of Jesus. Such a church often challenges the values of the larger society. Some Mennonite groups, especially the more traditional bodies, embrace this counter-cultural stance and maintain boundaries of symbolic separation from the larger society.

B. Scripture

The Bible is the essential book of the Mennonite Church. Mennonites believe that the Bible is inspired by God through the Holy Spirit. According to *Biblical Interpretation in the Life of the Church,* "The ultimate goal in interpretation is to allow the Bible to speak its own message with a view to worship and obedience." The same statement emphasizes that the "Bible is the Book of the people of God." As such, the scriptures are accepted as the "Word of God" and the standard for faith and life. Although Mennonites accept the Bible as the living, written Word of God, they acknowledge that His word was translated into a human language and is, therefore, open to interpretation. Mennonites view scripture as the guiding force in their lives, providing an authoritative source about faith and life, for guiding prayer and worship.

Mennonites do not publish their own translations of the Bible, but use Protestant translations of their country—Martin Luther for German; King James for English; etc. Several Bible translators have found Mennonite acceptance—Hans Denck (d. 1527), Christoph Froschauer (d. 1564), and Nikolaes Biestkens (d. 1585), though not officially sanctioned by a Mennonite body, have been widely used in Mennonite churches, homes, and classrooms.

Mennonites have produced translations in languages for missionary use: in Javanese (1892); two

Congolese languages (Kipende in 1935; Kikwango in 1950); Cheyenne (by Rodolphe Petter in the 1930s); and the Lengua dialect of the Chaco indians of Paraguay (by G.B. Giesbrecht in the 1950s).

C. Important Writers and Thinkers

John Howard Yoder (1927–1997)

John Howard Yoder, a seminary and university professor and author of important books, had a significant impact on contemporary Christian thinking in the last half of the twentieth century. Yoder, who died in 1997, was a professor at Associated Mennonite Biblical Seminary and then at the University of Notre Dame. He worked primarily in the areas of biblical scholarship, historical theology, and Christian ethics. In his most famous book, *The Politics of Jesus: Vicit Agnus Noster*, published in 1972, he argued that nonresistant love, nonviolence, and pacifism revealed by Jesus are the central ethical norms of the Christian life. He also claimed that Jesus's purpose was to establish a new community of people who embody forgiveness, sharing, and self-sacrificing love.

Gordon D. Kaufman

Gordon D. Kaufman, also a well-respected Mennonite theologian, began teaching at Harvard Divinity School in 1963. He published *In Face of Mystery: A Constructive Theology* in 1993. In this book, Kaufman studied the symbolic world of Christianity, noting how Christians have created religious symbolism in an effort to orient themselves in the world. In his latest book, *In the Beginning... Creativity*, Kaufman proposes a creative way of reconceptualizing God in a way that makes sense in a postmodern world. Kaufman's writings have had an important impact on the development of Protestant theology in the United States.

III. Rites and Rituals

A. The Calendar

Mennonites celebrate some of the holy days of the traditional Christian calendar; however, they do not strictly follow the liturgical calendar as do the high liturgical churches. Even among the Mennonites, the traditional and Old Order groups only observe the key Christian days such as Christmas, Easter, and Pentecost. More assimilated Mennonite groups also observe seasonal emphases such as Advent and Lent.

APRIL

• **Palm Sunday**—The sixth and last Sunday of Lent. Marks the entry of Jesus into Jerusalem and the start of Holy Week.

• **Maundy Thursday**—Held in remembrance of the night of the Last Supper, when Jesus washed the feet of his disciples and established the ceremony known as the Eucharist.

• **Good Friday**—Good Friday is the Friday before Easter. It commemorates the execution of Jesus by crucifixion.

• **Easter Sunday**—Celebrates the Resurrection of Jesus Christ (his return from death after the Crucifixion).

MAY

• **Ascension Day**—Commemorates Christ's last appearance on earth after his resurrection. It is celebrated forty days after Easter.

JUNE

• **Pentecost**—Celebrated the seventh Sunday after Easter. Commemorates the descent of the Holy Spirit upon the disciples.

DECEMBER

• **Advent Sunday**—The beginning of the ecclesiastical year on the Sunday closest to November 30. Advent is the season before Christmas.

- **Christmas Eve**—Day before Christmas Day.
- **Christmas Day**—The day when Christians celebrate the birth of Jesus Christ.

B. Worship and Liturgy

Mennonite Churches are typically not liturgical churches. Worship services vary in their degree of liturgical formality, but generally lean toward informal styles. Some congregations with recent immigrants from Latin America and Asia have a more Pentecostal style of worship.

The two most important rites in all congregations are believer's baptism and the Lord's Supper, often referred to as simply Communion. Some, but not all congregations practice foot washing as a rite of humility and service following the example and admonition of Jesus at the Last Supper with his disciples.

The Mennonite Church celebrates adult baptism rather than infant baptism. Baptism is viewed as a pledge before the church of a person's covenant with God. The Church believes that baptism is for those who confess their sins and commit themselves to follow Jesus. As such, baptism is for those who are old enough to know what they are doing and who freely request baptism. Believer's baptism (also known as credobaptism, derived from the Latin *credo*, meaning "I believe") is performed with youth and adults who have made a declaration of their personal faith in Jesus Christ. Mennonites use both forms of baptism: immersion and the sprinkling or pouring from a pitcher or bowl.

Mennonites do not subscribe to the idea that there is a bodily presence of Christ in ritually eaten bread and wine. The bread and wine are seen as symbolic: bread is simply bread; the wine is wine. Believers celebrate the Lord's Supper as a memorial, not a re-creation of Christ's sacrifice performed by priests on behalf of sinners. Jesus's words "Do this in remembrance of me" (Corinthians 1:11), indicated what the Supper was supposed to signify: a remembrance of Jesus's death and sacrifice.

For the most traditional Mennonite churches, foot washing and the Lord's Supper comprise the Mennonite ritual of Communion, which is observed twice a year. In some less traditional congregations, Communion only involves serving the bread and wine of the Lord's Supper. For these groups, foot washing may not be observed or is a separate service held once or twice a year.

Among those who observe it, foot washing is generally performed twice a year. The ritual of foot washing derives from language found in John 13:14–15: "Now that I, your Lord and Teacher, have washed your feet, you also should wash one another's feet. I have set you an example that you should do as I have done for you."

The most traditional mode of the observance is as follows: After the communion service is completed, one of the ministers or deacons reads and comments on John 13:1–17. Basins—usually plastic or metal tubs filled with warm water—and towels are provided in sufficient quantity to permit a fairly rapid observance. In traditional meetinghouses these are placed in either the front of the church or in the "amen" corners, and in the ante-rooms, or in some cases in the rows between the benches. The sexes then separately wash (more properly rinse or lightly touch with water) feet in pairs, concluding with the greeting of the holy kiss and a "God bless you." In some localities towels are furnished in the form of short aprons to be tied by cords around the waist, in presumed imitation of Jesus "girding himself," though most commonly ordinary towels are used. In many contemporary church facilities the foot washing rite may be observed in a fellowship hall or other sizeable room to facilitate ease of movement.

Although the interpretation of the ordinance may vary, it is always held to be symbolic of a spiritual lesson, and is never considered to have any religious value per se, or to be a "good work." The most common interpretation is that it teaches humility, equality, and service to others.

Out of the nineteen confessions of faith produced by European Anabaptists and Mennonites from 1527 to 1874, twelve speak of the ordinance of foot washing as a Christian practice, while nine omit it altogether. The first one to mention it (Dutch Waterlander Confession of 1577) indicates that it is to be done for visitors from a distance, particularly refugees, but is not prescribed as a church ordinance for a worship service. The same is true for the Concept of Cologne (1591), the Twisck thirty-three Articles of about 1615, and the George Hansen Flemish Confession of 1678 (Danzig area). The other seven that mention it (Olive Branch of 1627 in Holland, Dordrecht eighteen Articles of 1632, Jan Centsen of 1630 in Holland, the first Prussian confession of 1660, the Prussian confession of G. Wiebe of 1792, and the confession adopted in Russia in 1874 by the Mennonite Brethren) treat it as a general ordinance of the church. The Cornelis Ris' Dutch Confession of 1773 does not mention it, probably because it was already dying out in Holland. The widely used Elbing-Waldeck catechism of 1778 includes it, as does the Russian Mennonite catechism of 1870.

Many traditional Mennonite women—such as these, photographed in October of 1988—dress in simple, modest clothing, with white caps covering their hair.

C. Daily Life

Clothing

Many contemporary Mennonite churches have no restrictions regarding clothing, jewelry, or hair; however, many emphasize the biblical principles of simplicity and modesty. More traditional and Old Order Mennonites dictate plainness in dress, believing that a person's true worth does not lie in their clothes or appearance. It is this aspect of their beliefs that regulates the dress style, giving more traditional Mennonites their distinctive look with straw hats, bonnets, plain dresses, and coats.

More traditional Mennonite groups expect adult women to wear a white cap-like head covering in obedience to Scripture in Corinthians 1:11.

Dietary

Mennonites are discouraged from smoking cigarettes, overeating, and using recreational and addictive drugs. Some groups prohibit drinking alcohol, but others do not.

D. Life Cycle Events

Birth

Mennonites do not practice any specific religious rites related to childbirth. Some less traditional congregations observe baby dedications for young children typically under one year of age. The child is dedicated to God and the parents and congregants promise to nurture the child in the ways of faith. Confirmation is not a rite in the Mennonite church, but adult baptism, typically between the ages of fourteen and twenty-one, is a central and important ritual in the public affirmation of a believer's faith.

Education

As with many customs, educational practices vary widely across different Mennonite groups. However, general patterns do emerge among Old Order, conservative, and assimilated Mennonites.

Old Order Mennonites operate about 300 one- or two-room schoolhouses throughout the United States. These schools promote Mennonite values and bolster Mennonite identity. They also prevent assimilation into mainstream culture. Most old orders end their formal schooling with the eighth grade. They worry that too much formal education will lead youth away from the church and into the secular world; it may lead to pride and unacceptable ideas and also expose youth to worldly people and lifestyles. Higher education threatens the well-being of the community because it encourages individualism, critical thinking, and professional occupations. For these same reasons, Old Orders do not support formal theological education. Instead, they ordain lay members from within their congregations. Conservative Mennonites tend to support private elementary and secondary church schools but typically avoid higher education.

In contrast, most assimilated Mennonites value formal education. They operate schools at all levels of education—elementary and secondary schools, two- and four-year colleges and universities, bible colleges, and seminaries. Many Mennonites in the more assimilated groups also attend public schools for all levels of education.

Nuptials

Weddings of more modern Mennonites are very similar to other Protestant weddings. They are usually held in the church and are complete with gowns, tuxedos, candles, and flowers. There is usually a short meditation; the usual Protestant vows (or vows written by the couple) and wedding music are used. The couple has usually received premarital counseling.

The weddings of Old Order Mennonites are usually held in the bride's home and may last two hours. They include singing, a long sermon, simple vows, testimonies from church leaders, and an extended prayer. There are no kisses, rings, photographers, florists, or caterers. A large reception, prepared by the family, friends, and neighbors, follows the ceremony.

Death and Burial

Funeral practices vary greatly among and within Mennonite groups. All of the groups use the service of a mortician to embalm and prepare the body for death. Some funerals are very simple, without flowers and with the use of a plain coffin; others are more elaborate with flowers, and a commercial casket. In some cases, cremation may be used.

E. Family Life

Husband and Wife

The family is central to life in a Mennonite community. Large families are common among traditional groups, but among assimilated Mennonites the family size mirrors that of national trends with two or three children being typical. Gender roles vary. More traditional roles are embraced in the Old Order Mennonite communities, whereas flexible expressions of gender roles are found in the more assimilated churches.

Divorce

Within the more progressive Mennonite churches, divorce is discouraged. Until the 1960s and 1970s, divorce was in fact quite rare. In recent times, divorce is more common.

Within the Old Order Mennonite communities, marriage is considered a lifetime commitment and, as such, divorce is not permitted and separation is very rare.

IV. Denominations and Demographics

A. History

Although Mennonites in the U.S. today claim a common heritage and a similar theological identity, differences between types and groups of Mennonites abound. While most of these groups affirm the core convictions mentioned above, others choose to emphasize different aspects or prioritize some convictions over others. Even during the earliest years of the Anabaptist movement, the members did not all speak with one voice. Individual congregations were largely autonomous, and geographical barriers and strong leaders often led to differences and divisions between congregations. Divisions have occurred for theological and cultural reasons, as well as practical reasons, such as language barriers. The most serious division of the Mennonite community occurred in the 1690s in Switzerland. A small group of Swiss Anabaptists, who advocated a strict shunning of excommunicated members, broke off from the main body and became known as Amish, named after their leader, Jacob Amman. The chart below illustrates the divisions and mergers of selected Mennonite groups in the United States.

The U.S. contains more than thirty different Mennonite groups, which can be loosely sorted into three categories: Old Order, Conservative, and Assimilated (ranging from the most traditional to the most progressive). These groups differ in how they interact with the larger society and where they place the locus of moral authority. Does the group remain separated from the larger society, or does it actively participate in mainstream culture? Who holds the key to moral authority—the group, the individual, or some mix of both? Are members free to follow their individual consciences and make their own decisions, or does the church speak for heaven on such matters as dress, divorce, abortion, television, and financial investments? The answers to these questions generally indicate whether a particular Mennonite group is classified as Old Order, Conservative, or Assimilated.

B. Comparisons of Tenets and Practices

Old Order Mennonites

Old Orders are the most traditional Mennonite groups. They concentrate on preserving religious and cultural traditions, making little effort to engage in the dominant culture. In many ways, Old Order history can be read as an attempt to hold the forces of modernity at bay. They look to the past for their moral compass. Old Order groups find spiritual renewal in the reaffirmation of traditional customs, not in innovative practices from outside. Indeed, most Old Order groups separated from the main Mennonite Church from 1872–1901, the period of the (third) Great Awakening. These groups rejected the changes that the Great Awakening brought to America's religious institutions, especially Sunday

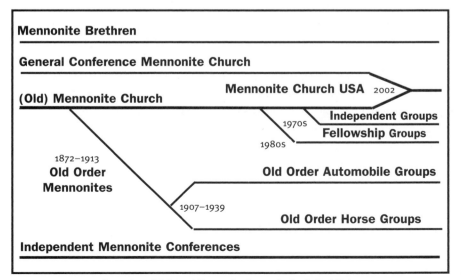

Formation of Selected Mennonite Groups in the United States

schools and evangelistic meetings. Instead, Old Orders cling to the old customs of worship and church life. They continue to affirm the 1632 Dordrecht Confession of Faith.

Old Order groups also maintain older cultural practices. These groups are predominantly rural and use technology selectively. Some use electricity and telephones in their homes, but not in their churches. Several groups use horse-and-buggy transportation while other Old Orders drive cars. None of them permit the ownership of television or the use of the Internet in their homes.

All Old Order groups seek to remain somewhat separated from the world. The social forces of modernity—specialization, discontinuity, mobility, and individualism—threaten to fragment the solidarity of closely knit Old Order communities. They feel that they can only preserve their redemptive community by keeping a social distance from the world because it threatens to splinter their bonds of ethnic solidarity. They prefer rural, isolated settings where face-to-face communication in a special dialect helps to preserve their way of life.

Old Orders typically have large, stable families, usually with six to ten children. Divorce is forbidden. Large families teach the children important old order values: obedience, cooperation, deferring to others, and accepting authority. Sizeable families are incubators of communal values, the perfect setting for learning humility and deference.

Patriarchy infuses Old Order communities and families. Children are to obey their parents; wives are to be submissive to their husbands; and everyone accepts that the church (which only ordains men as leaders) has ultimate authority over the individual. In Old Order families, men take the lead in interactions with the outside world; the pattern of decision-making inside the family varies by family unit. Wives do not work outside the home, especially if they have young children. Women wear plain dress, which consists of dresses (usually of a modest-color fabric), a cape (an extra layer of fabric over their upper torsos), prayer coverings, and bonnets.

Most Old Order Mennonite groups are ethnically homogeneous, with Swiss-German roots. This homogeneity is cultivated by their separateness from the world. Bishops will only marry members of the church. This practice of endogamy strengthens kinship ties across the community and enhances the growth of the church. These communities rely on biological reproduction for church growth instead of evangelism. With nearly 40,000 members, Old Orders (children and adults) account for about 20 percent of Mennonites in the United States.

Old Order Mennonites fall into two groups: those who drive automobiles and those who rely on horse-drawn carriages. The two largest Old Order Mennonite groups are the Groffdale Conference Mennonites and the Weaverland Conference. The Groffdale Conference (also known as Wenger Mennonites after their first bishop, Joseph O. Wenger) has a population of about 18,000 children and adults. The Wengers are fairly rural and more traditional than the other Old Order groups. They speak Pennsylvania German, drive horse-drawn carriages, and use steel-wheeled tractors in their fields. In contrast, the Weaverland Conference Mennonites are a more progressive Old Order group. They are centered in Pennsylvania and claim about 12,000 members. They speak English rather than a German dialect, and they drive automobiles.

Members of the Weaverland Conference were often nicknamed "Black Bumper Mennonites" because they painted the chrome parts on their cars black. Ministers still observe this practice, and even though the requirement is relaxed for members, most of them still drive dark-colored cars.

Conservative Mennonites

Conservative Mennonite groups hold the middle ground between the Old Orders and the more assimilated groups. They are a bit more engaged with modern, mainstream society than Old Order groups, but they remain fairly traditional in both doctrine and cultural practice.

There are about twenty conservative Mennonite groups, and they constitute nearly 25 percent of Mennonites in the United States. There is no central structure or organization that holds all of the conservative groups together. Some members of these groups grew up in Old Order communities and later joined the conservatives. Others left assimilated groups because they considered them too involved in the dominant culture. Conservative Mennonites hold varying doctrinal beliefs and participate in a range of cultural practices, but most conservative groups forbid military service and the holding of political office.

Although most of these groups affirm the eighteen articles of the Dordrecht Confession of Faith, some conservative Mennonites identify seven specific practices that set them apart from more assimilated groups. "In these days of moral decadence and spiritual apostasy, it is our desire to uphold the doctrines of the Scriptures as historically taught by the Mennonite church; such as separation from the world, nonresistance, separation of church and state, permanence of marriage, the Christian women's veiling, moral purity, and leadership of men." Conservative groups respect traditional practices and decry the moral and spiritual trends of mainstream culture.

Conservative groups value the structures of patriarchy and affirm traditional gender roles. They forbid divorce and the ordination of women. Women wear plain dress and have long hair covered by a veil, whereas conservative Mennonite men are less distinguished by their clothing. In 1988, the Council on Biblical Manhood and Womanhood, a conservative Mennonite group, released the "Danvers Statement," which affirmed that men and women are created for different roles and that these distinctions are ordained by God. Men are to be leaders and heads of households while women are to assume submissive and limited roles. Conservative Mennonites also view homosexuality as a sin and a corruption of the natural created order.

Despite their affinity for traditional customs and beliefs, conservative Mennonites do engage in mainstream culture. They speak English and drive cars. Their homes and churches have telephones and electricity, but they may restrict or forbid television and internet usage. They have few restrictions on technology for agriculture or business purposes.

There are many small, independent conservative Mennonite groups, but two groups contain the largest percentage of conservative Mennonites. The Church of God in Christ (Holdeman) Mennonites has 111 congregations with 12,000 members. This group emphasizes evangelical conversion, strict church discipline, and shunning of the excommunicated. The Conservative Mennonite Conference, formed in 1910, comes from Amish roots and claims 9,600 members.

Assimilated Mennonites

Over half of all Mennonites in the United States fall into the assimilated category. These groups accept technology, higher education, and many typical American values. They tend to embrace mainstream views on dress, gender roles, theological training, and political involvement. Because they usually grant authority to the individual conscience, members in these groups differ on a host of issues, including the ordination of women, homosexuality, abortion, capital punishment, and peacemaking. Assimilated Mennonites operate colleges and seminaries and manage national programs and organizations such as publishing houses, mission boards, and service agencies.

The largest group of assimilated Mennonites is the Mennonite Church USA This group formed in 2002 from the merger of the Mennonite Church and the General Conference Mennonite Church. In 2005, the Mennonite Church USA claimed 109,000 members in 965 congregations.

By the middle of the twentieth century, assimilated Mennonites felt it necessary to restate the church's doctrinal position in terms relevant to contemporary social issues. The 1963 Mennonite Confession of Faith reaffirmed most of the doctrinal positions of the Dordrecht confession, but it adds statements on more contemporary matters. For example, Article 9 states, "The church should witness against racial discrimination, economic injustice, and all forms of human slavery and moral degradation." Article 14 stipulates that although men and women are created as equals, men have been given a primary leadership role, while women are especially fitted for nurture and service.

Assimilated Mennonites restated their beliefs again in 1995, when the General Conference Mennonite Church and the Mennonite Church adopted the Confession of Faith in a Mennonite Perspective. As with previous Mennonite confessions of faith, the twenty-four articles of the 1995 document incorporate the historic creeds of the early church, as well as biblical texts. Also like previous confessions, this statement highlights some particularly Anabaptist convictions. For example, Article 17 echoes the historic Anabaptist understanding of discipleship:

Conformity to Christ necessarily implies nonconformity to the world. True faith in Christ means willingness to do the will of God, rather than willful pursuit of individual happiness. True faith means seeking first the reign of God in simplicity, rather than pursuing materialism. . . . True faith means giving first loyalty to God's kingdom, rather than to any nation-state or ethnic group that claims our allegiance.

An Anabaptist affirmation of peacemaking finds expression in Article 22: "We witness to all people that violence is not the will of God. We witness against all forms of violence, including war among nations, hostility among races and classes, abuse of children and women, violence between men and women, abortion, and capital punishment." Despite their partial integration into mainstream society, assimilated Mennonites continue to value core Mennonite teachings related to social justice and peacemaking.

The Mennonite Brethren are the second largest assimilated Mennonite group. This group emigrated from Russia to Kansas, Nebraska, and the Dakotas in the 1870s. Today they maintain 168 congregations in the central and western parts of the United States. More than a third of the Mennonite Brethren congregations in the United States are now located in California. They also have numerous congregations in Canada. The Mennonite Brethren are slightly different from other Mennonite groups because their ancestors were influenced by Pietism, which leads them to value heartfelt devotion and to practice immersion baptism. Overall, the Mennonite Brethren tend to favor more evangelical expressions of faith than other Mennonites do.

C. Organization and Distribution

The broad categories of Old Order, Conservative, and Assimilated Mennonites may not fit any particular Mennonite group perfectly, but they do help to clarify differences and identify common themes. The table on the next page highlights common traits associated with each of the categories.

V. Organization and Infrastructure

The propensity to build institutions reflects a combination of theological, social, and ethnic impulses, as well as a group's position in the larger world. In other words, Mennonite groups that are more comfortable with the larger culture will more likely use the institutions of the broader society than build their own. The more traditional Mennonite groups have fewer bureaucratic organizations than do the assimilated groups.

A. Education and Hierarchy of Clergy

Historically Mennonites have strongly rejected a hierarchical view of leadership. Ministers were ordained from the laity and often had no formal or

Assimilated Mennonite Groups	Conservative Mennonite Groups	Old Order, Traditional
• Widely use technology	• Use technology except television	• Use horse-drawn transportation
• Participate in cultural activities	• Promote individual religious experience	• Speak a special dialect
• Hold professional jobs	• Emphasize rational, formal, doctrine	• Use technology selectively
• Hire professional, salaried pastors	• Engage in evangelism	• Preserve older religious rituals
• Support peacemaking	• Forbid divorce	• Forbid divorce
• Support social justice activities	• Forbid the ordination of women	• Forbid the ordination of women
• Support higher education	• Discourage higher education	• Discourage higher education
• Value individualism	• Ordain lay pastors	• Ordain lay pastors
• Emphasize evangelism	• Practice nonresistance	• Emphasize traditional customs
• Operate large church organizations	• Wear plain clothing	• Stress collective church authority
• Participate in politics	• Involved in individual churches	• Uninvolved in politics
• Dress in modern attire	• Dress conservatively	• Wear "plain" clothing

Table 1. Typical Traits of Mennonite Groups Compared

specialized theological training. This is still the pattern among the more traditional groups. Assimilated churches, however, have moved toward a more professional and Protestant model for selecting and training pastors. While a single educational standard is not prescribed, a level of formal ministerial preparation through educational programs is encouraged in the more progressive churches. The Mennonite Church USA recommends the Master of Divinity seminary degree as the ideal expectation.

Licensing Toward Ordination

In the assimilated groups becoming a Mennonite minister requires that a candidate complete a licensing and ordination process. The format and process for the licensing varies from region to region. The typical procedure may include the following elements. In order to receive a licensing credential, one must participate in a licensing interview. Typically one to two hours in length, the licensing interview with the area conference ministerial leadership committee focuses on three points: (1) the candidate's call to ministry; (2) their theological understanding of the Christian faith; and (3) their commitment to serving within a Mennonite/Anabaptist community.

A candidate must provide to the committee: (1) a letter of request from the candidate's congregation

for the person to be licensed; (2) a copy of the Ministerial Leadership Information form; and (3) a theological statement as requested by the committee.

If the committee grants licensing, the credential is given for a two-year period of time and can be renewed for a second two-year term. A licensing ceremony is held to publicly acknowledge the committee's decision. The ceremony generally occurs as a special part of the regular worship service of the congregation, following the sermon. During the licensing ceremony, the conference minister or overseer asks the candidate particular questions in order to affirm commitment to Jesus, devotion to the church, and faithful service in ministry. A prayer of blessing, a statement of declaration, and a handshake follow the questions.

Ordination Interview

After the first complete year of licensing toward ordination, but no later than six months prior to the end of the licensing period, the ordination process begins. As preparation for the interview, the candidate must provide:

1. A letter of request from the candidate's congregation for the person to be ordained;

2. A statement of the candidate concerning the meaning of ordination, its privileges and

responsibilities, and the accountability relationship contingent upon it;

3. A written report and statement of support from the pastoral mentor;

4. An updated theological statement and response as requested by the area conference committee;

5. Statements from ministerial colleagues and/or peer group;

6. Report from the overseer, bishop or conference minister, and/or

7. A report from a qualified therapist, psychologist, or vocational counselor.

Following a positive ordination interview and approval for ordination, the ordination ceremony—a full worship service—will be held. Ordinations may range in tone from solemnity to holy celebration dependent on the individual being ordained and the minister's congregation.

The pattern for an ordination service includes: hymns, Scriptures, a sermon (or a series of shorter meditations), litanies and prayer. The ordination ceremony includes the presentation of the candidate, examination questions, the laying on of hands while the candidate kneels, a prayer of consecration, and presentation of a Bible.

Seminaries

Associated Mennonite Biblical Seminary
3003 Benham Avenue
Elkhart, IN 46517
800-964-2627
574-295-3726   Fax: 574-295-0092
admissions@ambs.edu

Eastern Mennonite Seminary
(on campus of Eastern Mennonite University)
1200 Park Road
Harrisonburg, VA 22802-2462
540-432-4260   Fax: 540-432-4598
TTY: 540-432-4599
admiss@emu.edu

Mennonite Brethren Biblical Seminary
Fresno Campus
4824 East Butler Avenue
Fresno, CA 93727
800-251-6227
559-251-8628   Fax: 559-251-7212
fresno@mbseminary.edu
Langley Campus
7600 Glover Road
Langley, BC V2Y 1Y1
Canada
604-513-2133
langley@mbseminary.edu
Winnipeg Campus
500 Shaftesbury Boulevard
Winnipeg, MB R3P 2N2
Canada
Toll free: 877-231-4570 ext. 350
winnipeg@mbseminary.edu

B. Shrines and Houses of Worship

Two Unique Congregations

Calvary Community Church
2311 Tower Place
Hampton, VA 23666
757-825-1133   Fax: 757-825-0567
The largest Mennonite church in the United States, with nearly 2,000 members, Calvary Community is a multicultural, interdenominational parish founded in 1985.

Germantown Mennonite Church
21 West Washington Lane
Philadelphia, PA 19144
215-843-5599
Founded in 1683, Germantown Mennonite is the oldest Mennonite church in the United States. The Germantown settlers began meeting in private homes, but eventually erected a log meetinghouse in 1708. In 1770, the log building was replaced with a

stone structure that was the regular meeting place for the congregation until the early 1890s. In the mid-1950s, with most of the regular attendees coming from the rural suburbs, this historic meetinghouse was almost sold.

The church's revival began in the mid-1970s, when the congregation began to grow numerically. A growing congregation soon made the 1770 meetinghouse obsolete. In 1993, the Congregation purchased the present site at 21 West Washington Lane.

For much of its history the congregation has been associated with the Eastern District of the General Conference Mennonite Church (GCMC). In the earliest years, until a schism in mid-nineteenth century occurred, the congregation was loosely connected with the Franconia Conference of the (old) Mennonite Church (MC). In the 1970s, Germantown Mennonite Church was reunited with the Franconia Conference.

The relationship with Franconia lasted until October 1997, when Germantown was removed as a conference member, due to the membership of homosexual parishioners in the Germantown congregation. For similar reasons, the Eastern District also removed Germantown as a member congregation in November 2002. In February 2002, the MC and the GCMC in North America merged as the Mennonite Church USA and Mennonite Church Canada.

C. Governance and Authority

Organization

The Mennonite Church is not a hierarchical or centralized church. Fraternal organizations in geographical regions, often called Conferences, provided the primary form of collaboration in the nineteenth and twentieth centuries. The first world-wide organization of congregations and regional groups emerged in 1925. Named Mennonite World Conference (MWC), this organization has gathered for fellowship, worship, and celebration every five to six years.

The MWC makes no binding decisions, but many of the more conservative Mennonite groups refuse to participate in or recognize this body.

The Mennonites have always maintained an adamant position of separation of church and state, seeking to minimize the influences of outside non-Mennonite forces. Ecclesiology and separation from the world are key issues for Mennonites. The tendency is to emphasize the local congregation and to build wider fellowships based on a commonality of belief.

The area conference is the basic membership unit of Mennonite Church USA. It is through the area conferences that congregations are also members of the Mennonite Church. Each area conference has the authority to determine which congregations may join the area conference in their region, taking into account the common vision, commitments, and membership guidelines of Mennonite Church USA. With this authority, an area conference can determine the criteria for membership and additional procedures, including the process for withdrawal and dismissal. As the area conferences function in a near-autonomous manner, they do retain the privilege of withdrawing their conference, and its member congregations, from the Mennonite Church USA. In addition to providing resources and assistance to congregations, the conferences are also responsible for credentialing ministers.

Each area conference participates in the planning and decision-making of the larger body through its representatives (delegates) to the Delegate Assembly. Each area conference is represented at every session of the Delegate Assembly and actively seeks to further the interests of the church during and between sessions.

Within the Mennonite Church USA, there are twenty-one area conferences:
• Allegheny Mennonite Conference
• Atlantic Coast Conference
• Central District Conference

- Central Plains Mennonite Conference
- Eastern District Conference
- Franconia Mennonite Conference
- Franklin Mennonite Conference
- Gulf States Mennonite Conference
- Illinois Mennonite Conference
- Indiana-Michigan Mennonite Conference
- Lancaster Mennonite Conference
- Mountain States Mennonite Conference
- New York Mennonite Conference
- North Central Conference of the Mennonite Church
- Ohio Conference of the Mennonite Church
- Pacific Northwest Mennonite Conference
- Pacific Southwest Mennonite Conference
- South Central Mennonite Conference
- Southeast Mennonite Conference
- Virginia Mennonite Conference
- Western District Conference

MISSION

Despite being victims of terrible persecution, early Anabaptists were active missionaries. Mennonites today undertake mission efforts to varying degrees. Some groups have vigorous outreach and church planting programs while others do not. The more traditional groups tend to shy away from missionary work, while conservative and assimilated groups are much more active in such activities.

Old Order groups do not engage in active evangelism. Instead, they strive to live faithfully so that their community will serve as a light on the hill to guide others. They believe that a pure church, untainted by worldly contamination, is the best and most enduring witness to the larger world.

Conservative Mennonites do engage in mission activity but embrace conservative standards of doctrine and practice. They emphasize personal salvation and individual religious experience.

Nearly all the more assimilated churches have active mission programs. Some members, however,

have more passion for peace and social justice programs than for evangelistic endeavors. Most Mennonite missionaries employ a "third way"—a holistic approach that blends spiritual ministry with social justice, physical care, and economic development.

D. Social Service Organizations

More often than not, Mennonite mission activity takes the form of service work. The early Mennonite leader, Menno Simons, described the Anabaptist commitment to service with the following words:

> True evangelical faith cannot lie dormant.
> It clothes the naked.
> It feeds the hungry.
> It comforts the sorrowful.
> It shelters the destitute.
> It serves those who harm it.
> It binds up that which is wounded.
> It has become all things to all people.

The commitment and willingness to serve the needy near and far varies from congregation to congregation. Nevertheless, concern for the needy and a commitment to service persists across most sectors of the Mennonite world. Mennonite churches engage in a host of service ministries ranging from relief and refugee work abroad to disaster service at home, from victim/offender programs to foster care, and from disability programs to elder care.

Mennonite Central Committee
21 South 12th Street
PO Box 500
Akron, PA, 17501-0500
717-859-1151
888-563-4676
http://mcc.org

Mennonite Central Committee (MCC) is the largest Mennonite service agency. Founded in 1920, it engages in refugee work, material aid, international development, and peace and justice efforts. While many Old Order groups do not embrace institutionalized service agencies, they do support MCC and participate in some of its program activities.

Mennonite Economic Development Associates
800-665-7026
meda@meda.org
www.meda.org

1821 Oregon Pike, Suite 201
Lancaster, PA 17601-6466
United States of America
717-560-6546   Fax: 717-560-6549

155 Frobisher Drive, Suite I-106
Waterloo, ON N2V 2E1
Canada
519-725-1633   Fax: 519-725-9083

302-280 Smith Street
Winnipeg, MB R3C 1K2
Canada
800-665-7026   Fax: 204-942-4001

Mennonite Economic Development Associates (MEDA) is another important Mennonite service agency. It provides access to savings and credit for those living in poverty around the world. Its members share their faith and resources in order to address human needs through economic development.

Mennonite Disaster Service
MDS Binational Office
1018 Main Street
Akron, PA 17501
717-859-2210   Fax: 717-859-4910
mdsus@mds.mennonite.net
http://mds.mennonite.net
Mennonite Disaster Service (MDS) responds to natural disasters in the United States and Canada. Its main focus is on cleanup activities after a disaster strikes and on repairing and rebuilding homes.

Mutual aid is a special kind of service. The practice emerges out of the Mennonite view of church as community. In early Anabaptist congregations, voluntary sharing of goods for needy members was the norm. The practice of mutual aid in times of disaster, distress, and special circumstance was a spontaneous response that was deeply woven into the fabric of the church. Spontaneous forms of mutual aid continue in almost all Mennonite communities: assistance with moving, childcare, elder care, medical care, and other special needs. More institutionalized forms of mutual aid have emerged in the twentieth century. Regional aid societies provide automobile, fire, and health insurance. Large national organizations, such as Mennonite Mutual Aid (MMA), offer financial and insurance resources to more assimilated Mennonites. Many Old Order groups reject these institutionalized forms of aid. These groups do not depend on commercial insurance agencies but rather trust that the community will support them during times of financial hardship.

E. Media and Communications

Mennonite Publishing Network

The Mennonite Publishing Network (MPN) produces publications from the Anabaptist perspective. MPN produces material for two divisions: Faith & Life Resources and Herald Press.

Faith & Life Resources
Waterloo, ON Offices:
490 Dutton Drive, Unit C7
Waterloo, ON N2L 6H7
519-888-7512   Fax: 519-884-5824
616 Walnut Avenue
Scottdale, PA 15683
724-887-8500   Fax: 724-887-3111

718 Main Street
Newton, KS 67114
316-283-5155   Fax: 316-283-0454

Faith & Life Resources produces materials for use by Mennonite congregations, Bible study, and missions. Products are available for adult and youth populations.

Herald Press
616 Walnut Avenue
Scottdale, PA 15683
724-887-8500
Ordering: 800-245-7894
info@mph.org
www.heraldpress.com
Herald Press is the trade publishing division of Mennonite Publishing Network, publishing and marketing books with an Anabaptist perspective for adults (e.g. general readers, academics, and pastors), youth, and children.

The Mennonite
Goshen Office:
1700 South Main Street
Goshen, IN 46526
574-535-6052   Fax: 574-535-6050

722 Main Street
PO Box 347
Newton, KS 67114
316-283-5100   Fax: 316-283-0454
Editor@TheMennonite.org
www.themennonite.org
The Mennonite is a semimonthly magazine for members of Mennonite Church USA and others interested in the Mennonite church and the Anabaptist movement. Issues feature articles, news of the church (both national and international), commentary, letters, columns, and editorials.

The Mennonite Quarterly Review
Goshen College
Goshen IN 46526
574-535-7433   Fax: 574-535-7438
mqr@goshen.edu

Founded by Harold S. Bender and the Mennonite Historical Society in 1927, *The Mennonite Quarterly Review* is a quarterly journal devoted to Anabaptist-Mennonite history, thought and affairs. Edited by leading scholars, this interdisciplinary publication features discussion of topics in the areas of the Radical Reformation, Amish, Mennonites and Hutterites. *The Mennonite Quarterly Review* is a cooperative publication of Goshen College, the Associated Mennonite Biblical Seminary and the Mennonite Historical Society.

FURTHER READING AND RESOURCES

Anabaptist (Mennonite) Directory, 2008
   2008: Sword and Trumpet

The Bloody Theater or Martyrs Mirror of the Defenseless Christians
   Thieleman J. van Braght, compiler
   1950: Herald Press

Two Kingdoms, Two Loyalties: Mennonite Pacifism in Modern America
   Perry Bush
   1998: Johns Hopkins University Press

Classics of the Radical Reformation (vols 1–9)
   1973–1999: Herald Press

Confession of Faith in a Mennonite Perspective
   1995: Herald Press

Confession of Faith of the Mennonites: Church Forms and Guidelines for the Weaverland Conference
   1996: Weaverland Conference

Mennonite Peacemaking: From Quietism to Activism
   Leo Driedger and Donald B. Kraybill
   1994: Herald Press

The Believers Church: The History and Character of Radical Protestantism
Donald F. Durnbaugh
1985: Herald Press

An Introduction to Mennonite History: A Popular History of the Anabaptists and the Mennonites. 3d ed.
Cornelius J. Dyck
1993: Herald Press

The Anabaptist Story: An Introduction to Sixteenth-Century Anabaptism. 3d ed.
William R. Estep
1996: Eerdmans Publishing Co.

Separate People: An Insider's View of Old Order Mennonite Customs and Traditions
Isaac R. A. Horst
2000: Herald Press

Anabaptist World USA
Donald B. Kraybill and C. Nelson Hostetter
2001: Herald Press

Horse-and-Buggy Mennonites: Hoofbeats of Humility in a Postmodern World
Donald B. Kraybill and James P. Hurd
2006: Penn State Univ. Press

Who Are the Anabaptists?
Donald B. Kraybill
2003: Herald Press

Through Fire and Water: An Overview of Mennonite History
Harry Loewen and Steven M. Nolt
1996: Herald Press

Mennonite Church Directory, 2008
2008: Christian Light Pub.

Mennonite Church USA 2008 Directory
2008: Mennonite Pub. Network

Mennonite Encyclopedia, The: (vols. 1–5)
1955–1959, 1990: Herald Press

The Mennonite Experience in America (vols. 1–4)
1985–96: Herald Press

Mennonite Society
Calvin W. Redekop
1989: Johns Hopkins Press

An Introduction to Old Order and Conservative Mennonite Groups
Stephen Scott
1996: Good Books

Anabaptist History and Theology: An Introduction
Arnold Snyder
1995: Pandora Press

Becoming Anabaptist: The Origin and Significance of Sixteenth-Century Anabaptism. 2nd ed.
J. Denny Weaver
2005: Herald Press

HISTORICAL LIBRARIES AND INFORMATION CENTERS

- Archives of the Mennonite Church, Goshen College, Goshen, Indiana
- Center for Mennonite Brethren Studies, Fresno Pacific University, Fresno, California
- Lancaster Mennonite Historical Society, Lancaster, Pennsylvania
- Menno Simons Historical Library, Eastern Mennonite University, Harrisonburg, Virginia
- Mennonite Brethren Center, Tabor College, Hillsboro, Kansas
- Mennonite Historical Library, Bluffton College, Bluffton, Ohio
- Mennonite Historical Library, Goshen College, Goshen, Indiana
- Mennonite Library and Archives, Bethel

College, North Newton, Kansas
- Muddy Creek Farm Library, Denver, Pennsylvania
- The Young Center for Anabaptist and Pietist Studies, Elizabethtown College, Elizabethtown, Pennsylvania

PERIODICALS

The Mennonite, Scottdale, Pennsylvania
Mennonite Life (online):
    www.Bethelks.edu/menonitelife
The Mennonite Quarterly Review, Goshen College, Goshen, Indiana
Mennonite Weekly Review, Newton, Kansas

WEBSITES

Global Anabaptist Mennonite Encyclopedia Online (GAMEO):
www.gameo.org

Links to Mennonite resources:
www.thirdway.com/Menno

Mennonite connections on the Web:
www-personal.umich.edu/~bpl/menno.html

Mennonite Church USA website:
www.mennoniteUSA.org

Mennonite World Conference:
www.mwc-cmm.org

Young Center for Anabaptist and Pietist Studies:
www.etown.edu/centers/young-center/

THE AMISH

In 1693, heated controversy among Swiss Anabaptists over the strict shunning of excommunicated members resulted in the emergence of a small faction of immigrant Alsatian Anabaptists who are now known as the Amish. Taking their name from Jakob Ammann, a Swiss Anabaptist leader who had immigrated to Alsace, France, this tiny group followed Ammann's call for change. Because many of Ammann's proposed changes reflected the early teachings of Menno Simons—such as literal foot washing during Communion services, the role of church discipline, the salvation of Anabaptist sympathizers, and the shunning of excommunicated members in daily life—Ammann's approach to Anabaptist observance can be considered a renewal movement in the church.

The division caused by the shunning controversy would be permanent, and, eventually, members of the opposing factions came to differ not only in practice, but also in appearance. Ammann, a tailor, advocated a distinctive mode of dress and appearance for his followers: hook-and-eye fasteners rather than "ostentatious" buttons; plain clothing; and untrimmed beards. As Ammann left very little writing of his own regarding his purported beliefs and practices, followers mostly look to pre-Ammann Anabaptist literature for guidance.

The Amish first notably arrived in America in 1737, settling in eastern Pennsylvania, at the behest of William Penn's "holy experiment" in religious tolerance. Today, over 250,000 Amish people (children and adults) reside in twenty-eight states, representing numerous branches of the sect. The most populous of these branches is the **Old Order Amish** (220,000), largely the most traditional sector of the religion. Most Old Order Amish adhere to the practices of driving horse-drawn buggies; favoring horses and mules over tractors in farming; wearing plain dress; speaking in the Pennsylvania German dialect; worshipping in the home; providing schooling for their children through the eighth grade; abstaining from the use of television and computers; among males, wearing a beard and shaven upper lip; and among females, donning a prayer cap.

The **Beachy Amish** (15,000) are the second largest branch. These Amish use cars, television, electricity, and telephones, and wear less plain clothing. Their religious observance tends to include more evangelizing than the other groups.

New Order Amish (10,000) occupy the third largest branch. This group accepts more of technology. Although they still drive horse-drawn buggies for local transportation, they fly in airplanes for some long-distance trips and use electricity and telephones in their homes. New Orders place greater stress on seeking salvation on an individual level, and are more heavily involved in youth education and public outreach.

Comprising the last group are the Amish **Mennonites** (5,000). These adherents have broken in practice from Old and New Order Amish; their observance of the religion more nearly emulates that of conservative Mennonites and the Beachy Amish. Amish Mennonites more fully embrace modern technology, and tend to distrust church-centralized programs, supporting privately operated service programs instead.

FURTHER READING

Plain and Simple: A Journey to the Amish
Sue Bender
1989: HarperCollins

The Riddle of Amish Culture
Donald B. Kraybill
2001: Johns Hopkins University Press

Plain Diversity: Amish Cultures and Identities
Steven M. Nolt and Thomas J. Meyers
2007: Johns Hopkins University Press

THE BRETHREN

Sixteen years after the emergence of the Amish, a tiny group called the Brethren united in the German village of Schwarzenau. Brethren beliefs are an admixture of early Anabaptism and Radical Pietism, emphasizing a life of discipleship that follows the teachings of Jesus, and advocating the practice of adult baptism, service to others, pacifism, and church discipline. In 1708, eight adults, including leader and baptizer Alexander Mack Sr. were baptized in the Eder River. These separatists of the official German church (Protestant) were dissatisfied with the hollow symbolism and ritual of church dogma, and longed for worship and relationships more alive with spirit and love. When news of the illegal baptisms erupted, Mack was banned from several regions of Germany, and his followers faced persecution and imprisonment. In fleeing to a German town near the Dutch border named Krefeld, the Brethren found fellowship Mennonites who would join their movement, which now claims about 200,000 members in several denominations.

Only a decade after their formation, Brethren arrived in America by way of the ship *Allen*, seeking religious freedom and economic opportunity. Over time, several affiliated groups have emerged within the comprehensive Brethren World. The four largest affiliations are the Church of Brethren, the Fellowship of Grace Brethren Churches, the Brethren in Christ, and the Brethren Church. Adherents of the movement represent the spectrum of traditionalism, from conservative to progressive observance of orthodox Anabaptist directives. Over 90 percent of Brethren have eschewed plain dress for contemporary clothing, and an even greater percentage drive cars. Despite outward differences, all Brethren live in witness to the gospel's decree "for the glory of God and our neighbor's good." The emulation of love and truth are central to Brethren worship, superseding literal obeying of dogma or creed. The lyrics of Kenneth I. Morse's "Move in Our Midst," the unofficial Brethren anthem, capture such sentiment:

Move in our midst, thou Spirit of God...
Walk with us through the storm and the calm...
Teach us to love with heart, soul, and mind...
Kindle our hearts to burn with thy flame...
Spirit of God, Thy love makes us strong...

FURTHER READING

The Brethren Encyclopedia, (4 Vols.)
 1983, 2005: The Brethren Encyclopedia, Inc.

Brethren Society
 Carl F. Bowman
 1995: Johns Hopkins University Press

The Church of the Brethren: Yesterday and Today
 Donald F. Durnbaugh
 1986: Brethren Press

THE HUTTERITES

With a dedication to communal life and isolation from worldliness, the Hutterites are the most economically distinct sect of the Mennonite religion. Hutterites establish colonies—complete with apartment buildings, a dining hall and church, a butcher and electrical shop, other shops, livestock barns, a truck garage, storage space, thousands of acres of rolling farmlands, and their own public school—on land far removed from what is regarded as urban vice. First arriving in the United States in the 1870s, the Hutterites sought to escape decades of persecution in Europe. The suffering endured by Hutterite forbears remains alive today in the teachings of the religion, which convey a deep-rooted suspicion of the outside world and the assurance that tribulation marks the way to salvation. Hutterites are taught to resist self-will and the desire for material possessions—to surrender themselves to communal good and find joy in selflessness. Exposure to worldly influence is discouraged—whether by way of television, literature, or social interaction, and children are carefully schooled in strict accordance with Hutterite values. It should be noted that Hutterites do make use of modern technology for the sake of agricultural productivity and the many businesses that they operate on their colonies.

Because the new planting of a Hutterite colony tends to disrupt the property value, consumer markets, and school systems of the surrounding secular community, conflicts often arise between Hutterites and civil authorities, sometimes resulting in vandalism or arson. However, once established, a Hutterite colony contributes to the local and regional economy. The Hutterites refuse government-offered Social Security, as they see to the well being of their own elderly. The number of Hutterite colonies in North America is about 450 each with approximately 100 children and adults. Slightly over one quarter of the Hutterites live in the United States, which claims approximately 140 colonies and a Hutterite population of 14,000, with a preponderance of members in South Dakota.

FURTHER READING

Hutterite Society
 John A. Hostetler
 1997: Johns Hopkins University Press

Hutterite Beginnings: Communitarian Experiments During the Reformation
 Werner O. Packull
 1999: Johns Hopkins University Press

11 Methodists

I. Origins and Early History

A. The Religion in America

METHODIST ORIGINS HAIL BACK TO THE EIGH-teenth century and the teachings of Church of England clergyman John Wesley. Methodism was first organized as societies under lay leadership within Anglicanism, but developed into a separate denomination after the American Revolution.

In 1729, John Wesley joined a small association of Oxford University students who were seeking to deepen their religious faith. They methodically met at a stated time for "prayer and religious exercises." Because their practices were so methodical—they met precisely on time and systematically engaged in a strict regimen of prayer, fasting, Bible reading, and

ministry—the group soon acquired the derisive name "Methodists." John Wesley and his brother Charles, a hymn writer, ventured to America as missionaries in 1735, a trip that would ultimately be a failure. But during the journey to the colonies, the brothers Wesley met some Moravian Christians whose simple piety and morality greatly impressed him. A relationship was established while in America, and John sought them out in England upon his return in 1738.

After returning to England, Wesley experienced a spiritual awakening while attending a meeting of a Moravian society in London. He claimed later to have "felt my heart strangely warmed," and said he finally knew that God truly loved him. He came to understand the revolutionary concept of justification by faith alone, and became convinced that salvation was possible for every person who exercised faith in

This engraving of a Methodist camp meeting was created by Matthew Dubourg around 1819.

Jesus. He immediately realized he needed to spread his new beliefs, but because his new methods seemed unorthodox, Wesley was not welcomed in Anglican pulpits. After the encouragement of evangelist George Whitefield, Wesley began traveling around the country preaching to large crowds of common people in the open air. He preached to the poor, the downtrodden, and the dispossessed, in open fields, on street corners, and in town squares. He preached on repentance, regeneration, justification by faith, on sanctification and the need for holiness.

British clergyman John Wesley (1703–1791)—founder, with his brother Charles, of Methodism—remained a member of the Church of England throughout his life.

His meetings led to a revival of religious fervor throughout England, especially among the poor.

Wesley's converts did not organize themselves into churches, but rather into "societies" that met in private homes. Within these societies, members supported each other and were accountable to each other. Members were honest in sharing their weaknesses and failings, and they encouraged one another to stay true to their faith.

During the 1760s in the new American colonies, Methodist societies had begun to meet regularly in Maryland and New York. In 1766, Phillip Embury organized a small class of Methodists in New York, marking one of the first organized Methodist groups in America. In 1769, Wesley sent his first missionaries to America, including in 1771, Francis Asbury, who was instrumental in establishing the American Methodist church.

The American Revolution forced many Anglican priests to return to England, leaving the Methodist societies without Anglican clergy, and thus without access to baptism and Holy Communion. The first annual Methodist conference was held in Philadelphia in 1773. In December 1784, a conference for all preachers was held in Baltimore, Maryland. It was during this "Christmas Conference" that the Methodist Episcopal Church was established

as a body separate from the English Methodist structure. Francis Asbury and Thomas Coke were the new church's first bishops. Wesley sent the new church his Twenty-four Articles of Religion, which was adapted from the Thirty-nine Articles of the Church of England. (Americans later added one more, making twenty-five articles all.) This document still serves as a doctrinal standard for the United Methodist Church and other Methodist bodies.

Soon after the official creation of the church, the Second Great Awakening (see Introduction to Protestantism on page 114) began. Asbury was the Methodists' most aggressive leader, traveling almost incessantly, preaching the gospel, and building his denomination. From roughly 1784 to 1816, he and other circuit-riding preachers spread Methodism across the Appalachian Mountains and into what was then frontier. They preached distinctively Methodist sermons with an emphasis on the need for conversion and regeneration. Asbury believed in the value of "circulation" and urged clergy to seek converts in even the most remote locations. He was also an advocate of "camp meetings," the extended outdoor revivals that helped establish Methodism as the most vigorous denomination of the period. The Methodist emphasis on personal religious experience and practical ethics attracted large numbers of people. By the mid-1800s, there were about 1.3 million Methodists in the United States.

Despite the spread and growth of the denomination, conflicts began to emerge within the church, most prominently regarding race. African Americans began to form their own independent churches. In 1845, delegates of the Methodist Episcopal Church from the southern conferences gathered in Louisville, Kentucky, to form the Methodist Episcopal Church, South, following a dispute at the 1844 General Conference over Bishop James O. Andrew owning slaves.

After the Civil War, northern and southern Methodists began to work toward unity and eventually, in 1939, a merger between the Methodist Episcopal Church, the Methodist Episcopal Church, South, and the Methodist Protestant Church formed the Methodist Church.

In 1968, a union of the Methodist Church with the Evangelical United Brethren Church, a denomination of German Pietist origin, formed the United Methodist Church.

B. Important Dates and Landmarks

1729 John Wesley and his brother Charles begin methodically meeting with a group of like-minded people at a stated time for "prayer and exercises."

1735 The Wesley brothers venture to America as missionaries and meet Moravian Christians while on the journey.

1738 John Wesley attends Moravian service in London; experiences spiritual awakening.

1766 Minister Philip Embury starts a class of Methodist societies in New York.

1769 Wesley sends the first missionaries to America.

1771 Francis Asbury arrives in America.

1773 The first annual Methodist conference is held in Philadelphia.

1784 The Methodist Episcopal Church is formally organized as a body separate from the English Methodist structure at a conference in Baltimore, Maryland—known afterward as the "Christmas Conference"; Asbury and Thomas Coke are the presiding bishops of the new church.

1791 John Wesley dies.

1790s–1820s The Second Great Awakening; evangelist Francis Asbury spreads Methodism across the Appalachian Mountains and the frontier until his death in 1816.

1794 The Republican Methodist Church is formed by James O'Kelly.

1816 The African Methodist Episcopal Church is organized by Richard Allen.

1816 The African Union Methodist Protestant Church is formed.

1820 The African Methodist Episcopal Zion Church is organized in New York City by Peter Williams and James Varick.

1830 The Methodist Protestant Church is formed.

1843 Orange Scott organizes the Wesleyan Methodist Church.

1845 The Methodist Episcopal Church, South, is created.

1846 The first General Conference of the Methodist Episcopal Church, South, meets in Petersburg, Virginia.

1852 The Congregational Methodist Church founded in home of Mickleberry Merrit.

1860 The Free Methodist Church of North America organized in western New York State.

1869 The Zion Union Apostolic Church is founded in Virginia.

1870 The Colored Methodist Episcopal Church is founded in Jackson, Tennessee; in 1954 the denomination later changes its name to the Christian Methodist Episcopal Church.

1881 The New Congregational Methodist church is founded in Georgia.

1886 The Evangelist Missionary Church is organized in Ohio by members of the African Methodist Episcopal Church.

1922 The Evangelical Congregational Church is founded.

1939 The Southern Methodist Church is founded in Columbia, South Carolina.

1939 The Methodist Episcopal Church, the Methodist Episcopal Church, South, and the Methodist Protestant Church merge to form the Methodist Church.

1946 The Evangelical Methodist Church is organized in Memphis, Tennessee.

1946 The Evangelical Association and the Church of the United Brethren in Christ unite to form the Evangelical United Brethren Church.

1968 The Evangelical Church of North America is founded in Portland, Oregon.

1968 The United Methodist Church is founded in Dallas, Texas, when the Methodist Church unites with the Evangelical United Brethren Church.

C. Important Figures

Church Leaders

John Wesley (1703–1791)—Founder of Methodism.

George Whitefield (1714–1770)—Methodist evangelical minister during the First Great Awakening.

Philip Embury (1729–1775)—Organized the first Methodist class in America in 1766.

Francis Asbury (1745–1816)—Missionary sent to America by Wesley in 1771; instrumental in establishing the American Methodist Church.

Thomas Coke (1747–1814)—Along with Asbury, one of the first bishops in authority over the new Methodist Church in America.

Absalom Jones (1746–1818)—Discrimination against Jones led to the formation of the African Methodist Episcopal Church.

Richard Allen (1760–1831)—Led the African-American membership of St. George's Church in Philadelphia away from the church in protest; began a new church for African-Americans, the Bethel Church for African Methodists in Philadelphia; organized other groups into the African Methodist Episcopal Church in 1816.

James O'Kelly (1738–1836)—Methodist minister who wanted an egalitarian governing structure in the church; when his protests failed, he withdrew from the main church and organized a new denomination, the Republican Methodist Church, later choosing the name Christian Church after a merger with the Disciples of Christ.

Orange Scott (1800–1847)—New England minister who organized the Wesleyan Methodist Church in 1843, after 1836 and 1840 General Conferences failed to adopt a strong antislavery position.

James O. Andrew (1784–1871)—Bishop of Georgia who refused to free the slave he owned, leading to the formation of the Methodist Episcopal Church, South, in 1845.

Jacob Albright (1759–1808)—Founder of the Evangelical Association movement.

Philip William Otterhein (1726–1813)—Founder of the United Brethren in Christ.

Dr. J. H. Hamblen (1877–1971)—First General Superintendent of the Evangelical Methodist Church.

Prominent Americans

Four presidents have been Methodists (**Polk, Hayes, McKinley**, and **G.W. Bush**); three vice-presidents (**Humphrey, Mondale, Cheney**); and many senators and representatives, including former First Lady and U.S. Secretary of State **Hillary Clinton** and recent presidential candidate **John Edwards**.

A list of famous Americans who were Methodists can be found on the following website: www.adherents.com/largecom/fam_meth.html

II. Tenets and Beliefs

Methodists followed Wesley's lead in rejecting the Calvinist emphasis on predestination, and instead espoused "Arminianism," which emphasizes human ability to respond to God's grace, and the belief that the death of Christ provided atonement for all human beings. Methodists also advocate belief in God's "prevenient grace." This is the idea that God reaches out to every person, providing each person with prevenient, or anticipatory, grace, offering him or her salvation through faith in Jesus Christ. Those who use free will as empowered by God's grace to positively respond by faith in Jesus become justified.

Most Methodists pay more attention to quality of life than to defending specific doctrines. Many, however, subscribe to some form of Wesley's doctrine of perfectionism—the idea that believers can be enabled by the Holy Spirit to say no to sin and become perfect in love in this present life if they completely surrender to God.

A. Statements of Faith

The *Book of Discipline* is the instrument for setting forth the laws, plan, polity, and process by which United Methodists govern themselves. The book includes the Constitution of the United Methodist Church; Doctrinal Standards and the theological task

A Tree of Life has been used in religious art, and particularly in Methodist missions and educational programs, for more than two hundred years. This one, published in 1896, features branches loaded with fruit, each of which bears the label of a spiritual virtue.

of the church, Social Principles, the mission and ministry of the church, organization, and administration.

The Twenty-five Articles of Religion is the official doctrinal statement of general Methodist bodies as adapted by John Wesley from the Thirty-nine Articles of the Church of England. The Articles can be found in paragraph 103 of the United Methodist *Book of Discipline* and have remained relatively unchanged since 1808.

The first fifty-three of **Wesley's** published sermons and his "Notes on the New Testament" are regarded as standards of doctrine.

The Social Creed of the UMC was originally adopted in 1908 as a statement on "the Church and

Social Problems." The Creed expressed the church's outrage over the lives of the millions of workers in factories, mines, mills, tenements, and company towns. The Creed was continually expanded and revised until 1972, when it was completely redesigned and renamed the Social Principles. The Social Creed now follows the Social Principles in the *Book of Discipline*.

B. Scripture

The doctrine of the Trinity and the Divinity of Jesus Christ are upheld by all Methodists. The universality of original sin and the consequent partial deterioration of human nature find their efficacious remedy in the universal distribution of grace. Humankind's free cooperation with the Divine gift is necessary for eternal salvation, which is offered to all, but may be freely rejected.

Methodists, according to Wesley's practice of theological reflection, make use of tradition as a source of authority—a lens through which Scripture is interpreted. Theological discourse for Methodists almost always makes use of Scripture read inside the great tradition of Christendom. The church believes that any disciplined theological work requires the careful use of reason. By reason, it is said, one determines whether one's Christian witness is clear. By reason one asks questions of faith and seeks to understand God's action and will.

In the UMC, the Bible is the primary source and criterion for Christian doctrine. Scripture is an authority in matters of faith. It reveals everything humankind needs to know about salvation. High value is given to human reason, for it is by reason that one reads and interprets the Bible.

The UMC does not have an "official" version or translation of the Bible. Only the General Conference can designate specific ritual texts or other liturgical or teaching resources as official. United Methodists affirm the usefulness of several translations and versions as being helpful for study, teaching, memorization, and other purposes, since each

sheds a slightly different light in translating or paraphrasing the original languages and manuscripts.

Other denominations in Methodism have more liberal or conservative views on the Bible.

III. Rites and Rituals

A. The Calendar

The United Methodist Church observes standard Christian holidays of Easter, Pentecost, and Christmas. The Church also observes Trinity Sunday, All Saint's Day, and Christ the King Sunday.

A unique feature of the American Methodist Church is its observance of the season of Kingdomtide, which encompasses the last thirteen weeks before Advent, thus dividing the long season after Pentecost into two distinct segments. During Kingdomtide, Methodist liturgy emphasizes charitable work and alleviating the suffering of the poor.

B. Worship and Liturgy

Methodism affirms the traditional Christian belief in the Trinity of God: the Father, the Son, and the Holy Spirit. Methodists also believe in the consubstantial humanity and divinity of Jesus. Methodists affirm the Apostles' and Nicene Creeds, which are said to embrace the biblical witness to God's activity in creation, encompass God's gracious self-involvement in the dramas of history, and anticipate the consummation of God's reign.

Methodists confess one holy, catholic, and apostolic church. They understand themselves to be a part of Christ's universal church. The local church is the community of believers, which the Spirit has brought into existence for the healing of nations. The church should be a community in which all persons, regardless of racial and ethnic background, can participate in every level of its connectional life and ministry. One is initiated and incorporated into this community of faith by baptism.

Baptism is a sacrament that initiates a covenant that connects God, the church, and the person being baptized. The mode can be sprinkling, pouring, or immersion. Persons of all ages are eligible for baptism.

Baptism is performed on infants soon after birth because they are already members of the Kingdom of God. Baptism does not produce sanctifying grace in the soul, but rather strengthens faith and is the sign of a regeneration which has already taken place in the recipient.

The Lord's Supper, or the Eucharist, or Communion, is a sacrament of redemption. People who partake of the elements spiritually receive bread and juice as the body and blood of Christ. Communion may be celebrated as often as desired and is open to all Christians.

The popular expression of Methodist theology is in the hymns of Charles Wesley. Since enthusiastic congregational singing was a part of the Evangelical movement, Wesleyan theology took root and spread through this channel.

Covenant Services encourage Methodist churches to annually follow the call of John Wesley for a renewal of their covenant with God. It is not unusual in Methodism for each congregation to normally hold an annual Covenant Service on the first convenient Sunday of the year, and Wesley's Covenant Prayer is still used, with minor modification, in the order of service. It is a striking and sobering piece of liturgical writing that calls all Methodists to be faithful Christians and devote their lives to Christ's cause.

Methodism has been aggressive in its work of conversion and **camp meetings and revivals** have been important forms of evangelization in America.

Methodist **love-feasts** recall the agape of Christian antiquity (in which Jesus broke bread with his disciples other than at the Last Supper). In these gatherings of believers, bread and water are handed around in token of brotherly union, and the time is devoted to singing and the relating of religious experiences.

C. Daily Life

Wesley imposed a few practices upon his followers, including the strict observance of the Lord's Day, the use of few words in buying and selling, and abstinence from all intoxicating drinks, from all purely worldly amusements, and from costly apparel.

The Free Methodist Church forbids its members from using tobacco and wearing rich apparel.

IV. Denominations and Demographics

A. History

In addition to the United Methodist Church, there are over forty other denominations that descend from the Methodist movement. Some, such as the African Methodist Episcopal Church, the Free Methodists, the Wesleyan Church (formerly Wesleyan Methodist), the Congregational Methodist Church, and First Congregational Methodist Church, are explicitly Methodist. Others do not call themselves Methodist, but are related to varying degrees. The Evangelical Church was formed by a group of Evangelical United Brethren congregations who dissented from the merger that formed the United Methodist Church.

The Wesleyan Methodist Church was organized in 1843, by advocates of a more radical attitude against slavery than found in the Methodist Episcopal Church.

The Methodist Protestant Church was founded on November 2, 1830, in Baltimore, Maryland, by members of the Methodist Episcopal Church who had been expelled or had freely withdrawn from that body. The separation was due to the refusal to extend the governmental rights of laymen. It divided in 1858 on the issue of slavery, but reunited again in 1877 and was a part of the 1939 merger forming the Methodist Church.

The African Methodist Episcopal Church was formed by Richard Allen, a man who organized his own church after an act of racial discrimination in his home church, Saint George's Church in Philadelphia. His new church was called the Bethel Church. Allen organized the African Methodist Episcopal Church in 1816. He was elected as the denomination's first bishop.

The Congregational Methodist Church was founded in 1852 as a result of dissatisfaction with certain policies of the Methodist Episcopal Church, South, among the lay members. The three primary objections were that lay members had no voice in the government of the church, that they believed the church should have more autonomy and be allowed to own its own building and call its own ministers, and finally, they wanted more reasonable requirements for lay individuals to become ordained as pastors. In 1852, a group of lay people and lay ministers from Georgia decided to sever their relationship with the Georgia Conference of the Methodist Episcopal Church, South, and organize a new church that acquiesced to all of the lay people's concerns. The church met in the home of Mickleberry Merrit on May 8, 1852, and elected William Farbough as its chairman.

The Free Methodist Church of North America was founded in 1860 in western New York by ministers and lay people who had been expelled from the Methodist Episcopal Church for insubordination. These people, under the leadership of Reverend Benjamin Titus Robert had voiced concern that the church had departed from the doctrines of early Methodism. On August 23, 1860, they formed their own church in order to address the issues that had caused them concern, including slavery, segregation in churches, freedom of worship style, and secret societies. The new church believed that all people, including African Americans, should be free and that all seating in churches should be free (the Methodist Episcopal Church rented and sold pews to wealthier members, forcing the poor to sit in the back). They also believed that there should be no participation in

The First Methodist Church of Oviedo, Florida, seen in this 2007 photograph, features an architectural style found in the central squares of many towns and small cities across the United States.

secret societies because truth should be shared openly and freely.

The Christian Methodist Episcopal Church was formed in 1870 after the emancipation of the slaves. African-American members of the Methodist Episcopal Church, South, (about 80,000 people), amicably split off from the white members and organized the Colored Methodist Episcopal Church in Jackson, Tennessee. At the 1954 General Conference in Memphis, Tennessee, the name of the denomination was changed to the Christian Methodist Episcopal Church. It now reaches not only across the United States, but also into Haiti, Jamaica, Nigeria, Ghana, and Liberia.

The Evangelical Congregational Church has its roots in the Evangelical Association, a movement founded by Methodist itinerant preacher Jacob Albright in 1796. In 1891, the Association suffered a division because of differences of opinion and practice, especially relating to episcopal authority, and in 1894 the United Evangelical Church was formed. In 1922, the two groups reconciled and reunited, but a small group did not approve of the merger and remained separate. They took the name Evangelical Congregational Church in 1928.

The Southern Methodist Church was founded in 1939 in Columbia, Georgia, by congregations that did not wish to go along with the merger of the Methodist Episcopal Church, South, with the Methodist Episcopal Church (North). They believed the northern body was tainted with apostasy and heresy. They also believed that such a merger would overly centralize ecclesiastical control in one body.

The Evangelical Methodist Church was founded in 1946 in Memphis, Tennessee, in reaction to the modernism that had infiltrated their parent body, the Methodist Church. Many people believed that there was a distinct separation between the liberal and conservative aspects of the church and so founded the Evangelical Methodist Church in order to preserve the distinctive biblical doctrines of the historic Wesleyan position.

The Evangelical Church of North America was established in 1968 by members of the Evangelical United Brethren. Those members objected to the planned merger of their denomination with the Methodist Church, which would result in the formation of the United Methodist Church. The denomination was organized in Portland, Oregon, and although its affiliate churches can be found throughout the country, the highest concentration can be found in the Northwest.

The United Methodist Church emerged in Dallas, Texas, on April 23, 1968, as a result of a union of the Methodist Church and the Evangelical United Brethren Church. When Bishop Reuben H. Mueller, representing the Evangelical United Brethren Church, and Bishop Lloyd C. Wicke of the Methodist Church joined hands at the constituting General Conference, and said, "Lord of the Church, we are united in Thee, in Thy Church and now in the United Methodist Church," the merger became a reality. Both churches shared similar doctrines and had similar books of discipline. Their preachers even spoke in each other's pulpits. Theological traditions steeped in the Protestant Reformation and Wesleyanism, similar ecclesiastical structures, and relationships that dated back almost 200 years facilitated the union. In the Evangelical United Brethren heritage, for example, Philip William Otterbein, the principal founder of the United Brethren in Christ, assisted in the ordination of Francis Asbury to the superintendency of American Methodist work. Jacob Albright, through whose religious experience and leadership the Evangelical Association was begun, was nurtured in a Methodist class meeting following his conversion.

B. Comparisons in Tenets and Practices

Most of the Methodist denominations have much commonality. Some of the more notable differentiations are:

• The Methodist Protestant Church has no bishops.

• The Wesleyan Methodist Church has neither episcopate nor itinerancy and debars members of secret societies.

• The Free Methodist Church has no bishops, excludes members of secret societies, and prohibits the use of tobacco and the wearing of rich apparel.

• The Independent Methodists maintain no central government. Each congregation enjoys supreme control over its own affairs.

• The African Union Methodist Protestant Church rejects the episcopacy, itinerancy, and a paid ministry.

• The Evangelist Missionary Church has no creed but the Bible and inclines to the admission of only one person in God, that of Jesus Christ.

C. Organization and Distribution

The African Methodist Episcopal Church has about 1.9 million members spread out through almost 8,000 congregations.

The Christian Methodist Episcopal Church has about 850,000 members and maintains 2,980 congregations.

The Congregational Methodist Church has about 15,000 members and 187 congregations.

The Evangelical Church of North America has about 13,000 members and 164 congregations throughout the United States, with heaviest concentration in the Northwest.

The Evangelical Congregational Church has about 22,000 members and 168 congregations.

The Evangelical Methodist Church has about 9,000 members and 105 congregations.

The Free Methodist Church of North America has about 62,000 members and 971 congregations.

The Southern Methodist Church has about 8,000 members and 82 congregations and is centralized in the southern United States.

The United Methodist Church has over 8 million members and over 24,000 congregations throughout the United States.

V. Organization and Infrastructure

A. Education and Hierarchy of Clergy

Methodists observe two orders of ministry: the deacons and the elders, or presbyters. The term "bishop" is a title of office, not of order. It expresses superiority to elders not in ordination, but in the exercise of administrative function. Bishops are not "ordained" as bishops but are clergy who are elected and consecrated to the office of bishop.

B. Seminaries

Contact information for the following seminaries and colleges may be found at this web address: www.gbhem.org.

UNITED METHODIST THEOLOGICAL SCHOOLS
Boston University School of Theology: Boston, MA
Candler School of Theology, Emory University:
    Atlanta, GA
Claremont School of Theology: Claremont, CA
Drew University, The Theological School:
    Madison, NJ
Duke University, The Divinity School:
    Durham, NC
Gammon Theological Seminary: Atlanta, GA
Garrett-Evangelical Theological Seminary:
    Evanston, IL
Iliff School of Theology: Denver, CO
Methodist Theological School in Ohio:
    Delaware, OH
Perkins School of Theology, Southern Methodist
    University: Dallas, TX
Saint Paul School of Theology: Kansas City, MO
United Theological Seminary: Trotwood, OH
Wesley Theological Seminary: Washington, DC

UNITED METHODIST-RELATED PRECOLLEGIATE
    SCHOOLS
Carrollton Christian Academy: Carrollton, TX
Kents Hill School: Kents Hill, ME
Lydia Patterson Institute: El Paso, TX
McCurdy School: Espanola, NM
The Pennington School: Pennington, NJ
Randolph-Macon Academy: Front Royal, VA
Red Bird Mission School: Beverly, KY
Robinson School: San Juan, PR
Tilton School: Tilton, NH
Wyoming Seminary College Preparatory School:
    Kingston, PA

UNITED METHODIST-RELATED COLLEGES AND UNIVERSITIES

Two-Year Colleges

Andrew College: Cuthbert, GA

Hiwassee College: Madisonville, TN

Lon Morris College: Jacksonville, TX

Louisburg College: Louisburg, NC

Oxford College of Emory University: Oxford, GA

Spartanberg Methodist College: Spartanburg, SC

Young Harris College: Young Harris, GA

Four-Year Colleges and Universities

Adrian College: Adrian, MI

Alaska Pacific University: Anchorage, AK

Albion College: Albion, MI

Albright College: Reading, PA

Allegheny College: Meadville, PA

American University: Washington, D.C.

Baker University: Baldwin City, KS

Baldwin Wallace College: Berea, OH

Bennett College for Women: Greensboro, NC

Bethune-Cookman College: Daytona Beach, FL

Birmingham-Southern College: Birmingham, AL

Boston University: Boston, MA

Brevard College: Brevard, NC

Centenary College: Hackettstown, NJ

Centenary College of Louisiana: Shreveport, LA

Central Methodist University: Fayette, MO

Claflin University: Orangeburg, SC

Clark Atlanta University: Atlanta, GA

Columbia College: Columbia, SC

Cornell College: Mount Vernon, IA

Dakota Wesleyan University: Mitchell, SD

DePauw University: Greencastle, IN

Dickinson College: Carlisle, PA

Dillard University: New Orleans, LA

Drew University: Madison, NJ

Duke University: Durham, NC

Emory and Henry College: Emory, VA

Emory University: Atlanta, GA

Ferrum College: Ferrum, VA

Florida Southern College: Lakeland, FL

Green Mountain College: Poultney, VT

Greensboro College: Greensboro, NC

Hamline University: Saint Paul, MN

Hendrix College: Conway, AR

High Point University: High Point, NC

Huntington College: Montgomery, AL

Huston-Tillotson University: Austin, TX

Illinois Wesleyan University: Bloomington, IL

Iowa Wesleyan College: Mount Pleasant, IA

Kansas Wesleyan University: Salina, KS

Kendall College: Chicago, IL

Kentucky Wesleyan College: Owensboro, KY

LaGrange College: LaGrange, GA

Lambuth University: Jackson, TN

Lebanon Valley College: Annville, PA

Lindsey Wilson College: Columbia, KY

Lycoming College: Williamsport, PA

MacMurray College: Jacksonville, IL

Martin Methodist College: Pulaski, TN

McKendree College: Lebanon, IL

McMurray University: Abilene, TX

Methodist College: Fayetteville, NC

Millsaps College: Jackson, MS

Morningside College: Sioux City, IA

Mount Union College: Alliance, OH

Nebraska Methodist College: Omaha, NE

Nebraska Wesleyan University: Lincoln, NE

No. Carolina Wesleyan College: Rocky Mount, NC

North Central College: Naperville, IL

Ohio Northern University: Ada, OH

Ohio Wesleyan University: Delaware, OH

Oklahoma City University: Oklahoma City, OK

Otterbein College: Westerville, OH

Paine College: Augusta, GA

Pfeiffer University: Misenheimer, NC

Philander Smith College: Little Rock, AR

Randolph-Macon College: Ashland, VA

Randolph-Macon Women's College: Lynchburg, VA

Reinhardt College: Waleska, GA

Rocky Mountain College: Billings, MT

Rust College: Holly Springs, MS

Shenandoah University: Winchester, VA

Simpson College: Indianola, IA

Southern Methodist University: Dallas, TX

Southwestern College: Winfield, KS
Southwestern University: Georgetown, TX
Syracuse University: Syracuse, NY
Tennessee Wesleyan College: Athens, TN
Texas Wesleyan University: Fort Worth, TX
Union College: Barbourville, KY
University of Denver: Denver, CO
University of Evansville: Evansville, IN
University of Indianapolis: Indianapolis, IN
University of Puget Sound: Tacoma, WA
University of the Pacific: Stockton, CA
Virginia Wesleyan College: Norfolk, VA
Wesley College: Dover, DE
Wesleyan College: Macon, GA
West Virginia Wesleyan College: Buckhannon, WV
Wiley College: Marshall, TX
Willamette University: Salem, OR
Wofford College: Spartanburg, SC

FMC:

Azusa Pacific University: Azusa, CA
Central Christian College: McPherson, KS
Greenville College: Greenville, IL
Northeastern Seminary at Roberts Wesleyan College:
    Rochester, NY
Seattle Pacific University: Seattle, WA
Spring Arbor University: Spring Arbor, MI

AMEC:

Payne Theological Seminary: Wilberforce, OH
Turner Seminary-ITC: Atlanta, GA
Wilberforce University: Wilberforce, OH
Allen University: Columbia, SC
Morris Brown College: Atlanta, GA
Paul Quinn College: Dallas, TX
Edward Waters College: Jacksonville, FL

WESLEYAN CHURCH
Seminaries:

Asbury Theological Seminary: Wilmore, KY and
    Orlando, FL
Azusa Pacific Graduate School of Theology:
    Azusa, CA

Evangelical School of Theology: Myerstown, PA
George Fox Evangelical Seminary: Newberg, OR
Nazarene Theological Seminary: Kansas City, MO
Tyndale Seminary: Toronto, Ontario, Canada
Wesley Biblical Seminary: Jackson, MS

Colleges and Universities:

Bethany Bible College: Sussex, New Brunswick,
    Canada
Houghton College: Houghton, NY
Indiana Wesleyan University: Marion, IN
Oklahoma Wesleyan: Bartsville, OK
Southern Wesleyan University: Central, SC

C. Governance and Authority

The government of the United Methodist Church is very similar to that of the United States. The General Conference serves as the top legislative body, with the nine-member Judicial Council acting as the "supreme court," and the Council of Bishops as the executive branch.

The General Conference is the legislative body for all matters affecting the United Methodist Church but has no administrative or executive power. The *Book of Discipline* defines the composition of the Conference as no less than 600 and no more than 1,000 delegates, half of which are to be laity and half of which are clergy. These delegates are elected by the Annual Conferences. The Conference meets on a quadrennial basis (every four years) but special sessions may be called by the Council of Bishops.

The Judicial Council determines the constitutionality of acts or proposed acts of the various conferences held annually, and also decides whether these acts conform to the *Book of Discipline*. The Council of Bishops consists of all active and retired bishops in the UMC and meets twice a year. There are fifty active bishops from the United States and eighteen representing Europe, Asia, and Africa, as well as ninety-six retired bishops worldwide.

Admission to full membership in the Methodist bodies was until recently usually granted only after the successful termination of a six months' probationary period.

D. Social Service Organizations

The UMC runs a variety of global missionary and ministry programs, including the South Asia Emergency Fund, which is dedicated to aiding tsu-nami victims. The local parishes and congregations of the UMC run a variety of community-based service ministries and programs on the local level.

The Free Methodist Church operates a large number of national and international service organizations, including:
- Women's Ministries International
- Men's Ministries International
- The Free Methodist Foundation
- The King Trust Company
- The Free Methodist Chaplains
- Free Methodist Bible Quizzing
- International Child Care Ministries
- Parish Nursing, Inc.

The FMC also runs the African American Consulting Network, the Free Methodist Urban Fellowship, and the National Student Ministry Team, all of which are specifically dedicated to serving Methodists in the United States. Within the Free Methodist Association of Human Service Ministries (FMAHSM) are the Birth Connection; the Butterfield Memorial Foundation; Clawson Manor/New Life, Deaconess Pregnancy and Adoption Services; The Heritage Group; Life Line Homes, Inc.; Oakdale Christian Academy; Olive Branch Mission; Warm Beach Senior Community; and the Woodstock Christian Life Services.

E. Media and Communication

UMC

The United Methodist Church maintains a website through which many aspects of communication with UMC congregants can be achieved. Many of the publications listed below can also be found online. In addition to magazine and newsletter publications, the UMC has several television spots and commercials and produces and distributes informational DVDs and CDs. The United Methodist Publishing House is the official publisher of the denomination and produces books and other media. The United Methodist News Service and United Methodist Communications are responsible for maintaining communication throughout all United Methodist connections.

Alive Now is a devotional magazine that seeks to nourish those who are hungry for a sacred way of living in the world.

Circuit Rider is a bi-monthly professional magazine to address the spiritual, intellectual, and practical needs of pastors.

Devo'Zine is a devotional magazine designed just for youth.

El Intépete is a ministry magazine for Spanish-speaking and Hispanic/Latino congregations.

Interpreter is a ministry magazine for United Methodists.

Leader in Christian Education Ministries is a magazine of practical ideas, training advice, inspiration, and encouragement for Christian educators.

Mature Years is a quarterly leisure-reading magazine and Bible study for older adults.

New World Outlook is the mission magazine of the UMC.

Newscope is a concise, late-deadline weekly update on news of interest to United Methodist leaders.

Orientation is an annual for graduating seniors, first-year collegians, and their parents to help with the transition from high school to campus life.

Pockets is a fun magazine for children ages six to twelve.

Response is the official magazine of United Methodist Women.

UMMen is the official magazine of United Methodist Men.

United Methodists in Service is a ministry magazine for Korean-speaking and Korean congregations.

Upper Room is a daily devotional guide.

Weavings is a journal of Christian spiritual life.

Worship Arts is a publication of The Fellowship of United Methodists in Music and Worship Arts.

AMEC

The-christian-recorder.org—official organ of the African Methodist Episcopal Church.

The Storehouse—the Amen Network news website—www.amennetwork.com.

Forministry.com—ministry web builder.

FMC

Light and Life Communications is the official publishing arm of the FMC. It is a nonprofit corporation that exists to serve in partnership with its parent body, and to enable the church to fulfill its mission.

Light and Life Magazine is a bi-monthly publication also available online. The FMC website, www.freemethodistchurch.org, also offers "The Gospel"—a three-minute video Gospel designed for kids. And the "Thinking It Through" page offers e-counseling on prayer and advice.

Real Fusion: What's Real Today is a daily video podcast that helps guide and inspire Christians in spiritual growth throughout the week and to help Christians become active in living out their faith every day, using cutting-edge multimedia resources to partner with local churches.

WESLEYAN CHURCH

News is available online at the church's website: www.wesleyan.org and through an e-zine electronic newsletter subscription of bi-monthly e-mails.

Wesleyan Life is a quarterly available online.

The Wesleyan Hour is a series of radio sermons that can be broadcast locally and nationally.

The Wesleyan Publishing House (WPH) is the denomination's official publisher, producing educational-liturgical resources for the Wesleyan Church.

FURTHER READING AND RESOURCES

Methodist Experiences in America
Rowe Richey and Miller-Schmidt, eds.
2000: Abingdon Press

Recapturing the Wesleys' Vision
Paul Wesley Chilcote
2004: InterVarsity Press

The United Methodist Book of Worship
Staff of Worship Committee (Editor)
1992: Abingdon Press

The United Methodist Hymnal
1996: United Methodist Publishing House

WEBSITES

African Methodist Episcopal Church:
   www.amecnet.org
Christian Methodist Episcopal Church:
   www.c-m-e-.org
Congregational Methodist Church:
   www.congregationalmethodist.net
The Evangelical Church of North America:
   www.theevangelicalchurch.com
Evangelical Congregational Church:
   www.eccenter.com
The Evangelical Methodist Church:
   www.emchurch.org
Free Methodist Church of North America:
   www.reemethodistchurch.com
Southern Methodist Church:
   www.southernmethodistchurch.com
The United Methodist Church:
   www.umc.org

12 Presbyterianism

I. Origins and Early History

A. Introduction

THOUGH PRESBYTERIANISM IS A DIRECT PRODUCT of the European Reformation movement, its developmental history as an established church is distinctively American in nature. Its highly pluralistic expression, historically fierce nationalism, organization as a representative democracy, and emphasis on knowledge and education are all highly reflective of the culture in which it formed. Though Presbyterianism shares similarities with other evangelical denominations involved in the formation of America's religious landscape, the movement's propensity for internal splitting conveys that penchant for individualism and initiative that are so characteristic of traditional "American spirit."

Presbyterianism traces its theological roots to the Protestant Reformation of the sixteenth century and the teachings of John Calvin. John Knox, a Scotsman who studied under Calvin in Geneva, is regarded as the founder of the movement. After finishing his studies in Switzerland, Knox returned to his native Scotland, where he became renowned for his thunderous denunciations of the Roman Catholic Church. In 1567, Knox's work culminated in Parliament's legal recognition of the Reformed Church of Scotland, a presbyterial organization founded upon a Confession of Faith partially authored by Knox. Ireland followed suit with their Presbyterian Church, formed from the Church of Scotland. But the rise of Presbyterianism was more belabored in England. Established in secret in 1572 toward the end of the reign of Queen Elizabeth I, the movement would not be openly embraced until 1647, when an act of the Long Parliament under the control of the Puritans acknowledged its acceptance in the eyes of the Church of England. In 1688, under the leadership of King William II, Knox's Reformed Church of Scotland was reorganized into the Established Presbyterian Church of Scotland.

In 1643, the English Parliament commissioned the Westminster Assembly to develop the creed of

John Knox was a leader of the Reformation and is considered the founder of Presbyterianism. In this engraving, he is seen reproving the ladies of Queen Mary's court.

the Church of England. The resulting confession was the collaborative effort of 121 English Puritan ministers, who met over a thousand times over three years. The Westminster Confession of Faith strongly stresses the sovereignty of God as well as the five points of Calvinism, often represented by the acronym TULIP: total depravity, unconditional election, limited atonement, irresistible grace, and perseverance of the saints. The creed was eventually adopted by existing Presbyterian churches as their primary confession of faith.

B. The Religion in America

Though traces of Presbyterianism were present in the seventeenth century, it first notably surfaced in the New World in 1706, when an organized presbytery was formed in Pennsylvania. Reverend Francis Makemie, ordained in the Presbytery of Laggan in Northern Ireland, spearheaded the formation with the help of six others. Initially known as The Presbytery, Makemie's organization was a fellowship of likeminded worshippers from England, Scotland, Ireland, and Wales. Dutch, German, and French Reformed Christians would soon join.

By definition, "Presbyterian" denotes a dependence upon regional gatherings of representatives. The church is so structured today, inclusive of multiple levels of representation that increase in both size and authority. At the highest level, a general assembly governs an entire nation. A synod wields regional jurisdiction. A presbytery usually presides over one portion of a state, and a session governs at the congregational level. Lastly, a stated clerk coordinates the meetings of a synod or assembly. Thus, Presbyterianism's growth in popularity and reach may be measured by its developing need for each increasing level of jurisdiction in America.

By 1716, the movement was sufficiently large enough to warrant the organization of its first synod, composed of three presbyteries from Maryland, Delaware, and New York–New Jersey. Uniting the few bodies only highlighted their differences in doctrine and practice, however. On one side were the Scots and Scotch-Irish, who felt focus should lie on precise theology and church governance. On the other were the English and Welsh, who upheld the pious religious experience as most important. It became necessary in 1729 to instate the Adopting Act, which sought to smooth over contention with a compromise. The act stated that all ministers must agree with the aforementioned Westminster Confession of Faith and the long and short catechisms. However, if a minister should disagree with some other portion of the Westminster Standards (inclusive of the confession, catechisms, rules of church government, and discipline, and guidelines for worship), the presbytery would consider and rule on the verity of the objection. This approach would seem to provide enough flexibility to enable cohesion among ministers and united growth in the religion—but it was not to prove a lasting solution. The Great Awakening would give too great a shaking to the young movement.

Divisiveness Within

In the year 1740, preachers George Whitefield and Jonathan Edwards sparked a craze that sent a shock wave of "awakening" sermons coursing through America. Their message emphasized the need for conversion of sinners—spiritual revival. The theology preached was Calvinist in basis, but its insistence on the conversion experience was embraced only by English and Welsh Presbyterians. When Presbyterian minister Gilbert Tennent established himself as a leading proponent of revivalism with the sermon, "On the Danger of an Unconverted Ministry," the Scots and Scots-Irish faction rebelled. Tennent's comparison of antirevivalistic ministers to the biblical Pharisees resulted in his immediate ejection from the church. His followers left with him. Thus, in 1741, Presbyterianism suffered a split between the New Side (supporters of revivalism) and the Old Side.

Gilbert Tennent and his father, William Tennent, had founded in 1726 the first American Presbyterian theological seminary, called "Log College." Located in Neshaminy (now Warminster), Pennsylvania, the seminary produced several influential preachers of the Great Awakening who followed Tennent's lead. This college is today considered the predecessor of Princeton University (many of its faculty and graduates would be integral figures of Princeton's early years).

As New Side Presbyterians increased in number while Old Siders found themselves decreasingly popular, the latter denomination revoked their prohibition of pro-revival worshippers from their congregations, and the two sects celebrated a reunion in 1758. This resulted in an overall flourishing of Presbyterianism throughout the northern and middle colonies, and an expansion into the South. In 1788, the first General Assembly was gathered, consisting of 200 congregations and sixteen presbyteries. In 1789, the newly formed Presbyterian Church in the United States of America (PCUSA) adopted a constitution that provided for national governance. However, this example of nationwide cooperation among adherents would not prove the norm.

Questions of patriotism would next plague the religion. Though enough Presbyterians forcefully supported the Revolutionary War to inspire King George III to call it "the Presbyterian War," loyalists did exist in the Presbyterian Church. These latter, many of them Seceders, had never joined the general synod. Furthermore, they would later object to other adherents' pledge of allegiance to George Washington because the United States Constitution did not declare its country a strictly Christian nation. The Seceders and "Covenanters" united in 1782 to form the Associate Reformed Church. Other Seceders formed the Associate Presbyterian Church in 1843. In 1858, some members of both the ARC and the APC defected from their churches because of issues with church government, closed Communion, and the singing of psalms during services. These members formed their own United Presbyterian Church of North America. The UPNA was mostly conservative in theology, and strongest in western Pennsyl-

vania. Those who did not defect—mainly belonging to the Synod of the Carolinas—continued on as the Associate Reformed Presbyterian Church.

Observance of the "Puritan Sabbath" was still important to all Presbyterians at this time. In fact, believers felt that state laws should support the moral imperative to "Remember the Sabbath Day, to keep it holy" (Exodus 2:8). Presbyterians were not the only religious worshippers to feel this way. Baptists, Methodists, and Congregationalists, especially, agreed to uphold Sunday laws. This led to the Plan of Union in 1801, according to which churches of both Congregationalist and Presbyterian leanings could be served by the same pastors. As a result of the union, Presbyterians concentrated on expansion throughout the South and West because New England was already well covered by Congregationalism.

The Presbyterian Church was destined to suffer more divisiveness over yet another awakening period. The Second Great Awakening commenced in 1790, and though its major effecter, Charles Grandison Finney, was in fact a Presbyterian minister, his advocating of emotionalism and inattention to theology was met with distrust by conservative Presbyterians. Those who deplored the vogue of barking, dancing, "melting" (crying), jumping, and shouting characteristic of conversion experiences frowned upon those who engaged in such activities. As a result, pro-revivalists abandoned what they regarded as the cold formality and intellectualism of their denomination for Baptist and Methodist churches. Revivalist Presbyterians in Tennessee and Kentucky formed their own Cumberland Presbytery.

In 1837, the culmination of conflicts over revivalism, the Plan of Union, slavery, and various social reform initiatives caused an abrogation of the Plan of Union and expulsion of four synods that had been formed under its clauses. This time, the two factions on either side of the split were called New School and Old School. The major proponents of the division were not only religion-specific; they also encompassed issues that reflected the growing tensions of the nation preceding the Civil War. In fact, the Civil

War would cause further divisions among the Old and New School factions. One important development of the New School movement was the founding of Union Theological Seminary, located in New York City, which temporarily served as the center for the movement. Regarding the Old School, some Southern Presbyterians withdrew from their churches in 1861 over issues of loyalty to the United States, and formed the Presbyterian Church in the Confederate States of America (PCCSA). In 1870, all was healed among northern Protestants when Old Schoolers and New Schoolers reunited under the old name Presbyterian Church in the United States of America. At about the same time, the PCCSA expanded into the Presbyterian Church in the United States. In 1869, the first black Presbyterian denomination was formed when the Cumberland Presbytery split along racial lines. Blacks now worshipped at the Second Cumberland Presbyterian Church.

Expansion and Modernism

The Reconstruction Period in America following the Civil War was characterized by fervent missionary efforts among all Presbyterians. The PCUSA instituted new schools and colleges to educate freed blacks, and all denominations contributed to missionary work abroad. But even as Presbyterian expansion occurred throughout the western frontier, the Midwest, and even Alaska, it met with the restricting force of scientific theory, which assertions threatened biblical inerrancy. Darwinism caused an uproar at Princeton University, where the biblical account of creation was traditionally taught. Furthermore, Calvinism came under attack for its claims that man was inherently sinful. A great number of Presbyterians desired that their confession be revised to accommodate the new scientific explanations of existence. Also, many wished to advocate God's love and forgiveness of all humanity, rather than focus on natural depravity.

Traditional Presbyterians battled the pull of these "modernists" by gathering "evidences" in support of the Princeton-taught theology. They insisted on their possession of objective proofs of Bible inerrancy, and defended the Westminster Standards. Traditionalists argued that if some sections of the Bible could be called into question, the book would lose authority altogether as an inspired source of truth. The trials of Charles A. Briggs (a professor at Union Seminary) and Henry P. Smith (of Lane Seminary) illustrate the strength of the proponents of the Princeton theology at that time. Both men were brought up on charges of heresy when they denied the authenticity of biblical passages while teaching. They were convicted and suspended from the ministry. These events led to the beginnings of what would become the Fundamentalist movement.

Several institutional changes were made in response to the new pressures brought about by science. Firstly, Union Seminary disassociated itself with Presbyterianism after the Briggs trial, allowing Briggs to keep his position there. Secondly, Princeton University lost one of its most prominent professors, John Gresham Machen. Decrying what he sensed as increasing liberalism at the university, Machen left and founded Westminster Theological Seminary, a bastion of ultraconservative thought. In 1936, Machen's followers founded a new denomination, now known as Orthodox Presbyterian Church.

Reunion

From this point on, reunion would be more common than fragmenting within Presbyterianism. The PCUSA grew in the North when it agreed to include five fundamentals: the inerrancy of Scripture, the virgin conception of Jesus Christ, a satisfaction theory of the atonement, physical resurrection, and the veracity of Christ's miracles. Over 100,000 members of the Cumberland Presbytery found they could once again support the PCUSA under these new terms, as did Welsh Calvinist Methodists and many newly initiated blacks.

The PCUSA membership grew in the South, as well, from nearly 80,000 to more than one million members from 1869 to 1962. Its success was widely due to the fact that it refrained from making formal statements on political or social matters—even issues regarding Sabbath observance and temperance. The last major defection would occur in 1970, when a number of right-wing conservative Southern congregations formed the Presbyterian Church in America. This sifting of conservatives from PCUSA ranks helped furnish its growth, however.

Unsuccessful attempts were made in the 1940s to unite the PCUSA and PCUS. The two branches tried again in the 1950s, this time including the UPNA in the plan. Again, the PCUS demurred out of fear of liberalist influences in the PCUSA. But in 1958, the PCUSA and UPNA joined to become the United Presbyterian Church in the United States (UPCUSA). These 250,000 members added to the 3 million of the former PCUSA reinforced its standing as the largest Presbyterian denomination in America. Finally, in 1982, the PCUS dropped its previous antipathies with the former PCUSA and voted affirmatively to join the UPCUSA.

In 1983, the two denominations convened at the General Assembly in Atlanta, Georgia, creating the Presbyterian Church (U.S.A.), or PC(USA). As of 1990, this denomination claimed 3.8 million members; recent reports set the number at about 2.3 million members, 10,900 congregations, and 14,000 ordained ministers—making it one of the largest mainline Protestant denominations in the United States.

C. Important Dates and Landmarks

1685 Protestants emigrate to England, Prussia, the Netherlands, and America.

1688–1689 "Glorious Revolution" deposes Catholic King James II of England; English Presbyterians are given limited toleration outside the (Anglican) state church.

1706 First organized presbytery in America is formed—Francis Makemie its convener.

1738 First Reformed Presbyterian congregation in North America is organized in Octorara (Lancaster Country, Pennsylvania).

1774 First Reformed presbytery is formed by four immigrant Irish and Scottish Reformed Presbyterian ministers.

1782 Associate Reformed Presbyterian Church is formed with merger of the Associate (Seceder) and the Reformed Presbyterian (Covenanter) churches in Philadelphia.

1789 First General Assembly of the Presbyterian Church in the U.S. held in Philadelphia, convened by Reverend John Witherspoon, one of the original signers of the Declaration of Independence.

1810 Cumberland Presbyterian Church is organized in Tennessee in the log cabin home of Reverend Samuel McAdow, together with Reverend Finis Ewing and Reverend Samuel King.

1858 United Presbyterian Church is formed by synods defecting from the Associate Reformed Synod in Philadelphia; the remaining synod continues on as the Associate Reformed Presbyterian Church.

1861 Presbyterian Church in the Confederate States of America is formed by southern Presbyterians after a split from the original PCUSA over issues of slavery and federal union (later becomes the Presbyterian Church in the United States).

1906 Presbyterian Church in the USA is joined by the majority of the Cumberland Presbyterian Church.

1920 Welsh Calvinist Methodist Church is absorbed by the Presbyterian Church in the USA.

1924 General Assembly adopts five "essential and necessary" pillars of Christian belief, prompting the Auburn Affirmation—a document embracing modernism and "liberty of thought and teaching."

1929 J. Gresham Machen is joined by a group of other conservative Presbyterian ministers and theologians in forming the Westminster Theological Seminary.

1933-1934 Many of churches of the Reformed Church in the United States (RCUS) merge with the Evangelical Synod of North America, which later merged with the Congregational Christian Churches to form the United Church of Christ.

1936 Machen and a group of conservative ministers, elders, and laymen form the Presbyterian Church of America in Philadelphia (the denomination's name was changed to the Orthodox Presbyterian Church in 1939).

1937 Bible Presbyterian Church is organized.

1938 First General Synod of the Bible Presbyterian Church is held in Collingswood, New Jersey.

1958 United Presbyterian Church of North America merges with the Presbyterian Church in the USA and forms the United Presbyterian Church in the USA.

1967 General Assembly adopts the Confession of 1967—the first new confession in 300 years.

1973 Presbyterian Church in America (PCA) is formed when a group of churches left the southern Presbyterian church because it was becoming too liberal.

1981 First general assembly of the Evangelical Presbyterian Church is held during which the new denomination drafts a list of essential beliefs.

1983 Reunion between the Presbyterian Church in the US (PCUS), the "southern branch," and the United Presbyterian Church in the USA (UPCUSA), the "northern branch," results in the formation of the Presbyterian Church (USA) or PC(USA).

1983 Association of the Reformed Presbyterian Church in the United States established.

D. Important Figures

John Calvin (1509–1564). A French Protestant theologian during the Protestant Reformation and a central developer of the system of Christian theology called Calvinism, or Reformed theology. In Geneva, Calvin rejected papal authority, established a new scheme of civic and ecclesiastical governance, and created a central hub from which Reformed theology was propagated.

John Knox (1513–1572). Scotsman who studied under John Calvin in Geneva; led the Parliament of Scotland to embrace the Reformation in 1560; father of the Protestant Reformation in Scotland and the Church of Scotland.

Francis Makemie (1658–1708). Organized the first presbytery in America and served as the convener of their organizational meeting. After the gathering of the Presbytery in 1706, Makemie went to New York, where he was arrested for leading worship illegally in a home. His incarceration and exoneration are often considered milestones in the process that led to religious freedom in America.

John Calvin, above left, was a prolific writer who produced a remarkable oeuvre of books, sermons, commentaries, and treatises. He also wrote many letters, including several to religious and political leaders. On July 4, 1552, in his letter to King Edward VI of England (a facsimile of which appears above right), he said, "It is a great thing to be a king...yet I have no doubt but that you esteem it incomparably better to be a Christian."

William Tennent Sr. (1673–1746). Founded the first Presbyterian institute of higher learning in New Jersey; this college would eventually become Princeton University.

Gilbert Tennent (1703–1764). Son of William Tennent Sr.; Irish-born American Presbyterian clergyman; founder of the theological school at Warminster, Pennsylvania called the Log College (the precursor to Princeton University); one of the leaders of the Great Awakening in colonial America.

John Witherspoon (1723–1794). Became the president of the College of New Jersey (later Princeton University) in 1768; also served in the Continental Congress for several terms; the only minister to sign the Declaration of Independence, which he did as a representative of New Jersey.

J. Gresham Machen (1881–1937). Founder of the Orthodox Presbyterian Church; led a conservative revolt against modernist society while teaching at Princeton University; formed the Westminster Theological Seminary as an orthodox alternative; one of the last "Princeton theologians"—the founders of the Princeton Theology, a conservative and Calvinist form of evangelical Christianity.

Carl McIntire (1906–2002). Fundamentalist radio preacher and founder of the Bible Presbyterian Church.

This portrait of clergyman John Witherspoon was painted by the American artist Rembrandt Peale after a 1794 original by his father, Charles Willson Peale.

II. Tenets and Beliefs

Presbyterianism has a strong emphasis on the sovereignty of God in all things, including human salvation, a high regard for the authority of the Scripture, and an emphasis on the necessity of personal conversion by grace through faith in Jesus Christ alone.

The Five Solas ("alones") of the Presbyterian church are: Scripture alone, faith alone, Christ alone, grace alone, glory to God alone.

According to PC(USA):

God is the supreme authority throughout the universe. Our knowledge of God and God's purpose for humanity comes from the Bible, particularly what is revealed in the New Testament through the life of Jesus Christ. Our salvation (justification) through Jesus is God's generous gift to us and not the result of our own accomplishments. It is everyone's job—ministers and lay people alike—to share this Good News with the whole world. That is also why the Presbyterian Church is governed at all levels by a combination of clergy and laity, men and women alike.

A. Articles of Faith

Some Presbyterian traditions adopt only the Westminster Confession of Faith as the doctrinal standard to which teaching elders are required to subscribe, in contrast to the larger and shorter catechisms, which are approved for use in instruction. Many denominations have adopted all of the Westminster Standards as their standard of doctrine, subordinate to the Bible. These documents are Calvinistic in their orientation, although some versions of the Confession and the catechisms are more overtly Calvinist than some other, later revisions.

The PC(USA) has adopted the **Book of Confessions**, which reflects the inclusion of other Reformed confessions in addition to the Westminster documents. These other documents include ancient creedal statements (the Nicene Creed, the Apostles' Creed), sixteenth-century Reformed confessions (the Scots Confession, the Heidelberg Catechism, and the Second Helvetic Confession, all of which were written before Calvinism had developed as a particular strand of Reformed doctrine), and twentieth-century documents (the Theological Declaration of Barmen and the Confession of 1967).

The **Westminster Confession of Faith** is a Reformed confession of faith, in the Calvinist theological tradition. It gives great prominence to the question of predestination and favors the infralapsarian ("after the fall") view of reprobation, which holds that God decreed election to salvation after the Fall, rather than before. It teaches the total depravity of fallen man and the exclusion of the non-elect from the benefits of Christ's atonement. In recent years, nearly all of the larger Presbyterian churches have officially disavowed the doctrines of total depravity and limited redemption. Some have even gone so far as to state a belief that all who die in infancy are saved.

The original Confession was altered many times since its conception in 1646. During 1787–1789, American Presbyterians revised the Confession and removed certain powers of the civil government over the church, which might be called theocratic principles. They also removed explicit identification of the pope as the Antichrist. In 1903, while the northern Presbyterian church (PCUSA) was separated from the southern church (PCUS), the PCUSA adopted revisions to the Confession that were intended to soften the church's commitment to Calvinism. In 1910, the PCUSA attempted to specify that a supernatural perspective is necessary and essential, according to the Bible and the Westminster Standards. This perspective was articulate in terms of five doctrinal issues: the divine inspiration and inerrancy of the Bible; the pre-existence, deity, and virgin birth of Jesus; the satisfaction of God's justice by the crucifixion of Christ; the resurrection, ascension, and intercession of Jesus; the reality of the miracles of Jesus.

The **Scots Confession of 1560** was written by John Knox, John Winram, John Spottiswoode, John Willock, John Douglas, and John Row. There are twenty-five chapters in the confession that spell out a contemporary statement of the Faith as understood by the followers of Calvin during his lifetime.

The **Heidelberg Catechism** is a document taking the form of a series of questions and answers, for use in teaching Reformed Christian doctrine. It was written in the sixteenth century by Zacharius Ursinus and Caspar Olevainus, who were appointed by the sovereign of Palentine, to be a Reformed catechism based on input from leading Reformed scholars of the time. It was approved in 1563 by the Synod of Heidelberg. In its current form, the Catechism consists of 129 questions and answers. They are divided into three main parts: "Of the misery of man"; "Of the redemption of man"; and "Of the gratitude due from man."

The **Confession of 1967** is a confessional standard or guide of the PC(USA) written as a modern statement of the faith of the then Northern Presbyterian Church (the United Presbyterian Church in the United States of America) to supplement the Westminster Confession and the other standards of faith in their Book of Confessions. The Confession is considered to be heavily influenced by modernism and the neo-Orthodox views of Karl Barth, the Niebuhr brothers, and other theologians of the age, especially regarding its view of Scripture.

The **Book of Order** describes the organization and functioning of the church at all levels. It is divided into three sections: Form of Government, The Directory for Worship, and The Rules of Discipline. The Form of Government describes the polity of the PC(USA), which is the adopted form of Presbyterian polity. The Directory for Worship includes the theological guidelines for worship within PC(USA) churches. In order to allow for a diversity of expression in worship, the Directory for Worship does not provide set orders for worship, but instead suggests the boundaries of worship that is in line with Reformed Christianity and the Scriptural warrants for worship. It is concerned more with standards and norms than any particular way or formulation of a liturgy or order of worship. The Rules of Discipline provide the standards for discipline within the church for matters that the secular judicial system does not address. The Rules of Discipline concerns itself with matters of preserving the purity of the church, achieving justice and compassion for all participants involved, correcting or restraining wrongdoing, upholding the dignity of those who have been harmed by disciplinary offenses, restoring the unity of the church by removing the causes of discord and division, and securing the just, speedy, and economical determination of proceedings.

The **Book of Confessions** outlines the beliefs of the PC(USA) by giving the creeds to which the Church adheres. It is the book of doctrinal statements of the church and is designated Part 1 of the Constitution. It consists of several ecumenical, Reformed, and modern statements of the Christian faith. None of them are required to be subscribed to point-by-point, and the newer confessions are said to take precedence over the older ones in points of conflict. Taken together, they as a body represent the official belief of the church.

B. Scripture

The Bible is considered sacred Scripture and is inspired by the Holy Spirit. The Bible is believed to contain all that is needed to be understood regarding how God has been present with humanity since the beginning of time and continues to be present today.

C. Secondary Sources

THEOLOGIANS, SCHOLARS, AND THINKERS

Samuel Davies (1723–1761). An itinerant preacher in Virginia, Davies constantly traveled by horseback to serve seven congregations scattered about the countryside. He became well known as an advocate of civil rights and religious liberties, and as one of the great pulpit orators of the eighteenth century. On July 26, 1759, Davies was elected fourth president of Princeton University, succeeding Jonathan Edwards. He died only eighteen months later of pneumonia.

Charles Hodge (1797–1878). Considered one of the greatest American apologists of the Calvinist theology in the nineteenth century, Hodge earned great distinction as a teacher, exegete, author, preacher, controversialist, and theologian. As principal of Princeton Theological Seminary between 1851 and 1878, he is credited with training almost 3,000 ministers. Hodge also wrote prolifically. He is most lauded for his 1835 work *Commentary on the Epistle to the Romans*, considered one of the most masterly commentaries on that work ever written.

Andrew Jackson (1767–1845). The seventh president of the United States, Andrew Jackson was the first Presbyterian president, but not the last. He was succeeded by seven other Presbyterians, the last of which was President Ronald Reagan.

Mark Twain (1835–1910). His birth name Samuel Langhorne Clemens, Twain gained much prominence as a humorist, satirist, and writer of works such as *The Adventures of Huckleberry Finn* and *The Adventures of Tom Sawyer*. Twain was raised as a Presbyterian, but was very critical of organized religion in later life.

David Brinkley (1920–2003). Brinkley was a popular American television newscaster from 1956–1997. He first co-anchored NBC's top-rated nightly news program *The Huntley–Brinkley Report*, renamed *NBC Nightly News* in 1970. In the latter part of his career, Brinkley hosted the Sunday morning program *This Week with David Brinkley*, and was a fixture on election nights on ABC News. Brinkley won ten Emmy Awards for his work, as well as a Presidential Medal of Freedom from President George W. Bush. Bush famously called him "the elder statesman of broadcast journalism." Brinkley was a practicing Presbyterian.

III. Rites and Rituals

A. The Calendar

Dates below are for a typical liturgical year.

January 1	New Year's Day
January 6	Epiphany of the Lord
January 13	Baptism of the Lord
January 18	Week of Prayer for Christian Unity begins
February 3	Transfiguration of the Lord
February 6	Ash Wednesday
February 10	First Sunday in Lent
February 17	Second Sunday in Lent
February 24	Third Sunday in Lent
March 2	Fourth Sunday in Lent
March 9	Fifth Sunday in Lent
March 16	Passion/Palm Sunday
March 17	Monday of Holy Week
March 18	Tuesday of Holy Week
March 19	Wednesday of Holy Week
March 20	Maundy Thursday
March 21	Good Friday
March 22	Great Vigil of Easter
March 23	Easter/Resurrection of the Lord
March 30	Second Sunday of Easter
April 6	Third Sunday of Easter
April 13	Fourth Sunday of Easter
April 20	Fifth Sunday of Easter
April 27	Sixth Sunday of Easter
May 1	Ascension of the Lord
May 1	National Day of Prayer
May 4	Seventh Sunday of Easter
May 11	Day of Pentecost
May 11	Pentecost Offering
May 18	Trinity Sunday
May 25	Presbyterian Heritage

September 21	International Peace Day
October 19	Children's Sabbath
October 26	Reformation Sunday
November 1	All Saints' Day
November 23	Christ the King/Reign of Christ
November 27	Thanksgiving Day
November 30	First Sunday of Advent
December 7	Second Sunday of Advent
December 14	Third Sunday of Advent
December 21	Fourth Sunday of Advent
December 21	Christmas Joy Offering
December 24	Christmas Eve
December 25	Nativity of Jesus Christ/ Christmas Day

B. Worship and Liturgy

The Session of the local congregation has a great deal of freedom in the style and ordering of worship in the PC(USA). Worship varies from congregation to congregation. The order may be very traditional and highly liturgical, or it may be very simple and informal. Many congregations offer a form of contemporary worship or emerging worship. It is very common to see churches use the Service for the Lord's Day.

The Directory of Worship in the *Book of Order* provides the rules for what must be, or may be included in worship. During the twentieth century, Presbyterians were offered optional use of liturgical books: *The Book of Common Worship* of 1906, *The Book of Common Worship* of 1932, *The Book of Common Worship* of 1946, *The Worship Book* of 1970, and *The Book of Common Worship* of 1993.

Services are generally characterized by extreme simplicity and consist of hymns, prayers, and readings from Scripture. In some churches instrumental music is not allowed, nor is the use of any other songs than those contained in the Book of Psalms. Many Presbyterians sing traditional hymns accom-panied by an organ. A number of ARP churches still sing psalms with no accompaniment.

Presbyterian worship services are characterized by the centrality of the Christian Scriptures. Bible readings and sermons that explain and apply its teachings are a central focus of each service. The Presbyterian Church (U.S.A.) arranges its services around five actions centered on the Bible: gathering around the word, proclaiming the word, responding to the word, the sealing of the word, and bearing and following the word into the world. Services also include prayer, music, the sacraments (the Lord's Supper and baptism), and an optional offering. In the PC(USA) the Session determines the order of worship.

Baptism is performed on infants and adults. Presbyterians disregard the Catholic notion of tran-substantiation and the Lutheran concept of consub-stantiation. Instead they view the Lord's Supper, or Communion, primarily as a memorial of Christ's death. Christ is present in the Lord's Supper not merely symbolically, nor substantially, but dynami-cally or effectively and for believers only. Communion is administered at stated intervals or on days appointed by the church officers.

C. Daily Life

The Reformed Presbyterian Church of North America (RPCNA) no longer prohibits alcohol use for all its members, but Chapter 26 of the RPCNA Testimony states that abstinence from alcohol is still a fitting choice for Christians.

D. Life Cycle Events

Birth

Infants are baptized in Presbyterian churches. "The Baptism of children witnesses to the truth that God's love claims people before they are able to respond in faith." Baptism is necessary to salvation not as a means, but only as something that has been commanded. Baptism can be celebrated among Presbyterians using modes of immersion, effusion, or sprinkling. Many Presbyterians continue to present their infants for baptism. Many others wait until their children are able to make personal professions of faith to receive a believer's baptism.

Confirmation

Hailing back to the earliest days of Christianity, adults who wished to follow the Christian faith were baptized to signify their conversion. Often, the rite included questioning by one or more of the apostles to glean the converted person's understanding of and dedication to Christ's teachings. Finally, an apostle would lay his hands on the baptized person in an act of "passing on the gift of the Holy Spirit": endowing the person with divine guidance. As time went on and the practice of baptizing infants became common, the laying on of hands was eliminated from the rite. It was conducted at a later date, when the child had grown to an age of spiritual awareness, and could more understandingly "confirm" the promise of his conversion as an infant. Bishops, regarded as successors of the apostles, now assumed the role of questioning and laying on of hands. This later ritual, distinguished from the baptism, became known as "confirmation."

In the PC(USA), it is understood that the endowment of the Holy Spirit is not dependent on the laying on of hands of a clergy person, but is carried out by God. Therefore, more emphasis is placed on the accruing of spiritual knowledge that precedes bestowment of the Holy Ghost. According to the church's Directory of Worship, the church nurtures those baptized as children and calls them to make public their personal profession of faith and their acceptance of responsibility in the life of the church. When these persons are ready, they shall be examined by the Session (G-10.0102b). After the Session has received them as active members, they shall be presented to the congregation during a service of public worship. In that service the church shall confirm them in their baptismal identity. They shall reaffirm the vows taken at baptism by:

a. professing their faith in Jesus Christ as Lord and Savior;
b. renouncing evil and affirming their reliance on God's grace;
c. declaring their intention to participate actively and responsibly in the worship and mission of the church.

They are commissioned for full participation in the mission and governance of the church, and are welcomed by the congregation.

Adolescents of the Presbyterian Church who are usually in their junior high school years attend classes on the theology, history, and role of their church. The pre-confirmation period may also include "retreats," or group withdrawals from ordinary activities, which are meant to foster spiritual reflection and a sense of communion among the teens. After examination by a session of church elders, during which the teens write a statement of faith, those students who are deemed "believers" and of sufficient religious understanding are welcomed into the church as adult members. They are consequently expected to carry on the ministry of the church, both locally and internationally.

Nuptials

Though each Presbyterian church has its own guidelines for the wedding ceremonies they hold, the order of service and various elements of the wedding reflect the stipulations proscribed by the *Book of Order*. In that book we find:

Marriage is a gift God has given to all humankind for the well being of the entire human family. Marriage is a civil contract between a woman and a man. For Christians, marriage is a covenant through which a man and a woman are called to live out together, before God, their lives of discipleship. In a service of Christian marriage a lifelong commitment is made by a woman and a man to each other, publicly witnessed and acknowledged by the community of faith (W-4.9001).

Often, a church will only marry couples in which one person is either a member of the church, or related to a member of the church. Usually, the pastor will meet with the engaged couple for one or more consultations before agreeing to marry them. The *Book of Order* states that a pastor may decline to officiate at a wedding where he "is convinced after discussion with the couple that commitment, responsibility, maturity, or Christian understanding are so lacking that the marriage is unwise."

Though each couple may plan their own order of service for the wedding in collaboration with the pastor, a typical order for a service may include the entrance of the family, pastor, groom, groomsmen and bridesmaids into the sanctuary; the processional of the bride; greeting and call to worship by the pastor; a hymn; a short sermon on the meaning of Christian marriage; prayer; vows; exchange of rings; dedicatory prayer; declaration of marriage, exchange of a kiss; benediction; recessional.

The Sacrament of the Lord's Supper may or may not be celebrated during the ceremony. Should it be conducted, its significance must be made clear during the ceremony, and the whole congregation must be invited to receive Communion. Prior approval by the church's governing body is required for wedding ceremonies to include the celebration of the Sacrament.

According to The *Book of Order,* "Music suitable for the marriage service directs attention to God and expresses the faith of the church" (W-4.9005). Usually, music selections must be chosen in advance and in consultation with the pastor. Flowers and decorations also should "enhance the worshipper's consciousness of the reality of God, and reflect integrity and simplicity of Christian life."

Some Presbyterian churches refuse to marry homosexual couples; others are willing to do so.

∽

The following section compares various groups and denominations of the Presbyterian Church with respect to issues of practice, worship, and daily life.

IV. Denominations and Demographics

A. Organization and Distribution

Most presbyteries center in metropolitan communities and draw surrounding country churches into their urban spheres.

The largest Presbyterian denomination in the United States is the Presbyterian Church (USA) PC(USA). The PC(USA) has 2.3 million members, about 10,900 congregations, and 14,000 ordained ministers. Its national offices are in Louisville, Kentucky.

The Presbyterian Church in America (PCA) is the second largest Presbyterian denomination in the United States. It has about 330,000 members and 1,600 congregations. The PCA has its greatest concentration in the states of the Deep South, with more scattered strength in the South Atlantic, the upper Ohio Valley, and the Southwest. The church maintains headquarters in Atlanta, Georgia.

The Orthodox Presbyterian Church (OPC) currently operates 255 churches and 63 missions in the United States. There are 27,990 members, of whom there are 449 ministers, 19,968 communicants, and 7,573 baptized members. The denominational headquarters is located in Willow Grove, Pennsylvania.

The Evangelical Presbyterian Church (EPC) has about 70,000 active members in 180 churches that can be found in 29 states. The Office of the General Assembly is located in Livonia, Michigan.

The Associate Reformed Presbyterian Church (ARPC) contains more than 200 churches in 10 presbyteries and has over 30,000 members. The denominational office is located in Greenville, South Carolina. There is also a denominational conference center, Bonclarken, in Flat Rock, North Carolina. There are churches in most states and Canada, but ARPC congregations are found mainly in Georgia, North Carolina, and South Carolina.

The Reformed Presbyterian Church of North America (RPCNA) has congregations in twenty states and two Canadian provinces. It has about 6,200 members and 71 congregations. Its "stronghold" areas are in northeastern Kansas, central Indiana, and western Pennsylvania.

The Cumberland Presbyterian Church (CPC) has about 86,000 members and 544 congregations in the United States, most of which are located in the southern and western states. The Cumberland Presbyterian Center is located in Memphis, Tennessee, and houses church boards and agencies.

The Reformed Presbyterian Church in the United States (RPCUS) has 74 churches in the United States.

B. Comparisons in Tenets and Practices

Some of the splits that have occurred in the history of the Presbyterian Church have been due to doctrinal controversy between the more liberal and the more conservative members. Some have also been caused by disagreement concerning the degree to which those ordained to church office should be required to agree with the Calvinist Westminster Confession of Faith, which historically serves as the main confessional document of Presbyterian churches. Those groups that adhere to the document most strictly are typified by baptism of the infant children of believers, a common Communion cup, limiting eligibility for ordination to the offices of pastor of elder to men only, and a fully Calvinist doctrine of salvation.

Women may be ordained to the ministry in the PC(USA) and the CPC. The CPC was the first Presbyterian denomination to ordain female clergy when they ordained Louisa Mariah Layman Woosely as a minister in 1889.

The conservative Presbyterian denominations believe in the inerrancy and infallibility of the Bible. Some, like the PCA, adhere closely to TULIP: total depravity, unconditional election, limited atonement, irresistible grace, and perseverance of the saints. The conservative churches are the ARP, EPC, OPC, PCA, RPCUS, RPCNA, and the BPC.

The ARP does not ordain women as ministers or elders, but does permit female deacons.

The RPCNA follows the Regulative Principle of Worship and requires a cappella singing of Psalms only in worship. The church also interprets the Bible as requiring all elders to be male, but deacons may be either male or female. Deaconesses have been permitted since 1888.

The BPC believes Christians should abstain completely from alcohol. They also use the Scofield Reference Bible which teaches the theological system called Dispensationalism rather than Covenant Theology, which is the historic theology of Reformed churches. The BPC has always maintained the unity of the Covenant of Grace (a nondispensational position) and has passed resolutions against dispensationalism at annual meetings. Bible Presbyterians do not have synod-controlled boards for missions and education, but annually approve independent agencies for mission work as well as colleges and seminaries.

The EPC allows individual churches and believers to decide on "nonessentials" such as worship styles, spiritual gifts and ordination of women. The denomination declares all Scripture to be "self-attesting and Truth," requiring our unreserved submission in all areas of life. They deem the sixty-six books of the Old and New Testaments the infallible Word of God, a complete and unified witness to God's redemptive acts culminating in the incarnation of the Living Word, the Lord Jesus Christ. The Bible, uniquely and fully inspired by the Holy Spirit, is the supreme and final authority on all matters on which it speaks. From this, the EPC derives their "essentials of faith," seven doctrinal points.

The PCA professes a strong commitment to evangelism, missionary work, and Christian education. The church declares its goal to be "faithful to the Scriptures, true to the reformed faith, and obedient to the Great Commission." The PCA is generally less conservative than the OPC and more conservative than the EPC. Some churches within the

PCA allow women to do what a nonordained man can do, such as teaching co-educational Sunday school classes. The more liberal denominations are the PC(USA), which contains the majority of all Presbyterians in America, and the CPC.

V. Organization and Infrastructure

A. Education and Hierarchy of Clergy

Presbyterians place great importance on education and continuous study of the scriptures and theological writings, and understanding and interpreting church doctrine embodied in several statements of faith and catechisms formally adopted by various branches of the church. The point of such learning, Presbyterians believe, is to enable one to put one's faith into practice; Presbyterians endeavor to exhibit their faith in action as well as words, by generosity, hospitality, and the constant pursuit of social justice and reform, as well as proclaiming the gospel of Christ.

Presbyterians have historically sought a thorough education for their clergy, especially as an article of faith. In fact, most considered literacy of all people important for human accountability to the demands of the Gospel as set forth in Scripture. The proclamation of the Gospel and its application to contemporary life demanded knowledge of God, knowledge of the languages in which the writers of Scripture had worked, knowledge of church history, and knowledge of the world in all its complexity. The Presbyterian "log colleges" prepared ministers for the American milieu by encouraging them to begin new congregations and to evangelize the un-churched.

The church offices are: pastor, elder, and deacon. All officers are elected by the congregation and the election of the pastor is also subject to the approval of the presbytery. The elders with the pastor as pre-

siding officer form the session which supervises the spiritual affairs of the congregation. Elders are both elected and ordained. An elder remains ordained after his or her term is complete. The Book of Order describes the job of an elder this way:

"Together with ministers of the Word and Sacrament, they exercise leadership, government, and discipline and have responsibilities for the life of a particular church as well as the church at large, including ecumenical relationships."

Teaching elders (pastors) have responsibility for teaching, worship, and performing sacraments. Pastors are called by individual congregations. A congregation issues a call for the pastor's service, but this call must be ratified by the presbytery. The deacons have charge of certain temporalities and are responsible to the session.

Women may be ordained to the ministry in many Presbyterian churches, but not all. They may be ordained in the PC(USA), but not in the Presbyterian Church in America or the Reformed Churches of the United States.

SEMINARIES AND COLLEGES

Alma College (Alma, Michigan)
Austin Presbyterian Theological Seminary (Austin, Texas) (PC[USA])
Auburn Theological Seminary (New York, New York) (PC[USA])
Bahnsen Theological Seminary (California)
Belhaven College (Mississippi) Bethel College (McKenzie, Tennessee) (CPC)
Columbia Theological Seminary (Decatur, Georgia) (PC[USA])
Covenant College (Lookout Mountain, Georgia) (PCA)
Covenant Theological Seminary (St. Louis, Missouri) (PCA)
Dubuque Theological Seminary (Iowa)
Erskine College (Due West, South Carolina) (ARP)
Erskine Theological Seminary (Due West, South Carolina) (ARP)

Evangelical Seminary of Puerto Rico (San Juan, Puerto Rico) (PC[USA])

Faith College of the Bible (BPC)

Geneva College (Beaver Falls, Pennsylvania) (RPCNA)

Greenville Presbyterian Theological Seminary (South Carolina)

Hampden-Sydney College (Virginia)

Johnson C. Smith Theological Seminary at the Interdenominational Theological Center (Atlanta, GA) (PC[USA])

Louisville Presbyterian Theological Seminary (Louisville, Kentucky) (PC[USA])

McCormick Theological Seminary (Chicago, Illinois) (PC[USA])

Memphis Theological Seminary (Memphis, Tennessee) (CPC)

Mid-America Reformed Seminary (Indiana)

Montreat College (Asheville, North Carolina)

New Geneva Theological Seminary (Colorado Springs, Colorado)

Northwest Theological Seminary (Lynnwood, Washington)

Pittsburgh Theological Seminary (Pittsburgh, Pennsylvania) (PC[USA])

Princeton Theological Seminary (Princeton, New Jersey) (PC[USA])

Reformed Presbyterian Theological Seminary (Pittsburgh, Pennsylvania) (RPCNA)

Reformed Theological Seminary (campuses across southern U.S.)

San Francisco Theological Seminary (San Anselmo, CA) (PC[USA])

Schreiner University (Texas)

Union Theological Seminary and Presbyterian School of Christian Education (Richmond, Virginia, and Charlotte, North Carolina) (PC[USA])

University of Dubuque Theological Seminary (Dubuque, Iowa) (PC[USA])

University of Tulsa (Oklahoma)

Westminster Theological Seminary (Philadelphia, Pennsylvania)

Westminster Seminary California

Western Reformed Seminary (Tacoma, Washington) (BPC)

Whitefield Theological Seminary (Florida)

Union Theological Seminary

Union Theological Seminary, founded in 1836 by a group of New School Presbyterians, is an independent multi-denominational seminary devoted to instilling in its students a critical understanding of the wide variety of Christian traditions, as well as finding insight from other faiths. Its location in New York City, near Columbia University, and across the street from Jewish Theological Seminary, reflects the founders' belief that training ministers in an urban context will help them better respond to the needs of the city.

The Union Theological Seminary in New York City is seen from above in this 1910 photograph.

B. Shrines and Houses of Worship

National Presbyterian Church
4101 Nebraska Avenue NW
Washington, D.C. 20016
202-537-0800
www.nationalpres.org

The National Presbyterian Church in Washington, D.C., has a history that spans four congregations since 1795, and is a traditional mainline church of the Reformed faith.

Fourth Presbyterian Church

126 East Chestnut Street
Chicago, IL 60611
312-787-4570
www.fourthchurch.org

Today, Fourth Church claims more than 5,700 members, and up to 2,000 people attend each Sunday service. The church was designed by Ralph Adam Cram, American's leading Gothic revival architect of the early twentieth century. Cram is most famously known for his work on the Cathedral of St. John the Divine in New York City—the world's largest Gothic cathedral.

The cornerstone of Fourth Church was laid in 1912, and the building dedicated in 1914. Its original interior and exterior have been preserved over the last near century. Cram stated that Fourth Church is not a "copy" of any one building, but instead combines what he saw as the best of English Gothic and French Gothic styles.

As part of their mission statement, the Fourth Presbyterian Church in Chicago affirms, "We are a light in the city reflecting the inclusive love of God."

Madison Avenue Presbyterian Church

921 Madison Avenue   (at East 73rd Street)
New York, NY 10021
212-288-8920   Fax: 212-249-1466
www.mapc.com

The predecessor of the present-day Madison Avenue Presbyterian Church, established in 1834, was dubbed "the church in the swamp" because of its location near the Lower East Side shipyards. Formally designated the Manhattan Island Presbyterian Church, the small congregation was not to last. However, in 1838 several of its members united with a contingent from the old Seventh Presbyterian Church to form the Eleventh Presbyterian Church of the City of New York. Eleventh church sustained quite the colorful history. During the Mexican War era, members locked horns over the introduction of organ music to services, which was considered by some a dangerous theatrical diversion. In the period of the Civil War, one member was brought up on charges by the governing body for reading Sunday newspapers, as well as for objecting to legal penalties for not attending church services. But all the while, the church was growing. In search of a larger venue, in 1864, the church moved to 55th Street between Lexington and Third Avenues (becoming the Memorial Presbyterian Church), then moved to Madison Avenue and 53rd Street, where it became the Madison Avenue Presbyterian Church. It would move one last time, in 1899, uniting with another congregation called Phillips Church, and a new structure was built to accommodate both congregations on its present site.

The Cathedral of Hope

PO Box 35466

5910 Cedar Springs Road

Dallas, TX 75235

214-351-1901 or 800-501-HOPE

www.cathedralofhope.com

Another work of architect Ralph Adams Cram, this church was built in the European Gothic style. Cram was given freedom by those who hired his services to build the grandest structure he could, and he felt he achieved it. Cram said, "Of all the cathedrals and churches I have built this is my masterpiece. This church has been the most profound spiritual experience of my life." At a construction cost of approximately $4 million, the building occupies an entire city block. Groundwork was commenced August 18, 1931. Construction concluded on May 12, 1935.

Bel Air Presbyterian Church

16221 Mulholland Drive

Los Angeles, CA 90049

818-788-4200

www.belairpres.org

Construction of a church in the mountain town of Bel Air, California, required seven months of rock

One of the former pastors of the Bel Air Presbyterian Church in Los Angeles, Donn Moomaw—who served from 1964 to 1993—gave the invocation and benediction at Ronald Reagan's 1981 inauguration. The church appears above in a 2008 photograph.

blasting and grading before the foundation could be laid. Such work began in October 1956. Four years later, the award-winning chapel opened its doors for services. On January 17, 1994, a 6.8 magnitude earthquake caused extensive damage to the church. Repair work commenced and, over a two-year period, restored the church's original unique beauty.

C. Governance and Authority

Presbyterian churches use a representational form of Church government in which authority is given to elected laypersons known as elders. The word "presbyterian" comes from the Greek word for "elder." Teaching and ruling elders are ordained and convene as a "Kirk Session," commonly referred to as simply Session, and are responsible for the discipline, nurture, and mission of the local congregation. Sessions are charged with representing the members of the congregation as well as "discovering and representing the will of Christ as they govern."

Several sessions constitute a presbytery, several presbyteries form a synod, and the General Assembly encompasses the entire denomination. Some churches, such as the PCA, do not have synods as part of their governing schema.

D. Social Service Organizations

The PC(USA) has a variety of mission outreach programs and social service organizations, including youth ministries; young adult ministries; women's ministries; men's ministries; older adult ministries; the Hunger Program; family and intergenerational ministries; urban ministries; the Rural Ministry Network; National Health Ministries; Presbyterian Disaster Services—helping Lebanon, Pakistan, Sudan, Northeast flood regions, and areas hit by U.S. hurricanes Katrina, Rita, and Wilma, and by tsunamis.

Presbyterian Church (USA) Foundation

200 East Twelfth Street

Jefferson, IN 47130

800-858-6127   Fax: 502-569-5980

The PC(USA) Foundation serves as a fiduciary for church-related trusts and endowments. It also invests and administers gifts, and distributes proceeds according to the direction of trust founders.

The Presbyterian Church (U.S.A.) is a partner in the Campaign for Children's Health Care, a multi-year campaign to raise awareness about the problem of uninsured children in America.

Reformed Presbyterian Home

22344 Perrysville Avenue

Pittsburgh, PA 15214

412-321-4139 or 800-RP-HELLO

Fax: 412-321-4661   rphome@rphome.org

The RPCNA runs the Reformed Presbyterian Home in Pittsburgh, Pennsylvania, a nonprofit institution that provides nursing care and residential living to elderly persons. It was established in 1897 to serve the aging members of the community.

The ARP's Board of Benefits provides opportunities for meaningful security to individuals and families in the areas of benevolence, insurance, and retirement. The ARP also runs the William H. Dunlap Orphanage.

William H. Dunlop Orphanage, Inc.

Associate Reformed Presbyterian Center

1 Cleveland Street, Suite 110

Greenville, SC 29601

www.arpsynod.org/wmhdunlap.html

The CPC's Board of Missions lists a variety of Christian Service Ministry Opportunities every year. The listings vary from opportunities for volunteer translators to GROUP, an interdenominational organization offering service opportunities for youth and the leaders of youth.

E. Media and Communication

Crown and Covenant

7408 Penn Avenue

Pittsburgh, PA 15208

www.crownandcovenant.com

The RPCNA publishes the *Reformed Presbyterian Witness,* a monthly magazine. Crown and Covenant Publications is the publishing house of the Board of Education and Publication. It promotes, encourages, and defends the Reformed faith and testimony of the denomination.

The Associate Reformed Presbyterian Church publishes *The ARP*, a monthly periodical, and maintain the electronic ARP News Update.

Christian Education and Publications

1700 North Brown Road, Suite 102

Lawrenceville, GA 30043

678-825-1100   Fax: 678-825-1101

cep@pcanet.org

The PCA publishes its own magazine, *By Faith* (www.byfaithonline.com). *Equip for Ministry* is a bimonthly periodical of the Christian Education and Publications branch of the PCA.

Great Commissions Publications

3640 Windsor Park Drive

Suwanee, GA 30024

770-831-9084 or 800-695-3387

Fax: 770-271-5657   www.gcp.org

Great Commissions Publications (GCP) is the joint publishing arm of the OPC and the PCA. It releases a full line of biblically faithful Sunday school curricula, adult Bible studies, the *Trinity Hymnal*, along with other products.

The OPC maintains a website at www.opc.org., which offers audio sermons and publications of the OPC. The Committee on Christian Education publishes the *Book of Church Order* and *The Confession of Faith and Catechisms with Proof Texts*. The OPC historian has released a number of historical books that keep alive the story of the denomination. *New*

Horizons and *Ordained Servant* are monthly and bi-monthly OPC periodicals, respectively, available online.

The Bible Presbyterian Church maintains its website at www.bpc.org. *The Christian Observer* is the official record of the BPC; the website is www.christianobserver.org. *Presbyterians Week* is an electronic summary of news of the Presbyterian community, published weekly by the *Christian Observer.*

The CPC publishes *The Cumberland Presbyterian,* a monthly magazine that serves to disseminate the news of the Cumberland Presbyterian Church to promote its faith, programs, and activities, and to provide open discussion of theological and denominational issues. *The Missionary Messenger* is a free bi-monthly periodical also produced by the CPC.

EPC publishes the *EPC Children's Ministries Network*, which serves as a forum for idea sharing among EPC Children's Ministries leaders.

Presbyterian Publishing Corporation (PPC)
100 Witherspoon Street
Louisville, KY 40202-1396
800-672-1789   Fax: 800-541-5113
cokes_serv@cokesbury.com
www.ppcbooks.com

PPC—PC(USA)'s publishing arm—publishes periodicals: *Call to Worship, Church and Society, Horizons, Hungryhearts News, Ideas! For Church Leaders, Mission Yearbook for Prayer and Study, Children's Mission Yearbook for Prayer and Study, OGA Perspective,* and *Presbyterians Today*; and editions of the *Book of Order,* the *Book of Confessions,* and the *Annual Report to the Church.* The PC(USA) website has many resources, including: the *Book of Order,* the *Book of Confessions, Daily Devotions, Social Witness Policy Compilation,* and a directory of websites for ministry with gay, lesbian, bisexual, and transgendered persons. The PC(USA) has also made available a variety of multimedia resources online, including the "Here and Now" Campaign to raise awareness of PC(USA) among eighteen to twenty-five-year-olds.

PCA Historical Center
12330 Conway Road
St. Louis, MO 63141
314-469-9077
www.pcahistory.org

A remarkably rich resource on matters pertaining to Presbyterian history in the U.S. and abroad.

FURTHER READING

The Presbyterians
Randall Balmer and John R. Fitzmier
1994: Praeger

Presbyterian Beliefs: A Brief Introduction
Donald K. McKim
2003: Geneva Press

A Brief History of the Presbyterians
James H. Smylie
1996: Westminster/John Knox

13 Quakers

I. Origins and Early History

A. Introduction

THE HISTORY OF THE GROUP POPULARLY KNOWN as the Quakers (but self-referred to as the Religious Society of Friends) began in 1643 when a serious and soul-searching young man by the name of George Fox set off on foot across England seeking spiritual truth. The son of an Anglican weaver from Leicester, England, Fox's Puritan upbringing left him spiritually uninspired, and at the age of nineteen a deep disillusionment overtook him. He left home in search of those who shared his dissatisfaction with existent Puritan sects—usually called Seekers.

Mid-seventeenth-century England roiled with numerous movements to purify the Anglican church of its "popish" trappings. Subsequent to King Charles I's defeat in the English Civil War (1642–1646), Puritans gained political and social control of the country, and used their newly won freedom of religious practice to promptly splinter into a variety of Presbyterian, Congregationalist, and Baptist groups. The teachings of John Calvin fundamentally united these groups. However, additional sects followed a more radical bent—deigning to find their own spiritual understanding through direct guidance from the Holy Spirit. It was these roaming Seekers that young Fox would ultimately unite.

Striking out in 1643, Fox sought out prominent Seekers and began "declaring Truth." This was often carried out in the middle of Protestant church services, when Fox would stand up and denounce the preacher, challenging him to debate. Such behavior was not long tolerated, and from 1650 to 1651, Fox was imprisoned for public disturbance and blasphemy. Those who chose to follow Fox were known as Friends of Truth or Children of Light—referring to the light, or inspiration, of the "inner Christ." Quakers believed that all manner of humanity was receptive to such revelation. This stood in

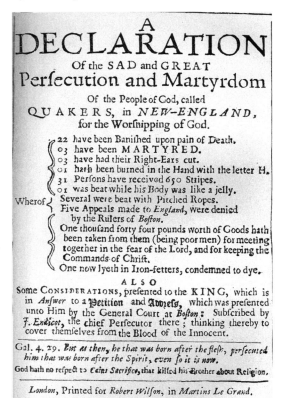

Quakers were persecuted in Europe and in the New World as well. Edward Burrough describes the events Quakers endured in New England in his 1661 book. Above is its title page.

direct opposition to Calvinistic beliefs that only a predestined elect could experience salvation.

The Quakers experience, above all, called for a strict demarcation between "inward" and "outward" forms of religion, with everything "outward" being viewed with suspicion.

Even Jesus's legacy as a physical man who had died on the cross should not be focused on so much as his unprecedented indwelling of the Holy Spirit. Other outward forms to be discarded were the Bible, theological creeds, clergy, and ecclesiastical sacraments. "Carnal" knowledge was contrasted with "inward" or "spiritual" knowledge, resulting in a spiritual-physical dualism. Quakers believed that it was only when one silenced all human thoughts, desires, and activities that Christ could be heard. Thus, meetings were largely characterized by long periods of silence, sporadically interrupted by utterances of members who felt led by God to speak. When under the influence of the Spirit, the speaker would tremble and quake, therein earning the sect their name.

Fox attributed the development of his reliance on the Spirit alone to his utter dissatisfaction with the human, or outward, religious experience:

"But as I had forsaken all the priests, so I left the separate preachers also, and those called the most experienced people; for I saw that there was none among them that could speak to my condition. And when all my hopes in men were gone, so that I had nothing outwardly to help me, nor could I tell what to do, then, oh then, I heard a voice which said, 'There is one, even Christ Jesus, that can speak to thy condition'".

There can be no doubt that Fox's vision of a radical turn to inward spirituality would have had little appeal and remained a minor movement had it not been for the historical events that surrounded it.

Following the Puritan Revolution of 1642 came a decades-long experiment in bloodletting and strife that led to the eventual restoration of the monarchy and the absolutism epitomized by the bleak political theory of Thomas Hobbes. Fox seemed to offer a third way that was neither monarchical nor revolu-

Of George Fox (1624–1691), right, the founder of the Religious Society of Friends, poet Walt Whitman wrote: "Fox stands for something too—a thought—the thought that wakes in silent hours— perhaps the deepest, most eternal thought latent in the human soul. This is the thought of God, merged in the thoughts of moral right and the immortality of identity."

tionary, that repudiated Puritan forms as well as those of the high church. The war that Fox preached was not the revolution of Oliver Cromwell, but what he called the Lamb's War, an inward conquest of the impure elements of the human soul. Religious wars, according to Fox, were not to be fought outwardly with swords and arrows, but inwardly through sitting in silence and "waiting upon the Lord"—a practice which liberal twentieth-century Quakers have come to identify with meditation.

This attitude ultimately led to the best known and most central tenet of the Quaker faith: the Quaker Peace Testimony. Although Cromwell, along with the parliamentary government, was never fond of the Friends and frequently accused them of being spies, the King held even less esteem for them, considering them to be religious dissidents. Yet, in the face of what was to become a general persecution, the Quakers released a document known as the Quaker Peace Testimony in which they declared all wars unchristian, and made it clear that they had neither fought for or against Cromwell and would not participate in any plot to overthrow the new king.

This did not appease the restoration government; it demanded loyalty oaths and was scarcely prepared to accept that the will of God did not completely authorize the monarchy. Moreover, although the Quakers called themselves an "unwarlike people," they rejected such common social conventions as swearing oaths, removing one's hat when addressing one's social betters, and used the formal mode of speech ("thou" instead of "you").

Each of these small factors led to the continual imprisonment of individual Quakers, including Fox, who served on repeated charges of contempt of court. Two acts of Parliament were enacted in an attempt to stifle disturbances caused by the Friends. The Quaker Act of 1662 banned the option to refrain from taking the Oath of Allegiance, and prohibited religious gatherings not authorized by the Anglican Church. The Conventicle Act of 1664 more rigorously instated the latter prohibition. These new restrictions led many Quakers to choose to emigrate to the New World.

The role of women in early Quakerism was unparalleled in any religious movement of the time and, after George Fox, one of the most influential leaders of the early Quakers was the woman who eventually became Fox's wife, Margaret Fell. Thus it is perhaps unsurprising that the first Quaker missionary to set foot in the New World was a woman, Elizabeth Harris, who arrived in America in 1652.

It was believed that the Spirit communicated indiscriminately through man, woman, or child; therefore, women spoke freely at meetings. However, this is not meant to imply that women were granted special rights of equality outside of the religious sphere. They were still regarded as the "weaker sex" and were expected to subordinate themselves to their husbands.

B. Quakers in America

Numerous other Quakers followed Harris, and George Fox himself visited colonial America between 1671 and 1673. But the Quaker pursuit of religious freedom was not initially more fruitful in the New World, as Quakers heterodoxy challenged the high hopes that Puritan colonists set for themselves of establishing bastions of religious unanimity and purity. The claims that the Quakers made about the "inner light" and that human teachers or authorities in religious matters are unnecessary often struck Puritans as a defense of religious anarchy, leading to

the banishment of Quakers from the colonies of Virginia and Massachusetts. The Friends fared better in outlying areas like Rhode Island, the first colony in the Americas to codify freedom of religion into law. Fox himself was challenged to a theological debate by Rhode Island founder Roger Williams. The contentious Fox accepted, and a three-day theological battle ensued in Newport, with the event concluding a week later in Providence. Both sides believed they had won, but the event certainly gave the Quakers a firmer footing in Rhode Island, especially after the "Cart and Whip" Act of 1661 allowed Massachusetts to ship unwanted Friends to Rhode island. By 1670, Quakers had achieved a majority in the General Assembly.

The overall status of the Quakers in America took a profound turn for the better with the land grant of 1681 to an influential Quaker convert by the name of William Penn. King Charles II owed a large debt to Penn's Anglican father, and, on the father's death, this charter became a means of settling accounts. Pennsylvania became the first Quaker colony, and thousands of Quakers had emigrated to the colony by the time of Penn's death in 1718. The colony, although at least partially a moneymaking venture by Penn, sought to embody the Quaker values of pacifism, freedom of conscience (Penn himself once went as far as shrugging off the charges of witchcraft brought against a woman), and consensus. The Quaker penchant for peacemaking led to good relations with the Native American populations, and the new colony avoided war for most of its early history.

Quakerism and Politics

On the whole, the Quakers were opposed to the American Revolutionary War, and only one of the men who signed the Declaration of Independence in 1776 had any Quaker ties—though he was later disowned by the Friends for buying a slave. The reasons for this fact lay once again in the Quaker dichotomy between the inward and the outward. Government as an outward form was to be left alone as a God-ordained means of restraining evil. Although it was permissible, and even highly encouraged, for Friends to raise a voice against injustice, participation in armed strife would result in expulsion from one's meeting. Given that the beginnings of Quakerism lay in civil war, the Quaker struggle for peace was widely seen as incompatible with taking the revolutionary side of this new battle. Thus, Quakers were sometimes jailed as loyalists, and some were even considered to have aided the forces of the crown.

For the Friends, the period from the death of George Fox in 1691 to the first steps of the U.S. abolitionist movement can be thought of as one long embrace of quietism. The inward turn during this period came to signify a radical disengagement with politics. Thus, while early Quakers refused to take sides in the English Civil War, they nonetheless were active in preaching against it and later in arguing for prison reform and religious tolerance. During this period, Quakers became more cautious and less committed to the political issues of the time.

The renewal of Quaker political engagement came with the rise of the abolitionism. John Woolman (1720–1772) was an important figure in shaping Quaker views on slavery. Woolman, at the age of twenty-three, had been asked to write up a bill of sale for a slave and yet could not conscionably bring himself do it. After that event, he became an itinerant preacher who traveled through the colonies speaking out against slavery. Woolman eventually authored two important works, "Some Considerations on Keeping Negros" (1753) an antislavery pamphlet, and *The Journal of John Woolman*, a book that has been seen as an important American spiritual classic. Although many influential men and women would come to oppose slavery on Christian grounds, no other major group of Christians committed themselves to opposing slavery as a body at such an early date. During the period from 1758 to 1784, every meeting of the Friends in America voted to ban slave holding by its membership.

Hicksites vs Gurneyites

This relative unanimity on the question of slavery, however, did not protect the Quakers from experiencing internal difficulties over this new turn toward politics.

Perhaps the history of Quakerism in America can best be viewed as a reflection of the dichotomy between the ideal of an inwardly focused spirituality of peace and equality and the desire to bring this ideal to the world at large. In and of itself this represents a paradox: When does the search for self perfection need to become a struggle to perfect the world around one?

The most influential figures in the Quaker world during the nineteenth century answered this question in different ways, leading to the first major splits in the Quaker organization. The important question centered around whether Quakers needed to blend in with their Christian neighbors, to stand aloof from them, or to offer a radical social critique particularly around questions of the equality of women, slavery, and rights for Native Americans. Quakers who felt that Quakerism was only one of the Christian denominations followed Joseph John Gurney, an educated British preacher who toured in America, and adjusted many of the traditional Quaker practices to bring them more in line with those of other Protestant denominations.

Other Quakers followed Elias Hicks, a prominent Long Island "recorded" minister (so-called because they were recognized for their inspired speech at monthly meetings). Followers of Hicks came to be known as the Hicksite Quakers. They described themselves as "liberals" and considered themselves closer to the Unitarians than to mainstream Christians. Some Hicksite Quakers, such as the feminist preacher Lucretia Mott (1793–1880), offered radical critiques of the doctrine of the Trinity, and Elias Hicks himself preached that Jesus had not been born the Christ, but had become God through the discovery of the light within. These Quakers in particular saw themselves as standing against the culture at large, fighting against slavery and for the rights of women. Lucretia Mott was a founding member of the American Anti-Slavery Society, and in 1848 she organized the first women's rights convention in the U.S. with several other Quaker women.

The Hicksites remained true to quietism: emphasizing silent meetings, quieting fleshly impulses, devotion to the inward Christ, and the peculiar dress and speech of early Quakerism. Many quietists found a commonality with the Enlightenment concept of Reason, in which they recognized parallels with their own concept of "inner light."

Gurney's followers, on the other hand, reflected the influence of the Second Great Awakening of nineteenth-century America, initiated by Charles Grandison Finney. Thoroughly educated at Oxford University, Gurney introduced to Quakerism critical study of the Bible. It should be remembered that early Quakers rejected the Scriptures as an "outward" form of worship. Gurney changed that with his assertion that the Bible should be considered the doctrinal authority. Furthermore, Gurney urged Quakers to focus more intensely than previously deemed appropriate upon the atonement of Jesus Christ, which, he claimed, was responsible for reckoning Christians to God. Finally, he overturned the Quaker notion that their sect held primacy among Christians, and himself engaged in a traveling ministerial tour much like those of Finney. Urban Friends found Gurney's innovations appealing, distinguishing themselves as Orthodox Friends from liberal Hicksites—mainly those in rural areas who retained their observance of quietism.

Quakerism and Civil Rights

During the American Civil War, Quakers remained officially committed to pacifism even as many Friends personally saw the fight to end slavery as a cause worthy of taking up arms. The American Civil War is the only American war in which a large number of Quakers chose to fight, and many meetings that had traditionally banned members who sought to go to war, quietly overlooked the fact that some of their young men fought in the Union army. Quakers of all forms were overwhelmingly pro-

This photograph of suffragist Susan B. Anthony (1820–1906) was taken by Frances Benjamin Johnston some time after 1890.

Union, so much so that southern Quakers found themselves, as it were, behind enemy lines.

At the close of the nineteenth century many Quakers remained committed to working for the rights of former slaves even as the well-known Quaker Susan B. Anthony (1820–1906–*shown above*) fought for women's right to vote. Anthony co-founded the National Women's Suffrage Association (NWSA) in 1869, influential in the passage of the Nineteenth Amendment in 1920.

Although Quakers would shrink as a proportion of the population during the twentieth century, it was during this period that Friends saw the first two Quaker presidents sworn into office: Hoover in 1929 and Nixon in 1969. The history of twentieth century Quakerism is, in many ways, parallel to that of mainline Protestant denominations in America. As with other denominations, the culture wars over women's rights, civil rights, and gay rights have been seminal in shaping the stances of the group. So, too, has been the rise of biblical literalism and fundamentalism and the Vietnam War. Quaker history differs from the history of these denominations only in the strength and radicalism of its liberal wing. While Quakers who followed Gurney's path eventually came to embrace the evangelical movement, the liberal Quakers put more and more faith in the "inner light" and inward spirituality, so much so that many today no longer consider Quakerism Christian and

call the Bible one inspired book among many at best and uninspired and patriarchal at worst.

Through the nonprofit organization the American Friends Service Committee (AFSC) the Quakers have been at the forefront of antiwar demonstrations since WWI, offering soldiers and other Americans strategies for avoiding the draft and obtaining conscientious objector status. The organization also played an instrumental role in the American civil rights movement through printing pamphlets and organizing marches. The Quaker emphasis on pacifism and nonviolence was also key in shaping the thoughts of Dr. Martin Luther King.

Aside from a few small conservative Quaker meetings, Quakers today remain firmly engaged with history and politics. A liberal Quaker meeting often resembles a radical political meeting, and may close with calls to political activism—a peace march, a vigil against the death penalty, or pro-choice lobbying. By contrast, evangelical Quakers, though officially antiwar and for women's equality, have largely adopted the politics of the political right.

Nevertheless, Fox's vision of an inwardly directed spirituality remains vital to many Quakers, and as a body the Quakers remain fiercely independent, antiauthoritarian, and firm in their defense of freedom of conscience.

C. Important Dates and Landmarks

1624 Birth of George Fox.

1642 The English Civil War begins.

1647 Fox's religious "opening."

1649 Cromwell's Parliament orders the execution of Charles I.

1655–1656 Elizabeth Harris becomes the first Quaker to visit the New World.

1660 The restoration of the monarchy in Britain.

1662 The Quaker Act forbids Quakers to meet in Britain.

1671–1673 George Fox tours America.

1681 William Penn receives charter for the colony of Pennsylvania.

1691 Death of George Fox.

1758–1784 Meetings of Quakers throughout the colonies vote to ban slave holding by members.

1827–1828 The first major splits in Quaker polity occurs with the Hicksite Quakers' separation from the orthodox Quakers.

1837–1840 Joseph Gurney preaches in the United States.

1848 Lucretia Mott leads the first women's rights convention in America.

1861–1865 American Civil War is fought.

1869 Susan B. Anthony cofounds the National Women's Suffrage Association (NWSA).

1917 The American Friends Service Committee (AFSC) formed.

1920 Women's right to vote established.

1947 Friends awarded Nobel Peace Prize.

1960s AFSC fights for civil rights in America.

1987 The first gay marriage performed by liberal Quakers.

D. Important Figures

Margaret Fox (1614–1702)

Margaret Askew was born in Lancashire, England. At the age of eighteen, she became the lady of Swarthmoor Hall when she married barrister Thomas Fell. Twenty years later, in 1652, Margaret first heard of the teachings of George Fox, and became convinced of his discovery of truth. The lady immediately devoted herself to the movement, taking on a secretarial role from Swarthmoor Hall in managing the written communications of traveling Friends. She also wrote theological texts for the movement, and collected funds for missionary ventures. Swarthmoor Hall would serve as a seat of refuge for persecuted Quakers after Margaret's husband died in 1658. This—and her failure to take an oath—led to her arrest in 1664. Margaret was imprisoned for six years, during which time she wrote additional texts, including "Women's Speaking Justified," a justification for women's ministry based on scriptural imperative. This writing played an integral role in women's right movements of the seventeenth century.

Margaret married George Fox one year after her release from prison, in 1669. The marriage would mainly be spent in separation, however, as Mrs. Fox was again arrested for breaking the Conventicle Act shortly thereafter. George left for American upon her release, only to be imprisoned himself when he returned to England. After George's release in 1675, he traveled constantly between Europe and the New World. Margaret remained at Swarthmoor for the rest of her life, taking an active part in the affairs of the Society.

John Wilbur (1774–1856)

Born to the Quaker majority of Rhode Island, John Wilbur climbed the religious ranks to elder in 1802, and minister just four years later. In 1822, he became widely known as an expounder of traditional Quaker theology while traveling in New England for the purpose of investigating the New Light move-

ment in Lynn, Massachusetts. It wasn't until Wilbur traveled overseas, however, that he found the impetus to historically impact the Quaker movement.

While in England, Wilbur noticed the British Friends' tendency toward evangelicalism. These Friends, Wilbur deduced, were overcompensating for Elias Hicks's heterodoxy. Their desire to pursue a more relatively orthodox Christian course had caused them to drop the essential Quaker reliance on the inward Christ. Wilbur lamented their unfeeling, intellectual approach to study of the Bible.

Upon his return to America, Wilbur discovered that the evangelical influence had touched Friends there, as well, mostly through the writings and ministry of Joseph Gurney. Wilbur made derogatory statements about Gurney's teachings that resulted in his disownment by several meetings. However, Wilbur had gained supporters. In 1845, a body of 500 members—to be called Wilburites—separated from "Gurneyites." The former would eventually join another branch of Quakerism called Conservative Friends.

David Updegraff (1830–1894)

David Updegraff's innovations to Quakerism made him one of the most highly controversial ministers in Quaker history. A proponent of Finney's "new measure" revivalism, Updegraff's meeting eschewed silence for scriptural readings, testimonies of conversion experiences, singing, inspired exultations, and long sermons. Indeed, after such sermons, Updegraff invited members who wished to be saved to approach the altar. Even his theology departed drastically from Quaker precedent. Updegraff disregarded the idea that all men were endowed with a persistent inward light, instead insisting that this light was God's wrath against sinners, and only appeared when one desired repentance. He also preached "entire sanctification," which necessitated a second baptism following one's conversion. Updegraff's viewpoints stemmed from premillennialism, the idea that the earth was ridden with increasing sin, to be purged upon Christ's imminent return.

Therefore, as many souls as possible must be saved before the advent of Christ's judgment.

Followers of Updegraff became known as "Waterites" because of their practice of a water baptism as a symbol of rebirth. The Waterites were not many, however, and indeed—Updegraff did not aim for a complete reformation of the Society; rather, he asked for mere tolerance. This was not granted, however, and was rebuked at the Indian Yearly Meeting of 1879. Updegraff continued to engage in water baptisms, even receiving a baptism himself—which action caused great contention. Many Friends believed baptism prevented one from serving as a minister. After a meeting that included a vote on the issue (highly uncharacteristic of Quaker meetings), another division nearly ensued among the Society. However, Updegraff's main opponent, John Butler, died before the split could occur.

II. Tenents and Beliefs

A. Basic Beliefs

No organized American religion is so pluralized when it comes to belief as that of the Quakers'. What do Quakers believe? Throughout most of their history, and certainly today among the liberals, Quakerism remains a religion that eschews all creeds and statements of faith as merely the "outward" trappings of religion and as having little worth. The earliest Quakers saw these as dry forms that had lost all the spirit of true religion. Worse, such creeds led to the debate and strife which George Fox dismissed as mere "jangling." What was needed was silence—a deep and profound silence in which the individual could approach God face-to-face. This fact led the influential Quaker historian Howard H. Brinton to describe Quakerism as being primarily a "method or a practice."

Many would agree with Brinton, at least to the degree of noting that Quakerism is unique among Christian denominations in that it does not hold the belief in a given creed to be the key factor in human salvation.

Central to this turning against creedalism has been Fox's doctrine of the "inner light," a belief, in Fox's words, that "Christ has come to teach His people Hisself." Taking cues from the prologue to the Gospel of John, Fox argued that Christ was "the light that enlightens all men," and that God dwells in all humans in such a way that the search for truth outwardly, in rituals, dogmas, or religious education, is useless. In order to find God, Fox argued, one must abandon all hope and reliance on these externals and look inward.

While the earliest Quakers saw themselves as returning to a true primitive Christianity, liberal Quakers, since the early nineteenth century, have drifted more and more from their Christ-centered roots. Today many liberal Quakers would describe themselves as Buddhist, Jain, Sufi, or even as Jewish Quakers. These liberals and universalists have wondered why the "inner light" should be thought of as Christian at all. In fact, such universalism dates back to the earliest attempt at a Quaker theology. Robert Barclay in his 1678 opus, *Apology for the True Christian Divinity*, argues that the "inner light" resides among those of all religions and in all nations and that these people, too, without knowing the name Christ, can be saved by him.

Not surprisingly, a minority of the most right-wing Quakers today have dismissed Fox's doctrine of the inner light as dangerous and contrary to Scripture. Nevertheless, it remains the fundamental Quaker belief to be reckoned with and is chiefly responsible for the immense diversity one finds among the Quakers today.

Of key importance to understanding Quakerism is the Quaker take on Scripture. Fox's inward turn led him to affirm the danger of prioritizing the Bible over "the spirit that inspired it." Although Fox clearly believed in the truth of Scripture and seemed to have had most of the Bible memorized so that he could counter every complaint against the Quakers with a proof text of his own, he believed that the spirit was still at work in the world and that Christians could, even now, be inspired to say words that were of equal spiritual profundity and worth. The Bible, for Fox, was useful in the way that it pointed toward God, but it should not be mistaken for God. The Bible, according to Fox, was not the "Word of God"; the Word was rather that inner voice which had been implanted in all of us.

Today many liberal Quakers have little patience for the Bible and find it patriarchal, antifeminist, and archaic. In a liberal meeting, the reading of a scriptural passage can often give way to heated debate over its relevance or may be countered with a Zen koan or Buddhist sutra. Such Quakers often claim that there is a universal mystical truth that lies deeply concealed beneath the words of all great religious texts and that the text is, to use the Buddhist phrase, merely "a finger pointing at the moon" and not the moon itself. Evangelical Quakers, on the other hand, may still believe in the continuing revelation of the Spirit, while at the same time holding to biblical inerrancy and the belief that the Bible represents a privileged stratum of God's revelation. These Quakers are more likely to see faith in Jesus Christ as savior to be central to truth and human salvation.

B. Secondary Sources

In the end, little can be said about Quaker belief without looking at the issue of peace and pacifism. The twentieth century had many moments in which the Quaker Peace Testimony rose to the surface of political thought. The great Russian novelist and author of *War and Peace,* **Leo Tolstoy**, became fixated on the question of pacifism toward the end of his life and this led him to write the work *The Kingdom of God Is Within You* (1908), a book which had an immense impact in Western intellectual circles. In this book, Tolstoy took up material from American Quakers and Russian pacifist sectarians and argued for a kind of religious anarchism, in which Christians would resist the power of government

The Quaker painter Edward Hicks (1780–1849) was occupied in his work by the notion of Inner Light, based in part on Paul's formulation of "Christ in you" (Colossians 1:27). Hicks's painting The Peaceable Kingdom, *of which he did several versions, is for some viewers a stirring visualization of Christ's eventual reign on a transformed earth. Note the artist's rendering of William Penn's treaty with Native Americans at left.*

through nonviolence. This book in turn was given to Mohandas Gandhi by Quaker missionaries, and Gandhi himself, although he rejected Christianity as hypocritical, claimed in his autobiography that this book and the Quaker peace witness was central to the development of his practice of nonresistance. Gandhi, in turn, influenced Martin Luther King, and the policy of peaceful marches and nonresistance to police and governmental brutality has become the hallmark of much activism in America today.

Another non-Quaker author who took up this theme was **Aldous Huxley**, who wrote the pacifist novel *Eyeless in Gaza* in 1936, in which a Quaker missionary plays a key role in converting the narrator toward a mission of peace. Huxley himself became somewhat of a mystic in his later life, writing the nonfiction work *The Perennial Philosophy,* which espoused a universalistic take on world religion. His novel *Island* became his most influential pacifist novel, arguing for a nonresistance to violence in the world and that this peace could be obtained through mystical states of religious awakening.

The most influential Quaker writers to take up the pen during the twentieth century have followed in this mystical vein. Writers such as **Thomas Kelly**, **Douglas Steere**, and more recently **Parker Palmer** have all written works urging that the practice of meditation and spiritual awakening lead to powerful self-transformation.

III. Rites and Rituals

To speak of "rites and rituals" as having a place within the Quaker life would surely offend some Quakers today, and the very mention of such words would have been an anathema to the early Quakers. The Quaker life, for many, stands in contrast to the very idea of all sacred forms, sacred days, or sacred practice. If the period between the beginning of Lent and Easter Sunday is central to Roman Catholicism, a Quaker might well say that, for a Quaker, every day is Lent. There are no holy days for a Quaker because every day is supposed to be holy. There are no days of prayer because every last one is supposed to be a day of prayer. Today, among liberal Quakers, the greatest acknowledgment of a holiday one might find on an Easter Sunday is an admission that other Christians view that day as holy. Otherwise, a meeting on this Sunday would be the same as any other.

A. The Calendar

To consider any day especially holy smacked, for the early Quakers, of idolatry. Idolatrous also was the very notion of a "church" which had been built by human hands, a concept which Quakers contrasted with the temple of the human heart. The Quakers called their services "meeting for worship" and their buildings "meeting houses," so as to carefully note that the building itself and the outward form of worship had no sanctity. Fox had always maintained that spirituality could be found or discussed in any environment—an orchard, for instance—and preferred to use the phrase "steeple house" in lieu of "church." Even the names of days of the week threatened Quakers with idolatry. Wednesday was named for the god Wodin; worse, the etymology of the name Sunday was linked to the worship of the sun. Thus for much of Quaker history Sunday became "First Day;" Monday, "Second Day;" and so on. Although most Quakers do not keep to this distinction today, it

crops up from time to time, and Quakers rarely talk of offering Sunday School for religious education, instead calling it "First Day School."

B. Worship and Liturgy

The Quaker "meeting for worship" in its most basic form is utterly tied to this notion of anti-idolatry and the thought that everything and everyone is equally sacred. The oldest Quaker meeting houses have no stained glass, no upholstery, no musical instruments, and no cross or crucifix. No art adorns the walls, which are painted stark white. There is no pulpit for a preacher, and the pews often face one another so that there is no front of the meeting house where someone can perform. Indeed, in its most traditional form, the Quaker meeting has no official or paid preacher; any Quaker (ideally) can be called by God to speak and to perform the role of minister. George Fox himself once said that he felt that the role of Quakers in the world was to bring an end to all preaching, and, at its most simple form, the Quaker meeting is simply a period of silence in which Quakers gather together in an empty place to reflect on God, to pray, and to meditate.

This meditation differs from that of Buddhists in that there is usually the expectation that someone at the meeting may be guided by the Spirit to offer a

This undated illustration reminds viewers that the communal dimension of prayer is heightened in a Friends prayer meeting, as the task at hand is as much communion with one's fellow worshippers as it is communion with God.

The Oblong Friends Meeting House in the Quaker Hill neighborhood of Pawling, New York, was built in 1763, and has been on the National Register of Historic Places since 1973.

"message." During this period of silence anyone in attendance, even nonmembers and non-Quakers, can rise and deliver a sermon. The only guideline is that such "messages" be inspired and one is "moved" to say them. Amidst the silence, which can last as long as an hour, Quakers occasionally burst into spontaneous song and sometimes recite passages from the Bible. Often, particularly in smaller meetings, this period of silence is the sum total of a Quaker service. If no one speaks, the meeting remains a wholly quiet time of reflection which is followed by a brief period of socializing and coffee.

Although the name Quaker originated as an insult thrown at the religious group by an unsympathetic judge, and the name preferred by this group was the Religious Society of Friends, "quaking" has been a part of Quakerism since the early days. Even today one will occasionally see a man or a woman begin to tremble uncontrollably during a meeting, before rising to his or her feet to speak.

Quaker meetings today can be grouped into two basic categories: the "programmed meeting" and the "unprogrammed meeting." The unprogrammed meeting is identical to the traditional form just described. The programmed meeting is more like what a non-Quaker might expect from a Protestant service. Although Quakers were traditionally very skeptical of music, the movement of Gurneyite Quakers toward assimilation with the larger Protestant culture has led to the acceptance of hymn singing and musical accompaniment among some Quakers. Similarly, the prohibition on hired ministers and prepared sermons has been eased among Quakers of the evangelical persuasion, so that some programmed meetings only allow short period for silence and "messages" from believers. Nonetheless, even in the programmed meetings there has been no movement toward sacramentalism. Following the thought of Fox and the early Quakers, the sacraments are thought to be spiritual and to be bestowed only by God. There is thus no baptism by water, but only the "baptism" through prayer; communion is communication with God and with other Quakers; and there are no priests to whom one can confess, although many meetings have committees on worship and pastoral care made up of congregants.

Meeting locationss in the U.S., whether conservative or liberal, programmed or unprogrammed, can be found at www.quakerfinder.org.

C. Daily Life

No doubt the most pervasive image that most Americans have of the Quakers arises from Quaker Oats and the dour face and black and white clothing of the man on the carton. Thus many Americans, when they think of Quakers at all, associate them with the Amish or the Mennonites. Although most Quakers today no longer wear "plain dress," for much of their history there was a spoken and unspoken prohibition on wearing bright or ornamented clothing. The Quaker focus on plainness and simplicity was nonetheless always distinct from that of the Amish and Mennonites, and the reason for this lies in the fact that Quakers were often rich as well as poor, often businessmen as well as farmers. When one looks back over nineteenth century Quaker dress, one finds that the costumes of Quakers changed with the times. A Quaker woman's gown differed from those worn by non-Quaker women not in cut, but only in the fact that it was white and lacked luxuriant dyes and trimmings.

Plainness and simplicity remain important Quaker values today, and nearly all Quakers pay lip service to it. But simplicity at the beginning of the twenty-first century can be variously interpreted and, although for many Quakers it means a commitment to owning less, it may or may not have anything to do with eschewing jewelry, color, or the latest technological innovation. Still, especially among Friends at the unprogrammed meetings, it is rare to see any member dressed in "church clothes." Instead one finds men and women in t-shirts, in sweat shirts, and in jeans——often in clothes which are weathered and well-worn and may belie the prosperous middle class status of their owners.

For much of their history Quakers could be distinguished by their unwillingness to use the informal mode of speech, referring to each other as "thou" instead of "you." This practice continued far into the nineteenth century, sounding archaic when that formal mode of speech fell away. Most Quakers today use "thee" and "thou" only as a joke, but, for a small number of Quakers, this remains a part of their religious identity.

D. Life Cycle Events

A Quaker congregation is divided between those who are members and those who merely attend the meeting on a regular basis, or, in more traditional terms, between those who are "attenders" and those who are "convinced Friends."

Both attenders and full members share many of the same duties in nonprogrammed meetings, and both can share messages and take positions on some of the minor committees for guiding the meeting. But only full members can become clerks, treasurers, and overseers, and become responsible for the business decisions of the meeting. The Quaker dislike of formal rituals plays a role here, and a written petition for entrance into the meeting, along with several prayerful consultations for discernment with a small group of experienced Quakers called a "clearness committee," takes the place that baptism plays in most Protestant denominations. Quaker children, particu-

larly among nonprogrammed and liberal Friends, are not urged to become Quakers or even to embrace Quaker values. They are instead encouraged to explore in the hope that they will one day return to Quakerism and become convinced Friends themselves.

Among programmed meetings, nuptials are much the same as they would be in most churches and include a processional, the recitations of vows, and the customary formalities performed by a minister. But the traditional marriage rite among Quakers as it is still preserved among the unprogrammed Friends is unique to Quakerism. This unique quality no doubt derives from the fact that the Quakers had no hierarchy or ordained leaders who could marry the couple.

Historically, local meetings instated their older or more prosperous members as overseers, who were granted regulative authority over such concerns as membership, education, burials, and marriage.

Today, the would-be bride and groom are invited to address a letter to the meeting in which they state their intention of being married. This in turn is followed by a period of soul-searching and discernment with a small group of members who oversee and aid the process. This "clearness committee" is invited to explore issues of finance, alcohol abuse, sexual preference, and commitments to extended family before they ultimately approve the wedding. The ceremony itself takes place in the meeting house and begins with an extended period of silence. After a suitable time the bride and groom clasp hands and stand together to recite their own vows. The Faith and Practice of the New York Yearly Meeting asks that the vows be words "to the following effect":

In the presence of God and before these our friends, I take thee_____, to be my wife/husband, promising with Divine assistance to be unto thee a loving and faithful wife/husband so long as we both shall live.

This declaration is followed by another period of silent worship, during which other members of the meeting or extended family who feel called to speak may do so.

A Quaker funeral is likely to follow a pattern of simplicity. A memorial meeting held within a week or two of the death is likely to have no set program and to open and close in silence even as all those gathered are given the opportunity to speak.

E. Family Life

Family life and values are among the most contested battlegrounds of contemporary Quakerism. Friends historically were very much opposed to premarital sexual activity and out-of-wedlock births, and were more opposed to divorce than most Protestants, considering it grounds for disownment by the meeting and refusing to permit marriages between divorcees.

Homosexuality, if and when it came up, would have been universally decried for much of Quaker history. All of this began to change, however, first with the movement of some orthodox Quakers toward integration with the Protestant mainstream, and second with the movement of other Quakers toward liberalism throughout the nineteenth and twentieth centuries. Thus, Quakers on both ends of the spectrum are likely to permit (but not encourage) divorce, while liberal and evangelical Quakers stand at opposing poles when it comes to homosexuality, premarital sex, and abortion.

IV. Denominations and Demographics

A. History (Schisms, Mergers, etc.)

For most of their history, and certainly today, the Quakers have never boasted a numerically expansive membership. One can only marvel at the comparative degree of influence that they have had, especially when one considers that Quakers in America today number only around 100,000, or less than 1/30th of one percent of the population as a whole. The greatest period of growth for the Quakers was during their ear-

liest period, and many estimate that by the time of Fox's death, there were more than 50,000 Quakers in Britain alone. But since this initial period of expansion, Quaker membership has not grown significantly. Although the population of the United States increased dramatically between 1900 and 2000, the number of Quakers in the population has remained stable.

Two key factors can be identified as contributing to this stability in numbers: The first is the Quaker tendency to quietism and the dislike of evangelizing, and the second is the Quaker tendency to schism. Even a single medium-sized meeting may, during the nineteenth century, have split numerous times, while reunions between branches have tended only to happen when each of the bodies had decline in numbers to such a degree that a reunion was necessary. The lack of an ordained clergy and the notion of the "ministry of all believers" has made it easy for Quakers groups to split off and to form meetings of their own. Unlike other denominations, the Quakers have no conception that spiritual power is something invested through a ritual laying on of hands by one authority to another. Spiritual "light" is something that can only come from God. This belief has made it difficult for one group to call into question the legitimacy of another after the manner of denominations who focus on apostolic succession through a council of bishops.

The culture wars in America have also played a role in shrinking and expanding the Quaker flock. Particularly in more liberal meetings, the lack of an executive authority to decide for or against steps such as the acceptance of gay marriage has entailed endless discussions of the question and frequent strife and alienation. Although, as with the Episcopal Church today, such meetings have also become a refuge for those who have been cast out by other more conservative denominations. One statistic estimates that as many as 87 percent of Quakers in these liberal meetings came to Quakerism as converts.

The branches of Quakerism today reflect the continual internal battle between radical liberalism and conservatism among Quakers that has raged since the early nineteenth century, as well as the equally important distinction between assimilation with other types of Christianity and the distinctiveness of the Quaker tradition. Today, it would seem that both these battles have stabilized, with Quakers content to maintain their differences and different meetings, and with little tendency toward reunion.

B. Comparison of Tenets and Practices

Four of the key inheritors of the different aspects of the Quaker tradition are the Friends General Conference (FGC), the Friends United Meeting (FUM), the Evangelical Friends International, and the Ohio Yearly Meeting of Conservative Friends. This last group, although very small in number, reflects the most traditional of all the strains of American Quakerism. These Quakers practice plain dress in a way that recalls the Amish, refuse to introduce music into their services or hire a minister, and continue to hold entirely unprogrammed meetings that are focused on silent worship. Moreover, these Quakers, unlike other Friends who meet in an unprogrammed style, are most likely to identify the "inner light" with Jesus and to consider themselves to be Christians rather than Buddhists or humanists.

The Friends General Conference represents the other strand of unprogrammed Quakerism in America. This group can largely be seen as the inheritors of the Hicksite liberal tradition in American Quakerism. These Quakers tend to be universalists who are theologically closer to Unitarians than to their unprogrammed brethren of the Ohio Yearly Meeting of Conservative Friends. It is among these Friends that one will find the claim that Quakerism need not be exclusively Christian. These Quakers maintain the traditional lack of hierarchy in meetings, and lack a paid leadership or ministry. They keep close to the traditional forms of practice while inviting theological pluralism and focusing on the claim that there is "that of God" in all humans and that this "light" may be reflected in numerous ways. Within meetings of the FGC there is often tension between "mystical" and "political" Quakers, between those Quakers who have been attracted to the meetings because of Quaker nonviolent political resistance, and those who have been attracted by the promise of silence, soul-searching, and meditation. As a whole, this group is politically liberal, and it is here that one will find an openness to gay marriage and other nontraditional unions.

The Friends United Meeting represents a more Christ-centered conception of the Quaker faith, and its members are much more likely to see an explicit creedal statement of Christian belief as central to their faith. This strain of Quakerism, along with that of the Evangelical Friends, is a result of the trend toward assimilation with other Protestant Christians in America. Friends of this strain are more likely to refer to their house of worship as "churches" rather than "meeting houses," and to speak of attending church rather than "meeting." The majority of services within this organization are programmed, having music and a pastor who delivers sermons such as one would find in other Protestant churches. However, many of these programmed services still retain a place for silence and for "messages" from other believers. Politically, these Quakers range across the entire spectrum from conservative to liberal, and this, as with the Episcopalians and the Methodists, has often led to dissent, controversy, and protracted battles over gay rights. However, one practice universally opposed is discrimination on the basis of sexuality by employers. Many members of the Friends United Meeting remain politically active in traditional Quaker causes such as ending the death penalty and opposing war.

Evangelical Friends come the closest to assimilation with the broader trends in Christianity today, and the majority of these Quakers see themselves as closer to other evangelical Christians than to other Friends. Such Friends rightly point out that their belief in the salvific power of faith in Jesus is closer to the beliefs of the early Quakers than the beliefs of most unprogrammed Friends today. Politically, Friends who identify as "evangelical" are more likely to embrace rightwing causes such as the pro-life movement than to struggle against war. The Quaker evangelical movement dates back to nineteenth-century revivalism in America, and these Quakers are much more likely than other Quakers to see salvation and the spiritual quest as something to be solved instantaneously when the believer is "born again" through a faith in Jesus Christ as the personal savior. Churches who belong to the Evangelical Friends International have official pastors and are more likely to feature music of all types, including pop and electronic music. As in other evangelical churches, multimedia Powerpoint slides may be projected during a service as an aid to the congregants, and stained glass windows are an accepted norm.

Of the 100,000 or so Quakers in America today, two thirds belong to programmed pastoral meetings, while the other third continues to worship in silence. The sound and color of Evangelical services differs as radically from that of nonprogrammed meetings as the politics and theology of its membership contrasts with that of more liberal Friends. Thus, although the Quakers are a small group numerically, in faith and practice they are one of the most plural and diverse religious denominations in America.

V. Organization and Infrastructure

A. Education

The Quaker stance on religious education remains very much under the influence of George Fox's rejection of the educated clergy of his time. Fox argued that Jesus Christ, in the form of the inner Word and light, could be the only teacher of religious truth. Fox had only disdain for Oxford educated divines, and his autobiographical journal is very

much a record of his triumph in debate over these learned figures. When one considers that the charter of Harvard College, founded in 1636, states that the sole purpose of the foundation is for the formation of an "educated clergy," and that other institutions such as Yale and Princeton were originally founded for a similar purpose, one can only conclude that the Quaker approach to education could not have been more divergent from that of the seventeenth-century Protestant mainstream.

Firstly, the Quakers, for much of their history, did not have a clergy at all. Because God was thought to reveal himself through, and dwell within, all humans beings, there was no need to pick out members of a congregation and to educate them especially for the role of ministry. Moreover, Fox dismissed the debates of the Oxford dons as mere "contention" and "jangling." The finer points of theology were all irrelevant in comparison to the silence of worship, a silence in which Fox believed God revealed himself. Even today among unprogrammed Friends, one often discovers an utter disdain for theological training. "Quakers don't have a theology," many will say. Quakers do, however, seek out higher religious education, particularly when it reflects social concerns such as spiritual direction or prison ministry, and teaches skills necessary for participation in nongovernmental organizations.

Eventually the Quakers did come to found a small number of Quaker institutions of higher learning, but they did so more to promote the general good of education than to offer training in Quaker theology. The most prestigious of these institutions today are Swarthmore, Bryn Mawr, and Haverford—Ivy League level institutions situated near one another west of Philadelphia. The Quaker belief in the equality of women meant that Swarthmore was originally founded as a coeducational school, while Haverford found a counterpart women's institution in Bryn Mawr, where several world-class women scientists and mathematicians have taught.

Swarthmore College

500 College Avenue

Swarthmore, PA 19081

610-328-8000

webeditor@swarthmore.edu

www.swarthmore.edu

Bryn Mawr College

101 North Merion Avenue

Bryn Mawr, PA 19010

610-526-5000

www.brynmawr.edu

Haverford College

370 Lancaster Avenue

Haverford, PA 19041

610-896-1000

www.haverford.edu

Among pastoral and programmed Friends, a theological education is now the norm for pastors. Would-be pastors now attend Quaker schools such as Earlham in Indiana or George Fox in Oregon, while Quakers of a more conservative bent may attend evangelical Bible colleges.

Earlham College

801 National Road West

Richmond, IN 47374

800-EARLHAM or 800-327-5426

www.earlham.edu

George Fox University

414 North Meridian Street

Newberg, OR 97132

503-538-8383

www.georgefox.edu

But even those Quakers today who have elected to hold programmed meetings make a distinction between "ordaining" clergy and "recording" them. Quakers do not ordain clergy, meaning that no human can give someone else the power to be a minister of God. Instead, they simply "record" the fact that a man or a woman has been called by God to do the work of a minister, and has received the education necessary to do so.

The Quakers have also founded a number of other institutions of higher learning, including Whittier College, the alma mater of President Richard Nixon.

Whittier College

13406 East Philadelphia Street

PO Box 634

Whittier, CA 90608

562-907-4200   Fax: 562-907-4870

Quakers have also been instrumental in founding two other universities of wide repute: Cornell University, founded in 1865 by Ezra Cornell—born a Quaker but later ejected for marrying outside the Faith; and Johns Hopkins University, founded in 1876 by Johns Hopkins, who left the university a bequest of $8 million, the equivalent of over $140 million today and believed to be the largest single bequest to a philanthropy for over a century.

The Quakers have also established many secondary schools across the country, usually with "Friends" as part of the school's name. In many areas, the highest ranked and most prestigious secondary schools bear the Friends name. Names and locations of Friends schools can be found on this website http://friendscouncil.org

B. Governance and Authority

The traditional Quaker form of doing business and reaching decisions as a body represents one of the most unique facets of Quakerism. Here Quaker anti-authoritarianism is seen in its most extreme form. Even the name of this form, "a meeting for worship with a concern for business" may seem paradoxical. Lacking an official institutional hierarchy who is in any way invested with the ability to discern truth or come to a decision about what is right, the Quakers come together as a body of all members that are willing to take the time and sit in silence to try to inter-

The Plymouth Friends Meeting House in Plymouth Meeting, Pennsylvania—the interior and exterior of which are seen above—was built in 1708 and enlarged in 1780. It is the first Quaker place of worship in the United States.

pret the will of God. This type of meeting, which can take place monthly or weekly in individual meeting houses, and quarterly and yearly among the larger denominational bodies, has very much the same form as a traditional meeting for worship. It is punctuated by silence and a prayerful attitude, and all who attend may speak when they feel called. Topics of discussion can range from political activity to loan payments, property holdings, membership, and the keeping of the grounds. It was at meetings such as these that the Quakers first elected to ban slavery. Although Quakers sometimes describe the process as one of reaching a "consensus," this is not strictly accurate. The process is, in fact, more theocratic than this, and the goal is not to reach an agreement between all those present, but rather to discern the "will of God for the meeting." The Quakers do not vote during meeting, and topics on which there is a large degree of dissent may be postponed until the next meeting and may even be raised again and again during meeting for many years.

Although members may certainly disagree during these meetings, argument is discouraged, and one is not supposed to directly address another's message in an argumentative tone. Members instead rise to speak the truth as it is revealed to them, and it is the clerk's job to read the signs and to interpret how God is working through those who speak.

The names of Quaker bodies are often difficult for outsiders to interpret. For example, Brooklyn Monthly Meeting, a meeting held in an old meeting house in downtown Brooklyn meets twice a week, on Tuesdays and Sundays, but holds a business meet-

ing only on the first Sunday of each month. This body in turn belongs to the New York Quarterly Meeting, a body which contains the unprogrammed meetings in New York City and holds a meeting once every three months to tend to business concerns. This body, in turn, represents a large portion of the New York Yearly Meeting, the members of which are invited to come together once a year to deal with larger, denomination-wide issues, while all of the bodies together belong to the Friends General Conference, the largest and most liberal group of unprogrammed Quakers in the United States.

Within a given meeting there are smaller committees dedicated to dealing with issues such as finance, ministry, evangelism, politics, and community outreach. Each of these committees meet separately in a prayerful manner to discern the direction that the meeting should take in these respective areas.

Among many types of Quakerism, policy and rules for faith are set down in a guidebook known as the *Faith and Practice of the Religious Society of Friends* or as *The Book of Discipline*. This book, which differs from yearly meeting to yearly meeting, offers first a series of questions or "queries" to lead the believer toward a higher spirituality. These queries can run from "Do we make time in our daily lives for communion with God. . . ?" to "Do we support measures to avoid pollution of air and water?" The practice section of the volume offers guidelines for worship, membership, marriages, ministry, and corporate practice. It is repeatedly rewritten under the continual discernment of the yearly meetings.

The two most influential and important Quaker social service organizations today are the American Friends Service Committee, which works for peace, promotes contentious objection to war, and strives for civil rights, and the American Committee on National Legislation, a group that works to lobby Congress on issues such as the death penalty, the draft, and Native American issues.

The four well-known figures seen here—from left: Herbert Hoover, Edward R. Murrow, John Greenleaf Whittier, and Bonnie Raitt—were all born to Quaker parents.

Quakers often feel that they must struggle to make their voices heard in America. Yet, their aversion to evangelism means that those efforts are usually aimed at Quaker insiders or address only secular political issues. Small Quaker periodicals include *Friend's Journal*, a monthly magazine representative of unprogrammed and liberal friends; the *American Friends Service Committee Quaker Service Journal*; and the *Friend's Voice*, published by Evangelical Friends International. *Quaker History* is a historical quarterly. The Quaker study center, Pendle Hill, in Wallingford, Pennsylvania, publishes books and pamphlets on spirituality and worship.

Material on the works of early Quakers is offered by the website Quaker Heritage Press Online Texts (www.qhpress.org). Meetings, whether conservative or liberal, programmed or unprogrammed, may be found at www.quakerfinder.org.

C. Some Notable American Quakers

Jane Addams, sociologist

Whittaker Chambers, *Time* editor, accused Alger Hiss of espionage

John Conard, U.S. politician nick-named the "Fighting Quaker"

William Cooper, founder of Cooperstown; father of James Fenimore Cooper

James Dean, actor

Edward Hicks, painter

Herbert Hoover, U.S. President

Dolley Madison, first lady

Elizabeth Magie, inventor of "Monopoly"

Dave Matthews, musician (originally South African)

James Michener, author

Edward R. Murrow, journalist

Richard Nixon, U.S. president

Bonnie Raitt, musician

John Raitt, actor (and father of Bonnie Raitt)

Bayard Rustin, civil rights leader

Anna Sewell, author

Joseph Taylor, Nobel Prize winner in physics

Benjamin West, painter

Jessamyn West, novelist

Joseph Wharton, industrialist; founder of the Wharton School of Business

Barclay White, superintendent of Indian affairs during Grant administration

John Greenleaf Whittier, poet

FURTHER READING

Faith and Practice: The Book of Discipline of the New York Yearly Meeting of the Religious Society of Friends
2002: New York Yearly Meeting

Friends for 350 Years
  Howard H. Brinton
2002: Pendle Hill

An Introduction to Quakerism
  Pink Dandelion
2007: Cambridge University Press

The Journal of George Fox
  George Fox; John L. Nickalls, ed.
1997: Religious Society of Friends

The Quakers in America
  Thomas D. Hamm
2003: Columbia University Press

14 Seventh-day Adventists

I. Origins and Early History

A. The Religion in America

O N THE NIGHT OF OCTOBER 22, 1844, A GROUP referred to by outsiders as the Millerites, but referred to within as Adventists, climbed up onto their rooftops or stood waiting in the midst of vacant fields in prayerful anticipation of the return of Jesus

William Miller studied prophecies in Daniel and Revelation to determine that the Second Coming of Christ would occur in 1844, the year after this chart was published.

Christ. Many had disposed of all of their property; some left their families. Others had been expelled by their home churches, whether Baptist, Methodist, or Presbyterian, because of their attraction to the theories of a man named William Miller.

Miller himself was a Baptist minister who gave great heed to the prophecies of the biblical book of Daniel. Within these passages, God promises to set up a kingdom on this earth, of which he will ultimately assume reign himself. But, wondered Miller, when would it happen? The prophecy states that God will return (following Jesus's ascension) after a period of 2,300 days. Miller theorized that these days symbolized years, and applying this theory (now called the "day/year rule"), he estimated that the Second Coming would happen sometime during the year of 1843. But, when March 21, 1844, passed without the advent of the Lord, others in the movement performed recalculations, finally setting the date as October 22. The movement had attracted converts across America and as many as 100,000 people stood by in expectation.

This night came to be known as the Great Disappointment. The Messiah did not descend; God did not establish a new kingdom on earth. Believers scattered in confusion; many joined the Shakers, and few among them were prepared to set another date for the apocalypse. This event—or nonevent—and the struggles for faith that followed, gave birth to two of America's most fervent and fast-growing denominations, the Jehovah's Witnesses and the Seventh-day Adventists.

Those who remained in the movement offered a series of different interpretations of what had happened. Perhaps the date had simply been incorrect or perhaps the day had, in fact, been the Day of Judgment, so that all who were saved or lost had been saved or lost before this event in cosmic history. The time for conversion and repentance had come to a close, according to this belief. A third theory emerged, born of a man named Hiram Edson. Edson reported that, on the day after the Great Disappointment, he had been out walking in the fields when a vision had unfolded to him. In this vision it was revealed that Christ had passed into the second compartment of heaven, a heavenly sanctuary. October 22, 1844, had indeed been the correct date, but it had signified a celestial event rather than an earthly one. Christ was now beginning a period of "investigative judgment" and was preparing for the end of days. It was this last theory that was eventually embraced by the Seventh-day Adventist Church and became the basis for their continued expectation of the coming of the Lord.

The dedication of these early Adventists to thorough and complete studies of the Hebrew Bible eventually elicited many important questions concerning the ancient Jewish laws of Leviticus and Deuteronomy. How much had changed with the crucifixion, death, and resurrection of Christ? Many Adventists questioned the fact that Christians no longer worshipped on the Sabbath day (Saturday) and came to feel the shift toward Sunday worship among early Christians had been a mistake. Did not God demand that the Jews keep his day holy? What of the dietary restrictions and the many laws that now comprise today's kosher restrictions had God changed his mind about? In the days after the Great Disappointment many of these questions repeatedly surfaced. Sabbatarianism, or the idea that one should worship on Saturday rather than Sunday, remained a minority position among the Adventists—until a woman by the name of Ellen White transformed the movement.

Ellen White

Although White never explicitly claimed the title of prophet herself, the Adventist Church today officially recognizes her as such and considers her to have

William Miller (1782–1849) predicted that Christ would return to earth on October 22, 1844; when this didn't happen, the result was termed the Great Disappointment. Still, Miller believed until his death that the second coming of Christ was imminent.

been a recipient of the "spiritual gift" of prophecy. When in conversation with other Christians, today's Adventists are quick to point out that White herself claimed that all of her insights were to be checked and double-checked with Scripture and that the Bible should remain the highest authority on the will of God. However, White's influence on the history of the Adventist church and its present tenets can hardly be overestimated. When stating its current positions in the *Church Manual*, the Seventh-day Adventist organization is likely to first quote as proof passages from the Hebrew Bible; second, passages from the New Testament; and finally, passages from the visionary writings of Ellen White.

Ellen White was born Ellen Harmon in Maine in 1827. First pledging allegiance to the Methodist Church, she came to join the Millerite movement while still a young girl. Harmon's early education came to an end at the age of nine when she was hit in the head by a rock thrown by a schoolmate. After three weeks of unconsciousness, Harmon improved, but it was to this period of protracted illness that she would later point when describing her conversion to Christianity. Harmon's first visions would come later, shortly after the night of the Great Disappointment, when she was seventeen. These visions were central to bringing together Adventists who suffered spiritual disillusionment from the failure of the Edson theory to correctly identify the date of a profound shift in the celestial realm. Two years later, Harmon met the man she would marry, James Springer White, another influential early Adventist, and over the next fifteen years Ellen White gave birth to four children. Meanwhile, her visions received a wider audience through the ex-tensive publishing network that had grown up around the Millerites. In 1851, she published the first of what would be some forty volumes of her writings printed in her lifetime. Today with the addition of collections of her essays and works in manuscript to her canon, more than a hundred volumes of her writing are in print. Fervent Seventh-day Adventist evangelism has made White the most translated female nonfiction author in world history and the most translated American nonfiction author of either gender.

The themes of White's visions ranged from celestial events, places, and realms, to social reform, marriage and the family, and health. Her firm visionary conclusion that God had intended the Sabbath Day as the day of worship proved decisive for many, and she and her husband were influential in establishing the Seventh-day Adventist Church as an organized body in 1863. Many of White's most influential visions centered around what she called the Great Controversy. This controversy signified the continual battle between the forces of good and the forces of evil, between Christ and the devil, the angels of light and the angels of darkness. White expounded on this theme throughout many of her works, giving Adventism much of its unique character as a thoroughly apocalyptic branch of American Christianity. Although today many Catholics, Lutherans, and Anglicans have come to the conclusion that the book of Revelation is to be interpreted symbolically as a veiled political statement concerning Rome and the early Christians, the Seventh-day Adventists remain committed to the belief that the events described in Revelation and Daniel will transpire in human history and have begun to transpire today. White's other unique and influential doctrines concern the role of health in the spiritual life of the believer. For White it was clear that "the body is the temple of the Holy Spirit," and that, as such, it is the religious duty of members to care for their bodies. This fact led White to advocate that Christians follow strict kosher dietary laws, including the proscription on eating pork and shellfish. She insisted that a vegetarian diet is integral to the Christian life.

White herself helped found the first Adventist hospital in 1866. And over the history of Adventism, this insistence on healthful living has led to the foundation of numerous clinics, hospitals, sanitariums, and medical research centers. Some of the most influential Adventists have been medical doctors and nutritionists, two of whom were the Kellogg brothers, John Harvey Kellogg (1852–1943), a noted nutritionist, the inventor of cornflakes, and an avid advocate of holistic medicine; and W. K. Kellogg (1860–1951), the founder of Kellogg foods. When the brothers feuded over the introduction of sugar into the cereal (John did not want to allow it), John left to found another company dedicated to promoting foods made from soy. Today an extensive network of Adventist health centers extend around the globe and much of Adventist missionary work focuses on health and healing.

The Adventist world view has always held evangelism central to religion. It is important for Adventists to proclaim Christ's impending return and the true day of worship throughout the world. Worldwide, Seventh-day Adventists now number over 15 million.

Other Adventist beliefs have also been seminal for the history of the church, the most important of which is the Adventist mistrust of organized government in general and particularly insofar as it is linked with religious authority. This has often led toward a quietist stance toward politics and has been influential in shaping the Seventh-day Adventist opposition to war and the religion's strong support for religious toleration and the separation of church and state. The early church was strongly pacifist in belief and was part of the antiwar effort surrounding the

John Harvey Kellogg (1852–1943) was a physician and Seventh-day Adventist who is perhaps best known for inventing cornflakes cereal. His obituary in the New York Times *said that he died at the age of 91, "nine years short of the century goal which he had set for himself."*

Spanish American War and World War I. Historically, many Seventh-day Adventists have sought and received conscientious objector status in times of war, and the Adventist focus on health and well-being led many Adventists to become medics and battlefield doctors during World War II, the Korean War, and the Vietnam War. Many of these Adventists preferred to be called "conscientious participants" rather than "conscientious objectors," and some volunteered for Army medical experimentation, as a way of showing their willingness to die for America without taking up arms.

The Branch Davidians

In 1993, an Adventist splinter movement popularly called the Branch Davidians was surrounded by the U.S. Bureau of Alcohol, Tobacco, and Firearms (ATF) at their compound in Waco, Texas, after an attempted arrest of their leader, David Koresh, on a series of firearm violations. The Davidians had been disfellowed from the mainstream Adventist Church in 1929, and Koresh's own group, the Students of the Seven Seals, was a further splintering of this movement. Koresh, like Miller and White before him, was obsessed with the book of Daniel. He saw himself as an important symbolic figure in the book, a figure who was destined to usher in the end of days. As the events in Texas played out, Koresh became more and more convinced that what was transpiring there in Waco was nothing less than one of the last battles described in Revelation. Koresh's fanatical beliefs coupled with the failure of the FBI and the ATF to comprehend the symbolic and religious implications (as touted by Koresh) of their every movement, ultimately led to a showdown in which the majority of the Davidians burned to death inside of their compound. Controversy still rages over how the fire started.

The Seventh-day Adventist Church and Adventists as a whole do not identify with the Davidians and point out that they were an extremely small group (in comparison with the Church's millions-strong membership) and had no affiliation with the mainstream denomination. On the other side, critics have pointed to Waco as a chief example of the danger of apocalyptic religion, and some have argued that Adventism itself is a cult. This last charge has little basis in reality as the church has not been led by a charismatic figure for over a hundred years, and Adventists are in no way prohibited from contact outside of the group. Nonetheless, apocalyptic spirituality in general, and in Adventism in particular, does foster a sense of separateness and a mistrust of the powers that be. At the beginning of the twenty-first century, many Adventists still look forward to the "time of trouble," a period of strife in which organized religion and the government of the Antichrist will join together to persecute true Christians—particularly those Christians unwilling to worship on Sundays.

One of the paradoxes of the Adventist faith is that, like many conservative denominations, and despite their early history of strong female leadership, the Seventh-day Adventists have been resistant to the ordination of women to the pastorate. Because many of the major positions in the church hierarchy can be filled only by ordained clergy, this has excluded women from positions of power in the Church. Controversy on this issue continues today, with many North American churches supporting the ordination of women and those from Central and South America (where many Adventists are converts from Catholicism) opposing it. In 1995, the North American Division of the Adventist Church introduced a proposal that would have allowed each church division to decide the issue for itself. For better or for worse, this proposal was defeated with the vote running heavily against ordination.

B. Important Dates and Landmarks

1827 The birth of Ellen Gould White (née Harmon) in Gorham, Maine.

1832 William Miller publishes the first of his writings on the coming Advent in a Baptist paper.

1840 White's family joins the Millerites.

1843–1844 The predicted year of the Second Coming passes between March 21, 1843, and the same date a year later. A revised date is set for October 22, 1844. This becomes the date of the Great Disappointment.

1844 Hiram Edson claims to have had a vision in which he saw Christ beginning his period of investigative judgment. In December, White has her first visions revealing the changes that have taken place in heaven.

1863 The Seventh-day Adventist Church is established.

1866 The first major Adventist health center opens at White's behest in Battle Creek, Michigan.

1898 Adventists conscientiously object to the Spanish American War.

1905 A sanitarium is established in Loma Linda, California, which eventually becomes Loma Linda University, a major center for Adventist medical research.

1915 Death of Ellen White.

1941–1945 Adventists participate in WWII as doctors and medics.

1993 Seventy-six Branch Davidians are killed in a fifty-one-day standoff with the ATF and FBI in Waco, Texas.

1995 The General Conference of the Seventh-day Adventist Church votes to oppose the ordination of women.

II. Tenets and Attitudes

A. Articles of Faith

Seventh-day Adventists affirm and hold many of the traditional creedal statements of the Christian Church. They affirm that there is one unique God and that this God is a Trinity: The Father who created all things; the Son and Redeemer Jesus; and the Holy Spirit who works in the world through prophecy and inspired the Bible. As do most Christians, the Adventists consider the death and resurrection of Christ to be the unique salvific event in human history for the purpose of atoning for human sin. According to Adventists, one can be saved and receive eternal life only through accepting Jesus as savior, and Adventists, following roots which date back to the Protestant Reformation, affirm that salvation is through faith alone and cannot be obtained through human actions.

Adventists' beliefs become especially unique regarding the question of the Second Coming and the perpetual struggle between good and evil. The world and the whole cosmos are, for the Adventists, in a state of war and upheaval. Satan, the great enemy, opposes the true Church of God, and on his side he has many fallen angels and human subjects who have surrendered to him. Because Adventists believe that these are the final days of this world order, they claim that Satan is even now playing a part not only in corrupting the souls of individual humans but also in human history at large.

In the "times of trouble" that lie ahead many Adventists expect to see the separation between church and state collapse both in the United States and in Europe. When this happens, an Antichrist will rise to power who, in the guise of Christianity, will pass laws that proscribe true Christian belief. What will be left will be a small "remnant" of believers who have an integral role in proclaiming the truth symbolized by the three angels in the book of Revelation. At the end of days, this remnant of believers will join resurrected believers in heaven, where they will dwell for a thousand years. Meanwhile, the earth will remain desolate, inhabited only by Satan and his angels. After the millennium expires, Christ will return to earth with all believers, and the wicked will be resurrected and destroyed by fire along with all of the demonic powers.

The view of the dangers of church-state relations and the religious persecution to come has placed Adventists at the forefront of the struggle for religious tolerance. Although most Adventists are conservative enough to believe that salvation can only come through Christ, organized Adventist lobbies continue to fight for such issues as the rights of Muslims to hold prayers in schools and in the workplace, and the right of American Indians to use peyote as part of their religious practice—a fact which is all the more remarkable considering that the Adventist church bans the use of mind-altering substances by its own congregants.

Two of the Seventh-day Adventists' unique beliefs concern the afterlife and immortality. Hell, for Adventists, is not an eternal place where sinners are punished. Instead, when God purges the earth of the wicked, nonbelievers, Satan's angels, and Satan himself will be burned to oblivion instantaneously, after which they will no longer exist. The wicked will be resurrected and judged, but will not receive immortality, as eternal life is conditional based on one's faith in Christ. Furthermore, Adventists believe in the "unconscious state of the dead," a concept that humans who die do not immediately pass on to heaven, hell, or purgatory. Instead, the dead rest in a sleep-like state until the resurrection.

Healthful Living

Other unique views concern the role of bodily health in Christian spirituality. White herself advocated a return to many of the dietary restrictions listed in the Hebrew Bible that forbid eating pork and shellfish and added to this the recommendation that all Adventists practice vegetarianism. Her 1897 book *Healthful Living* revealed the full extent of these beliefs for the first time. The official position of the organized church is that taking good care of the physical body is the duty of every Christian, and forms a significant part of good "Christian behavior." The body is considered the "temple of the Holy Spirit," and before becoming a member of the church Adventists must recite and sign a vow committing to abstinence from alcohol and tobacco and to exercising and eating a healthy diet. The Adventists also sponsor numerous studies on vegetarianism, nutrition, and longevity. The town of Loma Linda, California, which is the center of Adventist health study, was featured on CNN and in *National Geographic* in 2005 as one of only three places in the world where the average life spans of its citizens significantly exceed the norms for the population at large. Today, many of the Adventist positions on health and nutrition have entered the mainstream, but in the late nineteenth century such positions were radical indeed.

Historically, the Adventist belief in strict standards of Christian behavior has extended to include prohibitions on the theater, dancing, and on Hollywood movies. Although Adventists today are unlikely to feel that it is acceptable to view or listen to secular entertainment on the Sabbath Day, many Adventists are closer to mainstream Americans on these questions than they were in the past. On the question of jewelry and adornment, the Adventist Church retains the strict belief that these items should be forbidden. In a concession to mainstream culture the Adventists now permit the exchange of wedding bands. Adventists greatly support Christian music, and officially recognize the role that music and hymns play in leading believers toward God.

Medicine and Transportation

It is in the medical world that Seventh-day Adventists have had the greatest influence on American culture. In 1984, Loma Linda University became a center of worldwide controversy when surgeon **Leonard Bailey** transplanted a baboon heart into the body of an infant known to the world only as Baby Fae. Although the girl's immune system rejected the transplant of the foreign tissue after twenty-one days, and this was one of the last animal-human grafts attempted by medical researchers, the attempt was a seminal moment in the history of organ transplants. Perhaps even more widely known is the surgeon and best-selling author **Ben Carson**. Carson became the director of pediatric neurosurgery at Johns Hopkins at the age of thirty-three and first received extensive attention when he performed an operation to separate two Siamese twins who were conjoined in the head. The surgery marked the first time that such an operation was successful, and Carson went on to perform a number of other highly publicized surgeries. In 1996, Carson published the autobiography *Gifted Hands* with the evangelical publishing house Zondervan. The work went on to become the first of Carson's three best-selling volumes.

Peace and Pacifism

A chief point of contention and controversy in the Adventist church today revolves around the question of peace and pacifism. In the opening days of the current Iraq conflict the official organs of the Adventist Church failed to come out strongly against the war, and, while recognizing that war is a tragedy, seemed also to acknowledge the inevitability of war and in no way urged Adventists to return to their historical role of peace advocates.

The minority of Adventists today continue to see the pursuit of peace as central to Adventist belief and point to historical Adventists such as Desmond Doss, who became the first noncombatant to receive a Congressional Medal of Honor in 1945 for his role in saving lives as an army medic. These Adventists often turned to the internet (the "blogosphere") as a means of protesting the war, and numerous sites have sprung up on the web as these Adventists have sought to push the church toward a firmer commitment to the mission of peace.

B. Scripture

Concerning the role of the Bible, the vast majority of Seventh-day Adventists are fundamentalists and biblical literalists. Although Adventists consider the New Testament to be the highest and most privileged expression of God's truth, they also pay more than average attention to the writings of the Hebrew Bible and are much less likely than other Christians to see the New Testament as dramatically altering what was said in the Old. The Seventh-day Adventist Church believes that biblical books were written when they claim to be written, so that, for example, the book of Daniel is believed to have been written around 600 BCE rather than in the mid-second century BCE (when most secular historians believe it was written). The vast majority of Adventists are creationists, but are much less likely to endorse theories, such as Intelligent Design, which posit the guided evolution of life on this planet. Instead, Adventists believe that the biblical account of the creation of the earth in seven days is literally true and that the earth is only 9,000 years old. Adventists have founded the Earth Science Institute in Loma Linda in an effort to establish these ideas as facts, and are also highly involved in biblical archeology, where they are likely to seek evidence to establish the historical truth of biblical accounts.

Adventists see no conflict between the biblical fundamentalist stance and a belief in the inspiration of their prophetess, Ellen White. All of White's positions, including those surrounding the Second Coming, conditional immortality, and the unconscious state of the dead, are believed to have a scriptural basis, and, although Adventists believe that White was a recipient of the spiritual gift of prophecy, they hold that her visions are less authoritative than those within the biblical canon. Nonetheless, her books hold the highest possible place next to the Old and New Testament writings, and no other nonbiblical writer within the Church and church history is quoted in the Seventh-day Adventist *Church Manual*, the authoritative document on the rules and beliefs of the faith. Adventists hold that White was the final prophet sent by God to usher in the end times. The canon is thus closed in this respect and the Adventists will not introduce new writings into their corpus any time soon.

III. Rites and Rituals

A. The Calendar

Adventists hold that the period from sundown on Friday night to sundown on Saturday was set aside by God as a day of rest and worship and that those who fail to keep this day holy violate one of the Ten Commandments. Seventh-day Adventists are forbidden to work on the Sabbath day, as well as forbidden to enjoy secular entertainments. Many Adventists consider all commercial activities to be problematic as well. Adventists spend this day in worship service, Bible study, and prayer, and often hold potluck dinners in the early afternoon, the food for which has been prepared the day before.

Adventists view historical religious holidays such as Easter and Christmas with some skepticism, seeing them as pagan and Catholic innovations. This stance derives, in part, from the negative view that Adventists take toward Sunday worship. By and large, the Adventists hold that early Christians made many dangerous compromises, reflected in Christmas and Easter, with the original Christian faith in order to attract more believers. Yet, though Adventists do not consider these holidays sacred days, they have never been vehemently opposed to them. Adventists today may celebrate Christmas, Easter, and even Halloween at home, but they do not do so in church. Although Adventists do not believe that Christ was born on Christmas, they spend the Sabbath before Christmas singing hymns related to the birth of Christ and reflecting on these events. No special service is held on the holiday itself, and Adventists may observe it as they wish.

B. Worship and Liturgy

Seventh-day Adventist church services, although they vary from church to church, nearly always include a period for extended Bible study. While the children separate from the adults to attend "Sabbath school," where they memorize Bible passages and listen to religious stories, the adults often separate into various groups for their own version of religious education. This separation is often according to interest, with one group holding a weekly discussion of the writings of the Apostle Paul, and another, for example, studying passages which relate to prophecy. This period of study can range from twenty minutes to well over an hour.

The worship service itself often differs little from the practices of most Protestants. A large place is given to music, which can range from traditional Christian hymns to pop and folk music, depending on the congregation. Key scriptural passages are read from the Hebrew Bible and the New Testament, and the pastor gives a sermon on a preselected topic. Some pastors today are not adverse to using multimedia presentations and bullet point slides of key topics. Public prayers are also offered during the service, and a time is set aside to pray for those in the congregation who are ill. Many Seventh-day Adventist churches also incorporate a children's story into their service and have children gather around a deacon or an elder at the front of the church to hear a story drawn from the Bible, history, or from life. In larger churches, the average service may include the baptism of new members as well.

Seventh-day Adventists (like most Protestants) offer a Communion service in remembrance of the Last Supper four times a year. While in traditional Christian practice this ritual entailed the sharing of

Photograph taken on June 25, 1912, in Wausau, Wisconsin, at the annual convention of the state's Seventh-day Adventists.

blessed bread and wine by congregants, Adventists eschew alcohol even in this instance, and insist that as the bread used must be unleavened, so must the grape juice be unfermented.

Adventists differ from the Catholics and the Eastern Orthodox in that they do not see the Communion ritual as literally transforming the bread and wine into the body and blood of Christ. The ritual, for Adventists, is merely a symbolic remembrance of the life and death of Jesus. As part of the quarterly Communion service, Adventists ritually reenact another important part of the Last Supper story: the washing of the disciples' feet by Jesus. During this part of the service, men and women move to separate sides of the church and congregants take turns in going down on bended knee and washing each other's feet as a symbol of humility.

C. Daily Life

Seventh-day Adventists practice Christian behavior, vegetarianism, Sabbatarianism, beliefs concerning jewelry and adornment, and healthful living. Despite such distinguishing characteristics of their daily lives, Seventh-day Adventists are closer to the American mainstream culture than they have ever been before. For instance, it would be difficult on the basis of dress to separate them as a group from other evangelical Protestants. In many ways, Adventists today have softened the lines that separate them from the Christian mainstream and have embraced an identity where creationism and biblical fundamentalism often trump Adventist specific concerns and lead them to find commonalities rather than differences across denominational lines.

The Adventist focus on morality, the family, and sexual ethics have led them to embrace many of the causes of the political right, particularly concerning abortion and homosexuality. The majority of Adventists and the official organs of the church remain opposed to the toleration of homosexuality, which they judge to be a species of the biblical sin of forni-

cation. This opposition to homosexual behavior has led many Adventists to believe that homosexuality can be "cured," and a number of Adventists today consider themselves "former homosexuals."

However, the Adventist relationship with the political right remains an uneasy one because of Adventist fears that the distinction between church and state may collapse. Many Adventists, for example, opposed the candidacy of Governor Huckabee for president in the 2008 election due to the fact that he had been a Baptist minister.

Today's Adventists may attend movies and the theater, and watch television much in the same manner as other Christians. But like many other socially conservative denominations, the Adventists have put great effort into developing alternative media outlets and producing entertainment that is in keeping with their values. Adventist churches may also advocate outdoor recreation and hiking as an alternative form of entertainment, and an organization called the Pathfinders is a specifically Seventh-Day Adventist version of the Boy Scouts and trains children in survivalism and outdoor sports.

Both adults and young adults are expected to be active in charitable and evangelical work, and all members of the church are encouraged to offer Bible study sessions for any non-Adventists who are willing to listen. Such sessions often center on the prophecies from Daniel that were so fundamental to the foundation of Adventism. Adventists continue to hold revival meetings and public lectures on the book of Revelation as a means of attracting converts.

D. Life Cycle Events

Adventists have always had a deep interest in the education of children, and Ellen White herself was not only instrumental in organizing many Adventist schools, but wrote a great deal in advocation of education reform. Life in the church for the youngest Adventists revolves around Bible study, Bible camps, and outdoor summer camps. The Seventh-day

Adventists do not recognize the baptism of infants and argue that true baptism can only be performed on those who have had a deep conversion experience, understand the important tenets of the Adventist faith, and have received the grace from God that will allow them to be "born again." Young children who demonstrate a great eagerness to be baptized may be baptized at a young age, but, for most Adventist children, full life and membership in the church does not begin until sometime around the age of twelve. At this time, those children who feel ready to be baptized attend regular classes in which they must show that they understand the central creeds of the church. When these classes are completed, children are baptized during the regular Saturday church service.

Baptism. According to the Adventists, baptism must take place in running water and must involve the full immersion of the human body. Converts to Adventism who have been baptized in this manner need not be rebaptized. They can be accepted into the church after what is called "a profession of faith," which involves a formal submission of a statement of belief to the Church Board. But the Adventists do not recognize as valid the baptisms of the Catholics, Anglicans, and other denominations who baptize infants or do not baptize by full immersion. Most Adventist churches in America today have a built-in baptistry that lies somewhere in the paneling at the front of the church. This paneling can be drawn back to allow the baptism to occur in full view of the congregation as they sit in the pews. Typically the pastor and the convert dress in baptismal robes that evoke nineteenth-century paintings of biblical life. Before being submerged in the water, the convert recites a "baptismal covenant" in which he or she promises to uphold the faith, abstain from smoking and drinking, and to fulfill the mission of the church as the divinely appointed remnant. At this point the pastor baptizes the convert and welcomes him or her into full membership.

This baptism signifies the forgiveness of all sins through a faith in Christ, and such forgiveness is believed to be for life so long as the convert continually turns back in repentance toward God.

Adventist weddings do not differ significantly from most Protestant or secular American weddings. They tend to involve music, a processional, prayers, and the exchange of vows. The only significant difference lies in the fact that Adventists traditionally did not exchange wedding rings due to prohibitions on jewelry and adornment. But even this has begun to change, and the church now officially recognizes the exchange of wedding bands as the single instance in which jewelry is permissible. Adventists have no trouble accepting the marriage ceremonies of other denominations, and those Adventists who find themselves in some part of the world where there is no ordained Adventist pastor are encouraged to be married in a civil ceremony.

Adventist funerals are much like those of most Protestants, and Adventists do not believe that the rituals that surround death and burial have any real effect on the state of the dead. Adventists hold that one will meet one's deceased loved ones again, but unlike other Christians, they do not believe that those loved ones have moved on to "a better place." The dead remain asleep until Jesus's return.

Marriage. Seventh-day Adventist connections with other biblical fundamentalists and the political right have led Adventists to value family and the married state even more highly than they have in the past. Like many conservative Christians, Seventh-day Adventists often see the family as contested ground coming into the twenty-first century, and have adopted a very negative stance toward sexual liberation and homosexuality. Biblical literalism has also encouraged them to take seriously Pauline injunctions which speak of the submission of the wife to the husband. Nonetheless, Adventists are more likely to consider marriage a partnership between equals than other fundamentalists, and in the official *Church Manual* passages from Paul and the prophetess Ellen White are quoted to the effect that "submission" in marriage runs in both directions, and that the man must submit to the woman as well. Adventists, like many other Christians, quote passages to the effect that marriage symbolizes the union between Christ and the

Church, so that the man in his submission takes as his model the "self-sacrificial love and service that Christ gives to the Church." Marriage for the Adventists is divinely mandated and recognized, and through marriage the husband and wife become "one flesh."

Intermarriage. Of special concern to Adventists are marriages between believers and nonbelievers, or more particularly, between Seventh-day Adventist Church members and other believing Christians. Adventists stop just short of entirely prohibiting such marriages, urging that pastors in their churches not perform them and that members who ultimately decide to marry outside the faith understand that the official ministers of the church can play no role in sanctioning this choice. The Adventist focus on healthful living and the keeping of the Sabbath as a day of worship and rest are of crucial significance to the belief that outside marriages are unlikely to succeed without the compromise of practices central to the Adventist life.

Sexuality. Seventh-day Adventists, like many Protestants, do not condemn sexuality so long as sexual relations take place between married couples. According to the *Church Manual*, sexual intimacy in marriage "is a sacred gift from God to the human family" that "promotes ever-increasing closeness, happiness, and security, and provides for the perpetuation of the human race." Human sexuality can be strongly positive, but only when it finds outlet in monogamous heterosexual relationships. Homosexuality, for the Adventists, represents a false and tainted use of this "gift."

Although Adventists take the biblical injunction to "be fruitful and multiply" seriously, Adventists, like other American Protestants, are not opposed to the use of birth control by married couples. Abortion, on the other hand, is considered on par with murder by many Adventists who are strongly "pro-life" in sentiment. But while the church is committed to "respect" for unborn life, Adventists are, nonetheless, more circumspect than other fundamentalist denominations—a fact, no doubt, that is closely related to Adventist medical research. The Center for Christian Bioethics at Loma Linda University, for example, urges that Christians not give into the urge for simplistic answers to questions such as stem cells and the frozen embryos used in surrogate parenting.

Divorce. On the whole, Adventists are strictly opposed to divorce and believe that marriage has meaning only as a lifetime commitment in the eyes of God. Adventists quote passages from Jesus's ministry which prohibit divorce and speak strongly of God's "abhorrence" of the practice. Nonetheless, Adventists do recognize that not all marriages are permanent. When a husband or wife violates the principles of trust, loyalty, and "exclusiveness" that are central to marriage, such marriages are in danger of being "destroyed." For the Adventists, this means that there are only two possible grounds for a divorce: adultery and/or fornication, and abandonment by an unbelieving partner. Fornication in the Adventist view extends to include incest, child abuse, and homosexuality, while abandonment centers on the question of marriages in which one member or the other apostatizes from the church.

As for remarriage, Adventists consider there to be a difference between one who was guilty of betraying the original marriage and one who was innocent. The spouse who has remained faithful may remarry without sin, while the unfaithful one must remain unmarried at least until the point when his or her partner has remarried. In some instances, more liberal Adventists will overlook the letter of the law when it comes to divorce and remarriage, but for most Adventists, divorce and remarriage are seen as sinful, and a divorce must always assign guilt to one spouse for destroying the marriage bond.

IV. Denominations and Demographics

A. Schismatic History and Comparisons in Tenets and Beliefs

Throughout the almost 150 years since the church came into being, the Seventh-day Adventists have remained remarkably unified and resistant to the splintering that has affected many other American Protestant denominations. This is in part due to the fact that most Adventists are socially conservative, and a progressive or liberal faction has never been a serious threat to the right-oriented majority.

Those splits that have occurred have been on the conservative side and have come from those reform-minded Adventists who have believed that the church organization had become too worldly. Occasionally this type of conservatism has led individual pastors and congregations to split off from the larger Adventist body, but they have rarely become a force in their own right.

The Davidian Seventh-day Adventists, started by renegade pastor Victor Houteff in 1929, would have been only a minor exception to this rule, were it not for David Koresh's standoff with the ATF and FBI in 1993. The Davidians differed from the mainstream Adventist church in the intensity of their apocalypticism, but also in their belief that the spirit of prophecy remained alive and well in the world and that White was followed by other visionaries (including Koresh) who were important in these "times of trouble."

The Davidian Seventh-day Adventists have always remained a minority movement, and Koresh's own sect has not survived its encounter with the government. Nonetheless, Koresh recruited members exclusively from Seventh-day Adventist churches, and tapes of his sermons were circulated in apocalyptic Adventist circles and Adventist theological institutions well before his death. Apocalyptic theology, in fact, remains a powerful force in the church as a whole, though many Adventists were embarrassed by the officially unsanctioned advertising campaign of some Adventists during Pope John Paul II's visit to North America for Catholic World Youth Day in 1993, when Adventist apocalyptic groups took out billboards and sent out mass mailings warning that the pope was the Antichrist.

B. Centers and Distribution

Adventists in the United States are a culturally and racially diverse group due to worldwide Adventist evangelism. Church statistics for the year 2006 showed that more than 90 percent of all Adventists now reside outside of the United States, and the church at large continues to grow. Of the more than 15 million Adventists worldwide, more than five million of them reside in South and Central America and five million in Africa, in comparison with the just over one million members in the United States. Immigration of Adventist converts to this country have greatly increased the diversity of American Adventism as a whole. Today major cities in the United States tend to contain one or more Spanish-language Adventist churches, and even the most parochial Adventist churches often have members born overseas.

The North American Division of the Adventist Church has members across every state in America both in rural areas and in cities. Adventism continues to be strong in the Midwest and West, especially California, the site of many Adventist hospitals.

V. Organization and Infrastructure

A. Education and Hierarchy of Clergy

Seventh-day Adventist churches on a local level feature a clear hierarchy in which pastors, elders, deacons, and deaconesses play a central role. The pastor is the head of the local church and is officially invested with the powers of clergy through a laying-on of hands. The pastor serves an executive function within the local church and on the Church Board and is also chiefly responsible for baptisms, Communion, leading prayer, and giving sermons. Candidates for pastor must attend one of the Adventist seminaries around the world, the best known of which is the

Seventh-day Adventist Theological Seminary at Andrews University in Berrien Springs, Michigan. While in seminary, students take courses on the Bible and Adventist theology and often serve in other supporting roles at a local church. After earning a Master in Divinity (MDiv) or a Doctor of Ministry (DMin) degree, candidates must pass examinations before being ordained and assigned to lead a church. The General Conference of the Seventh-day Adventist Church officially prohibits the ordination of women to the pastorate (a position reaffirmed in 1995), but allows them to serve as pastors.

B. Governance and Authority

Elders and deacons are chosen from among the congregants of the local church to support the pastor and to aid in church ritual and decision-making. An elder is a congregant who embodies Adventist values; he is elected by the church congregation for a period of one to two years depending on local bylaws. Traditionally all elders were men, but in 1984 the General Conference voted to ordain women as elders. In some quarters, this remains controversial: even where women may be elected to office, their ordination rites are not the same as men's.

The elders play an important role as leaders of the local church and, in places that lack a minister, they are considered the chief authorities in the church, and may perform baptisms and marriages, and hold worship services. In larger churches they function as assistants to the pastor and aid in ministering to the sick and fulfilling other pastoral duties. Deacons and deaconesses are also elected for one to two years by and from the local congregation and play a role in visiting local congregants at their homes, preparing for the baptismal and Communion services, collecting offerings during the service, and serving on the Church Board. In this respect, governance of the local church combines the executive authority of the pastor (who is appointed by the conference) with representative democracy.

This democratic element can also be found throughout the church's higher levels. Unlike other denominations, the Adventist Church does not ordain bishops. Churches, divisions, and conferences instead elect delegates to represent the respective bodies at regional and worldwide conferences. An individual church votes to elect all of its own officers except for the pastor, and the elected officers of the church, in turn, appoint the officers of the state conference, and the officers of the state conference appoint the members of the united conference. The largest of these bodies, and the one granted ultimate authority on Adventist doctrine and practice, is the General Conference.

At a General Conference, delegates from every division in the world gather to vote on matters from theology and doctrine to social behavior and norms. A majority vote by this body is necessary to alter teachings contained in the *Church Manual of the Seventh-day Adventists,* a work of more that 200 pages that provides a rule of orthodoxy for the faith.

General Conference of Seventh-day Adventists
12501 Old Columbia Pike
Silver Spring, MD 20904
301-680-6000   www.adventist.org

Even at the local level, Adventist commitments to health, the separation of church and state, and the education of children have led them to form numerous organizations dedicated to these matters. In the realm of heath care, local leaders are encouraged to appoint a Health Ministry Council and conference directors may organize a Health Ministries Society, while the church Public Affairs and Religious Liberty Department (PARL) fights to safeguard religious liberty for all believers, no matter what their faith, and holds "freedom of conscience" as the highest principle. According to the *Church Manual,* every local church should consider itself an "informal Religious Liberty Association," and every Church member is a member of this association. Each church elects a "religious liberty leader" to monitor current events relating to religious freedom and appoints youth leaders and ministers to educate younger members.

Many host a branch of the Pathfinders, Adventist equivalent to the Boy Scouts.

C. Social Service Organizations

Maranatha Volunteers International
1600 Sacramento Inn Way, Suite 116
Sacramento, CA 95815

Maranatha Volunteers International Assoc.
45175 Wells Road, Unit 20
Chilliwack, BC V2R 3K7 Canada
916-920-1900   Fax: 916-920-3299
www.maranatha.org

Much of the money raised in tithes by local churches is used to found new churches, health clinics, schools, and orphanages abroad. Maranatha Volunteers International was founded in 1969 as an Adventist version of the Peace Corps, operating in Africa, South and Central America, and Asia. Maranatha often sends entire high school classes to impoverished areas, and Adventist doctors often spend years abroad as missionaries in remote areas.

D. Media and Communications

Since the earliest days of the Advent movement, believers have held it vitally important to witness to as many people as possible. Some of these early periodicals are still published today.

Review and Herald Publishing Association
55 West Oak Ridge Drive
Hagerstown, MD 21740
301-393-3000
info@rhpa.org
www.reviewandherald.com

Important periodicals are the *Adventist Review* and *Liberty Magazine*, dedicated to promoting the cause of religious liberty in America.

Hope Channel
PO Box 4000
Silver Springs, MD 20904
301-380-6689   Fax: 301-680-5147
888-446-7388
info@hopetr.org   www.hopetr.org

Three Angels Broadcasting Network
PO Box 220
West Frankfort, IL 62896
618-627-4651   Fax: 618-627-2726
www.3abn.org

Modern Adventists use television, radio, and the internet to teach and preach. Hope Channel, It Is Written Television, and the Voice of Prophecy broadcast worldwide. Three Angels Broadcasting Network (3ABN) is a cable television network created in 1986 to provide alternative Christian programming. The church's online organ is www.adventist.org

FURTHER READING

Seventh-day Adventists Answer Questions
1957: Review & Herald Publishing

This We Believe: An Overview of the Teachings of Seventh-day Adventists
Erwin Gane and Leo Van Dolson
1993: Pacific Press

Prophetess of Health: Ellen White and the Origins of Seventh-Day Adventist Health Reform
Ronald L. Numbers
1992: University of Tennessee Press

The Great Controversy
Ellen White
1950: Pacific Press

15 Unitarian Universalists

I. Origins and Early History

A. Introduction

I N SUBJECTIVE AMERICAN MEMORY, THE PURITANS ARE seen as dour, joyless, intolerant, and bigoted. We remember the witch trials in Salem and recall Hawthorne's *The Scarlet Letter* and Arthur Miller's *The Crucible,* which we read in school. We contrast the stuffy convictions of these Puritan ancestors with modern values of open-mindedness, pluralism, and cross-cultural sympathy and understanding. But while this impression is not completely inaccurate—the witch trials did indeed occur, and Puritans were guilty of crimes against the "pagan" Indians—it tells only one side of the story. The other side of the story relates the role Puritanism played in giving birth to American liberal religion, Massachusetts liberalism, and the call for openness and tolerance that are so much a part of the American religious scene today. This side of the story is the story of Unitarianism and Universalism in America.

B. Unitarianism in America

From the earliest days of Puritanism in England, the Puritan movement carried within it a strong anti-Catholic flavor. "Papism" was the enemy, along with all of the rituals of the Catholics and the 1,500-year history of Catholic dogma. The revelations of the Catholic saints were thought of not as revelations at all, but rather as human inventions at best and demonic corruptions at worst. Puritans ridiculed the obscurity of the Latin Mass and Eucharist ceremony by calling it "hocus pocus," a corruption of the words from the Mass, *hoc est corpus,* "this is my body." The goal of these Puritans—along with other Protestants —could be summed up by the phrase of Martin Luther, so often echoed by John Calvin: *sola scriptore,* "by Scripture alone." All of the accumulated theology had to be stripped away in order to return to the fount of religious truth, the biblical writings. These, and these alone, were to be the guide of true Christians. This new emphasis on Scripture carried with it a new emphasis on translations, study of Hebrew and Greek language, and methods of interpretation. For the first time since the fall of the Roman Empire, Western Christians began to read

All Souls Church, a Unitarian church in Washington, D.C., whose founding members include John Quincy Adams, was located in a building at D and Sixth Streets until it moved to a new home in 1923. This interior elevation of the original building was prepared by its architect, Charles Bulfinch, around 1821.

the New Testament in Greek, and to question the ideas that tradition had handed down to them about the life and work of Jesus.

Historically, liberalism can be seen as the enemy of tradition. A liberal is someone who calls tradition into question in the name of human reason and the ability of individuals to find truth by their own light. Puritanism, with its strong anti-Catholic flavor, gradually took on a liberal bias due to the desire of the Puritans to free themselves of the "Catholic yoke." With the rise of Enlightenment thought in the seventeenth and eighteenth centuries, the movement toward scriptural analysis and literary and historical criticism of Scripture was renewed and transformed.

The philosopher Baruch de Spinoza (1632–1677), an excommunicated Jew living in Calvinist Amsterdam, was central to this process. In a work he called the *Theological-Political Treatise*, Spinoza launched a dozen arguments that would become central to the definition of liberalism and liberal religion. He argued, among other things, for freedom of conscience and freedom of religion, but more importantly he argued that one should read the writings of the New Testament and Hebrew Bible as historical documents written by historical authors. Spinoza pointed out dozens of contradictions in Scripture and tradition, noting that portions of the Bible said to have been written by Moses could not have been written by him as the Bible itself claimed that Moses was dead by the time these events occurred. Spinoza further argued that Jesus had not been born God, but rather had attained the "mind of God" through his life and goodness. To support this thesis, he adduced passages from the Bible itself that seemed to support the thesis that Jesus was only God's "adopted" son.

Thus, the claim that Scripture was the fount of all truth paradoxically raised questions about the most fundamental of Christian ideas, and even, at times, about the validity of Scripture itself. In 325 CE, at the council of Nicaea, Christian bishops from across the Roman Empire had gathered together to vote on the much-contested question of the Holy Trinity. Was

God a Trinity made up of coequal substances? In other words, was Jesus God, and God Jesus, in such a way that both were equal? The opinions of the dissenting party, led by a bishop named Arius, were disallowed even though many of the earliest Christians, like Arius, seemed to have believed that Jesus was divine and yet still subordinate to God the Father and in no way equal to the one true God. Now the influence of the Enlightenment and the belief that Scripture had to be considered more authoritative than tradition caused many to question the validity of Trinitarianism. Did the New Testament describe a Trinity or was this only a later belief that Christians now read back into the Bible? If Jesus was a Trinitarian, why did he never directly claim such a thing? Why didn't he give Christians a Trinitarian creed?

The Great Awakening

In the 1730s and 1740s, this issue came to a head during what was known as the Great Awakening. Led by charismatic preachers, such as Jonathan Edwards, whose sermon "Sinners in the Hands of an Angry God" has become a classic work of English literature, New England became the home of a new breed of revivalism that called for a return to Calvinistic purity and a direct experience of salvific grace. Numerous New Englanders were "born again" in this new wave of enthusiasm. Those who resisted the movement came to be known as the Old Lights as opposed to the New Lights of the Great Awakening. These Christians judged the enthusiasm of their brethren as unhealthy and emphasized the value of reason and temperance.

More importantly, these Old Lights were uncomfortable with the Calvinist doctrine of predestination, and came to argue that human will had a place in religious salvation and that there was more to being saved than being emotionally swept off one's feet. Calvin, and the Puritans who had followed his dogmas, had interpreted passages from Paul to the effect that God unilaterally chose whom to save and whom to damn so that some were predestined to hell and some to heaven.

The Old Lights, centered in Boston, and lead by Jonathan Mayhew and Charles Chauncy, led an assault on this dogma. But perhaps more importantly, this new movement questioned the Calvinist doctrine of the "fallenness" and depravity of humankind. The strength of the doctrine of predestination lay in the notion that, since the time of Adam and Eve, humans had been too contaminated by evil to do anything that was genuinely pleasing to God or to discern truth by their own light. The dark cloud that lay over the human soul prevented humans from choosing the good on their own so that humans could become good only by the unilateral intervention of the divine being.

William Ellery Channing (1780–1842), born in Rhode Island, was one of Unitarianism's leading theologians.

This concept stood directly opposed to the humanism of Enlightenment thought. These thinkers argued that the "natural light" of human reason, however it might differ from the divine light, remained healthy and true, and that one could ignore the role that strong and thorough reasoning played in discerning truth only at the peril of becoming a slave to superstition. Thus, by way of Enlightenment thought, many of the Old Lights mounted an attack on the notion of human wickedness, an attack that was to be seminal in the development of Unitarianism.

Universalism

Toward the end of the eighteenth century another movement came to light, one which had a number of similarities to the Unitarian position. Like the Unitarians, the Universalists had difficulty with the doctrine of predestination. The name Universalism stood for the belief that everyone would eventually be saved and that God was too good to ever condemn a thinking and feeling human being to eternal damnation.

As with the Unitarian position, this dogma had historical roots that dated back to the earliest days of Christianity. The Alexandrian theologian Origen had supported such a theory when he wrote in the second century. But, as with anti-Trinitarian formulations, the notion of universal salvation had been proscribed by church council and had lain dormant for well over a millennium. The Universalist churches that emerged on the East Coast of New England differed from those of their Unitarian brothers in that they were primarily rural rather than urban, and made up of those less educated and less sophisticated Christians who were nevertheless attracted to theological liberalism. Although one critic would joke that the difference between the Unitarians and the Universalists lay in the fact that the Universalists thought that God was too good to damn them, while Unitarians thought that they were too good to be damned, nonetheless, each of these two groups were similar in their beliefs and in their faith that human sin and evil was nothing so dire that it could not be repaired.

Unitarianism eventually became the religion of the upper class and the educated in Boston, taking control of the Divinity School at Harvard almost as soon as it was founded in 1806. The Congregationalists who opposed Unitarianism, such as Jedidiah Morse, were replied to in kind. In 1819, William Ellery Channing delivered a seminal sermon in which he espoused many of the chief Unitarian beliefs, including a denial of the Trinity and what would later be called biblical "fundamentalism," and the Christian liberal tenet par excellence: Exemplarism. Exemplarism involves a rejection of the traditional Christian tenet that Jesus's death on the cross represents the single most important moment in salvation history. According to this belief, Jesus's life and ministry is more important than his death, and each of his actions and sermons saves by providing a moral example to Christians. This belief continues to be central to American liberal Christianity, and was raised most recently in response to Mel Gibson's film *The*

Passion of the Christ, when liberal theologians gathered at Harvard to denounce the film for focusing so exclusively on Jesus's death at the expense of his life.

In 1825, the Unitarians first came together as a loosely knit group with the formation of the American Unitarian Association. This event was followed in turn by the creation of the General Convention of the Universalists in 1833. Throughout the nineteenth century Unitarians and Universalists increased in numbers and strength across New England. And the influence of Unitarianism on culture at Harvard can hardly be overestimated. What was once a bastion of Puritanism that had been founded for the purpose of providing an "educated clergy" in 1636 now became equally a center of Enlightenment values, rationalism, and Scottish commonsense philosophy.

Romanticism and Transcendentalism

However, with the rise of Romanticism as a school of thought in the mid-nineteenth century the Unitarians began to experience some of their first internal battles. Romanticism as a teaching was thoroughly liberal and supported the battle of the individual against the forces of the state, the church, and all tradition. But, in defiance of Enlightenment thinking, the Romantics taught that intuition, rather than reason, was the most important human faculty, and that religious truth in particular could be discovered only by those who developed an intuitive and direct connection to the divine. These became the central questions of the controversy that surrounded Transcendentalism, a school of thought favored by Henry David Thoreau and Ralph Waldo Emerson. The Transcendentalists, following the philosopher Immanuel Kant and the German theologian Fredrich Scheliermacher, argued that truth and the real transcended the limits of reason. But, although this dispute cut to the very core of Unitarianism, it never caused any institutional splits, and Unitarianism today continues to be influenced by both types of thought.

Following a decline in numbers and influence after the Civil War and throughout much of the twentieth century—which was at least partially due

This portrait of Transcendentalist poet and writer Ralph Waldo Emerson was engraved in 1878 after an original drawing by Samuel W. Rowse.

to the fact that many of the core ideas of liberal religion had become more mainstream—the Unitarians and the Universalists increasingly began to look toward the union of their two churches. In 1931, a joint convention of the Unitarian and Universalist churches began meeting with the goal of a merger. When this did not succeed, the Free Church of America was founded which included churches from both sides. This movement was, however, unsuccessful, and by 1939 the Free Church movement had folded. But in 1947, the Unitarian General Conference voted to explore the possibilities for merger once more, and in 1953 the Council of Liberal Churches was established to gradually bring together institutional elements of the church.

The merger was finally completed in 1961 and the new church came to be known as the Unitarian Universalist Association, or the UUA.

B. Important Dates and Landmarks

1509 Birth of John Calvin.

1620–1640 Colonies established by New England Puritans.

1670 Baruch de Spinoza composes the *Theological Political Treatise.*

1692 Salem witch trials.

1730s–1740s The Great Awakening shakes New England. The Old Lights in Boston begin to teach and preach positions that will become central to Unitarianism.

1741 Jonathan Edwards delivers his famous sermon, "Sinners in the Hands of an Angry God."

1779 First Universalist Congregation in America, Gloucester, Massachusetts—with John Murray as minister.

1806 Harvard Divinity School established as a nondenominational seminary.

1819 William Ellery Channing preaches sermon against biblical literalism, arguing for "example" of Jesus's words and deeds.

1825 American Unitarian Association founded.

1833 The General Convention of Universalists holds its first meeting.

1838 Ralph Waldo Emerson delivers his seminal "Divinity School Address," which highlights for the first time the tension between Transcendentalist romanticism and Enlightenment rationalism.

1933 Humanist Manifesto I published; II will be published in **1973**; III in **2003**.

1961 The Unitarian and Universalist churches merge to create the Unitarian Universalist Association, or UUA.

1995 Statement of principles and purposes amended to include a sixth source, the spiritual teachings of earth-centered and nature-based religions.

C. Important Figures

Ralph Waldo Emerson (1803–1882)

One of the most famous of all Unitarians was Ralph Waldo Emerson, one of the founders and seminal figures of the Transcendentalist school of thought. Born in 1803, Emerson intended to follow his father and grandfather by becoming a minister. He completed his theological education at Harvard and attained the position of minister in one of Boston's major Unitarian churches. But Emerson's own liberalism differed from that of "orthodox" Unitarians. In 1832, he came to wonder at the validity of the Congregational Communion rite, and ultimately resigned his position in order to dedicate himself to the world of letters.

Nonetheless, in 1838 Emerson was chosen by the graduating class at Harvard Divinity School to deliver the commencement address. The result is still remembered today as one of the most important events to take place in those halls. From the first sentence of the address, Emerson's romantic tendencies were apparent. The staid call for reason was nowhere to be found. Instead, Emerson launched into a florid description of natural beauty:

In this refulgent summer, it has been a luxury to draw the breath of life. The grass grows, the buds burst, the meadow is spotted with fire and gold in the tint of flowers. The air is full of birds, and sweet with the breath of the pine, the balm-of-Gilead, and the new hay. Night brings no gloom to the heart with its welcome shade. Through the transparent darkness the stars pour their almost spiritual rays.

This natural beauty called forth, for Emerson, a whole host of religious questions and a sense of profound wonder, which Emerson contrasted with the doctrines of established religion. Established religion focused on the person of Jesus and the miracles that Jesus was said to have performed, instead of the miracles that were to be found everywhere in nature, Emerson claimed. Worse, the very notion of the Scripture as Christian revelation seemed to say that God had stopped speaking, and that communication with the divine was not an open channel to be discovered in the present. According to Emerson, one had to be free of the past in order to find God in the present.

Emerson's address caused an immediate reaction from the Unitarians at Harvard, who repudiated Emerson and published pamphlets and articles against him. Unitarian theologians up to this point had been careful to show that Unitarianism was still a brand of Christianity and that Unitarians believed in Jesus's miracles as much as any group of Christians. Emerson himself remained somewhat on the fringes of Unitarianism for much of his life, but today, many Unitarians look to Emerson for inspiration, and follow Emerson in his belief that God can be found in nature and through intuition, and that Christians lose out on the fullness of divine truth through their exclusive focus on the person of Jesus.

William Ellery Channing (1780–1842)

William Ellery Channing was a spokesman for liberal and Unitarian churches within Massachusetts's Standing Order of churches during the Unitarian controversy that embroiled Christian theology in New England during the first quarter of the nineteenth century. He published many sermons that served to illuminate a middle ground between orthodoxy and infidelity. He championed human dignity and human rights, fostering social reform in the areas of free speech, education, peace, antislavery, and relief for the poor. Channing entered Harvard College at age fifteen and graduated at the head of his class in 1798. In 1801, Channing was appointed regent, or student supervisor, for Harvard College, allowing him to study for the ministry under Professor David Tappan. Channing was ordained in 1803 and became the minister of Boston's Federal Street Church.

It was soon after his ordination that the Unitarian controversy began with the conflict over the appointment of David Tappan's successor. Within the Standing Order of Massachusetts churches, orthodox ministers refused to exchange

pulpits with liberal ministers, making it clear that the Unitarians would have to become a separate communion. In his landmark sermon, "Unitarian Christianity," Channing defined and clarified what it was this new communion believed. He defended the use of reason within religion and the reading of the Bible in the same manner one would read any other book. He criticized Trinitarian doctrine and the doctrine of predestination, arguing instead for a belief that emphasizes the likeness of humankind to God and the ability of humans to make their own moral choices.

John Murray (1741–1815)

John Murray was considered by early American Universalists to be the founder of American Universalism as well as a pioneer minister and inspirational figure. Murray came to Universalism when he went, as a member of a Methodist congregation in London, to attempt to bring back to the fold a young woman who had been won over by the Universalist teachings of James Relly, a Methodist minister turned Universalist. Instead of convincing her of Methodism, she answered all of his objections to Universalism and convinced him to believe in Universalism himself. After being excommunicated from his Methodist church for his change of heart, Murray traveled to America, where he was persuaded to take up preaching once again, this time as a Universalist. The agent of his persuasion was Thomas Potter (1689–1777), an illiterate farmer and Univeralist who, in 1760, built a church in the woods of New Jersey and who believed that Murray had been sent by God to preach in this Church. Murray established the first Universalist congregation, the Independent Christian Church, in Gloucester, Massachusetts. The Independent Christian Church played a central role in one of the landmark court cases on the separation of church and state. As a Universalist, Murray believed in a doctrine of universal salvation, because he saw all of humankind united in Christ and thus all saved through his sacrifice.

II. Tenets and Beliefs

A. Articles of Faith

The notion of universal salvation that formed the basis of Universalist belief raised a number of important questions, not the least of which was: If *everyone* is saved (not only those who believe in Jesus as a personal savior), should congregations open themselves to all types of believers, including those who are atheists or who espouse another, alien creed, such as, for example, a Hindu one?

By the middle of the nineteenth century there was already significant controversy around this issue. And today, Unitarians embrace all sorts of creeds and beliefs, and very few would identify as exclusively Christian. Indeed, it is a formal point of Unitarian theology that no one religion is exclusively true and that people of all creeds and faiths are to be welcomed into the congregation. All of this does not, however, mean that Unitarians have no fundamental beliefs that unite them. Officially, all Unitarian Universalist congregations have agreed to affirm the following seven principles:

1. **The inherent worth and dignity of every person;**
2. **Justice, equity and compassion in human relations;**
3. **Acceptance of one another and encouragement of spiritual growth in our congregations;**
4. **A free and responsible search for truth and meaning;**
5. **The right of conscience and the use of the democratic process within our congregations and in society at large;**
6. **The goal of world community with peace, liberty, and justice for all;**
7. **Respect for the interdependent web of all existence of which we are a part.**

Many of these principles echo traditional American and British liberal thought by claiming, in effect, that one is free to do and believe as one wishes, so long as one causes no harm. The last principle, that of respect for the "interdependent web of all existence" takes language from Hinduism and Buddhism. Unitarian Universalists also relate this last principle to Native American and nature-based religions, which, according to the web site of the UUA, "celebrate the sacred circle of life and instruct us to live in harmony with the rhythms of nature."

Many Unitarian Universalists continue to follow the teachings of the Transcendentalists and believe that the divine can be experienced directly by all human beings. Many place a faith in this experience of wonder above any and all historical teachings and believe that, at best, creeds can merely point to this place of mystery.

B. Scripture

In the most vigorous sense of the word, today's Unitarians repudiate "Scripture"——which is not to say that Unitarians lack a great deal of reverence and appreciation for the writings that other religions consider sacred. Modern Unitarian Universalists simply do not find it necessary to subscribe to one single religious text or body of texts and to consider it or them authoritative and final on matters of truth. The Unitarian Universalist position on sacred writings is rather one of extreme pluralism. The religious writings of all religions are considered to have truth and to offer opportunities for spiritual growth.

Concerning the Bible, Unitarians consider it an important piece of religious history and one that offers important truths about the necessity of loving one's neighbors. That said, very few Unitarians today would subscribe to those portions of the Bible that make claims about the divinity of Jesus. The religious writings of other religions are as important or more important to the Unitarian faith today than the Bible. Indeed, the Unitarian call for a continuous spiritual search and spiritual learning guarantees that the entire body of world religious writings finds a place within the religion. As early as Emerson, Thoreau, and the Transcendentalists, Hindu texts such as the *Upanishads* and the *Bhagavad Gita* were mined for insights by Unitarians. The emphasis on divine transcendence of all forms in the *Gita* has been very attractive to Unitarians, particularly those Unitarians who focus on religious pluralism.

A sermon today at a Unitarian church may well contain passages from these texts, the Buddhist sutras, Islamic Sufi writings, and even popular culture, such as songs by the Beatles.

C. Secondary Sources

The links between Unitarianism and Harvard, and the overall trend toward the ideals of tolerance, pluralism, and liberal religion in America, makes it difficult to single out any one thinker or set of thinkers that has influenced or been influenced by Unitarian Universalism. Instead, one needs to look at American culture as a whole and to take note of the ways in which basic Unitarian beliefs have become seminal for religious discourse and controversy in America today.

Jefferson and Unitarians

Thomas Jefferson is often cited as an inspiration by Unitarians for the way that he redacted the New Testament, creating a work that is known as the Jefferson Bible. Jefferson translated the New Testament into both English and Latin, but, as he did so, he trimmed and purged the work, so that all threats of hell and damnation were eliminated, and what was left were only those portions of Jesus's own words which gave a moral and ethical teaching. Jefferson then had this Bible privately printed and handed out copies to the United States Senate.

The trend toward liberal religion at Harvard and in the culture at large has been met with equal force by the reaction of evangelical fundamentalism. In many ways, Unitarian pluralism is the flip-side of the coin when it comes to this fundamentalism. If the Unitarians have argued for a looser, more flexible and

historical reading of the Bible, other Christians have reacted by claiming that every word of the Bible is not only inspired, but literally true. Schools such as Harvard, which concentrate on historical criticism, are opposed by Bible colleges that reject this methodology and seek a reading of the Bible that is based solely on faith. Today, works such as scholar John Dominic Crossan's *The Historical Jesus,* which offers a wholly human Jesus as a moral and "revolutionary" example, have attained bestseller status, even as conservatives decry any Christianity that does not focus on Christ as savior.

The notion of Universalism, or the belief that everyone will be saved, has also been taken up by liberal Christians in other denominations, from Eastern Orthodoxy to the mainline denominations such as the Methodists and Episcopals. Theologian S. Mark Heim raised both ire and enthusiasm in the academy with his 1995 book, *Salvations*, in which he argued that a plural and postmodern understanding of truth points to a reality in which everyone may not only be saved, but saved according to his or her own particular views and faith tradition.

William James

Another notable thinker who looked into these issues was the philosopher and Harvard professor William James, whose 1902 work, *The Varieties of Religious Experience*, became an essential textbook on world religion. James argued for another type of universalism, a universal religious experience. According to James, when theology and dogma were stripped away, there could be found in all religions a universal experience that stood beyond language. This universal religious experience, James argued, was important and life changing, and even those who had pulled away from religion should admit its existence on a psychological, philosophical, and scientific basis. James's theories have been integral to shaping both academic and popular conceptions of religion, and many writers on popular religion, including Aldous Huxley and Huston Smith, followed his lead throughout the twentieth century, influencing Unitarian belief and American discourse on religion as a whole.

Another avenue of influence that relates to Unitarianism is the line that runs between liberal American religion and civil rights issues. In the nineteenth century, many Unitarians were active in the abolitionist and women's rights movement, although some, like Emerson himself, believed that one's time was better spent in "inward" religious conquests than in protests and rallies. Today, the Unitarian Universalists as a body are fully committed to social action and change, and many consider leaders such as Gandhi and Martin Luther King Jr. to be examples of excellence in religious life in much the same way that earlier generations considered Jesus to have been a perfect moral example.

III. Rites and Rituals

A. The Calendar

Any discussion of the Unitarian Universalist calendar is complicated to say the least. Their Puritan forebears disapproved of nearly all rituals and had only scorn for the Catholic liturgical year and the numerous days of the saints. Today, however, with their strong bent toward pluralism, most Unitarians would argue that more instead of fewer days of religious celebration are necessary. When one adds the emphasis Unitarians place on religious education and learning about other cultures, it is hardly surprising that many Unitarian congregations embrace a wide variety of religious celebrations.

During the Jewish Passover, one congregation might read passages from the Hebrew Bible and study Jewish spirituality. Hindu ceremonies in India might well be echoed in a Unitarian congregation in New England. Many Unitarians today identify as having been influenced by Neo-Paganism and Wicca, and some congregations hold ceremonies to mark the spring and autumn equinoxes. Each congregational calendar differs depending on the choices of the minister and the interests of the congregation. Unitarians are always looking for new ways to incorporate other types of spirituality into their repertoire, and this fact has sometimes caused Unitarians to fall under fire from within and without. Some critics have alleged that, however one might respect such religions, it is very difficult to borrow ceremonies and holidays from the Native Americans in a culturally sensitive way. These critics have wondered whether the predominately white congregations were not "playing Indian."

In defense of the Unitarians, their statement of principles makes it very clear that they consider Native American "earth-centered" religions to be very serious indeed, and recognizes in them a number of vital ideas that seem to be missing from the Judeo-Christian heritage.

B. Worship and Liturgy

As was the case with the liturgical year, it is nearly impossible to set down the precise shape of the Unitarian worship service. Services can differ widely by congregation and by geographical location. Unitarian candidates for the ministry are likely to take courses in liturgy and ritual and to fully explore possibilities for creating new types of ceremonies and services, incorporating music of many types, preaching, art, and theater.

That said, many Unitarian services still bear more than a passing resemblance to old New England Calvinist services. One is unlikely to find anyone standing up to shout "Amen!" during a service, and many Unitarians would still agree with their Old Light ancestors in finding "enthusiastic" religion distasteful and overemotional. Many services still follow a traditional Protestant outline, with a place for music, a sermon, and religious readings. What differs is chiefly the content of the music, the sermon, and the readings. Today one would be unlikely to find two sermons on the same group of Scriptures in consecutive weeks, and the music might range from folk music to African chants.

C. Daily Life

Unitarians do not have the types of dietary restrictions and prohibitions on certain types of dress that characterize many religions. An individual Unitarian might incorporate veganism, vegetarianism, or fasting into his or her religious practices, but no such restrictions are considered mandatory or are shared by a wide cross-section of Unitarian congregants. Dietary practice might be borrowed from the Jains, and fasts from the Muslims, but no such practices are integral to Unitarianism itself.

In place of these prohibitions, Unitarians are likely to consider it mandatory that one uphold certain liberal values such as tolerance and respect for others in all aspects of one's daily life. Much in the way that thinkers such as John Stewart Mill argued that one should be free to do and believe whatever one wished, so long as one did not harm others, the Unitarians have few commandments regarding religious practice, but instead subscribe to an ideal of religious freedom. Unitarians have nothing like the laws of Leviticus, which describe what one should and should not do; rather they hold that all such practices should be permitted and respected. Tolerance and a search for common religious understanding are to be prioritized at all times, and congregants are encouraged to do their utmost to oppose ignorance and bias based on religious creed.

Unitarians are also strongly urged to make involvement in political and social issues a part of their daily life, and to strive for better democracy, civil rights, and progressive values.

D. Life Cycle Events

Birth

When a child has been born to Unitarian Universalist parents, the parents are encouraged to bring the child to a regular Sunday service for a ceremony that is sometimes called "baptism" but more often, in an attempt to distance the ritual from its Christian roots, "child dedication."

Part way through the service the parents bring the child forward, and the minister presides over the ceremony. The parents pledge to cherish the child and to bring up the child to uphold UUA values, and the congregation pledges to aid the parents in this role. The ritual of baptism is by no means considered essential, and adults who wish to join a Unitarian congregation do not need to be baptized regardless of their prior religious affiliations.

Confirmation

The Unitarians place special emphasis on educating teenagers and young adults about other religions and different systems of belief. Young adults are encouraged to "build their own theologies" and to evolve and grow spiritually by their own clock.

For Unitarian youths at the cusp of maturity, the church offers what they call a "coming of age ceremony." This ceremony differs from congregation to congregation and even according to the wants and needs of individual teenagers. The emphasis is both on learning and on celebration, as well as finding a way of marking the struggles entailed in becoming an adult. For this ceremony, congregations may borrow from Christian confirmation rituals, Jewish bar mitzvahs, New Age, Wicca, and the ceremonies of tribal religions, including Native Americans. For this ceremony many congregations ask the young adult to compose and give a talk explaining his or her beliefs and where they are rooted.

Nuptials

The Unitarian Universalist marriage ceremony, although it will differ slightly from congregation to congregation and couple to couple, strongly resembles the secular or Protestant service with which most Americans are familiar. A processional, music, the recitation of vows, and the exchange of rings are all a part of the standard service. That said, couples who wish to develop markedly different or alternative ceremonies are encouraged to do so, and the Unitarian notion of a marriage ceremony is large enough to incorporate many diverse elements.

Ministers are expected to meet with the couple numerous times in the months before the wedding in order to test the compatibility of the couple and to look for future problems that might arise in the marriage, including drug and alcohol abuse, before agreeing to perform the marriage.

Death and Burial

The Unitarian Universalists consider death and the loss of a loved one to be a personal matter that needs to be interpreted subjectively depending on the beliefs of the deceased and of his or her family.

Many Unitarians believe in an afterlife, but some do not. Some Unitarians are agnostic humanists, while others may worship the Great Goddess or the Christian God. In recognition of this fact, every memorial service is designed by the minister and the family to fit the desires and beliefs of those involved.

E. Family Life

Husband and Wife

The Unitarian stance on marriage does not differ greatly from that of most liberal Americans. Unitarians emphasize the need for freedom in making personal decisions, and consider marriage a partnership between equals. Unlike most Christian denominations, the Unitarians do not urge young men and women to marry, and cohabitation by unmarried adults is not prohibited by church guidelines. The openness of the UUA to all creeds and beliefs also means that Unitarians are not worried when members of their faith choose to marry partners who subscribe to other faith practices.

The Unitarians also perform and sanction gay marriages even in those states and regions where such marriages are not legally binding. For the Unitarians, such unions have equal validity to more traditional marriages.

Child-rearing

Unitarian ideals of freedom, tolerance, and respect play a role in Unitarian ideas about child-rearing and education. Unitarians are quick to argue that education cannot be mere indoctrination, but that children have to learn to become thoughtful, reasoning adults capable of guiding their own lives spiritually and politically.

As part of the regular weekly program, Unitarian congregations offer religious education for children. This program focuses on teaching children tolerance for others and helping them understand the plurality of religious belief that exists in the world.

Divorce

Unlike their Puritan forebears, Unitarians today are open to divorces, and recognize that sometimes the dissolution of a marriage is best for both parties. This position again reflects the influence of theological and political liberalism, and the belief that individual and personal freedom needs to be respected.

IV. Denominations and Demographics

A. History

Although this chapter focuses primarily on those Unitarian and Universalist groups that eventually came together to form the Unitarian Universalist Association, a number of other Unitarian groups exist in the United States today. Contemporary Unitarians often see historical analogues of Unitarianism in radical reformation figures such as Servetus and Socinus, who put forward anti-Trinitarian ideas, and relate the foundations of their own church to Transylvanian Unitarianism.

In the United States, other groups who use the name "Unitarian" include the American Unitarian Conference and the Unitarian Universalist Christian Fellowship. Each of these groups promote theological and political liberalism that seeks to remain closer to its Christian roots than the more explicitly pluralistic UUA. Still, these more Christian Unitarians are also likely to remain fully committed to the idea of Universal salvation, and to believe that many paths exist for arriving at religious and spiritual truth.

B. Variations on the Theme

One cannot complete a discussion of American Unitarianism without taking note of the fact that denominations which use the Unitarian name are not the only denominations in this country to espouse Unitarian beliefs. In the beginning of this chapter, we took especial note of the way that Unitarianism evolved out of Puritan and Protestant anti-Catholicism and the desire to return to a more primitive form of Christianity. We also noted that intensive study of the Bible, and the desire to uphold the Protestant ideal of *sola scriptore*—"by Scripture alone"—led some Christians to question the idea of the Trinity.

Given this reality, it is not surprising that a number of other denominations have evolved along similar lines, albeit with very different results. Many modern Pentecostals reject the notion of the Trinity and feel that this doctrine is merely a Catholic invention that obscures the Unity of the Godhead. Other groups, such as the Jehovah's Witnesses, also reject the dogma of the Trinity and argue for a position that is closer to the subordinationism of the third-century bishop, Arius. Nonetheless, these groups are very unlikely to use the name Unitarianism to describe their theology as they do not wish to associate themselves with Unitarian pluralism and liberalism.

Thus, somewhat paradoxically, anti-Trinitarianism as a dogma is found both among the most liberal and socially progressive Americans and among the most conservative and fundamentalist groups. Both groups reject the trappings of "theology" in the belief that one can have a more direct experience of spiritual reality.

C. Organization and Distribution

As is the case with many liberal religious denominations in America, it is a matter of extreme difficulty to provide concrete figures on the number of practicing Unitarian Universalists today. Many who identify in the census as Unitarians no longer attend Unitarian congregations, a fact that might well be explained by the belief that one is assured salvation and does not have to attend church weekly to attain it. Although more than 600,000 Americans today identify as Unitarian Universalist in religious surveys, perhaps as few as a quarter of these believers actually attend regular services.

Unitarian Universalism remains centered around Boston and New England, but churches exist across America, in the West and Midwest, and Seattle has a particularly large number of Unitarian congregants. The UUA currently represents over a thousand congregations.

V. Organization and Infrastructure

A. Education and Hierarchy of Clergy

SEMINARY

The Unitarian Universalists have what they call an "educated clergy," as opposed to the "called clergy" of other denominations. This means that Unitarians place emphasis on learning and theological training, and reject the notion, prevalent in many denominations, that God calls certain members of the congregation who are said to have a "religious vocation." Unitarians believe that spirituality is something that has to be studied and worked for, and tend to see religiosity as a lifelong path of growth rather than something that is perfected by a lightning, bolt born-again experience from God. Much of this

Andover Hall at Harvard Divinity School, built in 1906, holds a chapel and classrooms as well as several administrative offices.

emphasis goes back to the earliest days of Unitarianism when the Old Lights opposed the born-again enthusiasm of the Great Awakening.

Harvard Divinity School
45 Francis Avenue
Cambridge, MA 02138
617-495-5761
www.hds.harvard.edu

Harvard Divinity School today remains a center of Unitarian learning. Since its inception, the Divinity school (*above*) has been nondenominational, and modern students come from many faiths, including Buddhism and Islam, and study with professors from many of the world religions. The Harvard program offers academic degrees for those who wish to teach on world religion at secular institutions, as well as degrees such as the MDiv, or Master of Divinity, which is required for those who wish to become ministers in the UUA.

CLERICAL BODIES

The congregational and Puritan roots of Unitarian Universalism have left a strong mark on today's Unitarian church polity. The congregational system was itself designed to prevent hierarchy, centralized authority, and the coercion of conscience through the accumulation of dogma. It was, at its roots, anti-Papist, and rejected those forms of polity, then current in England, in which power was placed in the hands of bishops. Each congregation was to be left to make its own decisions and to raise up its own regional hierarchy.

Today's Unitarianism is very close to this form. Major decisions are made by the Unitarian General Assembly, which is made up of delegates from each congregation. Each congregation is allowed at least two voting delegates at the meeting: one delegate assigned for every fifty members, plus an additional delegate for any remaining fraction. For a meeting to count as a General Assembly of the church invested with decision-making power, at least 300 delegates must be present, representing no less than 100 separate congregations.

A board of trustees is elected at the General Assembly for staggered two-year terms in order to oversee the affairs of the denomination when the Assembly is not in session. Other permanent and special committees are also made up of elected officials. The General Assembly of the UUA elects a president of the denomination who serves for four years. The president is directly responsible to the board of trustees.

B. Shrines and Houses of Worship

Like many Protestant denominations, the Unitarian Universalists do not believe in the sanctity or particular holiness of any of their own churches or sites of religious history. The post-Christian slant of many UU congregations has also meant that some groups of Unitarians no longer use the word "church" at all to describe their places of worship or what takes place there. Instead they will speak of a "fellowship" or simply of the "congregation."

Because the Unitarians are the inheritors of much of the legacy of New England Puritanism, one finds (particularly in the environs of Boston and throughout New England) that many of the oldest and most venerable churches are now in Unitarian hands. These churches include Arlington

This photograph of the interior of King's Chapel in Boston was taken around 1898.

Street Church in Boston, which was the home church of William Ellery Channing, and King's Chapel, which is one of the oldest standing colonial churches in the Americas. Also notable is the First Church of Cambridge, a classic structure that stands across from Harvard University and dates back to the seventeenth century.

The building for the First Unitarian Society in Madison, Wisconsin, one of the larger UU congregations, was designed by master architect and Unitarian Frank Lloyd Wright, as was Unity Temple in Oak Park, Illinois.

> **Unitarian Universalist Association**
> **of Congregations**
> 25 Beacon Street
> Boston, MA 02108
> 617-742-2100
> info@uua.org
> www.uua.org

C. Governance and Authority

When the General Assembly of the Unitarian Universalist Association comes to important decisions for the guidance of the church, the principles are set forth in the book *Bylaws and Rules*, a twenty-plus page document that records both religious principles of the organization and the rules for church political organization and voting. The UUA empha-

sis on personal freedom and on congregational autonomy means that this document is very slender indeed, and several short pages on dogma take the place of what for most denominations is several hundred pages or even many thousands of pages.

D. Social Service Organizations

> **Unitarian Universalist Service Committee**
> 689 Massachusetts Avenue
> Cambridge, MA 02139-3302
> 617-868-6600   Fax: 617-868-7102
> 800-388-3920
> www.uusc.org

Most important among Unitarian Universalist social service organizations in America is the Unitarian Universalist Service Committee, founded in 1939 to advance the cause of Jews in Nazi-controlled Europe, and which today works for progressive causes such as the advancement of civil rights all over the world. The organization Promise the Children is an independent affiliate of the UUA and works to advocate for youth.

> **Promise the Children**
> 11939 Manchester Road, Suite 136
> St. Louis, MO 63131
> ptcstaff@swbell.net
> www.promisethechildren.org

As was the case historically, Unitarians today are reticent about missionizing and evangelical work. This means that Unitarians will often be active in cross-denominational or secular nonprofits that strive for common goals of democratic freedom and social justice. Unitarians have often joined together with Quakers and other religious and nonreligious liberals to work for important causes such as the abolition of slavery, women's rights, and gay rights. The UUA emphasis on social justice issues means that one is just as likely or more likely to find Unitarians working in nonreligiously affiliated nonprofits as in those that are specific to the denomination.

William Ellery Channing was called to the pulpit at the Arlington Street Church in Boston (left). He served as minister there from 1803 to 1842. The Unitarian Meeting House in Madison, Wisconsin (above), was designed by the celebrated Unitarian architect Frank Lloyd Wright and completed in 1951.

UU Ministry for Earth
PO Box 11
Lyme, NH 03768
503-595-9392
office@uuministryforearth.org
uuministryforearth.org

Unitarian Universalist Women's Federation
25 Beacon Street
Boston, MA 02108
617-948-4692
www.uuwf.org

Other important UUA organizations include the Unitarian Universalist Ministry for Earth and the Unitarian Universalist Women's Federation.

E. Media and Communication

UUA print periodicals include the magazine *UU World*, which reaches out to all Unitarians and is also available on the web at www.uuworld.org, and *InterConnections*, a quarterly bulletin aimed at leaders and lay officials within the church. Skinner House publishes ten to fifteen new books on the faith every year and has a backlist of more than a hundred titles on church history, social justice, and spirituality.

The Unitarian Universalists have also put considerable effort into electronic media, and the main Unitarian site, www.UUA.org, now includes over 18,000 pages of information. There are also numerous UU blogs, started by individuals or by Unitarian youth organizations. The site UUblogsearch.com offers a database of these sites. The Unitarian Universalist Wiki, www.uuaism.net, also offers a wealth of information about the faith.

FURTHER READING

An American Reformation: A Documentray History of Unitarian Christianity
Sydney E. Ahlstrom and Jonathan S. Carey, eds.
1985: Wesleyan Press

The Larger Hope: The Universalist Church in America (2 vols.)
Russell E. Miller
1979; 1985: Unitarian Universalist Association

A Stream of Light: A Sesquicentennial History of American Unitarianism
Conrad Wright, ed.
1975: Skinner House/Unitarian Universalist Assoc.

III. ISLAM

Historical Introduction

1. The Islamic Faith

2. Islam in America

III ISLAM

Historical Introduction

CONSIDERING HOW FEW MUSLIMS—ADHERENTS OF the religion of Islam—were found in North America at the beginning of the twentieth century, and comparing that with how many Americans now consider themselves Muslims (numbering several million and growing faster than any other religion in the United States), one cannot help but be impressed by the extent of the religion's appeal and the speed with which it has attracted followers. This success is all the more remarkable when one considers the factors that one might think would make American soil *in*hospitable to Islam, and would render the United States a land in which the religion of Muhammad would have great difficulty taking root successfully.

These obstacles exist on two levels: on the one hand, events of the past century, and of the past two

Each year for the past six decades, a steadily increasing number of Muslims have made the Hajj pilgrimage to Mecca, Saudi Arabia, to fulfill their religious duty. This nighttime photograph shows the Ka'ba, a cube-shaped structure covered with a black-and-gold curtain, located inside the mosque of Masjid al-Haram in Mecca. The Ka'ba is the holiest site in Islam.

decades in particular, have made the impediments to acceptance of Islam by Americans formidable, including decades of overbearing American political and military engagement in Muslim-dominated lands, coupled with terrorist attacks on American military and civilian enclaves (climaxed by the attacks by Islamic extremists on the World Trade Center on September 11, 2001); support by the American government of Israel in its wars with Arab states and in its treatment of Palestinians, as well as American support of governments around the world that have suppressed or restricted indigenous Muslim populations; and persistent negative stereotyping of Muslims in American literature, journalism, and popular entertainment.

These social and historical challenges can be addressed, however, by well-known (if not-so-well understood, and perhaps even less well-practiced) social and political tools and instruments: political activism; diplomacy; education; communication; intellectual and artistic exchange—all the methods by which groups defend their place in American society and through which they come to understand and learn to accommodate one another. In the relatively open society that the United States has presented to Muslims over the past century, many of the advances the Islamic community has seen have been the product of determined efforts by both Muslims and non-Muslims to find a congenial place for Islam and its adherents in the American social, economic, and political landscape.

The other obstacle, however, is more serious and more problematic, as it exists on the level of ideology: there may well be some elements of basic American values ingrained in America's national consciousness by its historical experience and woven into the fabric of its constitutional and historical underpinnings that may be at odds with fundamental Islamic principles and values—elements such as the separation of church and state, tolerance for individual choice and self-determination, and the ongoing goal of creating an egalitarian and secular society based on the application of secular law and constitutional principles. In

this sense, one hastens to add, Muslims are no less challenged by the "American experiment" than are other religious groups—than are *all* other religious groups, for that matter—for this is a fundamental difficulty that the American experiment in participatory democracy poses to any doctrine that places the highest authority over one's life in the revelatory hands of a deity and the ministers of a faith.

Yet, while other faiths have managed one degree of accommodation or another, either because they are very much a part of the prevailing power structure, or because the faith permits a level of accommodation that allows an assimilation of sorts to take place, the absolutist quality of the Islamic religion, its uncompromising adherence to theological principles, and its commitment to the values of Islam (the very word means "submission" to what is understood to be the will of God in every aspect of life), poses persistent challenges to the integration of Islam into the spirit, if not the mundane society and body politic, of the United States. Once again, even a casual observer must, in light of this, admire how well the Islamic faith has taken root on American soil in spite of these many obstacles.

In what follows, we will attempt to explore the history of the Muslim community in the United States from its earliest introduction to the present day. In order for this to be useful and to be appreciated in its historical context, we will briefly examine the history of Islam from its roots in seventh-century Arabia through its history to its current state in the world. We will present as clear and unbiased a picture as possible of the tenets and principles of the religion in a way that will make the faith clear to an American reader. We will attempt to explain the differences and commonalities that exist between different sects, schools, and ethnic expressions of Islam, around the world and particularly in the United States. And we will attempt to unravel the complex history of Islamic faith, culture, and society in the United States and its relationship with Islamic groups and constituencies around the world.

At this juncture in our history, it has become exceedingly important that these basic facts be understood, and that American readers of all religious faiths and political orientations have a firm grasp of the basic teachings and principles of Islam, a firm grasp on the place of Islam on the world scene and in American life—to know, for example, the difference between Sunni and Shi'ite; to integrate the simple fact that not all Arabs are Muslims and that the Muslim community worldwide encompasses more—many more—non-Arabs than Arabs; to understand the essence of the relationship between the African-American Islamic communities and movements on the one hand, and the mainstream Muslim faith community on the other; and to come to grips with the increasingly important role American Muslims play now and will continue to play in American life—in business, culture, politics, and quality of life—in the years ahead, as that group grows in numbers and influence to possibly become (if it is not already) the second-largest religious group in the United States.

The Life of Muhammad

The celebrated author and scholar, Karen Armstrong, begins her book, *Islam: A Short History*, with the following sentence: "During the holy month of Ramadan in 610 CE, an Arab businessman had an experience that changed the history of the world."

It is difficult to imagine a greater understatement. The man Armstrong is referring to is Muhammad ibn [son of] Abdallah. She refers to him as a businessman, because that is exactly what he was: he managed a business for his wife, a woman about fifteen years his senior who had inherited her father's successful caravan enterprise, though under Muhammad's management, it became even more successful. At this period in human history, caravans were part of a network of trade and transport that was only then coming into its own. The technology of transportation had been developed in shipbuilding and overland transport during the Roman period, but one more piece was necessary for trade to be carried out effectively, and this element could not be provided by the Romans, who, powerful as they might have been, could still not be in more than one place at any one time.

This element was the city—urban centers that could provide the financial services needed for the trading of goods from foreign lands; that could provide the security needed to see the goods safely (and profitably) on their way to their destinations; and that could maintain (feed, house, support, and entertain) the caravans and shipping that was the lifeblood of the entire system. To be sure, there were great cities in the ancient world, but they were few and literally far between. In the area of the eastern Mediterranean, there arose great cities—Baghdad, Basra, Beirut, Cairo, Damascus, Istanbul, Tehran, Tripoli, and others—that became sophisticated centers of learning, commerce, the arts, and technology—primarily as a result of Arab and Muslim groups who relied more on trade than on the unpredictable agriculture of the area for their livelihood.

In Muhammad's day, Mecca was a prosperous city at the middle of the western coast of the Arabian peninsula. It was ideally situated as a hub of the trade routes from east to west and from north to south, but it also had what one might call a "major attraction"—the Ka'ba ("cube"), a shrine that had been venerated for over 2,000 years by Arabs throughout the area as the place where the biblical Patriarch Abraham (Ibrahim in Arabic), with his son Ishmael (Ismail in Arabic), had built the first structure dedicated to worshipping the God that had revealed his existence to Abraham. Located near a fresh-water spring, Zamzam—the putative well that God had provided to Ishmael and his mother Hagar (Hajar), as recounted in the Bible and the Qur'an. The shrine had over the centuries become a center of idol worship; some 360 idols filled the area around the black stone (probably the remnant of a fallen meteorite) that father and son held as a sacred sign from above. The yearly influx of pilgrims who came to pray at and kiss the stone in the Ka'ba added much to the prosperity of the city.

Predictably, secularists and historians have questioned many aspects of Muhammad's life and career, as they have the founders and key figures of virtually every other religion on the map. Yet, the documentation and record—made for religious purposes, one must remember, and not to fulfill a degree requirement—of Muhammad's life are of a clarity and richness that other religions can only envy. Muhammad was orphaned at an early age and was raised in the home of his paternal grandfather. He was an introspective young man with a reputation for both intelligence and integrity; he acquired the nickname *al-Amin*—the trustworthy one. After his grandfather died, he was taken in by his uncle. As an orphan, he received little formal education. (When he sent letters, the sources report, he always dictated them.)

His reputation attracted the attention of Khadija bint [daughter of] Khuwaylid, a widow who belonged to the same clan as Muhammad, the Banu Hashim, and the same Arab tribe, the Quraish. She first made him manager of her business (he had shown his business acumen in many trips with his uncle, Abu Talib), but then she made the unusual move of offering him her hand in marriage. Though Khadija was fifteen years older than Muhammad, she bore him at least one daughter—possible three other daughters and two sons, though only one daughter—Fatima, survived him. They were married for twenty-five years and Muhammad relied on Khadija for her advice and wisdom right up to the year of her passing in 619 (known in Islamic tradition as the Year of Sorrow because it was also the year Abu Talib died).

But what about what happened to Muhammad in 610 that changed history? On the seventeenth day of Ramadan, Muhammad, then about forty years of age, went to a cave near the summit of Mount Hirah just outside Mecca to pray, fast, and meditate. He was contemplating what he regarded as the sorry state of Meccan society, with its unend-

This photograph shows the entrance to the Cave of Hira, where Muhammad received his first divine revelation.

ing cycles of vendetta killings and feuds, with its ruthless capitalism that trampled the poor and helpless, and with the rampant idolatry that seemed to betray the legacy that had been left them by the Patriarch Ibrahim and Ismail, ancestor of the Arab people. Suddenly, Muhammad was overcome with a presence that, he felt, brought him to the very edge of death. This presence demanded that Muhammad repeat what he was about to tell him, but Muhammad was dumbstruck and could not utter a sound until the presence seized him and said:

Recite in the name of your Lord who creates
Created man from a "clot of blood,"
Recite, for your Lord is most beneficent,
Who taught by the pen,
Taught man what he did not know.

(Qur'an, Sura 96, verses 1–5—throughout, Qur'anic citations will appear in this form: "Q 96:1–5"; the translation of Ahmed Ali will be used whenever possible).

Muhammad was overwhelmed and at first terrified, and remained so even after he learned that the presence was the Angel Gabriel (Jibril), even after the revelations continued over the next twenty-three years in 114 episodes—and even when (perhaps especially when) he learned in those later revelations that he was being spoken to by God directly. Muhammad was instructed to recite these messages verbatim (the word *qur'an* means "recitation" and "recording"), for the purpose of instructing humankind.

Throughout his life, Muhammad believed he was instructing humanity through these messages about a faith they had already been given: the monotheistic faith of Abraham and the moral code that went with it—a faith that had been the underlying message of many prophets of many nations since, but which had been distorted and corrupted, either by theological overanalysis or simply by greedy rationalization.

It took two years (and the encouragement of Khadija and others) for Muhammad to recite in public the verses he had heard and to preach the ideology that he derived from them. The religion of Islam that Muhammad preached was characterized by:

• A profound belief in the unity and dominion of God—the same "Allah" worshiped by Arabs for generations, but absent recognition of His dominion, uniqueness, and power as Creator of the universe;

• An acceptance of the obligation to submit (the very meaning of the word *islam*) oneself to God and to prostrate oneself—physically and emotionally—before Allah, the Creator;

• Acknowledgment of Muhammad as God's Prophet who has received the message and conveyed it (without embellishment or commentary) to humankind as a gift from a benevolent Almighty;

• Acceptance of the moral code of behavior derived from these facts, one that purges the human personality of hubris, greed, lust, and power.

• And one final element: a commitment to extending the influence and very presence of God and God-consciousness to every aspect of life, from the most mundane and personal to the most global and political. From this comes (to use Armstrong's term) the "sacrilization of history" that is one of Islam's most distinguishing characteristics.

As one might imagine, the message that Muhammad conveyed to the people of Mecca, challenging as it was to the status quo and to the very basis of the entire economy, was not generally well received. While some converts to the new religion were to be found there, it was not until Muhammad accepted an invitation from the strife-torn people of Yathrib, a city some 250 miles to the north, that the message of Islam was heard, and its amazing utility as a unifier of diverse factions of people and a motivator of concerted and coordinated action was realized. Muhammad's migration (more of an escape from the murderous intentions of the Meccans) to the city that would be henceforth called Medina (short for Medinat al-Nabi—the City of the Prophet) in 622 would prove a boon to his fortunes and his mission, and would make Medina the second most holy city to Muslims. There then ensued a number of battles where Muhammad displayed a combination of cunning, strategic prowess, daring, and ruthlessness that resulted in his unifying all of the Arabian peninsula under the banner of Islam, thus becoming the religious leader of Arabia.

The Growth of the Islamic Religion

And then Muhammad was gone! He died unexpectedly on June 8, 632, in the arms of his beloved wife Aisha, the young daughter of Abu Bakr whom Muhammad married after the death of Khadija. Though the tradition has him delivering what seems very much like a "farewell sermon"—in which he urged the pursuit of justice for all people; fair and respectful treatment of women; the equality of all believers in the eyes of God; and resisting adding "leap months" so as to align the lunar and solar calendars—the Prophet's passing seemed to have been sudden. It also threw the faithful into a state of disarray, since Muhammad had not indicated whom he wanted to assume leadership of the faith—now a position with far larger ramifications for the future. At least some believed he had not, for on the way back from Mecca to Medina on what was to be his final pilgrimage (Hajj), Muhammad said (Q 5:3):

> Today I have perfected your religion, and completed (or "bestowed") my favors upon you and chosen Islam as a religion for you.

Some believed this verse was the "seal" on his prophecy, and, in fact, on all prophecy, telling his followers that all prophets after Muhammad are false. But others emphasized the ambiguity of the language and, relying on traditions that were more explicit, believed this was an act in which Muhammad designated Ali ibn Abi Talib, his cousin and the husband of his beloved daughter, Fatima, as his successor. The supporters of Ali became known as the Shi'at Ali—the "Party of Ali"—or Shi'ites, while most of the followers (then and right to the present day) recoiled from anything that smacked of a dynasty and believed the leadership should be determined by popular decision; that is the way (*Sunna*) the Prophet would have wanted it and, in fact, what he urged when he urged all religious matters to be decided by consensus and without rancor or contention.

Hence was born a split that was to characterize Islam for more that 1,400 years: The Shi'ites believe the leadership belongs to the blood line of the Prophet, which begins with Husayn, the son of Ali and Fatima; and the Sunnis believe the leadership belongs in the hands of the men whom the people—the *ummah*, or the wide consensus of the faithful—deem most learned and most worthy, regardless of their lineage. Subsequent divisions of Islam into sects and subsects derive for the most part from this question of whence derives religious authority in Islam.

Lying underneath the surface of this dispute is a profound difference that may account for (if, perhaps, not justify) the centuries of bitterness that divides these two factions. The Shi'ites would say that Muhammad was clearly chosen by God to be the Prophet and messenger of the Qur'an, and was thus a man imbued—as, Muhammad tells us, many others of many nations throughout history had been—with special qualities of spiritual sensitivity and mystical insight. It follows that Muhammad's blood descendants are most likely to be imbued with these same special qualities and, thus, it is they who should lead the Islamic faith (and serve as *imam*—"leader").

The Sunnis would argue that the very idea of people having "special qualities" runs counter to exactly what Muhammad was teaching and is a distortion and corruption of the concept of God as the "wholly other" and supremely powerful Creator; it smacks of the notion that human beings can "partake" of the divine nature and essence, something Muhammad recoiled at, and insisted it not be said of him. In spite of Islam admitting a rich pantheon of angels and ethereal beings as part of the universe God created, including a human soul that survives death and stands to be resurrected (or not, if unworthy) on the Day of Judgment, flesh and blood is just that; anyone with the right training and the proper values and piety can achieve the highest level of holiness and station in Islam possible, no matter his pedigree. (How, one wonders, is so fundamental a dispute like this *ever* to be resolved?)

At the time (in 632), the group that had assembled around Muhammad chose Abu Bakr, his closest friend and (as was pointed out to dissenters) the one Muhammad asked to lead prayers in his absence, to be *khalifa*, or caliph ("representative," meaning representing the Prophet in his absence). Abu Bakr served for only two years, but they were fateful ones in which he refined the concept of the *ummah*—the community of the religion of Islam—to transcend ethnic and national boundaries, allowing it to encompass a wide populace loyal to the faith and its tenets above all else.

As a result of Abu Bakr's formulation—supported by the Qur'anic admonition that "There is to be no compulsion in matters of faith" (Q 2:256)—the Muslim armies were able to conquer lands in the name of Islam without worrying about what their new subjects believed. Jews and Christians were already honored in the Qur'an and by Muhammad as *ahl al-kitab*—usually translated as "people of the book," meaning, presumably, the Bible, but more likely meaning "people of an earlier revelation." The prophets of the Jewish and Christian Scriptures are honored and revered (in some ways, it has been noted, more than in the biblical books), and Jews, Christians, Hindus, Buddhists, Zoroastrians, Sikhs—in short, any monotheistic faith—were given protected status (*dhimmi*), which required them to pay a poll tax in return for the state's protection and services, but subject to no conversion, forced or otherwise. As a result, Jews experienced a minor "golden age" in Muslim Spain that came to a harsh end with the Inquisition and the Crusades, both enterprises associated with Christianity.

As for Islam, under Abu Bakr and his three successors, Umar ibn al-Khattab, Uthman ibn al-Affan, and, ironically, Ali ibn Abi Talib. These first four caliphs are known as *al-khulfa ar-rashidun* (or simply the Rashidun—the "rightly guided caliphs"), who expanded the Muslim empire over the next thirty years deep into the Persian and Byzantine Empires.

The Ebb and Flow of Imperial Islam

The Rashidun period ended with the massacre of Husayn ibn Ali, the Prophet's grandson, on the plains of Karbala in 680, at the hands of the forces of Yazid I, son of Muawiyyah (I) ibn Abu Sufyan. (Abu Sufyan was once a leading and vociferous antagonist of Muhammad in Mecca before he converted). This established the Umayyad Dynasty (660–750), under which Islam achieved its greatest size, from India to the Iberian peninsula (until Tours, where the spread of Islam was stopped by Charles Martel at the Battle of Poitiers in 732). The Umayyads ruled their empire from Damascus and engaged in ambitious construction projects—notably the Dome of the Rock and the Al-Aqsa Mosque complex in Jerusalem—but their lack of piety and their penchant for luxury disheartened devout Muslims of all persuasions.

One reaction to what was seen as the rampant materialism of the Umayyads was the development of a mystical tradition in Islam known as Sufism. The Sufis were named after the wool (*suf*) shirts they wore as an ascetic practice; others said they were named after the edge (*sufa*) of the mosques where they spent private hours in meditation; and still another origin of the name (conveyed by a modern Sufi master) is that it is a reference to the straight reed (*suf*) or line directly behind the Prophet where the earliest Sufis insisted on praying. Whatever their origin, the Sufis grew steadily in the spiritually barren environment of the Umayyads and by the tenth century were a force for spreading and developing Islam in far-flung areas. Many nations that later turned to Islam had their first exposure through Sufi mystics—this in spite of the persistent questions (enduring to the present) about the exact place of Sufism in Islamic orthodoxy.

The Umayyads were overthrown in 750 by the more devout faction of Muslims led by descendants of Muhammad's uncle, Abbas ibn Abd al-Muttalib, giving the empire the name Abbasid.

The Abbasid Empire was not able to retain control of Spain (al-Andalus)—that remained under tenuous Umayyad control; but they took control of virtually every other area with the help of a master strategist, General Abu Muslim (a Persian who came from what is today Afghanistan). From its new capital in Baghdad, the Abbasids extended the Islamic reach to India and around Africa to the western coast. More importantly, they ushered in a Golden Age of science, art, philosophy, and learning that was to endure for over 500 years, and was to bequeath to the West not only what was salvageable from Classical Greek and Roman culture (knowledge that would otherwise have been lost), but new systems of mathematics, philosophy, medicine, literature—and virtually every other area of human intellectual activity.

The Islamic interest in science and academic pursuits is long-standing and consonant with the Islamic ethos. "The ink of scholars," goes an old

In the arid environs of Arabia, the efficient use of water was a matter of survival. Arab engineers showed remarkable ingenuity in maintaining dams, pumps, cisterns, aqueducts, and all manner of water conveyances—using only gravity and hydraulic pressure for power. The drawing at right comes from a book by al-Jazari, a thirteenth-century Islamic scholar and inventor.

Islamic aphorism, "is holier than the blood of martyrs." Investigating the world is, for Muslims, a sacred duty, part of the service one renders to God and one way of understanding the God being served. With a long cultural tradition of practical, utilitarian thinking (which can be a life-and-death necessity in a desert environment), the scholars of the Abbasid courts poured out a trove of knowledge unrivaled since ancient Athens, Rome, and Alexandria, and unmatched (one may argue) even today. (*Skeptical readers are invited to look into this for themselves in titles in the* "Further Reading" *section at the end of this Introduction.*)

Such an empire was going to be difficult to maintain—given how deep the divisions that ran even among Shi'ite factions, it is remarkable that it lasted as long as it did. Three forces exerted what was ultimately fatal pressure on the Abbasids: Internally, independent mini-kingdoms sought their autonomy and were often able to get it with little more than minor tribute and lip service to the caliphate in Baghdad. Thus arose the Fatimids in Egypt (909–1171); the Samanids (819–999) in Iran; and a dozen other smaller kingdoms across the face of the Mediterranean rim, each promoting a particular brand of Islam and each resentful of Abbasid rule, particularly when Baghdad employed mercenaries—slaves, known as Mamluks ("owned ones"), who converted to Islam and were placed in the service of the caliph—to maintain military control. Eventually,

even the Mamluks themselves were able to carve out a kingdom of their own in Egypt, ruling there from 1215 to 1517.

The second pressure was being mounted by the northern European Christian kingdoms, led by the Franks and the Normans, that were just then emerging out of their antiquity and becoming civilized, powerful political entities. Beyond the normal empire-building instincts, they were driven by a powerful mission—the Reconquista (reconquest) of lands formerly Christian and wrested by the Muslims. As with many passionate missions in history, this one went to the limit and spawned the Crusades, the war to recapture the Holy Land from the Muslims. Either the Crusaders were unaware of the stakes in play for the Muslims, or they simply didn't care, but the initial successes of the First Crusade were emphatically overturned in the Second Crusade by Saladin, and the Crusader States became a footnote in the history of the Eastern Mediterranean.

The third force came from the Far East—the Mongols, an empire forged by the unification of tribes in the Asian steppes and grew to be either the first or second largest empire in world history. The Mongols were formidable soldiers; their conquests were accomplished with little fanfare and with seeming ease because they were united, organized, and hardy. They took Baghdad in six rather effortless days, and this was typical of their conquests. But the Mongols did not have a religion that could stand up to, well, any well-developed Eastern or Western faith. When they conquered Buddhist lands, they became at least nominally Buddhist; when they conquered Muslim territory, they were easily persuaded to convert to Islam; and when they encountered Christianity, they became devout Christians. Besides, the Mongols were, to put it plainly, in the empire-building game for the money: for the booty they would capture, the trade they would establish, the tribute they would exact, and the routes they would control. The Eastern Mediterranean was clearly not going to become a Mongol outpost, nor a Crusader state, nor, with the end of the Abbasids, an Arabian kingdom. It was time for a new player to enter the world stage—but meanwhile, how was Islam faring as a religion?

The Modern Period

As the face of Europe and Asia was scarred repeatedly by invasion, war, repulsions, and exhausted survival, the religion was, under the circumstances, faring well. The foundations laid during the Abbasid Golden Age provided much to work on and think about, and the congenial reception Islam kept receiving from each new conquering lord was, to put it simply, flattering. What were on the face of it defeats turned into spiritual victories and an indication of the mysterious ways Allah works His will on behalf of the *ummah*—His people. When the new force in the area, the Turks, took control—first as the Seljuks (1037–1153), and then, for the long haul, as the Ottomans (1299–1923)—and these were Islamic kingdoms (of one sort or another) as well—the majority of Islam turned inward and attended to the care and feeding of the religion itself.

Two groups were beneficiaries of this introspective turn: One was the Sufis, who saw a revitalization through the work of the prolific philosopher-mystic al-Ghazali (1058–1111), a man who blended science, logic, psychology, law, and sophisticated skeptical philosophy to recast Sufism into a mainstream Muslim discipline and sect. This proved enormously important and effective in creating interest in Islam in foreign lands (including in the New World) when the time was right.

The other group consisted of the followers of a little-known theologian from a small village in central Arabia who effected a revolution in Islamic thinking almost as influential as the one forged by the Prophet himself a thousand years earlier. He is Muhammad ibn Abd al-Wahhab (1703–1792), born in the town of Uyayna in the very center of the

Arabian peninsula. al-Wahhab studied theology in Basra in the Hanbali school, noted for its orthodoxy and extreme veneration of text and precedent. Upon his return to Uyayna, he became a popular orator and a favorite of the local shaikh, Uthman ibn Mu'ammar.

Much has been heard about Wahhabism in the past decade (in a moment we'll see why), but in its authentic form, Wahhabism calls for an orthodoxy that combines Sunni popularism with strict adherence to the Shariah—the day-to-day application of Islamic law to real-life situations. It is sometimes called fundamentalist because it advocates following the laws of Islam as set forth in the Qur'an and the Hadith (noncanonical traditions about, and sayings of, Muhammad), unless there is a compelling reason not to. In this sense, al-Wahhabi was advocating a revivalism of authentic Islamic law, which had been (in his view) abandoned amid all the empire-building and court-academics of the previous half-millennium. His call to a return to the model of the "early generations" (*salafi*) of Islam has a long tradition and makes Wahhabism part of the Salafi school of theology, a school with a long and distinguished tradition.

Al-Wahhabi convinced Ibn Mu'ammar to carry out two reforms that drew the disapproval of the area potentate, Sulaiman ibn Muhammad ibn Ghurayr. One was the razing of the grave of Zayd ibn al-Khattab, a companion of the Prophet, whose grave had been widely venerated. The reason was that the Qur'an explicitly forbids grave worship, which was what al-Wahhab claimed the local practice had become. The other was enforcing the Qur'anic punishment for adultery, which was stoning, a practice that had ceased among Muslims long before. Which action irked Sulaiman more is not known, but ibn-Mu'ammar was first ordered to execute al-Wahhab, then allowed to simply exile him from the town.

Several members of a prominent family in neighboring Dir'iyya had studied with al-Wahhab and prevailed on the head of the family to invite him to settle there. He did so, and soon that fam-

The photographs on this page illustrate some of the many sources of Islamic thought in all its diversity. From left: King Saud (1876–1953) was the first monarch of the consolidated nation of Saudi Arabia; Mustafa Kemal Ataturk (1881–1938) is considered the founder of modern Turkey; Ayatollah Ruhollah Khomeini (1902–1989) was the leader of the 1979 Iranian Revolution; the Shi'ite imam Abdul Aziz al-Hakim (1950–2009) was the president of the Islamic Supreme Council of Iraq, its largest political party; and Benazir Bhutto (1953–2007), a former prime minister of Pakistan, was until her assassination considered a liberal influence in that nation's politics.

ily—who happened to be the Ibn Saud family—became supporters and disciples of al-Wahhab. The relationship became a very close one and resulted in a pact of sorts between the theologian and the family that they and their descendants would be faithful adherents to the Wahhabi school. This would have ended the story, except that the Ibn Saud family would, over the course of the next 200 years, become the absolute rulers of Saudi Arabia, the site of both Mecca and Medina, and the richest oil-producing area in the world. With the financial and political support of the Saud family and Saudi government (much the same thing), since the very founding of Saudi Arabia in 1932, Wahabbism has become the dominant force in the educational systems of several Muslim countries, beginning with Saudi Arabia.

While there have been several movements in Islam in addition to Salafism that may be characterized as "revivalist," perhaps even "fundamentalist" (if we can, for a moment, not be scandalized by that word), fundamentalism, as many have pointed out, became a widespread and ubiquitous religious movement in faiths of all kinds in the late twentieth century. In Islam, groups such as the Muslim Brotherhood in Egypt and Jamaat-e-Islami in Pakistan, advocate an uncompromising theocratic alternative to secular political ideologies. In countries like Iran (after the Revolution) and Afghanistan (under the Taliban), revolutionary movements replaced secular regimes with states that saw Western cultural values as a threat, and Islam as the sole comprehensive solution to every public and private question. Transnational groups like Osama bin Laden's al-Qaeda have engaged in terrorism to further their goals—to the condemnation of Islamic religious leaders the world over. While these actions are considered grave misdeeds in the American mind, it should be remembered that the Taliban were once supported by the United States and stood on the front lines against the Soviet incursion into Afghanistan. The popular mythology (promoted by the film *Charlie Wilson's War*) that the Afghan *mujahideen* brought down the Soviet Union is a gross exaggeration, but the fact remains that they were once allies of the United States.

In contrast, liberal Islam attempts to reconcile religious tradition with modern norms of secular governance and human rights, believing that there are multiple ways to read the sacred texts of Islam, and that there is a place for independent thought on religious matters. As in many areas of religion, there are points of agreement and disagreement on these matters, gradations and shades that separate schools and positions. What is vital at this juncture is for the Islamic community to discuss this seriously and fully, and for that discussion to then be engaged in by interested parties in the West.

In a chapter in Professor Armstrong's history entitled "What Is a Modern Muslim State?" the various attempts made since World War II to establish a state in a land with a predominantly Muslim population are recounted. How to reconcile conflicting views of human rights and civil responsibilities, reconcile fidelity to principle with defense of human self-determination—these are difficult questions, and the complicated history in virtually every country bears witness to Armstrong's conclusion: "The fact that Muslims have not yet found an ideal polity for the twentieth century does not mean that Islam is incompatible with modernity."

The book ends with these words:

To cultivate a distorted image of Islam, to see it as the enemy of democracy and decent values, and to revert to the bigoted view of the medieval Crusaders would be a catastrophe. Not only will such an approach antagonize the 1.2 billion Muslims with whom we share the world, but it will also violate the disinterested love of truth and the respect for the sacred rights of others that characterize both Islam and Western society at their best.

Important Dates in the History of Islam

ca. 570 CE Birth of Muhammad.

ca. 610 Muhammad receives first vision while at a retreat in a cave near Mecca. His wife, Khadija, encourages him to regard it as authentic Divine Revelation.

ca. 610-622 Muhammad preaches (first to family; then publicly) in Mecca. The Meccans impose an embargo on family and followers that may have resulted in Khadija's death.

622 Hijira-Muhammad and 70 families of followers flee to Medina. Islamic calendar (AH = *Anno Hegirae*) begins.

624 Muslims successfully attack Meccan caravans at Badr.

625 Muslims are defeated by Meccans at Uhud, near Medina. Jewish tribes of Medina expelled as collaborators.

627 Muslims defeat larger Meccan force at "Battle of the Trench." Muslims massacre the Jewish Qurayzah tribe for support of the Meccans.

628 Muhammad's heroic and daring march (unarmed) into Mecca and the ensuing Treaty of Hudaybiyyah makes Muhammad leader of all Arabia.

630 Meccans violate Treaty of Hudaybiyyah; Muslims capture Mecca without bloodshed. Amnesty granted; Ka'ba cleansed; pilgrimage rites are Islamicized, tribes of Arabia vow allegiance to Muhammad.

632 Death of Muhammad. Abu Bakr chosen as Caliph.

632-633 Wars of *ridda* (rebellion) end with Abu Bakr restoring control by Islam.

633 Muslim conquests (Futuhat) begin.

633-642 Muslim armies take Fertile Crescent (Egypt, Syria, Palestine, Mesopotamia), North Africa, Persia, and Byzantium.

633 Muslims conquer Jerusalem; it becomes the third holiest city in Islam.

ca. 650 Caliph Uthman arranges for Qur'an to be written down.

656 Uthman is murdered; Ali becomes fourth caliph.

657 Battle of Siffin. Mu'awiya, governor of Syria, claims the caliphate.

659 Arbitration at Adruh opposed by Ali's supporters.

661 Ali is murdered; Mu'awiya becomes caliph. Umayyad caliphate (661–750).

680 Death of Husayn marks beginning of Shi'at Ali ("party of Ali") or Shi'a sect.

685–705 Reign of Abd al-Malik. Centralization of administration. Arabic becomes official written language (replaces Greek and Persian); Arab coinage established.

late 600s Ruling classes in East and West Africa convert to Islam.

700–800s Groups of ascetics and mystics form.

710 Arabs invade Spain from North Africa.

732 Muslim empire reaches its furthest geographical extent. Charles Martel (at Battle of Tours) prevents further advance.

747 Revolt defeats the Umayyads.

750 Abu l'Abbas becomes caliph in Iraq; founds the Abbasid Dynasty.

754 Baghdad (Madinat al-Salam, "city of peace") becomes the new Abbasid capital.

755 Abd ar-Rahman restores an Umayyad Dynasty in Cordoba, Spain.

765 Division within Shi'ites: majority are Imamiyya ("twelvers"), co-exist with Abbasids; minority are more extreme Isma'iliyaa ("seveners").

786–809 Reign of Harun ar-Rashid, best known through *The Thousand and One Nights*.

800s Written collections of Hadith (sayings of the Prophet) are compiled. Sicily comes under Muslim rule.

813–833 Reign of Ma'mun. Theological controversy: Is the Qur'an "created" or "uncreated" and eternal? Center for translation of Greek texts founded in Baghdad.

869–883 Uprisings of Black slaves (Zanj) eventually defeated.

908 First Fatimid caliph in Tunisia.

928 Umayyad Abd ar-Rahman III declares himself caliph in Cordoba.

940 Muhammad al-Mahdi, twelfth imam, disappears. Twelvers still await the return of the "hidden imam."

945 The Buyids (Persian) invade Baghdad.

969 Fatimids gain power in Egypt and attack Palestine, Syria, and Arabia. Cairo (Al-Qahira, "the victorious city") founded.

972 Fatimids establish *medrasah* (seminary) of al-Azhar for Shii studies in Cairo.

980–1037 Avicenna, Iranian physician and Aristotelian philosopher.

996–1021 Fatimid al-Hakim Hamza ibn Ali is basis of esoteric Druze religion.

late 900s West Africa converts to Islam.

1030 Umayyad caliphate in Cordoba defeated by the Christian Reconquista.

1055 Seljuk Turks take Baghdad; Abbasids now only nominal rulers.

1000s Reconquista takes more of Spain, Sicily falls to Normans, Crusader kingdoms briefly established in Palestine, Syria.

1071 Seljuk Turks defeat Byzantines at Battle of Manzikert.

1090 Hasan-i Sabbah takes Alamut in the Persian mountains; forms Assassin sect.

1099 Christian Crusaders take Jerusalem.

1100-1200s Sufi orders (*turuq*) founded.

1126–1198 Averroës, Muslim philosopher from Cordoba, sought to reconcile Islam with Greek thought.

1171 Saladin ends Fatimid rule in Egypt; declares himself sultan in 1174.

1193 Death of Saladin; most Crusader states return to Islam.

1200s Assassins defeated by the Mongols. Indian rulers in Delhi take title of Sultan. Spanish mystic Muhyi al-Din ibn al-Arabi (1165–1240) flourishes.

1221 Genghis Khan, Mongols enter Persia; take Punjab in 1241, Baghdad in 1258—sack city, end Abbasid caliphate.

1281–1324 Uthman (Osman) founds the Ottoman Empire. Muslim merchants and missionary Sufis travel to Southest Asia; exert influence on local populations.

mid-1300s Ottomans move into Europe through capture of Bursa and Iznik.

1366 Capital of Ottoman Empire moved from Bursa to Adrianople.

late 1300s Ottomans take control of Balkans.

1400s Islam reaches the Philippines.

1453 Mehmet Fatih (ruled 1451–1481) conquers Constantinople—unites Ottoman Empire; becomes Byzantine emperor.

1492 Castile and Aragon capture Granada. All Muslims (and Jews) expelled from Spain.

1501 Ismail (1487–1524) claims he is Hidden Imam; proclaimed Shah of Persia; makes Twelver Shi'ism official religion of Persia.

1516 Ottomans conquer Syria and Egypt; control Mecca and Medina following year.

1520–1566 Under Suleyman the Magnificent, Ottoman Empire reaches zenith. Hungary, Algeria, Tunisia under Ottoman rule.

1526 Babur (Mongolian) seizes Delhi sultanate and takes control of northern India.

1556 Akbar founds Mughal dynasty in India.

1600–1700s Venetians, Habsburgs, and Russians divide Ottoman lands in Europe.

1625 Java comes under rule of Muslim kingdom of Mataram.

1699 Treaty of Karlowitz: first substantial loss to Ottoman Empire in Europe.

1700s Muhammad Abd al-Wahhab rejects Sufism and all innovation (*bid'a*). Founds Saudi Arabian kingdom. Hindus regain power from Mughals in northern India.

1738 Mughal empire invaded by the Afghans.

1779 Afghans ousted by Qajar dynasty, which will rule Persia until 1925.

1798 Napoleon's expedition to Egypt.

1805 Muhammad Ali becomes governor of Egypt—independent of Ottomans, gains control of western Arabia and Sudan.

1807–1876 Tanzimat period. Ottoman Empire undergoes extensive modernization.

1830 Greek independence from Ottomans.

1850s Non-Muslim Ottoman citizens granted equality with Muslims.

1858 Last Mughal in India deposed as India comes under British rule.

1876–1908 Reign of Abd al-Hamid II; religiously conservative Ottoman rule.

1878 Congress of Berlin grants independence to previously Muslim Balkan states.

1882–1952 British occupy Egypt.

1908–1918 End of Ottoman rule. "Young Turks" introduce nationalistic, liberal policies.

1912 Founding of Islamic Union (*Sareket Islam*), modernizing influence in Asia.

1918 Fall of Ottoman Empire. League of Nations gives Britain mandatory control over Palestine and Iraq, France control of Lebanon and Syria.

1923 Republic of Turkey established. Mustafa Kemal ("Atarturk") first president.

1927 Tablighi Jamaat reform movement founded in India.

1928 Ikhwan al-Muslimun (Muslim Brothers) founded in Egypt.

1941 Jamaat-i Islami reform movement founded in Lahore, India, by Sayyid Abul Ala Mawdudi (1903–1979).

1945 Indonesia becomes independent republic.

1945–1960s Islam spreads West with mass migrations from Asia, Africa, and India.

1947 Pakistan founded as Islamic nation, making Islam minority religion in India.

1957 Independent Malayan state established with Islam as official religion.

1979 Shah of Iran overthrown; Ayatollah Khomeini establishes Shi'ite state.

1979–1981 American hostages held in American Embassy in Tehran.

1989 Ayatollah Khomeini issues fatwah (condemnation) of Salman Rushdie *The Satanic Verses*. Forty-eight of 49 Islamic states condemn the fatwah as un-Islamic.

1990 Iraq, led by Saddam Hussein, invades Kuwait; U.S. and allies launch Operation Desert Storm in retaliation. Iraqi forces are expelled from Kuwait by 1991.

1992 Serbian and Croatian nationalists kill and expel ("ethnically cleanse") Muslims of Bosnia and Kosovo.

1993 Israel and Palestinians sign Oslo Accords.

late 1990s Taliban takes control of Afghanistan; country divided beween radical and liberal factions.

2001 Muslim extremist terrorists attack United States on September 11.

2003 Saddam Hussein ousted by Western forces.

2005 Mahmoud Ahmadinejad wins Iranian presidential election.

Dec. 7, 2007 Benazir Bhutto, former prime minister of Pakistan, assassinated just prior to national elections.

Further Reading on Islamic History

Basic Works:

Islam: A Short History and
Muhammad: A Biography of the Prophet
    Karen Armstrong
    2002: Orion Books; 1993: Harper San Francisco

Islam: Past, Present & Future
    Hans Küng
    2007: Oneworld–Oxford

Muhammad: His Life Based on the Earliest Sources
    Martin Lings
    2006: Inner Traditions

The Children of Abraham: Judaism, Christianity, Islam
    F.E. Peters and J.L. Esposito
    2006: Harvard University Press

The World of Islam
    John Alden Williams
    1994: University of Texas Press

Science and Culture:

The Middle East: 2,000 Years of History and
The Muslim Discovery of Europe
    Bernard Lewis
    2001: W.W. Norton; 1997: Scribner;

God's Crucible: Islam and the Making of Europe, 570–1215
    David Levering Lewis
    2008: W.W. Norton

Peace Be Upon You: 14 Centuries of Muslim, Christian and Jewish Conflict and Cooperation
    Zachary Karabell
    2008: Alfred A. Knopf

Science and Civilization in Islam
    Sayyed H. Nasr
    1968: Harvard University Press

Science in Medieval Islam
    Howard R. Turner
    1995: University of Texas Press

Reference:

Islam: The Straight Path (3rd edition)
    John L. Esposito
    1998: Oxford University Press

The Oxford History of Islam
    John L. Esposito
    2000: Oxford University Press

Makers of Contemporary Islam
    John L. Esposito and John O. Voll
    2001: Oxford University Press

The Cambridge Illustrated History of the Islamic World
    Francis Robinson
    1999: Cambridge University Press

1 The Islamic Faith

I. Roots and Background

A. Introduction

MOST PEOPLE HAVE ENOUGH TROUBLE UNDER-standing and dealing with the tenets and beliefs of their own religion. Why, they ask, should we bother to understand another one, and why this one—Islam—specifically? This work has argued that understanding the teachings and history of other religions can inform one's own faith; as one author puts it, understanding more about Buddhism can make you a better Catholic. Still, intense study of a faith that is not one's own generally entails stretching

mental "muscles" already well-worn from dealing (and wrestling) with one's own religious tradition.

In the current historical context, however, learning about Islam and knowing it in as authentic and complete a way as possible seems a prudent thing to do for some very compelling reasons, namely:

1. One in five people on earth—1.2 billion people in all—is Muslim. No faith considers popularity a valid argument for its validity, but it *is* a good reason to learn about it. Having a knowledge of the basic tenets and beliefs of Islam allows for some dialogue to take place with a rather large portion of the people with whom we share this pale blue dot.

2. Islam is the fastest-growing religion in the United States—reliably estimated to be between 4 and 7 million, and, because of a high birth rate and increased immigration, is growing faster than any other religious group. It is already larger than many Protestant denominations, and possibly equal in size to the American Jewish population.

3. The image that has been created over four decades of absurd, demeaning, and insulting depictions of Muslims in the news and entertainment media has left many Americans with a distorted view of Muslims and of the Islamic religion. Any

The holy book of Islam is called the Qur'an (and may also be spelled Koran or Quran). It is believed to have been revealed to Mohammed by the angel Jibril (or Gabriel).

time would be a good time to correct this; now is an especially good time. Images from the Middle East tend to portray Muslims as violent and overwrought, but these images are selected and at times designed to bolster a stereotype and confirm a prejudice that (it is believed) results in good ratings. This work is, it is hoped, a small corrective step toward presenting the faith of Islam and the life and history of Muslims in the world and in America in a way that is true to the standards of objectivity, but faithful to the truth, wherever it may lead.

4. And here is another reason for learning about Islam—one that is just dawning on the world community and just now beginning to be realized by the American and world Muslim communities:

Muslims in the United States may be expected to have a profound influence in the future on the development of Islamic thought and the policies of Islamic-oriented nations around the world, just as members of many religions have influenced the development of their faiths as well as political developments relating to their religions in foreign lands. When the Muslim community in the United States was small, both in relation to the U.S. population and relative to the world Muslim community, American Muslims exercised little influence on thought and actions overseas. But that is going to change as the Muslim population grows in numbers, in political sophistication, and in cultural influence.

B. The Metaphysical Background

The belief background of Islam plays an important role in the details of the faith and in its practices. Rising out of a highly compromised form of monotheism rampant during the days of Muhammad, the Prophet rejected a great deal of what he saw as a corruption of the teachings that had been bequeathed to humanity by many earlier holy men and women who spoke of God as an Almighty, singular creator and admonished the people regarding their behavior. It was thus necessary for Muhammad to remind his listeners of truths that had already been taught but forgotten, of realities that were known and would be accepted once the distracting and misleading elaborations of the various religions were set aside. In this sense, Muhammad was reacquainting his disciples with what had been taught by Noah, Abraham, Moses, and Jesus, and a great many (as many 120,000) other saintly people, some known in Muhammad's part of the world and some preaching these truths in remote lands unconnected and thus unknown to the Mediterranean world of late Antiquity.

What the universe looks like from this perspective is elegantly simple; yet it calls upon humanity to accept, unequivocally and with vigor, the consequences of these metaphysical beliefs:

1. Almighty God created the universe. He did so out of a sense of love for His creation, and particularly for human beings. While He is completely unique and without equal, the universe that He created has many sorts of beings, including angels and ethereal entities. There is no way, however, in which God—designated simply as "Allah," which is a deliberately general, all-encompassing term for "god"—shares any of His majesty or power with any other being, physical or ethereal. No human, not even Muhammad, can, in Islamic thought, in any way partake of or share any similarity with God. The notion that any human being could possibly transcend material existence and participate in a divine plane of existence, or could possibly be the "son of God" or be identified with God in any way, is totally alien to the Islamic way of thinking. One of the challenges, in fact, of Islamic mystical thought such as Sufism (for which, on the face of it, there should be no room in Islamic theology), is to develop a mysticism that does not compromise the unity and majesty of God, or impugn God-like attributes to flesh-and-blood human beings.

2. The proper attitude of all of creation to God the Creator is one of grateful submission. The term *islam* (often mistakenly thought to be derived from the Arabic for "peace," with which it has only a distant etymological relationship), means "submission" and "obedience." The practices of Islam are designed to express human submission to God, to further the Divine Will, and to accept His love for His people, and, in fact, for all humankind.

3. **The universe created by God operates under the principles of justice and goodness.** The universe follows the dictates of God's will—which is why the study of the natural world has a religious dimension in Islam—and the underlying principle that directs life is Divine benevolence and mercy. In Islamic thought, human suffering has no positive or redeeming quality, and the fortunes of the individual and the nation—in fact of all humanity—are the result of Divine justice, applied as reward and punishment. Enjoying a wholesomely pleasurable quality of life is considered a blessing and an indication of righteousness and Divine favor.

4. **For each human being, as well as for nations and ultimately for humanity as a whole, there will come a Day of Judgment.** That day may come only at the end of days, the day the Angel Israfil signals with a trumpet blast the resurrection of the dead, or it may come in the afterlife—but it *will* come. In Islam, suffering is a sign of disfavor by God and signals a need for introspection and self-examination.

The strict accountability that every human being has for his or her actions is sometimes seen as at odds with the equally cherished idea that everything that happens in the universe is directed by God and is the product of His will and design (*al-Qadar*). How, then, can humanity be held accountable for actions if everything that happens is divinely preordained? Islam has over the centuries expended a great deal of energy and thought to the resolution of this paradox; it remains under investigation. But the two horns of the dilemma remain uncompromised in Islamic theology: the universe operates by Divine command; but human beings are free to choose their path, and are thus morally responsible for their actions.

5. **Muhammad is the prophet of God and is, in fact, the "seal of prophecy"**—meaning, the final and quintessential prophet. In spite of the many times

God has communicated to humankind through gifted and righteous individuals in the course of history, Muhammad taught, the wayward human mind has persistently found ways to confound the Divine intention and pervert the will of God.

The introduction of pomp and grandiose ceremony; the elevation of some humans to higher stations of sanctity (e.g., sainthood) over others; the overintellectualizing of doctrines and precepts; the autonomy that the devout or scholarly assume to determine proper ritual only for themselves, and, by contrast, the antinomian exclusion others believe they merit by virtue of their birth, attainments, or station; the class distinction that the wealthy or powerful translate into special status in the faith and among the faithful; the exclusion of the popular consensus and acclimation of the people in determining practice and leadership—all of these common corrupting practices were rejected by Muhammad's career and the message he conveyed in the Qur'an.

In Islam, the career of Muhammad and the existence of the Qur'an have metaphysical, existential import—that career and the Prophet's message is the basis of the Shari'a—the law or code by which Muslims lead their lives. By virtue of the revelations Muhammad shared with the world in the Qur'an, the observations and teachings he conveyed as recorded in the Hadith, and through the example of his closely watched and examined life, Muhammad is the foundation on which the Islamic faith rests.

II. Tenets and Beliefs

A. The Five Pillars

The core beliefs of Islam are contained within the "Five Pillars" of Islam (*arkan al-islam*); the practices through which Muslims live in accordance with the will of Allah. The following are the pillars adhered to by Sunni Muslims; Shi'ites have introduced minor additions and amplifications based on their adherence to their sect, but their Five Pillars will not differ significantly from that of the Sunnis'.

1. Shahada

A Muslim is required to utter the central creed of Islam, the Shahada, aloud at least once in his lifetime, though in practice, Muslims will recite the formula ("There is no God but Allah, and Muhammad is His messenger") many times. Belief in this creed is one of the defining characteristics of a Muslim, and the Shahada is repeated often in prayer. The Shahada is recited by those converting to Islam; a Muslim wants this to be the last words he or she utters; and there is a belief that a special place in Heaven is reserved for those who die a martyr's death with the Shahada on their lips. (*See below for more on Islamic prayer practices.*)

The Qur'an (4:48) also prohibits maintaining or espousing the contrary belief: "Though God may forgive all else, He will not forgive anyone who asserts that there are equals to God." In Muhammad's day, there was a widely held pagan belief that the supreme Almighty creator of the universe (who was known as Allah even then) had three daughters and a male co-deity, all of whom held equal position, much the way the gods of Greek mythology did. Rejecting this idea and ridding the Ka'ba of the idols representing these deities was a major part of the reforms and message of Muhammad. It is for this reason that Muslims

The Shahada appears on the flags of several countries with dominant Muslim populations and cultures—including Saudi Arabia, whose flag is shown here. Underneath the Shahada is a sword, symbolizing justice.

took such offense when the Indian-British (and sometime Muslim) novelist Salman Rushdie published the novel *The Satanic Verses* in 1988, which depicted Muhammad acknowledging the reality and godliness of the three goddesses of ancient legend. Non-Muslims in the West regarded with disdain the outcry and the violent protests in the Muslim world regarding the book, as well as the *fatwa* (decree) issued by Ayatollah Ruhollah Khomeini, the spiritual leader of Iran at the time, calling for Rushdie's execution. (The incident, in fact, led to Britain and Iran breaking diplomatic relations.) The degree to which Muslims regarded this a blasphemous insult needs to be compared with reactions Christian, Jews, and adherents of other faiths have had to similar insults—Jewish reactions to Nazis marching in Skokie; Christian objections to paintings of the Virgin Mary smeared with elephant dung, to cite two examples—to appreciate the depth of the outrage. If nothing else, the episode underscores how important the belief in the incomparable unity of God is in the Muslim mind.

2. Salat

Salat is the requirement for Muslims to pray. At first there were three daily prayer times, but then five times were instituted. Below we will describe the manner of Muslim prayer, but in terms of the place of prayer among the Five Pillars, the objective is to demonstrate through prayer the total and unequivocal submission of the individual to God. This calls for not simply the recitation or affirmation of the words, but physical prostration, with head touching the ground in a position of total subservience to God. The prayers may be said privately or in concert with others, but even when communal, care is taken to maintain the atmosphere of supplication to God, and not to use the gathering as a setting for ceremonial pomp and posturing. The effect on the individual—especially in the context of Western values of personal independence, personal decorum, and individual dignity—is both humbling and reverence-inspiring. Making this submission to the sovereignty

This sign in a Turkish mosque reminds worshippers when it is time to pray.

of God a critical element, and not a mere ceremonial addition or enhancement, separates Islam in a crucial way from other faiths.

Prayers (which we now understand to include the bowings, kneelings, prostrations, and recitations) are to be performed facing the Ka'ba in Mecca, and it has become customary for worshippers to gather, especially on Friday, for mid-day prayers, lending a communal and community-building component to Salat. Islam has maintained a remarkably (and enviably) consistent standard of preparation for prayer, insisting on both facilities for ablution (washing), as well as periods of mental and spiritual preparation, before prayer. (No doubt the sparse simplicity of the procedure has allowed focus to be maintained over the centuries on elements of the service that are most meaningful and important.)

3. Zakat

In addition to his revulsion at the pagan idolatry and polytheism of his fellow Meccans, Muhammad was outraged by what he saw as the exploitation and subjugation of the poor and helpless—the widow and orphan, the elderly, the sick and infirm—by the wealthy merchants of Mecca.

In response, Muhammad taught (and conveyed in the message of the Qur'an—Q 9:60) the requirement of Muslims of whatever station or income to provide 2.5 percent (per lunar year) of their accumu-lated wealth, including money in hand, savings, and all assets. But more important than this specific percentage is the act of giving itself, which helps to both ease the financial strain of the needy, while fostering an awareness of the inequalities of the world. In the same way it was necessary to intro-duce a form of prayer that would curb human hubris and vanity, it was necessary to introduce a means of showing compassion and charity toward the less fortunate. Those who are able to do so are strongly encouraged to give more than the minimum to charity (*sadaka*); the Qur'an is clear that the wealthy have a responsibility to help the needy and to use their wealth to create a stable, healthy, and admirable society (*ummah*).

Shi'ites, being devotees of the lines of specific religious Muslim leaders, give an additional amount (*khums*—a fifth of earnings) to the scholars (*ulama*) and spiritual leaders (*imam*) descended from the founder of their sect. In whatever land Muslims have lived, and whether they were a majority, a minority, or even a marginal part of the population, they have always established well-managed charitable organiza-tions to allow for the performance of Zakat.

4. Sawm

During the holy month of Ramadan (the ninth month of the Islamic calendar, during which Muhammad had his first revelation from God— Q 2:183–185), Muslims abstain from food, drink, tobacco, and sexual activity during daylight hours. This is a means of fostering empathy and compas-sion toward the hungry, poor, and less fortunate. It is also a time of reflection and self-examination (which disciplined fasting has the demonstrated power to inspire), and those who fast are enjoined to pay closer attention to their thoughts, words, and actions. Certain circumstances may exempt Muslims from the Sawm, including extended travel, pregnancy, and illness. (The poor are also exempt—their opportunity to eat being curtailed—provided they feed another poor individual during the day.) Fasting is not permitted for prepubescent children or menstruating women, and is not advised for the elderly (though they may fast, if they are up to it).

The effect of the Ramadan fast on the individual is profound, but even greater is the unifying effect the Sawm of Ramadan has on the world Islamic community. Knowing that tens of millions (if not hundreds of millions) of people are denying themselves the common pleasures of life in order to contemplate their lives, the welfare of their fellow Muslims, and the plight of the poor and needy is a powerful observance (and taxing on one's physical constitution). Shortly after sunset, the fast is broken in a meal known as the Iftar, often a communal meal, where the first item eaten is a date. Muslims in different countries traditionally prepare special foods for Iftar eaten only on the evenings of Ramadan.

The night between the twenty-sixth and twenty-seventh day of Ramadan is the Night of Power (*laylat al-qadr*), commemorating the night Muhammad first received a revelation from God through the Angel Gabriel (Q: 97:1–5. The exact night of the month was deliberately kept secret by Muhammad, so that Muslims would not restrict their prayer to that night alone. He only indicated that it was in the last third of the month.) It is customary to stay up all night and study sacred texts and recite the Qur'an and special prayers. It is also the night, tradition has it, that the fate of each individual, of the Islamic people, and the whole world, is determined in the Heavenly Court, warranting special prayers and devotions.

At the conclusion of Ramadan, Muslims around the world celebrate a festival—Eid al-Fitr—during which there is great jubilation, feasting, and exchanging of gifts. Prayers are abbreviated and Muslims don fine clothing and spend time with their families. It is also customary to provide a special meal—Zakat al-Fitr—during Eid al-Fitr for the needy. Devout Muslims observe six fast days of their choosing during the month after Ramadan (*Shawaal*) as a means of maintaining the contemplative habit beyond the holy month.

5. Hajj

Every able-bodied Muslim must arrange to make a pilgrimage to Mecca at least once during his or her lifetime, specifically during the month of Dhu al-Hijjah, the twelfth month of the Islamic calendar. The Hajj is a symbolic journey which consists of several rituals, including circling the Ka'ba seven times, traveling a space between two mountains seven times, throwing stones at pillars representing the Devil, and a ritual haircut. If the pilgrimage is performed at any time of year other than the time designated during the month of Dhu-al-Hijjah (between the tenth and fifteenth), the journey is known as Umra ("lesser Hajj") and while it may be performed for personal betterment, it does not fulfill the obligation of the Hajj.

Among the most important objectives of the Hajj, and the reasons it is placed among the Five Pillars of the Islamic faith are:

• It fosters solidarity and unity in the Umah (world Islamic community) by bringing together Muslims from all over the world in one place for the sake of communal prayer and celebration.

• It is a tangible act of honor and commemoration to Muhammad for his prophecy as contained in the Qur'an, for his leadership, for the example he set, and for his founding of Islam.

• It connects all Muslims to the tradition and legacy of the Patriarch Abraham (Ibrahim) and his son, Ishmael (Ismail)—both as builders of the Ka'ba and as the first human beings to recognize, acknowledge, offer prayers to, and vow obedience to God.

• It is a profoundly moving, life-altering experience that Muslims remember their entire lives and which makes them effective teachers and ambassadors of Islam when they return to their homelands.

Each year, some 2 million pilgrims make their way to Mecca and to the Masjid al-Haram, the mosque around the Ka'ba, which poses formidable logistical and safety challenges to the Saudi authorities. Yet, in spite of the crush of humanity (and assisted by the spirit of camaraderie that pervades the city during this period), untoward incidents have occurred far less than might be expected.

6. The "Sixth Pillar"

In addition to these Five Pillars, Shi'ites and the the more devout sects of Islam consider an additional concept, Jihad, as deserving of being considered a sixth Pillar of Islam. The term has a long and provocative history, with many unpleasant associations in the West: It is conventionally used to mean the spread of Islam through military force or through violent means. A careful analysis, however, shows this to be an oversimplification, and more careful definition (and less hysteria) will be required if we are to understand what the concept really means.

The word *jihad* means "struggle," and in its most colloquial sense, it denotes a personal striving, and connotes more an inner struggle than outer contention. Islamic theologians most often use Jihad to refer to the *inner* battle that the individual must wage to achieve righteousness, to perform acts of charity, and to conquer personal "demons" and habits that prevent one from doing one's moral or religious duty.

Islam, throughout its history, has eschewed the use of force to convert people to the faith. Unlike Judaism, which actively discourages and thwarts prospective converts; and unlike Christianity, which has several times over the course of the last 2,000 years used force and duress to bring people into the fold, the attitude of Islam has been to welcome converts, but to consider conversion by force of little value. "Let there be no compulsion in religion" is the oft-quoted verse in the Qur'an (2:256) that shows that Muslims are not prone to force people to convert, and this is borne out in a fair and comprehensive survey of Islamic history.

Muslim empires of the last 1,500 years have been interested mostly in being able to conduct their affairs, including large-scale social matters and affairs of state in accordance with the Shari'ah—code of Islamic law. Members of other religions, especially monotheistic religions (such as Judaism, Christianity, Zoroastrianism, Hinduism, etc.), were permitted to practice their faiths in the Muslim state, provided they pledged (through affirmation and by paying a tax—the Jaziyah) their loyalty and cooperation with the efforts of the ruling Muslim state to create a pervasive and durable Muslim society for its own people. Within the confines of these restrictions (which Muslims viewed as necessary for their survival), the religious lives of other religions went unfettered and was allowed to enjoy unparalleled periods of religious, intellectual, and cultural achievement, often called a "golden age."

The idea that there should be (or that there ever *could* be) a separation of church and state—the notion that a religion is not obligated to provide a social order and civil institutions that promote, enhance, and facilitate religious precept and sacred duties—is, frankly, from a Muslim point of view, nonsense. Espousing such values is regarded as a romantic delusion of Enlightenment philosophy, at best, and self-serving hypocritical propaganda, at worst—but most often rationalizations selectively applied to justify what for Muslims appear to be assaults on belief.

Herein lies the challenge for Islam, one with which it has wrestled since its very founding: unlike religions created and developed away from the stage of human affairs, in seclusion and isolation (often, it seems, requiring just such personalities to come into existence), Islam attempts to apply Islamic principles and categories to all aspects of life, including the social and political. In the difficult world of international diplomacy and realpolitik, this has called upon the use of warfare and other military devices that nations use in the course of their history.

What is significant is that the example set by Muhammad during his own lifetime has been (in most instances by far) to offer amnesty and peace to a defeated enemy and to spare noncombatants from the scourge of war.

B. Islamic Values

As with any faith, an important question to be asked is, what are the human values and traits that the religion seeks to inculcate and nurture within its adherents? Which values does the religion seek to promote and perpetuate through its rituals, precepts, and prohibitions? Among the values that Islam cherishes and prizes most highly (the converse of which it finds detestable—*makruh*) are:

Honesty. Scrupulous care and forthrightness in business is a cherished value, and the failure to exercise that value is regarded as despicable and revolting. Westerners often feel Islamic justice is cruel and barbaric in the manner it punishes theft and corruption. Without making any judgments in this area, it is certainly the case that the extremes of punishment that are exacted for such infractions indicate the degree of revulsion Muslims have for theft and dishonesty of any kind.

Generosity. That which a person acquires or possesses is to be considered a gift from God and an indication of being favored by the Almighty. It is thus incumbent on such an individual to share that gift and see himself as an instrument for sharing with others the gifts that God has given to him.

Hospitality. Welcoming friend and stranger alike into one's home to partake of that which God has granted is a blessing and a sign of righteousness. This is a quality that is traced back to Abraham, who kept his tent open on all sides (according to both the Islamic and Jewish traditions) so as to encourage strangers to partake of his hospitality.

Charity. The persistence of poverty and the plight of those who have fallen on hard times as victims of war, famine, disaster, sickness, or business reversals presents the Muslim with a personal challenge, not simply a social inconvenience.

Fairness. The lengths to which Muslims will go to be fair and to find the equitable resolution of a business dispute are remarkable—having more in keeping with the Jewish legalistic tradition of justice, in which "doing the right thing" is valued as highly by the powerful and advantaged as it is by the harmed and disadvantaged, than it has with the Roman system (supported by the Catholic church and the basis of what became Anglo-Saxon and then Anglo-American law), in which order and power can sometimes overshadow fairness and equity.

Humility. The value of humility is nowhere so evident as it is in the practice of Islamic prayer, in which the individual submits totally to the sovereignty of God, acknowledging that all that he has accomplished or acquired has been a gift from God. The worth of a person, in Islam, is determined not by the grandness of his accomplishments, but in the purity and depth of his piety and understanding. This stands in stark contrast with Western values, which place greater emphasis on individual accomplishment and "bankable" skills.

Modesty. This value has created problems in the West, both in terms of the perception on the part of the West of how the implementation of this value indicates the Islamic attitude toward women, and in terms of real-life issues of conformity in dress in places under government control.

Islam has deep revulsion for the public display of lewdness and sexuality, and regards such behavior as arrogant and a deliberate corruption of public values, particularly of young people. The manner of dress prescribed for women in public (and similarly for men, though less well publicized and less divergent from Western fashion than for women), has prompted local school districts in France and in the United States to ban the wearing of a *hijab*—headscarf—in state-supported schools. The reactions of these two governments have been very different, however: since 1944 the French government has supported the expulsion of over 100 schoolgirls from French state schools for wearing a hijab (though in virtually every case the decision was overturned by the French courts); while the U.S. government has, through the U.S. Justice Department, opposed school districts that ban or restrict legitimate religious dress, including the hijab.

This difference was highlighted in the case of

eleven-year-old Nashala Hearn, a sixth-grade student who was suspended by the Muskogee, Oklahoma, Public School District for refusing to remove her hijab, because it violated the dress code of her school, the Benjamin Franklin Science Academy. The United States Assistant Attorney General and a team of Justice Department lawyers fought for Hearn's right to wear her headscarf and attend school without restriction; while France, at almost the same time (spring of 2004), enacted a law that forbade "dress with overt religious identification," citing large crosses, skull caps, and headscarfs as examples, but clearly seeking to restrict the wearing of the hijab in schools.

As discussed below, the precise manner in which this value is expressed is determined as much by ethnic and national mores and values as by Islamic religious law. But the value that lies behind all these practices—the dignity of the individual, man or woman, and the inappropriateness of public displays of lewdness through provocative dress, speech, or behavior—is a value that is firmly and universally embraced by Islamic religious thought.

Islam and the Pleasures of Life

One value that Islam does *not* embrace—one that often plays a central role in other religious value systems—is denying oneself the pleasures of life. In Islam, the story of Adam is told in the Qur'an (Q 2: 30–39) with many of the same elements of the account in Hebrew Scriptures, but with two important differences: first, it is not Eve (who is barely mentioned) who leads Adam to sin, but Satan; and second, Adam and "his spouse" are banished from Paradise (Q: 7:19–25) with no taint of Original Sin." While this concept found its way into both Jewish and Christian theology, it is flatly rejected by Islamic thought—even deemed sacrilegious and a negation of the power and blessedness of God.

In the Qur'an, this concept is found at least four times (Q 3:104, 110; 7:157; 9: 71) with the formulation that God (through the Prophet) has "enjoined what is good" (Amr Bil Ma'roof) and "forbidden what is bad" (Nahi Anil Munkar). Muhammad

clearly enjoyed the pleasures of life—food, friendship, the company of women, sex, fine dining, and living—though he was acutely aware of the corrupting influence and even the intoxicating effect certain pleasures (especially in excess) can have on people.

Some items are clearly prohibited for this reason—alcohol, tobacco, or any intoxicants, or items that are likely to lead to overindulgence. Other activities, such as music, are considered intoxicating per se by some Muslims and thus banned, while others think it wrong to deprive oneself of the pleasure of music, especially when it can open a pathway to a higher spirituality.

An Additional (Controversial) Value

Shi'ite members of the various sects that adhere to different descendants of Ali and Fatima (Ahl-ul-Bait—"people of the house") also place a high value on *tawalla*—love and respect for the descendants of the Prophet (even if a Muslim does not accept their dynastic claims). Conversely, these Muslims also believe the Qur'an demands *tabarra*—rejection of and enmity toward those who do not love Ahl-ul-Bait. As with the phrases in Muhammad's Farewell Address that are ambiguous about the verse's intention, the verses in the Qur'an that deal with the "people of the house" (such as Q 42:23, or 33:33) are not unequivocally clear as to their intent. This is also a source of friction between Sunnis and Shi'ites. Regardless of these differences—and in spite of how heated these disputes have historically been—Muslims regard their primary spiritual allegiance is to the Ummah—the world community of Muslims. This identity is what makes it possible for members of very divergent sects and schools to assemble each year in performance of the Hajj in Mecca.

C. Islamic Doctrines about God, the Universe, and Humankind

A number of other theological concepts play important roles in the development and substance of Islamic thought and theology.

God and Creation

The Qur'an contains a Creation account that is similar to the account in Genesis, but differs in several interesting ways:

• The purpose of thinking about Creation at all is only to understand that God is the Almighty master of the universe. The Qur'an seems in several places to understand that the account is not to be taken literally (Q 45:3–5).

• Sura 21 contains the fullest Creation account. Though the event takes place over six days, the text uses language that indicates the word "day" (*youm*) is not to be understood literally.

• Conspicuously absent from the Qur'an's Creation account is a day of rest. After the sixth day, God "sits on His throne and oversees His Creation" (57:4) without feeling any "weariness" (50:38), or even with a sense of completeness, for God continues the Creation process with the birth of each human being (57:4).

God and Humankind

Though life is seen as having sprung from water (21:30; 24:45), the Qur'an views the creation (and birth) of every human being an act of Divine Creation and benevolence.

Yet, the entire human race is descendant from two people, Adam and his mate (unnamed in the Qur'an, but known as Hawwa, the Hebrew for Eve—in tradition. See 7:189—"[God] made his [Adam's] mate of like nature, in order that he might dwell with her in love.")

The special qualities that God imbued in Adam and imbues with every birth in humans is accompanied by the realization that the beginning of human life, like all other life, is in a lowly "drop of semen [others translate 'blood']" (53:46—in the celebrated chapter known as "The Star," thought to be the account of the Prophet's first Revelation).

Humans have been accorded a special place in creation by virtue of being given free will, an honor and gift to which other parts of Creation, namely, the angels, objected. The angels ultimately accepted God's decision—all but one, Satan (also called "Iblis"), who now is devoted to testing that decision by continually attempting to lead humankind astray.

God and the Nations of the World

The development of many nations is part of the Divine Plan for Creation—again, in contrast to the biblical account of a multitude of nations arising in the aftermath of the episode of the tower of Babel (Genesis 11), and thus a result of human failing.

The Qur'an also contains a decidedly pluralistic undercurrent, showing profound respect for other nations and religions, insofar as they (a) have come to recognize the existence of a singular, Almighty God; and (b) have developed the ability to produce and be taught by prophets with whom God has shared His truths and revelations. For this reason, some have suggested, Islam has found many nationalities and ethnicities receptive to its message.

God, History, and the Hereafter

Islam, like many Abrahamic religions, contains a strong belief in the ultimate fulfillment of the kingdom of God on earth through an apocalyptic event, the End of Days, the final judgment in which God will mete out justice upon all the inhabitants of the world. Islam has a firm belief in the ultimate resurrection of the dead (though some later Islamic theologians believed what was meant was a resurrection of the soul, not the physical body) to bear witness to the ultimate Final Judgment. Fully a third of the Qur'an is devoted to this subject.

In the meantime, Islamic doctrine goes on to say, the righteous and faithful will reside in Paradise (*jannah*—literally "garden"), where they will enjoy the pleasures of the world to an unimaginable degree. The language used is clearly a poetic description of a utopian state, and the descriptions fairly beg to be interpreted as symbolic of elements of life as it is lived.

Reports that Islam promises the righteous, particularly martyrs, an afterlife in which the reward will be the carnal services of seventy-two virgins is puerile nonsense—comparable to childish belief in the tooth fairy. To further report that young men are induced to perform acts of terrorism by being assured that such will be their reward in the afterlife is more nonsense, playing to the Western preconceptions of Muslims as pretechnological primitives incapable of being motivated by anything more sophisticated.

What the Qur'an *does* say (in four places) is that the rewards of Paradise will encompass heavenly versions of all the wholesome pleasures that are available to humankind on earth, including the pleasure of the companionship of the opposite sex—an appreciation of which Muhammad had to an especially advanced and healthy degree. The use of the term *houri*, translated as "comely maidens," clearly (and especially in the manner in which the term is used in 56:22) refers to a Paradise not unlike that depicted in other religious traditions.

III. Important Figures in Early Islamic History

A. The Prophet and the Rashidun

Islamic history begins with the leadership of the Prophet Muhammad, and the first four leaders of the faith in the wake of Muhammad's death in 632. The reigns of these "caliphs" were known as al-Khulafa' ar-Rashidun—the "rightly guided caliphates" who ruled effectively and with the consent of the faithful (though not without some dissent), who had been friends and confidants (*sahaba*) of Muhammad (and relatives through marriage), and whose loyalty, devotion, and service were unquestioned. In centuries to come, the period of the Rashidun would be looked upon as an idyllic time, when the Prophet, or people who had been instructed and inspired by him, led the Ummah, the Muslims, to victory and empire, though there would be many other periods of glory to come, and there

was no lack of divisiveness and contention during this period. We begin with Muhammad.

The Prophet Muhammad

The central human figure of Islam, Muhammad was born around the year 570 CE in Arabia in the wealthy and mostly pagan city of Mecca. The son of Abdullah and Amina, he was a member of the ruling Quraysh tribe and became an orphan around the age of six after his mother's death (his father having died before his birth). He was raised primarily by his uncle, Abu Talib, and in time acquired the skills of a merchant and camel caravan trader. By the age of twenty-six, he had married his employer, the widow Khadija, but it was not until he reached his forties that he is believed to have had his first "revelation."

A pious man throughout his early life, Muhammad would often retreat to the mountains surrounding Mecca for reasons of religious meditation. Upon returning from one such retreat in 610, he informed his family and friends that he had been visited by an angel who urged him to "recite" the words of the one true God, Allah. This would be the first of many revelations (114 in all) which continued over a span of twenty-three years, throughout which Muhammad's companions wrote down and memorized what they believed to be the literal word of God emanating from the Prophet's lips. For the remainder of his life, he spread the message of "Islam," meaning "submission" to the will of Allah. His revelations would be compiled into the Qur'an (meaning "recitation") shortly after his death in 632 in the city of Medina.

Muhammad is revered by Muslims as the holiest man who ever lived, and is believed to be Allah's final prophet. Throughout his lifetime he had several wives—two he seems to have held dear, while others were widows of fallen adherents who needed his protection and patronage. He had several children, though no male heirs survived him. The closest thing to a male heir is Ali ibn Abi Talib, his cousin and son-in-law, husband of his beloved daughter (by his first wife, Khadija), Fatima.

Though venerated, Muhammad was never deified

by Muslims, nor imbued with divine-like powers. Rather he is seen as the perfect manifestation of a faithfully submissive servant of Allah. His sudden death left no clear successor, though some believe his intention (expressed in the Qur'an) was that Ali be the heir to the leadership of Islam.

Khadija

The widow Khadija was the daughter of a wealthy merchant and inherited her father's business after his death. She met Muhammad when he was twenty-five and she was nearly forty, and employed him as an agent for one of her trade caravans. The two quickly grew fond of one another and were married a year after their first meeting.

Khadija is thought by many to have been the first convert to Islam after immediately believing in the revelations of her husband, and aiding him in his quest to spread the message. Their marriage, during which Muhammad had no other wives, was the longest of all of his unions.

Bilal ibn Rabah

Notable for being both the first African Muslim and the first *muezzin* (prayer caller), Bilal was an Ethiopian slave born in Mecca and freed by Abu Bakr. After becoming a Muslim, Bilal walked enthusiastically throughout the streets of the city calling others to convert as he had. The Prophet Muhammad admired his voice so much that he designated him as the official muezzin of the early Islamic community. The position remains active as muezzins call for and lead prayers from the minarets of mosques.

Abu Bakr

Abu Bakr (ca. 573–634) was a wealthy trader and cloth merchant, as well as a neighbor of the Prophet Muhammad during the early years of

Bilal ibn Rabah, Islam's first muezzin, stands atop the Ka'ba in this thirteenth-century miniature, calling the faithful to prayer.

his marriage to Khadija. The two maintained a very close friendship, and after Muhammad's revelations began, Abu Bakr was among the very first converts to Islam. Abu Bakr accompanied Muhammad on the Hijra—Muhammad's flight from Mecca to Medina in 622. After the death of Muhammad, the search for a successor began. The Prophet left no male heirs, which left the decision up to the popular vote of his followers.

Abu Bakr, who had often been instructed by Muhammad to lead prayers in his stead, was eventually elected to the position of caliph (*khalifa*—"substitute" for Muhammad), the civil and religious ruler of the Muslims. This decision infuriated those who believed that Muhammad's son-in-law, Ali, was the rightful successor, and became the cause of Islam's first schism. Sunni Muslims recognize the authenticity and authority of Abu Bakr's caliphate, and believe the Prophet's will was certainly that the caliph should be someone chosen by the people from among those most worthy, and not a member of any dynastic line.

Abu Bakr was from an aristocratic family, so that his conversion to Islam and his friendship and support of Muhammad meant a great deal to the Prophet and to his mission. He no doubt advised Muhammad on many practical and political matters with which the young religion had to deal.

Though Abu Bakr ruled as caliph for only two years (632–634), his tenure was extremely important in Islamic history for three reasons:

1. He fought the Riddah (Apostasy) Wars with the Muslims of Arabia, who had claimed that the teachings of Muhammad did not extend beyond the Prophet's life, and that they were absolved from the precepts and prohibitions that he had promulgated. It took armed conflict to bring these rebels to heel, so that in a real sense, it was Abu Bakr who ensured the continuation of the Islamic religion beyond the life of the Prophet.

2. He began the earnest collection of verses and the text of the oral recitations of Muhammad's revelations—the Qur'an—and committed them to written form for the first time. Believing the longest chapters (Suras) were the most reliable and the most sacred, he arranged them according to length.

3. He appointed a successor while he was still alive, thus avoiding much of the rancor and confusion that followed the passing of the Prophet.

Abu Bakr was succeeded by Umar ibn al-Khattab, another member of Muhammad's inner circle.

Umar ibn al-Khattab

Umar (also called Omar the Great—ca. 583–644), reigned as caliph for ten years—from 634 to 644, during which period the Muslim empire spread beyond the borders of Arabia, north into Palestine, Syria, and Persia, and became poised to challenge the Byzantine Empire.

In 637, Umar laid siege to Jerusalem and eventually took control of the city peacefully—however, the Orthodox Christian patriarch, Sophronius, insisted that the treaty be signed by Umar personally in the city. Umar came to the city (humbly walking through the gates beside his donkey) and signed the Treaty of Umar, under which Christians and Jews would be permitted to live in the city and worship as they wished, provided they paid the reasonable tax (*jizya*) for the maintenance of the city. The treaty was hailed for its magnanimity and became the model of many future Islamic conquests.

Legend has it that Umar asked the patriarch to show him the site of the Temple of Herod in Jerusalem. When he arrived and saw how the Romans had turned the site into a dung heap, Umar, overcome with emotion, knelt down on his knees and, before the astonished assembled, began to clean the site with his bare hands. In a moment, everyone else present joined the caliph, and in a matter of a few hours the site was clear once again. He ordered that a mosque be built on this site; a later caliph replaced the modest structure Umar had erected with the al-Aqsa Mosque, a sacred site in Islam.

Umar is also said to have asked a local rabbi who had converted to Islam to show him the location of the Foundation Stone—the boulder from which God had begun the creation of the world, on which Abraham had offered his son as a sacrifice (according to the Jews, that son was Isaac; according to Muslims, that son was Ishmael), and on which Solomon had placed the Ark of the Covenant in the First Temple. Umar cordoned the area off as a sacred place; later the Dome of the Rock was built on that site. (The Dome of the Rock is often mistakenly identified as the Mosque of Omar; the latter is near the Church of the Holy Sepulcher, where Umar knelt to pray after signing the Treaty of Umar.)

Umar's importance to the development of Islam and the robust growth of the Islamic empire is often underappreciated. As a devout and pious man with a strong sense of compassion and remarkable administrative and leadership skills, Umar was just the sort of caliph the young religion and empire needed so soon after the chaotic departure of the Prophet and the early passing of Abu Bakr. Umar was assassinated by a Persian slave during prayers. (Another legend has it that the assassin was so moved by the fact that none of the other Muslims present during the murder interrupted their prayers, that, overcome with remorse, he immediately stabbed himself to death.)

Uthman ibn Affan

The only member of the powerful and wealthy Umayyad family to become a member of Muhammad's inner circle, Uthman (b. 579) was an astute businessman, a consummate statesman, and a gifted administrator, able to maintain control over an empire that grew incredibly during the twelve years (644–656) of his reign as caliph.

As a man who supported the Prophet at great risk and cost to himself—the rejection of his family had profound economic as well as personal consequences for him—Uthman was a popular choice as caliph after the assassination of Umar; even Ali voted for him in the election that Umar had arranged to determine his successor. Uthman was a man of great charm and sophistication, an astute businessman, and generous to a fault. Though he was a devoted Muslim, he was not the simple pious man that Umar had been; neither was he a strong believer in ruling with an iron hand. As a result, Uthman instituted two practices that were to have long-range effects on the future of Islam: First, he continued Umar's policy of banning the usurping or sale of conquered territory by the army, insisting that the land remain in the hands of the Dhimmis—the non-Muslim citizens living in a Muslim state.

While Umar had enforced this policy strictly, because he was motivated by religious considerations, Uthman enforced it selectively, because he saw it as the key to his second great innovation, which was the division of the empire into provinces and districts ruled by local administrators, but overseen by governors appointed—in writing, with instructions read to the people—by the caliph. As the empire grew—stretching from Pakistan to beyond Gibraltar, and making the first Muslim foray into Iberia—Uthman had to draw upon members of his own family to serve as governors, and while Uthman himself took nothing from the swelling treasury, the Umayyad family, no strangers to luxury, lived in a manner that offended many Muslims, and appeared to have the trappings of a monarchy, which pleased neither devout Muslims nor the army. When Uthman lost the ability to protect his own governors from local insurrections, the die was cast and he was assassinated by Egyptian rebels who invaded Medina and besieged his palace.

Even Uthman's gesture to the religious element, that of sponsoring a committee of clerics to finalize the text of the Qur'an, a process that had been begun by Abu Bakr, backfired when the committee rejected (and destroyed) texts that were supported by some factions but rejected as spurious by others. (The fact that the dialect of the text that was finally approved and disseminated was decidedly Quraysh did not improve the authorized text's acceptability. The uniformity of the text from this point on did much, however, to unify Muslim people around the world.)

The funeral of Uthman was carried on in virtual secret and only a directive from Ali prevented rioters from stoning the small funeral procession of Uthman's casket to his simple, unadorned grave. At long last, Ali's time had arrived.

Ali ibn Abi Talib

Ali ibn Abi Talib (ca. 599–661) was the cousin and son-in-law of the Prophet Muhammad, having married his daughter Fatima, and tradition holds that he was the very first male convert to Islam. A highly skilled soldier, Ali was an active warrior in the service of Muhammad during nearly all of the religious wars fought in the defense and expansion of Islam during his lifetime.

After being passed over in favor of Abu Bakr as Muhammad's successor, Ali saw the office change hands two more times before he became the fourth caliph. His adherents are known as the Shia al-Ali—"the Party of Ali"—or Shi'ites for short; they consider Ali the first legitimate caliph and the first "imam"—leader of the Muslim people (not to be confused with the term *imam* used throughout Islam to signify anyone who leads prayers).

Ali's life is marked with remarkable military prowess and great piety—he was also a resourceful man capable of carrying out daring and complex schemes. According to tradition, he impersonated Muhammad and slept in his bed as a decoy for would-be assassins on the night Muhammad and Abu Bakr conducted the Hijra to Medina in 622. Another tradition has it that it was Ali who destroyed the idols in the Ka'ba when Muhammad marched into Mecca.

Following the assassination of Uthman, Aisha, the young daughter of Abu Bakr whom Muhammad took as a wife after the passing of Khadija, took exception to Ali's behavior, particularly the manner in which he negotiated for the caliphate. It seemed to her that he had fatally compromised the caliphate by allowing his selection to be determined by an election. She joined the Quraysh forces who had backed Uthman (a caliph of whom Aisha vigorously disapproved) and now demanded that Ali bring the assassins of Uthman (which may have included Aisha as an important instigator) to justice. It was an odd alliance that waged the first *fitna*—rebellion—against Ali and the famous Battle of Bassorah (the old name of Basra, Iraq), also known as the Battle of the Camel, because Aisha personally led the rebel forces riding a camel. Ali was victorious (for the moment), and the captured Aisha was forced to retire to Medina to live out her days.

Ali was an important source of many Hadith (traditions) regarding Muhammad; it was said that Ali possessed an amazing mind and committed to memory the verses of the revelations Muhammad received virtually the day the Prophet recited them. "I am the city of knowledge," Muhammad is reported to have said, "and Ali is its gate."

Ali was assassinated in 661, this time by a fellow Muslim, a Kharijite, who stabbed him with a poisoned sword while praying in the mosque of Kufa on the nineteenth day of Ramadan. He took two days to die, and his burial was kept secret at first to prevent its desecration by his enemies. Later, it was revealed that he had been buried in the Imam Ali Mosque in what is today the city of Najaf (seventy miles south of Baghdad), though it is also claimed (by a minority) that Ali's final resting place is a tomb in the famous Blue Mosque or Rawze-e-Sharif in the Afghan city of Mazar-e-Sharif, Afghanistan.

Ali's loyal followers kept his name and memory alive in the spirit of the Shia sect of Islam. Shia Muslims do not accept the validity of any of the caliphs preceding Ali, nor any after him who is not a member of the Prophet's blood-lineage household.

Aisha bint Abu Bakr

Said to be Muhammad's "favorite wife" and the person the Prophet was closest to after the death of his first wife, Khadija, Aisha (614–678) was a good deal younger than Muhammad, and it is possible that he initially married her because a previous betrothal was refused on the grounds that the groom's (pagan) family refused to be associated with Muslims. But Muhammad was won over by her charm, her beauty, and her intelligence—and probably also by her courage, as displayed at the Battle of the Camel. Muhammad is said to have used the curtain from Aisha's tent as his battle standard, and that he died in her embrace.

Aisha became an important source of Hadith—records of teachings and day-to-day habits of the Prophet that illuminated passages of the Qur'an. She never remarried after Muhammad's death out of devotion to Muhammad—and because the Qur'an explicitly (Q 33:53) forbids a Muslim from marrying a widow of the Prophet.

Most Muslims believe that Ali ibn Abi Talib is buried in this mosque in Najaf, Iraq (left). However, many Afghans believe that his tomb is in this famous blue-hued mosque, Rawz-e-Sharif, in Afghanistan (above).

Fatima

The daughter of Muhammad who was the wife of Ali (Muhammad's cousin, the fourth Caliph, the final of the Rashidun period, and founder of the Shi'ite line of Imams), Fatima was a defender of her father, particularly during the pre-Hiraj days in Medina. Many of Muhammad's followers sought Fatima's hand, but Muhammad, following a Revelation, gave his cherished daughter to Ali.

Their early married years were very difficult, as Ali was poor and unconcerned with wealth. Fatima is said to have worked with the servants and have had worn hands from housework. Once, when Fatima asked her father for a servant to help her with household chores, Muhammad asked her if she would prefer a much greater gift, something "worth more than everything in the world." When she agreed, Muhammad told her to end every prayer with the Great Exaltation, the Allahu Akbar (Great is Allah) thirty-four times; then recite the Statement of Absolute Gratitude, the Alhamdullah thirty-three times; and end with the Invocation of Divine Glory, the Subhan Allah thirty-three times—for a total of 100 recitations. This prayer is called the Tasbih e Fatima.

Husayn ibn Ali

After Ali's death in 661, a struggle ensued for the caliphate and for control of the sizable Muslim empire between Ali's two sons, Hasan and Husayn, on one side, and Yazid (I) ibn Muawiya ibn Abu Sufyan on the other. Muawiya had been an unlikely ally of Aisha in her revolt against Ali, and while Ali had been victorious, the Umayyad family and its supporters solidified their control of Arabia while Ali concentrated on Iraq and the northern conquests.

During this period, the phenomenon of Islamic sectarianism first appeared in the form of the Kharijites, a group of zealous Muslims who opposed both the rising Umayyad-backed forces of Muawiya and his son Yazid, but also (paradoxically) the forces of Ali and his sons. It was a Kharijite, it will be remembered, who assassinated Ali, and Kharijites who fought alongside Aisha at Basra.

Though both Ali's sons were content to sit by and allow Muawiya to take control as caliph (some believing that Hasan, the eldest, had been swayed by a large pension), Yazid was a different case, and Husayn in particular could not tolerate what was for him a repudiation of the principles of Islam. The garrison town of Kufa, meanwhile, had been looking for an opportunity to challenge the supremacy of Damascus, Yazid's capital, and to engage the Umayyad forces. During the first week of the twelfth Muslim month, Dhu al-Hijjah, in 680, Husayn set out for Kufa with a band of supporters, soldiers, and their families.

Realizing that if Husayn reached Kufa, he would have a formidable force with which to fight (and learning that a large armed contingent was heading toward Kufa from Basra to join Husayn), Yazid decided it best to force the confrontation before Husayn reached Kufa. He sent a contingent of 4,000 troops to pin Husayn's caravan down near the Euphrates River at a place called Karbala, a city about sixty miles southwest of Baghdad.

By blockading the camp and preventing them from accessing the waters of the Euphrates; by preventing Husayn from getting any messages through to Kufa or Basra asking for aid; by bombarding the camp with arrows, spears, and catapulted boulders, which terrified the women and children and created an atmosphere of panic; and by rebuffing overtures from Husayn for a negotiated settlement or a humanitarian truce, which Husayn made on the seventh day of Muharram as the camp's water was running out, Husayn was left with no choice but to fight with his small force against the, by now, overwhelming forces of Yazid.

On the tenth (Ashura) day of Muharram, the battle was joined; by nightfall, Husayn's forces had been massacred, Husayn himself beheaded with his dead infant son in his arms. The subsequent desecration of the bodies of Husayn and his family was deemed an additional sacrilege (these were, after all, descendants of the Prophet himself), and the imprisonment of Husayn's son, Ali, by Yazid in Damascus along with the periodic display of Ali in public in chains before the severed heads of his family inflamed Muslim sympathy for the fallen grandson of the Prophet and inspired the growth of the Shi'ite sect, especially in Iran and southeastern Iraq.

Looking back at this dramatic formative period of the Islamic religion and the growth of the Muslim peoples—we say "peoples" because in less than 100 years, over fifty different languages were spoken by the subjects of Muslim potentates and empires across the face of Europe, Africa, and Asia—a period taking up barely a single page of the summary four-page timeline on pages 406 to 410, above—we find the seeds of much of what developed over the next fifteen centuries, right to our own day. Though that history shows no lack of contention and enmity across borders and continents (for such is the life of nations), the Muslim community, with all its sects and denominations, looks back at the Rashidun as its most golden age.

B. The Growth of Sects

The basic distinction between Sunni and Shi'ite Muslims is simply that Sunnis accept the authority of the caliphs of the Rashidun and the subsequent chain of caliphs, irrespective of their connection to the family line of Ali. Shi'ites insist that the only leaders that are legitimate are those that have an acceptable claim of lineage to Ali, and, by virtue of the fact that Ali was the closest thing to being a male heir, from him to the Prophet Muhammad.

Worldwide, about 15 to 20% of the 1.2 to 1.5 billion Muslims there are in the world, meaning between 180 million and 300 million people, are Shi'ite. The rest are Sunni. Shi'ites make up a majority in Azerbaijan (85%), Iraq (65%), Bahrain (80%), and Iran (90%). Shi'ites constitute significant minorities in Lebanon (35%), Syria (17%), India (10% of the Muslim population), Pakistan (20– 35%—by including Ismailis and Moulai),

Afghanistan (18%), Turkey (25%), Albania (20%), and Yemen (45%). Shi'ites are also present in significant numbers in the smaller Persian Gulf states of Qatar, Kuwait (36%) and the United Arab Emirates (16%), and Eastern Province of Saudi Arabia (33%).

There are many divisions within Shi'ite Islam: the single largest sect is the **Ithna Ashari**—also known as **Imamis** (because of their belief in the imams who succeeded Muhammad) or **Twelvers** because they accept the authenticity of only twelve imam successors to Muhammad, beginning with Ali. These were known as imams and were infallible (as was Muhammad and Fatima). The line stopped at twelve when the twelfth imam, Muhammad ibn Hasan, or *al Muntazar* ("the awaited one") disappeared in 874 leaving no male heir. Twelvers believe he will return at the end of days as a messianic redeemer and serve as Mahdi, signaling the Final Judgment and establishing a perfect Islamic state. Clerical leaders of this sect are called *mutahids* (scholars), and the greatest of the scholars is called *ayatollah*, a contraction for the words that mean "sign from God." About 85% of world Shi'ites are Imamis—higher in Iran (where Shi'ites predominate).

Two smaller sects that are still part of the Shi'ite fold (in descending order demographically, yet still representing millions worldwide) are:

1. The **Ismailis**, known as the **Seveners** because they accept two additional imams after Muhammad ibn Hasan, the last being Ismail ibn Jafar al-Sadiq—the sixth imam. Ismail died in 765 and left no male heirs, thus ending the line of imams. The Ismailis were the dominant religious force behind the Fatimid Empire, created in Egypt in 909 (by a pretender to the imamate), and which ruled northern Africa until 1171. A series of imams were produced by the Fatimids, though the rest of the Shi'ite populace do not consider them true imams.

A large portion of the Ismailis are the **Nizaris**, so called because they accept the imamate of al-Nizar ibn al-Mustansir, a Fatimid imam who died in 1094. Al-Nizar was imprisoned by his younger brother when their father died and the younger al-Mustasil assumed control. The Nizaris were suppressed in Egypt and the brother's sect vanished with the fall of the Fatimid Empire, but one Nizari imam fled to India and established an imamate there, assuming the title Aga Khan. The first Aga Khan died in 1800, and there have been four altogether, including the current incumbent (who is also considered the forty-ninth Imam of the Fatimid line).

2. The **Zaydis** accept the imamate of Zayd ibn Ali (695–740), also known as Zayd the Martyr (Zayd ash-Shahid). He was the grandson of Husayn ibn Ali, the grandson of Muhammad, which places him as the fifth leader of Islam after Muhammad, Ali, Husayn, and his father, Ali (thus, they are also called Fivers). The Zaydis represent a very small portion of the Shi'ite minority, but are influential beyond their numbers because (a) they are a majority in Yemen, where they have ruled continuously from 893 to 1963; and (b) several important works attributed to Zayd have influenced the Shi'ite Mu'tazilite school of theology, a very strong influence on Sunni thought for centuries.

C. Shared Prophets

Muhammad recognized much of the authenticity of the Hebrew and Christian scriptures, although he believed the purity of their revelations had been altered and distorted over the years. Jews and Christians are both called "*ahl al-Kitab*"—people of the book (though "people of an earlier revelation" is a better translation). As a result, many Jewish and Christian prophets are shared and venerated in Islam, but perceived in unique ways.

Adam

Adam is believed by Muslims to be the first man, the first Muslim, and the first prophet of Islam. The Qur'an's account of the creation differs from the Bible's in specific details, and Adam's wife Eve is not mentioned by name, but the central themes of each story are very similar. Most important, it is Satan

who tempts Adam to sin, not Eve—and the result is not an eternal taint of "original sin." (See opposite page under Jinn.)

Nuh (Noah)

Nuh is mentioned often in the Qur'an as a servant of Allah whose faithfulness in building the Ark spared his life in the Great Flood (which is not depicted as a worldwide event, but as a local catastrophe—Q 23:23–32, and especially all of Q 71). Nuh was a righteous man who warned the people of his era of impending doom, and as such is revered as a true messenger of Allah, and an early Muslim.

Ibrahim (Abraham)

Ibrahim is a significant and holy figure in Islam. He is believed to have rebuilt the Ka'ba in Mecca together with his son Ismail, on its original foundation, first laid by Adam. It was the first house of worship of the one God, a concept first understood by Ibrahim. Ibrahim's footprint is displayed on a stone outside the Ka'ba, and sacrifices are offered at the end of the Hajj commemorating the substitute sacrifice made for Ismail. Ibrahim is loved for his faithfulness in his willingness to sacrifice his son Ismail, and respected as the spiritual ancestor of all Muslims.

Ismail (Ishmael)

Ismail is revered as a prophet of Islam, the ancestor of the Arabs, and the spiritual founder of the Muslim religion; Muhammad is said to be a direct descendant of Imail through Ismail's son, Kedar.

Musa (Moses)

Musa is the most-often mentioned prophet in the Qur'an. He is believed to have freed the Israelites from bondage in Egypt, revealed to them God's Ten Commandments, and was to have led them to the Promised Land. Upon reaching the Promised Land, however, the Qur'an states that the Israelites were too afraid to fight off its inhabitants. Musa warned them that if they did not fight, they would wander the desert for forty years. They did not fight, and suffered the consequences of being divided into many groups of nomadic tribes. Musa died a very old man, after having refused to accept an offer from Allah that would have allowed him to live longer.

Isa (Jesus)

The position of Isa/Jesus in Islam, while vastly differing from the Christian belief, is one of very high respect and appreciation. Muhammad preached that Jesus was born of the Virgin Mary, was a prophet of God, and performed many miracles during his lifetime. However, the Qur'an is clear that Muslims are not to equate Isa with Allah in any way, and must understand that everything good that Isa did was only so because Allah willed it to be so. Isa is believed to be the prophet immediately preceding Muhammad, and to have received a divine revelation from Allah (the Gospel) that would later be corrupted and misinterpreted by his followers.

The Qur'an says that Isa was sent by Allah to perform a service for humanity, but was unable to complete his mission. As a result, he was spared the pain of crucifixion and was raised into heaven, leaving behind a body that looked like him and that fooled his enemies into thinking they had actually killed him. This is in direct opposition to the Christian belief that Christ chose to die for the sins of humanity. Many Muslims believe that Isa will return in the end days to take part in the final war, which will bring peace to the world, but interpretations of the details surrounding this event differ widely among particular sects of Islam.

Maryam (Mary)

Maryam is believed to be the only human to have ever conceived a child solely through the will of Allah, and is the only female mentioned by name in the Qur'an; she is mentioned some thirty-four times and has an entire Sura (Sura 19) devoted to her. Several details regarding her early life and relationship to her son Isa are also mentioned, and it is believed by many that she will be among the first to enter paradise after the end times.

The Angel Gabriel

Muhammad reported to have received the revelations of the Qur'an through the intercession of the Angel Gabriel; another important figure shared in common by Judaism, Christianity, and Islam. At his first visitation of the Prophet, he commanded Muhammad to "recite" the word of God, an act that would continue over many years until the revelation was complete. Gabriel is given the same high level of respect due to a prophet of Islam.

Jinn

While angels in Islamic thought are not imbued by God with free will, other ethereal creatures are: the Jinn, described as composed of immaterial fire, are mentioned often in the Qur'an (Sura 72), sometimes as benevolent creatures (serving as the source of the folk figures known popularly as "genies"), and sometimes as malevolent adversaries of humanity.

The Islamic belief in the reality of nonmaterial entities goes beyond folk religion; it is an affirmation that there is more to the reality of the universe created by God than simply the material world.

IV. Sacred Writings and Sources

A. Scripture

THE QUR'AN

The Qur'an, meaning "recitation," is the central authority of Islam. It is believed that all that is necessary for life in this world is contained within the pages of this ever-evolving gift from Allah. Originally spoken by the Prophet Muhammad and memorized and transcribed by his companions on whatever material was available at the time, the Qur'an was formally collected and organized posthumously, in large part under the supervision of Muhammad's best friend, Abu Bakr.

Orthodox Muslims believe the Qur'an to be the literal, unaltered, perfect word of Allah, and no other written text is given this recognition. As the Qur'an was originally written in Arabic, translations into other languages are often categorized as commentaries rather than the genuine article. The text of the Qur'an is said to reflect a Heavenly Book (Q 43:3-4) or Tablet that God created along with the universe.

The 114 chapters (Suras) of the Qur'an are arranged in order of size and not chronologically. Since most of the early revelations (*wahy*) that Muhammad received in Mecca were short, while the later ones received in Medina were longer and dealt with more immediate practical concerns, one may regard the order as more or less reverse chronological (though note that Sura 53, "The Star," is said to be the first wahy received).

The exquisite poetry of the Qur'an was noticed immediately; it has often turned adversary to convert during Muhammad's time and since. It is certainly the most memorized and chanted work in the world today (perhaps in all of history). Several times in Islamic history, individuals who were expert and inspiring public chanters of the Qur'an, a group known as the Qurra, exercised influence in determining the course of events.

As with any text, interpreting the Qur'an—a discipline known as Tafsir— has been a major endeavor, as well as a major source of controversy and debate. But Muslims have leaned predominantly toward those schools of Tafsir that read and interpreted the text according to its most plain and direct meaning.

B. Secondary Sources

HADITH

After the Qur'an, the collection of Muhammad's sayings, habits, and teachings known as the Hadith, is the most revered work of Muslim literature. Originally an oral tradition, some 15,000 of these teachings were written down sometime during the eighth century, though many are believed to have been col-lected by Aisha and Ali. Many Muslims use the Hadith to supplement their religious lives—it contains valuable advice from the the Prophet that is specific and detailed. But except for use in adjudicating legal cases, offering interpretive guidance in understanding the Qur'an, and as a court of last resort in difficult questions, the Hadith are used with great caution, however venerated a particular collection (there are six main collections) may be by a sect.

SAHABA

One class of reports on the life and work of Muhammad are those created specifically by the companions of the Muhammad, which is sometimes liberally defined to include anyone who actually saw and heard the Prophet. That this source would be questioned even by devout Muslims is understandable, and there are those who call themselves Ahle Qur'an ("Qur'an aloners"), who accept Sahab and Hadith only for inspiration, but never for exegetical, juridical, or theological purposes.

HEBREW AND CHRISTIAN SCRIPTURES

Both the Hebrew and Christian Bibles are highly venerated in the Qur'an, and the Qur'anic term "people of the book" includes believers of the Tanakh (Hebrew Scriptures) and the Gospels. However, while respected and recognized as having originally been of divine origin, Islam teaches that the contents of both of these written traditions have been corrupted and misinterpreted by both Jews and Christians. In Islam, the Qur'an alone is Allah's pure and complete message to humanity.

SIRAH

In addition to Hadith and Sahaba literature, Muslim homes will often have a biography of the Prophet for educational purposes, and since Muhammad lived later than the founders of Judaism and Christianity (so that literary tools and standards were higher), and in a more publicly observed environment, many legends were apt to arise regarding Muhammad's life and career. Still, Islamic scholars, mindful of how imaginative inventions can get the better of sober judgment, have tried to restrict and control the level of embellishment that appears in such works, even when directed at the very young.

THE KALAM

It is no exaggeration to characterize the volume of philosophy and theology that Islam has produced over the course of 1,500 years as immense and monumental. Sensitive to the damage that can be done by the forces of ignorance (*jahaliya*); the seductive way human reason (*ijtihad*) can lead one astray; and the temptation to embellish (*bid'ah*) the teaching, but to thus weaken and distort it—all employed for the most noble of intentions (but just as often as an expression of human hubris)—the Islamic thinkers approached dialectic and philosophic thought with great care and even trepidation, reciting prayers asking for divine guidance before working even on dry technical matters like logic or geometry.

Following are some of the major practitioners of Kalam—the application of philosophical tools and thought to issues of Qur'anic interpretation and theological subjects. When the same techniques were applied to strictly philosophical or metaphysical matters (by the same people, and often with the same sense of responsibility), the enterprise was called (sometimes derisively) Falsafa.

This list is, of course, selective and inadequate; readers are invited to examine the larger histories (available in English) by Henry Corbin, Seyyed Hossein Nasr, and Majid Fakhry, as well as the shorter histories by Oliver Leaman and by Ignaz Goldhizer. We begin with the Mutazilite school:

Wasil ibn Ata (700–748) was born in Arabia and studied with a son of Ali ibn Abi Talib; later he studied in Basra, where he was expelled for an activity that often presages future greatness: asking embarrassing questions regarding the consistency of Muslim theology and political philosophy. He is credited with founding the Mutazilite ("dissenters") school of Islamic philosophy, the three fundamental tenets of which were:

1. No attributes can be meaningfully ascribed to God;
2. Human beings are free agents, and thus responsible for their actions; and
3. No human action is meaningful unless it stems from reason and understanding.

Throughout their history, the Mutazilites have been a paradox, using the suspected and "unsavory" methods of logic and reasoning to defend orthodox Islamic principles—but this is also one reason they found a receptive audience among so many Muslims.

Abu Yusuf Yaqub ibn Ishaq al-Kindi (known simply as **al-Kindi**—ca. 801–873) was born in Kufa, educated in Baghdad, and a favorite of Abbassid caliphs, though in his later years he was dismissed and persecuted (even beaten) for his liberal theories. Al-Kindi's range and depth of knowledge is astonishing—he contributed to every major science of his day and extended their boundaries in ways that left those who followed with a century or two of work in catching up. His most controversial position was his belief that reason was sufficient to reproduce what could be known by prophecy, raising the possibly heretical question: why is prophecy necessary?

Abu Nasr al-Farabi (ca. 872–951). Details of Al-Farabi's life are sketchy; even his origins are not known for certain. It is certain only that he lived and worked in Baghdad, spent the last years of his life in Aleppo, and died in Damascus. He was the founder of the great Islamic tradition of formal logic, extending Aristotelian logic into new areas, and he also developed physics beyond its Aristotelian confines. He was a prolific writer of over 100 works, virtually all of which were cherished, copied, and studied.

Al-Farabi's most lasting contribution was his theory of the imam, the perfect ruler, a blend of the Qur'an, Plato's *Republic*, and Aristotelian and Alexandrian eudaemonic (happiness-oriented) political philosophy that struck more orthodox readers as uncomfortably hedonistic.

Abu Ali al-Husayn ibn abd Allah ibn-Sina (ca. 980–1037), known as **ibn-Sina**, and by his Latin name **Avicenna**, was the foremost physician and Islamic philosopher of his time. Over half of his 450 works have survived, including over forty works in medicine. Ibn-Sina was born in Uzbekistan—which accounts for his familiarity with Indian mathematics—and raised a Twelver. He became a celebrated healer in Iran—so celebrated that he was at times imprisoned to prevent him from working for rivals.

Ibn-Sina's medical works were to be studied for centuries and were deemed the starting point of any serious modern study of medicine or pharmacology. He pioneered the application of experimentation and scientific testing in medicine. Though he advanced virtually every scientific field, his most lasting contribution may be in the area of psychology, in which he was the first to identify psychosomatic illnesses, diagnose depression (which he called "melancholia"), and intimate that there may be hidden "intelligences" at work in the human mind, anticipating the modern concept of the unconscious.

At the end of his life, he refused to shorten his long work day by famously saying, "I prefer a short life with width to a narrow one with length."

Abu al-Walid Muhammad ibn Ahmad ibn-Rushd—better known simply as **Ibn Rushd**, and by his Latinized name **Averroes** (pronounced a-*vair*-reez; 1126–1198)—was a Muslim philosopher-physician who was born in Andalusia (what the Muslims called Spain) in the golden city of Córdoba. He died in Marrakesh in modern-day Morocco, where he had been exiled by the Almohad caliph for supporting an nonorthodox rebel group.

Ibn Rushd founded a school that was widely influential in Europe in both Muslim and Christian circles. Known as Averroism, it amounted to taking Al-Kindi's support of reason to its ultimate conclusion: reason and revelation, Ibn Rushd said, were more than equivalent—they were identical. Ibn Rushd advanced this philosophy in two ways: he produced an enormous outpouring of works (num-

bering in the hundreds) in virtually every field known, advancing them all; but even more astonishing is his lifelong project of translating and writing commentaries on every Aristotelian work he could find. Many of the works were immediately translated into Hebrew and Latin, and for many works, these are all that survive. The complete Latin edition of Averroes's commentaries on Aristotle were published in Venice from 1562 to 1574 in sixty volumes.

Because of this work, and because of his influence on the proto-rationalists Aquinas and Maimonides, Ibn Rushd has been called the founding father of secular thought in Western Europe.

An outpouring of such brilliance was bound to give rise to a reaction. The adversaries who fought these thinkers on their own turf did not fare well—not nearly as well as those who took the battle to new territory and developed the mystical underpinnings of Islam. This took a giant leap with the work of al-Ghazali, whose work revitalized the Sufi mystical tradition and, ironically, gave rise (500 years later) to secular European philosophy.

Abu Hamid Muhammad ibn Muhammad al-Ghazali (known simply as **al-Ghazali**; 1058–1111), lived his entire life in the city of Tus in Persia (modern-day Iran; the city was virtually leveled by Genghis Khan in 1220). Al-Ghazali went through two periods in his life: the first was a reprise of the careers of the other great Islamic polymaths-scientists-philosophers already discussed; had he stopped working in 1095, his place among the top rank of Muslim thinkers would be assured. Because there are *two* al-Ghazalis, many (some 400) works that are attributed to him were not really his; still, seventy-two works have been verified as definitely of his authorship.

The influence of his later (post-1095) work is so great, that it seems pointless to dwell on his earlier writings. While they were important in the many fields in which he worked, the effect of his later work was to cast doubt on the entire philosophic enterprise and thereby usher in the skeptical turn of mind that would become critical for the development of the Enlightenment. Whether Descartes actually read a Latin edition of al-Ghazali is debated by scholars, but there is no doubt that the work in question, *The Incoherence of the Philosophers*, profoundly influenced the course of modern thought for centuries.

In that book, and in two subsequent works—al-Ghazali's autobiography, *The Deliverance from Error*, and a work in which he applied his skeptical approach and uncompromising analysis to Islamic disciplines, *The Revival of the Religious Sciences*—al-Ghazali presents an effective and emotional refutation of Aristotelian rationalism and lays the foundation for a mystical approach to religion that was to bring Sufism back into the Islamic mainstream.

Al-Ghazali went on several pilgrimages during his lifetime that were more aimed at finding inner peace and spiritual enlightenment than in visiting any shrine. The Islamic philosophers of the Kalam scrambled to answer the wandering al-Ghazali, usually pouring on more of the logical and empirical weaponry that had disillusioned al-Ghazali in the first place. His work is the cornerstone not only of Sufism, but of the philosophical tradition that developed in opposition to the Mutazilites, the Asharia, named after the Iraqi founder of that school, Abu al-Hasan al-Ash'ari (874–936).

C. Sufism

The inclusion of a section on Sufism in this chapter is itself controversial, insofar as many Muslims do not consider the Sufis authentic and legitimate Muslims, especially not the "New Age" forms Sufism has taken in the United States. Yet it is indisputably the case that Sufism proved to be a highly "exportable" version of Islam, one that the people of Central Asia and the Far East found not only endearing, but consonant with their own folk religious traditions.

Sufism placed great stock in direct personal transmission of the sect's teachings, so that a Sufi master (a *pir*, *shaykh* or *murshid*) would teach an apprentice (*murid*) for a number of years. This practice not only developed an effective pedagogy, it also allowed Sufi masters to attract adherents from powerful and influential families.

Sufism was also the Islamic order that emphasized the concept of Divine Love as a central concept. Credit for this goes largely to a slavewoman from Basra who became an ascetic and one of the great poets of the Arabic language. Rabi'a al-Adawiyya al-Basri (717–801), known as **Rabia**, was sold into slavery when her family fortunes were wiped out and her father died. Legend has it that she would go to the roof after a hard day's labor and sing, "O my Lord, the stars are shining and the eyes of men are closed and kings have shut their doors, and every lover is alone with his beloved, and here I am alone with Thee." One night, when her master heard these chants, he was so overcome with guilt that he freed her. She then led a life of asceticism and composed psalms of love poetry to God, some of the most beautiful ever put to pen.

There are many Sufi orders, but there soon developed two main types: one is known as the "intoxicated" form, by which is meant a group that engages in ecstatic chanting, singing, dancing, meditation, and trance-like incantations. This form claims as its founder Abu Yazid al-Bistami (known as Bayazid, d. 875). The other is the counterbalancing reaction to intoxicated Sufism, and is thus known as "sober" Sufism, founded by Junayrd of Baghdad (d. 910).

The sober Sufis engaged the religious leaders of Islam in debate over the many poetic passages of the Qur'an that intimate the possibility of cleaving unto God and of His sharing of His essence with His creation—a concept orthodox Islam regarded as *shirk*, heretical. Junayrd pointed out that the verse (7:172) "When you Lord took from the Children of Adam, from their loins their seed, and made them bear witness as to themselves: 'Am I not your Lord?' They said, 'Yes, we bear witness!'—lest you should say on the Day of Resurrection, 'Really, we were ignorant of this'" implies that all of humanity exists in God, for this verse refers to a time before there were people. The scholars replied that he was using a flawed text and that the verse is in the present tense, referring, therefore, to all human beings being born now.

And so the debate continued until 922, when a Sufi student of both Bayazid and Junayrd, Husayn ibn Mansur al-Hallaj, was tortured and crucified for espousing the heresy that Muhammad was divine, and that he shared some of that divinity himself. The Sufis were then cast out and sent into exile in all directions, which was how they appeared in such far-flung areas, bringing peoples of Asia and Africa into the Ummah. In retrospect, Islam was a great beneficiary of the persecution of the Sufi and their diaspora.

A Sufi who exercised great influence over Islam and in the world at large was Mawlana Jalal-ad-Din Muhammad Rumi (known as **Rumi** in the West; 1207–1273). The quintessential Muslim mystic, he took up residence in Anatolia, where he eventually founded the Mevlevi Order of Dervishes. Consumed by his love for Allah, as well as his concept of Allah's love for humanity, Rumi devoted much of his life to spreading his belief in the universality of God. His major works include a six-volume poem called "Spiritual Couplets" and "The Works of Shams of Tabriz," written in honor of his intimate friend and spiritual inspiration, "the Dervish Shams." Rumi's works are known around the world and are often praised for their inclusiveness, as Rumi himself believed

These "whirling dervishes" are performing the dance called the Sema, a choreographic affirmation of God's unity with all creation.

that God's love transcends all human boundaries. The spinning dancing that has become well known is actually symbolic of the *tawhid*—the singular unity of God. The use of music, poetry, and dance (*qawwali*), and the meditative (*muraqaba*) chanting and invocation (*dhikr*) of God's name—these have all become identified with Sufism and have greatly influenced culture far removed from Islam.

D. Islamic Law

At the other end of the spectrum are the schools of **Fiqh**—Islamic law and jurisprudence. The development of Islamic law is one of the monumental achievements of human society, occupying many of the best minds over many centuries, and, most importantly, with a continuity and consistency that is not to be found in other legal systems, secular or religious. When Islamic law was instituted as the state legal code of the Iranian republic with the return to Iran of Ayatollah Khomeini in 1979, the code was one that had been developed and analyzed for centuries and which spelled out proper behavior in virtually every conceivable area of life (again, secular or religious)—the Shari'ah—and not a hastily assembled, arbitrary set of regulations as Westerners were led or prone to believe.

There are five major schools of Islamic law: four are Sunni, holding sway in various countries with Sunni majorities; and one Shi'ite school that is accepted in countries that are predominantly Shia. The four Sunni schools are named after their founders; they are (with the area of their dominance): **Hanafi** (Turkey, Pakistan, the Balkans, Central Asia, India, Afghanistan, China, and Egypt); **Maliki** (North Africa, West Africa, and several Arab Persian Gulf states); **Hanbali** (Saudi Arabia); and **Shafi'i** (Indonesia, Malaysia, Egypt, Yemen, and parts of India). Hanbali law has a great deal of prestige by virtue of its association with the land in which Mecca is located, but the Shafi'i school is the one most widely accepted. It was founded by Abu

Abdullah Muhammad al-Shafi'i, or simply al-Shafi'i (767–820), a Meccan from a poor family that emigrated from Gaza a generation or two earlier. Details of his life are sketchy, but he was clearly versed in both the Maliki and Hanafi schools of law. His major work, *Al-Risala,* earned him the title "father of Islamic jurisprudence," and is the starting point of any serious Muslim legal education.

What made the Risala (as it is called) so remarkable, especially for so early a work, is that it showed profound respect for each of the legal traditions, sought areas of agreement, suggested acceptable resolutions for areas of disagreement, and codified the law with great clarity and precision. Al-Shaffi'i also clarified the *sources* of Islamic law and prioritized them: He placed the Qur'an at the first level (as determined by the accepted schools of *tafsir,* interpretation), followed by authoritative Hadith. He then placed consensus (*ijma*) above logic or sophistry, arguing (in a startlingly modern tone) that the objective was determining what was right action, not what was truth, which was elusive. He then placed a form of reasoning called *qiyas,* which can best be translated as "analogical reasoning." An example of *qiyas* is the extension of the prohibition of alcohol by analogy from the explicit mention of a prohibition of date wine in the Qur'an. Finally, he places reasoning—*ijtihad*—which he treated with suspicion, at the bottom.

Two principles of Fiqh ensure the continuing development and growth of Islamic law: one is the concept of *istihsan,* or fairness and equity, which looms over all legal systems like a stern, inscrutable taskmaster; and the other is *maslaha,* the public interest, also a frequently unforgiving consideration.

Shi'ites generally follow the **Ja'fari** school, founded by Ja'far al-Sadiq (702–765), the sixth infallible imam according to the Shia. This school is followed in Iran, much of Iraq, Azerbaijan, Lebanon, Bahrein, Pakistan, India, and parts of Afghanistan and Saudi Arabia. Two elements characterize Ja'fari law that make it unacceptable by the larger Muslim Umma (however much respect they may have for it): one is the reliance on the *fatwas,* rulings of previous imams, held by Shi'ites to have an authority derived from the connection with Muhammad; and the second is a reliance on individual reasoning and argumentation that strikes many as out of place with and unbefitting of the Shari'ah.

V. Rites and Rituals

A. The Muslim Calendar

Muslims follow a twelve-month lunar calendar of approximately 354 days. The years of the calendar are known as "Hijra years," as the first year marks Muhammad's Hijra, his emigration from Mecca to Medina in 622. As Westerners use CE and BCE to denote the years, Muslims, use AH and BH—"After" or "Before the Hijra"—to relate the years to the Hijra year of 622. The Qur'an (Q 9:36-37) explicitly prohibits the introduction of a "leap month" (known as an intercalary month) to align the Muslim year with the solar year (as the Jewish calendar does, in order to keep Passover a spring festival).

Originally, the new month was declared once witnesses observed the hilal—the first crescent of the new moon, which introduced some uncertainty about exactly when the month began, especially confusing when the new moon was observed on different days in geographically distant countries (which could be the case even without cloudy skies obscuring the moon). In some countries (mainly in East Asia), that method is still used, but in 1999 the Muslim communities in many countries (in the United States, this change occurred in 2007) adopted the Umm al-Qura (a term that means "center of villages" and is a reference to Mecca) calendar, whch is used by Saudi Arabia and determines the new moon, and thus the first day of the month, by astronomical calculations. This ensures that Ramadan will occur at the same time everywhere, and that the Hajj will be coordinated across the world.

The names of the Muslim months are:

1. **Muharram**
2. **Safar**
3. **Rabi' al-awwal (also known as Rabi' I)**
4. **Rabi' al-thani (also known as Rabi' II)**
5. **Jumada al-awwal (also known as Jumada I)**
6. **Jumada al-thani (also known as Jumada II)**
7. **Rajab**
8. **Sha'aban**
9. **Ramadan**
10. **Shawwal**
11. **Dhu al-Qi'dah**
12. **Dhu al-Hijjah**

B. Significant Dates and Holidays

The correlation between the Gregorian calendar used in the West and the Hijri calendar for any date can be ascertained at the websites: www.islamicfinder.org/dateConversion.php, and www.phys.uu.nl/~vgent/islam/islam_tabcal.htm.

Though some holidays are especially important to specific sects of Islam, all Muslims are aware of these dates and respect them, even if they are not members or adherents of the relevant sects.

MUHARRAM

• **1 Muharram** – The Muslim New Year. The beginning of the period of mourning for Husayn ibn Ali. It is also a time to recall the Hiraj (though it is not the date on which the Hiraj took place. That will be commemorated sixty-six days later on 8 Rabi' I.)

• **10 Muharram** – Ashurah ("the tenth"), the observance of the martyrdom of Husayn, Ali's son. (Also the the anniversary of Moses and the Children of Israel crossing the Red Sea.) The ten days from the first to the tenth of the month are, for Muslims, days of deep introspection and self-evaluation.

RABI AL-AWWAL

• **12 Rabi' al-awwal** – Milad un Nabi, Muhammad's birthday for Sunni Muslims.

• **17 Rabi' al-awwal** – Milad un Nabi, Muhammad's birthday for Shia Muslims.

RAJAB

• **13 Rajab** – Birthday of Ali ibn Abi Talib.

• **27 Rajab** – Isra and Miraj: The "Journey and Ascension" on which, according to the traditional interpretation of the Hadith, Muhammad was transported on the back of a winged beast from Mecca to the "furthest Mosque" (traditionally Jerusalem's Dome of the Rock) and then to heaven to meet with God and the prophets. See Q 53:7–14; 17:1.

RAMADAN

• **1 Ramadan** – Daytime fasting begins.

• **21 Ramadan** – Commemorates Ali's death.

• **A day in the last third of the month** – *Layl al-Qadr*, the Night of Power, or Night of Measures, commemorating the first revelation by the Angel Gabriel to the Prophet Muhammad. In many mosques, this is observed by all-night study, prayer, and contemplation. The date varies from one tradition to another.

SHAWWAL

• **1 Shawwal** – **Eid al-Fitr (Festival of Breaking the Fast)**: Marks the end of Ramadan's abstinence with feasting and celebration.

DHU AL-HIJJAH

• **8–10 Dhu al-Hijjah** – Period when the Hajj to Mecca is to be performed.

• **10 Dhu al-Hijjah** – **Eid ul-Adha (Festival of Sacrifice)**: Marks the completion of the Hajj—a joyous event for all Muslims, even those who did not make the pilgrimage that year; and a festival commemorating the prophet Abraham's faithful attempt to sacrifice his son. Unlike Jews and Christians who believe this son to be Isaac, Muslims believe that God instructed the prophet to sacrifice his first son, Ismail.

• **18 Dhu al-Hijjah** – **Eid al-Ghadeer (Festival of [Muhammad's] Final Sermon)**: Venerated by all Muslims, but especially by Shi'ites, who see in that

This mihrab *(niche) in the wall of a mosque in Delhi, India, indicates the Qibla—the direction to Mecca.*

address the appointment of Ali and the validation of the Imamate.

C. Worship and Liturgy

Place. Traditionally, Muslim prayers (Salat) are performed five times daily, usually with the aid of prayer mat or rug (a *musallah*, also a word used to describe a temporary or informal "storefront" space used for prayers, especially for Friday afternoon communal prayers, in areas where a full-fledged mosque is not available). The place of prayer, the *masjid* (or mosque, a variation derived from a Spanish rendering) must be kept clean and simple.

Preparation. Prior to prayers, a ritual ablution (*wudu*) is performed in which the hands, mouth, nose, face, arms, forehead, hair, ears, and feet are washed three times. Muslims also spend time before each prayer "cleansing the mind" from daily concerns and affirming the intention to pray (*niyya*) so they can concentrate and pray devoutly. During the ablutions and the mental preparations, they recite the Shahada repeatedly.

Orientation. The observant must face the general direction of the holy city of Mecca, with the Ka'ba imagined as a focal point—this direction is called the Qibla, and Muslims will often orient their lives and homes (even their graves) toward this direction. As was the case in the Prophet's time, a simple niche—a *mihrab*—is placed in the wall with a sign or wall hanging (but with no object) indicating that that is the Qibla, the direction to Mecca. (GPS devices are now available that show the Qibla on a wristwatch-type device.)

Praying in the proper direction is vital for the proper performance of Salat (prayer); it is preferable to miss the time of prayer because one was determining the Qibla than to pray in an uncertain or incorrect direction.

Times of Prayer. There are five daily prayers:
- **Fajr (dawn):** From first light on the horizon to sunrise.
- **Dhuhr (midday):** From noon till (according to many authorities) half the time until sunset. Often called for at noon.
- **Asr (afternoon):** From the end of Dhuhr until sunset (meaning, before the disc of the sun hits the horizon). The mention of the Asr prayer prominently in the Qur'an (2:238) makes it a significant prayer.
- **Maghrib (sunset):** From sunset to nightfall.
- **Isha'a (night):** From nightfall to midnight (but in any case, before first morning light.

Friday Prayer. Friday is a day of communal prayer (*jum'ah*), when Muslims congregate in a mosque for the Dhur prayers, pray, and hear a sermon from their religious leader (*imam*). It is not, however, considered a sabbath on which work is to be curtailed.

Order of Prayer. The *muezzin* calls the people for prayer with the Adhan, the call, *Allahu Akbar!*—"God is great." In Muslim lands, this function is performed by a *mu'adhdhin*, a caller specially trained and highly respected, calling from atop the minaret of the town mosque.

After the preparations and once inside the mosque, the worshipper begins by raising his or her hands toward Heaven (as if greeting a king) and declaring "Allahu Akbar." Then one lowers one's hands and stands erect, and the Fatihah is recited— the opening Sura of seven verses. All Suras of the Qur'an are prefaced with the phrase, "In the name of Allah, most benevolent and ever merciful," after which comes the text of the Fatihah:

> All praise be to Allah, lord of the worlds,
> Most beneficent, ever merciful,
> King of the Day of Judgment,
> You alone we worship, and to you alone [we] turn for help,
> Guide us, O Lord, to the path that is straight,
> The path of those you have blessed,
> Not of those who have earned Your anger, nor those who have gone astray.

Then the worshipper bows (ruku), placing palms on knees, reciting (self-selected) verses of the Qur'an.

Ruku is followed by standing erect again (Itidal), accompanied by recitations.

Itidal is followed by kneeling prostrations in which the worshipper falls to one's knees and then places the (bare) forehead on the ground while supporting the body with one's hands flat on the ground. During these prostrations, prayers (rakah) are recited.

The worshipper will then rise up but remain kneeling, reciting the Tashahhud—the "witnessing." The sequence requires three such declarations, each preceded by a prostration: one acknowledging Allah and His revelation to the Prophet, Muhammad; one acknowledging the Ummah and the special relationship the community has with God; and the final Tashahhud acknowledging the Prophets Abraham and Muhammad for their teaching and guidance.

The service is concluded by extending greeting to worshippers to the right and left: "May the peace, mercy, and blessings of Allah be unto you." (Some may recite a personal prayer (dua) it this point.)

This in outline and with variations (and no doubt, also with some oversimplifications) is the basic form of Islamic prayer; the main point made here is that the service is designed to maintain disciplined focus on the act of prayer, and not allow it to become an opportunity for performance, self-expression, and communal posturing, all of which have their place, *but not in prayer.*

• **Segregation.** Men and women are segregated during prayers, not only as a measure to maintain concentration, but to forestall the unseemly attention the physical aspects of the service (proximity and prostrations, etc.) would inevitably provoke.

D. Daily Life

Diet

The dietary laws of Islam (outlined in the Qur'an in Sura 5) distinguish first between that which is *haram* (forbidden) and that which is *halal* (permitted). Under the heading of dietary Haram (for the term also refers to improper activities) are:

• dead animals that were killed by anything other than an act of slaughtering (*dhabia*);

• pork or pork products and derivatives;

• blood (or meat out of which no effort to remove blood has been made);

• carnivores and predatory animals, but not including animals who eat fish (i.e., piscivores);

• alcohol or alcohol-derivatives (though permissible when used in medicine);

• insects (with the possible exception of locusts) and amphibians.

• fish with fins and scales are deemed halal by all Muslims, but shellfish and scaleless fish are considered haram by some (generally Shi'ites) and either halal or merely *makruh* (revolting) by others.

Kosher. The Islamic laws of proper slaughtering of an animal to render it halal (*zabihah*) are similar to those of Jewish slaughtering (*she'hitah*), except for the fact that halal meat must (in accordance with Q 5:4) have been slaughtered "in the name of Allah." The Qur'an explicitly (5:5) permits Muslims to eat food prepared by "people of the book," which includes Jews, who presumably have slaughtered the animal properly, but without invoking Allah, and

Christians, who, one presumes, did neither. The matter is the subject of considerable debate and there is wide diversity of opinion on the matter. It is fair to say that many Muslims, particularly in the United States, will avail themselves of kosher meat and will pronounce a benediction on the meat declaring that it is being prepared and consumed in the name of Allah. (Some take the additional controversial step by considering this valid even for meat not slaughtered kosher, but then only as a last resort.)

Dress

The Islamic value, *hijab*—"covering" if narrowly construed; "modesty" in its most general meaning—pervades much of Islamic culture and thinking, and gives rise to standards of behavior and dress that are often viewed as out of step with Western fashion. The Islamic standards of hijab extend not just to dress, however; they are equally applicable to language and all other areas of behavior where (a) men and women may come in close proximity, and (b) where there is a way behavior will influence young people in forming their values.

In this regard, the concerns of Islam are no different in kind from those of many other religions—and if they are perceived as more extreme in degree, then it should be noted that often such practices are dictated by a long ethnic and national tradition, and that the standards of hijab are always evolving and developing everywhere Muslims live and under all sorts of social contexts in which they find themselves.

Having said that, some observations are pertinent:

• The Qur'an enjoins men and women to dress modestly and to observe the rights and privacy of members of the opposite sex (see Q 24:31, regarding modest dress; 33:58–9, regarding maintaining distance and propriety; 33:32–3, regarding avoiding improper contact or familiarity). There is no mention of any specific garb or headcovering prescribed for women in the Qur'an; only the vague directive that they "draw their wraps over themselves" (33:58). Emphasis is clearly on values and substance.

• The entire tone and substance of the Qur'an is to place the responsibility for the code of dress in the hands of women. A double standard that has evolved and prevailed in many countries is clearly a product of male-dominated norms and practices, not of the Islamic faith—or any other religion, for that matter, however much proponents of male-dominated and chauvinist societies may claim it to be religiously dictated. Such a claim is belied (certainly in Islam) by the positive and egalitarian attitude of Muhammad and the Qur'an toward women, and the outstanding achievements and political leadership of women in Muslim-dominated countries in the last century.

• Islam considers various parts of feminine anatomy as having allure, sometimes in ways that are not immediately obvious or socially acknowledged, such as a woman's voice, hair, eyes, etc. A Muslim regards it as incumbent upon him- or herself to conduct one's affairs free of the *fitnah*—temptation—that will permit or encourage one party to use a position of power to abuse, harass, or otherwise extort sexual or other favors from the other. Muslims (again, consonant with the views of many other faiths) regards this as a practice that is tacitly allowed in the West, but that is unacceptable for Muslims and their families.

• Moreover, Islam (as is the case in many other religious traditions) takes special pains to maintain the privacy of a woman's natural cycle from public display or knowledge (because Islam regards it as either a condition of vulnerability or one that, like male emissions, requires ritual purification).

• Islam is highly critical of the public display of sexuality encouraged by the Western consumerist culture and paraded in public media and forums. Muslim countries are fully aware of the benefits the freedom that permits such behavior has provided the United States and the West—but is also mindful of the cost in terms of social upheaval and problems such unfettered expression can cause.

• Many people from a host of religious backgrounds (Christian, Jewish, Hindu, Buddhist, etc.), dissatisfied with what they perceive all around them in the United States and Europe as a lewd, libertine, and lascivious culture, have separated themselves and retreated to their own communities and enclaves in an effort to protect their families from the negative consequences of a chaotic and unregulated social environment. It is ironic (but characteristic of Muslim determination, and no doubt a legacy from centuries of being the majority in their native lands) that Muslims have been in the forefront of legally asserting the right to their cuisine and to practice their values of proper dress in the American public square, insisting that American society live up to its defense of personal freedom without hypocrisy.

E. Life Cycle Events

Birth

The birth of a child is considered a blessed event and a gift from God. It is customary to whisper the Adhan—the call to prayer—in both the newborn's right ear and left.

Aquiqa

In Middle Eastern countries, a feast is observed on the seventh day after a child (male or female) is born, at which an animal is sacrificed and then eaten by the assembled. A tradition has it that the child's head is shaven and the shorn hair weighed, and the weight of the infant's hair (in silver) is donated to charity. It is also customary to name the child at this feast. The Aquiqa has gained acceptance in many American Muslim communities.

Circumcision

Islam interprets the Qur'anic verse, "We commanded you to follow the way of Abraham the upright" (16:123) to refer to circumcision. In Middle Eastern countries, circumcision can occur for boys anytime between the ages of two and ten, and is deemed a rite of confirmation. In the United States, the overwhelming practice is to circumcise the child in infancy, preferably before coming home from the hospital, more often on the seventh-day cel-

ebration of the Aquiqa. (This is closer to the way circumcision was practiced in early periods of Islam.)

Ramadan

Ramadan is revered as the holiest month of the Islamic calendar. It is believed that the revelations of the Qur'an began during this month, and observant Muslims are instructed to abstain from eating or drinking (sawm) during daylight hours for the entire month. During the month, Muslims the world over rise before dawn to eat the Suhoor (predawn) meal and perform their Fajr (early morning) prayer. They break their fast after the fourth prayer of the day, Maghrib (sunset), is observed.

During Ramadan, Muslims avoid crude or vulgar sights and sounds. Sexual activities during fasting hours are also forbidden (Q 2:187). The act of fasting redirects the heart away from the mundane, instilling an inner peace and self-awareness. The fast is not an easy precept; it requires discipline and dedication—especially in environments in which Muslims are a minority. It is intended to make Muslims more sympathetic to the plight of the needy, and thus more generous, charitable, and dependent on material things (dunya). Muslims may eat after the sun has set. Pregnant women, the elderly, the sick, and children under the age of twelve are exempt from fasting (but not from the other spiritual tasks called for).

Muslims traditionally read the Qur'an systematically, a portion each day of the month. In some mosques, these recitations are formalized every night of Ramadan in prayers known as Tarawih. (As Tarawih services were instituted by Umar, the second caliph, they are not practiced by Shi'ites.) It is also during Ramadan that many Muslims perform Zakat—tithing—and bring themselves "up to date."

Muslims are prone to slow down during Ramadan, turning their attention from worldly affairs to matters spiritual. It is a time for prayer, devotion, charity, kindness, and philanthropy.

Muslims prepare special foods and buy gifts for their family and friends, including new clothes; they also provide such items for the poor. Special foods are prepared and a feeling of community is enjoyed at the Iftar meals (the meal at the end of the day when the fast is broken).

In many Muslim countries (or countries with large Muslim populations), markets close down in the early evening to enable people to attend prayers and partake of the Iftar meal. (Markets often reopen and stay open amid festivities well into the night.)

Nuptials

Muslim wedding customs vary widely according to country. Several elements are, however, found in many Muslim wedding traditions around the world:

• Muslim nuptials—*nikaah*—are celebrated over five days and are joyous occasions. The celebration feast—the *valimah*—can take place in the home of the bride or groom, though today it often takes place in a banquet hall. A *qadi* (a Muslim justice of the the peace) or an imam officiates, overseeing the two critical rituals: the *ijab*, the proposal by the groom; and the *qubul*, acceptance by the bride (who repeats the word "*qubul*"—I accept!—three times). Care is taken to make certain that all parties are entering into the marriage voluntarily.

• A *walima* (party at which the wedding is announced) is usually given by the groom's family, at which the prospective bride and groom meet each other's (and their new) relatives. At the walima, the bride's father presents the dowry (or its terms) to the groom's father in a ceremony known as Legan Chir. Similarly, gifts (*mahr*) are given (or offered) to the bride by the groom and his family at the wedding (and reiterated in the Nikaah Nama—see below).

• The Mehndi is an event (accompanied by traditional song and dance) in which henna is placed decoratively on the hands of the bride and groom in preparation of the wedding. A similar ceremony, Manjha, involves anointing the bride in preparation.

• The actual wedding is accomplished on the fourth day with a Nikaah Nama, or marriage contract, traditionally prepared by the bride's family and signed and duly witnessed in the presence of an imam. The groom arrives for this at the wedding venue where his bride awaits him amid dancing and rejoicing in a procession called the *baraat*.

• Days after the wedding, the father ceremoniously joins his daughter's hand with the groom's as the bride's family bids her farewell (*ruksat*); the groom's mother holds a Qur'an over her new daughter-in-law's head as she enters her new home; and on the fourth day, the bride returns to her parent's home for a congratulatory welcoming dinner (*chauthi*).

The joy and ceremony of the Muslim wedding is indicative of the great importance placed in Islam on the family and on the sanctity of marriage.

Hajj

Since every Muslim regards the Hajj, the pilgrimage to Mecca during the month of Dhu al-Hijja, a sacred duty and one of the Five Pillars of Islam, it stands to reason that each year, many tens of thousands of American Muslims may be expected to travel to Mecca for the sacred ritual. The effect this will have on the pilgrims themselves will be, as has often been reported, an enthralling and uplifting experience; what effect American Muslims will have on the world community of Islam with which it will mingle while on the pilgrimage, is less known.

The Hajj is steeped in tradition and symbolic ceremonies; its basic elements are:

• Upon arrival in Mecca, the pilgrims—now known as a Hajji (man) or Hajja (woman)—don *ihram* clothing (long, loose, plain, and white) and await the beginning of the ceremonies in the nearby town of Mina, in tents provided by the Saudi government. They have come to perform a series of ritual acts (*tawaf*) symbolic of the lives of Ibrahim (Abraham), his concubine Hajar (Hagar), and their son Ismail (Ishmael).

• On the first day of the Hajj, the eighth day of Dhu al-Hijjah, the pilgrims perform their first Tawaf, which involves all of the pilgrims entering the Sacred Mosque (Masjid al-Haram) and walking seven times counterclockwise around the Ka'ba, kissing (or pointing at, if the crowds are too thick) the Black Stone (Hajar al-Aswad) each circuit. Each circuit constitutes a "Shout"; only three Shouts are compulsory, but virtually everyone performs all seven for a complete Tawaf.

Eating is not permitted during the Shouts, but water may be drunk. The Tawaf is performed all at once, after which pilgrims offer two Rakaat prayers at the Place of Abraham (Muqaam E Ibrahim), an area near the Ka'ba (though they may pray anywhere in the Mosque if the crowds are too large).

• After Tawaf, on the same day, the pilgrims perform *sa'i*—running seven times between the hills of Safa and Marwah as a re-enactment of the frantic search for water by Hagar, before the Zamzam Well was revealed to her.

• The next morning, on the ninth of Dhu al-Hijjah, the pilgrims leave Mina for Mount Arafat, where they stand in meditative vigil near a hill from which Muhammad gave his last sermon. This is considered the highlight of the Hajj. No specific rituals are prescribed, but if a pilgrim does not spend the afternoon on Arafat, the pilgrimage is invalid.

• When the sun sets, the pilgrims leave Arafat for Muzdalifah, an area between Arafat and Mina, where forty-nine pebbles are gathered for the next day's ritual of the stoning of the Devil (Shaitan). Many pilgrims spend the night sleeping on the ground at Muzdalifah before returning to Mina. It is now the tenth of the month, the day of Eid ul-Adha.

• At Mina the pilgrims perform Ramy al-Jamarat, throwing stones to signify their defiance of the Devil and symbolizing Abraham overcoming the tests of his faith he endured at the hands of the Devil, a pillar marking the location of these tests.

• After the Stoning of the Devil, an animal is sacrificed (with its head facing the Ka'ba), symbolizing God's mercy on Abraham and His replacing his son with a ram, which Abraham then sacrificed.

• Previously, pilgrims slaughtered animals themselves, or oversaw the slaughtering. Today, pilgrims buy a "sacrifice voucher" in Mecca before the greater Hajj begins which allows an animal to be slaughtered in their name in Mecca on the tenth. The meat is then packaged and given to charity and shipped to poor people around the world. At the same time, Muslims worldwide perform similar sacrifices, in a four-day global festival called Eid ul-Adha.

• On the following days the pilgrims revisit the Masjid al-Haram in Mecca for another Tawaf, and then they perform another Jamarat (Stoning of the Devil) in Mina.

• Finally, before leaving Mecca, pilgrims perform a farewell Tawaf—Tawaf al-Wada.

• Though it is not required as part of the Hajj, many pilgrims then travel to the city of Medina and the Mosque of the Prophet, which contains Muhammad's tomb for prayer and meditation.

Death and Burial

When a Muslim is near death, friends and family recite verses from the Qur'an around him and it is recommended, if at all possible, that a Muslim's last words be the declaration of faith: "I bear witness that there is no god but Allah."

• Upon death, the family should not mourn immediately, but calmly attend to matters of the funeral. The eyes of the deceased should be closed, and the body covered temporarily with a clean sheet.

• Muslims try to bury the deceased as soon as possible after death, avoiding embalming or otherwise disturbing the body of the deceased. An autopsy may be performed, but only if legally required.

• The family or assigned members of the community wash and enshroud the body. (Martyrs, however, are buried in the clothes in which they died.) The deceased is washed with clean (scented) water, in a manner similar to ablutions for prayer. The body is then wrapped in a sheet (or sheets) of clean, white cloth (called a *kafan*).

• The deceased is then transported to a site of the funeral prayers (Salat al-Janazah)—outdoors or in a courtyard or public square, but not inside a mosque. The imam stands in front of the deceased, facing away from the worshippers and leads the bier (which is preferable to a casket, if allowed by law) to the cemetery, while the mourners follow behind and pray quietly.

- The deceased is then taken to the cemetery for burial (*al-dafin*). If possible, a cemetery (or section of one) should be set aside for Muslims. The deceased is laid in the grave on his or her right side, facing Mecca. Muslims do not as a rule erect elaborate tombstones, preferring simple markers.

- Loved ones and relatives observe a three-day mourning period, during which friends offering comfort and condolences are received. Widows observe an extended mourning period (*iddah*) of four months and ten days (in accordance with the Qur'an 2:234), during which time they may not remarry, move from their home, or wear decorative clothing or jewelry.

F. Family Life

Husband and Wife

The centrality of the family in Islam stems from two sources: (1) The profound respect that Muhammad had for women, enjoying their company and able to enjoy and appreciate their wisdom and perspective; and (2) Muhammad's appreciation of how important a wife and mother is to the health of the family, and thus to the promulgation and continuation of the religion. The faith depends on the loving attention that a mother provides a child and the husband depends on his wife to (in the Muslim view) attend to the matters of the home and provide a wholesome environment for the entire family. "The best among you," Muhammad is reported to have said to his disciples, "is the one best to his family," which expresses the Prophet's attitude as contained in hundreds of Qur'anic verses and in the Hadith.

Much has been made of a verse—Q 4:34—that according to some translations, seems to condone physically beating a recalcitrant wife. Not only have these been shown to be mistranslations, but the Tafsir (exegesis) of the verse and the overwhelming wealth of Hadith explicating it indicates clearly that the Qur'an was speaking only of admonishment, not corporeal response.

Polygyny

In ancient and early medieval Arabia, polygyny—a man having more than one wife—was commonplace and wives had diminished rights as a result. The Islamic reforms of this practice were radical; Muhammad himself had only one wife until Khadija died (after twenty-five years of marriage). After Khadija's death, the wives Muhammad married were the widows of fallen comrades who required a protector-patron; he was truly married to only one other woman, Aisha, for the remainder of his life.

The Qur'an (4:3) expressly forbids a Muslim having more than four wives and strictly enjoins that they all be treated equally and well. Islamic law provides that a woman can insist on a condition being placed in her marriage contract forbidding her husband taking another wife (which courts will uphold).

Treatment and Status of Women

The status of women in Islam is complicated by the social forces that are at play in the many nations and cultures where Islam is found. Historically, women were given vastly improved status by Islam throughout its formative period, and it has always evinced an almost worshipful attitude toward women, as evidenced by the central role women play in the early history of Islam. Khadija, Fatima, Aisha—these were formidable women who took leadership roles in the religion and the affairs of the Islamic state.

The negative attitudes of the Bible toward women, according to which women are to blame for Adam's Fall, are not repeated in the Qur'an, which instead speaks often of the importance of a wife's love and support and the mutual support husband and wife provide as "each other's garments" (Q 2:187).

Muslims—men certainly; possibly also women —view the "advances" that women have claimed in the West as illusory and misguided, turning them more into "sex-objects" and less into independent, full-fledged citizens, which is the goal of the women's struggle in modern Islam.

In Islamic law, to cite an example of evolving principles in this area, a woman inherits from her parents and husband. Although the text suggests strongly that a woman inherits equally to a man, the Qur'an places additional responsibilities on male heirs from which it absolves women, so that the law is that women inherit half-portions. This, along with other inequities that seem to reflect not Islamic thought but parochial social attitudes, are still being debated in Islamic circles. At a late 1980s conference of Christian and Muslim women at Harvard Divinity School, the observation was made that "in most Muslim marriages today, whatever lip service is given to male authority, the woman knows exactly how to exert power, as she has always known."

Divorce

Islam permits, but does not encourage, a legal divorce called Talaq. Talaq is considerably more difficult for Shi'ite Muslims than for Sunnis. Sunni Muslims traditionally require no witnesses, and a man may use a "triple Talaq," in which he can divorce his wife simply by repeating the word *talaq* three times. Shi'ites do not accept this, viewing divorce as a process rather than a decision, and requiring a waiting period during which the married couple must try to reconcile their differences.

If differences are irreconcilable, the woman must complete three menstrual cycles and have two witnesses present for each Talaq declaration for the divorce to be deemed valid. It has also become possible for a woman to petition a qadi to grant a divorce for cause; it is still the case that the husband need not provide a reason for his petition. This is one area where Sunnis have adopted a page from the Shi'ite notebook and have made divorce more difficult for all parties along Shi'ite lines. In any case, the rights of women to support and retain their *mahr* (wedding gifts) are strongly supported by the Shari'ah.

Child-rearing and Education

Education has been cherished in Islam for centuries (as has been pointed out above). Children who show early promise are nearly always provided with tutors and special opportunities. In the Qur'an

(Q 96:4–5), God is praised for being a teacher, and thus teachers (secular as well as religious) are shown great respect in Muslim cultures.

Extended Family

Muslims regard the Western practice of "depositing" the elderly in nursing homes with revulsion and amazement. The elderly are valued for their experience, knowledge, and sagacity. It is common for homes to include a family member who will serve as a guide and instructor. (See Q 46:15–17 for words regarding filial obligation.)

FURTHER READING

Al–Qur'an: A Contemporary Translation
   Ahmed Ali
   1994: Princeton University Press

*Islam: The Straight Path (3rd edition) and
What Everyone Needs to Know About Islam*
   John L. Esposito
   1998; 2002: Oxford University Press

*The Qur'an and its Exegesis: Selected Texts with
Classical and Modern Interpretation*
   H. Gätje (AT. Welch, translator)
   1996: Oneworld–Oxford

The Islamic Way of Life
   S.A.A. Maudoodi, K. Murad, et al.
   1986: Islamic Foundation

Islamic Life and Thought
   Sayyed H. Nasr
   1981: SUNY Press

Islamic Ritual Practices
   1983: American Council of Learned Societies

Mystical Dimensions of Islam
   Annemarie Schemmel
   1981: University of North Carolina Press

2 Islam in America

I. Roots and History

A. Introduction

IT IS OFTEN DIFFICULT TO WRITE A HISTORY OF WHAT has happened while it is happening; presumably, that is what journalism is all about. But although Muslims have been on American soil for centuries—in small numbers at first, but in recent times in numbers that rival those of many other religious groups—there is a sense that American Islam is still in its formative period. The story of the founding of the American Muslim community, in fact, is yet to be written for the simple reason that it is a story that is still unfolding. Muslims are today active in every corner of American society, in every theater contributing their talents, their conscientiousness, and their appreciation for the unique opportunities American culture has afforded them to make better lives for themselves and for their children.

Muslims in America will have some serious thinking to do over the coming decades, and some difficult questions to answer if they are to become fully part of American civilization:

• How will the ethnic and cultural differences that mark the various segments of the Muslim community allow it to coalesce into a unified or at least cooperative group that will permit it to participate in the American political and social conversation?

• How will the various sects of Islam interact with one another on the stage of American culture to present—to the society as well as to itself—an identifiable Muslim identity (that is, of course, the one that emerges after it has dispelled and refuted the negative stereotypes of Muslims that American popular culture keeps promoting and prolonging)?

• How will Islam and the African-American community interact to become either a wholesomely unified religious entity or (as has sometimes seemed the case) the estranged relatives one can't disown no matter how much one wants or tries to?

• How will American Islam interact with the world Muslim community, the Ummah, in responding to international events and in influencing (and being influenced by) the decisions, actions, and policies of Muslim communities, governments, and religious bodies in ways that enhance its stature in the world and in American society?

Islamic men bow for afternoon prayer on Madison Avenue at 41st Street in New York City during the United American Muslim Day Parade on September 28, 1997. The theme for the parade and related ceremonies was "Islam, the Religion for Humanity."

• How will American Muslims reconcile the difficulties and challenges posed by American culture to Islamic values, and how will that community forge its own way of life within that culture as a right to which their citizenship and service entitles them?

These questions seem to many so pressing and so palpably present in determining the identity of the American Muslim community that it would seem impossible to write a history of American Islam without answering them. As a consequence of not having firm and settled answers to these questions (and not even a conventional wisdom that one can revise and with which one can argue), this chapter looks very different than it would have looked ten years ago and very different, no doubt, than it will look ten years hence. We note that this subject was totally absent in the precursor of this volume that appeared a generation ago.

American Muslims are the inheritors of a multitude of cultural traditions, and it is important to note that ethnicity and nationality are two major factors which shape the perspective and thought of individual Muslims. Female Muslim immigrants are often visibly identifiable by their headdress, but the degree and even necessity of women covering their hair and head is dictated as much by specific culture than the law of the religion itself. Yet, Islam in America is no longer an "immigrant issue." As second-, third-, and fourth-generation Muslims are born in the United States, and as the religion continues to gain converts from among indigenous Americans, the roots of American Islam grow deeper and more vigorous with each passing year.

B. History of Islam in America

Early History: Pre-Civil War

The first recorded Muslim to set foot on American soil is reputed to be Estavanico of Azamor (also called Istafan), a Moroccan who was brought to America's shores in 1527 as a slave of the Spanish explorer, Alvar Nuñez Cabeza de Vaca, as part of the ill-fated attempt by Panfilo de Narvaez to recapture Florida. Estavanico had a remarkable gift for language that allowed him to pick up Native American languages and serve as a translator and good-will ambassador for the Spanish, first in Mexico and the Caribbean, and later in the American Southwest. Legend has it that he was killed by Zuñi Indians who were scandalized by his use of owl feathers, a bird that symbolized death to the tribe, to adorn his medicine pack.

There were, no doubt, other isolated instances of Muslim explorers (long famed for their adventurousness) who traveled across the Atlantic to the New World, and even some evidence that West Africans conducted a series of expeditions that reached well into the Gulf of Mexico and the Mississippi River. The year 1492 is noteworthy not only because that is the year of Columbus's voyage to the New World (on which, incidentally, he carried a Spanish Muslim record by one al-Idrisi of tenth-century voyages in the Atlantic that may have extended as far as the Caribbean), but also because it is the year Muslims and Jews were expelled from Spain. Like the Jews, most Muslims found refuge with coreligionists in other lands, but some explored the notion of settlement in the lands already known to exist across the Atlantic. Though some Muslims may have made tentative moves toward this end, no settlement took place during this period.

It is likely that the first Muslims to reach the New World in significant numbers were West African slaves removed forcibly from their continent beginning in 1530, and continuing to the mid-nineteen century. Had they arrived in any condition other than bondage, they may have been the pioneers of early Islamic communities similar to the Christian settlements of the Puritan Pilgrims.

What percentage of African slaves brought to America were Muslim? Earlier estimates were as high as 20 percent; today the number is believed to have been twice that. In Alex Haley's landmark 1976 book, *Roots*, Haley's ancestor Kunte Kinte invokes an Islamic prayer during his voyage across the Atlantic, and the *New York Times* reviewer, James Michener, criticized this as an unsubstantiated romanticization. Today, knowing how thoroughly Muslim the Mandika tribe, to which Kunte Kinte belonged, was, it is now considered probable (not just possible or plausible) that Kunte Kinte was originally Muslim.

Islam's history in the Americas is not at all similar to its contrastingly glorious envelopment of the Middle East, much of Europe, and northern Africa. The African slaves were the inheritors of their masters' religions, which meant that this first wave of "American Muslims" were almost immediately forced to become Christian.

Several noteworthy (though isolated) incidents dot the Colonial period and the years following Independence, including:

• Ayub ibn Sulaiman Jallon, a Muslim slave who became celebrated for maintaining his observance of Islam during two years of slavery in Maryland, was freed in 1732 by James Ogelthorpe, founder of Georgia, and returned to Africa.

• In 1770, two Muslim brothers named Wahhab were shipwrecked off the coast of North Carolina. They settled in North Carolina, became Christian, and began a clan that today runs one of the largest hotel chains in the Carolinas.

• In 1778, Morocco became the first government to officially recognize the newly formed United States of America. This act of friendship was commemorated in 1787 and 1790 with treaties between the two countries signed by the Sultan of Morocco and President John Adams.

• Abdul Rahman ibn Sori, a West African prince, was kidnapped in 1788 and sold into slavery. Known in America as the Prince of Slaves, he used his superior knowledge of farming techniques to become an indispensable manager of a large Mississippi cotton

This portrait of Abdul Rahman ibn Sori (1762–1829) bears an Arabic inscription that can be translated as "His name is Abd al-Rahman."

plantation. After nearly forty years of enslavement (and raising a family of nine children), he wrote a letter to the sultan of Morocco asking the Sultan to secure his freedom so that he and his family could return to Morocco to die. The sultan petitioned President John Quincy Adams, who issued an order freeing ibn Sori. A drawing of ibn Sori (by Henry Inman below), hangs in the Library of Congress.

• Another African Muslim who became celebrated at this time (and who was the subject of portraiture, this time by Charles Wilson Peale in 1819), was Yarrow Mamout, purported to have lived to the age of either 134 or 128 (the latter age documented), the oldest American on record (fourteen years older than the next documented longest-lived American). Peale's portrait (painted when Mamout was 100) hangs in the Pennsylvania Historical Society.

• The earliest memoir of an African Muslim slave was penned by Omar ibn Said (1773–1864), a scholar who was kidnapped from what is today Senegal and, after several escape attempts, found himself a slave to the wealthy Owens family of North Carolina. From the very start he was perceived to be educated and wise, and though he converted to Christianity, he continued to write about Islam and pray to Muhammad. He was still a slave to Owens when he died at the age of ninety-four, but he left behind fourteen manuscripts regarding his life and his recollections of Islam.

What these instances show is that there were many Muslims among the slaves who were brought to the Americas in the seventeenth century and that they were able in limited ways to exploit the portability of Islam and find ways of maintaining their faith.

From the Civil War to World War II

The earliest post-slavery Muslim settlers arrived in America in the late 1800s seeking business opportunities and a better quality of life, spurred on by the reports they received from Christian Arabs who had found a measure of success on American soil. But vast cultural differences and the lack of an established community conducive to a traditional Muslim way of life discouraged many of these pioneers. Those who were able (at least to some degree) to assimilate built houses of worship and founded Islamic associations, but it wasn't until much later in the century that words such as "mosque," "Ramadan," and "imam" became commonplace in the American vernacular.

In most cases, Muslims fled to the U.S. as a result of upheavals in their home countries: the deterioration and eventual fall of the Ottoman Empire in World War I resulted in a wave of immigration from Turkish-controlled countries. Eastern European Muslims arrived first and settled in New York, Albany, and along the Northeast coast, building mosques in their communities.

An Ahmadiya-supported mosque (with a mufti imported from India) was built in Chicago, complete with a magazine (*The Muslim Sunrise*) that is still published out of the movement's headquarters, which is today in Washington, D.C. The Ahmadiyas, a group from India founded in the early 1800s in Pakistan, were a persecuted minority in the Asian subcontinent, but were still able to send missionaries around the world to proselytize for Islam.

The earliest known American mosque (built as an addition to a private home) dates to 1900 in Ross, North Dakota; other mosques are known to have been built in Michigan City, Indiana, and in Highland Park, Michigan. The first serious concentration of Muslims in the U.S., necessitating not only a place to pray, but a locale in which to live and raise families, was in Dearborn, Michigan, where the large labor needs of the Ford automobile plant at River Rouge provided work opportunities for many immigrants. By the 1930s, the South End of Dearborn was reported to have had a clearly Arab-Muslim shopping area with coffee shops, groceries, and newsstands carrying goods directed at an Arab Muslim population. Similar communities arose in Cedar Rapids, Iowa, with the building of the first structure meant specifically as a mosque (still in use), and in Edmonton, Alberta, in the 1930s.

The influx of Muslims must have concerned East Coast Americans in the years after World War I, because two highly restrictive laws (one called the Asian Exclusion Act) were passed by Congress in the early 1920s which brought the flow of Muslims to the U.S. to a trickle between the World Wars. As a result, Canada recorded fewer than 3,000 Muslims in 1951, and an American estimate published in 1960 set the U.S. number at about 100,000.

It is during this period that the early engagement of the African-American community (many descendants of slaves, or else Africans who entered the United States during the last half of the nineteenth century) with Islam took place. (That story is told in Section V of this chapter.)

After World War II

The repeal of immigration quotas in 1965 (the Hart-Cellar Act) opened the gates of the U.S. to refugees from war-torn areas of the world, which the post-war period amply provided. Many of the immigrants came from upper-class families looking for better education for their children and a less restrictive environment for their businesses.

By 1980, a minaret was added to the mosque in Cedar Rapids (called the Mother Mosque of America), and mosques established in Brooklyn, New York, as far back as 1907 by Lithuanian and Polish immigrants (including one called the American Mohammedan Society) were revitalized by Indian and Middle Eastern Muslims in the 1960s.

A large contingent of immigrants to the U.S. came from Palestine as refugees displaced by the creation of the State of Israel in 1948. Additional waves of Muslim refugees came from Albania and Yugoslavia, escaping the new Soviet rule of those areas, which, though home to Muslims for centuries, had always presented Islam with a difficult environment.

The global state of Islam in the middle of the twentieth century was one of increasing political tension. The expulsion of Ruholla Khomeini from Iran, student uprisings in Pakistan, Indonesia, Egypt, and Algeria, and the worsening Israeli-Palestinian conflict contributed to Islam's reputation for hostility among Americans. This trend carried on into the beginning of the twenty-first century as Osama bin Laden was credited (including by himself) with masterminding the terrorist attacks on New York City's World Trade Center, publicly referencing Islamic principles as justifications for his actions.

At the beginning of the twenty-first century, Muslims are concentrated in seven areas of the United States:

Michigan and the Midwest. Centered in Dearborn and Cedar Rapids, with strong communities; the Midwest remains a strong population center with many well-developed Muslim institutions.

California and West Coast. Largely Indian and Southeast Asian, California has the largest Muslim concentration in the U.S., but is still young in development of local Muslim support institutions.

New York/New Jersey. As a center of culture and business, this area has attracted many of the best-educated and most culturally active Muslims from Arab and Asian lands, and many African Americans.

Chicago. Strong presence of Syrian and Palestinians; also an early center of African-American involvement in Islam.

Massachusetts and New England. Begun by Lebanese ship-builders in the late 1800s, the area attracted businessmen from Arab countries; centered in Boston, Quincy, and Sharon.

Washington, D.C. As a center of political activity and home of many diplomats and their families, the Muslim population of this area fluctuates.

Texas. Texas has the second-fastest-growing Muslim population in the U.S., showing strong appeal to fundamentalist Muslim communities.

Toward the Twenty-first Century

As the twenty-first century dawned, a number of trends were having their effect on the American Muslim demographic landscape as several Muslim groups were growing and finding (or struggling to find) their place in American society and an evolving, elusive American Muslim identity:

• Second-generation Muslims—either those who abandoned Islam for a secular Americanized life, or else those who maintained their observance but found ways of blending into American society—assumed a "low-profile" assimilationist strategy which, unhappily for their parents, was often seen by their progeny as license to abandon their faith altogether.

• Students who had come to the United States to avail themselves of the American university system entered the American social fabric upon graduation as professionals with a greater confidence and, more importantly, a greater understanding of the means of using information, networking, and organization to create communication channels and public- and government-relations institutions to improve the image, and thus the status, of Muslims in America.

• Americanized Muslims who were still either strongly identified with their Muslim roots or, in fact, still practicing Muslims, astutely used the political mechanism of American society to allow participation and enfranchisement, while dealing with the challenges this posed to their identities.

• African Americans began to turn toward orthodox Islam increasingly as a reaction to the earlier involvement, in which Islam and Islamic categories were used more as a device for couching civil rights concerns and inspiring action than as a genuine religious position. In this period, a serious commitment to Islam—or else abandoning the program entirely—was what was being called for.

• Muslims from different ethnic backgrounds and cultures were learning to work together, recognizing that some common issues override what separates them ethnically. In addition to Arab Muslims (who, as is the case in the rest of the world, constitute a minority of Muslims), significant numbers come from India–Pakistan and South Central Asia; Indonesia and Southeast Asia; Yugoslavia and Eastern Europe; Senegal and West Africa and sub-Saharan Africa; and a growing Latino Islamic community (looking to medieval Spain for its roots).

All of these elements were in full force when the calamities of September 2001 took place. In an earlier time, the events of that day would have driven any associated group underground into a low-profile existence, struggling to stay out of the limelight and avoiding drawing attention to itself. It is a measure of the vitality and health of the American Muslim community that such was not the case. American Muslims were quick to respond, first by condemning these attacks; then by mobilizing the effort to safeguard Muslim constitutional rights; and finally by moving to protect Muslim citizens and property from unwarranted and unjustified expressions of frustration and anger over the 9/11 attacks. This frequently called for outreach and cooperation with Christian, Jewish, and other religious and civil groups to join them in condemning stereotyping and combating discrimination.

C. Important Dates and Landmarks

Before 1492 Possible exploration of Western Hemisphere by West African Muslims.

1492 Fall of the "Moors" in Granada; expulsion of Muslims from Spain; some fleeing Muslims come to the Caribbean and South America.

1527 Estavanico of Azamor, a Muslim from Morocco, travels to the New World as the slave of a Spanish explorer in the ill-fated attempt to recapture Florida.

1530–1865 Slavery in America. It is estimated that 10 to 30 percent of the African slaves brought to America were Muslims.

1788 Abdul Rahman ibn Sori (1762–1829), a Fulani prince, is kidnapped and sold into slavery. Known as the Prince of Slaves, he is later freed by President John Quincy Adams after nearly forty years of enslavement in Mississippi.

1807 Omar ibn Said (1773–1864), a West African scholar, is captured and enslaved, brought to North Carolina and remains enslaved until his death. His autobiography, *Life of Omar ibn Said*, is earliest literary work by American Muslim.

1856 Failed experiment by Hajj Ali to introduce camels to the American Southwest.

1875 First wave of Muslim immigration to the U.S. from Syria.

1888 Journalist diplomat Alexander Russell Webb (1846–1916) converts to Islam. He becomes speaker, advocate of Islam; represents Islam at World Parliament of Religion in Chicago in 1893.

1889 Scholar and activist Edward W. Blyden tours eastern and southern U.S. promoting Islam for blacks.

1893 Muslims migrate to the U.S., largely from Lebanon, Syria, and Jordan.

1895 Muslims from India settle in the western U.S.

1900–1906 Bosnian Muslims settle in Chicago.

1907 The American Mohammedan Society founded in New York City.

1910 Hazrat Inayat Khan arrives in the U.S. from India; establishes Sufi order in the West and is one of the first Muslims to teach Sufism in the U.S.

1913 The Moorish American Science Temple is organized by Timothy Drew (Noble Drew Ali) in Newark, N.J. Drew preaches black nationalism, using Islamic concepts as well as beliefs of other religions to attract and unify African Americans.

1914–1922 Arab Muslims arrive in Detroit; they settle in the city and surrounding areas; find employment in the Ford Motor plant in Dearborn, Michigan.

1915 Albanian Muslims found one of the first American Muslim associations; build *masjid* in Maine and another in Connecticut in 1919.

1919 One of the first mosques in America is established in Detroit.

1920 Chapter of the Ottoman Red Crescent, modeled after the Red Cross, is established in Detroit. Mufti Muhammad Sadiq, first Ahmadi missionary, arrives.

1921 Johnson-Reed Immigration Act passed, limiting the number of Asian immigrants entering the U.S. Restrictions furthered in 1924 with passage of the Asian Exclusion Act.

First issue of the quarterly *The Moslem Sunrise* published; created to counter misrepresentations of Islam in the press.

1926 Universal Islamic Society founded in Detroit by Dusé Muhammad Ali—becomes mentor of Marcus Garvey.

1928 First Canadian mosque established in Edmonton, Alberta.

1930–1933 Wallace D. Fard founds the Black Muslim movement, the Lost-Found Nation of Islam—later Nation of Islam (NOI)—in Detroit. Fard urges African Americans to reject "the Christian religion of their white masters and return to the religion of their ancestors."

1934 Elijah Muhammad becomes the leader of the Nation of Islam after the disappearance of Fard. The NOI employs symbols and terms

from Islam, forging a new identity for African Americans. NOI headquarters moves to Chicago.

Mother Mosque of America completed in Cedar Rapids, Iowa.

1935 Arab American Banner Society established in Boston.

1939 Islamic Mission Society founded in New York by Sheikh Dawood; publishes *Islamic Sunrise* magazine.

1946–1952 Malcolm Little joins NOI while serving six-and-a-half year sentence for armed robbery. After his release, he rises in the ranks of the NOI and is henceforth known as Malcolm X.

1947 Muslim immigration from India, Pakistan, Russia, and Eastern Europe.

1950 Ahmadiyya headquarters moves to American Fazl Mosque in Washington, D.C.

1952 Muslim members of the U.S. Armed Forces sue and win the right to be identified as Muslims, and for Islam to be recognized as a legitimate religion.

The Federation of Islamic Associations (FIA) of the U.S. and Canada is established in Chicago.

1957 The Islamic Center of Washington D.C., which contains a mosque and library, opens. Ambassadors from all Muslim nations join President Eisenhower at dedication ceremony.

1961 Najeeb Halaby is appointed the head of the Federal Aviation Administration by President John F. Kennedy.

Malcolm X founds *Muhammad Speaks*.

1962 Dar al Islam movement begins in Brooklyn, at first promoting black separatism, but later strictly Sunni.

1963 The Muslim Student Association (MSA) of the United States and Canada is founded at University of Illinois.

1964 Champion boxer Cassius Clay joins the Nation of Islam and is given the name Muhammad Ali.

Malcolm X removed as minister of NOI Temple Number 7 in New York.

Allah's Nation of the Five Percenters founded in Harlem.

April 1964 Malcolm X makes the pilgrimage to Mecca. The experience is life-altering; he views Islam as a religion that can unite races and end bigotry; changes name to El Hajj Malik el-Shabazz.

1965 Malcolm X assassinated in Harlem at the Audubon Ballroom.

Repeal of immigration quotas signed by President Johnson. Increase of Muslim immigrants to U.S.

1968 Islamic Circle of North America (ICNA) founded.

Hanafi Madhdhab Center founded in New York City by Hamas Abdul Khaalis; moves to new center in Washington, D.C. Famed basketball star Kareem Abdul-Jabbar (born Lew Alcindor) becomes attracted to Islam through the Hanafi movement.

1971 Bawa Muhaiyaddeen Fellowship is founded in Philadelphia by Muhammad Raheem Bawa Muhaiyaddeen, a Sufi mystic who attracts many Muslim and non-Muslim disciples across the country.

1975 Elijah Muhammad dies; his son, Wallace Muhammad, assumes NOI leadership. Muslim Student Association headquarters established in Plainfield, Indiana.

Isa Muhammad establishes Ansaru Allah ("Allah's Helpers") movement—advocates Afro-centric attitudes and dress.

1976 Wallace Muhammad (to become Warith Deen Muhammad in 1980), changes Nation of Islam to the "World Community of Islam in the West," rejecting his father's separatist teachings and seeking to enter mainstream Islam (a process that will continue to 1985).

1977 Hanafi leader Hamas Abdul Khaalis and some followers occupy three Washington, D.C., buildings, taking hostages and demanding film depicting life of Muhammad (*Messenger of God*) be taken off market. One man killed in the 30-hour stand-off; resolved by intercession of Washington Muslim ambassadors, but Khaalis sentenced to life in prison.

1978 Louis Farrakhan breaks from Warith Deen Muhammad and reorganizes the Nation of Islam; founds *Final Call* newspaper.

1979–1980 Iranian hostage crisis. Following Iranian revolution and ouster of Shah, 70 Americans held by (government sanctioned) Iranian militants in the U.S. Embassy in Tehran, some for as long as a year. Resolution of the crisis at the end of 1980 a major factor in the election of Ronald Reagan as U.S. president and defeat of Democratic incumbent Jimmy Carter. Hostages are released virtually on Reagan's inauguration day.

1981 The International Institute of Islamic Thought (IIIT) is founded, with the involvement of Dr. Ismail al-Faruqi, a prominent Islamic scholar and activist who aided in the advancement of Islamic studies in the U.S.

The Islamic Society of North America (ISNA), offshoot of the Muslim Student Association, is established.

1983 American Islamic College established in Chicago.

1985 Prince Sultan Bin Salma bin Abdulazzi of Saudi Arabia—MBA degree from Syracuse University—first Arab and first Muslim to fly U.S. Space Shuttle.

mid-1980s PIEDAD Latino Community and Alianza Islámica founded in New York.

1986 Dr. Ismail al-Faruqi and his wife are murdered in their homes outside Philadelphia. (Murders still unsolved.)

1987 Muslim Alert Network (forerunner of Council on American Islamic Relations) established in Chicago to monitor media portrayals of Muslims.

1988 Jesse Jackson includes 50 Arab and Muslim Americans in his delegation to the Democratic National Convention; they are acknowledged by presidential nominee Michael Dukakis in his acceptance speech to the convention.

1989 Fatwah issued against Salman Rushdie by Ayatollah Khomeini for *The Satanic Verses*; American publishers threatened; forty-eight of forty-nine Islamic states reject fatwah.

1990 American Muslim Council (AMC), a Washington-based lobbying group promoting American Muslim domestic and foreign interests, established.

1991 Charles Bilal becomes first Muslim mayor in U.S.—of Kountze, Texas, a town of about

2,000, mostly Christian.

Imam Siraj Wahaj offers first Muslim prayer at House of Representatives.

1992 Warith Deen Muhammad first Muslim to offer opening prayer of U.S. Senate session.

1993 Captain Abdul-Rasheed Muhammad becomes first commissioned Islamic Chaplain in U.S. Army; hosts first Muslim American Military Chaplains Association (MAMCA) conference. Islamic Assembly of North America (IANA) founded.

First terrorist attack on World Trade Center as van filled with explosives is detonated in garage on February 26. In 1994 and 1998, six extremist Muslims are convicted for the bombings.

1994 Council on American Islamic Relations (CAIR) founded in Washington as nation's largest Islamic advocacy group.

1996 Denver's new international airport is first airport to provide a mosque.

First Lady Hillary Clinton hosts first Eid celebration in White House.

School of Islamic Social Sciences (SISS) founded in Virginia.

1997 A crescent moon and star representing Islam displayed with Christmas tree and Menorah on White House ellipse.

1998 Pentagon hosts Ramadan iftar meal for Muslims on active duty and for employees of the Department of Defense.

1999 Salam Al-Marayati, co-founder of Muslim Public Affairs Council (MPAC), participates in forming a code of ethics by Muslim and Jewish leaders fostering inter-faith relations between the two groups.

U.S. Postal Service issues stamp in Black Heritage Series honoring Malcolm X.

Osman Siddique sworn in as first Muslim U.S. ambassador (to Fiji).

Ahmad H. Zewail awarded the Nobel Prize in chemistry for revolutionary laser technique for observing atoms.

2001 First Muslim museum, the International Museum of Muslim Cultures, opens in Jackson, Michigan.

U.S. Postal Service issues stamp celebrating Islamic holiday, Eid al-Fitr.

September 11 attacks on Pentagon and World Trade Center, masterminded by extremist Osama bin Laden, Saudi-born leader of international terrorist group al Qaeda, results in death of nearly 3,000. U.S. retaliates by invading Afghanistan and removing Taliban from power.

2006 Several official estimates have U.S. Muslim population at 6 to 7 million.

2008 Barack Obama, himself a Congregationalist, son of a lapsed Muslim, mounts successful run for the U.S. presidency as the Democratic Party nominee.

D. Important Figures in American Islamic History

EARLY HISTORY

Alexander Russell Webb (1846–1916)

Webb is considered the first American convert to Islam. Born into a prominent Presbyterian family and the son of a leading journalist, Webb was a reporter for the Missouri *Republican* when he was appointed in 1887 by President Cleveland to be Consular Representative to the Philippines. In Manila, he met Muslims, became enthralled with

Islam, and studied it intensively. He converted in 1888 and toured India, and then spoke across the U.S., including at the World Parliament of Religions in Chicago in 1893. His major work, *Islam in America*, is a personal memoir of his conversion to Islam; it had a profound influence in the early twentieth century.

Abdallah Igram (b. ca 1920)

As a Muslim American soldier in World War II, Igram was distressed by the fact that an "X" appeared on his dog tags under "religion." This meant that if he were killed in battle, he would not be buried according to Islamic law. In 1953, Igram petitioned President Eisenhower, who, while sympathetic, showed no inclination to change the tags. Igram and other Muslims of his home town, Cedar Rapids, Iowa, home to a large Muslim population and one of the nation's first mosques, organized the Federation of Islamic Associations, forerunner of later Muslim American organizations. In 1954, a suit brought by the FIA was resolved with the Army agreeing to indicate "I" (for "Islam") on the dog tags of Muslim servicemen.

Omar ibn Sa'id (1770–1864)

Sa'id was captured in 1807 during a military skirmish and sold into slavery, remaining a slave until his death. He had been a student of Muslim scholars for some twenty-five years when he was enslaved, and had the good fortune of being the slave of a man who recognized Sa'id's abilities and allowed him ample time to write. Sa'id left behind fourteen extensive manuscripts (all written in highly literate Arabic) on his life as a slave, his memories of Africa, and his comments on Islam and the Qur'an. This material is still being translated and analyzed; it is housed at the University of North Carolina at Chapel Hill.

Two other figures from the period of slavery are **Ayuba Suleiman Diallo** (1701–1773), also known as Job ben Solomon, a Senegalese aristocrat who was captured while on a trip to buy paper. Diallo was placed in an Annapolis, Maryland, jail after one of his many escape attempts, where he met a lawyer, Thomas Bluett, who recognized immediately that Diallo was an educated individual. Bluett bought Diallo's freedom and took him to England, where he became a celebrity. His memoirs contain important information (plus a fair amount of hyperbole).

Another important document, the Bilal Document, was left behind by **Bilali Mohammet** (d. 1857), a Fula Muslim who was known for observing Islamic ritual all his life. He wore a fez and served as the imam of the other Muslims on his plantation, making his the first functional mosque on the continent. The Bilal Document, housed in the University of Georgia, is a *risala* (survey) of Islamic law and history as he remembered it late in life.

MODERN TEACHERS AND SCHOLARS

The scholars described below have (at least) one thing in common: they have developed their scholarship in Islam with uncompromising integrity and within the context of American (and Western) values of scholarship. Where those values have led them has not always been pleasing to the Islamic religious establishment—not in the United States, and certainly not in the Middle East and Asia, and neither was it always received well by Jewish and Christian colleagues, nor by pundits in the media and on campuses. But the manner in which they have developed their thought has struck a consonant chord with both Muslims exposed to Western intellectual traditions, and with Americans interested in exploring Islamic thought and values.

Ismail al-Faruqui (1921–1986)

Ismail al-Faruqui was a Palestinian-born Muslim who received high academic honors for his scholarship and for his work on behalf of the cause of Islamic scholarship from McGill and Temple Universities, where he was professor of religion and chair of Islamic studies. On May 27, 1986, he and his wife, Lois Lamya al-Faruqi, herself a renowned expert on Islamic art, were stabbed to death in their home in Wyncote, Pennsylvania. The crime may have been a robbery attempt gone wrong, or it may have been a deliberate assassination; the murders remain unsolved. But with it, the American Muslims lost tireless and dedicated workers for the cause of education and furthering appreciation of Islamic culture and learning.

Yusuf Estes (b. 1944)

The family of Ohio-born Estes were long-time members of the Disciples of Christ. Estes made his mark as a successful producer of music programs, musical instruments, and live concerts. He attributes his interest in and conversion to Islam to his business dealings with an Egyptian Muslim around 1991. Since then, most of the Estes family has joined him and he has embarked on an intense course of study. He has applied the latest information technologies to convey the teachings of Islam to young and old.

Seyyed Hossein Nasr (b. 1933)

Born in Tehran in 1933 and receiving his PhD from Harvard in Islamic studies, Nasr has been a source of insight and information about the depth of Islamic culture, from Sufi mysticism to Islamic cosmologies. He began his academic life as a physics student at MIT, and was studying with the celebrated Harvard historian of science, George Sarton. Sarton passed away before Nasr could finish his dissertation, so he was forced to finish it under the supervision of three illustrious scholars: I. Bernard Cohen, Hamilton Gibb, and Harry A. Wolfson. One of the few Muslim academicians to win a Templeton Prize (1999), Nasr's work has broadened the appreciation of the sophistication of Islamic thought, and he has been an outspoken expositor of the tradition in all its complexity and nuance. Today he is University Professor of Islamic Studies at the George Washington University.

Fazlur Rahman (1919–1988)

Fazlur Rahman was born in India's Punjab and was educated at Oxford, where he wrote his PhD dissertation on Ibn Sina. The tenor of his work, whether conducted in Pakistan or at the University of Chicago, was always to look carefully with a modern eye at the great, traditional texts of Islamic religion and literature. When, in the late 1960s, as head of the Central Institute for Islamic Research in Pakistan, he was (falsely) accused of questioning the existence of angels, his life and those of his family were threatened by radical Islamists, and he was forced to return to the U.S. and continue as the only Muslim scholar on the faculty of the University of Chicago Divinity School.

Edward Said (1935–2003)

Born in Jerusalem to a wealthy Protestant Palestinian family and educated at Princeton and Harvard, Said was a fixture both at New York's Columbia University, where he was a University Professor, the university's highest faculty rank; and on the pages of *The Nation*, *New York Review of Books*, and many other leading journals. He was an outspoken critic of U.S. policy in the Middle East, Israel's policy toward the Palestinians, and the West's demeaning Eurocentric view of the Arab world, a view he famously elaborated in his controversial book, *Orientalism*. It was sometimes said of Said that he was one of the few academics who could "out-Chomsky Chomsky," referring to his ability to infuriate the establishment with his baldly stated, provocative positions, much like his friend and colleague, the MIT linguist Noam Chomsky.

Yet, Said supported a "two-state solution" to the Palestinian problem, which meant he supported Israel's right to exist, a key element of the Zionist program that radical Muslims abhorred (and abhorred him for supporting). And he was an ardent supporter of music, writing music criticism for *The Nation* for many years. In 1999, he and Argentinian-Israeli pianist Daniel Barenboim founded the East-Western Divan Orchestra, an Arab-Israeli ensemble dedicated to promoting peace through the arts.

Hamza Yusuf (Mark Hanson) (b. 1960)

Born Mark Hanson in Walla Walla, Washington, to a Greek Orthodox family, he converted to Islam at seventeen while recovering from a near-fatal car accident. Yussuf teaches at the Zaytuna Institute in Berkeley, California, which he founded. He has studied abroad for years with eminent Islamic scholars, including at Cairo's Al-Azhar, the foremost institution in the Muslim world for higher Islamic theological studies. He has inspired enmity from many Muslim quarters for saying publicly that he believed the West a more conducive environment for some forms of Muslim theological development than many Muslim-dominated countries.

POLITICS, BUSINESS, SPORTS, ETC.

Muslims have made their mark in American society in a variety of fields. Two examples are **Zalmay Khalilzad** (*opposite right*), former U.S. ambassador to Iraq, Afghanistan, and the United Nations; and **Elias Zerhouni** (*opposite left*), director of the National Institutes of Health in the Bush administration from 2002 to 2008. Dr. Khalilzad was born in Afghanistan and received a PhD from the University of Chicago. Presently a counselor at the Center for Strategic and International Studies in Washington, D.C., he has worked closely with Albert Wohlstetter, a prominent nuclear deterrence theoretician, and with Zbigniew Brzezinski, with whom he was the architect of the U.S.-supported resistance of the Afghan *mujahideen* (freedom fighter) in their guerrilla war against the Soviet occupation. Dr. Zerhouni, a native of Algeria, is a world-respected researcher in CAT technology, having taught the subject at Johns Hopkins Medical School for twelve years since 1988 before accepting the NIH appointment. He has now returned to Johns Hopkins Medicine as a senior adviser.

Many Muslims have contributed to American business and, thus, to the quality of American life. Two examples are: **Farooq Kathwari,** chairman and CEO of Ethan Allen Interiors and a frequent commentator on financial and policy matters affecting Muslims and the economy. Born in Kashmir and

Elias Zerhouni (b. 1951) is the former director of the National Institutes of Health under President George W. Bush. He now serves as senior adviser to Johns Hopkins School of Medicine in Baltimore, Maryland.

Zalmay Khalilzad (b. 1951) served as U.S. ambassador to Afghanistan, U.S. ambassador to Iraq, and U.S. ambassador to the United Nations in the Bush administration. He is now a counselor at the Center for Strategic and International Studies in Washington, D.C.

receiving his MBA from NYU Business, Katwari has been a leader in civil rights and interfaith communication. And:

Anousheh Ansari, an Iranian-American, is part of the new generation of Muslims who have been innovators in the software development field as well as being a participant in the Russian space program as a (self-funded) passenger on the International Space Station in 2006 (just prior to her fortieth birthday).

Muslim Americans have had stellar careers in professional sports. Two who have been, arguably, the very best in their sports are heavyweight boxing champion **Muhammad Ali** and **Kareem Abdul-Jabbar**, star center for the three-time NBA champion Los Angeles Lakers. Ali, born Cassius Clay in 1942 in Louisville, Kentucky, converted to Islam in 1975 under the influence of Malcolm X. An Olympic gold medalist, Ali went on to have one of the most illustrious careers in world boxing, but not without controversy. In 1966, Ali refused induction into the U.S. Armed Forces as a conscientious objector. Though then stripped of his World Heavyweight Championship title, Ali continued to fight, regaining his belt in some of the most memorable bouts in boxing history, becoming an admired spokesman and symbol for Islam and the African-American community.

Abdul-Jabbar was born Frederick Lewis Alcindor in the Inwood section of Manhattan in 1947. After a stellar career at UCLA, winning three consecutive NCAA National Championships, he went on to win six MVP Awards in the NBA. He converted to Islam around 1971, and has been an outspoken

advocate for human rights and tolerance, as well as an author and sometime film actor.

II. American Muslim Life

American culture presents a number of significant problems and challenges to anyone attempting to lead a life consistent with Islamic law, the Shari'ah. Islamic society in the U.S. presents a virtually monolithic view of acceptable behavior for a Muslim; there is no great variety within the religious community as there is in Protestant denominations, in Judaism, and in Eastern faiths. This means that for any Muslim serious about maintaining good standing in the American Muslim community, most requirements regarding daily life, dress, ritual, and personal behavior are not negotiable.

Here we describe briefly only several issues:

Diet. The availability of genuine halal (permissible) food has been a problem for some time, though the number of companies, food retailers, and restaurants serving certified halal has grown over the past twenty years. Reliance on the highly developed kosher marketplace in Jewish areas was used by many Muslims as a stopgap measure, but the rules for kosher and halal, while similar, are not identical, plus the dedication of the slaughtering (*zebihah*) of the animal for religious purposes is not easily accomplished for kosher-prepared meat. The rules regarding the prohibition of alcohol (which is not per se prohibited in kosher food) are strict in Islamic law, and the prohibition of intoxicants may, according to some, extend to caffeine, which include caffeinated soft drinks, like colas.

An ongoing survey of halal providers and establishments across the U.S. (and the world) can be found at www.zebihah.com. The U.S. Armed Forces have arranged for halal rations to be distributed to Muslim personnel, and hospitals in Muslim areas are increasingly offering halal meals to patients and staff. Following the lead of Kentucky Fried Chicken, the first fast-food chain to offer halal in KFC outlets in Muslim areas, fast-food chains are increasingly looking into either openly halal establishments or, at least, such outlets under different names.

Dress. Though one might have thought that the court rulings and the support of the U.S. Justice Department would have laid to rest difficulties Muslim women have had with wearing a hijab, some prejudices die hard, and Muslims are still experiencing discrimination and harassment when wearing head-coverings. The problem has spilled over onto the playing field as a February 2007 Canadian junior league soccer tournament in Quebec was disrupted, first by a ruling banning a teenage girl from participating while wearing a headscarf, and then by the girl's teammates withdrawing from the tournament in support.

Several retailers and websites (e.g., www.thehijabshop.com) offer both styles and advice on headwear for Muslim women. Currently, an undercurrent has arisen in which the hijab has become a statement of solidarity and ethnic pride; surveys indicate that in many professions (such as hospitals), the public has greater confidence in the competence and conscientiousness of women wearing a hijab.

Discrimination and Harassment. The problems experienced by Muslims in the years following 9/11 have not eased appreciably, according to both government and Muslim monitoring organizations. Generally speaking, the problems exist on two levels: the "local" level of day-to-day indignities, slurs, and discrimination that Muslims experience on American streets and in American shops; and the "global" level of the violation of the civil rights of Muslims,

and withholding the machinery of due process in defending themselves legally. This latter type does not always take the form of improper detention and incarceration, and there are fears that "rendition"—transfer of people arrested by U.S. law enforcement to countries where torture is known to be used, without any legal recourse—is still taking place in spite of the assurances of Secretary of State Condoleza Rice in April 2006 that the U.S. has ceased this practice.

Gender and Family Issues. The status of Muslim women is, arguably, higher in the U.S. than in virtually any other country in the world, yet several issues remain intractable, including:

• **Domestic violence** is still swept under the rug by many Muslims, who will shun women who avail themselves of police protection or court orders.

• **Divorce and child custody** judgments that are rendered by the civil courts are sometimes ignored or circumvented in the community.

• **Polygamy**, though illegal, is still practiced (as a holdover from native countries), placing spouses in unfavorable family positions.

• **Isolation and exclusion** of women from the community when they have sought redress outside religious institution makes it difficult for them to connect with potential marriageable Muslim mates.

III. Distribution and Demographics

The Muslim population in the U.S. is uncertain, because even the most meticulously and impartially conducted surveys of the last decade have been disputed. Of the most reliable and respected sources, the numbers vary significantly (following are estimates with percentages of the U.S. adult population in brackets):

• 1.1 million (2001) CUNY/ARIS [0.5%];
• 1.6 million (2000) Glenmary Research Ctr. [0.5%];
• 1.9 million (2001) NORC(U of Chi)/AJC [0.6%];
• 2.0 million (2000) Hartford Institute [0.7%];
• 2.4 million (2007) Pew Research Center. [0.8%];

- 3.0 million (2002) CIA World Factbook [1.0%];
- 4.7 million (2005) Encyclopedia Britannica [1.5%];
- 5.0 million (2007) American Muslim Council [1.8%];
- 6.7 million (1997) Ba-Yunus/Bagby [2.2%];
- 7.0 million (2007) Council on American-Islamic Relations [2.0%].

These variations are largely the result of vastly different methods of collecting data. Since the U.S. Census Bureau is prohibited from inquiring about religious preference in its surveys, the government uses indirect methods of determining populations, which in the case of Muslims entails surveys of memberships made public by mosques and civic and religious organizations, as well as immigration records and statistics. (Estimates made by partisan organizations have been notoriously unreliable in the past, showing little reluctance to use the survey to further a political agenda.)

It now seems virtually universally agreed (by competent, objective observers) that there are between 5.5 and 7.5 million Muslims in the United States, which is by far the greatest increase of any religious group in the past quarter century. What is much more interesting is the ethnic makeup and distribution of that population.

Of the 32% of American Muslims that are South Asians—17% are Pakistani (the largest country of origin); 7% are Indian; 4% each are Afghan and Bangladeshi. African Americans comprise 20%. (AMC figures are twice that.) Arabs and Middle Easterners (including Iran and Turkey) comprise 18%; all others comprise 14% of the American Muslim population.

Geographically, Muslims are concentrated in ten states (in descending order of population, followed by percentage of the total U.S. Muslim population/percentage of total state population):

1. California (20.0/3.4);
2. New York (16.0/4.7);
3. Illinois (8.4/3.6);
4. New Jersey (4.0/2.5);
5. Indiana (3.6/3.2);
6. Michigan (3.4/1.8);
7. Virginia (3.0/2.4);
8. Texas (2.8/0.7);
9. Ohio (2.6/1.2);
10. Maryland (1.4/1.4).

In terms of impact on presidential politics, the Muslim vote may be expected to have its greatest influence in the four states where the Muslim population is more than 3 percent of the state's total population: California, New York, Illinois, Indiana.

IV. Organization and Infrastructure

A. Enclaves, Centers, and Major Houses of Worship

Some 2,000 mosques and Islamic centers are currently serving communities across the U.S. Many centers also operate or are critical for the functioning of Islamic schools, of which there are nearly 200—half of which are full time. (These numbers are higher than figures published in 2000 and 2001, reflecting the precipitous rise in the founding and operation of Islamic institutions.

Many mosques in the U.S. have communal services (*jum'ah*) on Fridays at which a sermon is delivered by the imam, frequently in English. Where an independent school cannot be provided by the community, the mosque will have either afternoon or full-time educational facilities. Separate areas for men and women are virtually universal, and only in the largest urban areas do women have a place in the mosque's leadership.

In many American cities, storefront "*musallah*" facilities are created to allow local Muslims to observe prayer times close to home or work.

The location of mosques can be found online at www.salatomatic.com and www.islamicfinder.org.

There are large and active Islamic centers in many major cities in the United States. At left is the Islamic Cultural Center of New York City (often called the 96th Street Mosque); below left is the Islamic Center of America in Dearborn, Michigan, the largest American mosque, which is located in the heart of one of the first Muslim communities in America; and on the opposite page is the Islamic Center on Embassy Row in Washington, D.C., which has 6,000 worshippers for Friday prayers.

4,000 worshippers for Friday *jum'ah* prayers. The Friday sermon (*khutbah*) is delivered in English. The services follow the Sunni tradition.

Islamic Center of America
19500 Ford Road
Dearborn, MI 48128-2404
313-593-0000
www.icofa.com
Imam: Sayed Hassan Al-Qazwini

The mosque was founded mainly by Shi'ite Arabs, though every effort is made to welcome Sunnis and all other denominations. Men's and women's *wudu* (ablution) spaces radiate conveniently off a circular corridor that wraps around the central hall. Women pray in the main space behind the men, though there is a separate, comfortable balcony area for women who want to pray separately. There are signs throughout the *masjid* reminding people to dress Islamically and directing them to things they might need. Prayer garments for women are available in niches all around the main and balcony prayer spaces for women who want to use them. Qur'ans, prayer beads, and Shia prayer tablets are available at the prayer space entrances.

Islamic Cultural Center of New York
1711 3rd Avenue (corner of 96th Street)
New York, NY 10029-7303
212-722-5234
Imam: Omar Abu-Namous

Opened in 1989 and sometimes referred to as the 96th Street Mosque, the Center occupies an entire city block on Manhattan's Upper East Side and is currently the largest mosque in New York City. The mosque was designed by the prestigious architectural firm of Skidmore, Owings & Merrill and financed mainly by the Kuwaiti government. The main hall of the mosque regularly draws over

B. Important Organizations

Islamic Society of North America (ISNA)
6555 South 750 East
PO Box 38
Plainfield, IN 46168
Washington Office:
110 Maryland Avenue NE, Suite 304

Washington, D.C. 20002

317-839-8157   Fax: 317-839-1840

ISNA is an association of Muslim organizations and individuals that provides a common platform for presenting Islam. It is composed mostly of immigrants, as well as some African-American converts. Its membership may have recently surpassed that of the ASM, as many independent mosques throughout the United States are choosing to affiliate with it. ISNA's annual convention is the largest gathering of Muslims in the United States. It publishes the popular bi-monthly magazine *Islamic Horizons*.

Islamic Circle of North America (ICNA)

166-26 89th Avenue

Jamaica, NY 11432

718-658-1199   Fax: 718-658-1255

www.icna.org

ICNA describes itself as a nonethnic, open-to-all, independent, North American, grassroots organization. It is composed mostly of immigrants and Caucasian and African-American converts. It is growing as various independent mosques throughout the United States join, and it may now be larger than the ASM. Its youth division is Young Muslims. A major focus of its activities is *dawah*—outreach and education to individuals investigating Islam as a religious possibility.

Islamic Assembly of North America (IANA)

PMB # 270

3588 Plymouth Road

Ann Arbor, MI 48105

iana@iananet.org

IANA is a leading Muslim organization in the United States. It is devoted to "unifying and coordinating the efforts of the different dawah-oriented organizations in North America and guiding or directing Muslims of North America to adhere to the proper Islamic methodology." IANA organizes and sponsors conventions, general meetings, and dawah-oriented institutions and academies. It also has a well-developed program of providing reading materials and counseling to the prison population.

Muslim Students Association (MSA)

PO Box 1096
Falls Church, VA 22041
703-820-7900   Fax: 703-820-7888
manager@msanational.org
www.msanational.org

The Muslim Students Association (MSA) is a group dedicated to "Islamic societies on college campuses in Canada and the United States for the good of Muslim students." The MSA provides Muslims on various campuses the opportunity to practice their religion and to ease and facilitate such activities. It is also involved in social activities, such as fundraisers for the homeless during Ramadan. The founders of MSA would later establish the Islamic Society of North America and Islamic Circle of North America. MSA was begun in 1963 by a group of students at the University of Illinois at Urbana who had been members of the Muslim Brotherhood, considered by some a radical Sunni organization. The profile of the organization has been decidedly communal and aimed at forstering intra- and inter-faith dialogue and cooperation.

Council on American-Islamic Relations (CAIR)

National Headquarters:
453 New Jersey Avenue, SE
Washington, D.C. 20003
202-488-8787   Fax: 202-488-0833
info@cair.com   www.cair.com

CAIR is the largest Muslim civil rights and PAC/advocacy group in the U.S., originally established in 1994 to promote a positive image of Islam and Muslims in America. CAIR is seen as the voice of mainstream, moderate Islam on Capitol Hill and in political arenas throughout the United States. It has aggressively condemned acts of terrorism, and has been working in collaboration with the White House on "issues of safety and foreign policy." The group has sometimes been criticized for alleged links to Islamic terrorism, but its leadership has strenuously denied any involvement with such activities, pointing out that International Muslim organizations have myriad connections, and that CAIR's concern is strictly advocacy, information, and community support. The organization is responsible for producing the excellent resource *The North American Muslim Resource Guide*, edited by CAIR Director of Research Mohamed Nimer.

Muslim Public Affairs Council (MPAC)

MPAC Washington, D.C.
110 Maryland Avenue NE, Suite 210
Washington, D.C. 20002
202-547-7701   Fax: 202-547-7704
mpac-contact@mpac.org

MPAC Los Angeles

3010 Wilshire Boulevard, Suite 217
Los Angeles, CA 90010
213-383-3443   Fax: 213-383-9674
www.mpac.org

MPAC is a national American Muslim advocacy and public policy organization headquartered in Los Angeles, with offices in Washington, D.C. Founded in 1986, MPAC has participated in a number of coalitions and networks, and recently worked with Japanese-American organizations. The mission of MPAC "encompasses promoting an American Muslim identity, fostering an effective grassroots organization, and training a future generation of men and women to share our vision. MPAC also works to promote an accurate portrayal of Islam and Muslims in mass media and popular culture, educating the American public (both Muslim and non-Muslim) about Islam, building alliances with diverse communities and cultivating relationships with opinion- and decision-makers."

Fiqh Council of North America (FCNA)

PO Box 1250
Falls Church, VA 22041
703-575-7737   Fax: 703-575-8755

fiqh@fiqhcouncil.org
www.fiqhcouncil.org

The FCNA traces its roots back to the Religious Affairs Committee of the then Muslim Students Association of the United States and Canada in the early 1960s. This Religious Affairs Committee evolved into the Fiqh Committee of the Islamic Society of North America (ISNA) after the founding of ISNA in 1980. As the needs of the Muslim community and the complexity of the issues they faced grew, the council was transformed into the Fiqh Council of North America in 1986.

The council continues to be an affiliate of ISNA, advising and educating its members and officials on matters related to the application of Shari'ah in their individual and collective lives in the North American environment.

C. Media and Communications

The American Muslim

The American Muslim was published as a quarterly print journal from 1989 to 1995; it was revived in 2002 and continues as an online "e-zine" publication. The founding editor (and still editor-in-chief) is Sheila Musaji. Its content was diverse and thought-provoking, and the editors were devoted to making it visually arresting. Produced entirely by volunteers, each issue included an original piece of calligraphy by Mohamed Zakariya as an insert.

FURTHER READING AND RESOURCES

Muslims in the United States
Ilyas Ba-Yunus and Kassim Kone
2006: Greenwood Press

Muslim Communities in North America
Yvonne Y. Haddad and Jane I. Smith
1994: SUNY University Press

The North American Muslim Resource Guide
Mohamed Nimer
2002: Routledge Publishing

Islam in the United States of America
Sulayman Nyang
1999: Kazi Publications

Islam in America
Jane I. Smith
1999: Columbia University Press

Muslims in the United States
Phillipa Strum and Danielle Tarantolo
2003: Woodrow Wilson Center
(Available at www.wilsoncenter.org)

V. Islam and African-American Religion

A. Introduction

QUESTION: How will the history of the religion of African Americans develop in the century ahead: will African Americans find a spiritual home in Christian Black Liberation theology and "reside" in one or another denomination (or several) that has been reconstituted to address satisfactorily the issues that the history of American race relations raises vis à vis religion—*or*—will African Americans find their spiritual home in Islam, seeing it as genuinely conducive to the self-actualization of African Americans in their spiritual lives?

ANSWER: We don't know yet.

Another way the same question could have been asked is: who has called it right—James H. Cone or Sherman A. Jackson? (Same answer, though.) Of course, it is also possible that a century hence, the situation will be no more clear or resolved than it is today (making this a "three-horse race").

The involvement of African Americans with Islam is by now over a century old, though immigrant Muslims often discount that history as an aberration—at best a flirtation for the sake of expediency and political currency; at worst, a wildly imaginative misinterpretation of any reasonable understanding of the faith through the misapplication of creativity where and in ways imagination and creativity are unwelcome.

That leaders of these movements keep coming back to more orthodox and mainstream brands of Islamic thought and practice, however circuitously, gives many the expectation—some with hope, others with foreboding—that Islam will be the dominant religious language of the American black community. Or—one cannot help but wonder, is there a "fourth horse" out there, one that represents some as-yet-unrealized amalgam of Islam and Christianity that American blacks may yet come to embrace?

B. History

In 1913, a poor twenty-seven-year old black from North Carolina named Timothy Drew, dissatisfied with the Christian churches founded in the nineteenth century (like Richard Allen's African Methodist Episcopal Church), and influenced by the "back to Africa" rhetoric of Marcus Garvey, founded the Moorish Science Temple of America in Newark, New Jersey. Drew preached that American

blacks needed to have "a name and a land," and he provided them with both: he said that American blacks were "Asiatic" or "Moors," and that their true religion and spiritual homeland was Islam. Drew changed his name to Noble Drew Ali and established temples in Chicago (where he made his headquarters) and, by 1928, in Philadelphia, Pittsburgh, and Detroit.

Marcus Garvey (1887–1940) had come from Jamaica, where he had been a printer's apprentice for his uncle. He availed himself of his uncle's vast library and impressed virtually everyone he was to meet with his eloquence and his erudition. From 1912 to 1914, Garvey lived in London and frequently spoke from atop a chair at Speaker's Corner in Hyde Park. In 1914, he returned to Jamaica and founded the Universal Negro Improvement Association (UNIA). Garvey always claimed that his primary purpose was to unite blacks and only secondarily to lead a mass exodus of blacks to Africa. In 1916, he arrived in the U.S. to raise money for a school in Jamaica modeled after the Tuskegee Institute. Working as a printer's apprentice by day and speaking from street corners (as he had in London) by night, Garvey attracted a large following, especially after he spoke out in protest of government inaction following the 1917 East St. Louis (Illinois) riots, directed at black laborers who whites

The Moorish Science Temple of America in Chicago, Illinois, seen in this 1928 photograph, was founded by Noble Drew Ali, who stands, wearing white, in the front row center.

believed had taken their factory jobs. Garvey established several businesses aimed at uniting blacks and funding his projects, and a newspaper, *Negro World*. By 1920, UNIA claimed a membership of 4 million, and Garvey spoke to a packed Madison Square Garden crowd of 25,000 that August 1.

Garvey had, however, made some dangerous enemies during the course of his work, including an assistant Manhattan district attorney, and J. Edgar Hoover, then head of the Bureau of Investigation (or BOI, which in 1935 became the FBI). Hoover clearly solicited the aid of men in the black community to help him have Garvey declared an "undesirable alien" and deported. This finally happened in 1927, after Garvey had served four years of a sentence for mail fraud. (The evidence against him at his trial was an empty, unmarked envelope which the prosecution alleged had been used to hand-deliver a stock certificate, that could not be produced, bearing a photo of a boat that Garvey's Black Star Shipping Line was buying, but did not yet fully own.)

Meanwhile, Noble Drew Ali had developed his organization and published a magazine, *The Moorish American* (still in limited circulation). In 1929, following an arrest, Drew died mysteriously, though his supporters blamed a beating he had received while in police custody. During his life, Drew had introduced many elements of Islam, which he claimed to have learned during a visit to Morocco that he may have made in 1902. Many of the practices seemed to orthodox Muslims like theatrical variations of genuine Islamic practices.

Nation of Islam

On July 4, 1930, a silk peddler appeared in Detroit and announced that he had just returned from Mecca where he had been told that the blacks of America are actually Muslims, the lost tribe of Shabbaz. Wallace Fard (also known at various times as W. D. Fard, Ali Fard, and W. F. Muhammad) was a man of uncertain race, though he said he was born of a Turkish father and European mother. He established the Allah Temple of Islam in Detroit, preaching an amalgam of Sufism, Islam, and Theosophy, and showing the political influence of Garvey and Nobel Drew Ali. He established an organization he called the Lost-Found Nation of Islam in the Wilderness of North America, or Nation of Islam (NOI) for short, and created a stolid, black-suited, male security contingent called the Fruit of Islam, and several other elements that lent the mission a theatricality that drew adherents.

One of his adherents was one Elijah Poole (1876–1975), born to a family of Georgia sharecroppers. Poole recounted that in his teens he had eyewitnessed three lynchings of blacks in Georgia. In 1917, he married Clara Evans (later known as Mother Clara Muhammad), and in 1923 he settled in Detroit and worked in the Ford plant. He came to be a devoted believer in Fard, who told the young man (now calling himself Elijah Muhammad) that he, Fard, was the long-awaited Mahdi (which in Muhammad's eyes made Fard a kind of deity), and that Elijah was the Messenger of God.

Fard was arrested and released for inciting unrest a number of times until he agreed to leave Detroit in 1933. When he disappeared without a trace, Elijah Muhammad assumed leadership of the group, now headquartered in Chicago. The management of NOI under Muhammad took on some Islamic features, but also elements that were completely rejected by mainstream Islam. In these early days, services were an amalgam of Baptist spirituals and teachings of Wallace Fard, whom Muhammad called the "incarnation of Allah" and himself the "prophet of Allah." He may well have been speaking metaphorically when he said these things, so that later adherents might still maintain the group's good standing in orthodox Islam. But the teachings Elijah Muhammad promulgated about race—that whites were evil descendants of Satan; that blacks must take their futures into their own hands, work hard, and separate themselves from evil whites; that blacks were a superior race that ought to establish a nation of their own, on the American continent, or else in Africa—could not be easily reconciled with Islamic thought.

Yet, these messages attracted hundreds of thousands of blacks who had been exploited and downtrodden for generations, and soon the Nation of Islam had thriving temples in over a hundred American cities.

One of the places NOI reached into was American prisons, whose population was disproportionately black. The message of the supremacy of blacks over whites and the satanic character of whites appealed to many black prisoners, and one, in particular, became an important member of the group.

Malcolm Little (1925–1965) was born in Omaha, Nebraska, and led a difficult life in his youth. By the age of thirteen, he was a member of the Boston underworld and was arrested and sentenced to six years in a Massachusetts prison for hardened criminals. There he met a self-educated man, James Elton Bembri, who convinced him to educate himself in prison. He did, and at his brother's urging, Little began a correspondence with Elijah Muhammad.

After he was paroled in 1952, Little went to Chicago to meet with Elijah Muhammad. Little joined the Nation of Islam, changed his name to Malcolm X, and through his eloquence and understanding of the media, he rose in the ranks of the organization until he was its chief spokesman.

In 1963, Malcolm X made some intemperate remarks regarding the assassination of President Kennedy that forced Elijah Muhammad to remove him from leadership. Malcolm went on a pilgrimage to Mecca, which turned into a Hajj, during which his commitment to Islam deepened. Upon his return, he announced his resignation from the NOI. He was assassinated in 1965 by two NOI members.

After Elijah Muhammad

In 1975, Elijah Mu-hammad died, and the NOI leadership was assumed by his son, Wallace D. Muhammad (b. 1930), who changed his name to Warith Deen Mohammed. Even earlier, he worked to move his father's organization closer to traditional Islam, first by becoming a *mujtahid* (an Islamic theological scholar) himself; and second, by introducing more and more authentic Muslim practice and ritual into the services and practices of the temples. Most importantly, he abandoned the group's separatist and supremacist stands and brought the group's racial philosophy closer to orthodox Islamic tolerance and respect for the "People of the Book;" namely, Christians, Jews, and other monotheistic faiths.

This resulted in a deep schism which led to Muhammad founding an organization in 1985 for African-American Muslims known as the American Muslim Mission, which is now fully integrated into the American Muslim community. What became of the Nation of Islam, on the other hand, is less clear. Minister Louis Farrakhan (b. 1933) took over (or, more accurately, reformed) the organization after an absence of three years. At first, the new NOI adopted many of the positions espoused by Elijah Muhammad, and Farrakhan found that many of those provocative positions were no longer what blacks supported. Gradually, Farrakhan has moved NOI closer to traditional Islam—this is reflected in the organization's newspaper, *Final Call*, and is found often on its website, www.noi.org.

In addition to a reconciliation with Warith Deen Mohammed in 2000, Rev. Farrakhan has also reconciled with the widow of Malcolm X, Betty Shabbazz, in 1995. In 2006, Farrakhan stepped down from leadership of NOI due to poor health.

In October 1995, the Nation of Islam, under Farrakhan's leadership, organized and sponsored the Million Man March, a rally of African-American men in Washington, D.C. to promote volunteerism, community activism, and voter registration. The successful event marked the completion of a radical transition of the controversial organization and its leader. (For an encore, Farrakhan has returned to his love of music, which he abandoned for a life of communal service some forty years earlier, and, in April 1993, performed the Mendelssohn Violin Concerto in concert to rave reviews. He has since performed concerti of Beethoven, Tchaikovsky, and Brahms.)

C. Major Organizations

American Society of Muslims (ASM)

ASM is the successor organization to the Nation of Islam, once better known as the Black Muslims (though that organization virtually never utilized that term), under the leadership of Warith Deen Mohammed. This group evolved from the Nation of Islam (1930–1975) in a transition that took twenty-three years of religious reorientation and organization, during which period the group was known by other names, such as the American Muslim Mission. It is not clear just how many Americans belong to ASM. The vast majority of ASM adherents are African Americans, all integrated into their local mosques.

Nation of Islam

7351 South Stoney Island Avenue
Chicago, IL 60649
773-324-6000   www.noi.org

The website of NOI and the newspaper *Final Call* contain much material on the history of the organization; there are, however, some inconsistencies between the section "Official Statements," which seems to contain material of a more moderate, conciliatory tone, and the standard, permanent material that still calls for a separate black country and a tax boycott. The material on the site regarding Islam and the beliefs of NOI are in keeping with other Muslim organizations.

FURTHER READING

American Islam
Paul M. Barret
2006: Farrar, Staus and Giroux

Martin & Malcolm & America
James H. Cone
1992: Orbis Books

Islam and the Black American
Sherman A. Jackson
2005: Oxford University Press

Malcolm X: A Life of Reinvention
Manning Marable
2011: Viking

African American Islam
Amina Beverly McCloud
1995: Routledge Publishing

Islam in the African-American Experience
Richard Brent Turner
1997: Indiana University Press

INTERNET RESOURCES

University-Based:
www.ucblibraries.colorado.edu/govpubs/
us/ilamus.htm
(University of Colorado–Boulder)

www.uge.edu/islam
(University of Georgia)

Sectarian:
http://islamworld.net
http://islamtoday.net
www.discoverislam.com
www.understanding-islam.com
www.IslamCity.com
www.Islamonline.net

General:
www.Beliefnet.com/Faiths/Islam/index.aspx

IV. JUDAISM

IV JUDAISM

Historical Introduction

In the Beginning

THOMAS CAHILL, THE BEST-SELLING AUTHOR AND, for many years, the venerated religion editor at Doubleday, begins his book, *The Gifts of the Jews,* with the following sentence: "**The Jews started it all—by 'it' I mean so many of the things we care about, the underlying values that make all of us, Jew and Gentile, believer and atheist, tick.**"

Cahill then goes on to show how the entire idea of history—that there is a beginning, a middle, and an end to the story of a person, a family, a nation, an empire, a period...even the universe and all of creation!—is a concept invented by a small band of people whose precise origins and identity are lost in the mists of antiquity because, well, because no one had invented history yet!

To be sure, there were many things before the Jews invented history. There was power—great empires swept across the landscape and conquered other great empires; there was law—with the increasing complexity of society and trade, some ground rules needed to be put in writing and societies did just that; there was science—royal courts had astronomers and naturalists who proposed how the cosmos worked and how nature functioned; there was technology (quite a lot of it, in fact)—civilizations built great edifices and developed agricultural methods that ensured prosperity and order, and weapons that protected them from invasion; and there was culture—works of art and sculpture

graced palaces and homes of the aristocracy while musicians played music on instruments. There was even literature—writing had been invented in Sumer and epics and poems were recited for the entertainment and inspiration of people, who also went to the theater (perhaps more than they do today)...but there was no history. Kings who carved their exploits onto the marbled palace walls

The crucial event in the book of Genesis, the Akeida (literally the "binding" of Isaac), in which Abraham displays his willingness to sacrifice his only son at God's command, is depicted in this fifth-century floor mosaic of the synagogue discovered in 1929 at Kibbutz Beit Alpha in northeastern Israel. Behind Abraham is the ram, caught in the bushes, that will be sacrificed instead.

did so for their own aggrandizement, and to impress (and intimidate) others, but (ironically) not to leave a lasting record and not to tell future generations about themselves. Of the many thousands of tablets excavated at the ancient city of Ebla, hardly any deal with anything that could remotely be called a historical record. Tablet after tablet of contracts, accountings, tax rolls, and financial receipts—the "books," but nothing resembling history.

And why would there be? Why, after all, should anyone care what is going to happen in the future? A parent loves a child and one feels a bond with one's own blood relatives, perhaps even with one's neighbors and fellow subjects, but, really, why should anyone care what is going to happen long after he or she is gone?

The Hebrews (the ancestors of the Jews and creators of the chain of thought that eventually became Judaism) arrived at an odd and interesting but satisfying answer to that question: caring about the future, seeing one's life in the context of a destiny that has been "written into creation" from the very beginning of time—that is what makes us human, what makes us more than animals that live only in the here and now, what makes us civilized and noble beyond our mortality… what makes us tick.

When God promises Abraham that he will have countless descendants who will worship God and follow his teachings, why should Abraham care? When God asks Abraham to leave his native land after he has challenged the pagan gods and lived to tell the tale, why does he go? And when he is asked to sacrifice his beloved son, Isaac, now that he has a revulsion of human sacrifice that comes from his newly created moral refinement, why does he obey?

He obeys because his life, his entire being, is bound up in the eternity that God has promised him. He makes what looks like a bad career move because he realizes that what he does in the narrow temporal confines of his life will have implications for generations, eons into the future. And he accepts God's promise because he has already begun the process himself—when he leaves his birthplace, he takes his possessions, his family and *ha-nefesh asher asu b'haran,*—"the souls they had made in Haran" (Gen. 12:5). There are many interpretations of that phrase (that Abram and Sarai took their servants, or their family, or their possessions), but the plain meaning is how we rendered it: they took the disciples who had learned a new way of thinking, of acting—of being. Abraham is already creating an oral tradition and body of teaching—about God, the universe, the nature of man, the nature of good and evil, and most important at this stage, about justice.

Abraham and the early Hebrews (they were called Hebrews, *Ivrim* because they had "come over"—from the lands of Mesopotamia, from the hills of Canaan, but, more importantly, they had sojourned from the pre-civilized thinking of the pagan world) understood how one's personal identity is bound up in a chain—of blood and of thought—that provides us with a context that extends beyond our years and to the extreme ends of time, whenever that may be.

The Bible follows the wanderings of the family of Abraham—his encampments, his battles, his engagements with the surrounding cultures, the ups and downs of his children and grandchildren, relatives who try to get the better of one another, brothers who don't get along because they are jealous of a parent's affection, brothers who take matters into their own hands when a sister is wronged. Seems like a pretty average family, except that this family has something else: God has given this family a destiny, a plan for the future in the form of a covenant, a bargain, if you will, struck between God and Abraham. The covenant promises Abraham that his descendants will be as numberless as the stars, and that all humankind will one day bless them and bless knowing them.

That was the good news; now the catch: They would have to spend 400 years in bondage as slaves, worked and persecuted to within an inch of their lives, until they would be redeemed and led out of bondage to the land that God has promised Abraham. Nowhere does it say why the Hebrews had to endure the bondage of Egypt before enjoying the benefits of the covenant, but the question must have been asked, and for many, the sermonic answers ("adversity builds character" and "you have to walk before you crawl") did not satisfy. The Hebrews may have grown great in number during the days of Joseph (Ex. 1:7), but when the bondage began, there were defections, escapes, rebellions, attempts to disappear and meld into the surrounding culture—perhaps even a savior or two who tried but failed to lead the Hebrews out of Egypt. The story of Moses—a child placed in the home of an Egyptian woman (who happened to be of the royal house), who rescued the child from the genocidal intentions of the monarch by raising the child as her own—was probably replayed in one form another many, many times in ancient Egypt. (We know this because in our own time, loving desperate parents frantically did the very same thing in the dark days of the Holocaust.)

The Hebrews Become a Religion

The tradition has it that the Hebrews were led out of Egypt amid great miracles (plagues, pillars of fire, sea-partings), and that they then encountered their God in the desert at the foot of a mountain, where they pledged their uncategorical loyalty to Him and to His commandments, as set forth in the Torah—the Five Books of Moses (the Pentateuch portion of the Hebrew Bible).

At first, there were but ten precepts (commandments—*mitzvot,* plural of *mitzvah*), but soon there were 613 of them, complete with a complex and carefully argued set of laws and details. The biblical account calls these the ten "utterances" (*aseret ha'dibrot*), to drive home the point that the nation of Israel—what the Hebrews could now be called—were in direct contact with God, who imparted these ten precepts in an act of Revelation. That the precepts were special was further emphasized by their being inscribed on two stone tablets "by the finger of God" (Ex. 31:18), making them the Two

Tablets of the Covenant (and thus making the case in which the tablets were carried the Ark of the Covenant, which became the focus of all prayer).

The Ten Commandments have become important in many religions and in world culture because they seem to encapsulate the full spirit of the Jewish religious ethos and value system. There are different ways of seeing ten precepts in the text of the Ten Commandments in the Bible (Exodus 20 and Deuteronomy 5), even in the Jewish rabbinic sources. Here is one traditional enumeration:

1. I am the Lord Your God, who took you out of the land of Egypt, the house of bondage.

Belief in one God is couched in the form of a personal communication from that God, to emphasize the idea that the Jewish belief is in a personal God to whom one may relate as to a father, a king, another person, as it were—and not as an unreachably abstract, distant entity unmindful of human events or concerns, nor as an omnipresence that is so identified with all of nature as to render prayer to that God no different from prayer to oneself. On the most basic level, the God who is speaking is the one who freed the Hebrew slaves from Egypt.

2. You shall have no other Gods besides me. You shall not make for yourself a sculpted image or any likeness of what is in the heavens above, or on the earth below, or in the water under the earth. You shall not bow to them and serve them, for I the Lord your God am an "impassioned" God [*eil kanah*], visiting the guilt of the parents on the children, upon the third [generation]—and even upon the fourth generation of those who reject Me. But showing kindness to the thousandth generation of those who love Me and keep My commandments.

The rejection of idolatry extends not simply to statuary and images, but to ethereal beings who may be adjuncts or "partners" in a divine pantheon or "underworld," or to powers, being, or concepts "unfathomable." The God concept is further defined in terms of consequences: His universe may be relied

Above, Charlton Heston portrays Moses in Cecil B. DeMille's 1956 production (his second) of The Ten Commandments. *The writing on the tablets is paleo-Hebrew, but represents only a small portion of the full text of the commandments.*

upon to deliver bad ends for the sinful, and (*very*) good ones for the righteous. God describes Himself here as an "impassioned" God—a better translation than the old "jealous." What is described is a God who is engrossed and involved in human affairs.

3. You shall not swear falsely by the name of the Lord your God, for the Lord will not clear [absolve] one who swears falsely by His name.

This precept is not about bearing false witness; that's covered in the tenth commandment. The commandment is often interpreted to prohibit the use of God's name in magic, the black arts, and divination—in other words, in frivolous or malicious pursuits. But at a very basic level and at the very least, the precept defends the sanctity (even godliness) of the pursuit of truth.

4. Remember the sabbath day and keep it holy. Six days shall you labor and do all your work, but the sabbath day is a sabbath for the Lord your God: you shall not do any work—you, your son or daughter, your male or female servants, your cattle, or the stranger who is in your settlements. For in

six days the Lord made heaven and earth, the sea and all that is in them, and He rested on the seventh day; therefore the Lord blessed the sabbath day and made it holy.**

Observance of the sabbath is tied to recognition of God as Creator and of the universe as a completed, and thus benevolent, work, of that Creator. The seven-day cycle seems totally arbitrary and if there are natural human and animal seven-day rhythms, as some naturalists think there may be, they could not be very overpowering since other cultures have adopted weeks of varying numbers of days. By the same token, the preponderance of a seven-day week all over the world today and throughout much of history suggests a connection. Anthropologists have argued that the weekly cycle and the opportunity to replenish on a day of rest has been a boon to culture and civilization, and this seems to be a device created by the ancient Hebrews, and which provided great social and palpable benefits. This may be what the Hebrew/Yiddish poet H. N. Bialik meant when he noted that, more than the Jewish people have kept the Sabbath, the Sabbath has kept the Jewish people.

5. Honor your father and your mother, that you may long endure on the land that the Lord your God is giving you.

This is a rare instance in the Bible when a practical reward for the performance of a precept is given. The tone is one of "good advice," lacking the dire consequences implicit in the other commandments. Perhaps, some suggest, the Torah hopes that honoring parents will follow from love of parents, best promoted with a softer approach.

6. You shall not murder.

The Bible makes a sharp distinction between killing and murder: the former can possibly be permissible, as in the administration of justice or in war. But reasons given in the rabbinic literature for why taking a human life is wrong—the desecration of the "image of God" in which humankind is created; the loss of all the victim's future generation; the usurpation of God's prerogative as giver of life—apply equally well to supposedly justified taking of a life.

7. You shall not commit adultery.

Unlike other ancient codes of law, in which adultery is a "great crime" committed against the property rights of the husband, here for the first time it is a sin—a desecration of the sacred bond of marriage and an affront to God. Adultery in the rabbinic tradition is one of only three sins (idolatry and murder being the other two) for which one must be prepared to give up one's life rather than commit (presumably because these misdeeds are irremediable).

8. You shall not steal.

Theft is prohibited so often elsewhere in the Torah, that these covenental precepts seem to require truly heinous acts beyond stealing. Thus many interpreters believe this refers to stealing *people*—kidnapping or dealing in the trade of human slavery. Others believe it refers to lawmakers and officials who sanction theft by allowing it to take place or go unpunished. In societies that persecute the helpless, an effort will be made to enact laws that support persecution, depriving victims of justice and recourse.

9. You shall not bear false witness against your neighbor.

Is this an elaboration of the previous commandment, extending the prohibition of stealing from lawmakers who give it the patina of respectability to the judges who implement the law; or does it tell us that both the judge and the witness are equally guilty of subverting justice? Regardless, the precept enjoins using the law as an instrument of inflicting harm, and sees it as a despicably destructive wrong against man and God.

10. You shall not covet your neighbor's house; you shall not covet your neighbor's wife, or his male or female slave, or his ox or his ass, or anything that is your neighbor's.

This commandment is the most difficult in the interpretive literature, yet it is the most direct and simplest to understand. It says, don't be envious of another's good fortune. The problem is: how can one legislate against how one reacts viscerally to a fine object or a beautiful person? Some commentators say, therefore, that the precept enjoins *acting* on those urges and reactions (in all the unpredictable ways people do). In a recent popular Hollywood film, a financier says to an audience of stockholders that "greed is good"—this commandment begs to differ.

This marked the beginning of Judaism as a religion, adhered to by an entire nation that entrusted its destiny and fortunes in this set of laws and rituals, however imperfectly they understood it and however far or frequently they would stray from it. A comparison of ancient Judaic law with the few codes we have from the ancient Near East shows the Hebrews possessing a much more sophisticated and analytical legal system than even the mightiest powers of the day. Was this a legacy of Sumer, where Abraham's family had been (according to tradition) members of the priestly class? Or was it a product of nomadic practicality, a knowledge of local laws and business practices being an important tool for a nomadic trader? Or is this a legacy of Egypt, where Moses (again, according to tradition) carried out his princely duties (before he was banished) by focusing on the cultures on Egypt's borders that could serve as useful allies? Or perhaps (and likely) a combination of all three. Whatever the source, the Israelites showed early on a predilection for legal analysis and for detailed argumentation that informed everything from ritual to civil law to family matters to affairs of state. Habits like that do not develop overnight.

There thus developed a dual track for the Nation of Israel—one devoted to the analysis of the Law: the Torah and the continuing body of knowledge—the so-called "chain" (*shal'shelet*) of the tradition; and the other played out in the life of the people: their life in the Land of Israel; their vicissitudes in their various adopted countries (as emigrants or as expatriates); their migrations; their golden ages; their periods of

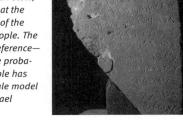

Little remains of antiquity, but some small clues point to a past that we now know was no fantasy. The Merneptah stele, at left, was inscribed by an Egyptian king who ruled at the beginning of the thirteenth century BCE. The bottom of the stele contains the earliest reference to Israel as a people. The Tel Dan stele, at right, contains the earliest known reference— ninth century BCE—to the House of David. Above, the probable layout and structure of much of the Second Temple has been pieced together by modern historians. This scale model of the Temple and its environs can be seen in the Israel Museum in Jerusalem.

decline and persecution. At certain points in its history, the Jewish people survived and endured because of the efforts of ordinary people fighting, striving, enduring hardships while remaining true to their identity. And at other points, the continuance of the nation was in the hands of the extraordinary few who maintained the vitality of Israel by studying, developing, codifying, and analyzing further the corpus of Jewish learning in all its various forms. The interplay of these two "Judaisms" is (we submit) the defining characteristic of Jewish history, from antiquity to our own day.

The Hebrews Become a People: Israel

What exactly happened next is still being debated and pieced together by experts, but the story that informed the development of the Jewish people over the next several millennia was that the Israelites spent some years wandering in the desert, presumably preparing for nationhood once they entered Canaan, the land that they believed had been promised to their ancestors. They entered that land under the leadership of Joshua, disciple of

Moses, and conquered it, mostly through military means. They spent some 170 years under the rule of "judges" and settling the land until a royal family was able to consolidate the various tribes and create a cohesive unified nation.

During some decades of the twentieth century, there was much doubt about whether there ever was a King David, whether there was a conquest of the land of Canaan, whether there was a Joshua or a Moses—whether there was, in fact, even anything called the nation of Israel in antiquity. These debates continue today, though little by little, pieces of the puzzle of the past are being found, deciphered, and understood. In any case, this is what the people who became the Jewish people believed and it was what informed their rituals, laws, and dedication to the Torah and its laws over many centuries.

In the tenth and ninth centuries BCE, Israel becomes a monarchy, and, in 966 BCE, Solomon builds a temple in Jerusalem. But Israel is soon a divided nation, with Judah (later called Judeans) in the south and the other tribes of Israel in the north. The nation is rife with idolatry and the influences of the surrounding pagan cultures; it is the heyday of the Kings of Israel, while prophets and scholars desperately struggle to preserve their lives and the teachings they have received.

And then catastrophe: The Assyrian king Sargon II conquers the Northern Kingdom and, as is the Assyrian strategy with conquered peoples, carries them off into exile to disappear. These are the Ten "Lost" Tribes of legend and history. Somehow, by chance or by a miracle (or, more likely, because Judah was too minor a kingdom to bother conquering), Judah escapes the Assyrians, but the vacuum left by Sargon's retreating armies is filled by the other tribes and political entities always on the border, and there follows a period of decline in the fortunes of Judah.

In spite of the rancor that existed for decades between the Northern Kingdom and Jerusalem, the sudden loss of a large number of co-religionists in the north stunned the Judeans and it was inevitable that they would, under the right king, turn back to their roots and revive their traditions. This came in the person of Josiah, during whose reign a book is "found" in the Temple by Hilkiah, the High Priest. Its authenticity is vouched for by one Huldah the Prophetess, and reading it to a throng assembled outside the Temple brings the people to tears and back to the Laws of Moses.

That book was probably the book of Deuteronomy, though it might have been the complete Torah—all Five Books of Moses—and during this period begins a movement away from the pagan-corrupted form of Judaism practiced throughout the land (north and south), back to a form that is recognizably Mosaic. This is also the period of the Prophets, who, though they were persecuted and as frustrated as any teacher has ever been, still chastised and attempted to inspire the people and set them in the right path—an enterprise that in earlier times would have been, frankly, wasted breath.

When the end of the First Temple came in 597 BCE, it was at the hands of the Babylonians, who had vanquished the Assyrians with the help of the many small tribal and political groups that the Assyrians had dispersed, but which had not forgotten who they were and were not about to be forgotten by their conquerors. With the promise to the nobility that each conquered group would have a place in the royal court, the Babylonians cut a swath through the ancient world and ruled supreme—until the Persians came along with a better offer: return to one's homeland in exchange for tribute, political loyalty, and military cooperation.

Thus, in less than a century, the First Temple was destroyed, the Judeans were carried off to Babylon (to weep next to its waters), and (quicker than one could say "Blessed is Mordecai and cursed is Haman," the antagonists in the book of Esther, which tries to explain this amazing reversal of fortune), the Judeans are back rebuilding the walls of Jerusalem and laying the foundation of a Second Temple, thanks to the Edict of Cyrus in 537 BCE.

It is also during this period that the "other Judaism" was on the ascendancy—the Scribes, led by Ezra, were able to establish norms of Jewish ritual: times and forms of prayers; public reading of the Torah; even changing the letters of the Torah scroll (so it would not be confused with the objectionable Samaritan version). Scholarly enclaves had been extant in Israel and in Babylonia for some time; now they grew in size and earnestness.

And so, after 600 years of Hebrew–Israelite–Judean civilization, over half that period ruled by a monarch, followed by a hiatus of about half a century, the Jews were back for a "second commonwealth" that would last another 670 years, complete with kings, wars, narrow escapes, assassinations, rebellions, glorious victory, ignominious defeat—but never again total sovereign independence, as first the Persians, then the Greeks, and then the Romans ruled over every square inch of the reachable world that they could conquer and control.

The community of the scholars—the rabbis, and later the Pharisees, or *perushim*, which literally means "separatists," meaning, separating as much from the decadence and paganism of the Temple priesthood and its sponsors, the Judean ruling class, as from the idolatrous nations everywhere in the Levant—

sometimes were able to reach the people and were protected by them, and sometimes they were hunted and slaughtered by the hundreds.

The history of the Second Commonwealth reads like a roller-coaster ride through history—euphoric victory followed by devastating defeat; glory and heroism (as with the Hasmonean victory of Judah Maccabee) followed by the slaughter of 800 rabbis by Judah's own great-grandnephew, Alexander Yannai, who feasted with his court as they watched the rabbis crucified and their wives and children slaughtered before their eyes. Each time the pendulum swung, the stakes were raised and the chaos in the land became greater.

Finally, in the year 69 CE, one man makes a fateful decision that will affect the course of Jewish history for the next twenty centuries—perhaps much, much longer. Faced with the decision to save one of the two Judaisms—the sovereign land of the people or the sacred domain of the Law, and knowing he cannot save both, or perhaps believing the land and the lives of the people on it are irretrievably lost—he elects to save the Law, the Torah and its defenders.

Judaism Becomes a Religion. . . Again

That man is Rabbi Yochanan ben Zakai and the scene is his audience with Vespasian, the Roman general who is laying siege to Jerusalem. Vespasian is just days away from victory; the partisans inside the walls have destroyed each other's storehouses, making it impossible for anyone to survive for any length of time. The rabbi, head of the Sanhedrin, had to fake his own death and was smuggled out in a coffin. Standing before the general, the rabbi addresses him as Emperor—perhaps as a ploy or as a bit of flattery, but just as Vespasian is about to reprimand the rabbi for his impertinence, a messenger arrives informing him that Emperor Nero has committed suicide and the Senate has made him emperor.

Vespasian is so impressed that he turns to Yochanan and grants him three requests. Yochanan

does not ask that Jerusalem be spared, for he knows that now the emperor will be loath to return to the Senate empty-handed. So he makes three "modest" requests: He asks that the family of Rabbi Gamli'el be spared (at the time, perhaps 200 strong); he asks that doctors be permitted to treat Rabbi Zaddok, the old sage who has fasted for forty years and is at death's door. By now, Vespasian was wondering if the rabbi hadn't become completely addled by the trauma of the siege. Yochanan then made his third request, what he really hoped for: "Give me Yavneh and her scholars." Yavneh was a coastal town of little financial or strategic importance, but which had an academy in which the best young students were taught Torah by the nation's leading rabbis.

Rabbi Yochanan's thinking is clear: he wishes to save the family of Rabban Gamli'el because, as direct descendants of Hillel, they are the only certain members of the Davidic household; and he wishes to save Rabbi Zaddok because he is the one man he knows for certain is a *kohein*—a member of the priestly class. As for Yavneh: it was not the only scholarly enclave, but it was not in a large city and it was isolated, so Vespasian would not have to answer for sparing it. With it and with the other rabbinic scholars who had escaped the tragedy of the destruction of Jerusalem, Rabbi Yochanan hoped there would be enough to maintain the "other Judaism" while the physical nation recovered. Meanwhile, the rabbis, the texts, the rituals—facing Jerusalem wherever they prayed; recalling the service of the Temple; waiting for the return, led by a messiah (and sometimes attempting to return without the benefit of a messiah)—would keep the memory and longing for the land of Israel alive.

Jewish Civilization in Europe

Now began a remarkable sojourn of the Jewish people through many lands, in a diaspora that reached to the far corners of the earth and took them to triumph and travails they could not have imagined in ancient Israel. At first, the Jews were taken (by ship or by the simple directions of the compass) to one of four places where they were to try to make a life. They either headed west to Rome and Italy; or they headed south, to Egypt and the Jewish settlements that had existed there since the First Temple; or they headed north to Mesopotamia and the enclaves in Babylonia, where there had been Jewish settlements since the Babylonian captivity; and some headed east, but not very far east; just into the desert of Transjordan and the Arabian peninsula. And some very few managed to stay in Israel (now called Palestine), hounded by the local Arabs and Romans, in constant fear of being arrested and sold into slavery.

Remarkably, each of the migrating groups persevered and endured to see their number increase and to experience periods of success and satisfaction, even if only momentarily. The Jews who went to Italy become the core of Sephardic Jewry, though they would not reach their pinnacle until they emigrated to Spain (Sepharad) and enjoyed the benefits of a tolerant Muslim caliphate there.

The Jews who went north and made a home in Mesopotamia were comfortable with the regimentation that was to become characteristic of early Christendom, and so became part of the Byzantine Empire, and from there eventually entered northern Europe. These were the Ashkenazim (named after the early medieval name of Germanic Europe, the area around the Rhine Valley), or Ashkenazic Jewry.

These two pictures of Jewish emigration patterns that account for the development of robust Jewish communities in Spain, Italy, North Africa, Germany, and later in eastern Europe, are speculation based on the supposition that people seek the familiar, even if it is not the most congenial environment. There are other markers that could trace migration patterns—linguistic, anthropological, ritual, even genetic. What they show is that over the course of 1,500 years, Jews traveled to virtually any place there were other Jews and found a home and spiritual comfort in those ostensibly foreign lands.

There was a cross-pollination of ideas, values, language, and folk forms that is unique in human history. The camaraderie that Jews of one "type"—be they Ashkenazic or Sephardic, German or Italian, light-skinned or dark—naturally had with all others was noted by and became a source of suspicion and envy on the part of the Gentiles around them. It may well have been the sympathy Jews felt for the stranger and the refugee that allowed them to mingle and accept Jews from other cultures; then again, it was also, no doubt, the commonality of their ritual and their belief system that bound Jews of diverse nationalities and ethnicities together. It is no accident or happenstance that the foundational codes of Jewish law are a blend of the work of Maimonides and Joseph Caro, Sephardic rabbis *par excellence,* with the work of Moses Isserles and Meir of Rothenberg, dyed-in-the-wool Ashkenazic Jews.

The Middle Ages for the Jews of Europe was a tragic period. The dominance of the Catholic church in Europe, looking constantly to the East and the Holy Land while staking its claim on the newly settled and civilized areas of the North and West, created a continually tense environment that periodically erupted into such episodes as the Crusades, the Inquisition, pogroms, and a paranoid suppression of Jewish life, culture, and enterprise. In retrospect, all the vitriol and mayhem that decimated whole communities in the name of ill-conceived beliefs and on the basis of ridiculous canards. The contribution that the Jewish people have made to humankind is testimony to "the pity of it all" (to use the title of Amos Elon's history of German Jewry)—the loss of this immense reservoir of industry and talent in century after century of hate and death.

Yet, in the midst of the maelstrom, great centers of life and learning arose in the cities of Western Europe and in the plains of Eastern Europe, within both a religious context and a secular one. The *yeshivot* (Talmudic seminaries) of Europe established a standard of erudition and analysis that rivaled the academies of Babylonia. The contributions of Jews to medical and other sciences made German medicine the finest in the world. Every symphony orchestra in Europe was the beneficiary of the Jewish love of and acumen in music, and every academic discipline was advanced by the relentless pursuit of excellence and knowledge that had Jewish participation far beyond its numbers. One wonders what American science, medicine, music, literature, culture, business, technology—virtually every field of human endeavor—would be like had Jews not come to these shores, *forced* to come to these shores by the events of the 1930s and 1940s.

The Holocaust (*Sho'ah* in Hebrew)

It would be facile to try to summarize the events denoted by the term "holocaust" in so short a space. We are still learning the full dimensions of the horror, the full extent of the duplicity of the so-called civilized world, and we are still evaluating the totality of the loss. But here it is, simply put: in spite of decades of progress and assimilation of the Jews of Europe into the fabric and polity of European society, virtually the entirety of European Jewry was exterminated, wiped off the face of the earth in the space of less than half a decade. The path from the Enlightenment of the eighteenth century, through the Emancipation of the nineteenth century, ended at the gates of the death camps of Auschwitz, Dachau, and dozens of others in which six million Jews and another four million non-Jews—ethnic Poles and Russians; Roma, Gypsies, and gay men; Freemasons and Jehovah's Witnesses; the mentally disabled, the elderly, and political "undesirables"— were killed ruthlessly, efficiently, and without recourse to law or redress.

That this could happen in a culture that prided itself for being liberal and sophisticated gives one pause and should make every human soul shudder at the evil that people are capable of. One observation that has become all too clear is that genocide—the crime of exterminating people for no reason other than they are members of a certain ethnicity, religion, nationality, or physical characteristic—has become a crime associated with the twentieth century; if we are not mindful and careful, it may well become a feature nearly as common in the twenty-first century.

The destruction of European Jewry is by no means the only "crime against humanity" ever perpetrated, but it has certain special characteristics that place it at the core of Jewish identity and consciousness—in America, and everywhere Jews live and for some time to come. Though we

Petr Ginz, a Czech boy of Jewish descent, was deported to the Terezin ghetto in 1941, at the age of fourteen. While there, he made a drawing entitled Moonscape, *which depicts the planet Earth as seen from the moon. The following year, Ginz was moved to the Auschwitz concentration camp, where he died at the age of sixteen. Ginz's drawing, which survived him, was taken into space by the Israeli astronaut Ilan Ramon (above), who perished during the re-entry of the ill-fated space shuttle* Columbia *in 2003. In 2005, the Czech government issued a stamp featuring a likeness of Ginz and his haunting work of art.*

want to believe that there are things people can do to prevent such catastrophes from happening, and we are determined not to sit by and *allow* it to keep happening, the seemingly inexorable course of history, cultural forces, and course of events that gave the Holocaust a patina of inevitability sends a shudder through Jews everywhere. There is no point denying it and no reason to avoid it. The aim of this tome is to provide readers with the tools to understand people of all religions. Anyone who wants to understand the Jews must learn about and come to grips with the Holocaust. Not even the birth of the state of Israel in the aftermath of World War II can assuage the unease that is a part of the modern Jewish psyche, including in America. (As Henry Kissinger famously used to say, "Just because you're paranoid, doesn't mean people *aren't* after you.")

And Then... America

In the next chapter, we will review the basic elements of the Jewish faith, and in the following chapter, we will look at the story of the Jewish religion in the United States. It is, for the most part, a history with many shining moments, though not without episodes the Jews of America would rather forget. In these pages, we would like to suggest several general principles that might help us understand that experience better and see it for the unique episode it is, not only for Jews, but also on a fundamental human level that may make the lessons learned applicable to others.

First, America is different—very different. Jews who came to these shores attempted to assimilate—culturally if not spiritually—as they never have before, because the allure was irresistible. America claimed to be an experiment in self-governance and in citizenry, a country that could work only if its people let it and made it work. Centuries of powerlessness and inconsequence were shed in an instant when the opportunity arose to be able to affect change and enter into the running of things. The

Israel Independence Day Parades in American cities—such as this one down New York's Fifth Avenue in 2008—often serve as much as a show of solidarity of the American Jewish community as a demonstration of support for the State of Israel.

Jews took to this novelty with energy and zeal; other immigrant groups have encountered this as well, but for none, it may be said flatly, was this as radically different from their historical experience as it was for the Jews.

Second, America is in a constant state of flux. Change is a defining characteristic of Americans; Jews, who have had to adapt to changing landscapes, rights, political standing, fortunes, and social status, are comfortable with this element of American life and are more than happy to help it along. In this, Jews draw upon a wide range of experience that permits them to view things from the skewed angle that gives rise to innovation and creativity. Jews, for all the jokes made about their sedentary proclivities, hate stagnation and love change.

Third, America belongs to... Americans! The very idea that the forests, mountains, and wilderness of the American landscape belong, not to a potentate or a lord, but to the people is a concept that

Jews could scarcely believe when they arrived. That sense of proprietorship extends to the city streets and neighborhoods, and it has allowed Jews to move out of the enclaves they first settled in and live, well, wherever they wanted to. To be sure, this idealization was not always practiced in the real world. Even Bess Myerson, the first Jewish Miss America, found herself barred from staying in many hotels across the country *while on tour as Miss America!* But the concept was there in black-and-white in the Constitution, and if the reality did not measure up to the ideal, then it was up to "us" to fight for it. This was a novel concept for Jewish immigrants to the U.S., which is why American Jews may well be ahead of much of the country in understanding the full implications of this idea.

Fourth, America cares about doing, and being, right. The American desire to "do the right thing," even when it is contrary to its own interest—to look squarely at misdeeds and injustices of the past, even though committed in innocence, or done under the duress that history is apt to put on nations, is a character trait that bewilders (or amuses and is derided by) the rest of the world, but is appreciated by Jews virtually without equal. What is considered "fair play" in the American psyche, however coarse its contours, is simply unknown elsewhere—and Jews know this probably better than anyone else.

Finally America celebrates being different— almost as much as it fears it. Coming from long experience in societies where conformity was the only passkey to acceptance, Jews appreciate the American embrace of the new, the independent, and the different as few other groups can. But the very human fear of the unfamiliar is also part of the American ethos. This is why and how the alliance between the American Jewish and the African-American communities came into being. Jews resonated with the black insistence that rights were not to be bought through cultural self-denial. This paradoxical tension remains a pressing issue for both.

Important Dates in Jewish History

Jewish History in Antiquity

1800 BCE Abraham founds the Hebrew nation.

1300–1250 BCE The Israelites in Egypt. Moses leads them out of bondage and takes them right up to the Promised Land.

ca. 1200 BCE Joshua invades Canaan.

1030–930 BCE First Saul, then David and Solomon rule a still-united Israel. Solomon builds his Temple in Jerusalem, 966.

931 BCE Israel is divided into "Israel" to the north and "Judah" to the south. Later called Judea, from which "Jew" derives.

721 BCE Assyrian king Sargon II conquers Northern Kingdom but is thwarted when attacking Judea. The Ten Tribes of the North are "lost" to Assyria (and to history).

640–609 BCE Reign of Josiah over Judah. Return to tradition and the task of collecting and correcting biblical texts begins.

597 BCE Nebuchadnezzar, king of Babylonia, captures Jerusalem and deports Jews to Babylon. He will level the Temple in 587.

539 BCE Cyrus and the Persians conquer the Babylonians. Cyrus allows captured nations to return (in return for their loyalty), including the Judeans in 537.

520–515 BCE Foundation laid for the Jerusalem ("Second") Temple; rebuilt over 5 years.

450–400 BCE Reforms of Ezra and Nehemiah; text of the Bible (Torah) reconstructed.

438 BCE Achashverosh becomes king of Persia.

ca. 426 BCE The Purim story—decrees of Haman; fast ordered by Esther; Haman's downfall and execution—recounted in Megillat (Scroll of) Esther.

331 BCE Alexander the Great conquers the land of Israel; is met outside of Jerusalem by high priest, about whom Alexander dreams the night before.

ca. 250 BCE Septuagint ("of the 70") translation of Torah into Greek, in Alexandria.

ca. 230–146 BCE Rome supplants Greece as the dominant empire in east Mediterranean.

175 BCE Antiochus, king of Syria, plunders Jerusalem and Temple; begins persecutions.

166–160 BCE Maccabean revolt against restrictions on practice of Judaism and pagan desecration of the Temple. Achieve victory at Battle of Emmaus, 166.

142–129 BCE Jews rule Israel "autonomously" under the Hasmoneans.

63 BCE Rome (Pompey) annexes land of Israel.

66-73 CE First Jewish Revolt against Rome.

69 CE Vespasian allows Yochanan ben Zakkai to establish a Jewish academy at Yavneh—center for rabbinic reinvention of Judaism.

66–70 The Great Jewish Revolt against Rome ends with destruction of the Second Temple and the sacking of Jerusalem.

70–200 The rabbis (called *Tannaim*–redactors) reorganize in the wake of the disaster. They codify oral traditions as the Mishnah, essential text of Jewish law, along with other (lesser) compilations. Process takes nearly 150 years; sealed by Judah HaNasi (The Prince) in 200.

73 Masada falls; Rome's victory is complete.

131 Roman emperor Hadrian renames Jerusalem Aeolia Capitolina; bars Jews.

132–135 Bar Kokhba revolt against Emperor Hadrian fails, and province of Judea is renamed Syria Palaestina, or Palestine.

220–500 The rabbis (called *Amoraim*—reviewers) in Babylonia and Israel analyze the Mishna and form basis of Talmud.

315–337 Roman Emperor Constantine I enacts new restrictions. Conversion of Christians to Judaism outlawed, meeting for religious services curtailed, but Jews may now enter Jerusalem (but only on the anniversary of the Temple's destruction).

358 Hillel II creates a perpetual calendar for calculating the Jewish dates. After adopting it, the Tiberias Sanhedrin (which had set the calendar monthly) is dissolved.

361–363 Julian, the last pagan Roman emperor, allows Jews to return to Jerusalem, and grants permission to rebuild the Temple.

438 Empress Eudocia removes ban on Jewish prayer at the Temple site. Heads of the Community in Galilee call for return.

450 Redaction of the (lesser) Talmud of Jerusalem.

550 Redaction of Babylonian Talmud by rabbis Ravina and Ashi, though text will continue to be modified for 200 years.

550–700 Period of the *Savoraim* ("analysts"), sages in Persia who put the Talmud in its final form. Jews in Israel are living under the oppressive rule of the Byzantines. After several revolts, expelled again in 628.

MEDIEVAL JEWISH HISTORY

7th century The rise of Islam, first in the Arabian peninsula; complete removal (or conversion) of that Jewish community.

700–1250 Period of the *Gaonim* (the "great ones")—the Gaonic era. Jews in southern Europe and Asia Minor live under the oppressive Christian kings. But most Jews live in tolerant Muslim Arab lands (Andalusia, North Africa, Palestine, Iraq, and Yemen), despite periodic persecution.

711 Muslims invade, occupy most of Spain. Jews (who were persecuted by Christians) enjoy "golden age" under Muslims.

846 *Siddur* (prayer book) of Rabbi Amram Gaon, dean of Sura Academy in Iraq.

900–1090 Height of Golden Age of Jewish culture in Spain. Abd-ar-Rahman III becomes caliph of Spain in 912; great tolerance. Muslims grant Jews and Christians exemptions from military service, right to courts of law, guarantee of safety of property. Jewish poets, scholars, scientists, statesmen, and philosophers flourish. Period ends with Almoravide invasion of 1090.

940 In Iraq, Saadia Gaon compiles his *siddur* (prayer book), which becomes standard.

1040–1105 Rabbi Shlomo Yitzhaki (acronym: Rashi) writes important commentaries on Hebrew Bible and Talmud.

1095–1291 The Crusades. Warfare with Islam in Palestine results in Crusaders temporarily capturing Jerusalem in 1099. Many Jews killed by European crusaders throughout Europe and the Middle East.

1107 Moroccan Almoravid ruler Yoseph Ibn Tashfin expels Moroccan Jews who refuse to convert to Islam.

1135–1204 Rabbi Moses ben Maimon (Maimonides or Rambam) is leading rabbi of Sephardic Jewry. He writes an important code of law (*Mishneh Torah*) as well as, in Arabic, an influential philosophical work (*Guide for the Perplexed*).

1141 Yehuda Halevi calls for Jews to emigrate to Palestine; eventually dies in Jerusalem.

1250–1300 Moses de Leon of Spain authors the *Zohar*, purported to be a second century work of esoteric interpretations of the Torah by Talmudic rabbi Shimon bar Yochai and disciples. Thus begins the modern Kabbalah (Jewish mysticism).

1250–1550 Period of the Rishonim—the "early" medieval rabbinic sages.

1267 Nahmanides (Ramban) settles in Jerusalem and builds the Ramban Synagogue.

1270–1343 Rabbi Jacob ben Asher of Spain writes the *Arbah Turim* ("Four Rows"), to become basis of all later Jewish law.

1290 Jews expelled from England by Edward I.

1300 Heyday of Rabbi Levi ben Gershom, (Gersonides), French Jewish philosopher, author of *Sefer Milhamot Adonai* ("The Book of the Wars of the Lord").

1306–1394 Jews are repeatedly expelled from France, then readmitted after payment.

1343 Jews in Western Europe invited to Poland by Casimir the Great.

1478 King Ferdinand and Queen Isabella of Spain begin Spanish Inquisition.

1486 First Jewish prayer book published in Italy.

1488–1575 Rabbi Yosef Karo compiles the mammoth *Beit Yosef*, a comprehensive guide to Jewish law; later a somewhat concise version, *Shulkhan Arukh* ("Set Table") that becomes the standard legal guide for the next 400 years. Originally from Spain, he lives and dies in Safed.

1492 The Alhambra Decree: Over 200,000 Jews expelled from Spain relocate in the Netherlands, Turkey, Arab lands, and Judea; some go to South and Central America, most to Poland. In two centuries, half the world's Jews live in Poland. Jews who remain in Spain publicly convert to Christianity while living as crypto-Jews (Marranos).

1492 Bayezid II of the Ottoman Empire issues formal invitation (and ships) to the Jews expelled from Spain and Portugal.

1493 Jews (over 130,000) expelled from Sicily.

1496 Jews expelled from Portugal and many German cities.

1501 King Alexander of Poland readmits Jews to Grand Duchy of Lithuania.

1516 Ghetto of Venice established—first Jewish ghetto in Europe. Others follow.

1525–1572 Rabbi Moshe Isserles (acronym: Rama) of Cracow writes extensive gloss to the *Shulkhan Arukh* for Ashkenazic Jewry.

1534 King Sigismund I of Poland abolishes law requiring Jews to wear special clothes.

1534 First Yiddish book published, in Poland.

1534–1572 Rabbi Isaac Luria ("the Arizal") teaches Kabbalah in Jerusalem and Safed. Some (like Chaim Vital) commit his teachings to writing.

1547 First Hebrew Jewish printing house, Lublin.

1550 Kabbalah academy founded in Safed by Moses ben Jacob Cordovero.

1567 First Jewish rabbinical academy (*yeshiva*), after 500 years, founded in Poland.

1577 Hebrew printing press established in Safed—first in Palestine or Asia.

EARLY MODERN JEWISH HISTORY

1580–1764 Council of Four Lands (Va'ad Arba' Aratzot) meets in Lublin, Poland, to discuss taxation and other issues important to the Jewish community.

1626–1676 Period of False Messiah Sabbatai Zevi.

1648 Jewish population of Poland reached 450,000 (4% of population). Worldwide Jewish population estimated at 750,000.

1648–1655 Ukrainian Cossack Bohdan Chmielnicki leads massacre of 65,000 Polish Jews.

1655 Jews readmitted to England by Oliver Cromwell.

1700–1760 Period of Israel ben Eliezer—the Ba'al Shem Tov—founds Hassidic movement, a way to approach God through meditation and fervent joy. He and his disciples attract many followers, and establish numerous Hassidic sects. Jewish opponents of Hassidim (known as Mitnagdim) follow more scholarly approach to Judaism.

1720 Arabs burn Jerusalem synagogue of Rabbi Judah the Pious and expel all Ashkenazic Jews from Jerusalem.

1720–1797 Rabbi Elijah, the gaon of Vilna.

1729–1786 Period of Haskalah (Enlightenment) movement and Moses Mendelssohn. Haskalah opens the door for the development of modern Jewish denominations and revival of Hebrew language; but also results in many conversions to Christianity.

1740 Parliament of Great Britain permits Jews to be naturalized in the American colonies. Previously, several colonies had also permitted Jews to be naturalized without taking a Christian oath.

1740 Ottomans invite Rabbi Haim Abulafia (1660–1744), Kabbalist and rabbi of Izmir, to Holy Land to rebuild city of Tiberias—spurring Messianic hopes.

1740–1750 Thousands immigrate to Palestine under the influence of messianic predictions, greatly increasing size and strength of Jewish settlement.

1747 Rabbi Abraham Gershon of Kitov (brother-in-law of Rabbi Israel Baal Shem Tov) begins the Hassidic aliyah (emigration to Israel). He first settles in Hebron, but later relocates to Jerusalem.

1772–1795 Partitions of Poland between Russia, kingdom of Prussia, and Austria. Privileges of Jewish communities revoked.

1775–1781 American Revolution.

1789 The French revolution. France grants full right to Jews in 1791 and allows them to become citizens (with restrictions).

1790 U.S. president George Washington sends letter to the Jewish community in Rhode Island, envisioning a country "which gives bigotry no sanction . . . persecution no assistance." Jewish number is limited.

MODERN JEWISH HISTORY

1791 Russia creates Pale of Settlement—includes land acquired from Poland with a large Jewish population; later that year, Crimea. The Pale's Jewish population tops 750,000.

1798 Rabbi Nachman of Breslov (mystical Hassidic master) emigrates to Palestine.

1799 Napoleon prepares proclamation making Palestine independent Jewish state, but abandons plan when siege of Acre fails.

1800–1900 Golden Age of Yiddish literature; revival of Hebrew language literature.

1808–1840 Active aliyah in anticipation of calculated arrival of the Messiah in 1840.

1820–1860 Development of Orthodox Judaism—traditionalists who resist influences of modernization and adhere strictly to traditional Jewish law (Halakha).

1831 Jewish militias defend Warsaw against Russians.

1837 Moses Montefiore, first Jew knighted by Queen Victoria; earthquake devastates Jewish communities of Safed, Tiberias.

1838–1933 Rabbi Yisroel Meir ha-Kohen (the Chofetz Chaim) opens important yeshiva; writes definitive Halakhic work, *Mishnah Berurah*.

Mid-1800s Rise of Reform Judaism; Rabbi Israel Salanter's Mussar (ethics-centered) movement; and Conservative Judaism.

1841 David Levy Yulee of Florida is elected to the United States Senate, becoming the first Jew elected to Congress.

1858 Jews emancipated in England.

1860 Alliance Israelite Universelle, international Jewish organization is founded in Paris with goal to protect Jewish rights.

1860–1875 Moshe Montefiori builds Jewish section outside Old City of Jerusalem.

1860–1864 Jews take part in Polish national movement, followed by January rising.

1860–1943 Henrietta Szold: educator, author, social worker, and founder of Hadassah.

1861 Zion Society formed in Frankfurt am Main, Germany.

1862 Jews are given equal rights in Russian-controlled Congress Kingdom of Poland.

1868 Benjamin Disraeli becomes prime minister of England. Converted to Christianity as child, yet he is first Jew to become a leader of a government in Europe.

1870–1890 Russian Zionist group Hovevei Zion (Lovers of Zion) and Bilu (est. 1882) set up a series of Jewish settlements in Palestine, financially aided by Baron Edmond James de Rothschild.

1875 Hebrew Union (Reform) College founded in Cincinnati by Rabbi Isaac Mayer Wise, architect of American Reform Judaism.

1877 New Hampshire becomes last state to give Jews equal political rights.

1878 Petah Tikva founded by religious pioneers from Jerusalem led by Yehoshua Stampfer.

1880 World Jewish population estimated at 7.7 million, mostly in Eastern Europe; 3.5 million in former Polish provinces.

1881–1884, 1903–1906, 1918–1920 Three major pogroms kill tens of thousands of Jews in Russia and Ukraine. More than 2 million Russian Jews emigrate in the period 1881–1920.

1881 First Congress Zionist Unions for the colonization of Palestine held at Focflani, Romania, December 30.

1882–1903 The First Aliyah, major wave of Jewish immigrants to Palestine.

1886 Rabbi Sabato Morais and Alexander Kohut lead Conservative Jewish reaction to American Reform and establish the Jewish Theological Seminary of America as a school of "enlightened Orthodoxy."

1890 Term "Zionism" coined by Austrian Jewish publicist Nathan Birnbaum in his journal *Self*

Emancipation; defined as the national movement for the return of the Jewish people to their homeland, resumption of Jewish sovereignty in land of Israel.

1897 In response to the Dreyfus affair, Theodore Herzl writes *Der Judenstaat* (The Jewish State), advocating creation of free and independent Jewish state in Israel.

1897 The Bund (General Jewish Labor Union) formed in Russia.

1897 First Russian Empire census: 5,200,000 Jews, 4,900,000 in the Pale. Poland has 1,300,000 Jews, or 14% of population.

20TH- AND 21ST-CENTURY JEWISH HISTORY

1902 Rabbi Dr. Solomon Schechter reorganizes the Jewish Theological Seminary as flagship of Conservative Judaism.

1903 St. Petersburg's *Znamya* newspaper publishes literary hoax "The Protocols of the Elders of Zion." Kishinev Pogrom caused by libel that Jews practice cannibalism.

1905 Albert Einstein's *Annus Mirabilis* Papers published. 1905 Russian Revolution accompanied by pogroms.

1907–1972 Rabbi Abraham Joshua Heschel, significant Jewish theologian of 20th century.

1910s–1980s Art of Marc Chagall, often dealing with Jewish cultural and historical topics, makes him world-renowned.

1915 Yeshiva College (later University) and its Rabbi Isaac Elchanan (Orthodox) Rabbinical Seminary is established in New York.

1917 The British defeat the Turks and gain control of the land of Israel. The British issue the Balfour Declaration, which gives official British support for "the establishment in Palestine of a national home for the Jewish people."

1917 February The Pale of Settlement abolished; Jews get equal rights. The Russian civil war leads to over 2,000 pogroms with tens of thousands murdered, and hundreds of thousand made homeless.

1918–1939 Period between the two World Wars often referred to as "golden age" of *hazzanut* (cantors). Some greats include Abraham Davis, Moshe Koussevitzky, Zavel Kwartin, Jan Peerce, Yossele Rosenblatt, Gershon Sirota, Laibele Waldman.

1920 At the San Remo Conference, Britain receives the League of Nations' British mandate of Palestine.

1920s–Present A variety of Jewish authors, including Gertrude Stein, Allen Ginsberg, Saul Bellow, Adrienne Rich, and Philip Roth, sometimes drawing on Jewish culture and history, flourish and become influential.

1921 British military administration of the mandate is replaced by civilian rule.

1921 Britain proclaims that all of Palestine east of the Jordan River is henceforth closed to Jewish (but not Arab) settlement.

1921 Polish-Soviet peace treaty in Riga. Citizens of both sides are given rights to choose their country. Hundred thousands of Jews, especially small businesses forbidden in the Soviets, move to Poland.

1922 Reform Rabbi Stephen S. Wise establishes the Jewish Institute of Religion in New York. (It merges with Hebrew Union College in 1950.)

1923 Britain gives the Golan Heights to the French mandate of Syria. Arab immigration is allowed; Jewish immigration is not.

1930 World Jewry: 15,000,000. Main countries: USA (4,000,000); Poland (3,500,000); Soviet Union (2,700,000); Romania (1,000,000); Palestine 175,000 (or 17% of total 1,036,000).

1930s-1940s Marx Brothers, a former American Vaudeville act, make series of successful films, becoming arguably the most famous comic entertainers of all time.

1933 Hitler takes over Germany; his antisemitic sentiments are well known, which prompts numerous Jews to emigrate.

1937 Adin Steinsaltz born, author of first Babylonian Talmud commentary since Rashi.

1939 British government issues "White Paper" reversing support of Balfour Declaration. Announce absolute limit of only 75,000 on future Jewish immigration to Palestine.

1938-1945 The Holocaust (Sho'ah): Destruction of 6 million European Jews by Nazis.

1945-1948 Post-Holocaust refugee crisis. British detain many Jews making aliyah to Palestine in detention camps.

1946-1948 Struggle for the creation of a Jewish state in British mandate of Palestine is resumed by Jewish underground movements: Haganah, Irgun, and Lehi.

November 29, 1947 United Nations approves creation of a Jewish state and an Arab state in British mandate of Palestine.

May 14, 1948 Israel declared independent nation. Andrei Gromyko, Soviet Union's UN ambassador, calls for UN to accept Israel as member state. UN approves.

May 15, 1948 Arab-Israeli War: Syria, Iraq, Transjordan, Lebanon, and Egypt invade Israel; attack fails; Israel becomes a state.

1948-1949 Almost 250,000 Holocaust survivors arrive in Israel. Operation Magic Carpet brings Yemenite Jews to Israel.

1956 The 1956 Suez War: Egypt blockades the Gulf of Aqaba, and closes the Suez canal to Israeli shipping. Egypt's President Nasser calls for the destruction of Israel. Israel, England, and France go to war and force Egypt to end the blockade.

1964 Jewish-Christian relations revolutionized by Roman Catholic Church's Vatican II.

1966 Shmuel Yosef Agnon (1888–1970) becomes first Hebrew writer to win the Nobel Prize in literature.

May 16, 1967 Egyptian President Nasser demands the UN dismantle the UN Emergency Force I (UNEF I) between Israel and Egypt. The UN complies.

Nasser then closes the strategic Straits of Tiran to Israeli shipping and states that Egypt is in a state of war with Israel.

June 5-11, 1967 Six-Day War; Israel victorious, but a tense peace follows with larger borders more difficult to defend.

September 1, 1967 Arab Leaders meet in Khartoum, Sudan. The Three No's of Khartoum: No recognition of Israel. No negotiations with Israel. No peace.

1968 Rabbi Mordechai Kaplan formally creates Reconstructionist Judaism movement by setting up Reconstructionist Rabbinical College in Philadelphia suburb.

1972 Mark Spitz sets the record for most gold medals won in a single Olympic Games (seven) in the 1972 Summer Olympics, site of the Munich massacre. Record to stand for over thirty-five years.

Oct. 6–24, 1973 The Yom Kippur War. Syria, Egypt, and Morocco launch surprise attack against Israel. Subsequently, OPEC reduces oil production, driving up oil prices, triggering a global economic crisis.

1975 President Gerald Ford signs Jackson-Vanik amendment, which ties U.S. trade benefits for Soviet Union to Jewish emigration.

1975 United Nations adopts resolution equating Zionism with racism. Rescinded 1991.

1976 Israel rescues hostages in Entebbe, Uganda.

September 18, 1978 Israel and Egypt sign Camp David Accord, which includes the withdrawal of Israel from the Sinai.

1978 Yiddish writer Isaac Bashevis Singer receives Nobel Prize.

1979 Prime Minister Menachem Begin, President Anwar Sadat share Nobel Peace Prize.

1979–1985 Operations Elijah, Moses, and Joshua rescue much of Ethiopian Jewry.

June–December, 1982 The Lebanon War. Israel invades to drive out the PLO.

1983 American Reform Jews accept patrilineal descent in defining who is a Jew.

1986 Elie Wiesel wins the Nobel Peace Prize.

1986 Nathan Sharansky, Soviet Jewish dissident, is freed from prison.

1987 Beginning of First Intifada against Israel.

1989 Fall of Berlin Wall between East and West Germany, collapse of the Communist East German government. Germany reunified.

1990 The Soviet Union allows 3 million Soviet Jews to leave; many move to Israel.

1990–1991 Iraq invades Kuwait; First Gulf War. Israel hit by thirty-nine Scud missiles from Iraq.

1991 Operation Solomon: Rescue of remainder of Ethiopian Jewry in twenty-four-hour airlift.

September 13, 1993 Israel, PLO sign Oslo Accords.

1994 Lubavitcher (Chabad) Rebbe (leader), Menachem Mendel Schneerson, dies.

October 26, 1994 Israel and Jordan sign peace treaty; open official diplomatic relations, open borders and free trade.

December 10, 1994 Arafat, Rabin, and Israeli Foreign Minister Shimon Peres share Nobel Peace Prize.

November 4, 1995 Israeli Prime Minister Yitzhak Rabin is assassinated.

1996 Peres loses election to Benyamin ("Bibi") Netanyahu (Likud Party).

1999 Ehud Barak elected Israel prime minister.

May 24, 2000 Israel unilaterally withdraws from security zone in southern Lebanon to international border, fully complying with UN Security Council Res. 425.

July 2000 Camp David Summit.

Summer, 2000 Senator Joseph Lieberman becomes first Jewish-American to be nominated for a national office (vice president) by a major political (Democratic) party.

September 29, 2000 The al-Aqsa Intifada begins.

2001 Ariel Sharon elected Israel prime minister.

March 31, 2005 The Government of Israel officially recognizes the Bnei Menashe people of northeastern India as one of Ten Lost Tribes of Israel, opening door for thousands to immigrate to Israel.

2005 August Israel withdraws military forces and Jewish settlers from Gaza Strip.

FURTHER READING IN JEWISH HISTORY

For ancient history and the biblical period:

The Gifts of the Jews
Tom Cahill
1998: Doubleday

How to Read the Bible
James L. Kugel
2007: Free Press

Understanding Genesis and *Exploring Exodus*
Nahum M. Sarna
1970, 1996: Schocken Books

Ancient Israel
Hershel Shanks, ed.
1999: Prentice-Hall

For excellent general, panoramic histories:

A Historical Atlas of the Jewish People
Eli Barnavi
2003: Schocken Books

A History of the the Jewish People
Hayim Ben-Sasson
1985: Harvard University Press

The Jew in the Modern World
Paul Mendes-Flohr and Jehuda Reinharz, eds.
1995: Oxford University Press

For excellent surveys of Jewish thought:

To Be a Jew
Hayim H. Donin
1991: Basic Books

Living Judaism
Wayne D. Dosick
1998: HarperOne

Essential Judaism
George Robinson
2001: Atria

The Sabbath World
Judith Shulevitz
2010: Random House

Jewish Literacy
Joseph Telushkin
1991: William Morrow

1 The Jewish Faith

I. Defining Judaism

A. Introduction

THE WAY OF LIFE THAT HAS COME TO BE CALLED Judaism has been some 5,000 years in the making. Religions have come and gone; empires have marched across continents only to then march off into oblivion as they were replaced by others. Judaism has been written off many times, yet it persists and endures, sometimes under inhumanly difficult circumstances. If ever a long shot in history has come through, it's the Jewish people and their faith.

Judaism, to paraphrase Mark Twain, is much like other religions—only more so. Having had more time to develop; having to adapt to radically different circumstances, epochs, and situations; and

The word "Torah" comes from the Hebrew for "to teach," and can refer both to the first five books of the Old Testament (sometimes called the Pentateuch) and, more generally, to Jewish law.

having been built on a foundation of a teacher telling a student, who then tells another, thereby becoming a teacher himself or herself—these are what accounts for the richness and vitality of Judaism and Jewish learning.

The central document of Judaism is the Torah, which is usually translated as "Bible," but the word "Bible" comes from the Greek for "book," and that conveys something all wrong from a Jewish point of view. Books are static, inert, inanimate. That is not what Torah means to Jews at all. The word comes from the word "to teach" and it conveys the idea of teaching and transmission, of the quest for knowledge and understanding, of the need to transmit what has been learned so that it can be reviewed and reformulated. In Judaism, early sages may be venerated, but the law is determined by the later scholars. The analysis of text, concepts, arguments, principles—these are the essence of Jewish civilization. Observance is important, to be sure, but in Judaism, no human failing is worse than ignorance.

Readers may be forgiven for being skeptical of the claim now being made that they will read the essential element of all of Judaism before they leave this page! Yet, that is the case, for the basic principle behind all of Judaism can be summarized in one word: study. The essence of Judaism and the Jewish way of life is that the paramount value is study—study of the law; study of the tradition; study of the intricacies of God and Creation;

study of what has been said by those who studied what was said before; study of how Jews lived and coped; study of the world and the intricacies of nature (because there is no such thing as irrelevant knowledge); study of—*everything*! Religions are frequently based on a single core value or concept—it might be obedience to God; love of God; harmony with the world; and so on. For Judaism, that core value is simply study—love of study, pursuit of study, support of study, conveying what is studied, building on study. This is put simply by a Rabbinic aphorism: *Talmud Torah k'ne-ged kulam*—"The study of Torah is comparable to all the rest."

B. What Other Torah?

The beginnings of Jewish learning are lost in the mists of early human history, before the invention of the tools and mechanisms by which developments are recorded and achievements are preserved. As was pointed out earlier, Jewish civilization is believed to be the source of many of these very elements that we today take for granted: history; documentation; oral traditions; putting ideas and rules into unambiguous, understood words. At a certain point in the history of the Jewish people, a document was created that was known as the Five Books of Moses (or the Five Books of the Torah), and just exactly what it consisted of and what was in it were of some question even to the people of the Bible itself. II Kings 22 recounts how a scroll was found in the Temple of Jerusalem during renovations ordered by King Josiah, and how the king sent the high priest, Hilkiah, to inquire of Huldah the Prophetess if the scroll was authentically the Torah. (According to some, what was found was the book of Deuteronomy, the Fifth Book of Moses.)

The incident underscores first the likelihood that during periods when the people were ruled by kings who led them away from adherence to the practices of the Torah (about which the prophets of Hebrew Scriptures chastised them often enough), they be-

came estranged from the document that was held in the Temple and which was bequeathed to them since antiquity—since the days of Moses. More importantly, however, it tells us that the sages who studied and ruled on Jewish law were also estranged from the sacred text of the Torah. The laws of the festivals and the Sabbath; the laws of the tithing and the Temple sacrifices; the laws of the prayers and service; the dietary laws and myriad others—all evidence indicates these were practiced, studied, transmitted, and developed all through the First Temple period. How, one may ask, is it possible that scholars would be so unfamiliar with the text of the Bible, that it would require a prophetess (presumably utilizing her prophetic gifts) to authenticate a biblical text?

The answer is an important one for understanding Judaism as a religion: There are, in fact, *two* Torahs. There is the written Torah that we know as the Bible, and traditionalist Jews and nontraditionalist Jews can (and do) "agree to disagree" on its provenance and composition—traditionalists believing the Torah was given at Sinai to the Israelites following their exodus from the bondage of Egypt under the leadership of Moses; and nontraditionalists believing the work was composed later (possibly during the days of that same King Josiah, or even later). It is not a trivial argument, but it is not the decisive issue in Judaism. It's the provenance, composition, content, and authority of the *other* Torah that is what all the real (and really heated and interesting) arguing is about.

The "other" Torah? "*What* other Torah?" one may ask. Judaism teaches that there was a second set of teachings—an Oral Law—that had its origins in antiquity and is the real source of and authoritative basis for behavior, ethics, ritual, jurisprudence among people, and service to God. The laws that are in written form in the Pentateuch are only summaries, mere allusions to larger principles and formulations, the surface of which the written law barely scratches.

The traditional viewpoint is that the Oral Law was given to Moses and the Israelites at the Revelation at Sinai (described in Exodus 19), though the traditionalists also believe that the Patriarchs observed the Law and studied and transmitted it. The process of analysis that engaged the Rabbis of the Talmud and later generations was part of a process that was carried out from teacher to student to student's student and so on for generations.

And what do the nontraditionalists believe? They say that the oral tradition was the invention of human beings and that the authority of that body of law is temporary and changeable—subject to reformulation and revision, and even radical overhauling. The categories, the nontraditionalists may say, have been established by history; there's nothing anyone can do about that. But what the law is and how one should behave is to be determined by people during their own time—and, of course, that means during *our* own time—using what we understand of ethics, what we know of the workings of the physical world, what type of social organization we believe will bring about human happiness and fulfillment, using all that to determine the law and the best way to live.

Notice, however, that both the traditionalist and the nontraditionalist (and later we will survey who falls into each category) undergo similar processes of analysis of text, synthesis of ideas, organization of principles, and applications of reasoning, as they both search for consistency with their logic, their history, and with the edifice of the laws of behavior and the rules of ritual they have created. In this sense, both the traditionalist and the nontraditionalist are engaged in a *Jewish* argument. This is not to say these differences are trivial, but they are Jewish, in ways that, say, the Karaites were not. By dismissing the Oral Law in any form and by not accepting rabbinic tradition as binding in any way—not even accepting knowledge of the traditions in any way relevant—immediately takes them out of the Jewish conversation and thus out of Judaism.

The same will be true of syncretic movements that adopt superficial Jewish names or artifacts (and often not even that much), but who espouse doctrines that cannot even be discussed within any sort of context that engages the rabbinic tradition: these

are simply not Jewish. (They may be something else, and no judgment is being made about their worth or value—but Jewish they are not.)

Into this category fall the various Jewish messianic movements: Jews for Jesus; Hebrew Christians; Judeo-Paganism (so-called Jewitchery); and systems that blend Judaism and Buddhism, Hinduism, or other religions. A significant number of Jews have adopted Buddhist elements into their thinking, seeing some common threads with certain Hassidic strains of thought. Known popularly as "Jubus," they often will select only those elements from the two traditions that promote personal notions about self-fulfillment and personal actualization. But if the combination introduces elements that are extraneous to the tradition (i.e., where no attempt is made to show that the tradition may be interpreted to include such beliefs and practices), then the belief system is simply not Jewish (again, however interesting and worthwhile it may be).

Even branches of Judaism that do not profess a belief in God or in Revelation, or who discount the authority of the rabbinic tradition, but which examine both of these for their spiritual content and personal enlightenment in devising their practices and beliefs—such as Reconstructionism and Humanistic Judaism—are still Jewish systems insofar as they *engage* the tradition in forming their tenets, beliefs, and practices. The disagreements between different branches of Judaism are not trivial, to be sure, but they are still all branches of the Jewish faith—because the discussion begins with the tradition.

II. Tenets and Beliefs

A. Articles of Faith

In traditional Judaism, there are 613 commandments—*mitzvot* (singular, *mitzvah*); that number seems to have been a tradition from antiquity. In lore, it equals the sum of the days of the solar year

(365), which is the number of negative commandments—"thou shalt not's"; and the bones and major organs in the human body (248), which is the number of positive commandments—"thou shalt's." Rabbinic scholars have debated about the exact list of the commandments, though there is agreement regarding most of them and about the number.

Less certain are the basic principles that underlie the commandments. Among the most revered rabbis and biblical commentators in Jewish history is Moses Maimonides (1135–1204; also known as Rambam, an acronym of his full Hebrew name, Rabbi Moses ben Maimon). Maimonides was perhaps the most influential rabbinic sage of the entire post-Talmudic period, brilliant in both rabbinics and Aristotelian philosophy (and evidently a first-rate physician). In his "Commentary on the Mishnah," Maimonides proposed Thirteen Principles of Faith that he considered essential tenets for leading a faithful Jewish life—in fact, for being considered part of the Jewish people at all! Earlier such "catechisms" were created to educate the general public about the essentials of Jewish belief, and later ones were designed to defend Judaism from challenges from Christian, Muslim, and other schools. Neither seems to have been the case with Maimonides and today we are not certain what he had in mind. (Perhaps he thought it possible to derive all of Jewish law from a Euclidean-like application of these "first principles," but that's just one man's speculation.) But the thirteen Principles became the most popular and oft-cited summary of Jewish faith, expressed in a thirteenth-century liturgical poem, "Yigdal," which is part of the daily morning service and is sung at the conclusion of the morning services on Sabbath and holidays.

Here in summary are those principles, along with some elements of Jewish practice, ritual, and law that incorporate and implement each ideal. Not all of Jewish law will be covered, but hopefully it will provide a sense of what Judaism is all about.

1. God is omnipotent creator of everything.

The universe did not happen by accident, Judaism teaches, neither did it always exist, nor did it come about through a natural consequence of physical law. It was created by an Almighty God, who is the author of all that exists. This is the monotheistic principle that set Judaism apart from other religions and which has set the tone and agenda for the remarkable human journey we know as religion.

The precept in Judaism that implements and symbolizes this belief is the Sabbath day (*shabbat*), the one day in seven on which one is to refrain from labor. The idea that one day in seven should be set aside for rest, resuscitation, and spiritual renewal may not have originated with the ancient Hebrews — modern theories connect the seven-day cycle to the early observation of the seven visible planets of astrology, or else to the phases of the moon. Regardless of its origin, it was certainly the ancient Hebrews and their heirs—from the Israelites of antiquity to the Jews of today—who have carried the banner of the Sabbath throughout history.

The Sabbath. In Judaism, the Sabbath contains two elements: the cessation of work; and the sanctification of life and home. The cessation of work (*melacha*) does not mean simply refraining from toil or labor, but from any creative, constructive work, regardless of the effort. Thus, writing, which may require very little physical labor, is prohibited, but what is interesting is that what is prohibited is the writing of two letters—a single letter would be a mere unintelligible mark, but two letters constitute a word or word element.

The rule is derived from the fact that two letters were required to label the beams used to erect the Tabernacle that traveled with the Israelites through the wilderness (Ex. 25–31). Thirty-nine such types of work were required in the construction and operation of the Tabernacle, and these are the thirty-nine main categories of work prohibited by rabbinic tradition on the Sabbath.

The Sabbath is also "an island in time," during which the human being not only recovers strength for the workweek, but discovers the dignity and beauty of home, hearth, and family. The day is to be one of rest, but also of familial conviviality—the home is to be light (starting with the lighting of Sabbath candles, generally done by the woman of the house), and warmth, with a fire burning from Friday afternoon and warm food that has steeped on a fire overnight. The Karaites, rejecting the rabbinic law, interpreted Exodus 35:3—"You shall kindle no fire throughout your settlements on the Sabbath day"—to mean that no fire could be burning, even if lit before the Sabbath. They thus spent Sabbath in the cold and dark. The lighting of candles and the eating of hot food on the Sabbath (properly prepared) thus became a way of rejecting this view and showing adherence to the rabbinic law.

But much more was meant: the Sabbath is to be a day of contemplation and spirituality; the home is to be a serene and dignified sanctuary; the day is to be honored with special foods, special attire, and the joy of family and friends. The Jewish Sabbath in the many settings in which it has been observed has been one of the most beautiful religious observances ever known, and it is responsible for that modern (though more frenetic) secular contrivance—the weekend.

2. God is One.

The biblical expression of the unity of God—the Shema, named after the first word of the Hebrew sentence (Deut. 6:4), "Hear, O Israel, the Lord is our God, the Lord is One."—is the most sacred sentence in Judaism. It has been recited by Jewish martyrs with their last breath; it was recited loudly by Jewish victims of the Holocaust as they were led to the gas chambers of Auschwitz. Traditionally, the verse is recited at least twice a day along with the three paragraphs that accompany it: Deut. 6:4–9 ("And you shall love the Lord your God with all your heart, with all your soul, with all your might…"); Deut. 11:13–21 ("And if you will obey My commandments…"); and Num. 15:37–41 (the section regarding *tzitzit*—fringes). Tradition has it that the eyes are covered when reciting the verse of Shema, and that the "d" ending of the final word, *echad* (one) is said with special emphasis (first, so it is not con-

fused with *acher*—"other"; and, second, to drive home the verse's monotheistic intent.

The first two paragraphs of the Shema are written on scrolls, then placed in small receptacles and affixed to the door posts of Jewish homes. This is known as a *mezuzah* and it has been a feature of Jewish domiciles for centuries. (Only in recent times has the mezuzah become an article of jewelry, serving as an amulet-like identification of the wearer as a member of the Jewish people.)

Judaism's strict and uncompromising monotheism gave Jewish and Muslim philosophers much to discuss, and separated them both from dualistic Zoroastrianism and from trinitarian Christianity.

(An odd sidelight of this principle is that Maimonides applies it also to the belief in many universes, where there may be other gods, or where God would have no dominion. He regards this as heretical, but such theories have usually been dismissed in the past as mystical and gnostic nonsense—until the idea was revived by, of all places, modern cosmological physics.)

3. God is not a material, corporeal being.

The obvious intent of this principle is to prohibit the worship of statuary and images, a mainstay of pagan religions, but one might have thought this principle superfluous after the previous one, for how can something singularly unique have a corporeal or material form, which would make it immediately like everything else, namely, material? Maimonides is here interested in addressing two problems: first, how is one to understand all the passages of the Bible in which God is described as having physical attributes and traits, even parts of a body (hand, eye, etc.)? Maimonides expends much of his masterpiece *The Guide for the Perplexed* (*Moreh Ne'vuchim*) to explaining these as anthropomorphisms that are not to be (and *may* not be) taken literally.

The second problem is a bit more difficult, as it arises from the biblical assertion (Gen 1:27) that humans (beginning with Adam) were created "in the image of God." What image is that if God *has* no image? A great deal of philosophic energy has been spent on understanding this phrase, but on its most basic level, it means (at least) that there is something about the human being that is Godlike, that bears a meaningful resemblance to the God who has no likeness or material appearance. (In fact, the logic might go: God has no image; humans have something about their physicality that resembles God, is in His image; thus, there must be *something* about human physical existence that is divine and Godlike.)

From this comes the very central Jewish value regarding the sanctity of the human form, the human body. Jews have since antiquity abhorred mutilation of the body in any form. The Bible already indicates (Deut. 21:22–33) that a criminal who is executed by hanging should not be allowed to be left hanging overnight, but must be buried the same day, "for a hanged body is an affront to God." This is the rationale behind the prohibitions of body incision (Lev. 19:28), scarification, and tattooing. It is also the basis of allowing the beard to grow: shaving with a straight razor against the skin is deemed a mutilation. It is also the reason Jewish tradition has been opposed to autopsies, even when mandated for a criminal investigation or for medical research. What about organ donation (both for deposit in an organ bank or for immediate use in either non-life-threatening or life-threatening situations)? The opinions vary widely from branch to branch (and even within each branch), but the underlying consideration is clear and universal in Jewish thought: what is or is not to be considered defacement or mutilation of the human body. Human history (and newspaper headlines) are more than adequately filled with episodes where an appreciation of this value would have prevented a great deal of human misery.

4. God is eternal.

We humans have some idea about what it means to create something, and we have some idea about what it means to be "one of a kind." We even have (or imagine we have) a notion about what non-corporeal existence might be like. But when it comes to eternity and infinity, our minds are simply not up to the challenge. It is therefore not surprising that, of the names of God that appear in the Bible and in Jewish literature, the one that is most revered and regarded as the most sacred is the one that alludes to the concept of the eternity of God. This is the four-letter name of God formed by the Hebrew letters *yod, hey, vav,* and *hey,* known as the Tetragrammaton (sometimes symbolized by "YHVH" or mispronounced "Yahweh" or "Jehovah").

This name is the one that is used in every Jewish blessing, as in *boruch atah*—and then the name, and translated as "Blessed art Thou or Lord..." In fact, the name is never pronounced; in Jewish tradition, the name is substituted with the word *adonai*, which means "my Lord," and strict Jews will never even pronounce that word except in prayer or while reciting a blessing, using the substitute *hashem,* which means simply "the name," in ordinary discourse. The name was inscribed on the miter (headplate) of the high priest in the Temple and was properly pronounced (the exact pronunciation a closely guarded secret) only once a year by the high priest at the climax of the service for the Day of Atonement. In many prayer books and Hebrew texts, a substitute form—two *yod*s or simply a lone *dalet*—will be used. Other names of God are viewed as descriptive; the Tetragrammaton is regarded as a personal name, though it is also indicative of the Divine quality of mercy in the rabbinic tradition. The list that appears in the Mishnah (Sanhedrin 10:1) of those who have no share in the "world to come" includes, "he who uses the [four-letter] name of God [presumably for magical purposes]." Yet, the name appears in the Bible over 6,800 times.

Why all the mystery? Possibly because of the verses in Exodus in which God appears to Moses in the Burning Bush, during which Moses asks what he should say if he is asked what is the name of the God who has sent him to take the Israelites out of Egypt. God's reply (Ex. 3:14–15) is: "I am that I am (*ehyeh asher ehyeh*—more correctly translated, "I will be the one who will be"); tell them, '[the Tetragrammaton], the God of your fathers... has sent me to you,' and this shall be My name forever." Later (6:3), God tells Moses, "I appeared to Abraham, Isaac, and Jacob as 'El Shaddai', but I did not make myself known to them as '[the Tetragrammaton]'." The message (or code) that Moses is given clearly establishes God as the deity who transcends time—the very name is clearly a contraction of sorts of the Hebrew for the three verb forms of "was," "is," and "will be." This identification of God and God's name with the *temporal* eternity of God and making that the most sacred form of address and appellation, and the consequent reverence that is accorded that name in Jewish life and ritual, may be viewed as an application of Maimonides's fourth principle.

Biblical criticism. The Tetragrammaton plays another important role in Jewish life: It is the name of God used in what Bible critics call the J Document. The J Document ("J" stands for *Jah-weh*, the German rendering of *Yahweh*) is purported to be one of the four documents that were combined to create the Biblical text (of the Pentateuch) that we know. The J Document used the Tetragrammaton to refer to God; the E Document used *Elohim* to refer to God; the P Document is the Priestly Code, largely comprising the book of Leviticus; and the D Document is Deuteronomy, with both the P and the D Documents contributing small bits to the other biblical books. The basis for thinking the Bible text consists of a redacted (edited) amalgam of the four sources is (mainly) the repetition of various stories and segments in the text.

Traditionalists in Judaism reject this Documentary Hypothesis, believing that the source of the Pentateuch is Moses, and that there are adequate explanations for the repetitions. Nontraditionalists may or may not accept the Documentary Hypothesis, in some cases believing the text has been corrupted over generations; in other cases believing the text was created anew the late First Temple or Second Temple Period; or believing the text is a historical "echo" of earlier oral versions that were set to writing in the mid- to late Second Temple Period. In any case, this matter is still hotly debated and rigorously inves-

tigated. Two historical problems that biblical criticism must deal with, however, is (a) how the Septuagint (the translation of the Bible into Greek in the third century BCE) was so revered if it was virtually a newly created text; and (b) how a document that used the most venerated name of God was treated equally with the other documents in the editing process—*if* such a redacting ever, in fact, took place.

5. God alone should be worshipped.

The quintessential prayer in Judaism is the Amidah ("standing"), so-called because it is said while standing erect, with feet together. All Jewish prayer revolves around this highlight of the liturgy. It is also called the *Shemoneh Esrei* ("eighteen") because it has eighteen blessings (or, more correctly *had* eighteen, until another was added). This prayer is often called the Shemoneh Esrei even on those days when there are fewer than eighteen blessings in the prayer, because the prayer always starts with the same three opening blessings, ends with the same three closing blessings, and is always said while standing erect. And one other thing, something that makes this a unique prayer not only in Judaism, but in religion in general: it is said silently. Worshippers mutter, or whisper, or sometimes even just mouth the words of the prayer. In synagogues around the world and for many centuries, at the climax of services that are marked with cantorial outcries and loudly fervent prayer, everything comes to a halt and the congregation stands in place, often swaying back and forth devotionally, as is often the custom in Jewish prayer, reciting the Amidah in hushed silence.

The remarkable reason for this is that the Sages took a lesson from a woman named Hannah, who came to the sanctuary at Shiloh in the period of Israelite settlement in Canaan, but before the era of the Kings, beginning with Saul. She came to pray for a child. The custom was for supplicants to call out their names and their needs to the priests (*kohanim*) offering sacrifices, so that the *kohein* (singular) would think of them when offering the sacrifice. The opening of the book of Samuel tells the poignant story:

The Western Wall in Jerusalem—seen at night in this 2005 photograph—is a holy site where Jews from all nations come to pray.

As Hannah prayed for a child, the high priest, Eli, saw her at the gate, and while everyone there was yelling at the top of their lungs, Hannah was standing and praying silently, only moving her lips. Eli, thinking she was drunk, chastised her for coming to the House of God inebriated. Hannah answers (I Sam. 1:15) that she has had nothing to drink: "I have been pouring out my heart to the Lord." Eli simply sent her away with the assurance that her prayer would be answered, but one can almost feel his stunned reaction (the "aha!" moment) between the lines. Prayer, he realizes, must be a private and intimate thing, between the person and God—not through intermediaries and not through loud outcries or priestly sacrifices.

It probably took some time for this manner of prayer to become universally accepted in Israel. (A persistent problem, once the Temples were built and the walls were high enough to shield the priests from calls from outside, was priests being pelted by stones being thrown over the walls wrapped in parchment, on which were the names and needs of the people outside. To solve this, the Temple administrators agreed to collect daily any notes left in the crannies of the wall and bring them to the priests—a custom—the note-leaving part—still observed today.) But by the Second Temple, this form of prayer, if not the full eighteen-blessing formula, was well established.

In spite of the firm Jewish belief that one should not pray to God in any way other than directly, and never through an intermediary, it has been customary to at times pray to an angelic or spiritual essence (the soul of a righteous departed, or an angel who pleads for humans in the mystical Heavenly Court, called *machnisei rachamim*—"emissaries of mercy" in the liturgy), or even to a flesh-and-blood righteous individual who will pray on one's behalf. This practice, however, was viewed as, at best, supplementary prayer, and not the primary form. In fact, the reliance of Hassidic adherents on the *tzaddik*—their rabbi and leader—to intercede with God on their behalf was practice non-Hassidic theologians found particularly objectionable.

6. God spoke to humanity through prophets.

Though quite the rationalist, Maimonides still believed thoroughly in prophecy. He believed, in fact, that all insight and ideas were gifts from God, bestowed upon humankind through what the Islamic philosophers called the "active intellect." For Maimonides, therefore, prophecy was a (very) heightened version of something that happens all the time—thinking. It follows, therefore, that prophecy is attainable by anyone with enough training, innate talent (though Maimonides might have taken that for granted), and righteous character.

Other Jewish thinkers objected to this "egalitarian" approach to prophecy (wondering why, if so, the era of prophecy ever came to an end); but they object even more to including this principle among the basic tenets of the faith (however important a belief they agreed it was). That this principle really is, as Maimonides proposed, critical in Judaism is indicated by the fact that *the* most important element of the Jewish liturgy and worship service—the Kedushah—is nothing more or less than the report of two biblical prophets of how they saw the angels worshipping God in their prophetic visions.

Isaiah reports (6:1–3) how he beheld the Seraphim (angels) in attendance around the Heavenly Throne of God turn to each other and call out, "Holy, holy, holy is the Lord of Hosts! All the world is filled with His presence." And Ezekiel reports (3:12) that he heard (but did not see) the angels praising God by saying, "Blessed is the Glory of the Lord in His Place." These two verses are recited by the congregation (for they may only be recited by a *minyan*—a quorum) during the reader's public repetition of the Amidah. The worshippers stand at attention, their feet together—because that's how the angels appeared to Ezek. (1:7), their legs fused. During the responsive recitation of these verses, worshippers bow from side to side as if addressing one another, because so did the angels (Isa. 6:3), and they lift themselves on their toes three times, one for each "holy," and once again for "blessed," to symbolize the worshipper's aspiration to join the angels in praising God.

The Kedusha service is brief and not given to very much embellishment, so it is often overlooked in the course of the many prayers and elements of the synagogue service, but its centrality and importance is as direct an affirmation of the Jewish belief in prophecy as one can imagine.

7. Moses was the greatest of the prophets.

The next three principles are interconnected: Moses is the greatest of the prophets *because* he is the means by which the Torah was given at Sinai, and that Torah is important *because* it was complete and immutable. Jewish attitudes toward Moses are not without misgivings—he is seen as not without his flaws and at times short-tempered and difficult, even in his relationship with God. (It has appeared to

more than one exegete that Moses is really trying God's patience, as it were, in their conversation at the Burning Bush of Exodus 3–4.)

But it is the quality of Moses's relationship with and perception of God that is crucial. The vision that Moses is purported to have had was direct and unmediated: he spoke to God, it is said in the Bible, "face to face" (Ex. 33:11), though when God Himself describes the relationship (Num.12:8), He characterizes it as "mouth to mouth." Both phrases mean "directly," however, as opposed to in a dream or in a hazy vision, as was the case with other prophets. (The latter description leaves room for Moses's request to God to show him His "presence" (Ex. 33:18).) The importance of this for Jewish faith is that the clarity and completeness of Moses's vision—of God, of Creation, of, simply, *everything*—provides reason to believe that the Torah and its laws as taught by Moses are consistent and in harmony with the world as it really is.

The opaque quality of the personality of Moses is consistent with his determination that Judaism not become a cult of personality—"Mosaism." Thus, his burial place is not known "to this very day" (Deut. 34:6). In the synagogue, when the Torah scroll is lifted and shown to the congregation after being read, the congregation says in unison: "This [motioning toward the scroll] is the Torah that Moses placed before the children of Israel, in accordance with the Lord's command, through Moses" (Deut. 4:44; Num. 9:23).

8. God's law was given on Mount Sinai.

What exactly happened at Sinai? We are not certain—how could we be, speaking as we are of extraordinary experiences of a mystical and otherworldly nature? It is an element of Jewish faith that the Israelites stood at the foot of Mt. Sinai and beheld, in some fashion, the presence of God—for this, the term *shechina* is often used, and this term is used often in Jewish literature to refer to the experience of the palpable (as it were) presence of God.

But that's not what this Principle is about; this is about the Law, and the Principle of Faith here is that the Law as it is understood, studied, and developed by generations of Jewish scholars, students, and Jews young and old immersed in the texts and ideas of the Torah and all its literature—this begins at Sinai.

The assertion that "the Law is from Sinai" presents an immediate problem, because the Torah also discounts Revelation as an arbiter of what the Law is. The verse "It is not from heaven" (Deut. 30:12) is used in the Talmud (Bava Metzia 59b) to dismiss extraordinary heavenly indications in support of a view by the saintly Rabbi Eleazar. The law has to appeal to the reasoning of the majority of the rabbis (Exodus 23:2), and not be determined by miracles or visions. For this reason, the coherence and reasoning of the argument is not the sole determinant; the provenance of the law and its logic is just as important. Frequently in Talmudic literature, the certainty of the source outweighs the quality of the argument.

9. The Torah is complete and immutable.

The legal framework of 613 Mitzvot; the oral traditions as contained in the rabbinic texts; and the entire chain of the tradition, stretching from antiquity to the present time—all this is to be considered complete and immutable. The examples given in the literature are: one may not add or detract the number of stands that make up the *tzitzit* (fringes), or add or subtract the number of species of vegetation one handles on Sukkot. The principle calls for having profound respect for the "thin encroaching wedge"—the seemingly minor addition or subtraction that will lead to the compromising of the law and its eventual abrogation. The rabbis adduce the story of the Garden of Eden for this idea: As soon as Eve erroneously framed the prohibition regarding the Tree of Knowledge as including touching it as well as eating from its fruit (Gen. 3:3), she became vulnerable to the snake's tempting.

Faith in the "chain of the tradition" depends intimately on being a part of that chain. Until one has experienced or witnessed the sacrifice and dedication

(and, often, persecution and martyrdom) that has been called upon in order to preserve and transmit the Torah from one generation to another, one cannot understand what these principles really mean. In the Jewish calendar, there are four fast days associated with the destruction of the two Temples, but they are also days that commemorate the many times teachers and transmitters of the Torah were persecuted and executed. On Tisha B'av, a dirge accompanies the reading of lamentations for the Ten Martyrs—ten rabbis of the Talmudic period who, during the Hadrianic persecutions that followed the unsuccessful Bar Kokhba revolt against Rome (in 135 CE), were executed heroically. The dirge combines several incidents separated in time, but the martyrdom of these sages is documented and their loss represented a tragic interruption of the transmission of the law. The quality and integrity of that process has been, throughout history, a major preoccupation of the Jewish people.

10. God knows all human actions and our innermost thoughts.

The next two of Maimonides's principles are also connected: *Because* God knows the deeds and thoughts of human beings—even when they do not know their inner thoughts themselves—good will be rewarded and evil will be punished. An interesting and poignant institution of Jewish law is the *eglah arufah*—gruesomely translated as the "decapitated calf." If the body of a murder victim is found in a field, the law states (Deut. 21:1-9), and there is no hope of finding the murderer, the elders of the nearest town or jurisdiction must offer a heifer as a sacrifice, wash their hands over it, and declare, "Our hands have not shed this blood, neither have our eyes seen it. Forgive, O Lord, Thy people Israel."

The Talmud (Sotah 46b) asks, does it occur to us that the elders of this town are responsible for the murder? The answer given: the elders must be able to say, in good conscience, that the victim did not: come to them or to the townspeople in search of protection while traveling; come in need of a place to stay for the night or food to eat; fail to find a lawful and secure environment that would permit a stranger to pass through unharmed.

This concept of collective responsibility, developed in Jewish law and ethics to a degree unknown in the West, became a hallmark of Jewish society and ultimately of the Jewish social conscience that was so evident during the American civil rights struggle. This principle in effect eliminates ignorance as an excuse for failing to act to prevent injustice to the disenfranchised and persecution of the stranger, the "other," *whoever* that might be.

11. Good is rewarded; evil is punished.

The world often poses serious challenges to this principle—the problem is known as the problem of theodicy: how to reconcile the existence of evil (sometimes crushingly heinous evil) and the concept of a benevolent and all-powerful God. A Talmudic tale (Berachot 5a) illustrates the Jewish approach: Once, Rabbi Huna suffered a financial setback when 400 of his jugs of wine went sour. His colleagues came to console him, and they told him that he ought to examine his actions to make certain he hadn't done something to deserve this calamity. "Why," he asked, "have you heard anything against me?" They said they had heard that he does not give his tenant his lawful share of the wine twigs. Rabbi Huna replied, "But he steals more than his share of the grapes." They answered with an old proverb: "Stealing from a thief gives one a taste for stealing." That the tenant was dishonest in one respect did not absolve Rabbi Huna from being scrupulously correct in any other. The story has a moralistic ending, with Rabbi Huna vowing to treat his tenant properly irrespective of the tenant's behavior, and recovering from his financial disaster.

The Jewish faith avails itself of the hope that justice will ultimately prevail, in the afterlife or in some future "end of days," as do other religions, but more important is the personal Jewish *response* to evil and to disaster: The Jew looks upon his or her own

behavior and asks if he or she hasn't behaved improperly. Taken to extremes, this can be seen as the source of the Jewish sense of guilt that is fodder for comedy and neuroses, but looked at seriously and soberly, and without excusing the evil of others, it betokens a profoundly honed sense of responsibility and individual involvement in the moral vicissitudes of the world.

12. One day, the Messiah will come.

Maimonides lays out his views of the Messiah and the messianic era in chapters 11 and 12 of "The Laws of Kingship," in his monumental and magisterial legal code, *Mishneh Torah*. For one thing, he does not see the Messiah as a wonder worker (or else Rabbi Akiva would not have thought Bar Kokhba the Messiah); for another, the Messiah has as his main task the ingathering of the Jewish people into their Promised Land and the rebuilding of the Temple. This presupposes that the Messiah will be, in addition to a descendent of the House of King David, also a defender of the Torah, written and oral.

"Messiah" (*moshi'ach*), literally means "anointed one," and is reference to the fact that the ancient kings of Israel were (as was the ancient royal custom) anointed with oil at their coronation. This underscores the role of the Messiah as a "king of the Jews." The idyllic vision of the messianic era in Isaiah 11 (in which peace extends right into the most predatory corners of the animal kingdom), is, for Maimonides, only an allegory. The Messiah will certainly be an inspiration for other nations, but his main concern will be the restoration of the Davidic kingdom.

In the formulation of this principle in the daily liturgy (the Ani Ma'amin in the Siddur), there is mention made of the fact that faith in the Messiah is held in spite of his tarrying. (No such equivocation appears for any other principle.) This may be why this principle (as opposed to the next one) became an oft-recited formula when Jews were martyred, including during the Holocaust.

Jewish history has had many pseudo-messiahs, from antiquity (in Judaism, Jesus is regarded as a false prophet/messiah, as is Muhammad), through medieval and Renaissance periods (e.g., Sabbatai Zevi and Jacob Frank), and, surprisingly, into modern times.

13. The dead shall rise when the Messiah comes.

Maimonides held the unusual (for a rabbi) view that after the dead are resurrected, there would be a great day of judgment, in which the righteous will be vindicated and the wicked will be destroyed (utterly). After that, the survivors would live out their lives—and then die. (Maimonides was evidently not able to conceive flesh-and-blood people living eternally.) The souls of the righteous would then resume their ethereal existences as before, and the world would similarly continue its natural course. It has been suggested that the concept of resurrection being widely disseminated during the period of persecution by the Romans (as a means of buoying the flagging spirits of the Judeans) was responsible for the story of Jesus and the belief in his resurrection.

An indication of the importance of the doctrine of resurrection is the fact that in the Amidah, the third of its eighteen benedictions is devoted to this principle, and is placed immediately prior to the recitation of the Kedusha. Branches of Judaism that do not take this belief to be literally true or no longer a foundational tenet have revised their liturgy accordingly. A belief in resurrection of the body is one reason Orthodox Judaism prohibits cremation (the other being it violates the sanctity of the body).

B. Scripture and Sacred Literature

The Hebrew Bible, known in the Jewish tradition by its Hebrew acronym **Tanakh**, is composed of three parts: **Torah** (consisting of the Pentateuch); **Nevi'im** (Prophets); and **Ketuvim** (Writings). The Torah is the same text which Christians and Muslims read and refer to as the Old Testament of the Bible. According to Jewish tradition, the Torah was revealed by God to the prophet Moses at Mount Sinai.

Orthodox tradition puts the date of this revelation at 1280 BCE, although interpretations differ as to whether the entire Torah was revealed to Moses in one event on Mount Sinai or over a period of many years during his life.

Many modern biblical scholars contend that the Torah is in fact the result of an oral tradition whose many versions were woven together by an unknown editor or multiple editors. Regardless, the divinity of the Torah is undisputed in classical Jewish tradition. For Orthodox and Conservative Jews, every word of the scripture is understood to be the infallible word of God; Reform and Reconstructionist Jews, on the other hand, may not regard the Torah as the literal word of God, although it is still the central text for their religious life and worship.

Also highly regarded are the rabbinic commentaries on the Torah, called the **Midrash**. Many of these were written with one of two purposes in mind: to cull from the text the origins and details of received Jewish law; or to interpret ambiguities in the biblical text and search for deeper meanings. The former category is referred to as **Halakhic**, or legal, Midrash; the latter is called **Aggadic**, or nonlegal, homiletical, Midrash.

Division of the Tanakh. The division of the Torah follows the standard Bible. The Nevi'im (Prophets), contains the visions and experiences of some fifteen prophets to whom God spoke and conferred divine knowledge, according to Jewish tradition. The books of the Nevi'im are divided into the Former Prophets (*Nevi'im Rishonim*), which contains Joshua, Judges, Samuel, and Kings; and the Latter Prophets (*Nevi'im Acharonim*), which contains Isaiah, Jeremiah, Ezekiel, and the Trei Asar ("Twelve"), or Minor Prophets—a single collection relating the shorter stories of the prophets Hosea, Joel, Amos, Obadiah, Jonah, Micah, Nahum, Habakkuk, Zephaniah, Haggai, Zechariah, and Malachi. Selections from the Nevi'im are known in the Jewish liturgy as the Haftarah and are read after the Torah portion of the Sabbath service, as well as on Jewish festival and fast days. Unlike the Torah, the Nevi'im are not considered to be written by God and revealed to the prophets, but rather are relations of the experiences of the prophets themselves and therefore are imbued with divine understanding but are not the direct word of God.

The final part of the Tanakh is the Ketuvim, or Writings, which is comprised of the following: the Three Poetic Books, which are Psalms (*Tehillim*), Proverbs (*Mishlei*), and Job (*'Iyyov*); the Five Scrolls (*Hamesh Megillot*) including the Song of Songs (*Shir ha-Shirim*), the book of Ruth, Lamentations (*Eikhah*), Ecclesiastes (*Kohelet*), and the book of Esther; and the other historical books, Daniel, the books of Ezra-Nehemiah, and Chronicles (*Divrei ha-Yamim*). The Poetic Books are, as their designation suggests, in the form of poetry and are presented in masoretic (i.e., of traditional origins) manuscripts in a special-two column form, with a system of cantillation notes to designate how they should be chanted during services. The scrolls (*megillot*) are read on specific holidays throughout the Jewish liturgical calendar, with the Song of Songs being read on Passover, the book of Ruth on Shavuot, Lamentations on Tisha B'av, Ecclesiastes on Sukkot, and the book of Esther on Purim. The other books of the Ketuvim are ostensibly historical narratives describing events such as the Babylonian captivity and the restoration of Zion.

The Apocrypha, Deuterocanonical, and Pseudepigraphal books are simply not recognized as having any authority or legitimacy in Jewish thought, though they may be of some historical interest.

C. Other Jewish Religious Literature

In addition to the written law and commentaries on it, Judaism has an oral tradition of legal and exegetical commentary on the Bible and its implications. These recorded opinions are collectively called the **Talmud**. The Talmud has two parts: the **Mishnah**, a compilation of the legal opinions and debates of various rabbis; and the **Gemara**, a compilation of rabbis' discussions and analysis of the Mishnah and related works.

The Mishnah contains six "orders" (*sedarim*), each of which deal with different areas of oral law. Within these orders are the recorded opinions of the rabbis of the Mishnah, known as **Tannaim**, on such parts of life as prayer and blessings, agricultural laws, civil and criminal law, laws of the Sabbath and the festivals, marriage and divorce, sacrificial rites, and dietary law. It is believed that the Mishnah was redacted around 200 CE, by Rabbi Judah HaNasi (the Prince), though the debates and discussions among the Tannaim took place over many generations, beginning as early as ca. 40 BCE with Rabban Yohanan ben Zakkai. Mishnaic traditions that Rabbi Judah did not include, but which may have been authentic, were collected in a secondary work known as the **Baraitha**.

The debates and viewpoints are generally presented without attributing statements to particular rabbinical interlocutors. Orthodox Jewish tradition holds that the Mishnah was given to Moses at the same time as the written Torah and meant to contain a complementary set of information and ideas, to elucidate the Torah despite not being included in the actual written text. Since its redacting, the Mishnah has been commented upon by scholars and rabbis from Maimonides in 1168 to present-day students, and some of this commentary was subsequently redacted into the Gemara.

The Talmud was compiled twice: once in Palestine, by scholars from schools in Tiberias and Caesaria—this Talmud is known as the Jerusalemite Talmud (a misnomer) and was redacted in about 350 CE, traditionally by Rabbis Muna and Yossi, but their editorship is uncertain. The second time was in Babylonia: this time producing a much more extensive and authoritative work called the Babylonian Talmud. The work was redacted by Ravina and Rabbi Ashi, and was based on the teachings of the academies of Nehardea, Mahoza, Pumbeditha, and Sura, all leading centers of Jewish learning since the Babylonian Exile in 586 BCE.

The Babylonian Talmud is more extensive and more authoritative than the Jerusalemite Talmud because the former was developed over a longer period of time; was developed in more academies, and ones that were larger and better endowed; was developed in a more tranquil political climate; devoted considerable attention to civil matters, which would be applicable anywhere Jews lived; and devoted less energy to laws involving the Temple and the tithes of the land of Israel, which became irrelevant once the Temple was destroyed and the Jews were exiled.

We classify the Talmudic corpus under religious literature because, as the repository of the Oral Law, its volumes carry a measure of the sanctity that is accorded biblical books. The general term for the talmudic literature is "*Shas*," an abbreviation of *Shisha Sedarim* or "six orders," referring to the six orders of the Mishnah.

D. Rabbinic (Halakhic) Literature

Following the completion of the Talmud, there followed a long line of commentaries and supercommentaries, as Jews in the Diaspora looked to the Talmud for direction in all areas of civil, ritualistic, and religious law. Thus was born the Halakhah—the "way" of life that was directed in every detail by the discourse and analysis of the Talmudic text.

The earliest commentators were known as the *Rishonim* ("first"); and subsequent commentators were called *Acharonim* ("later"). Among the Rishonim, important figures include:

Rashi (acronym for Rabbi Shlomo Yitzchaki; 1040–1105) was born in Troyes, France, and attended the *yeshiva* (academy) in Worms. Rashi was still a boy when his father died, so he was forced to attend the yeshiva only sporadically, having to attend to his family's business (a winery). In that time, although the Talmud had been committed to writing, there was still a hesitation to commit any more of the oral tradition (now contained in the discourse and analysis of the Talmud) to writing. But Rashi was forced to make notes (perhaps surreptitiously) so he could study during the long periods he was at

home, away from yeshiva. Rashi also attended the yeshiva in Mainz, the leading rabbinical seminary in the world at the time, still making brief notes of the teachings of his rabbis, who were themselves students of the great Rabbeinu Gershom, the greatest European rabbinic authority of the age.

In 1096, the People's Crusade swept through Europe and the academies of Worms and Mainz were destroyed, the scholars and students massacred. Rashi's notes now took on a special importance and he developed them further with the students of the yeshiva he helped to rebuild in Worms.

Rashi wrote additional commentaries on virtually the entire Tanakh and on the entire Talmud—they are masterpieces of brevity and clarity; they helped preserve a wealth of learning and educate many generations of students and scholars. Rashi had three grandsons who composed commentaries (often in opposition to his interpretation) known as *Tosephot*—"additional" comments. On the standard page of the printed Talmud, the text of the Talmud is flanked by Rashi's commentary on one side (the inside), and the comments of Tosephot on the other.

Other Rishonim wrote legal summaries of the Talmud—some, like Isaac Alfasi (1013–1103), following the order of the Talmudic text; and some, like Maimonides and Jacob ben Asher, author of the *Arbah Turim*—"four rows" or volumes, or Tur for short (1270–1340), creating their own logical-thematic order, used by later codifiers of Jewish law.

III. Rites and Rituals

A. Calendar

The Jews have, since antiquity, followed a lunar cycle in which each month begins on the appearance of the new moon and is either twenty-nine or thirty days long. Since the refrain in Genesis 1 places the evening before the day, in Jewish practice, the day begins with the night and continues to the end of the next daylight period. Since the Bible demands that Passover always be celebrated in the spring (Deut. 16:1), it was necessary to intercalate (i.e., add a lunar month) to the 354-day lunar year so that the lunar and solar year could more or less coincide. Adding seven lunar years during a cycle of nineteen years accomplishes this alignment. (This method is still off by six minutes per year, so that in 8,000 years, it will be necessary to add two additional months to one year to bring the lunar and solar calendars into alignment.)

The names of the months are taken from Babylonian and appear only in later biblical books (such as Esther). They are (beginning with the month on the first of which is the Jewish New Year, Rosh Hashanah: Tishri; Heshvan (called Marheshvan—"bitter Heshvan"—because no holidays occur in that month); Kislev; Tevet; Shevat; Adar; Nissan; Iyyar; Sivan; Tammuz; Av; Elul. The leap month is always an extra month of Adar (added before Nisan, the month of Passover, and thus called Adar *sheni*—"second" Adar).

B. Holidays and Festivals

Rosh Hodesh (First of the Month)

The first of each month was once an important festival (see II Kings 4:23, where it is comparable to Sabbath), but now work is permitted. A custom has it that women do not work on Rosh Hodesh as a reward for refusing to participate in the Golden Calf.

Sabbath (Shabbat)

The Jewish liturgical calendar revolves largely around the Sabbath, or Shabbat, which occurs each week from sundown on Friday to nightfall on Saturday. Shabbat is a day of rest observed in order to symbolize God's period of rest after He created the universe in six days. Jews are prohibited from doing any form of *melachah* (work) on Shabbat, though different branches of Judaism interpret this prohibition in differing ways. The Talmud identifies thirty-nine categories of work, including sowing, reaping,

grinding, kneading, weaving, tying, sewing stitches, slaughtering, writing (or erasing) two or more letters, or transporting an object between a private and a public domain, or carrying it more than four cubits (about twelve feet) in public.

Observing Shabbat includes attending services, praying, refraining from prohibited activities, eating festive meals, being joyous, and avoiding unpleasant things. A festive meal is cooked prior to Shabbat, usually on Friday afternoon, and it is customary to don one's best clothing, use the best tableware, and eat challah (braided loaves of bread) in honor of the Shabbat. Candles are lit (by women, but by men if there are no women present) ushering in the Shabbat, and Kiddush—a blessing sanctifying the day and made over wine—is recited at the beginning of the Friday night meal. Songs are sung at this meal, including *Shalom Aleichem*, welcoming the Shabbat "angels" that grace the home, and *zemirot* songs (that are sung only on that day).

Services in the synagogue are longer and include reading the weekly portion of the Torah, an additional (*musaf*) Amidah, and frequently a sermon by the rabbi. There are special Sabbaths during the year, either preparatory for an upcoming holiday, or commemorating a special event that appears in that week's Torah reading. Three meals are to be eaten on the Sabbath (Friday night, Saturday noon, and Saturday afternoon); the final meal, *Seudat Shelishit*, has great mystical significance in Kabbalistic and Hassidic lore. The day ends with a candle ceremony and a blessing (again recited over wine) called Havdalah—"separation" (from the mundane week).

The High Holy Days (Tishri 1–10)

The most significant holidays in the Jewish calendar are the High Holy Days—Rosh Hashanah and Yom Kippur. Often, American Jews who do not observe Shabbat or other Jewish holidays still go to services on the High Holy Days (*Yamim Noraim*—literally, "days of awe").

Rosh Hashanah is the Jewish New Year. It falls on the first and second days of the Jewish month of

Tishri, usually in September. According to Jewish tradition, God judges all humankind for the coming year on Rosh Hashanah. For this reason, it is customary, in addition to an extended prayer service that involves sounding the shofar (made from a ram's horn, shown below), to engage in *tashlikh*. Tashlikh is performed on the afternoon of the first day of Rosh

The shofar is traditionally sounded at Rosh Hashanah, the Jewish New Year, among other occasions.

Hashanah; it involves reciting prayers near a flowing body of water and is often accompanied by throwing pieces of bread into the water to symbolize the casting off of sins.

Despite this focus on God's judgment for the year, Rosh Hashanah is a celebratory holiday, with feasts of foods such as apples and honey, symbolizing the hope for a coming sweet year; a round challah, symbolizing the cycle of life; and pomegranates symbolizing the many *mitzvot* that Jews will perform. The customary greetings on Rosh Hashanah are *Shana tova,* meaning "A good year," or *Ketiva ve-chatima tovah,* meaning "May you be written and sealed for a good year."

Yom Kippur, the Day of Atonement, is one of the holiest days of the year for Jews. It falls on the tenth day of the Jewish month of Tishri. Before the holiday begins, it is customary to eat at least one large, festive meal, and some Jews eat more than one. It is also customary, before Yom Kippur, to ask for forgiveness from friends, family, or acquaintances whom one may have wronged or hurt over the past year. This is done during the *Aseret Yemei Teshuva,* the Ten Days of Repentance between Rosh Hashanah and Yom Kippur. Yom Kippur itself is observed with a twenty-five-hour fast and a day of intense prayer, traditionally in a synagogue. The prayer services on Yom Kippur begin with a prayer called Kol Nidre and involve other prayers called *selichot,* which ask forgiveness from God. In addition to the twenty-five-hour fast, no work is to be done on Yom

Kippur—as on Shabbat and many other Jewish holidays. The day ends with Ne'ilah ("closing of the gates") and blasts of the shofar.

Sukkot (Tishri 15–23)

Just a few days after Yom Kippur comes Sukkot, the Festival of Booths. Two main observances occur then:

1. Small huts (*sukkot*) with thatched roofs open to the sky are built near the home, and Jews will either eat their meals or in some cases actually live in the Sukkah, commemorating how the Israelites lived under the Pillar of Glory when they wandered through the desert after the Exodus.

2. Four species of vegetation—a palm frond (*lulav*); a citron (*etrog*); branches from a willow (*aravah*); and myrtle (*hadass*)—are held together, waved, and shaken. The combination symbolizes the unified elements of a person (spine, heart, mouth, and eye, respectively, which each physically resembles) in service to God; the different kinds of Jews, all unified on this holiday; the different ways vegetative growth obtains water, in prayer for an abundant crop.

On the latter days of the holiday, two additional days are observed: Sh'mini Atzeret (the eighth day of

The Sephardic Bikur Holim congregation in Seattle, Washington, erected a sukkah between their synagogue and social hall for the 2009 Sukkoth holiday. At right are the Four Species of vegetation eaten on Sukkoth. The citron (left) is a rare fruit that, because of its thin peel, does not rot but rather slowly dries out.

the Festival) and Simchat Torah (the "joyous celebration" of the Torah). On the last day, the cycle of
the annual (or tri-annual) Torah reading is renewed
and the last and the opening portions of the Torah
are read, amid much celebration. Prior to the Torah
reading during the day and at night (the only time
the Torah is read at night), the Torah is paraded
through the synagogue in circuits (*hakafot*) amid
much singing and dancing, which often spills out
into the street. In the evening, some of the final portion in the Torah is read; it is finished the next day
and the opening section of Genesis is begun.

Passover (Nisan 15–22)

Although the High Holy Days are the most
sacred days in Judaism and are often observed by
otherwise secular Jews, the most commonly observed
Jewish holiday by far is Passover, or *Pesach*. This is
especially true in America, where even Jews who do
not attend services in synagogue at any time during
the year will often attend a Passover *seder* ("order").
Passover commemorates the Exodus of the Jews from
Egypt after centuries of slavery there, as related in the
Torah. The Exodus is commemorated with the seder,
a traditional meal eaten on the first two nights of the
holiday (one night for Jews living in Israel), during
which family and friends gather and retell the story
of the Exodus. The instructions for the seder as well
as the Exodus story itself are written in the
Haggadah, which is used to conduct the prayers and
the ritual meal, including the reading of the story at
the table. The prayers and the story are traditionally
sung in Hebrew and Aramaic, although many more
secular Jews conduct the seder in the vernacular, or
in some combination of both. Often in more religious households, the seder involves discussion and
debate between segments of the Exodus story, leading the seder to last well into the night.

The meal is full of symbolic foods and rituals,
one of the most important of which is the eating of
matzah, unleavened bread. This practice is meant to
commemorate the quick escape from Egypt, when
the Jews did not have time to wait for their bread to

At the seder table, the matzah
lies under the cover in the middle of the table above, while the
ke'arah, *the seder plate,*
is positioned at the lower right.
Included on the plate are bitter
herbs, shankbone, and
charoset—the mortarlike spread.

rise and therefore ate unleavened bread on their journey. Observant Jews spend weeks before Pesach
cleaning their houses to rid them of leavened foods,
or *chametz*, and sell any remaining, or utensils used
to handle it, to a non-Jew for the holiday. Pesach lasts
eight days for Jews outside of Israel, with the first two
days and the last two days celebrated as full festival
days, involving special prayer services and abstention
from work, in addition to the traditional meals. On
the intervening days, known as Chol Ha-Moed,
work may be done. On the last day of Passover (as on
Shemini Atzeret, technically the last day of Sukkot)
Yizkor, the memorial prayer for the departed, is said.

Chanukah (Eight Days, from Kislev 25)

Another holiday celebrated by many American
Jews, even those who are otherwise quite secular, is
Chanukah. Chanukah commemorates the victory of
the Maccabees over the Syrians and the rededication
of the Temple in Jerusalem around 167 BCE.
According to the traditional story, upon rededicating
the Temple, the Maccabees and their followers
wanted to light the oil lamp in the sanctuary but
only had enough sanctified oil to burn for a single
day. This oil, it is said, lasted for eight days (while
new oil was pressed), and Chanukah, the Festival of

This giant electric Chanukah menorah adorned the White House lawn in 1995.

Lights, lasts for eight days in order to commemorate this miracle. The story is found not in the Torah but in the Talmud, and in the books of Maccabees.

The holiday begins on the twenty-fifth day of Kislev, usually in November or December. The festival is observed by lighting either oil lamps or candles in a candelabrum properly called a Chanukiyah, sometimes referred to by Ashkenazic Jews as a "Chanukah menorah." One new light is lit each night of the holiday, so that the number of lights increases each night until the candelabrum is full on the last night. It is also traditional to give small presents on each night of the holiday, especially to children, and to play a game with a top called a Dreidl, on which are inscribed the letters *nun*, *gimmel*, *heh*, and *shin*, which stand for *nes gadol hayah sham*— "a great miracle happened there."

Other Holidays

There are numerous other Jewish holidays, some of which hold more religious significance than those above, but which are observed less widely by American Jews (not at all by secular Jews). One of these is **Tisha B'Av**, a fast day commemorating several tragic events in Jewish history, including the destruction of both the First and Second Temples in Jerusalem, Bar

Kokhba's revolt against Rome, and the razing of Jerusalem after the Roman siege.

Likewise, **Shavu'ot** (Sivan 6–7) commemorates the receiving of the Torah by the Jewish people at Mount Sinai. It also has agricultural significance as it is connected with the end of the grain harvesting season in ancient Israel. The forty-nine days between Passover and Shavu'ot are counted—it is called "Counting of the Omer," the Omer being a measure of barley that was brought as an offering in the Temple on Shavu'ot, to sanctify the new harvest.

C. Worship and Liturgy

Jewish services are held in a synagogue, or *shul*, in addition to individual prayers and blessings (or *brachot*) said by Jews on a daily basis outside the synagogue. Community prayer, which is the preferred form, requires ten adults, called a *minyan*. Orthodox Judaism maintains that ten adult men must be present to form a minyan, although Reform congregations and some Conservative ones consider ten Jewish adults (either men or women) to make a minyan. Halakhah dictates strict times when certain prayers and services can be performed and attended. On weekdays, organized prayer is required three times a day: the morning prayers are called Shacharit and are to be said within the first three or four hours of the day; the afternoon prayers, Mincha, are to be said from half an hour after halakhic noontime until two-and-a-half (halakhic) hours before nightfall; the evening prayers, Ma'ariv, are traditionally recited after nightfall, although many congregations hold afternoon and evening services back-to-back on weekdays for convenience.

Before attending shul in the morning, various prayers are recited upon waking up, at which time *tzitzit* (fringed garments) are put on. Before or during the service in synagogue, a *tallit*, or prayer shawl, and *tefillin*, or phylacteries (two boxes containing Biblical verses—the Shema—with leather straps attached) are worn. In Orthodox Judaism, only men are permitted to put on tefillin, while in Reform and some Conservative traditions, women are permitted to do so. The morning service consists of blessings, psalms, the Mourner's Kaddish (the prayer for those mourning the dead), and on certain days a reading from the Torah.

The afternoon prayers vary by ethnic tradition, but all involve the reading of several psalms and the Mourner's Kaddish. The evening prayers begins with the Barechu, the public call to prayer (also present in the morning and afternoon prayers in various capacities), and some prayers relating to the Shema

The tallit (prayer shawl) and tefillin (prayer boxes) worn by this man while praying at the Western Wall are worn by Orthodox Jewish men during daily prayers. Only the head tefillin is visible; the arm tefillin is hidden beneath the tallit.

Yisrael. Once again, services vary by ethnic custom, with Ashkenazim outside of Israel adding some biblical verses and Sephardim adding Psalm 121. The Mourner's Kaddish is once again recited.

Shabbat Services

Shabbat services on Friday night begin with the weekday Mincha, with the addition of the Song of Songs in some communities and the Kabbalat Shabbat (a mystical prelude to the Sabbath) in most communities. This is followed by the recitation of several psalms and the Mourner's Kaddish. Services on Saturday morning begin as the weekday Schacharit services do, omitting psalms that are not appropriate for Shabbat, such as Psalm 100, an offering of Thanksgiving. A Torah reading is added, after which in many congregations the rabbi delivers a sermon on the topic of the Torah reading. There is then an additional service, called the Musaf, which begins with a silent recitation of the Amidah (standing prayer), several other prayers, and a reading from the book of Numbers. The Mourner's Kaddish is also recited, and Orthodox congregations follow this with a reading from the Talmud. The Saturday evening service is the same as the weekday Ma'ariv and then concludes with the Havdalah, which marks the end of Shabbat.

The book used for daily worship is the Siddur (order of prayer); the prayer book for the High Holidays and festivals is the Machzor. In addition to biblical texts required for following a reading, a worshipper might also have need for a Selichot for penitential prayers during the period of the High Holidays; and a Kinot, with Lamentations for Tisha B'Av.

In a tradition that goes back to antiquity among Jews, Psalms (*Tehilim*) is recited (responsively when recited by a group in the synagogue) in times of personal trouble or when facing illness or any calamity.

D. Daily Life

Halakhah dictates very specifically what prohibitions and requirements exist for the everyday life of a Jewish person. Among the most significant and pervasive are the dietary laws, known as *kashrut*, and some clothing restrictions.

Dietary Laws

The laws of kashrut are set down largely in the Book of Leviticus in the Torah and expanded upon by the rabbis in the Talmud and the Rabbinic codes. Following the laws of kashrut, or "keeping kosher," involves refraining from eating certain foods and food combinations, slaughtering animals according to kosher methods, and many other requirements. Depending on their particular denomination, different Jews uphold different levels of kashrut. For instance, the prohibition on eating pork, or any other animal which does not chew its cud and have cloven hoofs, is a fairly basic law of kashrut and is followed by observant Jews of most branches, from Orthodox to Reform. The prohibition on combining dairy and meat products, on the other hand, lends itself to many interpretations, from those who wait an hour between dairy and meat consumption to those who wait five or six hours.

In addition to such straightforward prohibitions, there are more obscure kashrut laws such as the requirement that foods including cheese and wine be prepared in whole or in part by Jews. Due to the extensive and intricate nature of the laws of kashrut, very observant Jews do not eat in restaurants which are not deemed kosher by a satisfactory rabbinical authority; they will also refrain from eating in the home of one whose observance is uncertain or deficient. They also refrain from purchasing food products which are not certified as kosher by kashruth-certifying organizations—reading a list of ingredients may be sufficient for less observant Jews, but Orthodox Jews will not eat foods without these labels and designations.

Personal Behavior and Decorum

Jews also look to Halakhah for instructions on how to dress. One of the most universally recognized elements of Jewish dress is the *yarmulke*, or *kippah*—a small skullcap worn by Jewish men and boys in honor of God, to recognize that God is above mankind. It is worn at all times by Orthodox Jews, although some Conservative or Reform Jews may wear it only when eating or praying. Some Jewish women of the Reform denomination have recently started wearing kippot as well. Jewish men are also required to wear *tzitzit*, fringes worn on the corners of four-cornered garments.

Both sexes are required to dress modestly, which means that Orthodox women are not permitted to wear pants, and most wear skirts of modest length. Shirts must not be low-cut, and many Orthodox women will only wear shirts which cover their elbows. For Conservative Jews, these rules of modesty may be relaxed, and many Reform Jews do not observe them at all. The same is true for the practice of women covering their heads once they are married, whether with a wig or a kerchief of some sort.

A similar sentiment is behind Jewish codes for the relations between men and women in Judaism; some Orthodox (and Conservative) Jews are *shomer neggiah*, meaning that they do not touch members of the opposite sex (except relatives) until after marriage. This is meant to protect people from being tempted by sexual desires. The daily life of a religiously observant Jewish person also entails going to synagogue, if not each day, then certainly each week for Shabbat services.

Religious Jews also pay close attention to their language, refraining from gossip, as well as profanity.

In addition to community prayer, there is also individual prayer and there are blessings to be said at appropriate times throughout the day, such as upon awakening, before eating food or drinking a beverage, upon finishing eating, when *birkat hamazon*—grace after meals—is recited, and upon embarking on a trip, when *tefilat ha'derekh*—traveler's prayer—is recited.

E. Life Cycle Events

Birth and Circumcision

Every aspect of the life cycle has a Jewish ceremony or practice to accompany it. When a baby is born, for instance, there are very specific Jewish customs, both halakhic and purely traditional. It is customary, for instance, not to have a baby shower or announce the pregnancy to anyone other than immediate family until the fifth month. Once the baby is born, if it is a boy the Hebrew name is not to be announced until the *bris* (circumcision and accompanying ceremony) a week later. If the baby is a girl, the name is not to be announced until the father can go to synagogue, have an *aliyah* (called to a reading of the Torah), traditionally as soon as possible after the birth. Among Ashkenazic Jews, the custom is to name the child after a relative who has passed away—never after a living relative, which is considered extremely bad luck. Sephardic Jews, on the other hand, do not observe this custom and often name the child after a parent or living relative.

Bar and Bat Mitzvah

One of the most important milestones in the life of a Jewish person is the process of becoming an adult, or a Bar or Bat Mitzvah (male and female, respectively). This ritual is traditionally gone through when a Jewish person is thirteen years old, and involves reading from the Torah and giving a speech about the Torah portion during synagogue services in front of the congregation. The Bar or Bat Mitzvah prepares and studies for this ceremony for months if not years beforehand. According to Jewish law, a person becomes a Bar Mitzvah regardless of whether or not he (or she, in those communities which perform the ceremony for women) is called to the Torah to read, but the custom is universal in Judaism and is mentioned in the Midrash. The ritual itself (and the party which customarily accompanies it in modern Judaism) has come to be called a Bar or Bat Mitzvah, but the word actually refers to the person, the Jewish adult him- or herself, the literal translation being "son (or daughter) of the commandment." Orthodox Jews only perform the ritual for boys, but most Conservative, and all Reform and Reconstructionist congregations, hold equivalent rituals, complete with Torah readings in synagogue, for female congregants as well.

Many Reform and Conservative congregations in America now also perform ceremonies called Confirmations when a child is sixteen or eighteen. The tradition was developed by the Reform movement, and is often used less as a replacement for the Bar or Bat Mitzvah than as a way to keep children involved in the congregation and in Jewish education past the age of thirteen.

Nuptials

Marriage is another life milestone which comes with many Jewish customs and rituals. The custom of veiling the bride, called the *badecken*, involves the groom checking before the veil is lowered to make sure that the bride is in fact his intended. The *chuppah*, or bridal canopy, is another essential custom in Jewish wedding ceremonies. The chuppah is meant to symbolize the home which the bride and groom will build and share, and is open on all sides (symbolic of hospitality). The chuppah is fairly universal among Jewish weddings, as opposed to some of the other more esoteric traditions such as fasting for the bride and groom on the day of the ceremony.

The chuppah, above, and the ketubah, right, are integral elements of the Jewish wedding ceremony.

Also unique to Orthodox weddings (*chatunah*) is the custom of holding separate receptions (*kabbalat panim*) for the bride and groom in different rooms before the actual wedding ceremony. At the ceremony itself there is a Kiddush (blessing of wine), a plain gold ring is given to the bride by the groom, and several blessings are recited. The *Ketubah* (marriage contract) is also read in the original Aramaic, and the groom breaks a glass under his foot to express sadness at the destruction of the Temple in Jerusalem, marking the end of the ceremony.

The couple then repairs to a private room for the *yichud* ("sequestering") for their first moments alone as husband and wife, and to break their fast. This is followed by a party with family and friends at which it is meritorious to entertain the newlyweds.

Death, Burial, and Mourning

Judaism has specific instructions relating to death. The dead are to be buried as soon as possible —no later than three days after death. Cremation is not acceptable in traditional Judaism because Jews believe in the eventual resurrection of the dead in the Messianic Era. At a Jewish burial service, it is customary for attending friends and family to participate in the burial by taking turns shoveling dirt onto the coffin after it is lowered into the grave.

Immediately after the funeral, mourners observe a period of mourning called *shiva*, literally "seven," after the seven-day period of mourning observed for an immediate family member who has died. The family members gather in one home and visitors pay "shiva calls," comforting the family and often bringing food for them to eat. The mourners customarily sit on low stools or boxes, and more observant Jews will not bathe or shower, not wear jewelry, cut their hair or shave, and will often keep household mirrors covered, all to express their grief.

After the shiva period is over, the mourning continues at a lesser level for a thirty-day period called *shloshim* ("thirty"), during which it is customary not to cut one's hair or shave, and to abstain from celebrations or social occasions. The mourner continues

to recite the Mourner's Kaddish in synagogue for this period of time, and for up to eleven months for a parent. The Kaddish is also recited at services on the anniversary of the death, and memorial prayers for the dead (Yizkor) is recited on the three major festivals and on Yom Kippur.

In the United States, an unveiling takes place about one year after the death, at which time a headstone (*matzeivah*) is set in place and is visited by friends and family, often with the reading of psalms and eulogies. When visiting a Jewish person's grave, it is customary to leave a small stone on the headstone, thereby adding to the marking of the grave.

A Jew who has survived a brush with death (such as surviving a terrible accident; living through a plague or a serious operation or illness; returning from a battlefield—or some such close call), goes to the synagogue and, following an aliyah (being called to the Torah), publicly recites the "Blessing of Deliverance" (Birkat HaGomel) in which he thanks God for having delivered him through the danger. The congregation responds with an amen, and then expresses the hope aloud that God may always favor this person by seeing him or her through such straits in the future.

FURTHER READING ABOUT THE JEWISH FAITH

What Do Jews Believe?
   David S. Ariel
   1995: Schocken Books

Contemporary Jewish Religious Thought
   Arthur P. Cohen and Paul Mendes-Flohr, eds.
   1988: Free Press

To Be a Jew: A Guide to Jewish Observance
   Rabbi Hayim Halevi Donin
   1972: Basic Books

The Jewish Religion: A Companion
   Louis Jacobs
   1995: Oxford University Press

2 Judaism in America

I. Origins and History

A. Introduction: The "Golden Land"

IT IS A SOBERING THOUGHT TO REALIZE THAT WHEN Jews in nineteenth-century Europe thought about America (when they thought about it at all), they believed it to be a *traifeneh medina*—an unkosher, heathen land with no religion, a place in which no Jew would want to be caught under any circumstances. "Sobering" because, in light of the disaster that befell European Jewry in the Holocaust of the mid-twentieth century, it is frightening to imagine what the state of world Jewry would be today had Jews and Judaism not taken root in American soil.

One might have thought that Europe's Jews felt as they did because they had it so good. Perhaps there were a deluded few who thought that, or that things were going to get (*had* to get) better. But most Jews knew full well the obstacles that stood in the way of them leading happy, enfranchised lives. Jew-hatred was so rife, it had acquired a name: "Antisemitism" was coined in 1873 by a German journalist-agitator,

On December 16, 1880, the Young Men's Hebrew Association staged a Chanukah celebration at the Academy of Music in New York City. This illustration, published in Frank Leslie's Illustrated Newspaper, *depicts a tableau dramatizing the dedication of the Temple.*

Wilhelm Marr, who wrote pamphlet after pamphlet reeking with pseudoscience about race and inflammatory conclusions about national character—about how Jews were subverting the national identity of Germany and the racial purity of the Aryan German race. Marr may have been dismissed by the more enlightened Jews and non-Jews of the day as a crank, but there was no dismissing the popularity of his work among the common people who eagerly devoured every word of it.

When, in 1850, the German composer Richard Wagner pseudonymously wrote an essay on "Jewishness and Music," in which he claimed Jews were detrimental to German culture (and their music was terrible), few could ignore the signs, and a sense of foreboding descended on the Jews of Europe—but few considered the United States a viable alternative. If they had, Herzl might not have had to develop a Zionistic alternative of his own.

By the beginning of the twentieth century, America in the eyes of European Jewry went from being a desert to a jungle. Jews found it increasingly difficult to gain entry, and once here, experienced severe discrimination in everything from jobs to education. The 1915 lynching of Leo Frank by an angry mob shouting antisemitic slurs sent a chill through American Jewry. Frank had been kidnapped out of a Marietta, Georgia, jail after being found guilty of murdering a young factory-worker girl solely on the testimony of a man who later was viewed as the most likely culprit. Add the virulent antisemitic diatribes of Henry Ford in his Dearborn newspaper, and the huge crowds who came to hear "America's hero," Charles Lindbergh, at America First rallies denouncing the Jews for pushing the U.S. into war (or the wrong war, since Lindbergh did favor joining Germany in waging war with Russia)—all made the future of Jews in America a questionable proposition.

How America Became "Golden"

Yet, the economic opportunities for Jews (or anyone else with drive, talent, and ambition) allowed them to prosper in ways that had never been open to them anywhere or at any time in Europe. As Jews prospered, and Jewish entry into the cultural, economic, and political fabric of American life became deeper and more intense, a distinction arose that had been previously unknown: between the history of *Jews* in America, and the history of *Judaism* in America. For centuries, the two had been identical, as Jews, who had been ghettoized physically, psychologically, and economically, clung to their monolithic religion for solace and protection.

In America, all that changed. Jews who "made it" in American society—who attained positions of wealth and power in the business world; who achieved high academic or professional status in America's growing educational, medical and legal establishments; who captured America's attention and imagination through dominance in entertainment, the arts, media, and culture (high, middle, and low) now had a power they never had before. They could direct the course of Jewish *religious* life, locally and nationally, through the synagogues, the social, communal and fraternal orders, and through the media—all devolving from the true source of this power: the power of the pocketbook.

As America became a *goldeneh medina*—a golden land, of opportunity and free of the old persecutions—it also ushered in a new force in Jewish religion, the effects of which are still being seen in American Jewish life today: the *ballabos*—the lay Jewish congregant or constituent who provided the funding and vocal support for the rabbi, the organization, the institution, the politician, in short, virtually every aspect of Jewish life. In the egalitarian environment of America, where anyone can build a synagogue or form a society anywhere they want (on land or in a building they own or rent), and hire (and fire) anyone they want as their rabbi, leader, or functionary—or hire none at all—the *ballebattim* (plural of *ballabos*) determine religious life of American Jewry in ways that were not possible in Europe.

How did this come about? In Europe, Jews conducted all their religious functions at the pleasure of the Christian (i.e., church) authorities, and this begrudging sanction given by the Gentile government gave the Jews of the *shtetl* (village) or city the right to establish their institutions—and nothing else. No one could open their own synagogue, school (*cheder*), academy (*yeshiva*), ritual bath (*mikveh*), slaughterhouse or butcher—not even a *mohel* (ritual circumciser) could function in Europe without permission from the Gentile authorities.

Judaism Meets the Free Market

But America was different. No such authorization was necessary, and the First Amendment of the U.S. Constitution guaranteed that none ever would be. Now the synagogue would hire the rabbi, and more often than not select a rabbi who had oratory skills, not a command of the laws of what makes a chicken kosher; who appealed to the young people and the women of the sisterhood; and who was willing to yield when the financial interests of the synagogue were at stake. This in effect reduced the rabbi to a transient employee, and the same was true of every director in the Jewish organizational world. (Even the Hassidic community in America has experienced insurrections unthinkable in the Old World.)

There were drawbacks to this populist, free-market brand of Judaism, yes, but there were also some advantages, to be sure. With *ballebattim* in charge in every meaningful way, important decisions that could affect the welfare of millions of Jews would not be solely in rabbinic hands, hands that generally had little real-life "hard-ball" business experience, hands often swayed by irrelevant ("pesky") ideology.

The effect of this boardroom approach to Jewish religious and communal life was profound. It informed every aspect of Jewish organization from Hassidic outreach programs on American campuses, to the way federations managed hospitals, to the way synagogues paid off their mortgages. And given the phenomenal extent to which Jews have integrated into American life, one would have to say that (so far) this approach has been vindicated. (Still, one can't help but wish some measure of rabbinic values would occasionally seep into that boardroom.)

B. The Religion in America

Early Period: To the Late Nineteenth Century

The "free-for-all" chaotic quality of Jewish life became apparent from the very beginning. The twenty-three Jews who disembarked in New Amsterdam Harbor in 1654, marking the beginning of American Jewish history, were not made to feel very welcome by the governor, Peter Stuyvesant. He complained to the directors of the Dutch West India Company about having to accept such "a deceitful race," as he put it, into his colony. The directors reminded him that many Jewish investors had made his colony possible in the first place. The new arrivals arranged first for a cemetery (always the first order of business in many religious communities), and then for a place of worship.

The ancestry of these Jews was Sephardic (their ancestors had been exiled from Portugal in the 1490s), so it was a Sephardic order of service that was followed. There were minor variations in the text of the service, but a very significant difference between the Iberian Sephardic service and the Franco-German Ashkenazic one was the direction the *hazan* (cantor) faced. In the Sephardic service he faced the congregation, directing them in prayer; in Ashkenazic services, he faced the Ark on the eastern wall of the synagogue, praying along with the rest of the congregation. When Ashkenazic Jews arrived in New York and Philadelphia, they accepted the Sephardic service (if only because the custom of a place once established takes precedence), but when they were much more numerous than the Sephardic Jews, they established Ashkenazic synagogues of their own, as happened in Philadelphia in 1802 and in New York in 1825.

But while the issue in the North was which way the cantor should face, more serious issues were being debated in the largest Jewish concentration in the late 1700s and early 1800s, which was in the South, centered in Charleston, South Carolina. These Jews, originally from Prussia and Central Europe, were busy grappling with the issues of Reform Judaism.

Ironically, America proved much more fertile soil for the Reform movement than Germany, the land of its birth. Two larger-than-life figures helped nurture its growth into a major American religious movement. One was **Isaac Mayer Wise** (1819–1900), whose love for everything American was matched by his prodigious organizational skills. Wise was dreaming about the freedom he imagined he would find in America while still serving in a traditional synagogue in Bohemia. He finally moved to the United States in 1846 and eventually became rabbi of a congregation in Albany, New York. Wise's reforms antagonized the traditionalists, boiling over one year in a riot during High Holy Day services. Wise was forced to resign, and in 1854 he accepted an invitation from a synagogue (B'nai Jeshurun) in Cincinnati, Ohio. He would serve there for nearly fifty years, creating three institutions that made Reform Judaism the strongest branch of Judaism in nineteenth-century America: the Union of American Hebrew Congregations (UAHC) in 1973; Hebrew Union College (HUC) in 1875; and the Central Conference of American Rabbis (CCAR), the professional organization of the American Reform rabbinate, formed in 1892.

The word "reform," one may note, does not appear in the name of any of these organizations, nor in the name of the English-language newspaper he founded (*The Israelite*) or the prayer book he issued, which he characteristically called *Minhag America* ("American Custom"). This was deliberate on Wise's part, because he believed these institutions would serve all of American Jewry. Wise always tried to accommodate his more traditional colleagues, though he openly mocked the kashruth laws and urged American Jews to abandon all elements of Judaism that could not be adopted universally. Wise genuinely thought Reform Judaism would win over the hearts of Jews from Eastern Europe who had settled in the Northeast, in spite of his promoting "family" (i.e., mixed) seating and organ music, and abandoning head covering and prayer shawls at services. In this he was hopelessly naive. Yet, under his guidance, all three organizations prospered, as did Reform

Isaac Mayer Wise was rabbi of the Plum Street Temple—now the Isaac M. Wise Temple—in Cincinnati, Ohio, from 1866 until his death in 1900. The Moorish-style temple, designed by James Keyes Wilson, appears in this 1951 photograph.

Judaism itself, becoming by far the most dominant form of Judaism in the nineteenth century.

As capable an organizer as Wise was, he was outshone in the field of theology by a reformer even more radical than he. **David Einhorn** (1809–1879) had been virtually thrown out of Europe by both the Jewish community, who regarded him as a danger to traditional Judaism (in spite of, or possibly because of, his deep Orthodox training), and by the Hungarian government, who regarded him a dangerous political provocateur. In America, Einhorn became a voice of radical Reform, though he did not have the political skills to fare any better in a rabbinical post, being forced to resign his pulpit in Baltimore for his abolitionist views.

Unlike Wise, he did not believe America was the fulfillment of Mosaic Judaism, but modeled Reform principles on the German model. If Wise was Reform Judaism's father, Einhorn was its spiritual leader (its "rabbi"), promoting a universalist version of Reform Judaism that was uncompromising. At the prompting of Einhorn's son-in-law, **Kaufman Kohler** (1843–1926), Wise's successor as president of HUC, a set of principles was adopted at a conference of Reform rabbis held in Pittsburgh in 1885. The conference was not well attended, had no official standing, and was not even recognized by the Reform organizations (though it was chaired by Wise). Nonetheless, out of it came the Pittsburgh Platform, which was to be the classic statement of American Reform ideology for the next seventy years (until repudiated in 1937 by the CCAR in the Columbus Platform). The Pittsburgh Platform was vintage Einhorn, and it slowly became adopted as the essential statement of Reform principles. A feature that Wise supported (though perhaps not as radically as Einhorn intended) was the principle that every Reform congregation—in fact, every Reform *congregant*—could determine for themselves exactly what elements of traditional practice suited them. This was to become the hallmark of American Reform Judaism, a principle that would be tested again and again as the American penchant for experimentation (especially evident on the West Coast) kept devising new practices and deviations from the tradition.

Middle Period: To World War II

At a fateful dinner in 1883 celebrating HUC's first graduating class, the first course—decidedly unkosher shrimp cocktail, along with a half-dozen other gross violations of kashruth—deeply offended some attendees, Orthodox rabbis and supporters who had been assured by Wise that the meal would be kosher. This was not the first time Wise had been the seemingly unwitting victim of a "mishap," and though attempts to salve the wounds were made, a group who saw the break with Reform as irrevocable met in New York to find an alternative. Led by **Sabato Morais** (1823–1897), hazan of Mikveh Israel, Philadelphia's Sephardic center, and **Henry Pereira Mendes** (1852–1937), rabbi of New York City's Sephardic synagogue, Shearith Israel, the groundwork was laid for what eventually became Conservative Judaism. The Jewish Theological Seminary (JTS) was formed in 1887 in New York City, designed to provide more traditional rabbinical training, but it would be some time before JTS was on firm enough financial footing. The ideology of JTS was inspired by the scholars of Europe who had (respectfully) applied academic scholarly methods to Jewish studies, creating a discipline known as *Wissenschaft des Judentums* (Science of Judaism). Known as the Historical School and exemplified in the work of Dresden's Rabbi Zechariah Frankel. the fit was not always an easy one, and most rabbinic authorities looked upon them with suspicion.

It took some time for the new Conservative movement to take root, and had it not been for the work of Arkansas-born Philadelphian **Cyrus Adler** (1863–1940), the Conservative movement might never have survived. Adler had received the first PhD degree in Semitics in the U.S. in 1887, awarded him by Johns Hopkins, He served as assistant secretary of the Smithsonian Institution, then became president of a struggling Dropsie College in Philadelphia, turning it into a first-rate academic institution in Semitics. At the age of twenty-three, he helped create JTS, and subsequently also helped create the Jewish Publication Society (1888) and the American Jewish Historical Society (1892). He was also instrumental in creating two major synagogue organizations: the Union of Orthodox Jewish Congregations in 1898 (at a time when Orthodoxy barely existed in the U.S.) and the United Synagogue of America in 1913, the major organization of Conservative congregations.

But perhaps his most important accomplishment was convincing **Solomon Schechter** (1847–1915), the dean of world Judaica studies, then a professor at the University of London, to leave England and assume the presidency of JTS. Schechter had come from a Hassidic family and been educated in Berlin and at Cambridge; he had attained world recognition for uncovering and retrieving the contents of the Cairo Geniza—the boarded-up anteroom of the abandoned Cairo synagogue in which discarded doc-

This undated photograph shows four major figures of American Judaism. From left to right, they are: David Philipson (1862–1949), author of the Reform Movement in Judaism; Solomon Schechter; Cyrus Adler; and Samuel Schulman (1864–1955), a founder of the Association of Reform Rabbis.

uments, some going back to antiquity, were respectfully stored when they became unusable.

Schechter's tenure, though only thirteen years, electrified American Judaism—so much so, that JTS became known simply as "Schechter's Seminary" and Conservative Judaism became the dominant form of Judaism in the period leading up to World War II. Conservative synagogues proliferated in the American landscape, particularly in the suburbs, where American Jews found homes once they worked their way out of the ghettos of New York, Philadelphia, and Boston.

Conservative Judaism found the perfect middle ground between the somewhat gothic (and elitist) formalism of Reform Judaism, and the unbending rigors of Orthodoxy, then known only in its European, shtetl-oriented form. The synagogue life that Conservative congregations forged made many accommodations to the American lifestyle: the partition (*mechitzah*) that separated men and women was dispensed with, and men and women either sat together or across an aisle. Friday night services were scheduled late in the winter (convenient for working people getting home after the early sunset), and the service itself, while based on the traditional liturgy, was shorter, oriented more to communal singing, less melodramatic than the Orthodox service, and much less "ecclesiastical" than the Reform. The enshrouding woolen *tallit* (prayer shawl) was replaced with a simpler, less cumbersome silken prayer shawl, and the synagogue itself was transformed into a facility with luxury-resort appurtenances.

Did Conservative Judaism permit driving to synagogue on Shabbat (something strictly forbidden in Orthodoxy)? Perhaps, but the full parking lots in suburban Conservative synagogues was proof enough that people were going to drive to services in any case, because that was the only way they could get there (and, after all, it's a free country, isn't it?). Women began to have increasingly important roles in synagogue life, which translated into being counted to a *minyan* (quorum) and given the same status as men in all the functions of the synagogue, including (as of 1985) serving as rabbis.

In all the many discussions that took place at JTS or by the Committee on Jewish Law and Standards, the central authority of Jewish practice, a committee of the Rabbinical Assembly, the Conservative movement's rabbinical association, very little time was spent discussing what seemed to be the single most important issue: what the traffic will bear. The movement had created a form of Judaism that was perfectly suited to the lives people were actually living in the U.S., and the Jewish populace had responded enthusiastically. The pronouncements of the Committee were (within reason) immaterial; Conservative congregations were going to practice Judaism as they saw fit, mindful of the tradition (to the extent they knew it), taking direction from their rabbi (whom they had chosen for his compatibility and conviviality), and aware that even in the area of attracting members, their synagogue was in a "competitive situation."

So successful was this brand of Judaism, that JTS could not keep up, and many men with Orthodox ordination accepted Conservative pulpits, sometimes rationalizing that their intent was to move the congregation closer to Orthodoxy (or at least to reinstate the *mechitzah*. Not surprisingly, few such synagogue "conversions" ever took place.)

Another area where Conservative Judaism took the lead was with regard to Israel. The Reform movement viewed the elements of the liturgy hoping for a return to "Thy [God's] city Jerusalem," and a rebuilding of the Temple, complete with sacrifices and a Davidic kingdom, as irrelevant and antiquated, and formally rejected Zionism in 1897, and then again in 1919, denouncing the British government for ever issuing the Balfour Declaration. Some Reform rabbis, like Abba Hillel Silver and Steven Wise, objected to this stand, and Orthodox Zionism was slow to develop first because of the overt secularism of the Zionist hierarchy (beginning with Herzl), and second because of the claims of the ultra-Orthodox (mainly, but not exclusively Hassidic) that a true return to the land of Israel could only be accomplished by a Messiah (who, alas, had clearly not yet arrived). It remained for the Conservative movement to bring Israel to the forefront of the American Jewish agenda, through fundraising, consciousness-raising, and in more than a few instances, arranging for or pitching in and helping ship arms and supplies to fighting Jewish soldiers on the front lines in Palestine.

Modern Period: After World War II

The big story of Judaism in America in the Postwar period is the extraordinary revival of Orthodoxy in America. Prior to WWII, Orthodox Jews in the U.S. were a distinct minority of the Jewish population (even if they weren't in the minority when disembarking at Ellis Island). Except for a few enclaves in New York and Boston, American life was not conducive to Orthodox practice, particularly Sabbath observance, which made employment difficult, and kashruth, which made eating anywhere but at home

impossible. There was very little in the way of education of Orthodox Judaism at any but the most elementary level. Some yeshivot organized on the European model existed, but they were small and struggled as much for funding as for students and rabbinic instructors. Americans seeking European rabbinic learning were more likely to travel to Europe and attend yeshivot like those in Nevardok or Slabodka, or even Hebron in pre-mandate Palestine.

World War II and the decimation of the Jewish community of Europe had a profound influence on Orthodoxy in America. Four men symbolize the Orthodox renaissance, though each had many extraordinary men and women supporting them. Further, each represents a different segment of Orthodox Jewry in the late twentieth century.

Rabbi Aharon Kotler (1891–1962) was a product of the Slabodka yeshiva and arrived in America in 1941, barely escaping the invading Nazis. In 1943, he established a high-level yeshiva—Bais Medrash Gavo'ah—in Lakewood, New Jersey, then a popular Jewish resort. Though the yeshiva had much interaction with Jews who vacationed in the many local hotels, the yeshiva was founded in a remote town so that it could be dedicated to the highest level of Jewish learning. The yeshiva today has several branches (in the U.S. and Israel) and over 5,000 students studying Talmud and rabbinics at a level comparable to the best yeshivot of Europe. Rabbi Kotler (perhaps taking a page from the notebook of Rabbi Yochanan ben Zakai) believed he and his yeshiva served American Jewry best by concentrating on learning, and avoiding when possible involvement in politics and communal affairs. As a result, the institution, though isolated, has provided American Jewry with thousands of learned and committed scholars who are today's teachers and leaders.

Rabbi Moshe Feinstein (1895–1986) was educated in Slotsk, Russia, and forced to emigrate to the U.S. in 1936. He founded a yeshiva on the Lower East Side, but his lasting influence was as a *posek*—an adjudicator of Jewish law, usually in the form of responsa to specific problems or questions, many of which required careful scientific elucidation, which he sought from experts, including some of his students and relatives. Many rabbis (of all branches) were privy to Rabbi Feinstein's private telephone number at his home on the Lower East Side and he took calls at all hours from all over the world. Rabbi Feinstein's legacy was first to bring the *Halachah*—Jewish Law—to the forefront of modern life, particularly of modern technology (including several controversial cases, such as the question of separating conjoined twins where one is certain to die in the process, which he permitted.) His other legacy is a body of responsa and rabbinic commentaries that will be studied and analyzed for generations. Rabbi Feinstein participated in Hillel Kook's ill-fated 1943 "Rabbi's March" in Washington, D.C., urging President Roosevelt to save Europe's Jews.

Rabbi Menachem M. Schneerson (1902–1994) was the seventh rebbe (Hassidic master) of Lubavitch, a sect named after a town in Russia, the sect is also known as Chabad, an acronym for the Hebrew for wisdom, understanding, and knowledge. Schneerson was educated in secular studies (engineering) at the Sorbonne and in Liverpool. In Berlin, he met Rabbi Joseph Soloveitchik at the home of their teacher, Rabbi Chaim Heller, and they became lifelong friends. When his father-in-law, the sixth Lubavitcher rebbe, Yosef Yitzchok Schneersohn, died in 1950, he became rebbe. Under his guidance, Chabad has grown enormously over the last fifty years, reaching out worldwide to alienated and disaffected Jews, especially young college students.

Rabbi Joseph B. Soloveitchik (1903–1993), scion of the illustrious family of rabbis of Brisk, Lithuania, came to be called simply "the Rav"—the master—and venerated as "JB" by others. He received a PhD in Kantian philosophy from the University of Berlin before emigrating to the U.S. in 1936. He succeeded his father as the dean (*rosh hayeshiva*) of the Rabbi Issac Elchanan Theological Seminary of Yeshiva University. In that capacity, he supervised the ordaining of several thousand rabbis schooled in "Modern Orthodoxy," the view that rabbinic learning must be combined ("synthesized") with secular knowledge. His students were to have a profound effect on American Jewry, serving as articulate (and often clean-shaven) rabbis and communal leaders, armed with both a rabbinic and a university education. Soloveitchik was a champion of higher Jewish education for women, founding Maimonides, a progressive Orthodox day school in Boston (where he was the unofficial head of the Jewish community), and promoting the study of Talmud by women in Yeshiva University's Stern College. Rabbi Solovei-tchik's public lectures in New York and Boston, always SRO events, conducted over four decades, had a profound effect on American Orthodox Jewry.

3. Rabbinic Activism

In addition to *ballabattim*, America has also spawned a new breed of activist rabbis who were not content to sit in their studies lost in Talmudic tomes, but who went out and campaigned, protested, and marched on behalf of an ideology or a cause they cherished. The three examples presented here are very different in their religious orientation, but they had this in common: they acted (sometimes at great personal cost) to further goals, ideals, and, they believed, the welfare of American Jewry. Their influence extended far beyond the immediate causes for which they worked, fulfilling in many American Jewish minds the proper prophetic role of the religious leader.

Abraham Joshua Heschel (1907–1972) was a theologian at JTS, but he made an even greater impact with his participation in social causes, such as marching with Martin Luther King Jr. in the Selma Freedom March of 1965. The cause of Jewish feminism is now (aptly) led by his daughter, Dartmouth professor Susannah Heschel.

Mordecai Kaplan (1881–1983) founded a branch of what might be called radically humanistic Judaism known as Reconstructivism, which is now an established fourth denomination of the faith, with a rabbinical seminary in suburban Philadelphia and many congregations across America.

Avraham "Avi" Weiss (b. 1944), rabbi of the Orthodox Hebrew Institute of Riverdale (in the Bronx, New York), has protested at Auschwitz and in front of the U.N., defending Israel against attacks by media, diplomats, and politicians, and countering the Holocaust-denial rhetoric of antisemites and of Iranian president Ahmadinejad.

C. Important Dates and Landmarks

1654 Portugal recaptures Brazil from Holland; expels Jews and Protestants. Most return to Holland; twenty-three sail to New Amsterdam; over Stuyvesant's objections, Jews granted the right to settle in New Amsterdam.

1730 New York Jews build first New York synagogue, Shearith Israel.

1733 Savannah establishes a Jewish community; will become permanent in 1790s.

1740s–1750s Philadelphia Jewry establishes a cemetery. Newport, Rhode Island, and Charleston, South Carolina, establish organized Jewish communities. New York founds an all-day Jewish school.

1760s Philadelphia and Montreal have organized Jewish communities. Newport builds its first synagogue (1763).

1787 The Northwest Territory Act grants Jews equality in all future territories and states.

1788 The United States Constitution ratified; Jews given full rights under federal (but not all state) laws.

1791 Bill of Rights, with First Amendment (freedom of religion) clause, ratified.

1802 The first U.S. Ashkenazic synagogue, Rodeph Shalom, founded in Philadelphia.

1824 First Reform Jewish religious group in U.S., the Reformed Society of Israelites, formed in Charleston.

1829 Isaac Leeser installed as *hazzan* (minister) of Cong. Mikveh Israel in Philadelphia.

1837 The first passover Haggadah is printed in America and published by S. H. Jackson.

1838 Rebecca Gratz establishes first Jewish Sunday school (Orthodox) in Philadelphia.

1841 Charleston's Beth Elohim first permanent Reform Jewish synagogue in the U.S.

1843 Isaac Leeser, hazzan of the Sephardic synagogue of Philadelphia, publishes *The Occident*, advocate of Orthodoxy. B'nai B'rith aid and fraternal order, established.

1852 The first East European congregation in New York City is organized. The following year, Isaac Leeser publishes an English translation of the Bible.

1854 Isaac Mayer Wise becomes rabbi of Cong. B'nai Yeshurun in Cincinnati. He publishes *The Israelite*.

1860 Morris Raphall first rabbi to open a session of the U.S. Congress with prayer.

1862 The United States government appoints army chaplains to serve Jews. General Grant expels Jews from Tennessee, charging collusion with the South; decree quickly revoked by President Lincoln.

1869 Reform rabbis, led by Samuel Hirsch and David Einhorn, meet in Philadelphia, publish first statement on Jewish Reform position in America.

1873 Union of American Hebrew Congregations (UAHC) established in Cincinnati.

1875 The Hebrew Union College is established in Cincinnati, intending to prepare rabbis for all types of synagogues.

1880 UAHC conducts first census of American Jewry. Estimate: 250,000.

1881 Pogroms in Russia force many East European Jews to flee to U.S. First Yiddish play performed in New York City, 1882.

1883 HUC "Treifa" (shrimp) Banquet.

1885 Pittsburgh Platform adopted by left-wing Reform rabbis. *Tageblatt*, first U.S. Yiddish daily paper, in New York City.

1886-1887 Jewish Theological Seminary (JTS), cornerstone of U.S. Conservative movement, is established in New York City.

1888 The Jewish Publication Society (JPS) of America is founded in Philadelphia. Rabbi Jacob Joseph elected chief rabbi of New York Orthodoxy; proves ineffective.

1889 Central Conference of American Rabbis (CCAR) founded by Isaac M. Wise.

1895 CCAR rejects authority of the Halakhah, Jewish rabbinic (oral) law.

1897 The first American yeshiva of a European type (Rabbi Isaac Elchanan Theological Seminary) is founded in New York City. At CCAR meeting Rabbi Isaac M. Wise denounces Zionism of Theodor Herzl. The socialist *Jewish Daily Forward* begins publishing first issue in New York City.

1898 The Union of Orthodox Jewish Congregations of America is established. The Federation of American Zionists is established in New York City.

1900 The *Arbeiter Ring* (Workmen's Circle) and ILGWU formed.

1901 The Rabbinical Assembly, organization of Conservative rabbis, established.

1902 The Union of Orthodox Rabbis (OU) is formed. Solomon Schechter, new JTS head, promotes Conservatism as separate denomination.

1903 Massacre of Jews in Kishinev, Russia, stirs American Jewry. Kaufmann Kohler named president of Hebrew Union College.

1906 Jewish Encyclopedia is published. American Jewish Committee, a secular (elite) organization, established.

1907 Rabbi Stephen S. Wise establishes the Free Synagogue. Dropsie College in Philadelphia grants PhD degree in Judaica and Jewish studies.

1909 Jacob H. Schiff's philanthropy bolsters educational programs at Jewish Theological Seminary and Hebrew Union College. Unsuccessful efforts by Judah L. Magnes to create New York

Kehillah. Hebrew Sheltering and Immigrant Aid Society (HIAS) formed.

1912 Young Israel organized on New York's Lower East Side. Henrietta Szold founds Hadassah, Women's Zionist Organization.

1913 The United Synagogue of Conservative Judaism is organized.

1914–1915 Joint Distribution Committee unites American Jewish ethnic groups to rescue East European Jewry in wake of WWI.

1915 Leo Frank lynched in Marietta, Georgia. Rabbi Isaac Elchanan Theological Seminary led by Bernard Revel.

1916 Louis D. Brandeis is appointed to the U.S. Supreme Court.

1917 English translation of the Hebrew Bible published by Jewish Publication Society. United States enters WWI; 200,000 Jews serve. National Jewish Welfare Board created to aid American Jewish servicemen. British government issues Balfour Declaration promising Jewish homeland in Palestine. Bolsheviks control Russia.

1918 First American Jewish Congress meets in Philadelphia; sets out to convince great powers in Paris to establish a Jewish homeland in Palestine. Yiddish Art Theater founded by Maurice Schwartz. Women's League for Conservative Judaism is formed.

1921, 1924 Immigration Acts of 1921, 1924 close America to East European Jews.

1922 Mordecai Kaplan creates Reconstructionist's Society for the Advancement of Judaism. The Orthodox Agudath Israel of America established. Zionist-oriented American Jewish

Congress founded. Stephen S. Wise founds (mainly Reform) Jewish Institute of Religion.

1923 First B'nai B'rith Hillel Foundation established at University of Illinois.

1925 Synagogue Council of America organized.

1927 Survey reports U.S. Jewish population at 4,228,000; 3,118 congregations.

1928 The National Conference of Christians and Jews is established. Rabbi Isaac Elchanan Yeshiva becomes Yeshiva College, first Jewish institution of higher education.

1933 Nazis gain in Germany, spurring antisemitic activity in U.S.

1934 Jewish Labor Committee is established. *Judaism as a Civilization* by Mordecai Kaplan published; *The Reconstructionist.*

1935 Rabbinical Council of America, organization of "Modern Orthodox" rabbis, formed.

1937 Central Conference of American Rabbis adopts more-or-less pro-Zionist position.

1939 The British White Paper on Palestine reduces immigration severely; World War II begins in Europe; first reports of mass killing of Polish Jews heard in America. The United Jewish Appeal founded.

1941–1945 Over 500,000 American Jews serve in WWII (many of them officers).

1942 American Zionists adopt Biltmore Program, demanding creation of Jewish State. Anti-Zionist American Council for Judaism formed by some Reform rabbis.

1943 Jews learn of the Holocaust. American authorities, and most Jewish leaders ineffective in convincing FDR to admit more Jewish refugees. CCAR adopts pro-Zionist resolution. Samuel Belkin becomes president of Yeshiva College. Maurice N. Eisendrath becomes president of UAHC.

1944 FDR establishes the War Refugee Board. The National Society of Hebrew Day Schools (Torah Umesorah) is founded.

1945 Yeshiva College becomes Yeshiva University. A-bomb dropped on Hiroshima. Jews prominent among scientists who made it.

1945–1952 President Truman allows hundreds of thousands of displaced persons into U.S.

1947 November 29: UN General Assembly votes for partition plan for Palestine.

1948 Brandeis University established as first secular university in U.S. under Jewish auspices. May 14: Israel declares independence. U.S. government recognizes Israel.

1950 The Hebrew Union College and the Jewish Institute of Religion merge.

1951 UAHC moves to New York City. Rabbi Menachem Mendel Schneersohn succeeds his father-in-law as Lubavitcher Rebbe.

1952 Germany agree to pay Holocaust survivors $822 million as reparations.

1954 Stern College for Women opens, first women's college under Jewish auspices.

1955 The Conference of Presidents of Major American Jewish Organizations formed.

1964 Congress passes the Civil Rights Act.

1965 Abraham Joshua Heschel marches with Martin Luther King in Selma, Alabama.

1967 Israel emerges victorious from the Six-Day War against Arab enemies.

1968 Reconstructionist Rabbinical College is established Philadelphia suburb.

1972 HUC-JIR ordains first woman rabbi, Sally Priesand.

1973 The Yom Kippur War—Egypt and Syria attack Israel. Israel again victorious.

1974 Jackson-Vannick amendment allows large numbers of Soviet Jews into U.S.

1975 UN General Assembly declares Zionism a "form of racism and racial discrimination."

1979 Camp David Accords: Pres. Jimmy Carter helps Israel, Egypt sign peace treaty.

1983 The Jewish Theological Seminary faculty votes to ordain women as rabbis.

1984 Central Conference of American Rabbis accept patrilineal Jewish identity.

1985–1990 The USSR falls. Many Russian Jews emigrate to Israel and the U.S.

1993 Rabin and Arafat shake hands on September 13 under the beaming eyes of President Bill Clinton after signing of Oslo Accord two days earlier.

1993 Opening of the U.S. Holocaust Memorial Museum in Washington, D.C. Release of Steven Spielberg film *Schindler's List*.

1994 Death of Menahem Mendel Schneerson, seventh Lubavitcher rebbe, without heir.

1999 New Statement of Principles for Reform Judaism calls for dialogue with tradition.

2000 Senator Joseph Lieberman nominated by the Democrats for the U.S. vice-presidency.

2001 September 11th terrorist attacks on U.S. result in heightened security by Jews.

2002 Surveys report decline in America's Jewish population, first since colonial times.

> The contribution of Jews to secular American culture is beyond the scope of this chapter. Readers are referred to resources at the end of this chapter for more on that subject.

II. Demographics and Distribution

The U.S. Jewish population over the past two decades has plateaued at between 5.5 and 6.2 million. A Jewish Federation–commissioned National Jewish Population Survey of 2002 reported the first decline in American Jewish population in 350 years, though some of the criteria used were questioned. The intermarriage rate, which rose from 8.0% in 1950 to over 40.0% in the 1990s, was offset by a "return rate" that did not

Yeshiva College in New York City, the undergraduate college for men at Yeshiva University, was founded in 1928.

manifest itself until the population lost had children. What was genuinely alarming, however, was that the replacement rate per Jewish woman had dropped from about 2.1%—the population-stasis rate—to a low of 1.8% (because Jewish women were marrying later and having fewer offspring).

New York City and Greater New York Area

Of the 5.8 million Jews in the United States, nearly 40.0% live in the Greater New York City area (including southern Connecticut, Long Island, Westchester and Rockland Counties, and Northeastern New Jersey). In New York City proper, Jews comprise as much as 13.0% of the general population; over the entire area, the figure is closer to 9.5%

The very high birth rate is indicated in the Hassidic enclaves in Brooklyn and Upstate New York (Monroe, Spring Valley)—as high as 3.4 per family. This may be expected to have significant political ramifications in the years ahead.

The many agencies that oversee social services in the over 400 communities in the United States with significant Jewish populations are united under one umbrella organization, United Jewish Communities. A complete directory of these agencies is downloadable at the website: www.ujc.org.

Many Jewish communities across the U.S. and Canada are served by a network of Jewish community centers, also called YMHAs. Manhattan, for example, has two large facilities, one on the Upper East Side, the 92nd Street Y, with a long and distinguished history; and a new institution, the Manhattan JCC, on the Upper West Side. The names and contact information for all JCC/YMHA (and similarly designed) facilities is downloadable at the website: www.jcca.org/jccdirectory.pdf

The Northeast: Boston-Washington Corridor

Boston area Jewry has shifted its center from the city to suburban areas, west (Brookline, Newton), north (Marblehead), and south (Randolph, Sharon). In Philadelphia, a similar migration has seen the center shift from northeastern Philadelphia to the west

The Beth Sholom synagogue in Elkins Park, Pennsylvania, was designed by Frank Lloyd Wright, who accepted the commission in 1953. The structure was consecrated in 1959. It is the only synagogue designed by Wright, and was the last project he completed before his death.

(Main Line) and north (Elkins Park). Only Germantown has remained a major Jewish enclave. The Washington, D.C. area centers of Jewry have similarly migrated away from urban to suburban communities. Today, the major centers are Silver Spring/Kemp Mill and Pikesville, Maryland, and the Shephard Park/Cleveland Park areas of suburban D.C., once heavily Jewish areas that lost large numbers of Jews, but which are experiencing revivals of Jewish life. (*See* www.shalomdc.org)

The South and Midwest

The Jews of the South and the Midwest have a fascinating history (See www.cofc.edu/~jhc/). A half-million Jews live in the southeastern Miami–Dade–Palm Beach strip, making it the third largest Jewish concentration in the country. Miami Beach has long been a favorite for retirees, but today many young Jews are finding South Florida a congenial area to raise a family.

Jewish merchants have dotted the South and Great Plains since the early 1800s, and by the mid-twentieth century, large Jewish communities were developed in Detroit, Minneapolis, Chicago-Skokie, Cleveland, and St. Louis. The U.S. economic downturn of the late twentieth century caused many Jews in these areas to seek opportunities elsewhere. (See www.jhsum.org and www.umm.edu/umja for more.)

The West and Northwest

California is second only to New York as the state with the most Jews; Los Angeles and San Francisco areas contain over 1 million, with average incomes generally higher than the national norm. The Jewish involvement in the entertainment industry has resulted in high-profile Jewish presence in Los Angeles, but significant Jewish communities are also to be found in Las Vegas, Houston, and Dallas, and in Seattle and Portland.

III. Organizations

Religious Organizations

Agudath Israel of America (AIA)
The Jewish Observer
www.shemayisrael.com/jewishobserver
Ultra-Orthodox organization.

Central Conference of American Rabbis (CCAR)
CCAR Journal
www.ccarnet.org
Reform rabbinical organization.

CLAL: National Jewish Center for Learning and Leadership
www.clal.org

Hillel Foundation for Jewish Campus Life
www.hillel.org
Originally a B'nai Brith project, now interdenominationally servicing major U.S. college campuses.

National Council of Young Israel
Viewpoint
www.youngisrael.org
Orthodox.

Rabbinical Council of America (RCA)
Tradition
www.rabbis.org
Modern Orthodox rabbinical organization.

Rabbinical Assembly (RA)
Conservative Judaism
www.rabbinicalassembly.org
Conservative.

Torah Umesorah: National Society of Hebrew Day Schools
Olomeinu/Our World
Orthodox day school organization.

Union of American Hebrew Congregations
Reform Judaism
www.uahc.org

Union of Orthodox Jewish Congregations (OU)
OU Kosher Directory
www.ou.org
Widely provides kashruth (OU) certification.

United Synagogue of Conservative Judaism
United Synagogue Review
www.uscj.org

Social and Political Organizations

American Jewish Committee (AJC)
Commentary
www.ajc.org

American Jewish Congress
Congress Monthly
www.ajcongress.org

Anti-Defamation League of B'nai Brith (ADL)
www.adl.org

Conference of Presidents of Major American Jewish Organizations
www.conferenceofpresidents.org

American Sephadi Federation (ASF)
Sephardic Today
www.asfonline.org

Zionist, Israel-Related Organizations

AIPAC: American-Israel Public Affairs Commission
Near East Report
www.aipac.org
Major Washington political group.

Theodore Herzl Foundation
Midstream
www.midstreamthf.com

Zionist Organization of America (ZOA)
www.zoa.org

Museums and Holocaust Memorialization

Center for Jewish History
www.cjh.org
Manhattan center housing AJHS, ASF, YIVO, Leo Baeck Institute, and Yeshiva University Museum.

The Jewish Museum (of JTS)
www.the jewishmuseum.org
On Manhattan's "Museum Mile."

Memorial Foundation for Jewish Culture
www.mfjc.org
Funds research and memorialization efforts.

Museum of Jewish Heritage
www.mjhnyc.org
Battery Park, Manhattan; houses Shoah Project.

National Museum of American Jewish History
www.nmajh.org
Near Liberty Bell in Philadelphia.

Skirball Cultural Center
www.skirball.org
Museum in Los Angeles affiliated with UHC.

U.S. Holocaust Memorial Museum
www.ushmm.org
Smithsonian Institute museum and research center, just off Mall in Washington, D.C.

FURTHER READING

General Histories:

The Jews of the United States
  Hasia R. Diner
  2004: University of California Press

Judaism in America
  Marc Lee Raphael
  2003: Columbia University Press

American Judaism: A History
  Jonathan D. Sarna
  2004: Yale University Press

A People Divided: Judaism in Contemporary America
  Jack Wertheimer
  1997: Brandeis University Press

Regional Histories:

Jews of the Pacific Coast
  Eisenberg, Kahn, and Toll
  2010: University of Washington Press

World of Our Fathers
  Irving Howe
  1989: Schocken Books

The Wonders of America
  Jenna Weissman Joselit
  1994: Hill and Wang

American Jewish Women's History
  Pamela Nadell
  2003: NYU Press

Pioneer Jews: A New Life in the Far West
  Harriet and Fred Rochlin
  2000: Mariner Books

Focused Works:

The Chosen People in an Almost Chosen Nation
  Richard John Neuhaus, ed.
  2002: Wm. B. Eerdmans

Jews and the Civil War
  Jonathan Sarna and Adam Mendelson, eds.
  2010: NYU Press

FURTHER READING AND RESOURCES

American Jewish Yearbook
  American Jewish Committee
  Annual: AJC/JPS (www.ajcarchives.org)

The Cambridge Companion to American Judaism
  Dana Evan Kapla, ed.
  2005: Cambridge University Press

Jewish Continuity in America
  Abraham J. Karp
  1998: University of Alabama Press

Judaism in America
  Marc Lee Raphael
  2003: Columbia University Press

American Judaism: A History
  Jonathan Sarna
  2004: Yale University Press

WEBSITES
  www.ajhs.org
  www.dinur.org
  www.temple.edu/feinsteinctr
  www.jewishvirtuallibrary.com
  www.myjewishlearning.com
  www.simpletoremember.com

V. EASTERN FAITHS

V EASTERN FAITHS

Historical Introduction

THE TERM "EASTERN FAITHS" REFERS TO RELIGIONS that originated in India and China and then spread to East and Southeast Asia. India gave birth to Hinduism, Jainism, Sikhism, and Buddhism; China was responsible for Taoism. These religions, which share many traits, are best known for a focus on individual enlightenment and growth. The notion that even the unlettered could achieve the highest religious reward made these religions attractive to all levels of society. Buddhism and Taoism, in particular, spread quickly throughout south and East Asia, quickly becoming localized by each country.

In addition to having wide popular appeal, these religions were tolerated by independent governments because (and as long as) they remained apolitical.

Located in the Valley of the Temples on the island of Oahu, Hawaii, the Byodo-In Temple is a replica of a Buddhist temple in Kyoto, Japan.

They did not advocate any particular social form or structure; they suggested instead how each person should act within one's respective society. In many ways, Eastern faiths have often appeared to Westerners as not strictly religions at all, but more like philosophies of how to live. This has allowed these religions to find hospitable environments in many different cultures.

Though there are striking similarities among these faiths, each has a distinct history and a very specific set of beliefs that makes each of them unique. In the chapters that follow, they are presented independently (and in the arbitrary order of the alphabet); but another way of approaching them would be to examine how their histories, impact, and teachings interact with one another. Here, a brief summary of these religions will highlight their inimitable features and point to some of the contours of these interactions:

Hinduism is the oldest of the Eastern faiths, having first taken shape during the Vedic period in India. It cannot be traced to a single founder, and instead formed over time, with the constant addition of scriptures. Since its inception, the body of scriptures has grown, and now Hinduism is praised for a vast number of books detailing theology, philosophy, and mythology, along with those teaching dharma, or how to lead a better, more spiritual life. Hinduism has many schools, and cannot therefore be classified as monotheistic, polytheistic, or even henotheistic. Instead of focusing on god(s), the focus of the religion is on the self, which is eternal. Through highly ritualized meditation practices the Hindu goal is to gain full awareness of this inner self, thus freeing it from the material world.

These shrines of Eastern faiths show a remarkable diversity of architectural styles. From left, they are: the Saimyo Buddhist temple in Mima, Japan; a detail of the ceiling in the Jain temple in Ranakpur, India; and the Hindu temple of Swaminarayan Akshardham in New Delhi, India.

Buddhism also originated in India. It quickly divided into two main schools: Theravada and Mahayana. Theravada Buddhism is the oldest, most conservative strand of Buddhism. It relies solely on the Pali Canon and related writings. Theravada Buddhism is mainly practiced in Southeast Asia. Mahayana Buddhism differs from Theravada in that it incorporates more texts into its teachings. Overall it is considered the more inclusive and less strict sect, and therefore has a greater following than Theravada. Mahayana Buddhism spread to East Asia, taking a slightly different form in each country that adopted it. In China, Mahayana Buddhism laid the groundwork for what is called Pure Land Buddhism; in Japan it became Zen Buddhism.

Jainism, another religion with roots in India, can be traced to the ninth century BCE, though many claim it is older. Jainism is loosely based on Hinduism, in that a central focus of the religion is on dharma—how to live a better life. Jains follow Jinas, or saints, who adhere to the rules of dharma, become fully liberated, and then teach others how to achieve this state. Jainism and its Jinas can be compared to Buddhism and the concept of the Bodhisattva. Jains have a small following, mainly in India, but membership continues to grow and spread.

Sikhism is a newer religion, dating to the late fifteenth century. Unlike Hinduism and Buddhism it has one founder, Nanak, who became the first of many gurus. Sikhism is a monotheistic religion but the Sikh god is nonanthropomorphic. The ten Sikh gurus, along with a body of texts, teach how to be less self-centered and more god-centered; in other words, how to practice humility and humanity. Sikhism represents the history, ideology, and culture of the Punjab; as a result its membership is greatest in the Punjab state in India.

Taoism is an ideology, philosophy and religion that is accredited to Laozi (or Lao-Tzu), a philosopher in China who lived sometime between the sixth century BCE and the fourth century BCE (although some say he never existed at all and is just a myth). Lao-Tzu is considered the author of the main Taoist text, the Dao De Qing. This book describes the concept of Dao (Tao): Dao is not seen but it is felt; it is the way. Humans have the choice every day to act against their natural state, which is Dao, and instead often make choices based on desire. Taoism encourages nonaction over action, stating it is this approach that will lead to a return to nature. Taoism shares many traits in common with Confucianism; however, the latter is strictly an ideology and philosophy whereas the former is also a formal religion. This distinction is often difficult to grasp, and so Taoism is sometimes wrongly brushed aside in discussions of Eastern faiths.

The **Baháʼí Faith** is another religion that enters the fold of Eastern faiths. Although its origins lie in Persia, and it is argued to have stemmed from Shiʼa Islam, its faith has a great number of followers in

Above left, the Harmandir Sahib (Abode of God) in Amritsar, India, is known to Sikhs as the Golden Temple; above right, the Cebu Taoist Temple in Cebu City, Philippines, is a popular tourist attraction; at right, the Shrine of the Báb, an important holy site for the Bahá'í Faith, sits atop Mount Carmel in Haifa, Israel.

South and Southeast Asia. Like Sikhism, the Baha'i Faith is monotheistic, yet unlike Sikhism, God's teachings are taught through a series of divine messengers starting with Abraham and Moses and ending with the Báb and Bahá'u'lláh. The Bahá'í Faith is least like the other Eastern faiths because it does not focus on individual liberation, but instead its focus lies in establishing peace and unity worldwide.

Whereas Western faiths are primarily Abrahamic faiths, most Eastern faiths do not subscribe to a Western history, chronology, or the same God. Western faiths are often linked closely with the state and its laws; whereas Eastern practices are less political, emphasizing individual growth instead. The nonpervasive nature of Eastern religions is precisely why they were able to spread so quickly throughout East and Southeast Asia. It is also why the import of Eastern faiths into the Western framework is relatively subtle, allowing the former to rest within the latter without imposing new rules and ordinances. This quiet blending of lifestyles and faiths can be witnessed in America.

The import of Eastern religions into the American landscape brought a refreshing new perspective on how to live. Americans, having primarily come from places with rigid religious laws, discovered a new vocabulary in these Eastern faiths. In today's America, it is not uncommon to find someone who outwardly

claims affiliation with and practices a Western religion, but whose ideology and spirituality is drawn from an Eastern faith. This is the allure of the Eastern faiths: they are private religions that do not overstep public law, or interfere with any other religion.

Even though many casually adopt Eastern faiths into their lives by making narrow (some may say superficial) personal choices, there are still a large number of people who practice and perpetuate the Eastern faiths on more serious levels. The growing number of shrines, temples, and houses of worship, along with personal shrines, attest to a devotion that goes beyond merely viewing the religions as an abstract ideology, a spiritual enhancement, or a self-help program. For immigrants, for their children, and for converts, these religions become a way of life, not just a series of disjoint personal choices. That so many can practice their faiths without hindrance shows that America has, in many ways, provided a tolerant and congenial home for Eastern faiths.

— REBECCA FINEMAN
SECTION EDITOR

1 Bahá'í Faith

I. Origins and Early History

A. Introduction

THE BAHÁ'Í FAITH, THE YOUNGEST MAJOR WORLD religion, is an outgrowth of Babism, which originally stemmed from Shia Islam. Babism emerged in the mid-nineteenth century, a period of high messianic expectation among many Muslims in Persia. On May 23, 1844, a young Iranian Shia Muslim from the city of Shiraz, Mírzá 'Alí-Muhammad, proclaimed himself the long-awaited successor to Muhammad. He called himself the Báb, meaning the "Gate." Babism was unequivocally denounced by Muslim leaders, yet the Báb succeeded in attracting thousands of devotees. The Báb's declaration ushered in the Bahá'í Era, which Bahá'ís believe will last approximately 1,000 years, after which point the Bahá'í Faith will be superseded by a religion more suited to the current era.

Among the Báb's disciples was Mírzá Husayn Alí Núrí. A favorite of the Báb, he continued to promulgate his teachings after the Báb's death. In 1863, he declared himself the next great prophet—Bahá'u'lláh, or Glory of God. This was a declaration of great significance: Bahá'u'lláh said he was the most recent in a line of manifestations of the Divine, of which Abraham, Moses, Jesus, Muhammad, the Buddha, and the Báb were part. This claim contradicted Muslim doctrine, which recognizes Muhammad as the last great prophet.

Bahá'u'lláh's assertion of divine authority was readily accepted by the majority of Bábís. Bahá'u'lláh actively promoted the new religion through letters to followers and encouraging Bahá'í pilgrims, spreading it as far as was practicable. Like the Báb, Bahá'u'lláh was persecuted; his followers, the Bahá'ís, were like-

Bahá'u'lláh (1817–1892), the founder of the Bahá'í Faith, was born in Persia. His passport, seen above, depicts the lion, sun, and saber symbol that was the country's emblem from 1423 through 1979.

wise persecuted and ridiculed. While imprisoned in Palestine in 1868, along with some of his followers, Bahá'u'lláh wrote the *Kitáb-i-Aqdas*, the Most Holy Book, an authoritative statement of Bahá'í laws and beliefs. During his forty years of ministry Bahá'u'lláh produced thousands of letters, essays, prayers, poems, treatises, and books, all of which are considered Bahá'í scripture.

Despite harsh and often violent persecution by both the government and parts of the Muslim community, the Bahá'í Faith continued to grow and had, by the late nineteenth century, spread throughout the Middle East and India. Before Bahá'u'lláh's death he named his son 'Abdu'l-Bahá (1844–1921) successor and head of the Bahá'í community.

The Shrine of Bahá'u'lláh, the founder of the Bahá'í Faith, contains the leader's remains. It is located in Acre, Israel.

B. The Religion in America

In 1892, a Lebanese Bahá'í convert named Ibrahim George Kheiralla moved to the United States and began to establish a Bahá'í community. A year later, at the World Parliament of Religions in Chicago, the first public mention of the Bahá'í Faith occurred when a Presbyterian missionary who had had firsthand experience with the religion spoke of it. A year after that, Thornton Chase (1847–1912), a Chicago businessman, became the first American convert to the religion.

Kheiralla's version of the Bahá'í teachings was tinged with his Christian background, and some of the ideas he propounded, such as 'Abdu'l-Bahá being the son of God and a latter-day incarnation of Jesus, are not completely faithful descriptions of Bahá'í doctrine. Nevertheless, his ideas were appealing to his followers, most of whom had Christian backgrounds. Among these was Marian Miller, an English immigrant who, in 1895, became Kheiralla's wife.

Female converts initially outnumbered male, perhaps because the faith gave them considerable freedom to organize and teach it. Though women in Bahá'í communities were, at first, restricted to serving on local Bahá'í governing bodies, all such restrictions ended in 1910–1912, and today women serve on all American Bahá'í governing bodies, including the National Spiritual Assembly.

Among other prominent early American believers were Dr. Edward and Louisa Getsinger, William Hoar, Henry Goodale, Charles Greenleaf, Paul Dealy, and Arthur Pillsbury Dodge, prominent lawyer and founding editor of *New England* Magazine. Phoebe Apperson Hearst, widow of Senator George Hearst, also added to the number of American Bahá'ís, as did her butler, Robert Turner, who became the first African-American Bahá'í. Many wealthier converts made pilgrimages to Akka.

In 1896, Kheiralla published *Za-ti-et Al-lah: The Identity and Personality of God*, condensing his teachings for the layperson. The book attracted new followers, and, by 1898, there were 225 Bahá'ís in the Chicago area. By this time Kheiralla had established Bahá'í classes in other cities in the Midwest and later on the East Coast, including New York. It is relevant to note that most of the early Bahá'í converts did not renounce their original faiths, as the Bahá'í Faith did not demand this of them.

Small groups of followers began springing up around the country. Kheiralla was seen as having a fair amount of power in these circles, for he knew the secret of the Greatest Name, Alláh-u-Abhá, or "God is Most Glorious." Kheiralla only taught this interpretation of Bahá'u'lláh's name to converts, never to those who were merely curious.

In 1899 Stoyan Krystof Vatralsky, a Bulgarian-born, Harvard-educated Protestant was asked by Christian churches in Kenosha, Wisconsin, to counter Bahá'í teachings. He gave a lecture at the Park Avenue Methodist Episcopal Church entitled "The Kenosha Truth Knowers: The Few Truths They Know and the Many Errors They Teach." This speech was met with anger and criticism from Bahá'ís and illustrated the extent of the Christian dismissal of the Bahá'í Faith.

A bigger controversy stemmed from the return of the first American Bahá'ís from a pilgrimage to meet `Abdu'l-Bahá. During the encounter, they came to believe that many of Kheiralla's teachings had been his personal ideas, rather than Bahá'í principles. Kheiralla felt his authority was being undermined and began to speak against `Abdu'l-Bahá. Eventually he broke with `Abdu'l-Bahá and set up his own rival Bahá'í community. Within a decade, however, it withered away and Kheiralla himself ceased to be active in it. To strengthen the Bahá'ís, `Abdu'l-Bahá sent a series of Persian teachers to deepen their knowledge of the Bahá'í teachings and commanded the election of governng councils.

By 1900, at the time of this fracture, there were approximately 2,000 Bahá'ís in the U.S. Kheiralla's defection shook the community, and, for a time, many confused converts drifted away from the faith. Eventually the situation began to right itself, and once again membership increased.

By 1908, fifteen African Americans had joined the Bahá'í Faith, including Louis Gregory, a lawyer, who later became a spokesperson for racial unity.

In 1908, Louise Waite wrote *Bahai Hymns of Peace and Praise*, which, despite its clear Christian influence, was distinctly Bahá'í. In 1909, the first National Bahá'í Convention took place. It was attended by thirty-nine delegates from thirty-six different cities.

`Abdu'l-Baha spent the greater part of 1912 visiting North America. On May 29 he gave a speech regarding the Oneness of Religion, in which he emphasized Jesus and His divine nature, a nature shared by many subsequent prophets rather than limited to one man. He spoke at Columbia and Stanford, and the press's coverage of these talks helped increase public awareness of the Bahá'í Faith. It was on this tour that `Abdu'l-Bahá laid the cornerstone for what was to become the Bahá'í House of Worship in Wilmette, Illinois.

In 1925, the National Spiritual Assembly of the Bahá'ís of the United States and Canada was officially recognized by Shoghi Effendi as the spiritual guardian of the Bahá'í Faith from 1921 to his death. In 1927, there were forty-seven local spiritual assemblies in North America.

In 1937, Shoghi Effendi gave the North American Bahá'ís a seven-year plan. It achieved three major goals: electing at least one local spiritual assembly in every state of the United States and Canada, opening every country in Latin America to the Bahá'í Faith, and completing the exterior of the Bahá'í temple in Wilmette. Nine years later, he gave them a second seven-year plan. In 1953, Shoghi Effendi gave twelve National Spiritual Assemblies a ten-year global crusade. At the end of the crusade Bahá'í membership in the United States numbered around 9,600.

In the 1960s, as civil rights issues raged, African-American Bahá'ís played a part in the fight for equality. Though some dissent existed within the faith as to whether Bahá'ís ought to involve themselves publicly in civil rights—largely due to the Bahá'í prohibition against involvement in politics—younger Bahá'ís tended to choose active roles.

From 1964 to 1972, the Universal House of Justice launched a nine-year plan, the goal of which was to increase the number of global conversions. It was a success: in 1964 the number of Bahá'ís in the United States had reached 10,000; by 1972 it was 59,372.

The Seat of the Universal House of Justice in Haifa, Israel, serves as the headquarters of the Bahá'í Faith. The shrine on page 532 is located on the hill above.

In 1992, the second Bahá'í World Congress was held at the Jacob Javits Center in Manhattan, at which 30,000 Bahá'ís gathered to honor the 100th anniversary of Bahá'u'lláh's passing. President George H. W. Bush sent his regards in the form of a laudatory letter to the Bahá'ís in attendance.

Diversity in the Bahá'í community is today at an all-time high, and the faith is found in every part of the U.S.; there are now over 157,000 Bahá'ís in over 7,000 American localities.

C. Important Dates

1817 Bahá'u'lláh is born.

1819 The Báb is born.

1826 Death of Shaykh Ahmad. Siyyid Kázim is appointed leader of the Shaykhi sect.

1828 Death of Mírzá Muhammad Ridá, the father of the Báb. Hájí Mírzá Siyyid `Alí, the Báb's maternal uncle, assumes care of the Báb.

1835 Marriage of Bahá'u'lláh and Navváb.

1843 Siyyid Kázim sends his students (including Mullá Husayn) to find the Promised One (the Mahdí). He then dies.

1844 The Báb declares his mission to Mullá Husayn in Shiraz, Iran.

1847 The Báb is imprisoned at Mákú.

1850 The Báb is publicly executed.

1853 Bahá'u'lláh is exiled from Tehran to Baghdad.

1857 Bahá'u'lláh writes the *Hidden Words*.

The 1980s saw growth slow as the country moved into a more conservative mood. The same shift toward conservatism was witnessed in Iran, where, with the 1979 revolution, large numbers of Bahá'í refugees fled, many seeking refuge in America, along with Europe, Canada, and Australia. Though Bahá'ís have always suffered from persecution and mistreatment in their native land, the revolution institutionalized it; the Islamic Republic destroyed or confiscated all Bahá'í properties. Today, Iranian Bahá'ís are not only stripped of many rights of citizenship, but are imprisoned and sometimes tortured and executed by their government.

During the 1980s and 1990s, Congress issued a number of official statements condemning Iran's treatment of its Bahá'í community. The Bahá'í Office of External Affairs was created to foster closer relations with governmental agencies and nongovernmental organizations.

In the 1980s, Bahá'í refugees also entered the U.S. from Vietnam, which helped diversify the religion, despite a relatively slow growth in membership. Though there was tension among different ethnic groups within the Bahá'í community, the issues were resolvable.

1862 *The Book of Certitude* is written in January, in only two days and nights.

1863 On the eve of his exile to Constantinople (Istanbul), Bahá'u'lláh declares himself to be "He whom God shall make manifest" in the Garden of Ridván in Baghdad. After four months in Constantinople, Bahá'u'lláh is moved to formal confinement in Adrianople (Edirne).

1865 Bahá'u'lláh writes the *Tablet of Ahmad*.

1867 Bahá'u'lláh begins writing and sending his Tablets to the kings.

1868 Bahá'u'lláh and a large group of followers are sent from Edirne to the penal colony of Akká, Palestine, Ottoman Turkey (now Acre, Israel).

1869 Bahá'u'lláh sends a letter to the shah of Persia, Nasser al-Din Shah; the letter's deliverer, Badí', is put to death.

1873 Bahá'u'lláh writes the *Kitáb-i-Aqdas*.

1889 E.G. Browne mentions the Bahá'í Faith as part of a series of academic talks and papers in England.

1892 The death of Bahá'u'lláh. His mortal remains are placed in a shrine dedicated to him next to the Mansion of Bahjí outside Akká, where he spends his final years. Before dying, Bahá'u'lláh appoints `ayn `Abdu'l-Bahá, his son, head of the Bahá'í Faith.

1893 First mention of the Bahá'í Faith in America at the World Parliament of Religions in Chicago (and in local newspapers).

1894 Thornton Chase becomes the first Bahá'í in the United States.

1898 The first Western pilgrims arrive in `Akká, including Phoebe Hearst and first African-American believer, Robert Turner.

1902 Cornerstone of first Bahá'í House of Worship laid in `Ishqábád, Turkmenistan.

1903 Significant persecution of Bahá'ís in Iran; resulting in over 100 Bahá'í deaths.

1908 `ayn `Abdu'l-Bahá is released from a lifetime of exile and imprisonment at age 64.

1909 After 59 years in hiding, mortal remains of the Báb are laid to rest in the Shrine of the Báb.

1910 Mary Maxwell, later known as Rúhíyyih Khanum, is born in New York City.

1911 `ayn `A'bdu'l-Bahá travels across Europe, visiting London, Bristol, and Paris. While in London, gives his first address to Western audience (with English translation) in City Temple.

1912 `ayn `Abdu'l-Bahá arrives in New York City for his visit to North America. During a stop in Wilmette, Illinois, `Abdu'l-Bahá lays the cornerstone of the planned North American Bahá'í House of Worship. Trip ends in December; he returns to Europe.

1916–1917 `ayn `Abdu'l-Bahá writes the 14 Tablets of the Divine Plan.

1920 `ayn `Abdu'l-Bahá is knighted in recognition of his humanitarian work during WWI.

1921 `ayn `Abdu'l-Bahá dies in Haifa; Shoghi Effendi is appointed guardian in his Will and Testament.

1937 Shoghi Effendi launches the first seven year plan for the spread of the Bahá'í Faith across the globe. He also marries Mary Maxwell, daughter of a prominent Canadian Bahá'í. She comes to be known as Rúhíyyih Khánum.

1944 Shoghi Effendi commemorates 100th anniversary of Bahá'í dispensation by releasing *God Passes By*, a history of Bahá'í.

1951 Eleven National Spiritual Assemblies exist at this point; Shoghi Effendi appoints 9 Hands of the Cause of God. By 1957, he raises the number to 27. He also appoints the first multinational Bahá'í body, the International Bahá'í Council.

1953 Shoghi Effendi launches the Ten Year Crusade. The North American Bahá'í House of Worship is dedicated in Wilmette, Illinois. The superstructure of the Shrine of the Báb is completed.

1957 On November 4, Shoghi Effendi dies without children and without appointing a successor guardian. Consequently, the role of Head of the Faith is temporarily assumed by 27 Hands of the Cause. They complete the Ten Year Crusade and establish the Universal House of Justice.

1963 The Ten Year Crusade culminates with the centenary of the Declaration of Bahá'u'lláh in the Garden of Ridván. The election of the first Universal House of Justice by representatives of 56 National Spiritual Assemblies held in Haifa. The first Bahá'í World Congress takes place in London.

1979 Iran's Islamic Revolution triggers a systematic long-term persecution of Iran's Bahá'ís; over 200 casualties by 2008.

1983 The Universal House of Justice takes up residence in its permanent seat.

1985 The Universal House of Justice publishes *The Promise of World Peace.*

1992 The Second Bahá'í World Congress takes place in New York.

1993 The *Kitáb-i-Aqdas* is released in English.

2001 By this point, 182 National Spiritual Assemblies exist, in almost every country.

2006 Iranian Islamic Revolution government documents are released by the Special Rapporteur of the United Nations. The Anti-Defamation League notes that these government policies signify steps toward Nuremberg-type laws.

On December 16, the Supreme Administrative Council of Egypt rules against the Bahá'ís—key event in the Egyptian identification card controversy.

D. Important Figures

Mirza 'Ali Muhammad (the Báb) (1819–1850)

Known as the Báb ("the Gate") `Alí-Muhammad was the founder of Babism, the direct precursor to the Bahá'í Faith. A revered prophet, he is considered a manifestation of God, in the same way as Jesus and other great religious prophets are.

The Báb was born in 1819 in Shiraz. He was a descendent of Muhammad, on both his father's and mother's sides.   In May 1844 he encountered a young religious seeker, Mullá Husayn, who told the Báb that he was searching for the Promised One. The Báb listened to Husayn's criteria—"of a pure lineage, is of illustrious descent, is endowed with innate knowledge and is free from bodily deficiency"—and declared himself the Promised One. He then spontaneously dictated the first half of one of his most important scriptural texts. Mulla Husayn became Babism's first adherent. Many others soon followed, including Mírzá Husayn-'Alí, the founder of the Bahá'í Faith.

The Iranian government and Muslim clergy found the Báb's teachings threatening to their understanding of Islam, and made aggressive attempts to curtail his influence. He was arrested several times, and finally, in 1850, was ordered to be executed by firing squad. The execution required two attempts. The first time, the Báb vanished in the cloud of gunsmoke after the shots were fired; the bullets had merely cut his ropes. He was found and a second firing squad executed him. The Bahá'ís believe the Báb's first disappearance was a miracle.

Mírzá Husayn-'Alí Núrí (Bahá'u'lláh) (1817–1892)

The Báb's most important disciple, Bahá'u'lláh, was founder of the Bahá'í Faith. He was born on November 12, 1817, to a wealthy, cosmopolitan family. Bahá'u'lláh devoted himself to the Báb at the age of twenty-seven, after having been converted to Babism by Mullá Husayn. Though Bahá'u'lláh never met the Báb in person, the two men corresponded.

After having been falsely accused in 1852 of participating in an attempted assassination of the Shah, he was sent to prison in Tehran. There he had a revelatory vision that indicated he was the prophet whose appearance had been predicted by the Báb, and who was destined to lead the Bábís to even greater glory.

Bahá'u'lláh faced the same persecution the Báb had, and was similarly resolute in the face of threats, arrest, and mistreatment. The wealth and political influence of his family ensured he was never executed. In 1853, the Iranian government exiled him to Baghdad. There he attracted more converts and revitalized the Bábí community, efforts that attracted similar controversy as in his native country. The Ottoman government ordered him to leave Baghdad for Istanbul in April 1863. Before his departure, he spent twelve days in the Garden of Ridván, where he publicly declared himself the successor to the Báb on April 22, 1863. Those who believed him called themselves Bahá'ís.

The Ottoman government sent Bahá'u'lláh to Akká in 1868, fulfilling Muslim and Jewish prophecies about the city's religious significance. He was released from imprisonment in 1877, after the sultan was deposed, but remained technically under house arrest. Eventually he moved to a large mansion called Bahjí several miles outside the city walls, where he died of natural causes in 1892.

'Abdu'l-Bahá (1844–1921)

'Abdu'l-Bahá (Servant of God), Bahá'u'lláh's oldest son, was born in Tehran on May 23, 1844, the day of the Báb's declaration. He was the leader of the Bahá'í Faith from 1892 until his death in November, 1921. His given name was 'Abbás. His childhood was fraught with poverty and hardship after Bahá'u'lláh was imprisoned and all his property confiscated by the government. 'Abdu'l-Bahá was a spiritual child, and eager to carry the Bahá'í torch to the next generation of believers. His father appointed him head of the faith in several texts. Upon assuming the role of head of the faith, he asked everyone to refer to him as 'Abdu'l-Bahá, "servant of Bahá."

'Abdu'l-Bahá was a capable and charismatic leader. A compelling speaker and an eloquent writer, he traveled extensively and greatly increased the number of Bahá'ís throughout the world. He was a prolific writer, producing some 16,000 letters, all of which are considered authoritative Bahá'í scripture; they have been published in *Selections from the Writings of 'Abdu'l-Bahá* and other volumes. 'Abdu'l-Baha's efforts were largely responsible for the spread of the new religion to the Western world; by the turn of the century it had spread to thirty-five different countries, and there were several thousand adherents in North America. Before his death 'Abdu'l-Bahá named his grandson, Shoghi Effendi Rabbani, as his successor.

Shoghi Effendi Rabbani (1897–1957)

Shoghi Effendi, the oldest son of 'Abdu'l-Baha's oldest daughter, was the official guardian of the Bahá'í Faith from 1921 until his death in November 1957. He was educated at American University of

Beirut and later at Oxford University. He was fluent in English, which proved to be a vital means of spreading the Bahá'í Faith throughout the Western world. The translator of many of Bahá'u'lláh's writings, Shoghi Effendi was also the only living individual with the authority to interpret them officially. Shoghi Effendi was author of *God Passes By*, a highly influential history of the Bahá'í Faith, and his letters have been collected in several volumes.

Shoghi Effendi is not considered a messenger of God, like Bahá'u'lláh, or a perfect human being, like `Abdu'l-Bahá. He was, however, an able leader, revered among Bahá'ís. In addition to his extensive translation work, he took `Abdu'l-Bahá's Will and Testament as a blueprint for building the system of local and national spiritual assemblies that became the Bahá'í Faith's principal means of organization. Once the administrative bodies were established, he used them to implement `Abdu'l-Bahá's Tablets of the Divine Plan, which commanded that the Faith be spread around the world. Under his tenure as guardian, membership in the Bahá'í Faith increased from 100,000 to 400,000, and the number of countries represented leapt from 35 to 250. Finally, Shoghi Effendi built up the Bahá'í World Centre in what is today Haifa, Israel, in spite of disruptions caused by World War II and the Israeli War of Independence.

Shoghi Effendi's guardianship was not without personal tragedies. He had to expel numerous family members from the faith when they opposed him or the organization of the Bahá'í community. He died suddenly of a virulent strain of flu in 1957, without naming a successor. This caused a confused state of affairs and an effort to split the faith, which had little effect on the Bahá'í community.

II. Tenets and Beliefs

A. Articles of Faith

The Bahá'í Faith does not have any sacraments or formal creeds. Often described as syncretistic, it is believed by its followers to encompass and embrace all the great religions of the past and present, including Hinduism, Buddhism, Judaism, Christianity, and Islam. According to Bahá'í scripture, all these religions, despite their apparent differences, teach certain essential ethical teachings. The idea of the oneness and unity of humankind is the central truth and guiding principle of the Bahá'í Faith. Bahá'ís believe their faith is the perfect modern expression of God's intentions for humanity.

The Báb, Bahá'u'lláh, and `Abdu'l-Bahá did not minimize the divine authority of the founders of other religions—called manifestations of God by the Bahá'í Faith—but instead claimed to represent a continuation of their messages and goals. Bahá'í scripture recognizes Zoroaster, Abraham, Moses, Jesus, Krishna, the Buddha, and Muhammad as previous manifestations. Bahá'u'lláh claimed to be God's appointed manifestation for the contemporary world. The Bahá'ís believe that in little more than a thousand years, God will send a new manifestation with a refinement of the message of God to make it intelligible to a new age. This concept is known as progressive revelation.

The Bahá'í Faith is a monotheistic religion. God is seen as essentially unknowable, though it is possible to know his attributes, such as love, mercy, compassion, and justice. Eternal life is attainable through acceptance of the manifestation and obedience to his laws. Bahá'ís believe in the immortality of the soul. They do not believe in reincarnation; however, a concept similar to karma is advocated in the belief that positive actions yield positive results and negative actions yield negative results (a law which applies to both the spiritual and material planes). Evil is nonexistent. That which seems evil is simply the lack of good; good can otherwise be thought of as God (the greatest power and, ultimately, the only existent force in the universe). Heaven is seen as oneness with God, Hell as separation from Him.

The Bahá'í Faith decries prejudice, violence and inequality based on class, race and gender. Bahá'í leaders—particularly Bahá'u'lláh—have promoted peace and condemned killing and warfare, in contrast with Islam and Babism, which permit jihad under special circumstances. The Bahá'í scriptures also assert the full equality of women and men:

. . . The female sex is treated as though inferior, and is not allowed equal rights and privileges. This condition is not due to nature, but to education. In the Divine Creation there is no such distinction. Neither sex is superior to the other in the sight of God. Why then should one sex assert the inferiority of the other . . . If women received the same educational advantages as those of men, the result would demonstrate the equality of capacity of both for scholarship.

(*See* www.h-net.org/~Baha'i/docs/vol3/wmnuhj.htm.)

In the Bahá'í view, each individual should focus on the development of his or her spiritual and moral qualities that constitute his or her true nature; this is one purpose of life on earth. Bahá'u'lláh thus referred to human beings as a "mine rich in gems of inestimable value." Other purposes of human life are to "know and worship God" and to "carry forward an ever-advancing civilization."

Bahá'ís believe in individual independent investigation of truth. Education is therefore strongly encouraged for everyone, male or female. Literacy (not common in Persia in the nineteenth century) is highly valued since literacy lends adherents the skill to read sacred writings for themselves rather than having to take another's word. Scientific research is seen as a valid complement to spirituality.

Like Protestants, Bahá'ís value a strong work ethic. They see work performed in the spirit of service to others as a form of worship. The Bahá'í Faith emphasizes ending extremes of wealth and poverty, using any wealth one has for the good of humanity, and securing a decent, moderate standard of living for everyone.

Conversion to the Bahá'í Faith is effected merely through acceptance of its tenets; no formal rituals are required, though in some countries, such as the United States, declarants are asked to sign a card indicating that they accept Bahá'u'lláh. Ten major principles enumerated by the Bahá'í Faith are:

(1) the independent search for truth;
(2) the unity of all people;
(3) the harmony of religion and science;
(4) the equality of female and male;
(5) the compulsory education for all;
(6) the establishment of one global language;
(7) the creation of a world governing system;
(8) harmonious relations of all people in work and love;
(9) the condemnation of prejudice; and
(10) the abolition of poverty and extreme wealth.

Bahá'ís feel very strongly about environmental awareness, and consider themselves culturally and technologically forward-thinking.

Life After Death

Bahá'ís believe that after death, the soul separates from the body and enters a timeless realm that is an extension of, but not separate from, the physical universe. The soul goes through many planes of existence, during which it moves closer and closer to God, based on divine grace. "Hell" is departure from God; "Heaven" is closeness to Him. Ultimately, for the Bahá'ís, the nature of an afterlife—beyond these basic generalities—is unknowable.

B. Sacred Literature

The scriptures of all of the world's major religions are considered, by members of the Bahá'í Faith, to be scriptures in the context of worship, but only the Bahá'í scriptures are used to determine how one lives one's life. The Qur'an is considered to be the most reliable of the non-Bahá'í scriptures in that it represents a true record of the revelations received by Muhammad. The scriptures specific to the Bahá'í

Faith are the writings of the Báb, Bahá'u'lláh, and `Abdu'l-Bahá. Even though only a small portion of their writings have been translated from Arabic and Persian into English, there are two dozen books of Bahá'í scripture available in that language. The *Kitáb-i-Aqdas* (the Most Holy Book), which Bahá'u'lláh wrote in 1868, is the most important work; it contains the Bahá'í laws.

Other writings of Bahá'u'lláh include *The Four Valleys*, describing the four types of religious seekers, and *The Seven Valleys*, relating to the seven stages that are passed through on the quest for truth. Both of these works were written for Sufi leaders during Bahá'u'lláh's time in Iraq. During these years he also wrote *The Hidden Words*, a work of aphoristic advice and wisdom, and the *Kitáb-i-Íqán* (Book of Certitude) a work about the nature of religion, symbols in the Qur'an and Bible, and the spiritual development of the individual. Altogether, 15,000 works by Bahá'u'lláh are extant, mostly letters to individuals.

`Abdu'l Baha wrote three important works in the late nineteenth century: *The Secret of Divine Civilization*, *A Traveler's Narrative*, and *Risáliy-i-Siyásiyyih* (Treatise on Politics). He also wrote letters, some 16,000 of which are extant, and some of which have been published in various compilations. He gave a series of talks about a variety of subjects in 1904–1906 that were compiled into a volume called *Some Answered Questions*. Because `Abdu'l-Bahá reviewed the transcripts for accuracy and approved them, the work is considered Bahá'í scripture. Several volumes of his talks in the West have been published, though they are not considered Bahá'í scripture because `Abdu'l-Bahá never reviewed all the transcripts for accuracy.

Shoghi Effendi Rabbani produced many writings—the estimate is 36,000, mostly letters, which are still being collected—the most important being *God Passes By*, a history of the Bahá'í Faith from 1844 to 1944. Important compilations of his letters include *The World Order of Bahá'u'lláh*, *The Advent of Divine Justice*, *The Promised Day Is Come*, *Messages to Canada*, and *Messages to India*. Shoghi Effendi's writings are considered authoritative and binding, but are not scripture, because Shoghi Effendi's theological status is that of an ordinary man granted divine authority to protect and guide the faith and interpret the scriptures, not produce new scriptures.

The Universal House of Justice is the highest Bahá'í authority since Shoghi Effendi Rabbani's death. The writings of `Abdu'l-Bahá and Shoghi Effendi give the Universal House of Justice the authority to clarify and elucidate the meaning of Bahá'í texts but not to interpret them authoritatively. They can also legislate on matters about which the Bahá'í texts are silent (such as birth control), can make decisions to protect the Faith from attacks, and can guide its expansion through the promulgation of teaching and development plans. Since its formation in 1963, the Universal House of Justice has overseen the composition of over one hundred thousand letters, and several compilations of their salient messages have been published.

C. Secondary Sources

Thornton Chase (1847–1912)

Chase was the first Westerner to convert to the Bahá'í Faith. Chase's early life was characterized by hardship: his mother died when he was eighteen days old, and after his father's remarriage, Chase was sent to live with a Baptist foster family. This childhood experience of family loss and abandonment may have sparked his subsequent quest for love and acceptance, which he would largely seek in religion.

After stints in college, the military, and as a salesman, Chase married and had two children. When his new specialty business in lumber failed, Chase moved to Boston to try his hand at acting. In 1873, the novice actor found himself deeply entrenched in poverty, hopelessness, and an old familiar loneliness. It was in the midst of this personal rock bottom that Chase experienced a sudden revelation of love "unspeakable," of "absolute oneness." He believed he'd been granted a glimpse of God's love, and, hope renewed, immediately set out upon a search for the "true" religion.

It would take Chase twenty-one more years to find what he was looking for. While working as a life insurance agent in Chicago in 1894, Chase heard of the Bahá'í Faith from a colleague. Its tenets striking a chord with him, he eagerly enrolled in a class on the religion. By 1895, Chase had completed the class and was considered an adherent of the religion—the first occidental member of the Bahá'í Faith.

Chase traveled widely to teach the religion and played an important role in organizing the early Chicago Bahá'í community. Chase's writing skills came to good use when he and three partners established what would become the Bahá'í Publishing Society in 1900. This society soon emerged as the primary publisher of Bahá'í literature in the English language.

In 1908, Chase wrote *In Galilee*, an account of his pilgrimage to Akká to meet `Abdu'l Bahá. The latter was very impressed with Chase, granting him the name Thábit, or "steadfast." Less than one year later, the American Bahá'í embarked on a new literary project, composing an introductory book, which emphasized the religion as a vehicle for spiritual regeneration. Entitled *The Bahai Revelation*, it was published in 1909.

Robert Hayden (1913–1980)

Hayden was raised by a foster family in a Detroit ghetto facetiously nicknamed "Paradise Valley." His childhood was marked by abusive parenting, the fighting of his foster parents, and a struggle between

Bahá'í poet Robert Hayden was the first African American appointed to the position of Consultant in Poetry to the Library of Congress.

his biological and foster mothers for his attention. Though raised by Baptists, Hayden converted to the Bahá'í Faith in the 1940s as a result of his marriage to Erma Inez Morris, who was Bahá'í.

In 1975, Hayden was elected to the American Academy of Poets. In 1976, he became Consultant in Poetry to the Library of Congress, a position now known as Poet Laureate Consultant in Poetry to the Library of Congress. Hayden served in this office for twelve years. He is widely regarded as one of America's most notable poets; certainly one of the greatest to emerge from the Bahá'í Faith, the influence of which can be seen in his work. Some of his most famous poems are "Those Winter Sundays," "Middle Passage," "Runagate Runagate," "Frederick Douglass," and "The Whipping."

Firuz Kazemzadeh (1924–)

Kazemzadeh was born in Moscow, Russia, and there spent his youth until immigrating to America at the age of twenty. In 1944, he entered Stanford University, graduating with a master's degree in 1947. Three years later, Kazemzadeh received a PhD in Russian history from Harvard University. He taught at the latter school from 1954 to 1956 before accepting a position at Yale University as a professor of history. In 1992, he retired from Yale as a professor emeritus.

Kazemzadeh's accomplishments include authorship of numerous books and scholarly articles on Russian and Iranian history, an appointment by President Bill Clinton to the position of commissioner on the United States Commission on International Religious Freedom in 1998, and reappointment to that post in 2001 by U.S. Senate majority leader Thomas Daschle. Kazemzadeh served as a member of the National Spiritual Assembly of the Bahá'ís of the United States from 1963 to 2000.

Robert Stockman (1953–)

Stockman became a Bahá'í in 1973 and received a doctoral degree from Harvard University in 1990 in the history of religion in the United States. He put this expertise to use as an instructor, teaching world religions at DePaul University and primal religions, Zoroastrianism, Judaism, Christianity, and the Old and New Testaments at the Wilmette Institute. Stockman is director of the Wilmette Institute and coordinator of the Institute for Bahá'í Studies in Wilmette. His literary works include *Thornton Chase: The First American Bahá'í,* two volumes of *The Bahá'í Faith in America,* and many scholarly articles on the Bahá'í Faith.

III. Rites and Rituals

A. The Calendar

The Bahá'í calendar begins on the vernal equinox and has 19 months, each of 19 days (totaling 361 days). In addition, the calendar includes four intercalary days (five in a leap year), which are known as Ayyám-i-Há, a holiday extending from February 25 to March 1 and celebrated by merrymaking, gift giving, and acts of charity.

The Nineteen-Day Feast is a festival that occurs once every Bahá'í month. Local Bahá'ís gather for the three portions of the feast: devotions, discussion of community business, and socializing.

Years in the Bahá'í calendar are counted from March 21, 1844, the beginning of the Bahá'í Era (BE). Days begin and end at sundown. The week begins on Saturday and ends on Friday, the Sabbath.

There are no specific practices or rituals that must be performed on holy days. Nine require Bahá'ís to abstain from work and school; two associated with `Abdu'l-Bahá do not require suspension of work.

Holy Days Requiring Suspension of Work

March 21 (Vernal Equinox) – Naw Rúz, the Bahá'í New Year

April 21 – First day of Ridván. The Festival of Ridván is a twelve-day period that commemorates Bahá'u'lláh's time in the garden of Ridván when he

declared himself a messenger of God. The first, ninth, and twelfth days are holy days.

April 29 – Ninth day of Ridván

May 2 – 12th day of Ridván

May 23 – Anniversary of the Báb's declaration

May 29 – The Ascension of Bahá'u'lláh

July 9 – Anniversary of the Báb's Martyrdom

October 20 – Birthday of the Báb

November 12 – Birthday of Bahá'u'lláh

Minor Holy Days

Work need not be suspended.

November 26 – The Day of the Covenant; a minor holy day in celebration of `Abdu'l-Bahá's status as Center of the Covenant.

November 28 – Anniversary of `Abdu'l-Bahá's passing.

Other Important Bahá'í Days

February 25–March 1 – Ayyám-i-Há, the intercalary festival, commemorated by gift giving, charitable deeds, and social gatherings.

March 2–March 20 – The Fast, a period during which adult Bahá'ís fast from sunrise to sunset, if they are able to do so.

B. Daily Life: Precepts and Restrictions

The Bahá'í sacred writings contain hundreds of possible prayers for Bahá'ís to use in their daily devotions, addressing many different life situations; however, Bahá'u'lláh wrote three obligatory prayers—one short, one medium, and one long—at least one of which must be recited every day. The obligatory prayers are to be recited while facing the shrine of Bahá'u'lláh. Cleanliness is obligatory, as it reflects a state of inner purity; thus ablutions are required before prayer, and prayers are to be recited in a clean area.

Bahá'u'lláh also urged his followers to recite the word of God every morning and evening and to bring themselves into account each day.

THE SHORT OBLIGATORY PRAYER

I bear witness, O my God, that Thou has created me to know Thee and to worship Thee.

I testify, at this moment, to my powerlessness and to Thy might, to my poverty and to Thy wealth.

There is none other God but Thee, the Help in Peril, the Self-Subsisting.

Children, the elderly and the ill are exempted from both fasting and the obligatory prayer requirement. Alcoholic beverages are forbidden in the Bahá'í Faith, as are all drugs that impair the mind and body. The Bahá'í Faith advocates a simple diet, in which moderation is key. Vegetarianism is not required, though `Abdu'l-Baha said it would one day be the diet of humanity.

Idleness is forbidden and begging is not allowed. Gambling is prohibited. Work performed in the spirit of service is also regarded as a form of worship. Bahá'ís are not permitted political careers, as participation in politics is seen as divisive, and world unity is the goal of the faith. Spreading the Bahá'í message is considered another sacred obligation, though no Bahá'í should ever pressure another to convert. The Bahá'í Faith promotes respect for animals and warns against forcing animals to do excessive work. Premarital sex is forbidden, as are adultery and bigamy. Homosexual unions are not allowed. As there is no monastic life in the Bahá'í Faith, every Bahá'í is encouraged to marry.

Nuptials

Individuals choose their mates, but parental permission must be obtained before marriage. A relatively short engagement—no more than ninety-five days—is recommended. Bahá'ís may marry non-Bahá'ís.

Bahá'í marriage ceremonies are generally simple. There is one required marriage vow that must be exchanged in front of at least two witnesses: "We will all, verily, abide by the Will of God." To this vow, Bahá'ís can add music, recitation of Bahá'í prayers and verses from the world's scriptures, brief talks, and anything else they wish.

Bahá'u'lláh, in order to eliminate the discord that may come with dowry negotiations, set fixed dowry amounts for urban and rural populations. The amounts are small (less than the value of most wedding rings).

Death and Burial

Bahá'ís are supposed to write a will, and distribute their wealth as they see fit. After death, the body must be treated with dignity, which means it cannot be cremated and should instead decompose naturally in the ground. According to scripture, the body should be buried within an hour's journey of the place of death. A ring should be placed on the deceased's finger on which is inscribed: "I came forth from God, and return unto Him, detached from all save Him, holding fast to His Name, the Merciful, the Compassionate."

The following passage by Bahá'u'lláh is called the Prayer for the Dead, which is to be recited by one Bahá'í on behalf of the others present at the funeral of anyone over the age of fifteen:

O my God! This is Thy servant and the son of Thy servant who hath believed in Thee and in Thy signs, and set his face towards Thee, wholly detached from all except Thee. Thou art, verily, of those who show mercy the most merciful.

Deal with him, O Thou Who forgivest the sins of men and concealest their faults, as beseemeth the heaven of Thy bounty and the ocean of Thy grace. Grant him admission within the precincts of Thy transcendent mercy that was before the foundation of earth and heaven. There is no God but Thee, the Ever-Forgiving, the Most Generous.

(Let him, then, repeat six times the greeting "Alláh-u-Abhá," and then repeat nineteen times each of the following verses:)

We all, verily, worship God.
We all, verily, bow down before God.
We all, verily, are devoted unto God.
We all, verily, give praise unto God.
We all, verily, yield thanks unto God.
We all, verily, are patient in God.

(If the dead be a woman, let him say: *This is Thy handmaiden and the daughter of Thy handmaiden, etc.*)"

One Bahá'í tablet details that cemeteries ought to be kept in good condition and look attractive, and gravesites should be respectfully maintained.

D. Family Life

Husband and Wife

Marriage is given great emphasis in the Bahá'í Faith, as it is symbolic of the spiritual oneness that is central to the religion. Marriage is, above all, a spiritual union, in which each partner supports the spiritual growth of the other. Equality between marriage partners is considered essential in keeping with the Bahá'í emphasis on gender equality. Sexuality in marriage is important, but Bahá'ís understand that physical sexuality is inherently less important than the nonphysical union of souls, which lasts beyond death. Premarital sex is forbidden, as are adultery and open marriage.

Childrearing

In one of his marriage prayers, Bahá'u'lláh said, "Marry, O people, that from you may appear he who will remember Me amongst My servants; this is one of My commandments unto you; obey it as an assistance to yourselves." Hence producing and raising at least one child is considered an important goal of marriage. Birth control methods that prevent the fertilization of the egg are permissible to determine the timing and spacing of children (though birth control methods that kill a fertilized egg are not).

The faith dictates that children should be respected, loved, and cherished; children, in turn, should respect their parents. Parents have the responsibility of setting an example of Bahá'í values for their children. Education is among the highest of these values; therefore, children must be offered the best education available. Any type of domestic violence is forbidden, as is corporal punishment of children.

Divorce

Divorce is allowed, but strongly discouraged, and Bahá'ís are admonished to make every possible effort to save a troubled marriage. Before a couple divorces, they must live apart for one year while making continuing efforts to reconcile their differences.

IV. Divisions and Demographics

A. Divisions

Whenever the Bahá'í Faith has seen a change in the head of the Faith, an attempt to split the Faith has occurred. The first split occurred in the late 1860s when the majority of Bábís accepted Bahá'u'lláh's claim to be the promised one predicted by the Báb, but a few others accepted Bahá'u'lláh's younger half brother, Mírzá Yahyá Azal as the head of the Bábí Faith (calling themselves Azalís), and a few others continued as Bábís awaiting the promised one (calling themselves Bayánís). A few members (perhaps hundreds) of both groups still exist in Iran. They have no widespread organization and do not publish literature.

When Bahá'u'lláh passed in 1892, the vast majority of Bahá'ís accepted `Abdu'l-Bahá as Bahá'u'lláh's appointed successor, but a small number, mostly family members, attempted to argue that Bahá'u'lláh's second son, Muhammad-`Alí, was the rightful successor, arguing that `Abdu'l-Bahá had disqualified himself by making exaggerated claims of his status. When `Abdu'l-Bahá died, some of Shoghi Effendi's family allied themselves with the remnants of Muhammad-`Alí's group and were also expelled from the faith. But there was no successful effort to recruit followers from the mainstream Bahá'í community, and no opposition group was formally organized. Only scattered individuals, mostly elderly, remain of either group.

When Shoghi Effendi died unexpectedly on November 4, 1957, he had not appointed a successor because `Abdu'l-Bahá's Will and Testament required that the successor be a male descendant of Bahá'u'lláh, and there were no male descendants left in the faith (Shoghi Effendi never had children). Shoghi Effendi, however, had accomplished three things: (1) he gave the Bahá'í world a Ten Year Crusade of detailed goals to accomplish through April 1963; (2) he appointed twenty-seven individuals as Hands of the Cause of God and gave them the title "chief stewards" on Bahá'u'lláh's world order; and (3) he had established detailed goals for the election of fifty-seven National Spiritual Assemblies, which, according to `Abdu'l-Bahá's Will and Testament, were the bodies to elect the Universal House of Justice. As a result, the Hands of the Cause of God continued the crusade with great care and energy, brought about the election of fifty-six National Spiritual Assemblies (it was impossible to form one in Afghanistan because of circumstances), and called for the members of the National Spiritual Assemblies to elect the Universal House of Justice (they disqualified themselves as members, also, so that they could continue their work as Hands). The election occurred in April 1963. Since then, the Universal House of Justice has been reelected by the members of the National Spiritual Assemblies every five years.

One Hand, however, chose to dispute this plan for giving the Bahá'í Faith the elected leadership called for by `Abdu'l-Bahá. Charles Mason Remey argued that Shoghi Effendi had in effect appointed him the second Guardian by appointing him president of the International Bahá'í Council, a forerunner to the Universal House of Justice. Of the 400,000 Bahá'ís in the world at the time, several hundred accepted his claim. Subsequently, Remey's group broke into at least three major divisions, two of which—the Orthodox Bahá'í Faith and the Bahá'ís Under the Provision of the Covenant—still exist. Neither group has more than a few hundred members.

The Bahá'í Faith's success in preserving its unity can partly be attributed to the detailed written instructions about organization and successorship, which made it virtually impossible for an attempted schism to achieve legitimacy. It can also be traced to the remarkably self sacrificing nature of its leadership, who inspire selflessness and a spirit of sacrifice among the followers. Bahá'ís also attribute its unity to the Covenant, which consists of the written guidance about organization, the divine principle of unity the texts entail, and the holy spirit guiding and protecting the Faith's unity.

B. Demographics

The Bahá'í Faith claims approximately 6 million members worldwide, including approximately 157,000 in the United States.

V. Organization and Infrastructure

A. Education and Hierarchy of Clergy

The Bahá'í Faith does not have a priesthood. Bahá'ís believe every individual is responsible for his or her own relationship with God, and mediation of that relationship through another person is inappropriate.

B. Governance and Authority

The Bahá'í administrative system works on a local, regional, national, and international level. At the local level, individual Bahá'ís elect nine-member local spiritual assemblies, which address all issues of importance to the local Bahá'í community (enrolling new members, overseeing Bahá'í marriages and divorces, counseling members, owning a local Bahá'í center, coordinating the education of children and adults, proclaiming the Faith to the local population, etc.). Local spiritual assemblies are often grouped together in larger divisions called clusters.

Every year, in countries with regional councils, the members of all local spiritual assemblies in a region elect a nine-member regional council. The regional council coordinates plans for growth and consolidation of the faith in the region. In 1997, four regional Bahá'í councils, in the northeast, southern, central, and western regions, were formed in the United States in order to decentralize organization. In 2006, the western region was split and councils for the northwestern and southwestern areas were elected.

Each national division (usually an entire country, like Canada, but in some cases a geographically distinct area, such as Alaska or Hawaii) is divided into districts, and every year all the Bahá'ís in the district elect one delegate to the national Bahá'í convention, though districts with very large populations, such as a large city like Los Angeles, may elect more than one delegate. Every year the delegates meet and elect the nine-member National Spiritual Assembly. It sets the overall direction of the Bahá'í Faith in that country, publishes literature, maintains relations with the national media and government, etc.

Every five years, the members of all the National Spiritual Assemblies vote for the nine individuals who serve in the Universal House of Justice. It is the supreme governing body of the Bahá'í Faith, answers difficult questions, legislates on matters not covered in the Bahá'í writings, coordinates the defense of the faith against attacks and persecution, and encourages the Bahá'ís through messages and letters. Occasionally, it expels individuals from the faith if they are causing disunity. Unlike local and national Bahá'í governing bodies, only men can serve in the Universal House of Justice, for a "wisdom of the Lord God's, which will erelong be made manifest as clearly as the sun at high noon." This exclusion of women has occasioned considerable anguish and some disunity in the Bahá'í community.

The Universal House of Justice has its headquarters on Mount Carmel in Haifa, Israel, near the burial places of the Báb and Bahá'u'lláh. It is served by a staff of over 600 people from 60 different countries.

The Universal House of Justice also oversees another wing of the Bahá'í administrative system. Every five years it appoints nine experienced Bahá'ís to the International Teaching Center as international counselors. The International Teaching Center coordinates the work of ninety-nine counselors, who serve in five continent-sized areas and are appointed to five-year terms. The continental counselors in turn appoint Auxiliary Board members, who serve parts of countries or small countries. The Auxiliary Board members in turn appoint assistants for localities and clusters. The purpose of the entire institution of appointed individuals is to encourage the Bahá'ís, direct their energies toward the teaching and consolidation priorities of the faith, bring news to them of national and international developments, and report back to the national and international bodies about the strength of the grass roots work.

The institution of the counselors was created to continue the functions of the institution of the Hands of the Cause of God. Bahá'u'lláh appointed the first Hands; `Abdu'l-Bahá and Shoghi Effendi appointed more. In his Will and Testament, `Abdu'l-Bahá said that only Guardians of the Faith could appoint Hands, so with the death of Shoghi Effendi it was not possible to appoint any more. The last Hand of the Cause of God died in 2006. Counselors do not have the spiritual rank of a Hand, but do carry out some of the same responsibilities, such as coordinating Auxiliary Board members.

The Bahá'í teachings reject all partisanship. Bahá'í elections occur in a spiritual atmosphere of prayer where each individual votes according to his or her conscience, uninfluenced by ideas from and arguments made by others. All campaigning and mentioning of names is prohibited, and all elections are done by secret ballot. Though assembly membership does not have term limits, members can resign or be expelled.

Scholarship

Since the Bahá'í faith lacks a formal ministry, it also lacks formal seminaries. Scholarship and learning are of paramount importance in the Bahá'í Faith; all Bahá'ís are encouraged to read and study the Bahá'í sacred texts and those of the other world religions, relate them to their own life, and relate them to world conditions. They are also encouraged to spread knowledge of the faith to those ignorant of it. However, knowledge should never be used to separate Bahá'ís from one another or to elevate particular members as special.

A quote from the International Teaching Center illustrates the Bahá'í attitude towards scholarship:

It is evident that Bahá'í scholarship is an endeavour accessible to all members of the Bahá'í community, without exception. All believers can aspire to the attributes described by the Guardian and can strive to relate Bahá'í teachings to the thinking and concerns of the non-Bahá'í community around them (International Teaching Centre, Scholarship 3; Source: Bahá'í-library.com; Parris article on Bahá'í scholarship).

C. Shrines and Houses of Worship

The building of temples is encouraged in the Bahá'í Faith. These temples are known as *mashriqu'l-adhkár* ("the place where the name of God arises at dawn"). The Bahá'ís hope to someday create temples in every community.

Bahá'í temples represent a variety of architectural styles. However, all have a large central dome and nine sides, with a door on every side. The number nine being the largest single-digit number, it is a symbol of unity. The Lotus Temple in New Delhi, India (*next page, top*) is among the most architecturally admired religious structures in the world.

Because there are no clergy, there are no sermons in the temples, nor do specific Bahá'í rituals occur there. Services, or devotional programs, are held daily; the sacred writings of the Bahá'í Faith and other major world religions are recited. Devotional programs are open to Bahá'ís and non-Bahá'ís alike.

Seven Bahá'í temples exist worldwide; however, there is only one temple in the United States—the

The Wilmette Bahá'í House of Worship is one of seven Bahá'í houses of worship worldwide, and the only one in the United States. It is located in Wilmette, Illinois, a suburb of Chicago.

Bahá'í House of Worship, located in Wilmette, Illinois. Abdu'l-Bahá broke ground for this temple in 1912, but it was not completed until May 1, 1953. The temple is architecturally ornate and surrounded by fountains and gardens. It is listed in the National Register of Historic Places.

Bahá'í House of Worship
100 Linden Ave.
Wilmette, IL 60091
847-853-2300
www.bahai.us

D. Social Service Organizations

Individual Bahá'ís are required to contribute to the Faith as they can afford. Bahá'ís are very conscientious about world issues and have developed over 1,000 grassroots social and economic aid projects, with the goal being to promote world peace. Links to Bahá'í social causes and projects may be found at www.bahai.us/social-action.

The Bahá'í House of Worship in New Delhi, India, is popularly known as the Lotus Temple. The building was completed in 1986.

Bahá'u'lláh and the New Era
J. E. Esslemont
2006: Bahá'í Publishing

Bahá'í Faith in America, Vols. 1 and 2 and
Thornton Chase: First American Bahá'í
Robert A. Stockman
1985; 1992; 2001: Bahá'í Publishing

E. Media and Communication

The headquarters of the National Assembly of the Bahá'ís of the United States is in the vicinity of the Bahá'í House of Worship in Wilmette, Illinois. The Assembly maintains an administrative staff of about 300, supervises a publishing trust, operates three retreat and conference centers, owns dozens of historic properties, and publishes several periodicals including a quarterly magazine, *World Order;* a children's magazine, *Brilliant Star;* and a bi-monthly news magazine for Bahá'ís, *The American Bahá'í.*

FURTHER READING

The Hidden Words
Bahá'u'lláh
2004: OneWorld Publications

The Kitab-i-Iqan Book of Certitude
Bahá'u'lláh and Shoghi Effendi
2003: Bahá'í Publishing

God Speaks Again: An Introduction to the Bahá'í Faith
Kenneth E. Bowers
2004: Bahá'í Publishing

2 Buddhism

I. Origins and Early History

A. Introduction

BUDDHISM'S INITIAL DEVELOPMENT OCCURRED IN the fifth and sixth centuries BCE in India. Its parent religion Hinduism had, by that time, split into numerous sects, and included those that were dissatisfied with traditional religious and social practices. Buddhism was introduced by Siddhartha Gautama (the Buddha), a nobleman of Kapilavastu, in the Sakya republic, which is located in modern-day Nepal, near its border with India. Buddhism thus grew out of a tradition of privilege and wealth, as this was the world to which the Buddha and his first followers belonged.

An early influential event in the history of Buddhism was the conversion of Indian emperor Ashoka in the second century BCE. This conversion played a pivotal role in increasing the religion's influence, and it ushered in a golden age for Buddhism that persisted through the middle of the coming millennium.

Buddhism eventually split into two schools, a schism that officially took place at the historical Buddhist Council of Vesali approximately one hundred years after the Buddha's death. The new divisions were: the Mahasanghika school (the newer and more liberal of the two), and the original Sthaviravada school.

Further divisions followed. Mahayana Buddhism, a variety of Buddhism less ascetic than the "original" school, came into shape, as did Theravada or Hinayana Buddhism. This split into Mahayana and Theravada was arguably the most significant schism in Buddhism's history. Mahayana attracted more adherents, since it allowed them to integrate their own traditions with this newer form of Buddhism. It became particularly popular in Nepal and the northern areas of India.

Early in the first century, a sect called the Sarvastivadins began traveling abroad, eventually reaching the Greco-Roman empire. During the second and

This text is from commentary on the Lotus Sutra, *an important Buddhist scripture. The commentary is believed to have been written by Prince Shōtoku (573–621), who supported Buddhism throughout his reign.*

third centuries, Mahayana Buddhism spread north-west to the Middle East, and from there it quickly moved to China. At this time many Chinese were disillusioned with Confucianism; consequently, the travelers were successful in planting Buddhism in China. By the year 700, Buddhism had taken root in Korea and Japan; each country practiced Buddhism in its own characteristic way, combining it with local traditions. Zen Buddhism, an outgrowth of Mahayana, soon became influential in China and later in Japan.

Buddhism eventually reached all of Asia, though it was often met with high levels of resistance and persecution from the ruling classes; this resistance is one reason Buddhism has not remained influential in the Middle East.

In the third and fourth century in India, Tantric or Vajrayana Buddhism developed. This sect emphasized mysticism over more formal intellectual practices, and became highly influential in Tibet and Nepal over the next few centuries.

By 1200, Buddhism disappeared almost entirely in India, due perhaps to an increasing influence from other religions, including Islam. At this time, there were numerous Muslim invasions, the most significant of which occurred in the twelfth century and resulted in the destruction of the last of the major Buddhist monasteries. Buddhism had also by then fallen out of favor with India's ruling class, a fact that surely contributed to its demise, as it had always been a religion whose influence was expanded primarily by the wealthy and powerful.

Modern Buddhism remains divided into two schools. The followers of Theravada consider their school to be truer to the original teachings and intentions of the Buddha, while followers of Mahayana believe their school to be more inclusive and egalitarian. Theravada Buddhism is the more influential sect in Southeast Asia, and Mahayana is more popular in northern areas, like Tibet. In the United States, Mahayana is the more popular of the two, and therefore it has had a great influence on art, literature and popular culture.

Buddhism has had a widespread effect in India, leading to permanent changes in the culture. Hinduism, for example, was profoundly influenced by the Mahayana school. In Ladakh and the Himalayan region, Buddhism survives as the majority religion to this day. During the twentieth century, Buddhism experienced a revival in India, due in part to dissatisfaction with socioeconomic discrimination in the Hindu tradition.

During recent centuries, colonialism has gradually severed the connection between Buddhism and the ruling classes of Asian nations, creating a somewhat more grassroots orientation—a style often associated with the faith today. Despite its uneven history, Buddhism is presently the fourth largest religion in the world.

B. The Religion in America

In recent decades, the Buddhist population of the United States has grown exponentially. This can be explained partly by the arrival of ever-growing numbers of East Asian immigrants, the presence of whom altered the spiritual landscape. However, it could also be argued that America's intellectual movement propelled its citizens toward Buddhism.

America's literary history includes many writers who have expressed an interest in Buddhism and other Eastern traditions, with Emerson Thoreau and the Transcendentalists as prime examples. This group of writers influenced the birth of the Theosophy movement, a Buddhist-tinged blend of Eastern and Western faiths that appeared late in the nineteenth century. The movement was spearheaded by Buddhist converts, Henry Steel Olcott and Helena Petrovna Blavatsky.

It is impossible to state as fact the cause of this zeitgeist, but it was likely fueled by a desire for an alternative to Protestantism. Another likely contributor was Chinese and Japanese immigration to America. By the end of the nineteenth century, over 400 Chinese temples had been constructed on the West Coast. Even though these were not exclusively

This bronze representation of the Buddha, cast in 1252, is located on the grounds of the Kotoku-in Temple in Kamakura, Japan. The statue weighs 93 tons and stands 13.3 meters (43.6 feet) tall.

Buddhist temples, most represented an integration of various Eastern religions, offering a catch-all option for immigrants from different Asian nations.

In 1893, the World's Parliament of Religions was held in Chicago. The conference was attended by delegates from countries throughout the world, among them Buddhist monks from China, Japan, Sri Lanka, and Thailand. These monks spoke convincingly of the applicability of their traditions to contemporary problems, planting seeds of synthesis between Western and Eastern philosophies. During the conference, C. T. Strauss, an American Jew, publicly converted to Buddhism, becoming the first known American to officially do so.

In 1943, anti-immigration laws were repealed, allowing an influx of Chinese immigrants into America. These immigrants built Buddhist temples so that they could practice their faith comfortably in their new land.

In July 1944, at the height of American prejudice against Japanese-Americans in World War II, followers of a Japanese Buddhist sect called Jodo Shinshu (True Pure Land Buddhism), who had been interned at the Topaz internment camp, met in Salt Lake City. At that meeting they decided to change the name of their organization to the North American Mission to the Buddhist Churches of America. A new constitution was adopted, and English was accepted as the primary language. The purpose of the meeting was in part to help facilitate tolerance of Buddhism. Eventually, Japanese Buddhism became a bigger influence than the Chinese on the Western idea of Buddhism. The two most practiced forms of Buddhism in America today—Jodo Shinshu and Nichiren—are both Japanese, as is Zen Buddhism.

In the mid–twentieth century, D. T. Suzuki, a Japanese Buddhist missionary, visited the United States and, in doing so, brought new ideas to a generation searching for alternatives to conventional Christian-influenced morality. At the same time, Alan Watts, an Episcopalian minister and academic, was writing popular books on Buddhism and its application to Western issues. These thinkers had a direct influence on the Beat poets and writers, who began blending Buddhism with popular culture. Buddhism, particularly Zen Buddhism, quickly became fashionable among the literati, a trend that crystallized in Kerouac's 1958 novel, *The Dharma Bums*. The trend trickled down to the general public and Zen centers opened on East and West coasts.

The countercultural movement of the 1960s and 1970s played a pivotal role in integrating Buddhism and other Eastern religions into American society. During these years, the number of young people was at an all-time high, with many seeking alternatives to a disunity they believed was aggravated by their parents' outmoded ideals of morality. Liberalized immigration policies in the mid-1960s also played a part in changing the nation's demographics, allowing East Asian Buddhists—many not belonging to Zen sects—to bring their unique perspectives to the front.

In recent decades, another school, Tibetan Buddhism, became popular due both to the media attention focused on Tibet's political situation and the Dalai Lama's part in addressing it. Even before the Dalai

Lama's first trip to the US in 1973, knowledge of Tibetan Buddhism was advanced by such figures as Chögyam Trungpa, a missionary, who settled in Colorado in 1970 and began to speak of both Tibetan Buddhism and the human rights issues faced by Tibet.

It is arguable that the Buddhism practiced by Americans today is distinct from traditional Buddhism. The Buddhism typically practiced by non-immigrant Americans is somewhat Protestantized; many Buddhist temples, for example, hold services on Sunday morning.

The Japanese term *bujizen* describes the phenomenon of the Zen practitioner who eschews traditional Zen observances in favor of a personal interpretation of its principles to suit his or her own needs. This term has been applied to American Zen practice—both as a compliment and as a criticism. Though Buddhism in America is refreshingly individualistic and progressive, it is also arguably dismissive of the rich Indian and East Asian history to which it owes its existence.

Demographically, Buddhism in the United States displays one very significant change from its ancient Eastern roots: here, women make up 50 percent of Buddhists. Another quality characteristic of American Buddhism is its association with glamour, arising largely from its connection with Western pop culture, from the Beats to today's Hollywood movie star converts. Nevertheless, as many as three-quarters of America's Buddhists are actually first-generation Asian immigrants.

C. Important Dates and Landmarks

ca. 566 BCE Birth of Siddhartha Guatama, the Buddha.

ca. 528 BCE Guatama attains enlightenment and becomes a buddha.

ca. 486 Death of the Buddha (the Parinirvana).

ca. 487 The First Buddhist Council is held at Rajagaha; the Buddhist canon is established.

ca. 386 The first official schism occurs in Buddhism at the Second Buddhist Council at Vesali, a major precursor of the Hinayana-Mahayana split. This might also be the council at which the Mahasanghika-Sthaviravada split occurs, known as the Great Schism. This schism is historically important due to the eventual development of the Mahasanghika school into the Mahayana school.

ca. 272–231 Emperor Ashoka rules India; he converts to Buddhism and works extensively to convert others.

ca. 247 Ashoka's son Mahinda, a missionary, establishes Buddhism in Sri Lanka.

ca. 250 The Third Buddhist Council is held at Pataliputra; the Sarvastivadin and Vibhajjavadin sects come into existence.

ca. 200 BCE Buddhism reaches central Asia.

ca. 68 CE Two Buddhist missionaries arrive in China and influence Emperor Ming. The spread of Buddhism to China begins.

ca. 30 CE The First Fourth Buddhist Council inscribes the Pali Canon.

2nd Century Numerous important Mahayana texts are written, such as the *Lotus Sutra*. By this time, as many as 500 different Buddhist sects exist.

ca. 150 Nagarjuna, an Indian philosopher, founds the Madhyamika (Middle Way) school, considered a highly influential early sect of Mahayana.

ca. 100 King Kaniska (78–101) organizes the Second Fourth Buddhist Council in Kashmir, where the Mahayana school is officially founded. The Theravadas do not recognize this council.

3rd Century The Yogacara school is founded (a subset of Mahayana).

3rd Century The Vajrayana school is founded; Buddhist texts are translated into Chinese by Kumarajiva and Hui-yuan.

ca. 372 Buddhism reaches Korea.

5th Century Buddhaghosa, a Theravadin, composes the *Visuddhimagga*; the influence of this work on Theravada Buddhism in Asia continues through the present day.

6th Century Numerous Chinese schools are founded, including Pure Land, which spreads to Japan and eventually becomes influential in twentieth-century United States.

6th Century Bodhidarma, an Indian Buddhist missionary, travels to China and teaches an interpretation of Buddhism that spawns the Zen school, which becomes influential in the U.S. in the twentieth century.

ca. 594 Buddhism is adopted as the official religion of Japan; in later centuries it struggles to maintain this place in the culture.

ca. 632 Tantric Buddhism becomes the state religion in Tibet.

8th Century The Nyingma school is established in Tibet.

ca. 1030 Atisa arrives in Tibet; establishes the tradition of Lamaism, made famous in West by the fourteenth Dalai Lama, Tenzin Gyatso.

12th Century Buddhism is established in Burma.

13th Century The True Sect of the Pure Land school is developed in Japan, along with the Soto Zen and Nichiren schools.

ca. 1200 Centuries of Buddhist persecution in India culminate in a major Muslim invasion, one of a series of invasions that result in decline in Buddhism's influence.

14th Century The Dalai Lama lineage begins in Tibet.

18th Century Colonial occupation in Asian nations causes a decline in Buddhism's power in this area.

1868–1871 The Fifth Buddhist Council takes place, during which the Pali Canon is revised.

1891 The Maha Bodhi Society is founded in Sri Lanka; among its goal is the spread of Buddhism to the West.

1907 The Buddhist Society of Great Britain is founded.

1949 Communism in China creates an inhospitable environment for Buddhism, with implications for immigration to Western nations.

1950 The World Fellowship of Buddhists is founded in Sri Lanka.

1954–1956 The Sixth Buddhist Council at Rangoon takes place, celebrating 2,500 years of Buddhism. The Pali Canon is again revised.

1989 The fourteenth Dalai Lama, Tenzin Gyatso, wins the Nobel Peace Prize for his efforts on behalf of freedom in Tibet.

D. Important Figures

The Buddha

Siddhartha Guatama (whose title was Buddha, or Awakened One) was born in approximately 566 BCE and died in approximately 486 BCE. More recent biographers propose his dates to be 490–410. Much of his life is shrouded in mystery and myth, but certain biographical information has been accepted, at least by Buddhists, as true.

Of royal parentage, Siddhartha was coddled as a child in the hopes of protecting him from painful experiences. It had been foretold that he was to become a Buddha (an "enlightened one"), and his parents wanted to prevent his exposure to any experience that might deter him from following this path.

On four separate trips outside his family palace, Siddhartha met an elderly man, a sick man, a religious ascetic, and a corpse. He was profoundly affected by these experiences, as he had not previously given thought to the realities of suffering, illness, and death. Realizing that these experiences awaited him, the Buddha left behind his wife and child, embarking at the age of twenty-nine on a lifestyle of self-denial.

For six years, Siddhartha wandered while practicing an ascetic lifestyle that included extreme fasting. This came to an end when, at thirty-five, nearly dead of starvation, he recognized that his self-mortifications had not led him to ultimate truth. Siddhartha then went to meditate beneath a pipal tree, resolving that he would stay there until the truth was revealed to him. (The pipal tree later became known as the bodhi tree, *bodhi* meaning "awakening" or "enlightenment.")

During the meditation he had a vision in which he saw all his past incarnations and the *karma* (exestential consequences) he had incurred though them; he then came to understand how one's past actions affect the present and future. He passed through four levels of insight during this meditation and became aware of the Four Noble Truths.

At this point, the Buddha recognized that the asceticism practiced by mystics was nothing more

This painting, on the wall of a Buddhist temple in Laos, depicts the Four Heavenly Messengers met by the Buddha on his journey from the family palace.

than the inverse of the self-indulgence of his youth. The avoidance of extremes by the "middle path," or the Noble Eightfold Path, was, the Buddha decided, the way to *nirvana* (*nibanna* in Pali)—"release" from *samsara*, the endless cycle of reincarnation. This revelation set the Buddha free from the bonds of samsara, but he chose to remain in physical form for a time in order spread his newfound wisdom.

Immediately after this event, the Buddha gave his famous first sermon in Deer Park at Sarnath to five close companions, explaining to them what had happened to him. Although initially doubtful, they became his first adherents. The Buddha lived for forty-five years after this, during which time he taught his wisdom (*dharma*), or "doctrine," to an ever-increasing number of disciples (*vinaya*)—the term "Buddhists" would be coined centuries later. He advocated the proselytization of his new religion, inspiring a generation of monks who spread its message to various parts of India and Nepal. His death in 486 (or 410) BCE is referred to as the Parinirvana.

According to Buddhist doctrine, Siddhartha Guatama was by no means the first buddha, and will not be the last.

II. Tenets and Beliefs

A. Articles of Faith

The basic articles of faith in Buddhism arose from a series of insights experienced by the Buddha during his meditation under the bodhi tree. The tenets of all Buddhist schools are based to varying degrees on these insights, and upon the subsequent teachings of the Buddha to his disciples. Though there is significant disagreement among the various schools, these differences are not equal in extent to those of, for example, the different subsets of Christianity, in which profound disagreements have arisen on fundamental points. The vast majority of Buddhists agree on certain essential elements of their faith.

The hallmark teaching of Guatama Buddha was delivered to five disciples at his first sermon, and it was committed to memory after his death.

It should be emphasized that the doctrines of Buddhism are intended to be practiced, and it is seen as contrary to Buddhism's vision to dissect its teachings. Similarly, a knowledge of the history of Buddhism is not considered essential to understanding it.

The Buddha's means of judging a person was based on the extent to which he or she was able to abide by the precepts; this indicated the level of spiritual maturity that the person had reached. He considered the caste system to be an unreliable gauge of enlightenment, and therefore promoted an egalitarian system which would abolish caste.

The Four Noble Truths (Arya-Satya)

These truths are the most essential of the Buddha's ideas; they underlie all his subsequent teachings. The first Noble truth is that the essence of life is suffering (*dukkha*). Suffering, therefore, is unavoidable; it is, in fact, often a necessary motivator (*samvega*) in life. The Second Noble Truth, arising from suffering, is that suffering is a result of desire (*tinha*)—the desire for power, possessions, and pleasures of the body, the sat-

isfaction of which can never bring true peace. The belief that desire can bring peace results from ignorance (*avidya*) of—or lack of acceptance of—the impermanent nature of existence (*anitya*) and the non-existence of a permanent self (*anatta*).

The Third Noble Truth (Nirodha) is that suffering can be eliminated by abandoning desire. The Fourth Noble Truth is that the abandonment of desire can be accomplished by following the Eightfold Path (Magga). Through the Eightfold Path, humans can free themselves from karma (the cause of samsara, or the repeating cycle of life, death, and rebirth). By this course of action, nirvana can finally be attained.

The Eightfold Path (Astangika-Marga)

The Eightfold Path is also known as the Middle Way, because it attempts to strike a balance between the extremes of self-denial and self-indulgence. Its doctrines are divided into three categories: morality (shila), comprising thought, speech, conduct, and livelihood; mental discipline (samadhi), comprising effort, mindfulness, and concentration; and intuitive insight (prajna), comprising views and intentions. The path consists of eight necessary aspects of existence that must be attended to; it is unclear whether these steps are intended to be progressive.

Right Views – seeing life accurately, which entails understanding impermanence, interdependence, and suffering and the Four Noble Truths.

Right Thought – the elimination of greed, anger, and delusion.

Right Speech – abstaining from falsehood, from tale bearing, from harsh and abusive speech, and from idle chatter. One should speak in an honest, kind and conscious way, recognizing that words, having power, produce good or bad karma.

Right Conduct – behaving appropriately; this entails following Buddhist precepts abstaining from killing, stealing, illicit sexual indulgence, lying, and intoxication, as well as a general obligation to be charitable and nonviolent. (For the Buddha, right and wrong conduct involves not just physical actions but also the intention behind them, which must be correct. A right action done accidentally, for example, does not yield good karma.)

Right Livelihood – abandoning wrong ways of living that bring harm and suffering to others: trafficking in (a) arms and weapons, (b) in animals for slaughter, (c) human beings, (d) intoxicating drinks, and (e) poisons. This is the obligation to earn one's living in a way that does not exploit others; fortune telling and stealing, for example, would on this account be unacceptable.

Right Effort – the obligation to attempt to attain an enlightened mental state, preventing and abandoning evil thoughts from arising, and developing and maintaining wholesome thoughts; and to continue to persevere in this effort despite obstacles.

Right Mindfulness – requires living in the moment, maintaining a clear and calm awareness of the self.

Right Concentration – the need to meditate, in the way prescribed by the Buddha, in order to achieve his results.

The Three Jewels and the Threefold Refuge

Attaining nirvana begins with taking refuge in the Three Jewels:

1. Faith in, and comfort from, the Buddha himself;
2. The Teaching, or dharma, of Buddhism;
3. The Community, or sangha, often referring to a community of Buddhist monks.

The Five Human Factors (Skhandhas)

These are the interrelated factors that make up human beings until their physical deaths. They are:

1. Physical form
2. Sensation
3. Perception
4. Volitions or dispositions
5. Consciousness

These attributes do not constitute a soul, but are rather the features that together create the illusion or worldly manifestation of permanent selfhood.

Dependent Origination

Essentially, this doctrine dictates cause and effect in the lives of human beings. All events arise from a previous cause; nothing can come from a vacuum. It is this fact that condemns humans to endure the cycle of karma, in which right actions lead to contentment and wrong actions lead to suffering.

Since nothing comes into existence except as a result of another thing, nothing has true, permanent, independent reality; all things are interconnected, all are part of a larger whole, and all are ultimately illusory.

The cycle of dependent origination is divided into twelve interdependent aspects, which follow one another: ignorance; predisposition; consciousness; name-form; the six senses; contact; craving; grasping; becoming; birth; old age and death; and ignorance.

The Doctrine of No-Soul (Anatman)

An essential teaching of Buddhism is *anatman*, or the idea that there is no such thing as a permanent self. This was one of the ways in which Buddhism sharply diverged from traditional Hindu thought, which claimed the existence of a soul, or atman (sometimes translated as "ego"). This Hindu belief in a permanent soul contradicted the Buddhist idea of anitya (impermanence). For a Buddhist, the mistaken belief in a self is part and parcel of a life of struggling to maintain and protect this "me," all of which ultimately leads to suffering.

Some Hindu thinkers of the period wondered what the motivation for right conduct would be if the idea of a permanent soul were removed. They reasoned that if there were no soul, there would be no ultimate personal reward, and thus no reason to strive. The Buddha, however, believed that this motivation came from the prospect of attaining nirvana, in which the temporary illusion of selfhood is lost and complete bliss achieved.

The Buddha did not address what occurs after death, nor did he ponder the ultimate fate of humanity. These types of inquiries were considered irrelevant to the teachings and practice of Buddhism, which place great emphasis on process. More importantly, since Buddhists believe nirvana is reachable during life, as the Buddha demonstrated, this can be reached at any time, making the question of what happens after death irrelevant (there need not *be* an after-death).

Nontheism

Buddhism does differ significantly from the monotheistic traditions of Christianity, Judaism, and Islam. The Buddha did not answer questions posed to him about the existence of God. In fact, the question is irrelevant to the concerns of Buddhism. The concept of the ultimate oneness of all things, as well as the doctrines of impermanence (anitya) and no-soul (anatman), are incompatible with ideas of a discrete, eternal, omnipotent deity. Yet Buddhism cannot be thought of as atheistic.

B. Scripture

There is a large body of sacred literature (*sutras*) in Buddhism, yet Buddhism emphasizes alternate ways of transmitting information. The knowledge attained through a student's interaction with his other teacher is considered superior to scholarly study; as a result, oral knowledge is more likely to result in rapid spiritual growth. This is especially true in the Mahayana tradition. Nevertheless, the reading of texts is considered a valid part of the path to nirvana, if such reading is kept in the proper perspective.

According to a commonly accepted account, the Buddha's words were recalled by his disciples at the First Buddhist Council, held in Rajagaha shortly after the Buddha's death. During this meeting, the *Tripitaka* ("three baskets," after the baskets the manuscripts were kept in) was created—resulting in the three-part Buddhist canon. This original version is known as the Pali Canon (Pali being the ancient language in which the canon was transcribed). It was not actually recorded in writing until the Fourth Council. This version is still accepted by the Theravada school.

The Tripitaka

The first part of the *Tripitaka*, the *Sutra Pitaka,* consists of the Buddha's discourses. The second, the *Vinaya Pitaka*, details the rules he laid down for the monastic life. The third part is controversial, as it may or may not have been recited at the Rajagaha council (the Theravadas believe that it was not). Known as the *Abhidharma*, it discussed the scholarly aspects of the Buddha's teachings.

From the time of Council of Vesali, the canon branches off into numerous versions, and today each of the many Buddhist schools has a canon that it considers authoritative, although most are based on the original *Tripitaka*.

The Mahayanas have several non-*Tripitaka* texts considered authoritative. Collectively called the *Buddhavacana* (Revelation of the Buddha), they include a collection known as the *Prajñaparamita* (Perfection of Wisdom), and a series of four sutras—the *Avatamsaka Sutra*, the *Lotus Sutra*, the *Vimalakirti Sutra,* and the *Nirvana Sutra*.

The *Avatamsaka Sutra* describes a universe of interdependence, in which all things contain one another. This sutra also extensively explains the process by which one may become a bodhisattva (a being of pure compassion, representing the ultimate state to which a Mahayana can aspire).

The *Lotus Sutra* describes the Buddha teaching to thousands of disciples, explaining his divine nature to them. Essentially, this text describes a Buddha who is nearer to the Christian conception of a Christ—that is, an incarnation of the Divine, in the sense that he was born as a perfectly enlightened being (rather than an ordinary man who later attained enlightenment). Like the *Avatamsaka Sutra*, the *Lotus Sutra* also discusses the bodhisattva concept, contrasting it with the Theravada focus on personal enlightenment.

The *Vimalakirti Sutra* takes the form of a narrative, in which the titular character, a revered teacher and contemporary of the Buddha's, is visited by Buddhist monks. Vimalakirti engages them in a conversation about the nature of emptiness (*sunyata*). The end result of this lengthy discourse is that

Vimalakirti discredits their dualistic notions, offering them an alternative to the monastic tradition. This is significant in that Vimalakirti is part of the laity, and is asserting the ability of lay people to attain enlightenment (a claim central to the Mahayana tradition).

The Mahayana *Nirvana Sutra* is believed to be a record of the Buddha's last night before his death (the paranirvana), when he gathered his followers around him and explained the nature of death to them. He emphasizes the ultimate nonexistence of the ego, and explains that his existence, though it will continue after death, transcends such mundane limits. He also comforts his disciples by assuring them that the Buddha nature (tathagatagarbha) that they revere actually exists in all things.

SACRED LITERATURE

Most of the many subsets of both the Theravada and Mahayana schools have noncanonical texts that they consider vital to the understanding of their traditions. However, it is Theravada that places the most emphasis on these texts, regarding certain noncanonical texts as sacred.

The most important of these are the writings of Buddhaghosa, a fifth-century Theravada monk. He wrote many texts, but his most important is the *Visuddhimagga* (The Way of Purity), a discourse on the methods a Theravada can use to attain wisdom, foremost among which is the proper practice of meditation. Buddhaghosa also wrote important works analyzing the *Tripitaka*.

C. Secondary Sources

THEOLOGIANS AND THINKERS

Nagarjuna (ca. 150–250 CE)

Nagarjuna was a philosopher and the founder of the Madhyamaka (Middle Way) school. He wrote a treatise, the *Mulamadhyamakakarika* (Fundamentals of the Middle Way), which discussed the main precepts of this branch of Mahayana Buddhism. Nagarjuna taught of the wisdom in emptiness (sunyata), advocating the attainment of a state beyond thought, contrary to the conventional Theravada view, which promoted thinking and reason.

Asanga (310–390 CE) and Vasubandhu (320–400)

Brothers Asanga and Vasubandhu together founded the Yogacara or Vijnanavada school (a Mahayana sect). They were writers of prose, poetry, and philosophy, as well as incisive critical works. Their Yogacara school advocated the nonexistence of all phenomena except consciousness, and marked a return to a more streamlined meditation-based practice of Buddhism.

Bodhidharma (ca. 440–528 CE)

Bodhidharma was a Mahayana monk who traveled from India to China to spread the doctrine of dhyana, or meditation. In China, his ideas blended with Taoism and became Zen Buddhism, which eventually spread to other areas, including Japan. In 1970, during the American vogue for Zen, D. T. Suzuki translated Bodhidharma's *The Two Ways of Entrance* into English.

Honen (Honen Bo Genku) (1133–1212)

Founder of the Pure Land (Jodo) sect in Japan, Honen's teachings were later to become very influential in America. Honen's highly controversial new form of Mahayana Buddhism taught that the simple recitation of the nembutsu—the calling on the grace of Amida Buddha, the Buddha of Infinite Light and Infinite Life, was sufficient for enlightenment. Jodo Shu, the Pure Land Way, was quickly followed by True Pure Land Way (Jodo Shin Shu), founded by a student of Honen's; both sects are now influential in America.

Nichiren (1222–1282)

Nichiren was a Japanese monk who founded the Nichiren school, based on the Tendai school. He taught the superiority of the *Lotus Sutra* over the other sutras, and emphasized the possibility of attaining enlightenment within one's lifetime.

Thomas Merton (1915–1968)

Thomas Merton was a Catholic priest who played a part in introducing Buddhism to the United States. Born to nonreligious American parents and raised in France, he had a conversion experience in 1938, and, shortly thereafter, became a Catholic monk.

An influential intellectual within his own religion, Merton became interested in Buddhism in the 1950s, particularly in the connections between the Zen sect and Christian mysticism, which has parallels to aspects of Zen practice such as focus on koans and the concept of emptiness (sunyata). Merton made numerous trips to Asia and at one point met with the Dalai Lama to discuss their religious commonalities. Throughout his life, Merton advocated monastic life and contemplation, both in the Catholic and Buddhist tradition. He wrote many books, including several on Buddhism.

Merton also engaged in a long-term epistolary friendship with D. T. Suzuki, the result of which was *Zen and the Birds of Appetite*, a collection of letters published the year of Merton's death.

D. Important Writers, Artists and Political Leaders

The Dalai Lamas (1391–)

"Dalai Lama" is a title bestowed upon a male Tibetan believed to be the latest incarnation of Avalokitesvara, a divine entity who epitomizes compassion (such entities, when in human form, are known in Mahayana as bodhisattvas). The Dalai Lamas are carefully chosen during early childhood by the monks of the previous incarnation, a search that takes several years and is based on various clues, including the perception of precocious wisdom and insight and recognition of the previous incarnation's personal effects. New incarnations are chosen among children

The Dalai Lama appears in this 2009 photograph, taken during a visit to the Massachusetts Institute of Technology in Cambridge, Massachusetts.

born forty-nine days after the previous incarnation's death. The first incarnation was born in 1391, but the Dalai Lama title was not used until the third was given this honorific in 1578. At first, the Dalai Lamas were simply spiritual leaders. The fifth Dalai Lama (1617–1682) changed this by taking on a more political role during a time of internal strife and threats from without, earning him the title "the Great Fifth."

Today, the best-known Dalai Lama is the current one, **Tenzin Gyatso** (b. 1935). He is considered to be the fourteenth incarnation of the Avalokitesvara, and is widely admired for his efforts in favor of a peaceful resolution to the problem of Chinese occupation in Tibet. In this type of activism, he followed in the footsteps of the thirteenth incarnation, who opposed European colonialism.

Gyatso's public role has garnered a great deal of attention from the Western press, drawing attention not only to Tibet's plight but also to the practice of Tibetan Buddhism. In 1989, the Dalai Lama received the Nobel Peace Prize for his work.

In 1997, the motion pictures *Red Corner*, starring high-profile Hollywood Buddhist Richard Gere; *Seven Years in Tibet*, starring Brad Pitt about the upbringing of the Dalai Lama and the fall of Tibet to the Chinese Communists; and *Kundun*, depicting the Dalai Lama's childhood and directed by Martin Scorsese were featured in a *Time* magazine cover story entitled "America's Fascination with Buddhism."

Daisetz Teitaro Suzuki (1870–1966)

Born and raised in Japan, D. T. Suzuki grew up in the Zen tradition, which he embraced with vigor as an adult. In 1897, he moved to Illinois and worked as a translator for Buddhist-oriented organizations. In 1911, back in Japan, he met and married Beatrice Erskine Lane, an American theosophist; together they founded *The Eastern Buddhist*, a Japanese magazine about Mahayana. Suzuki was particularly interested in the history of Mahayana as it traveled east from India, and how it had been adapted to traditional Japanese culture.

In the 1950s, Suzuki spent more time in the U.S., which included a teaching position at Columbia University and interaction with Beat writers interested in his ideas. Among his many writings, perhaps the most influential is *An Introduction to Zen Buddhism*, a beginner's guide to the school that includes discursive expositions of Christian objections to Buddhism.

Alan Watts (1915–1973)

Born to a middle-class family in England, Watts was raised as an Anglican, but became interested in Buddhism in his teens. After moving to America, he was briefly an Episcopalian minister, but eventually redirected his energies entirely to Buddhism, particularly Zen. Largely self-taught, he became an expert in the field. His contribution to American Zen was an encompassing spirituality that included elements of other Eastern religions; he also advocated a kind of Americanization of the Buddhist faith, of which the element of individuality and personal interpretation were a vital part. At the same time, he decried the kind of dilettantism he observed in some Beat poets, whom he believed were insincere in their efforts to be Buddhist.

Watts wrote more than twenty books on Buddhism, among them *The Way of Zen* (1957), *Beat Zen, Square Zen and Zen* (1959), and *The Book—On the Taboo Against Knowing Who You Are* (1966).

Jack Kerouac (1922–1969)

Born in Lowell, Massachusetts, to French-Canadian parents, Kerouac was to become the spokesperson for a generation of disaffected rebels. Author of *On the Road*, a novel based on his youthful experiences as a drifter, Kerouac (after reading Dwight Goddard's classic 1932 anthology *The Buddhist Bible*) embraced Buddhism in an attempt to find a set of contemporary ideals as an alternative to the conservative Catholic values with which he had been raised.

Having discovered Buddhism in 1954, Kerouac became fascinated by it. In 1955, he wrote a biography of the Buddha, which was published posthumously. During this time, Kerouac developed friendships with D. T. Suzuki, Alan Watts, and Gary Snyder, and these associations helped inspire *The Dharma Bums*, Kerouac's 1958 roman à clef.

Despite his admiration for Buddhism, Kerouac never converted. At the end of his life, when asked about his religion, he declared himself a Catholic; he can thus be said to typify a certain American sensibility regarding Buddhism, one in which it is embraced and used as inspiration without demanding abandonment of one's primary faith.

Allen Ginsberg (1926–1997)

Born to second-generation Russian-Jewish immigrants, Ginsberg was raised with liberal, even radical, values. A leading Beat poet, he is most famous for his book *Howl and Other Poems*, a titular work that addresses the damaging influence of increasing consumerism and conformity in American life. Like many of Ginsberg's poems, it also contains references to Buddhism.

Interested in the mystical since childhood, Ginsberg was influenced by Chögyam Trungpa, a Tibetian Buddhist and close friend, to explore the religion. Together with Anne Waldman, Ginsburg founded the Jack Kerouac School of Disembodied Poetics, at Naropa University, a Buddhist university Trungram had founded in Colorado. Ginsburg directed the program and taught in it for over twenty years.

Gary Snyder (1930–)

Gary Snyder is perhaps the Beat poet most closely identified with Buddhism. Born and raised in San Francisco, he grew up in the shadow of the Depression. After attending Reed College, he returned to his hometown, where he was influenced by D. T. Suzuki's writings. At the same time he began to develop friendships with Kerouac and Ginsburg, both of whom viewed him as exotic due to his experience as an outdoorsman and manual laborer. Snyder went on to study East Asian culture, first at U.C. Berkeley and then at the American Academy of Asian Studies. He became a dedicated Zen Buddhist in the mid-1950s.

Snyder's awareness of ecological issues led him to connect his Buddhist faith with his concern for the earth's condition. In addition to ecological concerns he had an abiding interest in mythology and traditional Native-American faiths. His Pulitzer Prize–winning 1974 poetry collection, *Turtle Island*, reflects this syncretistic mindset.

One of Synder's works, published in 1996, is *Mountains and Rivers Without End*, shaped in part by the *Mountains and Rivers Sutra*, which was originally written by thirteenth-century Zen master Dogen, founder of the Soto school. Snyder is currently Professor Emeritus of English at the University of California, Davis.

Robert Thurman (1941–)

One of the highest-profile Buddhist scholars today, Thurman is also a Buddhist practitioner. Born and raised in New York, he became disenchanted with American values in the early 1960s and left to

Writer and professor Robert Thurman, seen in this 2007 photograph, is the author of the 2008 book Why the Dalai Lama Matters.

explore India. At the age of twenty-four, he became a monk in the Tibetan tradition, a decision that was influenced by his friend, the Dalai Lama. He became the first known American to attain this status.

Thurman has authored numerous books on Buddhism and its relationship to American society today. He has written about the need to match the "outer modernity" of America with the "inner modernity" of Buddhist nations (*Buddhism in America*, p. 135), and has attempted to link American individualism with Buddhism's focus on the development of the inner self. He explored these themes in his 1998 *Inner Revolution: Life, Liberty and the Pursuit of Real Happiness*.

Thurman is president of the American Institute of Buddhist Studies and president and co-founder of Tibet House, a New York–based organization dedicated to preserving Tibetan religion and culture and sharing it with the West. He has been highly influential in raising the public's awareness of Tibet's current political and spiritual crisis and the threat it poses to the Buddhist tradition. Currently, Thurman is the Jey Tsong Kappa Professor in Indo-Tibetan Buddhist Studies at Columbia University.

III. Rites and Rituals

A. The Calendar

Theravada and Mahayana Buddhists celebrate different holidays, and those they share are celebrated in distinct ways. Theravada tends toward more elaborate and colorful rituals, but primarily the deciding factor is the country in which the ceremony is held—each incorporates its own unique details into celebrations. In general, though, for both Theravada and Mahayana, here and in Asia, holidays are marked by public celebration along with the observance of certain duties, such as the giving of alms and gifts to local monks. In addition, ceremonies often include attendance of a lecture on dharma offered by the monks. Aside from these firm duties holiday celebration varies. Some holidays, for example, involve the circling of a stupa, or Buddhist shrine, three times. Often, for many, there is chanting and meditation in the evening.

The dates of Buddhist holidays are not fixed, as they usually follow the lunar calendar; in recent years, however, the modern Gregorian calendar is sometimes used with the dates of full and new moons within those months as indicators of festivals. Much as every country performs Buddhist ceremonies differently, countries also choose festival dates based on their own systems.

Uposatha Days

In Theravada, every new, full, and quarter moon is celebrated, thus creating four lunar holidays each month. These days are minor holy days that entail a visit to a local monastery, and often involve a renewal of vows pledging commitment to the Eightfold Path and Five Precepts.

JANUARY

The Buddhist New Year

For Mahayana, this falls on the first full moon in January. For Theravada, it takes place on the first three days from the first full moon in April. Vajrayana celebrates New Year's Day on the first full moon in February. Traditions of celebration vary, but monastery visits, the giving of alms, and feasting are integral to the New Year celebration.

FEBRUARY

Parinirvana Day

In Mahayana sects, this day is a celebration of the Buddha's death (the parinirvana). It takes place on the full moon in February, the second lunar month, and is marked in different ways by different sects. Typically, the celebration involves a reading of the *Nirvana Sutra*, meditation on the continuing journeys of deceased loved ones, and the obligatory monastery visits and offerings of most holidays. Some sects may also hold celebratory feasts.

Losar

In Tibet, Losar is the Buddhist New Year. It is most often celebrated around the 19th of February, though the exact date varies according to the lunar calendar. Losar is a three-day holiday, the first day devoted to home-based celebrations, the second and third to calling on nearby friends and family, and exchanging gifts. Visits to monasteries are typical, and the monasteries are usually decorated elaborately. Some people volunteer to wash and paint local buildings, representing rebirth and renewal. The Dalai Lama plays an active and public part in this celebration, and he receives offerings.

MARCH

Magha Puja Day (Sangha Day or Fourfold Assembly)

Magha Puja Day celebrates the gathering of the Buddha at Sarnath with the 1,250 arhats who had come to worship him. This event first occurred after the first rains retreated and is noted because the arhats assembled spontaneously with no prior arrangement or agreement. It occurred on the full moon day of the third lunar month (March) and continues to be commemorated on that day. Sangha Day is considered the second most important holiday next to Buddha Day, as it honors the concept of spiritual community and monastic living, both structural components of Buddhism.

Avalokitesvara's Birthday

This holiday is generally celebrated in mid- to late-March, and honors Avalokitesvara, the bodhisattva who best embodied compassion. The Dalai Lamas are thought of as the incarnations of this deity. The holiday is observed only in Mahayana.

APRIL

Birth of Buddha

The Mahayana celebrate the birth of Buddha on April 8th. This day is a time to remember the Buddha, his journey, and his teachings, as well as to anticipate one's own personal attainment of nirvana.

Songkran

Many sects in Theravada celebrate Songkran, a festival that occurs in mid-April and goes on for three days. The most salient feature of this holiday is the traditional practice of spraying water on others; the rules are not strict and can mean anything from gently sprinkling perfumed water on someone's hands to unexpectedly turning a garden hose on them. This practice signifies renewal and the cleansing of one's spirit in preparation for the new year. Statues of the Buddha are also subject to this type of cleansing ritual on Songkran. As in Losar, house washing is another part of the celebration.

MAY
Vesak (Visakah Puja)

This feast, the most central in Buddhism, is known as Buddha Day and is the celebration of his birthday (and, in Theravada, his enlightenment and death). In Theravada it is celebrated with great fanfare on the full moon in the sixth lunar month.

In addition to chanting, prayer, and merrymaking, Vesak often involves pouring water over a statue of the Buddha as a symbol of the purification needed in order to reach his state; some followers leave gifts in thanks.

The Plowing Festival

The Theravada plowing festival, normally held in the second week of May, commemorates an event in the Buddha's childhood, wherein his father took him to watch the yearly plowing; this is when the Buddha first achieved a deep meditative state. This festival, in which oxen pull special plows and rice seeds are scattered from golden bowls, is believed to ensure a fruitful harvest.

JULY
Asalha Puja Day (Dharma Day)

Celebrated on the first full moon in the eighth lunar month (usually in July), this holiday marks when the Buddha first began his life of teaching. On this day he gathered his disciples at Sarnath and shared his truth (dharma) with them. This event is known as the Dharmachakra. Traditionally, this day marked the beginning of the rainy season.

Vassa

Vassa, occasionally called Lent, corresponds with the rainy season, which runs from July to October. It is observed by a retreat—rarely undertaken by the Mahayana in modern times—during which many of the laity take vows and lead an ascetic life until the rains stop, at which point there is merrymaking and feasting.

AUGUST
Festival of the Tooth

The Festival of the Tooth, a primarily Sri Lankan holiday, takes place on the full moon in August. In Kandy, a Sri Lankan city, there is a beautiful temple which purportedly houses one of the Buddha's teeth, encased within a number of ornate safes. On this day these are paraded through the streets of Kandy on the back of an elephant (the elephant is sacred in Buddhism). This elaborate parade involves a procession of many elephants, and lasts nine days.

Ulambana (Ancestor Day or All Souls' Day)

This holiday, central to the Mahayana tradition, is also celebrated by some Theravadas. It is embraced in Japan perhaps more than any other nation. It falls on the first to fifteenth days of the eighth lunar month and is a time to honor the dead, particularly those who have gone to hell; it is believed that these people are allowed back to earth for the two weeks of Ulambana. On the last day, their relatives visit their graves and offer gifts and prayers.

In Japan, Ulambana (known there as Obon) has less of an emphasis on hell, being merely a time to honor and communicate with ancestors. It lasts only three days, and is celebrated in July with fireworks and, in some areas, the setting of lightweight lanterns to sail in local bodies of water.

OCTOBER

Pavarana Day

Pavarana Day marks the end of the rainy season. This feast entails the fashioning of a large robe (mahakathina)—the creation of which occurs in one night and requires an entire village's participation—to be given to the local monastery in a ceremony known as kathina. This event commemorates the prodigious robe-making efforts of the Buddha's mother the night before he left on his journey of enlightenment.

Abhidharma Day

In Burma, this is a holiday commemorating the occasion when the Buddha visited Tushita Heaven (a level of paradise slightly below the final one that Buddha entered when he died). Here he found his mother and taught her the *Abhidharma* (roughly translated as "higher teaching"). Abhidharma Day usually falls on the first full moon in October.

NOVEMBER

Anapanasati Day

This holiday, usually falling in mid-November, commemorates an unusually long Vassa retreat during the Buddha's ministry. He had been so happy with his disciples' progress that he extended the retreat for an extra month. At the end of this time, he gathered them and offered them his advice on mindful breathing (anapanasati), which was later recorded in a special sutra.

Loy Krathong

This Theravada festival, popular in Thailand, occurs generally on the full moon in November. Falling after the rainy season, when the rivers are at their highest tide, this festival entails the floating of colorful paper bowls, often handmade, which contain flowers, incense, leaves, and other offerings. The practice is supposed to bring luck, and acts as an apology to Nature, and request for forgiveness, for the pollution suffered by the river.

The Elephant Festival

Falling on the third Saturday in November, this holiday symbolizes the value of friendship between generations, particularly the relationship between a student and mentor. According to legend, the Buddha described such relationships in terms of a wild elephant trained through being tied to a tame elephant.

B. Worship and Liturgy

Worship can take any number of forms, and there is little of the attention to formalized rites and rituals found in Christianity. Usually, services consist of monks presiding over the reading of sacred texts. There may also be chanting, prayer, or meditation, often led by monks.

In general, Buddhism does not require worship at temples and there is a fair amount of freedom offered to worship in whatever location one finds comfortable. Many Buddhists erect a shrine in their homes, complete with a small statue of the Buddha and candles or incense.

Different sects have differing types of praxis. Traditions vary among Theravada, Mahayana and Vajrayana, but meditation (dhyana) is a vital part of daily life for all three branches of Buddhism, and one can draw certain generalities about how it is approached.

For all Buddhist traditions, there are four stages of concentration (dhyanas) that should be reached in meditation; each leads to a greater purity of being:

1. detachment from the physical world, and a feeling of joy and effortless contemplation;

2. intense concentration, accompanied by liberation from attempts at reason or logic;

3. the fading of the sense of joy, leaving only peaceful contemplation;

4. the passing away of the sense of effortlessness, accompanied by pure equanimity.

The dyanas are followed by the samapattis:

1. Apprehension of the infinity of space;

2. Apprehension of the infinity of thought;

3. Apprehension of the unreality of all things;

4. Attainment of a nearly thought-free state.

Different sects offer different styles of meditation to reach this final state. Samatha ("calm") is a method used by both branches, but is more developed and emphasized in Mahayana. It entails focusing the mind intently on a single object, thought, or mantra, in the belief that, in order to rise above thought, the mind first needs a specific point to focus thought upon. This concept has been made famous partly by the popularity of Hinduism's recent gift to the West, transcendental meditation; samatha, in fact, predates the Buddha by centuries.

In Theravada, vipassana ("clear vision") is the main meditation style. Unique to Buddhism, it is considered an essential additional step, to samatha, and the main distinguisher of Buddhist meditation from its Hindu counterpart. Vipassana essentially entails the focus of consciousness on one's own thoughts to encourage an awareness of the consciousness beyond thought.

Other schools have various different techniques beyond, or as part of, samatha and vipassana. For example, Zen practitioners often focus on *koans*, or riddles, which have no right or wrong answer and help a meditator move beyond logical analysis into a state beyond it. Attainment of this state has nothing to do with solving the riddle; the riddle is merely a vehicle to a particular state. The archetypal koan is "What is the sound of one hand clapping?"

C. Daily Life: Precepts and Restrictions

It is difficult to generalize what Buddhism requires of its adherents. The first problem with attempting such a generalization is that the Buddha avoided the idea of setting down laws of conduct to which a follower must adhere in order to become enlightened, although he did offer guidelines in the form of the Eightfold Path and the Five Precepts.

Another difficulty in discussing requirements is that the Buddha's "laws" of behavior are more accurately described as wisdom, which, given sufficient incarnations, the individual comes to understand naturally, even if he does not undertake them as a form of specifically Buddhist devotion.

Guidelines vary widely among different subsets; there are also very different requirements for laity and monks, a difference particularly striking in Theravada. Despite the lack of firm laws, there are general principles that most Buddhists (from any school) make an effort to follow:

The Five Precepts (for the laity):

1. Abstain from harming any living being;

2. Abstain from stealing;

3. Abstain from sexual misconduct;

4. Abstain from lying;

5. Abstain from alcohol and mind-altering drugs.

Interpretations of these precepts varies widely among sects. Many see the first precept as necessitating vegetarianism; some do not. The third precept has also been the subject of several different interpretations, resulting in complete lifelong celibacy for some and, for others, mere restraint from sexual addiction, adultery, or mistreatment of lovers. The fifth precept is simply ignored by a few sects.

The Ten Precepts (for monks):

In addition to the above, monks must:

6. Abstain from solid food after noon;

7. Abstain from popular entertainments;

8. Abstain from excessive adornment, jewelry, or perfume;

9. Abstain from using raised or soft seats and beds;

10. Abstain from taking money except alms.

In general, adherence to these last five is not a matter of debate. However, in the U.S., liberalized monastic practice has changed the way Buddhist monks and nuns live. Some see this as a mutually beneficial syncretism of two cultures, but some see it as dangerous bastardization. Discussing the relaxation of monastic requirements, John Daido Loori, a well-known roshi (Zen teacher), commented, "...To me, this hybrid path—halfway between monasticism and lay practice—reflects our [American] cultural spirit of greed and consumerism. With all the possibilities, why give up anything? 'We want it all'" (*Buddhism in America*, p. 245).

D. Life Cycle Events

Buddhist life cycle rituals are not decided by the religion but by the individual's national culture. Thus, a Japanese Buddhist celebrates a wedding differently from a Sri Lankan Buddhist, who celebrates it differently from an American Buddhist. Even so, certain generalities can be made about the way Buddhists view many life events.

Birth

Buddhism does not advocate any particular ritual regarding birth, perhaps because human existence is seen as synonymous with suffering, and birth is generally regarded as a less important human event than death. The circumstances surrounding the Buddha's own birth are not regarded as a model, since the Buddha was of royal parentage and because his entrance into the world ended in the death of his mother, Mahamaya.

Many Buddhists, however, choose to have new babies blessed by a monk. Ceremonies surrounding such blessings depend on national and local customs. In many cases, a naming ceremony is held to select a name for the child. This ceremony need not occur directly after birth, but can take place any time until the child's eighth birthday. The procedure is simple: a monk creates a natal astrological chart for the child and determines which name best fits the child's character and destiny. The monk then cuts off a lock of the child's hair and announces the name.

Confirmation

Neither baptism nor confirmation exists in Buddhism. The decision to be a Buddhist is chosen freely and therefore cannot be predetermined by the family or culture. Buddhism is different from other religions in that it does not pass down through the family line. Buddhism is more a philosophy for living, which a person may either accept or reject as he or she sees fit, than a religion that one is born into.

Nuptials

In Buddhist countries, marriage is seen as a civil ceremony, not as a religious one. As a result, the rituals of weddings depend largely on the customs of the country where the wedding takes place. Nevertheless in many Buddhist weddings homage is paid to the Buddha, and also the Three Jewels and the Five Precepts are both recited. In most Buddhist countries it is customary to visit a monk after the ceremony in order to obtain his blessing for the marriage, and sometimes to ask his advice about how to make it a happy one.

The *Sigalovada Sutra* provides the traditional Theravada vows of the bride and groom:

Husband: Towards my wife I undertake to love and respect her, be kind and considerate, be faithful, delegate domestic management, provide gifts to please her.

Wife: Towards my husband I undertake to perform my household duties efficiently, be hospitable to my in-laws and friends of my husband, be faithful, protect and invest our earnings, discharge my responsibilities lovingly and conscientiously.

These vows, still popular in Southeast Asia, strike some American Buddhists as outmoded.

Death and Burial

Traditions vary widely, but Asian Buddhists tend to focus more on funerals than they do on weddings, perhaps due to the centrality of the Parinirvana in Buddhism and the belief in death as the portal to new pathways of learning. A basic tenet of Buddhism is that life is suffering; thus a funeral while not joyous is also not necessarily a somber affair.

In the Theravada tradition, family members of the moribund will encourage a focus on the Buddha and his teachings before death, sometimes even putting slips of paper in his or her mouth with relevant ideas written on them. After death the body is bathed. A long viewing period—about a week—is usual, wherein the body is surrounded by flowers and other decorations or offerings. Monks will visit during this time, chanting from the *Abhidharma*; the family, in turn, offers them alms. After the viewing period, most families, especially in Theravada nations, choose cremation, in part because the Buddha himself was cremated. It should be noted that cremation was common in his day as part of the effort to prevent the spread of disease.

E. Family Life

Husband and Wife

Though there is a common perception that Buddhism discourages marriage, as it is considered an aspect of worldliness, there are only a few sects that require that monks remain unmarried. The Buddha himself was married and had children. He left his wife and children, not out of disapproval for this path, but out of his own need to embark on a deeply personal journey of spiritual discovery. The Buddha later spoke highly of marriage and children, calling both a major source of human joy and enlightenment. Within a marriage, husbands and wives should treat spouses according to the Five Precepts, as they should all people.

Childrearing

There are no specific instructions on how to raise children. The Buddha spoke little about the subject, saying children should be taught about the Five Precepts and parents should help them understand the laws of karma. Corporal punishment of children is held unacceptable, as Buddhism is nonviolent.

In the *Ambalatthikarahulovada Sutra*, the Buddha teaches his son the importance of honesty after the boy tells a fib. The Buddha's technique is Socratic: he asks the child probing questions and draws out the flaws in his thinking that led to his decision to lie. The Buddha's focus here is the importance of carefully considering the origin, purpose, and consequences of our actions before we take them, to ensure they are in keeping with the Five Precepts.

In East Asia, often parents bring their children to temples for classes, similar to Sunday school in Protestantism, where they are taught about the Buddha and his teachings.

Abortion is considered a violation of the First Precept, since, in the Buddhist view, life begins at conception. Theravada countries tend to impose this injunction more stringently; in general, Buddhism allows many exceptions based on the health of the mother and other relevant components. Many Buddhists in America do not feel strongly about the issue, and some are even pro-choice.

Extended Family

The same principles that apply to the nuclear family apply also to the extended family. In the Buddha's time, there was little separation between the two, and the extended family was as much a part of one's daily life as one's child or spouse. In predominantly Buddhist countries, particularly those in Southeast Asia, this is still the case. Still, customs and practices regarding the extended family vary in each country, and so it is not uniform. Many Mahayana countries, in becoming Westernized in their thinking, do not view the extended family as a significant part of an individual's life.

Divorce

Divorce, in its modern form, did not exist in ancient India, and therefore the Buddha never spoke on the topic. Divorce is frowned upon in many Buddhist countries, particularly Theravada countries, simply because these cultures are fairly conservative about the role of marriage and the nuclear family in society. American Buddhists, however, tend to be more accepting of divorce.

IV. Denominations and Demographics

A. History (Schisms and Mergers)

The history of Buddhism is complex, which is well illustrated by the sheer number of sects in both the Theravada and Mahayana traditions. Despite the number of schools and beliefs, there remains a great deal of similarity among Buddhist groups.

Significant schisms in Buddhism began approximately 100 years after the Buddha's death (c. 383), at the First Buddhist Council. Here, controversies over different interpretations of the Buddha's teachings came to a head. Many issues were trivial, such as whether or not buttermilk could be consumed after meals, yet these debates ultimately addressed the importance of rules and rituals in the practice of Buddhism. The result was the Sthaviravada-Mahasanghika split, with the Sthaviravada the more conservative group, determined to hold to the traditions they believed had been set down 100 years earlier.

A deeper issue at stake was the question of how to attain enlightenment. The Sthaviravada believed only those who followed the precepts of the Buddha exactly as he described them could become arahants (*arhat* in Sanskrit)—an arahant is one who has reached the stage of enlightenment immediately below that of a buddha. For the Mahasanghika, not only was this belief inaccurate, but they thought the goal of arahant was too limited and personal, and therefore insufficient and misguided.

Other rifts quickly followed. The Sthaviravgada-Mahasanghika break holds a significant place in Buddhist history, often perceived as the initial split that would later direct the Mahayana–Theravada split.

The Mahayana-Theravada Split

The Mahayana-Theravada split occurred around 100 CE, during the Second Fourth Buddhist Council in Kashmir (the Theravadas do not acknowledge this council). At this time, eighteen official Buddhist schools existed, but they were still essentially divided into two general groups. The more conservative group, who became known as the Theravadas, focused on obeying specific laws and performing rituals to the exact specifications of the Pali scriptures. They concerned themselves with the laws of karma, and the ways in which an individual might finally overcome it—through strict adherence to the Buddha's laws of behavior. The liberals of the council were unhappy with what they saw as a shortsightedness of this mindset, and nicknamed the conservative sect Hinayana, meaning "lesser vehicle." Thus the Mahayana ("greater vehicle") school was born.

From the first century on, most of the major schisms occurred only within the Mahayana school. Around 150 CE, Nagarjuna founded the Madhyamaka (Middle Way) branch of Mahayana in an attempt to resolve the popular disputes between the Mahayana and the Theravada. Nagarjuna claimed that nothing is real except the Void, and that no "truth" can be ascertained other than the unattainability of truth itself. From this popular school arose Yogacara, centered on the writings of Asanga and Vasubandhu. This idealist sect declared that truth could be known, but truth was simply consciousness: What we perceive as truth may not exist, but what we are does. Thus Yogacara saw reality as subjective, based on each individual's experience. Much later, in the seventh century, the Yogacara school spread to Asia, and eventually became important both in China and Japan. Its idealism colors all Mahayana schools.

The next major development was the emergence of mysticism in Mahayana. It is uncertain exactly when this occurred, but it is likely to have developed in the third or fourth century with the appearance of the Vajrayana, or Tantric, sect. Vajrayana seems to have been founded partly in reaction to the general Mahayana focus on philosophical problems of being (as opposed to the experience of being). It was also probably influenced by a resurgence of Hinduism, with its focus on magical rituals and rites. Even today Vajrayana Buddhism resembles Hinduism in that it boasts a vast number of demigod-like beings, most with human characteristics.

Vajrayana quickly became an enormously influential school. In the seventh, eighth, and ninth centuries, its ideas were disseminated in Tibet and Nepal; there they combined with traditional Mahayana beliefs to form the Buddhist school known in the West as Tibetan Buddhism. During the mid-twentieth century Chinese occupation of Tibet, many Tibetan Buddhists—some with high positions within the faith—were forced to emigrate to Western nations; this accounts for some of Tibetan Buddhism's current influence in the United States.

Pure Land Buddhism

The sixth and seventh centuries saw still more schisms within Mahayana. Pure Land, a Chinese sect previously without much influence, was reanimated by the scholar T'an-luan. He promoted the idea that Amitabha (the Buddha of Infinite Light), had promised paradise in Sukhavati (the Pure Land) to all those who believed in him and called upon him. In the seventh century, Tao-ch'o went further than T'an-luan, saying the world was falling into decline, and all other previous Buddhist tenets were no longer valid for the present age; only Pure Land could save society.

Pure Land became popular in Japan in the ninth and tenth centuries, and eventually engendered True Pure Land (Jodo Shinshu) in the thirteenth century. True Pure Land, which included elements of the Tendai Buddhism, then popular in Japan, was seen as simpler than Tendai and thus more accessible to the common people; all that was required for enlightenment was calling upon the Amida Buddha. Pure Land and True Pure Land are still popular in their countries of origin, due to their ability to appeal to the proletariat (in contrast with Buddhism's general history of alignment with monarchies).

Cha'an (Zen in Japanese) Buddhism arose around the same time as Pure Land. Discussing the history of Zen is difficult, because this branch of Mahayana disavows scholarly study entirely, and it rejects even historical details. Zen considers such discussion unhelpful in the quest for nirvana and therefore unnecessary.

Ch'an Buddhism grew partly out of Yogacara. Ch'an's founder, Bodhidarma, approved of Yogacara's focus on idealism (the nonexistence of all but the self and its experiences). Bodhidarma offered Ch'an as an alternative to Pure Land; he enjoined his followers to believe that enlightenment was possible not just in the hereafter, as Pure Land claimed, but even in the present.

Ch'an was introduced to Japan in the twelfth century as Zen, where it later split into numerous subsets. All of them agreed that followers should abandon ritual in favor of meditation and similar practices intended to focus their minds on the now, rather than the nirvana they might attain in the future. This notion would later prove seductive to twentieth-century American artists and writers.

Nichiren Buddhism

In the thirteenth century, Nichiren, a Tendai monk, declared all existing forms of Buddhism void. He conceived an eponymous new sect, which was reviled by many in its infancy, but whose followers today number upwards of 30 million.

Nichiren Buddhism arose from Tendai, and, like Tendai, emphasized the superiority of the *Lotus Sutra*, declaring it the only one worth studying; Nichiren's ministry is seen as fulfilling the prophecy in the *Lotus Sutra* that, during Buddhism's decline, a great sage would appear to lead the faith back to its roots. Nichiren Buddhism was, and still is, a nationalistic sect, one that offered the Japanese a sense of hope and renewed pride during a time of political uncertainty. Despite areas of seeming rigidity and pedantry, it is essentially optimistic and egalitarian. It offers laypeople the same chance for enlightenment as monks, and it preaches, like many Mahayana sects, that enlightenment can happen before death.

B. Comparison of Tenets and Practices

Buddhism's long history has given birth to many sects, most of which have not been addressed here. Today's Buddhism can be divided into three primary schools: the Three Vehicles—Mahayana, Theravada, and Vajrayana (although Vajrayana is actually a school within Mahayana). Though usually classified under Vajrayana, Tibetan Buddhism is here considered separately, as it incorporates elements of all the Three Vehicles.

Despite manifold divisions within these four categories, certain essential ideas unify them, making it possible to discuss them as a major belief system.

Theravada

The first school, and perhaps the most quintessentially Buddhist, is the Theravada school, which came into existence officially after the Buddha's death. For about 500 years, it dominated the practice of Buddhism in India, and today it is the dominant form of Buddhism in Southeast Asia.

A salient feature of Theravada is its traditionalist character. Theravada Buddhists pride themselves on the fact that they practice Buddhism in accordance with the laws set down by the Buddha and recorded in the *Tripitaka*. Theravada demands self-discipline, and in contrast to the more liberalized Mahayana, claims nirvana can only be attained by those willing to live a monastic life.

Theravada centers on the individual and his or her eventual enlightenment. For a Theravada monk, the ultimate goal is to become an arahant, or completely enlightened individual—second only to a buddha, who has fully achieved nirvana. Becoming an arahant requires strict obedience to the precepts of the *Tripitaka*, which are believed to have been decided by the Buddha himself. In addition to meditation, these requirements include celibacy and adherence to dietary restrictions.

In Theravada, the Buddha, though greatly admired, is not deified. The Buddha's message and teachings, not the man himself, are the focus of the individual's journey toward enlightenment.

Mahayana

The Mahayana school rejects the Theravada goal of becoming an arahant. Instead, the Mahayana Buddhist focuses on the process of becoming a bodhisattva, one who has overcome his karma and attained nirvana, but who, like the Buddha, opts to remain in the world in order to help others achieve the same goal. Thus, while Theravada focuses on the individual and his quest for enlightenment, Mahayana's focus is on compassion for others.

In addition, Mahayana Buddhists consider themselves to be more egalitarian than Theravada buddhists. They consider Theravada a discriminatory practice, since it traditionally reserves enlightenment for monks; its rules are much more difficult for the lay people to obey. A Mahayana Buddhist, on the other hand, does not follow strict rules and laws.

Unlike Theravada, for the Mahayana, faith in the Buddha is paramount. Rituals, or other physical actions, are insignificant in comparison with the importance of one's ideology. Mahayana focuses on the Buddha and his transcendence, whereas in Theravada, the Buddha was merely a human teacher, no different from the average practitioner, except for his level of enlightenment.

The emphasis on the Buddha's transcendence in Mahayana is part of a larger focus on the esoteric, particularly in later centuries in East Asia. Mahayana stresses the idea that one cannot focus on the temporal in order to achieve an understanding of the transcendent, and over the centuries it began to further develop the esoteric and discard much of the ritual and ceremony, regarding them as superfluous to Buddhist goals. As a result, one can often determine whether a sect is Mahayana or Theravada based on the level of ritual—the former sparse while the latter is elaborate and colorful.

In contrast to Theravada, which relies heavily on a sharp distinction between samsara and nirvana, Mahayana emphasizes the idea of oneness. In fact, for most Mahayana sects, the distinctions between samsara and nirvana are blurred, and the two are considered part of the same overarching reality.

Mahayana became popular quickly, owing in part to the ease with which converts could practice it. It is now the dominant form of Buddhism in China, Korea, Vietnam, and Japan.

Vajrayana

Vajrayana (Vehicle of the Diamond) is the youngest major tradition in Buddhism, and one of the best known in the West due to popularization by the media in recent decades. Vajrayana, or Tantrism, is the form of Mahayana Buddhism currently practiced by most non-Chinese in Tibet, despite attempts on the part of the Chinese government to curtail its influence.

Like most Mahayana sects, Vajrayana encourages participation from the laity, and offers them a chance at becoming a bodhisattva. Vajrayana's initial emergence, however, represented a return to ritual, albeit in a very different form from that of Theravada. Vajrayana brought with it a Hindu-like attention to mantras and iconography to speed enlightenment. One of Vajrayana's claims to superiority was this speed; it offered converts an accelerated path to nirvana, by which one could become a bodhisattva within his or her lifetime. Many of the bodhisattvas worshipped in this sect are female Hindu-like deities. They serve as icons, which followers focus on in order to hasten their own journeys toward bodhisattva-hood.

Philosophically, Vajrayana continued on and eventually expanded the Mahayana tradition of reconciling opposing natural forces, thus working against Theravada's dichotomous view of the universe. Vajrayana philosophy, more than Mahayana, attempts to resolve all opposing principles within Buddhism. This resolution of opposing principles can be observed in the Tantric icons that employ sexual imagery, the purpose of which is to unite feminine and masculine forces.

Vajrayana's most noteworthy contribution was its innovative ways of overcoming everyday modes of thought. The tantras, which include special meditation practices, are intended to rouse followers from spiritual sleep. In some Vajrayana sects, for example, teachers will shock their students—both mentally and physically—out of intellectual apathy. It has thus found many adherents in artistic communities around the world.

Tibetan Buddhism

Although Vajrayana is a popular school in Southeast Asia and Tibet, the school known as Tibetan Buddhism is its own distinct tradition—distinct from Vajrayana, despite a frequent tendency to classify the two as identical schools. In reality, although Tibetan Buddhism is a sect within Vajrayana, it is more accurately described as Vajrayana plus the philosophy of several ancient (pre-Vajrayana) Mahayana sects and also the Theravada emphasis on traditional ascetic monastic practices. In this sense it is the most syncretic Buddhist school in existence today.

Tibetan Buddhism came into form in the seventh century and was shaped in part by Mahayana, particularly the Yogacara and Madhayamika sects. It also incorporated shamanistic elements of Bon, the primary indigenous faith of ancient Tibetan peoples. Tibetan Buddhism shares with other Vajrayana sects a focus on iconography and a remarkable number of deities, featuring contrasting good and wicked aspects.

Tibetan Buddhism has been referred to in the West as Lamaism, an outdated and misleading term that nonetheless captures the Tibetan focus on the incarnation of lamas, Tibetan spiritual teachers who continue to be reborn through reincarnation. Tibetan Buddhism is distinctive for its acceptance of continual emergence and reemergence of new great spiritual leaders, including new buddhas.

C. Population and Distribution

Currently, Buddhism has about 350 million followers worldwide, most of them living in Asia (including 102 million in China).

In 1998, one poll counted 2,445,000 (2000 *World Almanac*); another in the same year counted 2,400,000. Yet another study claimed there are 1,300,000.

In 2000 in North America, 0.8% of the population identified as Buddhist. Alternately, the website www.urbandharma.com cites the statistic 1.6%, and further claims that in the mid-1990s there were three to 4 million Buddhists practicing in the U.S.

Buddhistfaith.com claims Buddhism is currently the fourth most practiced religion in America. For 2004, it cites 1,527,019 believers and a national percentage of 5.

Below are statistics from 2001; states not named had no reported adherents.

California	2.0%
Colorado	1.0%
Florida	1.0%
Illinois	1.0%
Maryland	1.0%
Massachusetts (1990)	0.4%
Michigan	1.0%
New York	1.0%
North Dakota	1.0%
Oregon	1.0%
Washington	1.0%
Washington D.C.	4.0%

As reported on www.Adherents.com

V. Organization and Infrastructure

There are no priests in Buddhism, at least not as the term is understood within Christianity; the closest thing to true clergy is the vital monastic culture that, even before the Buddha's day, had long been an important aspect of Hinduism. Note, however, that Buddhist monastic conventions differ significantly from Hindu ones.

A Buddhist monastic community is known as a sangha. The rules that the monks (bhikshus) follow were set down in the *Vinaya Pitaka*, specifically in the section known as the *Patimokkha*. Essentially, it consists of a series of admonitions and prohibitions; the prohibitions, in addition to those required of any Buddhist, included the need to renounce all personal property and refrain from theft, murder, dishonesty, and sexual intercourse, though some Vajrayana schools allow monks to engage in ritualistic sexual activity, and celibacy requirements in general have relaxed somewhat in recent years. Some sects also require dietary restrictions, such as vegetarianism and abstinence from alcohol. Bhikshus take vows against committing these offenses, at the beginning of their life as monks and every fourteen days thereafter. The breaking of these vows is grounds for expulsion from the sangha.

In general, Buddhism requires training before a place in the sangha is offered. A year is usually required before ordination, during which time the aspirant offers his services as a laborer, while learning what is needed to pass the entrance test.

From the beginning, there was a focus in sanghas on student-teacher relationships, and monks considered such teaching to be an essential part of their quest for nirvana. These teachers were known as gurus, and such tutelage served as the training for those who aspired to join a sangha themselves.

Buddhist monks are not cloistered. A Buddhist monk is very much engaged in the community, and serves it though moral example. He also offers the same kinds of services as a Catholic priest, such as officiating at marriages and funerals and giving spiritual and emotional counsel. Bhikshus also provide more practical services, such as educating local children and, occasionally, acting as an intermediary between citizens and their governments. The community repays this debt by offering alms to monks, most of whom live on charity, including, in some sects, groups of wandering mendicants. Those laypeople who dedicate themselves to almsgiving are known as upasakas (men) and upasikas (women). They earn good karma through these practices, a step that advances their quest for nirvana.

Over the years, the element of hierarchy—strongly present in Buddhism's early history—softened, particularly in the Mahayana tradition. Within monastic communities, there is little sense of hierarchy. Order is maintained through what essentially amounts to a democracy, in which members resolve issues and create regulations based on periodic discussion meetings; disputes about specific problems might require a vote. Novices are not required to accept orders from anyone, though usually there is a desire to benefit from an elder's wisdom.

A distinction is made, particularly in Theravada, between a bhikshu and a novice, or samanera; and there is usually a senior monk or sthavira (in the West, occasionally referred to as a priest or minister), whose function is one of guidance and teaching. A samanera typically studies for a year or more before qualifying to become a bhikshu, though women must often study for five years or more before attaining this privilege. This varies, of course, across sects, as perception of women's roles differs greatly among sects. In the Theravada tradition women have been barred from joining sanghas (at least for the past millennium; ancient Theravada sects appear to have had less gender bias). However, some sects of Mahayana are more permissive in this regard. Buddhist nuns are known as bhikshunis.

In some branches of Theravada, which has traditionally reserved the promise of nirvana for monks, an option is offered to the laity that gives them the opportunity to lead a semimonastic life that is seen as a "second-tier" path to enlightenment. Theravada also encourages the Buddhist practice of temporarily joining a sangha, an option enjoyed by many who did not feel they could devote their lives to such an endeavor. Buddhism in general allows those who wish to renounce membership in the sangha to do so; the vows they take at their ordination are not considered permanently binding. Remaining a bhikshu is a matter of continual free choice.

A. Seminaries and Institutes

Maitreya Buddhist Seminary
1710 West Cornelia Avenue
Chicago, IL 60657
773-528-8685
www.chicagobuddha/programs/seminary
Founded in 1985 by the Venerable Samu Sunim and run under the auspices of the Buddhist Society of Compassionate Wisdom, the Maitreya Buddhist Seminary provides residential and nonresidential monastic training for those who aspire to become a dharma priest or teacher.

Naropa University
2130 Arapahoe Boulevard
Boulder, CO 80302
303-444-0202   Fax: 303-444-0410
www.naropa.edu
A Buddhist liberal arts university in Boulder, Colorado, Naropa University was founded in 1974 by Chögyam Trungpa, a noted monk of the Tibetan tradition. A small private school, Naropa advocates "contemplative education," an integrative philosophy

Among the undergraduate programs available at Naropa University in Boulder, Colorado—whose administration building appears above—are Contemplative Psychology, Environmental Studies, and Traditional Eastern Arts.

that combines the advantages of the Western liberal arts tradition with aspects of Eastern spirituality. It offers BAs and MAs in Indo-Tibetan Buddhism, as well as a Master of Divinity degree.

In 1974, Beat poets Allen Ginsburg and Anne Waldman founded Naropa's Jack Kerouac School of Disembodied Poetics, in which, in Waldman's words, "poets could learn about meditation and meditators could learn about poetry." Numerous well-known Beat writers, including William S. Burroughs, have taught seminars at the school.

Buddhist Churches of America
1710 Octavia Street
San Francisco, CA 94109
415-776-5600   Fax: 415-771-6293
www.buddhistchurchesofamerica.org
Founded by a group of Japanese Jodo Shinshu Buddhists, Buddhist Churches of America, an organization of American Buddhist temples, was, in part, an attempt to integrate Buddhism with the larger culture and ease xenophobic fears that helped keep Buddhism at the fringes of American religious life. The word "churches" in the name reflects this motivation.

The society quickly grew after the Second World War. Today, it is highly influential in American and European Buddhism. It encompasses 100 temples and has over 20,000 members. Based in San Francisco, it is the regional center of the World Fellowship of Buddhists, a powerful international Buddhist organization.

Hsi Lai Temple
3456 South Glenmark Drive
Hacienda Heights, CA 91745
626-961-9697
www.hsilai.org
Founded by the Fo Guang Shan Buddhist order, this is one of the world's largest Buddhist organizations. Relatively new, this temple is the largest in the Western Hemisphere. It is affiliated with the Ch'an (Zen, in Japanese) school of Chinese Buddhism,

The Arhat Garden at the Hsi Lai Temple in Los Angeles County, California, features statues of eighteen arhats, early followers of the Buddha.

though its goal is a synthesis of Buddhist schools, and it respects all Western traditions. Affiliated with the temple are a monastery and a university, the University of the West.

San Francisco Zen Center
300 Page Street
San Francisco, CA 94102
415-863-3136
www.sfzc.org
The San Francisco Zen Center, founded by Shunru Suzuki Roshi in 1962, belongs to the Soto Zen tradition. The center has three temples: the City Center in San Francisco, Green Gulch Farm in rural Marin County, and Tassajera Zen Mountain Center, a monastery and monastic teaching center in Big Sur.

This enclave flourished during the 1960s, contributing to the San Francisco counterculture. It is a member of Buddhist Churches of America and a regional center of the World Fellowship of Buddhists.

Tibet House
22 West 15th Street
New York, NY 10011
212-807-0563   Fax: 212-807-0565
www.tibethouse.org
Founded in 1987 by the Dalai Lama and Buddhist scholar Robert Thurman, Tibet House is a nonprofit organization whose headquarters function as a gallery, library, educational institute, and

Buddhist cultural society. The goal of Tibet House is to educate the public about the Tibetan Buddhist tradition and offer Buddhist-based public services.

Rubin Museum of Art

150 West 17th Street
New York, NY 10011
212-620-5000   Fax: 212-620-0628
info@manyc.org   www.rmanyc.org

The Rubin Museum was founded in 1999 by health magnate Donald Rubin and his wife Shelly Rubin for the purpose (it was thought) of exhibiting their extraordinary collection of Himalayan art, as well as other art and artifacts from that region. When the museum opened in 2004, many anticipated that it would find its place among the many niche art museums in New York and be of interest to a narrow field of connoisseurs of Asian art. But it has proven to be so much more than that. The Rubin has virtually rewritten the meaning of what a museum is, as well as providing new insight into the experience of the full range of Eastern thought and spirituality, as no institution has succeeded in doing before. Museums and institution throughout New York and, indeed, worldwide, are reevaluating their programs and missions in light of the extraordinary response the Rubin has received to its programs in which the arts, science, philosophy, literature, public policy, and virtually every area of human concern is explored and evaluated in light of Eastern religious and philosophical values—all in a stunning facility designed by renowned artist Milton Glaser and housed in a landmark New York building. Closed on Tuesdays and open late on Fridays, the Rubin manages a robust website and provides rich educational resources.

B. Governance and Authority

Buddhism does not have a "chain of command" of the type that is seen in the Judeo-Christian tradition. Certainly, one explanation for this is Buddhism's nontheistic nature. The principle of universality and equality in Buddhism, along with its acceptance of the uniqueness of the individual's path to enlightenment, seem at odds with the type of hierarchy in most traditionally theistic faiths. Buddhism's lack of a structured authority may also be partly a result of its roots in India, in which the religion was so aligned with the powerful and wealthy monarchy that it was unnecessary to establish this relationship officially. During this phase, the mythology of Buddhism included various explanations and justifications for the supremacy of the monarchy. Later, as Buddhism began to reach East Asian countries, the reverse was true—the ruling classes in these areas perceived the new faith as threatening, cultish, or as a cultural intrusion, preventing official hierarchies from forming. In most East Asian cultures, however, and during various times in history, the faith has been closely aligned with the state—though this situation was usually short-lived.

Religious circumstances in Tibet, on the other hand, have been unique. Before the Chinese invasion the government was essentially a Buddhist theocracy similar to that of ancient India during Ashoka's reign. This system began sometime in the twelfth century with the reign of the Mongol Khans, with whom the Tibetan sanghas were closely aligned. Starting in the seventeenth century the Dalai Lamas were official government leaders. This situation was uninterrupted until recently; Tibet eventually came under full Communist Chinese authority in 1959, thus ending its theocracy.

Despite this political change, the Dalai Lama remains the highest religious authority in TIbetan Buddhism. Referred to as "His Holiness," he is considered the spiritual leader of the Tibetan people. In addition to being the highest religious authority in Tibetan Buddhism, he is also an admired figure in all schools. He does not, however, hold the authority to alter the tenets of the religion by handing down official doctrine.

An influential school within Tibetan Buddhism, the Gelug school has its own leader, the Ganden

Tripa. While lacking the political power of the Dalai Lama, the Ganden Tripa retains significant spiritual influence. The office of the Ganden Tripa is attained through appointment, and is earned through merit (in contrast to the Dalai Lama, a position based on reincarnation).

C. Social Service Organizations

Buddhist Peace Fellowship
PO Box 3470
Berkeley, CA 94703
510-655-6169
www.bpf.org
The Buddhist Peace Fellowship, founded in 1978 by Nelson Foster and Robert and Anne Aitken, is dedicated to humanitarian efforts both in the United Sates and abroad. In the U.S., there has been a focus on political issues such as fostering democracy and encouraging political participation. BPF also supports antiwar causes. Since it is ecologically inclined, it supports research on alternative sources of energy as a solution to the dependence on oil, which it sees as a cause of war.

BPF advocates the abolition of the death penalty. Its prison programs address the issues of abuse within the prison system, as well as offering prisoners the education needed for them to participate in the Buddhist tradition.

Benevolent Organization for Development, Health & Insight (BODHI)
BODHI U.S.
2743 Portobello Drive
Torrance, CA 90505-7309
310-378-0260905
www.bodhi.net.au
BODHI, based in the U.S. and Australia, was conceived by Dr. Colin Butler. After the Los Angeles office was opened in 1989, his request to the Dalai Lama to be the founding patron was accepted, and BODHI's work began.

BODHI's international efforts focus on diverse issues faced by third-world countries, such as hunger, poverty, natural disasters, HIV/AIDS, overpopulation, and climate change.

Tzu Chi International Medical Association (TIMA)
USA National Headquarters
1100 South Valley Center Avenue
San Dimas, CA 91773
909-447-7799
www.tzuchi.org
Founded in 1966, Tzu Chi is an international nonprofit humanitarian organization focused on community services such as medical care, education, and relief efforts. It also addresses ecological concerns. Originally Taiwan-based, it began to set up chapters in the West in 1985, and now has over 30,000 members worldwide.

Tzu Chi operates on the teachings of Master Cheng Yen, a Buddhist nun who views love as the driving force behind life and the solution to all human problems. She was nominated for the Nobel Peace Prize in 1996.

Los Angeles Free Clinic
1000 South Garfield Avenue
Alhambra, CA 91801
626-281-3383   Fax: 626-282-5303
FreeClinic@us.tzuchi.org
http://tima.us.tzuchi.org
A project of TIMA, the clinic provides health services to the poor and disadvantaged. There also TIMA free clinics in Flushing, New York, and in Honolulu, Hawaii—check the website for details.

D. Media and Communication

Tricycle: The Buddhist Review
92 Vandam Street
New York, NY 10013
212-645-1143   Fax 212-645-1493

www.tricycle.com

Founded in 1991, *Tricycle* is a quarterly magazine that addresses Buddhism in the modern Western world, dealing with issues relating to all schools. The name of the journal refers to the three Great Vehicles—Mahayana, Theravada, and Vajrayana. Published by the Tricycle Foundation, whose goal is to disseminate information about Buddhism to the general public as well as to encourage dialogue among Buddhists and non-Buddhists, *Tricycle* deals particularly with Buddhism's application to other Western traditions and how Buddhism can augment and complement them.

Journal of Buddhist Ethics

www.buddhistethics.org

The *Journal of Buddhist Ethics* is a free online academic journal begun in 1994 that publishes on an ongoing, rather than periodical, basis. It addresses the modern problems of Western society from a Buddhist perspective. Topics include contemporary ethical issues (such as those that arise in medicine and technology), environmental and human rights problems, and timeless ethical dilemmas.

Turning Wheel Magazine

PO Box 3470
Berkeley, CA 94703
510-655-6169   Fax: 510-655-1369
www.bpf.org

Turning Wheel is the award-winning quarterly publication of the Buddhist Peace Fellowship. Initially a grassroots publication, its mission is socially engaged Buddhism, with a focus on international issues, human rights, and the environment. It also focuses on individual dharma practices, and the relationship of individual practice to global activism.

The Buddhist Channel

www.buddhistchannel.tv

Originally called the Buddhist News Network, the Buddhist Channel began operations in October of 2001, and is a nonprofit worldwide news service founded by Lim Kooi Fong. It is dedicated to disseminating news, issues, and information of interest to Buddhists.

FURTHER READING

Buddhist Faith in America
Michael Burgen
2003: Fact on File

How the Swans Came to the Lake: A Narrative History of Buddhism in America (3rd edition)
Rick Fields
1992: Shambhala

The Accidental Buddhist
Dinty W. Moore
1997: Algonquin Books

Mountains are Mountains and Rivers are Rivers: Applying Eastern Teachings to Everyday Life
Ilana Rabinowitz, ed.
2000: Hyperion

Buddhism in America
Richard Hughes Seager
1999: Columbia University Press

Essential Tibetan Buddhism
Robert Thurman
1996: HarperOne

3 Hinduism

I. Origins and Early History

THE ULTIMATE ORIGINS OF HINDUISM ARE LOST IN antiquity. The world's oldest major religion—with beginnings dating back over 5,000 years—it is also the only one with no single founder, central religious establishment, or sole authoritative scripture. This is partly attributable to the fact that it is, in an important sense, not just a religion but rather a way of life based on a rich and diverse collection of philosophical traditions and religious practices of the Indian subcontinent. Hindus have historically referred to their own religion as *Sanatana Dharma*, which translates to "eternal path" or "law." So broad and difficult to define is the term "Hindu" that the word was legally defined by the Supreme Court of India as any person who does not practice Islam, Christianity, Zoroastrianism, or Judaism.

The Orientalist or Western understanding of Hinduism's history attributes its origins to the invasion of the long-established ancient Indus Valley culture by Aryans from the North, sometime between 2000 and 1200 BCE. This view, originally theorized by F. Max Muller in 1848, holds that the Aryans brought with them the fundamental elements of what would become Hinduism, eventually rendering the traditional practices of the Indus Valley peoples obsolete. Beginning in the 1980s, this theory was challenged and has now been largely discredited by scholars who have presented compelling archaeological, anthropological, linguistic, and ethnological evidence that an invasion never occurred and that Hinduism is more likely the product of indigenous

traditions. Moreover, no such invasion is accounted for by the vast collection of sacred Hindu scripture of the time.

The earliest stages of Hinduism is referred to as the Vedic Age. The *Vedas*, composed in Sanskrit, are the oldest and most sacred texts of Hinduism and are still in use today. The Sanskrit word *veda* means "knowledge" or "wisdom," and is derived from the root word *vid*, which means "to know." Originally, the *Vedas* were passed down through a strict oral tradition, but over time, they were recorded in stages between 1700 and 500 BCE, although exact dates are uncertain. The *Vedas* are comprised of some 100,000 verses and prose.

The first collection of the *Vedas*, known as the Samhitas, which are a collection of mantras or poetic hymns, includes the well-known *Rig-Veda*,

Originally written in Sanskrit, the Rig-Veda *are among the sacred texts of Hinduism. This edition dates from the early nineteenth century.*

Sama-Veda, *Yajur-Veda*, and *Atharva-Veda*, and was recorded between 1700–1100 BCE. The second collection of the *Vedas*, known as the *Brahmanas* (900–700 BCE), are commentaries on the mantras of the Samhitas as well as the proper procedures for performing various rituals. Each of the Samhitas has one or more associated *Brahmanas*. The *Brahmanas* also advanced the concepts of karma, the various stages of human life and reincarnation.

The final collections are the *Aranyakas* (c. 700 BCE), which contain discussions of the inner significance of vedic rites, and the *Upanishads* (800–200 BCE), which document philosophical aspects of the human quest for Brahman, or the universal essence of existence. During this period, sacrifice and ritual began for some to recede in importance in favor of the philosophical search for the relationship between atman (the human soul) and Brahman. It was during this era, in the sixth century BCE, that Buddhism and Jainism—movements for reform within Hinduism—were born.

The years from 400 BCE to 400 CE is sometimes referred to as the Epic Age. Caste, first mentioned in the *Rig Veda*, began as a fluid system of designation based on an individual's nature and propensities, but became increasingly rigid and stratified. It was during this period that Hinduism as a specific faith took shape. Some believe that the word Hindu was coined, likely by Persian traders attempting to pronounce the word sindhu, referring to the river region in which Hindu civilization flourished. Others have cited to it as early as fourth century, where it is found in sections of the Talmud also referring to the region and its people.

The Sanskrit epic poems, *Ramayana* and the *Mahabharata*, both of which had been orally transmitted for generations, were finally written during this time; these epic tales were concerned with the responsibilities of nobility, which included maintaining social order and adhering to traditional Vedic principles. Also written down during this period was the *Bhagavad Gita* ("Song of the Lord"), detailing a conversation which took place in the Mahabharata

between Lord Krishna and his disciple, Arjun, on the eve of the epic battle. It is perhaps the most widely read of Hindu scriptures as many consider it to be a concise summation of the philosophy outlined in the *Vedas*. Specifically, the *Gita* highlights the importance of dharma, or one's duty in life; the immortal atman, or soul; and the three major forms of yoga: bhakti yoga (devotion), karma yoga (selfless action), and jnana yoga (knowledge of one's self). Yoga, as referred to in the Gita, implies the discipline which leads to uniting with or serving for eternity the Supreme Being, thereby liberating oneself from the cycle of birth and rebirth. The *Dharmashastras*, a collection of codes regulating personal, social, civil, and religious duties, composed by various authors, also came out of the Epic phase.

From the Puranic period, stretching from the fourth to the eighth centuries, came the *Puranas*, most notably the *Mahapuranas* and *Upapuranas*. These sacred texts, detailing five main topics, largely focus on the creation of the universe and the human race. Shakti or Devi (Mother Goddess) worship took shape around this time. This was also the phase during which the concept of trimurti, or the Hindu trinity of Brahma, Vishnu, and Shiva—fully materialized. Buddhism was firmly entrenched in India at this time, and for many years was closely aligned with Indian authority—the first of many challenges to Hinduism's continued existence.

During the period between the eighth and eleventh centuries, devotional Hinduism began to assume an important place in the culture. It was characterized by greater emotion and passion in worship, and the creation of the Bhagavata-Purana, which personifies and humanizes important avataras or incarnations of God such as Krishna. Devotional Hinduism also saw movements dedicated to Shiva, Devi and others.

During the Medieval period, Hinduism crystalized into six primary schools: Sankhya, Yoga, Nyaya, Vaisheshika, Mimamsa, and Vedanta. Some scholars, however, date these six schools to as far back as the turn of the millennium. The period also produced an increased focus on devotion in temples. During this phase the *Puranas* were composed, as well as the *Tantras* ("Disciplines" and "Rituals"), which emphasized a new set of rituals that promoted yet another path to enlightenment. This era was also the phase in which Buddhism largely disappeared from India after having had a profound effect on Hinduism, particularly within Vishnu worship and the beliefs and practices of the Bhakti movement (emergent for some time but established officially in the fourteenth century).

The first invasion of India by Muslims occurred during the tenth century. Muslim invaders made their own mark on Hindu culture, adding such traditions as segregation of women (*pardah*). Furthermore, numerous Hindus were converted to Islam by force. Out of this merging came change: Guru Nanak, Sikhism's founder, based much of his new religion on a blending of what he saw as the best of Islam and Hinduism.

In recent centuries, Hinduism, similar to all other world religions, has been influenced by contact with other nations. Imperialism informed modern Hinduism in numerous ways; it was a contributing factor to a fallow period for the religion that has given way in the latter half of the twentieth century to a Hindu revival. Various movements in support of traditional Hinduism have taken place since the eighteenth century. These movements have emphasized ancient Hindu practices and texts, and have had a marked influence on the twentieth-century campaign for Indian independence. The most recent of these movements was partly necessitated by the recent separatist tendencies of Sikhs and Muslims, which spurred Hindus to redefine and reaffirm their own faith, despite the traditionally inclusive tendencies of the religion.

Today there are approximately one billion Hindus. The vast majority live in India, Bangladesh, Sri Lanka, and Nepal. The remaining Hindu diaspora has reached as far as England, South and East Africa, Indonesia, other parts of Southeast Asia, and of course, the United States.

A. The Religion in America

American awareness of and interest in Hinduism predated the influx of Hindu immigrants by over two centuries. Merchants and missionaries, who returned from India with intriguing tales of the exotic religion practiced by the natives there, sparked much of this interest. It was not until 1784, however, that a sympathetic treatment of Hinduism appeared—Hannah Adams's *An Alphabetical Compendium of the Various Sects Which Have Appeared from the Beginning of the Christian Era to the Present Day*. Fifteen years later, Joseph Priestly, noted scientist and Utilitarian philosopher, published *A Comparison of the Institutions of Moses with Those of the Hindoos and Other Ancient Nations*. In the ensuing decades, several translations of Hindu texts were published, including the *Bhagavad Gita* and *The Laws of Manu*.

The most significant contributor to popular familiarity with Hinduism was the Transcendentalist movement of the early- to mid-nineteenth century. Ralph Waldo Emerson had an abiding interest in Hinduism and published works such as "Brahma" and "Over-soul," introducing Hindu concepts to an intrigued public. Henry David Thoreau also became deeply involved in Hindu philosophy; his reading of Hindu texts was a factor in his decision to live in the woods. Walt Whitman's exposure to the *Bhagavad Gita* was one inspiration for his poem "Passage to India," which deals with the path toward God and the after-death experience.

In the late nineteenth century, Theosophy, an esoteric spiritualist movement that originated in New York, credited Hinduism as one of its influences since its monastic perspective was influenced by Hindu thought. The movement's founders, Helena Petrovna Blavatsky and Henry Steele Olcott, actually traveled to India in order to experience the faith firsthand. Annie Wood Besant, an English immigrant convert to theosophy, was a highly public advocate of Hinduism as the ideal religion for contemporary Western cultures.

In the 1890s, railway transport innovations and agricultural advances meant sudden demand for laborers, a role filled primarily by recent immigrants. It was at this time that Indians began choosing to come to the United States, particularly California, and avail themselves of what they hoped would be economic opportunity. However, their presence was met with resistance, in part due to the fear that the cheap labor they offered would make native-born labor unnecessary. Only a few thousand Indians had arrived—many of them not Hindus but Sikhs—before the Asian Exclusion Act of 1917 made further immigration all but impossible.

The Trimurti—the Hindu gods Shiva, Brahma, and Vishnu—represent three aspects of the Divine Reality, or the personal presence of God. Shiva (left) is the destroyer, Brahma (center) is the creator, and Vishnu (right) is the preserver.

In 1893, the World Parliament of Religions was held at the Chicago World's Fair. Missionaries and religious leaders from all over the world attended, and the convocation did much to promote awareness of non-Christian faiths. Among the attendees was Swami Vivekananda, a representative of a nondual (advaita) Vedanta sect of Hinduism. Vivekananda founded the Vedanta Society, which still exists and has headquarters in several American cities.

Around the turn of the century, Chicago attorney William Walker Atkinson converted to Hinduism. Atkinson, an advocate of the fledgling New Thought movement, published numerous popular books on Hinduism and its connection with New Thought.

In 1920, Paramahansa Yogananda, a Hindu yogi, arrived as a delegate to the International Congress of Religious Liberals. He remained permanently in the U.S. and eventually founded the Self-Realization Fellowship, an organization with the goal of teaching the principles of the Yoga Sutras and the kriya yoga, both of which aim to help practitioners reach God-realization. The movement was very popular, and later proved a seminal influence on popular culture and New Age ideas.

The first few decades of the new century witnessed modernist poets like W.B. Yeats and T.S. Eliot incorpo-rating Hindu themes into their work. Colleges and universities were gradually beginning at this time to offer courses on world cultures, as well as Hinduism and other Eastern religions, opening younger thinkers to the ideas of unfamiliar traditions. Though America's nascent interest in and acceptance of Hinduism waned somewhat in the 1940s and 1950s, the plight of India in the late 1940s (and the part played by Mohandas K. Gandhi in its resolution) served to arouse American interest in the principle of nonviolence in Hinduism and Jainism. In the 1950s, writers like Allen Ginsburg, Jack Kerouac, and J.D. Salinger explored Eastern religious traditions in their work, paving the way for increased public acceptance of these faiths.

Interest in Hinduism surged with the influence of 1960s counterculture and, perhaps more importantly, the repeal of the Asian Exclusion Act in 1965. With this invitation, many Asian immigrants began streaming into the nation, including Indian Hindus, and it was then that varying schools of Hindu thought began to be represented demographically.

Many Hindu and Hindu-influenced religious movements played a part in changing popular attitudes towards Hinduism. The Transcendental Meditation movement emerged in the 1960s, promoted by Maharishi Mahesh Yogi. It became a pop culture phenomenon, largely due to the Beatles embracing the practice later in the decade.

In 1965, A. C. Bhaktivedanta Swami Prabhupada arrived and formed the International Society of

Krishna Consciousness (ISKCON), or "Hare Krishna," a group that, in contrast with most sects, worshiped Krishna not merely as an avatar but as the ultimate deity. In 1969, the Happy, Healthy, Holy movement began with the arrival from India of Yogi Bhajan, a Sikh and advocate of Kundalini (Sanskrit, literally "coiled"; this spiritual energy is thought to reside in the base of the spine) who wanted to spread his knowledge to the West. The movement, influenced by Sikhism as much as by Hinduism, began with a collection of communes and grew into a national organization.

In 1970, Maharaj-ji arrived in the United States, bringing with him the Divine Light Mission movement, which emphasized meditation and the attainment of world peace. The movement was met with some hostility and eventually dissolved, but it proved to be yet another way in which Hindu concepts were planted in the American landscape.

This period also saw the conversion to Hinduism of numerous native-born white Americans, some of them prominent intellectuals; among them was Richard Alpert, a Harvard academic who changed his name to Ram Dass ("God's servant") and wrote the influential *Be Here Now*.

In the 1970s, Swami Muktananda Paramahansa and his followers formed the Siddha Yoga Dham of America; in 1981, Bhagwan Rajneesh founded a commune in Oregon called Rajneeshpuram. Both of these groups generated much negative press and accusations of culthood, a fate suffered to varying degrees by many Hindu and Hindu-influenced movements during this time. Yet paradoxically, the controversial nature of these movements helped bring Hinduism and other Indian religions to the forefront of the counterculture, and indirectly promoted social acceptance of Hinduism and other Asian religions.

During the 1970s and 1980s, Hindu temples began proliferating throughout the country, serving the needs of an increasing number of Indian Hindus. Most of these temples are suited for general worship and transcend linguistic, cultural, rit-

ual, and deity differences these same Hindus may have had in India. Temples dedicated to a broad pantheon—ranging from widely worshipped forms of Vishnu, including Rama, Krishna, and Balaji to Ganesha, Shiva, and Devi and her various forms, and comprising a variety of Hindu traditions—have been established based on the needs of the community. Today, Hindu temples in the United States serve these needs not only as houses of worship, but also as religious cultural centers in which the community gathers to educate future generations on Hinduism, pass on the traditions of religious music and performing arts, celebrate festivals and holidays and serve as a place for social gatherings.

According to Harvard University's Pluralism Project, one of the most comprehensive information clearinghouses on data on the various faith communities existing in the U.S., as of 2007, there were close to 700 Hindu temples or organizations. Some regions in the U.S. which have a significant population of Hindu Americans, including California, Illinois, New York, New Jersey, and Texas, have a greater number of temples per capita and are thus returning to more traditional temples that are deity or sect specific and where the temple membership is linguistically, ritualistically or culturally more homogenous.

B. Important Dates and Landmarks

2800–1800 BCE Indus Valley Civilization thrives.

1700–1100 BCE The *Rig-Veda*, *Yajur-Veda*, and *Atharva-Veda* composed.

800–200 BCE The *Upanishads* are composed.

5th century BCE Buddhism and Jainism born.

4th Century BCE *Dharmashastras* are written.

400 BCE–400 CE Hinduism's Epic period, during which Brahmanism evolves into Hinduism. The *Ramayana* text appears.

200 BCE–100 CE The *Bhagavad Gita* written.

PURANIC PERIOD
300–1700 CE *Puranas*, early *Tantras* composed.

711–715 CE Muslims invade Southern India—first of a series of devastating invasions.

7th–11th centuries Main Tantras composed; and Tantrism becomes popular with both Hindu and Buddhist masses.

1210–1526 The Delhi Sultanate, Muslims from Afghanistan, rule India.

14th–17th centuries The Bhakti movement is officially established. Tantrism and Bhakti together add a populist appeal to everyday Hinduism, making it more personal and human.

15th century Sikhism, Hinduism's most recent major offshoot, founded by Guru Nanak.

1526–1707 The Mughal Dynasty, begun by Afghani conqueror Babur, in India.

1757 British forces defeat the Bengali Muslim dynasty.

18th–20th centuries Hindu Renaissance and reform movements. As Hinduism is threatened by European imperialism and industrialism, concerted national efforts to revive traditional Hinduism are partially successful. The nineteenth and twentieth centuries, paradoxically, bring waves of progressive reform, such as the Brahmo Samaj and Arya Samaj movements—intended to modernize Hinduism and rid it of what was seen as its classism and superstition.

1893 The World Parliament of Religions is held at the Chicago World's Fair; Swami Vivekananda speaks about Vedanta.

1906 The first American Hindu temple is opened in San Francisco.

1947 India gains its independence in the culmination of a liberation movement led by Mohandas Gandhi. Six months later, the Muslim nation of Pakistan is created, to Gandhi's sorrow. As he predicts, enormous bloodshed follows the partition.

1950 India becomes a secular republic, and caste discrimination is made illegal. However, the practice continues, to an ever-lessening degree, to the present day.

1965 The Asian Exclusion Act is repealed, allowing large numbers of Hindu immigrants to settle within U.S. borders.

1979 Sivaya Subramuniyaswami founds the international periodical *Hinduism Today*.

1986 Swami Satchidananda dedicates the Light of Truth Universal Shrine at Yogaville, Virginia. Shrine is dedicated to the oneness of all world religions.

C. Important Figures

Krishna Dwaipayana

Also known as Ved Vyasa, or "composer of the Vedas," Dwaipayana is a legendary figure who appears in the great Hindu epic *Mahabharata*, and is also believed to be its author. He is also accepted by most Hindus as the compiler of the *Vedas*, as well as many of the *Puranas*. However, since evidence indicates that the *Vedas* were recorded in stages over the second and first millennium BCE, Dwaipayana—

despite his status in Hinduism as a saint—is very likely representative of several scholars, perhaps living many years apart.

II. Tenets and Beliefs

A. Articles of Faith

Less an organized religion than a flexible and expansive culture of interconnected philosophies and practices, Hinduism does not have formal articles of faith. Instead, it encompasses a diverse group of beliefs about life, the universe, and balance, be it internal or personal and external or societal. Some core concepts can be identified, however, from these philosophies, particularly with regard to larger questions concerning the nature of reality and human existence.

Though the idea is alien to the Western mind, a passionate immersion in Hinduism does not exclude a belief in other chosen spiritual paths. As the *Rig-Veda* states, "The Truth is one, but sages call it by various names." The truth of Hinduism does not invalidate the truth of other faiths, but rather attempts to encompass them in order to enlarge its own understanding of reality. Also unfamiliar to many in the West is the way in which a Hindu's daily life is essentially identical to his or her religion; religion is not a separate aspect of life to be isolated and formalized, but instead a set of beliefs and philosophy that pervades every minute of life.

Atman-Brahman

Fundamental to Hinduism's worldview is an understanding of *atman* and Brahman. Atman is approximately synonymous with the term "soul" and refers to the aspect of the infinite reality encompassed by every individual. The concept of atman is also understood as jiva by some of the six major schools of Hindu thought. Brahman—sometimes referred to as God, though the concept is not syn-onymous with the God of the Judeo-Christian tradition—is the eternal, omnipresent, infinite, ever-changing yet changeless essence of all matter, energy, time, space, and being in the universe, whose true and exact nature is incomprehensible to humans. Brahman is the beginning and the ending of all things. It is often described as the reality of universal truth or wisdom, or simply as perfect bliss. Hinduism conceives of reality as constantly changing, yet permanent and fixed; time is like a pool, rather than the more common western perception of it as an ever-moving stream. The surface of the pool may form waves, but the pool itself does not change or move. Reality for Hindus is fully interconnected and interdependent, with all things being a part of Brahman, and Brahman being a part of all things:

"Thou art woman, thou art man; thou art youth, thou art maiden; thou, as an old man, totterest along on thy staff; thou art born with thy face turned everywhere. Thou art the dark blue bee, thou art the green parrot with red eyes, thou art the thunder-cloud, the seasons, the seas. Thou art without beginning, because thou art infinite, thou from whom all worlds are born." (from the *Upanishads*)

It is the goal of Hinduism to teach the realization that atman or jiva and the universal Brahman are inextricably linked. The degree to which they are linked depends largely on which of the six schools and numerous sub-schools of Hindu thought one ascribes to; each of which have described in remarkable depth a relationship between atman or jiva and Brahman, which ranges from total nondualism to complete dualism, and several descriptions occupying the spectrum between the two.

As such, many of Hinduism's sects have debated within the religion as to whether Brahman contains all things in the universe (nondualism), or transcends them (dualism). The Advaita philosophy (nondualism) believes that universe is consciousness and consciousness is Brahman. But humans are limited in their knowledge of Brahman, as most live within an illusion referred to as maya. And it is *avidya*, or the condition of ignorance or of being disillusioned by maya, that leads individuals to believe themselves to be limited by their physical manifestation and material experiences. It is also this avidya which causes people to see one atman as many, each in a different body. Thus, the cycle of rebirth is escaped when the atman merges with Brahman, i.e. when one truly realizes that atman is Brahman. On the other hand, the Dvaita school of philosophy characterizes Brahman as having a personal form, commonly Vishnu. Dvaita philosophy maintains that there is a difference between *jiva*, or an individual's soul, and Brahman.

A common metaphor used to illustrate these two philosophies analogizes Brahman as the ocean and a drop of water as atman or jiva. The Advaitist believes that the ocean is composed of drops of water; each drop is an entity and yet it collectively makes the ocean; the Dvaitist believes that while the drop of water and the ocean may share common qualities, the drop, can in no way, ever be mistaken for the vast ocean.

Most schools of Hinduism see Brahman as both *nirguna* and *saguna*. Nirguna refers to the impersonal, featureless Brahman, which can only be grasped by enlightened masters in the deepest states of meditation; saguna is the aspect of Brahman embodied in a beloved deity.

The Trimurti

Brahma, Vishnu, and Shiva together compose the Trimurti, Hinduism's sacred trinity. Brahma, not be confused with Brahman, serves the function of the cosmic creator, Vishnu, the cosmic preserver, and Shiva, the cosmic change. In a sense, however, they are all necessary for the work of creation. Creation cannot occur without preservation, lest a creation vanish the moment it comes into existence. Nor can creation happen without change, as the old must be cleared to make way for the new. The Trimurti is also accepted as the representation of earth, which is the mother of all beings; water, without which life cannot be sustained; and fire, which destroys all. While Brahma is very rarely worshipped, both Vishnu and Shiva are popularly venerated. Vishnu is most popularly worshipped in his *avataras*, or incarnations, of Balaji, Krishna, and Rama. Shiva, traditionally worshipped through the Shiva linga (a symbol for the worship of Shiva), is generally shown deep in meditation or in the form of Nataraja, dancing upon the demon of ignorance.

It is necessary to note the importance that Hinduism places on the feminine divine by examining the Trimurti of Goddesses: Saraswati, the Goddess of Knowledge (Brahma's counterpart); Lakshmi, the Goddess of Wealth (Vishnu's counterpart); and Durga, the Goddess of Power (Shiva's counterpart). Scriptures state that man is not complete without woman, so rarely will Vishnu (or any of his avataras) or Shiva be depicted or worshipped without their respective female counterparts (or her corresponding avatar). Interestingly, the same does not hold true for most temples honoring Devi in Her various forms, in which the feminine divine is often times worshipped exclusively of any male forms or counterparts. The concept of feminine divinity is also apparent in the Hindu understanding of primordial energy, supreme power, and nature; all of which are understood to be female in character.

Not Truly Polytheism

Brahman's mysterious and infinite nature, for most Hindus, demands the conceptual representation of Brahman into many gods—symbolically stated to be 330 million—which, by portraying the abstract as concrete, can aid in human comprehension of the Divine. An analogy would be the direction of white light through a prism to split it into infinite shades of color, rendering the light visible to the human eye. This anatomization of Brahman not only enables the human mind to meditate on its nature—otherwise too vast and ineffable to grasp—but also allows each individual Hindu to have a God, called Ishtadeva, to whom he or she can communicate and supplicate in a more personal, human way than would otherwise be possible.

Thus Hinduism, strictly speaking, is not truly polytheistic, as its many gods are all simply parts of one universal whole or God. It should also be noted that a few strictly monotheistic traditions do exist in Hinduism, in which only one form of God is worshipped and accepted as the supreme deity.

Ahimsa

Ahimsa is Sanskrit for nonviolence and became widely known in the Western world through the efforts of Mohandas K. Gandhi. The concept did not exist in its present form during the Vedic era, with its many sacrificial rituals. The earliest references to ahimsa, however, are found in the *Yajurveda* and the *Upanishads*. The concept is based largely on the monistic ideas so central to Hindu thought; since everything in life contains the essence of Brahman, and since Brahman is all things, harming another is not only harmful to the harmed person, but also to the harmer and all things in existence.

Maya

Maya is a concept first detailed in the *Upanishads*. As described by the nondualist worldview, it refers to the illusion of physical life and the age-old delusion that humanity is separate from Brahman. Maya leads to avidya, or the erroneous belief that we are beings separate from one another, God, and the universe and is based on our own human enchantment with ourselves and the physical world around us. Maya is inherently temporary and fleeting. Yet this fleeting nature makes life as we know it possible. It must eventually be recognized as an illusion in order for an individual to achieve *moksha*, or release from the cycle of birth and rebirth.

Maya, in the world of dualism, is not illusion but the mysterious power of God. With it, Brahman creates, sustains, and dissolves all of physical existence. Brahman may also use maya to cause ignorance and deception in the jiva, or soul, making escape from the cycle of birth and rebirth for eternal union with God or mukti impossible.

Karma

Karma is an elemental concept in Hindu life, inextricably tied with the Hindu belief in reincarnation (*samsara*). Simplified, karma is the law of cause and effect. The concept is not based on punishment; rather, karma simply dictates that all actions and thoughts have natural and inevitable consequences. These may manifest instantly, or may take lifetimes to appear; but they are never erased merely because one has left the physical plane. According to nearly all Hindu sects, souls reincarnate based on how well they have fulfilled their *dharma*, or duty, in the present lifetime.

There are three basic types of karma. Sanchita karma refers to the collective karmic load accumulated from all of one's previous lifetimes. Most people are assumed to have numerous lives behind them, and a good deal of sanchita karma to be resolved. Prarabdha karma refers to the, probably small, part of one's sanchita karma he or she must experience in the current lifetime. Kriyaman, or agami karma, is the karma that one is producing in the present lifetime and whose fruits will be handled in the future. It is also created by envisioning the future plans and actions. The success or futility of these future plans is determined by the current choices and actions of an individual.

Karma can result from not only individual, but also group, family, or national occurrences and actions. The idea of karma is uncomfortable for some Westerners, as it seems to suggest a lack of control over one's destiny. However, karma is not fate or destiny. It actually entails near-total ability to dictate one's fate, though the results of this control do not often manifest instantly, but instead tend to unravel gradually over one or many lifetimes.

Varna or Caste

Varna is the traditional system of general occupational division in India. There are four basic varnas, each of which contains a vast number of jatis, or subcastes:

Brahmins: teachers, intellectuals, and priests (or other individuals with arcane religious training and knowledge);

Kshatriyas: nobility and landowners;

Vaishyas: skilled workers—merchants and those involved in commercial enterprise;

Shudras: unskilled workers, laborers, and artisans.

The varna system involved the division of ancient Indic civilization based on four general occupational groupings. Within these four groups were thousands of sub-groups. In theory, caste is largely based on the assumption that individuals are born into the "correct" caste—in other words, caste does not compel people to do things not suited to them or not in tune with their innate characteristics and talents. The idea is that a fisherman's son is more likely to develop the skills of a fisherman than those of a warrior. But if the fisherman's son shows a greater aptitude for warfare, then the varna system did not prohibit him from becoming a warrior in the army.

Over the millennia, however, what was to be a skills-and-aptitude based guild system was rigidified into a hereditary hierarchy. This distortion was a result of certain social practices and taboos gaining acceptance over time and countless invasions by foreign civilizations. It lies on the very thin line between Indian culture and Indian religion, and it has often been debated whether caste is part of Hinduism at all, or merely an Indian social practice embraced by Hindus, as well as many individuals of other religions throughout Southeast Asia. Although, varna is discussed at length in many early Hindu texts, such as the *Manusmriti*, it should be noted that there is no basis for a discriminatory caste system in what is believed to be revealed in Hindu scripture, or *shruti*, as opposed to man-made religious literature, or *smriti*. Many Vedic and non-Vedic scripture advance the concept of equality of all mankind as prescribed in the ancient hymn, "No one is superior, none inferior. All are brothers marching forward to prosperity."

Perhaps the most controversial aspect of caste is its discriminatory practices. Outcastes, or untouchables—traditionally known as *panchamas*—are considered of the fifth or "beneath" caste, most often due to the individual's occupation that is considered impure, such as handling of carcasses, or cleaning of streets and sewers. In recent years, this group has been renamed the *harijan* (loosely, "God's people"),

as part of a widespread effort, encouraged by Gandhi and others, to eliminate the inequities of the traditional caste system.

Despite immense societal discrimination over several centuries, there have been countless saints and sages from the "lower" castes who have profoundly impacted Hindu philosophy and devotional practice. To name only a few, Sant Raidas, a cobbler, was the guru of Mirabai, the most famous of the women devotional poets of northern India; Sant Ramdev was a prominent devotional poet from central India important to both Hindu and Sikh traditions; and Sant Tiruvalluvar of southern India who wrote the Tirukkural, an influential scripture of sacred wisdom. Modern-day saints, with millions of followers worldwide include Mata Amritanandamayi, or Ammachi, who was born into a fishermen community, and Satya Sai Baba, who was born into an agrarian community.

There have also been Hindu spiritual leaders and organizations, starting as early as the time of Siddharta Gautama, or the Buddha, to contemporary leaders, including Raja Ram Mohan Roy, Mahatma Gandhi, Narayan Guru, Sri Shivamurthy Murugharajendra, Arya Samaj, and Sahayoga Foundation, that have been engaged in eradicating this system from Indian society. The caste system has been illegal since 1950, and its hold on Indian culture, though not by any means gone, is continually lessening. Shudras and harijans are now far freer to succeed professionally and socially, and are able, for the most part, to mix with the upper castes, particularly in metropolitan areas. Most of rural India still practices de facto caste discrimination of various kinds, and, in many cases, it is one "lower caste" discriminating against another caste perceived by them to be even lower.

The perception of some Indians who embrace the concept is that the life and work of the lower castes has its own dignity and worth, and that caste makes sense from a larger social and religious standpoint; others feel that while the original intent of the system, that being one of the division of labor, was appropriate as a fluid social structure in a particular historical context, the rigid and discriminatory system that took shape over the millennia is a distortion of that and should thus be eliminated.

The Three Paths, or *Margas*

The *Bhagavad Gita* describes the theory of the three yogas or *margas* as detailed in the introduction. Again, all three yogas aim to achieve the same goal: that is provide a path of righteous action that is conducive to the well-being of the world, and in turn, personal spiritual liberation or God-realization. The Bhakti marga refers to achieving *moksha* or *mukti* through love, devotion and service to God. Vishnu, Shiva, and Shakti devotees are particularly partial to this path. The Jnana marga is the process of gaining knowledge and understanding about the true nature of God and the distinction between one's soul and the mortal body. In the *Bhagavad Gita*, Lord Krishna explains the atman as "unborn, eternal, everlasting . . . not slain when the body is slain." Karma marga refers to achieving liberation through performing one's prescribed duties without thought or attachment to fruits of the action. Here, Lord Krishna says, "It is in action alone that you have a claim, never at any time to the fruits of such action . . . By performing action without attachment, a person attains the Supreme."

The Four Goals, or *Purusharthas*

Conventionally, Hinduism has proposed four goals that an individual soul strives to attain in its physical existence: *kama, dharma, artha,* and *moksha*. Kama, the lowest of these, refers largely to sensual and emotional pleasures. It is considered a necessary aspect of life, and a worthy one as long as it is kept in balance and done within the bounds of Vedic law. Types of kama range from sexual pleasure, to other physical and emotional pleasures, to aesthetic joys attained from the arts or nature.

Dharma is certainly the most basic to the daily life of a Hindu. It has been variously translated as "teaching," "rightness," and "duty." It refers to the rules that shape daily life, thought and action. The

idea behind it is that there is an appropriate path for everyone. The word has strong implications of universal order and the necessity for each aspect of nature to fulfill the function dictated by its innermost essence. There are several categories of dharma, including sanatana dharma, or Eternal Law, which encompasses the inherent laws of nature and the Divine; samanya dharma; and vishesha dharma. Samanya dharma includes general laws that govern all forms and functions, including one's duty to strive toward and achieve contentment, forgiveness, self-restraint, nonstealing, purity, control of senses, discrimination between right and wrong, spiritual knowledge, truthfulness, and absence of anger. Vishesha dharma, or special duties, expound upon social law or the laws defining an individual's responsibilities within the nation, society, community, and family law. This is according to life stage, or the laws governing age-appropriate duties related to the natural process of maturing from childhood to old age, and personal law or the individualized application of dharma according to an individual's sum of past karma, intelligence, aptitudes, tendencies, physical characteristics, and community.

Artha, often translated as "purpose," is the third goal. It refers to worldly success and prosperity, which may for some include striving toward fame, renown, and high social standing. Artha is considered the second most important goal largely because without material wealth, fulfillment of one's dharma—indeed, life on earth—would not be possible. Again, striving for artha must be done with dharma in mind.

Moksha—or release—is the ultimate goal of every Hindu, and is attained through successful navigation of the previous three. Moksha offers a soul release from samsara, or the cycle of birth and rebirth (and the suffering inherent in it). By the time a soul reaches this state, it has overcome avidya, or ignorance. The ultimate irony of moksha is that it can only be obtained when a soul recognizes the uselessness of desire—including, of course, the desire for moksha. Moksha can be obtained only when one ceases to grasp at it.

The Four Stages of Life, or *Ashramas*

The four stages of life, or *ashramas*, are believed to have been prevalent since the fifth century BCE. Males are assumed to move naturally through the four major stages. The first, *brahmacharya*, is the student stage lasting approximately until the age of 25, when one gathers knowledge from his guru or teacher. The second stage, *grihastha*, refers to the period of life in which a man marries and becomes a husband, father, and householder; during this phase the pursuit of sensual pleasure (kama) and material advantages (artha) is encouraged. The third phase, *vanaprastha*, refers to the slower, more contemplative life of older men, after about the age of 50, when material desires are to be abandoned and focus turns to devotional worship, spiritual introspection, and meditation. *Sannyasa* is the fourth and final phase. Ideally, at this time, a man has gained enough wisdom to be in touch with the need to become an ascetic, renouncing the pull of home and family and seeking only the final release of moksha. In the modern world, few dedicate themselves purely to the final two tasks. Notably, Hinduism, unlike most sects of Buddhism, does not demand asceticism or foregoing of life as a householder in order for an individual to be seen as being on the path towards enlightenment.

Women in Hinduism

While traditionally women are not held to the same expectations of the four ashramas, they play an important role in each stage and in daily Hindu life. The *Vedas* are replete with hymns extolling the spiritual sameness or equality of male and female deities and characters, while highlighting their differences in nature. Many themes center around courtship and marriage, while others focus on philosophical and educational engagement. The timeless role of male and female, whether divine or mortal, has thus been identified in Hinduism as one of setting aside innate differences and coming together for social and spiritual fulfillment like two halves of a whole. This understanding of complementary spiritual and religious halves is referred to as *ardhangi* (male) and *ard-hangini* (female). So important is this partnership, that most rituals require a married couple to perform them as a pair. There are few rituals that a married male may conduct without his wife; however, there are many rituals and fasts that are exclusively female, dealing primarily with marriage, reproduction, and familial well-being.

Despite belief in the feminine divine and examples of women occupying leading roles in the *Vedas* and *Epics*, since 200 BCE onward, efforts to institutionalize the suppression of rights previously enjoyed by women became prevalent. Access to education, which was only religious at the time, became limited and in later times prohibited. Rights to property were restricted if not eliminated. The perception of women as "impure" because of menstruation emerged, resulting in restrictions of access to temples and worship. The obsession with chastity rose with increasing foreign invasions, thereby leading to early marriage, which affected men as well, and prohibitions against widow remarriage. The treatment of women as property of first their fathers and then husbands also became common. Over time, the once more independent spiritual and religious role of women in Hinduism became one of supporting men in their pursuit of spiritual enlightenment. However, this attitude has begun to change significantly as a result of both Hindu reform movements and the influence of feminism.

Since time immemorial, Hindu women, albeit not in as great numbers as men, have profoundly impacted Hindu philosophy and practice. From philosophers of Vedic times to saints rebelling against all social mores during the Bhakti, or devotional movement, and from female renunciants to Hindu warrioresses, Hindu women have shaped and challenged the customary role of women. Hindu reform movements have also been working over the past century to correct or reverse some of the socio-religious practices that have adversely affected the rights of Hindu women, including advocating for limitations on age of consent for marriage, equal property rights, and protection from spousal and familial abuse.

Various *sampradayas*, or religious traditions, have also reopened their doors to provide religious education opportunities to women. Access to traditionally male monastic orders has been afforded. Interestingly, similar to the suppression of women in other cultures, many of the repressive practices that continue to be perpetuated are by other women, but unlike other feminist movements throughout the world, many of the reforms have been initiated by men.

B. Scripture

The immense body of sacred Hindu texts is a vital part of the religion. Hinduism's sacred texts can be categorized into two main categories, which are shruti and smriti. Shruti, literally translated as "that which is heard," is considered to be revealed and eternal. Knowledge of shruti scripture is the result of a long oral tradition that is believed to have been placed in written form between 1700 and 1200 BCE. It includes the *Vedas*. Some Hindus also include the *Agamas* and the *Bhagavad Gita*; however, the categorization of any texts other than the *Vedas* into shruti scripture is widely debated. Smriti is "that which is written" and is considered man-made, canonizing the practical applications of the eternal principles according in a particular cultural, social, and historical context. It includes the *Epics, Ramayana, Mahabharata, Puranas, Dharmashastras*, and the texts detailing the six schools of Hindu thought, among others.

No one Hindu text, not even the *Bhagavad Gita*, is seen as gospel in the way that the Bible is to a Christian. This would be impossible, due to the philosophical discourse in many of the scriptures that allows for opposing viewpoints and degrees of ambiguity, as well as many open admissions of human fallibility and ignorance. This scriptural humility illuminates the Hindu tolerance for ambiguity and mystery in discussions of religious truth. Moreover, scripture in Hinduism does not have the same place as it does in many other faiths in that Hinduism is premised on realization, not revelation.

Accordingly, to be enlightened, one must have personal experience of the truths set out in the *Vedas* and other revealed scripture. Notably, the words of a living, enlightened teacher, or guru, can be as valid as the words of scripture. The following list is necessarily incomplete, as the Hindu canon is staggeringly large and complex. However, there are several groups of texts that are considered central to an understanding of the Hindu religion.

THE VEDAS

Sometime between 1700 and 1200 BCE, the *Rig-Veda*—the monumental first Hindu scripture based on a long-established oral tradition—was written down. The first known major literary work written in an Indo-European language, the *Rig-Veda* is also the world's oldest living scriptural document. The *Rig-Veda*, like all the *Vedas*, is believed to have been revealed to multiple sages, or rishis, and compiled and edited by the respected Ved Vyasa.

The *Rig-Veda*, organized into ten books known as Mandalas, consists of over 1,000 hymns of praise to Vedic deities and to natural phenomena. Many of the deities central to the *Vedas*—such as Indra, the God of War and Weather and the King of the Devas—are no longer an active part of Hindu worship.

In addition to its praise of a pantheon of nature-deities, the *Rig-Veda* begins to tackle philosophical questions, such as that of creation:

> *There was neither non-existence nor existence then;*
> *There was neither the realm of space nor the sky*
> *which is beyond.*
> *What stirred? Where? In whose protection?*
> *Was there water, bottomlessly deep?*
>
> *There was neither death nor immortality then.*
> *There was no distinguishing sign of night nor of day.*
> *That one breathed, windless, by its own impulse.*
> *Other than that there was nothing beyond.*
>
> *Darkness was hidden by darkness in the beginning;*
> *With no distinguishing sign, all this was water.*

The life force that was covered with emptiness,
That one rose through power of heat.

Desire came upon that one in the beginning;
That was the first seed of mind.
Poets seeking in their heart with wisdom found the
Bond of existence in non-existence. (10.29)

These kinds of larger inquiries are more fully developed in texts such as the *Upanishads*. In upcoming centuries, the *Yajur-Veda*, *Sama-Veda*, and *Atharva-Veda* were composed. These were conceived primarily as supplemental texts to aid in understanding the first Veda. The *Yajur-Veda* offered hymns of ritual sacrifice and instructions for carrying these rituals out. The *Sama-Veda* offered music to accompany the *Rig-Veda's* verse. The *Atharva-Veda*, the last of the *Vedas*, offers practical advice for everyday life, such as medicinal recipes and spells to ensure love, success, and wealth.

THE BRAHMANAS

The *Brahmanas*, composed sometime between 900 and 700 BCE, are commentaries to the *Vedas*. They not only detail practical advice for performing and reciting Vedic rituals and hymns, but also give the reader backstories and biographies to help the Vedic devotee understand the hymns' origins and meaning. The *Brahmanas* also offer philosophical elaboration on some of the major Vedic hymns, and were instrumental in developing later Hindu philosophy, law, geometry, and linguistics.

THE ARANYAKAS

The *Aranyakas* (ca. 700 BCE) are sometimes grouped as a separate part of the Hindu canon (often mentioned in connection with the *Upanishads* because of their age or their similarity to the *Upanishads* in content), but are also sometimes viewed as a part of either the *Brahmanas* or the *Upanishads*. In addition, there is some disagreement over whether either the *Aranyakas* or the *Upanishads* should be called *Vedas*; though not usually grouped in this category, they are considered *Vedas* in the

larger sense of the word, since *veda* means "knowledge" in Sanskrit.

Aranya means "forest," and the *Aranyakas* were designed as companions for those ascetics who chose to isolate themselves from towns and villages in order to meditate in nature. The texts focus on rituals that are meant to be performed in the wilderness.

THE UPANISHADS

The *Upanishads* (ca. 800–200 BCE) have had a more profound impact on Hindu philosophy than any other group of texts; they have especially informed the highly influential nondual Vedanta strains of Hinduism. In the texts, we see evidence of the gradual movement away from ritual and toward contemplation of the meaning of Brahman. There are over one hundred *Upanishads*, with eleven being of central importance—the *Aitareya*, *Mandukya*, *Brihadaranyaka*, *Mundaka*, *Chandogya*, *Prashna*, *Isha*, *Shvetashvatara*, *Katha*, *Taittiriya*, and *Kena*.

The *Upanishads* are known as Vedanta, meaning the end of the *Vedas*. However, they branch off into entirely new directions, exploring theological problems and questions such as morality, the nature of Brahman, and the ultimate fate of the human soul. The essential idea of Brahman as the sum total of all things is first fully articulated in the *Upanishads*.

A quote from the *Chandogya Upanishads* illustrates its monistic perspective on the nature of life:

> *Those who see themselves in all the creatures go*
> *day by day into the world of Brahman hidden*
> *in the heart. Established in peace, they rise*
> *above body consciousness to the supreme*
> *light of the Self. Immortal, free from fear, this*
> *Self is Brahman, called the True. Beyond the*
> *mortal and the immortal, he binds both worlds*
> *together. Those who know this live day after*
> *day in heaven in this very life.* (192–193).

THE RAMAYANA AND MAHABHARATA

These two epic poems, originating in oral form from the eighth century BCE, were continually re-

recorded, retranslated, and augmented over the centuries. As a result it is impossible to firmly date either of these works; the first written records probably occurred before the year zero. These massive epics—the *Mahabharata* is the longest poem in history—have enormous importance in Hinduism. The *Mahabharata* describes the chain of events that culminate into a civil war between the five Pandava brothers and their 100 stepbrothers at Kuruksetra, a battleground near present-day Delhi. The *Ramayana* relates how Rama, an incarnation of Vishnu, rescues his wife Sita, an incarnation of Lakshmi, from the clutches of Ravana, the evil King of Lanka.

Though both epics are tales of bravery and hard-won victories over wickedness, their underlying purpose to explore the most profound beliefs of Hinduism—the pursuit of dharma and the possibility of attaining inner peace in the face of our inevitable mortality.

The *Bhagavad Gita*, or "Song of God," is a book of the *Mahabharata*, added sometime between 200 BCE and 200 CE. It is the most widely read text in Hinduism, and pivotal to the Bhakti movement. The *Gita* is a dialogue between Prince Arjuna and Lord Krishna, which takes place on a chariot in the middle of the battlefield on the eve of the epic war. The chariot placed between the two armies symbolizes an individual pausing to decide between right and wrong, between dharma and adharma. As the *Bhagavad Gita* begins, Arjuna, the greatest archer of his time, falters at the thought of having to kill his relatives despite the injustices they placed upon the Pandava family. In the process, Krishna explains the importance of adhering to dharma, the need for nonattachment to outcomes, and the way to maintain hope and joy in the face of the seemingly endless grinding cycle of death and rebirth. Krishna promises that faith in his power can be Arjuna's—and all humanity's—salvation from despair.

This page from an eighteenth-century Hindi manuscript of the Bhagavata Purana *describes how the god Krishna subdued the many-headed cobra Kaliya.*

THE PURANAS

The *Puranas* are a body of eighteen post-Vedic primary texts composed between the first and eleventh centuries CE. They consider such issues as the universe's creation and its cyclic nature; lineages of gods, sages, and rulers; and offer advice, prayers, and hymns for wisdom-seekers. The *Puranas* are written in couplets, and are still occasionally composed even in modern times, though none of the modern texts approach the importance of the original eighteen.

The most popular *Purana* is, and has always been, the *Bhagavata Purana*. This book narrates the mischief-filled childhood of Krishna, a Vishnu avatar who is currently one of the most widely worshipped forms of God in Hinduism.

C. Secondary Sources

THEOLOGIANS, SCHOLARS, AND THINKERS

There were five legendary a*charyas*—or teachers —whose ideas brought the scriptures and teachings of Hinduism back to the common people during the period between the eighth and sixteenth centuries. These people were broadly associated with the populist movement in Hinduism—the Bhakti movement; its aim was to bring Hinduism back to the people, who had grown disillusioned with the hollow pomp and ritual of the Hinduism that was being propagated by the priestly classes. The Bhakti movement has historically been associated with the Vaishnava (Vishnu-worship) sects; however, the contributions of these five philosophers are honored by all Hindus. There are also many Shiva and Shakti-centric Bhakti traditions.

The Bhakti movement was as much a path to liberation as it was a movement toward religious and spiritual equality. Caste and masculinity were, in many ways, looked upon as obstacles to liberation, while women and individuals of lower social status were seen as embodiments of humility and devotion. Devotional songs, even when composed by male bhaktas, were written primarily from the perspective of woman calling out to her adored deity.

A significant number of women inspired and partook in the Bhakti movement between the sixth and thirteenth centuries. But despite their suffering, social ostracization, and loss of family for their chosen path of complete devotion and surrender to God, it is still primarily the male acharyas who are credited with the movement's leadership.

The following five thinkers profoundly influenced the course that Hinduism would take in the coming centuries, making it more understandable and accessible to all Hindus, regardless of caste or gender, and paving the way for future reform movements of the nineteenth and twentieth centuries.

Adi Shankaracharya (ca. 788–820 CE), the first and perhaps most important acharya, lived only to the age of thirty-two, but the short duration of his life belies his great impact on the Hindu faith. His ministry took place during a time when Hinduism was threatened by Muslim forces. He worked to solidify the public's sense of themselves as Hindu, particularly the lower castes. Shankaracharya stressed Advaita philosophy (monism) and the identification of the self (atman) with universal reality (Brahman).

Ramanujacharya (ca. 1017–1137), the second great acharya, continued in the tradition of Shankaracharya, but modified Shankaracharya's monism to include the idea of a separate Brahman as a loving force from which atman issues, but which also has its own separate reality from atman. This qualified monism was known as vishishtad-vaita.

Nimbarkacharya, whose birth dates have prompted much confusion, promoted dvaitadvaita, a philosophy that claims the self is both identical with and separate from Brahman. Nimbarkacharya, how-

ever, pushed for greater dualism, assuming Brahman was a separate, supreme, and immanent being.

Madhvacharya (1238–1317), promoted absolute dualism, or the dvaita school, and was very influential in the Bhakti movement. He took Nimbarkacharya's qualified dualism and carried it to its full conclusion; his philosophy claims Brahman is independent and absolute, and also that physical reality is dependent on it. Madhavacharya's philosophy identified Brahman with Vishnu, the ultimate deity in this system. Vishnu worship is still the most common form of Hinduism today.

Vallabhacharya (1479–1531) brought monism back to popular thought. He refined it further than Shankaracharya had, to the point of pure monism (shuddha advaita). Of the five acharyas, he is perhaps the one most strongly associated with the Bhakti movement. The Bhakti movement is generally associated with the personal worship of a particular deity. Yet Vallabhacharya managed to reconcile the idea of oneness with the practice of worshipping an aspect of that oneness in order to achieve a greater understanding of it.

INFLUENTIAL HINDU WRITERS, ARTISTS, AND POLITICAL LEADERS IN AMERICA

Ralph Waldo Emerson (1803–1882)

Emerson is considered the founder of Transcendentalism, a movement begun in the 1830s in Massachusetts in reaction to the predominant realism. Acknowledging such influences as Romanticism, Kantian, and Neo-Platonic philosophy, it emphasized the divine nature of all beings, the ability to transcend everyday reality, the equality of all people, and the importance of the individual.

Originally a Unitarian minister, Emerson abandoned the church after he began to see it as passionless and moralistic. In the 1840s, as part of his search for new sources of wisdom, he began exploring Eastern sources, including such Hindu texts as the

Puranas and the *Bhagavad Gita*, which greatly influenced his beliefs regarding the nature of reality. In particular, Emerson was intrigued by monastic Vedantic ideas, as well as the general ideas of karma, maya, and Brahman. The theme of monism dominates his poem "Brahma":

> If the red slayer thinks he slays,
>   Or if the slain thinks that he is slain,
> They know not well the subtle ways
>   I keep, and pass, and turn again.
> Fear or forgot to me is near;
>   Shadow and sunlight are the same;
> The vanished gods to me appear;
>   And one to me are shame and fame.

Other Hindu-influenced works include his poems "Hamatreya," "Maya," and the essay, "Oversoul."

Hindu thought informs even Emerson's secular essays, as well as those works that advanced his Transcendentalist theories; however, works where the influence is explicit initially met with bewilderment and shock from his contemporaries and a public utterly unfamiliar with Hindu culture. Still, his open discussion of Hinduism laid the groundwork for the increasing acceptance that was to come later in the century with the arrival of theosophy and the Vedanta society.

Emerson's deep interest in Hinduism helped shape the thinking of his protégé, Henry David Thoreau, whose experiment in solitary living near Walden Pond in Massachusetts, owed a debt to Hindu scriptures' descriptions of forest-dwelling recluses seeking enlightenment.

Swami Vivekananda (1863–1902)

Chief disciple of Ramakrishna Paramahamsa, a beloved and influential Hindu saint, Swami Vivekananda was born Narendranath Dutta in Kolkata, West Bengal. He received a classical British education; according to legend, this derailed his spiritual mission until he was finally awakened at eighteen by Ramakrishna, who immediately recognized his student as a highly evolved spirit. They worked together intensively for five years until Ramakrishna passed away. Vivekananda then lived as a mendicant for several more years and traveled the Indian subcontinent.

This photograph of Swami Vivekananda was taken in Jaipur, India, some time between 1885 and 1895.

Encouraged by peers and teachers to visit the United States, Vivekananda represented Hinduism at the famed World Parliament of Religions in Chicago in 1893. His passionate and affecting lecture there is viewed by many as the symbolic beginning of Hinduism's acceptance in America.

Vivekananda was a proponent of the Vedanta school, a rich tradition in Hinduism. Based largely on the nondual ideas of the *Upanishads*, Vedanta deemphasizes the worship of multiple gods. After the assembly in Chicago, Vivekananda founded the Vedanta Society and spent several years in the U.S. promoting his ideas where he taught students for free and lectured at major universities. He then returned to India in 1897, where he founded the Ramakrishna Mission, one of the largest charitable organizations, and asked that they incorporate Western scientific advances, as the Americans were beginning to appreciate age-old Hindu wisdom. Vivekananda worked extensively to correct social injustice in his native land, focusing particularly on youth education.

Vivekananda wrote numerous works, the most important of which are the *Jnana-Yoga*, *Bhakti-Yoga*, *Karma-Yoga*, and *Raja-Yoga*, all meditations on Hindu philosophy. Today, he is still revered throughout India and amongst Hindus in America.

Paramahansa Yogananda (1893–1952)

Paramahansa Yogananda was born Mukunda Lal Ghosh in Gorakhpur, Bengal, and received his spiritual training under Sri Yukteswar, a descendant of a saint believed to be a reincarnation of Krishna.

In 1920, Paramahansa felt inspired to move to the United States and share his spiritual insights there. He promoted the path of Kriya Yoga, deep inner experience over religious belief, as truth cannot be merely believed, but must be felt: "Self-realization is the knowing in all parts of the body, mind, and soul that you are now in possession of the kingdom of God; that you do not have to pray that it comes to you; that God's omnipresence; and that all you need to do is improve your knowing." Numerous wealthy and well-known Americans became fascinated with his ideas; in 1927, he was received at the White House by President Coolidge.

The year of Paramahansa's arrival, he founded his famed Self-Realization Fellowship, which still thrives today in Los Angeles. It is dedicated to disseminating information about Paramahansa, Hinduism, and Kriya Yoga, a system of meditation and practice designed to speed the path to inner peace.

Paramahansa was a published poet, but by far his most influential work was *Autobiography of a Yogi*, a memoir that includes detailed descriptions of his spiritual experiences.

Controversial claims have been made about the circumstances surrounding his death; some say that even weeks afterward, his body displayed no visible sign of decay.

Mohandas Karamchand Gandhi (1869–1948)

The spiritual head of the movement for Indian independence (swaraj), Mohandas Karamchand Gandhi never held political office. Yet he had an enormous impact on India's political and religious fate, as well as its perception by the rest of the world.

Born in Porbandar, India, Gandhi was interested in religion from an early age, particularly Jainism and his own Hinduism. After attending law school in London, he was for many years a civil rights activist in South Africa, where blacks and Indians suffered severe discrimination.

Gandhi returned to India in 1914 and became deeply involved in the burgeoning independence

Mohandas Gandhi was one of the most influential spiritual and political leaders of the twentieth century. His life and work served as the inspiration for Philip Glass's 1980 opera, Satyagraha.

movement. He was a passionate and persuasive advocate of Satyagraha (nonviolent resistance), a philosophy inspired in part by his reading of Thoreau's *Civil Disobedience*. Gandhi eventually became President of the Indian National Congress, and his leadership inspired the populace and played a pivotal role in India's eventual emancipation from Britain. He was assassinated in 1948 by Nathuram Godse, who blamed him for the India-Pakistan partition, which Gandhi had opposed.

Gandhi's powerful message of religious equality and social justice made him a legend worldwide. In America, he helped promote appreciation of the Hindu and Jain concept of ahimsa (nonviolence) and shook the common American view of India as benighted and backward. And perhaps most notably, Gandhi's satyagraha deeply influence Martin Luther King Jr., who would eventually lead the U.S. Civil Rights Movement on behalf of African Americans. The memory of Gandhi's life and leadership continues to generate American interest in India.

Maharishi Mahesh Yogi (ca. 1915–2008)

Maharishi Mahesh Yogi—the Maharishi—was a Hindu teacher whose interactions with popular culture made him a celebrity in America and helped create a vogue for meditation that has yet to fade. Born in Raipur, India, the Maharishi was well educated and had early formal training in science; he abandoned this path, however, when he met Swami Brahmananda Saraswati, his teacher who inspired him to promulgate his spiritual ideas.

The Maharishi Mahesh Yogi was a spiritual guru to many celebrities, including the Beatles. This photograph of the Maharishi sitting next to a portrait of his own spiritual master, the Shankaracharya, was taken in December of 1967.

In the 1950s, the Maharishi began traveling in England and America, spreading the word about his Transcendentalist Meditation, a meditation system based on a combination of Vedantic philosophy, traditional Yogic practices, and the use of special mantras chosen for students by their gurus. Transcendentalist Meditation (TM) became very popular with a small cult of celebrities, including Mia Farrow, the Beach Boys, and the Beatles; on the basis of these celebrity endorsements, its popularity spread to the public and helped inspire a new interest in Hindu thought. Its unique appeal to Americans may have resulted from the Maharishi's vocal belief in a biological basis for meditation's efficacy, a theory that has since been confirmed.

In 1971, the Maharishi founded the Maharishi International University in Fairfield, Iowa. Though the Beatles eventually renounced their devotion to the Maharishi and his teachings, TM remained popular with many, and the Maharishi continued to find support in the West until his death in 2008.

III. Rites and Rituals

A. The Calendar

Holidays in Hinduism are dated according to a lunar calendar, which varies slightly by area and is sometimes combined with the solar calendar. A Hindu month goes from approximately the twentieth day of a modern Gregorian month to the twentieth day of the next. As the lunar year is shorter than the solar year, every three years a "leap month" is added to ensure holidays continue to fall in the same season. There is no Sabbath in Hinduism, as every day has the same potential for holiness. To paraphrase Lord Krishna in the Mahabharata, there is no good or bad day; there is only good or bad karma.

Rules for the Hindu New Year vary throughout India; it can fall anywhere from autumn to mid-spring. As with most faiths, major holidays in Hinduism are clustered near the solstices, reflecting ancient roots in the worship of natural phenomena.

Different areas of India follow different regional observances, and, beyond that, not all Hindus celebrate all holy days: those who worship Vishnu, Shiva, and Shakti will, for the most part, each observe different holidays, or observe the same ones in very different ways. Even though Hindu holidays usually involve fasting, they are also almost always festivals, and so they are celebrated with merrymaking.

JANUARY
Makara Sankranti, or Pongal

This holiday, based on the solar calendar, marks the sun's entrance into the sign of Capricorn, and the end of the harvest season. Pongal is largely celebrated in South India, and it may be marked by street fairs, kite-flying, feasting, and offerings of gifts and sweets to loved ones. Some Hindus honor cows on this day, bathing and adorning them with garlands or decorative shawls in thanks for their contribution to the success of the harvest. Renewal is the focus of this day, so an important aspect of the holiday involves discarding old items and obtaining new ones, or simply meditating on change. For some, this is considered the New Year.

FEBRUARY/MARCH
Maha Shivaratri

This day is dedicated to Shiva. Most worshippers fast, and some refrain from liquid intake; many keep a twenty-four-hour vigil. On this day the Shiva Lingam—a priapic figure, usually made of dark stone, representing Shiva—is worshipped and bathed with milk, honey, and perfume. Offerings are also made, and hymns of praise sung.

Some Hindus celebrate this festival in the February–March month.

Holi

Known as the Festival of Colors, Holi celebrates the arrival of Spring and is one of the most popular festivals as celebrant let loose by dancing, singing, eating sweets, and throwing colored powder and water at friends and family. According to legend, the evil king Hiranyakashipu tried to kill his son Prahlad, a devotee of Lord Vishnu, by making him sit in a bonfire on the lap of Holika, the demon king's sister who couldn't be burned by fire. But as Prahlad prayed to Vishnu, Holika was burned to death in the flames and the young boy survived without so much as a mark. The tale symbolizes the importance of *bhakti*, or "faith in God."

Holi also honors Krishna. Krishna is the most beloved and playful avatar of Vishnu, the form of God associated with the yearly renewal of spring.

MARCH/APRIL
Rama Navami

This is the celebration of Rama's birthday, a central holiday for the many Hindus. The story of Rama, the seventh avatar of Vishnu, is told in the epic tale of *Ramayana*. On Rama Navami, Hindus decorate temples and statues of Rama, fast until midday, pray to him, and make offerings. Many communities have dramatic performances of the *Ramayana* called Ramaleela. It is believed that, on this day, Rama will fulfill any requests made to him by the faithful followers.

AUGUST
Krishna Janmashtami

This is Krishna's birthday, one of the most important days for Krishna devotees. Krishna Janmashtami involves a week of musical performances. On the seventh day, there is a special ritual of worship that ends at the stroke of midnight—when Krishna was born—with singing, dancing, and feasting.

Raksha Bandhan

On this full-moon holiday, young girls tie colorful threads, known as *rakhis*, around the wrists of their brothers and other male relatives to celebrate the relationship between brothers and sisters. Brothers vow to protect sisters, and it logically follows that *raksha* means "to protect" and *bandhan* means "bond." The origin of Raksha Bandhan is traced back to various tales including one where Indra's wife tied a thread around his wrist to ensure his victory against an evil demon.

AUGUST/SEPTEMBER
Ganesha Chaturthi

This age-old harvest festival celebrates the birthday of Ganesha, the elephant-headed son of Shiva. On this day, worshippers take lightweight clay statues of Ganesha to the river, and let them dissolve in the water. This is a reference to the story of the creation of Ganesha; he is believed to have been molded by his mother Parvati from the clay of her own body as she bathed. It is also a symbol of the idea that each individual god dissolves back into the oneness of Brahman.

SEPTEMBER/OCTOBER
Navaratri or "Nine Nights"

Navaratri, or Nine Nights, celebrated throughout India, marks the end of the monsoon season. During this festival nine major avataras of the great Goddess Shakti are successively worshipped; each day's celebratory activities reflect the sphere of life ruled by her. Also associated with Navaratri is garba, a coordinated circular dance performed by both men and women that is particularly popular in the Indian state of Gujarat. Throughout southern India, the nine days are commemorated by kolu, which is a display, similar to the nativity scenes set by Christians during Christmas, where women set up decorated planks in a corner of the house and set up elaborate and rustic or religious themed scenes using dolls collected over the years.

OCTOBER
Vijayadashami

Also called Durga, Puja, and Dusshera, Vijayadashami is the tenth day following the ninth night of Navaratri. It honors Lakshmi, the goddess of good fortune, and celebrates the triumph of good over evil. Vijayadashami is considered a lucky time to begin a new venture.

OCTOBER/NOVEMBER
Diwali or Deepavali

Diwali (or Deepavali), the Festival of Lights, is a New Moon festival, and perhaps the biggest holiday in Hinduism. For many, it is the New Year. For southern Indians, it marks Krishna's defeat of the demon Narakasura; for those in the North it honors the return of Rama to Ayodhya after many years of exile.

Diwali continues on for five days and is celebrated with lights or lamps that represent the victory of good over evil and knowledge over ignorance. Many people fashion lamps and set them afloat in lakes and rivers. Gifts, particularly sweets, are often exchanged. In many areas, Hindus will rise before sunrise to take a ritual bath; water from the sacred Ganges is believed to be in all water during Diwali.

B. Worship and Liturgy

There are many ways to reach Brahman in Hinduism, and the remarkable variety of ritual and devotional activity reflects this. Some of this activity is private, to be conducted in a believer's home; some is very much shared and social. But all will depend on the tradition to which one belongs and upon the particular path one has chosen.

Thus, it would be impossible to describe all of Hinduism's expressions of worship (*puja*), not the least because such ritual is so central to the life of the average Hindu. Religion and daily life are not separate in this faith, so it can be argued that every activity is, on some level, a religious expression.

Daily rituals performed at the home altar or personal shrine by individual Hindus may not be liturgical in the Christian sense, in that there is no belief in the necessity of performing a ceremony in a precisely planned, stylized way. There is also a rich and ancient tradition of Vedic rituals that are still performed today either daily or for rites of passage, where the time, place, manner, and reason for performing are dictated by ancient texts in excruciating detail. The result is an intricate and perfected formula that has remained relatively unchanged for several millennia, involving prescriptions for the ideal planetary alignment and timing, appropriate deity form and location for the ritual, special ritual supplies, and specific mantras that will aid the seeker in overcoming a particular obstacle. Nonetheless, Hinduism sees humanity and all its conceits as lasting an infinitesimal moment in the vast eternity of Brahman. This attitude seems to prevent Hindus from any great egotism with regard to their own traditions, and contributes to individual's seeking their own path to salvation and tolerance and acceptance of other paths as valid.

Personal Shrines

Most Hindus maintain a personal shrine, home altar, or mandir in their homes, ranging from a simple table to more elaborate structures with murtis (representations of select forms of God), a diya (special lamp), and perhaps incense and rosary beads (a Hindu rosary has 108 beads). This is a central part of puja, or personal worship. As part of puja, a Hindu will generally light a diya and perhaps provide an offering such as food or fresh flowers every day. But the thought is the most important thing, so a Hindu who cannot afford to make an offering may simply think about the gift he or she would like to have given.

These personal mandirs took on great symbolic importance during periods of Muslim rule, when public worship was often denied Hindus.

Mandir (Temple) Worship

Worship in a Hindu temple, or mandir, is optional, but most Hindus attend them. Most Hindu temples can be visited on any day, but require certain expressions of reverence—for example, one must be freshly bathed, wearing modest attire; and shoes should be removed before entering. An offering of some kind should be brought, if possible.

There is often a central *murti*, or deity, in the temple, which a worshipper may kneel before or meditate upon. These statues, most commonly carved from stone, granite, marble, wood, or cast in precious metal, are carefully cared for and often clothed. Visitors generally take turns venerating a statue.

Unlike most western religions, worship in Hinduism is not usually scheduled and organized, although certain prayers at mandirs are performed at specific and regular times. On major festival days, worshippers will generally gather at their local mandir where special pujas and prayers will be performed. Some Hindu mandirs in America more congregational in style, reflecting adaptation of Hindu Americans to the demands and expectations of the Western work week and lifestyle.

Yoga

Yoga is a discipline designed to purify, focus, and balance the mind and body. Recent archaeological evidence reveals the practice of yoga from the time of the Indus Valley Civilization. It is one of the Hindu rituals most enthusiastically embraced by Hindus and Westerners alike, though in the case of the latter, not usually in traditional Hindu forms. Yoga's goal is to assist seekers in leading a mentally, physically, and spiritually balanced, Supreme Being-focused life, which ultimately leads to liberation.

Hatha Yoga and Raja Yoga—discipline through exercises—are considered essential elements of meditation. Not all Hindus are dedicated to these practices, but those who have achieved proficiency in them are called yogis.

Yoga, as it is currently known, is officially attributed to the sage Patanjali who wrote *The Yoga Sutras*

The classic Padmasana, or full lotus posture, is one of the more advanced Yoga Asana, or body positions.

of Patanjali. Patanjali's yoga is Raja Yoga but became the basis for Ashtanga Yoga, or Eight Limbed Yoga. The eight essential steps, or limbs (angas) are:

1. Yama–(Five abstentions) refraining from violence, deception, theft, irresponsible sex, and attachment to objects

2. Niyama–(Five observances) purity, contentment, austerity, self-study or study of scriptures, and surrender to God

3. Asana–physical position, i.e. the proper arrangement and alignment of the body

4. Pranayama–control of the life force (breath)

5. Pratyahara–control of the senses, leading to a diminished focus on outward things and greater focus on the inner self

6. Dharana–focus on a single object (such as a flame, one's breath, a mantra, or God)

7. Dhyana–contemplation of Brahman, in which the chosen form is gradually forgotten

8. Samadhi–elimination of the ego and oneness with Brahman

Pilgrimages

India and the surrounding areas are so filled with holy sites that it would be difficult for a Hindu to avoid making pilgrimages. In fact, such journeys are considered a joy and privilege rather than a chore, though some of them may require extraordinary personal, physical and financial sacrifice.

One of the holiest sites is Varanasi (formerly Benaras), a city on the banks of the sacred Ganges. There are over 1,500 temples there, mostly Shaivite, accommodating the constant influx of visitors and tourists. Hindus come to bathe in the river, considered to be spiritually purifying (its recent pollution notwithstanding). Because the Ganges is also a site at which many Hindus wish to die, some of its visitors are gravely ill, and pyres have been erected around the river for families to cremate deceased relatives.

C. Daily Life

The guidelines of Hindu life are complex, and vary greatly by caste, gender, stage of life, and, to an extent, sect. Volumes have been written on the topic, attempting to set in place officially the complex system of traditional Hindu ethics. Hinduism does not have the same concept of sin as Christianity, but focuses on an individual's karma, which is to always be guided by three core concepts (the five yamas of Patanjali are an expansion of these), namely, ahimsa or nonviolence, satya, or truth, and brahmacharya, or self-control. Though the rules have been relaxed, particularly in America, there are several vital behavioral laws and ethical principles that remain firmly in place for most Hindus.

The Five Yamas of Patanjali
Ahimsa—refraining from harming any living being. Thoughts of harming others are considered violations of ahimsa, albeit minor ones.

Satya—refraining from deception in thought and action;

Asteya—refraining from stealing;

Brahmacharya—refraining from overindulgence in bodily pleasures;

Aparigraha—refraining from greed—i.e., limiting possessions.

The Five Niyamas of Patanjali
Saucha–Cleanliness. This injunction is not limited to physical cleanliness. It also refers to keeping one's thoughts clear and pure;

Santosha–Contentedness; this is based largely on acceptance of life's conditions, rather than struggle and resistance;

Tapas–Literally, "heat," but refers to the passionate desire to connect with God, expressed through self-discipline and asceticism;

Svadhyaya–Study. This entails study of the scriptures, as well as of one's own inner self;

Ishvara Pranidhana–Surrender to God. This entails being open to God's will, rather than that of the individual, with its limited and narrow perspective.

Dietary Restrictions
For the greater part of Hinduism's history, the principle of ahimsa has been interpreted by many Hindus as excluding the consumption of meat, which is also traditionally considered unhealthful. However, this is not a hard-and-fast rule, and some allow more leeway with keeping meat in their diet.

Cows are sacred to the majority of Hindus; thus beef is not consumed. Cow's milk, however, is acceptable and a common ingredient in many foods. Alcohol is avoided in the more orthodox Hindu sects.

D. Life Cycle Events

Rites of passage (samskaras) are events marked with great fanfare in most sects of Hinduism. This is partly due to the fact that the idea of life stages and passages is enormously important in Hinduism, and seen as deeply related to personal spiritual progress; dharma dictates certain actions and occupations for different life stages, so the passage into one of them is particularly meaningful. Rites will differ by caste and sect.

Most rites of passage are performed before a sacred fire, a symbol that God is a witness.

Birth

Rites begin before conception, with parents saying ritual prayers before, during and after sex to ensure successful conception and pregnancy; many also say prayers to request male children, particularly in the conservative areas of India, which are still patriarchal. Tradition dictates that pregnant women be given all they desire to the best of the family's ability to provide them, because the unborn child is believed to be greatly influenced by the mother's mental, physical, and spiritual attitude and behavior. Many stories found throughout Hindu scripture describe this concept, such as in the story of Prahlad. Despite having a demon king as his father, Prahlad was said to have been born a great devotee of Vishnu because he was exposed in utero to stories, or *kathas*, praising the greatness of Vishnu when his mother stayed in an ashram while pregnant. Another story in the *Mahabharata* tells of a queen who fearfully closed her eyes during the conception of her child and later gave birth to a blind son, while a second queen, pale with fear during conception, gave birth to an extremely pale son.

Jatakarma is carried out just after birth, and is thought to bestow wisdom; the father places honey, ghee (clarified butter), and curds in a spoon and touches it to the baby's mouth, while whispering God's name in his or her ear. This is followed by mantras thought to guarantee long life.

The Hindu naming ceremony, namakarna, may occur anywhere from ten days to one year after birth. It is carried out at home or in a temple, and often involves a consultation with an astrologer to ensure an auspicious name is selected. The father then whispers the chosen name into the right ear of the child. Often, the baby already has a "secret name" given by the parents immediately after birth, told to the baby but not shared with family and friends.

Rituals of prayer accompany both the child's first trip outside the house (nishkarmana) and his or her first taste of solid food (annaprasana). This last ceremony, also known as the rice ceremony, is a social event, involving dressing the child in festive garb and offering him or her a tray covered with numerous small objects; the one the child chooses is thought to suggest his or her future talents and destiny. Afterward, the child receives a small amount of rice from the mother's finger.

Ear-piercing rituals for females (karnavedha) and haircutting rituals for males (mundan) come soon after; both are thought to promote good health and karma and symbolize the fleeting nature of the material world.

Confirmation

Boys of the Brahmin, Kshatriya, and Vaishya varnas undergo an initiation known as the *upanayana*, or a scared thread ceremony, which occurs anywhere from the age of eight to fifteen, and used to qualify a boy to begin his student life. His head is shaved, he is ritually bathed, and is given the sacred thread (upavita), consisting of three interlocking threads, tied in one knot, and worn over the left shoulder, under the right arm, and around the torso. The three threads have come to represent triads: the Trimurti (Brahma, Vishnu, and Shiva), the three gunas (sattva or purity; rajas or activity; passion; and tamas or darkness; and inertia). The thread is a constant reminder of one's dharmic duties. The single knot is symbolic of Brahman, illustrating that everything emerges from Brahman and merges back into Brahman. The boy is then introduced by his guru to the sacred Gayatri mantra of the *Rig-Veda*; formerly, the boy would then leave home to live as an ascetic, with the guidance of his guru, until ready for marriage, though such an undertaking is quite rare nowadays.

Nuptials

Family life is an integral part of the Hindu tradition, and therefore, the marriage ceremonies and celebrations carry great significance. In older times, the ceremonies and celebrations could last for days and took many months to prepare. In modern times, although preparation for the events takes just as long, they rarely last more than one or two days. The function is traditionally divided into three parts: pre-wedding ceremonies, the actual wedding, and post-wedding ceremonies. Each day and ceremony has an associated meaning attached to it. The wedding itself is held at the home of the bride's family, although in modern times, the weddings are held in a variety of locations such as hotel banquet halls. Before the ceremony, relatives from both sides of the family will offer blessings and presents to their soon-to-be in-laws and to the bride and groom.

Hindu grooms usually wear a cream colored traditional suit or dhoti and kurta (draped pants similar to a sari and top) while brides wear saris or lenghas (a long skirt and top) in a variety of colors, but primarily reds, oranges, or deep pinks. A bride's hands and feet have often been intricately adorned with mendhi, or henna—a natural dye—by female relatives the day before the wedding.

A priest officiates the ceremony, before which the father of the groom requests the daughter's hand of the bride's father. Flower garlands are exchanged, Vedic hymns chanted and offerings thrown into the *yajna*, the sacred fire, while the couple circumambulate it four times. One of the most important rituals of the ceremony is saptapadi, seven steps the bride and groom take together where each step corresponds with a vow of marriage. Toward the end of the marriage ceremony, the groom will mark his wife's forehead, or the part in her hair, with bright red kumkum powder so that her marital status will be public. In place of a wedding ring, a married woman is recognized by a mangalsutra, a necklace made of small black and gold beads. In southern India, a married woman is recognized by toe rings worn on the second toe of each foot.

After the wedding, the bride moves to her husband's family home. Before entering the house, she will step three times on the family's grinding stone, symbolizing

This Hindu bride's hands have been decorated with henna, a natural reddish dye.

her official entry into her new family; often, she will throw an oblation into the hearth of her new house.

The night of the wedding, a couple will often stand facing the direction of the North Star and vow to remain as steadfast in their love and devotion as the star is in its light.

Death and Burial

Death is particularly significant in Hinduism because of the beliefs in karma and reincarnation. The funeral rites are called *antyesti*. After death, a body will be bathed, shaved (if male), and generally dressed in white clothes; it will then be cremated. All of this happens quite quickly after death.

The funeral conducted by the eldest son, after he has led a procession to the cremation site which is called shmashana. The corpse is placed on a pyre, around which the son will walk while reciting prayers. Afterward, a pot of water is broken over the site, and the ashes are scattered into a body of water.

The cremation marks the beginning of the thirteen-days mourning period. Specific rites are performed by the mourning family for remaining days of the mourning period. The rites are meant to facilitate the soul's migrating from the dead body to the world of the ancestors and on to the next life.

E. Family Life

Husband and Wife

Marriage is traditionally arranged, though this practice is becoming less common, particularly in the West. Child marriage—once prevalent due to inescapable social and financial realities—is now rare, and has been outlawed in India since 1955.

For most of Hindu history, and for some today, passion, romance, and courtship were not seen as deciding factors in choosing a spouse; instead, caste, financial considerations, education, family background, and compatibility were paramount.

The issue of dowry has frequently been a troublesome one associated with Hinduism, despite the fact that it is not part of Vedic tradition. Females who marry leave their family of origin for their husband's; the practice of dowry is based on the assumption that this new member will prove a financial burden, and that this burden must be shared by both the protector (father), and provider (husband). What was intended as a distribution of economic burden between the two families eventually degenerated into ostentatiousness and debt. Dowry was outlawed in 1961, but remains a social ill that is practiced across several religious traditions throughout southern Asia.

Traditionally, wives have been subject to the rule of their husbands. The husband is the breadwinner; women are responsible for housework and childrearing. These attitudes are changing gradually, particularly for American Hindus.

Much of Hindu marriage revolves around a strong sense of family duty, and the need for selfless devotion to dependents. But marriage is also a sacred covenant between a couple, in which each party loves and supports the other, and each guides the other further down the path to moksha.

Childrearing

Children are seen as a sacred obligation and one of the most important products of marriage. For this reason, the use of contraception has historically been frowned upon, though never forbidden. In the past, couples who have only girls may continue trying to conceive until a male child is born. These two factors together have tended to produce large families.

Most Hindu children live with or near extended family and are raised not only by their parents, but by aunts, grandparents, uncles and older cousins. Relatives often take great pleasure in indulging children, who are seen as a blessing and a joy.

Traditionally, daughters are prepared to be good wives, sons to be responsible householders. Religious training has been considered important for both boys and girls. Corporal punishment has historically been an acceptable form of discipline; however, many today are abandoning it, particularly in the West, on the grounds that it violates the doctrine of ahimsa (nonviolence).

Children are brought up with the notion of duty and self-sacrifice, and they are expected to care for elders in their old age. As with much of Hindu tradition, these family values are gradually becoming more Westernized with the influence of emigration and globalization.

Extended Family

The interconnectedness and interdependence of family is seen as symbolic of society and, ultimately, the universe. Hindus see obligations to family as being of fundamental importance—perhaps more today than ever; with the influence of caste diminishing, the family unit has taken on a new importance as a microcosm of the larger social matrix.

A typical household will be large, particularly in India, and include a husband, his parents, paternal grandparents, uncles and brothers, and perhaps unmarried aunts or sisters, a wife, and children. As a result, cousins are often raised together in the same household. In general, younger family members defer to their elders, even in the case small age differences. The oldest male usually has the final say on major family decisions. In America, it is somewhat less common for several generations to live in the same house, though living in close proximity is common.

A man's family of origin is connected to him for the rest of his life, and he will typically never fully separate from them. He himself bears the responsibility of his own wife and children.

Divorce

The concept of divorce is, in many ways, foreign to Hinduism insofar as a marriage is viewed as sacred and is "predestined" because of karmic connections from a past life. In fact, a traditional belief is that couples are reunited after seven births. Divorce is thus viewed as an immature attempt to escape painful karma that should instead be faced and worked through. However, it has usually been possible for men to leave a marriag; in 1955, this right was extended to Indian women. Divorce is frowned upon in most Hindu communities and is still fairly uncommon.

Widowhood is a far more serious social issue than divorce. Many have heard of suttee—the self-immolation of widows on their husband's funeral pyre. The nineteenth-century Indian social reformer Raja Rammohan Roy campaigned against suttee on religious grounds. The practice was outlawed by the British in 1829, and remains illegal today.

While suttee has been exceedingly rare throughout history, it has occured occasionally, and speaks to the larger problem of widowhood in Hindu society. Many beliefs and historical realities regarding widowhood that have led to extreme cases of ostracization, including the belief of widows as cursed or seeing them as burdens. Remarriage was often not possible for women, though this is changing. Historically, faced with the prospect of being taken as a wife by foreign invaders, some widows chose death—particularly as this form of suicide has traditionally been viewed as an act of devotion and virtue.

IV. Denominations and Demographics

A. History (Schisms and Mergers)

From the beginning, Hinduism has consisted of various groups of interconnected belief systems. Therefore, it is difficult to speak of schisms within Hinduism. Forms of worship other than one's own are not seen as a problem in this religion, but simply a different perspective. Thus, there has been little need for dramatic schisms within the religion, a real-

ity that creates a sense of unity among Hindus despite the differences in worship style. Hinduism interprets varied styles of worship as individual attempts to apprehend Brahman, so relatively little fuss is made over what are generally seen as minor, surface variations in people who are all striving for an identical goal. This is not to say that intra-faith dissent has not arisen, but it certainly has not reached anywhere near the level of those of many other major world faiths.

Different sects do exist. But because of the size of Hinduism's sphere of influence and the length of its history, it is often difficult to say when certain sects or belief systems developed, or precisely which influences gave rise to them. Some sects did arise in reaction to long-established ways that were seen as objectionable by some, but others seemed simply to arise naturally out of a sense of yearning or lack on the part of the Hindu majority. This was the case with the Bhakti movement, which spanned the first millennium, but reached its peak in the medieval period. It promoted devotional love toward a particular aspect of Brahman—for most, Shiva, Vishnu, or Shakti. This new form of worship was seen as a more intimate, authentic path toward God, without the rituals that many Hindus increasingly felt were repetitious and unhelpful. They saw Bhakti as both earthly (in its focus on personal love for an anthropomorphic deity) and universal (in its new hope of oneness with Brahman). Bhakti was also a liberalizing force, encouraging women and those of the lower castes to join in worship.

It is impossible to say just when Shaivism, Vaishnavism, and Shaktism began, as they evolved over many, many centuries, changing shape as time went on. By the same token, the orthodox sect defined itself in relation to Bhakti, so its existence can be dated either to the beginning of Hinduism or the beginning of Bhakti.

The syncretistic denomination Smartism, on the other hand, can be approximately dated. It was popularized by Adi Shankaracharya, the famous ninth-century monist philosopher, who was distressed at the level of dispute arising within Hinduism at the time. His inclusive Smartism was intended as a solution to end in-fighting.

B. Comparisons of Tenets and Beliefs

Orthodox Hinduism and the Six Systems (*Darshanas*)

Hinduism's origins are in Vedic scripture, and those Hindus who still rely primarily on the *Vedas* and *Upanishads*—or who believe they are the only true and inspired Hindu texts—are considered strict adherents. Six philosophical systems have gradually crystallized, all of which attempt to interpret Vedic scriptures, though in very different ways. They are usually considered in sets of two.

Sankhya and Yoga are probably the oldest of the systems, dating from approximately 500 BCE. Sankhya was developed by an ancient thinker, Kapila, who, much like Aristotle, used logical principles to develop a complex system of organization and classification. He created twenty-five categories of existence, each of which fell into the class of either spirit or matter. His was dualistic philosophy, though he felt this dualism might ultimately be surmountable.

Yoga was a kind of addendum to Sankhya; it added a twenty-sixth element, God (ishvara), to the list. This is assumed as an ideal focus on which to meditate, and yoga has much to say on the proper methods.

Mimamsa and Vedanta came next. *Mimamsa* (ca. 200 BCE), a Sanskrit wording meaning "investigation," was the brainchild of philosopher Jaimini. Mimamsa is a school of Vedic exegesis that promotes rigid adherence to traditional Vedic ritual, and places great importance on karma or ritual action. Some may consider Mimamsa to be atheist, as it rejects God as a creator and focuses on proper action.

Vedanta is by far the most influential of the six systems. It denied that ritual had the vital importance Vedic religion had ascribed to it and instead focuses on self-realization through the understanding of Brahman. Associated with the *Upanishads*, the highly theoretical series of commentaries on the *Vedas*, it was not fully articulated until the great philosopher Shankara (ca. 788–820) described his theory of reality as the soul (atman), and ultimately Brahman. This is the central belief of most Hindus.

Vaisheshinka and Nyaya marked a return to scientific thought, and a return from the monism of Vedanta. The school of Nyaya introduced the idea of the value of knowledge in the study of religion, and marked Hinduism's first attempt to put faith under the microscope of logical thought. The philosopher Guatama developed this system sometime before 100 CE. His theory dictates that faulty logic is the source of all suffering, and that truth can be obtained by laborious dissection of these logical flaws.

The Vaisheshika school, promulgated by Kanada at around the same time as Nyaya and largely associated with Nyaya, offered an atomic theory which dictated that all matter can be reduced to indivisible atoms which were created by God. It is a dualistic school, which sees God as the creator and the human soul as fully and permanently separate.

Vaishnavism

Vishnu, over time, usurped the most powerful Vedic deities and developed his own following. Vaishnavism is now the largest school within Hinduism, with 70 percent of Hindus, known as Vaishnavas, belonging to it. This school is most closely associated with Bhakti and Bhakti Yoga. Vishnu, as the Preserver God, maintains the balance among the different forces of the universe; thus he can take on aspects representing any one of them. Traditionally, Vishnu is rendered as handsome and blue-tinted, where the blue color represents the infinite sky and ocean, with four arms, which represent his omnipresence and omnipotence. In his upper right arm, he holds a chakra (discus) that symbolizes the purified mind from which ignorance and ego have been destroyed. In his upper left arm, he carries a conch shell, from which the sound "om" is emitted (considered to be the sound of creation). In his lower right arm, he carries a gada (mace), which symbolizes the power to destroy materialistic or demonic tendencies, and in his lower left arm, he holds a lotus, the symbol of purity, eternity, and perfection. He is often portrayed laying on his side, usually with his consort Lakshmi, the Goddess of Wealth.

Vishnu has ten main avatars (incarnations); each corresponds to a subsect. Avatars take on particular importance in Vaishnavism. The two most commonly worshipped are Rama and Krishna. Rama, seventh avatar and courageous protagonist of the epic *Ramayana*, embodies persistence, devotion, and adherence to dharma. Krishna, Vishnu's incredibly popular eighth avatar from the epic *Mahabharata*, is often worshipped in his child form as beloved prankster. Buddha is considered the ninth avatar of Vishnu, and the tenth avatar, Kalki, is believed will appear at the end of the current time period.

There are an enormous number of subsects within Vaishnavism, and each has its own perspective. In general, however, Vaishnavism is a warm, personal school; its followers tend to see the world as an essentially friendly place, and God as a helpful companion, rather than a distant, awesome force. Feeling and devotion to God, rather than method, is emphasized in this denomination. Art is held in high esteem, and the works of great Bhakti poets are recited and enjoyed.

Many Vaishnavites wear tilak marks on their foreheads; depending on sect, they may be two vertical lines in parallel or resemble the letter U, drawn in white ash-based paint. A vermillion dot represents Lakshmi, Vishnu's female companion.

Vaishnavism, in general, is the school of Hinduism most welcoming to all people, regardless of gender or caste. This accessibility has contributed to its popularity among the masses.

Shaivism

Shaivism, a more challenging philosophy, is not as popular as Vaishnavism. Shiva, the God of Change, is responsible for clearing a path for new growth to emerge; he does the often painful yet always necessary work of death. For many Shaivites, however, he is also the original Creator, responsible for even Brahma's birth.

Shiva is commonly portrayed as sitting deep in meditation and with a third eye, which has numerous meanings, but commonly symbolizes his ability to destroy man's ego. Shiva is usually depicted in his ascetic form, wearing only a loin cloth, garlanded with snakes, and often sitting on a tiger-skin with a trident as his weapon. The snakes symbolize not only Shiva's power over desire, but also the evil in the world from which Shiva protects his devotees. The tiger skin represents Shiva's ability to control and transform animal nature and the three prongs of the trident represent the three gunas (sattva, rajas, and tamas) as well as the three aspects of time (past, present, and future). As Nataraja, Lord of the Dance, he dances in a ring of fire, since it is associated with destruction and rebirth. Many artists have interpreted him as a half-male, half-female being. He is sometimes worshiped in the form of Shiva linga, as a cylindrical object, emerging from a circular base resembling a female, thereby representing not only the generative union between a man and a woman, but the union of the mind and body.

Shiva's wife has both fearsome and nurturing personifications (Kali, Durga, Devi, and Parvati, among others). Their son, Ganesha, the elephant-headed god, is the Remover of Obstacles; he is worshipped before one embarks on a new endeavor.

Shiva is considered by his followers to be whole, all-encompassing, and self-sufficient. He is seen as embodying joy, yet also often as terrifyingly other. He is revered in a way Vishnu generally is not; not only is Shiva seen as awesome, but as the all-in-all. Shaivism generally promotes asceticism, and demands great attention to meditation and study. Shaivites can often be identified by three horizontal white lines painted across their foreheads.

Shaktism

Shakti is both a Goddess and a feminine principle. She is sometimes represented in physical form.

Her school originally developed after the fifth century. Her energy is associated with all female goddesses in Hinduism, including that of Shiva and Vishnu's wives, Parvati and Lakshmi, correspondingly.

Shakti is practiced in both Tantric and non-Tantric forms; it is also associated with Shaivism. Indeed, Shaivites—along with Vaishnavites—acknowledge the principle of bhakti in their worship, even when they are worshipping the male deity.

Some worship Shakti as a deity, and many of these see her as the all-in-all, the Creator, and the highest being. Those who do not, may worship her as Kali, Lakshmi, Parvati, or Durga. Still others see her as a lower manifestation of Shiva, through which Shiva's true nature can be indirectly reached.

Like Shaivites, Shaktis focus intently on duty and ritual. For example, *yantras* (amulets used to focus meditation) are popular in Shaktism, as is Tantric worship; animal sacrifice is not unheard of, even today. The extent of these activities will depend on the sect. In general, it is a tradition that demands great devotion and self-discipline. Notably, both Vaishnavas and Shaivites, despite strict worship of only one deity, do not worship Vishnu or Shiva respectively, without their female counterparts, Lakshmi or Parvati.

Smartism

This school belies the term; it is modern, inclusive and flexible. An attempt to synthesize Hinduism's different schools, Smartism was developed from an inchoate earlier form by Shankara, who refined and popularized it. A monist, Shankara developed the school as an expression of what he saw as the essential oneness of all Hinduism's factions.

Shankara based his theories on his exposition of the *Vedas*—the primary text of the Smartas—and allowed followers to choose their favorite deity (ishta devata) of six—Shiva, Vishnu, Shakti, Ganesha, Surya, and Skanda. Smartism teaches that the systems that developed around these deities are simply different paths to the same goal. This sect, with its diversity and inclusiveness, is popular with Western believers.

A notable aspect of Smartism is its focus on pure dharma (duty) as a path toward enlightenment. The simple act of engaging in the daily Vedic rituals and practices Smartism demands will, it is believed, lead eventually to clarity, even if there is little faith at the start of the spiritual journey.

Tantrism

Tantra was a post-Vedic movement probably begun sometime in the sixth or seventh century. It exists in Buddhism and Jainism as well, and gradually spread throughout Asia after its beginnings in India. Based partly in the *Vedas* and partly in the *Tantras*, a series of noncanonical sacred texts, Tantrism is an advaitic (monistic) school that attempts to help its followers transcend the dualities of ordinary existence, symbolized by the relationship between Shiva and his female companion Parvati. The tantric texts state that the philosophy of the Vedas is too difficult to grasp and follow in the current age, and thus, present an arguably easier method of achieving moksha.

Tantrism makes heavy use of both ritual and mantras. There is a strong history of teacher-student relationships in Tantrism, in part because the power of Tantric rituals is seen as necessitating guidance so that they are used properly.

As many Westerners know, Tantrism often involves sexual rites. In Tantric texts, sex has three specific purposes: procreation, pleasure, and liberation. For those seeking liberation, the acts balance the energies between both participants, and eschew orgasm as the act aims to unite both participants into cosmic consciousness. Ritual meat or alcohol consumption also occurs, sometimes in ways intended to produce physical distress. These activities attempt to use natural, inescapable corporal desires as part of one's spiritual advancement; in theory, these desires, through Tantric rituals, can be blissfully united with the higher desires of the spirit.

C. Population and Distribution

In 1995, approximately 0.2% of the U.S. population—about 910,000—was Hindu. It has continued to increase since. A 1998 reckoning placed the number at 1,285,000, and a 2004 USDOS estimate placed the number at 1,479 million, or 0.5%, of the total population. The only major accounting of Hindu population by state occurred in the 1990 census, the results of which are below. The Hindu population of any state is largest in major cities.

V. Organization and Infrastructure

A. Education and Hierarchy of Clergy

There is no clergy in Hinduism. Hindus receive religious authority through brahmins, or priests, who are usually, but not universally, male. They have always held the authority to officiate at rites, such as weddings and naming ceremonies.

As noted in the section describing the true varna system, those born into the brahmins were thought to be naturely inclined toward learning, thinking, and teaching.

The power of a brahmin was also contingent on a number of things, including lifestyle, certain rites of passage, such as the coming-of-age string ceremony and the long period of religious study that followed it. In addition, violation of dharma had the potential to strip a brahmin of his authority. Thus, brahmins lived under a burden of great responsibility. In America and modern India, brahmins and non-brahmins alike hold the authority to officiate rites and rituals.

EDUCATION

There are no formal seminaries in Hinduism. The passing on of knowledge happens from guru to student, a sacred relationship in which imparted wisdom penetrates more deeply than the mind.

The hierarchy of caste has also made the existence of seminaries impractical, since the percentage of individuals qualified to be brahmin priests has always been extremely small. It is important to note that many of the well-known sages and swamis of Hindu history were not born into the brahmin varna, or caste. In fact, Ved Vyasa, who compiled the *Vedas* and *Mahabharata*, was the son of a lowly fisherwoman.

A tradition of formal monasticism developed in Hinduism during the medieval period, inspired in part by the influence of Buddhism; these monasteries were, of course, enclaves of learning, but were open only to twice-born (upper-caste) men. Many such monasteries still exist today, and are hubs of study and meditation. Most of Hinduism's formerly

States in which Hindus represent at least 0.1% of the population*	
Colorado	0.2%
Connecticut	0.1%
Georgia	0.2%
Illinois	0.2%
Iowa	0.1%
Kansas	0.1%
Maine	0.1%
Maryland	0.2%
Michigan	0.2%
Minnesota	0.1%
Nebraska	0.2%
New Jersey	0.3%
New York	0.6%
Ohio	0.1%
Oklahoma	0.1%
Pennsylvania	0.1%
Virginia	0.1%
Washington	0.1%
West Virginia	0.1%
Wyoming	0.2%

*Provided by the Hindu-American Federation, based on the 1990 U.S. Census.

rigid class division has softened in the past century. Though becoming a priest still demands high caste, religious instruction is now available to all Indians who are interested in learning about Hinduism.

SHRINES AND HOUSES OF WORSHIP

Hindu temples (mandirs) in India are different in sizes, but usually have diverse sculptures and decorations covering the outside walls and doors. This tends to be less the case in the United States, however, where the architecture and decor of Hindu temples is often more streamlined and similar to the houses of worship of other faiths. In the West, it is the inside of a temple that is likely to feature many different murtis and depictions of Gods. As the Hindu community in the West grows, more mandirs resembling those in India are being constructed.

Mandirs are constructed in accordance with Vedic specifications, which describe the mandir to be square. A traditional Indian mandir is divided into an inner sanctum (garbha griha), where the central deity's murti is kept, and a worship hall, where worshippers gather to pray. Neither room has pews; worshippers stand, kneel, or sit before the figure of the central deity. There are also murtis of the deity's avatars. A large, ornate tower is often located in the back of the temple, representing the temple's connection with the Divine.

The Malibu Hindu Temple, owned and operated by the Hindu Temple Society of Southern California, was built in 1981.

MAJOR MANDIRS

Hindu temples began appearing in America in the 1960s and 1970s, and today there is at least one in nearly every major American city, and large cities like Los Angeles and New York often have many. Most are interdenominational, accommodating the many different sects represented in the US; however, a fair number are strictly Vaishnavite.

Hindu Temple Society of Southern California
1600 Las Virgenes Canyon Road
Calabasas, CA 91302
818-880-5552   Fax: 818-880-5583
hindutemplesoutherncalifornia@hughes.com
www.hindutemplesoutherncalifornia.org

The Hindu Temple Society of Southern California, established in 1977 and today popular with both native Californians and tourists, is located in the Santa Monica Mountains. One of the largest Hindu temples in the Western Hemisphere, it is dedicated to Venkateswara, a manifestation of Vishnu. The temple's ornate architecture is traditionally Indian, and the temple offers various shrines and meditation rooms, as well as rooms for Hindu local programs and cultural events.

Sri Venkateswara Temple
1230 South McCully Drive
PO Box 17280
Penn Hills, PA 15235
412-373-3380   Fax: 412-373-7650
rivaru@svtemple.org
www.svtemple.org

Built in 1976, Sri Venkateswara Temple is dedicated to Vishnu as Venkateswara. Its design is based on the ancient temple of the same name, Tirupati, India. It is meant to symbolize Vishnu's body. This large temple attracts many Hindus and curious visitors. It offers scheduled puja (worship), meditation instruction, and Sunday religious classes for children.

Murugan Temple of North America
6300 Princess Garden Parkway
Lanham, MD 20706
301-552-4889   Fax: 301-552-5043
info@murugantemple.org
www.murugantemple.org

Murugan Temple is a Shaivite temple devoted to the God Murugan, venerated by the Tamil minority of India. The temple was built in 1982, and is located ten minutes from the nation's capital. It features representations of numerous Shaivite avatars, such as Ganesha. The temple has a community center, serving the needs of the area, and a learning center that offers Sunday classes for children.

Sri Maha Vallabha Ganapati Devasthanam
45-57 Bowne Street
Flushing, NY 11355
718-460-8484   Fax: 718-461-8055
webmaster@nyganeshtemple.org
www.nyganeshtemple.org

Sri Maha Vallabha Ganapati Devasthanam, more popularly known as the Ganesh Mandir, was built in 1977 in order to accommodate an increasing influx of Hindu immigrants in New York. One of the largest temples in the West, the mandir is devoted to Ganesha, but the temple welcomes all worshippers.

More than just a mandir, Ganesh is a Hindu cultural center for the tri-state area. The community center, built in 1998, hosts a wide selection of community and cultural events and classes for both adults and children, as well as charitable fundraisers.

BAPS Shri Swaminarayan Mandir
30W015 Army Trail Road
Bartlett, IL 60103
630-213-2277   Fax: 630-213-2088

The majestic Shri Swaminarayan Mandir, dedicated in 2004, is affiliated with Bochasanwasi Akshar Purushottam Sanstha, a Vaishnavite sect founded in the nineteenth century and gaining popularity. One of the largest Hindu temples in North America, Shri Swaminarayan Mandir lies on thirty acres of land,

and was constructed using marble and limestone, in a traditional mandir architectural style.

Major Organizations

Vedanta Society of New York
34 West 71st Street
New York, NY 10023
212-877-9197
VedantaSoc@aol.com
www.vedanta-newyork.org

The Vedanta Society of New York is one of many Vedantic societies dedicated to promoting ancient monist ideals of oneness, universality and the equality of all religions, based on an Upanishadic interpretation of the *Vedas*. Promoted in the U.S. by Swami Vivekananda, this Vedanta school promotes meditation as among the most effective ways of attaining enlightenment.

American Institute of Vedic Studies
PO Box 8357
Santa Fe, NM 87504-8357
505-983-9385
vedicinst@aol.com   www.vedanet.com

The American Institute of Vedic Studies, founded in 1988, is an educational institution and cultural center that offers training, teaching, and publications relating to Vedic Hinduism. Vedic texts and philosophy, as well as Ayurveda, Tantrism, and Vedanta, can be explored here.

Hindu University of America
113 North Econlockhatchee Trail
Orlando, FL 32825
407-275-0013   Fax: 407-275-0104
staff@hua.edu   www.hindu-university.edu

A nonprofit organization founded in 1989, the Hindu University of America is an accredited institution that provides bachelor's, master's, and doctorate degrees in such subjects as Hindu philosophy, yoga, Sanskrit, and Ayurveda. The University aims to promote unity among Hindus, as well as to provide opportunities for Hindus and non-Hindus alike to explore Hinduism's ancient traditions and apply them to modern-day Western life.

Kauai Aadheenam Monastery
107 Kaholalele Road
Kapaa, HI 96746
808-822-3012   Fax: 808-822-4351
contact@hindu.org
www.himalayanacademy.com

This Kauai Aadheenam retreat, founded in 1970 by Satguru Sivaya Subramuniyaswami, occupies 458 acres on a beautiful tropical island in Hawaii. Also known as Kauai's Hindu Monastery, it includes a Hindu seminary, a temple, and the publishing headquarters of *Hinduism Today*. It is a popular pilgrimage site for Hindus, as well as curious tourists.

B. Governance and Authority

The topic of religious governance is not one that generally preoccupies Hindus, who understand the obligations of their religion as embedded in the culture. There is little need for an authority to reiterate these laws, which have already been recorded in the ancient scriptures and passed down orally.

In addition, Hinduism adheres to the belief that truth is contained within the soul (atman) of each of us. Thus, rules and regulations, while important from the standpoint of karma and dharma, are seen as merely guidelines that lead Hindus toward the truth already inside them, and facilitate their souls' inevitable release (moksha).

C. Social Service Organizations

Hindu American Foundation
5268G Nicholson Lane, #164
Kensington, MD 20895
301-770-7835   Fax: 301-770-7837
www.hinduamericanfoundation.org

The Hindu American Foundation (HAF) is a nonprofit advocacy organization providing a voice for Hindu Americans. The Foundation interacts with and educates leaders in public policy, academia, media, and the public at large about Hinduism and global issues concerning Hindus, such as the free exercise of religion, the portrayal of Hinduism, hate speech, hate crimes, and human rights.

D. Media and Communication

Hindunet (www.hindunet.org) features a vast array of Hindu-related resources for Hindus and anyone wishing to learn about Hinduism. The site comprises articles, news stories, links, and other resources related to Hindu philosophy, culture, history, and daily life. It offers special sections for children, as well as numerous forums and chat rooms.

Hinduism Today
107 Kaholalele Road
Kapaa, HI 96746-9304
808-822-7032   Fax: 808-822-4351
www.hinduismtoday.com

Hinduism Today is an award-winning quarterly periodical, appearing in both online and full-color print versions, dedicated to the exploration and analysis of Hinduism and Indian religion. Founded in 1979 by Satguru Sivaya Subramuniyaswami, the magazine attempts to promote universal appreciation of the Hindu tradition and to foster unity among today's Hindus in order to preserve and support the tradition in a changing world.

SELECTED REFERENCES ON HINDUISM

What is Hinduism?
  Editors of *Hinduism Today*
  2007: Himalayan Academy
The Essentials of Hinduism
  Swami Bhaskarananda
  2002: Viveka Press
Hinduism: A Cultural Perspective
  David R. Kinsley
  1993: Prentice-Hall

4 Jainism

I. Origins and Early History

A. Origins and History

JAINISM, ALSO KNOWN AS JAIN DHARMA, IS A RELIGION and philosophy with origins in ancient India. Jainism stresses spiritual independence (*jain* means "victory over the self") and equality of all life with particular emphasis on nonviolence. Self-control (*vratas*), compassion, and nonpossessiveness are vital for spiritual progress, which eventually leads to the realization of a soul's true nature and ultimate liberation of self. Jainism has significantly influenced the religious, ethical, political, and economic spheres in India for about three millennia.

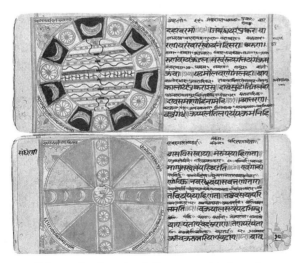

This seventeenth-century Indian manuscript of a work commonly called Trailokya Dipika, *or* The Illuminating Gloss on the Tripartite World, *describes the fundamentals of Jain cosmography and geography.*

The philosophy of the Jain religion is eternal, but, from time to time, the truth has been realized by various *tirthankaras*—self-liberated individuals who are also the spiritual teachers and have revealed the truth for the benefit of mankind. The tirthankaras are therefore not the founders of Jain religion, but they have continually modified its code of conduct and practices based on time, place, and society.

A tirthankara is an ordinary soul that is born as a human and attains the status of tirthankar as a result of intense compassion and equanimity toward all living beings, practice of penance, and meditation. As such, the tirthankar is not defined as an incarnation of God, but is rather believed to be the ultimate developed soul.

The primary objective of the tirthankar's teaching is to attain total freedom from the cycle of birth, life, pain, misery, and death, which results in the permanent blissful state of one's self. This state is also known as liberation, nirvana, absolute freedom, or moksha.

Jains believe that we are currently living in the "present age" and that up to now there have been twenty-four tirthankaras. The twenty-four tirthankaras of this age are: Rishabha, Ajita, Sambhava, Abhinandana, Sumati, Padmaprabha, Supärshva, Chandraprabha, Suvidhi, Shital, Shreyäns, Väsupujya, Vimala, Ananta, Dharma, Shänti, Kunthu, Ara, Malli, Muni-Suvrata, Nami, Nemi, Pärshva, and Mahävira. The word *Nätha* (meaning lord) is often added after their names in the Jainist literature.

Some of the early tirthankaras are mentioned in Hindu texts. The first tirthankar, Lord Rishabha, is mentioned in *Bhagavata Puräna*. In Mathura excavations, images of several tirthankaras from the Kushana period (71–178 CE) have been found. Significant historical information is available about the twenty-third tirthankara, Pärshva, who lived 250 years before Mahävira, the last tirthankara. Pärshva gave his followers four vows: nonviolence, truth, nonstealing, and nonattachment, and also a definite identity as a distinct sect of dedicated ascetics.

The final, twenty-fourth tirthankar, Mahävira, is regarded as the person who gave Jainism its present-day form, but is often is wrongly referred to as the "founder of Jainism" by historians. Mahävira was born a prince, but, at the age of thirty, he left his life of royalty and chose to live the life of an ascetic, renouncing all worldly pleasures and comforts. He spent the next twelve years in meditation, subjecting himself to extremely long, arduous periods of fasting. As a mark of utmost detachment and selflessness, he decided to stop wearing clothes and remain naked for the rest of his life. At the age of forty-two he attained *keval-jnän* (enlightenment) and thus the exalted position of *jina* (the conqueror, or the pure and equinimate, or Vitaräga soul). From then on Mahävira taught the path he had discovered to other seekers. He added the principle of chastity to the four Jain principles already given by Pärshva. He attained nirvana (liberation from cycles of birth and death) in 527 BCE, when he was seventy-two years old.

Over the next five centuries after Mahävira's nirvana (death), Jainism spread throughout India, from Punjab to Bengal, and as far south as Sri Lanka. During the Gupta dynasty (fourth to sixth century CE), Hinduism (Puränic tradition) grew more influential, yet Jainism continued to remain a major religion in several parts of India. During this time, however, Buddhism virtually disappeared in India. Jainism began to lose its strength during the Turkish conquest of India in the twelfth to thirteenth centuries CE. At this time, it was hard for Jain monks to wander freely, still Jainism survived in pockets of India. During the seventeenth to nineteenth centuries, several reformist movements arose which restored interest in Jainism.

At present, there are approximately 8 million Jains, whose presence continues to influence the culture and philosophy of India. Mahatma Gandhi, who adopted the Jain philosophy of nonviolence, is proof of the influence of Jainism on popular Indian culture and thinking.

The Jains are a well-educated business community in India and, in spite of their small population, they continue to be a major influence in India.

B. The Religion in America

The Jains started arriving in America in significant numbers in the early 1970s. The foundation of Jainism, however, was laid much earlier. In 1893, Virchand Gandhi, now considered to be the father of American Jainism, arrived in the United States and participated in Chicago's Parliament of World Religions conference. He remained in the U.S. for several years and propagated the message of nonviolence in the northeastern part of the country. A few years later, at the 1904–1905 World's Fair in St. Louis, Missouri, a wooden Jain temple was constructed by the British government, even though there were no Jains in the country at the time. Jains in the United States regard this temple as a herald of the later arrival of Jainism in the U.S. After the fair, the temple was dismantled and rebuilt in Las Vegas, though it was taken down again in the 1960s. The Jain Society of Los Angeles later acquired the temple and reassembled it at their Jain Center.

C. Important Dates and Landmarks

1850 American Vegetarian Society established.

1893 Virchand Gandhi arrives in America and participates in Chicago's Parliament of the World Religions.

1904 Jain temple is built at the St. Louis World's Fair.

1933 Barrister Champat Räi Jain visits Chicago.

1944 The first Jain settlers arrive in the U.S.

1959 First assembly of Jains informally organize in the New York and New Jersey area.

1965 The Jain Center of America is established in New York.

1972 The Jain teacher, Shri Chitrabhanu (a former Jain monk), arrives in the U.S.
Dr. Dhiraj Shah fights against being drafted for war in Vietnam and wins the right for Jains to avoid military conscription based on religious convictions.

1973 Jain Meditation International Center is built in New York.

1973 Jain Center of Greater Boston is established.

1974 A Jain monk, Muni Sushil Kumar arrives in the U.S.

1978 Jain Society of Greater Cleveland is established.

1979 The mayor of Cleveland declares the Day of Ahimsa (nonviolence).

1981 The first Jain convention is held in Los Angeles.

1984 JAINA, umbrella federation of Jain Associations in North America is organized.
A regular program inviting Jain Scholars from India is started by JAINA.

1990 Temple Pratishthä (ritual inauguration) is held by the Jain Sangh in Cherry Hill, New Jersey, and the Jain Society of Metropolitan in Washington, D.C.

1990 A nine-member Jain Delegation visits Buckingham Palace with H.R.H. Prince Philip to issue the Jain Declaration on Nature authored by Dr. L. M. Singhavi.

1991 Siddhächalam, the Jain tirtha of North America, is founded.

1993 Temple Pratishthä is held by the Jain Society of Metropolitan Chicago.

1994 First Young Jains of America (YJA) Convention is held in Chicago.
Young Jain Professionals (YJP) is formed and the first convention is held in Florida.

1995 Temple Pratishthä is held by Jain Center of Cincinnati/ Dayton and Houston.

1998 Jain Sunday school curriculum established and teacher's conference held in Boston.

1998 Temple Pratishthä is held by the Jain Society of Greater Detroit.

1998 Jain population in North America is estimated to be 75,00–85,000. First Pathshala (Sunday School) Teachers Convention is organized in Boston.

2000 Temple Pratishthä is held by the Jain Center of Northern California (JCNC).

2001 Jain Prayer for peace is recited at the opening of session of Ohio Senate (September).

2002 Sunday school student enrollment reaches 3,500.

2008 Jain Prayer said at opening of U.S. House of Representatives. JAINA (with many Jains) become founding member of Ahimsa Center at Cal Tech in Pamona, CA. Regular Sunday morning Jain TV program MANGALAM is launched on TV ASIA. U.N. Economic and Social Council grants consultative status to JAINA.

D. Important Figures

Lord Rishabha

(ca. end of Stone Age to Agricultural Age)
According to legend, Lord Rishabha existed before civilization began, and fathered over 100 sons. He was an integral leader of pre-civilization, teaching people valuable survival skills such as agriculture, raising livestock, and cooking. Rishabha is regarded as the first to realize "the truth," guiding people toward liberation through inner bliss, rather than indulgence in the sensual pleasures.

Lord Pärshva (ca. 9th century BCE)

Lord Pärshva, or Pärshvanätha, was the twenty-third tirthankara, and the earliest Jain figure for whom significant historical information can be found. He is credited with having attained nirvana through a life of asceticism and renouncement of worldliness.

Lord Vardhamän Mahävira (ca. 599–527 BCE)

Lord Vardhamän Mahävira was the twenty-fourth and last tirthankara. He established the tenets of Jainism that are in play today. His life as an ascetic was characterized by an unconditional and superior compassion for all living beings—humans, animals, insects, and vegetables—and an absolute practice of nonpossession and nonattachment by abstention from wearing clothes. His discourses were memorized by his disciples and compiled into many sutras that were transmitted orally for 1,000 years. These texts form the foundation of the vast Jain literature available today.

Aryikä Chandanä (ca. 6th century BCE)

Aryikä Chandanä was the first Jain nun and the leader of the Jain nuns. Her unbroken tradition continues today, and it has always occupied a major place in the Jain society.

Ächärya Haribhadra Suri (459–529 CE)

Ächärya Haribhadra Suri was a leader and author and is known for his authoritative works in Sanskrit and Prakit on Jain doctrine and ethics. He is best known for his *Shaddarshanasamuccaya*, which deals with six philosophical systems of India, and his various summaries of Jain thought and practice. He also wrote on Jain logic and yoga in Sanskrit and contributed to Prakit narrative literature.

Ächärya Kundakunda (2nd century CE)

Ächärya Kundakunda is the celebrated author of several Präkrit philosophical texts including the popular *Samaysär*.

Ächärya Hemchandra (1089–1172)

Ächärya Hemchandra was one of the most prolific and influential Jain authors, writing not only about philosophy and history, but also about grammar, poetics, and logic. The ruler of Gujarat, king Kumärpäl was his disciple.

Ächärya Ätmärämji (1837–1896)

Ächärya Ätmärämji was a reformer of a Tapägachha Shvetämbar sect, who revitalized Jainism in the nineteenth century by reintroducing rigorous practices. Today, more than 35 percent of monks and nuns belong to the lineage of Ätmärämji. He sent Virchand Gandhi to the United States to represent Jain religion in the Parliament of World Religions conference in 1893.

Virchand Gandhi (1864–1901)

Virchand Gandhi is considered the father of American Jainism. He represented Jainism at the Chicago World's Parliament of Religions in 1893, and lectured widely in the United States and

England for several years. He also founded several Jain societies in the United States.

Ächärya Shänti Sägarji (1872–1955)

Ächärya Shänti Sägarji reformed and revived the Digambar Jain monastic tradition. He was the first Digambar Jain monk to wander in northern India after a gap spanning several centuries.

II. Tenets and Beliefs

A. Articles of Faith

The following list summarizes the fundamental beliefs of Jainism:

• The universe is without a beginning or an end, and it is everlasting and eternal. No one created it and no one can destroy it;

• Six fundamental substances or entities known as *dravya* constitute the universe. The six substances are soul (jiva), matter (pudgal), Principle of Motion (dharma), Principle of Rest (adharma), space (äkäsha), and time (käl);

• All six entities are eternal. Although they undergo countless changes continuously, they do not transform from one substance to another, and they always retain their inherent qualities;

• The soul is the only living substance, which has consciousness. Every living being is a soul. Infinite souls exist in the universe, and they are all unique souls;

• From eternity, every soul is ignorant of its true nature and is bounded by karma. The ignorant soul, while remaining in bondage, continues to attract and bind new karma. It is due to karma that the soul migrates from one life cycle to another and passes through many pleasure and painful situations and suffers;

• A soul in its pure form (a soul without any anger, ego, deceit, and greed, or without karma attached to it) possesses infinite knowledge, infinite perception, infinite energy and power, unobstructed bliss, and no physical body;

• In its impure form (a soul with attached karma particles), each soul possesses limited knowledge, limited perception, limited energy, physical body and its limitations, and experiences pleasure and pain;

• The ultimate goal for the soul is to achieve liberation from suffering through the understanding and realization of its pure nature. Jains believes that the proper knowledge of reality, when combined with total conviction and proper conduct, leads the worldly soul to break the continual binding process of karma to the soul and attain liberation from karma;

• Jains believe that each living being is a master of his/her own destiny. They rely a great deal on self-effort and self-initiative for both their worldly requirements and their salvation or liberation;

• The whole truth cannot be observed from a single viewpoint. To understand the true nature of reality, it is essential to acknowledge and accept the positive nature of the multiple perspectives of each situation or idea. This concept is called anekäntaväda (nonabsolutism);

• The supreme ideals of the Jain religion are nonviolence, equal kindness, reverence for all forms of life, nonpossessiveness, and the philosophy of nonabsolutism (anekäntaväda).

Concept of God and Tirthankar

The concept of God as a creator, protector, and destroyer of the universe does not exist in Jainism. The concept of God's descent into a human form to destroy evil is also not applicable in Jain philosophy. Jainism is a religion of purely human origin. It is propagated by self-realized individuals who are believed to have attained total self-control, perfect knowledge, and omniscience by personal efforts. They have been liberated from the bondage of attachment, aversion, and of worldly existence, thus ending the cycles of life and death. These individuals are popularly viewed as human gods in Jainism.

They are also recognized according to their deeds by various names such as arihanta, arhat, tirthankar, jina, nirgrantha, or kevali. All these words depict various qualities of a Jain human god.

• Arihanta is one who has destroyed the inner enemies, such as anger, ego, deceit, and greed;

• Jina is one who has conquered the inner enemies of worldly passions such as desire, hatred, anger, ego, deceit, lust, and greed by personal effort;

• Nirgrantha is one who has removed all bondages of prejudice in life;

• Tirthankar is one who has showed the path of liberation from our misery and established the religious order of sädhus (monks), sädhvis (nuns), shrävaks (laymen), and shrävikäs (laywomen) out of total compassion. Tirthankars have revived the Jain philosophy at various times in the history of humankind;

• Kevali is one who has attained infinite knowledge, infinite perception, perfect conduct, and unlimited energy by eradicating all karma which subdued the original qualities of the soul (four ghäti karma).

In ancient times, Jainism was known by many names such as the religion of Nirgrantha, the religion of Jina, or the Saman tradition.

The arihantas or tirthankars are not gods in the sense of being the creators of the universe, but rather those who have accomplished the ultimate goal of liberation from suffering and desire through personal effort. In the past, these individuals were human beings like us. Many such individuals existed in the past and many will achieve such a spiritual stage in the future. All human beings have the potential to reach this spiritual stage.

When a person destroys all his karma, which subdues the true nature of the soul (known as ghäti karma), he attains infinite knowledge (keval-jnän), infinite perception (keval-darshana), perfect faith and conduct (happiness), and unlimited energy. At that time, he is known as arihanta (tirthankar), or sämänya (simple) kevali. However, he continues to live his human life until all his other karma, which are responsible for physical body, mind, social status, and life span (known as aghäti karma) are destroyed, which occurs at the time of death.

A tirthankar or arihanta is distinguished from a sämänya kevali by the foundation of a religious order.

They remain in a meditative state as part of the existing order established by the arihanta of that time.

At the end of life, both arihanta and sämänya kevalis attain liberation or nirvana, and all of them are known as siddhas. All siddhas are unique individual souls. They are pure consciousness. They possess infinite knowledge, infinite perception, unobstructed bliss, unlimited energy, and they do not possess a physical body. Hence, from the qualities and attributes point of view all siddhas are the same.

All arihantas (perfect human beings) and siddhas (pure souls) of the past and present are gods in Jainism.

Universe and Its Nature—Jain Reality

Jainism posits that the universe is without a beginning or an end and is everlasting and eternal. Six fundamental substances, or entities, known as *dravya* constitute the universe. Although all six entities are eternal, they continuously undergo countless changes known as paryäya. During these transformations nothing is created or destroyed, and fundamental properties or qualities (gunas) of the base substance remain unchanged.

The following are the six fundamental substances (dravya) that constitute the universe in Jainist thought:

Jiva	Soul or Consciousness
Pudgal	Matter
Dharma	Principle of Motion
Adharma	Principle of Rest
Äkäsha	Space
Käl	Time

Soul, or jiva, is the only living substance, while the other five substances are nonliving substances and they are collectively known as ajiva.

Jiva (Soul)

The soul is the only living substance which is conscious and possesses knowledge. Similar to energy, the soul is invisible. Infinite souls exist in the universe. In its pure form (without attached karma particles), each soul possesses infinite knowledge, infinite perception, infinite energy and power, and unobstructed bliss. In its impure form (a soul with attached karma particles), each soul possesses limited knowledge, limited perception, limited energy, a physical body and its limitations, and experiences pleasure and pain. In other words, a pure soul is expressed by infinite qualities and an impure soul is expressed by finite qualities.

Pudgal (Matter) and Karma Particle

Matter is a nonliving substance. All visible substances are matter, but certain types of matter, which are too subtle to experience through our senses, are not visible. Also, the other five substances (soul, Principles of Motion and Rest, space, and time), which are not matter, are invisible.

Many types of matter exist in the universe. Everything we see, touch, and feel is also matter, and hence Jainism states that sound, light, darkness, color, and smell are all various types of matter.

Extremely minute particles constitute karma. These particles are not visible though they are considered a form of matter. The entire universe is filled with karma particles known as karma varganä.

Doctrine of Karma Philosophy—Nine Tattvas

The group of nine *tattvas*, or fundamentals, is the single most important subject of Jain philosophy. This subject deals with the doctrine of karma, which provides the basis for the path of liberation. The proper knowledge of these tattvas is essential for spiritual progress.

The doctrine of karma provides a rational explanation to the apparently inexplicable phenomena of birth and death, happiness and misery, inequalities in mental and physical attainments, and the existence of different species of living beings.

It also explains that the principle governing the succession of life is karma. The karma that binds our souls is not only due to the actions of our body, mind, and speech, but also to the intentions behind our actions. Jainism strives for the realization of the highest perfection of the soul, which, in its original purity, is free from all pain, suffering, desire, and bondage to the cycle of birth and death.

Nine Tattvas (Nine Fundamentals)

Jiva	Soul or living being (consciousness)
Ajiva	Nonliving substances, which include all the remaining five universal substances
Äsrava	Causes of the bondage of karma
Bandha	Characteristics of the bondage of karma
Punya*	Merit, or karma of good deeds
Päp*	Sin or transgression, or karma of bad deeds
Samvar	Stoppage of attachment of new karma
Nirjarä	Exhaustion of the accumulated karma
Moksha	State of total liberation from all karma

*Some literature defines punya (merit) and päp (sin) as separate tattvas, while others include them in äsrava. In reality, punya and päp are the result of äsrava. Hence, while Jains always say nine tattvas, in truth there are only seven tattvas.

According to the theory of karma, the happiness of a being's present life is the result of the moral quality of the actions of the being in the past, perhaps its previous lives. Karma works without the intervention of any other being; gods, angels, and devils play no role in dispensing rewards or punishments.

Anekäntaväda, a foundation of Jain philosophy, literally means "nonsingular conclusivity" or equivalently, "non-one-endedness," or "non-one-sidedness." Anekäntaväda teaches the importance of overcoming any inherent biases on any topic. Anekäntaväda is defined as a multiplicity of viewpoints, for it stresses looking at things from others', and many, perspectives.

Path of Liberation—Jain Trinity

One can detach from one's karma and attain liberation by understanding the true nature of the soul and other reality and having a total conviction in this knowledge. This way one removes ignorance about one's own nature. This can be achieved by following the spiritual path of liberation, known as the Jain Trinity:

- **Right Conviction or Faith (Samyak-Darshan)**
- **Right Knowledge (Samyak-Jnän)**
- **Right Conduct (Samyak-Chäritra)**

Jainism states that a proper knowledge of reality includes the six universal substances, the nine tattvas, and the relationship between the soul and karma. This knowledge provides an understanding of the nature of all substances in the universe as they really are. The rationale and total conviction in this knowledge is called Right Faith. When faith is based on knowledge from experience, it becomes unshakable. Once a person has the Right Faith, then all his rational knowledge is considered Right Knowledge.

Hence *samyak darshana* is what Jains know as "rational and right faith or conviction." This means avoiding preconceptions and superstitions that obstruct clarity. Samyak darshana cannot be achieved unless one is determined to distinguish truth from untruth.

Samyak jñāna means "rational and right knowledge, viewpoint and insight," and involves having an accurate and sufficient knowledge of the real universe. This requires a knowledge of the five/six universal substances and nine tattvas or fundamental truths of the universe.

The realization of truth, or *samyaktva*, leads to Right Conduct. *Samyak chāritra* is "rational and right conduct," which means living one's life according to rational ethical rules, avoiding doing harm to all living beings, and freeing oneself from attachment and other impure attitudes and thoughts. It also includes pluralism of views (anekāntavāda or syādvāda), nonpossession (aparigraha) or limitation of possessions, and nonpossessiveness, self-purification, self-control, austerity, asceticism, penance, yoga, and meditation.

Various stages exist in practicing Right Conduct. Every living being starts at the spiritual stage, mithyātva. On the path toward spiritual progress, a person, after acquiring proper knowledge of soul and karma, attains Right Conviction or Faith. This stage is known as the Attainment of Samyaktva. The person then gradually progresses toward Right Conduct.

First, one adopts the twelve vows of conduct for laypeople and then gradually progresses toward the renunciation of worldly life and becomes an ascetic. One follows the five great vows of an ascetic and is slowly able to remove passions such as anger, ego,

deceit, and greed from his nature. At the perfection of Right Conduct, he becomes totally free from passions, which is known as the Attainment of Vitarāga. After this stage he attains keval-jnän—Omniscience State—and attains infinite knowledge, infinite perception, infinite happiness, and infinite power and energy.

A kevali continues to live a human life as a monk and delivers sermons at various places. This way he spreads the message of nonviolence, compassion, nonpossessiveness, and pluralism view. In the end, at the time of his death or nirvana, he attains total liberation; his purified soul remains in a permanent blissful state forever.

B. Scripture

Lord Mahāvir's preachings were memorized and orally compiled into many sutras (texts or books) by his disciples. These sutras are known as Jain Āgam or Āgam Sutras (called Jain scriptures). The Āgam Sutras promote great reverence for all forms of life, strict codes of vegetarianism, asceticism, compassion, nonviolence, and opposition to war.

These scriptures were not documented in any form but, instead, were memorized by ascetics and passed on orally to the next generation of ascetics. Over the course of time, many of the Āgam Sutras were forgotten, some were modified, and new sutras were added. About one thousand years after Lord Mahāvir's nirvana, the memorized Āgam Sutras were recorded on palm leaves (tädpatris). By that time, no living monk could remember any of the sutras of *Drashtivāda*, the twelfth Anga Āgam text.

The Āgam Sutras

The Āgam Sutras are divided into two major groups: The Anga Āgam and the Angabāhya Āgam Sutras.

The Anga Āgam Sutras

The Anga Āgam Sutras contain the direct preachings of Lord Mahāvir. The main disciples of Lord

Mahävir, known as Ganadhars, had compiled them after Lord Mahävir's first sermon. They consist of twelve textbooks. The twelfth text, known as *Drashtiväda*, which includes fourteen Purväs, is extinct. Hence, in reality, there are only eleven Anga Ägams. The names and contents of the Anga Ägam Sutras are undisputed among the various Jain traditions.

The major Anga Ägam Sutras are *Ächäränga*, *Sutrakritanga*, *Bhagavati*, *Sthänänga*, and *Sama-väyänga Sutras*.

This West Indian manuscript of the Kalpa Sutra and Kalakacharya-Katha dates from about 1400.

The Angabähya Ägam Sutras

Shruta Kevali monks, who possessed the knowledge of the twelve Anga Ägams, compiled the Angabähya Ägam Sutras. They were compiled orally within 160 years after Lord Mahävir's nirvana. They provide further explanation of the Anga Ägam Sutras.

Following is the summary of the Angabähya Ägam Sutras accepted as scriptures by various Jain traditions:

- Thirty-four texts according to the Shvetämbar Murtipujak tradition
- Twenty-one texts according to the Sthänakaväsi and Teräpanthi traditions
- Fourteen texts according to the Digambar tradition

The major Angabähya Ägam Sutras are *Dasvaikälik*, *Ävashyak*, *Kalpa Sutra*, and *Uttarädhyäna Sutra*.

Shvetämbar Literature

Shvetämbar Jains have accepted the recorded Ägam Sutras (eleven Anga Ägams and all Angabähya Sutras) as mentioned above as an authentic version of Lord Mahävir's teachings. In addition to the Ägam Sutras, they also follow *Tattvärtha Sutra of Umäsväti*, *Sanmatitarka of Siddhasen*, and six volumes of *Karma Grantha*.

Digambar Literature

Digambar Jains have not accepted the recorded Ägam Sutras (eleven Anga Ägams and any of Angabähya Sutras) as an authentic version of Lord Mahävir's teachings. They concluded that after one thousand years no monk remembered the true original Ägam Sutras.

In the absence of authentic Ägam Sutras, Digambars practice the Jain religion by following the literature written by the great Ächäryas from 100 to 1000 CE. It includes two main texts: *Shatakhand Ägam* and *Kashäya Pähuda*, and four Anuyogas, which consist of more than twenty texts such as *Samaysär*, *Panchästikäya*, and *Pravachansär of Ächärya Kunda-Kunda*, *Tattvärtha Sutra of Umäsvämi*, *Padma-Purän*, *Ädi-Purän*, *Mulächär*, and *Gommatsär*.

C. Sacred Literature

Saman Suttam

The *Saman Suttam* contains 756 verses, which were compiled in 1974 during the celebration year of 2,500 nirvana anniversary of Lord Mahävir from various Jain Ägams, Digambar Shästras, and some ancient texts. Hence, the book is itself as valid as the scriptures. It is a brief compilation of the essential principles of the Jain religion and philosophy.

There are four parts and forty-four sections in this book. This is a comprehensive book for the purpose of having a general acquaintance with the doctrines of the Jain religion, its code of ethics, and the process of gradual spiritual advancement of life in a traditional but devotional manner.

Tattvärtha Sutra

Ächärya Shri Umäsväti's or Umasvämi's (ca. 200–400 CE) creation of the *Tattvärtha Sutra* is considered the greatest gift to Jains and is accepted by all Jains. Most of the sacred literature of the Jains is written in the Präkrit Ardha-Mägadhi language. However, the *Tattvärtha Sutra* is the first Jain text written in terse aphoristic form in the Sanskrit language. The book has ten chapters, and 344 or 357 aphorisms. They are related to all the major theoretical and practical aspects of the Jain system.

D. Secondary Sources

Shared Texts:

- *Tattvärtha Sutra of Umäsväti*
- *Sanmati Tarka*
- *Pauma Chariu of Vimala Suri*
- *Bhaktämar Stotra*
- *Samana Suttam*, compiled by a council led by Jinendra Varani

Svetambara Texts:

- *Tattvaarthaadhigamasutra* by Umäsväti
- *Nyäyävatära* by Diwäkar Siddhasen
- *Saddarsanasamucchaya* by Haribhadra
- *Trishashti Salakapurusas Chäritra* by Hemchandra
- *Saddarsanavichara* by Merutunga

Digambara Texts:

- *Ratna Karanda Shrävakächär* by Samantabhadra
- *Mahäpurän* by Jinsen
- *Jainaslokavartika* by Vidyanand
- *Atmaanusasana* by Gunabhadra
- *Tattvärtha-sära* by Amitachandra
- *Syadavadamanjari* by Mallisena
- *Tattvardhasaradipika* by Sakalakirti

A great deal of literature is available in Indian vernacular languages. Some of the earlier literature in Kannada, Tamil, and Gujarati is of Jain origin. The Jain monks created their own narrative texts (Charitas and Puranas) comparable to Hindu Puranas. There are also considerably important Jain works in mathematics, politics, arts, and science.

III. Rites and Rituals

A. The Calendar

Paryushan and Dash Lakshana Parva

This is the holiest season of the year and is an eight- or ten-day period of fasting, complex rituals, review of Jain principles, and prayers for forgiveness from all living beings. The celebrations include a period of self-reflection, contemplation, self-introspection, repentance, austerity, penance, and moral and spiritual awakening granting forgiveness to others and requesting forgiveness from others for any pain or misunderstanding that may have been caused intentionally or unintentionally. It takes place during the monsoon month of August to September.

In the Shvetämbar Jain tradition this festival lasts eight days, while in the Digambar tradition it lasts ten days and is known as Dash Lakshana Parva.

In the Shvetämbar tradition, the scripture, *Kalpa Sutra*, is read in places of worship. The *Kalpa Sutra* contains a detailed account of Lord Mahävira's life. On the fourth day of the Paryushan, the *Kalpa Sutra* receives a very special reverence and may be carried in the procession. On the fifth day, at a special ceremony, the auspicious dreams of Mahävira's mother, Queen Trishalä, are demonstrated. The final day of Paryushan is the most important of all. On this day many Jains (young and old, men and women) observe fasts and do self-introspection by performing *pratikraman* (a systematized way of self analysis). Those who have observed the fasts are specially honored. This is also the day when Jains ask for and grant sincere and unconditional forgiveness to all living beings, the family, friends, and foes alike, for any acts they have or might have knowingly and unknowingly, mentally, verbally, and physically committed toward them in the previous year.

In Digambar tradition, the scripture *Tattvärtha Sutra* is read. The book has ten chapters, and one chapter is read every day.

Mahävir Jayanti (Janma Kalyänak)

This day, which falls sometime in March or April, marks the birthday celebration of Lord Mahävir. The day is celebrated with various festivities and cultural activities. Jains gather in temples, places of worship, and public places to listen to the teachings of Mahävira. Generally, there are lectures, public gatherings, processions, and parades in the main streets of the cities and villages, and images of the tirthankara are paraded through the streets. Often times, this becomes an all day cultural event.

Deepävali (Diwäli)

Diwäli is celebrated in October to November throughout India. This day is particularly important in the Jain tradition for it was on this day, in 527 BCE, that Lord Mahävira attained ultimate liberation or nirvana. To carry on the tradition, lamps are lit all over India during Diwäli. Jains visit temples, exchange gifts, and sweets are given to all visitors.

The day after Diwäli begins the New Year, an occasion for joyful gatherings in both Hindu and Jain calendars. Also on this day Gautam Ganadhar, the first disciple of Lord Mahavir, attained keval-jnän.

Jnän Panchami

The fifth day of the New Year is known as Jnäna Panchami, the day of knowledge. Jain scriptures are displayed in various religious places. Jains worship these sacred scriptures with devotion.

Kärtik Purnimä

Kärtik Purnimä commences in October or November. This is a time for pilgrimage to the sacred places associated with the Jain religion.

Mauna Ekädasi (Agiyäras)

Mauna Agiyäras is observed during the months of November and December. This is the most pious day of the year. As such, it is a day of fasting and complete silence, during which Jains mediate on the five great worshipful personalities, or supreme ones—arhat (the enlightened souls), siddha (the liberated souls), ächärya (the preceptors), upäd-hyäyas (spiritual teachers and guides), and sädhu (all mendicants and followers of paths of righteousness). Many people temporarily live the life of an ascetic by staying at an upäshray (temporary residence of traveling ascetics) on that day.

Akshaya Tritiya (Varsitapa Pärnä)

This marks the fast breaking day of a year-long fast by the first tirthankar, Lord Rishabhadev. Jains who have been fasting on an alternate day for a year, break their fast by drinking fresh sugar cane juice.

Some Jains fast as many as ten days in a given month and undertake other religious practices and vows on many auspicious days throughout the year.

B. Worship and Liturgy

Jains do not worship to please God or heavenly angels, nor do they do so with any hope of favoritism. Although Jains appear to worship the tirthankaras, they do not actually regard them as persons, but rather as the ideal of perfection. The physical form is not to be worshipped, but it is the virtues and qualities (gunas) that are praised. Jain worship provides the individual with a discipline that helps him or her concentrate on Jain ideals and cultivate detachment from worldly pleasure and material happiness.

Jains have built temples where images of tirthankars are venerated. Many Jain temples are ancient. There are several sacred pilgrimage centers, such as Palitana, in Gujarat, and Shravanbelgola, in Karnataka, which are considered to be temple cities because of a large number of temples.

Jain rituals may be elaborate, because symbolic objects are offered and the virtues and qualities of tirthankars are praised in song. Jain rituals include: Pancha-Kalyanak Pratishthä, Pratikraman, Guru-Vandanä, Chaitya Vandan, and many other rituals to praise tirthankar virtues, honor ascetics, and taking different vows to discipline the self.

The Shrävakächär is the Jain code of conduct for householders. This prescribed set of rules and restraints are essential to the practice of Jainism. Included in the Shrävakächär are thirty-five qualities leading to a noble life, right conviction and belief: sixty-seven qualities of a person having samyaktva, or realization of true knowledge; five minor vows (anu-vrata), three supporting restraints (guna-vrata), four disciplinary restraints (shikshä-vrata), and the sallekhanä-vrata meaning fasting to voluntarily and willingly end life when the body is no longer capable of doing its normal functions and one becomes a burden to society.

The five anu-vrata (minor vows) for householders are:

(1) Ahimsa (nonviolence to mobile living beings and minimum violence to plants);

(2) Satya (moral truthfulness);

(3) Asteya (nonstealing);

(4) Brahmacharya (no physical relationships other than with lawfully wedded spouse);

(5) Aparigraha (nonpossession, or nonpossessiveness and nonattachment).

The three guna-vrata (supporting restraints) are: (1) geographical restraints; (2) consumption restraints; and (3) avoidance of purposeless activities.

The four shikshä-vrata (disciplinary restraints) are: (1) forty-eight minutes of meditation and equanimity; (2) stricter geographical restrictions; (3) practicing the life of a monk; and (4) sharing what one has.

Worship and pujä can take many forms. The Pancha-Kalyanak Pujä takes place when a new tem-ple or image is consecrated with a "Pratishthä" ceremony. It is a ritual to commemorate the five great events of the tirthankar's life; namely conception, birth, renunciation, omniscience, and liberation. The ritual bathing of the image (Snätra Pujä or Abhisheka) is symbolic of the bathing of a newborn tirthankara by the heavenly gods. Antaräya Karma Pujä consists of a series of prayers to remove certain types of karma that obstruct the spiritual uplifting power of the soul. One symbolically touches one's own forehead with the liquid used to bathe the idol.

C. Daily Life: Precepts and Restrictions

Each day Jains should bow and say their universal prayer, the Namaskär or Namokär Mantra. Jains are expected to visit a temple every day and also bow to a monk if one is present at the temple.

Sämäyika, the practice of equanimity or meditation, is a ritual act undertaken early in the morning and often also at noon and night. It lasts for forty-eight minutes and involves sitting in one place in quiet meditation, not allowing the passions of attachment and aversion to rise in the mind. For this period of time, one contemplates the nature of self, examines as to how much purity of life he has attained, reads true religious works, and concentrates on the supreme soul.

Pratikramana is performed periodically, though precisely when is left up to the individual. It may be performed in the morning for the repentance of violence committed during the night and in the evening for the violence during the day. During Pratikramana, a person expresses remorse for any harm, wrong doing, or duties left unfinished. The exercise is for negating the karmic influx since the last Pratikramana. The Shvetämbar Jains perform a Pratikramana at least once during the year.

Pujä, a more elaborate form of worship, is a regular daily ritual usually performed in a temple. The worshipper enters the temple with the words "Namo

Jinänam" ("I bow to the Jina") and repeats "Nissihi" three times (to relinquish thoughts about worldly affairs). This form of worship is not exclusive to the temple, but can also be performed at home using a smaller household shrine. It is important to note that not all Jains perform these acts of worship because some Jain sects, like the Sthäna-kaväsi and Teräpanthi Shvetämbars and Tärana-pantha Digambars, regard the worship of the Jina image unnecessary, while still revering the Jinas.

All Jains follow the five anu-vrata, or minor vows. For the laity, chastity involves confining sensual pleasure to marriage, but for monks and nuns it means complete celibacy. Nonviolence includes being a vegetarian; some choose to be vegan because of the cruel practices on many modern dairy farms. Jains are expected to be nonviolent in thought, word, and deed, toward humans and every living creature. Jain monks walk barefoot and sweep the spot before sitting down to avoid harming or killing any insect.

Compassion for all life, human and nonhuman, is central to Jainism. Human life is valued as a unique, rare opportunity to reach enlightenment. The religion requires monks and laity, from all sects and traditions, to be completely vegetarian and observe nonviolence in every thing they do. Jains abjure food obtained with unnecessary cruelty. Many are vegan due to the violence of modern dairy farms. The Jain diet excludes most root vegetables because they destroy significantly more lives than other vegetables. Garlic and onions are avoided because they increase the passions of anger, hatred, and jealousy.

Eight Cardinal qualities

The eight primary or cardinal qualities of a lay follower are: abstinence from taking meat, including fish, eggs, and other animal products, (except milk and milk product); abstinence from drinking wine and other spiritual liquors; refraining from eating honey squeezed out of live honeycombs; avoiding indiscriminate and unchecked indulgence in the five sinful practices; injury to other living beings; falsehood; cheating and misappropriation; unlawful relations; acquisition of material possessions. Sometimes abstinence from indulgence in gambling, prostitution, adultery, and hunting of animals is also included among the eight cardinal qualities.

Jain monks practice strict asceticism and strive to lift their spirituality so that they will either be liberated in this life or in the next life. The laity pursues less rigorous practices, strives to attain rational knowledge and rational faith and conviction, and to do as much good as possible. Members of the laity usually choose professions that revere and protect life and avoid violent livelihoods.

Jains do not harbor ill will toward others, and they practice forgiveness. They believe that *atma* (self) can lead one to becoming *parmatma* (self with perfection and with absolute and permanent bliss), and this must come from one's inner self. The eighteen vices that should be eradicated are:

• Pränätipäta – violence
• Mrushäväda – untruth
• Adattädän – theft
• Maithun – unchaste behavior
• Parigraha – possessiveness
• Krodha – anger
• Mäna – arrogance
• Mäyä – deceit
• Lobh – greed
• Räg – attachment
• Dvesha – hate
• Kalah – arguing
• Abhyäkhyän – accusation
• Paishunya – gossip
• Rati-Arati – likes and dislikes
• Par-Pariväda – criticism
• Mäyä-Mrushäväda – malice
• Mithyätva-Shalya – wrong belief

Fasting is common among Jains and most Jains fast at special times—during festivals and on holy days. A Jain may fast at any time, especially if he or she feels some error or violation of certain vows has been committed. Variations in fasts encourage Jains to do whatever they can to maintain whatever self-control is possible for the individual.

Visiting a Jain Temple

Jain worship services are open to the general public. However, guests attending such services are expected to observe certain basic requirements, such as wearing clean clothes; leaving one's shoes at the entrance of the temple; not eating, drinking, or bringing items of a violent nature (meat or liquor) in or around the temple area; and having respect for all lives while in the temple area. A visit will reveal the inherent democracy of a Jain temple—different individual Jains might be found silently meditating, performing rituals, singing prayers, or studying scriptures all in the same space and without a priest or clergyman. Jainism is an eternal philosophy whose benefits can be taken up by anyone wanting to improve his or her spiritual life.

D. Life Cycle Events

Nuptials

Jain wedding rituals vary within every Jain community. Regardless of variance in rituals, marriage means a public declaration of a man and a woman's intention to be together for their entire lives. The Jain community condemns the practice of negotiating a dowry before marriage; Jains believe there should be no waste of money or time. (The steps described here are generally applicable to Jain communities in western India.)

There are a series of rituals that occur before a wedding ceremony. A typical Jain marriage begins with Vaganda, when the parents of the bride and groom declare the intention to marry them. After this the Pradana takes place, and the bride is gifted with ornaments. The engagement ceremony, also known as Sagai, is held at the groom's house where the lagna-patrika (document stating the intent of forthcoming marriage) is read. Gifts are given to the groom by the brother of the bride and the groom is presented and seeks the blessings of the elders. Sacred prayers are then recited to ensure the happiness and fertility of the couple. In the days before the wedding, the mandap, the structure under which the marriage will be held, and the vedi, the altar for the ceremonial fire, are made.

On the day of the wedding, the Ghudhchadi (riding the horse) Ritual takes place at the groom's house during which he is given a headgear and all of his relatives apply tikä to his forehead. After this is the baraat, the groom's procession, during which the groom traditionally rides on horseback. Upon reaching the destination, rites of welcome are performed. The women welcome the groom and offer him a length of red cloth. When the groom enters the mandap, he steps on two earthenware bowls in order to guard against evil spirits that may influence the ceremony. Mantras are chanted by the Jain priest presiding over the ceremony and a series of prayers are recited as the bride and groom enter the mandap.

The Kanyavaran ceremony involves the parents or the uncle of the bride balancing one dollar and twenty-five cents, along with rice, on the right hand of the bride. The father of the bride publicly proclaims a formal presentation of the bride in front of all the assembled guests. The priest pours water on the hands of the bride and groom. During the Hasta Melap (joining of hands), the priest places a single cloth garland around the couple's necks. The bride's parents wash the groom's feet, wipe them, and dress them, with flowers. The groom is then given special items to hold and the priest places the bride's hand into the groom's and recites a prayer linking them together for life. Following this, the priest gives gifts to the bride's parents and other prayers are recited.

A ceremonial fire is lit in a small vessel on the vedi (altar) and offerings are made in the presence of the fire god (agni-deva). After the offerings, the couple's heads are anointed with water during the first abhisheka. Then a married woman takes the corner of the pallu of the bride's sari and ties it to the shawl of the groom. Once this is done, the Agni Pradakshina begins. During this ritual the couple circles the sacred fire four times; specific mantras are spoken for each round. Before the final round, the giving away of the bride (kanyadaan) is performed. This is when the

Distribution of Jain Temples in the United States (JAINA)

STATE	NO.	TEMPLE LOCATION AND NAME
California	2	Milpitas: Jain Center of Northern California
		Buena Park: Jain Center of Southern California
New York	4	Elmhurst: Jain Center of America
		Crefzille: Jain Society of Buffalo*
		Londonville: Jain Society of Capital District*
		Pittsford: Jain Society of Rochester*
Texas	2	Houston: Jain Society of Houston
		Richardson: Jain Society of North Texas
Florida	1	West Palm Beach: Jain Society of S. Florida
Pennsylvania	2	Monroeville: Jain Center of Pittsburgh*
		Allentown: Jain Sangh of Allentown*
Illinois	1	Bartlett: Jain Society of Metro. Chicago
Ohio	1	Cincinnati: Jain Ctr. of Cincinnati & Dayton
Michigan	1	Farmington Hills: Jain Soc. of Greater Detroit
New Jersey	3	Essex Fall: Jain Society of New Jersey
		Blairstown: Siddhachalam/Int'nl Mahavir Mission
		Pennsauken: The Jain Sangh of New Jersey
North Carolina	2	Morrisville: Jain Study Center of N. Carolina*
		Charlotte: Jain Study Group of Charlotte*
Georgia	2	Augusta: Hindu Temple Society of Augusta*
		Atlanta: Jain Group of Atlanta
Massachusetts	1	Wellesley: Jain Center of Greater Boston
Maryland	1	Silver Springs: Jain Society of Metro. Washington
Minnesota	1	Minneapolis: Jain Center of Minnesota
South Carolina	1	Simonville: Jain Group of Greenville*
TOTAL:	**25**	*(Combined Hindu/Jain Temple)

father of the bride offers his daughter to the groom and the groom accepts. After the Agni Pradakshina, the priest sprinkles vasakshepa (a fragrant powder) on the couple's heads and the bride's father gives water and tal to the groom. After the second abhisheka is the Kar-mochan, during which the couple's hands are released. After the bride's father offers another gift to the groom, the wedding is concluded with final words spoken by the priest.

Death and Funeral

In Jainism, death is considered to be a natural part of life, and it is therefore accepted without fear. According to Jain thought, when a being dies, the soul (*jiva*) goes to its next body instantly. This body may not be human or even animal; the quality of its next life is determined by the karma one acquires during this and previous lives. The mental state of the being at the moment of death is also important: a calm and contented death with the mind focused on spiritual matters is best.

A final rite for Jains is an austere ceremony. The body is bathed and dressed in all white clothing in preparation for cremation. Cremation is generally performed without delay and often within hours of death though never after the sun sets.

Jain monks and some Jains practice Santhärä when death is considered to be imminent. In this ritual, the person who has completed all duties in this life and whose body is incapable of performing its routine duties, voluntarily, and with the specific permission of family and Jain saints, ceases to eat or drink and enters meditation until his death. This is a time-honored practice among Jains, but has led to controversy in India where some non-Jain activists are fighting to make Santhärä illegal.

IV. Denominations and Demographics

A. History (Schisms and Mergers)

The Jain Sangha is divided into two major sects: Digambar and Shvetämbar. The process of division was initiated in the fourth century BCE, when the Ächärya Bhadrabähu, the leader of the sangha, led 12,000 followers to southern India to avoid famine. Twelve years later they returned to find the remaining monks had adopted different practices under the leadership of Āchārya Sthuli-bhadra. The Digambars follow those who migrated, and Shvetāmbars follow the lineage of Sthulibhadra. The division became more pronounced in 453 CE, when the Vallabhi council compiled traditional Shvetāmbar scriptures.

The key difference is reflected in the names: the Digambar (literally, "sky-clad") do not wear clothes and the Shvetāmbar (meaning "white-clad") wear white clothes. In Gujarat (western India) , the majority of Jains follow the Shvetāmbar tradition, while in the south, the majority of Jains are Digambars. In north and central India, both sects are found.

B. Comparisons in Tenets and Practices

Both sects believe in ahimsa, asceticism, karma, soul, and the relation between soul and karma, but they disagree over details of the life of Mahāvira, the spiritual status of women, whether monks should wear clothes or not, rituals, and which texts are authentic. The Digambar monks follow the practices of Lord Mahāvira, while the Shvetāmbars consider some of their practices unsuitable for modern times.

Both of the major sects can be subdivided further into smaller sects—Shvetāmbars include Derāvāsi, Sthānakavāsi, or Terāpanthi; and the Digambars include Bisapantha, Terāpanthi, or Tāranpathis. Many simply call themselves Jains and follow general traditions rather than specific sectarian practices.

Some Jains are murtipujak (image worshippers) while others are "non-murtipujak" (non-image worshipper) who regard images simply as guides. Sādhumārgi Shvetāmbar Jains, such as the Sthanakvasi and Terāpanthi, believe statues and temple unnecessary.

Digambar monks do not wear clothes because they believe clothes, like other possessions, increase dependency and desire for material things, which ultimately leads to sorrow. Shvetāmbar monks wear white seamless clothes, believing there is nothing in Jain scripture that forbids wearing clothes needed to function in society.

Digambars believe that women cannot live a truly ascetic life because they have to possess clothes; it is impractical for them to live naked. Shvetāmbars believe that women may certainly attain liberation and that Mallināth, the nineteenth tirthankar, was female.

V. Organization and Infrastructure

The Jain Sangha (community) has four components: monks (sādhu), nuns (sādhvi), laymen (shrāvikās), and laywomen (shrāvikās). The monks and nuns are not expected to stay at the same place for more than a few days except during the rainy season. Serious believers simply choose to become monks or nuns and pursue enlightenment under ascetic circumstances. After being a monk (sadhu) for certain years and learning prescribed scriptures, a monk may rise to the level of an upadhyay (teacher) and ultimately to an acharya (head monk), who may than have his own followers. There is a strict code of conduct and a teacher-pupil hierarchy for monks.

Jain monks do not perform routine temple ceremonies. The head monk gives sermons in the morning and at other times they study scriptures or perform daily obligatory tasks like pratikraman. They may also teach aspects of the scriptures to those who go to them for that purpose. Junior monks visit homes of the nearby Jain families for alms twice a day. All the monks of a given group share the alms quietly. Jain monks are forbidden to travel in motorized vehicles. Because of travel restrictions, there are no traditional orthodox monks in the U.S.

Many Jain scholars and former monks from India regularly visit the U.S. and give discourses in religion at Jain centers. There are also home grown Jain scholars in the U.S. serving the community.

At every Temple there is someone chosen or elected leader of the group, known affectionately as a Sanghpati. He or she looks after the temple, arranges for scholar visitations, organizes Sunday school for the young. (In India women are never Sanghpati.)

The priests, known as Pujari, in the Jain temples are lay individuals (who may or may not be a Jain) who are familiar with the rituals; some may even conduct marriages. However, they are not monks.

A. Shrines and Houses of Worship

ORGANIZATIONS

The major influx of Jains to the U.S.A. began in the 1960s. Many came as students and a few came as skilled professionals like doctors or engineers. Initially they settled in big cities. Today there are approximately sixty-seven centers in the United States and Canada and more than 100,000 practicing Jains. Each center is autonomous and is managed by local Jains. In the U.S.A., almost all Jain centers are non-sectarian, with all the sects represented at each temple. The temples are designed in a way to accommodate both Digambar and Shvetämbar images and meditation and Swädhyäy rooms are provided for all Jains. This unity makes the Jain institutions in the U.S. significantly different than those in India, which are almost invariably affiliated with a specific sect. In some small cities, where the Jain population is not large, Jains have joined with Hindus to build a combined Hindu-Jain Temple, common in India.

Cities like New York, Boston, Cherry Hill (NJ), Essex Fell (NJ), Washington, D.C., Chicago, Detroit, Dallas, Houston, Phoenix, Los Angeles, and San Francisco have large Jain Temples to go along with its significant Jain population.

Siddhachalam, a unified Jain temple established by the late Acharya Shri Sushil Kumarji in the Poconos, PA, is considered a national place of pilgrimage (a teerth) for the Jains. Established in 1983, it is the first such place of pilgrimage for Jains outside of India. Siddhachalam Jain Tirth is located in an idyllic setting in rural Pennsylvania on 120 acres of hilly terrain. The main temple has magnificent marble idols of Lord Adinath, Lord Pärshvanätha, Lord Mähavira, Lord Chandraprabha, and Lord Shantinath. The smaller temple's main idol is of Lord Pärshvänatha, carved in magnificent black marble. The smallest temple is a meditation spot with several idols. Siddhachalam also has a Guru Mandir housed in the second floor of Acharya Sushil Kumar Ahimsa Bhavan and separate residences for visiting clerics, a library, and a study and meditation hall.

B. Governance and Authority

The Federation of JAINA (Jain Associations in North America), founded in 1983, is an umbrella organization of local Jain Associations in the U.S.A. and Canada. JAINA is a federation of sixty-seven Jain organizations representing more than 100,000 Jains living in the U.S.A. and Canada, without any distinction based on sect, language or region. It is not an authoritative organization, but rather serves to unite the various Jain societies located in the United States and Canada.

The goals of JAINA are to promote religious and educational activities related to the Jain religion, to develop better understanding of the Jain religion, to assist and promote charitable and humanitarian activities in North America and worldwide, to actively promote vegetarianism and nonviolence, to provide and promote academic and cultural exchanges amongst Jains everywhere, to assist existing Jain associations and support the formation of new Jain association in North America, to serve as a liaison with government agencies in pursuance of all JAINA objectives, and to foster cordial relationships with interfaith or multifaith organizations.

YJA and YJP are the Youth wings of JAINA with about 2,500 members. They hold biennial conventions drawing close to 600 youths for three days of networking and learning about their heritage.

JAINA Headquarters
PO Box 15790
Philadelphia, PA 19103
Phone/Fax: 215-561-0758
E-mail: jainahq@jaina.org
Website: www.jaina.org

C. Social Service Organizations

JAINA runs several social service organizations:

The **Jivadaya** organization collects and provides funds to food and shelters for animals.

The **North American Jain Families Assistance Program** evaluates and helps financially and socially troubled Jain families in North America.

The **JAINA Pilgrimage committee** organizes a pilgrimage to Jain Temples every year. The Teerthodhdhär Committee sponsors medical camps for Sädhu Sädhvis and funds restoration of Jain Temples.

The **Wheel of Hope** is an organization that helps the needy in India by supplying free medical equipment and supplies to hospitals and other institutions.

The **World Community Service** organization provides medical and emergency services to the needy all over the world, with emphasis on India.

The **JAINA Education** Committee prepares educational material to promote and encourage studies in Jainism and world religions. More than 3,000 students use this material in Sunday schools in Jain centers. Over 10,000 copies of the book *The Essence of World Religion* have been distributed

The **JAINA Interfaith** committee organizes and participates in Interfaith-related activities and represents Jainism in various world religion conferences.

The **JAINA Exhibition** committee has prepared an exhibition on all aspects of Jainism, displayed in many North American cities as well as in Singapore.

The **V.R. Gandhi Scholarship Fund** promotes studies in Jainism and in the message of Shri Virchand Räghavji Gandhi. Scholarships are awarded to needy students pursuing higher education in Jain studies at recognized universities and institutions.

D. Media and Communication

The *Jain Study Circular* is a quarterly magazine begun in 1980 that contains articles, stories, and poems about and related to Jainism. The first Jain publication in America, it has significantly influenced the practice of Jainism in the U.S. Articles as well as other media resources can be found online at **www.jainstudy.org**.

The *Jain Digest* is a free quarterly publication from the JAINA, it is mailed to more than 10,000 families in North America and worldwide. It contains news from the local society and religious articles affecting the life of the people in North America. The JAINA *Spectrum* is "the Jain Voice of North America," JAINA's monthly electronic newsletter featuring activities, events, and trends, and is also published by the JAINA. Anyone can subscribe at **www.jaina.org**.

Jinamanjari is an international research journal of Jain studies published by the Brähmi Jain Society in Canada/U.S.A. (Email: jinamanjari@hotmail.com)

There are several extensive Jainism related websites: **www.jainworld.com**, and **www.jcnc.org**.

There are a large number of Jain publications in India, several of which are dedicated to human and planetary nonviolence. Mahävira Vision, a U.S. foundation, in collaboration with JAINA, organized an International School for Jain Studies. For details: **www.jainstudies.org**.

FURTHER READING AND RESOURCES

The Jaina Path to Purification
  Padmanabh Jaini
    2001: Motilal Banarsidass
Jainism and The New Spirituality
  Vastupal Parikh
    2002: Peace Publications
Jainism: Religion of Compassion and Ecology
  Pravin K. Shah
    2007: Federation of JAINA

5 Sikhism

I. Origins and Early History

A. Introduction

SIKHI, NOW THE FIFTH LARGEST ORGANIZED religion in the world, began in Panjab (also called Punjab, a region in south Asia now divided between India and Pakistan) during the sixteenth century with the teachings of Nanak and nine successive human gurus. It is a system of religious tenets and expression also known as Gurmat (the teachings of the gurus), or Sikhi. (Note: Sikhi comes from the word *sikh*, which means "disciple" or "learner." Also, the proper name of the religion is Sikhi—since it is popularly known as Sikhism, we use that term.)

Guru Nanak was born in the village of Rai Bhoi di Talvandi, now Nankana Sahib, in present-day Pakistan. Nanak's fascination with religion and his desire to meet the guru-prophet inspired individuals led him to leave his home. It is said that during his time away from home, Nanak met Kabir, a saint revered by people of different faiths although no evidence exists of such a meeting.

Tradition states that at the age of thirty, Nanak went missing and was presumed to have drowned while bathing at the Kali Bein stream. He reappeared three days later, and in answer to questions about his disappearance, he said: "There is no Hindu; there is no Muslim." Thus Sikhi began. This was a result of direct confrontation with the One Universal Integrative Force (God) and was advent of revelatory divine mission.

It is believed that Nanak made four major journeys to share his message of integration and universalism. He first went east toward Bengal and Assam, then south toward Ceylon via Tamil Nadu. On the third journey he traveled north, toward Kashmir, Ladakh, and Tibet, and on the fourth went west, toward Baghdad and Mecca. He finally settled in the town of Kartarpur (City of the Creator), which he founded on the banks of the river Ravi.

Guru Granth Sahib *is the Sikh scriptures. This illuminated manuscript dates from the late seventeenth or early eighteenth century.*

Nanak had two sons. The elder son, Sri Chand, was an ascetic who had a considerable following of his own, a group that became known as the Udasis. His younger son, Lakshmi Das, was completely immersed in worldly life. Nanak believed in the ideal of *raj-jog*, activism in both spiritual and political affairs of life, and thought that both his sons were unfit to carry on the Guruship.

In 1538, Nanak chose Lahina as a successor to the guruship. Lahina was named Guru Angad. Sri Chand's Udasi followers believed that Chand should have been named the second guru because he was a man of pious habits and was Nanak's son. They therefore refused to accept Angad's succession. Angad moved from Kartarpur and founded Khadur on direct orders of Nanak to remain focused on the divine mission while Nanak dealt with distractions and detractors.

In 1552, Guru Amardas became the third Sikh guru at the age of seventy-three. He institutionalized equality for women by prohibiting *purdah* (the concealment of women from men, both socially and with the use of garb) and *sati* (the self-immolation of a woman on her late husband's funeral pyre). Of the twenty-two religious and administrators he appointed, three were women. He also upheld the practice of *langar* (the serving of free food in a manner that treats all diners as equals) and required his visitors attend langar before they could speak to him. He appointed his son-in-law, Jetha, as the fourth guru before he died in 1574.

Jetha became Guru Ramdas. He established the city of Ramdaspur, later named Amritsar. In 1581, his youngest son became the fifth guru of the Sikhs, Guru Arjun. Arjun built the Harimandir Sahib, commonly called the Golden Temple, and prepared the *Guru Granth Sahib*, the Sikh sacred text, which included writings of the first five gurus, among other Sikhs and non-Sikhs.

Guru Hargobind became the sixth guru of the Sikhs in 1606, after Arjun was executed by the Mughal ruler, Jahangir, for supporting an unsuccessful contender to the throne. Hargobind carried two swords,

This Tanjore-style painting of the late nineteenth century depicts the Ten Gurus, whose teachings form the basis of Sikhism, with Bhai Bala and Bhai Mardana. (Bhai is an appellation meaning "brother.")

the miri and piri, one to show spiritual sovereignty and other the political. The Sikhs grew as an organized nation under his leadership and had a trained fighting force ready to defend their independence. In 1644, Guru Harirai became guru followed by Guru Harkrishan, the youngest guru, in 1661.

Guru Teghbahadur became guru in 1665, and led the Sikhs until 1675. He was executed by Aurangzeb for helping to protect a delegation of Kashmiri Pandits, who sought his help when the Emperor condemned them to death for refusing to convert to Islam. Teghbahadur's son, Gobind Rai, succeeded his father and became the tenth guru of the Sikhs at the age of nine. He was initiated by the Panj Piare when he formed the Khalsa in 1699, after which he became known as Guru Gobind Singh. The Khalsa is a disciplined community that combines its religious purpose and goals with political duties. Guru Gobind Singh inaugurated the

Khalsa—the full-time revolutionaries—to uphold the Doctrine of Love and Doctrine of Justice.

Before his death in 1708, Gobind Singh ordered that the Guru Granth Sahib (the Sikh scriptural canon) be the ultimate spiritual authority for the Sikhs with temporary authority going to the Khalsa Panth, the Sikh Nation. Gobind Singh charged Banda Singh Bahadur with the duty of delivering justice to the persecutors in South Asia and formally establish the Khalsa Raj—the Sikh rule. Banda Singh Bahadur became the leader of the Sikhs and was responsible for the establishment of egalitarian society with a plebian mission. After his death and two major holocausts later, a loose confederation of Sikh commonwealth known as Misls formed.

Under the leadership of the Maharaja Ranjit Singh, the Mughal empire in the Panjab lost popularity while the Sikh empire grew. Its capital was in Lahore and the empire stretched all the way to the Khyber Pass and the borders of China. After Ranjit Singh's death, the Sikh kingdom fell into disorder and eventually collapsed with the Hind-Panjab (inaptly labeled as Anglo-Sikh) Wars, which brought the Panjab under British rule.

Sikhs supported and participated in the Indian National Congress—a major political party in India heading the Independence Movement—and formed their own groups, the Shiromani Gurduara Prabandhak Committee and the Shiromani Akali Dal in order to preserve the Sikhs religious and political organization. In 1947, Panjab was partitioned and thousands of Sikhs were killed in the violence that ensued. Millions were forced to leave their ancestral homes in West Panjab.

During the 1970s Green Revolution, Panjab became the most prosperous Indian state and many Sikhs enjoyed considerable prosperity. A group led by cleric Jarnail Singh Bhindranwale arose during this time demanding greater autonomy for all Indian states through the federal structure of the government. After the 1984 attacks on Sikhs and their culture, the movement for an independent Sikh state, named Khalistan, was launched. This resulted in state repression and human rights violations, as reported by Amnesty International and Human Rights Watch. This led to clashes between militant groups and government forces, resulting in communal violence and state repression.

B. The Religion in America

Worldwide there are about 26 million Sikhs, the majority of which (68%) currently reside in Panjab, India. Beginning in the 1960s, changes in immigration laws along with persecution and high rate of unemployment in Panjab led to an increase in emigration to western countries. There are approximately 600,000 Sikhs in America today. The number of Gurduaras in America has grown from only a handful in the 1960s to over 150 today.

Asian Indian immigrants came to the United States as early as 1820, but they did not arrive in significant numbers until the western railroad projects of the late 1890s provided them with employment opportunities. Most of the first wave of immigrants came from Panjab and most of them were Sikhs. They worked on farms, in lumber mills, or in railroad construction.

The first Sikh Gurduara in America was built in Stockton, California, in 1909, through the joint efforts of Sardar Basakha Singh and Bhai Jawala Singh. The second temple in America was built in El Centro, California, in 1948. In addition to these temples, the Sikhs established cultural organizations such as the Pacific Coast Khalsa Diwan Society and the India American Cultural Center.

The United States Congress passed the Asian Exclusion Act of 1917, thus limiting the immigration quota on Asian Indians. The Act was repealed in 1965, and in the late 1960s a second and much larger immigration wave commenced, carrying hundreds of thousands of Indian immigrants, many of them Sikhs, to cities across the U.S.

C. Important Dates and Landmarks

1469 Birth of Guru Nanak.

1499 Nanak disappears for three days during which he experiences a divine encounter that prompts him to begin his mission.

1538 Guru Angad becomes the second guru of the Sikhs.

1553 Guru Amardas becomes the third guru of the Sikhs.

1567 Emperor Akbar sits with ordinary and poor people of Panjab to have langar.

1574 Guru Ramdas becomes the fourth guru of the Sikhs.

1581 Guru Arjun becomes the fifth guru of the Sikhs.

1604 Guru Arjun compiles the first version of the Sikh scripture, the Adi Granth.

1606 Guru Harigobind becomes the sixth guru of the Sikhs after Arjun is tortured and killed for refusing to make changes to the Granth and for supporting an unsuccessful contender to the throne.

1644 Guru Harirai becomes the seventh guru of the Sikhs.

1661 Guru Harkrishan, the youngest guru, becomes the eighth guru of the Sikhs.

1665 Guru Teghbahadur becomes the ninth guru of the Sikhs.

1675 Gobind Rai becomes the tenth guru of the Sikhs.

1699 Gobind Rai inaugurated the Khalsa and is initiated by the Panj Piare as Guru Gobind Singh.

1845–1846 First Hind-Panjab (Anglo-Sikh) War.

1848–1849 Second Hind-Panjab (Anglo-Sikh) War.

1947 Partition of Panjab and formation of India and Pakistan.

1984 Modern day Holocaust of the Sikhs.

D. Important Figures

Kabir (1440–1518)—a saint revered by people of different faiths.

Guru Nanak (1469–1539)—the founder of Sikhi and the first guru; had a revelation and shortly thereafter uttered the words: "There is no Hindu; there is no Muslim"; laid forth three basic principles by which everyone should abide: (1) live in remembrance of the Divine; (2) earn an honest living; (3) share your earning before you consume.

Guru Angad (1504–1552)—second guru; widely credited for standardizing the Gurmukhi script as used in the sacred scripture of the Sikhs.

Guru Amardas (1479–1574)—third guru; organized the construction of twenty-two centers of learning, from religious to political.

Guru Ramdas (1534–1581)—fourth guru; founded the city of Amristsar, the religious center of Sikhi.

Guru Arjun (1563–1606)—fifth guru; began the construction of the Golden Temple in Amristar; complied the Adi Granth (Sikh scripture) with writings from all of the gurus up until that time as well as writings from Muslim and Hindu saints; was tortured and killed for refusing to convert to Islam (the first Sikh martyr).

Guru Hargobind (1595–1644)—sixth guru; maintained an army to assert sovereignty to protect the downtrodden; constructed Akal Takht as the center of temporal affairs in the Sikh religion.

Guru Harirai (1630–1661)—seventh guru; continued to organize the Sikhs into a sovereign nation.

Guru Harkrishan (1656–1664)—eighth guru; became a guru at the age of five; worked to alleviate the suffering of the common person during a smallpox epidemic, but succumbed to the disease and died at the age of eight.

Guru Teghbahadur (1621–1675)—ninth guru; killed for protecting Hindus from the Emperor.

Guru Gobind Singh (1666–1708)—tenth guru; formalized the Sikh initiation ceremony, to become the Khalsa; declared that the guruship would be a combination of the Khalsa Panth and Guru Granth Sahib. Banda Singh Bahadur was the leader of the Sikh nation after the death of Guru Gobind Singh. Maharaja Ranjit Singh established the first Sikh Raj, under whose rule the Sikh empire flourished.

II. Tenets and Beliefs

A. Articles of Faith

The principal belief in Sikhi is faith in One Universal Integrative Force, Vahguru, as revealed to humanity through the guru. The Sikh view of the Divine is summarized in the mul mantar—an expression used, in full or in abbreviated

form, at the start of every collection of verses in the *Guru Granth Sahib*. The mul mantar is:

One Universal Integrative Force, Eternal, The Reality, The Name, Creator and Doer, All-pervading, Without fear, Without rancor, transcending time, Unincarnate, Self-existent, (realized) through the Guru's Grace.

Sikhi advocates the pursuit of salvation through disciplined, personal meditation on the name and message of God.

The followers of Sikhi follow the teachings of the ten Sikh gurus, or enlightened prophets, who were leaders, as well as the holy scripture—the *Guru Granth Sahib*—which includes the works of many contributors from diverse socioeconomic and religious backgrounds that held the same vision of the Divine as an infinite prayer. The text was decreed by Gobind Singh, the tenth guru, as the final guru of the Khalsa Panth. According to the Sikh religion, the guru and the Vahguru (God) are equally important. While Vahguru is unknowable and unborn, the guru is the Perfect Being with whom people can communicate and from whom they receive advice. He manifests all divine attributes including immortality. According to Guru Granth Sahib: "My True Guru is forever; Guru does not come and go." The guru comes to the world for the freedom of humanity. A guru's mission is to help humanity to develop harmony with the Divine.

B. Scripture

The *Guru Granth Sahib* is the first Sikh scripture and was compiled by the fifth guru, Arjun, in 1604. It is written in the Gurmukhi script that was institutionalized by Guru Angad for use by the Sikhs. The Adi Granth is an authoritative scripture that was created to protect the integrity of hymns and teachings of the Sikh gurus and selected saints.

The *Guru Granth Sahib* was compiled by Guru Gobind Singh and consists of the original Adi

Granth with the addition of Guru Teghbahadur's hymns. It also contains the traditions and teachings of saints such as Kabir, Namdev, Ravidas, and Sheikh Farid along with several others. The bulk of the scriptural canon is classified into rags, with each rag subdivided according to length and contributor. The languages used in the *Guru Granth Sahib* are spoken hybridized forms of South Asia as well as the Middle East. There are also over 5,000 *sabads*, or hymns, which are poetically constructed and set to classical form of music rendition. The hymns can also be set to predetermined musical tal, or rhythmic beats. All text within the Granth is known as gurbani, which, according to Nanak, was revealed by Vahguru directly, and the contributors wrote it down for the followers. Along with declaring the line of the living gurus to be finished, Guru Gobind Singh also said that the *Guru Granth Sahib* should serve as the eternal guru, with its interpretation vested with the community.

No sacred text should ever touch the floor, be handled with unwashed hands, or read by a Sikh whose head is not covered. Pages should not be turned with a licked finger, and the utmost respect should be paid to all scripts from the gurus.

C. Secondary Sources

Janamsakhis, or birth stories, are biographies of Nanak. They are not considered scripture, but provide an interesting look at Nanak's life and the early start of Sikhi.

The Dasam Granth is an eighteenth-century collection of miscellaneous works partially attributed to Guru Gobind Singh. It does not hold guruship; the authenticity of some portions of the Granth, therefore, have been questioned, and the appropriateness of its content still causes much debate.

III. Rites and Rituals

A. The Calendar

Festivals in Sikhi mostly center around the lives of the gurus and Sikh martyrs. The Shiromani Gurduara Parbandhak Committee, or SGPC, a Sikh organization in charge of upkeep of the gurduaras (sikh temples), organizes celebrations based on the new Nanakshahi calendar. This calendar was highly controversial among Sikhs, but is now almost universally accepted. Before March 13, 1998, the Sikhs used a Indian lunar calendar to determine their feast days. The Nanakshahi calendar aligns with the Gregorian calendar. The era (1 Chet 1 Nanakshahi) is the Sikh new year. The Nanakshi calendar was established using the shared system of the *Guru Granth Sahib* and what could be substantiated historically. It has an obvious relationship with South Asian cultures, but, for simplicity, the dates in the Gregorian Calendar are used.

Baramaha is the name of a composition in the *Guru Granth Sahib* which mentions the twelve months (South Asian names of the months) in a calendar year. A famous Baramaha composed by Guru Arjan in Rag Majh is generally read in gurduaras on the day of Sangrand. Guru Nanak also composed a Baramaha in Reg Tukhari.

Sikh months begin:

Chet—March 14
Vaisakh—April 14
Jeth—May 15
Harh—June 15
Sawan—July 16
Bhadon—August 16
Asu—September 15
Katik—October 15
Maghar—November 14
Poh—December 14
Magh—January 13
Phagan—February 12

Gurpurabs are celebrations or commemorations based on the lives of the Sikh gurus. They tend to be either birthdays or celebrations of Sikh martyrdom. The Nanakshahi calendar is used for all the Gurupurabs except for three events, including the birthday of Guru Nanak, which is still celebrated according to the South Asian Lunar calendar on Katik Puranamashi.

Vaisakhi normally occurs on April 13th and marks the beginning of the new spring year and the end of the harvest. Sikhs celebrate it because on Vaisakhi in 1699, the tenth guru, Gobind Singh, began the Khalsa initiation tradition. Divali celebrates Guru Hargobind's release from the Gwalior Jail on October 26, 1619. Hola Mohalla occurs the day after Holi; the Khalsa Panth gather then at Anandpur to display their justice and military skills.

B. Worship and Liturgy

Worship in a gurduara consists chiefly of singing of passages from the *Guru Granth Sahib*. Sikhs will commonly enter the gurduara, touch the ground before the *Guru Granth Sahib* with their foreheads, and make an offering. The recitation of Ardas is customary for attending Sikhs.

Khalsa, meaning pure or sovereign, is the title given by Gobind Singh to all Sikhs who have been initiated by taking ammrit in a ceremony called *ammrit sancar*. Initiated Sikhs are bound to wear the articles of faith known as the Five Ks (panj kakar) at all times. These must be worn so that a Sikh can use them to make a practical difference in their own and others' spirituality. The five items are: kes (uncut hair), kangha (comb), kara (iron bracelet), kirpan (traditional sword), and kachihra (under-shorts).

Gurpurabs mark the culmination of Prabhat Pheris, the early morning religious procession, which goes around the localities singing sabads (hymns). These pheris generally start three weeks before the festival. Devotees offer sweets and tea

when the procession passes their homes.

The celebrations start with the three-day akhand path, in which the *Guru Granth Sahib* is read continuously from beginning to end without a break. The conclusion of the reading coincides with the day of the festival. The *Guru Granth Sahib* is also carried in procession on a float decorated with flowers throughout the village or city. Five armed guards, who represent the Panj Piares, head the procession carrying Nishan Sahibs (the Sikh flag). Local bands play religious music and marching schoolchildren form a special part of the procession. Free sweets and langar (community meals) are offered to everyone, regardless of religious faith. Local volunteers serve it with a spirit of seva (service) and bhakti (devotion). Sikhs visit gurduaras where special programs are arranged and kirtan (religious songs) sung. Houses and gurduaras are lit up to add to the festivities.

C. Daily Life

The Sikh Rahit Maryada, the Official Sikh Code of Conduct, states that discipline is the basic tool that is required to solve the problems and pains of life. A Sikh should live up to the discipline of Bani (living in remembrance of the divine) and Bana (wearing of the five Ks and keeping piety of outlook) to attain the ultimate goal. The code of conduct provides social, cultural, religious, and spiritual precepts for living life.

The ultimate aim of a human being is to overcome problems and lead a pure and pious life in order to attain harmony with Vahguru. According to Sikhi, the remedy of pain lies within. Human life is viewed as an opportunity to meet the Divine, and this opportunity is wasted if one chooses to pursue transitory gratification. Lust, anger, greed, attachment, and ego are impediments to understanding the Divine. Merely reading and reciting the scriptures, going on pilgrimages, bathing in holy rivers, fasting, renunciation, celibacy, various yogic routines, charity, etc. are seen as useless exercises. Skills of the mind and body only enhance one's ego unless one has understood the Guru's Word. One has to cleanse one's mind of the taint of ego and in humility seek the True Guru's help in understanding the purpose of life. The True Guru instructs the Sikh about the Divine, warns him of the impediments, and instructs him in a lifestyle that would prepare him for the ultimate union with the Divine and for eternal joy. Meeting the True Guru is possible only through Vahguru's grace.

The Sikh faith denounces idolatry and hypocrisy and holds that the ultimate joy is obtained through constant remembrance of the Divine, enabling one to see Vahguru in oneself and in all of creation. Once this is understood, there can be no inequality among people, and no intolerance. A Sikh's motto is, *nam japo, kirt karo, vand chako* ("Remember the Divine, engage in honest labor, and share the fruits of that labor").

The daily recitation of specific passages from the *Guru Granth Sahib*, especially the Japu hymns, is recommended immediately after rising and bathing. Family customs include both reading passages from the scripture and attending the gurduara (inaptly *gurd-wara*, meaning "thru the guru"). The five daily Banis are found in the pothis, or small books, that many Sikhs carry with them. The pothis are handled very carefully and are wrapped in a clean cloth; one must wash one's hands before handling them. The Banis (Japji, Jap, Savaye, Rahiras, and Sohila) are read every day. Additionally, banis such as Caupai and Anand, among others are also recited daily by many Sikhs.

When Sikhs are performing their daily prayers and meditation, they sit comfortably on the floor, bed, or sofa, cross-legged with their spine in a straight position. It is usually preferred to reflect, recite, or sing in a quiet place in the house. Prayers are either read quietly from the pothis or are recited from memory.

Adult males are required to wear turbans and leave their hair and beards uncut. The turban represents respectability, and is a sign of nobility in the Sikh culture. Guru Gobind Singh gave all of his Sikhs turbans to recognize the high moral status that the Khalsa has to adhere to. A turbaned Sikh stands out in a crowd and is easily recognizable. The dastar, as the Sikh turban is commonly known as, is an article of faith, and all initiated Sikhs are required to wear one. The turban is believed to be more than just a piece of cloth, but becomes one and the same with the Sikh's head. There are many reasons a Sikh may have for wearing a turban, the most important of which is as an expression of love for and obedience to the wishes of the founders of their faith. Sikh women usually keep their hair combed downward and covered with a flowing scarf, but some also wear turbans in a similar style to those of the men. Essentially, dastar is assertion of Sikh sovereignty.

In many families, when a boy (girls in some cases) reaches a certain age—usually between eleven and sixteen—he is taken to a gurduara and, in the presence of the *Guru Granth Sahib* and following Ardas, his first turban is ceremonially tied on by the Granthi or by a Sikh elder. The ceremony, Dastar Bandi, is usually attended by many family members and friends. The turban is a crucial article of faith, considered to be more important that the five Ks by some Sikhs. Turbans may be of any color and are tied in many different ways and styles.

There are two types of proper Sikh headcoverings for males. Boys wear a patka, while grown men wear the full turban, called a pagri. This Sikh family was photographed in Delhi, India, in 1989.

D. Life Cycle Events

Birth

The Sikh naming ceremony takes place in a gurduara in the presence of relatives and friends soon after the birth of a child. The family offers donations, Karah Parshad, sacred pudding, and a rumala, which is a covering for the *Guru Granth Sahib* made of high-quality silk, cotton, or embroidered cloth. Prayers are offered asking for a special blessing of good health, long life, and the Sikh way of life (Gursikhi) for the child. After reciting Ardas, the *Guru Granth Sahib* is opened at a random point and the child is named using the first letter on the top left-hand corner of the left page. All boys are given the middle or last name Singh, meaning "lion," and all girls are given the middle or last name Kaur, meaning "princess."

When the name is selected by the family, the congregation gives approval by a felicitation or Jaikara: "*Jo Bole So Nihal! Sat Siri Akal!*" The ceremony ends with the distribution of Karah Prasad, and the placing of the rumala over the *Guru Granth Sahib*. Sometimes, sweets or langar, free food from the guru's kitchen, is served, but this is not an official part of the ceremony.

Initiation

Anyone who can read and understand the contents of the *Guru Granth Sahib*, and is mature enough to follow the Sikh code of conduct, can be initiated into the Sikh religion. The initiation ceremony, Khande di Pahul, is held in a holy place, preferably a gurduara. Five initiated Sikhs, known as the Khalsa, conduct the ceremony.

During the ceremony the *Guru Granth Sahib* is opened in the ceremonious way. One of the five Khalsas offers the formal prayer in the presence of the *Guru Granth Sahib*. Then a random reading from the scriptural canon occurs. The candidates for initiation join in a formal prayer. Then they stand in front of the congregation and ask their permission for admission into the Guru Khalsa Panth. They are

Sikh men—and women—possess five articles of faith at all times. Among them are a wooden comb (kanga), an iron bracelet (kara), and a strapped knife (kirpan). Not shown in this photograph are the keshas (uncut hair) and the kachira, a type of undergarment.

then instructed by one of the Khalsa in the various things they may and may not do after taking Ammrit (see below). After the acceptance of these instructions, the Ammrit (literally, "Immortality") is prepared. The water is stirred by all five Khalsas with a double-edged sword, the khanda. Five Banis are recited while the water is being stirred. After this, a prayer is said and another random verse is read from the *Guru Granth Sahib*. The Ammrit is then administered to each candidate in a ceremonial fashion. Following this, another prayer and reading are recited and the Karah Parshad is distributed to all.

Once a Sikh is initiated as such, he must have on his person at all times the "five Ks": the keshas (unshorn hair), the kirpan (traditional sword), the kachira (under-shorts), the kanga (comb), and the kara (iron bracelet).

Khande di Pahul, now known as the Ammrit Sanskar, was introduced by Guru Gobind Singh in 1699. It is an initiation with a double-edged sword. Addressing the congregation, Gobind Singh asked for a volunteer willing to present his head. He is said to have taken the volunteer inside then come back out with a sword dripping blood, asking for another. He gave the Khande di Pahul to five volunteers and called them his Panj Piare (Five Beloved Ones). He then asked them to give him the Pahul. The initiates were called Khalsa, meaning the "sovereign ones" (of the guru). The Khalsa lifestyle was to be that of "saint-soldiers" exemplified by the gurus during their own lifetimes. They were to bear arms, to be trained in their use and to be prepared to fight against injustice whenever the occasion arose. The Khalsa were required to wear the five Ks. The most visible of these is the uncut hair (kes in Panjabi). The four major transgressions that must be avoided by all initiated Sikhs are: dishonoring the hair, eating sacrificial meat (such as halal or kosher), extramarital sex, and using recreational intoxicants (such as alcohol, tobacco, drugs). Any Sikh who after taking the Pahul violates the commandments is a patit, or "fallen" one.

The role of the Khalsa has been to defend their faith, protect the weak, and to fight unjust oppression. Sikhs believe in universal equality, freedom of worship for all, and have always been ready to fight oppression in defense of the downtrodden.

Nuptials

Sikhs are joined in wedlock through the Anand Karaj, meaning "ceremony of bliss." The ceremony is conducted in a gurduara or any other suitable place where the *Guru Granth Sahib* is duly installed. During the ceremony, the couple circles the *Guru Granth Sahib* four times. The purpose of the ceremony is to implore the husband and wife to become "one spirit in two bodies." While the couple is circling, with the groom leading in a clockwise direction with the bride following as nearly as possible in step, the Lava is sung. The four verses of the Lava explain the four stages of married life. The first verse emphasizes the performance of duty to the family and the community. The second verse refers to the stage of yearning and love for each other. The third verse refers to the stage of detachment, or Virag. The fourth verse refers to the final stage of harmony and union in married life during which human love blends into the love for Vahguru.

Sikh marriages are usually casually arranged by relatives and close family friends who might suggest a suitable match for an eligible Sikh. After a mutual discussion between the boy or girl on one side, and his or her parents and relatives on the other, an agreement to marry can be arranged. Several criteria are adopted before making a marriage proposal. Most importantly, the boy and girl must announce their willingness for marriage, after taking into account compatabilities in the various dimensions which are deemed important.

Usually before the wedding day the Kurmai or Shagan occurs at the bridegroom's house or at the gurduara. Though there is no formal ceremony, there is always a promise to marry, an exchange of rings, and other presents.

Death and Burial

The Bhog, or death ceremony, is split into two parts: Saskar, the cremation of the body, and the Antim Ardas, the final prayer at the end of the ceremony. If cremation is not possible, any means of disposing of the body may be employed. The ashes are collected after the cremation and later disposed of by immersion in the nearest river or sea. During the funeral ceremony, the antim sanskar, the kirtan sohila, and ardas prayers are performed. The Antim Ardas involves a complete reading of the *Guru Granth Sahib* either at home or in a gurduara. This is what is known as the Sahaj Path, and is usually completed within specified days.

Sikh doctrine regarding reincarnation is somewhat complex. Life is to be celebrated and therefore mourning is discouraged. Death is expected and can happen at any time. As a result, each Sikh must fulfill all duties during his life, not putting off anything until death. Death is seen as the cessation of life and the extinction of the body and sense organs; it is the antithesis of life. Salvation doesn't occur after death; freedom is to be attained while alive. Yet, the soul, as part of the spiritual universe, moves up and down a hierarchy of existence that leads ultimately to communion with God. This may entail an episode as a creature on earth once again—or it may not.

E. Family Life

Husband and Wife

Marriage in Sikhism is monogamous and is regarded as a sacred bond in attaining worldly and spiritual joy. The guru speaks about an ideal marriage saying: "They are not husband and wife who only have physical contact; rather they are wife and husband who have one spirit in two bodies."

Divorce

According to Sikh religious rites, husband and wives are not allowed to divorce. A Sikh couple that wishes to divorce may be able to do so in a civil court, but this is not condoned by religious law.

IV. Organization and Infrastructure

A. Education and Hierarchy of Clergy

The Sikhs have no priests. Any Sikh, man or woman, can officiate at religious ceremonies.

Though generally the most knowledgeable person present is given the honor.

B. Shrines and Houses of Worship

ORGANIZATION

The gurduara is the Sikh place of learning and worship. The sangat is the congregation. Committees, elected by the local membership, manage the Sikh places of worship.

MAJOR ENCLAVES

Sikhs maintain temples in New York, Washington, D.C., Chicago, Houston, and a number of California locations. The largest of these institutions is located in Yuba City, California, and is also the biggest Sikh temple in the world.

The most famous shrine is the Harimandir Sahib in Amritsar, also known as the Golden Temple. Groups of Sikhs regularly visit and congregate at the Harimandir Sahib. On specific occasions, groups of Sikhs are permitted to undertake a pilgrimage to Sikh shrines in the province of Panjab in Pakistan, especially at Nankana Sahib and the samadhi (place of cremation) of Maharaja Ranjit Singh in Lahore.

This Sikh temple, or gurduara, is located in El Sobrante, California, and serves the Sikh population in the San Francisco Bay area.

C. Governance and Authority

The Akal Takht is the seat of supreme temporal authority for Sikhs around the world. Sikh congregations elect committees to run their facilities. Their common link is allegiance to Guru Panth and the Sikh Rahit Maryada (Sikh Principles of Living). All disputes can be appealed to Siri Akal Takhat Sahib.

D. Social Service Organizations

The Sikh Coalition is a community-based organization that defends civil rights and civil liberties in the United States. Its main role is to educate the broader community both about Sikhs and about diversity, along with promoting local community empowerment, and fostering civic engagement among Sikh Americans. The Sikh Coalition website is www.sikhcoalition.org.

The Sikh American Legal Defense and Education Fund (SALDEF) provides legal assistance, educational outreach, legislative advocacy, and media relations for American Sikhs. The organization was formerly known as SMART (Sikh Media Watch and Resource Task Force). The SALDEF website is www.saldef.org.

The Sikh Research Institute (SikhRI) is a community development organization that "imparts Sikh values through training and development, creates global awareness of Sikhi, and delivers strategic solutions to key issues." SikhRI is an educational institution focused on the internal development of Sikh Americans. Their website is www. sikhri.org.

Other organizations (and their websites) are:
- Ensaaf (Ensaaf.org)
- Sikh Human Rights Group (www.shrg.org)
- Sikh Youth Federation, U.S.A. (www.sikhyouthfederation.org)
- The Sikh Foundation (www.sikhfoundation.org)
- United Sikhs in Service of America (www.unitedsikhs.org)

FURTHER READING AND RESOURCES

The Sikhs of the Punjab
J.S. Grewal
1990: Cambridge University Press

Sikhism
Gurinder Singh Mann
2004: Prentice Hall Series

Textual Sources for the Study of Sikhism
W.H. McLeod
1984: University of Chicago Press

The Sikhs
Patwant Singh
2000: Knopf

WEBSITES ON SIKHISM

- www.sikhspectrum.com
  quarterly online newsletter

- www.sikhnet.com
  The Sikh Network

- www.sikhphilosophy.net
  the Sikhi Philosophy Network

- www.allaboutsikhs.com
  "Your Gateway to Sikhi"

- www.sikhiwiki.com
  Sikh Wikipedia (online encyclopedia)

- www.sikhwomen.com
  information for Sikh women

- www.worldsikhcouncil.org

∽

6 Taoism

I. Origins and Early History

A. Introduction

TAOISM (OFTEN WRITTEN AS DAOISM*) IS A WEB OF interwoven disciplines; a conglomeration of various strands of meditation, spiritualism, astral projection, highly focused physical movements, holistic medicine, ancient alchemy, and the development of inner metaphysical potentials. "Tao" literally means "way" or "path," but is construed metaphorically to refer to the way human beings make their way through the world. Taoism places emphasis on an individual's achievement of perfection, with the promised reward of immortality. The religion, the principal religious system of East Asia and, specifically, China for over two thousand years, is founded upon a mythical structure—one in which deities and

Taiji Quan, sometimes called tai chi, is a form of Chinese martial art. Movements are often performed slowly, and can be a form of meditation.

immortals may be appealed to for blessings in their specific areas of salvation and wisdom.

Taoists divide existence into three sectors: Humanity, Heaven, and Earth. These sectors essentially correlate with the principles of mind, spirit, and body. A Taoist sage lives by his belief in the interrelatedness of these elements, acting in accord with a fundamental understanding of the universal cause of being, rather than reacting to phenomenal observation, or effect. Therefore, while Taoists do certainly adhere to a physically disciplined lifestyle of health and exercise, more focus is placed upon spiritual regeneration as a means of achieving true harmony. Such harmony is not transcendental; on the contrary, it is a lived oneness with the natural world.

B. The Religion in America

The transmission of Taoism to North America from China is very poorly documented. Within the first 100 years of Chinese immigration to America, which began in 1849, there is not one individual or teacher on record who claimed to be a Taoist. There is evidence of a talk on Taoism in 1893, but the speaker remains anonymous and many believe that he was not a Taoist.

The Taiji Quan (shadow boxing) and Qi gong (breath work, or energy work) teachers and organizations are credited as being the most important

---

Throughout this chapter, we use the modern conventions of the Pinyin system of transliteration in place of the older Wade-Giles system—except for one word: Tao. We look forward to the day when "Dao," the proper Pinyin designation, replaces the older, but still popular, name for the religion.

groups involved in the transmission of Taoism to North America. Da Liu is the first person documented as a teacher on the ethics of Taiji Quan in New York City in the 1950s. He taught classes and wrote many books on the subject of Taoist practices.

Other than these teachers, Taoism eventually came to America through Chinese immigrants, mostly from Hong Kong and Taiwan, many of whom had immigrated in order to flee the Communist take-over of China in 1949. The earliest Taoist priest to arrive was Share K. Lew in San Francisco. In 1970, he, along with Khigh Dhiegh, formed the Taoist Sanctuary in Los Angeles. This was the first Taoist organization to receive federal status as a church. Now it has become the Taoist Institute of Los Angeles, and it offers instruction, guidance, and practice in a variety of Taoist traditions including Chinese philosophy and religion, the Yi jing, Qi gong, Chinese internal yoga and meditation, internal martial arts, and Chinese medicine. This organization embraces and propagates an understanding of Taoism in terms of self-cultivation with an emphasis on health and healing.

Moy Lin-Shin, a Taoist monk and teacher, emigrated from China and founded the Taoist Taiji Quan Society in Toronto in the mid-1970s; the religious arm of this organization is Fung Loy Kok; it conducts classes in 437 cities worldwide with major branches in Tallahassee, Florida, and Denver, Colorado. Within Taoist temples, the separate arts of Moy's Taiji Quan and chanting are practiced.

Hua-Ching Ni, an author, teacher, and physician of traditional Chinese medicine, is the founder of Integral Way Society in Santa Monica, California. This society focuses on the teachings of Lao Zi and the ancient Taoist sages as interpreted through Hau-Ching Ni. The premise of the organization is to promote balance, health, harmony, and virtue through personal growth and spiritual development.

Master Ni and his organizations are at the center of the Taoist community in North America. He began his teachings with an ongoing seminar called the College of Tao. In January 1989, he established the Yo San University of Traditional Chinese Medicine, a non-profit educational institution and a degree-granting college. Ni's two sons, Daoshing Ni and Maoshing Ni, now run the college.

Another prominent Taoist is Mantak Chia. He originally received his Taoist teachings in Hong Kong, where he studied under master Taoist Yi Eng. He later formed the Natural Healing Center, then moved to New York in 1979 and established the Healing Tao Center. Since then, many such centers have opened up across America.

Also located in New York City is the American Taoist and Buddhist Association. Created in 1979, this association provides both Taoist and Buddhist alters, offering members and the surrounding community a variety of rites and services, religious ceremonies, cosmic renewal rituals, and Taoist seminars and training. The association is committed to the community and offers a free Sunday vegetarian lunch for those in need.

Hsien Yuen, an immigrant from Taiwan, heads the Association. In his book *The Taoism of Sage Religion: True Principle*, Yuen describes himself as the "heir to the wisdom and tradition as transmitted through an unbroken succession of the Lungmen sect . . . fully empowered as a true Master of traditional Taoist disciplines, including all aspects of Taoist science and metaphysics." He is also one of the few American Taoists who claims to have an open communication with immortals and deities. With the American Taoist and Buddhist Association, he advocates and represents a ritual model. Through cosmic renewal and purification rites, Yuen ensures harmony and wellbeing in both the family and community.

C. Important Dates and Landmarks

ca. 550 BCE Daode Jing is written by Lao Zi.

ca. 350 BCE Zhuang Zi further develops Taoist philosophy.

ca. 150 BCE Immortality Taoism is developed; Taiping Jing is compiled.

226–49 CE Wang Bi introduces Taoist concepts into Confucian learning.

251–334 Wei Huacun becomes the first female leader of the Shangqing sect.

365–448 Kou Qianzhi revives Taoism of Heavenly Masters.

456–536 Tao Hongjing develops the Shangqing School.

618–626 Emperor Gaozu builds a great temple at the birthplace of Lao-Tzu.

637 Emperor Taizong (r. 626–649) issues an edict placing Taoists over Buddhists.

691 Empress Wu, Buddhist, reverses Taizong's policy and builds Buddhist temples.

712–756 Rule of Taoist Emperor Xuanzong; questions on Taoist texts become a feature of civil service examinations.

768–824 Emperor Han Yu opposes Buddhism.

845 Emperor Wu-zong persecutes Buddhists and all other non-Taoist religions.

960–1279 During the Song dynasty, Perfect Truth Taoism and Orthodox One Taoism arise and the Taoist canon is edited.

1500s Sanyi Jiao (Three-in-One Religion) is founded by Lin Zhaoen (1517–1598) as synthesis of Confucianism, Buddhism, and Taoism.

1584 Temple of the Three-in-One Religion built.

1644–1911 During the Manchu Qing dynasty, new movements founded within Taoism, Buddhism, and Christianity. Followers of "Three-in-One Religion" are persecuted.

1851 Hong Xiuquan founds the Heavenly Kingdom of Great Peace movement based on Christian ideas.

late 1800s Violent clashes arise between Christian missionaries and the Chinese people.

1912 China becomes a republic.

1919 The Fourth of May movement founded; uses science to stamp out religion.

1920s–1930s National Taoist organizations are founded.

1928 Taoist and Buddhist temples dismantled.

1950s–1960s Religions are tightly controlled by the Chinese government. Temples damaged during Cultural Revolution, 1966.

1970 First Taoist Sanctuary formed in Los Angeles by Share K. Lew and Khigh Dheigh.

1979 American Taoist and Buddhist Association is created in New York City. Taoism recognized (but tightly controlled) by PRC.

1989 Yo San University of Traditional Chinese Medicine is founded by Master Hua-Ching Ni.

D. Important Figures

Lao Zi

(Also spelled Laozi, Lao Tze, and Lao Tzu.)
Lao Zi is credited for having written the most important text in the Taoist religion, the *Daode Jing*.

It is thought that he lived in the sixth century BCE, though some historians believe he actually lived in the fourth century BCE—and others contend that he never lived at all, but is only a mythical figure.

According to legend, Lao Zi was a contemporary of Confucius and worked in the Imperial Library of the Zhou Dynasty. Confucius heard of Lao Zi's wisdom and decided that he wanted to travel and meet him. During this meeting they talked of ritual and propriety. It is said that these discussion proved more educational for Confucius than did the entire library.

Perceiving that the kingdom's affairs were disintegrating, Lao Zi decided to move elsewhere. On his journey, he came to Han Gu Pass, which was heavily guarded. The keeper of the pass noticed that Lao Zi was leaving the kingdom for good and asked him to write down a few of his philosophies. Lao Zi immediately wrote what became the *Daode Jing* and was never heard from again.

The legend goes on to say that Lao Zi lived for 900 years, which logistically accounts for the possibility that he was both Confucius's senior and contemporary.

Zhang Daoling

Zhang Daoling founded the Tianshi Dao (Way of the Celestial Masters) sect of Taoism. It is said that Lao Zi appeared to him and told him that the world was coming to an end and would be followed by an era of great peace. Lao Zi told him that those following him would go on to another life, which was part of the "Orthodox One Covenant with the Powers." Through this covenant, Zhang and his followers would have access to the celestial powers of those who control the fate of mankind.

The major change that Zhang made to the Taoist religion was the rejection of food and animal sacrifices.

Legend surmises that Zhang Daoling did not die, but rather, he ascended to heaven with his wife and two of his disciples, where he became deified as an Immortal. He is now known as the "Ancestral Celestial Master."

At some point during the Song Dynasty (960–1279), this statue of Lao Zi in Quanzhou, China, was carved into a rock at the foot of Mount Qingyuan. The figure is five meters (more than sixteen feet) tall—the biggest statue of Lao Zi in China.

Chen Bo

Chen Bo was an eminent Taoist of the later Five Dynasties and early Song. He was an exceptional personage who greatly contributed to Inner Alchemy and the Science of Changes. The Diagram of the Supreme Ultimate was originally transmitted by Chen Bo, who called it the Diagram of the Infinite.

Zhuang Zi (Chuang-Tzu)

Zhuang Zi was a philosophical Taoist in the Warring States period. He once worked as an official in a varnish tree farm, but decided that he wanted to live as a hermit instead. He despised fame and fortune and lived a simple life immersed in the Tao. He was an inheritor and promoter of Taoist thought, and believed that one should lead a nourishing life instead of being caught up by peripheral matters and being destroyed by desires.

During his lifetime he wrote many essays and poems important to the Taoist faith. His most important work, the *Zhuang Zi*, is believed to have been written mostly by his disciples, himself authoring only the first seven chapters. Nevertheless, his teachings have left a significant impact on Taoism.

Guanyin

Guanyin is a highly-ranked bodhisattva, alternately depicted as male or female. In English, "guan" may be translated as "to look on," while "yin" is "sound"; therefore, Guanyin is acknowledged as an Immortal who is receptive to all prayers. This has earned her the title Goddess of Mercy. Guanyin, in the masculine sense, is considered a savior and deliverer (especially of sailors on stormy seas); in the feminine, she is looked to as an ideal of graceful womanhood. It is said that Guanyin was the gatekeeper who asked Lao Zi to write down his philosophy; these writings later became the *Daode Jing*. (It is important to note that while Guanyin is worshiped in Taoist temples, she is primarily a Buddhist deity.)

Wei Boyang

Born into a distinguished family, Wei Boyang was reluctant to follow his relatives in securing an official gentry position, but rather immersed himself in the study of the Tao. He dedicated his life to the practice of perfection and secretly worked to attain to nothingness. Wei is most notably one of the greatest Chinese contributors to the science of alchemy, writing the earliest book on theoretical alchemy in the year 142 CE entitled *The Kinship of the Three*.

Ge Hong

Ge Hong developed the early immortal theories of the Tao. In his book *Inner Book of the Master Who Embraces Simplicity*, he wrote that the keys to obtaining immortality were to practice keeping the oneness, breath dirigation, gymnastics, and sexual arts. He stressed that those seeking immortality must have the fundamental virtues of loyalty, piety, gentleness, obedience, benevolence, and righteousness. He believed that one should practice nourishing life and the arts of immortality for the inner life, and the Confucian way for the outer, social life. He also believed that writing should contribute to enlightenment.

Ge Hong also wrote a book on the achievements of alchemy, and recorded a large number of ancient scriptures on alchemy and methods of alchemical fabrications of elixir. This work would hugely influence later developments in alchemy.

Ge Hong believed that Taoist priests should study medical skills in order to benefit mankind. His records contain the earliest treatment of smallpox on record. He also attained a vast knowledge of tuberculosis almost one thousand years earlier than Western science. His detailed accounts of the properties of medical plants greatly influenced the future development of the national medical science and pharmaceuticals.

Kou Qianzhi

Kou Qianzhi was given the commandments on the New Ordinances of the Clouds by an Immortal called the Supreme Venerable Sovereign. These commandments addressed the techniques of Gymnastics, Ingesting Vital Breath, and Oral Formulas. The Immortal also ordered him to abolish false Taoist techniques, attach the greatest importance to rituals and ordinances, maintain a dietetic regimen, and practice inner refinement.

Several years later, Kou was given the knowledge of golden alchemy, as well as secret Taoist techniques of summoning the gods and interrogating ghosts. He published these in his work *The Perfect Book of Registers and Charts*. Through his works, the Northern Celestial Masters Tradition was born.

During his life, Kou advocated ordaining only the worthy to official positions—individuals who observed the Five Eternal Virtues (the father's righteousness, the mother's affection, the elder brother's friendliness, the younger brother's respect, and the son's piety), followed the commandments, and cultivated good behavior. He also revised and increased several fast rituals and rites, which laid the foundation for those of later years.

Lu Xiujing

During his lifetime, Lu Xiujing rectified certain things that he felt were going wrong in Taoism. He forbade the self-ordination of Taoist officials and instituted a system of promoting rank according to one's merits and virtues. He maintained that the cultivation of Tao included recitation of scriptures and meditation to purify one's spirit and behavior, and that the supreme Tao can only be obtained whence the spirit and behavior are pure. He founded the Southern Celestial Masters Tradition.

Lu Xiujing also sorted and classified the Taoist cannon. He created a system for the classification that involved three grottoes, twelve sections, and four supplementary sections. This system was used during various periods following the Sui and Tang dynasties.

Tao Hongjing

Tao Hongjing is credited for being the founder of the Highest Clarity Sect as well as the Mount Mao sect. He sorted out materials about the missionary work of Yang Xi, Xu Mi, and other missionaries, and used his findings to compile the book *Declarations of the Perfected*. This was the systematic exposition of the history of the Highest Clarity Sect. He also compiled the *Illustrated Ranking of the Immortals*—the first Taoist book on theogony—in an effort to clarify theogonic confusion that had originated in the Wei and Jin dynasties.

Tao was also proficient in the art of healing and wrote many commentaries on the subject. The classification of medicine that he used on such topics as nourishing life and medicines are still used today.

Sima Chengzhen

Sima's Taoist theories influenced the development of Taoist Cultivation and Refinement theories. He believed that human beings are gifted with the qualities of Immortals; one must simply cultivate the "Vital Breath of Emptiness," fulfill one's nature, and keep in harmony with Tao to fully experience the realization of immortality. He also published a book in which he illuminated the seven stages for cultivating Tao and organized the process of attaining immortality into five "Gates of Progress." There Sima writes that the five gates and seven stages can be summed up in three rules: decrease involvement in human affairs, eliminate desire, and clear the mind.

Du Guangting

Du Guangting contributed to the establishment of Ritual Offerings of the Golden Registers, Yellow Registers, and Jade Registers, as well as the setting up of the altar, and conducting rituals. He also sorted and annotated the Taoist cannon. Through his writings, Du was a major contributor to the spread and development of Taoism.

Zhang Sanfeng

Zhang is a legendary, not historical, figure in Taoism. His major contribution was the invention of Taiji Quan (or Taij quan, shadowboxing) as a method of cultivating the Tao while keeping fit. Taiji Quan is still popular and widely used today. Zhang also founded the Wudang sect on Mount Wudang. He cleared the land and built the sect's temple himself, predicting even before its establishment that it would one day flourish.

II. Tenets and Beliefs

A. Articles of Faith

The Great Tao

Tao is the eternally existing origin of the world. It knows no limits in space or time, and is the source of all being. It is an undifferentiated whole preceding the existence of heaven and earth. It is empty, silent, and formless; it grows independently and is inexhaustible; it eternally revolves, never halting its movement. This force is so ancient, and so fundamentally different from all other forces, that it cannot be described in ordinary language. However, mortals must have some means of referring to it; hence, it is called "Tao," or "Great."

Tao is non-being, an existence that follows no earthly laws. Tao's transcendent and unlimited nature sets it apart from all beings possessing form, matter and a specific place in space-time. Tao is formless, and therefore unbound by concrete laws.

It is pure emptiness, while simultaneously the origin of the world and the generator of all movement and evolution in the universe.

The avatars of Tao are the Lordly Spirits and deities: Tao is emptiness and non-being, but it also has a divine nature. In a state of dispersion, it is formless and imageless Vital Breath; in a concentrated state, Tao forms Deities. Because Tao can transmute itself into deities, and man can cultivate the state of Tao within himself, man can become a deity through his attainment of this state of being. Within Taoism, deities are simply men who have achieved immortality through their cultivation of Tao. Attaining immortality is possible for all people; hence, the Taoist pantheon is open and limitless.

The creative function of Tao does not express itself through specific orders for mankind. It does not interfere with earthly life, but allows each person to follow one's own nature and path of growth and development from non-being to being and from being to non-being. This is called "Non-Interference." Though Tao does not interfere, it is not inactive. The Great Tao gives birth to all, but does not assume possession of mankind; it is the fundamental source of accomplishment, but claims no credit for it.

Tao is in a process of constant cyclical motion, always following the law of return to the opposite. Reciprocal concepts such as being and non-being, high and low, long and short, before and after are all relative and mutually generating. Fortune and misfortune depend on each other, each perpetually becoming its opposite. Tao will never rest in a state of normality, because even normality has its reciprocal: abnormality.

The Taoist concept of virtue is rich in meaning. Generally speaking, virtue and Tao are two aspects of a single concept: virtue is the reflection of Tao, and Tao is the root of virtue. Tao begets all things, and virtue fosters them. Tao is the fundamental origin of all beings, while virtue is the reflection of Tao in all beings. Tao is formless and imageless; virtue, as the manifestation of Tao in all concrete things, is also formless. However, while Tao is emptiness and governs non-being, virtue exists in all concrete things and governs being. This latter statement is not meant to indicate a disparity or separation between the two concepts; rather, it reflects the different functions of each element within different situations. Indeed, Taoists often refer to Tao and virtue as a single concept that is absolutely void and still, and the ultimate abstruse ancestor of all beings. As the reflection of Tao in all beings, virtue can be said to be each concrete being's attainment of Tao.

According to Taoism, a man of genuine virtue is not actively conscious of his virtue. Alternatively, a man who prides himself on his own virtue is not truly virtuous. A seeming disparity arises here when one considers the Taoist belief that all men inherently possess virtue. The religion explains this conflict with the example that human beings are subject to many external stimuli over the course of their lives, resulting in a mental attraction to external glory and splendor. This distraction by fame and wealth distances a person from virtue. Therefore, Taoism counsels men to eliminate selfish desires, explore one's inner nature, and embrace one's spontaneous Tao. Such feats require indifference to fame or gain, and abstinence from seeking comfort in material desires. If the mind is free of preconceived ideas, free of pressure, free of confused desires, is magnanimous and big-hearted, empty, still, and unsullied, then it will be in natural harmony with Tao, and will manifest true virtue.

Mentally eliminating vulgar attachments for the sake of cultivating virtue does not imply that one should ignore society and the sufferings of people. On the contrary, Taoists do care for the collective good of all people, and advocate universal salvation. Taoists are therefore advised to accumulate merit through community service, and this action is the first state of virtue cultivation. Taoists do not seek reward for establishing merit in service of needful humanity, and do not desire to be known for their good deeds; instead, they believe that the spirits in heaven and earth will naturally recognize their good works. This type of merit is called "hidden virtue" or "hidden merit." Taoism advocates a broad accumulation of hidden merit.

Spontaneity is an attribute of Tao. Lao Zi says: "Man follows earth, earth follows heaven, heaven follows Tao, Tao follows spontaneity." Tao is the ultimate existence; no other existence is above it or precedes it. Therefore, it does not follow anything but itself. Heshang Gong's Han dynasty interprets this idea as, "The nature of Tao is spontaneity; it is ruled by nothing."

"Spontaneous" is often substituted for the word "natural," as in, "all beings have their own nature," which is spontaneous. When man becomes consumed with fame and material substance, he loses his natural spontaneity. Spontaneity also has the quality of non-interference. Tao does not interfere and does not give orders, but spontaneously generates the myriad beings of earth. To achieve non-interference and to unite with Tao is to achieve a state of spontaneity.

The concept that "Tao follows spontaneity" and the principle of non-interference do not imply that one should remain inactive, but rather that he should avoid excessive human interference. Observation is recommended as a preferable alternative.

Cosmogony

Taoism has developed a rich literature regarding the process of the creation of the world. The notion of universal cycles is an important concept in Taoist cosmogony. A single universal cycle includes both the creation of a universe and its destruction. An easy way to picture this creation and destruction is yin-yang (see page 652 for more on yin-yang and dualities). Existence is comprised of an endless process of such repeating cycles. The major universal cycles are named in sequence; for example, "Dragon Han," "Extended Well-Being," "Crimson Light," etc. This succession of cycles has been recurring for an indeterminable number of ages.

Upon the completion of a cycle, the extinguished universe plunges into a period of darkness, across which the mighty "Diamond Wind" blows through a world of chaos—a space of infinite emptiness and absolute darkness in which no light, form, or image may be found. Only the most accomplished deified immortals are capable of surviving such apocalypse, and will continue to exist through the formation of a new cycle.

It is at this point of cycle termination that existence will undergo a new birth and growth of nature and the new cycle will begin. As the space-time in which we presently live is considered by Taoists to be part of the cycle of Crimson Light, the past formation of our present universe is referred to as "The Appearing of the Crimson Light."

According to the ancient legend of Taoist cosmogony, the formation of a new cycle originates with the commingling of the Vital Breaths of Tao, during which an octagonal book—symbolizing "Essential Truth"—suddenly emerges from the void. Rays of light stream forth from the eight corners of the book, which serve as an indication to the Primeval Lord of Heaven (the highest divinity of Taoism) that a new cycle must be inaugurated. The Primeval Lord of Heaven subsequently places the book—written in jade characters—into the "Forges of Heaven," heating the book until its jade characters emit crimson rays of light. At this point, they have officially become "Crimson Characters." These Crimson Characters are said to be the source of the heavens, and are called the "Original Matrix"—the "root of the world." *The Book of Salvation* (formally known as *The Lofty and Sublime Book of the Limitless Salvation of the Supreme Pervasive Mystery and Numinous Treasure*)—anonymously written but considered "the leader of all scriptures" and given primary placement in the Daoist canon of the Zhengtong Era—describes this period of cycle and rebirth as, "The Crimson Characters of the Grotto of Chaos are the word of essential truth arising from the absolute void. At the very beginning of the cycle, it forms the cosmos and makes the sun, the moon and the stars send forth their light. It is the origin of the heavens. It has no ancestor; its essence is of Tao."

The Original Matrix weaves itself in all directions, creating thirty-six heavens: eight in each cardinal direction, and one each in the directions of Northeast, Northwest, Southeast, and Southwest. Thirty-five of these heavens exist within the thirty-sixth heaven, called the Great Overarching Heaven. Taoism names the Great Overarching Heaven as the home of the Primeval Lord of Heaven, who resides on Jade Capital Mountain. This latter heaven is believed infinite, while the thirty-five heavens comprising it are said to be finite. At the completion of the creations of the heavens, which compose the new universe, the Primeval Lord of Heaven opens the Perfect Script of the Five Divine Tablets—a document integral to the formation of various spirits. He also reveals holy scriptures, through which he teaches Tao, or "the way," offering salvation to newly reincarnated humanity. Those who possess superior spiritual affinity, allowing them to attain salvation, may ultimately join the ranks of Immortals. It is said in Taoism that the scriptures revealed by the Primeval Lord of Heaven at the beginning of a cycle are the most mysterious of all Tao scriptures.

Taoist cosmogony divides the thirty-six heavens of the universe into distinct worlds. Twenty-eight of the heavens are divided between three worlds: the World of Desire, the World of Forms, and the World of Formlessness. Each being born into one of these three worlds is subject to reincarnation through the cycles and karma. The remaining eight heavens house the Immortals—those who have achieved salvation through the cultivation of Tao, and may therefore escape cyclical apocalypse and reincarnation.

The World of Desire includes six heavens. Visible form and desire comprise this world; men and women have intercourse and procreate. The World of Form includes eight heavens. Here, there is form but no desire. Humanity does not engage in sexual intercourse, and the creation of new human beings occurs through the conglomeration of Vital Breath. In the World of Formlessness—comprised of four heavens—there exists neither form nor desire.

The humanity of the World of Formlessness cannot be seen by the humanity of other worlds; only Immortals have the capability of recognizing formless humans.

Taoism further divides the universe into nine levels, which are called the Nine Realms: Realm of Colorful Brilliance; Realm of Diamond Brilliance; Realm of Paraffin Brilliance; Realm of Humid Brilliance; Realm of Golden Millet Brilliance; Realm of Diamond and Iron Brilliance; Realm of Water Brilliance; Realm of Great Wind Brilliance; Colorless Diamond-Link Realm of the Pervasive Abyss. Each of these realms can further de divided into four realms, for a total of thirty-six realms—each governed by an Emperor of the Soil.

The Taoist underworld of hell is believed dark and obscure. Mortals cannot enter the netherworld, but the souls of the mortal dead, as well as ghosts and goblins, are "locked up" there—specifically, in a place the Chinese call "Supreme Yin." The underworld is governed by the Five Kings of Hell.

Vital Breath

In Taoist doctrine, "Vital Breath" is defined as the source and fundamental substance of all beings—both phenomenal and spiritual. Hence, it is considered "the unified foundation of the universe." Vital Breath exists in different densities and states of order: the clearest and least dense forms of Vital Breaths float upward to form heaven, while heavy and dense Vital Breath sinks downward to form Earth. Harmoniously ordered Vital Breath coagulates to form man, while dispersed and disorderly Vital Breath disperses to form all other beings.

Taoism states that man is composed of three elemental states of Vital Breath: Essential Matter (the material essence of Vital Breath), Vital Breath, and Spirit. Vital Breath is also held responsible for the creation of spirits, and for this process may also exist in varying forms. For example, Proper Vital Breath transforms itself into "proper spirits," while Deviant Vital Breath transforms itself into malicious demons and monsters. Therefore, Daoism advocates purifying

Vital Breath, disseminating Proper Vital Breath, and eliminating Deviant Vital Breath.

A person who wishes to unite with Tao is advised to strive to master the unlimited powers attributed to Vital Breath. Once achieved, these powers are said to grant a person long life and eternal vision, as well as the ability to perform feats considered impossible by ordinary people.

Returning to the Infinite

Tao has never not existed. It preceded heaven and earth, and will succeed the termination of all universal cycles. Furthermore, it occupies infinite space. Hence, Tao is denoted as "the Infinite."

This phrase is sometimes used in juxtaposition with the present existence of Tao; however, when used in discussions of universal evolution, "the Infinite" often describes the period of time preceding Heaven and aarth's formations, whereas "Tao" describes the chaos that directly produced heaven and earth. From this perspective, the Infinite is the origin of "the Supreme Infinite" (present Tao). Therefore, to fully unite with Tao, humans must seek a spiritual return to the essential origins, or roots of Tao. This process is called "Returning to the Infinite."

The Five Supremes

Between the Infinite and the evolution of heaven and earth from chaos, Tao passes through five qualitative stages, which Taoists refer to as the "Five Supremes." The first is the Supreme Change, or the infinite void before Yin and Yang divide and Vital Breath appears. As the Supreme Change, Tao is silent and formless. Following Supreme Change is Supreme Origin. This stage marks the origin of Vital Breath. Tao next evolves into the Supreme Beginning, which initiates the development of form in the universe. At this point, Yin and Yang begin their intercourse. The Supreme Simplicity follows, during which substance emerges from the establishment of form. However, neither form nor substance yet constitutes body. After this fourth stage, Tao reaches the state of chaos requisite to the formation of heaven

The traditional symbol of Yin and Yang has become an almost universally recognizable visual representation of opposing yet complementary forces.

and earth, or the Supreme Ultimate (the fifth and final stage). From the Supreme Ultimate emerge heaven and earth, and all beings inhabiting them. Illustrations depict the Supreme Ultimate and give rise to mystical interpretation and analysis that remind many of Kabbalistic musings of the Jewish tradition. This affinity has been noticed by many authors in both traditions and has spawned a dialogue between the two communities.

Yin-Yang

Another diagrammatic depiction of the Supreme Ultimate is the Yin-Yang symbol (*shown above*). In the Yin-Yang, a curved line divides the circle into two halves, one half white and the other black. The white represents Yang and the black represents Yin. There is a black dot in the white part and a white dot in the black part, signifying that there is Yin in Yang and there is Yang in Yin. If the two halves are separated they resemble two fishes; therefore, the diagram is popularly called the "Yin-Yang Fishes."

It deeply and visually indicates that everything in the universe forms a unified whole made up of the two opposite and complementary forces of Yin and Yang. If one cuts this circle in half with a straight line through its center, both halves will always contain both Yin and Yang elements, showing that none of its components can ever be independent and free of internal tension.

Yin-Yang is intrinsic to the universe. The source of Yang is Tao. The Laozi states that Tao gave birth to the primordial organic unity, from which are derived the two opposite forces that interpenetrate each other, giving birth to the myriad beings. The backside of all beings is Yin while their front side is Yang; the Vital Breaths of Yin and Yang cross-penetrate until they reach a harmonious state. The generation of Yin and Yang by Tao creates the most fundamental forces of the universe, which are both in opposition and in unity. These Vital Breaths are both mutually opposite and mutually generating. At the same time, they are intrinsic to everything. Ying-Yang's unity in opposition manifests itself in countless ways. As expressed in humanity, it may be found in the relationship between the male and female genders, and the dual human dimensions of the spiritual (Yang) and the material (Yin). Regarding the physical universe, heaven is Yang and earth is Yin; mountains are Yang and waters are Yin, etc. Taoists believe that mountains, water, grass, wood, earth, stones, ghosts, spirits, and so on all contain Yin and Yang aspects.

The Five Agents

The Five Agents are a fundamental classification system for all things. The relationships between the Five Agents represent the basic relationships between all things. The Five Agents are wood, fire, earth, metal, and water, each having manifold meanings, which it would be impossible to fully enumerate. Below is a brief list of the meanings most commonly used in Taoist religious practice and Scriptures:

- Five Agents: Wood, fire, earth, metal, and water
- Five Directions: East, south, center, west, and north
- Five Colors: Green, red, yellow, white, and black
- Five Flavors: Sour, bitter, sweet, acrid, and salty
- Five Planets: Jupiter, Mars, Saturn, Venus, and Mercury
- Five Viscera: Liver, heart, spleen, lung, and kidney

Mutual generation and mutual control characterize the relationships between the Five Agents. "Mutual generation" is the birth of one agent from another according to a specific order. Mutual generation occurs is an endless cycle. "Mutual control" is the restriction of one agent by another agent, also according to a specific (though different from that of generation) order. The cycle of control is also endless: each controlling agent is also under the control of another agent in a different situation.

The order of mutual generation is as follows: wood generates fire; fire generates earth; earth generates metal; metal generates water; water generates wood. The order of mutual control is as follows: wood overcomes earth; earth overcomes water; water overcomes fire; fire overcomes metal; metal overcomes wood.

When the Five Agents are enumerated in the order of wood, fire, earth, metal, water, one can say that in the cycle of mutual generation each agent generates the next agent down the list; while in the cycle of control each agent overcomes the next agent down the list.

The Supreme Ultimate gives birth to Yin and Yang, which, through their intercourse and transformations, give birth to the Five Agents, each of which, in turn, has Yin and Yang aspects. For example, the Agent Fire is expressed in man as his Spirit, which can be divided into Yin Spirit and Yang Spirit, and hence Yin Fire and Yang Fire. Earth expresses itself as man's consciousness. But consciousness can be divided into correct knowledge and confused thoughts. Correct knowledge is Original Spirit, and is also called the male (Yang) earth, while the confused thoughts are called female (Yin) earth. The latter is one element of humanity that must be eliminated through the process of self-refinement.

The Immortals

The highest-ranking divinities of Taoism are called the Three Pristine Ones. They are as follows:

1. The Primeval Lord of Heaven. The Primeval is one of the highest divinities of Taoism. It is believed that he exists eternally. He occupies the highest position in heaven, called the Jade Clarity Realm, where all Immortals must go to pay their respects to him. At the formation of each new heaven and earth, the Primeval Lord of Heaven inaugurates the new kalpa (cycles) and offers salvation to humanity by teaching them the secret Tao.

2. The Heavenly Lord of the Numinous Treasure. This lord is second to the Primeval Lord of Heaven. He is the ruler of the Sun Palace of Stamen Pearls, and governs the Seven Purple Chambers of Light. According to the Pervasive Mystery's Book of Original Deeds, the Heavenly Lord of the Numinous Treasure saves people by using the Laws of the Numinous Treasure. Whenever an inquisitive man with affinities raises questions, the Heavenly Lord of the Numinous Treasure teaches kindly and generously. He has the ability to transform into thirty-six different forms and seventy-two different apparitions, which skill allows him to immediately attend to the wishes of the people in tens of thousands of places at once.

3. The Heavenly Lord Of Dao. This lord is also known as the oft-mentioned Lao Zi. It is said that he was born before heaven and earth, after a seventy-two-year-long stay in his mother's womb. He was born under a plum tree with the ability to speak, and took his surname "Li" after the tree. His position in the heavens is in the middle of the fourth rank, in the Supreme Ultimate Palace of the Supreme Clarity Realm. The Seven Slips of a Cloudy Satchel says, "[Lao Zi] is the venerable sovereign and avatar of Dao. He is the ancestor of original Vital Breath and the root of heaven and earth . . . He is called the highest true perfect Dao, numinous and subtle beyond name."

4. The Jade Emperor. This Immortal is the emperor of ten thousand spirits and of all heavens—the King of all Immortals. All the spirits follow and attend to him in queue, in the same manner an emperor is ministered to in the human world. He is said to be the incarnation of the Three Pristine Ones, and as such, he is the master of the three fundamentals in change: heaven, earth, and man.

5. The Heavenly Lord of Supreme Oneness and Salvation from Misery. This Immortal is also the "Great Benevolent One of the Heavenly Court's Eastern World of Eternal Happiness." It is said that he is everywhere—in the Heavenly Palace, the human world, and in hell, as the powerful governor of the devils. It is believed that he can transform into anything in response to a human appeal for salvation. He serves to save those sentient beings who express the highest forms of holiness, benevolence, extreme kindness, and love. According to legend, a man in distress need only recite the name of the Heavenly Lord of Supreme Oneness and Salvation from Misery, and he will receive help and relief in response to his cry for help. As for those who have accumulated merits perfectly, this Heavenly Lord will descend on his immortal cart of nine masters and, shining forth the auspicious lights of the hundred treasures, lead those perfect beings to their ascension to Immortality.

The Officials

1. The Heavenly Official. This official is in charge of all of the emperors of all the heavens. It is said that on every fifteenth day of the first month of the lunar calendar, he descends to the human world and inspects and decides the sins and blessings of men, and thus is also called the "Heavenly Official Who Confers Blessings."

2. The Earthly Official. This official is in charge of the Five Emperors of the Five Sacred Mountains and the Earthly Immortals of all places. It is said that every fifteenth day of the seventh month of the lunar calendar he comes to the human world, inspects the sins of men, and absolves them.

3. The Water Official. The Water Official is in charge of all of the Immortals who reside in water. It is said that every fifteenth day of the tenth month of the lunar calendar he comes to the human world to inspect sins and good fortune and eliminates the misfortunes of men.

4. The Four Heavenly Ministers. These ministers are the Great Jade Emperor, the Middle Heaven

Great Emperor of the North Pole Star of Purple Subtlety, the Great Heavenly Emperor of the Highest Palace of Polaris, and the Imperial God of Earth. The Heavenly Emperors of the four poles have their respective functions: The North Pole Emperor of Purple Subtlety is in charge of all stars; the South Pole Emperor of Longevity is in charge of all spirits; the Heavenly Emperor of the Supreme Ultimate is in charge of the longevity of all spirits; and the East Pole Emperor of Blue Essence is in charge of the salvation of all sentient beings.

5. **The Emperors of the Soil.** These are the thirty-six earth spirits of Taoism. The Emperors of the Soil are the spirits in charge of the earth realms in all directions. Taoism regards the emperors of the Soil as subordinate spirits to the Imperial Goddesses of Earth, with the task of mastering Yin and Yang, eliminating darkness and elevating divinity.

6. **The Queen Mother of the West.** The Queen Mother is the ancestor of the female Immortals. All women who have attained immortality in the three realms and ten directions, in heaven or in the human world, are under the rule of the Queen Mother of the West. She commands all spirits and perfected saints, and is in charge of the attendants of all the heavens as well as the inspector of the higher saints.

7. **The Thunder Patriarch.** The ninth son of the Primeval Lord of Heaven, the Thunder Patriarch is in charge of thunder and rain. He also leads the twenty-four law-protecting heavenly sovereigns who bring wind and rain. Placed before the Heavenly Lord are thirty-six thunder drums in the charge of thirty-six spirits. When the time has come for thunder, the Thunder Patriarch beats the drum once, after which Grandpa Thunder and the Master of Thunder throw out thunderbolts. It is also believed that the Thunder Patriarch announces fortune or misfortune and confers life or death after the evaluation and inspection of the people.

The Stellar Sovereigns

1. **The Great Perfect Warrior Emperor.** Also known as the "Mysterious Warrior," this emperor

consists of the seven northern constellations, among which is the Dipper Constellation. In Taoism, the southern Dipper decrees life and the northern death; hence, worship of the Dipper stars takes on special import.

2. **The Imperial Sovereign Wenchang.** This is a collective name for the six stars of the Wenchang constellation, each possessing its own name: Highest General, Assistant General, Noble Premier, Controller of Destinies, Controller of the Middle, and Controller of Wealth. Wenchang is a model for filial piety and benevolence. According to the *Book of Hidden Virtues of Imperial Sovereign Wenchang*, Imperial Sovereign Wenchang was incarnated as a high official in the human world seventy-three times. As an honest and clean official, he was never cruel to people. Instead, he "helped people in need, forgave others their mistakes, was merciful to the orphans, and moved the heavens with many merits."

3. **The Stellar Sovereign of the Five Planets and Seven Stars.** This name refers to seven Taoist deities: the Year Star (Jupiter), the Sparkling Deluder (Mars), the Grand White Star (Venus), the Chronographic Star (Mercury), and the Quelling Star (Saturn). Along with the sun and the moon, these deities make up the Seven Stars, or Stellar Sovereigns. The sun is the essence of Yang (male) and the moon is the essence of Yin (female).

4. **The Four Numinous Animals and Twenty-Eight Constellations.** The Four Numinous Animals are the figures formed by the stars in the four cardinal directions: the Blue Dragon in the East, the White Tiger in the West, the Red Phoenix in the South, and the Black Warrior in the North. The twenty-eight constellations are the ancient astronomers's distinctions and signs of the fixed star areas where the sun and moon pass by. These are the guardians of the greater divinities.

5. **The Big Dipper.** The Big Dipper is known as the mother of the stars of the Dipper. According to the Fundamental Destiny Life-Prolonging Heart Scripture of the Great Sagely Primordial Sovereign of the Supreme, Mysterious, and Numinous, the Big

Dipper, "with her great merit of medicine and healing, manages and harmonizes the Five Agents, balances the Vital Breaths of Yin and Yang, dissolves the stagnant and eliminates the evil and dark. Under her mercy, those who miss the time of salvation catch up with the time of salvation. In charge of the safety of pregnancy and birth, as well as the healing of diseases, she takes the important role of Heavenly Healer." She is in charge of the production and life of Heaven, Earth, and all things.

6. The Sixty Daily Spirits of the Heavenly Stems and Earthly Branches. A cycle of Twelve Terrestrial Branches correlated with Ten Celestial Trunks forms sixty units to mark the year, month, day, and hour. In Taoism, each of the sixty units has a year spirit, who is called the Supreme Year Star on Duty. The Supreme Year Star on Duty is in charge of people's luck or misfortune during the year. It leads the spirits, decides their direction, runs the order of time, and takes responsibility for the years.

Spirits of Mountains, Rivers, Seas, Thunder

1. The Emperor of the Sacred Mountain of the East. This deity is Emperor of Mount Tai, located within the Shandong province. People worship Mount Tai because they considered it the way to heaven and equal to heaven in height. As it lies in the east, it is said to be where all things begin at the intercourse between Yin and Yang. Taoists believe that the Emperor of the Sacred Mountain of the East knows the length of each man's life.

2. The Primordial Lady of the Emerald Cloud. The Primordial Lady commands the heavenly generals and divine soldiers in the mansion of Mount Tai to inspect all the virtuous and evil deeds in the human world by order of the Jade Emperor. She holds vast magic powers, cures the sick, and protects the affairs of farming, trade, travel, and marriage.

3. The Five Supreme Commanders of the Thunder Agency. The Five Supreme Commanders of the Thunder Agency are frequently seen in Taoist scriptures and books and have portraits enshrined in some Taoist temples. Their names are Deng, Bi, Liu, Xin, and Pang. Deng is the chief among laws and decrees and of the interrogation and summoning of the Thunder Agency. Bi is the master of dragons, is in charge of the Thunder court, controls the dryness and wetness of heaven and earth, checks the activities of demons, and attacks those who are not benevolent or upright. Liu can summon wind and rain, and is in charge of various kinds of affairs of the prince palace of the Thunder Agency. Xin is responsible for the affairs in the five directions, traveling back and forth in the heavens, and eliminating the evil ghosts and demons in this world and the netherworld. Pang guards the gate of heaven in order to vanquish the demons in the netherworld and exterminate the old evils.

4. The Father of Thunder and the Mother of Lightning. The Father of Thunder is in charge of thunder, and the Mother of Lightning is in charge of lightning. Thunder and lightning avenge wrongs committed in accordance with heaven's decree, punishing hidden misdeeds and striking miscreants to death.

5. The Dragon King. The functions of the Dragon King are to conjure up clouds and rain, rid people of scorching weather, and regulate rivers and watercourses.

6. The Master of Rain. The Master of Rain can appear as a spirit, or in human form. As his name implies, he controls the rain.

7. The Earl of Wind. The Earl of Wind governs the rising and fading of wind in the eight directions and exerts mastery over the clouds.

Spirits of the Soil and Local Protector Spirits

1. The City God. The City God protects the common people in his own city, which entails maintenance of the safety and peace of the common people and supervision of the officials, including the redressing of errors. The City God governs in heaven's name, dispels villains, benefits all things, judges his subjects' lives and deaths, and bestows happiness and longevity upon them. He also manages the household registers of the netherworld.

2. The Earth Spirit. The Earth Spirit carries and gives birth to everything on Earth. She blesses the safety of houses, the birth of babies into families, the thriving of domestic animals, and just behavior.

3. The Door (Gate) Spirits. The spirits who guard the doors of houses ward off evil spirits, demons, harassment, and invasion.

4. The Kitchen Spirits. The Kitchen Spirits are in charge of cooking in the human world. They also supervise human evils as well as a family's lives and deaths, misfortune, and happiness. In return for burnt incense and candles, the Kitchen Spirits protect a family's health and safety. They also inspect the family's good and evil deeds and present the family's merits and misdoings to the Jade Emperor at the end of each month.

Spirits of Wealth and Longevity

1. Spirit of Wealth This spirit controls thunder and lightning, dominates wind and rain, eliminates plague and disease, resists disasters and bad luck, brings justice to the victims of wrong verdicts, bestows wealth on fair business practices, and rewards pious prayer.

2. The Stars of Luck, Wealth, and Longevity. The Star of Luck refers to the Heavenly Official. He confers good luck on people. He is also the commander of all ghosts and spirits, the "Great Sage of Spontaneity," controller of the heavenly world, and protector of the eternity of heaven. The Star of Wealth refers to Wenchang. This deity is a bundle of six stars who rewards contributions and encourages well-educated people. He is also considered responsible for the careers of the literati. The Star of Longevity refers to the Venerable Old Man of the South Pole. He foretells the lifespans of the emperors.

The Guardians of Hell

1. The Great Emperor of Fengdu. This is the divinity that controls hell and the dead, also known as the king of all spirits. Upon death, each person's soul travels to hell to be judged by the King of Spirits. He discriminates between the souls based on the evils their persons committed while alive. Family members of the deceased may benefit the fate of guilty souls by atoning for its sins through ritual offerings. If appeased, the Great Emperor of Fengdu may decide to pardon the sinful souls, sentencing them to endure hardships—after which they may go to heaven—rather than remain in hell.

2. The Yamas of the Ten Halls. These deities are also known as the "Kings of Hell," or the "Kings of Souls." Each resides in his own hall. In the first hall resides King Qinguang, who rules over man's birth, life, death, and luck. King Chujiang lives in the second hall, and the ruler of the Ice Hell. King Songdi, resides in the third hall, and rules over the Black Rope Hell. In the fourth hall lives King Wuguan, who is the ruler of the Blood Pool Hell. In the fifth hall, King Yanluo runs the Wailing Hell. In the sixth hall, King Diancheng runs the Grand Wailing Hell, as well as the City of Innocent Deaths. King Taishan directs the Human Flesh Jam Hell from the seventh hall. The eighth hall contains King Dushi, who controls the Suffocation Hell. In the ninth hall, King Pingden rules the Avici Hell of the Iron web. The tenth hall houses King Zhuanluan, who is in charge of discriminating between ghosts according to their behavior, and deciding affairs such as grades and transmigration. When transmigration occurs, human affairs such as pregnancy, birth, sex, wealth, and lifespan are notated each month and sent to King Qinguan, who files this information away.

3. Mongpo. When a soul is reincarnated as a man, the deity Mongpo forces the man to imbibe a potion that erases the memory of his previous life.

Perfect Men and Immortals

1. Three Mao Perfect Sovereign Brothers. These brothers are considered to control men's destiny and wealth. The Elder Sovereign Mao acts as assistant of the Supreme Ultimate; the Middle Sovereign Mao and the Younger Mao are only earth immortals.

2. The Eight Immortals. The Eight Immortals represent eight aspects in the Taoist's daily life: men and women, wealth and poverty, youth and old age, and nobility and lowliness.

This relief sculpture of the Eight Immortals comes from a temple in Hue, Vietnam.

4. The Motherly Matriarch. The Motherly Matriarch is the protector of the sea. She saves wrecks, those in danger, and innocent souls seeking release. She also saves businessmen, farmers, craftsmen, soldiers, women suffering from difficult labor, and patients—if they call her name piously and state their wishes.

5. Numinous Official Wang. This Immortal is considered to be the protector of Taoist skills and altars. He has a special affinity for determining truth and falsehood. Many Taoist temples place statues of the Numinous Official Wang at their gates in hopes of reaping his special protective skills.

B. Social Ideals

Taoism calls for supreme peace, which it holds may be attained through the dissemination of Tao. Tao's essential peacefulness reflects its harmony with nature; stable societies and peaceful relationships must be supposed in alignment in Tao. By this reasoning, troubles, quarrels and riots occur when people rebel against Tao, or live their lives in opposition to natural laws.

One may find the meaning of Tao and virtue through meditation and specific insight, rather than in subjective statements or fabrications. Tao exists universally, and changes as the world changes. In order to remain in agreement with the ever-changing Tao, then, one must seek its essence in one's own inner simplicity. As one realizes his innermost nature, he also realizes his perfection, and begins to live in accord with this perfection, or virtue. Therefore, seeking Tao also serves to enhance one's morality.

In the Tao, all beings are equal and have no differences. This equality includes a general concern for others. In the *Book of Salvation*, this concern is enumerated as the Ten Prohibitions:

1. No murdering
2. No injuring
3. No envying
4. No hating
5. No indulging in promiscuity
6. No stealing
7. No indulging in greed
8. No indulging in corrupt desires
9. No abominating
10. No suspecting others

In addition to the above, one should never lie or use offensive language, and should treat others as they would their own family members. Taoism states that if everyone were to follow these guidelines, each member of society would experience a universal love, and supreme peace would be established. Furthermore, social classes would be abolished, and the world's wealth shared among the people.

Taoism opposes war. A Taoist will only fight in defense, when attacked. But he does not delight in the killing or hurting of others.

A harmonious relationship between nature and humanity is a prerequisite to social stability and prosperity. Taoism stresses the importance of this relationship, which includes the protection of nature. Taoism believes that wealth is generated in accord with the natural state of the environment, rather than through human exploitation of the earth's natural resources.

Purity, Tranquility, and Non-Interference

Tranquility is more powerful than unrest because it is the abode of Tao. Every man must inevitably return to original purity and tranquility, which is called, "returning to the origin," a state of eternity. According to Lao Zi, this state is the essence of Tao and the only reliable way to observe and understand the movements of the Great Tao. In order to align oneself with the Great Tao, one must maintain inner emptiness and tranquility.

A man can obtain tranquility by mentally purging his desires and ambitions. According to the *Sublime Book of the Supreme Venerable Sovereign's Teachings on Eternal Purity and Tranquility*, a man's original spirit is inclined to purity, but his heart disturbs it; a man's inner nature is inclined to tranquility, but his sensual desires mislead it. A man misled by his desires is likely to produce evil passions, which is described as the Three Poisons: the Poison of Negative Spirit, the Poison of Negative Essential Matter, and the Poison of Negative Vital Breath.

Salvation of Humanity

Taoists take great interest in the preservation of Chinese culture and civilization, and Taoism is viewed as an important vehicle for the transmission of that culture. Therefore, evidence of the religion may be found in almost every Chinese community.

Life and salvation are inherent to Taoism. The medical field is highly valued because of its goal to heal the sick and restore life. Many Taoists devote themselves to medicine and provide their services free of charge. In fact, many temples establish clinics to provide medical assistance to those in need.

Ethical Education and Practice

In Taoism, the good or evil one does is believed to directly determine the length of one's lifespan. All deeds are known and evaluated by the spirits of heaven and earth, who keep careful track. No good or evil deed can escape the principle of retribution, for, although the personal merits and evil deeds are hidden from mortals, they are known by the spirits of heaven and earth. Taoists assert that each evil thought decreases one's lifespan by three days; the penalty for an evil deed that harms others is 300

days. But a decreased lifespan is not the only punishment. The spirits responsible for retribution will ensure that evil doers will experience impoverishment and exhaustion, suffering, and societal disgust, and will withhold auspicious occasions from their lives so long as evil is committed. If the penalized span of time taken away from one's lifespan exceeds his lifespan, his descendants will inherit the penalty.

Karma

Karma is a Buddhist concept that later became an integral part of Taoism. Taoist karma works on a cause and effect basis (because cause cannot exist without effect, and vice versa). Karmic causes are the words, thoughts, and actions done; karmic effect is the result of such words, thoughts, or actions. This effect does not affect only the cause's targets—the people influenced by the doer's actions; to the contrary, every deed done also affects the doer. Good deeds accumulate within the doer, bringing him nearer to perfection and perfecting the society surrounding him.

In Taoism, there are two types of karma: worldly karma, and karma that occurs outside of the human world. Worldly karma's causes are good and evil; its effects are joy and sorrow. Extra-worldly karma's cause is wisdom, and its effect is detachment (called "Tao Fruit").

Experiencing karma in one's life is inevitable, and cannot be escaped—even through death. If one should die before experiencing the effect of his karma, he will experience it in the netherworld, Fengdu Hell.

Norms and Methods

In Taoism, there are expected norms of good and proscribed methods for achieving good. Norms include showing kindness and consideration to all, remaining steadfastly good even in trivial matters, showing enthusiastic concern for public welfare, practicing ethics in one's business and career, and remaining aware that the criteria of good and evil change with time. The methods for doing good include recognizing one's centrality in the conferring of good or evil, continually exhorting and examining one's thoughts and motives, and reducing one's selfishness and false desires. Among the clergy, Taoists priests are admonished to hold higher moral expectations of themselves than of the laity.

Philosophy of Life

Tao cannot be understood through or directly grasped by the material senses, and for this reason, it cannot be taught—only discovered, or "received." Tao cannot be humanly logically analyzed, or realized through common sense or human reasoning. Others can try to explain their understanding of Tao, and their experience as a Taoist, but one cannot himself understand Tao until he personally experiences it. To best prepare oneself for the reception of Tao, one must empty his mind of attachments to concrete things and of material desires and ambitions. Because emptiness houses Tao, Tao will gradually creep into the mind that is emptied.

The Taoist does not confine himself to the concepts of existence or non-existence. He remains open to the mysterious and abstruse, does not have preconceived notions of the Tao, or make assumptions. He remains calm, mild of manner, pure and desirous of enlightenment—and never seeks first place or priority over others. There are nine norms of studying Tao:

1. Maintain Harmony
2. Maintain Spirit
3. Maintain the Vital Breath
4. Maintain Benevolence
5. Maintain Simplicity
6. Maintain Constancy
7. Maintain Pureness
8. Maintain Fullness
9. Maintain Gentleness

There are also nine predicted difficulties:

1. Surviving the burden of life
2. Fulfilling obligations to elders
3. Avoiding quarrels with wife and family
4. Anxiety about fame and gain
5. Surviving unexpected calamities
6. Practicing restraint
7. Overcoming incorrect views
8. Overcoming weak will
9. Avoiding wasting time

However, these difficulties are just small obstacles when compared to the human barriers one faces in studying Tao. The barriers are intelligence, disputation, non-persistence, disbelief, illusion, bookishness, lack of definite views, life and death, wilfulness, the physical body, lust, delusion, karma, hidden evil, attachment to appearances, complacency, wealth and gain, the female elixir, coldness and hotness, destitution, craft, flaunting, stove fire, fear of hardship, excessive drinking, disrespect, glory and rank, decline in aspiration, fear of difficulty, disgrace, deep love, loftiness, quick results, suspicion, carelessness, heavy debt, waste of time, emptiness, nothingness, arrogance, false understanding, pretense, envy, giving oneself up, irritability, anger and hatred, laziness, cowardice, and adversity. It is believed that overcoming these barriers will make the Taoist a healthier and better person, and enable them to hear the whisperings of the Great Tao.

A person's decision to study Tao actively should be founded on a desire for virtue, acted upon firstly by gaining merits, and secondly by eliminating demerit. Those who wish to achieve immortality must practice the qualities of loyalty, filial piety, harmony, obedience, benevolence, and fidelity. If one is merely on a quest to gain the Taoist skills of magic and gives no heed to virtue, he will never achieve immortality.

In studying and practicing Tao, one needs to learn the basic skills of refining the Vital Breath, dietetics, gymnastics, and so on. Inner alchemy is also a highly valued skill. The Taoist must always remember that no matter how many skills are gained, the foundation of being a Taoist is to accumulate merits.

Those who have obtained Tao lead a simple life free of worldly desires, regard position and health as fleeting clouds, care not for fame or gain, and disdain from preoccupying themselves with worldly affairs. The perfect man has risen above "self"; the divine man does not believe in worldly achievement; the sage has no human identity—no "name." Tao is obtained through the accumulation of merits and gain of a higher spiritual state. The cultivation of Tao, as described in *Discourse on Sitting in Oblivion*, is divided into seven steps. Here, "oblivion" means total detachment from human affairs.

The steps are:

1. **Respect and faith.** One should respect the Tao and hold firm to his belief that sitting in oblivion (forgetful meditation) will grant him Tao;

2. **Interception of karma.** Separate oneself from the bonds of the world, including karma;

3. **Taming the mind.** The mind is master of the body; the key to sitting in oblivion is restraining the mind's tendency to focus on material cares and worries;

4. **Detachment from affairs.** Handle affairs in a leisurely and unconcerned manner. Life and death are a matter of destiny and one should not pursue things that are not destined. One should excise all trivial matters from his life;

5. **True observation.** One should perceive good and bad luck, fortune and misfortune, prior to their occurrence, "know the branch through perception of the root," and reduce human business on a daily basis. Not until one's body is quieted and his mind calm can he perceive sublimity;

6. **Intense concentration.** Quietness and concentration need not be sought out, but merely harnessed, for they naturally occur ubiquitously and at all times;

7. **Realizing the Tao.** One's body is one with Tao, therefore, he is immortal; his mind is one with Tao, therefore, he has infinite capability. One cannot be harmed, because life is eternal—there is no death.

C. Scripture

The Taoist canon is open, and has, over time, become the largest religious canon in the world. The first Taoist text was *Diode Jingo* by the Great Master,

Lao Zi. Since then, many texts (numbering in the hundreds) have come to be venerated in the Taoist canon.

D. Secondary Sources

THEOLOGIANS, SCHOLARS, AND THINKERS

Wang Changyue (?–1680)

Wang was a Taoist priest who preached the word of Tao in Nanjing. He stressed a particular methodology of Tao cultivation: first, one must and find a master and proclaim himself a Taoist believer. Second, one must believe in the Three Jewels of Taoism: Tao, Taoist scriptures, and the community of Taoist masters. Third, one must confess his sins, dispose of obstacles, and eliminate passions and attachments. Finally, one must endure the humiliation brought on by strict adherence to these commandments, and thereby receive peace and tranquility of mind and purity of bodily life. Wang's works include the five-volume *The Alms Bowl Mirror*, *Commandments for Primary Perfection* (preserved in *Selections of the Taoist Canon*), and *The Book of the Azure Garden Altar*.

Liu Yiming (1734–1821)

Liu Yiming was a famous Master of inner alchemy and Chinese traditional medicine in the Qing Dynasty. Liu turned to Taoism in his twenties as a result of serious illness, through which tribulation he claimed to have discovered the meaning of life. In his works, he combined elements of Buddhism, Confucianism, and Taoism. He insisted that "one cannot become an immortal unless he cultivates Spiritual Nature and Bodily Life in an integrated way," and held that bodily nature should be perfected before one attempts to cultivate the spiritual.

His works include *Inner Chapters on Comprehending the Mind*, *Outer Chapters on Comprehending the Mind*, *Nine Essentials for the Cultivation of Perfection*, *Book of Passing through Barriers*, *Three Ways Unified and Normalized*, *On Realizing Perfection*, and *Book of Secret Correspondences*.

Min Yide (1758–1836)

Min Yide is responsible for the prosperity of the Dragon Gate Sect. An eleventh-generation disciple of the sect, he lamented the lack of successors to the Dragon Gate Sect, as well as its collapsing religious buildings. He determined to revitalize its prosperity, and did so by making the means of spiritual practice more accessible to others. Min realized that Confucians inquired into the truth through reading, managing state affairs, and harmonizing the family; Buddhists awoke to the truth by sitting in deep meditation, realizing spiritual nature, and enlightening the mind; and Taoists found truth through cultivation of moral character, reducing sins, and behaving beneficently to things and people. Clearly, there were many ways of discovering truth, and therefore one could choose the method that most conveniently suited him. He could equally practice commandments, magic arts, worship, or doctrine; likewise, he could either stay at home, go out into the world and worship, or join a sect. Min's works include *Light of the Mind on Mt. Jingai*, *Supplementary Taoist Canon*, and *Collection of Ancient Books from the Tower of the Bookish Hermit*.

Tan Qiao (10th century)

Tan was an important scholar of the Tang Dynasty/Five Dynasties. Even as a child, he was an avid reader and accrued much information at a very early age. When he felt called to devote his life to Taoism, he left his family to pursue his interests in it. Eventually, Tan determined to become an Immortal. He wrote extensively during his lifetime and contributed much to the Taoist way of thinking. His main work is *The Book of Transformation*.

E. Important Leaders

Fu Xi (mid-2800s BCE)

Fu Xi is known as the first of the mythical Three Sovereigns (god-kings, or demigods, who served extremely long reigns and utilized magical powers to improve the lives of their subjects) of ancient China. He is a cultural hero among the Chinese, credited with having invented animal trapping, fishing, and writing. More importantly, he is said to have created the *I Ching*, a classic Chinese text that serves as a symbol system for divination of events that occur by chance. The text elucidates symbols and provides rules for manipulating them. Taoists believe that Fu Xi may be the original author of the *Book of Changes*.

Wu Yun (d. 778)

Wu Yun was a priest and poet. He wrote works on anti-Buddhism, and inspirational works for Taoists. He was a defender of reclusion and a philosopher of immortality. His surviving works include *On the Possibility of Learning to be Immortal*, and *On the Mysterious Matrix*, and many poems.

Wang Chongyang (1113–1170)

Wang was a Taoist in the Song Dynasty. He is accredited for founding the Quanzhen School in northern China. His teachings are known as "the teachings of the Great Perfection." He was an author of many poems for Taoist instruction, as well as *An Anthology on Complete Perfection by Chongyang*, *Chongyang's Anthology on Teaching Transformation*, *Chongyang's Anthology of the Ten Transformations by Dividing Pears*.

Li Daochuan (1170–1217)

Li Daochuan was a Taoist teacher and master. He advocated the integration of Taoism, Buddhism, and Confucianism. His main area of expertise was inner alchemy, which he discusses in *Essays on Harmony*.

Sun Simiao (581–682)

Sun Simiao was a famous clinician and alchemist. He traveled a great deal and spread the word of the importance of medicine. He followed Taoist thought, but combined it with Buddhism and Confucianism. Though Sun was frequently requested by emperors to accept official court positions, he always refused, preferring a rural life. Sun devoted himself to the teachings of the *I Ching* and the *Diode Jingo* and pursued an interest in alchemy. He advocated that all patients should be treated equally, regardless of age, rank, wealth, or beauty. His works include *Prescriptions Worth a Thousand Gold, Inscription on Visualizing Spirits, Refining Vital Breath*, and many books on various disorders and their treatments in the medical field.

Zhang Guo (Tang Dynasty)

Zhang Guo, or Master Comprehension-of-Profundity, was a Taoist occultist-alchemist who is now considered one of the Eight Immortals. He had a love for wine and winemaking, and the other Immortals professed that his wine had healing attributes. Zhang was one of the most eccentric of the Immortals, making liquor from various shrubs and herbs, practicing the Kung Fu style of gymnastics, and fasting for days at a time. By the time Empress Wu came into power, he claimed to be several hundred years old. Zhang's major work is *The Sublime Book of the Mind's Correspondence with the Nine Supreme Essentials.*

Zhang Junfang (11th century)

Zhang was an historian of the Song Dynasty who was responsible for compiling the *Precious Canon of the Heavenly Palace of the Great Song*. Over the course of this project, he engaged in discussions with Taoist priests on stylistic rules and varying versions of Taoist books, and he selected and arranged them in the order of the Three Grottoes and the Four Compliments. This work resulted in *Seven Slips of the Cloudy Satchel*, a 122-volume reference book on Taoism.

Zhong Liquan (Han Dynasty)

Zhong Liquan is the fifth member and leader of the Eight Immortals. His teachings on Tao inspired the Emperor to give him the title "Imperial Sovereign Zhengyang of Manifold Teachings Who Enlightens and Transmits Tao." His works include *The Song of the Reversion Elixir* and *The Song of Dispelling Illusion* and *Rectifying Dao.*

Shi Jianwu

Shi was a famous poet after the Tang and Song Dynasties. His writing includes well-known scenic spots, particular views on how to cultivate Tao, and his beliefs about immortality. Because Shi was infamously reclusive, little else is known about him. His main work is the *Record of the Realization of Perfection by the Concourse of Immortals of West Mountain*, and his poems and prose are found in the *Complete Poetry of the Tang* and *Complete Prose of the Tang.*

Chen Nan (Southern Song Dynasty)

Legend has it that Chen Nan employed his "thunder skills" in order to save people from monsters and that he healed people with talismanic water. Chen taught disciples of his work on inner alchemy, who in turn had great success in their own work. Chen claimed that Master Xue Zixian imparted the Tablet of the Reversion Elixir and Return to Life to him, and that a spirit imparted the Daoist Book of Great Thunder and Auspicious Clouds to him.

Zeng Zao (Southern Song Dynasty)

Zeng was an inner alchemist and famous scholar who published many works on the Tao. His books focused on the obtaining of immortality and alchemy. His main work was *The Pivot of the Dao.*

Qiu Chuji

Qui Chuji is one of the Seven Immortals of Wang Chongyang, and a Taoist monk and alchemist. Genghis Khan requested that Qui teach him Taoism. In his teachings, Qui advocated that Taoists should lead an ascetic personal life, benefit other people, do good deeds, and cultivate their virtue. His works include *On Nourishing Life by Waxing and Waning, Direct Pointers to the Great Elixir, Pan Stream Essays, Record of the Auspicious Gathering with Daoists*, and *Essays on Advocating Dao.*

Ying chanzi Li Zhichun

Ying chanzi wrote the *Book of Changes*—a work integral to Taoist inner alchemy. He organized the book into four sections: the first section explains inner alchemy in mathematical terms; the second section is a chart illustrating the Golden Elixir; the third section explains the Buddhist Heart Sutra as interpreted through Taoism; the last section is a commentary on the *Book of Secret Correspondences*. He explains in this last section that Buddhism, Confucianism, and Taoism are all the same.

Wu Shouyang (1573–1644)

Wu Shouyang was a major contributor to the systemization of inner alchemy. In *Essential Formulas of the Golden Elixir*, he writes that one can only attain immortality by combining inner and outer alchemy. The inner elixir forms the pure Yin body needed, and the outer elixir forms the pure Yang breath.

The Yellow Emperor (27th-century BCE)

The Yellow Emperor is a legendary Chinese figure who is sometimes believed to be the forbearer of all Han Chinese. He was a major sovereignistic deity of Taoism during the Han Dynasty, and is now a revered culture hero. The Yellow Emperor is credited as one of the earliest great thinkers on the art of medicine, supposedly inventing the principles of traditional Chinese medicine. He practiced excellent health, and lived to the age of 100 before gaining immortality. Many books have been written in honor of his name.

III. Rites and Rituals

A. The Calendar

This calendar is for the Chinese 2005–2006 year as observed in America. Each Taoist temple has its own calendar, so this is to be considered merely an example. Exact dates for the current year are found at http://www.daoistcenter.org/homepage.html and at other websites listed at the end of the chapter.

FEBRUARY

Vegetarian Days: 9, 16, 22, 23.
Taoist Holidays:
Yuan Shi Tian Zun's (One of the Three Immortals) Birthday: 9.
Cai Shen's (God of Wealth) Birthday (Lantern Festival): 13.
Yu Huang Da Di's (Jade Emperor) Birthday: 17.
Shang Yuan Tian Guan's (One of the Three Guan) Birthday: 23.
The Day for Qiu Chuji (Student of Wang Chong Yang): 27.

MARCH

Vegetarian Days: 3, 4, 8, 9, 10, 17, 23, 24, 27.
Taoist Holidays:
Tudi Gong (Land of God) Festival: 11.
Wen Chang Di Jun's (God of Culture and Literature) Birthday: 12.
Dong Hua Di Jun's (Eastern King) Birthday: 15.
Ge Xianweng's (Immortal Pill Maker) Birthday: 24.
Tai Shang Lao Jun's (Laozu - Celestial Worthy of the Tao and It's Virtues): 24.

APRIL

Vegetarian Days: 1, 2, 6, 7, 8, 9, 16, 22, 23, 26.
Taoist Holidays:
Zhong Yue Da Di's (Central Mountain Emperor) Birthday: 26.

MAY

Vegetarian Days: 1, 2, 6, 7, 8, 15, 25, 30, 31.
Taoist Holidays:
Ma Zu's (Goddess of Longevity) Birthday: 1.
Dong Yue Da Di's (Eastern Mountain Emperor) Birthday: 6.
He Xiangu's (One of the Eight Immortals) Birthday: 17.
Lu Dong Bin's (Patriarch Lu) Birthday: 21.
Han Zhong Li's (Lu Dong Bin's Teacher) Birthday: 22.

Goddess of Midwifery's Birthday: 24.

Hua Tou's Birthday: 25.

JUNE

Vegetarian Days: 4, 5, 6, 7, 14, 20, 21, 24, 29, 30.

Taoist Holidays:

Nan Ji Chang Sheng Da Di's (South Pole Long Life Emperor) Birthday: 7.

Dragon Boat Festival (Duan Wu Jie): 11.

Zhang Tian Shi's Birthday: 24.

Ma Dan Yang's Birthday: 26.

JULY

Vegetarian Days: 4, 5, 6, 13, 19, 20, 23, 28, 29.

Taoist Holidays:

Ling Bao Tian Zun's Birthday: 5.

Lu Pon's Birthday: 18.

Wang Ling Guan's Birthday: 20.

Guan Gong's (Diefied General Representing Virtue) Birthday: 29.

Lan Caihe's (One of the Eight Immortals) Birthday: 30.

AUGUST

Vegetarian Days: 2, 3, 4, 5, 12, 18, 19, 22, 27, 28.

Taoist Holidays:

Festival of the Seven Sisters (Jade Emperor's Daughters): 11.

Tie Guanli's (One of the Eight Immortals) Birthday: 14.

Zhong Yuan Di Guan's (Emperor of Exorcism) Birthday: 19.

SEPTEMBER

Vegetarian Days: 1, 2, 3, 4, 11, 17, 21, 26, 27.

Taoist Holidays:

Di Zhang Wang's (King of the Dead) Birthday: 3.

The Day for the Plough God to Descend to Earth: 6.

Zao Jun's (Stove/Kitchen God) Birthday: 6.

Bei Yue Da Di's (Northern Mountain Emperor) Birthday: 13.

Chang E Festival (Moon Goddess Festival): 17.

OCTOBER

Vegetarian Days: 1, 2, 3, 10, 16, 17, 20, 25, 26, 30, 31.

Taoist Holidays:

The Nine Plough Gods Descend to Earth (Seven Stars of the Big Dipper, Fire God, and Earth God): 3-11.

The Day for the Nan Dou Star God to Descend to Earth: 3.

Birthday for Zhang San Feng, Dou Mu Yuan Jun, Chong Yang Di Jun, Feng Du Emperor: 11.

Guan Yin Remembrance Day: 21.

Tai Yi Zhen Ren's Birthday: 24.

Sa Zu Zhen Ren's (Temple Protector) Birthday: 25.

NOVEMBER

Vegetarian Days: 1, 2, 9, 15, 16, 19, 24, 25, 29, 30.

Taoist Holidays:

San Mao Zhen Jun's (Three Mao Brothers) Birthday: 4.

Zhang Guolao's (One of the Eight Immortals) Birthday: 11.

Xia Yuan Shui Guan's (One of the Three Guan) Birthday: 15.

The Day Qiu Zu Ascends to Heaven: 28.

Bei Ji Zi Wei Da Di's (One of the Four Emperors) Birthday: 28.

Festival of the North Pole Star: 28.

DECEMBER

Vegetarian Days: 1, 8, 14, 15, 18, 23, 24, 28, 29, 30, 31.

Taoist Holidays:

Xi Yue Da Di's (Western Mountain Emperor) Birthday: 6.

Special Day for Tai Yi Jiu Ku Tian Zun (The Blue Emperor): 11.

The Day for the Nan Dou Star God to Ascend to Heaven: 23.

JANUARY

Vegetarian Days: 7, 13, 14, 17, 22, 23, 27, 28, 29.

Taoist Holidays:

Han Xiangzi's (One of the Eight Immortals) Birthday: 8.

Nan Yue Da Di's (Southern Mountain Emperor) Birthday: 15.

Wang Chong Yang's (One of the Seven Perfected Ones) Birthday: 21.

The Day for the Stove God to Ascend to Heaven and Report the Good and/or Bad Actions of People to the Jade Emperor: 23.

The Day for all Gods to descend to Earth: 29.

B. Worship and Liturgy

RITUALS

Taoist rituals generally serve to harmonize existence on three levels: on the large scale of the cosmos; on the smaller scale of human society; and on the personal scale of an individual's life. Rituals are highly complex in Taoism, consisting of chanting, the burning of incense, playing instruments, making offerings to spirits, purification rites, and meditation. Because of the intricacy of the rituals, participation by the laity is minimal; most ceremonies are performed under the direction of a High Priest—an eminent Taoist master of notable character and high prestige—and his team of assistants.

Six chief specialists conduct Taoist rituals, three of them presiding under the title of "Three Master." Sharing this ranking with the High Priest is the Chief Cantor, who regulates the chanting and co-leads the rituals. The Chief Cantor and High Priest must both have great familiarity with and command over the ceremonies, and a facility for disseminating Tao. The third member of the Three Masters is The Fast Inspector. The Inspector supervises the conduct of the rituals, monitoring them according to official Taoist rules and commandments. He corrects the mistakes made by ritual practitioners without partiality. Under the supervision of the Three Masters, a Taoist ritual attendee fills the role of Incense Attendant. The attendant begins his preparations before each ceremony begins. He arranges the incense burner, decorates it, and keeps it clean. He also makes sure that the incense sticks continue burning throughout the entire ritual. The Incense Attendant must be very fastidious in his tasks, for if a mistake is made he may be levied a fine of incense or oil by the temple, or docked twelve years of his life expectancy by the deities.

Another Taoist ritual attendant serves as the Lantern Attendant. Lanterns and candles are widely used in Taoist rituals, and it is the Attendant's job to keep the temple looking bright and magnificent. He must extinguish the candles and lanterns come morning, but report to a master priest in stormy weather (who may ask him to keep the lanterns burning under such circumstances). A negligent Lantern Attendant may be levied a fine of incense or oil. A third Taoist attendee fills the role of Scripture Attendant. The Scripture Attendant has a number of duties. He in charge of general cleanliness and order—cleaning the desks and chairs and Scripture covers, arranging the exhibition of the Scriptures, keeping the rolls in order, and organizing the temple's books. Following the ritual he gathers the Scriptures, straightens up, and keeps the laity away from the ritual alter. Scripture Attendants who fail in their duties are subject to blame and punishments.

Prescribed sets of ritual objects are used within each ceremony. These include magical swords, magical seals, commandment plaques, magical staffs, bells, inverted bells (the latter two may require their own official attendants), tablets, S-shaped ornamental objects, streamers, shallow pans, wooden fish, large cymbals, and horsetail whisks.

The Yellow Register Ritual

This ritual is part of the "Three Register Fasts." It serves to benefit the living and save the dead. A Taoist may conduct this ritual in times of great tribulation and distress for the purpose of restoring peace and harmony within his life.

The Great Ritual Offerings to the All-Embracing Heavens

Three Pristine Ones, the Lofty Saints of the Ten Directions, the Heavenly Lord and Perfect Man of the Jade Capital and Gold Palaces, the Masters of the Ten Directions, the Officials of the Three Realms, and all other deities between heaven and earth are invoked in this ritual. The ceremony is very significant—performed to ensure the peace of the state and the security of its people, repentance of sins, prayer for longevity, and salvation for the dead. The ritual lasts from three to seven days, and varies each day.

Anterior Heaven Ritual for Feeding, Saving, and Refining Ghosts

This ritual is mainly performed by Taoists from Hong Kong. It provides a means of seeking relief from sufferings by appeasing the spirits (or ghosts) who can end them. The ghosts are invoked, fed, relieved of restlessness, appealed to, and "refined"—reintegrated into the Taoist cycles of transmutations. The ritual may be led by up to three people, and involves three parts: feeding ghosts, saving ghosts, and refining ghosts. The usual agenda is as follows: opening prayer, offering of incense, purifying with water, visualization, petition to the Five Hells, breaking the hells, triple invocation, invocation of spirits, taming of ghosts, odes to Taoist fasts and offerings, prostrations to the ten directions, extinguishing grievances, reciting the Five Kitchen Book, feeding ghosts, refining ghosts with water and fire, taking the Three Refuges, transmitting the Nine Commandments, and singing hymns to see off the dead. This ritual lasts about four hours and is done while sitting and singing poems and odes, which recitations are paired with certain talismans and incantations.

Ritual of Scattering Flowers and Communicating with Spirits through Lanterns

A popular ritual with Taoists from Hong Kong and Guangdong, it is performed to release sin and save the souls of the dead. The Master of the ritual begins by chanting the Scriptures and scattering flowers, coins, and rice. This is followed by hanging of lanterns; invoking the Sages; memorializing, petitioning and communicating with spirits by singing hymns; praying; and leading the souls of the dead out of the Gate of Hell. The flower-scattering element of the ritual includes offerings: incense, flowers, lanterns, water, and fruits, plates containing flowers, rice, and nine ancient coins plaved on a table.

Ritual of Refinement and Salvation

This ritual serves to save the dead by means of the living—to help the souls of the dead obtain new healthful physical bodies. There are many different versions of it, the differences mainly lying in which spirits are summoned and the means of granting them new bodies. The ritual begins with prayers and offers of incense in petition to the Highest Emperor. Talismans are burned to summon Immortals and spirits. The High Priest takes his seat and summons heavenly generals and officials, then visualizes their descent to Earth. Next, the souls of the dead are summoned and refined with fire and water. The Taoist Commandments are preached, the Three Jewels of Tao are eulogized, talismans are read and proclamations made. The High Priest then leaves his seat and sends the invoked souls to "cross the bridge." Taoists believe in three bridges to the underworld: the golden bridge, the silver bridge, and the naihe bridge. The first two bridges are for the souls of sages and righteous people; the last used by the souls of commoners. It is also known as the "river of endless sorrow bridge," because it is believed to span a river made of the blood of sinful people and inhabited by snakes and other fearsome creatures. The High Priest guides the souls across their requisite bridges with the use of a candle to illuminate the way. Afterwards, music of the Three Pristine Ones is played.

Lantern Ritual for the Destruction of Hell

A commonly practiced ritual in Taoism, it serves

to light the way for the souls of the dead through the darkness of hell and helps them see the root of life. This in turn will enable them to have their sins eliminated and good fortune restored. In preparation for this ritual, the Taoist scatters clean sand in an octagon (representing the nine hells) and lights the divine lanterns of the nine hells. These lanterns may be arranged so that nine lanterns occupy nine different spots in nine trees, for a total of eighty-one lanterns. Sometimes, nine stages of lanterns are erected on each tree, and nine wine vessels are placed on each stage. The Master of the ritual lights the lanterns after sunset, then conducts summoning practices to illuminate the Nine Hells to save the souls of the dead.

Memorial-Presenting Rituals

These rituals are the most important of the Taoist tradition of fasting and making offerings. Their purpose is to communicate the wishes of Taoists to the Heavenly Court, who may fulfill the wishes. "Memorials" are texts made by Taoist priests that eulogize spirits and appeal to them. When engaging in the Memorial-Presenting rituals, priests present the memorial documents to the spirits, thereby transmitting the wishes of mortals to spirits, reporting matters of earth to heaven, inviting the deities to the offering altars, and requesting salvation of the souls of ancestors. There are three parts to this ritual: commencement; invoking the sages; and presenting memorials. In commencing the ritual, the ritual Master and his servants enter the altar to burn incense and kneel down in prayer. To invoke the sages, effigies of the deities of the five directions are respectfully arranged, incantations are spoken, and the sages made to descend to earth. When presenting memorials, the ritual Master and his servants ask the invoked spirits to protect the memorials in their journey up to heaven. The Master then paces a Big Dipper diagram on the floor while reading the memorials. The Master and servants conclude by giving thanks to the deities and offer sacrifices, then leave.

C. Daily Life

Taoists conduct morning and evening rites on a daily basis for the sake of cultivating Tao. The morning rite includes incantation, reading the Scriptures, and making exhortations. Evening rites include only incantations and the Scriptures. The Taoist does not eat before the morning rite; the evening rite serves to renew energy lost over the course of the day.

Fasting is an integral part of the Taoist tradition, both for therapeutic purposes, and to purify the mind and body, thereby allowing for a greater imbibition of Tao. The Taoist diet usually consists of whole grains, organic vegetables, fruit that is in season, seeds, nuts, tofu, soy, herbs, and tea. Intake of red meat, refined products (white sugar, etc.), artificial additives and preservatives of any kind, dairy products, and cold drinks and foods is severely limited. Taoists believe that they must be frugal in their diets, and base it primarily on cereals.

Ideally, Taoists live their daily life with one thing in mind: emptiness and oneness with the Tao. They constantly seek opportunities to do good deeds and accumulate merits. They are peaceful beings who strive to avoid quarreling.

D. Life Cycle Events

Birth

When a Taoist couple wants to have a child, they respectfully pray to the Water-Margin Lady, asking that the birth be healthy and natural. After the child is born, the parents show their gratitude to the Water-Margin Lady by erecting a statue of her in their home. This is repeated at the child's first shower, one-month birthday, and one-year birthday.

Nuptials

A family elder must acknowledge a wedding in order for it to be officially recognized. Upon such recognition, an official directs the bride and groom to pray first to heaven and earth, then to respectfully acknowledge the groom's parents or family elders, and finally to bow to each other. The official then announces that the union is successful and the wedding party escorts the bride and groom to the bridal chamber to consummate the wedding.

Death and Burial

Taoists take death and burial very seriously. Funerals serve to secure peace for the souls of the deceased and to separate the dead from the living so the shadow of death will not linger among the living. "Relieving Rituals" are performed at the gate of the tomb to ensure separation. Because it is believed that a Taoist priest can make the dead ascend to heaven quickly and spare them the sufferings of the nether world, a priest is often called on to work with the family in eliminating the soul's bad deeds, enabling its ascendancy to heaven.

A Taoist funeral usually consists of four stages. The first stage is the chanting stage. It is believed that chanting sutras for the dead will release them of the sufferings in darkness. The second stage involves litanies and water and land rituals. Litanies are confessions made to the gods in which one admits one's sins and implore forgiveness. Funeral litanies are made for the sake of the deceased: family members hope to gain pardon for the guilt of the dead and thereby grant him access to heaven or allow him a good reincarnation. The water and land ritual may take over a week to complete. It is highly complex, including the feeding and refining of ghosts in the three worlds and many deliverance rites.

The funeral's third stage involves lighting lanterns and disposing of water lanterns—encompassed in the Nine Darkness Lantern Ritual. It is believed that this ritual causes divine light to shine over hell, helping the deceased soul find its way to heaven. The lantern altar is arranged according to the locations of the sun, moon, and constellations above, and the Eight Trigrams and Nine Palaces below. The ritual allows sunshine into Hell to break up the darkness, and an oil lamp is placed at the feet of the dead corpse to illuminate the dark path. Because it is

believed that the dead must cross a river, the family provides lanterns— paper lamps folded in the shape of a ship or lotus and floated in lakes—to help guide the soul safely over the river.

The fourth stage of the funeral consists of feeding hungry ghosts—relieving dead souls from hunger or thirst; and refining them—freeing them of spiritual suffering. A Taoist Master uses positive energy and his own good spirit to achieve the latter. While the Master is at work, mourners construct a pond and fire basin called zhao—water is for cleansing; fire for refining.

E. Family Life

Husband and Wife

The relationship between husband and wife is seen as an equal partnership in which life energy is mutually shared. The husband possesses yang energy and the wife possesses yin energy.

IV. Denominations and Demographics

A. History

There are formal sects within Taoism. The two surviving denominations of Taoism—Quanzhen and Zhengyi dao—are widespread and popular. In getting to this place, though it is important to understand Taoism and its history. Taoist history may be divided up into four periods. The period from antiquity to the second century CE, there were no formal Taoist organizations or groups; however, it was during this time that the main Taoist texts were written, such as the *Diode Jingo* and *Zhuang Zi*.

Scholars of the religion classify the second period as that of Classical Taoism, because it was an era during which many Taoist practices, texts, and rituals took shape. It began in 142 CE when Zhang

Daoling founded the first successful organized Taoist religious system called the Way of the Celestial Masters. Two other important organizations formed during this time were the Way of the Highest Clarity and the Way of Numinous Treasure. It was also during this Classical period that Buddhism was brought to China, which did influence the ideas and practices of Taoism. An intense rivalry developed between Buddhism and Taoism, but Taoism surfaced as the official religion of the Imperial Court. This period ended with the conclusion of the Tang Dynasty.

The period of Modern Taoism began with the Song Dynasty. During this time, the boundaries between Buddhism and Taoism became so blurred that it was hard to differentiate between Taoism as a religious category and Chinese culture. The most significant event during this time was the forming of the Way of the Complete Perfection under Wang Zhe. This group was devoted to the knowledge of inner alchemy in which the ways of the body were refined by breathing and other forms of meditation—promoting longevity. The Way of the Complete Perfection sought to create peace between Buddhism, Taoism, and Confucianism. Despite their efforts, many heated debates arose between Taoists and Buddhists, resulting in the burning of important Taoist texts. This period also saw the completion of the Taoist canon in 1445, and the adoption of Taoist ideas and practices in popular religious culture. Taiji Quan and Qi Gong, for example, became increasingly widespread.

The last and current period began in 1949, and is referred to as Contemporary Taoism. When the Great Proletarian Cultural Revolution was instated by Mao Zedong in 1966, many Taoist temples were destroyed and overt functions of the religion were stifled in China. However, starting in 1980, Taoists began to rebuild their shattered temples and practice openly again in China. Thanks to the immigration of the Chinese to Europe and America, Taoist temples now exist across the world. The religion is once again flourishing in China and elsewhere.

B. Population and Distribution

Approximately 30,000 Taoists may be found in America. Taoism claims 20 million followers worldwide, most of whom reside in Taiwan and China.

V. Organization and Infrastructure

A. Seminaries and Institutions

The Center of Traditional Taoist
PO Box 134
Weston, MA 02193
webmaster@tao.org   www.tao.org

World Medicine Institute
(Formerly Tai Hsuan Foundation)
College of Acupuncture & Herbal Medicine
PO Box 11130
Honolulu, HI 96828
808-949-1050   Fax: 808-955-0118
worldmedicine@cs.com
www.acupuncture-hi.com

The Taoist Center/Zhi Dao Guan
3824 Macarthur Boulevard
Oakland, CA 94619
510-336-0129
info@thetaoistcenter.com
www.thetaoistcenter.com

The Taoist Institute
10630 Burbank Boulevard
North Hollywood, CA 91601
818-760-4219
www.taoistinstitute.com

Taoist Studies Institute
225 North 70th Street
Seattle, WA 98103
206-784-5632
www.taoiststudiesinstitute.org

B. Shrines and Houses of Worship

American Evergreen Taoist
(known as the Taoist Association of America)
644 Broadway
San Francisco, CA 9413
415-837-1285

Fung Loy Kok Taoist Temples
1060 Bannock Street
Denver, CO 80204
303-623-5163
1833 Dr. MLK Jr. Street North
N. St. Petersburg, FL 33072
727-521-3336   Fax: 727-521-3336

Hsien Taoist Monastery
760 Cathedral Drive
Aptos, CA 95003
(831) 688-5514

Taoist Sanctuary in San Diego, CA
4229 Park Boulevard
San Diego, CA 92103
(619) 692-1155
www.taoistsanctuary.org

C. Media and Communications

The Empty Vessel: A Journal of Contemporary Taoism is a quarterly dedicated to nonreligious Taoist philosophy and practice.

The website www.topix.net/religion/taoism posts articles by Taoists of many locations.

Three scholarly and dependable websites with up-to-date information are:
www.daoistcenter.org/homepage.html
www.daoiststudies.org
www.stanford.edu/~pregadio/index.html

ADDITIONAL REFERENCES ON TAOISM

Early Daoist Scriptures
Stephan R. Bokenkamp
1997: University of California Press

The Inner Teachings of Taoism
Po-Tuan Chang and Thomas Cleary
1986: Shambhala Publications

Practical Taoism
Thomas Cleary
1996: Shambhala Publications

Taoism: The Enduring Tradition.
Russell Kirkland
2004: Routledge

Daoism and Chinese Culture
Livia Kohn
2001: Three Pines Press

Tao Te-Ching
Lao Zi
1997: Vintage Books

VI. OTHER RELIGIOUS GROUPS

VI OTHER RELIGIOUS GROUPS
Historical Introduction

༄

We've Got Some Nerve Calling These "Other Religions"

OUR AGE IS ONE IN WHICH THE WAY WE VIEW AND treat our world has become increasingly important. We live in a world beset by global warming, pollution, vanishing habitats, decreasing species diversity, and increasing natural disasters. And we know that much of this is our own fault. Environmentalism and environmental conservation, once considered by many to be liberal issues if not "hippie" indulgences, have now become matters literally of life and death for all of us. The earth and the damage done to it can also have religious significance. For is it not because of our most vital concerns—the survival of our species and with it the survival of the life of this planet—that we are drawn to religion in the first place?

One of the significant elements of most traditional Native American religious practices is the emphasis on place. The land itself and its specific features—trees, rocks and rivers—are infused with spiritual significance. These are not religions that can be practiced anywhere. Beyond merely designating some places as sacred and sanctified, this religion is rooted in a specific place and the specific natural elements of the place. It is for this reason that these faiths place emphasis on respect for the earth and its creatures. Nature-based worship and New Age spirituality mingle old and new practices, from witchcraft, shamanism, and Hermetic philosophy to the awakening of a cosmic consciousness

and visits from other planes. They are bringing back (or creating anew) a focus on personal spiritual growth and learning to live in harmony with the world. In much of nature-based worship, the elements of the earth are themselves embodied as gods and goddesses, which are revered in the world and in the self. Some philosophies even view the biosphere of earth in its entirety as a living entity, conscious and sacred, for which we must show respect.

Pueblo and Hopi cultures identify more than four hundred kachinas, or spirits, in their religious practice. These illustrations of seven different kachina dolls made by the Pueblo Indians of the southwestern Unived States appeared in an 1894 anthropology book.

Much of what these religions strive for harkens back to an older time, before Christianity, and prior to the patriarchal organization of society, when humans were more able to relate to the natural world around them—and, perhaps, even to each other. The traditional Native American faiths are indeed old. Nature-based worship tends to draw on old practices in synthesis with modern values, while New Age philosophy (as the name suggests) is often of unabashedly recent vintage. However, they all show a way of viewing the world different from that which has led to much of the destruction humanity has caused in recent years. Perhaps this accounts for the upsurge in faiths grounded more in nature.

And perhaps part of it is a reaction to the society in which we live. We in America are proud of our mobile culture, our ability to pack our bags and move to a new place. We are proud of our cities full of shining towers where one cannot see all the way to the ground from the top floors. But, perhaps this, too, is what draws people to these faiths—a sense of disconnection with the world around them, a loss of roots. This culture of dislocation leads, for some, to a renewed desire to connect with the land, to be its steward. Native American religions have always felt this bond with the land and drawn strength from localization—from being not just of a time, but also, and more importantly, of a place. Nature-based worship is in some ways less geospatially dependent, since it can be practiced anywhere, but, because it views the entire world as sacred, it encourages a sense of reconnection to the earth. Much of New Age philosophy is, in fact, about awakening to the ties between our world and ourselves.

These faiths are not simply intellectual exercises; they are ways of life. From stewardship of the earth through ecologically sound behavior in every day life, to a living space organized to bring harmony into the home, to personal alignment through chakra work, these are religions that become part of a person's way of being in the world. Furthermore, these are faiths that believe in the capabilities of human beings to positively affect the world. This

can be through Magick (given the extra "k" to distinguish practical magic from stage magic), where the will of the individual is made manifest in the world or through actively making oneself a part of natural cycles—or even just making one's habits gentler to the earth. The connection to this world in each of these religions also means an emphasis on one's impact here and now—in the community, in the home, and in life. This emphasis on the individual's connection to the community and the world around him or her and the ability to influence the world for good, are all distinguishing elements of the faiths in these next two chapters.

And perhaps this is something we need now more than ever. Our world is changing, and it is changing because of us. Species that have existed since long before apes walked upright are dying. The global temperature is increasing, bringing storms that destroy cities. Pristine arable land is vanishing. We are running out of some of the natural resources on which we base our society and upon which we depend for life. This may be a practical concern that is dawning on humankind at last, but for some it is, as it has been since before recorded history, a spiritual obligation to undo the damage.

In this section, section VI, three major groups will be covered—Native American religions; nature-based religions; and secular, nontheist belief systems such as Atheism, Agnosticism, and Humanism. The chapter on Native American religions focuses on traditional Native American religion, both in overview and in the case of specific tribal practices. The complexity, richness, subtlety, sophistication, and wisdom of these belief systems is richer than anyone ever imagined—at least anyone not a part of one of these cultures. Only a small sampling is possible here, and the task is further complicated by the Native American encounter with European Christianity, an encounter that is still being played out by a beleaguered people.

In the chapter on Nature-based religion, Wiccan, Neopagan, Shamanistic, and New Age movements, practices and beliefs will be discussed. We will exam-

The Salem Witch Trials—one of which is depicted in this 1876 illustration—gripped an area of Massachusetts around the town of Salem in 1692 and 1693. More than 150 people were tried for the capital crime of witchcraft, and twenty-five people (including six men) were executed or tortured to death in efforts to extract a confession. Medical investigators now theorize that the hysteria was caused by wheat infected with a fungus that had hallucinogenic properties.

ine their history, the founders of different faiths, and the connections to other cultural and political movements, such as Eco-activism, Environmentalism and Feminism. We will touch upon the occult dimensions of the religions, and look into religious practices that are a hybrid of Nature-based and Christian religious practices such as Vodou and Santeria.

The third chapter covers belief systems that have developed as alternatives to religion. The history of Atheism, Agnosticism, and Humanism in America will be reviewed, as will the various landmark events involved in the prejudice against and acceptance of these groups in America and their rise to respectability in American culture. The chapter will explore the tensions between science and religion, the separation of church and state, and survey the authors, philosophers, and activists who have championed American nontheism. Finally, we will explore humanistic and human-centered branches of religions such as Judaism and Christianity.

This chapter is also a testament to the originality and creativity of religion in America. With freedom of religion comes the birth of new religions, homegrown and imported, many of which are controversial. Just two will be examined briefly: Scientology, the religion founded by the science-fiction author L. Ron Hubbard, and the Unification Church founded by Reverend Sun Myung Moon.

We have gathered all of these serious human concerns and endeavors into a category we labeled "other groups" and "other religions," not to be dismissive or belittling, but because we have not been able to think of a better term. It is a clumsy device we use fully mindful of the following observations: That there was a religion called Zoroastrianism (still practiced by many adherents today, though not by many in the United States) that could once lay claim to being the largest religion in the world, and the state religion of three empires. And that the religions that dominate the world today were once preached by solitary prophets and sages to small bands of persecuted followers in remote corners of the world. So, we ask, which "other religions"— perhaps too small now to even be described in this work—will ignite human passion, imagination, and devotion, and one day lay claim to millions— perhaps billions—of members of the human race?

— JESSICA SIRKIN
SECTION EDITOR

1 Native American Religions

I. Origins and Early History

Introduction

TRADITIONAL NATIVE AMERICAN RELIGION CAN hardly be classified as "religion" within the context of Euro-American Christianity. It is more nearly a spiritually infused way of life, reflected in the culture, lives, ceremonial occasions, and day-to-day rituals of its practitioners. Furthermore, Native Americans did not all practice one form of religion with a universal set of beliefs, but instead had a diverse array of religious practices that varied primarily based upon the geo-spatial location of the tribe's homeland. In its heyday, Native American spirituality spanned both the North and South American continents—

Pedro de Gante, also called Pieter van der Moere, was a Franciscan missionary to Mexico in the sixteenth century. This image is from a facsimile edition of his Indian Catechism, *originally published around 1520.*

tip to tip and coast to coast—encompassing over 500 tribes and 250 indigenous languages (about 100 of which are still spoken today); yet, common values and strains of thought can be discerned in this tapestry of beliefs. Today, having weathered half a millennium of persecution, war, genocide, land displacement, and forced conversion, traditional Native American religions have managed to survive, though often in hybridized strains.

A. The Encounter of Native American and European Religions

When Columbus landed on the shores of the New World in 1492, an estimated six to ten million indigenous peoples inhabited what is now the United States. They were presumably of Asian origin, having arrived some 25,000–75,000 years ago by way of a land bridge that once existed in what is now the Bering Strait. These people came to exist in nations composed of multiple tribes, each bearing its own unique cultural tradition. Looked at collectively and in the broad view, visible forms of religious expression show shared aesthetic and ideological values through the practice of elaborate rituals, in an overarching reliance on the natural world for sustenance, and in the organization of society primarily around kinship ties. Thus, the reliance on the tribe for establishing personal identity and the powerful connection Native Americans feel to the land they inhabit make it difficult, if not impossible, for a Native American's belief system to exist independent of his or her particular

In 1860, the German-American artist Emanuel Leutze (1816–68)—who also painted the famous 1851 painting Washington Crossing the Delaware—received a commission from Congress to decorate a stairway in the Capitol. This painting is a study for the mural he eventually created, entitled Westward the Course of Empire Takes Its Way, also popularly known as Westward Ho! It celebrates the idea of America's manifest destiny, or westward expansion.

geographical, social, and historical setting. A tribe's religion cannot exist independent of that particular land and that particular tribe in that particular epoch, and are therefore not portable or transferable.

Unlike Euro-American Christianity, which is a direct outgrowth of the Bible, Native American religions originally relied mainly upon oral traditions for the transmission of values. Because no written historical records or spiritual treatises exist, the religion could only be determined from its visible manifestations in Native American lifestyle. To ensure the longevity of spiritual beliefs and their accuracy in translation to future generations, those members of the society demonstrating special proficiency in language and communication were identified and trained to memorize and pass on such information.

The pioneering Europeans who first happened upon the Native Americans in 1492 soon realized that they were not, as had been assumed, dealing with Asians, and long debated over what to make of this unexpected population. Those Europeans who looked to the Bible to explain the existence of such peoples determined them to be descendants of Noah. Those who looked to popular folklore saw them as *l'homme sauvage*, or "the wild man." Either way, Columbus's catchall term, "*los indios*" ("the Indians"), was adopted for the whole. This tendency to homogenize the entire population of Natives extended likewise to Native religions. Europeans did not recognize cultural differences among Native Americans and sometimes dismissed all Native religions as primitive, or even diabolic. The common Native American practice of recognizing the presence of sacred power in persons, places, and objects struck some European Christians as irreverent and vulgar. Though most European Christians believed Native Americans were descended from Adam, and therefore redeemable through conversion, a dismissal of Native American religions as primitive sometimes led to a regard of Native peoples as somehow less than fully developed humans.

The advent of Europeans in North America had a devastating effect upon Native American culture. Because a tribe's geospatial location in the environment served as a foundation for religious meaning, land displacement by encroaching whites resulted in a tragic loss of identity and religious orientation. The many rituals and ceremonies born of home landscapes suddenly lost viability in a new environment. It is no wonder that one forced removal was frequently referred to as "The Trail of Tears." The fact that Native American religions varied from tribe to tribe at first inhibited the indigenous people from banding together against white opposition, because different tribes felt they had nothing in common. Furthermore, it allowed Europeans to set tribes against each other in a strategy of divide-and-conquer. However, ironically, the white tendency to homogenize the Native Americans ultimately served to help unite them against their common enemy, as a myth arose concerning the common origin of all "red men." First significantly breaking out in the early nineteenth century, Native American resistance appeared in both militant and peaceful forms, occurring in raids of white villages and outright battles, and also ritualistic dances in prayer that the white man would leave. Nevertheless, brutal killings, disease, alcoholism, President Jackson's removal policy after 1830, and a drop in birth rate among indigenous peoples caused their population to plummet to an estimated twenty percent of its original size, and cultures and entire languages—and with them oral libraries of history, religious beliefs, lore, narratives and humor—were lost.

By the 1870s, the United States government's new policy was to "kill the Indian to save the man," and both intermarriage (to dilute native blood concentration) and religious conversion were employed to achieve this goal. Missionaries had been directing their attention to North American Natives as early as the sixteenth century, but efforts reached only a handful of Native peoples. In the seventeenth century, a small pocket of "Praying Indians," composed of members of the Massachusett, Pequot, Wampa-noag and other Algonkian-speaking nations, adapted the Puritan lifestyle by turning from hunting to farming and establishing fourteen permanent towns in which the model Christian "godly life" was adhered to. The eighteenth-century colonial period was characterized by missionary ventures on behalf of the Germans, Spanish, French, and English. In England, Thomas Bray, a commissary for the bishop of London, established the Society for the Propagation of the Gospel in Foreign Parts (SPG), an organization for the subsidization of Anglican missionary work counter to Congregational and Methodist efforts. However, the SPG was only one of the latter manifestations of the European missionary effort. The French and Spanish had engaged in vigorous missionary efforts starting in the sixteenth century and German pietists had also been active since that time. However, the latter proved far more vigorous than the more than 300 missionaries sponsored by the SPG. By the time Jackson took office in 1828, white Americans viewed Native Americans as merely "in the way" of Manifest Destiny, and land displacement undid much of the missionary work of those priests and evangelists who had earned Native American trust. The majority of whites still did not appreciate the idea of cultural pluralism, leaving Native Americans with two choices: assimilate, or face elimination.

Many Native Americans chose to assimilate—by either adopting European-Christian beliefs in their entirety or by combining elements of Christianity with Native religion. Some chose to be extremely selective in their acceptance of European-Christian practices, so as to preserve as much as possible of their native religions. One of these was Quanah Parker, the founder of The Native American Church, or the Peyote Church, now the most widespread religious denomination among American indigenous peoples. Formally incorporated in 1918, this religious practice uses the enthogenic peyote cactus, or Lophophora williamsii, to induce altered states of consciousness, perceived as spiritual or mystic experiences. Quanah Parker advocated the Half Moon Way of Religion, which unlike the Christianized Cross Fire Way, was less influenced by Christianity. Another who strived to preserve Native American religions was Handsome Lake. After a vision, he developed the Code of Handsome Lake, which advocated learning from the Europeans and adopting some of their lifestyle without losing their essential Iroquois religion. Wovoka, inspired by a vision, created and spread what has come to be known as the Ghost Dance, and advocated a way of life that preserved tradition while still cooperating with Europeans. Other Native Americans chose allegiance to Protestant sects, or adopted a Catholic-based hybrid religion. One of the most well known of these is the Yaqui Nation.

B. Important Dates and Landmarks

ca. 3700 BCE Native Americans in the Rio Grande discover the peyote plant, a small cactus, with psychedelic effects, that can be used for medicinal purposes and for religious insight.

1000 BCE Peyote usage commences in what is now Mexico and Texas. Heyday of massive mounds and associated earth works at modern-day Poverty Point.

500 CE Animal-shaped earthwork mounds are common in upper Great Lakes area.

900 CE Foundation of what is now called Moundville, a site covering three hundred acres centered around a one-hundred-acre plaza surrounded by twenty paired mounds.

1000 Rise of communities based on corn agriculture.

1492 Europeans arrive in America in the person of Christopher Columbus.

1500 Abandonment of Moundville.

1521 Europeans in Mexico forbid use of hallucinogens. Religious practices involving peyote become covert ceremonies.

1560s–1600s Jesuit and Franciscan priests establish missions in what are now Canada, Maine, Upstate New York, Florida, and Georgia; later in present-day Arizona, California, New Mexico, and Texas.

1646 Colonist missionary John Eliot begins delivering sermons to Native Americans in rudimentary Massachuset, an Algonkian language. Eliot's efforts will result in the formation of fourteen permanent towns of "Praying Indians," who follow a Christian way of life.

1663 Eliot completes a Massachuset translation of the Bible.

1680 Franciscan missionaries seek to suppress Tewa, Taos, and Picura religious practices by flogging their priests, destroying sacred Native American artifacts, and desecrating *kiva*—special areas for religious activities. A Tewa holy man named Popé initiates a revolt that results in the death of over 400 Spanish colonists and the destruction of every church in New Mexico. Spain will restore authority by 1686, but only upon promising to protect Tewa, Taos, and Picura lands from exploitation and tolerating the local religions. In return, natives must pledge loyalty to the Spanish crown.

1701 Commissary of the Bishop of London Thomas Bray founds the Society for the Propagation of the Gospel in Foreign Parts.

1743 Congregationalist minister Eleazar Wheelock enrolls Native American youths in his academy, Moor's Charity School, disseminating gospel thought and practice. Few Native Americans graduate from this school; even fewer return to their tribes as missionaries.

1759 Mohegan Indian and Moor's Charity School graduate Samson Occom is fully ordained as a Presbyterian minister and conducts preaching services, teaches in schools, counsels natives on practical matters, and performs marriages and funerals. Occom wins great acclaim among the British as a model of Christian scholarship and piety.

1803 Louisiana Purchase provides whites land for expansion and spurs removal of Native Americans.

1810 The American Board of Commissioners for Foreign Missions (ABCFM) founded to direct interdenominational evangelical activity among Native Americans. This organization sends exemplary citizens to set up model farms and households amid Indian settlements. The ABCFM hopes to instill values of industry, sobriety, Christian piety, and discipline. The Tennessee Cherokee are most responsive to this venture, ultimately emulating most aspects of European culture.

1829 President Jackson presses Native Americans to accept white government or relocate west of the Mississippi River.

1867 At the Battle of Adobe Walls, Quanah Parker refuses to sign the Medicine Lodge Treaty, which would assign the Kiowa, Comanche, Plains Apache, Cheyenne, and Arapaho tribes to reservations that provided few natural resources.

1869 President Grant creates the Board of Indian Commissioners for the sake of rooting out corruption in the government's procurement of missionary activity and assignment of missionaries to reservations. Plan allows missionaries of only one denomination on any reservation.

1874 Guided by the prophet Isatai, Chief Parker and Kiowa Chief Big Bow lead their tribes to a successful battle against buffalo hunters at Adobe Walls.

1883 The Bureau of Indian Affairs for the Indian Courts creates the Indian Religious Crimes Code. Responsible for the development of these laws is Secretary of the Interior Henry Teller. He prohibits dances and feasts and demands Native Americans revise their beliefs regarding medicine and medicine men.

1887 The General Allotment Act authorizes the president to carve up reservation land and apportion one quarter-section to the heads of native families. Surplus land is allocated to white use.

Late 1800s Peyote use increases in the U.S. among Native Americans. After suffering life-threatening injury, Chief Quanah Parker is treated with peyote tea. Upon ingesting the drug, Parker claims he experiences a vision of Jesus Christ, who told him to spread the peyote religion to his people as atonement for having led a life of war and killing.

1890 Originally taught to Native Americans by native seer Wovoka, a ritual known as the Ghost Dance—stressing loyalty to traditional native values—is performed with such vigor by Native Americans in South Dakota that white authorities become anxious and call in reinforcements. This leads to the deaths of 200 Dakotas—or the "Wounded Knee Massacre."

1892 The Rules for Indian Courts is established by commissioner Thomas J. Morgan, prohibiting Native American religious practices, such as sun dances, scalp dances, war dances, or other feasts. Violation punishable by imprisonment.

1918 James Mooney, an archeologist from the Smithsonian Institute, travels to Oklahoma and engages in several Peyote Ceremonies. He feels driven to unite the Native American people, and aids in developing the charter for the Native American Church.

1978 The American Indian Religious Freedom Act (AIRFA) is passed by Congress, guaranteeing constitutional protection of First Amendment rights for Native Americans. Act intended to redress past wrongs inflicted on Native Americans by the federal government or its agents.

1994 The United States government, supported by the Drug Enforcement Agency, rules that the First Amendment covers and protects the right of Native Americans to use peyote for religious purposes.

C. Important Figures

Quanah Parker

Born circa 1850, Quanah Parker is a leading figure in the formation of the Native American Church. Half Comanche and half white, Parker's dual heritage symbolizes the ultimate duality of his loyalties:

to both white and Native American culture. This adoption of acculturation lay at the end of a long and arduous road of both personal and public conflict, however. Quanah first battled the discrimination he experienced from the Comanche as a "half-breed" to earn his peoples' respect, then battled against white invasion of the Staked Plains to determine his people's fate.

Quanah Parker (ca. 1850–1911) appears in the undated photograph above left before his "Europeanization"; in the photograph above right, taken in the 1880s or 1890s, he stands at the far right wearing a three-piece suit.

The territory of the Great Plains that is now Texas and Oklahoma was first occupied by the Comanche Nation in the early 1700s. A little over a century later, the Comanches were no longer alone. White settlers moved into the area around 1836, and the Comanche resorted to raids on white settlements in an effort to drive them out. It was during one of these raids that Quanah's mother, Cynthia Ann Parker, was abducted by the Comanche and adopted into their tribe. Cynthia would ultimately marry a Comanche chief, Peta Nocono, and bear him three children: Quanah ("fragrance"), Pecos ("peanuts"), and Topsana ("prairie flower"), the latter two dying at a young age.

Quanah's adolescence largely consisted of warrior training. Spurred by the need to overcome the tribe's prejudice against his half-white heritage, he showed an unparalleled dedication to the study of soldiery and horsemanship, and often accompanied his father on raids of white villages. When the tribe's leader was killed during a raid, Quanah saw an opportunity for immediate promotion: in a deft display of leadership and competence, he rounded up the confused band and led them to safety. His reputation as a military leader was thus established.

Quanah eventually formed his own band, the Quahadi, which quickly gained a reputation for military excellence. Harboring a great distaste for the white settlers who would displace his people from their own land, Quanah resolved to resist this incursion by force. It was said of him that he had "never lost a battle to a white man." But Quanah would eventually compromise with the white man. After a particularly devastating battle at Adobe Walls in 1874, Quanah began to believe the pressures on the Comanche were too great. As Quanah now saw it, he was faced with a simple choice: he could continue to fight, and ultimately witness the annihilation of his people; or he could accept assimilation, but witness the disappearance of the Comanche culture. Parker chose the latter, and in May 1875, he marched into Fort Sill, Oklahoma, and agreed to move his people onto a reservation.

Once on the reservation, Quanah worked to improve the quality of life of the relocated Comanche. He made himself useful to the reservation agent, and demonstrated great diplomacy in representing the needs of his people in peaceful collaboration with white law. He gained the respect of the whites in his dealings as a cattle rancher, which made him prosperous. As a result, in 1890 he achieved the title of Principal Chief of the Comanche Nation. Soon thereafter, his leadership would take on a new direction, as he founded Peyotism and the Native American Church, which offered a unique blend of Christianity and indigenous spiritual belief.

According to one account, Quanah was first administered Peyote tea by a Mexican *curandera* (healer) after suffering severe injury in battle; in another, the curandera attended to him during a serious illness. Both accounts, however, assert that Quanah experienced a vision of Jesus, who commanded him to devote his life to peace and teach his people Christianity. Quanah began to commend the teachings of Jesus to his people, as well as to develop the Half Moon ceremonial style of all-night peyote prayer vigils. According to Quanah, God gave whites the Bible for the sake of learning about him; and to Native Americans, he gave the peyote cactus fruit for this same purpose. Quanah is famously quoted as saying, "All the same God, both ways good"; and, "The white man goes into his church and talks *about* Jesus. The Indian goes into his Tipi and talks *with* Jesus."

In 1911, the War Chief-turned-priest contracted rheumatism, and died of heart failure on his ranch in Cache, Oklahoma. The Native American Church was formally founded by anthropologist James Mooney in 1918, seven years after Quanah's death.

Jack Wilson (Wovoka)

"Wovoka" to Native Americans and "Jack Wilson" to whites, this nineteenth-century prophet of the Paiute tribe was a leading proponent of the Ghost Dance, or "round dance," among indigenous peoples.

Born circa 1850, Wovoka reportedly experienced many visions as a child, but had difficulty interpreting them. Wovoka's father placed the promising youth under formal training by an established holy

This illustration of a Sioux Ghost Dance ceremony appeared in an 1891 issue of The Illustrated London News.

man. In 1889, Wovoka, then revered as a talented medicine man and weather doctor, claimed to receive directions from God on the governance of his fellow Native Americans. According to Wovoka, God promised the return of the bison, a life of abundance and reunion with deceased loved ones in return for his peoples' dedication to brotherly love, peace, hard work, and cooperation with whites. God forbade gratuitous warfare, any form of lying, and stealing. He then presented Wovoka with the Ghost Dance, and said that if it were to be performed by all Native Americans, evil would be obliterated, and universal love and happiness would ensue. God, it was claimed, ordained Wovoka deputy of the Western United States—while President Harrison retained leadership of the East.

Jack Wilson's message of peace and dancing was eagerly adopted by Native Americans, and the new religion, called "Dance in a Circle," spread rapidly throughout the West. In this ceremony, the entire community danced in a circle around a single individual who led the dance. The name "Ghost Dance" developed among Europeans, who first encountered the phenomenon through the Sioux, and mistranslated their term "Spirit Dance."

As tensions mounted on reservations due to further appropriation of previously allotted Indian land, failures in agriculture, and the diminishing of previously guaranteed government food rations, Native Americans danced the Ghost Dance ever more fervently. In the face of such frustration, Wovoka's pledge for peaceful collaboration with the whites was forgotten by many, and the Ghost Dance was performed with the intent of removing the white man from the West. White reservation agents became alarmed at the heightened display, and troop reinforcements were sent in. The situation deteriorated and white troops reacted with disproportional violence at any sign of Native American rebellion or unrest (real or imagined), resulting in the spiral of violence that culminated in what is known as the Wounded Knee Massacre.

John "Moon-head" Wilson

John Moon-head Wilson of the Caddo-Delaware tribe contributed to the spread of the Ghost Dance in 1890, a year after Wovoka, or Jack Wilson, initiated it among western Native Americans. He promoted ingestion of the hallucinogenic fruit of the peyote cactus for the purpose of spiritual trances, and developed the "Cross Fire" style of ceremony for all-night peyote prayer vigils.

Catherine Tekakwitha

Catherine Tekakwitha was born in 1656, in the Mohawk stronghold Ossernenon, now known as Auriesville, New York. The daughter of a Mohawk father and an Algonquin Catholic mother, her life would reflect her diverse spiritual heritage. At the age of four, Catherine contracted the smallpox virus that had infected her entire family. The disease claimed the lives of Catherine's parents and siblings and ravaged her appearance, causing severe scarring on her face and compromising her eyesight. The orphan was adopted by her uncle, a Mohawk chief who openly professed his opposition to the Christian faith.

In the Autumn of 1666, Ossernenon was burned at the hands of a punitive expedition from Quebec, led by the Marquis Alexandre de Prouville de Tracy, who had declared war on the Mohawk nation in the name of France. Begging for clemency, the Mohawks complied with de Tracy's demands that they accept the Roman Catholic faith, and Jesuit missionaries were assigned to the nation.

Catherine worked closely with the priests, and was quickly won over by their gentle meekness, purity of mind, and consecrated nature. She eagerly sought to adopt their ideals, and though—as the adopted daughter of the chief—she received many proposals of marriage, Catherine chose chastity, embarking on a quest to emulate her idol, the Virgin Mary. In 1675, Catherine requested baptism from missionary Jacques de Lamberville, and received it on Easter Sunday, 1676. In the ceremony, she took the name Catherine.

Catherine's life would change drastically after this episode. Her dedication to the Catholic faith

Catherine (or Kateri) Tekakwitha (1656–1680), depicted in this statue at the Basilica of Sainte-Anne-de-Beaupré near Quebec City, was a Mohawk-Algonquin woman who formally converted to Catholicism in 1676.

brought severe censure from her people, including death threats. De Lamberville recommended she pray unceasingly, and, although Catherine interpreted her trials as necessary for her development as a Christian, she ultimately accepted De Lamberville's suggestion that she relocate to Kahnawake, Canada, a town with many Christian Native Americans. Catherine flourished in her new setting.

Though her own tribe had driven her from her home, Catherine remained committed to them, continuing to join them on winter hunting expeditions, nearly until her death. She became noted for her purity and charity of heart, and spent much time caring for the sick. Catherine was also interested in the practice of corporal mortification. She subjected herself to sleep deprivation, fasting, wearing painful metal belts, extreme cold, burning her legs, scourging, and rolling in branches of thorns. These mortifications were, according to the recent biography by Allan Greer, ritual actions undertaken to gain sacred power in Mohawk terms, not simply in Catholic ones. Catherine was a member of a group of Native American women who employed these ritual practices and who wished to be allowed to incorporate themselves as a community of Catholic nuns. In 1679, Catherine was granted permission to take the vow of chastity, which, in Catholicism, symbolizes consecrated virginity. One year later, at the age of twenty-four, Catherine died of a "slow fever."

She is now referred to as "The Mohawk Maiden," the "Lily of the Mohawks," and "Fairest Flower Among True Men." A Jesuit priest who looked upon her in her coffin reported that Catherine's scars had disappeared after her death, revealing a young woman of astonishing beauty. In 1884, the move to canonize Catherine began. In 1943, she was declared Venerable by Pope Pius XII, and was beatified by Pope John Paul II on June 22, 1980. Catherine is the first Native American to be referred to as "Blessed" by the Roman Catholic Church. There is much support among Catholic Native Americans for Catherine's full canonization, which is awaiting verification of a miracle. In 1830, a convent was opened in Mexico, where Native American nuns pray daily for her sainthood.

James Blue Bird

Born in 1889 to a Sioux Episcopal minister, James Blue Bird became a follower of the Peyote religion in 1902, at the age of fourteen. He attended services at the Pine Ridge Reservation in South Dakota from 1904–1907. After graduating from the Carlisle Indian Industrial School of Pennsylvania, James returned to his homeland, where he played a significant role in founding the Native American Church of South Dakota. The church was formally incorporated on October 5, 1922, and James served as one of the initial trustees. His leadership included instituting the Cross Fire ceremonial style of Peyotism, introducing the Bible as the main reference for worship, and suggesting the inclusion of ministers within the church's organization. James remained heavily involved with the NACSD for over fifty years.

Black Elk

Born in 1863, Black Elk committed himself to preserving Lakota culture. During his young adult-

hood, missionaries attempted to convert his people, the Oglala Lakotas, to Christianity. Black Elk was among the converted, but his Lakota spirituality remained strong and he became part of an underground traditional religious movement. He led his people in outwardly accepting Christianity, in order to survive U.S. policy, but worked to preserve Lakota traditional beliefs. Fearing that U.S. intended to wipe out the Lakota tribe, and with it its culture and religious heritage, he dictated his life story to John Neihardt. This became the book *Black Elk Speaks,* which was widely circulated and urged the Lakota to never fully assimilate and lose their unique identity. After the passage of the Indian Religious Freedoms Act in 1978, Black Elk's teachings were influential in creating a renaissance of traditional Lakota spirituality, which led to the decline of Lakota membership in Christian churches and an increase of traditional spiritual practices amongst the younger generation.

Handsome Lake

Handsome Lake was born in 1753 in the village of Ganawagus, in present-day New York State. In 1799, after a near-death experience, he had three visions in which he was told that he had been chosen by God for a mission and given a series of instructions that came to be called the Code of Handsome Lake. This code specified abstinence from alcohol, the use of witchcraft solely for healing, an end to the usage of "love medicine," and the importance of family and children. He also counseled his people to learn the ways of the white man but also to keep their traditional clothing for ceremonies. He advocated the preservation of traditional rituals and prayers and his code proscribed four specific sacred rituals. He made predictions about the future, which included signs of the end of the world.

In 1802, Handsome Lake traveled to Washington to meet with President Thomas Jefferson and Secretary of War Henry Dearborn. Almost a decade after his death in 1815, his teachings were revived with the help of his grandson, Jimmy Johnson, and nephew, Owen Blacksnake. Since then, meetings have been held at various reserves to maintain the Iroquois traditions of the Code of Handsome Lake.

Smohalla

Sometime between 1815 and 1820, Smohalla was born into the Shahaptian Wanapum tribe in the Columbia Plateau region of what is now Washington State. Smohalla quickly grew to prominence as a spiritual leader, at which point he received his name, meaning "preacher." He developed what is now called a "revitalization" doctrine, which called for a return to the traditional practices and beliefs of his people's forbears. Widespread preaching of revitalization resulted in the formation of a united confederation of Pacific Northwest Natives opposed to white expansion. When it was learned by members of this confederation that the United States government intended to push their tribes onto tiny reservations, the Native Americans militantly mobilized against government forces in what is now called the Yakima War of 1855–1856.

Smohalla ultimately became known as a prophet, amassing nearly 2,000 followers of revitalization. He took spiritual journeys during which he was said to be in touch with the spirit world, and revived the Washani religion and its corresponding rituals in relating his spiritual visions to his disciples. Smohalla died in 1895, but was succeeded as a religious teacher by his son, Yoyouni.

II. Tenets and Attitudes

A. Articles of Faith

TRADITIONAL ROOTS

Traditional Native American religion rests upon a communal framework: it exists to benefit the community as a whole, rather than to serve the individual. Unlike Euro-American religious practices, a Native American cannot choose his or her religion; rather, one is born into the specific way of life that will dictate it. Each tribally-unique manifestation of spirituality is connected to the community as a whole and, in turn, to the specific geographical locale where it is observed. Land is believed to possess a religious character; terrestrial elements are ascribed specific powers, and deities are experienced as alive. Native Americans found life lessons within every geographical and spatial aspect of their world. A certain rock might remind one of a personal experience; a tree may teach a moral lesson; a particular cardinal direction oriented one towards life, happiness, goodness, and health.

Tribal territories were established as swaths of "bound land" delineated by natural barriers such as mountains, marshland, or rivers. The spatial relations of a tribe to its locale took on paramount importance in dictating the directional elements of ceremonies, prayers, town layouts, and architecture. For example, Osage towns were bisected by a main road running East-West, the division symbolizing the duality of the two great fructifying forces of existence: "Wakonda Above" (Sky) and "Wakonda Below" (Earth). According to Osage custom, a marriage must include a representative from either side of the division to symbolize the unification of both forces inherent to life. However, even within marital unity, each spouse continued to recognize the customary practices of his or her birth division—for instance, which shoe is to be tied first. This served to remind the individual of the necessary role he or she played in constituting the communal whole.

The spectrum of deific figures varies widely within Native American religions. Some cultures recognize at least one major deity—of either gender or no gender at all. The outsider conception of the "Great Spirit" often attributed to Native American religions is actually a poor translation of the Lakota Wakan Tanka, or, more closely, "Sacred Power," and is usually mistakenly equated with the Christian God. In fact, Wakan Tanka is pantheistic in nature, believed to interpenetrate and animate all aspects of the natural world. The Sacred power is considered a great unknown, to be understood by humans through phenomenal spatial manifestations: in the land, nature, and astronomical constellations.

Traditional Native Americans mostly do not believe in a single cosmic creator who created the universe from nothing. Rather, they believe the primordial characteristics of the cosmos were specifically ordered according to the direction of mythological figures. Native American stories illustrate how the world was "found," emphasize its shape as spiritually significant, and describe the ways in which ancestral organization of the landscape imbued it with meaning.

Symbolism plays a fundamental role in elucidating spiritual meaning—both in tangible and abstract forms. For example, many physical objects, such as corn, tobacco, squash, beans, the eagle, and the bear, all serve as dominant symbols of various religious truths. However, (in a manner that has caught the attention of Western anthropologists) symbolism is also utilized pictorially (e.g., the open circle represents motion and interdependent relationships) and dramatically (often through symbolic reversal, in which a clown or trickster encounters hardship through rebellion against order, thereby representing the importance of following order). Symbolic rituals also occur commemorating transitions in the life cycle or calendar, interests of the community (for example, success in hunting), or the onset of illness.

Health is an integral part of Native American religion. Healing specialists, termed "medicine persons" or sometimes "shamans," utilize magico-religious power or objects of power to restore their patients' well-being. Native Americans recognize an interrelatedness (or holism) of all living and nonliving things within one's environment. Consequently, health determines the status of this relationship: sickness indicates an imbalance somewhere along the delicate web of interdependence. Thus, healing does not address the physical symptoms of a patient, but the possible causal factors in the system at large. Like all other aspects of Native American life, sickness is assigned a religious meaning.

Shamanism can involve a psychic trance, or ecstasy, by which the practitioner achieves higher spiritual status. Shamans initially come by their religious power through a power quest, inheritance, purchase, or election. Once acquired, they are believed to wield powerful spiritual influence over the world. Shamans restore health through one of two methods: restoration of a lost or stolen soul (life's vitality), or removal of an intruding object of malevolence. The lost soul is sought, located, and recovered, while the intruding foreign body may be removed through sucking, blowing, singing, or administering formulas.

PEYOTISM

Today, more than two-thirds of Native Americans characterize themselves as "somewhat Christian." Many combine Christian and Native American ideas, while others keep them separate but maintain ideas drawn from both. With at least 250,000 adherents, Peyotism now reigns as the most prevalent religion originated, founded, and currently practiced by Native Americans. Ingestion of the fruit (or button) of the peyote cactus began among indigenous peoples of Mexico 7,000 years ago. Today, its ceremonial use—mostly in the southwestern United States—incorporates many ancestral beliefs, tempered with hints of Christianity.

Like Christianity, Peyotism is monotheistic. Practitioners believe in one Creator, also referred to as God, the Great Spirit, or Wakan Tanka (in Lakota). All men and women are the children of this Creator, brought to existence and endowed with inalienable rights by the Creator's grace. Humankind's duty is to explore these rights and reclaim them—and God provided the peyote button for just that purpose. According to Peyotism, God gave the white men Jesus for the sake of divine revelation; to the Native Americans, He gave peyote. By this reasoning, peyote ingestion is deemed a sacrament.

Peyotists recognize a universal Truth that pervades existence. It is imperative that humankind align with this Truth—though many worldly forces would constantly fragment one's perception of it. Truth may be explored at the "Matrix of Harmonic Convergence" where Earth and Sky meet in harmony. This belief harkens back to the native belief in Wakanda Above and Wakanda Below, the two spiritual forces, the unification of which is inherent to earthly existence. According to Peyotism, man possesses "apertures of energy," which are always open and functioning (in the transference of energy). These apertures are in primal disarray, but may be thoughtfully aligned by people through intense focus of their spiritual energy. Once synergistically aligned, the apertures serve as portals through which one may enter the Matrix and immerse oneself in Truth; one is the open to receive the unique Gifts of Being, bestowed by the Creator. Peyote is employed to transport humans into this Matrix reality, beyond the limited, sensory world of matter. In his introduction to *Coyote Man and Old Doctor Loon*, Bob Callahan describes reality as the "mysterious, ubiquitous, concentrated form of non-material energy . . . loose about the world and contained in a more or less condensed degree by all objects."

Peyote is ingested during prayer vigils, which extend from sunset to sunrise, and include praying, singing, peyote ingestion (eaten in dried, fresh, or powdered form, or drunk as tea), and contemplation. Participants experience hallucinations in which they "travel down Peyote Road," the way to spiritual enlightenment, understanding of Self, and oneness with the Creator. The vigils are guided by shamans, or medicine people. Shamans are believed to possess superior spiritual powers through mastery of energy use and the ability to have visions. They are credited with special knowledge of divine being, for they frequently traverse the axes between matter and reality. Other official positions held by members of the church, which play specific roles in the peyote ceremonies, are Cedar Chief, Fire Chief, Drum Chief, Earth Mother, and Morning Water Woman. Materials used during the ceremony include an eagle bone whistle, feather fans, a water drum, and a prayer staff.

The simplest practice of Peyotism occurs on an individual level, for the purpose of a vision question. This is performed in a solitary, natural setting. The vision seeker engages in fasting, peyote ingestion, and contemplation, persisting in his vigil until he reaches a sense of physical and spiritual self-unity, or completeness, through communion with the Great Spirit. The process mirrors the ancient Creator Spirit Story, in which a man or woman was lost in the desert, suffering of starvation and thirst. On the very verge of death, the lost person suddenly heard the voice of the Spirit who commanded reaching out and picking the first succulent plant their fingertips touched. Upon eating this plant, the person found hunger satiated, thirst slaked, and their feet led home.

The tenets of the Native American Church are avoidance of alcohol or recreational drugs, devotion to family, unceasing work ethic, financial self-support, humility, and brotherly love. The church has historically accepted new members of any ethnicity, so long as they are deemed sincere adherents to the spiritual beliefs of Peyotism. However, on account of an overwhelming interest showed in Peyotism by the counter- (or "hippie") generation of the 1960s, a law was passed in 1978 prohibiting the possession of peyote by non-Native Americans. This law remains in effect today. Unless a card-carrying member of the Church of Native Americans is one quarter Native, he or she may not carry, cultivate, or possess peyote. This calls into question the legality of non-Native Americans as bona fide members of the Native American Church.

The largest problem facing the church today is the dwindling supply of available peyote. The peyote cactus is a slow-growing plant, requiring the same amount of time to produce fruit as most fruit trees (about five years). Improper harvesting of the fruit (cutting roots shafts too deep to allow regeneration) and loss of peyote habitat to ranching has resulted in an overall decrease in peyote production.

THE YAQUIS

One of a dozen nations currently practicing a hybrid Native American Christian religion is the Yaqui people. The Yaquis, or Haiki Nation, occupy territory in northern Mexico and Arizona surrounding the Yaqui River. The tribe numbers around

30,000 people, and observes a religion that incorporates both indigenous beliefs and sixteenth-century Jesuit teachings.

During the fifteenth-century European invasion of the Americas, Spanish conquistadors attempted without success to conquer the Yaquis. Jesuit missionaries, who practiced a more tolerant approach to Native traditions and culture, were welcomed by the tribe, and managed to coexist in peaceful harmony with them until the 1730s, when the Spanish colonial government ordered the Jesuits out of Mexico. This caused great upheaval among the Yaqui and severed their economic and religious ties with white settlers. Today, the Yaqui live on a 202-acre reservation near Tucson, Arizona, or farther north on territory in Guadalupe, Arizona. Over forty-four percent of the civilization's ethnic make-up is Native American, and the Yaqui traditional language, called "Yoeme," is still widely spoken and taught.

The Yaqui follow the Roman Catholic calendar, but use Native rituals to celebrate traditional Catholic holidays. Easter, for example, is the main holiday observed by the Yaqui. Beginning before Ash Wednesday and continuing for seven weeks, churches are decorated, symbolic masks are made, and crosses are set up. Public rituals and performances, such as the "deer dance," go on throughout the forty days preceding Easter Week. On Good Friday, it is claimed that "the flower world has died" and sadness is upon the face of the Earth. The Yaqui remove all flowers from homes and public places and attire themselves in dark clothing. The Passion of the Christ is enacted with a crucifixion of an effigy of Jesus. On Saturday, deer dancers and Pascolas ("Old Men of the Ceremony")—armed with flowers—battle the acting "Pharisees" until they are "defeated," at which point the actors throw their masks and an effigy of Judas into a large fire. When it is announced that Jesus has been resurrected, festivities resume in a community-wide celebration, including feasting, music, and more deer dancing. The grand occasion continues on through Easter Sunday.

The Yaqui World View

Yaqui tradition holds that the world is composed of four differentiations: the world of people, the world of animals, the world of flowers, and the world of death. Ritual is focused at perfecting these worlds by correcting human effacement of them. As previously mentioned, flowers are a very significant element of Yaqui symbology. They are said to have sprung up where the Virgin Mary's joyful tears dropped at Jesus's resurrection. Alternately, they are said to emanate from drops of Jesus's shed blood during his crucifixion. Either way, flowers are seen as manifestations of souls. They represent new life, new beginnings, happiness, and beauty.

The sun, moon, and stars are also important Yaqui symbols. The sun represents the home and energy of the Father of all Creation, "Achai Taa'ah"; the moon represents the Mother of all Creation, "Maala Mecha"; the stars are the ancestors of the living. It is said that when a person dies, he first passes through the sun, then becomes a star. The Yaqui believe themselves strongly connected to the natural world, and express a connectedness to animal life.

The "deer dance" is perhaps the most representative element of Yaqui spiritual practice. Performed throughout the year, it is meant to commemorate the Yaqui's relationship with the deer, which they traditionally hunted for food and skin, and continue to revere today. In this performance, "deer dancers" fasten a deer head complete with antlers and glass eyes upon their own heads. They cover their faces with white cloths, leave their chests bare, and wear loincloths. They may carry dried gourds or tie rattles to their ankles. The deer dancers act out the role of a hunted deer, displaying skittishness, fear, silence, and aloofness. The Pascolas, akin to hosts of the performances, "hunt" the deer. Musicians convey the deer's heartbeat with gourd drums, and labored breath with rasping sticks. When the deer dancer has been "captured" by the Pascolas, he dramatically enacts the deer's death with flailing, erratic movements.

B. Scripture

As Christianity is a major aspect of the Native American Church, the Bible serves as a primary scriptural source. Traditional Native American religions are orally transmitted, obviating the possibility of sacred texts. Yaquis concentrate on the sacred parts of the Catholic mass such as the consecration of the Eucharist as well as the Bible and the hymns. Other parts of the mass such as the priests' homily or the donations are not considered as sacred.

C. Secondary Sources

Vine Deloria Jr.

Vine Deloria Jr. was born in South Dakota in 1933 near the Oglala Lakota Indian Reservation. He attended school on the reservation as a child, then went on to undergraduate schooling at Iowa State University. Intending to become an Episcopalian minister like his father, Deloria next attended the Lutheran School of Theology in Rock Island, Illinois, where he earned a Master's Degree in Theology in 1973. But, Deloria's schooling did not end there. In 1970, he graduated with a law degree from the University of Colorado, then accepted the position of Executive Director of the Congress of American Indians. Deloria published over twenty books in his lifetime, beginning his writing career with *Custer Died for Your Sins: An American Manifesto* in 1969. This book would become one of his best-known in the field, eliciting a panel response from the American Anthropological Association. In the work, Deloria disputed widely-held views of American westward expansion, addressing the phenomenon from the Native American perspective. He also refuted Native American stereotypes held by whites. Through his books, Deloria served as a powerful spokesperson for Native American identity and social change, advancing his views on present-day religious and educational issues faced by his people. He won several literary awards for his work, and served as a professor at both the University of Arizona and the University of Colorado at Boulder. Deloria died on November 13, 2005.

Neolin

Neolin was a nativist prophet of the Delaware tribe in the mid-eighteenth century. He attributed the misfortunes of the Native Americans to European influence and advocated a return to traditional rituals, beliefs, and practices. Before their contact with the Europeans, the Delaware's religious world was governed by spirits with which an individual could commune through ritual. However, in the mid-eighteenth century, prophets such as Neolin began to identify European interference as the cause of spiritual anger. They believed that divine favor could only be restored through the rejection of all alien influences and beliefs.

In 1776, Neolin claimed to have experienced a vision in which a spiritual messenger warned him of what would happen should his people continue to stray from their traditional ways. According to Neolin, the route to heaven had once been clear and easy to access, but then it had become blocked by the Europeans. Because Native Americans had abandoned their traditional practices, wore European clothes, hunted beyond subsistence level for the purpose of trade, and allowed Europeans to occupy their land, their souls would now be shunted from heaven into the realm of the Evil Spirit. Neolin's message of reform, while it was a call to return to the traditional ways, contained Christian elements, such as the reference to the Evil Spirit.

Neolin was strongly anti-British and believed that the reformation would take seven years during which the British would be driven from Native land. Unlike many prophets, Neolin achieved widespread influence. Pontiac, an Ottawa chief, used Neolin's ideas to support his attack on the British in 1763. Neolin predicted victory over the British, but the uprising collapsed in 1764–1765.

John Eliot

John Eliot, known to Native Americans as the "Apostle," was born in Hertfordshire, England, in the early 1600s. He served a Puritan missionary to Massachusetts Native Americans, most notably translating the Bible into their native Natick language. The Natick Bible of 1663 was one of the first books printed in North America. Eliot's efforts at preserving Native American culture within a European context included his formation of towns for Native Americans governed solely by them, in which they were encouraged to lead Christian lives. Eliot succeeded in setting up fourteen such towns of "Praying Indians" before whites destroyed them in the King Philip's War. Eliot died on May 21, 1690.

John Eliot preaches to a group of Pequot Native Americans in this undated print.

III. Rites and Rituals

A. The Calendar

Though the Native American Church uses the traditional Gregorian calendar, it is understood that each tribe throughout the United States celebrates or observes holidays according to its own timeline and preferences.

The Yaquis, on the other hand, along with other hybrid Native American/Catholic religions such as the Sonoran Catholicism of the Tohono O'odham people, have uniformly adopted the ritual calendar of the Catholic Church. This liturgical calendar begins with Advent, the four week period in which Catholics anticipate the birth of Christ. Christmas, December 25, is observed in commemoration of Jesus's birth. "Ordinary Time" follows, during which no holidays are celebrated, until Lent, the forty-day period of Christian fasting in anticipation of Easter. Lent begins on Ash Wednesday and ends on Palm Sunday, after which Ordinary Time resumes. Addi-

tional important feast days are Christmas, All Saints Day, the Assumption of Mary, and other Saints days.

Among the Hopi Tribe, the Powamu Festival takes place in late January or early February. During this eight-day festival, the Hopis celebrate the six-month return of the spirits of their ancestors, or "Kachinas," from the mountaintops. Participants believe these spirits grant their families with health and prosperity. Several rituals are performed to honor the spirits of their ancestors, including the ingestion of bean sprouts, which are a symbol of fertility.

The Hodenosaunee (popularly called Iroqouis) Midwinter Ceremony is also held in January and February. Commencing with the appearance of a new moon and the positioning of the Big Dipper constellation at the sky's zenith, a new spiritual year is said to begin. Five days into the new year, a nine-day celebration is held during which new members of the council are chosen for the year. Also, ceremonial rituals are held in honor of the tobacco plant to promote its successful growth in the coming year.

The Kwakiutl Midwinter Ceremony occurs in February in honor of the connection human beings share with the supernatural world. According to Kwakiutl beliefs of human origins, this connection was acquired from the animals, who originally ruled Earth with supernatural powers. This Midwinter Ceremony consists of feasts, dances, and gift giving. Another important Kwakiutl ceremony is the Athabascan Stickdance, performed for a week in March, during which the deaths of male tribal members are mourned. The Stickdance also requires gift-giving, the preparation of which can be costly and time-consuming. For this reason, grieving family members may choose not to hold it on an annual basis.

Among the Diné (popularly called Navajo) the coming of spring is celebrated with a Mountain Chant. It is traditionally performed after the season's first thunderstorm but before warm, spring winds begin to blow. The Mountain Chant is meant to heal the ill, as well as those suffering from disharmony in life or relationships.

The Ute Bear Dance facilitates courting among tribal members, in addition to celebrating spring. The emergence of bears from hibernation serves as a Ute symbol of fertility. Traditionally, women choose their partners for the dance. This festival usually lasts four to five days, ending when a dancing couple collapses from exhaustion.

The Green Corn Dance is still performed by several nations, typically occurring in May. For the Seminoles, this dance marks the new year; for many other tribes it is held in honor of the corn crop. Eating corn before the dance is performed is considered blasphemous.

The Sun Dance was also traditionally performed by many Native American nations of the plains, who usually held it in accord with the summer solstice. It includes two weeks of preparation, followed by four to eight days of fasting, dancing, and ritual. During the Sun Dance male dancers affix themselves to a central pole by having their back or breasts skewered and tied with leather thongs to the pole. While dancing, they strain against the ropes until they eventually tear free from the skewers. These dancers sacrifice in order to forge a strong relationship with the Sacred Power, and for the benefit of their communities and families. Because of its violent nature, the Sun Dance was outlawed by the U.S. government in 1904. However, it continued to be practiced in secret until the ban was lifted and the Sun Dance could be practiced openly once more.

The Crow Fair is an agricultural fair hosted by the Crow Nation as a "giant family reunion under the Big Sky." Held the third weekend of every August outside of Billings, Montana, the Crow Fair is considered the biggest powwow of various Native Nations of the year. Women and men are invited to demonstrate their agricultural and domestic skills in adjudicated food and home goods displays, while children may try their hand at winning cash prizes in various games. The fair includes an expansive parade, rodeos, horse races, and dancing contests.

Every August, on the northeastern mesas of Arizona, the Hopi Nation prays for rain and an abundant corn crop in a nine-day affair called the Hopi Flute Ceremony. The event mainly consists of a ceremonial procession, during which Kokopelli—the god of rain and fertility—is appealed to through a succession of symbolic requests for rain and thunderstorms from all cardinal directions. A carved Flute Altar is used for rituals involving cornmeal, corn stalks, and ears of corn in prayer for a large harvest.

The Hopis also employ the Snake Dance in asking the deities for rain. The Hopi Snake Dance occurs every two years in August or September, and continues on for sixteen days. The actual dance—involving snakes—occurs on the last day of the event. Hopis regard the snake as man's "brother," and employ snakes in this ritual to carry a message to the gods of the underworld, where they believe their ancestors reside. Snakes are rooted from their burrows by adults and then gathered by children. A "snake whip"—a rod with two eagle feathers fastened to one end—is used to prevent the snake from coiling and subsequently striking. Once the hundreds of snakes are gathered, they are washed in herb-infused water, sprinkled with cornmeal, and released in a snake shrine. A few days preceding the Dance, one girl and one boy of fourteen years old are selected to represent Snake Youth and Antelope Maid. As the children stand in front of an illustrative sand painting, priests relate the legend of these iconic figures in a dramatic story-telling event that may extend for several hours. In this story, the snake symbolizes Mother Earth, while the antelope symbolizes fruitful reproduction. The antelope's antlers symbolize its ability to reach high into the heavens. Races between the two animals are held to represent the pathway to the union of Mother Earth, reproduction, and heaven. Priests traditionally perform dances with snakes in their mouths as the final stage of this ritual.

The Miwok, located in northern California, annually hold the Miwok Acorn Festival in the last weekend of September. Acorns were traditionally a major food staple of this people, and the festival is held in honor of their provision. During the festival, the acorns are gathered, crushed, and rid of tannins, then made into bread, mush, or soup.

The Eagle Dance is performed by many different Native Nations, and may be held any time of year. Traditionally, however, it is performed in the spring. Because the eagle can achieve great elevation in flight, it is regarded by Native Americans as sacred—in communion with both Earth and Heaven. As such, it is ritualistically employed to carry messages to the gods, especially in request of rain. The Eagle Dance portrays the life cycle of the eagle from birth to death. This bird plays a highly significant role in Native American symbology, representing wisdom, power, strength, and the sun. Eagle feathers are a popular gift for Native American boys, who are carefully instructed as to their handling. It is warned that an eagle feather must never touch the ground. Should a feather be dropped, a selected tribal elder must retrieve it and return it to its owner, who is expected to present the elder with a gift of thanks.

The Diné Night Chant is a nine-day ceremony held in the late fall or early winter, and incorporating sand paintings, prayer sticks, chants, songs, and dances as a means of restoring harmony and balance to the world and personal health. The Night Chant occurs within the homes of invalid Diné, and is conducted by a chanter, or medicine man. The chanter calls an entire community to participation, then instructs each individual patient to sit to the west of a fire. The first four days of elaborate chanting, dancing, and singing are devoted to purification; the following days are allotted to the work of Holy Men. On the ninth day, the patient is told to look east at the rising sun in a symbolic gesture of renewal.

The Shalako Ceremony of the Zuñi Natives occurs during the winter solstice on a date arrived at through careful calculations by a Sun Priest. The "Shalako" are believed to be God's messengers, and bringers of rain. The Sun Priest publicly announces the chosen date of the ceremony only eight days in advance, at which point the entire Zuñi tribe must burst into preparatory activity. Certain households of the Zuñi tribe are selected to host the Shalako impersonators, which, in housing, feeding, and entertainment costs, is often a great financial burden. On the day of the ceremony, the Shalako actors appear in a large field in giant masks held aloft on towering poles that are concealed with blankets. The masks are adorned with a feather headdress and moving eyes and beak. Three men are required to manipulate each heavy mask upon its pole, making it appear to dance, bow, blink, and snap its beak. All manipulation occurs under the blankets, where the men rotate their duties when fatigued. Near midnight, the dancers travel to their host homes, where they continue to perform. Twelve hours later, at noon, the Shalako dancers depart the house in a ritualistic procession. This departure is the final prayer for plenty of rain before the hot, dry summer months.

The Soyaluna is a ceremony held on December 22nd by the Hopi for the purpose of offering prayers for the New Year and persuading the sun to return to Earth. Hopis believe that the Sun God is closest to the Earth during the summer solstice, but that he is driven away by hostile forces as the summer wanes and fall commences. Also, Hopis hold the "black Plumed Snake" accountable for solar eclipses, claiming that it is swallowing the sun. The Soyaluna Ceremony is therefore an opportunity to make a peace offering to the Plumed Snake, and entice the Sun God closer to the earth.

B. Worship and Liturgy

The Native American Church's most popular form of worship and religious expression is singing, which composes sixty percent of their ritual rites. Dancing, drumming, praying, meditation, fasting, abstinence, and consumption of peyote are included among religious expression. The Native American Church has also adopted the traditional Sweat Lodge, which resembles a sauna, as part of their rituals for renewal, purification, and education.

The focus of worship for the Native American Church is the peyote plant. The fruit of this small cactus is believed to have medicinal value and is viewed as a sacramental substance with divine powers that can purify, heal, and enlighten those who ingest it. Because it is a hallucinogen, it is thought to provide a heightened spiritual experience through visions.

The Yaquis engage in singing hymns and performing dances as a form of spiritual expression. The Matachin Dance Society is composed of forty or more dancers and is run by the Church Governor. Matachin dances honor Jesus Christ and the Blessed Mother and are performed in accordance with prayers and chants. The characters portrayed include Moctezuma and Malintzin and the dance tells the story of the Spanish conquest.

During many traditional religious ceremonies, symbolic objects are often employed for their supposed religious powers. These objects are collected into "bundles" and may include: pipes; natural paints and dyes; plant materials (such as sweet grass and sage to be used as incense); animal and bird skins; hair and bones; stones; and other materials.

In preparation for worship, Native Americans may engage in acts of induced suffering to propagate dreams and visions. This includes fasting and causing harm to body parts or flesh. These practices are believed to facilitate spiritual visions that bring about stronger relationships with sacred powers.

C. Daily Life

Indigenous beliefs are so interwoven in the daily practices of adherents that Native American religion is better viewed as a "way of life" than as an isolated institution. Religious beliefs will likely influence every aspect of a tribe's culture and daily habits.

Members of the Native American Church are taught to follow the "Peyote Road," which advocates love and support of one's family, disciplined work habits, and avoidance of alcohol and drug use.

D. Life Cycle Events

Birth

Since each tribe of Native Americans has its own specific religious beliefs and practices, there is no way to generalize all of Native American birthing rituals. One can only provide examples.

The Blessing Way is a Diné rite lasting two nights. This ritual is intended to provide good luck, protection (most importantly, for women during childbirth), and to consecrate marriage. The ceremony includes a ritual bath, prayers, songs, sand painting, and stories.

Those born into the Native American Church and the members of the Yaqui religion as well as other sects of Native American Christianity such as Protestantism receive the sacrament of baptism to cleanse them from original sin. This is an aspect of the Native American Church that has been adapted from Christian beliefs and traditions.

Coming of Age

Traditionally, both male and female children go through a puberty ceremony which involves periods of isolation. Girls are isolated at the time of first menstruation. Isolation periods might last from several weeks to a year, during which an older woman tend to the girl and instructs her in her role as an adult member of the tribe. Following her isolation, the girl begins to wear adult dress. Boys undergo public rites of initiation for their first tooth, first steps, and first big game killed. Within some Native American cultures, when a boy nears adolescence, he journeys alone to a mountaintop or into a forest for the purpose of a vision quest, brought on by fasting. Upon his return to the tribe, he is regarded as an adult.

Confirmation is a Christian (usually Catholic) sacrament of initiation in which adolescents confirm their devotion to the religion in question. It is also defined as a "completion of baptismal grace," during which the Holy Spirit unites the confirming church member more closely with Jesus. Many Native Americans receive this sacrament in accordance with their belief in Christian traditions. Each denomination of Christianity varies in the ceremonial practices of confirmation; usually it involves anointing the newest confirmed member with oil.

Among the Apaches, a girl's entrance into womanhood is celebrated for four days in July with a celebration called Girls' Sunrise. Girls who have experienced their first menstrual cycle are included in the puberty rites, which involve symbolic face painting, dancing, and telling the story of creation.

The Wuwuchim Ceremony is enacted by the Hopi Nation as a means of inducting boys into adult society. For sixteen days in November, all fires are extinguished and all women and children retreat indoors, while coming-of-age boys and tribal men gather in a kiva, or underground home, to enact highly secret rituals. During this period, elders divulge Hopi religious traditions and beliefs to the initiated boys. Following initiation, the boys are treated as men and may take part in adult rituals.

Nuptials

According to the Algonquin wedding tradition, an engaged couple must solicit four sponsors of the marriage who are older, well-respected members of the tribe. These sponsors provide spiritual and marital guidance throughout the lives of the couple, and commit to helping it succeed. Before the ceremony, the bride must wash herself in a natural body of water in order to bless herself of the spirit of the Earth. The wedding itself is usually held outdoors and conducted by a Pipe Carrier, who reminds the couple that marriage is a lifelong commitment to one another and to the Creator. After the ceremony, the couple smokes his pipe to symbolize their union.

Marriages in the Delaware Traditions are prearranged by the parents of the bride. There is no formal ceremony; simply an exchange of jewelry or blankets, the acceptance of which marks the beginning of the couple's union. During the ceremony, the bride wears a deerskin skirt and is bare from the waist up, with white, red and yellow clay face decoration.

Hopi women are typically met with suitors between the ages of sixteen and twenty. The girl extends an invitation of formal courtship to the boy of her choice by presenting him with a loaf of gomi, or a bread made of sweet cornmeal. If the boy is interested, he accepts her gift. If he wishes to progress the courtship, he presents her with a bundle of fine clothing. The girl's acceptance of the clothing marks their engagement. The bride wears manta beads and a wedding blanket during the ceremony. She and the groom walk barefoot to the latter's house, where they must reside for three days. After the marriage ceremony, the bride presents her mother-in-law with cornmeal. To signify their union, the couple washes their entwined hair in a basin. They then pray to the rising sun, and move to the bride's home, which becomes their permanent residence.

In northern California, Native Americans enter different levels of marriage. In a full marriage, the groom pays the bride's family a dowry. The future social status of the family is dependent on the amount paid by the groom. In a half-marriage, the groom pays half the usual price and lives with the bride under his father-in-law's jurisdiction. This might occur if the groom is not wealthy or if he married against his father's will. Silver jewelry is worn by both the bride and groom and acts as a shield against evil, hunger, poverty, and bad luck.

Native Americans who follow Christian tradition are married in a church. The wedding ceremony is performed by a member of the clergy, as matrimony is viewed as a union blessed by God. The couple exchange vows and blessed wedding rings. Marriage is viewed as a lifelong commitment since most Christian denominations frown upon divorce.

Death and Burial

Native American burial rites vary from tribe to tribe and have changed over the years. Past burial practices have included encasement, which is similar to placing in a tomb, sub-surface interment, cremation, and exposure. These ceremonies could last several days depending on the social status of the deceased. The Creator is called upon for guidance of the deceased in the spirit world. Some tribes, such as the Lakota tribe, erect the corpse onto a scaffold with the deceased's belongings for a four-day mourning period before the burial.

The Spirit Keeping Ceremony is a year long custom during which the spirit of the deceased is honored. A tipi for the spirit is built, and there is no mourning, since the spirit is considered to be present. A lock of hair, considered sacred, is wrapped in a special cloth and placed in the tipi. A bowl is also provided, out of which the spirit may feed. After one year, the family is ready to let the spirit go, and they demonstrate this by painting a figure of the deceased on a pole. The family looks on while the painted pole is dressed in new garments. This dressing is accompanied by pipe ceremonies and prayers. The ceremony ends with a feast and gift-giving to all the poor and those who have helped the family.

The White Buffalo Ceremony is performed by the Lakota for special members of the tribe and is combined with the Lakota Spirit Keeping Ceremony. During this ritual, the deceased's family must obtain a white buffalo skin and hang it outside the spirit's tipi. This is a great honor as the white buffalo are a rare species.

Other burial traditions include music, dance, art, and storytelling. Many Native Americans believe in everlasting afterlife in the spirit world.

Native Americans who adopt European practices are provided burial grounds on church property. Some who follow Christian practices perform traditional Christian funeral rites for the deceased. For them, a wake is held in which the body of the deceased is put on display in a funeral home. This is followed by a funeral mass, held in a church.

E. Family Life

Husband and Wife

In the past, marriages within Native American circles were usually arranged, and often viewed as a social contract rather than an emotional commitment. The main goal of the union was to share responsibilities in child-rearing. In matrilocal nations, the couple usually lived with the wife's parents. Today, we have little information about indigenous Native American marriages, as their means of historical record-keeping was exclusively oral.

Child-rearing

Traditionally, women in Native American tribes are respected as life-giving creatures with the power to create future generations—the pride of Native American culture. Myths and songs have been passed down from generation to generation in praise of women and their embodiment of bounty and fertility. Accordingly, the ultimate goal of life for many Native American women is to have children and raise a healthy family.

In the past, many Native American women died in childbirth, despite their use of herbal medicines and other practices thought to ease them through the process. In many tribes, female relatives acted as midwives during the birth. In other tribes, women gave birth in solitude and then remained in isolation with the baby for quite some time. Some Native Americans today choose a Diné Blessing Way ritual. This ritual focuses on the story of creation, and that of the Changing Woman, who is the essence of the Earth and causes its seasonal change. It is a two-day ceremony used to grant peace, harmony, and success upon the honored event. The families of expecting parents may exchange Birth Beads—representing energy centers of the body, fertility, and motherhood—as a symbol that child-rearing is a family-wide responsibility.

Native Americans have a very high regard for children. The Lakota word for "child" also means means "standing sacred." Most Native Americans do not believe in punishment, but do believe that it is important to give children a sense of belonging to family and friends, to teach them skills as well as generosity and independence.

Extended Family

Most traditional Native Americans placed less emphasis on the nuclear family than the extended family or kin. Kin included not only blood relatives, but other individuals from the community who became close to the family by fulfilling sacred obligations of loyalty. Among Native Americans, the fulfillment of such obligations granted inclusion in a group, regardless of genetic background. Native Americans invite extended family to participate in decision-making regarding their children, and although independence is valued in youths, traditional Native American parents depend greatly on the members of their tribes and extended family to educate and act as role models for their children.

Divorce

The fact that the nuclear family was traditionally insignificant in lieu of kinship ties meant that many Indian societies were open to and provided means for divorce. Today, among Christian Native Americans, divorce is largely not condoned. Marriage is viewed as a lifelong union sanctioned under God the Creator. Therefore, ending such a union is considered breaking a covenant made with God.

IV. Denominations and Demographics

A. History

The various belief systems of Native American tribes were most often developed in direct connection with the environmental needs of each tribe and the natural resources available. For example, in the Dakota region, the buffalo played a distinct role in religious beliefs and rituals, mainly because of the Dakota's enormous dependency on the animal's food, skin, and bones. As another example, three Native American tribes of the Southwest—the Apache, Comanche, and Kiowa—created the Peyote religion after their relocation to Oklahoma.

As European Christian settlers gained influence, Christian ideology was incorporated into Native American belief systems. In many cases, this was merely an effort on the part of the Natives to escape from religious persecution. Many Native Americans hoped that the superficial appearance of Christianity within their religious practices would help them avoid negative attention from European Christians, allowing them to peacefully practice their traditional beliefs in secret. Others—such as those who joined the Native American Church or the Yaqui religion—found similarities between Christianity and the beliefs they had already held to be true—for instance, the Christian beliefs in one almighty Creator and eternal life.

Besides the Yaqui religion and the Native American Church, there are many, many others of more traditional practice. Each tribe has its own indigenous religion that focuses on the acquisition and maintenance of relationships with sacred powers.

B. Comparisons in Tenets and Practices

Beliefs vary greatly among Native American Tribes. Particular rituals and traditions differ due to their environmental conditions. However, they share the common practice of recognizing and imbuing the natural world with sacred power. For example, trees, animals, rocks, and human beings are all believed to be inhabited by spirits. However, many Native American religions contain a belief in one Great God that is in control of all the other spirits. Since natural resources and environments vary across America, it is inevitable that a religion based on such principles would vary as well. Despite differences, many Native American religions hold the belief that the universe is an interdependent system in which everything and everyone is unified and connected.

C. Distribution

The history of population estimates of Native Americans has long been characterized by deliberate prevarication, either to justify European confiscation of Native American land or to hide the extent of the various genocidal means that whites used to drive Native Americans from their territories or to depopulate them. As a result, nearly no estimates reported before the mid-twentieth century, when Native Americans first began participating in the demographic enterprise itself, can be considered reliable. The Native American Church claims a membership of about 300,000; the Yaqui people claim nearly 10,000; and some 500,000 Native Americans consider themselves Catholics.

The 2003 U.S. Census reported that there are a total of four million Native Americans, comprising 0.9 percent of the population. Most Native Americans live in California, Oklahoma, and Arizona, but Native people live throughout the United States in urban, suburban, and rural areas as well.

V. Organization and Infrastructure

A. Education and Hierarchy of Clergy

Medicine people are Native American religious leaders who are believed to have supernatural powers. They are believed to act as conduits of sacred power for purposes of healing, prophesying, and controlling natural events. To become a medicine man in most Native American tribes, one must directly inherit supernatural abilities or be recognized by one's community as having a relationship with one or more sacred powers. Medicine men are often

sent referrals and may belong to medicine societies.

Another form of Native American religious leader is the roadman. The roadman leads all-night peyote ceremonies during which followers of the "Peyote Road" ingest the cactus fruit while praying to and worshipping the Creator. A roadman obtains his position through experience; later he passes on his skills to others who wish to learn. For some, this office is a full-time position; however, roadmen are only paid in gifts. A roadman is accompanied in his role by three other leaders, which include the chief drummer (provides accompaniment to the singing of hymns), a cedarman (consecrates ritual objects), and a fireman (tends to the ceremonial fire rituals).

The Yaquis established a more complex church hierarchy. The leadership structure of the Church is composed of three levels:

1. To the first level belongs the eldest member of the church, the Maestro, who reads prayers, sermons, and other portions of the Catholic liturgy. Also belonging to this level is a group of officials known as the Temahatim, who are in charge of upkeep of the church, the male religious icons owned by the church, and the money that is donated. A second group, Kiyohtei, is responsible for the female religious icons of the church, the altar cloths, and other cloths used during ceremonies.

2. The second level consists of the Church Governor, the Pihkan Ya'ut, and the Matachin Dance Society. The Governor organizes activities and dances. The Pihkan Ya'ut is an educated instructor of the Yaqui doctrine, responsible for maintaining and spreading knowledge about the standard prayers while building relationships with adherents of the church. The Matachin Dance Society is a group of forty or more dancers who represent good forces. They perform the Matachin Dance, which is the most sacred of the Yaqui rituals.

3. Comprising the third level of the hierarchy are the Customs Authority, the Pahkome, and the Military Society. The Customs Authority is in charge of the Lenten and Easter celebrations. The Pahkome burn the dead during the fall and summer

and maintain religious obligations to the patron saints of the Yaqui town. The Military Society is comprised of Bow officers, military leaders who defend towns, and "Coyotes," who perform religious rituals, dances, songs, and other ceremonial obligations throughout the year.

Native Americans also have ministries in other traditional Christian Churches. In these, the hierarchy is consistent with that of Christian organizations.

SEMINARIES AND COLLEGES

Since traditional Native American religion relies on oral traditions for transmission, there is little opportunity to apply the mechanism of modern collegiate discipline-building. There are, however, several colleges throughout the U.S. that cater to the education of Native American Christian youths:

Indian Bible College
PO Box 30880
Flagstaff, AZ 86003-0880
928-774-3890   Fax: 928-774-2655
ibc@indianbible.org   www.indianbible.org

The American Indian College of the Assemblies of God
10020 North 15th Avenue
Phoenix, AZ 85021-2199
602-944-3335   Fax: 602-943-8299
www.aicag.edu

Cook School for Christian Leadership
708 South Lindon Lane
Tempe, AZ 85281
480-968-9354   Fax: 480-968-9357
www.cooknam.org/EducationalPrograms.html

American Indian Bible Institute (AIBI)
AIBI Main Office
PO Box 511
Norwalk, CA 90651-0511
www.aibi.org

Native American Theological Education Consortium (NATEC)
(at the University of Dubuque)
University of Dubuque Seminary
2000 University Avenue
Dubuque, IA 52001-5099
800-369-8387
udts.dbq.edu

Native American Bible College
PO Box 248
Shannon, NC 28386
910-843-5304   Fax: 910-843-9265
office@nativeamericanbiblecollege.org
www.nativeamericanbiblecollege.com

B. Shrines and Houses of Worship

ORGANIZATIONS
Tribes are the most local level by which Native Americans organize themselves. Each tribe, depending on religious affiliation, is a member of a larger community or parish. Each parish has a specific house of worship or church. Very little information is available about the technical breakdown of non-Christian Native American people.

SACRED SPACES
Traditional Native American religions are very much connected to the land as a manifestation of the sacred. Consequently, the holy grounds in traditional Native American religions are not churches, temples or shrines, but areas of nature with especial religious significance. Thus, these sacred spaces are as fragile as any other natural landscape and, unlike the enclosed spaces of many other religions in America, are often threatened with the encroachment of business interests and tourists.

There are many of these significant sites, since every tribal group found their own holy ground. These places are frequently areas of unusual natural beauty. Some are open land, some are national parks and some are sites of business interests. A complete list cannot be given, since it would be simply too long, so here is a small sample of traditional Native American sacred spaces:

Badger-Two Medicine Area has been the ancestral homeland and setting for myths and oral tradition of the Blackfoot Tribe since prehistory. It is located at the Rocky Mountain Front in Montana and contains one of the last free-range grizzly bear habitats, as well as moose, elk, mountain goats, gray wolves, wolverines, and harlequin ducks. In 1885, European immigrants exterminated the free-range bison herds and in 1895, weakened by small pox and famine, signed away the Badger-Two Medicine Area to the European-Americans. Since then, parts of Badger-Two have been transformed into nature conservancy, game preserve, and oil drilling sites. For the last, Badger-Two currently is under a moratorium—renewed annually—to prevent drilling. However, this provision only extends until the ecosystem is deemed less fragile and able to better handle the devastation of oil drilling.

Black Hills, for many of the plains tribes of Native Americans, is holy ground, a source of tribal pride and religious strength. The mountain chain links southwest South Dakota to Wyoming and forms a natural habitat for eagles, hawks, antelope, deer, elk, mountain goats, and bighorn sheep. The native Mandan, Arikara, Kiowa, Crow, Sioux, and Cheyenne tribes attempt to revive their religious beliefs and maintain their interconnection with each other and the natural world through annual gatherings in the Black Hills for athletic events, conferences, and research projects on their spiritual homeland. Unfortunately, hunters, herders, and tourists have despoiled much of the natural landscape of the Black Hills. Through the Religious Freedom Act of 1978 the Lakota and Tsistsista sued for relief and damages against the federal authorities who managed the Black Hills National Park, who built parking lots and campgrounds on their sacred space and opened a trail that intersected with the ancestral approach to the summit. However, they lost, and that loss was upheld when appealed.

Enola Hill is forty-five miles outside of Portland, Oregon, and named by mid-nineteenth century pioneer Elsie Creighton for "alone" spelled backwards. A shrunken population of coho salmon of the Lower Columbia still spawn in its waters and cougars make its precipices their territory. For the Umatilla, Warm Springs, and Nez Perce tribes, Enola Hill is a place of pilgrimage, oral history, and sacred power. However, it has received little protection from government agencies set up to protect native heritage. In 1995, the U.S. Forest Service gave to loggers the cutting rights to 4.8 million board feet of deciduous trees and old growth evergreens within 158 acres. Protests from both local and environmental activist groups attempted to halt the clear cutting, but were unable to stop the logging.

MAJOR ENCLAVES

Native American tribes can be found in every state. Population distribution varies from state to state, with California, Arizona, and Oklahoma hosting the largest number of Native Americans.

C. Social Service Organizations

American Indian Religious Rights Foundation
Brenda R. Chitwood
11363 South Highway 171
Covington, TX 76636
www.airr.org
The American Indian Religious Rights Foundation (AIRR) is a nonprofit organization working to represent the religious rights of Native American prisoners. Their assistance in legal affairs includes making formal inquiry into the religious treatment accorded to Native American prisoners by contacting prison, state, and federal officials, after which they will take corrective action to remedy problems.

American Indian Heritage Foundation

PO Box 6301
Falls Church, VA 22040
703-819-0979   www.indians.org

The American Indian Heritage Foundation was established in 1973 to provide relief services to Native peoples nationwide, and to build bridges of understanding and friendship between Native and non-Native people.

Native American Christian Fellowship

Stanford University
Stanford, CA 94305
www.stanford.edu/group/nacf/

Founded at Stanford University, the Native American Christian Fellowship exists to provide an environment of fellowship and encouragement for Native American Christians and those interested in Christianity and applying Biblical principles to the context of Native American culture.

National Congress of American Indians (NCAI)

1301 Connecticut Ave NW, Suite 200
Washington, D.C. 20036
202-466-7767   Fax: 202-466-7797
ncai@ncai.org   www.ncai.org

The National Congress of American Indians was founded in 1944 in response to assimilation policies forced upon tribal governments by the United States in contradiction of Native American treaty rights. Since 1944, the NCAI has been working to inform the public and Congress on the governmental rights of American Natives and Alaska Natives.

D. Media and Communication

The Native American people utilize all aspects of the media for widespread communication. Native American Newspapers include:

American Native Press Archives

Sequoyah Research Center
301A Ottenheimer Library
University of Arkansas at Little Rock
2801 South University Avenue
Little Rock, AR 72204-1099
501-569-8336   Fax: 501-371-7585
dflittlefiel@ualr.edu; jwparins@ualr.edu;
resanderson@ualr.edu; anpa.ualr.edu

Char-Koosta News

PO Box 98
Pablo, MT 59855
406-275-2830   Fax: 406-275-2831
charkoosta@cskt.org   www.charkoosta.com

Cherokee Observer

www.cherokeeobserver.org

Chickasaw Times

612 E. Arlington, Suite B
PO Box 1548
Ada, OK 74821
580-332-2977   Fax: 580-332-3949
times.Chickasaw@chickasaw.net
www.chickasawtimes.com

The Circle

PO Box 6026
Minneapolis, MN 55406
612-722-3686   Fax: 612-722-3773
circlempls@aol.com   www.thecirclenews.org

Indian Country Today

3059 Seneca Turnpike
Canastota, NY 13032
888-327-1013
www.indiancountry.com

Native American Journalists Association

at University of Oklahoma Gaylord College
395 West Lindsey
Norman, OK 73019
405-325-6945
info@naja.com   www.naja.com

Native American Times
PO Box 692050
Tulsa, OK 74169
570 East 141st Street
Glenpool, OK 74033
918-321-2323   Fax: 918-321-2326

Native Voice
9417 B. North Foothills Hwy
Longmont, CO 80503
303-449-1974   Fax: 303-443-9989
www.native-voice.com

The Navajo Times
Highway 264 & Route 12
Window Rock, AZ 86515–0310
928-871-6641   Fax: 928-871-6409
www.thenavajotimes.com

Other Media

Native Americans have also used television, radio broadcasting, and magazines to discuss issues of Native American life, news, heritage, and culture. These ventures include:

American Indian Radio on Satellite (AIROS)
AIROS Native Radio Network
1800 No 33 Street
Lincoln, NE 68503
402-472-3287   Fax: 402-472-8675
airos@unl.edu   www.airos.org

AccuRadio
400 North Wells Street, Suite 404
Chicago, IL 60610
312-527-3879
feedback@accuradio.com
www.accuradio.com

Aboriginal Peoples Television Network,
APTN Winnipeg Head Office
339 Portage Avenue
Winnipeg, Manitoba R3B 2C3 Canada
204-947-9331 / 888-278-8862 ext.358
Fax: 204-947-9307   www.aptn.ca

American Eagle Magazine
www.alphacdc.com/eagle

SPIRIT Magazine
PO Box 2
Parry Sound, ON P2A 2X2 Canada
www.spiritmag.ca

SAY Magazine
www.saymag.com

FURTHER READING AND RESOURCES

The Sacred: Ways of Knowledge, Sources of Life
Peggy V. Beck, Anna lee Waters
and Nia Fransico
1977: Navajo Comm. College Press/Northland
The Vanishing American: White Attitudes and
U.S. Policy
Brian Dippie
1982: Wesleyan University Press
Handbook of North American Indians, Volume
14: Southeast
Raymond D. Fogelson and William Sturtevant
2004: Smithsonian Institution
Black Elk Speaks
John Gneissenau Neihardt
1932: William Morrow and Company
1961: University of Nebraska Press
Native American Tribalism: Indian Survivals
and Renewals
Darcy McNickle
1973: Oxford University Press

2 Nature-based Religions

I. Origins and Early History

Introduction

UNDER THE BROAD CATEGORY OF "NATURE RELIgions," one may find a wide variety of beliefs and practices from New Age to Wiccan, from Neopagan to Spiritualist, from Santería to Crowlean Magick. In many ways, these different beliefs and practices have little in common both in terms of their roots and their modern manifestations. Often, what unites them is only a series of family resemblances that display a unique take on modernism, symbolism, and spiritual practice. At certain points all of these practices overlap in America today: Santería, an Afro-Caribbean practice, is currently informed by New Age practices and beliefs, even as students of magick and American Neoshamanism borrow from belief systems that range from Kabbalah and ancient Egyptian hermeticism to tantra and anthropological accounts of Native American and African sorcerers. For many of these religions the concept of nature is sacred, but for all of them the world is seen as permeated by spirit.

A. Origins

The religions covered in this chapter are, on one hand, the most ancient of all religions and, on the other hand, the newest. Modern practitioners of Wicca, Neopaganism, and Neoshamanism often point to prehistorical times as a source of inspiration,

Hermes Trismegistus, or "thrice-great Hermes," is a combination of the Greek god Hermes and the Egyptian god Thoth. Some modern occult and New Age believers think that Hermes Trismegistus was from Atlantis and may have designed the Pyramids.

and many believe that the practices in which they engage are as ancient as humanity itself. American Neoshamans who engage in the use of traditional hallucinogens such as peyote, psilocybe mushrooms, and ayahuasca often point to cave art such as the paintings in Tassili n'Ajjer in the Sahara desert, which date to the Late Neolithic period and show what seems to be a shaman holding a handful of mushrooms. Pre-Columbian art from the Americas in the form of rock carvings show mythological beings holding the San Pedro cactus, a mescaline-containing plant, suggesting that the use of this plant as a religious aid dates back at least to 1300 BCE. In a similar way, many modern practitioners of Wicca date their practices back to pre-Christian and pre-historical matriarchal culture, claiming that their form of worship is the original religion of Europe and the British Isles and has survived underground through

Christian-inspired persecution, only to emerge now, when religious strictures have relaxed.

Practitioners of many forms of modern magick date the origins of their beliefs to the Hermetic Corpus, a series of esoteric books from ancient Egypt that date back to the third century CE. Students of this belief often claim to be the descendants of a direct line of teachings handed down from secret society to secret society throughout millennia. On the other hand, many New Age practices point to an underlying universal religious experience of being "one" with the universe and connective with one's true or higher self. Many New Agers will claim that this vital experience is the heart and soul of true religion, but that it has been buried by dogma and tradition, only to reemerge now as a path of healing and fulfillment. The age of Christianity has passed away, according to some, and a new aeon of intuitive spiritual connection has reemerged to bring an end to a period of darkness and religious dryness.

Almost across the board, members of the religions that we have loosely dubbed "Nature Religions" claim that their practices are older and more primitive than Christianity, Islam, and Buddhism, and that they harken back to a time before patriarchy and civilization destroyed the connection to the divine and the immanent manifestation of the gods, goddesses, and spirits in nature. In order to understand the emergence of these practices in America, it is important that we separate New Age, Wiccan, and Neopagan beliefs about their origins from the more concrete and less mythical avenues of historical influence in the eighteenth, nineteenth, and twentieth centuries. It is only by doing this that we can begin to see this path as distinctly modern, and to recognize the remarkable amount of creativity that has surrounded this movement.

The Enlightenment

This history begins with the Enlightenment in Europe. In the eighteenth century, one saw the rise of a new emphasis on the "light" of reason coupled with a newfound fascination with the study of the natural world and other non-Christian societies. The goal of these philosophers, scientists, and men of letters, particularly in Britain and France, was the accumulation of empirical knowledge. Among French philosophers, Denis Diderot is best known for his massive encyclopedia—which featured thousands of entries on everything from social issues to the natural sciences. The enemy of the Enlightenment philosopher was the "darkness" of superstition in all forms. Paganism, magic, ritual, and even Christianity fell under fire.

What was to be avoided at all cost was "prejudice," where prejudice entailed anything that could not be proven through natural and scientific facts. Religion, above all, needed to be subjected to reason. And it was in Diderot's *Encyclopédie* that the notion of the "shaman" first emerged in European consciousness as symbolizing the primitive superstition that was the antithesis of everything enlightened and rational. The ideal of positive knowledge contained as its shadow the "ignorance" of the "primitive" or "savage." And, as the Enlightenment search for knowledge intensified, so too did inquiries into "uncivilized" tribal societies.

Romanticism

The rise of Romanticism in the early nineteenth century marked a cultural shift around questions of magic, religion, and intuition. During this time, the quest for rational and scientific knowledge continued unabated. But the increase in knowledge of the tribal other began to have a deep influence on romantic intellectuals and artists who sought an alternative to the rational scientific paradigm and the pursuit of industrial efficiency. This was coupled with an interest in "folk culture," fairy tales, and Celtic, Germanic, and Norse mythology. Many romantics believed that the religion and stories of the people represented a level of purity and authenticity that civilized life and storytelling could not attain. Romantic fiction and poetry, particularly in France and Germany, held up the ideal of poetic "vision" in which the artist, like a tribal shaman, directly witnessed the secrets of the

The Russian spiritualist Helena Blavatsky (1831–1891) and the British occultist Aleister Crowley (1875–1947) were iconic figures whose posed studio photographs were widely used to promote their appearances at entertainment events. Both came under intense criticism from the world's scientific community—criticism that sometimes enhanced their influence and reputation with their followers. The photograph of Blavatsky, above left, was taken in 1899; the photograph of Crowley, above right, was taken around 1930.

gods. Artists like Baudelaire, Gerard de Nerval, and Théophile Gautier indulged in the smoking of hashish and opium as a way of attaining the visionary powers of the "uncivilized" and ancient other, even as romantic writers on religion such as Novalis and Friedrich Schleiermacher wrote about contact with the divine through visionary intuition. Meanwhile, Hindu and Buddhist texts were increasingly being translated into English, French, and German, leading many intellectuals to consider ideas such as reincarnation and karma for the first time.

The most direct ancestors of many who would fall under the category of New Age today were the esoteric societies that emerged during the eighteenth and nineteenth centuries, such as the Rosicrucians and the Freemasons. These societies claimed to have a secret knowledge that dated back to ancient Egypt and offered many unique teachings about God and the self that were linked to alchemy and the "hermetic corpus." Although the function of these societies was often political, social, and economic in nature, many of their esoteric teachings were to have a great impact on the magical and theosophical

schools in Britain and France that appeared during the Victorian period.

Spiritualism

Theosophy was a blending of this western-style esotericism with the newly popularized teachings of the East. Founded by Helena Petrovna Blavatsky, William Quan Judge, and Henry Olcott in New York City in 1875, the Theosophical Society offered teachings on the chakras, consciousness, and Eastern religion alongside seances and other spiritualist gatherings designed to contact the spirits of the dead. Blavatsky herself, best known as "Madam Blavatsky," was a Russian immigrant who claimed to be a medium and to experience levitation and out-of-body travel as well as to be able to read minds and "materialize" psychic phenomena in the form of "ectoplasm." Blavatsky wrote numerous books on the teachings she claimed to have received from discarnate spiritual masters, the most famous of which was *Isis Unveiled*. Blavatsky moved to India in 1878, where she set up an esoteric school for western expatriots. During this time she challenged scientists and doctors to investigate her telepathic claims, and, in 1884, Richard Hodgson of the Society of Psychical Research—a committee of scientists, psychologists, and writers dedicated to studying psychic phenomena—traveled to India, where he exposed the fact that her compound contained hidden chambers and compartments, and that she stole her students' mail in order to discover their secrets and better manipulate them. This led the Society to deem Blavatsky "one of the most accomplished, ingenious, and interesting impostors in history." Despite this exposure, Blavatsky continued to have many adherents, and the Theosophical Movement continued to be strong in the United States into the 1920s and '30s. Some theosophical groups still exist today.

Meanwhile, the 1880s and 1890s were an era of unprecedented explorations into psychic and spiritualist phenomena both in the United States and Britain. Under the auspices of the Society for Psychical Research, luminaries such as Hodgson, William

Crookes, Fredrick Meyers, and William James (the founder of the first psychology program in the United States at Harvard) dove into the question of telepathy and sought to prove the existence of life after death though studying spiritualist mediums. Although they came across many frauds, scientists of the time including James and Hodgson were eventually convinced that some mediums, at the very least, exhibited the power of telepathy and clairvoyance and may indeed have had contact with discarnate spirits.

When William James began an investigation of the medium Lenora Piper in Boston, a skeptical Richard Hodgson traveled from England to investigate, telling no one that he was arriving. He barged into her living room wearing a mask only to find that she was able to speak about facts of his family life that no one else knew. He spent much of the next few years watching her and testing her, hiring detectives to follow her and everyone she came into contact with, and to open her mail to make sure that she did not have spies in her employ to gather information. Despite years of scrutiny, Piper, unlike Madame Blavatsky, was never shown to be a fraud or to have gotten information from any source other than her psychic powers.

Spiritualism was very much a phenomenon that was tied to the western Enlightenment project of attaining positive knowledge and empirical evidence. Despite the fact that, to many scientists and intellectuals, spiritualism seemed to reek of superstition and fraud and to be tied to "primitive" mediumship and shamanism, the movement thrived during this period of intense skepticism. If anything, wide-scale skepticism increased public interest in spiritualism. Mediums would dare scientists to investigate them and would hold public events at theaters in order to "prove" the existence of spirits and telepathy to a disbelieving audience. These events would attract much media attention, and the spiritualists themselves were rarely caught in acts of trickery. The dialectic between belief and skepticism that surrounded spiritualism filled a deep need felt by many Americans for a religion that was in conversation with science and

was subject to the scientific method. Traditional Christianity could not be proved or disproved through experiment, but a medium could be tested and the results of his or her "telepathy" could be exhaustively tallied. Although Victorian detractors often painted spiritualists as gullible and manipulated, the truth was that hard-nosed skeptics often surrounded mediums, attracted by the hope of proving once and for all the existence or non-existence of the spiritual realm. Interestingly, Arthur Conan Doyle, whose most famous creation, Sherlock Holmes, was a paragon of rationality, became one of the best-known adherents of spiritualism and was convinced that he had contacted his dead son through public seances.

As the disciplines of anthropology and sociology passed into the late nineteenth and early twentieth centuries, the project of exposing superstition and laying bare the "truth" about religion was made more complex by Émile Durkheim's work on the sociology of religion, *The Elementary Forms of Religious Life* (1893). Durkheim argued that religion was a "reality sui generis," a part of reality that was irreducible to scientific fact or mere politics. Durkheim was particularly fascinated by papers that spoke of life in totemic aboriginal societies and wrote at great length of the ways in which groups could come together and experience a sense of unity around symbols such as a frog, a snake, or the flag of a nation state. Durkheim's work did much to return academic discussions of religion to the realm of feeling and emotion, and proved a challenge to those who sought to reduce the religious question to merely that of truth and falsehood.

After Durkheim, the study of "primitive" religion came to focus more and more on the ways in which religious rituals functioned in tribal society. Such rituals were no longer dismissed as merely the superstitious manipulations of fraudulent actors, but were increasingly seen as playing an important sociological role. From the time of the Enlightenment through the end of the Victorian period, Protestant skepticism about the role of ritual and symbolism was the norm in the social sciences, but now thinkers began to wonder whether ritual was not necessary and to question whether modern alienation was not a symptom of a society that lacked religious ritual. Durkheim himself wrote a work on the question of suicide, arguing that suicides were likely committed by those who were unable to be ritually integrated into society.

In the intellectual world, the twentieth century stood in constant relation to the ideal of a past in which modern and industrial alienation from the natural and social world had not occurred. Critics dismissed this feeling as merely a "nostalgia for the mud," but nonetheless, particularly in the literary world, a longing for a past which was rich in symbolism and ritual became the norm. T.S. Elliot's influential poem, "The Waste Land," made constant references to the nature rituals of primitive England catalogued in James Frazer's sociological text, *The Golden Bough,* and William Butler Yeats worked to recreate the world of Irish myth, often pointing out the ways in which the lost world of Irish symbolism was preferable to the dead, industrial, materialistic world in which he lived. Yeats himself eventually became involved in a group known as the Hermetic Order of the Golden Dawn, an esoteric society which, despite the fact that it was relatively short-lived, has had an impact that continues to reverberate in the world of American occultism today.

Orders and Societies

The Hermetic Order of the Golden Dawn was part of the renaissance in occultism that has given us today's tarot decks, popular kabbalism, and much of today's ritual "magick." An early influential figure in this movement was Alphonse Louis Constant. Constant studied for the priesthood, but was expelled from seminary. Taking the name Eliphas Levi, Constant wrote numerous books in which he claimed to have uncovered the secrets of the Jewish Kabbalistic work, *The Zohar.* In Constant's unique interpretation, the twenty-two paths of God's emanation that led to the creation of the material world spoken of in *The Zohar* had a hidden correspondence to the twenty-two trump cards in the tarot deck. Constant claimed that one was necessary to illumi-

nate the other and that he had discovered this correspondence from ancient texts.

In truth, Constant most certainly invented many of his "ancient" sources, and today it seems highly doubtful that any links between the tarot decks used in fortunetelling and the Kabbalah existed before Constant's time. Nonetheless, Constant's invented tradition was brilliant, and by reading Zoharic symbolism into the tarot deck, Constant added whole new realms of meaning and depth to the deck. Constant (or Levi) became a prime innovator in what would become a significant movement in the late nineteenth and twentieth centuries. Many had argued and continue to argue that the age of myth has vanished and that new religions cannot emerge in an age of skepticism and scrutiny, but men and women such as Levi, A. E. Waite, Austin Osman Spare, Aleister Crowley, and Gerald Gardner would prove this thesis definitively wrong. Traditions were nothing so permanent and static as they seemed, and the work of remarkable individuals, drawing from ancient sources and inventing them when they were not available, came to create new traditions almost overnight—traditions that include today's Wicca, Druidism, Neopaganism, and Magick.

Constant's greatest avenue of influence was in Britain, where he was read and translated by A. E. Waite, the creator of the Rider-Waite Tarot deck, which has become the standard deck of tarot cards in America today. Waite adopted all of Levi's innovations, refining them in the process. This method of interpreting tarot alongside the Kabbalah eventually became the backbone of the teaching of the Hermetic Order of the Golden Dawn.

Among the adherents of the order was a young man named Aleister Crowley. Crowley, who also referred to himself as "The Beast," penned numerous innovative works on ritual magic that drew from the Kabbalah, alchemy, Renaissance-era works on black magic, gnosticism, and his own avid imagination. His work is as controversial today as it was in its own time, when many were scandalized by his teachings about sexual magic and channeling demonic powers, his occasional use of animal sacrifice, and his drug use. Crowley was eventually expelled from the Hermetic Order of the Golden Dawn, and went on to lead other secret societies including the Ordo Templi Orientis (OTO) and his own group the Argentinum Astrum. He died a penniless heroin addict in 1947. Nevertheless, his adherents in America today are many, and it is almost impossible to have a discussion of ritual magic without his name arising. His books can be found in most New Age shops and in the occult sections of many bookstores, but an aura of taboo often surrounds them, as they speak of the darker side of magical beliefs and practices rather than the healing-oriented practices that most New Agers prefer.

Wicca

The reinvention of Witchcraft as "Wicca," a nature-oriented religion that looked backwards toward ancient paganism and matriarchal culture, had to wait for the 1950s, when a retired British rubber planter and customs officer named Gerald B. Gardner published the book *Witchcraft Today* (1954). Gardner claimed to be an initiate of an ancient coven of Witches called the Forest Coven that had survived underground in Britain since before pagan times. Gardener himself, during his time as a rubber planter, had published anthropological works on Malay weaponry and had researched their traditional magical practices. On returning to Britain in 1936, he had become a member of the Rosicrucian order and also of Crowley's Ordo Templi Orientis. His account of the rituals of the Forest Coven draws from all of these sources, and there can be little doubt that the group Gardner was associated with was very much a product and extension of Victorian-era occultism and spiritualism rather than a straightforwardly ancient religion.

How much Gardner invented remains unclear. What is clear is that Gardner's new religion attracted immediate adherents across England and the United States and that this new uprising of Witchcraft was very much a grassroots occurrence. Many of Gard-

ner's readers followed his lead in founding their own covens based on ancient myths of the Great Goddess, modern anthropology, and Crowlean occultism. Wicca was particularly attractive to women and to the feminists of the 1960s and 1970s. Would-be witches combed historical and mythological texts in an attempt to fully "recover" the tradition, and many seem to have found that the newness and unstructured nature of the religion allowed for a great deal of creativity. An extension of the Wiccan revival is the practice of Druidism, a religious reinvention of the little understood ancient religion of England that today borrows from Arthurian legend, the bardic tradition, and Irish and Welsh mythology.

B. The Religion in America

The rise of Neoshamanism as a culturally influential movement in the United States is an even more interesting story. As is the case with the Wiccan religion, Neoshamanism as a movement is inseparable from anthropology and mythology as disciplines of study. Most American shamans are avid readers of anthropological case studies and look to cultures around the world for inspiration. In order to really understand this movement, one has to look back to William James's seminal work, *The Varieties of Religious Experience*. Besides investigating psychic phenomena, working to prove the existence of life after death, and pioneering the field of American psychology, James also dabbled in philosophy and epistemology (the study of knowledge), and it is in these fields that he is most well known today. James argued that theology was just an accumulation of dogma that had little bearing on truth but that truth in religion could be found only in religious experience. For James, religious experience was an expression of a psychological state of consciousness; it was, moreover, universal and to be found among all cultures and all beliefs. This meant that different religions had a common ground in experience and could be compared on that basis.

In many ways, James was the archetypal American philosopher. He had no patience for abstract questions of truth—he wanted results. James founded a school of thought called "Pragmatism," in which the pursuit of truth was reduced to the search for efficacy. James was also a pioneer in the exploration of consciousness through drugs, and would later claim that his deepest religious experiences came through the use of the drug nitrous oxide.

James' work, *The Varieties of Religious Experience*, gave birth to the phenomenological school of religious studies, a school whose focus lay entirely on the question of experience. The focus of this school was often on the mystics of the Middle Ages alongside Zen Buddhists and Hindu yogis who had begun to evangelize in the United States during the early twentieth century. Nonetheless, it was this school that was eventually to give birth to modern American shamanism. The key moment in this development was the publication in 1951 of Mircea Eliade's work, *Shamanism: Archaic Techniques of Ecstasy*. In this text, Eliade blended together a wide variety of sources to create a cross-cultural compendium of trance techniques and the beliefs that surround them. The word "shaman," a Tungus word, came to replace words such as "medicine man" and "witch doctor" in popular vocabulary, and the shaman as a type entered American pop culture for the first time. Eliade claimed that shamans across the world experienced similar things and underwent similar trials and experiences on the path to ecstasy and healing. Today, scholars are highly critical of Eliade's methods and believe that he ignored and glossed over the myriad differences that exist in the religious practices of different cultures, but nonetheless, Eliade's work captured the American imagination, aptly granting him consideration as the godfather of modern American Neoshamanism. Although Eliade, unlike Gerald Gardner, did not invent self-consciously and never claimed to be a shaman himself, his works occupy a similar place in the world of American shamanism as the works of Gardner in Wicca, and represent a moment of twentieth-century mythmaking. Eliade was the Chairman of the Department of the History of Religions at the University of Chicago and died in 1986.

Drug Culture

Despite Eliade's work, American Neoshamanism would never have emerged as a cultural force without the discovery of LSD and psilocybin and the popular account of the effects of mescaline written by Aldous Huxley in *The Doors of Perception*. Huxley, a popular British novelist and intellectual, had taken mescaline under the direction of psychologist Havelock Ellis, and, during his "trip," he claimed to have suddenly understood all the myriad religious texts that he had read and studied during his life, from the writings of the Christian saints to the sacred writings of the East. He had been interested in religious experience from a young age, and as early as 1936 had conceived of the project of creating a Jamesean study of religious experience. However, his experiences with mescaline transformed his religious beliefs and led him to embrace the hope that psychedelic drugs could gradually enlighten the world and lead to world peace.

The discovery of the effects of LSD in 1943 and the drug's eventual study at Harvard during the 1960s marks one of the seminal moments in American cultural history and was undoubtedly one of the key factors in the cultural upheavals of the late 1960s. The experiments done by Timothy Leary and Richard Alpert (a young scientist who eventually transformed himself into the spiritual leader Ram Dass) were widely known. Leary and the others were highly inspired by Huxley and consulted with him on the question of the connection between religion and drug-induced ecstatic states. Also well known was the Good Friday Experiment, in which Harvard researcher and doctoral candidate Walter Pahnke dosed divinity students with the drug psilocybin only to discover that the majority of these students experienced what they considered to be religious ecstasy. Among those present at the experiments was Huston Smith, who was to become a popular author on, and a philosopher of, religion.

Baba Ram Dass—born Richard Alpert in 1931—is a psychologist, spiritual leader, and former Harvard professor who experimented with altered states of consciousness through the use of mind-altering substances. His most widely known book is Remember, Be Here Now.

These experiments, and the eventual escape of LSD from its laboratory confines, led to increased interest in traditional religions that used drugs as a sacrament. The publication of Carlos Castaneda's best-selling book, *The Teachings of Don Juan,* brought even more attention to the world of psychedelic shamanism. Castaneda claimed to have studied under a Yaqui shaman and sorcerer who had given him psychedelic mushrooms, peyote, and an ointment made from the roots of the datura plant. Although many of his stories were later discredited as a patchwork of stories from other anthropologists and his own fantasy, Castaneda continued to write best-selling books and to hold training sessions in the path that he had developed. Meanwhile, Jim Morrison had founded the band The Doors, taking the name of his band from Huxley's book *The Doors of Perception.* Morrison self-consciously styled himself as a modern shaman and wrote and sang about shamanism. Even the style of dancing that Morrison performed aped Native American ceremonial dances. It was by way of Jim Morrison that the "shaman" once and for all staked out a place in the American landscape.

Varieties of Practitioners

Differences between the beliefs and practices of these religions will be discussed later in the chapter, but for the moment let it suffice to say that Neoshamans and Wiccans in America today share many underlying beliefs. What differs most dramatically is that Wicca is primarily a matter of ritual magic while the root of shamanism is ecstasy and trance. Some Wiccans may, however, engage in ecstatic practices, and many Witches believe that this is an essential part of magic as well. The third wheel in the revival and reinvention of earth-based religion in America is the movement known as Neopaganism. The sine qua non of Neopaganism is the festival. Descendent from the 1960s Love In, Grateful Dead Concerts, and Rainbow Gatherings, today's Neopagan festivals celebrate nature, often around a bonfire with dancing, chanting, and drumming. But although the festival is an important part of Neopaganism, other Neopagans describe themselves as "solitary practitioners." These pagans may engage in ritual and worship at home and spend time studying historical paganisms. Neopaganism may also be associated with the "Modern Primitive" movement, which practices body modification techniques and ritual scarification in ways that imitate initiation rituals in tribal societies. One of the key founders of this movement was Roland Loomis (b.1930), better known as Fakir Musafar, whose techniques in scarification, tattooing, and the suspension of the human body from meat hooks began to emerge in popular culture in the 1980s.

Santería in Court

Some academics have argued that Wicca, Neoshamanism, and Neopaganism are religions made up primarily of those of Protestant Anglo-Saxon descent, theorizing that the lack of ritual in Modern Protestantism is a decisive influence in the development of these groups. Others have argued that this phenomenon is more generally representative of the U.S. population. The history of Santería, Vodou, Santo Daime, and the União du Vegetal differ greatly from this history in that these religions are primarily practiced in the United States by immigrants from the Caribbean, Mexico, and South and Central America. Santería and Vodou are syncretic religions that developed in the Caribbean from African roots and represent a blending of Catholic and African symbolism. The iconography of Catholic saints is transposed onto that of African spirits so that, in Vodou, Saint James doubles as the spirit Ogun. Santería and Vodou have a great many similarities, and many of their practices and beliefs overlap, but these religions developed semi-independently; Santería in the Spanish-speaking world and Vodou in French-speaking Haiti. New Orleans has long been regarded as a central hub of Vodou practice because of its location, the slave trade, and its French history; but today, practitioners of Vodou can be found in any city with a large population of immigrants from the French-speaking Caribbean.

Santería is popular in Cuba, Mexico, and across much of Spanish-speaking Central America and is found among the Mexican, Cuban, and Caribbean immigrant population in the United States. Most major cities in the United States have at least one *botanica*—a Santería-influenced store that sells magical goods, medicinal plants, and New Age and magical literature from the Spanish-speaking world.

The Santo Daime and the União do Vegetal are twentieth-century religions that emerged among urban populations in Portuguese-speaking South America. Both of these religions combine Christian belief with the nature-oriented, earth-centered beliefs of South American tribal shamans. These religions borrow more than just their ideas from shamanism. They are unique in that they both use magical psychedelic potions as part of their ceremonies, potions that contain what is perhaps the most powerful of all hallucinogenic drugs, the chemical DMT (dimethyltryptamine). Both of these religions have emerged in the United States only recently and have remained more or less underground due to the illegality of their sacrament. However, after the seizure of their sacrament in 1999 by the government, the União du

Vegetal emerged into the spotlight when it was revealed that the acting head of the religion in the United States was an heir to the Seagram's fortune, Jeffery Bronfman. Using Bronfman's money, the U.D.V. fought the government and, in 2006, won the right to use their sacrament in the Supreme Court decision *Gonzales v. O Centro Espirita Beneficente Uniao do Vegetal*.

C. Important Dates and Landmarks

1765 Diderot publishes an article on the shaman in his masterpiece, *Encyclopédie*.

1855 Eliphas Levi publishes *Transcendental Magic*.

1875 The Theosophical Society is founded in New York by Madam Blavatsky, Henry Olcott, and William Quan Judge.

1882 William James experiments with nitrous oxide, and claims that under the influence of the drug he can understand mysticism and the philosopher Hegel.

1884 Richard Hodgson issues a report to the Society for Psychical Research exposing Blavatsky as a fraud.

1893 Durkheim publishes *The Elementary Forms of Religious Life*.

1890s W.B. Yeats and other intellectuals join the Hermetic Order of the Golden Dawn.

1900 Aleister Crowley is expelled from the Hermetic Order of the Golden Dawn on the insistence of Yeats and others.

1909 A.E. Waite publishes the Rider-Waite deck of tarot cards.

1951 Mircea Eliade publishes *Shamanism: Archaic Techniques of Ecstasy.*

1954 Gerald Gardner publishes the influential *Witchcraft Today*. Aldous Huxley publishes *The Doors of Perception* on religious impact of his mescaline experiments.

1960 Timothy Leary and Richard Alpert (Ram Dass) begin their experiments with LSD and psilocybin at Harvard.

1968 Carlos Castaneda publishes *The Teachings of Don Juan: A Yaqui Way of Knowledge*. The rock band The Doors releases its first album. Both events popularize the idea of the shaman.

2006 The União do Vegetal win case *Gonzales v. O Centro Espirita Beneficente Uniao do Vegetal*, gaining the right to use their hallucinogenic sacrament in the U.S.

II. Tenants and Beliefs

A. Articles of Faith

Many New Agers offer healing treatments from Eastern Reiki to the psychoanalytic-inspired body-based technique of Rolfing. Others draw on Chinese energy healing and practice what is known as Polarity Therapy, a technique that involves holding one's hands above the body of the patient and "helping the energy flow throughout it." But here again the question is not whether or not one believes in this type of psycho-physical energy. Instead, what is at stake is how one feels, or the idea that one can literally feel this energy flowing through oneself. The body and materiality are quite important to many New Agers, who argue that Christianity undervalues bodily health and the effect of the body on the spiritual life.

Perhaps what most unites all of these disparate religions is that they do not rely heavily on the Christian category of belief or faith. These are instead religions of power and of experience. Wiccans do not have a faith or belief that the Great Goddess will save them; instead they use ritual practice to heal themselves and others and draw upon the power of the Goddess to alter their lives and the world around them. Similarly, America Neoshamans do not so much "believe" in the spirits and entities that they contact as they "confront them," "learn from them," and ask them to help them heal others. Some American shamans believe that these spirits are inhabitants of the astral realm, a nonphysical plane that lies "above" the physical world, while others believe that they contact spirits of the natural world; but still others believe that these spirits are unconscious sides of the human personality, or "higher selves." The question here again is not so much what one believes about religion, but what one experiences and whether the religion works.

In the world of ritual magick today, one is likely to encounter a great deal of disagreement over what magical practices can and cannot do. Can magick cure cancer or kill an enemy at long distance? Is it possible to change oneself into an animal? Are the effects of magick merely mental and emotional, or does it operate on the material and physical level as well? On all of these questions one can encounter believers at both ends of the spectrum. However, all practitioners would agree that within their given realms, the magical spells and rituals have (or should have) measurable concrete effects.

Magic, Gods, and Godesses

In the world of channeling, spiritualism, and fortunetelling, however, the question of belief is constantly at stake. Much in the fashion of spiritualists of the Victorian era, today's spiritualists entertain a skepticism that constantly draws them to seek out new mediums, palm readers, and psychics. Many of those who visit psychics withhold information much in the fashion of Richard Hodgson in the story cited above. Some may not reveal that they have children, or if they reveal that, they may withhold the fact that the children are girls in order to test the perspicacity of the medium. Later, when they speak of a session, they may note that, while they are unsure if the medium was indeed psychic and telling the truth, nonetheless, the psychic did know that they had had children in college, for example, despite the fact that the client never mentioned such details.

Beliefs about gods, goddesses, and spirits differ from person to person and group to group even among those who practice a certain discipline such as Wicca. Some practitioners will see gods and goddesses primarily as powerful symbols that unlock the power of the natural universe, while still others may believe more literally in certain goddesses and spirits and believe that it is important to have a personal relationship with a higher being who will serve as a spiritual "guide." Many Neopagans and Wiccans will speak of the Gaia, or the earth itself conceived of as an entity, and believe that it is possible to commune and become one with the natural world in the form of this goddess. Gaia can also be conceived of as the "overmind," or the world soul, a fusion of all the minds of living beings from plants and animals to humans. The goddess, in this sense, is life itself, a life that has its own cosmic purposes and seeks a balance that will repair ecological and industrial destruction.

Many who practice Crowlean ritual magick at least nominally embrace and seek out the Judeo-Christian God. Following a particular Victorian interpretation of the Jewish Kabbalah, which is a descendant both of the inventions of Eliphas Levi and the seventeenth-century Latin work *Kabbalah Denudata* (The Kabbalah Unveiled) by Knorr von Rosenroth, these practitioners seek to harness the power of God's emanations for the purposes of changing the self and the world. But for these believers, the Judeo-Christian God is not so much a personal God as he is the force, power, and ideation that shapes reality itself. Crowley and those who follow him in America today map Egyptian and Greek mythology onto the Godhead as well, and believe

that religious symbolism is a method of understanding reality and the self. This type of work also borrows heavily from the work of alchemists such as Paracelsus who used astrology to map out the dimensions of the spirit and the self.

Additionally important here is the idea of consciousness. Especially among those who are attached to the New Age movement and those who embrace Neoshamanism, the notion of consciousness can serve much in the way the concept of God serves in other religions. The goal of many practices, at least since the time of the theosophists and William James, is to attain a "higher level of consciousness." Certain states of consciousness are thought to reveal reality more fully and to help the individual attain a sense of oneness and communion with other humans and the entire cosmos. These theories are often heavily influenced by the science of psychology as well as by the dialectical philosophy of Hegel.

Practitioners of Santería and Vodou hold a complex series of beliefs that are heavily influenced by both Catholic and African religion. The name Santería itself was originally a derogatory term used to describe those who ignored the worship of God only to concentrate on the saints. Both practitioners of Vodou and Santería do indeed believe in a singular powerful God, but like eighteenth- and nineteenth-century English deists, they see this God as distant and uninvolved. For religious practice to work, it must not reach so high. The saints or spirits are much like humans, and are therefore more susceptible to praise, food, and sacrifice and more likely to aid humans and to understand human needs. Practitioners of these religions associate certain saints such as Saint James, Saint Isidore, and Saint Mary with African spirits such as Ogun, Yansan, and Oshun, and believe that those who practice Santería and Vodou can contact and even become possessed by these entities. The practice offers power to the individuals involved, and the spirits can help one to attain knowledge, heal sicknesses, and attain wealth and financial success. These spirits are seen as having very real material and physical effects, and practitioners believe that it is to them, rather than to a distant God, that one must look if one wishes to alter and improve one's material life.

B. Scripture

None of the religions in this chapter utilize anything like scripture or a work of sacred writings to which individuals submit. Those who subscribe to New Age, Wiccan, Neopagan, and Neoshamanic beliefs and systems are often avid readers of historical documents, anthropological works, mythology, world religious texts, and self-help bestsellers; but the relation of the reader and practitioner to these texts is not one of submission but rather one in which texts are mined for inspiration and ideas.

These religions are very much an extension of the liberal American belief in choice and freedom of conscience. Rather than restricting themselves to a single tradition or culture, the hope is that people can "explore" as deeply as one must until they discover the methods and beliefs that work for them as individuals. Even those involved in popular magical practices such as kabbalism, which is entirely text-based, lack the same sort of commitments to the Biblical texts that is found among Jewish practitioners of Kabbalah. The religious texts are seen as having great symbolic value and power, but this belief does not lead magical practitioners to follow the text literally or to believe that the laws given in the Bible are applicable to themselves.

Certainly on a case-by-case basis, individuals in these religions may attach themselves to a text or series of texts and use them as a religious rule. But more often, particularly among Wiccans, practitioners comb through numerous books and documents in order to compile a "grimoire," or spell book, of their own. Nonetheless, Renaissance-era grimoires, such as the Grand Grimoire and the Clavicles of Solomon (a text which offers techniques for harnessing the powers of demons and which is attributed to the Biblical king Solomon), often receive a great deal of respect due to their antiquity. Occultists and New Agers may also place their faith in documents they believe have been "channeled," or brought down to earth from higher planes through the possession of the human writing the text. Aleister Crowley, for example, claimed that many of his books were dictated to him by beings from another plane. Numerous other such books exist today including works that the human authors claim were dictated by angels or alien beings from planetary systems near the Pleiades.

Practitioners of Vodou and Santería are often faithful Christians who may respect and hold the Bible to be true. Nonetheless, the Bible itself is not particularly important to either religion.

C. Secondary Sources

One could argue that the center of New Age religion in any American city is the New Age bookstore. Such bookstores offer opportunities to buy magical supplies such as crystals, tarot cards, and tuning forks for healing treatments that involve sound vibrations; many stores also have in-house psychics. But more importantly, these bookstores serve as community centers, the sites of networking and lectures. The lack of a single set of scriptures only encourages spiritual literacy, and New Agers are constantly on the lookout for books on new techniques and ideas.

It is impossible to create an adequate list of influential New Age books; each year brings new bestsellers. But some figures are worth noting. The classic work on astral projection, *Journeys Out of the Body*, was written by former advertising executive Robert Monroe (1915–1995). Monroe claimed to be able to separate his soul or astral body from his physical body during the process of falling asleep. He claimed that during his flights he could see the physical world and that he had tested himself numerous times by, for example, checking the dates on coins while "traveling" and writing them down when he awoke, only to find that the dates that he had seen in the astral state were correct. He also claimed to have traveled to the "astral realm"—a realm above the earthly experience—and to have met and interacted with numerous astral beings.

Other influential works, such as *The Search for Omm Sety* by Jonathan Cott and *Winged Pharaoh* and *Life as Carola* by Joan Grant, purport to contain accounts of remembered past lives. Both Grant and Dorothy Eady, the subject of Cott's investigations, claimed to have lived lives in Ancient Egypt and were insistent on the fact that their memories were historically accurate in ways that they never could have anticipated.

The work *A Course in Miracles* is a best-selling treatise of spiritual instruction. Author Helen Schucman claimed that the text came to her entirely though the rapid dictations of a voice she eventually came to identify with Jesus Christ. Another important genre of New Age literature is that of spiritual autobiography. Many such autobiographies are (perhaps fictionalized) accounts of studying with spiritual masters. An influential book in this genre is Dan Milman's autobiographical novel *Way of the Peaceful Warrior*, a work in which he recalls studying with a gas station attendant and sage whom he calls "Socrates."

As was the case with the spiritualist ancestors of the New Age movement, today's New Agers remain very interested in science and the scientific method. Many attempts are made to prove that New Age healing techniques work, and even Robert Monroe was subjected to numerous scientific tests as he sought to prove the reality of astral projection. Later in his life, Monroe worked with scientists to create "hemi-synch" technology, a method that utilizes the technique of "entraining" brain waves to make astral projection available to all. Important on the scientific front are works such as *Healing Words: The Power of Prayer* by Larry Dossey, M.D. In this book, Dossey showcases studies he has performed in which prayer and meditation were shown to be effective in fighting cancer and other illnesses. New Agers are also likely to be interested in the work of America Buddhists who seek to chart the brain waves of meditation masters. Another intersection between New Age and popular science can be found in the works of Gary Zukav, such as *The Dancing Wu Li Masters*. Zukav notes numerous parallels between modern quantum science and the holistic spiritual worldview.

Wiccan and Shamanic Writers

One of the more notable authors on Wicca writes under the name Starhawk. Starhawk, born in 1951, wrote the volume *The Spiral Dance* in 1979. This book and others have served as a primer for many would-be Wiccans, and represents a fruition of the feminist promise that a Goddess-centered nature religion has held since its inception. "Goddess feminism" represents one of the more important aspects of Neopaganism in America today. Cynthia Eller and Wendy Griffin are two important thinkers who combine feminism, spirituality, and academic prowess. Eller is a professor of Religion at Montclair State University while Wendy Griffin is a professor of Women's Studies at California State University, Long Beach. Susan Greenwood's *Magic, Witchcraft and the Other-World* represents a serious study by a modern anthropologist on Wicca. Greenwood studied with an English coven for a number of years, and in her work she attempts to uncover and explain the power of ritual and magic in a way that social scientists can appreciate and understand. Also of note in the formation of modern Wicca is science fiction and fantasy author Marion Zimmer Bradley. Bradley drew upon historical research and Arthurian legend to write her best-selling work, *The Mists of Avalon*, a novel that describes the gradual replacement of the goddess-oriented religions of ancient Britain by Christianity. Today her works serve as a source of inspiration for Wiccans and Neopagans interested in reinventing the ancient Celtic practices of Druidism.

The world of Neoshamanism in America today is almost inconceivable without the work and teaching of two figures: Michael Harner and Terrence McKenna. Their work represents different avenues of Neoshamanic thought, and Neoshamans are likely to embrace the writings of one or the other, but rarely both. Harner began his career as an anthropologist in the 1960s and worked among the Jivaro (Shuar) Native Americans. These Natives used the psyche-delic potion ayahuasca, which contains the potent hallucinogenic drug DMT. Harner himself soon used the drug and was eventually drawn in and initi-ated into shamanism himself. In much the fashion of Mircea Eliade, Harner saw shamanism as a universal phenomenon. Borrowing the motif of the "wounded healer," Harner writes of how a prospective shaman may become ill with an illness that can only be healed in the spiritual world. If this proto-shaman survives and makes it through the difficult process of healing himself, he will then be able to heal others.

In 1980, Harner wrote the best-selling book, *The Way of the Shaman,* in which he published his views on the universal shamanic experience for a popular audience and briefly described his own experiences Soon after, Harner started the Foundation for Shamanic Studies in Hartford, Connecticut in order to offer workshops and training sessions to spread and disseminate shamanic practices in the modern United States. His organization also works to support and preserve the practices and teachings of traditional shamans around the world. Harnerian shamanism eschews the use of all psychedelic drugs and seeks to develop the practitioners' abilities for spontaneous trance through drumming and dance. The emphasis here is very much on the New Age category of heal-ing. A shaman for Harnerians is someone who has been spiritually healed and can spiritually heal others.

Shamanism a la Terrence McKenna is something else entirely. McKenna first sampled DMT in a labo-ratory where he encountered what he called "self-repli-cating machine elves." These entities, theorized McKenna, represented language itself, the logos of Greek philosophy. McKenna combined the writings of the Neoplatonist Jewish philosopher Philo with the numerology of the *I Ching* and numerous other sys-tems of belief to create a philosophy that was decidedly his own. Rather than forming a self-consistent system of beliefs, McKenna preferred a method of speaking and writing that was free form and expressive. Among McKenna's most influential theories was that history

was going to end in 2012, at the end of the Mayan cal-endar. He spoke of what he called the "ingression of novelty." History, according to McKenna, was speed-ing up, and change was becoming ever more rapid; at some point this wave would reach its apex and humans would be liberated from their history through a kind of apocalypse or revelation. The experience of tripping on DMT or psychedelic mushrooms repre-sented this moment on a personal level. McKenna also theorized that UFO sightings were the effect of a cos-mic event ahead of us. The event would be so dramatic that it would create ripples backward in history. Central to McKenna's beliefs was the idea that the modernized Western world was in the process of expe-riencing what he called an "Archaic Revival." Patriarchal "dominator culture" was once again being replaced by vital practices that brought humans in touch with the collective "Gaian mind."

McKenna, when he considered it at all, felt that shamanic "healing" was of secondary importance. What matters instead is knowledge, revelation, and experience. The role of the shaman, according to McKenna, is to travel to other realms in order to bring back knowledge of the cosmos and of the world. He was fascinated by tribal shamans who used visionary trance to discover the locations of herds of animals for the hunt, and felt that the social effects of shamanism in the modern world had to be looked for in an overall change of consciousness rather than in self-help style healing. McKenna traveled greatly and spent time in the South American rain forest seeking out shamans who used the drug DMT in their potions. Among these indigenous peoples, he sought to find daring explorers of the other worlds. But in his search McKenna was disappointed. He was unable to find shamans who took large "heroic doses" of the plant materials. It his writing, he won-ders aloud whether "true shamanism" did not die out in other parts of the world even as it was revived in the United States.

Other important thinkers for McKenna-style Neoshamans include the scientists Rick Strassman and Alexander Shulgin. Shulgin represents a forgotten type: The independent researcher and scientist. Working on his own in a small ranchette in California, Shulgin single-handedly invented hundreds of psychedelic drugs including STP or DOM and the rave drug 2C-B. He is perhaps best known as the man who discovered the psychoactive properties of MDMA or Ecstasy. His works *Phikal (Phenethylamines I Have Known And Loved)* and *Tikal (Typtamines I Have Known and Loved)* tell the story of his personal experimentation with psychoactive chemistry and religious experience. Strassmann, on the other hand, is one of the few scientists affiliated with a major research institution to work with hallucinogenic drugs. The book, *DMT: The Spirit Molecule,* gives a popular account of research in which he administered the drug DMT to fifty subjects at the University of New Mexico Medical center and has attained must-read status among drug-oriented members of the Neoshamanic fold.

Also of note when considering sources on shamanism is the work *Shamanism, Colonialism, and the Wild Man* by leftist anthropologist and Columbia University professor Michael Taussig. Taussig examines at great length the phenomenon of modern shamanism in Colombia, shows how shamanism relates to political power, and describes how shamans manipulate and use symbols of the state.

Another important thinker for both the Neoshamanic and New Age worldviews is the Czech psychoanalyst Stanislaw Grof. During the 1960s, Grof was one of the researchers to undertake the study of LSD for the treatment of neurosis. Like William James, he theorized that it was possible to have psychological "breakthrough experiences" that could change one's life in ways that standard analysis could not. Giving his patients doses as much as five times as strong as the standard street dose of LSD, Grof sought to guide his patients through marathon therapy sessions that could last twelve to fourteen hours. Eventually, political pressure and the desire to have a method that could be self-induced and did not last so long led Grof to develop a technique of breathing that induced LSD-like states. He coined the term

"Holotropic Breathwork" to describe this technique, and breathwork today is practiced among numerous New Agers as a method of contacting "non-ordinary" states of consciousness. Grof is also well known for theorizing that many neuroses are tied to the trauma of birth. For Grof, the motif of rebirth that is found in so many of the world religions and in shamanism expresses the human need to work through the birth trauma and to experience being "born again" in a fairly literal sense. Today, rebirthing techniques are an important part of the New Age movement.

Occult Writers and a New Medium

In the realm of ritual magic and occultism, the most remarkable figure alive today is undoubtedly Allan Moore. Moore is best known as the author of numerous comic books including "The Watchmen," "V for Vendetta," and "The League of Extraordinary Gentleman." His character John Constantine recently appeared in the movie *Constantine* starring Keanu Reeves, in which Reeves played the title character, a hard-boiled British occultist who owes his soul to the devil. But for Moore, the comic book genre has proved not only an avenue for producing entertainment, but also for the expression of his unique yet highly influential views on magic and the occult. Other comic book authors such as Grant Morrison have followed Moore's lead, so that today many American practitioners of ritual magic first became interested in the occult through reading graphic novels or watching the films that are based on them. Moore's magical opus is the graphic novel Promethea, in which Moore interprets the Kabbalah and the tarot while telling the highly entertaining story of a teenage girl who realizes that she is destined to bring an end to history.

Regarding books on Santería and Vodou, it is difficult to find works on these religions written in English for an American audience. In the English-speaking world, two works are of note for the ways in which they have shaped popular interpretations of Vodou: *The Serpent and the Rainbow* by Wade Davis, and *Mama Lola* by Karen McCarthy Brown. The first book records a young ethnologist's travels in Haiti and his discovery of the practice of making humans into zombies by drugging them with tetrodotoxin (TTX), a drug found in the uncooked flesh of the blowfish. This work had a deep impact on pop culture and was eventually made into a movie. *Mama Lola,* on the other hand, is the work of an anthropologist who spent many years studying with the Vodou priestess "Alourdes" in Fort Greene, Brooklyn. Brown presents these practices sympathetically, showing ways in which spirits help give meaning to family and community while describing her own personal initiation into the Vodou life.

III. Rites and Rituals

A. The Calendar

Within all of the religions described in this chapter, rites and rituals are given a central place. These religions focus on right practice, or orthopraxy, as opposed to right belief, or the orthodoxy of such religions as Christianity. In each of these religions importance is given to the movements of the heavenly bodies and the changing of the seasons, and key religious rituals are performed on the dates when the planets, the stars, the sun, and the moon are properly aligned. Of chief importance to Wiccans are the vernal and autumnal equinoxes—the nights in the spring and the fall where the hours of daylight and night are equal—and the winter and summer solstices—those nights when the sun is at the furthest and closest points from and to the earth, respectively. Some Wiccans correlate this shifting of the seasons with the tale of the horned god from British mythology. The horned god is said to be the lover of the Great Goddess. In the fall, at the autumnal equinox, the horned god dies and the Goddess goes into mourning. But in the spring, at Beltane, the god rises again, and summer represents the full bloom of their love. For many Wiccans, an under-

standing of this myth is also influenced by the Egyptian myths of the Goddess Isis and her lost and yet returned love Osirus, and the Greek myth of Persephone and Demeter.

Also important for Wiccans is the lunar calendar. The movements of the moon are central to Wicca, partly because they play such a central role in surviving Medieval and Renaissance era magical texts, but also because the moon is often associated with femininity and the cycle of women's menses. Many spells purport to be effective only during the full moon, and certain herbs can only be picked at midnight on these nights if they are to have magical potency. The night of the full moon was traditionally seen as the night of the witches' sabbat: the night when witches would take flight on the backs of animals and broomsticks to fly off to meet the goddess or the devil. Today covens may also celebrate their sabbats on the equinoxes, the solstices, and the midpoints between those solar events, which they call the Samhain, Imbolc, Beltane, and Lammas.

Like Wiccans, other Neopagans are likely to hold the equinoxes and the solstices as central to their practices. Practitioners hold festivals or gatherings on or around these dates to celebrate the changing of the seasons and the shifts that occur in the natural world. Sources for Neopagan festivities may reflect everything from Greek Mythology to European harvest festivals and Native American ceremonies. For many Neopagans, these celebrations are very much celebrations of the natural world and differ from the Christian calendar in their connection to the earth. These festivals are often steeped in the history of religions from Charles Frazer to Mircea Eliade, and one can see in them another concept popularized by Eliade, The Myth of the Eternal Return, or the sense that history and life is not a linear progression, but rather an eternal cycle.

In the Neoshamanic world, one can observe a split in orientation around the question of the calendar. Adherents to Harnerian shamanism are likely to observe the equinoxes and solstices along with others of a Neopagan orientation, while those influenced by

Terrence McKenna may hold a unique vision of time in which time is seen to progress ever more rapidly through history toward a great moment of revelation or apocalypse which marks the end of history. This view of history also informs the writings of Allan Moore and, more recently, of Daniel Pinchbeck, who authored the work *2012: The Return of Quetzalcoatl*, which, following McKenna, takes especial note of the ending of the Mayan calendar in that year. Neoshamans who follow this style of belief are unlikely to be interested in marking out a religious calendar as a series of recurrent holidays. They are far more interested in the coming singular event of human awakening.

Among New Agers, the question of a religious calendar can range from disinterest to utter and complete attention to astrological dates. Belief among those who follow astrological systems differ depending on the system one follows and whether it is influenced by Native American, Egyptian, Chinese, or alchemical beliefs about the planets and stars. Modern astrology has many sources and is greatly complicated by the discovery of planets that were unknown in the ancient world. Astrology as a system assigns each individual a specific "sign" according to the month in which the person was born. This sign is further ramified by the precise date and time of the person's birth, so that each person can be said to have a unique destiny marked out for them by the cosmos. New Agers who are interested in astrology go to astrologers to have their "charts done," meaning that they have an astrologer analyze the patterns of the heavens at their time of birth. This chart can then be used to make important decisions, given the idea that the ordering of the planets at any given moment has a unique effect on each individual depending on his or her sign. Certain months or days will be bad for making business decisions for some people, while, at other times, the effect of a given planet may be thought to invigorate them.

In Santería and Vodou, rituals, feasts, and sacrifices are held on certain days to commemorate and celebrate certain saints or spirits. Alourdes, the sub-ject of Karen McCarthy Brown's work, *Mama Lola,* refers to these events as "birthday parties" for the spirits. At one time these festivities would have been linked to the Catholic holidays associated with the spirits or saints, so that, for example, the celebration of Ogun would have been held on the feast day of Saint James. Some practitioners of Vodou link certain spirits to the natural elements; for example, Danbala and Lasyrenn with water and Azaka with the peasant who works the land.

B. Daily Life

Practitioners of Wicca, Neoshamanism, Neopaganism, and many of those attached to the New Age movement are generally social liberals who seek personal and religious freedom while supporting increased regulation of business around questions of the environment and international free trade, which many of them see as harmful to traditional shamanic and tribal cultures. The belief in the importance of physical and material life, as well as the desire to respect and protect animals, has led many from these groups to practice vegetarianism or veganism.

Some New Age practices stress the importance of fasting, while others focus on the fine-tuning of the body through nutritional supplements. New Age practice is very much a lifestyle, and many New Agers practice daily meditation based on Hindu or Buddhist beliefs, or utilize hypnotic relaxation techniques that derive from nineteenth- and early twentieth-century psychoanalysis. New Agers may also be interested in practices such as Feng Shui, which involves the arrangement of household furniture in a way that is "balanced" so as to bring joy and luck. Others may consult spirits, the tarot deck, or the astrological chart daily in search of advice.

Few of these practices are associated with any particular restrictions on dress on a day-to-day basis, and practitioners usually do little to differentiate themselves otwardly. Certainly among modern primitive Neopagans, one finds many whose scarification or piercing practices differentiate them from others.

Thick gauge earrings or nose, tongue, and lip rings, will stand out, as will more radical practices such as cleaving one's tongue down the middle to create a fork, or filing one's teeth to points. But Neopagans are generally anonymous professionals who transform into their pagan alter egos only during festivals.

Among practitioners of Vodou, Santería, and forms of ritual magic, certain taboos and restrictions may be necessary on certain days, and certain types of fasts may be thought enhance magical powers. In Vodou, a priest or priestess who channels or is possessed by a certain spirit may have to abstain from the foods that the spirit dislikes. Rarely does any of this spill over into daily life.

C. Life Cycle Events

Birth

Among Neopagans and Wiccans, life cycle events represent one of the most important parts of ritual practice. Practitioners of these religions often criticize modern American Protestant-influenced culture for having lost spontaneity in these events, and for having reduced many of these events to a merely materialistic exchange of gifts. On the other hand, many New Agers, despite a commitment to the idea of ritual, do not have traditions in place around these events. Indeed, this is one of the points which separate practitioners of Wicca and Neopaganism from other New Age-influenced pursuits: Wiccans and Neopagans are more likely to emphasize the importance of communal rituals and traditions over the merely individual pursuit of spiritual well-being. Given the fact that these nature-oriented religions derive so many of their ideas from the study of the history of religions and anthropology, it is little surprise that these rituals have so much diversity and are so rich in ideas.

Today's Wiccans often refer to the events surrounding the birth of a child as a "Wiccaning." The word Wiccaning is, of course, a usage derived from the term "Christening" and serves as a reminder of the ways in which Wiccans and other Neopagans view themselves in contradistinction to what they perceive as a dominating patriarchal Christian culture. Also important for Neopagans and Wiccans is the absence of a concept of original sin. This means that while Wiccans creatively draw from many sources in the invention of their rituals, they are highly resistant to the idea of the baptism of a child or other "cleansing" rituals.

A Neopagan Wiccaning serves much the same role that child presentation ceremonies do in some modern churches. A child is introduced to the community and also to the divine—in this case the Great Goddess or other natural spirits. The ritual may also include an invocation of natural beings such as the winds, the forests, or the spirits of the waters. On the whole, one can expect such services to be highly individualized and to make full use of the creative powers of the parents and the community. Also of note here are the ways in which Neopagans have sought to revive the practices of midwifery and folk healing. Many in the Neopagan community seek knowledge of traditional herb lore, specifically around questions of women's health.

Confirmation

Coming-of-age ceremonies, as in many of the traditional cultures that these new communities look back toward, are an important part of Neopagan and Wiccan religious life. Wiccans and Neopagans seek to mark this event in the life cycle of a young adult in ways that American Protestantism, with its lack of ritual, does not. Most coming-of-age ceremonies among Neopagans involve celebration and teaching. This can include talks with elders about sexuality and religious beliefs. Many Neopagans use this time to take a camping trip that, in some ways, is symbolic of the rituals found in tribal societies where youths take vision quests or are secluded from society for a time to mark the passage to adulthood. As in many tribal and traditional cultures, Neopagans and Wiccans usually separate the sexes for coming-of-age rituals. Men initiate young men into adulthood and women initiate young women.

Particularly among Neopagans of a shamanic bent, this period is ideally one in which the young adult seeks out initiation into the spiritual world, often through vision or a time alone in the wilderness. Among more Harnerian shamans, a vision quest may be a time in which a young adult seeks out a power animal or totem, the spirit or guide who will help him or her become a healer.

In general when considering coming-of-age ceremonies, one must take care in differentiating them from other magical initiation ceremonies. The coming-of-age ceremony is designed to mark out a physical event in the cycle of life, while magical initiation ceremonies can often take place at any time during the religionist's lifetime and mark instead the progress of learning or the fact that one has been called to serve a certain spirit. This type of initiation ceremony will be discussed later in the chapter under the heading of Education and Hierarchy of Clergy.

Nuptials

Among New Agers and Neopagans, the nuptial ceremony is likely to be a blend of individual creativity and appropriation. Couples will often write their own vows or ask artistic or spiritual leaders of the community to work with them to create a ceremony that is the ideal expression of their tastes and beliefs. Many New Agers mistrust authority and tradition, and are not likely to desire to be married in a traditional setting. These weddings may simply be a form of an American secular wedding. It is also important to note that, given New Age individualism, it is frequently the case that couples do not share beliefs about religion, the divine, and the soul.

Today's Wiccans and Neopagans often refer to the rituals that surround marriage in their communities as "Handfasting." This name reflects a common ritual practice among Wiccans and Neopagans that involves wrapping the hands of the new couple together with a ribbon in order to, quite literally, "tie the knot." The word "Handfasting," like " Wiccaning" above, also serves as a marker to separate ideologically the practices of Wiccans and Neopagans

Wiccan weddings often take place at the center of a labyrinth, which sometimes consists of a stone pathway—such as the one at top, in Ivins, Utah—or a pathway laid out among tall grass or weeds. At bottom is the symbolic "Handfasting," a ritual in Wiccan weddings in which bride and groom become bound to one another spiritually.

from those of Christianity. "Handfasting," unlike the words "marriage" and "wedding," does not carry with it connotations of patriarchy and the submission of women to their husbands. It is also important to note that couples may or may not choose to have their new status as a couple recognized by secular authority. The rite is thought to have value in itself without it becoming a government-sanctioned marriage. The vast majority of Wiccans and Neopagans, as religious and political liberals, are open to performing a Handfasting ritual with same sex couples.

Croning, Eldering, Death and Burial

Many Neopagans and Wiccans, when asked about their rituals for death and burial, are quick to respond that, in their world view, another important stage in the cycle of life must first be recognized—one which is often missed by modern Western society—the stage of the elder or crone.

Wiccans recognize menopause as an important event in the lives of women. It is seen as just as important as the process of coming of age. A crone is a woman who has passed into this period of life and deserves to be recognized as one who holds wisdom and learning. The rituals surrounding a "croning" may be as simple as a birthday party or as complicated as a coming-of-age initiation, but what is symbolically important is that the community recognizes this transition into a new phase of life. This ceremony carries with it the common Neopagan and Wiccan theme of valuing each stage of life and recognizing the changes that take place in the natural world, whether they occur in the human body or the changing of the seasons. The idea of the crone also carries with it important connotations for Wiccan feminism. These feminists argue that mainstream Western culture values women primarily as objects of men's sexual desire, and that the importance of independent, strong, elderly women is often overlooked or ignored. The ritual of eldering symbolizes a similar point in the late life of men, but the role of the elder carries with it little of the matriarchal and political meaning of the role of crone.

Neopagan and New Age groups are unlikely to have a series of highly structured rituals around the death and passing of a group member. Such rituals may be individualized and reflect the personal beliefs and ideals of the deceased. Memorial services are likely to be simple and to focus on memorializing the individual who has passed on. Here it is important to note that New Agers, more than any other group, are likely to place emphasis on the processes of grieving among those who have survived the lost individual. The popular self-help book, *On Death and Dying,* by Dr. Elizabeth Kübler-Ross, is often invoked, and New Agers speak of "working through the stages of grief." This process may last several years in the eyes of many New Agers, but what is important here is that one not "repress" one's sense of loss and anger.

Among New Agers of a spiritualist orientation, attempts may be made to contact the spirit of the dead through a medium, through dreams, or through the use of a pendulum which, when dangled from the hand, is thought to answer yes-and-no questions by turning clockwise or counterclockwise at the spirit's whim. Tools such as the planchette, a device on wheels that holds a pencil lead, or a Ouija board may be used for the purpose of receiving messages through the involuntary movements of one's own body. Some spiritualist New Agers also use similar processes to contact the spirits of dead pets including cats and dogs Making contact with the dead in this fashion can often offer reassurance that the loved one has gone on to a better place, but it can also be used to make sure that the loved one had no unfinished business on this earth that is holding him or her back from spiritual liberation. Some New Agers believe that the spirits of deceased humans may become guides or teachers to those who remain below. In these instances an attempt is made to enter into an ongoing conversation with the spirit in order to receive advice on matters that range from spirituality to business and love.

The majority of New Agers and many Wiccans and Neopagans believe in life after death. These beliefs may range from the notion of reincarnation (perhaps the dominant belief) to the idea that there are many realms or heavens into which one can pass on one's journey; but a significant portion of those who follow these religions are materialists or hold a spiritual world view in which the individual experiences dissolution at the point of death. For these materialists and naturalists, death may still be viewed as a positive event in the life cycle, and the passing of individuality may be thought of as a kind of reunion with nature, a return to the oneness of all being, or a becoming-all-things. Believers of this stripe often point out that, when we die, our material bodies pass naturally into the bodies of plants and animals, and thus the cycle of life goes on.

D. Family Life

Husband and Wife

As noted above, Neopagans, Wiccans, and many in the New Age movement may have more than average skepticism about marriage and marriage practices and are likely to feel that marriage in general carries with it connotations of patriarchy and the oppression of women. It is also important to note that some of these religious practices have roots in the Free Love era of the 1960s, and that, therefore, Neopagans and New Agers are more likely to feel comfortable with sexual relationships that fall outside of the mainstream Western tradition.

Among Neopagans, the notion of "polyamory" has many supporters. This type of relationship views monogamy as unduly restrictive and believes one can have many loves at the same time. Polyamorous households may include multiple men and women who share sexual relations with one another. Some Neopagans also support the idea of non-exclusive, open marriages and look toward tribal societies in which times of festival were also times of orgy.

In the New Age movement, many who believe in reincarnation hold that we often find ourselves together with the same souls as we move through our lifetimes. One often marries a person with whom one has lived many past lives—in short, one's "soul mate." In this view, one may have tried and failed to resolve certain spiritual and emotional issues with one's mate in past lives, and this new life represents a chance to try again.

Child-rearing

Most New Agers and Neopagans have liberal attitudes toward child-rearing and education and believe that children should be allowed to explore different ideas and practices on their way to spiritual maturity. Children are encouraged to question dominant cultural attitudes, in particular the attitudes and beliefs of traditional Christianity. This liberal attitude toward child-rearing and education may also mean New Age and Neopagan parents are less likely to punish children for fear of inhibiting their natural curiosity and desire to question authority. Many groups offer child-oriented activities, including yoga for children. Neopagan and Wiccan parents will seek out activities that will bring about a love of nature and the natural world in children.

Attitudes toward myth in Neopaganism and Wicca lead many parents to strongly believe in the power of storytelling. Such parents may try to create a sense of magic in children's lives by reading them tales of Merlin or King Arthur and his knights.

Extended Family

The New Age emphasis on the individual search for spiritual truth is often very much at odds with the emphasis of many traditional cultures on shared practices and beliefs among extended family. New Agers (and Neopagans as well) are very likely to have come from conservative or mainstream Protestant backgrounds, and their religious orientation often marks a rejection of the Christianity of their parents and family. The acceptance of doctrines such as reincarnation and the practice of magic can often lead to partial or complete alienation from family members who remain committed to other traditions.

In Santería and Vodou this tension may be evident as well, although in different ways. These cultures are both highly tradition-oriented, and family history may play a great role in deciding what spirits to worship. Indeed, in Santería, the spirits of the deceased are welcomed and supplicated in many ceremonies—a practice many mainstream Catholics and most Protestants remain opposed to and view as both pagan and Satanic. This can create severe alienation in families where one member becomes attracted to Santería or Vodou and the others remain mainstream Christians, or in families in which one or more members convert to Protestantism, an event that is increasingly common among the hispanic population in the United States and in South and Central America.

Divorce

Among virtually all New Age and Neopagans, divorce is seen as a normal part of modern life. The individual quest for religious, emotional, and intellectual fulfillment is often seen as more important than any commitment between individuals. This is particularly true given New Age and Neopagan skepticism of marriage and its general suspicion of patriarchal society.

Within the New Age movement, especially given its connections to modern psychotherapy, much emphasis is likely to be placed on personal healing in relationships, and couples may attempt numerous different types of therapies before settling finally on divorce. These therapies may also be seen as useful for healing the emotional traumas of a marriage after it is dissolved, in particular those traumas incurred by women in relationships in which the male was dominant.

As noted above, practitioners of Santería and Vodou may or may not see themselves as committed to upholding Catholic tradition in areas like marriage. The Catholic tradition, of course, prohibits divorce and remarriage.

IV. Denominations and Demographics

A. History

It is not possible to present a thorough account of all of the different branches of New Age, Neopagan, Wiccan, and occult religions in groups in America and their schisms and mergers. The reasons for this stretch far beyond the problem of mere pluralism and the fact that many thousands of such groups exist without having any larger organizational affiliations. The deeper problem lies in the mythologizing nature of many of these religions. Founders of occult and pagan groups have traditionally laid claim to a host of secret knowledge and occult initiations that may or may not be fictitious. In the world of occult magic, many groups lay claim to the heritage of the Hermetic Order of the Golden Dawn, the Rosicrucians, and the Ordo Templi Orientis, whether or not any genuine historical connection exists.

In the New Age world, on the other hand, history and tradition—though they may lend authority to a practice or belief—are less important than they are in other religions. There is no stigma attached to newness and innovation among New Agers, and founders of new practices often disregard historical analogs, preferring to credit their teachings to angels, aliens, or disembodied spiritual masters. Many New Age groups do not so much split from other older groups as they do spring up, almost spontaneously, around the latest best-selling New Age author.

Recent New Age moments of interest include the popular movie *What the Bleep Do We Know*, a film which combines the theories of quantum physics with the ideas of positive thinking and self-actualization, and the video and best-selling book *The Secret*, by Rhonda Byrne. Byrne claims the authority of ancient Egyptian texts such as the *Emerald Tablets of Hermes Trismegistus* and alchemists such as Paracelsus as a historical basis for her method, called the "Rule of Attraction." According to the rule of attraction, what is inside of one is mirrored in the outside world, so that if oneself wants to be rich in the outside world, one needs to first "attract the wealth" by imagining oneself as wealthy and taking on the confidence of a wealthy person. Although Byrne's thought does have superficial similarities to Renaissance-era alchemy, a more immediate but uncredited source is American "New Thought."

Covenant of the Goddess
CoG, Correspondence Officer
PO Box 1226
Berkeley, CA 94701
www.cog.org

On another note, such groups do not carry with them the Christian ideal of unity. Pluralism in and of itself is valued, and few groups see the need to strive toward institutionalization, especially given Neopagan and New Age objections to Christianity as "organized religion." Some leaders have attempted to build larger organizations of Wiccans and Neopagans. The largest of these organizations among Wiccans is the Covenant of the Goddess, a loosely organized interdenominational polity that was founded in 1975 for the purpose of guaranteeing religious freedom for Wiccans and helping Wiccan groups receive tax-exempt status with the IRS.

Other issues that are of importance to Neopagan polity include representation in the World Parliament of Religions; the need for army, prison, and hospital chaplains who are members of nature-based religions; and the recent Supreme Court decision that permitted Wiccan soldiers to have their graves marked with a pentacle rather than a cross.

Foundation for Shamanic Studies
www.shamanism.org

Also of note is the fact that many in the Unitarian Universalist church today identify as Neopagan, Wiccan, or as having an "Earth Centered" spirituality. CUUPS (The Covenant of Unitarian Universalist Pagans) is the most significant Pagan Unitarian group. In the Neoshamanic world, the most influential group is Michael Harner's Foundation for Shamanic Studies, founded in 1985 after the publication of his popular book *The Way of the Shaman*. This group offers training in "core shamanism" all across the world.

Santería and Vodou are decentralized religions in the United States and practitioners may have no affiliations with each other, but rather may be centered around local influential practitioners who work with the spirits. These religions, like many occult groups, tend to work in secret. This is particularly the case among those groups that practice animal sacrifice, a practice that has been (unsuccessfully) challenged by animal rights groups in the United States.

B. Organization and Distribution

In the case of all of these religions, attempting to determine concrete statistics as to the numbers of practitioners in the United States is futile. The reasons for this lie in the decentralized and pluralized nature of these religions. Wiccans and Neopagans may or may not belong to organized covens or pagan groups of which there are many thousands—many of which are not affiliated with any larger bodies. Practitioners may also be solitary magicians or dabble in paganism in secret. The concepts of Neopaganism and Wicca overlap and differ. An individual may identify as both Neopagan and Wiccan or only one or the other. Given these factors, it is of little surprise that different methods of taking statistics have posited different numbers for Neopagans in the United States. Some of the better surveys have estimated that there are between 250,000 and two million Neopagans and Wiccans in the U.S.

One runs into even greater methodological problems when it comes to estimating the number of New Agers and spiritualists in America. These names can cover thousands of different organizational bodies that have little or nothing to do with one another. Then again, one practitioner of a certain type of yoga may identify more heavily with the New Age and another with Hindu beliefs. Many New Agers may also identify as American Buddhist, despite the fact that their interests include many beliefs and practices that fall outside of traditional Buddhism. Furthering the difficulty is the fact that, for many, "New Age" does not constitute an identify so much as a series of ideas and methods. An individual may receive New Age psychic and astrology readings or New Age healing treatments without considering the "New Age" to be part of one's identity. Indeed, the entire phenomenon of self-help literature, which includes many of each year's nonfiction bestsellers, is connected to the New Age focus on self-realization and healing. Nearly a fifth of Americans identify as "Spiritual not Religious," a category that includes many of those who engage in New Age practices.

One runs into similar problems when examining the statistics for practitioners of Vodou and Santería in the U.S. Exactly who counts as a practitioner? Perhaps the majority of immigrants from Haiti and Cuba have had some contact with these religions and practices. Many may have bought charms or had their fortunes told and yet still do not consider Santería or Vodou to be their religion. They may identify as Catholic, as, in fact, may many who have been fully initiated into these religions. Because of this tendency, estimates of the numbers of Santería and Vodou practitioners in the U.S. range from several thousand to upwards of three million.

The largest population centers for Vodou practitioners are in urban areas that have a high population of Haitian immigrants, including the boroughs of New York City. New Orleans has also traditionally been a site of Vodou activity, and many homegrown traditions. Similarly, Santería is largely an immigrant urban phenomenon with centers in places with a high number of immigrants from Cuba and, to a lesser degree, other Latin American countries. New York, Miami, and Los Angeles stand out as areas with a high concentration of Santería botanicas.

Practitioners of Neopaganism, Wicca, and Neoshamanism are more evenly distributed across the country and many covens exist in the Midwest and South as well as on both of the coasts. New England stands out as an area with a higher than average Wiccan population, and the town of Salem, the historical site of the Puritan witch trials, offers much for the Wiccan enthusiast, including numerous Wiccan bookshops and weeks of festivities around Halloween. Northern California and Los Angeles are also centers with a large Neopagan population.

V. Organization and Infrastructure

A. Education and Hierarchy of Clergy

Most religions discussed in this chapter are initiatory religions, meaning that they are, by nature, religions of the few rather than of the many. They are also elective religions rather than religions into which one is born. But we recall that Christianity itself was once an initiatory mystery religion, that the ceremony of baptism was once one of initiation. Nearly all of this flavor was lost to Christians with the introduction of infant baptism and the reality of a dominant mainstream Christian culture.

Among Wiccans and Neopagans, the attempt to recover the mystery of initiatory religions is a self-conscious effort, and many Wiccans and Neopagans look back toward the mysteries of Ancient Egypt and Greece for inspiration—at perhaps the Eleusinian mysteries or the mystery cults of Isis and Osirus. Many Neoshamans also look back to the mysteries of Eleusis with interest and reverence, given that many historians believe that the initiations that took place there involved the use of a hallucinogenic drink.

Wiccan and pagan initiations may involve the choosing of a new religious name, and, as in many other religions, there is often a motif of death and rebirth involved in the ceremonial liturgy. Groups that stem more directly from the English occult tradition may have many levels of secret occult initiations. A secret hierarchy may exist in these organizations made up of a number of "grades" from acolyte or novice to master. In some organizations even the number of grades is kept secret from outsiders and those of lower grades. Typically in initiatory religions of this sort, the levels of initiation are thought to reflect the proficiency and knowledge of the individual. Individuals who are more proficient and knowledgeable may move through the grades quickly while some will not be offered advancement at all. The initiation ceremonies in some of these traditions may be linked to the Rosicrucian and Masonic initiation ceremonies, which involve the blindfolding of the candidate and a series of oaths to secrecy that a new brother must take.

On the whole, the separation in initiatory religions is between outsiders and insiders to the religion rather than between clergy and laity. All initiates have, in some measure, embraced a sacred role, regardless of the grades of initiation that may exist above them.

Rights of initiation into Santería and Vodou vary greatly from place to place and depending on what spirit is to be "seated upon" or to "ride," or possess the candidate. A candidate for initiation into Santería must spend a great deal of money buying new clothing, sacrifices, and food for the spirits. After meeting with the Babalawo, or the high priest, he or she is informed of the past sins that he or she has committed against the spirits and what types of sacrifices will be necessary to propitiate them. These sins are then transferred into birds, doves, chickens, and pigeons, by rubbing the fowls on the body of the initiate. The birds are then sacrificed and the initiate tastes the blood of the sacrificed animals. If the novice is then accepted by the spirits, he or she may receive a full immersion baptism. Further rituals make sure that the guardian angel or the Eleda of the individual accepts his or her new role as a Santero or Santera. After this process, the initiate must enter into a trance in which the spirit that has been seated upon him or her manifests itself so that the ritual is shown to have been successful. He or she is now prepared to serve the spirit and to practice and perform ritual actions that involve the intervention of the spirit seated upon him or her.

SEMINARIES

Members of these religions, in general, do not attend formal seminary after the fashion of Christians in order to obtain the privilege of administering religious rites. Among Wiccans, Neopagans, and occultists, as well as among those who practice Santería and Vodou, the process of religious education is likely to be one in which teachings are handed down on a one-on-one basis by religious masters.

Grof Transpersonal Training, Inc.
PMB 516
38 Miller Avenue
Mill Valley, CA 94941
415-383-8779   Fax: 415-383-0965
gtt@holotropic.com   www.holotropic.com

On the other hand, in the New Age world, paying for training is the norm. Many organizations offer certificates and licenses that individuals may obtain after logging numerous hours of coursework. Adepts at a given practice such as Reiki or Polarity Therapy may travel across the country offering training. When one has completed enough coursework and logged enough hours of practice, one can be officially endorsed as a licensed practitioner by various bodies such as, for example, Stanislaw Grof's Grof Transpersonal Training, Inc.

Although no concrete numbers exist, one might estimate that there are tens of thousands of these types of training and licensure opportunities currently available in the New Age community. Nearly all New Age teachers and authors have introduced these types of programs, including Michael Harner, who offers a program in "core shamanism." These programs often cost many thousands of dollars and may take years to complete. That said, many practice these New Age techniques without being licensed by an organization and claim instead that they have a sacred or psychic "gift" for a certain type of practice. Many of these organizations exist on a for-profit basis and serve to enrich charismatic members of the community who author successful books or pioneer new healing techniques. Some Wiccans have also begun to offer for-profit courses.

Integral University
www.integraluniversity.org

Naropa University
2130 Arapahoe Avenue
Boulder, CO 80302
303-444-0202   Fax: 303-444-0410
www.naropa.edu

At the university level, two programs that offer degrees in New Age style theology, metaphysics, and healing are author Ken Wilber's Integral University (through partnership with Fielding Graduate University and John F. Kennedy University), and Naropa University, a school in Boulder, Colorado. The latter was founded by Tibetan Buddhists but has long been a center for New Age as well.

Cherry Hill Seminary
PO Box 5405, Columbia, SC 29250-5405
888-503-4131
www.cherryhillseminary.org
Cherry Hill Seminary offers a distance education degree for those who are interested in becoming licensed pagan ministers.

Also of note in the New Age world are medical programs that offer training for doctors in "integrative medicine," or medicine that attempts to treat the entire lifestyle of the individual rather just specific illnesses, and emphasizes nutrition, exercise, and stress reduction. The first of these programs in the United States was started by best-selling author Andrew Weil at the University of Arizona in Tucson. Numerous other programs now exist including those at Harvard, Duke, and Columbia.

American Polarity Therapy Association
122 N. Elm Street, Suite 512
Greensboro, NC 27401
336-574-1121   Fax: 336-574-1151
APTAoffices@polaritytherapy.org

North American College of Gnostic Bishops
www.nacgb.org

B. Shrines and Houses of Worship

Many of these religions believe certain places in the world to be the loci of special power. Among Wiccans, Neopagans, and some New Agers, these locations may be thought to be related to the lines of powerful earth energy that are said to circulate around the globe. These lines, called ley lines, are believed to offer natural power to those who are sensitive to it. Those who map out ley lines across the world often say that they intersect at places like Stonehenge and the Great Pyramids, and at mountains and other places held sacred by ancient societies. Several other important sites include Sedona, in Arizona, and Glastonbury in Britain. These intersections, called nexuses, are the best sites for holding religious rituals and practicing meditation. Certain New Age groups offer world tours of sacred sites for those who seek enlightenment and can pay the fee.

However, many Wiccans and Neopagans are emphatic that everywhere in the natural world is sacred. Places where nature is particularly preserved and beautiful are believed to be excellent sites for festival and ritual. On the whole, Wiccan, Neopagan, and New Age religions in the U.S. are often practiced in the home. The same can be said of Santería and Vodou where simple home altars often take the place of elaborate temples. New Age trainings and workshops may also be offered in bookstores, dance and yoga studios, or public and hotel convention centers depending on the popularity of the author or master giving the training.

C. Governance and Authority

Authority in New Age religions may be thought, in some cases, to lie in the hands of unaffiliated individuals on a spiritual quest. In other cases, the individual may belong to a larger commercial organization that follows a corporate structure and is designed to promulgate the teachings and practices of a given author or teacher; such organizations may also be non-profits which are beholden to a board of trustees. In still other cases, the organization may be wholly owned by a teacher or individual. It is worth noting that perhaps the majority of "cults" started by charismatic leaders in the United States fall loosely under the heading of "New Age." These "cults" may offer radically countercultural teachings and center around a leader who is said to have access to aliens, angels, or spiritual beings who pronounce the rules and regulations for the community.

On the other hand, in the Wiccan and Neo-pagan world, organizations may be tiny and contain no governing structure aside from the consensus of the community. Organizations such as the Covenant of the Goddess have sought to bring a loosely knit congregational style polity to Neopaganism in order to offer pagans and Wiccans some of the benefits that greater numbers bring for official recognition and lobbying purposes.

The practices of Santería and Vodou are also highly decentralized in the United States. Larger communities of Santería practitioners may gather around a high priest or Babalawo, while in other areas believers may gather in small, unaffiliated groups to practice their rituals.

Occult groups are by nature extremely hierarchical, with numerous levels marking one's spiritual progress. Some of these groups, influenced by Catholicism and Neognosticism, ordain priests and bishops. The organization North American College of Gnostic Bishops includes bishops from many occult groups who gather together to vote in a synod on religious and social service issues.

D. Social Service Organizations

New Agers, Wiccans, and Neopagans are involved in numerous social causes. Particular causes for Wiccans and Neopagans center around the preservation of the environment and advocate holding nature sacred. Other issues, especially for Wiccans, include feminism and women's health.

Reclaiming
PO Box 14404
San Francisco, CA 94114
rcorrespondence@yahoogroups.com
www.reclaiming.org

Perhaps the best known of all Neopagan social service organizations is the eco-feminist activist group Reclaiming, founded by Wiccan writer, Starhark.

Neoshamans of all stripes are likely to work for the preservation of traditional culture around the world and to see globalization and free trade as a threat to these cultures. Of particular note here is Michael Harner's Foundation for Shamanic Studies, but Neoshamans are just as likely to be involved in other organizations that fight for the same aims.

Center for Cognitive Liberty & Ethics
PO Box 73481
Davis, CA 95617-3481
Fax: (205) 449-3119
www.cognitiveliberty.org

In the New Age world, a central cause for lobbying is natural health, with New Agers fighting to keep herbal and mineral medicines unregulated by the FDA and to gain funding for programs in alternative medicine. Another issue for Neoshamans in particular is freedom of religion and its relation to the war on drugs. Lobby groups such as the Center for Cognitive Liberty and Ethics defend "freedom of consciousness," and the right of an individual to use mind-altering plants and drugs. Although the CCLE cannot be identified as a Neoshamanic group, many Neoshamans take a great interest in its causes.

It is difficult to identify social service organizations as particularly New Age or Neopagan given that many secular organizations endorse some New Age beliefs. This is particularly true of environmental groups, many of which argue for the sacredness of nature and for health issues, where alternative medicine has been increasingly embraced by mainstream America. The radical environmental group Earth First! has been known to embrace Neopagan ideas. (Each issue of the organization's journal corresponds to a Neopagan holiday.)

E. Media and Communication

Many heavily promoted New Age books are published by mainstream publishing houses. These books reach a broad swathe of the American public, and authors may receive attention from mainstream media outlets. Nonetheless, numerous specifically New Age and occult publishing houses exist.

Llewellyn Worldwide, LTD.
2143 Wooddale Drive
Woodbury, MN 55125
1-800-THE-MOON / 651-291-1970
Fax: (651) 291-1908

Weiser Books
Red Wheel/Weiser/Conari
65 Parker Street, Suite 7
Newburyport, MA 01950
978-465-0504   Fax: 978-465-0243
www.weiserbooks.com

Two of the better-known houses are Llewellyn, which publishes tarot cards, books on psychic phenomena, and volumes on Wicca and Neopaganism; and Weiser, which focuses on books that relate to the English occult tradition, including classics by authors such as Aleister Crowley and books on Kabbalah. One Spirit (www.onespirit.com) is a popular book club company that caters to a New Age audience.

Shaman's Drum
PO Box 270,
Williams, Oregon 97544
541-846-1313
drum@shamansdrum.org
www.shamansdrum.org

The New Age world also has numerous periodicals such as the *Whole Life Times* and, in Southern California, the biweekly newspaper *Awareness*. In the Neoshamanic world, one of the best-known magazines is *Shaman's Drum*, a periodical devoted to traditional shamanism.

For many Neopagans, Neoshamans, and Wiccans, online communities offer the best prospect of meeting others who share their interests. For Neoshamans, this often means sharing tips on the preparation of drugs and herbs on sites such as www.erowid.org and www.ayahuasca.org, while for Wiccans and Neopagans this may mean setting up blogs to share rituals, spells, and art. Those looking for an online introduction to Neopaganism and Wicca should check out the Internet Book of Shadows, a compendium of user-generated online material (www.sacred-texts.com/bos/index.htm). The site www.newageinfo.com offers much information on New Age practices.

For Spanish speakers, the site www.olofin.com offers information on and by Santeros and Santeras.

FURTHER READING AND RESOURCES

Drawing Down the Moon: Witches, Druids, Goddess Worshippers and other Pagans in America Today
Margot Adler
1979: Viking

Magic, Witchcraft and the Other World
Susan Greenwood
2000: Macmillan

The Doors of Perception
Aldous Huxley
1977: HarperCollins

New Age and Neopagan Religions in America
Sarah Pike
2004: Columbia University Press

3 Atheism, Agnosticism, Humanism, and Other Groups

I. Origins and Early History

A. Nontheism in America

WHEN AMERICANS LOOK BACK ON THEIR EARLY history, two distinct moments come into focus. We see first the arrival of the Pilgrims in this country and of other settlers seeking a land in which they can practice their religion openly. Catholics arrive, as do Quakers, each of them hoping for religious toleration. America, at this moment, appears as the home of devout religionists of different stripes. Colonies are founded; a few—such as Rhode Island—offering freedom of conscience as the right of all. Others, founded as theocracies, offer their citizens a chance at purity and hope for a life they believe God has intended for them. Such is a portrait of America in the seventeenth century.

The second moment comes with the signing of the Declaration of Independence in 1776. At this juncture Americans no longer appear as devout refugees fighting to survive in an inhospitable land. Instead, the men gathered together to debate this document are successful men of business, traders, and landowners—the educated elite of the nation to be. Their concerns are no longer religious dogmas, but rather taxation, the appointment of the judiciary, and property rights. They are not uninterested in religion, and indeed some are religious men, but their immediate business concerns the natural rather than the supernatural. Their hope is not just for religious toleration, but for the end of the sort of "superstition" that allows for the government of kings and prevents the free exercise of reason and the unfettered exercise of commerce.

The chief author of the Declaration of Independence was Thomas Jefferson. Jefferson has sometimes been called an atheist, sometimes a deist, and sometimes a Unitarian, but rarely has he been called a Christian. Jefferson undoubtedly admired Jesus as a thinker. He wrote in glowing terms of his maxims and reflections, and argued, somewhat justly, that, while the teachers of the ancient world focused their philosophies on the self and tranquility of the secularly-absorbed mind, the teachings of Jesus focused instead upon selflessness and loving others.

Mather Brown painted this oil-on-canvas portrait of Thomas Jefferson sometime around 1786; the painting hangs in the Smithsonian Institution's National Portrait Gallery.

Nonetheless, for Jefferson, the teachings of Christianity were mostly myth and superstitious absurdity. Jefferson's firm hope was that the United States would eventually be a country ruled by reason and cleansed of traditional myths. He wrote to John Adams, "The day will come when the mystical generation of Jesus by the supreme being as his father in the womb of a virgin will be classed with the fable of the generation of Minerva in the brain of Jupiter. But we may hope that the dawn of reason and freedom of thought in these United States will do away with all of this artificial scaffolding and restore the primitive and genuine doctrines of this the most venerated reformer of human errors."

For Jefferson, Jesus was not God and the doctrine of the Trinity was merely "Eastern" mysticism engrafted onto Jesus's "simple teachings." Jefferson, however, did not deny the existence of a creator God. For Jefferson, the existence of such a God could be proven by reason. A first cause was necessary to explain the generation of the world. But the God of belief and faith, particularly the God of John Calvin and those who followed him, was to be abhorred. To worship this God, argued Jefferson, was to be an "atheist," or worse, a believer in a superstition that fell far short of the true God. Jefferson saw God as thoroughly rational and accessible to rational thought. He ridiculed those who read the prologue to the Gospel of John as stating that the Word—*logos* in Greek—or Jesus had created the world. For Jefferson, it was clear that the Greek word "logos" needed to be understood as reason. The world was intrinsically reasonable, as were the teachings of Jesus, he thought, and reason was what would lead to proper ethics and good government. Eventually, Jefferson would translate the Gospels from Greek, expunging as he did so all mention of hell, miracles, and the supernatural. He would then have this work printed and would give a copy of the document to every senator in order to demonstrate what he felt religion in America should be.

On the whole, the founding fathers, whether religious or otherwise, were committed humanists

Thomas Paine (1737–1809), influential writer-pamphleteer of the American Revolution, advocated deism and an end to organized religion. This engraving of Paine was made after a painting by George Romney.

and believed that lawmaking and good citizenship were independent of religion and religious belief. What needed to be taken into account was not whether a law was in accordance with the will of God, but whether it lent itself to the health, freedom, and prosperity of human beings. Today, many continue to debate the religiosity of these figures. Alexander Hamilton, for example, was known to make jokes about God and religion, and to some, his later expressions of faith seemed to reflect his political belief that religion was necessary for good citizenship. This same belief was expressed by Niccolò Machiavelli among others, a man who had an immense influence on the Federalist Papers and regarded talk of God as an aid to patriotism and little more. Those who would gauge the state of religion in early America would also do well to examine the inauguration speech of our first president. Here Washington makes reference to the "Almighty Being who rules over the Universe" and the "Great Author of every public and private good" in a manner that unmistakably reflects piety and humility. However, these are not traditional Biblical titles for God, and Washington makes no mention of Christ or Christianity. Like Jefferson, Washington seems to have believed that the God of tradition had no place in American government. The God of the American state was instead to be a God of reason and of inalienable human rights, a humanistic and philosophical God. Washington himself, although born into the Church of England, no longer attended communion in his later life.

Ideologically, all of these figures were steeped in the recent history of political thought both in England and the Continent. Figures including Hobbes, Spinoza, Montesquieu, Jean-Jaques Rousseau, and John Locke had sought to establish the basis for government upon the idea of nature rather than upon any divine right. Even figures such as Hobbes, who were staunch supporters of the monarchy, began to see that reason, rather than tradition, ought to be the basis for government. Taking a dim view of human nature, Hobbes had argued that the best thing for humans was that they be ruled over by the iron sword of a king. But even this was a departure from the argument that God had set up all kings and governments and that to defy them was a crime against God. Rousseau and Locke, men who believed in the primacy of human nature, argued that any government had to improve human life in order to be considered just. For the founding fathers, this meant that religion was something to be guarded against and even feared insofar as it claimed a right that was not based on reason and human nature, but upon tradition and revelation instead.

Important for the early foundation of nontheism in America was the establishment of secular universities. Universities such as Harvard, Yale, and Princeton had been established as institutions for the training of clergy. But even as these schools became ever more liberal under the influence of Enlightenment thought, Thomas Jefferson founded the University of Virginia with the hope that it would represent a new type of institution, one which was both secular and public. Although most universities at the time offered degrees only in theology, law, and medicine, Jefferson decided not to have a theology department at all. Instead the university would offer degrees in architecture, botany, political science, astronomy, and philosophy. Jefferson himself laid out the ground plan for the university. At the center of the campus, in the place hitherto reserved for a chapel, would stand a grand library in a style that would recall a classical temple. No longer would the university appear as a place oriented toward God and the Divine. Knowledge instead would take position as the highest good. Over time, most universities would follow Jefferson's lead both in terms of the academic structure of the university and the ground plan. Schools such as Princeton and Yale would separate from their divinity schools and ever grander libraries would rise up as secular houses of worship.

Although America would remain a country ripe for religion, the establishment of Enlightenment humanism in the Constitution and the separation of church and state would always leave a large space open for disbelief and a secular and naturalistic understanding of the cosmos. Over time, secularism in the academy would become the rule, and theology as a discipline would be rejected in favor of the sciences and humanities.

B. Important Dates and Landmarks

1774 Thomas Paine arrives in America—he will play an influential role in the American Revolution, but even more influential as a writer. His book, *The Age of Reason*, attacked Christian doctrine and belief in the Bible as revelation.

1776 Thomas Jefferson drafts the Declaration of Independence.

1787 Drafting of the Constitution of the United States.

1788 Ratification of the Constitution of the United States.

1870 Robert Ingersoll begins lecturing and writing essays. Ingersoll was to become the foremost agnostic of his time, likening organized religion to slavery and urging people to trust in science and human reason rather than in God.

1872 Ingersoll publishes *The Gods*, which states: "Each nation has created a god, and the god always resembles his creators." Ingersoll becomes an controversial figure and a prime target for apologetics.

1925 In what would become a landmark court case, John T. Scopes, a Tennessee (substitute) science teacher accused of illegally teaching evolutionary biology. The Christian statesman William Jennings Bryan spars against defense attorney Clarence Darrow over the truth of the biblical account of creation and the descent of humans from apes. Bryan wins the trial and Scopes pays a small fine, but Darrow wins popular opinion.

1933 Signing of the Humanist Manifesto.

1941 Foundation of the American Humanist Association.

1963 Madelyn Murray O'Hair, angered by her son being forced to pray in public school, successfully brings suit to U.S. Supreme Court that eliminates "sectarian opening exercises" from Baltimore public schools, setting an important precedent.

1965 Madelyn Murray O'Hair founds the American Atheist Center.

1973 Signing of the Humanist Manifesto II.

1980 Signing of the Secular Humanist Manifesto.

1987 U.S. Supreme Court rules in landmark *Edward v. Aguillard* case that Louisiana's legislation in the "Balanced Treatment for Creation-Science and Evolution-Science in Public School Instruction Act," which would force schools to teach creation science if they insisted on teaching evolutionary biology, is unconstitutional because it sought to advance a religious agenda, but leaves the door open for intelligent design.

2003 Signing of the Humanist Manifesto III.

2005 The U.S. Supreme Court rules in the landmark Dover Trial that the law requiring Intelligent-Design creation science to be taught alongside evolutionary biology is unconstitutional, since the teaching of intelligent design is intended to promote a particular religious agenda.

☙☙

ATHEISM

A. Introduction

Atheism is a curious inclusion in a book on religion. Atheism is not a religion. It is, in fact, the absence of religion—*dis*belief in God. [However, to be an atheist is not to be without faith, for atheists need to have faith in a world that works without the need of divine intervention.] They need to believe in an explicable world, where nothing is beyond what humankind was meant to know. Yet, many atheists are interested in the big questions, but without religion's easy answers, they prefer to explore these issues and come up with answers on their own.

However, atheists in America have a long history of being mistrusted. Some of this can be traced back to the original colonization of America. As every school child in America knows, the first colonists came to America in search of a place to practice their religion, a religion that was at odds with the state religions of their former homes. These were devoutly religious people, people willing to cross the sea to an unknown land for their faith. Consider the shipboard speech of John Winthrop, the oft-reelected governor of the Massachusetts's Bay Colony, to his people. He told the new colonists that they, in their undertaking, had entered into a covenant with God and it was God who would determine whether they would succeed or fail. Thus, it was of utmost importance that all of the colonists be God-fearing men and the colony be a place ordered in accordance with their God. Not only that, but this colony was going to be watched by the world. It would be an example to the world, either held up as the pinnacle of success through obedience to God or of failure through lack of piety. In the most famous lines of his speech, Winthrop wrote, "For we must consider that we shall be as a city upon a hill. The eyes of all people are upon us. So that if we shall deal falsely with our God in this work we have undertaken, and so cause Him to withdraw His present help from us, we shall be made a story and a by-word through the world."

So, from its founding, America has considered itself a religious endeavor and, beyond that, a light of Christianity intended to serve as an example for the rest of the world. This was perhaps never more obvious than during the Cold War, when the enemy was "Godless Communism." Communism was anti-religious; communists saw religion as an antiquated tradition intended to suppress the lower classes. Karl Marx himself referred to religion as "the opiate of the masses." Thus, it was easy to make the Cold War not just a contest of political ideologies, communism versus democracy, but about faith. Thus, the crime of the communists, in the mind of Americans, was not just their alternate political system with its expansionist policies, but their turning away from belief in

God. If the defining characteristic of the enemy is godlessness, then it is easy to make the defining characteristic of a fellow citizen godliness.

It is easy to see why this made life difficult for even the most patriotic American atheists. However they supported their country, they still had, in the minds of those around them, something in common with the enemy. Thus, atheists during the Cold War years were forced to defend themselves against accusations of having communist sympathies.

However, America is still a country founded on the firm belief that one should not enforce religious beliefs and that the state should not have any say in a person's religion. So, atheists, regardless of people's suspicions, still had the legal right to their beliefs and to the respect of those beliefs by public institutions. One example was the case of Madelyn Murray O'Hair. She was an atheist and mother living in Baltimore. She attempted to get her son exempted from saying prayers in public school, but that led only to harassment of the whole family. So O'Hair took her case to court. And even during the Cold War, when tensions were at their height against atheism, O'Hair won and prayer was banned in public schools across Baltimore. It was praying in public school, not O'Hair's atheism, that had been declared unconstitutional, because it forced a particular set of religious practices on everyone, practices with which those who were not part of that religion—atheists and theists of a different stripe—could not agree. This was a landmark court case that set the standard across the country.

Perhaps the other most important court case in the history of American atheism is the Scopes Trial, sometimes also referred to as the Monkey Trial. This was the trial of John T. Scopes, a science instructor accused of illegally teaching evolutionary biology in a Dayton, Tennessee school. However, what was really on trial for most of America was fundamentalism and the literalist approach to reading the Bible. Christian statesman William Jennings Bryan faced off against defense attorney Clarence Darrow, arguing whether it was legal to ban a subject from school because of religious views. However, Darrow, during the course of the trial, called Bryan to the witness stand to testify about his own beliefs and interpretations regarding the Bible. While this portion of the trial was removed from the court proceedings, it was witnessed by television viewers across America. The fundamentalist reading of the Bible was as much on trial here as evolutionary biology. While Bryan won the case, it was quickly overturned and banning the teaching of evolutionary biology was deemed unconstitutional.

In some ways, what it took for atheism to become respectable was for religion to go on trial. For many people, the argument against atheism was one of moral character. A religious person could be counted on to be a good person, the thinking went, because they knew if they were not, God would punish them. An atheist, not believing in God, would feel no compulsion to be moral. While many atheists argued that in fact they had a deeper morality founded on principles rather than fear of God, they were still frequently less trusted.

But then, slowly, it began to come to light that religious people were also capable of being very untrustworthy. Probably the most well-known of these scandals was that of child abuse by priests. Clergy members whom people trusted unequivocally—after all, they were men of God—were found to be committing heinous acts and, moreover, were being protected by their institutions of faith. Rather than dismissing priests who performed these criminal acts, the church had simply been moving them to other parishes where their pedophilia was unknown and letting them begin again. This scandal and others like it shook people's faith in religious people and the institutions of religion. If religious figures could not be trusted to behave like God-fearing people ought, then perhaps, people thought, they were no better than atheists. Or perhaps, it was that atheists were no worse than them. Thus, atheists and atheism gained a measure of respectability.

B. Important Figures

Madelyn Murray O'Hair

In the years following World War II, Madelyn Murray O'Hair (1919–1995) became the world's most famous atheist. Born Madelyn Mays in Pittsburg, Pennsylvania, the daughter of a Lutheran mother and a Presbyterian father, she read the bible cover-to-cover at age thirteen—and determined that its view of the world was impossible. She served as a cryptographer in the Women's Army Corps during World War II, but spent most of her career as a psychiatric social worker. Her fame derived from the 1963 Supreme Court case of *Murray vs. Curlett*. O'Hair had requested that her son, William, be excused from prayers at school. When students and adults began harassing the family, O'Hair brought the issue to court. She won, eliminating "sectarian opening exercises" from Baltimore public schools.

After her victory, O'Hair continued to campaign against organized religion. She challenged the inclusion of the phrase "under God" in the Pledge of Allegiance (not added until 1954), attacked the Federal Communications Bureau for not forcing stations to sell airtime to atheists, and challenged the tax-exempt

Madelyn Murray O'Hair stands in front of the Supreme Court with her sons, William J. Murray, then sixteen, and Garth Murray, then eight, on February 27, 1963. On that day, the High Court began hearing arguments on O'Hair's attempt to get a court order discontinuing the use of the Lord's Prayer and the reading of the Bible in Baltimore schools.

status of religious organizations. In 1965, she founded the American Atheist Center and served as its director until 1973, when she vanished, along with members of her family, under mysterious circumstances. Many believed that she and her family absconded with her organization's money, but it was later found that they had been robbed and murdered. Despite this, the American Atheist Center, now an organization called American Atheists, continues to this day.

Christopher Hitchens

Christopher Hitchens (1949–) is a controversial English-American political polemicist, with views that have ranged throughout his career from socialism to his current staunch support of the war in Iraq. He was educated at the Leys School, Cambridge, and Balliol College, Oxford, where he studied philosophy, politics, and economics. He has written for the *New Statesman*, *The Nation*, *Vanity Fair*, and *The Atlantic Monthly*, and has been interviewed on numerous current affairs television programs. He is also the author of the best-selling book *God is Not Great: How Religion Poisons Everything*, which attacks all forms of religion, not just the three best-known monotheistic religions. He argues that the belief in a God or Supreme Being is inherently totalitarian and destroys personal freedom. He is also the editor of *The Portable Atheist*.

Ellen Johnson

Ellen Johnson was president of the American Atheists from 1995–2008, drafted to lead the movement after the disappearance of Madelyn Murray O'Hair and her family. She is a self-described soccer mom and second-generation atheist. Her educational background consists of Bachelor's degrees in environmental studies and political science and a Master's degree in political science. As president, she continued O'Hair's legacy by making the separation of church and state within public school a priority, attempting to prevent religious recruitment programs from occurring on school grounds or as part

Ayn Rand used her novels to promulgate her philosophies of "rational selfishness" and objectivism.

of athletic events. Johnson also co-hosts the television show "The Atheist Viewpoint" and is the executive director of the Godless Americans Political Action Committee. This group grew out of the 2002 Godless American March on Washington, an effort to promote civil rights, the separation of church and state, and the full recognition of atheist Americans as a part of American culture and politics.

Frank Zindler

Frank Zindler is the current president of American Atheists and the manager of American Atheist Press. His background is in science, as he was a professor of biology, geology, and psychobiology at a branch of the State University of New York for almost twenty years. For the past twenty-five years, he has worked for the scientific society as a linguist and editor of chemical research literature. He is the author of *The Jesus the Jews Never Knew*, which posits that ancient Jews had never heard of Jesus. He also writes articles for the *American Atheist* on logic, language, Bible historicity, flood geology, creationism and evolution, and first amendment rights.

Ayn Rand

Ayn Rand (1905–1982) was a Russian-American best-selling novelist and influential philosopher. She was born in St. Petersburg, Russia, but emigrated to the United States in 1926. Her two master works of literature were *The Fountainhead*, a novel about the conflict between free thinkers and the old guard in the world of architecture; and *Atlas Shrugged*, a novel set in dystopian America where industrialists and other creative individuals leave society to set up a free-economy paradise in the mountains. Both novels, as well as her plays, novellas, and other writings, relate to her philosophy, which she dubbed "objectivism." Rand was famously quoted as saying that the individual "must exist for his own sake, neither sacrificing himself to others nor sacrificing others to himself. The pursuit of his own rational self-interest and of his own happiness is the highest moral purpose of his life." This became a concise, though incomplete, summary of objectivism—a philosophy based on reason and based in objective reality. It advocates self-interest over self-sacrifice, as well as a free market economy and a government that protects the rights of individuals, but does little more.

Ayn Rand founded a group called (jokingly) the Collective, which published the *Objectivist*, a newsletter containing her writing and that of her compatriots. The Collective helped promote her philosophy through the Nathaniel Brandon Institute, named for a Collective member. Her work continues to be influential today.

Sam Harris

Sam Harris is the author of two *New York Times* best-selling nonfiction books, *The End of Faith* and *Letter to a Christian Nation.* He graduated from Stanford University with a degree in philosophy and is completing a doctorate in neuroscience. His book, *The End of Faith,* proposes Harris's theory of how religious belief leads to the suspension of reason and acts of violence. *Letter to a Christian Nation* is a reply to his critics, of which he has many, which addresses current topics such as the controversy over stem cell research, Intelligent Design, and religiously motivated violence. He has also written many articles on religion, politics, and neurobiology. Harris is the founder and chairman of the Reason Project, an organization dedicated to advancing knowledge and secular values in society that aims to encourage critical thinking and wise public policy and offer material support to religious dissidents and intellectuals.

C. Major Events: Atheism on Trial

Many of the major events in the history of atheism in America played out on the courtroom floor. Atheism has always been a controversial belief, bound up in America with the separation of church and state. Whether directly or indirectly related to atheism, these court cases sometimes advanced the rights of atheists and other times lost atheists the hard-earned respect of their fellow Americans. Here are a few examples of landmark court cases that altered the popular opinion of atheism in America.

Leopold and Loeb (1924)

The Trial of Leopold and Loeb (1924) may not seem at first to be related to atheism. After all, it is a murder trial. Eighteen-year-old Richard Loeb (1905–1936) and nineteen-year-old Nathan Leopold (1904–1971) were on trial for the murder of fourteen-year-old Bobby Franks, a crime without a motive. Leopold and Loeb both considered themselves superior to the majority of humanity. They were both exceptionally bright and came from exceedingly wealthy families. They met when they were fourteen and thirteen respectively; both, despite their youth, were attending the University of Chicago. They quickly became friends and then lovers. Leopold was an avid reader of the philosopher Friedrich Nietzsche. Misinterpreting Nietzsche's idea of the superman, Leopold came to the conclusion that he and Loeb were supermen, so that the rules of ordinary society did not apply to them.

Crime was an important part of their relationship, especially for Loeb. So, they decided that when the time came for them to go their separate ways, they needed something to permanently cement them to each other and a perfect crime, or better yet, a perfect murder, seemed ideal. The perfect murder was to be in cold blood and leave not a clue. The victim was not chosen ahead of time, so the murder had nothing to do with the identity of the victim. The plan was to kidnap and kill a victim and then collect a ransom from the dead boy's family. The collection of the ransom after the murder was important, because it would prove to the two young men that they had risen above emotions like compassion.

The crime was far from perfect and the body of Bobby Franks was quickly found in the culvert where Leopold and Loeb had left it. The pair continued to maintain their innocence until conclusive evidence forced them to confess. Loeb's parents were friends with the well-known trial lawyer, Clarence Darrow, and begged him to come to their son's aid and work to lighten the killers' sentence from the death penalty to life in prison. As a staunch opponent of the death penalty, he agreed.

The prosecution focused on the mercilessness of the crime, while the defense focused on the youth of the killers and their upbringing, claiming that neither of the young men had been "normally socialized." The age of the two criminals was what finally convinced the judge to suspend the death penalty and sentence Leopold and Loeb to life in prison. However, what many members of the public attached most importance to the philosophy of the youthful murderers. Their sense of self was deeply predicated on their interpretations of the philosophy of Nietzsche, a philosophy that believed that "God is dead" and mankind was now the highest authority. Thus, many people interpreted the killings as resulting from a lack of religion. In a sense, Leopold and Loeb put atheism itself on trial, setting atheism back and increasing the suspicions people had toward atheists.

Loeb died in prison, killed by a fellow inmate, but Leopold was eventually released for good behavior and went on to marry and live a normal life. He died in bed with his wife by his side.

The Scopes "Monkey Trial"

The Scopes Trial (1925) may have been one of the most important court cases in the history of American atheism, but it had its beginnings in a conversation in a drugstore in Dayton, Tennessee. George Rappelyea, a local coal company manager, brought to Fred Robinson's drugstore a copy of the

One of the most celebrated cases of lawyer Clarence Darrow (above left, in 1922) was the trial of schoolteacher John Scopes (above center, in 1925), who taught evolution—a violation of the Butler Act—in a Tennessee high school science class. The trial pitted Darrow against evangelist orator William Jennings Bryan (above right, in 1908).

American Civil Liberties Union's announcement that they would be willing to sponsor anyone who wanted to challenge the new anti-evolution statute in Tennessee. This statute, the Butler Act, made it unlawful "to teach any theory that denies the story of divine creation as taught by the Bible and to teach instead that man was descended from a lower order of animals." George Rappelyea wanted to challenge the Butler Act and asked the well-liked new general science teacher at Dayton High School, John Scopes, to be the defendant. John Scopes had taught evolutionary science in the high school when he was substituting for the regular biology teacher, as well as briefly in his own general science course. Admitting this publicly in Fred Robinson's drugstore put him in violation of the Butler Act.

The ACLU took on the case and John Scopes traveled to New York to meet with them. The defense team was Clarence Darrow, a famous trial lawyer known for his oratorical skill and controversial stances, Arthur Garfield Hays, a prominent free speech advocate, and Dudley Field Malone, an international divorce lawyer. The prosecution was William Jennings Bryan, a well-known Christian statesman, stentorian speaker, and three-time presidential candidate (though never president); the former attorneys general of East Tennessee, A.T. Stewart and Ben B. McKenzie; and William Jennings Bryan's son, William Jennings Bryan, Jr.

The first day of the trial, July 10, 1925, saw the Rhea County Courthouse packed with nearly one thousand people, many of whom had to stand. Radio announcers were also in attendance, making the Scopes Trial the first to be broadcast over live radio. The presiding judge was a conservative Christian, John T. Raulston, and of the twelve-man jury, eleven were regular churchgoers. John Scopes had little chance of acquittal, which was precisely the point. The hope of the defense was for the case to reach the Supreme Court, where it could be ruled that the Butler Act, and any other laws like it, were unconstitutional.

The opening statements of the trial made it clear that more was at stake than a $100 fine for John Scopes. The fundamentalist reading of the Bible was on trial, as was the separation of church and state. The prosecution saw the trial as a struggle between good and evil, religion and atheism. The defense saw the trial as a contest between knowledge and willful ignorance. Bryan is famously quoted as saying, "If evolution wins, Christianity goes." Darrow, meanwhile, contended that, "Scopes isn't on trial; civilization is on trial." This trial was, for Bryan, necessary in the defense of American Christianity and, for Darrow, a chance to give atheists and agnostics a hearing in court.

While Bryan did inevitably win the court case, his reputation, and that of the fundamentalist interpretation of the Bible, was severely undermined. When Dr. Maynard Metcalf, a zoologist from Johns Hopkins University, testified on the validity of the theory of evolution, Bryan mocked him and his exposition of the theory of evolution. This led defense lawyer Dudley Malone to make his famous speech in which he accused Bryan of the same kind of ignorance that led to the conviction of Galileo for heresy. Finally, the defense called Bryan himself to the witness stand as a Bible scholar. Darrow questioned Bryan about the specifics of the Bible in a manner that attempted to undermine a literalist interpretation of the Bible, eventually forcing Bryan to concede that not everything in the Bible should be interpreted literally. (The confrontation was dramatized in the celebrated play and film *Inherit the Wind*.)

While the prosecution won the case, it was soon overturned by the Tennessee Supreme Court, though not on the constitutional grounds the defense hoped for, but rather on a technicality. However, the Scopes Trial was still a major setback for the opponents of evolution. Of the fifteen states in 1925 with anti-evolution legislation pending, only Arkansas and Mississippi actually enacted laws restricting the teaching of evolution.

The Dover Trial (2004–05)

The Dover Trial was, in some ways, the successor to the Scopes Trial. In 2004, the school board of Dover, Pennsylvania, voted to include the teaching of Intelligent Design in the science curriculum. Intelligent Design claims to be an alternative to Charles Darwin's theory of evolution, which posits the necessity of a creator, because the complexity of life on Earth, the theory believes, could not have occurred "by chance." U.S. District Judge John E. Jones ruled that Intelligent Design was not science, but creationism in disguise, and that the teaching of Intelligent Design in Dover schools was thus unconstitutional.

The policy in Dover required students to hear a disclaimer before learning about the theory of evolution, which stressed that Darwin's ideas were "not fact" and had many inexplicable "gaps." It then referred students to the Intelligent Design textbook, *Of Pandas and People*. Judge Jones ruled that this was not an attempt to balance the students' scientific understanding, but rather to single out the theory of evolution for special treatment, misrepresent its status in the scientific community, and present students with a religious alternative.

In response, Richard Thompson, president and chief counsel of the Thomas More Law Center in Ann Arbor, Michigan, who defended the school board, said, "What this really looks like is an ad hominem attack on scientists who happen to believe in God." Thus, it is clear that for Thompson this case was a contest between religion and atheism. However,

Judge Jones was himself a churchgoer, and his ruling purposefully says nothing about the truth or falsehood of the existence of a creator. Instead, Judge Jones ruled that Intelligent Design had no place in the science classroom because it was not science. Intelligent Design violated one of the ground rules for categorization as science by invoking supernatural causes. Furthermore, the various claims of Intelligent Design had, according to Judge Jones, already been refuted by the scientific community. He further believed that the board members had lied as to their real reasons for advocating the teaching of Intelligent Design, and that far from trying to improve science education by exposing students to alternative theories, they were attempting to promote a religious agenda.

The case was not appealed because all of the members of the school board who were up for reelection and had advocated the teaching of Intelligent Design were voted out of office. This marked a major change in the way the separation of church and state was viewed in America since the Scopes Trial.

D. Media, Communication, and Organization

Atheism is not a heavily organized belief system, yet there are many explicitly atheist organizations and publications.

American Atheists
PO Box 5733
Parsippany, NJ 07054-6733
908-276-7300   Fax: 908-276-7402
info@atheists.org
www.atheists.org

Atheist Alliance International
PO Box 234
Pocopson, PA 19366
1-866-HERETIC
info@atheistalliance.org

Freedom From Religion Foundation
PO Box 750
Madison, WI 53701
(608) 256-8900   Fax: (608) 256-1116

A prominent atheist organization in the U.S. is American Atheists, which is a rights advocacy group. The Atheist Alliance International aims to help democratic atheistic societies grow and to advance rational thinking through education. Another organization, the Freedom from Religion Foundation, has as its goal to promote freethought and defend the principle of the separation of church and state.

There are also many atheist publications and resources. Three of the most well-known are the *American Atheist Magazine* (atheists.org), a journal of atheistic news and thought; Ethical Atheist (www.ethicalatheist.org), a website that offers resources on scientific education and ethical living; and *Secular Nation*, a magazine published by Atheist Alliance International.

AGNOSTICISM

A. Introduction

The important difference between atheism and agnosticism is that while an atheist believes that there is no God, an agnostic simply says that he or she does not have enough evidence to decide either way. Thus, while many atheists call themselves freethinkers, because they consider the world without recourse to God, agnostics are more bound up in the skeptical movement. Like skeptics, agnostics refuse to take anything on faith and insist upon proof.

However, not all agnostics are alike. Agnosticism is sometimes broken down into the categories of strong and weak agnosticism, with the strong agnostic believing that proof of God's existence or non-existence is impossible, and weak agnostics believing that such proof is merely unavailable at the present. "Ignosticism" is the view that the concept of God is meaningless because it has no verifiable consequences. Science as a whole today takes this ignostic view in presuming that the concept of God simply does not have a useful role to play in a description of the universe. Thus, while in the scientific view God may or may not exist, the concept of God cannot be used as an explanation for natural events since the scientific community as a whole does not allow the invocation of supernatural forces as part of the premise of a theory.

This often sets agnosticism and the scientific worldview in opposition to faith and religion, at least in popular opinion. However, this is not strictly the case. It is not so much that agnostics are opposed to religion—as some, but not all, atheists are—but that agnosticism simply has no need of religion. Perhaps the most famous example of this is French mathematician and astronomer Pierre Laplace (1749–1827), who translated geometrical study of mechanics, as used by English physicist, mathematician, and alchemist Isaac Newton (1643–1727), into a study of mechanics based on calculus. He also wrote the *Mécanique Céleste*, which, among other things, attempted to prove the dynamic stability of the universe. His translator, Bowditch, claimed that after reading the *Mécanique Céleste,* Napoleon questioned Laplace on his neglect to mention God. Laplace is said to have replied that he had no need of that hypothesis. That is perhaps the core of agnosticism—the idea that while God may or may not exist, without evidence it is irrelevant.

However, this leads to the question of whether science has, or will, render the belief in God obsolete. Think of the idea of the "God of the gaps," which is to say the God that explains that which humans do not understand. This is the basis of many of the arguments for the existence of God—that the universe needs to have had something to provide the initial impetus to start everything, or that life is too complex for it to have come into being without prompting from a designer. However, science offers explanations of how either of these things and many others, once

attributed solely to divine intervention, could occur. Science seems to encroach further and further into the questions that were once answerable only by faith. Thus, while science and religion were once reconcilable disciplines, they now appear in some quarters to have little to share or contribute to each other.

With America so rich in religious traditions and denominations, it is not surprising that it is fairly often religion that interferes with scientific research. The adoption of Laplace's attitudes by much of the scientific community has set them somewhat in opposition to religion and religion-influenced moral opinions in America. Certain modern scientific advances have met recently with religious disapproval, some of which has been translated into law. There is fear that this attitude is holding America back in the world of science and that the U.S. will be eclipsed by a country like India or China. Current conflicts on topics such as stem cell research and Intelligent Design simply add fuel to the fire.

B. Important Figures

Robert Ingersoll

Robert Ingersoll (1833–1899) was the most widely known agnostic of his day. He grew up in Dresden, New York, in the religiously fertile area known as "The Burned-Over District." His father was a Calvinist minister in the Congregational Church and his mother a secret reader of Thomas Paine. While only intermittently formally taught, Ingersoll read voraciously and educated himself. He began practicing law prior to the Civil War, but was commissioned into the Union Army and was captured

Of the noted agnostic Robert Ingersoll, his friend the poet Walt Whitman wrote: "[He is] American-flavored—pure out of the soil, spreading, giving, demanding light." Ingersoll delivered the eulogy at Whitman's funeral in 1892.

and imprisoned by the Confederacy. Upon his release in 1862, he became well-known for his legal practice, became active in the Republican Party, and was appointed attorney general of Illinois.

In 1870, Ingersoll began, in addition to practicing law, lecturing, and publishing essays that were to make him both famous and infamous. Ingersoll was a brilliant speaker with a rapier wit and often took on prominent members of the religious orthodoxy. He likened organized religion to slavery and called for the American people to put their trust in science and human achievement rather than religion and God. He also wrote controversial essays, such as "The Gods," where he claimed that each nation created its Gods in its own image; "Ghosts," where he depicted the limitless potential of humankind without religion; and "Some Mistakes of Moses," where he examined scathingly and in detail the idea of the divine origin of the Bible. He also was committed to human intellectual freedom in the political arena and advocated for the extension of the rights of citizenship beyond the adult white male.

Carl Sagan

Carl Sagan (1934–1996) was a writer, astronomer, and popularizer of science. He was also an agnostic. While he himself did not believe in God, he was famously quoted as saying, "Absence of evidence is not evidence of absence." This meant that, just because there is no proof of God does not mean that there is no God. It is still possible that not all methods of attempting to find evidence of God have been exhausted. Among his accomplishments, Sagan was instrumental in the discovery of the high surface temperature of Venus and among the first to hypothesize that Saturn's moon, Titan, and Jupiter's moon, Europa, might possess oceans (that could support life of some kind). He co-founded the Planetary Society, the largest space-interest group in the world, and was a member of the board of trustees for the Search for Extra Terrestrial Intelligence (SETI) Institute. He became famous for his television series, *Cosmos*, on the nature of the universe.

Sagan was a prolific writer on the subject of science and the perception of science. He often advocated the usage of the scientific method in his books. Among his better-known works are: *Broca's Brain: Reflections on the Romance of Science; The Dragons of Eden: Speculations on the Evolution of Human Intelligence; Cosmos; Pale Blue*

This photograph of the agnostic astronomer Carl Sagan was taken in 1981.

Dot: A Vision of the Human Future in Space; and his posthumously published *The Varieties of Scientific Experience.* The book most directly related to his work as an agnostic and skeptic was *A Demon Haunted World: Science as a Candle in the Dark,* which presented tools for testing arguments and determining if they were fraudulent. It promoted the scientific method and provided a toolkit for skeptics as they attempted to think critically about the world around them. Sagan himself promoted skepticism and a critical agnostic outlook on the world and did much to popularize the scientific method as a part of everyday life. On the subject of God, he is famously quoted as saying, "The idea that God is an oversized white male with a flowing beard who sits in the sky and tallies the fall of every sparrow is ludicrous. But if by 'God' one means the set of physical laws that govern the universe, then clearly there is such a God. This God is emotionally unsatisfying . . . it does not make much sense to pray to the law of gravity."

Martin Gardner

Martin Gardner (1914–2010) did not describe himself an agnostic. While not subscribing to an organized religion, he did claim to believe in God. However, he was a very prominent skeptic and his way of thinking had a profound influence on agnosticism in America. Gardner was a remarkably prolific writer with published works in numerous fields, especially science, mathematics, philosophy, religion, and the occult. He was well-known for his math and science journalism, including his column on recreational mathematics, which he wrote for *Scientific American* for twenty-five years. He was also known for his work as a debunker of frauds, turning his eye on occultists and scientists alike. His book *Fads and Fallacies in the Name of Science* has become a seminal text of the skeptic movement. It examines and debunks numerous ideas he considered pseudoscientific, including Fletcherism, creationism, organic farming, Charles Fort, Rudolf Steiner, Dianetics, unidentified flying objects, dowsing, extra-sensory perception, the Bates method, and psychokinesis. Another classic of his that debunks pseudoscience is *Science: Good, Bad and Bogus*. He also wrote such popular science books as *The Ambidextrous Universe* and *The Relativity Explosion,* plus works of fiction and literary criticism.

He was the founding member of the Committee for the Scientific Investigation of Claims of the Paranormal (CSICOP) and wrote a regular column called "Notes from a Fringe Watcher" for their magazine *The Skeptical Inquirer*. He also took public and prominent religious figures, such as Mary Baker Eddy, to task for being unable to support their religious claims. Gardner cast a critical eye on every aspect of life, thus popularizing the skeptical outlook and bringing skepticism and its attendant agnosticism to public attention and respectability.

A New England rabbi who wrote a positive review of one of Garner's science books was asked by a reporter how he could support the work of one so ardently agnostic. The rabbi replied, "Give me a congregation of Martin Gardners and I'll have the Messiah here by Wednesday."

James Randi

James Randi (1928–), a close friend of Martin Gardner, has used his training as a professional magician to debunk pseudoscientific and paranormal claims. As a professional magician he hosted his own radio show, "The Amazing Randi Show," and numerous television specials. He once escaped from a straight jacket while suspended over Niagara Falls,

and became nationally prominent through his many appearances on *The Tonight Show* and his repartee with host Johnny Carson.

Randi began his career as a skeptic when he publicly challenged Uri Geller on his claim to psychokinetic powers. He became known for infiltrating and revealing the lack of scientific rigor in paranormal investigation institutes and exposing several faith healers as frauds. Randi was awarded a MacArthur Foundation Fellowship for his work in debunking the paranormal. He is the author of many books on the subject, including *The Truth About Uri Geller; The Faith Healers; Flim-Flam!;* and *An Encyclopedia of Claims, Frauds, and Hoaxes of the Occult and Supernatural.* He also founded the James Randi Educational Foundation, which provides information on paranormal frauds and has presented an ongoing challenge, with a prize of one million dollars, to anyone who can demonstrate—under proper, verifiable observational conditions—evidence of supernatural, paranormal, or occult powers or phenomena. Randi's skepticism and devotion to finding "the truth behind the illusion" has made him an inspiration to skeptic and agnostic movements in America and worldwide.

Michael Shermer

Dr. Michael Shermer (1954–) is the founding publisher of *Skeptic* magazine, the executive director of the Skeptics Society, and the host of the Skeptics Distinguished Science Lecture series at the California Institute of Technology. He also authors a monthly column for *Scientific American* and is adjunct professor of economics at Claremont University.

He is a prolific writer whose work focuses on the evolution of the mind and how it affects human behavior today. His books include: *The Mind of the Market; Why Darwin Matters: Evolution and the Case Against Intelligent Design; Science Friction: Where the Known Meets the Unknown; The Borderlands of Science* and books on the subject of science, psychology, and religions, such as *The Science of Good and Evil: Why People Cheat, Gossip, Share, Care, and*

Follow the Golden Rule, which takes as its subject the evolutionary origins of morality and how one can be good without God; and *How We Believe: Science, Skepticism and the Search for God,* which presents his theory on the origin of religion and why people believe in God. Shermer is a vocal proponent of the skeptical outlook, especially in terms of religion. He looks for scientific answers to the questions of religion and considers a belief in God and unnecessary hypothesis for a rational, moral human being.

C. Agnosticism and Science

To be agnostic literally means (in Greek) to be "without knowledge." So, it might seem strange how connected agnosticism is to science—which literally means "knowledge" in Latin—and the scientific worldview. However, the scientific worldview is an essentially agnostic one. It does not claim to have certain knowledge of anything, only evidence for theories that have not yet been falsified. Science calls for skepticism, not faith. Agnosticism, thus, often means an application of the scientific method in place of faith. Since an agnostic has no evidence for or against God, he or she does not believe one way or another. Thus, with the scientific method so much a part of agnostic thinking, it is unsurprising that the concerns of many agnostics are related to science and the interference of religious belief in scientific research.

A case in point is the current controversy surrounding stem-cell research. Stem cells are cells that can renew themselves through division and differentiate into a variety of types of cells. In adults, these stem cells may be used as a repair system for the body and can generally only differentiate into cells of a similar type, limiting their usefulness. However, stem cells taken from embryos four to five days old (embryonic stem cells), are "totipotent," meaning they can divide to form many types of cells, which may, medical researchers hope, be used to cure illnesses such as Parkinson's disease, Alzheimer's disease, and diabetes.

The embryos cannot survive at this point outside of the mother's body. Furthermore, in vitro fertilization creates more embryos than it can use, which are frozen and stored, since they have no immediate use. In August 2006, President Bush vetoed (the first of his administration) the lifting of the ban on creating new stem-cell lines from frozen embryos, because while in cold storage the embryos can still be revived, but after being harvested for stem cells they are irreversibly dead. Since it is highly unlikely that any of these embryos will ever leave cold storage, many scientists advocate using these stem cells.

However, stem-cell research is still a controversial issue in American life, to the point where the government limits the funding of research on new stem-cell lines, greatly limiting the availability of stem cells for research. Much of this opposition is religious in nature, based on the belief that an embryo receives a soul at the moment of conception and is thus a full person even when it consists of only a few cells. This leads some to believe that using stem cells is tantamount to murder, and to opposition to stem cell research, despite the possibility that it may save lives. This was the basis for President Bush's policy in regard to stem-cell research, as well as the official position of the Catholic Church.

Agnosticism takes the view that while we have no evidence for the existence of souls, we do have evidence that this breakthrough may save lives. Agnosticism is concerned with what we can and do know, and using that knowledge to improve the human condition, thus challenging the morality of desisting from stem-cell research.

D. Media, Communication, and Organization

Agnosticism is not an organized belief system. However, there are many publications and organizations designed to encourage skeptical thinking and provide agnostics and skeptics with information and community. Here are a few examples:

The American Rationalist
Center for Inquiry/AR
PO Box 741
Amherst, NY 14226-0471
1-800-818-7071
kazd@nmia.com   www.therationalist.net

The Skeptic Society and Skeptic Magazine
626-794-3119
skepticsociety@skeptic.com
www.skeptic.com

Committee for Skeptical Inquiry
The Skeptical Inquirer
CSICOP
PO Box 703
Amherst, NY, 14226
716-636-1425
www.csicop.org

Center for Inquiry Transnational
3965 Rensch Road
Amherst, NY 14228
716-636-4869   Fax: 716-636-1733
www.centerforinquiry.net

The James Randi Educational Foundation
201 S.E. 12th Street (E. Davie Blvd.)
Fort Lauderdale, FL 33316-1815
954-467-1112   Fax: 954-467-1660
jref@randi.org   www.randi.org

HUMANISM

A. Introduction

Humanism is a movement that aims to place humanity and human accomplishment, rather than God, at the center of the spiritual universe.

Humanists believe in the dignity and worth of all people and that the ability to discern right from wrong is an inherent quality in humans, part and parcel of reason, and not dependent on religious belief. They believe in a universal morality derived from the common human experience and that the solution to humanity's problems must come from humanity. Humanists focus on self-determination and reject the religious ideal of belief based on faith and without reason.

However, unlike atheism and agnosticism, humanism, though a secular movement, is not necessarily without religion. Humanism can be a part of an individual's religion, since while humanists reject the idea that the resolution of human affairs should come through the belief in a higher power, they do not necessarily reject the higher power itself. Thus, humanists, while they are often atheists or agnostics, are not necessarily either. Instead, many humanists believe simply that humanity, and not God, is the most vital part of religion.

Perhaps religious humanists have the hardest task of all. They practice a religion that not only does not need God, but also exists without *reference* to God. Religious humanists practice a religion, but often without belief in the God of that religion. Instead, they celebrate the unique culture and traditions of that religion. They do not believe that their religious traditions are divinely inspired, but rather that they are products of a purely human effort to understand and live within the world.

For some, religious humanism is very difficult to understand, and in some religious circles the title of "humanist" is used as a disparagement. After all, what is religion without God? According to the humanist movement, religion without God is still religion, just refocused—rather than concentrating on God and prayer to the deity, humanistic religion concentrates on the religious traditions and accomplishments of humans and keeps alive religious traditions, even among nonbelievers.

B. Important Figures

Charles Francis Potter

Charles Francis Potter (1885–1962) grew up in an evangelical Baptist family and began his career as a Baptist minister. Potter was ordained at the age of seventeen and began preaching while he attended Bucknell University in Pennsylvania. He earned a B.D. and an S.T.M. from Newton Theological Seminary, as well as an M.A. from Bucknell University. However, during his time as a Baptist preacher, Potter began to question many of the tenants of Orthodox Christianity, which led to his conversion to Unitarianism in 1914. Potter served as the minister of the West Side Unitarian Church in New York City as well as at others, where he taught modern, liberal Bible interpretation. In 1924, Potter came to national attention when he debated the fundamentalist Baptist preacher Rev. John Roach Straton, bringing the fundamentalist-modernist conflict in Bible interpretation to public interest. In 1929, Potter left the Unitarian Church, to found the First Humanist Society, which he declared would have no creed, clergy, baptism, or prayers. The First Humanist Society had as board members such luminaries as Albert Einstein, Thomas Mann, John Dewey, and Julian Huxley. Potter was known to have said, in regard to the foundation of the Humanist Society, "I was leaving not only Christianity—if Unitarianism is Christianity—but Theism as well."

Potter began to write books on religion and humanism, including *The Story of Religion, Humanism: A New Religion* (which he co-wrote with his wife Clara Cook) and *Humanizing Religion*. Potter also became an advocate of social reform, campaigning for "civil divorce" laws, women's rights and birth control, and against capital punishment. He also founded the Euthanasia Society of America in 1938, which brought the issue of euthanasia before the American public. In 1958, he published what was probably his most popular book, *The Lost Years of Jesus Revealed*, interpreting the Dead Sea Scrolls. On the subject of humanism he was quoted as saying, "Humanism is not the abolition of religion, but the beginning of real religion. By freeing religion of supernaturalism, it will release tremendous reserves of hitherto thwarted power. Man has waited too long, for God to do what man ought to do himself and is fully capable of doing." Humanism would be, he said, "A religion of common sense; and the chief end of man is to improve himself, both as an individual and as a race."

Edwin Wilson

Edwin Wilson (1898–1993) was the primary author of both the *Humanist Manifesto I* and the *Humanist Manifesto II* and received the prestigious American Humanist Association's Humanist Merit Award. During World War I, Wilson served in the Army Signals Corps. In 1922, he graduated from Boston University with a Bachelor's degree in business administration, but he returned to school in 1924 to attend the Meadville Theological School, which was at that time exclusively Unitarian. He was ordained as a Unitarian minister in 1928. However, it was in 1929 that Wilson began his career as a humanist, when he began writing for *The New Humanist*, a mimeographed newsletter published by the Humanist Fellowship. Wilson became the managing editor of the no-longer mimeographed *New Humanist* in 1930. In 1933, the *Humanist Manifesto*, of which he was the primary author, was published in *New Humanist*. The manifesto was explicitly not a doctrine or a creed, but rather a statement of purpose for the humanist movement. When *New Humanist* was forced to close because of a lack of funding, Wilson continued to spread the message of humanism with his own *Humanist Bulletin*, which has become the publication *The Humanist*. Wilson is famously quoted as saying that "Humanism has time, science, and human need on its side."

Sherwin T. Wine

Sherwin T. Wine (1928–2007) founded the first humanistic Jewish congregation in Birmingham, Michigan, in 1963. Wine earned degrees in philosophy and political science from the University of

Michigan and then enrolled in the most liberal rabbinical school at the time, Hebrew Union College in Cincinnati. He was ordained as a reform rabbi in 1956, but a study of Jewish history led him to the conclusion that God was irrelevant. According to Wine, in the wake of the Holocaust, it is hard to believe in a God who was just and all-powerful, because it is difficult to see how such a God could allow the Holocaust to happen. Consequently, God was, in Wine's mind, "either cruel, incompetent—or didn't exist." Wine founded the Birmingham Temple in 1963, because he had become uncomfortable addressing a God he did not know existed.

In 1969, Wine founded the Society for Humanistic Judaism. Jewish humanism embraces secular Jewish culture and Jewish history, rather than a belief in God, as the foundation of a Jewish identity. Humanistic Judaism, as Wine describes it, is "horizontal" rather than "vertical." Traditional Judaism is vertical, because it is oriented up toward a higher power; humanistic Judaism is horizontal because it relies not on a higher power, but on the self and on others. There is no prayer or worship in humanistic Judaism, though the Torah is studied as an important ethical and historical document.

Kurt Vonnegut

Kurt Vonnegut (1922–2007) was a prolific writer of science fiction and satire, known for his ability to strike a balance between cynicism and humanistic optimism in his writing. He attended Cornell University and, while there, was drafted into the army, which sent him to the Carnegie Institute of Technology (now Carnegie Mellon University). He fought in World War II and survived the firebombing of Dresden as a prisoner of war. He is a self-described humanist, skeptic, and freethinker, all of which strongly informs his writing. Some of his most popular books are *Cat's Cradle; Slaughterhouse-Five;* (or *The Children's Crusade*); *Breakfast of Champions* (or *Goodbye Blue Monday*); *Galapagos; Bluebeard; The Sirens of Titan*; and *Player Piano*. His short story about the dangers of limiting human excellence in

favor of an artificial concept, "Harrison Bergeron," has been influential and widely read. Many humanist themes appear repeatedly in his writing, such as the struggle for self-determination, the value of humanity, and the irrelevance of a divine power.

Isaac Asimov

Isaac Asimov (1920–1992) was a Russian-American author, scientist, and professor of biochemistry, best known for his science fiction writing and works of popular science. He attended Columbia University, graduating in 1939, and earned a Ph.D. in chemistry from there in 1948. He then joined the faculty of Boston University, where he taught until he found success as a writer. He has had books published in nine out of ten categories of the Dewey Decimal System—every category except philosophy—although his most well-known books are the future histories in *the Robot, Foundation,* and *Galactic Empire* series.

He is considered one of the three greatest science fiction writers of the twentieth century, along with Arthur C. Clarke and Robert A. Heinlein. His short story "Nightfall" was voted in 1946 by the Science Fiction Writers of America to be the best science fiction story of all time. In his science fiction writing, he addressed what it means to be human, often by showing robots in contrast to humans. He was, at one point, the president of the American Humanist Association, and was voted the American Humanist Society's Humanist of the Year in 1984. He did not oppose specific religious belief, but was vocal in his opposition to unfounded superstition.

C. Religious Humanism

Because humanism is not opposed to religion and is often consonant with many religious philosophies, many religions have humanistic branches.

Humanistic Judaism takes as its fundamental principle that a belief in God is not integral to a Jewish identity. Instead, a Jew is defined as a person who identifies with Jewish history and culture, and that this Jewish identity is best preserved in a pluralistic environment. Jewish Humanists believe that Jewish history is a human story, attesting to the power and responsibility of people, not God, and that it is people who have the power to decide the course of their own lives, not a supernatural authority. Ethics and morality, according to humanistic Judaism, should serve the needs of humankind, and thus the freedom and dignity of all people is integral to the freedom and dignity of the Jewish people.

Like all humanists, humanistic Jews believe that the solution to human problems lies within humanity and that it is thus important for people to be free of the influence of a supernatural authority. They see Judaism as an ethnic culture, not a product of divine intervention; Jewish holidays and ceremonies are seen as responses to and celebrations of the experience of Jewish life and the Jewish people, not a worship of God. The founder of the modern humanistic Jewish movement and the Society for Humanistic Judaism was Rabbi Sherwin T. Wine (*see* page 747). For more information, see www.shj.org.

(It is often thought that Reconstructionist Judaism, especially as espoused by its founder Mordecai Kaplan, is a form of agnostic humanistic Judaism. Though Reconstructionist theology bears many elements of humanistic philosophy, the manner in which it is practiced and espoused through its seminarians and in its publications and houses of worship clearly places it closer to the three main branches of Judaism than to Humanistic Judaism and other agnostic forms of religious thought.)

Humanistic Christianity is not the same as modern Unitarian Universalism, which has grown to contain religious practices and beliefs from many different faiths. Unitarian Universalism is essentially creedless, while humanistic Christianity maintains the same creed as other branches of Christianity. Like all humanistic beliefs, humanistic Christianity places humans at the center of the faith. The struggle to maintain Christlike behavior in the modern world is at the core of Christian humanism. Some Christian humanists do not see a belief in God as integral to a Christian identity and consider a good Christian to be someone who emulates in his or her life the teachings of Jesus. Others do not see the principles of humanism and more traditional Christianity to be at all contradictory.

Humanistic Islam is less visible than humanistic Judaism and Christianity. However, many of the values of American Muslims are also reflected in humanistic values. Especially for those who have immigrated from repressive Middle Eastern governments, the right to freedom of religion and form of religious practice without government interference is highly valued. This religious freedom is supported by the Qur'an, which states (Sura 2, verse 256), "There is no place for compulsion in religion," an injunction taken very seriously by American Muslims especially.

D. Media, Communication, and Organizations

American Humanist Association
1777 T Street, NW
Washington, D.C. 20009
202-238-9088/800-837-3792
Founded in 1941, the American Humanist Association was established to increase public awareness and acceptance of humanism; to establish, protect, and promote the position of humanists in society, and to advance humanist thought and action.

The Council for Secular Humanism supports rational inquiry, ethical values, and human development through secular humanism.

The Church of Spiritual Humanism promotes the licensing of secular ministers to provide services such as weddings in many states. Also important when considering humanist organizations in the United States is the Unitarian Universalist church. Although not all Unitarian Universalists identify as humanist, the values of the church promote freedom of thought, freedom of conscience, and human rights, and Unitarians are likely to be involved in many of these organizations both locally and abroad.

Institute for Humanist Studies

www.humaniststudies.org

Notable media outlets for American humanists include: *Humanist Network News,* an e-journal published by the Institute for Humanist Studies; *New Humanist Magazine* (Email: webcontact@newhumanist.org.uk), published by **The Rationalist Association** in Britain; and the *International Humanist News,* published by the **International Humanist and Ethical Union**. Two other notable humanist publications are *Free Inquiry* and *The Humanist.*

This chapter ends with a brief discussion of two other religious groups that operate in the United States: Scientology and the Unification Church.

SCIENTOLOGY

SCIENTOLOGY IS THE BRAIN CHILD OF AMERICAN science fiction writer L. Ron Hubbard (1911–1986). It began with the publication of *Dianetics, The Modern Science of Mental Health* in 1950. In this book, Hubbard described how "engrams"—brain records of past experiences, including past lives—affect the mind, forcing people to repeat negative behaviors from their past. Happiness, according to Hubbard, can be achieved by eliminating these engrams. This is done through a process of "auditing," in which the participant is asked a series of questions that will allow him or her to go back through past experiences and undo the damage. At the end of this process, a person is said to be a "clear."

In 1960, Hubbard added to this therapy an elaborate system of metaphysics that became the foundation of Scientology. According to this metaphysics, the spiritual essence of a human being is a "thetan," derived from the Greek letter theta. The thetan survives a person's death and is able to take on new bodies and live new lives. Scientologists work toward becoming "Operating Thetans," which are thought to be free from the ill effects of engrams and to possess extraordinary power, including the ability to bring into existence matter, energy, space, and time.

Scientology has come under criticism by religious groups and the media for cult-like behavior and its secretive practices. Unlike many mainstream religions, Scientology does not have an established creed accessible to all. Instead, the church's beliefs are revealed slowly over time to the initiate as they progress through levels of auditing. The auditing sessions are also expensive, costing up to $6,000 for a single course, and the expense increases as one approaches the pinnacle of Scientology's teachings. According to court documents made public by *The Times* in the 1980s, one of the secret beliefs among Scientologists is that many of the troubles of humankind stem from an intergalactic battle that took place 75 million years ago. In this battle, the evil tyrant Xenu captured the thetans of his enemies and electronically implanted into them false concepts, including the beliefs of most of the world's major religions, before imprisoning them on Earth. These alien thetans supposedly latch onto human thetans, adding the trauma of their encounter with Xenu to the human suffering of the individual.

In 1967, the Internal Revenue Service ruled that Scientology did not qualify for tax-exempt status; this was upheld by the U.S. Supreme Court in 1988. Scientology did not achieve its status as a tax-exempt religion until 1993. In the meantime, during the early 1980s, Hubbard's wife and ten other leading Scientologists were charged with illegally interfering in investigations of the Church of Scientology by government agencies, and were briefly imprisoned.

Scientology has weathered its scandals and remains a growing religion with 700 centers in 65 countries. There are "Advanced Organizations" specializing in advanced training, located in Los Angeles; Clearwater, Florida; Great Britain; Sydney, Australia; Copenhagen; and a 440-foot cruise ship ("Freewinds") based in Curacao in the Caribbean.

In 1986, Scientology's founder, L. Ron Hubbard,

died, and David Miscavige (b.1960) took over leadership of the organization. During his tenure, a number of celebrities have reportedly become Scientologists, including John Travolta, Kirstie Alley, Juliette Lewis, Isaac Hayes, Anne Archer, Jenna Elfman, Beck, and Chick Corea, and, most prominently, Tom Cruise (b.1962), who has become a friend of Miscavige, a vocal supporter of Scientology, and has reached one of the highest levels of study within the Church—Operating Thetan VII.

National Headquarters of Scientology
6331 Hollywood Boulevard, Suite 1200
Los Angeles, CA 90028-6329
323-960-3500   Fax: 323-960-3508
www.scientology.org

FURTHER READING
The Church of Scientology and L. Ron Hubbard
June D. Littler
New York: Garland Publications, 1992

UNIFICATION CHURCH

THE UNIFICATION CHURCH WAS FOUNDED BY Reverend Sun Myung Moon of Korea in 1945, and was brought to the United States by Moon's followers in 1959. The movement was officially named the Holy Spirit Organization for the Unification of World Christianity, though in the 1990s the name was changed to the Family Federation for World Peace and Unification. Moon himself came to the United States in the early 1970s, where his movement quickly grew, attracting well-educated young people in search of religious solutions to the cultural and social problems brought to light in the 1960s.

Moon's followers, often referred to derogatorily as "Moonies," far from resembling "hippies" of the 60s counter-culture, were clean-shaven, clean-living, and refused recreational drugs and sex before marriage—in keeping with Moon's emphasis on the family, as outlined in the Church's holy book, *The Divine Principle,* originally published in 1957.

According to Unificationists, Jesus was sent into the world not simply to save humankind from sin, but to marry and create a God-centered family with perfect children and restore the divine lineage. Jesus was unable to found a family and thus the construction of the kingdom of God on Earth was not begun. The mission of the "Lord of the Second Advent"—generally considered to be Moon himself—is to succeed where Jesus failed and found a perfect family. Moon's followers thus refer to him as "Father" and his second wife Hak Ja Han as "Mother."

The Unification Church has come under fire with accusations of cultist activity, especially related to Moon's practice of mass weddings—in 1975 he wed 800 couples—and alleged brainwashing of devotees. This latter accusation led to anti-cult activists attempting to "deprogram" Moon's followers, though in 1977, a Californaia state appellate court overturned a lower court ruling granting custody of certain Unification Church members to their parents. Moon's tendency to mix religion and politics—as in his support of Richard Nixon during the Watergate Scandal, and his reported connection with the anti-communist intelligence agency of South Korea—has been regarded as inappropriate for a religious leader. Thousands continue to be influenced by Moon's teachings, however. The Unification Church has a seminary in Barrytown, New York; controls the Washington *Times* newspaper; and has recently bought Bridgeport University.

Unification Church of America
4 West 43rd Street
New York, NY 10036–7408
212-302-6216
www.unification.org

FURTHER READING

Sun Myung Moon and the Unification Church
Frederick Sontag
1977: Abingdon Press

PART TWO

Issues in American Religion

To America's Community of Faith

BY HIS HOLINESS, POPE BENEDICT XVI

O*n Thursday, April 17, 2008, in the Rotunda Hall of the Pope John Paul II Cultural Center of Washington, D.C., Pope Benedict XVI encouraged interreligious leaders to work not only for peace but for the discovery of truth. Speaking to 200 representatives of Islam, Jainism, Buddhism, Hinduism, and Judaism, he asked them "to persevere in their collaboration" to serve society and enrich public life. Each interfaith representative also received a small memento from the pope.*

Pope Benedict's visit to the United States, April 15–20, included public Masses in Washington and New York City, a meeting with Jews in a New York synagogue, a meeting with other Christian religious leaders, and various talks to groups of Catholics—as well as an historic address to the United Nations.

Here is the complete text of his remarks to the representatives of the various religions.

M Y DEAR FRIENDS,
I am pleased to have this occasion to meet with you today. I thank Bishop [Richard John] Sklba [from Milwaukee, Wisconsin] for his words of welcome, and I cordially greet all those in attendance representing various religions in the United States of America. Several of you kindly accepted the invitation to compose the reflections contained in today's program. For your thoughtful words on how each of your traditions bears witness to peace, I am particularly grateful.

Thank you all.

This country has a long history of cooperation between different religions in many spheres of public life. Interreligious prayer services during the national feast of Thanksgiving, joint initiatives in charitable activities, a shared voice on important public issues: these are some ways in which members of different religions come together to enhance mutual understanding and promote the common good. I encourage all religious groups in America to persevere in their collaboration and thus enrich public life with the spiritual values that motivate your action in the world.

The place where we are now gathered was founded specifically for promoting this type of collaboration. Indeed, the Pope John Paul II Cultural Center seeks [in its mission statement] to offer a Christian voice to the "human search for meaning and purpose in life" in a world of "varied religious, ethnic and cultural communities." This institution reminds us of this nation's conviction that all people should be free to pursue happiness in a way consonant with their nature as creatures endowed with reason and free will.

Americans have always valued the ability to worship freely and in accordance with their conscience. Alexis de Tocqueville, the French historian and observer of American affairs, was fascinated with this aspect of the nation. He remarked that this is a country in which religion and freedom are "intimately linked" in contributing to a stable democracy that fosters social virtues and participation in the communal life of all its citizens. In urban areas, it is common for individuals from different cultural backgrounds and religions to engage with one another daily in commercial, social and educational settings. Today, in classrooms throughout the country, young Christians, Jews, Muslims, Hindus, Buddhists, and indeed children of all religions sit side-by-side, learning with one another and from one another. This diversity gives rise to new challenges that spark a deeper reflection on the core principles of a democratic society. May others take heart from your experience, realizing that a united society can indeed arise from a plurality of peoples—"*E pluribus unum*": "out of many, one"—provided that all recognize religious liberty as a basic civil right (cf. *Dignitatis Humanae*, 2). The task of upholding religious freedom is never completed. New situations and challenges invite citizens and leaders to reflect on how their decisions respect this basic human right. Protecting religious freedom within the rule of law does not guarantee that peoples—particularly minorities—will be spared from unjust forms of discrimination and prejudice. This requires constant effort on the part of all members of society to ensure that citizens are afforded the opportunity to worship peaceably and to pass on their religious heritage to their children.

The transmission of religious traditions to succeeding generations not only helps to preserve a heritage; it also sustains and nourishes the surrounding culture in the present day. The same holds true for dialogue between religions; both the participants and society are enriched. As we grow in understanding of one another, we see that we share an esteem for ethical values, discernable to human reason, which are revered by all peoples of goodwill. The world begs for a common witness to these values. I therefore invite all religious people to view dialogue not only as a means of enhancing mutual understanding, but also as a way of serving society at large. By bearing witness to those moral truths which they hold in common with all men and women of good will, religious groups will exert a positive influence on the wider culture, and inspire neighbors, co-workers and fellow citizens to join in the task of strengthening the ties of solidarity. In the words of President Franklin Delano Roosevelt: "no greater thing could come to our land today than a revival of the spirit of faith."

A concrete example of the contribution religious communities make to civil society is faith-based schools. These institutions enrich children both intellectually and spiritually. Led by their teachers to discover the divinely bestowed dignity of each human being, young people learn to respect the beliefs and practices of others, thus enhancing a nation's civic life.

What an enormous responsibility religious leaders have: to imbue society with a profound awe and respect for human life and freedom; to ensure that human dignity is recognized and cherished; to facilitate peace and justice; to teach children what is right, good and reasonable!

There is a further point I wish to touch upon here. I have noticed a growing interest among governments to sponsor programs intended to promote interreligious and intercultural dialogue. These are praiseworthy initiatives. At the same time, religious freedom, interreligious dialogue and faith-based education aim at something more than a consensus regarding ways to implement practical strategies for advancing peace. The broader purpose of dialogue is to discover the truth. What is the origin and destiny of mankind? What are good and evil? What awaits us at the end of our earthly existence? Only by addressing these deeper questions can we build a solid basis for the peace and security of the human family, for "wherever and whenever men and women are enlightened by the splendor of truth, they naturally set out on the path of peace" (Message for the 2006 World Day of Peace, 3).

We are living in an age when these questions are too often marginalized. Yet they can never be erased from the human heart. Throughout history, men and women have striven to articulate their restlessness with this passing world. In the Judeo-Christian tradition, the Psalms are full of such expressions: "My spirit is overwhelmed within me" (Ps 143:4; cf. Ps 6:6; 31:10; 32:3; 38:8; 77:3); "Why are you cast down, my soul, why groan within me?" (Ps 42:5). The response is always one of faith: "Hope in God, I will praise him still; my Savior and my God" (Ps 42:5, 11; cf. Ps 43:5; 62:5). Spiritual leaders have a special duty, and we might say competence, to place the deeper questions at the forefront of human consciousness, to reawaken mankind to the mystery of human existence, and to make space in a frenetic world for reflection and prayer.

Confronted with these deeper questions concerning the origin and destiny of mankind, Christianity proposes Jesus of Nazareth. He, we believe, is the eternal Logos who became flesh in order to reconcile man to God and reveal the underlying reason of all things. It is he whom we bring to the forum of interreligious dialogue. The ardent desire to follow in his footsteps spurs Christians to open their minds and hearts in dialogue (cf. Lk 10:25–37; Jn 4:7–26).

Dear friends, in our attempt to discover points of commonality, perhaps we have shied away from the responsibility to discuss our differences with calmness and clarity. While always uniting our hearts and minds in the call for peace, we must also listen attentively to the voice of truth. In this way, our dialogue will not stop at identifying a common set of values, but go on to probe their ultimate foundation. We have no reason to fear, for the truth unveils for us the essential relationship between the world and God. We are able to perceive that peace is a "heavenly gift" that calls us to conform human history to the divine order. Herein lies the "truth of peace" (cf. Message for the 2006 World Day of Peace).

As we have seen then, the higher goal of inter-religious dialogue requires a clear exposition of our respective religious tenets. In this regard, colleges, universities and study centers are important forums for a candid exchange of religious ideas. The Holy See, for its part, seeks to carry forward this important work through the Pontifical Council for Interreligious Dialogue, the Pontifical Institute for Arabic and Islamic Studies, and various Pontifical Universities.

Dear friends, let our sincere dialogue and cooperation inspire all people to ponder the deeper questions of their origin and destiny. May the followers of all religions stand together in defending and promoting life and religious freedom everywhere. By giving ourselves generously to this sacred task—through dialogue and countless small acts of love, understanding and compassion—we can be instruments of peace for the whole human family.

Peace upon you all!

The American Clergy

BY SUE E. S. CRAWFORD

AS LEADERS OF RELIGIOUS ORGANIZATIONS, CLERGY reflect and shape the nexus between religion and American society. American culture and political institutions create opportunities and constraints on clergy leadership. Clergy, in turn, influence American culture and politics in a variety of ways.

It is hard to imagine any other single type of voluntary community organization that involves more Americans than religious congregations. Nearly half of Americans report attending some local religious organization at least once a month and over a quarter of Americans report attending a congregation once a week (General Social Survey 2004). Even more Americans report belonging to some congregation. Of those who report belonging to some congregation, over half also belong to other specific church related groups such as a choir, board, or fellowship group (General Social Survey 2004). Clearly, congregations in America provide an important conduit that links Americans to one another and to their communities. Moreover, congregations shape political attitudes and actions (Gilbert 1993; Wald, Owen and Hill 1988). As leaders of these congregations, clergy have the opportunities to engage in moral education and community leadership that impact citizen attitudes and public policy.

Demographic Patterns

Congregational clergy are well situated to exert social and political leadership. In addition to the moral legitimacy and organizational resources that come from their leadership of religious organizations, most are well-educated. Well over half of clergy in senior or sole leadership positions in congregations in the United States have a master's degree or a doctoral degree (Pulpit & Pew 2001). Increasingly, clergy also bring expertise from prior professions. Over half of clergy report having other careers prior to becoming clergy. The aging of the population and the surge of second-career clergy results in a strong tilt towards older clergy. Over half of congregational clergy leaders are over fifty (Pulpit & Pew 2001).

The profession remains heavily male dominated (Olson, Crawford and Deckman 2005; Zikmund et al. 1998). Several Christian and Jewish religious traditions began female ordination in the twentieth century. The timing of these advances in women's ordination had more to do with the timing of broader women's movements in American society than with clergy shortages or other religious shifts in doctrine (Chaves 1997). Two of the largest religious traditions in America (Roman Catholic and Southern Baptist) currently ban ordination of women as priests or ministers. Mainline Protestant and Jewish traditions and some Pentecostal traditions have been more open to women clergy, but women still comprise less than 25% of clergy in most traditions (Olson, Crawford, and Deckman 2005). In spite of, or perhaps because of, their professional struggles, women clergy in Mainline Protestant and Jewish traditions regularly speak out on discrimination issues at higher rates than their male colleagues (Olson, Crawford and Deckman 2005).

Over 80% of clergy who lead congregations in America are white with almost 2% identifying themselves as Hispanic. African Americans comprise the other major racial group at 13% (Pulpit & Pew 2001). These clergy serve congregations in a variety of religious traditions with fewer than 10% of African American clergy reporting serving in historic Black denominations in 2001 (Pulpit & Pew 2001). African American clergy historically led segregated congregations. Some congregations retained affiliation with majority white denominations while others affiliated with black church denominations such as African Methodist Episcopal and Missionary Baptist. In the face of racism and exclusion in mainstream institutions, black churches provided vital alternative institutions and necessary community leadership for African Americans (Lincoln and Mamiya 1990). Black clergy served as key liaisons between governments and the black community. This role placed prominent black clergy in the position of directly negotiating with government officials. The central role of clergy and the church in the Civil Rights movement illustrates the importance of the black church in mobilizing their own members for social change.

As blacks gain electoral power, the clergy mediation role evolves. Elected officials speak at prominent black churches at the invitation of pastors and prominent black clergy press elected officials to make choices that support the interests of African American constituents. Alongside the very public leadership of black clergy in many Protestant traditions, a strong other-worldly emphasis in Holiness-Pentecostal church traditions discourages this kind of civic leadership. Recently, some African American clergy have returned to developing alternative institutions with an emphasis on providing economic opportunities in African American communities through credit unions, economic development projects, and affordable senior housing for predominately African American communities.

Although religious diversity is growing, Christianity still dominates the religious landscape in America. Over three quarters of Americans identify themselves as Christians (Heclo 2007, p. 65). Fewer than 5% of congregations report a non-Christian religious tradition (Pulpit & Pew 2001). Christian clergy clearly outnumber clergy from other religious traditions, which translates into a strong Christian voice in much social and political action by American clergy. However, individual clergy from other faith traditions can gain access to greater numbers of opportunities for public dialogue about faith and social issues. Their small numbers put them in high demand given a common emphasis on including multiple faith perspectives in community dialogue and national media coverage.

Denominational Institutions

Nearly 90% of congregations report a denominational or associational affiliation (Chaves 1998). These denominational organizations often provide a wide array of opportunities and resources for clergy (and lay) leadership on religious and social issues, including offices in Washington, D.C., and advocacy websites to facilitate political engagement by clergy and laity.

Two important trends in American religion are often cited as heralds of the demise of denominational influence. Growing similarities in worship styles and increasing accommodation to individualism across traditions reduces denominational distinctiveness (Wolfe 2003). Also, the progressive–orthodox divide across denominations increasingly leaves progressive Christians of different denominations more similar to one another than their fellow orthodox members, and orthodox Christians more similar to one another than to their progressive co-religionists (Wuthnow 1988).

The view of denominational influence from the pulpit, however, differs from the view from the pews. As leaders of affiliated congregations, clergy are more directly linked into denominational networks and organizations than most members of the denomination. Denominational officials play strong roles in the placement of clergy into congregations, particularly in Catholic and some mainline Protestant traditions. A little over 25% of clergy report receiving direct performance reviews by denominational officials (Pulpit & Pew 2001).

The influence of denominations goes beyond clergy job evaluations and placement, though. Only 15% of clergy who serve in denominationally affiliated congregations report that the denomination is of little or no importance for the organization of programs and ministries within the congregation (Pulpit & Pew 2001). The connection to denominations by clergy is also evidenced by the 85% of these clergy who report being satisfied or very satisfied with the support that they receive from denominational officials.

Denominational institutions tend to be important in the initial training of clergy and continuing education opportunities. They also provide resources for congregational work and access to leadership opportunities beyond the congregation. In denominations with affiliated hospitals, social service agencies, and educational institutions, the denomination provides valuable networks to link congregations to these other institutions. These denominational links make it easier for clergy to access partners and resources for congregational programming and community leadership.

American Adaptations

America's unique non-establishment stance toward religion allows clergy to play visible roles in public debate without being government spokespersons. This legal stance combined with constitutional free speech protections provides a setting in which clergy have had a free space to challenge government policies. However, clergy have also often played roles in supporting governments and government legitimacy. Prayer has frequently been a part of government ritual and many government officials have had clergy advisors or clergy taskforces.

The U.S. tax code grants tax-exempt and tax-deductible status to congregations on the condition that the organization avoids explicit campaigning. This legal constraint, along with professional socialization that often stresses political neutrality, results in very few clergy endorsing candidates. However, sizable numbers of clergy exercise moral leadership roles through educating and challenging their members to consider important social issues. About half of white Protestant and Roman Catholic clergy report speaking on social issues from the pulpit in 2000 (Smidt 2004). Although the specific social issues differ, clergy tend to stress either a social justice agenda or a moral reform agenda (Guth et al. 1997). The social justice agenda stresses equality, stewardship, and inclusiveness, and includes issues such as economic equality, reduction of discrimination, and environmental protection. The moral reform agenda calls members to take back the culture and to fight for respect for life, and stronger religious expression in the public square. It includes issues such as abortion, homosexuality, and public expression of religion.

From the perspective of the role of clergy in American society, the most striking American adaptation of religious life has been the dominance of the voluntary (congregation) organizational form. The legal context of separation of church and state removes government coercion to compel financial contributions or membership to these congregations. This legal context combined with a social context of religious pluralism creates a mix of religious congregations in most communities to which community members can belong. The strong tradition of voluntary congregation organizations with a building, weekly worship, education, and other programming in American society, creates strong organizational expectations for clergy leaders, even in religious traditions that do not structure their religious life this way in other nations. Clergy are expected to develop and build strong congregational organizations with effective worship, education, visitations, and programming. These organizational responsibilities take on even greater importance for congregations that see themselves in competition with other congregations for membership. Decisions concerning appropriate social and political messages in the congregation and appropriate community leadership responsibilities outside of the congregation occur in the shadow of these central organizational imperatives.

Discussions of when or how to engage in broader social and political leadership often come back to organizational imperatives. Concerns about driving members away or keeping members from hearing core religious teachings because of political disagreements can reduce involvement, while confidence that community engagement strengthens the organization through greater visibility and opportunities for members can increase involvement (Jelen 1993; Olson 2000; Olson, Crawford, and Deckman 2005). However, other factors usually exert stronger influences on clergy civic engagement than these organizational pressures (Djupe and Gilbert 2003; Guth et al. 1997; Olson, Crawford and Deckman 2005; Smidt 2004).

American Contexts of Clergy Activism

Several factors that drive clergy social and political engagement reveal the influence of the American context in which clergy work. Clergy with stronger affiliations with either of the two main American political parties and clergy with stronger ideological commitment participate at higher rates. Similarly, personal identification with various political issue groups such as pro-life groups, environmental groups, and anti-poverty groups increase engagement (Djupe and Gilbert 2003; Guth et al. 1997; Olson, Crawford and Deckman 2005; Smidt 2004). The immediate secular political contexts in which clergy work, including the issues on the national agenda at the time and political concerns and opportunities at the local level, also shape clergy involvement (Crawford and Olson 2001; Olson 2000).

As would be expected, theology and religious tradition strongly shape clergy involvement in social and political leadership. The legacies of a theological split in white Protestant responses to modernity and the legacy of the unique African American religious experience can be seen in patterns of clergy social leadership. Clergy from those Protestant traditions that eschewed modernity (evangelical and fundamentalist traditions) largely backed away from political leadership outside of the church in the mid-twentieth century while clergy from those traditions that accepted modernity (mainline traditions) heightened commitment to public leadership (Marty 1970). The former group embraced an orthodox theology while the latter adopted a progressive theology. This theological split remains relevant in shaping political attitudes and participation of Protestant clergy (Guth et al. 1997; Smidt 2004). Although mainline clergy engaged in higher rates of political activism for most of the twentieth century, conservative mobilization in the past two decades has resulted in levels of activism among evangelical and fundamentalist clergy that match those seen by mainline clergy (Smidt 2004). Meanwhile, commitment to social leadership and engagement with government remains strong among Black Protestant clergy.

Growing media attention to conservative Christian influences in politics results in media coverage of conservative Christian clergy. These clergy are rarely congregational clergy, but instead are clergy leaders of para-church and interest group organizations. The development of 24-hour television news channels opens even more opportunities for these clergy to reach audiences through secular television while cable television and radio also provide direct media outlets for many of them. The internet provides additional opportunities for these clergy leaders to educate and mobilize others towards political action through websites, electronic petitions and ready-to-send letters to elected officials, and email alerts to supporters. Similar clergy political leadership also appears at the state level through state denominational and interest group organizations. State political debates over same-sex unions, gambling, stem-cell research, and minimum wage laws have given clergy in such groups much reason to mobilize at the state level.

On the tails of Catholic involvement in the Civil Rights movement, American Bishops produced pastoral letters on peace and economic justice. These statements and resulting church teachings establish a foundation for progressive leadership by Catholic clergy. However, visible Catholic clergy have become very assertive in advocating conservative positions against abortion and same-sex marriage. In the current American party system, Catholic social teachings on economic justice, peace, dignity of life and sanctity of marriage leave Catholic clergy with no clear political party ally and leave Catholic laity a key swing vote constituency.

Perhaps the most overlooked form of clergy leadership in American communities is the local ministerial association. On the surface, these associations appear to engage mostly in professional networking and occasional community worship services. However, this network serves as a powerful source of social capital in a community. When an emergency strikes or a new social issue becomes pressing, this network can pull together resources to construct a community response, particularly in communities where other community networks are sparse. Countless established social service organizations and community entities sprang from initial responses to community crises by ministerial associations.

American clergy have been shaped by the adaptation of religious institutions to various aspects of American culture, and clergy in turn have shaped American politics and culture. Legacies of religious responses to the separation of church and state, modernity, women's rights movements, and the Civil Rights movement continue to shape the views and actions of American clergy. Clergy, and their religious institutions, are currently struggling with questions that come from increasing social acceptance of homosexuality. This struggle has exacerbated tensions between orthodox and progressive factions within many religious traditions, and heightened tensions between Black clergy and liberal clergy who have been allies in the past. The issues surrounding the acceptance of homosexuality also have direct implications for clergy in America as one of the key questions is whether to ordain homosexuals. The implications of this struggle for clergy influence as social leaders in American society remain to be seen.

SOURCES

Chaves, Mark. 1998. *National Congregations Study. Data file and Codebook.* Tucson: AZ: University of Arizona, Department of Sociology.

Chaves, Mark. 1997. *Ordaining Women: Culture and Conflict in Religious Organizations.* Cambridge, MA: Harvard University Press.

Crawford, Sue E. S., and Laura R. Olson. 2001. *Christian Clergy in American Politics.* Baltimore, MD: The Johns Hopkins University Press.

Djupe, Paul A. and Christopher P. Gilbert. 2003. *The Prophetic Pulpit: Clergy, Churches, and Communities in American Politics.* Lanham, MD: Rowman & Littlefield Publishers, Inc.

General Social Survey. 2004. General Social Survey Data file and Codebook. Accessed through The Association of Religion Data Archives (www.thearda.com).

Guth, James L., John C. Green, Corwin E. Smidt, Lymann A. Kellstedt, and Margaret M. Poloma. 1997. *The Bully Pulpit: The Politics of Protestant Clergy.* Lawrence, KS: University of Kansas Press.

Heclo, Hugh. 2007. "Is America A Christian Nation?" *Political Science Quarterly,* 122: 59–87.

Jelen, Ted G. 1993. *The Political World of Clergy.* Westport, CT: Praeger.

Lincoln, C. Eric, and Lawrence H. Mamiya. 1990. *The Black Church in the African American Experience.* Durham, NC: Duke University Press.

Marty, Martin. 1970. *Righteous Empire: The Protestant Experience in America.* New York: Dial Press.

Olson, Laura R., 2000. *Filled with Spirit and Power: Protestant Clergy in Politics.* Albany, NY: State University of New York Press.

Olson, Laura R., Sue E. S. Crawford, and Melissa M. Deckman. 2005. *Women with a Mission: Religion Gender, and the Politics of Women Clergy.* Tuscaloosa AL: University of Alabama Press.

Pulpit & Pew. 2001. National Opinion Research Center Data file and Codebook. Accessed through The Association of Religion Data Archives (www.thearda.com).

Smidt, Corwin E. 2004. *Pulpit and Politics: Clergy in American Politics at the Advent of the Millennium.* Waco, TX: Baylor University Press.

Wald, Kenneth D., Dennis E. Owen, and Samuel S. Hill. 1988. *Churches as Political Communities.* American Political Science Review. 82: 531–48.

Wolfe, Alan. 2003. *The Transformation of American Religion: How We Actually Live our Faith.* New York: Free Press.

Wuthnow, Robert. 1988. *The Restructuring of American Religion: Society and Faith since World War II.* Princeton, NJ: Princeton University Press.

Wuthnow, Robert and John H. Evans. 2002. *The Quiet Hand of God: Faith Based Activism and the Public Role of Mainline Protestantism.* Berkeley, CA: University of California Press.

Zikmund, Barbara Brown, Adair T. Lummis, and Patricia M.Y. Chang. 1998. *Clergy Women: An Uphill Calling.* Louisville: Westminister John Knox.

The New Convergence

The ancient covenant is in pieces: Man knows at last that he is alone in the universe's unfeeling immensity, out of which he emerged only by chance. So pronounced the Nobel Prize-winning French biologist Jacques Monod in his 1970 treatise *Chance and Necessity*, which maintained that God had been utterly refuted by science. The divine is fiction, faith is hokum, existence is a matter of heartless probability and this wasn't just speculation, Monod maintained, but proven. The essay, which had tremendous influence on the intellectual world, seemed to conclude a millennia-old debate. Theology was in retreat, unable to explain away Darwin's observations; intellectual approval was flowing to thinkers such as the Nobel Prize-winning physicist Steven Weinberg, who in 1977 pronounced, "The more the universe seems comprehensible, the more it also seems pointless." In 1981, the National Academy of Sciences declared, "Religion and science are separate and mutually exclusive realms of human thought." Case closed.

And now reopened. In recent years, Allan Sandage, one of the world's leading astronomers, has declared that the Big Bang can be understood only as a "miracle."

Charles Townes, a Nobel Prize-winning physicist and coinventor of the laser, has said that discoveries of physics "seem to reflect intelligence at work in natural law." Biologist Christian de Duve, also a Nobel Prize winner, points out that science argues neither for nor against the existence of a deity: "There is no sense in which atheism is enforced or established by science." And biologist Francis Collins, director of the National Human Genome Research Institute, insists that "a lot of scientists really don't know what they are missing by not exploring their spiritual feelings."

Ever so gingerly, science has been backing away from its case-closed attitude toward the transcendent unknown. Conferences that bring together theologians and physicists are hot, recently taking place at Harvard, the Smithsonian, and other big-deal institutions. The American Association for the Advancement of Science now sponsors a "Dialogue on Science, Ethics, and Religion." Science luminaries who in the 1970s shrugged at faith as gobbledygook, including E. O. Wilson and the late Stephen Jay Gould and Carl Sagan, have endorsed some form of reconciliation between science and religion.

Why the renewed scientific interest in spiritual thinking? One reason is the cyclical nature of intellectual fashions. In philosophy, metaphysics is making a comeback after decades ruled by positivism and analytical theory of language. These restrained, empirically based ideas have run their course; now the pendulum is swinging toward the grand vision of metaphysics; someday, surely, to swing away again. Similarly in science, the pure materialistic view that reigned through the twentieth century, holding that everything has a natural explanation, couldn't keep other viewpoints at bay forever. The age-old notion that there is more to existence than meets the eye suddenly looks like fresh thinking again.

Meanwhile, decades of inconclusive inquiry have left the science-has-all-the-answers script in tatters. As recently as the 1970s, intellectuals assumed that hard science was on track to resolve the two Really Big Questions: why life exists and how the universe began. What's more, both Really Big Answers were assumed to involve strictly deterministic forces. But things haven't worked out that way. Instead, the more scientists have learned, the more mysterious the Really Big Questions have become.

Perhaps someday researchers will find wholly natural explanations for life and the cosmos. For the moment, though, discoveries about these two subjects are inspiring awe and wonder, and many scientists are reaching out to spiritual thinkers to help them comprehend what they're learning. And as the era of biotechnology dawns, scientists realize they're stepping into territory best navigated with the aid of philosophers and theologians. We are entering the greatest era of science-religion fusion since the Enlightenment last attempted to reconcile the two, three centuries ago.

Look up into the night sky and scan for the edge of the cosmos. You won't find it; nobody has yet. Instruments such as the Hubble Space Telescope's deep-field scanner have detected at least 50 billion galaxies, and every time the equipment is improved, more galaxies farther away come into focus. Space may be infinite—not merely vast, but infinite, encompassing an infinite number of galaxies with an infinite number of stars.

All this stuff, enough to form 50 billion galaxies, maybe fantastically more, is thought to have emerged roughly 14 billion years ago in less than a second, from a point with no physical dimensions. Set aside the many competing explanations of the Big Bang; something made an entire cosmos out of nothing. It is this realization, that something transcendent started it all, that has hard-science types such as Sandage using terms like "miracle."

Initially, scientists found the Big Bang's miraculous implications off-putting. When, in 1927, Catholic priest and astronomer Georges Lematre first hypothesized that existence began with the detonation of a "primordial atom" of infinite density, the idea was ridiculed as a transparent ploy to place Genesis on technical grounding. But Lematre enclosed a testable prediction: that if there had been a bang, the galaxies would be rushing away from one another. This idea, too, was ridiculed, until Edwin Hubble stunned the scientific world by presenting evidence of cosmic expansion. From Hubble's 1929 discovery on, science has taken Big Bang thinking seriously.

In 1965, another sort of Big Bang echo, the cosmic background radiation, was discovered. Soon, it was assumed, cosmologists would be able to say, "Here's how everything happened, steps one, two, and three." Today cosmologists do think they know a fair amount about steps two and three, what the incipient cosmos was like in the instant after the genesis, how matter and energy later separated and formed the first galaxies. But as for step one, no dice. Nobody knows beyond foggy conjecture what caused the Big Bang, what (if anything) was present before that event, or how there could have been a prior condition in which nothing existed.

Explanations of how the mass of an entire universe could pop out of a void are especially unsatisfying. Experiments announced in July this year (1999) by the Brookhaven National Laboratory in New York measured properties of subatomic particles known as muons, finding that they behave as though influenced by other particles that seem to have materialized from nothingness. But no object larger than the tiniest subatomic particle has been observed to do this, and these "virtual" particles are volatile entities that exist for less than a second, while the Big Bang made a universe that is superbly stable, perhaps even permanent.

About ten years ago (1989), just as scientists were becoming confident in Big Bang theory, I asked Alan Dressler, one of the world's leading astronomers, and currently a consultant on the design of the space telescope scheduled to replace the Hubble, what caused the Big Bang. He scrunched his face and said, "I can't stand that question!" At the time, cosmologists tended to assert that the cause and prior condition were unknowable. The bizarre physics of the singularity that preceded the explosion, they explained, represented an information wall that blocked (actually, destroyed) all knowledge of the prior condition and its physical laws. We would never know.

The more scientists testily insisted that the Big Bang was unfathomable, the more they sounded like medieval priests saying, "Don't ask me what made God." Researchers, prominently Alan Guth of MIT, began to assert that the Big Bang could be believed only if its mechanics could be explained. Indeed, Guth went on to propose such an explanation. Suffice it to say that, while Guth asserts science will eventually figure out the cause, he still invokes unknown physical laws in the prior condition. And no matter how you slice it, calling on unknown physical laws sounds awfully like appealing to the supernatural.

The existence of 50 billion galaxies isn't the only mystery that's prompting scientists to rethink their attitudes toward the divine. Beyond this is the puzzle of why the universe is hospitable to living creatures.

In recent years, researchers have calculated that if a value called omega, the ratio between the average density of the universe and the density that would halt cosmic expansion, had not been within about one-quadrillionth of one-percent of its actual value immediately after the Big Bang, the incipient universe would have collapsed back on itself or experienced runaway-relativity effects that would render the fabric of time-space weirdly distorted. Instead, the firmament is geometrically smooth, rather than distorted, in the argot of cosmology. If gravity were only slightly stronger, research shows, stars would flame so fiercely they would burn out in a single year; the universe would be a kingdom of cinders, devoid of life. If gravity were only slightly weaker, stars couldn't form and the cosmos would be a thin, undifferentiated blur. Had the strong force that binds atomic nuclei been slightly weaker, all atoms would disperse into vapor.

These cosmic coincidences were necessary to create a universe capable of sustaining life. But life itself required an equally unlikely fine-tuning at the atomic level, yielding vast quantities of carbon. Unlike most elements, carbon needs little energy to form exceedingly complicated molecules, a requirement of biology. As it happens, a quirk of carbon chemistry—an equivalence of nuclear energy levels that allows helium nuclei to meld within stars—makes this vital element possible.

To the late astronomer Fred Hoyle, who calculated the conditions necessary to create carbon in 1953, the odds of this match occurring by chance seemed so phenomenally low that he converted from atheism to a belief that the universe reflects a "purposeful intelligence." Hoyle declared, "The probability of life originating at random is so utterly minuscule as to make the random concept absurd." That is to say, Hoyle's faith in chance was shaken by evidence of purpose, a reversal of the standard postmodern experience, and one shared by many of his successors today.

This web of improbable conditions, making not just life but intelligent life practically inevitable, came to be known as the anthropic principle. To physicist Charles Townes, an anthropic universe resolves a tension that has bedeviled physics since the heyday of quantum theory. "When quantum mechanics overthrew determinism, many scientists, including Einstein, wanted the universe to be deterministic," he points out. "They didn't like quantum theory, because it leaves you looking for a spiritual explanation for why things turned out the way they did. Religion and science are going to be drawn together for a long time trying to figure out the philosophical implications of why the universe turned out favorable to us."

Of course, not every scientist is ready to don choir robes. Hard science's attempt to explain our anthropic universe without any reference to the divine has led to the emerging theory of the multiverse, or multiple universes. Andrei Linde, a researcher at Stanford, has argued for a decade that the Big Bang wasn't unique. Universes bang into existence all the time, by the billions. It just happens in dimensions we can't see.

Linde starts from the assumption that if the Big Bang was a chance event driven by some natural mechanism, then such events can be expected to happen repeatedly over eons. Ergo, billions of universes. With each bang, Linde supposes, physical laws and constants are determined anew by random forces. Huge numbers of universes end up with excessive gravity and are crushed out of existence; huge numbers end up with weak gravity and no stars; huge numbers lack carbon. Once in a while, an anthropic cosmos comes about.

Several variations on the multiverse theory are popular in academia because they suggest how our universe could have beaten the odds without a guiding hand. But the multiverse idea rests on assumptions that would be laughed out of town if they came from a religious text. Townes has said that speculation about billions of invisible universes "strikes me as much more freewheeling than any of the church's claims." Tenured professors at Stanford now casually discuss entire unobservable universes. Compare that to religion's proposal of a single invisible plane of existence: the spirit.

Linde admits that we can't observe or verify other universes in any way; for that matter we can't

even explain how they might occupy alternate dimensions. (As a scientific concept, extra dimensions are ambiguous at best; none beyond the familiar four have ever been observed, and it's far from clear that a higher number is possible.)

Thus, the multiverse theory requires as much suspension of disbelief as any religion. Join the church that believes in the existence of invisible objects 50 billion galaxies wide! To be fair, the dogmas embraced by science tend to be more flexible than those held by theologians. If empirical evidence of God were to appear, science probably would accept it eventually, if grudgingly; while religion, if presented with an empirical disproof of God, might simply refuse to listen. Nevertheless, while cosmology seems more and more to have a miraculous aspect, the scientifically approved alternatives require an article of faith.

Numerous other areas of contemporary science sound like supernaturalism dressed up. Researchers studying the motions of spiral galaxies have found that the stars and gas clouds within them behave as though they're subject to 20 times more force than can be explained by the gravity from observed matter. This has led to the assumption, now close to a scientific consensus, that much of the cosmos is bound up in an undetectable substance provisionally called dark matter. The ratio of dark to regular matter may be as high as 6 to 1.

Other experiments suggest that as much as two-thirds of the content of the universe may crackle with an equally mysterious dark energy. In 1998, astronomers were surprised to discover that, contrary to expectations, cosmic expansion isn't slowing as the momentum of the Big Bang peters out. Instead, it appears to be speeding up. Something very powerful is causing the galaxies to fly apart faster all the time.

Then there's the Higgs field. In an attempt to explain the ultimate source of mass, some theorists propose that the universe is permeated by an undiscovered field that confers mass on what would otherwise be zero-mass particles. The Superconducting Supercollider project, cancelled in 1993, was intended to test this hypothesis.

These and other mystery forces seem to function based on nothing. That notion, now a fact of life among physicists and cosmologists, would have been considered ridiculous just a few generations ago. Yet Judeo-Christian theology has been teaching for millennia that God made the universe ex nihilo, out of nothing. Maybe these forces work in a wholly natural manner that simply hasn't yet been determined. Certainly, there's a better chance of finding observational evidence for theories of physics than theories of theology. But for the moment, many believers find physics trending in their direction, while physicists themselves are left to ponder transcendent effects they can't explain.

Physicists and theologians hold chummy conferences and drink sherry together, but most biologists still want little to do with spiritual thought, and the feeling is mutual on the part of many believers. More than three-quarters of a century after John Scopes stood trial for teaching evolution, Darwin's theory remains a flash point. Only last September (1998), creationists urged Congress to enact legislation supporting the teaching of alternatives to evolution in public schools.

The battle between evolutionary biology and faith isn't inevitable. As genome researcher Collins says, "I am unaware of any irreconcilable conflict between scientific knowledge about evolution and the idea of a creator God. Why couldn't God use the mechanism of evolution to create?" Mainstream Protestant denominations and most branches of Judaism accept Darwin, and in 1996, Pope John Paul II called Darwin's work "more than just a hypothesis."

Even Christian fundamentalism wasn't always anti-Darwin. When the American movement began at the start of the twentieth century, its trumpet call was a popular series of pamphlets called "The Fundamentals," which were to the decade of the 1910s what the "Left Behind" series of evangelical novels is today. According to The Fundamentals,

evolution illustrated the subtle beauty of God's creative power.

The tide began to turn a decade later, however, when William Jennings Bryan began preaching against Darwinism. He was influenced by a 1923 book, *The New Geology*, which argued that Earth's apparently ancient age was an artifact created by God to test people's faith. Moreover, Bryan had just spent a year in Germany and was horrified by the incipient Nazi movement, which used social Darwinism, now discredited, but then fashionable on the left as well as the right, to assert that it was only natural for the strong to kill the weak. His crusade against evolutionary theory led to the Scopes trial in 1925, which cemented into American culture the notion that Darwin and religion were opposing forces.

Espousing a theory known as intelligent design, molecular biologist Michael Behe and others are attempting to forge a synthesis. Often, though inaccurately, described as creationism lite, intelligent design admits that evolution operates under current conditions but emphasizes that Darwin is silent on how those conditions came to be. Science doesn't have the slightest idea how life began. No generally accepted theory exists, and the steps leading from a barren primordial world to the fragile chemistry of life seem imponderable.

The late biologist Gerald Soffen, who oversaw the life-seeking experiments carried out by NASA's Viking probes to Mars, once outlined the early milestones in the evolution of living processes: development of organic compounds; self-replication of those compounds; appearance of cells isolating the compounds from their environment; photosynthesis enabling cells to use the sun's energy; and the assembly of DNA. "It's hard to imagine how these things could have happened," Soffen told me before his death in 2000. "Once you reach the point of a single-cell organism with genes, evolution takes command. But the early leaps, they're very mysterious."

Intelligent design trades on this insight to propose that only a designer could create life in the first place. The theory is spiritual, but it's not bound by Scripture, as creationism is. A designer is a nondenominational, ecumenical possibility, not a dogmatic formula.

Did a designer set Earth's life processes in motion? Few questions are more interesting or intellectually rich. Because the evolution debate is so rancorous, however, the how-did-life-begin question is usually lost amid shouting matches between orthodox Darwinians and hard-line creationists.

The biotech era may change this. Biologists and fundamentalists may still want to hurl bricks at one another, but there's no dodging the immediate questions of biological engineering, stem-cell research, transgenic animals, and so on. What is life? Do individual cells have rights? Do human beings have the right to alter human DNA? Is it wise to reengineer the biosphere?

The need to grope our collective way through such quandaries may force theologians, church leaders, biologists, and philosophers to engage one another. Perhaps this debate will get hopelessly hung up in doctrine, for instance on the question of whether life begins when sperm meets egg. But there is at least an equal chance that the pressure of solving biotech questions will force science and theology to find the reasonable points of either field. Unlike cosmology, which poses fascinating questions whose answers have no effect on daily life, biotech will affect almost everyone in an immediate way. A science-and-religion reconciliation on this subject may be needed to write research rules, physician ethics, and, ultimately, law.

Oh, and what did Einstein think about this issue? He said, "Science without religion is lame, religion without science is blind." Einstein was neither convinced there is a God nor convinced there is not; he sensed that it's far too early in the human quest for knowledge to do more than speculate on transcendent questions. Science, which once thought the case for higher power was closed, is now trending back toward Einstein's view.

Is America a Hospitable Land for Islam?

By John L. Esposito

IF MUSLIMS WERE INVISIBLE IN THE WEST ONLY A few decades ago, today the landscapes of most cities and towns include mosques and Islamic centers alongside churches and synagogues. Within a span of a few short decades, Islam has emerged as the third largest religion in America. Major Muslim communities of the world of Islam today reflect this major demographic shift: not only Cairo, Damascus, Islamabad, Kuala Lumpur, and Khartoum, but also New York, Washington, Detroit, Chicago, and Los Angeles are major centers of Islam.

Muslims in America are far from monolithic in ethnic and racial composition, religious beliefs, and politics. Islam, like Christianity, globally and in America, is a mosaic of many ethnic, racial and national groups: African-American, Arab, South Asian, Iranian, Southeast Asian, African, and Central Asian. The majority of American Muslims are immigrants or children of immigrants who came in pursuit of political and religious freedom, economic prosperity, or education. The minority are predominantly African-Americans, descendants

of slaves, and converts shaped by the civil rights struggle and issues of economic and social justice.

Muslim issues, like those of other religious minorities, are those of identity (assimilation vs. integration); the preservation and practice of religious faith in a society based upon Judeo-Christian or secular values; and empowerment in politics and culture. The identity of immigrants has been shaped by the Muslim societies from which they come, as well as their subsequent experience in the West and with other Muslims. Living as a minority in a dominant culture often ignorant of or hostile to Islam, many have experienced a sense of marginalization, alienation, and powerlessness. Those who were born and raised in predominantly Muslim countries have been challenged to find their place in an American mosaic that, despite separation of church and state, retains a Judeo-Christian ethos and a profound secular bias. The tendency of some in America to sharply contrast American (or a Judeo-Christian) "national culture" with Islamic values further complicates the process of integration or assimilation.

Muslims, like previous generations of non-Muslim immigrants in the West, face questions of integration or assimilation. Can Muslims retain their Islamic heritage and do so in a manner that enables them to also function within the secular, pluralistic traditions of America? The pluralism of countries in the West is likewise being tested. Is Western pluralism a limited form of pluralism? Is it inclusive or exclusive, primarily secular or Judeo-Christian? Can Muslims (as well as Hindus, Sikhs, Buddhists, and others) come to be fully accepted as fellow citizens and neighbors with equal political and religious rights?

However different their ethnic and racial backgrounds and experiences may be, Muslims in America have common concerns about practicing their faith, retaining an Islamic identity (in particular for their children), and preserving family life and values. Specific religious issues include the ability to take time out from work to pray daily, to attend mosque on Friday for the weekly congregational prayer, and to celebrate the two great feasts of Islam (Eid al-Adha and Eid al-Fitr), as well as the availability of halal foods in schools, chaplains in the military and in prisons, and, for those women who wish, the right to wear a headscarf (hijab).

For Muslims, as for other religious minorities such as Jews before them, how to simultaneously retain distinctive religious values and also become part of the majority culture, part of the fabric of society, is a major challenge in the mosaic of our multicultural and multireligious secular societies.

The vast majority of Muslims *have*, in fact, become economically and increasingly politically integrated into mainstream American society. Like many other communities before them, Muslims span the socioeconomic spectrum. They are seen in the professions (education, entrepreneurship, medicine, engineering, law) and in the business world as corporate executives, small business owners, blue collar workers, and laborers. They have built institutions—mosques, Islamic centers, schools, professional and social associations, advocacy groups,

PACs. The freedoms of America have also enabled a number to become major voices for Islamic reform. Their writings, and their training of students, both Americans and foreign, have enabled them to make major contributions in Islamic thought that address the many religious and cultural issues confronting Islam and Muslims today.

Muslim integration in American society has been reflected in major polls. A CAIR 2006 poll of American Muslim voters found that 89 percent of Muslims said they vote regularly; 87 percent said Muslims should financially support worthy non-Muslim political candidates; 86 percent said they celebrate the Fourth of July; 64 percent said they fly the U.S. flag; and 42 percent said they volunteer for institutions serving the public (compared to 29 percent nationwide in 2005). Ninety-seven percent of Muslims believe they should donate to non-Muslim social service programs like aid for the homeless. A formidable 90 percent say Muslims should participate in interfaith activities.

A Project MAPS 2004 survey further revealed that, contrary to the conventional wisdom, domestic policy is a more important factor than foreign policy in influencing the Muslim vote: 44 percent said domestic policy was the most important factor while 34 percent said that foreign policy was the most important factor in deciding how to vote.

If many Muslims in America at the turn of the century were integrated into America and progressing in society, 9/11 created new and major obstacles and challenges. The impact of the attacks in New York and Washington, as well as in Madrid and London and the ongoing threat of global terrorism, have raised fresh questions about the religion of Islam and the loyalty of Muslims. While former President George W. Bush called upon Americans to distinguish between the religion of Islam and the acts of a terrorist minority, preachers of hate (right wing politicians, political commentators, media personalities, writers and religious leaders) have conflated mainstream Islam with terrorism, and thus have fed an increase in discrimination against

Muslims ("Islamophobia"), leading to hate crimes and widespread suspicion of mainstream American Muslims.

A significant consequence of the Bush administration's declared war on global terrorism has been domestic anti-terrorism legislation, and a proliferation of new agencies and policies. Beyond targeting violent extremists and eradicating or containing terrorism, critics have charged that racial profiling, the controversial use of secret evidence, and the mechanism used to implement the Patriot Act have led to indiscriminate detention and arrests of thousands and the erosion of Muslims' civil liberties.

As David Cole, a prominent civil liberties expert, noted in *Less Safe, Less Free* (2007: New Press), of the more than 5,000 Muslims held in preventive detention after 9/11, the vast majority were never even accused of any terrorist act, and not a single individual was found guilty of having committed a terrorist act. While more than four hundred persons were charged in "terror-related" cases by the Justice Department, "the vast majority involved no charges of terrorism whatsoever, but only minor nonviolent offenses, such as immigration fraud, credit card fraud, or lying to an FBI agent."

Cole concludes: In the name of preventing terrorism, the administration has locked up thousands of individuals without trial—within the United States and abroad—the vast majority of whom have never been accused, much less convicted, of any terrorist act. The recent Supreme Court ruling that such actions are unconstitutional is gratifying (especially in light of the Court's recent record on such matters), but the Bush Administration's continued insistence on the legitimacy of this practice is seen by many Muslims as a continued targeting of the Muslim community by the American government, in spite of that government's insistence that it is not waging the war on terrorism against the Islamic religion or against American citizens who are its adherents.

American Muslim experiences post-9/11 were reflected in responses to an open-ended question in a Project MAPS/Zogby 2004 poll: "What do you consider to be the most important issue facing the Muslim American community today?" Twenty-eight percent said constitutional issues and 24 percent said bias and racism. The poll also found mixed experiences in Muslims' relations with other Americans. Slightly more than a third of Muslims say that in their own experience, Americans have been respectful of Muslims, but that American society overall is disrespectful and intolerant of their culture. Another third take the unqualified position that Americans have been tolerant and respectful of Muslims.

Major polls also confirm American Muslim concerns about a changing climate in American society regarding the image of Islam and Muslims. When asked what they most admire about Muslim societies, the answer "nothing" was the most frequent response to a December 2005 Gallup Poll of American households. The second most frequent response? "I don't know." Combined, these two responses represented the majority (57 percent) of Americans surveyed.

The majority of Americans (66 percent) also admit to having at least some prejudice against Muslims; one in five say they have "a great deal" of prejudice. Almost half do not believe American Muslims are "loyal" to this country, and one in four do not want a Muslim as a neighbor.

Americans' lack of knowledge and resultant negative impressions of Islam and Muslims were also reflected in the Gallup World Poll of 2007, which found that 72 percent of Americans disagreed with the statement: "The majority of those living in Muslim countries thought men and women should have equal rights." In fact, majorities in even some of the most conservative Muslim societies directly refute this assessment: 73 percent of Saudis, 89 percent of Iranians, and 94 percent of Indonesians say that men and women should have equal legal rights. Majorities of Muslim men and women in dozens of countries around the world also believe that a woman should have the right to work outside the home at any job for which she is qualified (88 percent in Indonesia, 72 percent in Egypt, and even 78 percent in Saudi Arabia), and to vote without interference from family members (87 percent in Indonesia, 91 percent in Egypt, and 98 percent in Lebanon).

Ignorance of another people's beliefs, history, and culture have time and again led to gross miscalculations in governmental policy at home and abroad and allowed for demagoguery in the media and in the election process. If for no other reason than to know what we and our elected officials are talking about—and to hold them to an appropriately high standard of knowledge and reasonableness—it is vital for Americans and their leaders to learn more about Islam.

Yet, despite an environment in post-9/11 America that has been problematic for numbers of Muslims, their overall assessment of living in America remains more positive than negative. While a majority of Muslims say a friend or family member has suffered discrimination since the September 11 attacks, a majority (51 percent) say this is nevertheless a good time to be a Muslim in America. Slightly more than a third (36 percent) say it is a bad time.

Whether America will be a hospitable land or not for Muslims is in some ways a moot and irrelevant question: the American Muslim community is already larger than many Protestant denominations. There are, for example, more Muslim Americans than Presbyterians and Episcopalians combined; soon there will be about as many Muslim Americans as Jewish Americans. The current demographics indicate that this will certainly be the case by 2020. Utilizing their prodigious talents and drawing upon a centuries-long tradition of intellectual, business, and scientific excellence, Muslims are quickly becoming a part of the fabric of American society and are learning to assert their citizenship and their fundamental rights as the American constitutional heritage encourages and demands.

In the current environment, Muslims seek more than simple tolerance; too often in the past, tolerance has meant the power-structure of the populace "suffering" the existence of others while believing them and their belief systems to be inferior. As a people proud of its history and its contributions to the betterment of humankind, Muslims are neither likely nor inclined to accept anything less than full participation and citizenship—anywhere.

In the end, the insistence of American Muslims on being treated with respect and with full access to the rights and opportunities the United States offers its citizens, may (as has happened so often in American history) result in an America that is stronger, better, more hospitable, and more congenial a place to live for everyone.

∽

Religion and American Politics

By Jo-Renee Formicola

ORGANIZED FAITH COMMUNITIES ARE INCREAS-ingly becoming a stronger voice in American politics. This is because specific Christian denominations have been using many of their financial and spiritual resources to articulate and inject their moral values into the U.S. political debate, to influence specific public policies, and to impact political appointments and elections—all with the intention of implementing an American, Christian, values-oriented political agenda.

This phenomenon has evolved, in spite of constitutional strictures within the First Amendment of the Bill of Rights that forbid the establishment of a national church or government interference into the free exercise of religion. Jefferson reiterated these notions in his "Letter to the Danbury Ministers" by calling for a high wall of separation between church and state; but tradition, practice and Supreme Court decisions throughout American history have resulted in varying relationships between church and state. They have, at different times, reflected the principle of strict separation, as well as the idea of a government-neutral position toward religion, and even a zone of accommodation with religion.

Historically, America was founded by Protestant Christians, namely "Puritans," who were seeking religious freedom and economic advantages that had been denied to them in England. They brought with them covenant theology, a belief in the work ethic, and a respect for individualism, all of which translated into notions of government by consent and accountability, economic competition, human rights, and a sense of belief in the providential destiny of America. Subsequently, Protestants controlled American culture, education, and politics during early U.S. history, a situation that assured and insulated them from government intrusion into their religious affairs. However, as Catholics immigrated in larger numbers to America at the turn of the twentieth century, and began to attain critical mass, they began to challenge Protestant power at all levels of society, seeking government protection, especially through the courts, to preserve their own spiritual, social, economic and political interests.

Catholics and mainstream Protestants—that is, Episcopalians, Presbyterians, Methodists, Congregationalists, Lutherans and American Baptists—were mutually concerned about issues such as temperance, creationism, and control of the American educational system. But, the public schools were a *de facto* Protestant construct, and their federal funding, practice of school prayer and reading of the King James version of the Bible, along with a commitment to a Protestant values-oriented curriculum, were an immediate matter of contention between Catholics and Protestants.

Seen by Catholics as a means to stifle their own religious freedom and exercise, Protestant educational policies were challenged in the Supreme Court. In 1920 in *Pierce v Society of Sisters*, Catholics were allowed to send their children to schools of their choosing. Other cases, such as *Cochran v Louisiana* (1930) and *Everson v U.S.* (1947), granted Catholics the right to receive public monies to pay for textbooks and to transport students to parochial schools. During the 1960s, other Supreme Court decisions dealt a blow to Protestants, particularly fundamentalists, when it ruled in Engle v Vitale (1962) and *Abington Township School District v Schempp* (1962) that school prayer and Bible reading in public schools are unconstitutional.

Through those early church-state decisions, the Supreme Court tried to balance church-state interests. In fact, in *Everson*, it also set explicit parameters delineating what was meant by the establishment clause of the Constitution, and drew clear lines as to what both church and state could and could not do with regard to each other's affairs. *Everson* held that the federal and state governments could not set up a church, or pass laws that aided one religion or all religions, or that preferred one religion over another. It said that the government could not force or influence a person to go to or remain away from a church, or profess a belief or disbelief; that no one could be punished for his or her beliefs or disbeliefs, or for church attendance or non-attendance. It forbade the government to tax people to support religious activities or institutions. It denied governmental participation in the affairs of religious organizations and vice versa.

As a result of *Everson*, a religious truce, of sorts, emerged between Catholics and mainstream

Protestants over education and other social issues. Catholics, who had also demonstrated their patriotism by serving their country in World War II, had dispelled fears of their loyalty to a foreign Pope, and proved their Americanism by supporting anti-Communist policies during the Cold War. Mainstream Protestants still controlled the social, economic, and political infrastructure in America in the aftermath of World War II, but a fundamentalist, conservative branch of its members, the Evangelicals, began to grow, uniting around common conservative religious, social and political concerns. This began to change the religious-political dynamic in America slowly over time.

Committed to personal salvation, religious revivalism, witnessing for Jesus and the belief in His second coming, Evangelicals advanced the notion of moral consistency: that is, they held that the literal teachings of Jesus must pervade every aspect of one's life and actions, even politics. In 1942, they established the National Association of Evangelicals (NAE), bringing together 147 ministers, close to 60 different like-minded religious organizations, and a membership that, today, boasts of close to 80 million adherents.

By 1960, Catholics felt accepted within the political process with the election of one of their own, John F. Kennedy, to the Presidency. Although he disavowed any Church influence on his political decisions, Kennedy represented political acceptance and credibility for Catholics, and a potential threat to other religious groups, particularly Evangelicals.

During the 1960s, the Black Church in America also became actively involved in the political process, an outgrowth of its traditional role as the sanctuary, social service provider and religious faith community for those in society who were racially, culturally, economically and politically marginalized in U.S. society. They provided a model to other religious groups, showing how they could have a critical impact on the American political agenda in the future. It was Black ministers who led demonstrations and protests; who led the fight for civil rights and integration—and whose efforts led to the passage of legislation that prohibited racial discrimination and assured voting rights for Blacks in America.

While the Black Church was the most active religious force during the 1960s, receiving some help from liberal religious denominations, it was not until 1973, when the Supreme Court handed down its decision in *Roe v Wade* that more traditional faith communities became involved in the American political process. *Roe v Wade* allowed a woman to exercise her privacy rights, trumping those of her fetus at various stages of a pregnancy. As a result, religious concerns over changed moral and social values resulted in *Roe v Wade* becoming a lightning rod; it politically energized religious groups and split them along theological, ideological, and even partisan political lines.

Social conservatives along with Evangelical denominations within the NAE and the Catholic Church were impelled to political activism to try to reverse what they believed to be a turning point in American moral behavior. More mainstream Protestant denominations, along with Jewish organizations, as well as secularists and feminists, hailed the decision and worked to protect reproductive rights.

From 1973 forward then, right to life and pro-choice activists have become more involved in the political process, attempting to have greater influence over the political agendas of both major parties; trying to have an impact on public policies that deal with issues that impinge on morality, and working to elect political candidates and appointees that best represent their own moral views on questions that often divide and polarize the electorate.

Today, political action by religious groups is justified as part of their unique spiritual mission: to save souls and bring people to God. Many religious organizations believe that they can and must accomplish this salvific goal within the contemporary, political process through a variety of non-partisan

ways. These include actions such as raising awareness about social and economic disparities, using their good offices to work for justice and peace, and injecting the moral imperative into the political debate.

Many groups, however, believe that their role is broader, and work to support specific political parties and ideologies. It is this movement toward greater politically involved religious groups that is leading to social, religious, and political divisiveness in the United States today.

The evidence of this is the growing political symbiosis between Evangelicals and the Republican Party. Evangelicals have had one clear, consistent religious and political message: that the current American way of life erodes traditional family values, that it is mired in moral relativism, and that it assaults Christianity. Today, Evangelicals represent about 25 percent of the American population—about the same number as Catholics—but they have been in political ascendancy since the 1980s, a result of organizational skills that made it possible for them to provide overwhelming support for Ronald Reagan in his quest for the Presidency.

At that time, Evangelicals led by Rev. Jerry Fallwell formed the Moral Majority and Rev. Pat Robertson founded the Christian Coalition. They were registering huge numbers of their adherents to vote, thus creating a new conservative religious constituency for the Republican Party. In return, they gained vital political access, secured appointments, and gained credibility with those in the White House and the rest of the government. Their concern for traditional family values, the culture wars, and a society that they believed was obsessed with materialism and hedonism became the basis for future Republican platforms and Evangelical support for candidates that were willing to advance their conservative moral values through the political process.

Catholics were working for their own spiritual agendas as well during this time. They supported the Carter administration and its foreign policy based on human rights; opposed the use of nuclear weapons and the Reagan military policy; and accepted the Republican President's notion of supply side economics. The United States Catholic Conference of Bishops issued major pastoral statements and spent a significant amount of time on Capitol Hill as monitors and educators about social justice concerns at home and abroad. But they were fragmented within their own ranks—the hierarchy and clergy supporting Vatican teachings within the context of American politics, and those in the pew who chose more liberal policies with regard to divorce, birth control, and even abortion. Their political support was, therefore, unreliable. Catholics could not be counted on to vote as a bloc, but rather represented the swing vote within a variety of religious constituencies.

Mainstream Protestants and others who were politically and socially in tune with Catholics found their political voice muffled by a liberal clergy trying to lead a more conservative, establishment-minded group of adherents. Ministers who had been committed to social justice, human rights, and other issues such as poverty, racism, sexism and oppression during the 1960s found themselves out of touch with many of their more conservative congregations in the decades that followed. Again, their votes were often difficult to read (and to count) as wealthier Protestants were cross-pressured by economic and social considerations as well as religious ones.

By the 1990s, the religious-political picture in America began to change further. The Clinton Administration did not have close ties with any specific religious group, but it had a broader agenda for economic globalization, universal health care, and welfare reform that appealed to more liberal religious groups. Many Black Christians in America, which had a history of political involvement on behalf of civil rights and social justice, became more politically active at the time to advance the economic well being of many marginalized within American society.

Of all these groups, however, it was the strength-ening symbiosis between the Evangelicals and the Republican Party that allowed religion to play a greater role in American politics, a phenomenon that has become pronounced during the Presidency of George W. Bush. Evangelicals provided the 43rd American President with overwhelming political support, expecting him to advance traditional Christian values on matters that were polarizing, known as wedge issues. These included their concerns over public policies regarding life, death, education, traditional marriage, stem cell research and cloning. Indeed, the President obliged, and appointed many government officials who supported the theological and cultural beliefs of social and religious conservatives.

From his earliest days as a candidate for the Presidency, George W. Bush engaged in a new type of politics designed to gain the support of Evangelicals, while also pursuing a policy of outreach to Catholics and those within Black faith communities. Bush's innovation, implemented by Karl Rove, the president's chief campaign strategist, can be called the "politics of values."

Rove's tactics included targeting Evangelical and other "values voters," and incorporating their moral agenda into Republican policy initiatives. It consisted of preparing and providing socially conservative ideological candidates for election, as well as framing and controlling the political debate within moral parameters. Most importantly, it was also designed to articulate the candidates' values while contrasting the moral flaws of the opposition. Taken together, the strategy of the politics of values was the successful means of winning the White House in both 2000 and 2004, close elections in which the Evangelical values voter made the difference.

The President showed his appreciation. In 2001, only nine days after his first election (and months before the earth-shattering events of September 11, 2001), the new President unveiled his signature, domestic, public policy: the Faith Based and Community Initiative (FBCI). Implemented by an Executive Order, it established faith-based offices in a number of cabinet departments—offices that were to give religious social and charitable agencies the same right to apply for federal funds as secular ones. Based on the principle of "compassionate conservatism," the FBCI completely shifted government funding for social services with the intention of leveling the playing field for religious organizations involved in providing such help. Within the course of his Presidency, Bush established federal, as well as state offices and a budget for the FBCI, setting up a bureaucracy that had the potential to exist long after he would leave office.

The FBCI was followed by other public policies that reflected the social and religious, conservative agenda. The President implemented pro-life policies: reinstating the Global Gag rule, a policy of both Ronald Reagan and Bush's father that prohibited any U.S. Government-funded international agencies to use its own private funds or public monies to perform or provide abortions, from lobbying their own government for a change in abortion laws, or conducting public education campaigns about abortion. Further, it prevented the referral of women to abortion providers or giving them counseling about abortion. In 2002, the President declared a "Sanctity of Life Day," and directed states to classify a developing fetus as an unborn child. With this new designation, funds for State Children's Health Insurance Programs could cover children from conception to age 19. In 2003, the President signed the Partial Birth Abortion Ban, in 2004 the Unborn Victims of Violence Act, and offered federal employees a "Catholic health plan" that excluded payments for contraceptives, abortion, sterilization, and artificial insemination. In that same year, he also signed the Teen Endangerment Act, a law that allowed only a parent to transport a minor across state lines for an abortion. The only pro-life battle that Bush lost was the right to ban the over-the-counter sale of emergency birth control known as Plan B, or the "morning after pill."

Other conservative moral values that the President worked to implement during his two terms in office were opposition to embryonic stem cell research, which he vetoed twice after Congressional passage; state legislation to oppose gay marriage; and efforts to involve the government in the debate over death with dignity as evidenced in the Terri Schaivo case.

By 2006, however, the Evangelical symbiosis with the Republican Party began to unravel. Internal scandals within the party involving sexual advances to House pages by Rep. Mark Foley (R–Fl.), another stemming from conflicts of interest between the influential Republican lobbyist Jack Abramoff and several Republican Congressmen, and ethical allegations against House Minority Leader Tom Delay (R–Tx.) showed the Party to be legally and morally vulnerable. This left the Evangelicals disillusioned, but then discredited as well when news of a sexual affair that involved the head of the NAE, Rev. Ted Haggard and a paid male escort became public. Values such as character and integrity, which had won the day for Republicans and their Evangelical supporters in the past, had eroded among their ranks, and were reflected in the 2006 mid-term elections. Democratic victories at the polls were attributed to the dissatisfaction with the war in Iraq, but exit polls actually showed that scandals and corruption were considered more important to most of the general electorate.

Since then, the Republican Party has been fighting for its values-oriented political life. Evangelicals have tried to re-group, but challenges from the Democrats, as well as from the religious left and center, portend a change in the power equation between religion and politics for the future.

A new political phenomenon is beginning to appear among socially progressive religious groups. Led by liberal and centrist theologians and clergy, they are working to establish broader, universal values that can be injected into the American political agenda. Moving beyond wedge issues that separate voters, to more transcendent values that unite them, they are committed to political action to bring attention to moral issues such as poverty, homelessness, environmental stewardship, and AIDS.

The Rev. Jim Wallis, for example, an activist minister who wrote *God's Politics: Why the Right Gets it Wrong and the Left Doesn't Get It* has set up *Sojourner*, a liberal religious magazine, established a policy organization known as "Call for Renewal" to overcome poverty, and rallied members to a new organization that he founded known as the "Red Letter Christians" who challenge the literal translation of the bible by Evangelicals. Wallis has held a Values Voter Summit, and set up a "Faith Forum" to question potential presidential candidates. Another influential progressive minister is the Rev. Rick Warren, founding pastor of the 22,000 Saddleback (mega-) Church in Lake Forest, California, and author of *The Purpose Driven Life*. He is working to serve those affected by AIDS and to train church leaders in developing countries to fight poverty, disease, and illiteracy. Rabbi Michael Lerner has written *The Left Hand of God: Taking Back Our Country from the Religious Right*, calling for the religious left to work with the secular left to advance a "politics of meaning" in the world of today. Dr. Ron Sider, the author of *Rich Christians in an Age of Hunger*, has brought together moderate Evangelicals and helped create the "Evangelical Call to Civic Responsibility," a document that sets out consistent religious and political goals for the future.

All of these leaders and the many more that are emerging have established a "prophetic agenda" of speaking truth to power. They have the potential to create a new relationship of their own with the Democratic Party, if either side were so disposed. Currently, however, both the religious and secular left are uninterested in creating a symbiosis similar to that of social, religious conservatives and the Republican Party.

Religious groups in America, whether on the left, center or right, are becoming more conscious of their ability to influence morality, as well as the voter in the political process. Megachurches and the ministers who preach to tens of thousands of values voters each week, as well as televangelists who reach millions, can provide a political platform for those who are seeking ways to counter the secular culture and politics that have pervaded American society. If they chose to do so, religion will move further into the political arena in an attempt to control public policies and elections, thus changing the tenuous, constitutional dynamic that exists between church and state in America in the future.

Can "It" Happen Here?

By Abraham H. Foxman

So much of the community activism of American Jews over the past decades has been based on the notion of "Never Again!"—that we can never allow a repeat of the great tragedy that befell the Jewish people in the 1940s, the Holocaust. When American Jews stand up for Israel under siege, "Never Again!" resonates. When American Jews combat the resurgence of anti-Semitism in Europe and elsewhere, "Never Again!" is heard. And when American Jews are in the forefront of the "Save Darfur" movement, once more it is "Never Again!" that is their motivation, both on moral and practical grounds. The community sees the need to stand up to any potential genocide because we know this evil from our own experience and because we know the value to our own community of different groups joining together.

The assumption of "Never Again!" generally relates to "over there." If it can happen again, it will happen to Jews in Israel or even in Europe. Rarely is there open discussion as to the possibility of it happening here. After all, America is the land of freedom and opportunity, the place often described as the best one for Jews in 2,000 years of Diaspora,

so to talk of a Holocaust here sounds inconceivable.

Still, it would not be honest to suggest that one never hears such conversation in Jewish circles. There are those who take the position that Jews are not safe anywhere, outside of Israel, and they cite the fact that so many German Jews felt completely at home in Germany, and then came Hitler.

It is also noted that anti-Semitism, which shares characteristics with other forms of racism and bigotry, has a unique core that makes it not only so lethal but also so enduring, so liable to thrive in many different cultures and societies. That core belief rests on the notion that Jews are not what they seem to be—that they have a secretive, poisonous, powerful hidden agenda that is iniquitous to the societies in which they live. This concept reached its height in Nazi Germany, but has been used elsewhere against Jews, even in America. Charles Lindbergh, in the period leading up to America's entry into WWII, blamed "powerful Jews" of trying to bring America to war against Germany in order to serve their own interests against those of America. And people like John Mearsheimer and Stephen Walt, professors at the University of Chicago and

Harvard respectively, have, in a more sophisticated fashion, blamed Jews for America's troubles in the Middle East, including the war in Iraq.

So there is a basis in history, and in the essence of anti-Semitism, to argue that even in America one can't rule out the possibility that large-scale anti-Semitism could become a reality. Studying the history of the Jews, there is never reason to be complacent about anti-Semitism. Nevertheless, it is correct, in my view, to say that America is different, and to suggest therefore that the likelihood of it happening here is indeed remote.

There are many reasons why America is different and it begins with the question: What does it mean to be an American? That question was being asked even before America declared its independence. Thinkers realized early on that something new and different was emerging in America. People were coming from different nations, were settling together, were becoming part of a new whole, or many new wholes. This meant there was automatically a fluid sense of identity on many levels which did not exist in Europe.

Listen to J. Hector St. John de Crevecoeur writing in *Letters from an American Farmer* in 1793: "What then is the American, this new man?... He is an American who leaving behind him all his ancient prejudices and manners, receives new ones from the new mode of life he has embraced, the new government he obeys, and the new rank he holds.... Here individuals of all nations are melted into a new race of man, where labors and posterity will one day cause great changes in the world.... The Americans, therefore, ought to love this country much better than that wherein either he or his forefathers were born."

Ever since, there have been many different answers to the question of who is an American. The multicultural answer is the latest. All are premised on the notion that one did not have to be born in America to be an American; one did not have to be of a particular religion or come from a particular place to become an American.

All of which forced Americans early on to address issues of both unity and diversity: how to keep a sprawling nation with many different people and religious perspectives together as one nation and—while there was a dominant culture and group, later identified as white Anglo-Saxon Protestant—how to give legitimacy and expression to the diverse cultures and customs that were characteristic of each ensuing immigrant population.

The European case is different. There, Jews have been at a disadvantage whether because of tendencies toward social unity or diversity. Historically, a united nation generally meant it was religiously and ethnically homogeneous, which led to centuries of exclusion, discrimination, and violence against Jews. Yet now, the rise of European "diversity," in part due to the large influx of immigrants, has produced a phenomenon in which Israel and Jews have become the targets of Muslim groups supported by European left-wing ideologies.

Not so in America, where both unity and diversity have given legitimacy to Jews. Even while such forces as nativism and racism led to laws and violence toward various ethnic groups, the concept of being an American—fundamentally different from European definitions of identity and nationhood—remained.

In 20th-century America, three stages developed in understanding the relationship between unity and diversity. Along the way, there was movement away from the unity pole and toward the diversity pole without, however, abandoning the overriding theme of unity. First came the melting pot theory of America, the notion that every new immigrant group melts into the existing American stew, changing it slightly with additional spices but leaving the basic makeup of a united America. The focus here was mostly on the new immigrant assimilating to American mores.

Then came the idea of cultural pluralism, where cultural differences became more visible to Americans. This concept compared America to an orchestra, where each group played its own instrument, while together they produced beautiful euphonic music. In many ways, cultural pluralism represents the ideal for American Jews. It does nothing to weaken the goal of American unity and American values, which have provided unique opportunity for Jews, but it also defines "Americanness" in a way that Jews can feel completely equal while still expressing and living their particular cultural and religious values.

More recently, multiculturalism has shifted the paradigm of unity and diversity more to the diversity side, and in some versions, by questioning the very values of Western culture, may pose a potential threat to American unity.

Still, the overwhelming thrust in American society is toward openness to newcomers becoming full-blown Americans. This has expanded to people of color from different parts of the world. The power of this idea mitigates the worst manifestations of multiculturalism. In one school in New York City, it is said that 130 languages are spoken. The city takes pride in this because these different languages represent people all looking to make it in America, as Americans. Tendencies in multiculturalism to Balkanization, to denigration of the West, to criticism of the majority culture and history, are not nearly as powerful as they are in Europe.

The condition of American Jews is different for other reasons as well. The historic tradition and constitutional provisions separating religion from government provide for a radically different climate for Jews here than abroad. The prohibition in the First Amendment against government establishing a state religion reinforced America's pluralistic ethos. Rather than have a government-imposed religion, which invariably would have marginalized Jews, what evolved was a broad neutral sphere in which people of all religious persuasions could participate as equal citizens and, at the same time, left ample room in society for a religious sphere that protected religion from government intrusion, while still encouraging religious expression. The result is a society where religions, including Judaism, flourish and are respected and where Jews, despite being a distinct minority, are an integral part of the broader society. This was unheard of in Europe and remains another anchor in the belief that "it can't happen here."

Other factors obtain as well. Because of America's diversity and because of the civil rights movement, there has been much more emphasis here in educating against prejudice and bigotry. Extensive anti-bias programs have been brought to schools, corporations, campuses, communities, and government institutions. And following the dramatic changes in the Catholic Church—on the heels of the Vatican Second Council adopting *Nostra Aetate*, which absolved Jews of the "deicide"—churches of all denominations have moved away from classical positions about Jews which were the basis for the most egregious anti-Jewish attitudes.

In the final analysis, one has to make a distinction between the question of whether anti-Semitism will in the future be a significant problem in America and whether a radical anti-Semitic experience will ever face American Jews.

On the question of normative anti-Semitism, much will depend on whether education against prejudice continues to be a priority and whether political, religious, and cultural leaders see it as obligatory to speak out against anti-Semitism wherever it occurs.

As to the more extreme question of whether "it can happen here," that is directly connected to what kind of a society America will be in the future. If we remain a society ruled by law, by the protections of the Constitution, including the Bill of Rights and separation of powers, if we respect the rights of the individual and maintain a balance between security and civil liberties, then it is impossible to foresee a situation where Jews would be targeted for pogroms, or worse. In other words, if America remains America, such a proposition is outlandish.

It seems, then, that only if America dramatically loses its way would it be possible to even imagine that "it" could ever happen here.

Transforming Tolerance:
American Religion and Sexual Diversity

By Jay Emerson Johnson

Religion, family, and politics have always been tightly woven together in American society, though the pattern of their weaving has undergone nearly constant change. The fluidity of religious practice (whether in New England Puritanism, colonial outposts of the Church of England, or Catholic missions lining the western edge of the continent) and the varying configurations of marriage and family life generated by these religious experiments contributed significantly to the resilience and malleability of American democracy. Historically, the tolerance of diversity woven into these patterns of American culture and religion advanced the daunting project of constructing a cohesive national identity in the United States. Ideals inherent to such tolerance, such as individual liberty and self-determination, likewise propelled moments of profound social change in American history, especially concerning race, ethnicity, and civil rights. Since the middle of the twentieth century, however, the limits of American tolerance have been tested by the increasingly visible presence of "homosexuals" in both civic and religious arenas.

Today, America's religious landscape exhibits deep fault lines over human sexuality and gender expression that suggest a turning point in the role played by religion in the evolving cultural dynamics of American society. As the tradition of tolerance has to a considerable degree transformed American institutional religion, some of those institutions are in turn trans-forming tolerance into an affirmation and welcome of sexual and gender diversity. This transformation of tolerance will only continue to reshape the multifaceted and, at times, turbulent relationship between religion and culture in American life.

The socio-religious contestations over "homosexuality" punctuating American society in recent years—from the "don't ask, don't tell" military policy enacted during the first term of the Clinton administration to the election of Gene Robinson as the Episcopal bishop of New Hampshire in 2003, and the galvanizing court rulings on same-sex marriage in Massachusetts and California—rightly belong to a longer history of America's cultural self-reinvention and the transformations of religion in American society. Catherine Albanese characterizes that history as exhibiting both the "manyness" and the "oneness" of religion in America. Tolerance of religious diversity, together with religion's freedom from state interference (within certain limits), created the conditions for wide-ranging religious and spiritual experimentation. The challenge of forging a single nation from a host of diverse ethnic, cultural, and religious populations, especially in the nineteenth century, energized the emergence of an American "public Protestantism," replete with its own creed, code, and cultus, as one of the primary means of constructing a unified social identity.[1]

One could then, when addressing diverse sexualities and gender expressions, turn to a number of religious traditions in America for a variety of responses, whether in Native American traditions (which are also significantly diverse) or American versions of East Asian spiritual practices (from Buddhism to Taoism) or "home grown" approaches to religion, such as the nineteenth-century New England transcendentalists. But by far American public discourse and social movements have been dominated by the rhetorical strategies, biblical arguments, and institutional policies of Christianity. For that reason, any analysis of religion in America with respect to sexual diversity must begin with and turn repeatedly to Christian traditions, even if the analysis eventually leads beyond those traditions.

The Protestant character of America's civil religion, which necessarily refrains from endorsing any particular institutional or sectarian expression, relies generally on the Bible and biblical argumentation for navigating times of profound social change or controversy. The abolition of slavery and the "first wave" of a women's rights movement in the nineteenth century illustrate well this reliance on biblical rhetoric. In both cases appeals to Enlightenment-era notions of individual rights and liberty proved far less galvanizing than arguments drawn directly from biblical texts.[2] Abolishing the slave trade and securing women's suffrage are but two among many social movements that provide examples of how religion, and especially biblical reasoning, operates in the dynamics of American cultural developments. For all three "religions of the book" (Judaism, Christianity, and Islam), not only in America but worldwide, the interpretation of scripture resides at the heart of each faith community's engagement with these wider social realities. Yet, this is particularly true in the United States, where the official disestablishment of religion and a historically unprecedented splintering of religious traditions into multiple denominations, communities, and sectarian groups gradually eroded the authority of institutional religion in the public square of American life. Rather than relying on the pronouncements of inherently unstable institutional sources, American Christians (among others) turned instead to sacred texts, to the apparently more reliable (read "unchanging") guidance of scripture.[3] However, as religious institutions more often reacted to cultural and scientific developments rather than leading the way, Christian churches were forced either to adapt or retrench. Scripture operated in both scenarios as warrants for a particular approach to configuring social patterns of interaction. The Bible, in other words, came to function not so much as the source of a particular ideology or social pattern in modern American life, but more often as the justification for already established sensibilities.

Today, after four decades of critical biblical scholarship on human sexuality and gender, and countless church task forces, committees, synods, and conferences, the intersection of religion and sexuality poses a new question concerning lesbian, gay, bisexual, and transgender (LGBT) people. It is no longer a matter of *if* LGBT people will be welcomed at the table of America's religious traditions, but how that will contribute to the ongoing development of those traditions. Transforming tolerance into acceptance and welcome will necessarily transform the communities in which such diversity is embraced.

More than a subtle turn of phrase, the transformation of tolerance with respect to sexual diversity points to as yet unexplored horizons for religious and spiritual practice in American society, the charting of which promises to transform religion itself. Appreciating the significance of those horizon lines requires first some familiarity with the modern emergence of diverse sexual identities in relation to religion (especially Christianity); and second, a consideration of the implications for social change of increasingly visible LGBT religious leaders.

Sexual Identity Politics and Christianity

Michel Foucault once famously observed that in the mid-nineteenth century "homosexuality" was invented.[4] He did not mean that same-sex sexual behavior did not exist prior to that date. Foucault instead wanted to highlight the discursive social practices of the modern period, especially in the fields of medicine and psychiatry, that constructed a unique identity for those who engaged in same-sex sexual acts. As Foucault and others have helped to demonstrate, prior to the modern period anyone was potentially vulnerable to the temptation of the sin known as "sodomy," the temptation to engage, even just occasionally, in same-sex sexual acts. This helps to explain in part the rather regular sermonic denunciations of sodomy from colonial-era American pulpits and the later stress on the "sanctity" of marriage and family life in American society.[5] Nearly half of the original English colonies, for example, insisted on the death penalty for those caught in the act of sodomy, or the "crime against nature." While capital punishment for such acts was removed from state statutes after the Revolutionary War, religious communities remained vigilant on this front, a vigilance inflected as much by fears over gender non-conformity as by objections to particular acts of sexual intimacy (or more precisely, their fear that some of those acts violated the gendered order of God's creation). One could note in that regard early Christian missionary encounters with diverse gender expressions in some Native American communities, especially androgynous or "transgender" behavior, which contributed to the development of American legal statutes requiring styles of dress to conform to a person's sex/gender.[6]

Significantly, the medical construction of a homosexual identity emerged along with similarly "scientific" categorizations of both gender and race. Arguments concerning the former, which included claims for the "natural domesticity of women," supported the cultural practice of "separate spheres" for men and women, and arguments in the latter for justifying cultural stereotypes of non-white people, which often contributed to their disenfranchisement in many social institutions. Rather than distinct moments of scientific discourse, gender, race, and sexuality should instead be understood as mutually informing modes of categorical classification. A homosexual identity, for example, was understood at first, in the late nineteenth century and the first half

of the twentieth, as a type of gender inversion (a man's compulsion to take on a woman's role), and later as analogous to ethnicity in the emerging identity politics of the 1970s and 1980s.

As Melissa Wilcox has argued, most if not all religious institutions and faith communities were entirely unprepared to address these modern social-scientific notions of distinct sexual orientations.[7] Neither the word "homosexual" nor the concept of a sexual identity it was meant to describe appear anywhere in the Bible, leaving only a handful of biblical texts that could be construed as condemning particular types of behavior. In 1955, Derrick Sherwin Bailey published the first historical-critical study of those particular texts as an attempt to reorient their traditional interpretations. The biblical story of God's destruction of Sodom and Gomorrah in Genesis, he argued, did not indicate a divine condemnation of "homosexuality" but of violent inhospitality.[8] Multiple scholarly interventions of this type since the mid-twentieth century have not, however, soothed the ferocity of religious debates over "homosexuality," which for many faith communities remains tied to gender roles and expectations.

The current sense of crisis over human sexuality in the worldwide Anglican Communion captures in microcosm the contours of this religious struggle, which extend well beyond the concerns of American Episcopalians. The decision in 2002 by the Canadian diocese of New Westminster to bless same-sex unions, and a year later, the election of Gene Robinson—an openly gay and partnered priest—as the bishop of New Hampshire, compelled some Anglicans (both in the U.S. and elsewhere) to draw a line in the ecclesial sand. This global ecclesial stand-off has exposed a rhetorical shift in how sexual diversity is adjudicated in contemporary religious terms. The objections made to the Canadian and American decisions retained their traditional reliance on biblical arguments, but mostly avoided citations that had been typical of twentieth-century debates. Rather than decrying the apparent approval of "sodomy" in New Westminster and New Hampshire, critics of these decisions instead objected to the violation of God's own gendered order of creation manifested by same-sex unions. The biblical arguments thus drew directly from the creation accounts in the opening chapters of Genesis to support the notion of "gender complementarity" as the divine intent in marriage.[9]

Here the controversy at the intersection of sexuality and religion turns not on loving and committed relationships, but instead, and as it did throughout early American history, on the perceived transgression of a properly gendered order of reality. George Chauncey's study of World War-era American society offers a particularly apt illustration of this mode of religious reasoning as he considered the gender implications of sexual behavior in the American military. Chauncey analyzed the 1919 naval investigation of "homosexuality" in Newport, Rhode Island, which had quickly spread to the local ministerial association. Some of the sailors staying at the Newport YMCA accused a prominent Episcopal priest of making sexual advances in the course of his pastoral care. The ministerial association, including the Episcopal Bishop of Rhode Island, vigorously defended the accused so as to prevent the accusations from spreading to other ministers. The concern here, however, had little if anything to do with a potential epidemic of "sodomy"; instead, as Chauncey argues, they worried mostly about their own gendered performance of ministry. As upper-class clergy offered compassionate care to working-class sailors, the sailors perceived this care as effeminate and therefore a solicitation of sexual relations. Significantly, the defense offered by these clergy relied on arguing that masculinity is not compromised in acts of compassion.[10] Put another way, just because a man is religious doesn't make him "more like a woman."

Chauncey's research points more broadly to the explicitly gendered construal of what male "homosexuality" implies for men and masculinity in American culture, which in turn infuses the ecclesial debates over church membership and ordination for differently gendered (i.e., "homosexual") people. This kind of gendered posture toward human relationships persisted in many American religious communities for decades (and still does in some), regardless of the social-scientific research available on questions of sexual and gender identity. Despite the 1972 decision of the American Psychiatric Association to declassify homosexuality as a mental illness or disorder, many religious institutions and faith communities continued to cite biblical texts as their basis for considering homosexuality "unnatural" and therefore sinful. Moreover, even explicitly religious and theological arguments in favor of changing those institutional policies often had little effect.

Historical-critical interpretations of the Bible have in some cases dealt effectively (at least eventually) with a range of highly charged issues, whether in terms of Darwinian evolution or the enslavement of Africans, but for decades such scholarship often left virtually untouched the supposed biblical condemnation of "homosexuality." When critical reassessments of that biblical material reached a wider audience it did so only in the context of broader societal change, especially when lesbian and gay people were willing to be more public and visible about their lives and relationships. Horace Griffin provides helpful illustrations of precisely this in his study of African American Christians in traditional black churches who treat biblical texts unevenly, critiquing Pauline passages concerning slavery on the one hand while uncritically citing Pauline passages concerning sexuality on the other.[11] Again, the Bible on its own does not usually generate social values; it is instead more often employed to support and justify already established cultural mores.

Religious institutions, no less than many LGBT people, may not have wished to grapple with the implications of modern sexual/gender classification schemes and the often fractious identity politics those schemes generated in the latter half of the twentieth century; yet that is of course what both were compelled to do. In spite of, and sometimes because of those wrenching engagements, American cultural sensibilities have been gradually but nonetheless profoundly changing over the last fifty years, especially in response to an increasing number of openly LGBT people engaging in public religious leadership. While many faith communities still wrestle with even the most basic approaches to the Bible and social science on sexual and gender diversity, the voices and relationships of LGBT clergy have already had a significant impact on the American religious landscape and in the courts of public opinion.

LGBT Religious Leadership and Social Change

Over the last 150 years, historical-critical interpretation of the Bible in concert with developments in the social sciences was necessary but not sufficient for transforming some religious institutions in America concerning their policies and postures toward diverse human sexualities and gender expressions. In the contested relationship between religion and culture throughout the modern period, religious leaders and faith communities at times pioneered movements for social change (such as the abolition of slavery or the emergence of a labor movement in the early twentieth century). On other fronts, religious institutions appeared to lag behind cultural trends. It wasn't until a full fifty years after women achieved the right to vote in the United States, for example, that they were granted both voice and vote in the Episcopal Church and even later, in 1976, officially admitted to ordained ministry. While wider societal influences on institutional religion are clearly important they are also difficult to measure and evaluate; religious institutions rarely if ever cite social movements or cultural developments as the rationale for changes in policy and practice, which demand instead explicitly biblical, theological, and religious reasoning. Nonetheless, on such highly charged issues as race, ethnicity, the role of women, and LGBT people, uniquely American cultural developments have contributed significantly to religious transformations.

Post-World War II American society witnessed unprecedented social change and compelled many faith communities to address new challenges. Increased visibility for lesbian and gay people, especially in urban centers, often necessitated a religious response. In 1964, the pastor of Glide Memorial Methodist Church in San Francisco helped to establish the Council on Religion and the Homosexual, which sought to initiate dialogue on homosexuality in churches but quickly shifted its attention to social justice advocacy (at first simply calling for an end to police harassment of homosexuals). The council's interdenominational work soon spread to other cities, including Dallas, Los Angeles, and Washington, D.C. In 1968, Troy Perry founded the Universal Fellowship of Metropolitan Community Churches (MCC), a year before the galvanizing Stonewall Riots in New York City that many consider a milestone in, if not the actual launching of, a gay liberation movement in the United States. Perry, an openly gay and ex-Pentecostal minister, founded MCC specifically for lesbian and gay people as an interim step toward their full inclusion in other denominations. Today MCC is international in scope with roughly 40,000 members in 300 congregations spread over eighteen countries. In 1972, William Johnson received widespread media attention as the first openly gay man to be ordained in a mainline Christian denomination, the United Church of Christ (UCC); Johnson later founded the gay caucus in the UCC.

These twentieth-century moments of highly visible, public expressions of sexual diversity, along with such equally provocative developments as divorced and remarried clergy, the invention of the birth-control pill, and "second wave" feminism, prompted wide-spread debate in nearly every American religious tradition and faith community. The result of these often contentious deliberations, with which we are still living today, was a patch-work of various institutional policies and guidelines on a gerrymandered religious landscape. These institutional debates, now stretching over more than three decades, further fragmented some denominations while establishing others as safe havens for LGBT people in the hard work of transforming tolerance into acceptance and welcome. Still others have reached an entrenched stalemate in their deliberations as openly LGBT members continue to lobby for institutional change, including access to ordination, even as their national policy-setting bodies repeat traditional arguments for their exclusion (examples of which include the United Methodist Church, the Evangelical Lutheran Church in America, and the Presbyterian Church USA).

Dawne Moon's study of two congregations in the United Methodist Church offers helpful insights here regarding the complexities of negotiating religious tradition and American culture on these potentially schism-producing questions. In her study of a generally liberal or progressive congregation and a more conservative or Evangelical one, Moon sought to understand better the social/cultural components of religious belief, especially how conflicts are negotiated in those contexts. In the course of her interviews, she found that both congregations mined a wide range of sources encountered in everyday life for articulating their theological positions, which she argues helped them to perceive their beliefs as universal and timeless, or just "natural." For these congregations, biblical texts and church teaching were only two of the many sources people consulted for their "everyday theologies," which renders the process of religious meaning-making far more complex than simply conforming to institutional norms. But she was surprised to discover that both congregations exhibited a nearly universal disdain for "politics," which she theorized as stemming from the perceived threat politics poses to "denaturalize" religious faith; in other words, political deliberation threatens to expose the contested and negotiated character of belief itself. This led Moon to her central thesis: homosexuality is so highly charged in today's churches not primarily because of the Bible, church teaching, or theological traditions, but because religious debates over human sexuality expose the inherently political character of church life. In that light, homosexuality remains explosive and potentially divisive to the extent that congregations perceive the church as "above" politics.[12]

The mutually affecting relationship between religion and culture in American society thus demands a broad range of analytical tools for assessing the prospects for a wider inclusion of LGBT people in faith communities. Statistical data on the sexuality of clergy, for example, is often difficult to collect, especially in the more restrictive traditions where homosexuality can lead to expulsion. That noted, many would argue that nearly without exception a certain percentage of the members as well as the clergy of every Christian denomination (including many non-Christian traditions) is lesbian, gay, bisexual, or transgender, whether openly or not. Roman Catholicism presents a further challenge in that regard given the requirement of clergy celibacy, which would seem to make the question of sexual orientation moot. Yet some studies have suggested that the number of Roman Catholic priests who are gay could be as high as fifty percent.[13]

Difficulties in data collection aside, high profile cases of ecclesial adjudication in various denominations continue to suggest a well-established presence of LGBT people across the American religious spectrum: in 1995, First United Lutheran Church in San Francisco was expelled from the Evangelical Lutheran Church in America for calling an openly gay man to be their pastor; a year later, Bishop Walter Righter faced a heresy trial in the Episcopal Church for ordaining an openly gay man (the charges were eventually dismissed); and in 2003—the same year Gene Robinson was elected as the Episcopal bishop of New Hampshire and the U.S. Supreme Court overturned state sodomy statutes—Irene Elizabeth Stroud came out in a sermon as a partnered lesbian to her Germantown, Pennsylvania, United Methodist congregation. This public declaration of sexual diversity from the pulpit prompted two church trials and she was eventually stripped of her ordination credentials.

Often at issue throughout these contestations is the extent to which sexual diversity receives sustained public attention in a religious venue. In the case regarding Gene Robinson, which now threatens to splinter the worldwide Anglican Communion, the broader public reach of a bishop's work played a key role. While hundreds of openly lesbian and gay people had been ordained as priests and deacons in the Episcopal Church prior to Bishop Robinson's election, the national as well as global reach of his new position begged the ecclesial question of sexual diversity in locales as remote from New Hampshire as Nigeria and Australia. Here the more centralized and globally networked polity of the Anglican Communion has contributed significantly to the high-stakes rhetoric coming from nearly all sides of the question. More "decentralized" or congregationally based denominations often but not always live with greater flexibility, or a "local option" policy regarding openly lesbian and gay clergy. Baptist churches are a notable exception as the American Baptist Church U.S.A. and the Southern Baptist Convention began in the 1990s to "disfellowship" congregations that welcomed homosexual members.

In short, the tradition of tolerance woven into the fabric of American life has in large measure transformed the posture of American Christianity toward sexual diversity even as some traditions continue to exclude LGBT people from full participation in their community's life of faith and spiritual practice. The trajectory of greater visibility for lesbian, gay, and bisexual people over the last fifty years, and more recently of transgender people, has been transforming tolerance itself into postures of acceptance and welcome. This transformation of tolerance has created the conditions for an ever-growing number of openly LGBT religious leaders, which, in turn, will make a significant impact on American society more broadly. Achieving full marriage equality for lesbian and gay couples is just one among many examples of that broader impact.

The tradition of tolerance has likewise carved out ample cultural space in American society for LGBT participation in a variety of religious traditions well beyond the confines of institutional Christianity. Given the history of "public Protestantism" in American culture, Christianity often receives the lion's share of media attention on a whole range of issues, and often for good reason. Yet institutional

church debates certainly do not describe without remainder the intersection of religion and sexuality in American life. Reformed Judaism, for example, has often shown a more progressive posture toward sexual diversity than some liberal Christian churches, and in 2007, the leading seminary of Conservative Judaism opened its admission procedures for lesbian and gay people who wish to study for the Rabbinate.

A recent collection of essays called, simply enough, "Gay Religion," explores the participation of LGBT people in a wide range of traditions (from Buddhism and Judaism to Santería and Native American rituals) as well as new and emerging spiritual practices and communities. Each of the essays demonstrates the religious diversity and spiritual vitality among LGBT people, both historically and presently. As the editors of this volume note, in mainstream media sources "one is hard pressed to find positive stories of gay religious life or tales of organizations harmoniously merging homosexuality and religion. Yet these stories abound."[14] LGBT people are not, in other words, by definition "irreligious," nor are they bereft of opportunities to engage in religious and spiritual practices despite the institutional policies of some traditions.

As this essay collection and other sources show, and contrary to the popular portrayals of religion in America, whether in film, television, or the news media, much more is happening religiously in the United States than what transpires on a Sunday morning in American churches. For a good number of LGBT people, the institutional policy decisions of a given church body matter little if at all as to whether they will engage fully in religious and spiritual practices. The transformation of tolerance, in other words, as Melissa Wilcox has noted, means at the very least that one's religious identity is no longer reliant "on the statuses that institutions confer."[15]

Mainline American Christians would do well to consider the implications of Wilcox's observation, especially in the light of a religious vitality and of thriving spiritual practices among remarkably diverse LGBT communities. In doing so, more than a few

Christian communities would likely find the stalemate they have reached in their debates over "homosexuality" broken open by new questions, including what "religion" itself entails. As Donald Boisvert argued in his contribution to "Gay Religion," some aspects of popular gay male culture (whether in dance clubs or at pride parade festivals) can become occasions for "apprehending the sacred, the transcendent, or the religious."[16] If so, then instead of (or perhaps in addition to) asking whether LGBT people can be "tolerated," Christian communities might reflect on the insights gleaned from LGBT people for the sake of revitalizing their congregational life.

The contestations over sexual and gender diversity, in both religious and civic arenas, are far from over. Yet I would agree with those who believe that the transformation of tolerance into a posture of embrace over the last fifty years marks an irreversible trend in American society. While no one can predict precisely the shape of its arc, this much seems clear: that trend has and will continue to transform religion in America.

❦

NOTES

1. Catherine Albanese, America: Religions and Religion (Belmont, Calif.: Wadsworth Publishing, 1992), see especially chapter 12. Albanese does not mean that all or even most Americans, either historically or today, would identify as "Protestant." Rather, as she puts it, "Whatever it meant in the personal lives of millions, public Protestantism meant acknowledged ways of thinking and acting that were supported by most institutions in society. . . " (398).

2. Prominent examples here would include the biblical critiques of institutional Christianity by Frederick Douglass after his emancipation from slavery (Frederick Douglass, The Life and Writings of Frederick Douglass, edited by Philip Foner [New York: International Universities Press, 1975]); Elizabeth Cady Stanton's biblical commentary written from the perspective of women's rights (Elizabeth Cady Stanton, The Woman's Bible: Comments on Genesis, Exodus, Leviticus, Numbers and Deuteronomy [New York: European Publishing Company, 1895]); and the galvanizing mix of both race and gender with reference to biblical texts in the life and work of Sojourner Truth (see Elizabeth Cady Stanton, Susan B. Anthony, and Matilda Joslyn Gage, History of Woman Suffrage, vol. 1 [New York: Fowler and Wells, 1881], 115-117).

3. See Mark A. Noll, The Old Religion in a New World: The History of North American Christianity (Grand Rapids, Mich.: Wm. B. Eerdmans Publishing, 2002), 267-274.

4. Michel Foucault, The History of Sexuality, vol. 1, trans. Robert Hurley (New York: Vintage Books, 1978).

5. While the relationship between behavior and identity is much contested in some academic disciplines, in my view Mark Jordan has argued convincingly that "sodomy" could describe a range of objectionable acts and, by extension, persons in Christian history until its near reduction in the eleventh century to anal intercourse between men. It was this categorical religious definition that crossed the Atlantic with the European colonizers of America, where virtually everyone needed to guard against the temptation presented by "sodomitical vices" (Mark Jordan, The Invention of Sodomy in Christian Theology [Chicago and London: The University of Chicago Press, 1997]).

6. See Jonathan Ned Katz, Gay American History: Lesbians and Gay Men in the U.S.A., revised edition (New York: The Penguin Group, 1992) and the historical documents collected here that illustrate how some Euro-Americans perceived links between gender non-conformity and "sodomy" in Native American communities (281-334).

7. Melissa Wilcox, Coming Out in Christianity: Religion, Identity, and Community (Bloomington and Indianapolis, Ind.: 2003), 39-46.

8. Derrick Sherwin Bailey, Homosexuality and the Western Christian Tradition (London: Longmans, Green, 1955), 2-4.

9. Andrew Carey, son of a former Archbishop of Canterbury, illustrates well this approach when he argued that objections to homosexuality rely on "an entire theology and anthropology arising from the creation narrative. . . . [and thus] "the bias of scripture towards the complementarity of men and women as the ideal of God's created order" (quoted in Stephen Bates, A Church at War: Anglicans and Homosexuality [London and New York: I. B. Tauris, 2004], 39). See also Edith Humphrey, "What God Hath Not Joined: Why Marriage was Designed for Male and Female," in Christianity Today, 48:9 (2006), 36.

10. George Chauncey, "Christian Brotherhood or Sexual Perversion? Homosexual Identities and the Construction of Sexual Boundaries in the World War I Era," in Hidden from History: Reclaiming the Gay and Lesbian Past, edited by Martin Duberman (New York: New American Library, 1989), 308.

11. Horace Griffin, Their Own Receive Them Not: African American Lesbians and Gays in Black Churches (Cleveland, Ohio: The Pilgrim Press, 2006), 73.

12. Dawne Moon, God, Sex, and Politics: Homosexuality and Everyday Theologies (Chicago: The University of Chicago Press, 2004), 5.

13. See Donald Cozzens, The Changing Face of the Catholic Priesthood (Collegeville, Minn.: The Liturgical Press, 2000).

14. Scott Thumma and Edward R. Gray, eds., Gay Religion (Walnut Creek, Calif.: Alta Mira, 2005), xi.

15. Wilcox, Coming Out in Christianity, 54.

16. Donald L. Boisvert, "The Spirit Within: Gay Male Culture as a Spiritual Venue," in Thumma and Gray, Gay Religion, 353.

Look to the Mountains:
Religion and the Environment

By Eric Kampmann

For many years now I have been a section hiker on the 2,175 mile-long Appalachian Trail. When you hike the trail, tradition dictates that you adopt a trail name which, in my case, is "Trail Thoughts" (abbreviated, "T2"). Let me explain why I picked that particular name.

For me, trail thinking happens when you venture outside on a clear, cold winter night and gaze into the heavens. It happens when you stop to see millions of tiny stars speckle the dark expanse, lighting up the world in all its glory, beauty and mystery. It happens when you face the natural world straight on without the clutter of diverting gadgets. It happens when you hear the music of the spheres while others hear absolutely nothing. "Let the rivers clap their hands, let the mountains sing together for joy; let them sing before the Lord…." (Psalm 98:8–9)

It boils down to this: among His many attributes, God seems to be an artist and He has placed within each of us a desire to experience the beauty, harmony, and grandeur of all His wondrous works.

In our own man-made, ultra-connected world, it is difficult to step back from the millions of electronic darts that besiege us everyday. We are forced to lash ourselves to our computers in an almost futile effort to stay ahead of the avalanche of data tumbling relentlessly out in our direction. As a result, the work world can become a cyber-prison that ties up our minds and our lives in ways that can separate us from the natural world we were born into. Eventually, we submit; or, alternatively, we devise ways to escape. For me, escape comes through periodically returning to the hills and mountains that exist beyond the shores of the wired city. This allows me the time and tranquility to contemplate the path I have been walking verses the path I need to walk. While I have not abandoned the city, it is on the trails that lead into the natural world where I regain the rhythm and pace that seems to exist beyond the helter skelter of our detonating civilization. It is there that authentic life often reveals itself in large and small ways. And it is there that my city thinking is transformed into trail thinking and I begin to actually become my trail name.

Don't get me wrong. Hiking the trail is more than mere walking and climbing. Nature is beautiful and alluring—and very hard. There will be sore knees, turned ankles, persistent thirst, lonely nights and lingering doubt. On the Appalachian Trail there will be blizzards in the Smokey Mountains, lightning strikes in Virginia, searing summer heat in Pennsylvania, downpours in the White Mountains of New Hampshire and everything you can imagine in Maine.

But, as you walk this or any other trail and become hardened by its challenges, you will experience a change of heart and mind. With time and miles, a veteran slowly emerges; the novice at Springer Mountain in Georgia becomes the confident and knowledgeable thru-hiker who is determined to face every adversity on the long trek to Katahdin. The postcard landscape of the armchair hiker has given way to a more profound understanding of what it means to step out into nature. What began as toil and trouble has become something akin to joy.

So join me here as I recollect a few of the many trips that have reconnected me to a world beyond the screen and keyboard. I would like to begin by telling you about my first extended trip on the Appalachian Trail in New Hampshire many years ago.

Late one afternoon, after an easy ten-mile hike, I began to search for a place for the night. About a mile or so beyond the small village of Glencliff, I found an open cabin slightly off the trail. Inside, it was dark and empty, so I resigned myself to another night in the woods alone. After a light dinner, I felt a strong desire to get out of the cold gloom of the shelter, so I left that place to take a walk toward an open field on a hillside surrounded by thick woods. The colors had turned to the deep contrasts and long shadows of a late summer day; stillness permeated the scene. It was as if I had walked into a beautifully painted landscape. And right in the middle of it stood three deer grazing on the hillside. They didn't notice me, and so I gazed in wonder on this scene of magical beauty and perfection—no noise, no breeze, just an intuited sense that God was there and that I was witnessing the magnificent splendor of His creation. Then a sound intruded and the deer lifted their heads. Sensing danger, they vanished and once again, I was alone.

Years later, I recollect that momentary scene as if it were an image painted by God Himself. I felt the warmth of God's presence that day, but I had to turn back to the shelter of the solitary cabin. I did not know then that the journey ahead would be hard and long. Yet, wherever life has taken me, I have carried with me that image as sustenance for the times I have experienced hunger and thirst.

On another extended trip, I took a wrong turn. I thought I was on the right track and I was comforted by the fact that the map showed a small body of water up ahead so I continued on. But as I climbed higher, the land became parched; trees and vegetation gave way to dust and unrelenting heat and my supply of water quickly dwindled to a few drops. I thought about turning back, but I foolishly decided to forge ahead to what became even dryer and more isolated ground.

Within an hour, the water on the map became a longing, then an obsession, then an urgent necessity. I was becoming desperate when I finally stumbled upon a shallow pool of still water. Without hesitation, I drank it as if it were the sweetest water I had ever tasted. I experienced great relief and great joy at something as common as water because my body desperately needed replenishment.

What is true for the body depleted of life-giving water is just as true for the soul of someone wandering in a spiritual wasteland. Our physical thirst mirrors a thirst deep within the human heart. Will we find drink to quench that thirst or will we continue farther into the dry land where there is little or no water to be found?

On another trip the trail took me up to a ridge on a low-lying mountain range in central Pennsylvania. Often, when walking the trail, I can hear the familiar noises of civilization: the distant rumble of a passing freight train, or the subtle hum of an interstate, or just the low-grade sounds of far-off activity. But on this day everything was different, for as I moved along the rocky path, I began to notice the absence of sound. It seemed as if I had walked into a vacuum. The feeling of isolation became palpable and the sense of sudden vulnerability was haunting and troubling.

It is at times like this that you feel a deep appreciation for the power of two. If I had fallen while alone, I would have been in trouble, but if a companion had been with me, I would have been helped. If I had become lost, my friend would have assisted in finding the way back to the trail. Alone, my chances of survival would have been greatly diminished.

This noiseless world, beautiful and intriguing as it was, reminded me of how powerless we really are, but it also reinforced the reality that you and I are built for relationships. So, while the walk was memorable, I was relieved, in the end, to hear all the familiar sounds of human activity once again. To me, these noises were the sound of companionship, friendship and most importantly, the sound of love. It felt good to be back.

The joy of the trail need not be found only in majestic sunsets or large panoramic mountain landscapes. You need to walk the earth to experience the tiny marvels that inhabit it. As you walk along, you can't help but notice whole worlds of small creatures going about their mysterious business. The big things like the mighty Susquehanna River, or the powerful midnight storm, or even the rolling hills of cultivated farmland prompt one to stop in wonder, but the small things of the land, the insects and small animals, are just as amazing and mysterious as the mighty rivers and panoramic vistas. The God of the universe is the God of both the large things of creation as well as the small.

Often when starting out on a backpacking trip, I am distracted by all of the unknowns: Where will I spend the first night? Who will I meet? Will it rain or snow? Have I forgotten something crucial? It takes time to unload all the civilizing baggage that I seem to want to carry with me into the wilderness. But with time I begin to peel off the layers of weight and anxiety that separate me from the world I am entering. Soon I am resting under the stars, looking up into the fathomless heavens as our earth sails silently through space. And it is at moments like this that I feel in my heart the truth of the psalmist's words: "(The Lord) determines the number of the stars and calls them each by name.... He covers the sky with clouds; He supplies the earth with rain and makes grass grow on the hills. He provides food for the cattle and for the young ravens when they call. His pleasure is not in the strength of the horse, nor his delight in the legs of a man; the Lord delights in those who fear him, who put their hope in his unfailing love."(Psalm 148:4–11)

I wrote the essay above several years ago; it was then offered as a meditation on experiencing firsthand the presence of God in the natural world. But here I offer it as a kind of advocacy against transforming nature into a mere political battleground. I feel as wounded as anyone when I see the natural environment being torn apart by needless development. I do not see a shredded world as a sign of progress; rather I see man's heedless devotion to subduing the land as an expression of a betrayal of God's directive to man to be good stewards of the earth. But does advocating good stewardship suggest a Luddite resistance to all change or to any progress? I think not.

Some of the environmental advocates of today have lost a sense of balance and proportion. Even worse, some of these same people preach their environmental sermons from air-conditioned forums in glass office buildings or from pulpits in far flung corners of the globe accessed by private jets and black Escalades. Earlier in this essay I state that "Nature is beautiful and alluring-and very hard." I say here, before we begin that sermon on saving nature and saving the world, we might consider taking a walk on the wild side. Taste and feel nature on a firsthand basis. Walk the trails; get off the road; slow down. Listen to the sounds of the trees and the winds that beat the sounds of any iPod pounding in your ears. If you do, you just might hear the voice of God just as Elijah did when the voice of God came to him as "a gentle whisper"(1Kings 19:12).

Contemporary American Spiritual Movements

By Don Lattin

AMERICA HAS ALWAYS BEEN A SPIRITUAL MELTING pot, a place where believers claim the right to concoct new theologies or modify old ones. So perhaps it should come as no surprise that the last half of the twentieth century offered fertile ground for the growth of spiritual movements not affiliated with major world religions.

Religious beliefs and spirituality have traditionally been viewed as the province of churches, temples, synagogues, and mosques. Yet spirituality and religious faith are increasingly viewed as individual, private matters with few connections to congregation and community. Surveys show that seven in ten Americans believe that one can be religious without going to church. Clergy and denominational leaders dolefully note rampant individualism even among members of their own congregations. They are particularly concerned about the growing number of "seekers"—those who have dropped out or never became institutionally involved, despite a keen personal interest in spirituality.

Most studies of American baby-boomers show declining church attendance and less adherence to church teachings. This does not mean that most baby-boomers became agnostics or atheists. Rather, they adopted a religion tailored to individual preferences and personal spiritual experience. In the past, spirituality was tied to a comprehensive belief system that valued intellectual agreement, authority, and tradition, along with personal faith experience. The modern emphasis on choice and the importance of the individual has often been translated into the view that beliefs and doctrine must be in sync with one's life experiences. An individual moved by experiential religion is not going to take the clergy's word that a particular belief is true. Though the breakdown of church authority can be traced back to the Protestant Reformation and the Enlightenment, spirituality has never been as centered around the individual as it is today.

Self-help and personal empowerment are central to the formation of these spiritual movements. The first self-help programs were based on a generic religiosity, as seen in Alcoholics Anonymous, which invokes a self-defined "higher power." Alcoholics Anonymous began in 1935, when a New York stock investigator, Bill Wilson, helped an Ohio physician, Robert "Dr. Bob" Smith, to stop drinking. Wilson had sobered up with the help of some men from a Protestant evangelical group known as the Oxford Group. But, in founding A.A., Smith and Wilson turned away from brand-name religion.

Seven decades after its founding, A.A. reports more than two million active members. That does not count hundreds of thousands of other people in similar "twelve-step" recovery movements designed to overcome addiction to heroin, cocaine, marijuana, gambling, shopping, food and even religion.

Sometimes called "the secret church," A.A. helps its members overcome addiction and rekindle a sense of the sacred by following a twelve-step path to sobriety and spiritual wholeness. Members are encouraged to "turn our will and our lives over to the care of God *as we understood him*." A.A. places those words in italics to emphasis the non-denominational, non-creedal spirituality of the movement.

In today's marketplace of religion, fewer Americans feel social pressure to stay within the confines of their religious heritage. The wide range of spiritual texts and self-help books comprise an endless menu of spiritual teachings that can be selected and combined. This personalized approach to religious truth is perhaps best illustrated in the many best-selling books in the eclectic library of contemporary spiritual movements. Reading and small group discussions around spiritual and religious books have replaced organized congregational worship for millions of Americans. Some of the major works in this genre include *The Road Less Traveled* by M. Scott Peck, *Care of the Soul* by Thomas Moore; *The Celestine Prophesy* by James Redfield and *The Power of Now* by Eckhart Tolle.

Much of this mix-and-match spirituality falls within the rubric of the so-called "New Age" movement. While few people actually identify their religious affiliation as "New Age," this reluctance to label themselves goes hand in hand with the diffuse and loose-fitting nature of the movement. Participants may have a primary religious affiliation, and then draw various practices and teachings from the movement. Although New Age terminology, prac-

tices, and personalities may be faddish, its eclectic spirituality will endure in the new millennium.

As with any well-publicized trend, the movement was judged to be over just a few years after the media discovered it in the late 1970s and early 1980s. Purists in the New Age vanguard disassociated themselves from crowds of initiates climbing on the bandwagon. While the diffuse nature of the New Age movement makes it hard to define, these unconventional spiritual stirrings have their roots in Eastern religions, occultism, neo-paganism, feminism, political activism, indigenous faiths, human potential teachings, new forms of psychotherapy, and environmentalism. Even its basic philosophy sends seemingly conflicting messages. While the movement stresses spiritual individualism, calling for individuals to discover their own path, it also proclaims a "world is one" communalism.

There is little that is truly "new" in this eclectic movement. Some of it is ancient—especially those elements taken from the Wicca, pagan, and goddess-worship traditions. Other beliefs and practices have their roots in Taoism, Transcendentalism, spiritualism, Mesmerism, parapsychology, New Thought, and Swedenborgianism.

Devotees of the New Age tend to follow the demographic journey of the baby-boom generation. During the 1980s, the New Age expressed itself in natural mystical experiences from channeling to meditation. When the baby boomers reached middle age in the 1990s, the emphasis again shifted, this time to social concerns, technology, environmentalism, and holistic healing. This intense interest in the spirituality of health, healing, and aging will continue as the baby boomers encounter frailty and death. The fact that the New Age is so closely tied to the baby-boom generation guarantees that it will continue to be a force in the coming decades.

In a national survey conducted in January 2002, pollster George Gallup found that one third of Americans now describe themselves as "spiritual but not religious." These are not just spiritual seekers and baby boomers stuck in the sixties. Other recent surveys have found personalized spirituality even more common among "Generation X," those Americans born between 1965 and 1980. Jackson W. Carroll and Wade Clark Roof surveyed more than a thousand Americans and found rising religious individualism in Generation X. For example, nearly 73 percent of the younger generation agreed with the statement: "An individual should arrive at religious beliefs independent of church groups." That compared to 65 percent for the baby boomers (those born from 1945 to 1965) and 60 percent for older Americans.

This eclectic spiritual approach can be found at places like the Esalen Institute in Big Sur, the birthplace of the human potential movement—a precursor to the New Age. This retreat center on the central California coast was founded on the belief that human consciousness and capabilities are evolving. Through a variety of spiritual disciplines, physical training, and psychological therapies, visitors seek to transform their consciousness, improve communication, and deepen compassion for other people. There is no doctrine, no exclusive claims to sacred truth. Esalen also helped popularize various forms of massage and bodywork, which deal with the physical form but are often infused with the sacred sense that they foster the integration of mind, body and spirit.

Other contemporary spiritual movements are based on the revelations of individuals claiming a direct connection to God. In the last half of the twentieth century, one of the most influential of these spiritual mediums was a Columbia University psychologist named Helen Schucman, who claimed that on October 21, 1965, she heard the voice of God telling her, "This is A Course in Miracles. Go take notes." Schucman and a colleague, William Thetford, did exactly that, and twelve years later published *A Course in Miracles*.

There are 750 biblical references in *A Course in Miracles*, but many of them radically reinterpret such familiar Christian terms as "Holy Spirit" and "Son of Man." Some see the Course as a return to the mystical teachings of Jesus—a New Age Christianity without the guilt, sin, fire, and brimstone. For them, the voice is the voice of Jesus. Others see it as a self-taught experiment in spiritual psychotherapy, a tool for personal transformation and a practical guide for improving day-to-day relationships with family, friends, and colleagues. Shortly before the voice ordered her to take notes, Schucman and Thetford visited the Association for Research and Enlightenment in Virginia Beach, the headquarters for followers of psychic Edgar Cayce. Bill Thetford had also been a favorite student of Carl Rogers, a leader in the humanistic psychology movement in the 1950s. Rogers believed humans had a natural impulse for "self-actualization" and personal growth.

Like many contemporary spiritual movements, the Course spread under the radar through countless small groups that regularly gathered to discuss the teachings. Those gatherings are just one example of the broader small group focus in contemporary American spirituality. "These groups see God as a deity that can be known fairly easily by following a few simple steps," observers sociologist Robert Wuthnow. "It's a God of acceptance and love, rather than a God of judgment, justice, or mystery."

Other spiritual movements in the post-World War II generation were fueled by the intense revelatory experiences sometimes produced by psychedelic drugs. Aldous Huxley, the novelist and influential author of *The Doors of Perception*, warned back in 1953 that psychedelic plants can give us a glimpse of heaven or a trip straight to hell. But it was two Harvard University faculty members, Timothy Leary and Richard Alpert, who led a generation that sought cosmic contact through LSD and other psychedelic drugs. Alpert shifted gears and went off to India, where he found a guru and a less-toxic method of mind expansion—meditation and religious devotion. He came back transformed into Ram Dass, the "servant of God," wrote *Be Here Now*, and inspired countless other spiritual seekers.

While the psychedelic drug movement advocated exploration of the inner space, another type of spiritual movement in the post-WWII era was finding religious meaning in outer space. UFO spirituality dates back to a June 24, 1947, report of "flying saucers" buzzing around Mount Rainier in Washington state. Organizations such as the Urantia Brotherhood and the Raelians promoted spiritual movements around extraterrestrial contact. Another UFO cult in Southern California, Heaven's Gate, received widespread media attention in the spring of 1997, when thirty-nine of its members dressed themselves in identical black jeans and Nike shoes, covered their heads in triangular purple shrouds and downed a deadly mixture of seconal and vodka. They believed they would posthumously rendezvous with a UFO trailing the Hale-Bopp comet.

That mass suicide by the followers of Marshall Herff Applewhite revived public concern over the dangers of new spiritual movements organized around charismatic individuals demanding total obedience. Those worries peaked during the "cult wars" of the 1970s when late in that decade more than 900 followers of the Rev. Jim Jones perished in the Peoples Temple mass murder/suicide in Guyana, South America. Those fears were rekindled in 1993 when a hellish inferno engulfed the Branch Davidian compound in Waco, Texas, killing seventy-two followers of David Koresh, an apocalyptic preacher whose sect was an offshoot of the Seventh-day Adventists. Applewhite, who proclaimed himself to be one of the "two witnessses" prophesized in the Book of Revelation, and Jones, a San Francisco-based minister with the Disciples of Christ, also drew heavily upon the apocalyptic visions of the New Testament.

Leaders of the anti-cult movement argue that Heavens Gate, Waco, and Peoples Temple show the potential dangers of religious cults. They began organizing in the early 1970s in response to the aggressive recruitment tactics and abusive behavior in the Children of God/Family International, a religious sect founded in 1968 by David "Moses" Berg, an apocalyptic preacher and free love advocate. Defenders of new religious movements—including many sociologists of religion and other scholars—counter that the vast majority of these groups are harmless and should be left alone to enjoy the benefits of religious liberty guaranteed in the U.S. Constitution.

In the 1980s, a new wave of spiritualists attracted fame, fortune, and significant followings in New Age circles. A Seattle businesswoman, J.Z. Knight, began channeling Ramtha, the 35,000-year-old warrior from the lost continent of Lemuria, and came to represent all that was wacky and weird about New Age spirituality on the West Coast. Ramtha's basic message was a kind of neo-Gnosticism: the idea that the physical world is an illusion and that enlightenment is achieved through various esoteric teachings and spiritual practices.

Another spiritualist guru, Elizabeth Claire Prophet, revived popular interest in Saint Germain, as alchemist, oracle, and semi-legendary "Wonder-man" who dazzled the royal courts of eighteenth-century France before his ascension as a heavenly prophet of God. Generations of occult leaders, including Prophet's late husband, Mark Prophet, have claimed to receive divine dictations from "le Comte de Saint Germain."

Both Prophet and J.Z. Knight draw heavily from Helena Petrovna Blavatsky, the infamous occultist who was born in Russia in 1831, and founded the Theosophy movement. Reacting to the stifling conformity of the Victorian age and the materialism of the Industrial Revolution, Blavatsky created a magical universe of disembodied spirits of white light, Hindu mantras, Buddhist saints and a Great White Brotherhood of heavenly masters. Prophet received divine dictations from ascended masters immortalized a century ago by Blavatsky, while Ramtha came from Lemuria, the mythical lost continent described in Blavatsky's 1888 opus, *The Secret Doctrine*.

Knight's rise in popularity was just part of a "channeling" craze that began in the 1960s that included Jane Roberts and the "Seth" material, continued in the 1970s with Kevin Ryerson as "John,"

Jach Pursel as "Lazaris," and began to die down in the late 1980s with Penny Torres as "Mafu."

Knight and Prophet also follow in the footsteps of Annie Besant. This Englishwoman succeeded Blavatsky as head of the Esoteric Section of the Theosophy Society and anointed a young Indian boy, Krishnamurti, as the new messiah to lead the world into the age of cosmic consciousness. Krishnamurti later renounced his role as New Age savior, and spent decades urging people to think for themselves and find their own path to salvation.

According to his widow, Mark Prophet had been a member of two other influential movements, the Rosicrucians and the Self-Realization Fellowship, founded in Los Angeles in the 1920s by the late Paramahansa Yogananda.

Many contemporary spiritual movements in America were spawned by gurus, yogis, and other spiritual teachers who came to the United States from India, Japan, and elsewhere in Asia in the decades following the immigration reforms of the 1960s. They are primarily covered in other sections of this work dealing with American Hinduism and Buddhism, but include Maharishi Mahesh Yogi, founder of TM (Transcendental Meditation); Swami Satchidananda, founder of the Integral Yoga Institute; Srila Prabhupada, founder of the International Society for Krishna Consciousness (Hare Krishnas); Bhagwan Shree Rajneesh; Shunryu Suzuki, founder of the San Francisco Zen Center; Swami Muktanada, who established Siddha Yoga; and last but not least the Tibetan Buddhist leader Tendzin Gyatso, the fourteenth Dalai Lama.

At the same time, a new openness to Eastern religion provided fertile ground for other East-meets-West synthesizers such as the Rev. Sung Myung Moon, the Korean evangelist and founder of the Unification Church. Eastern spiritual teachings can also be found in popular self-help movements founded by such spiritual entrepreneurs as L. Ron Hubbard, the founder of the Church of Scientology, and Werner Erhard, the man behind the Erhard Seminar Training (EST) phenomenon of the 1970s and 1980s.

Many of the spiritual movements of the late twentieth century were part of the larger counterculture crusade, the sexual revolution, and the environmental movement. The liberation movements of the 1960s and 1970s changed society as they reshaped individual lives. Feminism put women in the Senate and behind mainline Protestant pulpits, while the sexual revolution and the gay rights movement shook church and family to their foundations. A new awareness of the connections between mind and body, the values of meditation, and the benefits of more natural and wholesome foods began on the New Age fringe but spread to medical centers and supermarkets across America. That changed everything from the food we eat and the clothes we wear to the way we heal ourselves and the way we die. Powerful spirits moved the religious revolution of the era: idealism, innovation, empowerment, and the search for authentic experience, and they remain the hallmarks of an extraordinary time in American religious history.

Can an Atheist Be a Good Citizen?

By Richard John Neuhaus

I

THE QUESTION IS ASKED WHETHER ATHEISTS CAN BE good citizens. I do not want to keep you in suspense. I would very much like to answer the question in the affirmative. It seems the decent and tolerant thing to do. But before we can answer the question posed, we should first determine what is meant by atheism. And, second, we must inquire more closely into what is required of a good citizen.

Consider our late friend Sidney Hook. Can anyone deny that he was a very good citizen indeed? During the long contest with totalitarianism he was a much better citizen than many believers, including numerous church leaders, who urged that the moral imperative was to split the difference between the evil empire and human fitness for freedom.

On the other hand, Sidney Hook was not really an atheist. He is more accurately described as a philosophical agnostic, one who says that the evidence is not sufficient to compel us either to deny or affirm the reality of God. Sidney was often asked what he would say when he died and God asked him why he did not believe. His standard answer

was that he would say, "Lord, you didn't supply enough evidence." Some of us are rather confident that Sidney now has all the evidence that he wanted, and we dare to hope that the learning experience is not too painful for him. Unlike many atheists of our time, Sidney Hook believed in reason and evidence that yield what he did not hesitate to call truth. They may have been false gods, but he was not without his gods.

There is atheism and then there is atheism. The Greek *a-theos* meant one who is "without God." It had less to do with whether one believed in God than with whether one believed in the gods of the city or the empire. For his perceived disbelief in the gods, Socrates was charged with atheism. The early Christians were charged with atheism for their insistence that there is no god other than the God whom Jesus called Father. In the eyes of the ancients, to be a-theos was to be outside the civilizational circle of the civitas. To be an atheist was to be subversive. The atheist was a security risk, if not a traitor. Christians were thought to be atheists precisely because they professed the God who judges and debunks the false gods of the community. In the classical world, then, the answer to our question was decisively in the negative: No, an atheist could not be a good citizen. But those whom they called atheists then we do not call atheists today.

Those whom we call atheists in the modern period believe that they are denying what earlier "atheists," such as the Christians, affirmed. That is to say, they deny the reality of what they understand believing Jews and Christians to mean by God. This form of atheism is a post-Enlightenment and largely nineteenth-century phenomenon. It developed a vocabulary—first, of course, among intellectuals, but then becoming culturally pervasive—that was strongly prejudiced against believers. Note the very use of the term "believer" to describe a person who is persuaded of the reality of God. The alternative to being a believer, of course, is to be a "knower." Similarly, a curious usage developed with respect to the categories of faith and reason, the subjective and the objective, and, in the realm of morals, a sharp distinction between fact and value. Belief, faith, subjectivity, values—these were the soft and dubious words relevant to affirming God. Knowledge, reason, objectivity, fact—these were the hard and certain words relevant to denying God. This tendentious vocabulary of modern unbelief is still very much with us today.

Necessarily following from such distortive distinctions are common assumptions about the public and the private. One recalls A. N. Whitehead's axiom that religion is what a man does with his solitude. Even one so religiously musical as William James could write, "Religion...shall mean for us the feelings, acts, and experiences of individual men in their solitude" (*The Varieties of Religious Experience*, Lecture 2). In this construal of matters, we witness a radical departure from the public nature of religion, whether that religion has to do with the ancient gods of the city or with the biblical Lord who rules over the nations. The gods of the city and the God of the Bible are emphatically public. The confinement of the question of God or the gods to the private sphere constitutes what might be described as political atheism. Many today who are believers in private have been persuaded, or intimidated, into accepting political atheism.

Political atheism is a subspecies of practical or methodological atheism. Practical or methodological atheism is, quite simply, the assumption that we can get along with the business at hand without addressing the question of God one way or another. Here the classic anecdote is the response of the Marquis de Laplace to Napoleon Bonaparte. You will recall that when Napoleon observed that Laplace had written a huge book on the system of the universe without mentioning the Author of the universe, Laplace replied, "Sire, I have no need of that hypothesis." When God has become a hypothesis, we have traveled a very long way from both the gods of the ancient city and the God of the Bible. Yet, that distance was necessary to the emergence of what the modern world has called atheism.

In his remarkable work, *At the Origins of Modern Atheism*, Michael Buckley persuasively argues that the god denied by many moderns is a strange god created by the attempts of misguided religionists to demonstrate that god could be proven or known on philosophical grounds alone.

The extraordinary thing to note about this emergence of the denial of the Christian god which Nietzsche celebrated is that Christianity as such, more specifically the person and teaching of Jesus or the experience and history of the Christian Church, did not enter the discussion. The absence of any consideration of Christology is so pervasive throughout serious discussion that it becomes taken for granted; yet it is so stunningly curious that it raises a fundamental issue of the modes of thought: How did the issue of Christianity vs. atheism become purely philosophical? To paraphrase Tertullian: How was it that the only arms to defend the temple were to be found in the Stoa?

As Nietzsche's god had nothing to do with Christology, so, needless to say, the god that he declared dead had nothing to do with Sinai, election, covenant, or messianic promise.

In his notebook, after his death, was found

Pascal's famous assertion of trust in "the God of Abraham, the God of Isaac, the God of Jacob, not of philosophers and scholars." Modern atheism is the product not so much of anti-religion as of religion's replacement of the God of Abraham with the god of the philosophers, and of the philosophers' consequent rejection of that ersatz god. Descartes determined that he would accept as true nothing that could be reasonably doubted, and Christians set about to prove that the existence of God could not be reasonably doubted. Thus did the defenders of religion set faith against the doubt that is integral to the life of faith.

The very phrase, "the existence of God," gave away the game, as though God were one existent among other existents, one entity among other entities, one actor among other actors, whose actions must conform to standards that we have determined in advance are appropriate to being God. The transcendent, the ineffable, the totally other, the God who acts in history, was tamed and domesticated in order to meet the philosophers' job description for the post of God. Not surprisingly, the philosophers determined that the candidates recommended by the friends of religion did not qualify for the post.

The American part of this story is well told by historian James Turner (*Without God, Without Creed: The Origins of Unbelief in America*). "The natural parents of modern unbelief," Turner writes, "turn out to have been the guardians of belief." Many thinking people came at last "to realize that it was religion, not science or social change, that gave birth to unbelief. Having made God more and more like man—intellectually, morally, emotionally—the shapers of religion made it feasible to abandon God, to believe simply in man." Turner's judgment is relentless: "In trying to adapt their religious beliefs to socioeconomic change, new moral challenges, novel problems of knowledge, and the tightening standards of science, the defenders of God slowly strangled Him. If anyone is to be arraigned for deicide, it is not Charles Darwin but his adversary Bishop Samuel Wilberforce, not the godless Robert Ingersoll but the godly Beecher family."

H. L. Mencken observed that the great achievement of liberal Protestantism was to make God boring. That is unfair, of course, as Mencken was almost always unfair, but it is not untouched by truth. The god that was trimmed, accommodated, and retooled in order to be deemed respectable by the "modern mind" was increasingly uninteresting, because unnecessary. Dietrich Bonhoeffer described that god as a "god of the gaps," invoked to fill in those pieces of reality that human knowledge and control had not yet mastered. H. Richard Niebuhr's well known and withering depiction of the gospel of liberal Christianity is very much to the point: "A God without wrath brought men without sin into a kingdom without judgment through the ministrations of a Christ without a Cross." Absent our sin and divine wrath, judgment, and redemption, it is not surprising that people came to dismiss the idea of God not because it is implausible, but because it is superfluous, and, yes, boring.

It would no doubt be satisfying for Christian believers—and for Jews who identify themselves not by the accidents of Jewishness but by the truth of Judaism—to conclude that the God of Abraham, Isaac, Jacob, and Jesus has not been touched by the critiques of atheism. However, while it is true that the god denied by many atheists is not the God of the Bible affirmed by Christians and Jews, there are forms of atheism that do intend to preclude such affirmation, and certainly to preclude such affirmation in public. There is, for example, the more determined materialist who asserts that there simply is nothing and can be nothing outside a closed system of matter. This was the position of the late and unlamented "dialectical materialism" of Communism. It is the position of some scientists today, especially those in the biological sciences who are wedded to evolution as a belief system. (Physicists, as it turns out, are increasingly open to the metaphysical.)

Perhaps more commonly, one encounters varieties of logical positivism that hold that since assertions about God are not empirically verifiable—or, for that matter, falsifiable—they are simply meaningless. In a similar vein, analytical philosophers would instruct us that "God talk" is, quite precisely, nonsense. This is not atheism in the sense to which we have become accustomed, since it claims that denying God is as much nonsense as affirming God. It is atheism, however, in the original sense of a-theos, of being without God. Then there is the much more radical position that denies not only the possibility of truth claims about God but the possibility of claims to truth at all—at least as "truth" has usually been understood in our history. Perhaps today's most prominent proponent of this argument in America is Richard Rorty. This is not the atheism that pits reason against our knowledge of God; this is the atheism of unreason.

Rorty is sometimes portrayed, and portrayed himself, as something of an eccentric gadfly. In fact, along with Derrida, Foucault, and other Heideggerian epigones of Nietzsche, Rorty was the guru of an academic establishment of increasing influence in our intellectual culture. Here we encounter the apostles of a relativism that denies it is relativism because it denies that there is any alternative to relativism, and therefore the term relativism is itself "meaningless." They are radically anti-foundationalist. That is to say, they contend that there are no conclusive arguments underlying our assertions, except the conclusive argument that there are no conclusive arguments. They reject any "correspondence theory" of truth. There is no coherent connection between what we think and say and the reality "out there." Truth is what the relevant community of discourse agrees to say is true.

The goal, in this way of thinking, is self-actualization, indeed self-creation. The successful life is the life lived as a *novum*, an autobiography that has escaped the "used vocabularies" of the past. This argument has its academic strongholds in literary criticism and sectors of philosophy, but it undergirds assumptions that are increasingly widespread in our intellectual culture. If personal and group self-actu-

alization is the end, arguments claiming to deal with truth are but disguised stratagems for the exercise of will and the quest for power. Whether the issue is gender, sexual orientation, or race, we are told that the purpose is to change the ideational "power structure" presently controlled by oppressors who disingenuously try to protect the status quo by appeals to objective truth and intersubjective reason.

The only truth that matters is the truth that is instrumental to self-actualization. Thus truth is in service to "identity." If, for instance, one has the temerity to object that there is no evidence that Africans discovered the Americas before Columbus, he is promptly informed that he is the tool of hegemonic Eurocentrism. In such a view, the "social construction of reality" (to use the language of Peter Berger and Thomas Luckmann) takes on ominous new dimensions as it is asserted that all of reality, without remainder, is constructed to serve the will to power and self-actualization. Brevity requires that I describe this approach with broad strokes, but, alas, the description is no caricature.

But are people who embrace this view atheists? They brush aside the question as "not serious," for the theism upon which atheism depends is, in this view, not serious. As with relativism and irrationality, so also with atheism—the words only make sense in relation to the opposites from which they are derived. Of course privately, or for purposes of a particular community, any words might be deemed useful in creating the self. One might even find it meaningful to speak about "Nature and Nature's God." People can be permitted to talk that way, so long as they understand that such talk has no public purchase. Rorty's "liberal ironist" can employ any vocabulary, no matter how fantastical, so long as he does not insist that it is true in a way that makes a claim upon others, and so long as he does not act on that vocabulary in a manner that limits the freedom of others to construct their own realities.

There is indeed irony in the fact that some who think of themselves as theists eagerly embrace deconstructionism's operative atheism. Today's cultural scene is awash in what are called "new spiritualities." A recent anthology of "America's new spiritual voices" includes contributions promoting witchcraft, ecological mysticism, devotion to sundry gods and goddesses, and something that presents itself as Zen physio-psychoanalysis. All are deemed to be usable vocabularies for the creation of the self. The book is recommended by a Roman Catholic theologian who writes that it "turns us away from the 'truths' outside ourselves that lead to debate and division, and turns us toward the Inner Truth that is beyond debate." But theism—whether in relation to the gods of the civitas or the God of Abraham—is devotion to that which is external to ourselves. In that light, it is evident that many of the burgeoning "spiritualities" in contemporary culture are richly religionized forms of atheism.

There is additional irony. Beyond pop-spiritualities and Rortian nihilism, a serious argument is being made today against a version of rationality upon which Enlightenment atheism was premised. Here one thinks preeminently of Alasdair MacIntyre, and especially of his most recent work, *Three Rival Versions of Moral Enquiry*. MacIntyre effectively polemicizes against a construal of rationality that understands itself to be universal, disinterested, autonomous, and transcending tradition. Our situation, he contends, is one of traditions of rationality in conflict. MacIntyre's favored tradition is Thomism's synthesis of Aristotle and Augustine. If I read him correctly, MacIntyre is prepared to join forces with the Rortians in debunking the hegemonic pretensions of the autonomous and foundational reason that has so long dominated our elite intellectual culture. After the great debunking, all the cognitive cards will have to be put on the table and we can then have at it. Presumably, the tradition that can provide the best account of reality will win out.

If that is MacIntyre's proposal, it strikes me as a very dangerous game. True, in exposing the fallacious value-neutrality of autonomous and traditionless reason, the academy is opened to the arguments of eminently reasonable theism. But, in the result-ing free-for-all, it is opened to much else as well. It is made vulnerable to the Nietzschean will to power that sets the rules, and those rules are designed to preclude the return of the gods or God in a manner that claims public allegiance. For one tradition of reason (e.g., Thomism) to form a coalition, even a temporary coalition, with unreason in order to undo another tradition of reason (e.g., the autonomous "way of the mind") is, to my way of thinking, a perilous tactic.

And yet something like this may be the future of our intellectual culture. In our universities, Christians, Jews, and, increasingly, Muslims will be free to contend for their truths. Just as lesbians, Marxists, Nietzscheans, and devotees of The Great Earth Goddess are free to contend for theirs. It is a matter of equal opportunity propaganda. But—and again there is delicious irony—the old methodological atheism and value-neutrality, against which the revolution was launched, may nonetheless prevail.

In other words, every party will be permitted to contend for their truths so long as they acknowledge that they are *their* truths, and not *the* truth. Each will be permitted to propagandize, each will have to propagandize if it is to hold its own, because it is acknowledged that there is no common ground for the alternative to propaganda, which is reasonable persuasion. Of course history, including the history of ideas, is full of surprises. But there is, I believe, reason to fear that theism, when it plays by the rules of the atheism of unreason, will be corrupted and eviscerated. The method becomes the message. Contemporary Christian theology already provides all too many instances of the peddling of truths that are in service to truths other than the truth of God.

II

We have touched briefly, then, on the many faces of atheism—of living and thinking a-theos, without God or the gods. There is the atheism of the early Christians, who posited God against the gods. There is the atheism of Enlightenment rationalists who, committed to undoubtable certainty, rejected the god whom religionists designed to fit that criterion. There is the practical atheism of Laplace, who had no need of "that hypothesis" in order to get on with what he had to do. There is the weary atheism of those who grew bored with liberalism's god created in the image and likeness of good liberals. There is the more thorough atheism of Nietzschean relativism that dare not speak its name, that cannot speak its name, lest in doing so it implicitly acknowledge that there is an alternative to relativism. And, finally, there is the atheism of putative theists who peddle religious truths that are true for you if you find it useful to believe them true.

Can these atheists be good citizens? It depends, I suppose, on what is meant by good citizenship. We may safely assume that the great majority of these people abide by the laws, pay their taxes, and may even be congenial and helpful neighbors. But can a person who does not acknowledge that he is accountable to a truth higher than the self, external to the self, really be trusted? Locke and Rousseau, among many other worthies, thought not. However confused their theology, they were sure that the social contract was based upon nature, upon the way the world really is. Rousseau's "civil religion" was apparently itself a social construct, but Locke was convinced that the fear of a higher judgment, even an eternal judgment, was essential to citizenship.

It follows that an atheist could not be trusted to be a good citizen, and therefore could not be a citizen at all. Locke is rightly celebrated as a champion of religious toleration, but not of irreligion. "Those are not at all to be tolerated who deny the being of a God," he writes in "A Letter Concerning Toleration." "Promises, covenants, and oaths, which are the bonds of human society, can have no hold upon an atheist. The taking away of God, though but even in thought, dissolves all." The taking away of God dissolves all. Every text becomes pretext, every interpretation misinterpretation, and every oath a deceit.

James Madison, in his famed "Memorial and Remonstrance of 1785," wrote to similar effect. It is always being forgotten that for Madison and the other founders, religious freedom is an unalienable right that is premised upon unalienable duty. "It is the duty of every man to render to the Creator such homage and such only as he believes to be acceptable to him. This duty is precedent, both in order of time and in degree of obligation, to the claims of Civil Society." Then follows a passage that could hardly be more pertinent to the question that prompts our present reflection: "Before any man can be considered as a member of Civil Society, he must be considered as a subject of the Governour of the Universe: And if a member of Civil Society, who enters into any subordinate Association, must always do it with a reservation of his duty to the General Authority; much more must every man who becomes a member of any particular Civil Society, do it with a saving of his allegiance to the Universal Sovereign."

State constitutions could and did exclude atheists from public office. The federal Constitution, in Article VI, would simply impose no religious test. In reaction to the extreme secularist bias of much historical scholarship, some writers in recent years have attempted to portray the founders as Bible-believing, orthodox, even born-again evangelical Christians. That is much too much. It is well worth recalling, however, how much they had in common with respect to religious and philosophical beliefs. While a few were sympathetic to milder versions of Deism and some were rigorous Calvinists in the Puritan tradition, almost all assumed a clearly Christian, and clearly Protestant, construal of reality. In the language of contemporary discourse, the founders were "moral realists." This is amply demonstrated from many sources, not least the Declaration and the Constitution, and especially the preamble of the latter. The "good" was for the founders a reality not of their own fabrication, nor was it merely the "conventionalism" of received moral tradition.

The founders' notion of the social contract was

not a truncated and mechanistic contrivance of calculated self-interest. Their understanding was more in the nature of a compact, premised upon a sense of covenantal purpose guiding this *novus ordo seclorum*. That understanding of a covenant encompassing the contract was, in a time of supreme testing, brought to full and magisterial articulation by Abraham Lincoln. The Constitution represented not a deal struck, but a nation "so conceived and so dedicated."

In such a nation, an atheist can be a citizen, but, I would contend, he cannot be a good citizen. A good citizen does more than abide by the laws. A good citizen is able to give an account, a morally compelling account, of the regime of which he is part. He is able to justify its defense against its enemies, and to convincingly recommend its virtues to citizens of the next generation so that they, in turn, can transmit the regime to citizens yet unborn. This regime of liberal democracy, of republican self-governance, is not self-evidently good and just. An account must be given. *Reasons* must be given. They must be reasons that draw authority from that which is higher than the self, from that which is external to the self, from that to which the self is ultimately obliged.

An older form of atheism pitted reason against the knowledge of God. The newer atheism is the atheism of unreason. It is much the more dangerous because the more insidious. Fortunately, the overwhelming majority of Americans—and, I believe, the majority of our intellectual elites, if put to the test—are not atheists of any of the varieties we have discussed. They believe that there are good reasons for this ordering of the civitas, reasons that have public purchase, reasons that go beyond contingent convenience, reasons that entail what is just, the laws of nature, and maybe even the will of God.

The final irony, of course, is that those who believe in the God of Abraham, Isaac, Jacob, and Jesus, I believe, turn out to be the best citizens. Those who were once called atheists are now the most reliable defenders, not of the gods, but of the good reasons for this regime of ordered liberty. Such people are the best citizens not despite, but because their loyalty to the civitas is qualified by a higher loyalty. Among the best of the good reasons they give in justifying this regime is that it is a regime that makes a sharply limited claim upon the loyalty of its citizens. The ultimate allegiance of the faithful is not to the regime or to its constituting texts, but to the City of God and the sacred texts that guide our path toward that end for which we were created. They are dual citizens, so to speak, in a regime that, as Madison and others well understood, was designed for such duality. When the regime forgets itself and reestablishes the gods of the civitas, even if it be in the name of liberal democracy, the followers of the God of Abraham have no choice but to invite the opprobrium of once again being "atheists."

I am well aware that there are those who will agree with the gravamen of this argument, but for quite different reasons. They do not themselves believe, but they recognize the importance of religion as a "useful lie" essential to securing this kind of public order. It is true, and it is sad. It is sad because they do not believe, and it is sadder because they are prepared to use, and thereby abuse, the name of the God whom they do not honor.

But of course they are right about religion and this public order. It is an order that was not conceived and dedicated by atheists, and cannot today be conceived and dedicated anew by atheists. In times of testing—and every time is a time of testing for this American experiment in ordered liberty—a morally convincing account must be given. You may well ask, convincing to whom? One obvious answer in a democracy, although not the only answer, is this: convincing to a majority of their fellow citizens. Giving such an account is required of good citizens. And that is why I reluctantly conclude that atheists cannot be good citizens.

∞

Serenity at Last

By Harold Rabinowitz

God, give us grace to accept with serenity
the things that cannot be changed,
Courage to change the things that should be changed,
And the wisdom to distinguish the one from the other.

THIS IS A CLASSIC VERSION OF WHAT IS KNOWN as "The Serenity Prayer"—it is without doubt the most revered and most famous prayer of modern times and the only rival to the Lord's Prayer in popularity in the English– and German–speaking worlds in the last hundred years. As noted, it is named after the last word on the first line, although, as Elisabeth Sifton, the daughter of the man most closely associated with the prayer, the Protestant theologian Reinhold Niebuhr, points out in her book, *The Serenity Prayer* (Norton: 2003), it could just as easily have been named the "Grace" prayer, the "Courage" prayer, or the "Wisdom" prayer. But The Serenity Prayer is how it is known, and as widely known as it is, it is even more widely known as the Alcoholics Anonymous credo.

According to the AA history website, Bill W. himself was shown the prayer by a New York member, who saw it unattributed in a 1942 New York *Herald Tribune* obituary. "Never had we seen so much of AA reflected in so few words," Bill W. wrote, that he had Ruth Hock, the Fellowship's first secretary, have 500 cards printed with the prayer and distributed to members. Those cards did not attribute any authorship, but over the years, AA acknowledged Reinhold Niebuhr as the author and even set the date—1943—and the place where Niebuhr had composed the prayer—a little stone cottage in Heath, Massachusetts, where the Niebuhr family had indeed then resided. But over the years, AA also added many pieces of text to the original prayer, texts that may have reflected AA values, but which conflicted with the spirit of the original prayer (for reasons we shall see below), and the organization also wistfully entertained many fanciful theories about other possible origins of the prayer, none of which have stood up to scrutiny.

In 1944, a neighbor and friend of Dr. Niebuhr, Howard Robbins, received Neibuhr's permission to include the prayer in a booklet published by the Federal Council of Churches and distributed to army chaplains and servicemen. The USO published an additional printing of several hundred thousand copies which were distributed to servicemen worldwidw; in all the booklets, the prayer was attributed to Reinhold Niebuhr.

By the early 1960s, the Serenity prayer was ubiquitous on greeting cards, wall-hangings, embroideries, inspirational prints, candles, keychains...even Zippo lighters. Rarely did Dr. Niebuhr's name appear on any of it, but by then, the name Reinhold Niebuhr was internationally known. [*See his biography on page 213.*]

Making his mark speaking out for social justice from his pulpit in the working-class area of Detroit, Niebuhr spoke eloquently about such unnervingly new ideas as "applied Christianity" and "practical Christian realism," notions that made it impossible to ignore the plight of exploited workers, discriminated minorities, and, most of all, persecuted peoples wherever they where on this God's earth. While others in his own church and other denominations counseled isolationism and neutrality toward Fascism, Nazism in Germany and Communism in Russia, Niebuhr was strident in his condemnation and passionate in his appeal to the moral sense he believed (and prayed) existed in all human beings.

In the thirty-two years he taught at Union Theological Seminary in New York to 1960, he forged by all accounts one of the most important careers in American religious history, producing works that will stand as the finest examples of American theological thinking—and indeed, in many ways, defining what an American theology means. His works and words influenced important leaders in every field in American life and on the world stage. His influence was acknowledged by such diverse personages as Martin Luther King, Jr., Ronald Reagan, Robert Kennedy, and Barack Obama. He received many honors, including the Presidential Medal of Freedom from President Lyndon Johnson in 1964, and an honorary doctorate from the Hebrew University in Jerusalem in 1967. Niebuhr was eulogized at his funeral by Rabbi Abraham Joshua Heschel and honored by Arthur M. Schlesinger, Jr., and Lionel and Diana Trilling.

It was therefore not without some amusement that we witnessed the uproar that ensued when a law librarian at Yale University wrote a piece for the Alumni magazine in 2008 under the title, "Who Wrote the Serenity Prayer?" The man was Fred R. Shapiro, author of nine books, including the newly published Yale Book of Quotations (Yale University Press: 2006). Prof. Shapiro had made a reputation as a debunker of mis-attributions of famous quotes,

many of which he has corrected in his authoritative book. Shapiro, it should be noted is no ordinary debunker or author of popular reference books. His works are meticulously researched and he has greatly influenced such august reference institutions as the Oxford English Dictionary. His column for the Yale alumni magazine, "You can quote them," may be light and sprightly, but the scholarship is serious and the issues treated in earnest.

So it was not surprising that the piece he wrote in which he indicated that a computer search of archives had come up with a number of pieces that had appeared in the 1930s in which language that was similar (though not exact) to the language of the Serenity Prayer predating the previously accepted Niebuhr-authorship date of 1942, made the front page of the *New York Times*. Shapiro further indicated that Niebuhr himself had acknowledged in an offhand way that it was certainly possible that similar formulations had circulated in the 1930s. Niebuhr was quoted using what I suppose was a Mid-westernism, saying the language may have been "spooking around for years." Shapiro also reported, however, that Dr. Niebuhr was certain that he had composed and originated the prayer.

The battle that ensued was, well, a spectacle. The Internet and print publications were humming with arguments and counter-arguments about how *only* Reinhold Niebuhr could have written the Serenity Prayer, and anyone who uttered anything similar in the Thirties *must* have heard it from him at a sermon or lecture somewhere, and that the methodology of computer searches of archives was suspect because, well, just because. Rejoinders begat rejoinders—Shapiro asked for comments on the Freakanomics blog (to which he is a regular contributor) on the validity of his arguments. And Sifton appealed to her book, which provided an eye-witness account of the creation of the work in question by her father—albeit in 1943. One would never have guessed that the Serenity Prayer occupied barely a page in any of the biographies of Niebuhr, such as those by Richard W. Fox (1985) and Charles C. Brown (2002). Niebuhr, whom I did not know personally, was, by all accounts, a man with a "playful sense of humor." I believe he would have had a good chuckle over the row Shapiro's article had caused.

The entire circus came to an end in November 2009, when Duke researcher Stephen Goransen posted a message on the American Dialectical Society at 11:26 a.m. on November 19, that he had found an article in a Christian student newsletter dated November 1937, which cited the Serenity Prayer virtually as we now have it and attributed it to Reinhold Niebuhr. Although some of Shapiro's problem sources predated 1937, he was evidently so happy to discover *something* that showed Niebuhr had been credited with the prayer before 1942, that he quickly threw in the proverbial towel and magnanimously capitulated. I say "evidently" because he e-mailed his retraction to Laurie Goodstein, the *Times* reporter who wrote the original story, at 11:49 that same morning—just twenty-three minutes later.

For me, however, the issue was resolved the day it started. Among the comments that appeared to Fred Shapiro's original article in the Yale Alumni Magazine was one by (irony of ironies) the same Stephen Goranson who would settle the matter fifteen months later. His comment (appearing only on the magazine website, of course) cited a 1934 article from *Sewanee Review* by a June Purcell Guild, entitled, "Why Go South?" about the difficulties Northerners encounter moving to a southern state in the years after the Civil War. She wrote: "North or South, not all have [the] serenity to accept what cannot be helped." Goranson believed this was an example of a precursor of the Serenity Prayer, and the other examples he and Shapiro adduced were no better. But it seemed to me that Jane Guild had no more claim on the provenance of the Serenity Prayer than Abe Lincoln's butcher had a claim on the provenance of the Gettysburg Address for having once sold Lincoln four score and seven pounds of prime ribs for his Fourth of July barbecue.

Basically—posturing and carrying-on aside—Sifton was right: Niebuhr's contribution wasn't so much composing the prayer as it was recognizing its unique message and understanding its uniquely American character. For Niebuhr, the American religious temprament begins with serenity. Not with euphoric ecstasy or mindless hysteria. The responsible religious citizen must be able to first calmly and serenely assess the situation and determine what is given, unalterable, unchangeable. And just as calmly accept it. This responsible religious personality must then summon (through prayer) inner strength—let's call it courage—to address that which can, ought, and *must* be changed, determined just as calmly, just as serenely and just as deliberatively. And then that responsible religious person must maintain that calm vision, discernment—that wisdom—to constantly assess what can be changed, and what cannot.

Compare that with the frenzied mobs entranced by demagogues and driven to murderous zeal by hate and lurid lies; with goose-stepping armies of automatons trampling on the weak and powerless and satisfying blood-lust in the name of religion and in the name of the unholy, unsacred, masquerading as something sanctified by the logic of power and vengeance. Niebuhr saw nothing Godly in any of that—only pain, degradation, and evil. His gift to us was not only the Serenity Prayer, but also its message—only by calmly taking control of ourselves and our world can we, might we, fulfill our Godly missions on earth. That is why what has been added to the Serenity Prayer—submission to the Divine; complete trust in a Higher Power; abandonment of self-reliance—is contradictory to the Prayer, though it may be essential to the AA program.

As Niebuhr biographer Richard W. Fox wrote to the Times after the dust had settled, "Putting the spotlight on Niebuhr's authorship (whether he was the sole "originator" of the prayer" or the major "codifier" of fragments already floating in the homiletic air) may help redirect attention toward the social Gospel *meaning* the prayer conveyed to Niebuhr and his many liberal disciples…"—bringing serenity to us all, at last.

The Spirituality of Despair

By Ames K. Sweet

B Y THE TIME ALCOHOLICS ANONYMOUS (A.A.) HAD percolated its way into America's public consciousness in the late 1940s, '50s, and '60s, aided in part by critically-acclaimed films such as "The Lost Weekend" with Ray Milland and "The Days of Wine and Roses" with Jack Lemmon, it had been quietly at work behind the scenes since its founding in 1935, helping scores of alcoholics transform the pain and tragedy of active alcoholism into salvation and hope.

At its core, Alcoholics Anonymous, the fellowship that launched the modern-day recovery movement, has always been based on the lifesaving communication between one alcoholic and another. In late 1930s America, the era into which Alcoholics Anonymous was born, the idea of one alcoholic talking therapeutically with another, resulting in the betterment of both, was big news, changing the plane of alcoholism treatment forever. Traditionally a vertical relationship—with the communication going up and down between doctor and patient—A.A. brought a horizontal approach to alcoholism treatment that revolutionized the way people thought about alcoholics. This transmission

of hope, passing from one person to another, opened the way for a new kind of spirituality, the spirituality of despair, wherein fellow sufferers found that by reaching out to each other, they could accomplish what neither had been able to do alone: stay sober.

Often described in early A.A. literature as a "chain reaction," the active ingredient, the agent of change in this reaction was the particular identification between alcoholics, the recognition that another had gone through similar trials and had found a way to stay away from a drink.

From an historical perspective, this chain reaction got its start when Bill Wilson, A.A.'s eventual co-founder, received a visit from an old friend, a former drinking buddy, who had found a way to get sober with the help of the Oxford Groups, an evangelical movement which flourished in the 1920s and early 1930s and was led by one-time Lutheran minister Dr. Frank Buchman. This friend, a man named Ebby Thatcher, arrived one day on Bill's doorstep, with a message of hope he wished to impart to Bill, who was hungover at the time and floundering in the throes of his own alcoholism.

Yet, as Bill would later say, for some reason, he was ready to hear and accept what Ebby had to say:

> Ebby told me his story, carefully detailing his drinking experiences of recent years. Thus he drew me still closer to him. I knew beyond doubt that he had lived in that strange and hopeless world where I still was. This fact established his identification with me. At length our channel of communication was wide open and I was ready for his message.
>
> And what was his message? All A.A.s know what it was: honesty with oneself, leading to a fearless moral inventory of character defects; a revelation of these defects to another human being, the first humble and faltering steps away from isolation and guilt; willingness to face up to those we had harmed, making all possible restitution. A thorough house-cleaning inside and out was indicated, and then we were ready to devote ourselves in service to others, using the understanding and language of the heart, and seeking no gain or reward. Then there was that vital attitude of dependence on God, or a higher power.
>
> None of Ebby's ideas were really new. I'd heard them all before. But coming over his powerful transmission line they were not at all what in other circumstances I would have regarded as conventional cliches for good church behavior. They appeared to me as living truths which might liberate me as they had liberated him. He could reach me at depth. ("Language of the Heart", The AA Grapevine, Inc., NY, NY, p. 245)

This link, this connection at depth, while based on religious principles, has always been considered spiritual in nature, and, while much of its early membership was drawn from the ranks of America's predominantly white, middle-class, church-going population of the time, the program these alcoholics developed was clear in its separation between religion and spirituality.

Codified in its literature from the start, A.A. has always been careful not to present itself in religious terms and, while highlighting the healing benefits of an individual alcoholic's relationship with God, A.A.'s pioneers went to great lengths to keep the doors of A.A. as wide open as possible by not defining just what God they were talking about. With early membership claiming a number of agnostics and atheists, it was important to the early members to be inclusive rather than exclusive and they understood that religion was an element that could easily divide—and thus destroy—the fledgling fellowship.

One of the fundamental building blocks of the A.A. program, upon which the recovery of millions of alcoholics has been built, is the set of principles and actions known as the Twelve Steps. These steps, based on the trial-and-error experience of A.A.'s early members, outline just how an alcoholic can gain and maintain sobriety, and the concept of God is central among them.

Practiced as a way of life, the Twelve Steps include elements found in the spiritual teachings of many faiths. However, in the formulation of these steps, after considerable discussion within the small but growing group of autonomous alcoholics who were recovering in the 1930s, provisions were made to advance the separation between spirituality and religion, and God was referred to in the steps simply as a "Power greater than ourselves," and later, "God, as we understand Him," opening the door to individual rather than group determination of a "Higher Power."

Further, as A.A. began to consider its relations with the outside world and to develop a working public relations policy, the A.A. Preamble was developed, stating, in part, "A.A. is not allied with any sect, denomination, politics, organization or institution, does not wish to engage in any controversy, neither endorses nor opposes any causes." This Preamble is today read at the beginning of almost every meeting of Alcoholics Anonymous worldwide and serves as a constant reminder that A.A. is neither religious, political, nor controversial in any way.

As noted by a sober priest in the late 1970s in A.A.'s monthly magazine, The A.A. *Grapevine*, "One of the great liberating and reassuring elements of the whole Twelve Steps experience is the realization that I am making this journey of recovery hand in hand with the God of my understanding. I need not explain nor justify this relationship to anyone. In A.A., each member's belief has always been private, individual, sacred. The founding fathers of the program were at great pains to make this abundantly clear... If, then, there is the slightest insinuation in the Twelve Steps that this God of our understanding can be discovered, loved, and served only within the confines of a particular church or denomination, such an insinuation completely escapes me."

A.A. has had many friends in the world of religion, as it has in the worlds of medicine, psychiatry and business. Among them was Dr. Harry Emerson Fosdick, pastor of New York City's Riverside Church, a man whose face graced the cover of Time magazine in October of 1930. In the book *Alcoholics Anonymous Comes of Age,* Dr. Fosdick said of A.A., "The meetings of Alcoholics Anonymous are the only place, so far as I know, where Roman Catholics, Jews, all kinds of Protestants, and even agnostics get together harmoniously... They do not talk theology. Many of them would say that they know nothing about it. What they do know is that in their utter helplessness, they were introduced to a Power greater than themselves, in contact with whom they found a strong resource which made possible a victory that seemed incredible. I have listened to many learned arguments about God, but for honest-to-goodness experiential evidence of God, His power personally appropriated and His reality indubitably assured, give me a good meeting of A.A.!"

The spiritual chain reaction that grew from Ebby and Bill, to Dr. Bob Smith (to whom Bill car-

ried the message and who, along with Bill, is considered A.A.'s co-founder), has stretched to countless alcoholics in cultures as diverse as imaginable. A.A. today has an estimated 2,000,000 members, consisting of more than 106,000 groups located in more than 180 countries. A.A.'s literature has been translated into languages such as Afrikaans, Arabic, Hindi, Nepali, Persian, Swahili, and Vietnamese, among many others, and its twelve-step method has been adapted widely by fellowships of people recovering from various addictions, compulsive behaviors, and mental health problems. Today, the recovery movement includes such established organizations as Narcotics Anonymous, Overeaters Anonymous, Debtors Anonymous, Gamblers Anonymous, and the Al-Anon Family Groups (for the family and friends of alcoholics), along with such newcomers as Anorexics and Bulimics Anonymous, Clutterers Anonymous, and Sex Addicts Anonymous.

Turning addiction and despair into salvation and hope is a hallmark of the modern-day recovery movement. At its core is identification between one sufferer and another, a horizontal spiritual link in the long chain of recovery stretching around the world.

APPENDIX

The Twelve Steps of Alcoholics Anonymous*

1. We admitted we were powerless over alcohol— that our lives had become unmanageable.
2. Came to believe that a Power greater than ourselves could restore us to sanity.
3. Made a decision to turn our will and our lives over to the care of God as we understood Him.
4. Made a searching and fearless moral inventory of ourselves.
5. Admitted to God, to ourselves, and to ano-ther human being the exact nature of our wrongs.
6. Were entirely ready to have God remove all these defects of character.

7. Humbly asked Him to remove our shortcomings.

8. Made a list of all persons we had harmed, and became willing to make amends to them all.

9. Made direct amends to such people wherever possible, except when to do so would injure them or others.

10. Continued to take personal inventory and when we were wrong promptly admitted it.

11. Sought through prayer and meditation to improve our conscious contact with God, as we understood Him, praying only for knowledge of His will for us and the power to carry that out.

12. Having had a spiritual awakening as the result of these Steps, we tried to carry this message to alcoholics, and to practice these principles in all our affairs.

The A.A. Preamble[#]

Alcoholics Anonymous is a fellowship of men and women who share their experience, strength and hope with each other that they may solve their common problem and help others to recover from alcoholism. The only requirement for membership is a desire to stop drinking. There are no dues or fees for A.A. membership; we are self-supporting through our own contributions. A.A. is not allied with any sect, denomination, politics, organization or institution; does not wish to engage in any controversy, neither endorses nor opposes any causes. Our primary purpose is to stay sober and help other alcoholics to achieve sobriety.

Copyright © A.A. World Services, Inc.
 # Copyright © The A.A. Grapevine, Inc.

"Soup, Soap, and Salvation"
A Brief History of the Salvation Army

IN 1865, IN ENGLAND, A METHODIST MINISTER NAMED William Booth was traveling the country, preaching and sharing God's word to all who would listen, trying to persuade others to become Christians, too. One day he found himself in the East End of London, preaching to crowds of people in the streets. Some missioners heard him speaking and were so impressed by his powerful preaching that they asked him to lead a series of evangelistic meetings they were organizing.

Booth agreed to lead the meetings and this proved to be the end of his wanderings as an independent traveling evangelist. His renown as a religious leader spread throughout London, and Booth soon realized he had found his destiny.

Along with his wife Catherine, Booth hit the streets of London with the fervor of a military crusader. He preached hope and salvation to those assembled, most of whom were desperately poor and many of whom were drunkards. Realizing it was hard to interest people in religion when they were cold, hungry and dirty, he championed the cause of "soup, soap, and salvation," surmising that if you could fill a man's stomach and clean him up a bit, he might be more eager to hear your message.

Initially, Booth's plan had been to stabilize his converts then funnel them to London's established churches, but he soon discovered that former prostitutes, gamblers, and thieves were not welcomed by mainstream denominations. So, Booth formed his own movement, which he called The Christian Mission, where he continued giving his new converts spiritual direction, challenging them to save others like themselves.

The mission grew slowly, yet the results remained discouraging. The mission was just another of the many charitable groups trying to help the disenfranchised poor in London's East End. But, one morning in 1878, while reviewing the Christian Mission's Annual Report, Booth noticed a statement characterizing his organization. It read, "The Christian Mission is a Volunteer Army." Something about that phrase caught his attention and in a moment of inspiration, Booth crossed out the words "Volunteer Army" and wrote in "Salvation Army."

Spiritual Warfare

Responding to a recurrent theme in Christianity that saw the Church engaged in spiritual warfare against evil, the new name appealed to Booth's followers. The idea of an army fighting sin caught the imagination of the people and the newly-minted Salvation Army began to grow rapidly.

The Army utilized certain soldierly features such as uniforms, flags and ranks to identify, inspire and regulate its activities. Members called themselves soldiers and Booth himself was known by his followers as "General."

Despite its rapid increase in numbers and growing success, the Salvationists provoked opposition, attracting many enemies. Pub and brothel owners in particular were angered when many of their former customers were converted in Booth's Army. Their profits fell and business suffered.

Many people condemned Booth's methods, yet the Salvationists continued with the evangelical idea that if the sinful did not come to them, then they must take the gospel message into the streets. Many towns and villages were soon aware of the Army's presence as the Salvationists marched in procession

with flags and banners waving, searching for converts. Such processions often incited anger and all over the country Salvationists were faced with angry mobs often hurling dead rats and cats, rocks, rotten vegetables and even burning coals to show their hatred of the new movement.

Gradually, however, when people began to see the value of the Army's work and the beneficial effect on the lives of those who responded to the gospel message, attitudes slowly changed.

Coming to America

Meanwhile, the Army was gaining a foothold in the United States. Lieutenant Eliza Shirley had left England to join her parents, who had migrated to America. In 1879, she held the first meeting of the Salvation Army in America, in Philadelphia. The Salvationists were received enthusiastically and Shirley wrote to General Booth, begging for reinforcements. None were available at first, yet glowing reports of the work in Philadelphia eventually convinced Booth to send an official group in 1880 to pioneer the work in America.

On March 10, 1880, Booth sent a delegation of Salvationists to New York City. At their first official street meeting these pioneers were ridiculed, arrested, and attacked, as had happened in Great Britain. Yet, three years later, they had expanded their operation into California, Connecticut, Indiana, Kentucky, Maryland, Massachusetts, Michigan, Missouri, New Jersey, New York, Ohio, and Pennsylvania. In 1886, President Grover Cleveland received a delegation of Salvation Army officers and gave the organization a warm personal endorsement. This was the first recognition from the White House and would be followed by similar receptions from succeeding presidents.

General Booth's death in 1912 was a great loss to the Salvation Army. However, His eldest son, Bramwell Booth, succeeded him as "General."

TODAY'S MISSION

The Salvation Army serves in 113 countries and provides services in 175 different languages. The organization operates hundreds of rehabilitation centers for the physically and socially handicapped, provides education at every level in more than 1,700 schools and helps more than 32 million people annually in the United States alone.

Each recruit to the Salvation Army abstains from the use of alcoholic beverages, drugs and tobacco, and signs a membership document, known as the "Soldier's Covenant," before enrolling as a Salvation Army soldier. The covenant, originally called the "Articles of War," states allegiance to the Army's eleven articles of faith and recognizes the soldier's acceptance of Jesus Christ as his or her Lord and Savior.

The Salvation Army is an integral part of the Christian Church, although distinctive in government and practice. The Army's doctrine follows the mainstream of Christian belief and its articles of faith emphasize God's saving purposes. Its objects are the advancement of the Christian religion, of education, the relief of poverty, and other charitable objects beneficial to society or the community of mankind as a whole. In short, the Army seeks today, as it did in the beginning, to provide soup, soap, and salvation to the world's forgotten people.

According to David Giles, at the International Headquarters of the Salvation Army, "As Christians, we cannot opt out of society. We must engage with it, influencing it for good."

The theologian Karl Barth once said, "You need to have the Bible in one hand and the newspaper in the other." If we can imagine Jesus in the desperate situations we read about, we cannot be ambivalent. We cannot sit back and delude ourselves into thinking that human rights abuses in North Korea have nothing to do with us. We can't pretend that solving the issue of crippling poverty in sub-Saharan Africa is somebody else's problem. We must not convince ourselves that the melting of the polar ice caps just means we can enjoy a few extra days lazing around on the beach next summer.

"We must find solutions, campaign on behalf of those who have no voice, and support projects which strive to make the earth a better place—whether financially, prayerfully or in person."

Intelligent Faith

By Larry Witham

Without "intelligent faith," American believers could neither make wise moral choices nor master precise knowledge of a religious tradition. Increasingly, however, intelligent faith in America will hinge on reconciling religious and moral beliefs with the expanding frontiers of science.

The typical American response has been to separate religion and science into their own compartments. The science compartment, for example, contains Darwinian evolution, nuclear energy, neuroscience, genetic engineering and unlimited scientific experiments, with the prospect of "mad scientists" but also better televisions, a cure for Alzheimer's, and a booming economy. On the religion side, the compartment contains belief in God-given morals, human uniqueness, concern for justice, and a whole array of beliefs about God's supernatural intervention (or presence) in history, in nature, in the human body, and in the mind.

The intelligent faith of the future will require bridge-building between these two sides. The most durable bridges will be philosophical ones, for theology and science often do not speak the same language. Nevertheless, even the best bridges are no guarantee that the politics of science and religion in America will be settled. Intelligent faith may not stop political and legal battles, but it can enrich individual lives, thus affecting society in a positive way.

Besides politics, intelligent faith today must also deal with the great stories of the past, generated by encounters between science and religion. For Americans, the Galileo trial of 1633 and the Scopes Trial of 1925 are the two greatest war stories, an embarrassment, respectively, to Catholics and Protestants. The modern American debate may not have produced any legends on the scale of a Galileo and Scopes, but the last quarter century has produced plenty of small dramas to choose from. In 1999, for example, the fundamentalist preacher Jerry Falwell and agnostic evolutionist Stephen J. Gould faced off on CNN's "Crossfire" over teaching evolution in schools. That same year, two renowned physicists—one a Christian and one an atheist—verbally clashed at the National Museum of Natural History in Washington, D.C., over, "Is the Universe Designed?" John Polkinghorne said that science suggested it was, while Steven Weinberg countered that the universe was "pointless."

Other examples of divergent views abound. In 2005, a federal judge ruled that "intelligent design"—which argues that a higher "intelligence" explains complexity in nature—was not science and could not be mentioned in public school science classes. Over the next two years, President George Bush twice vetoed federal funding of stem cell research on human embryos. Former Vice President Al Gore, meanwhile, made a comeback by lecturing on global warming and attaching God and "stewardship" to the cause.

Even such compelling headlines tend to simplify the issues at stake, obscuring how complex the relationship between "science and theology" (two ways of knowing) and between "science and religion" (two groups and their cultural institutions) can be. These events at least suggest four areas in which the engagement between science and religion is most active: evolution, "life" issues, the environment—and the "meaning" of the universe.

The stage was set for the current evolution-creation debate in 1980. The Reagan Republicans pursued the White House and a new legal theory of mandating "balanced treatment" of "evolution-science." Consequently, "creation-science" took hold in Arkansas and Louisiana. In 1987, however, the Supreme Court declared that "scientific" creationism was not science and mandating it in the classroom violated the separation of church and state.

Most legal disputes since then have been about putting disclaimers in textbooks—that evolution is "only a theory"—at least until 2005. That year, in the longest creation-evolution trial in history, a federal judge ruled that a school board in Dover, Pennsylvania, had violated the constitution by mandating that students learn about "intelligent design" as an alternative to evolution. The ruling followed the precedents set by the Supreme Court in 1987, showing their likely permanence.

But the debate over evolution has three thorny issues still to contend with: public sentiment, public school curricula, and loopholes left by the Supreme Court. First, a large majority of Americans (around seventy percent) want creationism taught "somewhere" in public schools, since evolution is mandated. This public propensity for "fairness" frustrates evolutionists, but no one has yet decided where "creationism" or "intelligent design" can be taught: social science, history, or comparative religion? For now, it typically arises with student interest, or is bootlegged into a science class.

Finally, the Supreme Court said that it could not force states to ban "scientific critiques of prevailing scientific theories" (such as evolution) in the classroom. The high court also allowed that "teaching a variety of scientific theories about the origins of humankind to schoolchildren might be validly done with the clear secular intent of enhancing the effectiveness of science instruction." So far, however, efforts to teach a "variety" have arisen from religious motives in a community, and thus have no chance of surviving a constitutional challenge in court.

The public debate over "life issues"—how biological sciences affect the human body, sexuality, and life and death—is perhaps second only to evolution for involvement of American believers, both intellectually and politically. The political lines were drawn in the 1960s and 1970s over topics such as artificial birth control and abortion. As scientific techniques advanced, the life issues expanded to artificial insemination, genetic manipulation, euthanasia, and research on stem cells in human embryos. In all cases, a majority of Americans felt uncomfortable with the new technologies, worried about a "slippery slope" into a "brave new world." The public has invariably liberalized on each, however, and now draws a strict moral line only against late-term abortion, euthanasia, and cloning human beings (opposed by nine in ten Americans).

Despite two presidential vetoes of federal funding for research on human embryo stem cells, the public has become more accepting (opposition dropped from fifty-one percent to thirty-six percent), and new discoveries are making stem cell research less controversial as it grows in the public imagination as a miracle cure to illness. But Americans are still skittish at each new technology, and the same is true with genetically modified food and use of "nanotechnology." Americans want the first labeled, and they worry that the second will be used in tiny devices that might threaten privacy.

For religious Americans, environmental pollution is both a practical and moral issue. The faith traditions have introduced the slogans of "justice" and "stewardship" into an otherwise secular debate. The justice issue hinges on whether only the rich will benefit from new technologies, and only poor neighborhoods will be used as waste dumpsites. Similarly, religious Americans from evangelical to mainline traditions have offered "stewardship" of God's creation as the reason to stop pollution and deal with climate change. In all these areas, intelligent faith is challenged to obtain the best scientific facts and avoid the "apocalyptic" themes that run through every religion.

The topic that gains the fewest headlines is probably the deepest in the American search for intelligent faith: how to make sense of God, belief, and morals in a scientific age. Beyond the classroom, courtroom, and legislative chamber, this question hinges on how Americans view science and religion, what beliefs they hold, and the many ways they can reconcile them with scientific challenges.

In general, around ninety percent of Americans acknowledge belief in God or a "universal spirit." A healthy dose of "doubt" is always mixed into belief, and its size varies across traditions. While 86.5 percent of evangelical Protestants have "no doubts" that God exists, only forty-three percent of Jews claim that. Catholics (at seventy-five percent) and Mainline Protestants (at sixty-four percent) fall in between.

On the whole, scientists are more unbelieving than average Americans—but less agnostic than once thought. The nation's top natural scientists (members of the National Academy of Sciences), for example, report only seven percent belief in God. At the same time, however, forty percent of the nation's ranking scientists believe in an afterlife

and a God who answers prayers. More recent surveys have found still larger percentages of academics in sciences adhering to "spiritual" beliefs, and medical doctors seem the most likely to hold beliefs similar to those of average Americans.

Despite these stark differences in American scientific and religious cultures, Americans are as positive about science as they are about religion. They give science higher approval ratings (eighty-four percent) than do Europe (fifty-two percent) and Japan (forty percent). They give scientists a "confidence" rank in leadership up with the military and doctors. Most parents (eighty percent) would be proud to have a child enter a science profession. Americans also don't mind federal spending on science: nearly nine in ten say technology makes life "better" and that research should go forward "even if it brings no immediate benefits."

Still, science comes in low as an American interest compared to crime, politics, local schools, or wars. Medical discovery draws most interest, followed by new inventions. Interest in pollution is high, but for all its media attention, space exploration ranks surprisingly low in American interest. At the turn of the twenty-first century, more than half of Americans polled agreed with the statements that (1) "we depend too much on science and not enough on faith"; (2) "scientific research these days doesn't pay enough attention to the moral values of society"; (3) "scientific research has created as many problems for society as it has solutions."

Not surprisingly, Americans with strong religious commitments were far more likely than the general public to agree with these statements. One reason for the clash between the scientific and religious cultures in the United States is this degree of distrust (mixed with praise). But the science establishment is also embarrassed by America's lack of science literacy. Around forty percent of Americans, in rejecting evolution, accept that God created humans "pretty much in their present form" ten thousand years ago. In one study over fifteen years, the only "new" fact the public seemed to have learned was that antibiotics killed viruses. Learning about science comes mostly from headlines, with television the biggest source (fifty-one percent) followed by newspapers (twenty-two percent)—although the Internet is now the preferred public "research" tool.

The American scientific establishment may use "creationism" as its prime example of wrong-headed "pseudoscience," but American interest in non-scientific mysteries touches on several areas. More than two in ten Americans believe that UFOs are from outer space and about four in ten accept stories of an ancient Atlantis civilization. Five in ten Americans believe dreams foretell reality (fifty-two percent), and many more (seventy-five percent) say alternative medicine is at least as effective as Western reductionist medicine. Interestingly, the more orthodox believers and churchgoers are least open to paranormal belief, which flourishes most among Americans with no religious affiliation.

The division between science and belief in America also has roots in the nation's social stratification. Scientists are few and believers are many. There are an estimated 300,000 "scientists" at work in America, and another six million Americans at work in technical fields that require the study of science. In contrast, there are about 500,000 clergy of all faiths in the United States. While just five hundred science museums operate in the United States, the number of houses of worship is about 350,000. Each year, about thirty million American adults visit a science museum at least once, but the numbers of Americans who attend houses of worship each year exceeds all other social and public events, even sports.

For better or worse, science museums and conferences generally do not discuss religion, and houses of worship rarely take up scientific issues. Studies of sermons have shown very few references to natural science or scientific theory, and the most likely intersection is in the area of "activism": what a congregation is going to do about abortion, stem cell research, medical care for the needy and elderly, nuclear weapons, or the environment.

Nevertheless, backgrounds in science and education often do help define the memberships of various American religious denominations, and explain why wealthier Americans tend to be more theologically liberal (and more accepting of scientific authority), and why more liberal traditions (Jewish, Unitarian, Episcopal, Congregationalist and others) seem to produce a larger share of scientists, or have more such people in the pews.

The crux of this trend in religious affiliation usually comes down to how one believes in the Bible and how much supernatural intervention one can introduce into the natural world. The more orthodox, conservative, or evangelical religious groups place more literal authority in Bible statements and miracles. Hence, these traditions feel more challenged by science's claims to explain the "soul" by neuroscience, "creation" and morality by evolution, and "revealed" scriptures as secular and symbolic literature. More liberal churches accept scientific explanations and adapt their theology accordingly.

But the vaunted "secularization theory" of the mid-twentieth century is now being discarded by social scientists who find that higher education, and even a scientific profession, hardly leads to disbelief. In addition to surveys of scientists and academics showing spiritual interests, working scientists and ordinary Americans show one major overlap: about forty percent of both believed that God "guided" evolution, a view called "theistic evolution." This is probably the most typical bridge in what is being called "intelligent faith" today.

Theistic evolution by no means solves all the scientific debates and problems in evolutionary theory itself, or solves the ways that Christians, Jews, and Muslims try to explain "divine action" in the material world. But compared to atheism, on one side, and a literal biblical explanation on the other, theistic evolution offers a complex middle ground that some of the leading "science-and-religion" movements of recent years have occupied. This middle ground invariably adapts to the claims of science, while trying to keep intact the tenets of God, free will, immortality and the use of traditional religious language. The middle ground has also pointed out the uncertainties, and even philosophical biases, of science: that science also makes metaphysical claims about reality that must be taken on faith. This relativizing of science, and criticsm of its tendency to "reduce" all things to simple matter, has somewhat leveled the playing field between the claims of science and faith, both for modernist and orthodox solutions.

One of the most popular formats to explain the possible ways science and religion interact is a four-fold model: (1) a conflict model of "war" between the two sides; (2) a separation model of two kinds of knowledge; (3) an interaction model that compares beliefs of science and theology; (4) and an "integration" model that often leads to a "scientific religion" based on scientific facts and theories but using religious terminology.

Obviously, Americans do not consciously pick one of the four labels, which tend to more aptly describe more institutional and cultural approaches to the two ways of knowing. Probably most Americans keep religion and science separate. Others try to "harmonize" science and faith, for example saying that six "days" in the Bible were epochs and that Adam and Eve were early hominids. A smaller number of Americans adopt a "scientific faith," adding a spiritual reality to evolution. For those who want to accept all the findings of science, modern theologians have provided helpful tools, defining God as the "ground of being" and religion as "ultimate concern," not doctrines. Other theologians see God as evolving nature to an Omega Point (cosmic salvation), or God being in a "process" that gives nature and humanity freedom in a quest for a higher love, unity, and creativity.

The "science and religion" dialogue has always existed in the United States, especially at the level of intellectual groups, religious denominations, and individual scientists. Its modern version, prompted mostly by liberal Protestants, received a new infu-sion of energy in the late 1970s. One source was a new pope, John Paul II, who in 1979 celebrated Einstein's 100th birthday and called for a new decade-long study and report to exonerate Galileo. The other new source of energy has been the billionaire investor John Marks Templeton, whose foundation became dedicated to the quest "to explore and encourage the relationship between science and religion" in 1987. By the early 1990s, the Templeton Foundation was granting $50 million a year, much of it to such projects.

The papal rhetoric and Templeton funding stirred a reaction among secular scientists and groups, adding a more erudite debate to the otherwise populist one of evolution in schools and funding of biological research or sex education. Intelligent faith, while seeking these kinds of bridges—especially under the models of "interaction" and "integration"—faced a new challenge after the terrorist attacks by religious zealots on September 11, 2001. A Neo-atheist movement has gained momentum. This atheism is no longer just reacting to the "science and religion" dialogue, the Religious Right in politics, or anti-evolutionism in public schools. It now argues that 9/11 proves that religion per se is dangerous.

The vast majority of Americans have not been persuaded by or attracted to atheism, however. As the "baby boom" generation faces its mortality, questions of ultimate meaning, and even spiritual healing, will vie with every new scientific discovery. Science will produce new comforts, but also a new kind of "rat race," and Americans will likely seek religious traditions to humanize life in an age of nanotechnology, genetic engineering, biological experimentation, and environmental degradation. The future challenge of intelligent faith may be to offer a comforting faith as well as to reconcile theological doctrine with scientific fact.

Eastern Religion on American Soil

By Lili Zhang and Naoko Sasaki

American society of the past three decades bears witness to an increasing expansion of the presence of Eastern religions and a growing fascination with it. The visibility of Eastern religions such as Buddhism, Hinduism, Sikhism, Jainism, Taoism, Confucianism, and Shinto can be easily found across the nation's geographic landscape in the spectacular oriental temples in American cities as well as in thousands of small religious centers in rural towns. According to a 2006 national survey conducted by the Pluralism Project of Harvard University, there were 2150 Buddhist centers, 714 Hindu temples and 244 Sikhism centers across the United States. In addition to these religious centers, thousands of secular organizations teach techniques of self-cultivation, such as yoga, Taiji, Qigong, and meditations, many of which play an integral role in some Eastern religious traditions. Estimates suggest that there are four to five million practicing adherents of Eastern religions here.

The influence of Eastern religions in America is not just limited to the walls of those religious centers and their enrolled immigrant and American practitioners, but extends far into American daily life, appearing in literature, film, television, art, music, health therapy, diet, fashion, publishing, advertising, and sports. The widespread popularity of Eastern religions is made evident in American culture by the ubiquity of many terms such as yoga, karma, Tao, dharma, yin/yang, Taiji, and fengshui. Enthusiasm for Eastern culture, if not religion, has brought great profits to Hollywood with the marketing of a variety of oriental films in recent years such as "Crouching Tiger, Hidden Dragon," "The Forbidden Kingdom," and "Kung Fu Panda." For readers, bookstore shelves are flooded with many books about the application of oriental wisdom to various aspects of life, ranging from mental, psychological, and physical health to successful business practices in the Asian marketplace. These sensory impressions about the significant and growing impact of Eastern religions in the country are well supported by statistical data, providing a precise index about the popularity of Eastern religions in America. According to a 2003 report by Wendy Cadge and Courtney Bender, thirty percent of American adults (that is, sixty-three million people) say they are familiar with Buddhism; twenty-two percent (forty-five million people) with Hinduism; fifty-five percent of these surveyed indicated their personal encounters with Buddhism; and fifty percent of them with Hinduism.

The flourishing of Eastern religions in American society has changed the conventional image of America from a country of Western religions such as Christianity and Judaism to a country of diverse religions. This change is rooted in the ongoing struggles against racial and religious discrimination, the adaptation of Eastern religions to American social conditions, changes of American attitude to Eastern religions, and the development of information technologies.

1. The Historical Setting

The Statue of Liberty, an icon of freedom on the East Coast, symbolized for most nineteenth- and twentieth-century Americans a welcome to all immigrants regardless of nationality or religion, insofar as it related to Europeans. In reality, it took more than one century before America opened its doors to large numbers of Asians. Although they landed in America in significant numbers in the late nineteenth century, several Asian exclusion laws extending from 1882 to 1924 precipitously restricted immigration, and their numbers reached no more than 0.2 percent of the population by 1960. Not until 1965, with passage of the Hart-Celler Act, were the doors re-opened to Asians.

The Hart-Celler Act and others before it impacted the few Asian immigrants and those already here in significant ways, including the practice of their religious faiths. Prior to 1965, Asian immigrants established very few religious communities and organizations primarily within the concentrations of Asian immigrants on the West Coast. According to the U.S. Census of 1906, nationwide there were only sixty-two Chinese temples and 141 Shinto shrines. They brought organizational structures, beliefs, and rituals from their home countries, keeping them intact given their isolation from the other ethnic populations.

During this period, only limited communication between Eastern religious groups and Christian churches took place. These encounters, for instance, at the Chicago World Parliament of Religions in 1893, occurred primarily on the abstract, theoretical level,

and participants had little interest in engaging concretely with the existing Asian religious communities. In this environment, American understanding of Asian religions was superficial and flawed. Until very recently two stereotypical nineteenth-century representations of Asian religions have predominated: one chauvinistic and the other romantic.

Chauvinistic representations were primarily adopted by Christian missionaries and anti-Asian Americans, depicting Eastern religions as irrational, despotic, backward, passive, stagnant, debased, and inferior in contrast to the putatively rational, democratic, humanistic, creative, dynamic, progressive Western religions. As a result, in several anti-Asian movements at the end of the twentieth century Eastern religions were identified as a national threat and used to justify the Asiatic exclusion legislation at the sacrifice of America's foundational commitment to religious and human equality. Edward Said, the contemporary philosopher well known for his seminal study of orientalism, correctly points out that such demonic representations of Eastern religion as a whole have grown out of "a relationship of power, of domination, [and] of varying degrees of complex hegemony."

Romantic representations of Eastern religion have been adopted by some American elites who are attracted by Hinduism, Buddhism and other Asian religions, such as members in spiritualist transcendentalist movements and those in the occult oriented Theosophy movement. Learning Eastern religion from texts and itinerant teachers who disregard the firsthand experiences of Asian immigrants, they tended to read Eastern religions in the abstract, romanticizing Eastern religions as the source of genuine transcendental spirituality that was irretrievably lost to Western religion. Such a romantic vision of Eastern religions particularly impacted the American countercultural and alternative lifestyle movements associated with the Beat writers of the 1960s.

While the stereotypical representations of Eastern religions, chauvinistic or romantic, continue to exit in non-Asian Americans, this ideological construction of Eastern religions is perforce slowly giving way to complexity with the dramatic increase of Asian-American populations and with the concrete experiences of living religion in its diverse forms. According to 2008 U.S. Census data, the number of Asians grew elevenfold in 2008 since the 1960s, rising to fifteen million, to constitute 4.9 percent of the United States population. The burgeoning population of Asian immigrants has produced renaissance from within.

2. Eastern Religions Encounter America

Asian immigrants transplant their beliefs and practices from their home countries to the new land. However, transplantation always signals transformation. In their home countries, many traditional Eastern religions belong to cloister-centered communities, situated in secluded and remote regions and providing only religious worship services for the laity. These lay practitioners usually come to the temples by long pilgrimages on very few occasions throughout a year. The internal organizational structures in Eastern religions primarily keep the traditional hierarchical relationship of patriarchal domination between the elder and the younger. Such traditional structures obviously do not fit the conditions of Asian immigrants who need the ready availability of their religious institutions to help them retain their ethnic and religious identity in the new land and guide them to survive in a challenging social environment. Nor do these communities in the traditional form fit American democratic culture. To adapt to social and cultural conditions of the host country, Eastern religious communities have engaged in a reformation of their organizational structures, their ritual formality and the ways they interpret their religious tenets.

Eastern religious communities commonly, if not universally, undertake democratic reform by assimilating the American Protestant congregational model characterized as a community based on voluntary participation. Abandoning the hierarchies between monastics and laity, between masters and disciples, and between monks and nuns, reformed Eastern religious communities usually carry these features: focusing the local communities as a congregation; inviting voluntary and equal participation of members in religious functions; being open to laity and providing multiple services. Hundreds of Chinese Buddhist and Taoist centers, for example, stand in the Chinatowns of American metropolitan centers and share space with commercial markets in busy streets. While a few are established by monks, most are founded and administered by lay believers. These Buddhist sites are not only perceived as a place for religious worship and funerals, but also a space to conduct secular activities such as wedding ceremonies, job placement services, family counseling, and general cultural activities. Many of them have created official websites to market themselves.

Beyond external changes according to the Protestant structural procedures, ritual forms have similarly adapted. These reforms have affected formalities of ritual to include ritual times, procedure in worship and language of worship. Given the global predominance of the weekly cycle with its societal rhythm, which makes no exception for Asian immigrants, Eastern religions have had to compromise their traditional religious calendars and adjust their religious holidays and events to weekends. Following Protestant worship patterns, they also offer regular Sunday collective worship services with a procedure similar to Protestant churches: hymn singing, collective chanting and prayers, the affiliate's sermon, and so on. Instead of the sacred language, the service is bilingual—English and the ethnic language. Alter-natively, there may be two sections of Sunday service in each language.

Not only have Eastern religions reformed their religious organizational structures to accommodate lay members, they have also adjusted doctrinal interpretations of their authoritative scriptures to reflect and engage with new situations. Many Eastern religious doctrines have been traditionally colored with the negation of worldly affairs based on the dichotomy of the profane and the sacred, taking seclusive self-meditation as a means for the escape out of the sufferings of the secular world. While self-meditation still remains emphasized in Eastern religious communities, they are inclined to adopt a different doctrinal line for their heritages and to reorient individual spiritual transformation toward transformation of society as a whole. This change is exemplified by the "socially engaged Buddhism" movement in America, initiated by Thich Nhat Hanh, leader of Vietnamese Buddhists abroad. Drawing on inspirations from the teachings of the Buddha, the Bodhisattva ideal and expansive Mahayana world views, he expanded the application of the dharma from religious charity and philanthropy to large social issues such as peace and justice, not only with the scope of immigrant communities but also on a global scale. According to him, techniques of sitting and chanting are the means to a thorough and deep engagement with society rather than seclusion from society. With the same commitment to social work, Zen Buddhists successfully applied their philosophy and practice of meditation to the "good death" movement at two well-respected AIDS hospices in San Francisco.

The democratic reform of their organizational structures and the emphasis on social commitment in the understanding of their heritages unambiguously reflect a process of Americanization of Eastern religion in that these innovations developed in response to the general American contexts and specifically along the line of American Protestantism. However, Americanization has not weakened the vitality of Eastern faiths but has promoted the efficacy of these religions in solidifying their members' beliefs and guiding them to meaningfully engage with society in the new condition.

3. America Encounters Eastern Religion

Eastern religion in America is certainly not limited to Asian immigrants, but has already spread widely into non-Asian American communities, whose participation significantly contributes to Eastern religions' entrance into the American main-stream. While the attraction to Eastern religions differs for different Americans, their approaches may be divided in two ways: religious and secular. The former usually takes Eastern religions as an alternative to their inherited faiths as they felt dissatisfied with them. Some converts from Roman Catholicism, for example, found the meaning of life in Dalai Lama's teachings without the fear and guilt usually associated with their religion. For Protestant converts, meditation in Eastern religions allows them to have an immediate and bodily experience of the transcendent, mostly absent in Christian churches that place the emphasis on beliefs and doctrines.

While some American converts have joined Asian immigrants at religious centers and temples, most of them have established their own institutions apart from immigrant communities. This eclectic choice obtains not from differences in language, but from different orientations to the cultural and social appropriations of beliefs and rituals in Eastern religions. Some share the orthodoxy of Eastern religions concerning the soteriological faith and doctrines on the philosophical level, but have abandoned traditional temple-based ritual formalities. For instance, many Zen centers established by non-Asian Americans simplify the complicated ritual procedures characteristic of Zen temples in Japan into a few steps—bowing to the Buddha statue, lighting the candle, ringing a bell and sitting on cushions. Some may not take the soteriological notions or personal faith to deities, such as reincarnation and karma in Buddhism, but only follow selected ritual practices such as zazen in Zen, and yoga in Hinduism, and associate these practices alone with a religious transcendental goal. Even though traditionalists suspect that non-Asian immigrants' selective appropriations of Eastern religions may impoverish a given religious tradition, many still celebrate this freedom, in which they can find not only "a new standard and simple method of professing their [religious] commitment," but also "a renewed sense of seriousness" for all religious groups.

More numerous than the eclectic American converts who adopt Eastern religions in spiritual modes are Americans who accept Eastern religions in a lay sense and approach them in the secular mode. The techniques of self cultivation, traditionally viewed in Eastern religions as the means to spiritual liberation—yoga in Hinduism, meditation in Buddhism, Taiji, Qigong, Gongfu, acupuncture, and herbal dietetic in Taoism—are now translated into viable therapies to combat certain health problems or to engage in physical games. These are taught in fitness clubs, health clinics, hospitals, retirement centers, and physical education classes in public or private schools. Some, such are yoga classes, acupuncture, and herbal medicine have been accepted by many major health insurance plans. Whether such secular appropriations of Eastern religions in American society constitute among traditionalists marginally legitimate or inauthentic practices remains hotly debated. The efficacy of these techniques in the promotion of mental and bodily health is gradually enjoying independent corroboration as more and more scientific studies devoted to these techniques appear in the public sphere.

4. The Future of Eastern Religions in America

In the wake of Asian immigration of the 1960s, Eastern religions have undergone multifaceted, profound transformations in Asian and non-Asian communities alike. No longer intact religious communities isolated within the immigrant circle as they were during the early Asian immigration stage, Eastern religions have entered into the American spiritual and secular mainstream and redefined the culture of pluralism in contemporary America along with other religions in American. Not merely co-presenting with other ethic religions, Eastern religions have engaged in empathic dialogues with other religions to reform and improve themselves and society, and have carved a distinctive, creative and enriching life in America in yet more productive interactions.

However, Eastern religions find themselves in an unabated process in response to new conditions. One of the great challenges for Eastern religions today and in the future comes from the increasing expansion of cosmopolitan, transnational realities resulting from economic globalization and advanced media technology like the internet, email, and satellite video and telephones. Although it has a clear path ahead, Eastern religion in America still demands creative imagination. One innovation in particular is notable: the formation of a variety of globally based religious communities. There have already appeared, for example, worldwide network religious temples with their headquarters in America, resembling chain stores. Also, bearing much similarity to online e-commerce stores, many online e-religious temples have been spawned. They post their mission statements, religious doctrines, and guidelines to practice online. They recruit members across the world and hold online conferences to discuss religious matters and community issues. In addition to the new forms of religious institutions, with advanced technology in transportation and communication, individual experiences of Eastern religions have changed radically. People can find a communal religious experience firsthand through easy pilgrimages either to religious sites in their home countries, or to religious sites online, where they can communicate on religious beliefs and practices with practitioners in different countries via email, MSN, or Skype. They can also formulate internet-based mobile religious groups.

These visible changes herald the cosmopolitan move of Eastern religions and other religions. It is still too early to know how the shape, content, and practice of Eastern religions will be transformed in the digital age and the age of globalization. However, the pluralism that Eastern religions have contributed to America in the past will be an important factor in how Eastern religions adapt to these new situations. The longing for freedom, which once made Eastern religions congenial to American culture, will, it may be expected, continue to allow Eastern religion to find a home in America's cosmopolitan world in the future.

State __Oregon__
County __Marion__
Township or other division of county __Election Precinct 7__
Incorporated place __Salem City__
Ward of city __5 (part)__ Block No. _____
Unincorporated place _____
Institution _____

Enumeration District No. __24-67__
Supervisor's District No. __2__
Sheet No. __15__
Enumerated by me on __Apr. 24__, 1930 __Mrs. N. V. Greene__

Line	Place of abode		Name	Relation	Home Data		Personal Description						Education		Place of Birth (Person)	(Father)	(Mother)	Occupation	Industry
1	2590 409 421	McCarroll, Mabel C.	Head	O 4500		F W 40 M 22			Yes	Washington	Wisconsin	Iowa		None				
2		Evelyn	Daughter		F W 16 S			Yes	Washington	Iowa	Washington		None					
3		Lucille	Daughter		F W 13 S			Yes	Oregon	Iowa	Washington		None					
4		Gerald	Son		M W 11 S			Yes	Oregon	Iowa	Washington		None					
5		William	Son		M W 8 S				Oregon	Iowa	Washington		None					
6	2595 410 422	Presnall, Emory	Head	O 4500		M W 50 M 23			Yes	Indiana	North Carolina	Indiana		Laborer	Odd jobs			
7		Mary	Wife		F W 49 M 16			Yes	Indiana	Missouri	North Carolina		None					
8		John B.	Son		M W 53 S			Yes	Indiana	Missouri	Indiana		Laborer	Odd jobs			
9	2575 411 423	Keach, Lamberth	Head	O 8000		M W 61 M 36			Yes	New Hampshire	New York	New Hampshire		Operator	Elevator			
10		Maud	Wife		F W 53 M 25			Yes	Kansas	United States	United States		Laundry	Laundry			
11		Tonyers, Gretchen	Cousin		F W 65 Wd			Yes	New Hampshire	New York	New Hampshire		None					
12	2593 412 424	Schoneman, Martin L.	Head	O 1500		M W 49 M 25			Yes	Missouri	Germany	Germany		Laborer	Gas Co.			
13	2595 413 425	Long, Carroll	Head	O 4300		M W 32 M 29			Yes	Oregon	Oregon	Oregon		None	Garage			
14		Grace	Wife		F W 31 M 23			Yes	Oregon	Pennsylvania	Pennsylvania		None					
15	2595 414 426	Bickett, Earl M.	Head	O 7500		M W 39 M 19			Yes	Oregon	Oregon	Oregon		Gas Fitter	Gas Co.			
16		Minnie B.	Wife		F W 42 M 21			Yes	Washington	North Carolina	Oregon		Teacher	Rural			
17		Genevieve	Daughter		F W 18 S			Yes	Oregon	Oregon	Washington		None					
18		Chester D.	Son		M W 16 S			Yes	Oregon	Oregon	Washington		None					
19		Milton D.	Son		M W 12 S			Yes	Oregon	Oregon	Washington		None					
20		Lydia J.	Daughter		F W 10 S			Yes	Oregon	Oregon	Washington		None					
21		Evelyn	Daughter		F W 7 S				Oregon	Oregon	Washington		None					
22	918 415 427	Rhodes, John	Head	O 1300		M W 67 M 33			Yes	Unknown	Washington			Retired	Farmer			
23		Allie	Wife		F W 59 M 25			Yes	Washington	Illinois	Missouri		None					
24		Newell	Son		M W 21 S			Yes	Oregon	Ohio	Washington		Laborer	Camp			
25		Loren	Son		M W 19 S			Yes	Oregon	Ohio	Washington		Laborer	Odd jobs			
26	2597 416 428	Smith, Paul E.	Head	O 2000		M W 51 M 21			Yes	New York	New York	New York		Laborer	Paper Mill			
27		Ethel R.	Wife		F W 49 M 21			Yes	Illinois	England	Pennsylvania		Fancy Work	Cannery			
28		Paul E.	Son		M W 25 S			Yes	Iowa	Illinois	Illinois		None					
29		Robert E.	Son		M W 11 S			Yes	Oregon	Illinois	Illinois		None					
30	2515 417 429	Gamble, Marion A.	Head	O 4000		M W 82 M 32			Yes	Ohio	Ohio	Vermont		Janitor	Church			
31		Charity A.	Wife		F W 57 M 25			Yes	Indiana	Ohio	Indiana		Helper	Church			
32	44 430	Sims, Mary E.	Head R	15		F W 57 Wd			Yes	Utah	England	England		None					
33		William	Son		M W 26 S			Yes	Oregon	Utah	Utah		Machinist	Planing Shed			
34		James	Son		M W 24 M 21			Yes	Oregon	Utah	Utah		Planer	Planing Shed			
35		Cato L.	Daughter		F W 17 S			Yes	Oregon	United States	United States		None					
36	2590 418 431	Davis, Luther H.	Head	R 10		M W 66 M 29			Yes	Pennsylvania	Pennsylvania	Pennsylvania		Broker	Real Estate			
37		Jessie	Wife		F W 60 M 20			Yes	Michigan	Canada-English	Pennsylvania		Artist	Art House			
38	2580 419 432	Holwell, Frank	Head	O 4500		M W 56 M 20			Yes	Canada-English	Canada-English	Canada-English		Broker	Section			
39		Ida	Wife		F W 51 M 19			Yes	North Dakota	Canada-English	Michigan		Fancy Worker	Cannery			
40	226 420 433	Barber, Erma	Head R	20		F W 49 S			Yes	Idaho	United States	United States		Spinner	Linen Mill			
41		Dipman, Gwendolyn	Roomer		F W 19 S			Yes	Washington	Wisconsin	Minnesota		Spinner	Linen Mill			
42		Dipman, Irene	Roomer		F W 20 S			Yes	Washington	Wisconsin	Minnesota		Reeler	Linen Mill			
43		Leona, Mildred	Roomer		F W 21 M			Yes	Oregon	Wisconsin	Grade English		Spinner	Linen Mill			
44	4 434	Kneser, Earl	Head	O 10		M W 28 M 20			Yes	Oregon	Wisconsin	Canada-English		Checker	Wood			
45		Margaret	Wife		F W 20 M 20			Yes	Oregon	Canada-English	Oregon		None					
46	5 435	Reisers, Edmund A.	Head	R 19		M W 41 M 26			Yes	Wisconsin	Germany	Switzerland		Laborer	Odd jobs			
47		Elizabeth M.	Wife		F W 42 M 28			Yes	Minnesota	Germany	Germany		None					
48		Heath	Daughter		F W 11 S			Yes	Iowa	Wisconsin	Minnesota		None					
49	2261 421 436	Smith, Joseph M.	Head	O 6000		M W 67 M 40			Yes	Iowa	Ohio	Ohio		Bookkeeper	Sand & Gravel			
50						F W 67 M 22			Yes	Iowa	Ohio	Ireland		Teacher	Deaf School			

PART THREE

Faith, Facts, and Figures

Introduction

Contents of Part Three

1. Religious Affiliation/Geography

2. Religious Affiliation/Demography

3. Maps: Religious Distributions

4. Polls and Surveys

5. Sources and Methodology

Faith and Numbers

From batting averages to horsepower, Americans demand the numbers. Numbers are indicative of hard facts, of contrast and precision—but they also point to broad trends, similarities, and gray areas. Numbers inform; they lead to understanding and to action. America is home to over 300 million, and its religious landscape is too broad to fit into a single panorama. "Faith and Numbers" is a collection of data on a range of topics that concern American religious groups. Our intention is to create a mosaic of smaller snapshots that will help us to see the bigger picture of American religion.

Numbers spur business decisions; companies spend millions in search of consumer information. While demographic statistics are subject to margins of error, they come close to fact; if one million "choosy moms" choose a particular brand of peanut butter, it must be popular—to say nothing of nutrition, taste, or cost, but that's the beauty of numbers; they have the ability to convince.

Statistical studies are reviewed, re-sampled, re-mapped, and their results often point to success or to failure. Numbers are our proofs—they display options, making quick work of complex study. The election process speaks volumes of our trust in numbers. As we prepare to elect leaders, we focus on early polling results—how well a candidate does on his or her second hurdle largely depends on numbers from the first hurdle. With polls at the forefront of our minds, we march to caucus or primary. The results appear in the media, and, in turn, affect the vote.

Historically, the government has used the census to measure for representation, for taxes, for land distribution, and for the military. While the idea remains the same, its practical application has broadened considerably to provide information for government programs, for public services, and, of course, for taxes. The U.S. Census Bureau does not make questions of religious preference mandatory, but by tracking religious trends, we can learn a great deal about their influence on American history.

Our intent is to present a collection of religious numbers in order to understand America's religious landscape. Our information comes from private studies as well as public censuses, all of which aim to paint an accurate picture, yet they have different methods and reasons for polling. We sought as much information as possible from a variety of sources. We array the data side-by-side, with disparate sources in one place, and have hopefully made it possible to see the bigger picture. Moreover, we hope to provide a compendium of useful reference data in the form of tables, graphs, charts, and maps that can be understood by all levels.

As nearly 80 percent of Americans identify with a form of Christianity, we have unearthed a corresponding abundance of data on Christianity in America. Of course, having an overwhelming amount of information on one religious group is not necessarily positive; it may lead to the exclusion of data on other groups. However, we cite studies that have taken pains to produce numbers on smaller religious groups. A practical reality may be that form follows foundation; the view may be laden with information on Christianity since it is the most common religion in America.

Most of our data comes from five sources. The 2001 American Religious Identification Survey, described at its release as "the most comprehensive study of religion in America," was undertaken by the City University of New York. We used Baylor University's 2006 study, American Piety in the twenty-first century. We relied on the three major commercial polling organizations that are responsible for much of the polling statistics in America. Since the 1930s, the Gallup Organization has produced data on a range of topics. The Harris Poll has provided relevant data on religion since 1975. Recently, the Pew Foundation, a third polling organization, initiated the Pew Forum on Religion and Public Life, which provides information on religion and religious issues. They will publish The Religious Landscape Survey in 2008. We feel that these sources present non-partisan research that is both useful and interesting.

— ADAM ALEXANDER
EDITOR, PART THREE

Contents of Part Three

5. SOURCES AND METHODOLOGY

1 Religious Affiliation/Geography

AMERICA IS OFTEN CELEBRATED FOR ITS DIVERSITY. The following two chapters provide a glimpse of the variety of religious affiliation throughout the United States. In the past, religious affiliation has largely been determined by such factors as membership, participation, and attendance at religious services, but when people are asked to identify their religious affiliation, the results can differ significantly. In what follows, we explore the distribution of the major religions in America based on both institutional categories and individuals' self perception.

Although Americans differ in their degrees of religiosity, roughly seventy-five percent of the adult population regard themselves as religious in some way; this finding alone would indicate the importance of religious practice and belief in many citizens' lives.

Since Christianity and Protestantism, specifically, retain the highest number of adherents in the United States, we provide additional information on the diversity within those groups. Unaffiliated individuals also make up a significant portion of the U.S. population. From surveys deking with prayer and institutional participation, we observe that affiliation is not necessarily related to belief or to religiosity; about thirty percent of the unaffiliated sometimes pray, while only ten percent occasionally attend services.

In the second part of this section, the graphs illustrate the demographics of religious affiliation in the United States. The country's demographics are continuously changing, due to immigration patterns, generational replacement, and other factors. In turn, these demographic changes alter the religious landscape of the country. For instance, Protestants are more likely to be native born; they also make up a significantly larger proportion of the older generation. Nearly fifty percent of immigrants are Catholic, which reflects changes in religious affiliation among immigrant populations. Changes in the population of certain age groups are also reflected in religious identification surveys; younger people are more likely to identify as secular, and, correspondingly, they make up an increasing proportion of the population. While a greater percentage of women identify as religious than men, the difference is not numerically significant. By examining demographics such as marital status and number of children, we can observe trends in family life among different groups in comparison to the overall population.

At the end of this section, we take a look at the religious affiliation of the United States government, from its founding to the present. The data in those tables shows that, despite America's ever-present and growing diversity, its government is not representative of the population. In part, the disproportion results from recent immigration trends, but it also reflects gaps in education and income level between religious groups during the founding of this country. The disproportion of representation by certain groups in the U.S. government is slowly changing, as changes in the demographic landscape of this country are reflected in society. While it is difficult to generalize about the religious landscape of the United States, the tables and graphs in this section allow a closer look at the overall distribution among religious groups and the characteristics of their populations.

— Emily Feldman
Section Editor

A. National Numbers

The religious diversity in America can be difficult to visualize from a particular corner of the country. In this section, we take a look at the numbers, using graphs and tables to illustrate patterns of affiliation, by self-identification and by predetermined criteria such as church attendance or prayer frequency. Through the breakdown that these charts provide, we can better understand the geographic significance of religious affiliation in this country. While the sample size varied, the surveys are representative of the greater population of the United States.

1.01 U.S. Religious Affiliation

The following pie chart illustrates the distribution of some major religions in the United States. Not surprisingly, Protestants make up roughly sixty percent of the population, with more than half of that figure identifying as Evangelical Protestant. Catholics make up slightly more than twenty percent of the population, which reflects recent immigration trends as well as their historical presence in the United States. Unaffiliated individuals make up more than ten percent of the population; their presence serves as a reminder that not all Americans are religiously affiliated.

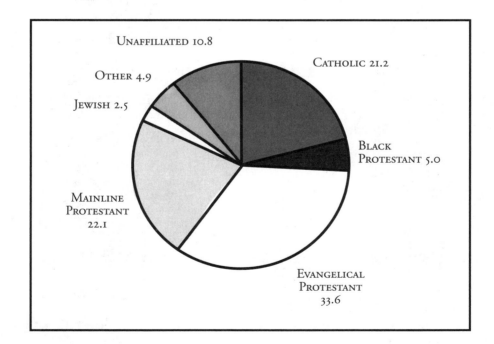

NOTE: N=1687; 34 INDIVIDUALS DID NOT PROVIDE SUFFICIENT INFORMATION TO BE CLASSIFIED INTO A RELIGIOUS TRADITION.
BAYLOR INSTITUTE FOR STUDIES OF RELIGION: *American Piety in the 21st Century*, 2006.

1.02 Religious Composition of the U.S.

This table shows the top twenty religions in the United States and how their populations compare to that of other religions. The numbers are derived from self-identification in the ARIS poll. The predominance of Christianity in America is clear from the percentage totals; there are only three groups in whole digits, and Christianity's numbers are more than five times higher than the runner-up.

EVANGELICAL PROTESTANT CHURCHES	26.3	Congregationalist in the Evang'l Trad.	<0.3
Baptist in the Evangelical Tradition	**10.8**	Conserv. Congregational Christian	<0.3
Southern Baptist Convention	6.7	Other Congreg. denom.–Evang'l Trad.	<0.3
Independent Baptist–Evang'l Trad.	2.5	Congregationalist–Evang'l Trad., unspec.	<0.3
Baptist Missionary Association	< 0.3	**Holiness in the Evangelical Tradition**	**1.0**
Free Will Baptist	<0.3	Church of the Nazarene	0.3
Gen'l Assoc. of Regular Baptists	<0.3	Free Methodist Church	0.3
Other (Evang'l) Baptist denom.	<0.3	Wesleyan Church	<0.3
Baptist/Evang'l Trad., unspecified	0.9	Christian and Missionary Alliance	<0.3
Methodist in the Evang'l Tradition	**0.3**	Church of God (Anderson, Indiana)	<0.3
Nondenominational/Evang'l Tradition	**3.4**	Other Holiness denom.–Evang'l Trad.	<0.3
Nondenominational Evangelical	1.2	Holiness-Evang'l Trad., unspecified	<0.3
Nondenominational Charismatic	0.5	**Reformed in the Evangelical Tradition**	**<0.3**
Nondenominational Fundamentalist	0.3	Christian Reformed Church	<0.3
Nondenominational Christian	<0.3	Other Reformed denom.–Evang'l Trad.	<0.3
Interdenominational–Evang'l Trad.	0.5	Reformed—Evang. Trad., unspecified	<0.3
Community Church–Evang'l Trad.	<0.3	**Adventist in the Evangelical Tradition**	**0.5**
Other nondenom. Group–Evang'l Trad.	<0.3	Seventh-day Adventist	0.4
Nondenom'l-Evang'l Trad., unspecified	0.8	Other Adventist Group–Evang'l Trad.	<0.3
Lutheran in the Evangelical Tradition	**1.8**	**Anabaptist in the Evangelical Tradition**	**0.3**
Lutheran Church, Missouri Synod	1.4	**Pietist in the Evangelical Tradition**	**<0.3**
Lutheran Church, Wisconsin Synod	<0.3	**Other Evangelical/Fundamentalist**	**0.3**
Other Lutheran denom. Evang'l Trad.	<0.3	**Protestant nonspecific—Evang'l Tradition**	**1.9**
Lutheran–Evang'l Trad., unspecified	<0.3	MAINLINE PROTESTANT CHURCHES	18.1
Presbyterian in the Evang'l Trad.	**0.8**	**Baptist in the Mainline Tradition**	**1.9**
Presbyterian Church in America	0.4	American Baptist Churches in U.S.A.	1.2
Other Presby. denom. Evang'l Trad.	<0.3	Other Baptist denom.–Mainline Trad.	<0.3
Presbyterian–Evang'l Trad., unspec.	<0.3	Baptist–Mainline Trad., unspecified	0.6
Pentecostal—Evang'l Trad.	**3.4**	**Methodist in the Mainline Tradition**	**5.4**
Assemblies of God	1.4	United Methodist Church	5.1
Church of God Cleveland Tennessee	0.4	Other Methodist denom. Mainline Trad.	<0.3
Four Square Gospel	<0.3	Methodist–Mainline Trad., unspecified	0.4
Pentecostal Church of God	<0.3	**Nondenominational–Mainline Tradition**	**0.9**
Pentecostal Holiness Church	<0.3	Interdenominational–Mainline Trad.	0.3
Nondenom., Independent Pentecostal	<0.3	Other nondenom. group–Mainline Trad.	<0.3
Church of God of the Apostolic Faith	<0.3	Nondenom.–Mainline Trad., unspecified	0.6
Apostolic Pentecostal–Evang'l Trad.	<0.3	**Lutheran in the Mainline Tradition**	**2.8**
Other Pentecost'l denom. Evang'l Trad.	<0.3	Evang'l Lutheran Church in America	2.0
Pentecostal-Evang'l Trad., unspecified	0.7	Other Lutheran denom.–Mainline Trad.	<0.3
Anglican/Episcopal-Evang'l Trad.	**<0.3**	Lutheran–Mainline Trad., unspecified	0.8
Restorationist–Evangelical Tradition	**1.7**	**Presbyterian in the Mainline Tradition**	**1.9**
Church of Christ	1.5	Presbyterian Church U.S.A.	1.1
Christian Churches, Churches of Christ	<0.3	Other Presbyterian denom. Mainline Trad.	<0.3
Restorationist–Evang'l Trad., unspec.	0.3	Presbyterian–Mainline Trad., unspecifd	0.7

Anglican/Episcopal in the Mainline Tradition	**1.4**
Episcopal Church in the U.S.A.	1.0
Anglican Church (Church of England)	0.3
Other Anglican/Episcopal–Main. Trad.	<0.3
Anglican/Episcopal–Main. Trad., unspec.	<0.3
Restorationist in the Mainline Tradition	**0.4**
Disciples of Christ	0.3
Restorationist–Mainline Trad., unspec.	<0.3
Congregationalist in the Mainline Tradition	**0.7**
United Church of Christ	0.5
Congregationalist–Mainline Trad., unspec.	<0.3
Reformed in the Mainline Tradition	**<0.3**
Reformed Church in America	<0.3
Other Reformed denom.–Mainline Trad.	<0.3
Reformed–Mainline Tradition, unspecified	<0.3
Anabaptist in the Mainline Tradition	**<0.3**
Friends in the Mainline Tradition	**<0.3**
Other/Protestant nonspecific–Mainline Trad.	**2.5**
HISTORICALLY BLACK CHURCHES	6.9
Baptist in the Historically Black Tradition	**4.4**
National Baptist Convention	1.8
Progressive Baptist Convention	0.3
Independent Baptist–Hist. Black Trad.	0.5
Missionary Baptist	<0.3
Other Baptist denom.–Hist. Black Trad.	<0.3
Baptist–Hist. Black Trad., unspecified	1.7
Methodist–Historically Black Tradition	**0.6**
African Methodist Episcopal	0.4
African Methodist Episcopal Zion	<0.3
Christian Methodist Episcopal Church	<0.3
Other Methodist denom.––Hist.Black Trad.	<0.3
Methodist–Hist. Black Trad., unspecified	<0.3
Nondenominational–Hist. Black Trad.	**<0.3**
Pentecostal–Historically Black Tradition	**0.9**
Church of God in Christ	0.6
Apostolic Pentecostal–Hist. Black Trad.	<0.3
United Pentecostal Church International	<0.3
Other Pentecostal denom.–Hist. Black Trad.	<0.3
Pentecostal–Hist. Black Trad., unspecified	<0.3
Holiness in the Historically Black Tradition	**<0.3**
Protestant nonspecific–Hist. Black Trad.	**0.5**
CATHOLIC	23.9
MORMON	1.7
Church of Jesus Christ of Latter-day Saints	1.6
Community of Christ	<0.3
Mormon, unspecified	<0.3
JEHOVAH'S WITNESS	0.7
ORTHODOX	0.6
Greek Orthodox	<0.3
Russian Orthodox	<0.3
Other Orthodox church	<0.3
Orthodox, unspecified	<0.3

OTHER CHRISTIAN	0.3
Metaphysical	**<0.3**
Spiritualist	<0.3
Unity; Unity Church; Christ Church Unity	<0.3
Other Metaphysical	<0.3
Other	**<0.3**
JEWISH	1.7
Reform	0.7
Conservative	0.5
Orthodox	<0.3
Other Jewish groups	<0.3
Jewish, unspecified	<0.3
BUDDHIST	0.7
Theravada (Vipassana) Buddhism	<0.3
Mahayana (Zen) Buddhism	<0.3
Vajrayana (Tibetan) Buddhism	<0.3
Other Buddhist groups	<0.3
Buddhist, unspecified	0.3
MUSLIM*	0.6
Sunni	0.3
Shia	<0.3
Other Muslim groups	<0.3
Muslim, unspecified	<0.3
HINDU	0.4
Vaishnava Hinduism	<0.3
Shaivite Hinduism	< 0.3
Other Hindu groups	<0.3
Hindu, unspecified	<0.3
OTHER WORLD RELIGIONS	<0.3
OTHER FAITHS	1.2
Unitarians and other liberal faiths	**0.7**
Unitarian (Universalist)	0.3
Liberal faith	<0.3
Spiritual but not religious	<0.3
Eclectic, "a bit of everything," own beliefs	<0.3
Other liberal faith groups	<0.3
New Age	**0.4**
Wica (Wiccan)	<0.3
Pagan	<0.3
Other New Age groups	<0.3
Native American Religions	**<0.3**
UNAFFILIATED	16.1
Atheist	1.6
Agnostic	2.4
No belief system in particular	12.1
DON'T KNOW	0.8

* "MUSLIMS AMERICANS: MIDDLE CLASS AND MOSTLY MAINSTREAM" PEW FORUM ON RELIGION AND PUBLIC LIFE: U.S. RELIGIOUS LANDSCAPE SURVEY, 2008.

1.03 Self-Described Religious Identification of Adult Population: 1990 and 2001

The table below summarizes the religious self-identification of U.S. adults and provides a sense of the diversity that characterizes the U.S. religious landscape. It compares findings from an earlier survey.

RELIGIOUS GROUP	1990 (1,000s)	2001 (1,000s)	RELIGIOUS GROUP	1990 (1,000s)	2001 (1,000s)
Adult population total [1]	175,440	207,980	Fundametalist	27	61
Total Christian	151496	159,506	Salvation Army	27	25
Catholic	46,004	50,873	Independent		
Baptist	33,964	33,830	Christian Church	25	71
Protestant (no denom.)	17,214	4,647			
Methodist/Wesleyan	14,174	14,150	Total Other Religions	5,853	7,740
Lutheran	9.110	9,580	Jewish	3,137	2,831
Christian (no denom. specified)	8,703	14,150	Muslim/Islamic	527	1,104
Presbyterian	4,985	5,596	Buddhist	401	1,082
Pentacostal/Charismatic	3,191	4,407	Unitarian/Universalist	502	629
Episcopalian/Anglican	3,042	3,451	Hindu	227	766
Mormon/Latter-day Saints	2,487	2,787	Native American	47	103
Churches of Christ	1,769	2,593	Baha'i	28	84
Jehovah's Witness	1,381	1,331	Taoist	23	40
Seventh-Day Adventist	668	724	New Age	20	68
Assemblies of God	660	1,106	Scientology	45	55
Holiness/Holy	610	569	Eckankar	18	26
Congregational/			Rastafarian	14	11
United Chuch of Christ	599	1,378	Sikh	13	57
Church of the Nazarene	549	544	Wiccan	8	134
Church of God	531	944	Deity	6	49
Eastern Orthodox	502	645	Druid	(N/A)	33
Evangelical [2]	242	1,032	Santeria	(N/A)	22
Mennonite	235	346	Pagan	(N/A)	140
Christian Science	214	194	Spirituaist	(N/A)	116
Church of the Bretheren	206	358	Ethical Culture	(N/A)	4
Born Again [2]	204	56	Other unclassified	837	386
Nondenominational [2]	195	2,489			
Disciples of Christ	144	492	Specified no religion–total	14,331	29,481
Reformed/Dutch Reform	161	289	Atheist	(N/A)	902
Apostolic/New Apostolic	117	254	Agnostic	1,186	991
Quaker	67	217	Humanist	29	49
Full Gospel	51	168	Secular	(N/A)	53
Christian Reform	40	79	No religion (general)	13,116	27,486
Foursquare Gospel	28	70	Declined reply	4,031	11,246

NA: NOT AVAILABLE [1]REFERS TO THE TOTAL NUMBER OF ADULTS IN ALL 50 STATES. ALL FIGURES ARE BASED ON PROJECTIONS FROM SURVEYS CONDUCTED IN THE CONTINENTAL U.S. [2]BECAUSE OF THE SUBJECTIVE NATURE OF REPLIES TO OPEN-ENDED QUESTIONS, THESE CATEGORIES ARE THE MOST UNSTABLE; THEY DO NOT REFER TO CLEARLY IDENTIFIABLE DENOMINATIONS AS MUCH AS UNDERLYING FEELINGS ABOUT RELIGION; THEY MAY BE MOST SUBJECT TO FLUCTUATION OVER TIME. 1990 DATA, BARRY A. KOSMIN AND SEYMOUR P. LACHMAN, "ONE NATION UNDER GOD: RELIGION IN CONTEMPORARY AMERICAN SOCIETY", 1993; 2001 DATA, THE GRADUATE CENTER OF THE CITY UNIVERSITY OF NEW YORK, BARRY A. KOSMIN, EGON MAYER AND ARIELA KEYSAR, AMERICAN RELIGIOUS IDENTIFICATION SURVEY, COPYRIGHT © 2001, TABLE FROM U.S. CENSUS 67.

1.04 Reported Household Membership in Church, Temple, Synagogue, or Mosque for Selected Religious Groups

The following table shows the distribution of religious institutional membership among the twenty-two largest religious groups, including "no religion," which, at nineteen percent, is highly rep- resented. Table 1.05 covers a civilian population of adults, with a more specific look at their religious preferences and institutional (church) attendance over a period of twenty-two years.

Name of Group	Percent Members
Catholic	59
Baptist	69
No Religion	19
Christian	60
Methodist	66
Lutheran	68
Presbyterian	64
Protestant	45
Pentecostal	68
Episcopalian/Anglican	64
Jewish *	53

*NOTE: THIS REFERS ONLY TO JEWS BY RELIGION

Name of Group	Percent Members
Mormon	75
Churches of Christ	71
Non-denominational	55
Congregational/UCC	69
Jehovah's Witnesses	55
Assemblies of God	78
Muslim/Islamic	62
Buddhist	28
Evangelical/Born Again	83
Church of God	68
Seventh Day Adventist	70
US TOTAL	54

1.05 Religious Preference, Church Membership, and Attendance: 1980–2002

YEAR	Protestant	Catholic	Jewish	Orthodox	Mormon	Other (specific)	None	Church/ Synagogue Members	Church/ Synagogue Attendees [1]
1980	61	28	2	(N/A)		2	7	65	40
1985	57	28	2	(N/A)	(N/A)	4	9	71	42
1990	56	25	2	(N/A)	(N/A)	6	11	65	40
1995	56	27	2	1	1	5	8 [2]	69	43
1998	59	27	2	2	1	4	8 [2]	70	40
1999	55	28	2	1	2	2	1 [2]	70	43
2000	56	27	2	1	1	5	8 [2]	68	44
2001	53	25	2	1	2	7	10 [2]	66	42
2002	53	25	2	1	2	8	9 [2]	65	44

• [1] PERSONS WHO ATTENDED A CHURCH OR SYNAGOGUE IN LAST 7 DAYS • [2] INCLUDES THOSE RESPONDENTS NOT DESIGNATING 1.04—GRADUATE CENTER OF THE CITY UNIVERSITY OF NEW YORK: AMERICAN RELIGIOUS IDENTIFICATION SURVEY, 2001. 1.05—THE GALLUP ORGANIZATION, PRINCETON, NJ, U.S. CENSUS 67.

1.06 Measures of Vitality: Half Full or Half Empty?

The bar graph below depicts the vitality of congregations within the United States in terms of congregational success. The poll covered both spiritual vitality as well as attendance and financial vitality as measures of congregation accomplishments. While 43% of congregations report that they are spiritually vital, only 24% report that they are financially vital to the population.

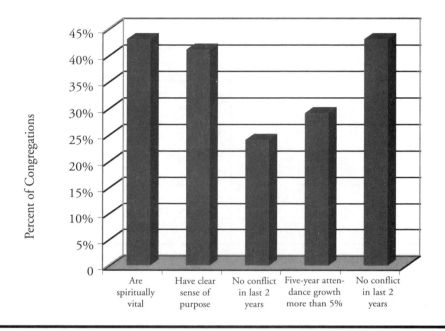

1.07 Size of Congregations: Small Still Dominates

The Hartford Institute for Religion Research polled for congregation sizes and found that the vast majority of congregations have a weekly attendance of between one and one hundred members, and 37% have a weekly attendance of between 101 and 350. The findings show that most American houses of worship are small or moderately sized; large attendance is less common.

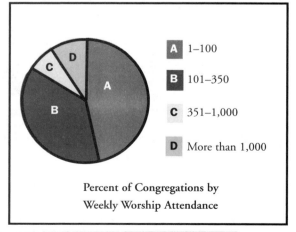

A 1–100

B 101–350

C 351–1,000

D More than 1,000

Percent of Congregations by
Weekly Worship Attendance

1.06, 1.07: Hartford Institute for Religion Research: American Congregations, 2005.

1.08 Number of Adults by Current and Prior Religious Identification, 2001

This table lists percentages of members of major religions who have switched denominations. The group with the highest percent switching in, Jehovah's Witnesses, also has the highest percent switching out. The next highest group in member gains, Evangelical/Born Again, has a low rate of loss.

Name of Group	Current Number	Switched In	Switched In (%)	Prior Number	Switched Out	Switched Out (%)	Net Gain (Loss)
Catholic	50,873,000	4,282,909	8%	56,084,003	9,493,912	17%	−9%
Baptist	33,830,000	4,401,587	13%	34,048,066	4,619,653	14%	−1%
No Religion	29,481,000	6,622,494	23%	23,976,587	1,118,081	5%	23%
Christian	14,190,000	2,873,155	20%	12,803,459	1,486,614	12%	11%
Methodist	14,140,000	2,631,703	19%	15,284,374	3,776,077	25%	−7%
Lutheran	9,580,000	1,755,644	18%	9,682,231	1,857,875	19%	−1%
Presbyterian	5,596,000	1,316,068	24%	5,712,050	1,432,118	25%	−2%
Protestant	4,647,000	316,587	7%	5,418,822	1,088,409	20%	−14%
Pentecostal	4,407,000	1,340,583	30%	3,796,957	730,540	19%	16%
Episcopalian/Anglican	3,451,000	899,908	26%	3,296,468	745,376	23%	5%
Jewish*	2,831,000	171,447	6%	2,950,943	291,390	10%	−4%
Mormon	2,787,000	441,317	16%	2,791,683	446,000	16%	0%
Churches of Christ	2,503,000	292,129	12%	2,556,519	345,648	14%	−2%
Non-denominational	2,489,000	721,683	29%	1,810,865	43,548	2%	37%
Congregational/UCC	1,378,000	183,916	13%	1,463,860	269,776	18%	−6%
Jehovah's Witnesses	1,331,000	517,540	39%	1,194,443	380,983	32%	11%
Assemblies of God	1,105,000	221,398	20%	1,028,116	144,514	14%	7%
Muslim/Islamic	1,104,000	182,859	17%	1,019,474	98,333	10%	8%
Buddhist	1,082,000	340,523	33%	962,512	221,035	23%	12%
Evang'cl/Born Again	1,032,000	384,339	37%	725,710	78,049	11%	42%
Church of God	944,000	241,296	26%	898,437	195,733	22%	5%
Seventh-day Adventist	724,000	247,780	34%	653,855	177,635	27%	11%

*NOTE: Only Jews by religion are included in the analysis.

1.09 American Religious Outlook, 2001

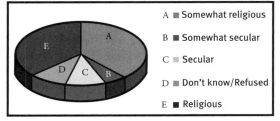

A ■ Somewhat religious

B ■ Somewhat secular

C ■ Secular

D ■ Don't know/Refused

E ■ Religious

The pie chart at left describes the "religious outlook" of the American population. Participants were asked, "When it comes to your outlook, do you regard yourself as . . . " The respondents who regarded themselves in any way religious totalled about 75% of the polled population.

1.08, 1.09: THE GRADUATE CENTER OF THE C.U.N.Y.: AMERICAN RELIGIOUS IDENTIFICATION SURVEY, 2001.

1.10 Best Describing Religious Identity Among Those Affiliated with Major Christian Traditions

The Baylor Institute's Survey of American Piety in the twenty-firtst century asked the four main denominations of Christians how they would describe their religious identity—whether they were Bible-Believing, Born Again, Evangelical or Mainline Christian.

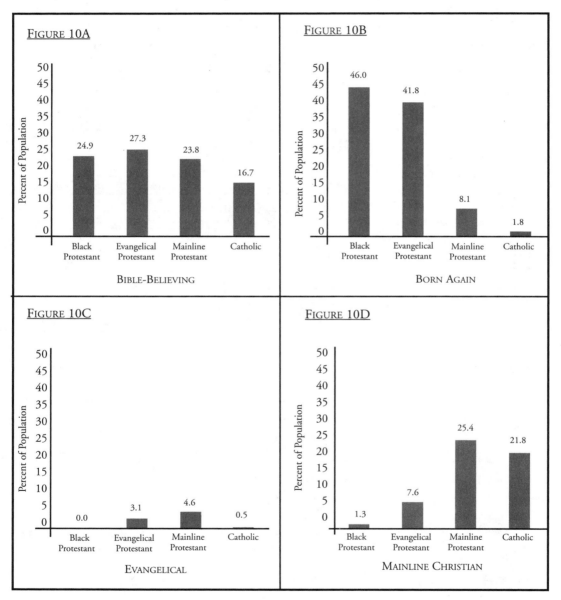

FIGURE 10A

BIBLE-BELIEVING

Black Protestant: 24.9
Evangelical Protestant: 27.3
Mainline Protestant: 23.8
Catholic: 16.7

FIGURE 10B

BORN AGAIN

Black Protestant: 46.0
Evangelical Protestant: 41.8
Mainline Protestant: 8.1
Catholic: 1.8

FIGURE 10C

EVANGELICAL

Black Protestant: 0.0
Evangelical Protestant: 3.1
Mainline Protestant: 4.6
Catholic: 0.5

FIGURE 10D

MAINLINE CHRISTIAN

Black Protestant: 1.3
Evangelical Protestant: 7.6
Mainline Protestant: 25.4
Catholic: 21.8

BAYLOR INSTITUTE FOR STUDIES OF RELIGION: AMERICAN PIETY IN THE 21ST CENTURY, 2006.

1.11 Frequency of Religious Service Attendance Among Those Unaffiliated with a Religious Tradition

The Baylor Institute polled Americans not affiliated with a church on their frequency of church attendance and of prayer. While only 10.7% of unaffiliated Americans attend church, 31.6% pray.

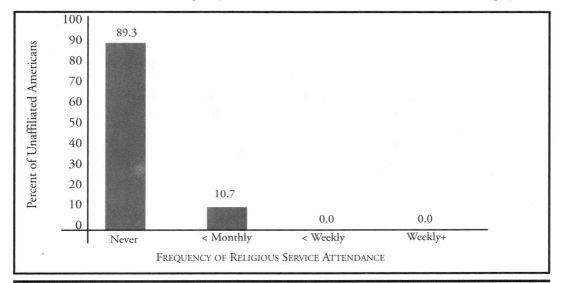

1.12 Frequency of Prayer Among Those Unaffiliated with a Religious Tradition

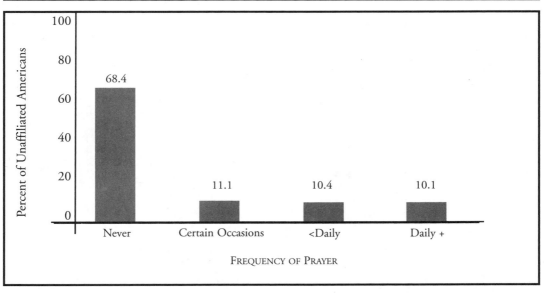

1.11, 1.12: BAYLOR INSTITUTE FOR STUDIES OF RELIGION: AMERICAN PIETY IN THE 21ST CENTURY, 2006.

1.13 Percentage of Adults in Mixed Religion Families for Selected Religious Groups, 2001

The American Religious Identification Survey found that of all households that contained either a married or domestic partner couple, 22% reported a mixture of religious identification. At the low end are the Mormon adults who are found in mixed religion families at 12% and such other groups as Baptists, those adhering to the Churches of Christ, Assemblies of God, the Evangelicals, and those adhering to the Church of God (all at about 18%). At the high end we find the Episcopalians at 42% and Buddhists at 39% living in mixed religion families. In all, about 28 million American married or otherwise "coupled" adults live in a mixed religion household.

RESPONDENT'S RELIGIOUS GROUP	MIXED HOUSEHOLDS
Catholic	23
Baptist	18
No religion	28
Christian	21
Methodist	24
Lutheran	28
Presbyterian	27
Protestant	33
Pentecostal	24
Episcopalian/Anglican	42
Jewish*	27
Mormon	12
Churches of Christ	18
Non-denominational	32
Congregational/UCC	24
Jehovah's Witnesses	30
Assemblies of God	18
Muslim/Islamic	21
Buddhist	39
Evangelical/Born Again	18
Church of God	18
Seventh Day Adventist	24
Percent in Mixed Households	**22****
Total Adults in Mixed Couples	**28,400,000**

*NOTE: CATEGORY REFERS ONLY TO JEWS BY RELIGION
**NOTE: BASE INCLUDES ADULTS MARRIED OR LIVING WITH A PARTNER WHERE THE RELIGIOUS SELF-IDENTIFICATION REPORTED BY RESPONDENT DID NOT MATCH THAT REPORTED FOR SPOUSE/PARTNER.
THE GRADUATE CENTER OF THE CITY UNIVERSITY OF NEW YORK: AMERICAN RELIGIOUS IDENTIFICATION SURVEY, 2001.

1.14 Percent of Population Identifying with Selected Religious Labels

The Baylor Institute reported, "Sorting people by where they attend worship is one way to create religious groups. Another way is to ask people to sort themselves. We give respondents this option." This particular technique brings to light the percentage of the population which agrees and disagrees with the religious labels commonly applied to people of faith. It is clear from these results that the popular or media-induced labels are not always accurate according to those within the supposed identification.

Religious Identity Labels	Percentage Identifying w. Label[A]	Pct. Indicating as Best Description of Religious Identity
Bible-Believing	47.2%	20.5%
Born Again	28.5%	18.6%
Mainline Christian	26.1%	12.9%
Theologically Conservative	17.6%	5.3%
Evangelical	14.9%	2.2%
Theologically Liberal	13.8%	9.1%
Moral Majority	10.3%	1.7%
Seeker	8.5%	3.9%
Religious Right	8.3%	1.2%
Fundamentalist	7.7%	1.0%
Charismatic	7.3%	0.3%
Pentecostal	5.8%	1.7%
None of these	—	21.8%

[A] RESPONDENTS ANSWERED YES/NO TO EACH LABEL. CATEGORIES WERE NOT MUTUALLY EXCLUSIVE;, THEREFORE, REPORTED PERCENTAGES DO NOT ADD TO 100.
BAYLOR INSTITUTE FOR STUDIES OF RELIGION: AMERICAN PIETY IN THE 21ST CENTURY, 2006.

1.15 Religious Beliefs and Practices by Religious Tradition

This table describes the various beliefs among different religious groups pertaining to simple questions of faith. Certain questions would clearly be answered differently among faiths—Catholics and Jews of course would fundamentally differ on the question of whether Jesus was the son of God or not—but there are also broader questions such as whether the Bible is literally true, where only Evangelical Protestants and Black Protestants show high numbers. Media induced labels are not always accurate according to those within the supposed identification.

Religious Affiliation	Black Protestant	Evang. Protestant	Mainline Protestant	Catholic	Jewish	Unaffil.
BELIEF ABOUT GOD						
No doubts God exists	100.0	86.5	63.6	74.8	42.9	11.6
Don't believe in anything beyond the physical world	0.0	0.4	0.7	1.1	7.2	37.1
BELIEF ABOUT JESUS						
Jesus is the son of God	95.1	94.4	72.2	84.9	9.6	11.0
Jesus is a fictional character	0.0	0.0	0.9	0.2	2.3	13.7
BELIEF ABOUT BIBLE						
Literally true	40.6	47.8	11.2	11.8	8.9	1.0
Ancient book of history and legends	1.5	6.5	22.0	19.8	52.6	82.3
PRAY						
Once a day or more	74.1	67.1	44.1	46.1	32.8	10.1
Never	3.7	3.6	11.6	6.9	16.6	68.4
READ SCRIPTURE						
Weekly or more	54.4	42.1	16.0	7.1	1.4	1.5
Never	3.7	9.3	21.9	33.1	27.0	67.3
ATTEND RELIGIOUS SERVICES						
Weekly or more	43.1	45.2	24.3	32.8	7.3	0.0
Never	10.6	11.8	13.5	9.3	28.9	89.3

The column group header above the percentage columns reads: PERCENTAGES

NOTE: DIFFERENCES IN PERCENTAGES FOR ALL BELIEFS AND PRACTICES ARE SIGNIFICANT ACROSS RELIGIOUS TRADITIONS. SAMPLE INTERPRETATION: THREE-FOURTHS OF CATHOLICS (74.8%) HAVE NO DOUBT THAT GOD EXISTS. BAYLOR INSTITUTE FOR STUDIES OF RELIGION: AMERICAN PIETY IN THE 21ST CENTURY, 2006.

1.16 Retention of Childhood Members Among Groups

Roughly half of children raised Protestant identify with the same affiliation in which they were raised, but this reflects movement between denominations. Eighty percent of children raised Protestant remained so, which includes individuals who retained their original affiliation or switched to another Protestant denomination. Most denominations lose a number of adherents to the unaffiliated category.

	PERCENT NON-CONVERTS	PERCENT CONVERTED TO ANOTHER GROUP/DK	PERCENT CONVERTED TO NO RELIGION
Total population	56.5	30.1	13.4
Among those raised...			
Hindu	84	8	8
Jewish	76	9	14
Orthodox	73	21	7
Mormon	70	15	14
Catholic	68	18	14
Buddhist	50	22	28
Jehovah's Witness	37	30	33
Unaffiliated	46	54	N/A

1.17 Retention of Childhood Members Among Protestant Religious Groups

	Did not change	New Prot. family	Evangelical churches	CHANGED TO... Mainline churches	Hist. Black churches	Non-Prot. Religion/ DK	No Religion
Among those raised...			PERCENTAGE				
Protestant	52	28	15	10	3	7	13
Largely Evangelical Families							
Baptist	60	23	12	8	4	6	11
Nondenominational	44	27	16	11	1	10	19
Pentecostal	47	35	23	8	3	6	12
Restorationist	46	35	21	13	1	6	13
Holiness	32	51	36	9	5	4	13
Adventist	59	23	10	6	6	7	10
Anabaptist	40	51	29	20	2	2	7
Largely Mainline Families							
Methodist	47	32	19	11	3	8	12
Lutheran	59	19	10	9	*	9	13
Presbyterian	40	36	16	18	1	9	14
Anglican/Episcopal	45	23	10	11	2	12	20
Congregationalist	37	35	15	17	2	9	20

Due to rounding, figures may not add to 100.

1.16, 1.17: PEW FORUM ON RELIGION AND PUBLIC LIFE: U.S. RELIGIOUS LANDSCAPE SURVEY, 2008.

1.18 Regional Distribution of Religious Traditions

The graph below illustrates the diversity of religious traditions in each region of the United States, in which each has its own pattern of religious affiliation. The South and West have the largest percentage of unaffiliated individuals (29%), and the Northeast has the largest percentage of Jews (41%). Catholics are evenly distributed among regions, but the majority reside in the Northeast. The largest percentage of Evangelical Protestants (50%) resides in the South, and 76% of Mormons are concentrated in the West.

U.S RELIGIOUS TRADITIONS	NORTHEAST	MIDWEST	SOUTH	WEST	SAMPLE SIZE
National Total	19%	23%	36%	22%	35556
Members of Evangelical Protestant Churches	10%	23%	50%	17%	9472
Members of Mainline Protestant Churches	19%	29%	34%	18%	7470
Members of Historically Black Protestant Churches	13%	19%	60%	8%	1995
Catholics	29%	24%	24%	23%	8054
Mormons	4%	7%	12%	76%	581
Orthodox	33%	19%	24%	25%	363
Jehovah's Witnesses	16%	19%	36%	29%	215
Other Christians	14%	23%	22%	41%	129
Jews	41%	12%	26%	21%	682
Muslims	29%	22%	32%	18%	1050
Buddhists	17%	15%	23%	45%	411
Hindus	29%	13%	32%	26%	257
Other Faiths	23%	20%	26%	31%	449
Unaffiliated	19%	23%	29%	29%	5048

DATA FOR MUSLIMS FROM "MUSLIM AMERICANS: MIDDLE CLASS AND MOSTLY MAINSTREAM," PEW RESEARCH CENTER, 2007.
PEW FORUM ON RELIGION AND PUBLIC LIFE: U.S. RELIGIOUS LANDSCAPE SURVEY, 2008.

1.19–1.22 Religious Affiliation by State for Each Region

The four tables that follow show the distribution of major religious groups by state in the four main regions of the United States. The tables reflect the percentages in the previous graph, and give a more specific look at where members of each religion are concentrated.

* FROM "MUSLIM AMERICANS: MIDDLE CLASS AND MOSTLY MAINSTREAM," PEW RESEARCH CENTER, 2007
PEW FORUM ON RELIGION AND PUBLIC LIFE: U.S. RELIGIOUS LANDSCAPE SURVEY, 2008.

1.19 Religious Affiliation by State in the Northeast

(PERCENTAGE)	National	Northeast	Conn./R.I.	Maine	Mass.	N.H./Vt.	N.J.	N.Y.	Penn.
Members Evang. Prot. Churches	26	13	10	15	11	11	2	11	18
Members Mainline Prot. Churches	18	19	13	26	15	23	13	16	25
Members Hist. Black Prot. Churches	7	5	4	<0.5	2	<0.5	5	5	7
Catholic	24	37	43	29	43	29	42	39	29
Mormon	2	<0.5	<0.5	1	<0.5	1	<0.5	<0.5	<0.5
Jehovah's Witness	1	1	1	1	<0.5	<0.5	<0.5	1	1
Orthodox	1	1	1	<0.5	1	<0.5	1	1	1
Other Christian	<0.5	<0.5	<0.5	<0.5	<0.5	<0.5	<0.5	<0.5	<0.5
Jewish	2	4	1	<0.5	3	1	6	6	2
Muslim	1*	1	<0.5	<0.5	<0.5	<0.5	1	1	<0.5
Buddhist	1	1	1	1	1	1	1	1	<0.5
Hindu	<0.5	1	<0.5	<0.5	1	<0.5	2	1	<0.5
Other World Religions	<0.5	<0.5	<0.5	<0.5	<0.5	<0.5	<0.5	<0.5	<0.5
Other Faiths	1	1	2	2	2	7	1	1	1
Unaffiliated	16	16	23	25	17	26	12	17	13
Don't Know/Refused	1	1	1	<0.5	1	<0.5	2	1	1
Total	100	100	100	100	100	100	100	100	100
N	5,556	6,556	482	245	748	320	932	1,933	1,896
Margin of Error (%)	±0.6	±1.5	±5	±7	±4	±6.5	±4	± 2.5	± 2.5

1.20 Religious Affiliation by State in the Midwest

(PERCENTAGE)	Nat.	Midw.	Ill.	Ind.	Iowa	Kans.	Mich.	Minn.	Mo.	Neb.	ND./SD.	Ohio	Wisc.
Members of Evang. Prot.	26	26	19	34	24	29	26	21	37	21	24	26	24
Members of Mainln. Prot.	18	22	17	22	30	27	19	32	18	27	35	22	23
Members of Hist. Bl. Prot.	7	6	9	6	1	3	8	1	6	3	<0.5	7	3
Catholic	24	24	32	18	25	23	23	28	18	31	25	2	29
Mormon	2	1	<0.5	1	1	1	1	<0.5	1	<0.5	1	<0.5	<0.5
Jehovah's Witness	1	1	1	1	<0.5	<0.5	1	<0.5	1	<0.5	<0.5	1	<0.5
Orthodox	1	<0.5	1	<0.5	<0.5	<0.5	<0.5	<0.5	<0.5	<0.5	<0.5	1	1
Other Christian	<0.5	<0.5	<0.5	<0.5	<0.5	<0.5	<0.5	<0.5	<0.5	<0.5	<0.5	<0.5	1
Jewish	2	1	2	1	1	<0.5	1	1	1	<0.5	<0.5	1	<0.5
Muslim	1*	<0.5	<0.5	<0.5	<0.5	<0.5	1	1	<0.5	<0.5	<0.5	1	<0.5
Buddhist	1	<0.5	1	<0.5	<0.5	<0.5	1	1	<0.5	0.5	<0.5	<0.5	<0.5
Hindu	<0.5	<0.5	1	<0.5	<0.5	<0.5	<0.5	<0.5	<0.5	<0.5	<0.5	<0.5	<0.5
Other World Religions	<0.5	<0.5	<0.5	<0.5	<0.5	<0.5	<0.5	<0.5	<0.5	<0.5	<0.5	<0.5	<0.5
Other Faiths	1	1	1	<0.5	1	1	1	1	1	1	2	1	1
Unaffiliated	16	16	15	16	15	14	17	13	16	16	12	17	16
Don't Know/Refused	1	1	1	<0.5	1	1	1	<0.5	<0.5	<0.5	1	1	1
Total	100	100	100	100	100	100	100	100	100	100	100	100	100
N	35,556	9,078	1,340	924	487	421	1,275	789	879	247	238	1,654	824
Margin of Error (%)	±0.6	±1.5	±3	±4	±5	±5.5	±3.5	±4	±4	±7	±7	±3	±4

1.21 Religious Affiliation by State in the South

(PERCENTAGES)	Nat.	South	Ala.	Ark.	Del.	Fla.	Ga.	Ky.	La.	Md./DC	Miss.	N.C.	Okla.	S.C.	Tenn.	Tex.	Va.	W.Va.
Members Evang. Prot. Ch.	26	37	49	53	15	25	38	49	31	15	47	41	53	45	1	34	31	36
Members Mainln. Prot. Ch.	18	17	15	16	18	15	16	17	9	20	11	21	16	18	18	15	20	32
Members Hist. Bl. Prot. Ch.	7	11	18	10	14	8	16	5	20	18	23	13	3	15	8	8	10	2
Catholic	24	16	6	5	27	26	12	14	8	18	9	9	12	8	7	24	14	7
Mormon	2	1	<0.5	<0.5	<0.5	<0.5	1	<0.5	<0.5	<0.5	1	<0.5	<0.5	<0.5	1	1	1	<0.5
Jehovah's Witness	1	1	1	1	<0.5	1	1	<0.5	1	1	1	<0.5	<0.5	1	<0.5	1	<0.5	<0.5
Orthodox	1	<0.5	<0.5	<0.5	1	1	<0.5	<0.5	<0.5	5	1	<0.5	<0.5	<0.5	1	<0.5	<0.5	1	<0.5
Other Christian	<0.5	<0.5	<0.5	1	<0.5	<0.5	<0.5	<0.5	<0.5	<0.5	<0.5	<0.5	<0.5	<0.5	<0.5	<0.5	<0.5	<0.5
Jewish	2	1	<0.5	<0.5	2	3	<0.5	<0.5	<0.5	5	<0.5	<0.5	<0.5	1	<0.5	1	1	1
Muslim	1*	<0.5	<0.5	<0.5	<0.5	1	<0.5	<0.5	1	<0.5	<0.5	<0.5	<0.5	<0.5	1	<0.5	<0.5	<0.5
Buddhist	1	<0.5	<0.5	<0.5	<0.5	<0.5	<0.5	<0.5	1	1	<0.5	1	1	<0.5	<0.5	1	1	<0.5
Hindu	<0.5	<0.5	<0.5	<0.5	<0.5	0.5	<0.5	<0.5	<0.5	1	<0.5	<0.5	<0.5	<0.5	<0.5	1	1	1
Other World Religions	<0.5	<0.5	<0.5	<0.5	<0.5	<0.5	<0.5	<0.5	<0.5	<0.5	<0.5	<0.5	<0.5	<0.5	<0.5	<0.5	<0.5	<0.5
Other Faiths	1	1	1	<0.5	4	1	<0.5	1	<0.5	1	1	1	1	1	1	1	1	<0.5
Unaffiliated	6	13	8	13	19	16	13	12	8	17	6	12	12	10	12	12	18	19
Don't Know/Refused	1	1	1	<0.5	<0.5	1	<0.5	1	<0.5	1	1	1	1	<0.5	1	<0.5	1	1
Total	100	100	100	100	100	100	100	100	100	100	100	100	100	100	100	100	100	100
N	35,556	12,643	681	378	110	1,694	967	599	528	756	333	1,166	46	570	837	2,266	997	296
Margin of Error (%)	±0.6	±1	±4.5	±6	±10.5	±3	±3.5	±4.5	±5	±4	±6	±3.5	±5	±5	±4	±2.5	±3	±6.5

1.22 Religious Affiliation by State in the West

(PERCENTAGES)	Nat.	West	Ariz.	Calif.	Colo.	Idaho	Mon./Wyo.	Nev.	N.M.	Ore.	Utah	Wash.
Members of Evangelical Prot. Churches	26	20	23	18	23	22	26	13	25	30	7	25
Members of Mainline Prot. Churches	18	15	15	14	19	16	21	11	15	16	6	23
Members of Hist. Black Prot. Churches	7	3	2	4	2	<0.5	<0.5	2	2	1	1	1
Catholic	24	25	25	31	19	18	23	27	26	14	10	16
Mormon	2	6	4	2	2	23	5	11	2	5	58	2
Jehovah's Witness	1	1	1	1	<0.5	1	2	<0.5	2	<0.5	<0.5	1
Orthodox	1	1	<0.5	1	1	<0.5	<0.5	2	<0.5	<0.5	<0.5	<0.5
Other Christian	<0.5	1	<0.5	1	1	<0.5	<0.5	1	<0.5	1	<0.5	1
Jewish	2	2	1	2	2	<0.5	<0.5	1	2	1	<0.5	1
Muslim	1*	<0.5	<0.5	<0.5	<0.5	<0.5	<0.5	2	<0.5	<0.5	<0.5	<0.5
Buddhist	1	2	1	2	1	<0.5	1	<0.5	2	2	<0.5	1
Hindu	<0.5	<0.5	<0.5	1	<0.5	<0.5	<0.5	1	<0.5	<0.5	<0.5	<0.5
Other World Religions	<0.5	<0.5	<0.5	<0.5	1	<0.5	<0.5	1	<0.5	<0.5	<0.5	<0.5
Other Faiths	1	2	2	2	2	2	2	3	1	2	1	1
Unaffiliated	16	21	22	21	25	18	20	21	21	27	16	23
Don't Know/Refused	1	1	2	1	2	<0.5	<0.5	2	1	<0.5	1	2
Total	100	100	100	100	100	100	100	100	100	100	100	100
N	35,556	7,279	578	3,574	590	196	272	252	228	521	323	745
Margin of Error (%)	±0.6	±1.5	±4.5	±2	±4.5	±8	±7	±7	±7.5	±5	±6	±4

* FROM "MUSLIM AMERICANS: MIDDLE CLASS AND MOSTLY MAINSTREAM," PEW RESEARCH CENTER, 2007
1.21, 1.22: PEW FORUM ON RELIGION AND PUBLIC LIFE: U.S. RELIGIOUS LANDSCAPE SURVEY, 2008.

1.23 The Bible Belt is Still Distinct

A portion of the South has commonly been referred to as the "Bible Belt" because of its high number of religiously active individuals. This graph suggests that the phrase continues to have a numeric basis; at 41%, the South's number of congregations is twice the national average.

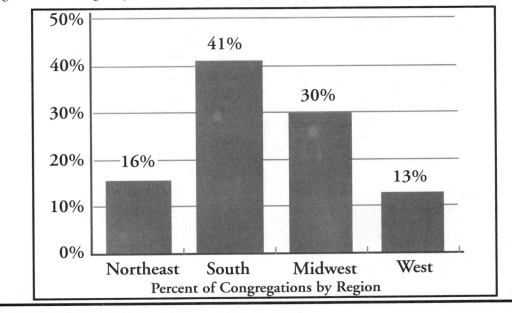

Percent of Congregations by Region

1.24 Will the Metro Areas Catch Up?

While most congregations are in small towns and country areas, the majority of Americans reside in cities with populations of more than 50,000 and related suburbs. The median size of small-town and country religious institutions is twice that of urban and suburban congregations.

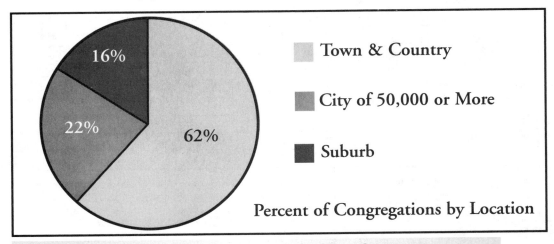

- Town & Country
- City of 50,000 or More
- Suburb

Percent of Congregations by Location

1.23, 1.24: HARTFORD INSTITUTE FOR RELIGION RESEARCH: AMERICAN CONGREGATIONS, 2005.

1.25 Christian Churchgoers, 2000; Jewish Population, 2004

The following table compares the distribution of Christian adherents and the Jewish population in each state in 2000 and in 2004. Christian church adherents were defined as "all members, including full members, their children, and the estimated number of other regular participants who are not considered as communicant, confirmed, or full members." The Jewish population includes Jews who define themselves as Jewish by religion as well as those who define themselves as Jewish in cultural terms.

STATE	CHRISTIAN ADHERENTS 2000		JEWISH POP. 2004		STATE	CHRISTIAN ADHERENTS 2000		JEWISH POP. 2004	
	NUMBER (1,000s)	% OF POP.	NUMBER (1,000s)	% OF POP.		NUMBER (1,000s)	% OF POP.	NUMBER (1,000s)	% OF POP.
U.S.	133,377	47.4	6,452	2.2	MO	2,813	50.3	59	1.0
AL	.2,418	54.4	9	0.2	MT	401	44.4	1	0.1
AK	210	33.6	3	0.5	NE	995	58.2	7	0.4
AZ	1,946	37.9	106	1.8	NV	604	30.2	70	2.9
AR	1,516	56.7	2	0.1	NH	571	46.2	10	0.8
CA	14,328	42.3	1,194	3.3	NJ	.4,262	50.7	480	5.5
CO	1,604	37.3	79	1.7	NM	1,041	57.2	11	0.6
CT	1,828	53.7	112	3.2	NY	9,569	50.4	1,618	8.4
DE	.299	38.2	14	1.6	NC	3,598	44.7	26	0.3
DC	331	57.8	28	5.1	ND	468	72.9	(Z)	0.1
FL	5,904	36.9	653	3.7	OH	4,912	43.3	145	1.3
GA	3,528	43.1	127	1.4	OK	2,079	60.3	5	0.1
HI	431	35.6	7	0.5	OR	1,029	30.1	32	0.9
ID	624	48.3	1	0.1	PA	6,751	55.0	285	2.3
IL	6,457	52.0	279	2.2	RI	646	61.7	19	1.7
IN	2,578	42.4	17	0.3	SC	1,874	46.7	11	(Z)
IA	.1,698	58.0	6	0.2	SD	510	67.6	(Z)	(Z)
KS	1,307	48.6	18	0.7	TN	2,867	50.4	19	0.3
KY	2,141	53.0	11	0.3	TX	11,316	54.3	131	0.6
LA	2,599	58.2	16	0.4	UT	1,659	74.3	4	0.2
ME	450	35.3	10	0.8	VT	230	37.8	6	0.9
MD	2,012	38.0	235	4.2	VA	2,807	39.7	98	1.3
MA	3,725	58.7	275	4.3	WA	1,872	31.8	43	0.7
MI	3,970	39.9	88	0.9	WV	646	35.7	2	0.1
MN	2,974	60.5	47	0.9	WI	3,198	59.6	28	0.5
MS	1,549	54.5	1	0.1	WY	229	46.4	Z	0.1

Z Fewer than 500 or .05 percent. 1 Based on U.S. Census Bureau data for resident population enumerated as of April 1, 2000, and estimated as of July 1, 2004. Source: Christian church adherents—Dale E. Jones, Sherri Doty, Clifford Grammich, James E. Horsch, Richard Houseal, John P. Marcum, Kenneth M. Sanchagrin, and Richard H. Taylor, Religious Congregations and Membership in the United States: 2000, Glenmary Research Center, Nashville, TN www.glenmary.org/grc, 2002 (copyright); Jewish population—American Jewish Committee, New York, NY, American Jewish Year Book (copyright). SOURCE: UNITED STATES CENSUS BUREAU.

2.01 General Demographics: Religious Affiliation by Demographic Characteristics

The table below shows the religious affiliation of Americans by demographic characteristics. It may come as no surprise that while 62.5% of Black Protestants are in the demographic group "African American," the demographic group "White" makes up 0.0% of the Black Protestant affiliation. On the other hand, it may seem surprising that the Evangelical Protestant affiliation has their highest numbers among young people (ages 18-30), though this age group is most likely to have no affiliation (more than 7% more likely to have no affiliation than any other age group).

RELIGIOUS AFFILIATION	BLACK PROTESTANT	EVANGELICAL PROTESTANT	MAINLINE PROTESTANT	CATHOLIC	JEWISH	OTHER	UNAFFIL-IATED
Total Sample *	5.0	33.6	22.1	21.2	2.5	4.9	10.8
Gender							
Male	2.8	30.0	22.1	23.8	2.5	6.0	12.8
Female	6.9	36.7	22.1	18.9	2.4	3.9	9.0
Race							
White	0.0	35.4	24.1	22.8	2.6	4.3	10.8
Afri. Amer.	62.5	9.5	7.7	5.0	3.7	6.0	5.7
Age							
18–30	3.8	39.0	20.1	10.1	2.7	5.7	18.6
31–44	5.4	34.9	17.6	23.0	1.9	5.8	11.4
45–64	3.9	31.3	22.5	23.7	2.7	4.8	11.1
65+	7.3	33.1	28.1	19.9	2.9	3.5	5.4
Education							
H.S. or less	5.0	45.4	18.0	22.0	2.3	2.1	5.2
College or more	3.0	23.5	29.0	21.4	3.6	6.7	12.8
Household income							
$35,000 or less	9.9	39.3	20.3	15.2	2.2	3.1	9.9
$100,000 +	0.0	26.9	22.0	27.7	5.1	7.7	10.7
Region							
East	5.0	13.1	26.0	35.1	4.7	4.6	11.6
South	7.2	50.3	19.3	11.5	1.9	2.7	7.1
Midwest	5.6	33.7	26.0	22.1	1.4	3.0	8.3
West	1.3	31.7	17.7	19.2	2.2	10.3	17.6

*NUMBERS ARE ROUNDED TO ONE DECIMAL PLACE IN ALL TABLES IN THIS DOCUMENT. NOTE: DIFFERENCES IN PERCENTAGES ACROSS RELIGIOUS GROUPS ARE SIGNIFICANT FOR ALL DEMOGRAPHIC CHARACTERISTICS. BAYLOR INSTITUTE FOR STUDIES OF RELIGION: AMERICAN PIETY IN THE 21ST CENTURY, 2006.

2.02 Religious Identity Labels by Religious and Demographic Characteristics

The table below looks at region, education, income level, and other demographic factors and their relation to religious identification. Roughly 20% of males consider themselves "theologically conservative," while only 14.6% of females identify with the same statement. 41.5% of Bible-believing individuals have completed college or a higher level of education. Individuals with household incomes of more than $100,000 a year are twice as likely to identify as "Theologically Liberal" than people with household incomes of $35,000 or less a year.

DO THE FOLLOWING TERMS DESCRIBE YOUR RELIGIOUS IDENTITY?	PERCENTAGE					
	BIBLE BELIEVING	BORN AGAIN	THEOLOGICALLY CONSERVATIVE	EVANGELICAL	MAINLINE CHRISTIAN	THEOLOGICALLY LIBERAL
Total Sample	47.2	28.5	17.6	14.9	26.1	13.8
Religious Tradition						
Black Protestant	69.5	57.3	7.3	16.0	14.8	7.3
Evangelical Protestant	68.6	62.4	27.3	32.6	23.1	5.6
Mainline Protestant	48.1	16.8	4.5	12.3	44.3	20.5
Catholic	38.4	4.7	21.0	2.8	34.9	13.9
Gender						
Male	41.7	23.6	21.1	12.1	28.1+	14.7+
Female	52.0	32.8	14.6	17.3	24.4+	13.0+
Race						
White	45.7	27.2	18.5+	15.3+	27.5	13.8+
African American	63.0	43.9	11.0+	13.7+	17.4	12.6+
Education						
High School or less	54.9	33.7	13.4	11.8+	19.5	6.1
College or more	41.5	22.9	20.6	15.2+	31.0	22.2
Household Income						
$35,000 or less	49.9	34.4	12.4	12.9+	20.6	9.4
More than $100,000	37.8	20.5	22.9	14.1+	32.6	21.7
Region						
East	36.4	14.5	13.1	8.5	27.3+	16.3+
South	52.8	43.9	20.7	19.2	24.8+	11.5+
Midwest	54.2	28.3	19.2	17.3	30.0+	13.5+
West	42.9	22.0	16.5	12.8	22.6+	14.9+

NOTE: DIFFERENCES IN PERCENTAGES ARE SIGNIFICANT FOR ALL DEMOGRAPHIC CHARACTERISTICS, EXCEPT WHERE NOTED BY PLUS SIGN (+). SAMPLE INTERPRETATION: HALF OF PERSONS WITH A HOUSEHOLD INCOME OF $35,000 OR LESS (49.9%) REPORT "BIBLE-BELIEVING" AS A TERM THAT DESCRIBES THEIR RELIGIOUS IDENTITY. BAYLOR INSTITUTE FOR STUDIES OF RELIGION: AMERICAN PIETY IN THE 21ST CENTURY, 2006.

2.03 Demographic Patterns of Religious Change

The chart below considers the demographics of respondents that have changed religions. The most significant differences in affiliation change exist among different racial and ethnic groups. Thirty-five percent of Latinos and thirty-seven percent of Asians report that they have changed their religious affiliation from that in which they were raised. These rates are lower than that of blacks (42%) and of whites (45%). While the rates of change in affiliation among different age groups are comparable, the generational differences in types of affiliation changes are interesting. For instance, in the seventy and older group, more than half of the people who have switched religious affiliations have switched from one denominational family to another. Among participants under the age of thirty, about 75% of respondents who changed affiliation switched religious traditions or left their religion for no religion.

| AMONG... | CONVERTS (NET) | PERCENTAGE | | NOT CONVERTS |
		CHANGED WITHIN TRADITION	CHANGED TO ANOTHER TRADITION	
Men	45	14	30	55
Women	42	17	25	58
Ages 18–29	42	11	32	58
Ages 30–39	44	13	31	56
Ages 40–49	45	15	29	55
Ages 50–59	45	18	27	55
Ages 60–69	43	19	24	57
Age 70+	40	22	18	60
Education				
High school or less	41	15	26	59
Some college	46	17	30	54
College graduate	45	17	28	55
Post-grad degree	47	16	31	53
Race/Ethnicity				
Non-Latino whites	45	17	28	55
Non-Latino blacks	42	20	22	58
Non-Latino Asians	37	9	29	63
Non-Latino mixed/other	54	18	36	46
Latinos	35	4	31	65

DUE TO ROUNDING, FIGURES MAY NOT ADD TO 100.
PEW FORUM ON RELIGION AND PUBLIC LIFE: U.S.
RELIGIOUS LANDSCAPE SURVEY, 2008.

2.04 Gender Composition of Religious Traditions

The graph below depicts the gender composition of the major religious traditions in the United States. National figures reveal that men are significantly less likely to identify with a religious affiliation than women. Women are a greater proportion of every Christian group. On the other hand, among Hindus, 61% of adherents are men, while only 39% are women.

U.S. Religious Traditions	Male		Female		Sample Size
National Total		48%		52%	35,556
Members of Evangelical Protestant Churches		47%		53%	9,472
Members of Mainline Protestant Churches		46%		54%	7,470
Members of Historically Black Protestant Churches		40%		60%	1,995
Catholics		46%		54%	8,054
Mormons		44%		56%	581
Orthodox		46%		54%	363
Jehovah's Witnesses		40%		60%	215
Other Christians		46%		54%	129
Jews		52%		48%	682
Muslims		549%		46%	1,050
Buddhists		53%		47%	411
Hindus		61%		39%	257
Other Faiths		54%		46%	449
Unaffiliated		59%		41%	5,048

DATA FOR MUSLIMS FROM "MUSLIMS AMERICANS: MIDDLE CLASS AND MOSTLY MAINSTREAM," PEW RESEARCH CENTER, 2007.   PEW FORUM ON RELIGIOUS LIFE: U.S. RELIGIOUS LANDSCAPE SURVEY, 2008.

2.05 "When it Comes to Your Religious Outlook, Do You Regard Yourself as . . ."

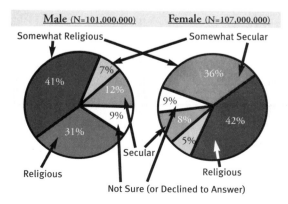

Male (N=101,000,000)

Female (N=107,000,000)

Somewhat Religious

Somewhat Secular

41%

7%

12%

36%

9%

9%

8%

42%

31%

5%

Secular

Religious

Religious

Not Sure (or Declined to Answer)

The charts at left highlight differences in religiosity between men and women. Though the numbers are similar, women are more likely to label themselves as "Religious" (42%>31%,) while men are more likely to identify as "Somewhat Religious" (41%>36%). Men are also more likely to label themselves as "Secular" (12%>8%.) The same percent (9%) of both genders was unsure or did not give an answer when surveyed.

GRADUATE CENTER, CITY UNIVERSITY OF NEW YORK: AMERICAN RELIGIOUS IDENTIFICATION SURVEY, 2001.

2.06 Age Distribution Within Religious Traditions

The graph below shows the distribution of ages among major religious traditions, using a sample size of 34,695 Americans. The Pew Landscape Survey found significant differences among different age groups in terms of religious affiliation. Younger age groups are also more likely to be religiously unaffiliated, and older Americans are more likely to be affiliated. The highest percentages of those affiliated with religion generally fall into the 30–49 age category.

U.S. Religious Traditions	18–29	30–49	50–64	65+	Sample Size
National Total	20%	39%	25%	16%	34695
Members of Evangelical Protestant Churches	17%	39%	26%	19%	9281
Members of Mainline Protestant Churches	14%	36%	28%	23%	7271
Members of Historically Black Protestant Churches	24%	36%	24%	15%	1942
Catholics	18%	41%	24%	16%	7856
Mormons	24%	42%	19%	15%	565
Orthodox	18%	38%	27%	17%	358
Jehovah's Witnesses	21%	39%	25%	14%	207
Other Christians	16%	35%	27%	22%	127
Jews	20%	29%	29%	22%	664
Muslims	29%	48%	18%	5%	1027
Buddhists	23%	40%	30%	7%	410
Hindus	18%	58%	19%	5%	250
Other Faiths	26%	37%	27%	10%	437
Unaffiliated	31%	40%	20%	8%	4947

DATA FOR MUSLIMS FROM "MUSLIMS AMERICANS: MIDDLE CLASS AND MOSTLY MAINSTREAM," PEW RESEARCH CENTER, 2007.
PEW FORUM ON RELIGION AND PUBLIC LIFE: U.S. RELIGIOUS LANDSCAPE SURVEY, 2008.

2.07 Religious Composition of Age Groups

In general, young Americans identify less with Protestant groups, and older Americans identify more with Protestant groups, and with religion in general. Middle-aged Americans seem to fall into a middle category; 52% of middle-aged Americans are Protestant, which is 9 points higher than adults under age 30, and 10 points higher than that of adults over age 70. Adults under age 30 are more likely to identify as atheist or agnostic. But while younger adults tend to be less religiously affiliated, more than a third of adults with no particular affiliation report that religion has some importance in their lives.

FAITH	TOTAL POP.	PERCENTAGE					
		18–29	30–39	40–49	50–59	60–69	70+
Christian	78	68	76	80	80	84	88
Protestant	51	43	47	52	54	57	62
Evangelical churches	26	22	26	28	27	29	30
Mainline churches	18	12	16	17	20	21	26
Historically black churches	7	8	6	7	7	7	6
Catholic	24	22	25	25	23	24	23
Mormon	2	2	2	2	1	2	1
Jehovah's Witness	1	1	1	1	1	1	1
Orthodox	1	1	1	1	1	<0.5	1
Other Christian	<0.5	<0.5	<0.5	<0.5	<0.5	1	<0.5
Other Religions	5	6	5	4	5	5	4
Jewish	2	2	1	1	2	2	2
Muslim	1	1	1	<0.5	<0.5	<0.5	<0.5
Buddhist	1	1	1	1	1	1	<0.5
Hindu	<0.5	<0.5	1	<0.5	<0.5	<0.5	<0.5
Other world religions	<0.5	<0.5	<0.5	<0.5	<0.5	<0.5	<0.5
Other faiths	1	2	1	1	1	1	1
Unaffiliated	16	25	19	15	14	10	8
Atheist	2	3	2	1	1	1	1
Agnostic	6	9	7	6	6	4	3
Religious unaffiliated	6	9	7	6	5	3	3
Don't Know/Refused	1	1	1	1	1	1	1
	100	100	100	100	100	100	100
Share of Total Population	(100)	(20	)	(19)	(20)	(18)	(12)

DUE TO ROUNDING FIGURES MAY NOT ADD UP TO THE SUBTOTAL INDICATED
PEW FORUM ON RELIGION AND PUBLIC LIFE: U.S. RELIGIOUS LANDSCAPE SURVEY, 2008.

2.08 Age by Protestant Denomination

In the table below from the Pew Foundation's Religious Landscape Survey, we get a picture of the age of religious adherents within the Protestant Denomination—one of the largest denominations in the United States, and, consequently, one of the largest denominations polled (around 18,000 out of 35,000.) The highest concentration of church members come from the 30–49 age range, while the lowest comes from the 18–29 range. The list of traditions is not exhaustive, but it gives a relatively accurate glimpse of the diversity of Protestantism among America's adult population.

	PERCENTAGE				
	18–29	30–49	50–64	65+	N
Total Population	20	39	25	16	34,695
Total Protestants	17	38	26	20	18,494
African Methodist Episcopal (Hist. Black Tradition)	14	31	30	25	120
American Baptist Churches in USA (Mainline Tradition)	18	36	23	23	404
Anglican Church (Mainline Tradition)	7	26	33	35	130
Assemblies of God (Evangelical Tradition)	14	41	33	12	473
Church of Christ (Evangelical Tradition)	22	32	24	22	552
Church of God Cleveland, Tenn. (Evangelical Tradition)	18	30	24	28	120
Church of God in Christ (Historically Black Tradition)	29	33	28	10	153
Church of the Nazarene (Evangelical Tradition)	16	31	25	28	102
Disciples of Christ (Mainline Tradition)	10	33	21	35	135
Episcopal Church in the USA (Mainline Tradition)	11	29	34	25	455
Evangelical Lutheran Church in Amer. (Mainline Tradition)	8	36	29	27	855
Free Methodist Church (Evangelical Tradition)	13	31	27	29	102
Independent Baptist (Evangelical Tradition)	15	39	27	19	897
Independent Baptist (Historically Black Tradition)	36	35	19	10	120
Lutheran Church, Missouri Synod (Evangelical Tradition)	11	32	31	26	582
National Baptist Convention (Historically Black Tradition)	14	35	29	21	538
Nondenominational Charismatic Churches (Evang. Trad.)	18	54	22	6	166
Nondenominational Evangelical Churches (Evang. Trad.)	19	51	22	8	406
Nondenominational Fundamentalist Churches (Evang. Trad.)	12	43	33	12	102
Presbyterian Church in America (Evangelical Tradition)	12	29	32	27	165
Presbyterian Church USA (Mainline Tradition)	8	31	30	32	534
Seventh-Day Adventist (Evangelical Tradition)	20	44	21	15	134
Southern Baptist Convention (Evangelical Tradition)	13	37	27	22	2,492
United Church of Christ (Mainline Tradition)	11	27	34	28	241
United Methodist Church (Mainline Tradition)	11	34	29	26	2,195

DUE TO ROUNDING, ROWS MAY NOT ADD TO 100.
PEW FORUM ON RELIGION AND PUBLIC LIFE: U.S. RELIGIOUS LANDSCAPE SURVEY, 2008.

2.09 Outlook of Older and Younger Adults: Religious or Secular

The remarkable bar graph below from the American Religious Identification Survey indicates a trend in religiosity when measured against the age of Americans. The image suggests that the younger Americans are, the more likely they are to consider themselves "Secular," "Somewhat Secular," or only "Somewhat Religious," as opposed to the more definite category, "Religious."

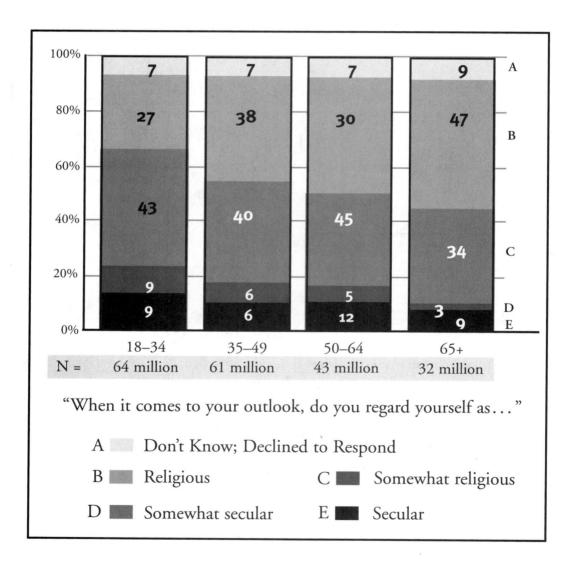

"When it comes to your outlook, do you regard yourself as..."

A — Don't Know; Declined to Respond
B — Religious
C — Somewhat religious
D — Somewhat secular
E — Secular

GRADUATE CENTER OF THE CITY UNIVERSITY OF NEW YORK:
AMERICAN RELIGIOUS IDENTIFICATION SURVEY, 2001.

2.10 Religious Affiliation of Racial and Ethnic Groups

The graph below gives a more detailed view of the religious affiliation of different racial and ethnic groups in America. Of the major racial and ethnic groups in the U.S., blacks are the most likely to identify with a religious affiliation. In contrast, Asians are the ethnic group most likely to be unaffiliated. Roughly a quarter of Asians have no religious affiliation, and more than three quarters of Asians are sec-

ular, atheist, or agnostic. 58% of Hispanics identify themselves as Catholic, but nearly a quarter of Hispanics belong to either evangelical or other Protestant churches. A third of all whites belong to evangelical churches, which is nearly two times the number of whites who identify as unaffiliated with a religious tradition. 22% of whites are Catholic, and 23% belong to mainline Protestant churches.

| | PERCENTAGE | | | | | |
| | | NON-LATINO | | | | |
	TOTAL POP.	WHITE	BLACK	ASIAN	OTHER/ MIXED RACE	LATINO
Christian	78	78	85	45	69	84
Protestant	51	53	78	27	51	23
Evangelical churches	26	30	15	17	34	16
Mainline churches	18	23	4	9	15	5
Hist. black churches	7	<0.5	59	<0.5	2	3
Catholic	24	22	5	17	14	58
Mormon	2	2	<0.5	1	2	1
Jehovah's Witness	1	<0.5	1	<0.5	1	1
Orthodox	1	1	<0.5	<0.5	1	<0.5
Other Christian	<0.5	<0.5	<0.5	<0.5	1	<0.5
Other Religions	5	5	2	30	9	2
Jewish	2	2	<0.5	<0.5	1	<0.5
Muslim	1	<0.5	1	4	1	<0.5
Buddhist	1	1	<0.5	9	1	<0.5
Hindu	<0.5	<0.5	<0.5	14	1	<0.5
Other world religions	<0.5	<0.5	<0.5	2	<0.5	<0.5
Other faiths	1	1	<0.5	1	5	<0.5
Unaffiliated	16	16	12	23	20	14
Atheist	2	2	<0.5	3	1	1
Agnostic	2	3	1	4	3	1
Secular unaffiliated	6	7	3	11	7	4
Religious unaffiliated	6	5	8	5	9	8
Don't Know/Refused	1	1	1	2	2	1
	100	100	100	100	100	100
Share of Total Population (Pct)	(100)	(70)	(11)	(2)	(3)	(12)

DUE TO ROUNDING, FIGURES MAY NOT ADD TO 100 AND NESTED FIGURES MAY NOT ADD TO THE SUBTOTAL INDICATED.
PEW FORUM ON RELIGION AND PUBLIC LIFE: U.S. RELIGIOUS LANDSCAPE SURVEY, 2008.

2.11 Race by Protestant Denomination

While the majority of Americans are Protestant, the Protestantism consists of many varied traditions. The table below shows the distribution of different races in a number of Protestant denominations. Evangelical churches show high numbers of white congregants, as do Presbyterian traditions. The Seventh-day Adventist tradition has the most Latinos, at 27%.

| | PERCENTAGE | | | | | |
| | NON-LATINO | | | | | |
	WHITE	OTHER/ BLACK	ASIAN	MIXED	LATINO	N
Total Population	71	11	3	3	12	35,101
Total Protestants	74	16	1	3	5	18,753
African Methodist Episcopal (Hist. Black Trad.)	1	93	0	5	1	125
American Baptist Churches in USA (Main. Trad.)	81	4	2	6	7	406
Anglican Church (Mainline Trad.)	92	6	2	0	0	130
Assemblies of God (Evang. Trad.)	72	2	2	6	19	477
Church of Christ (Evang. Trad.)	76	13	2	3	6	561
Church of God Cleveland, Tenn. (Evang. Trad.)	83	2	1	3	11	124
Church of God in Christ (Hist. Black Trad.	11	71	1	4	13	158
Church of the Nazarene (Evang. Trad.)	95	2	0	1	2	103
Disciples of Christ (Mainline Trad.)	79	8	0	3	10	137
Episcopal Church in the USA (Mainline Trad.)	92	4	1	1	2	468
Evang. Lutheran Church in America (Main. Trad.)	97	1	1	1	1	867
Free Methodist Church (Evang. Trad.)	86	7	5	3	0	103
Independent Baptist (Evang. Trad.)	91	0	1	4	3	905
Independent Baptist (Historically Black Tradition)	0	97	0	0	3	121
Lutheran Church, Missouri Synod (Evang. Trad.)	95	2	1	1	1	583
National Baptist Convention (Hist. Black Trad.)	0	98	0	0	2	549
Nondenom. Charismatic Churches (Evang. Trad.)	75	14	2	1	9	170
Nondenom. Evangelical Churches (Evang. Trad.)	73	10	4	4	9	412
Nondenom. Fundamentl'st Churches (Evang. Trad.)	79	7	3	1	9	103
Presbyterian Church in America (Evang. Trad.)	86	5	4	1	4	168
Presbyterian Church USA (Mainline Trad.)	91	4	2	1	2	542
Seventh-Day Adventist (Evang. Trad.)	43	21	5	4	27	134
Southern Baptist Convention (Evang. Trad.)	85	8	1	3	2	2,520
United Church of Christ (Mainline Trad.)	91	4	0	4	1	246
United Methodist Church (Mainline Trad.)	93	2	1	2	2	2,232

DUE TO ROUNDING, ROWS MAY NOT ADD TO 100.

QUESTION ASKED: "ARE YOU, YOURSELF, OF HISPANIC ORIGIN OR DESCENT, SUCH AS MEXICAN, PUERTO RICAN, CUBAN, OR SOME OTHER SPANISH BACKGROUND? [TO INTERVIEWER: IF HISPANIC, ASK:] ARE YOU WHITE HISPANIC, BLACK HISPANIC, OR SOME OTHER RACE? [TO INTERVIEWER: IF NON-HISPANIC, ASK:] WHAT IS YOUR RACE? ARE YOU WHITE, BLACK, ASIAN, OR SOME OTHER?"

PEW FORUM ON RELIGION AND PUBLIC LIFE: U.S. RELIGIOUS LANDSCAPE SURVEY, 2008.

2.12 Outlook of Selected Groups of U.S. Adults: Religious or Secular

The bar graph below shows the results of a survey in which participants were asked to identify as secular or religious, and to what degree they felt that they identified with either category. Out of 6 million surveyed, 21% of Asians identified as secular, nearly twice as much as any other group.

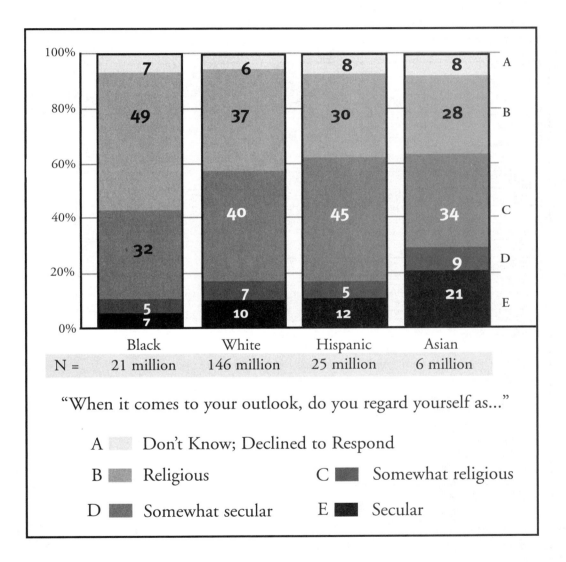

GRADUATE CENTER OF THE CITY UNIVERSITY OF NEW YORK:
AMERICAN RELIGIOUS IDENTIFICATION SURVEY, 2001.

2.13 Religious Affiliation of Educational Groups

The table below provides a breakdown of the religious affiliations of individuals with different levels of formal education. Nearly a third of adults who have less than a high school education belong to Evangelical Protestant churches, while nearly a tenth of those without a high school education belong to historically black Protestant churches.

Less than a quarter of college graduates belong to the Evangelical tradition, and only 5% of college graduates are members of historically black churches. Twenty-three percent of adults with post-graduate degrees belong to mainline Protestant churches, in comparison with the 11% that have less than a high school education.

	PERCENTAGE					
	TOTAL POP.	LESS THAN HIGH SCHOOL	HIGH SCHOOL GRAD	SOME COLLEGE	COLLEGE GRAD	POST-COLLEGE
Christian	78	83	81	78	76	68
Protestant	51	51	55	52	48	43
Evangelical churches	26	31	29	27	22	16
Mainline churches	18	11	17	18	22	23
Historically black churches	7	9	8	7	5	3
Catholic	4	29	24	22	24	21
Mormon	2	1	1	2	2	2
Jehovah's Witness	1	1	1	1	<0.5	<0.5
Orthodox	1	<0.5	<0.5	1	1	1
Other Christian	<0.5	<0.5	<0.5	<0.5	<0.5	1
Other Religions	5	2	3	5	6	13
Jewish	2	<0.5	1	1	3	6
Muslim	1	<0.5	<0.5	1	1	1
Buddhist	1	<0.5	<0.5	1	1	2
Hindu	<0.5	<0.5	<0.5	<0.5	1	2
Other world religions	<0.5	<0.5	<0.5	<0.5	<0.5	<0.5
Other faiths	1	1	1	1	1	2
Unaffiliated	16	15	15	16	16	19
Atheist	2	1	1	1	2	3
Agnostic	2	1	2	3	4	5
Secular unaffiliated	6	4	6	6	7	8
Religious unaffiliated	6	9	6	5	4	3
Don't Know/Refused	1	1	1	1	1	1
	100	100	100	100	100	100
Share of Total Population (Pct)	(100)	(14)	(36)	(23)	(16)	(11%)

DUE TO ROUNDING, ROWS MAY NOT ADD TO 100.
QUESTION ASKED: "WHAT IS THE LAST GRADE OR CLASS THAT YOU COMPLETED IN SCHOOL?"
PEW FORUM ON RELIGION AND PUBLIC LIFE: U.S. RELIGIOUS LANDSCAPE SURVEY, 2008.

2.14 Level of Education by Protestant Denomination

The chart below gives a more thorough breakdown of the Protestant tradition in terms of formal education attained by its members. It shows the educational distribution among denominations as compared to the total United States population with a sample size of 35,298.

	PERCENTAGE					
	LESS THAN H. S.	H. S. GRAD	SOME COLLEGE	COLLEGE GRAD	POST-COLLEGE	N
Total Population	14	36	23	16	11	35,298
Total Protestants	14	38	24	15	9	18,825
African Methodist Episcopal (Hist. Black Trad.)	10	35	29	17	9	127
American Baptist Churches in USA (Main. Trad.)	23	48	15	9	5	410
Anglican Church (Main. Trad.)	1	23	27	25	24	132
Assemblies of God (Evang. Trad.)	24	41	23	8	4	478
Church of Christ (Evang. Trad.)	18	39	23	14	6	562
Church of God Cleveland, Tenn. (Evang. Trad.)	28	43	20	4	4	122
Church of God in Christ (Hist. Black Trad.)	27	35	27	8	3	160
Church of the Nazarene (Evang. Trad.)	11	45	28	10	5	103
Disciples of Christ (Mainline Tradition)	10	31	24	18	17	137
Episcopal Church in the USA (Main. Trad.)	1	20	22	30	27	473
Evang. Lutheran Church in America (Main. Trad.)	6	38	26	19	11	867
Free Methodist Church (Evang. Trad.)	20	47	17	9	7	103
Independent Baptist (Evang. Trad.)	18	45	22	11	5	908
Independent Baptist (Hist. Black Trad.)	19	48	25	5	3	120
Lutheran Church, Missouri Synod (Evang. Trad.)	9	38	25	18	9	584
National Baptist Convention (Hist. Black Trad.)	22	38	22	11	6	546
Nondenom. Charismatic Churches (Evang. Trad.)	1	43	32	13	11	171
Nondenom. Evang. Churches (Evang. Trad.)	6	28	34	18	15	408
Nondenom. Fundament'lst Churches (Evang. Trad.)	5	35	31	19	11	103
Presbyterian Church in America (Evang. Trad.)	18	27	24	19	13	167
Presbyterian Church USA (Main. Trad.)	7	23	23	23	24	542
Seventh-Day Adventist (Evang. Trad.)	24	30	26	16	5	134
Southern Baptist Convention (Evang. Trad.)	15	42	22	14	7	2,525
United Church of Christ (Main. Trad.)	4	33	21	21	21	248
United Methodist Church (Main. Trad.)	8	34	23	21	14	2,229

DUE TO ROUNDING, ROWS MAY NOT ADD TO 100.
QUESTION ASKED: "WHAT IS THE LAST GRADE OR CLASS THAT YOU COMPLETED IN SCHOOL?"
PEW FORUM ON RELIGION AND PUBLIC LIFE: U.S. RELIGIOUS LANDSCAPE SURVEY, 2008.

2.15 Religious Affiliation by Income

Religious affiliation patterns among different income groups reflect divisions among educational groups; nearly 40% of Americans who earn less than $30,000 annually are members of evangelical or historically black Protestant churches. Twenty-four percent of Americans in that category are Catholic, and 15% identify as unaffiliated. A similar percentage (26%) of Catholics make more than $100,000 annually. Seven percent of Americans who make more than $100,000 are atheist or agnostic, which is more than twice that of the 3% of atheists and agnostics who make $30,000 or less.

	Total Pop.	Under $30,000	$30,000– $49,999	$50,000– $74,999	$75,000– $99,999	100,000+
			PERCENTAGE			
Christian	78	81	79	79	78	74
Protestant	51	54	54	52	49	45
Evangelical churches	26	29	29	29	24	20
Mainline churches	18	15	17	19	21	22
Historically black churches	7	10	8	5	4	3
Catholic	24	24	21	22	25	26
Mormon	2	1	2	2	2	2
Jehovah's Witness	1	1	1	1	<0.5	<0.5
Orthodox	1	<0.5	1	1	1	1
Other Christian	<0.5	<0.5	<0.5	<0.5	<0.5	<0.5
Other Religions	5	3	4	5	5	8
Jewish	2	1	1	2	1	4
Muslim	1	<0.5	<0.5	1	1	<0.5
Buddhist	1	1	1	1	1	1
Hindu	<0.5	<0.5	<0.5	<0.5	1	1
Other world religions	<0.5	<0.5	<0.5	<0.5	<0.5	<0.5
Other faiths	1	1	1	1	1	1
Unaffiliated	16	15	17	16	16	18
Atheist	2	1	1	2	2	3
Agnostic	2	2	3	3	3	4
Secular unaffiliated	6	5	7	6	7	7
Religious unaffiliated	6	8	6	5	5	4
Don't Know/Refused	1	1	<0.5	1	1	1
	100	100	100	100	100	100
Share of Total Population	(100%)	(31%)	(22%)	(17%)	(13%)	(18%)

DUE TO ROUNDING, FIGURES MAY NOT ADD TO 100 AND NESTED FIGURES MAY NOT ADD TO THE SUBTOTAL INDICATED. PEW FORUM ON RELIGION AND PUBLIC LIFE: U.S. RELIGIOUS LANDSCAPE SURVEY, 2008.

2.16 Income Level by Protestant Denomination

The table below shows the distribution of income level among different Protestant denominations. Like the income level of religious traditions, the percentages here closely reflect education levels. In cases where there wasn't enough of a sample population, responses were not included.

	INCOME LEVEL					
	Under $30,000	$30,000– $49,999	$50,000– $74,999	$75,000– $99,999	$100,000+	N
Total Population	31	22	17	13	18	29,435
Total Protestants	32	23	17	12	15	15,741
African Methodist Episcopal (Hist. Black Trad.)	40	24	13	9	14	108
American Baptist Churches in USA (Main. Trad.)	46	22	16	9	8	354
Anglican Church (Main. Trad.)	17	16	12	15	39	113
Assemblies of God (Evang. Trad.)	41	26	15	11	8	415
Church of Christ (Evang. Trad.)	37	24	17	11	11	483
Church of God Cleveland, Tennessee (Evang. Trad.)	41	27	19	6	8	100
Church of God in Christ (Hist. Black Trad.)	46	27	10	8	9	134
Church of the Nazarene (Evangelical Tradition)	Too few cases for analysis					
Disciples of Christ (Main. Trad.)	31	14	21	14	20	106
Episcopal Church in the USA (Main. Trad.)	16	19	11	18	35	394
Evangelical Lutheran Church-America (Main. Trad.)	24	24	21	15	17	713
Free Methodist Church (Evang. Trad.)	Too few cases for analysis					
Independent Baptist (Evang. Trad.)	37	25	17	11	11	798
Independent Baptist (Hist. Black Trad.)	55	19	13	5	8	104
Lutheran Church, Missouri Synod (Evang. Trad.)	24	20	20	18	17	478
National Baptist Convention (Hist. Black Trad.)	46	29	12	6	7	474
Nondenom. Charismatic Churches (Evang. Trad.)	22	23	26	17	11	153
Nondenomin. Evangelical Churches (Evang. Trad.)	15	22	21	18	25	360
Nondenom. Fundamentalist Churches (Evang. Trad.)	Too few cases for analysis					
Presbyterian Church in America (Evang. Trad.)	34	20	16	12	18	147
Presbyterian Church USA (Main. Trad.)	16	19	19	18	28	452
Seventh-Day Adventist (Evang. Trad.)	46	26	10	7	11	115
Southern Baptist Convention (Evang. Trad.)	30	25	19	11	15	2,107
United Church of Christ (Main. Trad.)	27	20	21	14	18	197
United Methodist Church (Main. Trad.)	23	21	19	16	22	1,876

DUE TO ROUNDING, ROWS MAY NOT ADD TO 100.
TEXT OF QUESTION: "LAST YEAR, THAT IS IN 2006, WHAT WAS YOUR TOTAL FAMILY INCOME FROM ALL SOURCES, BEFORE TAXES? JUST STOP ME WHEN I GET TO THE RIGHT CATEGORY. [INSTRUCTION TO INTERVIEWER: READ IN ORDER]: LESS THAN $10,000; 10 TO UNDER $20,000; 20 TO UNDER $30,000; 30 TO UNDER $40,000; 40 TO UNDER $50,000; 50 TO UNDER $75,00; 75 TO UNDER $100,000; 100 TO UNDER $150,000; $150,000 OR MORE."
PEW FORUM ON RELIGION AND PUBLIC LIFE: U.S. RELIGIOUS LANDSCAPE SURVEY, 2008.

2.17 Religious Affiliation by Marital Status

According to the Pew Survey, the religious affiliations of married people reflect that of the general U.S. population, with some exceptions. For instance, 29% of married people are members of Evangelical Protestant churches, in comparison to 26% of the total population. Members of historically black Protestant churches are a smaller proportion of married people than the general population (4% compared to 7%). Americans who have never married or who live with a partner are more likely to be unaffiliated than their married counterparts. Twenty-four percent of Americans who have never been married are religiously unaffiliated, and a third of this group is atheist or agnostic. Among married Americans, 14% are unaffiliated, and only 3% identify as atheist or agnostic.

	TOTAL POP.	MARRIED	LIVING W. PARTNER	DIVORCED/ SEPARATED	WIDOWED	NEVER MARRIED
			PERCENTAGE			
Christian	78	81	68	79	89	69
Protestant	51	52	40	56	64	45
Evangelical churches	26	29	19	28	30	19
Mainline churches	18	19	14	19	24	14
Historically black churches	7	4	7	9	10	12
Catholic	24	25	26	21	22	21
Mormon	2	2	1	1	1	1
Jehovah's Witness	1	1	<0.5	1	1	1
Orthodox	1	1	<0.5	<0.5	1	1
Other Christian	<0.5	<0.5	1	1	<0.5	<0.5
Other Religions	5	5	5	4	3	6
Jewish	2	2	2	1	2	2
Muslim	1	<0.5	<0.5	1	<0.5	1
Buddhist	1	1	1	1	<0.5	1
Hindu	<0.5	1	<0.5	<0.5	<0.5	<0.5
Other world religions	<0.5	<0.5	<0.5	<0.5	<0.5	<0.5
Other faiths	1	1	2	2	1	2
Unaffiliated	16	14	26	16	7	24
Atheist	2	1	3	1	1	3
Agnostic	2	2	4	2	1	5
Secular unaffiliated	6	6	10	6	3	8
Religious unaffiliated	6	5	9	6	3	8
Don't Know/Refused	1	1	1	1	1	1
	100	100	100	100	100	100
Share of Total Population	(100%)	(54%)	(6%)	(12%)	(8%)	(19%)

DUE TO ROUNDING, FIGURES MAY NOT ADD TO 100 AND NESTED FIGURES MAY NOT ADD TO THE SUBTOTAL INDICATED. QUESTION: ARE YOU MARRIED, LIVING WITH PARTNER, SEPARATED, WIDOWED OR HAVE YOU NEVER BEEN MARRIED? PEW FORUM ON RELIGION AND PUBLIC LIFE: U.S. RELIGIOUS LANDSCAPE SURVEY, 2008.

2.18 Marital Status by Protestant Denomination

The table below provides a detailed look at the marital status among Protestant denominations in comparison with the total population. At 3%, the Church of the Nazarene has the lowest rate of never-married adherents, in comparison with the national total of 19%.

	TOTAL POP.	PERCENTAGE				
		MARRIED	LIVING W. PARTNER	DIVORCED/ SEPARATED	WIDOWED	NEVER MARRIED
Total Population	54	6	12	8	19	35,308
Total Protestants	55	5	13	10	17	18,822
African Methodist Episcopal (Hist. Black Trad.)	39	2	16	16	27	125
American Baptist Churches in USA (Main. Trad.)	49	9	16	12	14	411
Anglican Church (Main. Trad.)	55	3	15	14	13	134
Assemblies of God (Evang. Trad.)	64	5	12	8	10	478
Church of Christ (Evang. Trad.)	52	6	13	11	18	561
Church of God Cleveland, Tenn. (Evang. Trad.)	60	0	13	13	13	124
Church of God in Christ (Hist. Black Trad.)	39	6	19	6	30	158
Church of the Nazarene (Evang. Trad.)	65	6	14	12	3	102
Disciples of Christ (Mainline Trad.)	56	2	14	14	14	137
Episcopal Church in the USA (Mainline Trad.)	55	5	11	10	18	474
Evang. Lutheran Church in Amer. (Mainline Trad.)	63	3	10	13	11	865
Free Methodist Church (Evangelical Trad.)	54	6	15	15	10	103
Independent Baptist (Evang. Trad.)	62	5	12	9	12	910
Independent Baptist (Hist. Black Trad.)	23	6	17	6	48	119
Lutheran Church, Missouri Synod (Evang. Trad.)	60	5	11	13	11	586
National Baptist Convention (Hist. Black Trad.)	35	7	16	15	26	547
Nondenom. Charismatic Churches (Evang. Trad.)	66	6	10	5	13	169
Nondenom. Evang. Churches (Evang. Trad.)	68	4	9	4	16	412
Nondenom. Fundament'lst Churches (Evang. Trad.)	61	4	18	7	10	103
Presbyterian Church in America (Evang. Trad.)	57	2	10	16	16	166
Presbyterian Church USA (Main. Trad.)	62	3	10	14	10	539
Seventh-Day Adventist (Evang. Trad.)	48	10	11	7	25	135
Southern Baptist Convention (Evang. Trad.)	61	4	13	10	13	2,525
United Church of Christ (Main. Trad.)	55	6	11	15	13	246
United Methodist Church (Mainline Tradition)	62	4	11	12	12	2,231

DUE TO ROUNDING, ROWS MAY NOT ADD TO 100.
QUESTION: ARE YOU CURRENTLY MARRIED, LIVING WITH A PARTNER, DIVORCED, SEPARATED, WIDOWED, OR HAVE YOU NEVER BEEN MARRIED?
PEW FORUM ON RELIGION AND PUBLIC LIFE: U.S. RELIGIOUS LANDSCAPE SURVEY, 2008.

2.19 Number of Children at Home for Religious Traditions

We often think of religion as related to family life, and, as a result, to family size. Mormons and Muslims are the most likely to have large families, while members of mainline Protestant churches, Jews, and Buddhists are less likely to have children living at home. Catholics and members of Evangelical Protestant and historically black churches are comparable to the general population in terms of family size. At a rate of 75%, atheists and agnostics are most likely to have no children living at home, and least likely to have three or more children.

NUMBER OF CHILDREN UNDER AGE 18 LIVING AT HOME					
	PERCENTAGE				
	0	1	2	3+	
Total Population	65	13	13	9	=100
Protestant	66	13	12	8	=100
Evangelical churches	65	13	13	9	=100
Mainline churches	70	12	12	6	=100
Historically black churches	64	15	11	10	=100
Mormon	51	14	14	21	=100
Jehovah's Witness	63	16	11	10	=100
Catholic	61	13	15	11	=100
Orthodox	70	9	14	6	=100
Jewish	72	9	11	8	=100
Muslim	53	13	19	15	=100
Buddhist	70	16	11	4	=100
Hindu	52	21	24	3	=100
Unaffiliated	67	13	13	7	=100
Atheist	75	11	10	5	=100
Agnostic	75	11	9	4	=100
Secular unaffiliated	67	15	13	5	=100
Religious unaffiliated	60	14	14	12	=100

DUE TO ROUNDING, FIGURES MAY NOT ADD UP TO 100 AND NESTED FIGURES MAY NOT ADD TO THE SUBTOTAL INDICATED. RESULTS HAVE BEEN REPERCENTAGED TO EXCLUDE NONRESPONSE.
PEW FORUM ON RELIGION AND PUBLIC LIFE: U.S. RELIGIOUS LANDSCAPE SURVEY, 2008.

2.20 Number of Children by Protestant Denomination

After looking at the breakdown of family size among different religions, it's helpful to see exactly how the many Protestant denominations measure up. Like the chart on the previous page, the table below focuses on family size in terms of how many children live at home in each household. There is an additional category for households with more than four children.

NUMBER OF CHILDREN UNDER AGE 18 LIVING AT HOME						
	PERCENTAGE					
	0	1	2	3	4+	N
Total Population	65	13	13	6	3	35,431
Total Protestants	66	13	12	5	3	18,883
African Methodist Episcopal (Hist. Black Trad.)	71	16	8	4	1	127
American Baptist Churches in USA (Main. Trad.)	64	14	13	7	2	441
Anglican Church (Main. Trad.)	78	7	11	4	0	132
Assemblies of God (Evangelical Trad.)	64	12	12	8	4	480
Church of Christ (Evangelical Tradition)	70	13	10	5	2	560
Church of God Cleveland, Tenn. (Evang. Trad.)	74	15	8	3	1	124
Church of God in Christ (Histo. Black Trad.)	63	12	11	6	8	160
Church of the Nazarene (Evang. Tradition)	70	10	12	4	4	103
Disciples of Christ (Mainline Trad.)	76	7	10	2	5	137
Episcopal Church in the USA (Main. Trad.)	73	12	12	2	1	474
Evang. Lutheran Church in Amer. (Main. Trad.)	70	11	13	5	1	868
Free Methodist Church (Evang. Tradition)	70	12	12	3	3	103
Independent Baptist (Evang. Trad.)	63	14	14	6	3	911
Independent Baptist (Hist. Black Trad.)	61	17	15	4	4	121
Lutheran Church, Missouri Synod (Evang. Trad.)	72	11	10	5	2	587
National Baptist Convention (Hist. Black Trad.)	68	16	7	6	3	549
Nondenom. Charismatic Churches (Evang. Trad.)	46	22	16	9	8	171
Nondenom. Evang. Churches (Evang. Trad.)	52	15	19	9	4	411
Nondenom. Fundament'lst Churches (Evang.Trad.)	59	20	12	5	3	103
Presbyterian Church in America (Evang. Trad.)	79	10	6	2	3	168
Presbyterian Church USA (Main. Trad.)	74	11	10	4	1	542
Seventh-Day Adventist (Evang. Trad.)	62	15	10	10	3	135
Southern Baptist Convention (Evang. Trad.)	67	13	13	4	3	2,537
United Church of Christ (Main. Trad.)	75	10	10	3	2	246
United Methodist Church (Main. Trad.)	72	11	12	4	1	2,238

DUE TO ROUNDING, ROWS MAY NOT ADD TO 100. QUESTION: "ARE YOU THE PARENT OR GUARDIAN OF ANY CHILDREN UNDER 18 NOW LIVING IN YOUR HOUSEHOLD?" IF YES, ASK, "AND MAY I ASK HOW MANY?" PEW FORUM ON RELIGION AND PUBLIC LIFE: U.S. RELIGIOUS LANDSCAPE SURVEY, 2008.

2.21 Percentage Divorced or Separated by Selected Religious Group, 1990–2001

The table below illustrates a comparison between percentages of divorced and separated adults in major religious groups in surveys conducted in 1990 and 2001. There were no dramatic changes in the eleven-year period; the similarities reflect constancy of divorce and separation patterns.

	1990		2001	
	TOTAL NUMBER OF ADULTS	PERCENT DIVORCED/ SEPARATED	TOTAL NUMBER OF ADULTS	PERCENT DIVORCED/ SEPARATED
Christian	8,100,000	10	14,190,000	9
Catholic	46,000,000	8	50,873,000	9
Protestant	17,214,000	7	4,647,000	9
Baptist	33,964,000	11	33,830,000	12
Methodist	14,174,000	8	14,140,000	9
Lutheran	9,110,000	8	9,580,000	7
Presbyterian	5,000,000	8	5,596,000	9
Pentecostal	3,116,000	11	4,407,000	14
Episcopalian/Anglican	3,000,000	10	3,451,000	12
Mormon	2,487,000	10	2,697,000	8
Churches of Christ	1,800,000	6	2,593,000	9
Congregational/UCC	599,000	8	1,378,000	8
Jehovah's Witnesses	1,400,000	11	1,331,000	6
Assemblies of God	617,000	9	1,105,000	10
Evangelical/Born Again	242,000	10	1,032,000	7
Church of God	531,000	6	944,000	7
Seventh Day Adventist	668,000	12	724,072	11
Non-denominational	195,000	17	2,489,000	9
Jewish *	3,137,000	9	2,831,000	7
Muslim/Islamic	527,000	10	1,104,000	7
Buddhist	401,000	11	1,082,332	8
No Religious Affiliation	14,331,000	11	29,481,000	9
TOTAL US ADULTS	**175,000,000**	**9**	**208,000,000**	**9**

*NOTE: ONLY JEWS BY RELIGION WERE TABULATED.
THE GRADUATE CENTER OF THE CITY UNIVERSITY OF NEW YORK:
AMERICAN RELIGIOUS IDENTIFICATION SURVEY, 2001.

2.22a U.S. Census 2000 Fact Box 1

When looking at how marital status varies among different religions, it's important to get a general understanding of the marital status of the total adult population. The United States Census reported marital statistics for Americans over the age of fifteen. ARIS 2001 defined its survey population in terms of adults over the age of eighteen; since its sample size is smaller, its results vary slightly from that of the 2000 Census. ARIS also added categories for individuals who are single but live with partners, and for respondents who refused to give information about their marital status. Both the U.S. Census and ARIS report that more than half of the American adult population is currently married, and that roughly a quarter have never been married before.

Married	15,580,691	54%
Single, never married	58,049,225	27%
Separated	4,795,275	2%
Divorced	21,365,741	10%
Widowed	13,887,524	7%
TOTAL	213,678,456	100%

U.S. Census AT-02 Profile of Selected Social Characteristics: 2000 (American Fact Finder)

2.22b ARIS 2001 Fact Box 2 (Weighted Estimate)

Married	122,053,785	59%
Single, never married	40,914,395	20%
Single, living with partner	11,101,951	5%
Separated	3,431,149	2%
Divorced	15,005,207	7%
Widowed	12,502,674	6%
Refused info	2,959,032	1%
TOTAL	207,968,192	100%

The Graduate Center of The City University of New York: American Religious Identification Survey, 2001.

2.23 Intermarriage Patterns

Of the major religions, Hindus and Mormons are most likely to be married to someone of the same religion. 78% of Catholics and 69% of Jews are also married to someone of the same religious affiliation, but the majority of unaffiliated individuals, members of other faiths, and Buddhists are married to people of different religions. 81% of married Protestants are married to Protestants, while 10% are married to Catholics and 6% to spouses who are unaf-

filiated. Intermarriage patterns vary among Protestant denominations. Table 2.27 explores intermarriage rates among married people that have changed religions. While one might expect intermarriage rates to be lower among those who practice a different religion, the rate of intermarriage among people who have changed their religious affiliation is 50%, close to twice as high as the rate of intermarriage among people that have not changed affiliations (28%).

2.23a Intermarriage Patterns among Major Religious Groups

SPOUSE IS...	SAME RELIGION	DIFFERENT RELIGION	PROTESTANT	ALL OTHER/ CATHOLIC	DK/REF	UNAFFIL- IATED	
Among married...*			PERCENTAGE				
Hindus	90	10	1	2	3	3	=100
Mormons	83	17	5	5	2	5	=100
Catholics	78	22	14	N/A	3	5	=100
Jews	69	31	7	12	3	8	=100
Orthodox Christian	65	35	12	16	4	3	=100
Jehovah's Witnesses	65	35	9	6	5	15	=100
Buddhists	45	55	15	7	6	27	=100
Other faiths	33	67	28	11	8	19	=100
Unaffiliated	41	59	28	22	9	N/A	=100

2.23b Intermarriage Patterns within Protestantism

SPOUSE IS...	SAME RELIGION	DIFFERENT RELIGION	DIFFERENT PROT. FAMILY	CATHOLIC	ALL OTHER/ DK/REFUSE	UNAFFIL- IATED	
Among married...*			PERCENTAGE				
Protestants	63	37	18	10	3	6	=100
Evangelical churches	68	32	17	8	2	5	=100
Mainline churches	55	45	19	15	3	8	=100
Hist. black churches	69	31	19	5	3	4	=100

* FIGURES INCLUDE RESPONDENTS WHO SAY THEY ARE MARRIED AND RESPONDENTS WHO SAY THEY ARE LIVING WITH A PARTNER. DUE TO ROUNDING, FIGURES MAY NOT ADD TO 100.
QUESTION: "ARE YOU CURRENTLY MARRIED, LIVING WITH A PARTNER, DIVORCED, SEPARATED, WIDOWED, OR HAVE YOU NEVER BEEN MARRIED?"
2.23A, 2.23B, 2.23C PEW FORUM ON RELIGION AND PUBLIC LIFE: U.S. RELIGIOUS LANDSCAPE SURVEY, 2008.

2.23c Intermarriage and Change in Affiliation

SPOUSE HAS...	SAME RELIGION	DIFFERENT RELIGION	
Among...	———————— PERCENTAGE ————————		
All married* people	63	37	=100
Married, has not changed religion	72	28	=100
Married, has changed religion	50	50	=100

2.24 Political Party Preference by Selected Religious Groups, 2001

NAME OF GROUP	NUMBER OF ADULTS	PERCENTAGE				
		REPUBLICANS	DEMOCRAT	INDEPENDENT	OTHER/ NONE	TOTAL
Christian	14,190,000	34	28	31	7	100
Catholic	50,873,000	28	36	30	4	100
Protestant	4,647,000	37	22	32	9	100
Baptist	3,830,000	33	39	22	6	100
Evangelical/Born Again	1,032,000	58	12	20	10	100
Church of God	944,000	38	28	25	9	100
Seventh-day Adventist	724,000	38	28	31	13	100
Methodist	14,140,000	36	32	27	5	100
Lutheran	9,580,000	39	26	31	4	100
Presbyterian	5,596,000	46	25	26	3	100
Pentecostal	4,407,000	32	34	27	1	100
Episcopalian/Anglican	3,451,000	35	35	26	4	100
Mormon	2,787,000	55	14	26	5	100
Churches of Christ	2,503,000	41	27	26	6	100
Congregational/UCC	1,378,000	34	28	33	5	100
Jehovah's Witnesses	1,331,000	2	10	34	54	100
Assemblies of God	1,105,000	59	16	19	6	100
Non-denominational	2,489,000	46	16	30	8	100
Jewish *	2,831,000	13	56	26	5	100
Muslim/Islamic	1,104,000	19	35	39	7	100
Buddhist	1,082,000	9	31	48	12	100
No Religious Affiliation	29,481,000	17	30	43	10	100
TOTAL US ADULTS	208,000,000	31	31	30	8	100

*NOTE: THIS CATEGORY REFERS ONLY TO JEWS BY RELIGION.
THE GRADUATE CENTER OF THE CITY UNIVERSITY OF NEW YORK:
AMERICAN RELIGIOUS IDENTIFICATION SURVEY, 2001.

2.25 More Conservative Than Many Think

The graph below compares the political and theological outlooks of the majority of participants in religious congregations, revealing parallels between political and religious conservatism and liberalism; similar numbers of individuals who are predominately conservative theologically are also politically conservative.

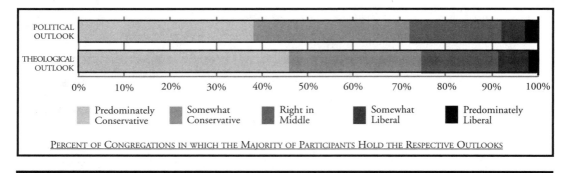

POLITICAL OUTLOOK

THEOLOGICAL OUTLOOK

0%　10%　20%　30%　40%　50%　60%　70%　80%　90%　100%

Predominately Conservative　Somewhat Conservative　Right in Middle　Somewhat Liberal　Predominately Liberal

PERCENT OF CONGREGATIONS IN WHICH THE MAJORITY OF PARTICIPANTS HOLD THE RESPECTIVE OUTLOOKS

2.26 President to Population

The table below uses current proportions of religious groups to examine the religious distribution of past U.S. presidents. A disproportionate number of American presidents were Unitarians; Unitarians are only 0.2% of the population, but four presidents were Unitarian. The group least represented in comparison to its proportion of the general population is Catholicism; John F. Kennedy was the only Catholic U.S. president, despite the fact that Catholics make up 25% of the current U.S. population.

RELIGIOUS AFFILIATION	NUMBER OF PRESIDENTS	PERCENT OF PRESIDENTS	PERCENT OF CURRENT U.S. POP.	RATIO: PCT OF PRES: PCT OF POP.
Episcopalian	11	26.2	1.7	15.4
Presbyterian	10	23.8	2.8	5.1
Methodist	5	11.9	8.0	1.5
Baptist	4	9.5	18.0	0.5
Unitarian	4	9.5	0.2	47.5
Disciples of Christ	3	7.1	0.4	18.7
Dutch Reformed	2	4.8	0.1	48.0
Quaker	2	4.8	0.7	6.9
Congregationalist	2	2.4	0.6	4.0
Catholic	1	2.4	24.5	0.1
Jehovah's Witness	1	2.4	0.6	6.0
TOTAL	42	100.0	57.0	

2.25: HARTFORD INSTITUTE FOR RELIGION RESEARCH: AMERICAN CONGREGATIONS, 2005.
2.26: ADHERENTS.COM

The table below provides the religious affiliations of each U.S. president. In cases where it was difficult to determine a president's religion, he is listed in both categories. For instance, sources give conflicting views as to whether Theodore Roosevelt was Episcopalian or Dutch Reformed. While he was raised in and identified with the Dutch Reformed Church, he was also affiliated with Episcopalian churches.

RELIGION	PRESIDENT
Episcopalian	
	George Washington
	Thomas Jefferson
	James Madison
	James Monroe
	William Henry Harrison
	John Tyler
	Zachary Taylor
	Franklin Pierce
	Chester A. Arthur
	Theodore Roosevelt *
	Franklin Delano Roosevelt
	Gerald Ford
	George H. W. Bush
Presbyterian	
	Andrew Jackson
	James Knox Polk *
	Ulysses S. Grant *
	Rutherford B. Hayes *
	James Buchanan
	Grover Cleveland
	Benjamin Harrison
	Woodrow Wilson
	Dwight D. Eisenhower
	Ronald Reagan
Methodist	
	James Knox Polk *
	Ulysses S. Grant *
	Rutherford B. Hayes *
	William McKinley
	George W. Bush

RELIGION	PRESIDENT
Baptist	
	Warren G. Harding
	Harry S. Truman
	Jimmy Carter
	William Jefferson Clinton
Unitarian	
	John Adams*
	John Quincy Adams
	Millard Fillmore
	William Howard Taft
Disciples of Christ	James A. Garfield
	Lyndon B. Johnson
	Ronald Reagan
no specific denomination	
	Thomas Jefferson
	Abraham Lincoln
	Andrew Johnson
Dutch Reformed	
	Martin Van Buren
	Theodore Roosevelt *
Quaker	
	Herbert Hoover
	Richard M. Nixon
Congregationalist	
	John Adams *
	Calvin Coolidge
	Barack Obama
Catholic	
	John F. Kennedy
Jehovah's Witnesses	
	Dwight D. Eisenhower *
River Brethren	
	Dwight D. Eisenhower *

*MEANS THAT HE'S LISTED IN 2 PLACES; RELIGIOUS AFFILIATION IS UNSURE
ADHERENTS.COM

2.28 Religious Affiliation of U.S. Founding Fathers

In the table below, the definition of "Founding Fathers" is restricted to give a representative view of the United States' founders. Less than 8% of the Founding Fathers switched denominations; double-counting is rare. Quakers are more likely to have switched than any other group; many Founding Fathers renounced or were expelled from the pacifist denomination after supporting war against the British.

RELIGIOUS AFFILIATION OF U.S. FOUNDING FATHERS		
RELIGIOUS AFFILIATION	NUMBER OF FOUNDING FATHERS	PERCENTAGE OF FOUNDING FATHERS
Episcopalian/Anglican	88	54.7
Presbyterian	30	18.6
Congregationalist	27	16.8
Quaker	7	4.3
Dutch Reformed/German Reformed	6	3.7
Lutheran	5	3.1
Catholic	3	1.9
Huguenot	3	1.9
Unitarian	3	1.9
Methodist	2	1.2
Calvinist	1	.6
TOTAL	204	

2.29 Religious Affiliation of Signers of Declaration of Independence

The signers of the Declaration of Independence were intelligent, ethically-minded, and had significant ties to religion. Four of the signers were preachers, and others were sons of clergymen. The remainder held secular professions, but they, too, had religious ties. The proportion of religious affiliation of the signers was significantly higher than that of the general population of the colonies.

RELIGIOUS AFFILIATION OF SIGNERS OF THE DECLARATION OF INDEPENDENCE		
RELIGIOUS AFFILIATION	NUMBER OF SIGNERS	PERCENTAGE OF SIGNERS
Episcopalian	32	57.1
Congregationalist	13	23.2
Presbyterian	12	21.4
Quaker	2	3.6
Unitarian or Universalist	2	3.6
Catholic	1	1.8
TOTAL	56	100

2.30 Religious Affiliation of First U.S. Congress Senators and Representatives

The table below provides a glimpse of the religious affiliations of the first United States Congress. Not surprisingly, there was more religious diversity within the House of Representatives, given its larger population. In comparison with current figures of religious affiliation in the United States Congress, these early figures seem small, and they do not reflect the same amount of diversity.

RELIGIOUS AFFILIATION OF THE FIRST U.S. CONGRESS				
RELIGIOUS AFFILIATION	NUMBER OF SEN.	PCT. OF SEN.	NUMBER OF REP.	PCT OF REP.
Episcopalian/Anglican	13	44.8	24	36.4
Congregationalist	4	13.8	7	10.6
Presbyterian	3	10.3	3	4.5%
Methodist	2	6.9	(NA)	(NA)
Catholic	1	3.4	2	3.0
Dutch Reformed Church	1	3.4	3	4.5
Quaker	1	3.4	3	4.5
Lutheran			2	3.0
German Reformed Church			1	1.5
Huguenot			1	1.5
Unitarian			1	1.5
Calvinist			1	1.5
unknown	5	17.2	20	30.3
TOTAL	29	100.0	66	100.0

ADHERENTS.COM

2.31 Affiliation of 109th Congress (2005–2006)

The 109th United States Congress reflects the growing diversity of the United States as well as the growing importance of religious affiliation in political campaigns. Catholics are the highest represented religious group, with 24 senators and 130 representatives. They make up 28.8% of Congress, a slightly higher proportion than their 24.5% of the general population. A number of groups that had, until recently, not been represented in Congress now have representatives.

RELIGIOUS AFFILIATIONS OF THE 109TH U.S. CONGRESS					
RELIGIOUS AFFILIATION	SEN.	REP.	TOTAL	PCT. OF CONGRESS	PCT. OF U.S. POP.
Catholic	24	130	154	28.8	24.5
Baptist	7	68	75	14.1	16.3
Methodist	11	50	61	11.4	6.8
Presbyterian	15	37	52	9.7	2.7
Episcopalian	10	32	42	7.9	1.7
Jewish	11	26	37	6.9	1.3
Lutheran	3	18	21	3.9	4.6
Latter-day Saints	5	11	16	3.0	1.9
UCC/Congregationalist	6	4	10	1.9	0.7
Stone-Campbell	1	6	7	1.3	1.8
Christian Scientist	0	5	5	0.9	0.0
Eastern and Greek Orthodox	2	2	4	0.7	0.3
Assemblies of God	0	4	4	0.7	0.53
Unitarian	1	2	3	0.6	0.30
Christian Reformed	0	2	2	0.4	0.04
Seventh-day Adventist	0	2	2	0.4	0.35
African Methodist Episcopal (AME)	0	2	2	0.4	0.58
Evangelical (unspecified)	1	1	2	0.4	0.5
Quaker	0	1	1	0.2	0.10
Community of Christ (RLDS)	0	1	1	0.2	0.05
Foursquare Gospel	1	0	1	0.2	0.10
Nazarene	0	1	1	0.2	0.26
United Brethren in Christ	0	1	1	0.2	0.01
Scientologist	0	1	1	0.2	.019
Community Church	0	1	1	0.2	N.A.
McLean Bible Church	1	0	1	0.2	0.005
"Protestant" (not further specified)	1	20	21	3.9	2.2
"Christian" (not further specified)	0	5	5	0.9	6.8
unspecified	0	4	4	0.7	13.2
TOTAL	100	435	535	100.0	

2.32 Religious Affiliations of US Governors in 2005–2006

The chart below shows the distribution of religious affiliations of United States Governors in 2005–2006. 44% of governors were Catholic, in comparison with its 24.5% of the total population. Methodists, Presbyterians, and Episcopalians were also significantly overrepresented compared to the total population. Baptists, at 12%, were underrepresented (compared with 16.3%). In fact, faiths represented by U.S. governors represent 75.8% of the religions in the total population.

RELIGIOUS AFFILIATIONS OF US GOVERNORS, 2005–2006			
RELIGIOUS AFFILIATION	NUMBER OF GOVERNORS	PERCENT OF GOVERNORS	PCT OF US POPULATION
Catholic	22	44	24.5
Methodist	6	12	6.8
Baptist	6	12	16.3
Presbyterian	4	8	2.7
Episcopalian	3	6	1.7
Church of Jesus Christ of Latter-day Saints	2	4	1.9
Jewish	2	4	1.3
Lutheran	1	2	4.6
Eastern Orthodox	1	2	0.3
United Church of Christ/Congregationalist	1	2	0.7
Protestant (not further specified)	1	2	2.2
Not stated	1	2	13.2
TOTAL	50	100	75.8

ADHERENTS.COM

2.33 Religious Composition of the Native Born and Foreign Born

The table below looks at the religious makeup of native born and foreign-born populations. 74% of immigrants are Christian, which reflects the total population. 46% of immigrants are Catholic, more than twice the percentage of native born Catholics. Adults born in the U.S. are more than twice as likely to be Protestant than adults born outside of the U.S. non-Western religions such as Islam, Buddhism, and Hinduism are highly represented among foreign-born adults.

RELIGIOUS COMPOSITION OF NATIVE BORN AND FOREIGN BORN AMERICANS			
	PERCENTAGE		
	TOTAL POPULATION	BORN IN U.S.	BORN IN FOREIGN COUNTRY*
Christian	78	79	74
Protestant	51	55	24
Evangelical churches	26	28	15
Mainline churches	18	20	7
Historically black churches	7	8	2
Catholic	24	21	46
Mormon	1.7	1.8	0.9
Jehovah's Witnesses	0.7	0.7	1.0
Orthodox	0.6	0.4	1.8
Other Christian	0.3	0.4	<0.3
Other Religions	5	4	9
Jewish	1.7	1.8	1.5
Muslim	0.6	0.3	1.7
Buddhist	0.7	0.6	1.6
Hindu	0.4	<0.3	3.0
Other world religions	<0.3	<0.3	<0.3
Other faiths	1.2	1.3	0.5
Unaffiliated	16	16	16
Atheist	2	2	1
Agnostic	2	2	2
Secular unaffiliated	6	6	5
Religious unaffiliated	6	6	7
Don't Know/Refused	1	1	1
Total	100	100	100
Share of Total Population	(100)	(88)	(12)

*INCLUDES RESPONDENTS WHO WERE BORN IN U.S. TERRITORIES (GUAM, U.S. VIRGIN ISLANDS, ETC.) AND PUERTO RICO. DUE TO ROUNDING, FIGURES MAY NOT ADD UP TO THE SUBTOTAL INDICATED. PEW FORUM ON RELIGION AND PUBLIC LIFE: U.S. RELIGIOUS LANDSCAPE SURVEY, 2008.

2.34 Religious Affiliation of Immigrants by Region of Origin

Sixty-one percent of immigrants to the United States are from Latin America, with more than half from Mexico. 72% of Mexican immigrants are Catholic, in comparison to 51% of Catholic immigrants from other Latin American countries. A significant number of immigrants from countries outside Latin America are Catholic. Immigrants from Canada are most likely to identify as atheist or agnostic, while 8% of immigrants from Western Europe and 7% of immigrants from Eastern Europe are atheist or agnostic.

	Canada	Mexico	Other Latin America	Eastern Europe	Western Europe	East Asia	South-Central Asia	N. Africa/ Middle East
Christian	65	88	82	70	65	57	16	43
Protestant	41	14	29	37	18	29	11	12
Evang. churches	19	11	19	15	13	18	9	3
Mainline churches	19	2	5	22	5	11	2	9
Hist. black churches	3	1	5	1	<0.5	<0.5	<0.5	<0.5
Catholic	19	72	51	28	27	27	3	9
Mormon	3	1	1	2	<0.5	1	<0.5	<0.5
Jehovah's Witness	<0.5	1	1	1	<0.5	<0.5	<0.5	<0.5
Orthodox	2	<0.5	<0.5	3	19	<0.5	2	21
Other Christian	<0.5	<0.5	<0.5	<0.5	<0.5	<0.5	<0.5	1
Other Religions	10	<0.5	2	8	15	15	71	43
Jewish	4	<0.5	<0.5	3	12	<0.5	1	18
Muslim	2	<0.5	<0.5	1	2	<0.5	12	24
Buddhist	<0.5	<0.5	<0.5	1	1	14	1	1
Hindu	<0.5	<0.5	1	1	<0.5	1	55	<0.5
Other world rel.	1	<0.5	<0.5	<0.5	<0.5	<0.5	3	<0.5
Other faiths	3	<0.5	<0.5	2	<0.5	1	<0.5	1
Unaffiliated	24	11	15	21	19	27	11	14
Atheist	6	<0.5	<0.5	4	4	2	2	4
Agnostic	7	<0.5	1	4	3	5	2	1
Secular unaffiliated	7	3	3	8	7	13	7	6
Religious unaffiliated	5	8	10	5	5	7	<0.5	3
Don't Know/Ref.	1	1	<0.5	1	<0.5	1	1	1
	100	100	100	100	100	100	100	100
Share of Immigrant Population (Pct)	(3)	(34)	(28)	(11)	(4)	(9)	(4)	(2)
N =	134	881	702	488	165	315	256	105

───────PERCENTAGE───────

PEW FORUM ON RELIGION AND PUBLIC LIFE: U.S. RELIGIOUS LANDSCAPE SURVEY, 2008.

2.35 Religious Affiliation of Immigrants by Time of Arrival

Over the past 100 years, the religious composition of the immigrant population has changed significantly. While Catholics have long had a presence in immigrant groups, they currently have a higher percentage of immigrants than in the 1970s (48% to 39% respectively). Hindus also make up a higher percentage of the immigrant population than they did in 1960. In contrast, Jews are less represented among immigrants; since 1960, the population of new Jewish immigrants has decreased from 3% to 1%.

	PERCENTAGE					
	1910–1959	1960–1969	1970–1979	1980–1989	1990–1999	2000–2007
Christian	78	78	68	76	74	74
Protestant	33	30	24	27	21	22
Evangelical churches	13	15	15	17	13	13
Mainline churches	19	14	7	7	5	5
Hist. black churches	1	1	1	3	3	3
Mormon	1	1	2	1	1	1
Jehovah's Witness	1	1	1	1	1	1
Catholic	42	44	39	45	49	48
Orthodox	2	2	2	2	2	2
Other Christian	<0.5	1	<0.5	<0.5	<0.5	<0.5
Other Religions	7	8	12	10	8	8
Jewish	3	3	3	2	1	1
Muslim	<0.5	<0.5	2	2	1	2
Buddhist	1	2	2	2	1	1
Hindu	<0.5	2	3	3	4	4
Other world religions	<0.5	<0.5	<0.5	<0.5	<0.5	<0.5
Other faiths	1	1	1	1	<0.5	<0.5
Unaffiliated	13	14	19	14	18	16
Atheist	1	2	1	1	2	1
Agnostic	2	2	3	2	2	1
Secular unaffiliated	5	6	8	4	5	6
Religious unaffiliated	5	4	9	6	9	8
Don't Know/Refused	2	<0.5	1	<0.5	<0.5	1
Total:	100	100	100	100	100	100
Share of Immigrant Pop. (Pct)	(6)	(8)	(12)	(20)	(28)	(19)
N	N=346	N=340	N=432	N=608	N=798	N=536

DUE TO ROUNDING, FIGURES MAY NOT ADD TO 100 AND NESTED FIGURES MAY NOT ADD TO THE SUBTOTAL INDICATED. PEW FORUM ON RELIGION AND PUBLIC LIFE: U.S. RELIGIOUS LANDSCAPE SURVEY, 2008.

2.36 Beliefs of Incarcerated Americans (Prison)

The table below shows the affiliations of Americans who are in prison. The highest proportion of inmates are Catholics, which is significantly more than their representation in the total population.

RESPONSE	NUMBER	PERCENTAGE
Catholic	29,267	39.164
Protestant	26,162	35.008
Muslim	5,435	7.273
American Indian	2,408	3.222
Nation	1,734	2.32
Rasta	1,485	1.987
Jewish	1,325	1.773
Church of Christ	1,303	1.774
Pentecostal	1,093	1.463
Moorish	1,066	1.426
Buddhist	882	1.18
Jehovah Witness	665	0.89
Adventist	621	0.831
Orthodox	375	0.502
Mormon	298	0.399
Scientology	190	0.254
Atheist	156	0.209
Hindu	119	0.159
Santeria	117	0.157
Sikh	14	0.019
Bahai	9	0.012
Krishna	7	0.009
Total Known Responses	74,731	100.001 (rounded to 3 digits)
Total Unknown/No answer	18,381	
Total Convicted	93,112	
Prisoner's religion known		80.259
Total Held in Custody	3,856 (not surveyed due to temporary custody)	
Total in Prisons	96,968	

3 Maps: Religious Distributions

THIS SECTION PROVIDES A VISUAL COMPILATION of the most recent religious distribution data as provided by numerous sources, including the latest census, as a companion to sections I and II of this book. We cover a variety of statistics—regional, national, and global—pertaining to religious numbers and numbers of religiosity. The primary objective of this book is to discuss the diverse religious groups and organizations of America, what they stand for, and their place in the country. In addition to focusing on such factors as organizational character, position in American society or culture, and size, this section centers on their geographical distribution across the country.

American society has served as fertile soil for the propagation of religious flora. There is a rich and colorful diversity that has characterized the United States dating back to, not the formation of the United States, but since the first peopling of what is now America, some tens of thousands of years ago. The United States is a land of immigrants and has thereby become home to most of the world's religions.

Several of the original thirteen colonies were established by English settlers who wished to practice their own religion without discrimination: Pennsylvania was established by Quakers, Maryland by Roman Catholics, and the Massachusetts Bay Colony by Puritans, not to mention the original territorial settlements of American Indian tribes. The United States was one of the first countries in the world to enact a separation of church and state and freedom of religion. The framers of the United States Constitution rejected any religious test for office, and the First Amendment specifically denied the central government any power to enact any law respecting either an establishment of religion, or prohibiting its free exercise.

When analyzing these maps there is a requirement when focusing on the religions and their geographic distribution across the country. America must be partitioned into a set of regions used for the examining and comparing of patterns of national dispersion or regional distribution. Regional patterns of the U.S. are numerous and include a general scheme with environmental characteristics, such as landforms or climate, taken into consideration. Many patterns within regions will also reflect cultural, economic, and population density factors. There will be numerous references, when discussing the territory of the lower 48 states, to the South, West, Midwest, and Northeast regions of the country; while concentrations within major urban cities, smaller population states, and Hawaii and Alaska will be referred to where appropriate for the analysis of each map.

These maps were collected from numerous sources including Wadsworth, a compilation of recent US Census Data, The Pluralism Project at Harvard University, and The Pew Forum on Religion & Public Life, and were collected for observations on belief allocation and religious temples, churches, or center distributions.

We first take a look at religions on a global level, then to religion in America and its distribution of religiosity, then to the demographics of Christian denomination by county and the demographics of Jewish, Islamic, and Eastern Religions, ending with American Indian tribes and their original territorial inhabitants on the North American continent.

— Catherine M. Stolfi,
Section Editor

A. Global Religious Outlook

When considering religion in America, it is necessary to think about trends throughout the world. While our focus is American religion, it is important that we place the American religious landscape in context with the world as a whole. America was founded, in large part, by immigrants that came to this country with the hope of freedom and acceptance of their diversity. The First Amendment to the Constitution prohibits the United States Congress from making laws that prohibit free exercise of religion. America's diversity is a reflection of global diversity.

3.01 World Religious Distribution

The following map of the globe reflects religious diversity throughout the world. For the most part, Roman Catholicism is found in South America, Central America, eastern Canada, Alaska, and most of Europe. Mostly Protestant sections include the majority of the United States, Canada, Australia, and northern European countries, such as Norway and Sweden. Eastern Orthodox regions include a good portion of Russia and some eastern European countries, including the Ukraine. Both types of Islam, Sunni and Shia, are spread over most of northern Africa and the Middle East. Hinduism is found mostly in India, while Buddhism claims high numbers of adherents in southwest China and all of Mongolia. Traditional and tribal beliefs are found in northern Asia, Canada, and most of Greenland. Tribal Christianity and Islam make up the rest of the African landscape, while Judaism appears in many regions of the world, including North and South America.

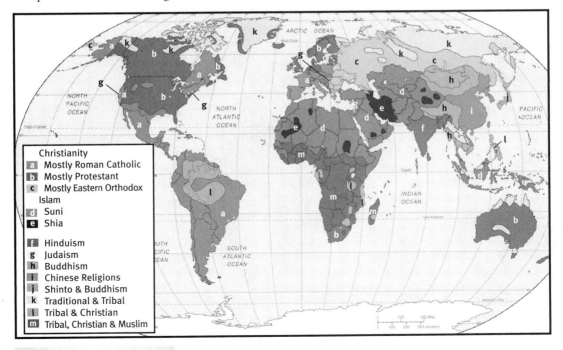

Christianity
- **a** Mostly Roman Catholic
- **b** Mostly Protestant
- **c** Mostly Eastern Orthodox

Islam
- **d** Suni
- **e** Shia

- **f** Hinduism
- **g** Judaism
- **h** Buddhism
- **i** Chinese Religions
- **j** Shinto & Buddhism
- **k** Traditional & Tribal
- **l** Tribal & Christian
- **m** Tribal, Christian & Muslim

SOURCE: WADSWORTH

3.02 U.S./North America Religious Belief Distribution

This image of North America displays the percentage of people by state in the United States, Central America, and Canada who identify with a religion, as opposed to "no religion." The color-coded map documents the percentage of the population with its corresponding religious beliefs (dark) by state, province, or country. Each state or province is color-coded based on the last available survey from that region. We can see from this data that the populations of Central America, eastern Canada, and parts of the midwest of America have a percentage of the population with religious beliefs at almost 100%. The percentage of the population of Central America that identify with religious beliefs never dips below 50%.

THE SURVEY OF THE U.S. IS FROM 2001 AND APPROXIMATELY 4 PERCENT OF THOSE ASKED DID NOT PARTICIPATE IN THE SURVEY. THE PROVINCIAL SURVEYS FROM CANADA ARE FROM 1991, 1998, OR 2001, WHILE MEXICO IS BASED ON COUNTRYWIDE DATA. SOURCE: COMPILATION OF RECENT U.S. CENSUS DATA

B. National Religious Outlook

This section brings the focus back to the religious landscape of the United States. We move from broad studies to more focused studies, that is, from numbers of total adherents, to interfaith specifics on the national level. The majority of the country identifies with a religion, and the most densely religious populations reside in the Midwest and in other middle parts of the country. The leading church bodies' distribution, however, has more of a concentration of Baptists in the South, with Catholics as the majority in the rest of the country. The most interfaith centers are distributed in California and New York, the west and east coast hubs.

3.03 Percentage of Religious Adherents

This map shows religious adherents as a percentage of all residents, with the darker regions representing the highest percentage of adherents. The darkest regions include northern Texas, western Minnesota, eastern Dakota, and Utah; all reported that their religious adherent population was greater than 75%. The least religious areas of the country are the far west, including Oregon and Arizona, and West Virginia on the east coast. The middle portion of America, which stretches laterally from Minnesota to the southern tip of Texas, is where the highest concentrations of over 50% of religious adherents reside.

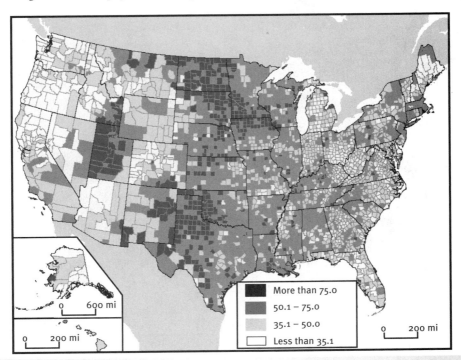

Legend:
- More than 75.0
- 50.1 – 75.0
- 35.1 – 50.0
- Less than 35.1

COUNTY PERCENTAGES BASED ON THE TOTAL NUMBER OF ADHERENTS REPORTED BY THE 149 RELIGIOUS BODIES THAT PARTICIPATED IN A STUDY SPONSORED BY THE ASSOCIATION OF STATISTICIANS OF AMERICAN RELIGIOUS BODIES DIVIDED BY THE TOTAL POPULATION IN 2000 REPORTED BY THE U.S. CENSUS BUREAU.
SOURCE: RELIGIOUS CONGREGATIONS AND MEMBERSHIP IN THE UNITED STATES, 2000.

C. Distribution of Religious Commitment

This section—still part of the national numbers—looks at the number of specific affiliations (including non-affiliations) and seeks to include as many religious groups as data is available for. Three states of the U.S. have a 51 to 100 percent population range that affiliates with U.S. Evangelical Protestants: Oklahoma, Arkansas, and Tennessee. Meanwhile, U.S. Catholics, those unaffiliated, the restoration movement, and mainline Protestants don't reach above 50 percent in any state of America; though, a concentration in each different region varies greatly throughout.

3.04 U.S. Distribution of Unaffiliated

The percentage of Americans unaffiliated with any religion never rises above 30 percent in this state-by-state census. All of the Midwest, parts of the South, the West, and the Northeast make up the percentage range from 11 to 20 percent while most of the West ranges from 21 to 30 percent. Even with the high percentage of religious Americans, there are still some widespread concentrations, though small, of those that don't connect themselves with any particular religion.

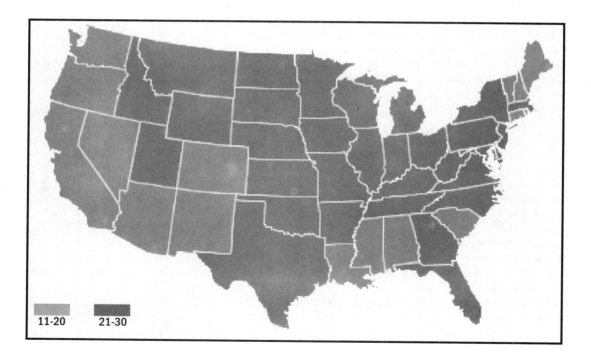

11-20   21-30

NOTE: EIGHT TRADITIONS (BUDDHIST, HINDU, JEHOVAH'S WITNESS, MUSLIM, ORTHODOX, OTHER CHRISTIAN, OTHER FAITHS AND OTHER WORLD RELIGIONS) CONSTITUTE 5% OR LESS OF THE POPULATION IN NEARLY EVERY STATE. IN THESE CASES, THE MAP WILL SHOW LITTLE OR NO VARIATION. SOURCE: THE PEW FORUM ON RELIGION & PUBLIC LIFE: U.S. RELIGIOUS LANDSCAPE SURVEY, 2008.

3.05 U.S. Restoration Movement

This map shows restoration movement Christians as a percentage of all residents in the U.S. This map shows the highest concentrations in the Southwest and southern Midwest, ranging from 3 percent to 37 percent. The rest of the states in the majority of the country make up no more than 3 percent. These findings were based on numbers reported by Restoration Movement church bodies, County percentages based on the total number of adherents reported by Restoration Movement church bodies, including the Christian Church (Disciples of Christ), Christian Churches, and Churches of Christ.

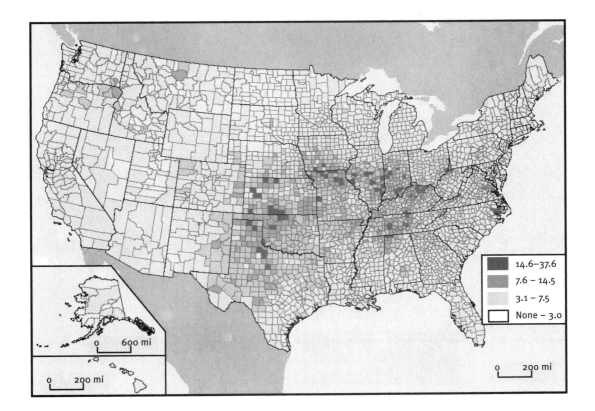

14.6–37.6
7.6 – 14.5
3.1 – 7.5
None – 3.0

0   600 mi

0   200 mi

0   200 mi

COUNTY PERCENTAGES BASED ON THE TOTAL NUMBER OF ADHERENTS REPORTED BY RESTORATION MOVEMENT CHURCH BODIES, INCLUDING THE CHRISTIAN CHURCH (DISCIPLES OF CHRIST), CHRISTIAN CHURCHES, AND CHURCHES OF CHRIST, AND CHURCHES OF CHRIST, DIVIDED BY THE TOTAL POPULATION IN 2000 REPORTED BY THE U.S. CENSUS BUREAU. SOURCE: RELIGIOUS CONGREGATIONS AND MEMBERSHIP IN THE UNITED STATES, 2000.

3.06 U.S. Evangelical Protestants

This map shows the percentage of each state's population that affiliates with the Evangelical Protestant tradition. The South makes up the high concentration, with ranges from 51 to 100 percent coming out of Oklahoma, Arkansas, and Tennessee. States such as Alabama, Georgia, Kentucky, and North and South Carolina are runners up with 41 to 50 percent of the states' populations being Evangelical Protestants. Texas, Louisiana, Missouri, and Virginia hold slightly more Evangelical Protestants than most of the midwest and western states with up to 40 percent in each.

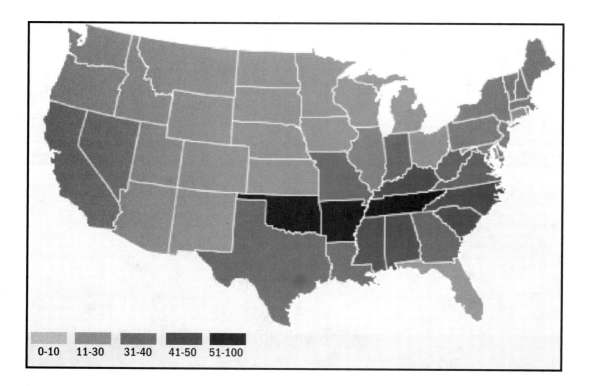

0-10   11-30   31-40   41-50   51-100

NOTE: EIGHT TRADITIONS (BUDDHIST, HINDU, JEHOVAH'S WITNESS, MUSLIM, ORTHODOX, OTHER CHRISTIAN, OTHER FAITHS, AND OTHER WORLD RELIGIONS) CONSTITUTE 5% OR LESS OF THE POPULATION IN NEARLY EVERY STATE. IN THESE CASES, THE MAP WILL SHOW LITTLE OR NO VARIATION.
SOURCE: THE PEW FORUM ON RELIGION & PUBLIC LIFE: U.S. RELIGIOUS LANDSCAPE SURVEY, 2008.

3.07 U.S. Mainline Protestants

The map below shows the percentage of each state's population that affiliates with the Mainline Protestant tradition. The highest percentage range, 31 to 40 percent, is reported in North and South Dakota, Minnesota, and West Virginia, with most of the South and the West in the 11 to 20 percent range. The remaining midwest states never go below 30 percent, such as Montana, Wyoming, Nebraska, and Iowa. Mainline Protestants are most widespread across the continental U.S., with no great concentrations in any one area.

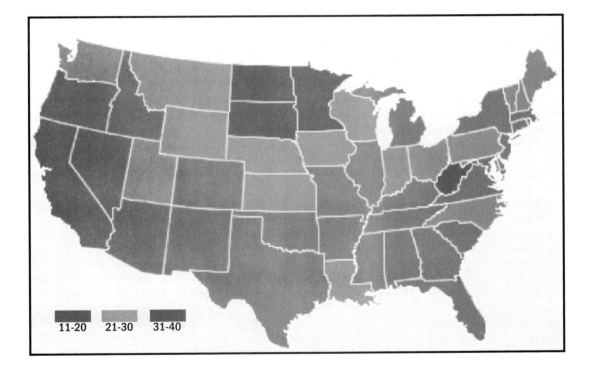

11-20   21-30   31-40

NOTE: EIGHT TRADITIONS (BUDDHIST, HINDU, JEHOVAH'S WITNESS, MUSLIM, ORTHODOX, OTHER CHRISTIAN, OTHER FAITHS, AND OTHER WORLD RELIGIONS) CONSTITUTE 5% OR LESS OF THE POPULATION IN NEARLY EVERY STATE. IN THESE CASES, THE MAP WILL SHOW LITTLE OR NO VARIATION.
SOURCE: THE PEW FORUM ON RELIGION & PUBLIC LIFE: U.S. RELIGIOUS LANDSCAPE SURVEY, 2008.

D. Demographic of Christian Denomination (By County)

As already noted, Christian denominations are the most widespread in the U.S., with Baptists and Catholics covering the majority of the country. Not far behind are Lutheran, Methodist, and Latter-day Saints with only certain sections of the midwest and east of the country having high densities of each particular faith. While Unitarians hold the smallest percentage of all the 50 states, Quakers, Pentecostals, Presbyterians, and Mennonites are surprisingly widespread. While their high concentrations are found mostly in the Midwest and in the South, their numbers are found in major cities from the east to west coasts. Amish and Unitarians find their highest concentrations on the east coast, with the Pennsylvania Amish clearly represented in that state. The detailed maps give a greater idea of how certain denominations are widespread while others occupy definite territories.

3.08 U.S. Baptists

The map below shows Baptists as a percentage of all residents as reported in 2000. The results were reported by more than two dozen church bodies and clearly show the demographic impact of Baptists in the south of the country. More than 50 percent call Oklahoma, northern Texas, Arkansas, Louisiana, and Mississippi home. The rest of the country shows only up to 10 percent that report Baptists in each region.

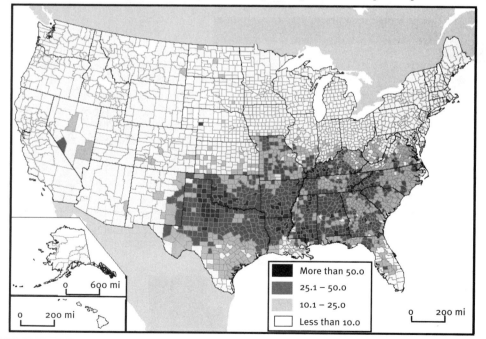

More than 50.0
25.1 – 50.0
10.1 – 25.0
Less than 10.0

COUNTY PERCENTAGES BASED ON THE TOTAL NUMBER OF ADHERENTS REPORTED BY MORE THAN TWO DOZEN BAPTIST CHURCH BODIES, INCLUDING THE SOUTHERN BAPTIST CONVENTION, DIVIDED BY THE TOTAL POPULATION IN 2000 REPORTED BY THE U.S. CENSUS BUREAU. SOURCE: RELIGIOUS CONGREGATIONS AND MEMBERSHIP IN THE U.S., 2000.; NASHVILLE, TN: GLENMARY RESEARCH CENTER.

3.09 U.S. Catholics

Catholics as a percentage of all residents is shown in the map below where they constitute more than 50 percent of southern Texas, most of New Mexico, and the southern tip of California. There are distributional spurts in Montana, New York, and Massachusetts. North Dakota and Wisconsin also show a fairly high amount of settling in certain regions of the states. The states with the least amount of Catholics are North and South Carolina, Idaho, Utah, Oregon, Kentucky, and many other southern states.

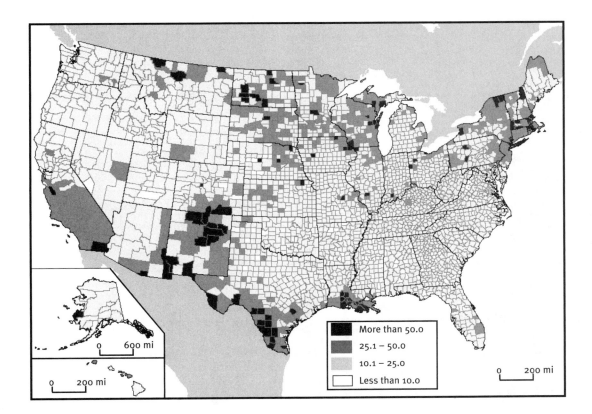

Legend:
- More than 50.0
- 25.1 – 50.0
- 10.1 – 25.0
- Less than 10.0

COUNTY PERCENTAGES BASED ON THE TOTAL NUMBER OF ADHERENTS REPORTED BY THE CATHOLIC CHURCH DIVIDED BY THE TOTAL POPULATION IN 2000 REPORTED BY THE U.S. CENSUS BUREAU. SOURCE: RELIGIOUS CONGREGATIONS AND MEMBERSHIP IN THE UNITED STATES, 2000. NASHVILLE, TN: GLENMARY RESEARCH CENTER.

3.10 U.S. Eastern Orthodox

Orthodox Christians as a percentage of all residents by county is displayed in the map below, with only a small concentration being in Minnesota, some parts of California, and Colora-do. We see the majority of the concentration is the eastern part of the U.S. in states such as New York, Massachusetts, and Pennsylvania. These counties are not even above 5 percent of all residents that affiliate with orthodox Christians. Yet, there is an almost 20 percent concentration of the population in certain counties in Alaska that are Orthodox Christians.

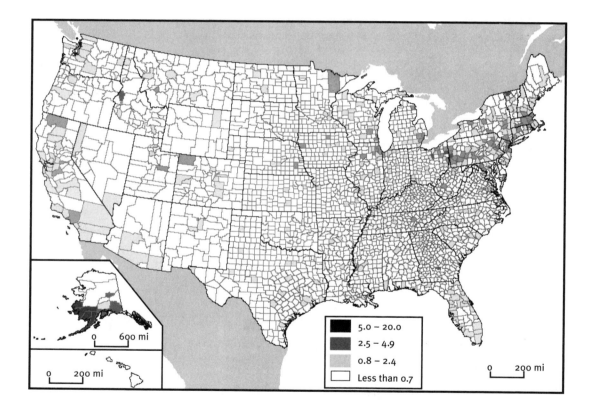

Legend:
- 5.0 – 20.0
- 2.5 – 4.9
- 0.8 – 2.4
- Less than 0.7

COUNTY PERCENTAGES BASED ON THE TOTAL NUMBER OF ADHERENTS REPORTED BY MORE THAN TWENTY ORTHODOX CHRISTIAN CHURCH BODIES DIVIDED BY THE TOTAL POPULATION IN 2000 REPORTED BY THE U.S. CENSUS BUREAU. SOURCE: RELIGIOUS CONGREGATIONS AND MEMBERSHIP IN THE UNITED STATES, 2000. NASHVILLE, TN: GLENMARY RESEARCH CENTER.

3.11 U.S. Lutherans

Lutherans are situated, for the majority, in the northernmost part of the country, with concentrations in North and South Dakota and Minnesota, as shown in the map below of the percentage of all residents, by county, of Lutherans. Also, up to 50 percent of all residents in certain counties are associated with the Lutheran religion. The rest of the country never reaches above 25 percent in any other county in the U.S. The information was based on what was provided by the leading Lutheran church bodies.

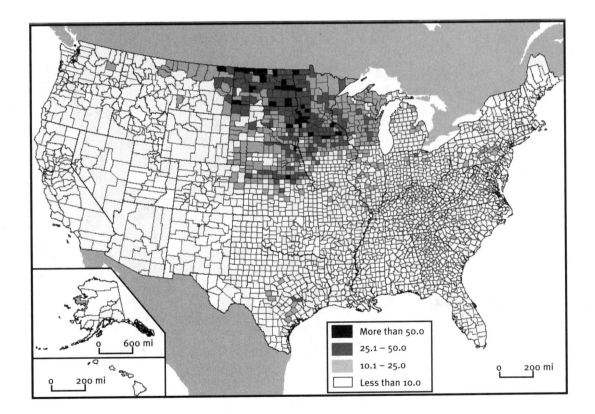

Legend:
- More than 50.0
- 25.1 – 50.0
- 10.1 – 25.0
- Less than 10.0

0 600 mi

0 200 mi

0 200 mi

COUNTY PERCENTAGES BASED ON THE TOTAL NUMBER OF ADHERENTS REPORTED BY THE LEADING LUTHERAN CHURCH BODIES, INCLUDING THE EVANGELICAL LUTHERAN CHURCH IN AMERICA, THE LUTHERAN CHURCH - MISSOURI SYNOD, THE WISCONSIN EVANGELICAL LUTHERAN SYNOD, AND THE ASSOCIATION OF FREE LUTHERAN CONGREGATIONS, DIVIDED BY THE TOTAL POPULATION IN 2000. SOURCE: RELIGIOUS CONGREGATIONS AND MEMBERSHIP IN THE UNITED STATES, 2000. NASHVILLE, TN: GLENMARY RESEARCH CENTER.

3.12 U.S. Methodists

When considering the percentage of the United States that affiliate with Methodists, a high concentration can be found in the eastern Midwest states, such as Nebraska, Kansas, and Oklahoma. Certain counties of these states can reach up to 46 percent while the majority of the eastern and southern U.S. is more in the range of 5 to 18 percent. These percentages are based on reports by six Methodist church bodies, accounting for the large amount of a small percentage and unreported counties in the U.S.

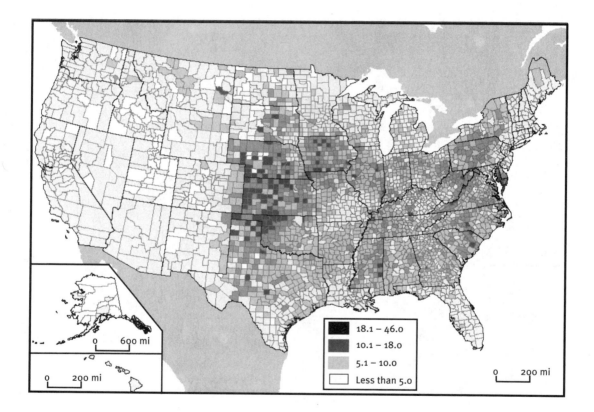

Legend:
- 18.1 – 46.0
- 10.1 – 18.0
- 5.1 – 10.0
- Less than 5.0

COUNTY PERCENTAGES BASED ON THE TOTAL NUMBER OF ADHERENTS REPORTED BY SIX METHODIST CHURCH BODIES, INCLUDING THE UNITED METHODIST CHURCH, DIVIDED BY THE TOTAL POPULATION IN 2000 REPORTED BY THE U.S. CENSUS BUREAU. SOURCE: RELIGIOUS CONGREGATIONS AND MEMBERSHIP IN THE UNITED STATES, 2000. NASHVILLE, TN: GLENMARY RESEARCH CENTER.

3.13 U.S. Mennonites

Mennonites as a percentage of all residents as taken in 2000 never reach above 28 percent in any county of the U.S. We see an almost 10 percent concentration of the population of certain counties in Montana, South Dakota, Kansas, and Pennsylvania, that affiliate with Mennonites. Only sixteen Mennonite church bodies were considered in this map of Mennonite distribution which would account for the high number of "none reported."

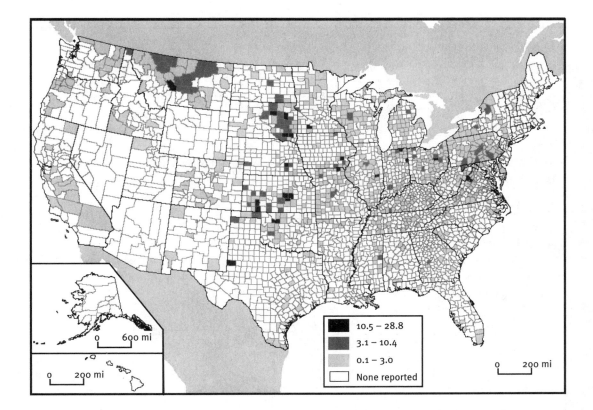

Legend:
- 10.5 – 28.8
- 3.1 – 10.4
- 0.1 – 3.0
- None reported

0   600 mi

0   200 mi

0   200 mi

County percentages based on the total number of adherents reported by sixteen Mennonite church bodies, including the Mennonite Church USA and the Old Order Amish Church, divided by the total population in 2000 reported by the U.S. Census Bureau. Source: Religious Congregations and Membership in the United States, 2000. Nashville, TN: Glenmary Research Center.

3.14 U.S. Latter-day Saints (Mormons)

U.S. Latter-day Saints as a percentage of all residents is shown in this map of the U.S. We see high concentrations reaching up to 50 percent in certain counties in the west of the country. Utah and Idaho, by far, have the highest concentrations out of all fifty states. The other surrounding states, such as Nevada, Arizona, and Idaho, can be as low as 10 percent in certain counties with the rest of the country barely reaching that 10 percent level.

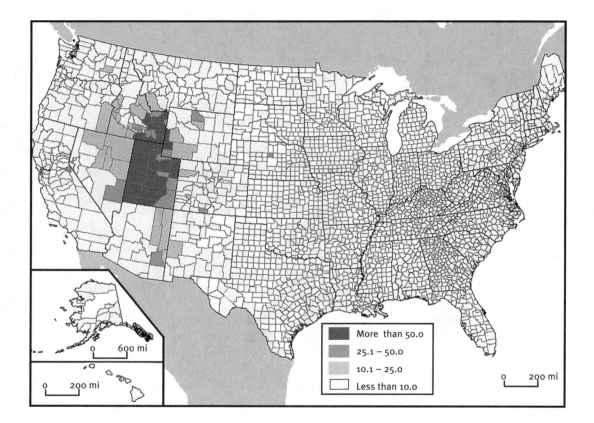

More than 50.0
25.1 – 50.0
10.1 – 25.0
Less than 10.0

COUNTY PERCENTAGES BASED ON THE TOTAL NUMBER OF ADHERENTS REPORTED BY THE CHURCH OF JESUS CHRIST OF LATTER-DAY SAINTS DIVIDED BY THE TOTAL POPULATION IN 2000 REPORTED BY THE U.S. CENSUS BUREAU. SOURCE: RELIGIOUS CONGREGATIONS AND MEMBERSHIP IN THE UNITED STATES, 2000. NASHVILLE, TN: GLENMARY RESEARCH CENTER.

3.15 U.S. Pentecostals

Pentecostals can be found dispersed over most of the continental U.S., though there is no county that reaches over 20 percent of the population. The highest concentrations are in the Northwest, the southern Midwest, and the South. Oregon, Washington, and Oklahoma have the highest concentrations with states like Florida, Georgia, and Texas trailing close behind. All areas of the fifty states see a concentration of at least 2 percent of the country with few counties that reported none.

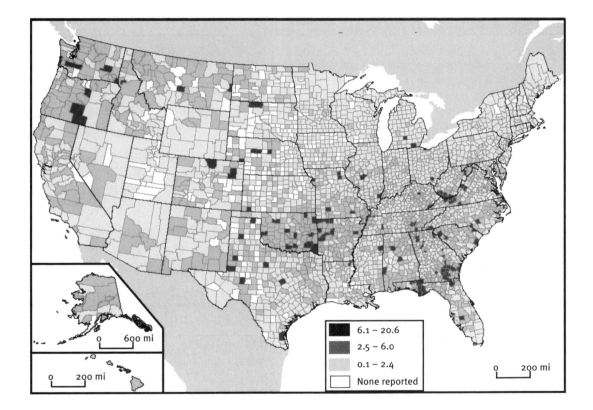

6.1 – 20.6
2.5 – 6.0
0.1 – 2.4
None reported

0   600 mi

0   200 mi

0   200 mi

COUNTY PERCENTAGES BASED ON THE TOTAL NUMBER OF ADHERENTS BY SEVERAL PENTECOSTAL CHURCH BODIES, INCLUDING THE ASSEMBLIES OF GOD, THE CHURCH OF GOD (CLEVELAND, TN), AND THE INDEPENDENT CHARISMATIC CHURCHES, DIVIDED BY THE TOTAL POPULATION IN 2000 REPORTED BY THE U.S CENSUS BUREAU. SOURCE: RELIGIOUS CONGREGATIONS AND MEMBERSHIP IN THE UNITED STATES, 2000. NASHVILLE, TN: GLEN-MARY RESEARCH CENTER.

3.16 U.S. Presbyterians

The map below shows the Presbyterians as a percentage of all residents, taken in 2000, which shows the highest concentrations by county not reaching past 16 percent. Small parts of the Midwest states, such as Montana, South Dakota, and Kansas, as well as sections of some eastern states, such as Pennsylvania and Virginia, both hold these low percentages ranging from 8 to about 16 percent. A higher amount is found in Alaska with the rest of the continental United States barely holding above 8 percent in each county.

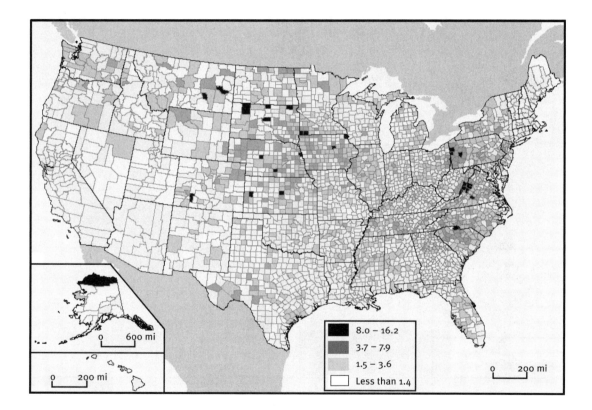

■	8.0 – 16.2
▓	3.7 – 7.9
░	1.5 – 3.6
□	Less than 1.4

0   600 mi

0   200 mi

0   200 mi

County percentages based on the total number of adherents reported by six leading Presbyterian church bodies, including the Presbyterian Church (U.S.A.), divided by the total population in 2000 reported by the U.S. Census Bureau. Source: Religious Congregations and Membership in the United States, 2000. Nashville, TN: Glenmary Research Center.

3.17 U.S. Unitarians

Unitarians make up the smallest percentages in the United States, seen within the procession of the maps in this section. The map below is of Unitarians as a percentage of all residents as taken in 2000. The highest percentages of 1.5 percent is seen in the Midwest in Wyoming and Colorado with the far Northeast having the heaviest densities, such as in states like Vermont, New Hampshire, and Maine. Most of the country has no reported data or ranges from 0.1 to 0.2 percent.

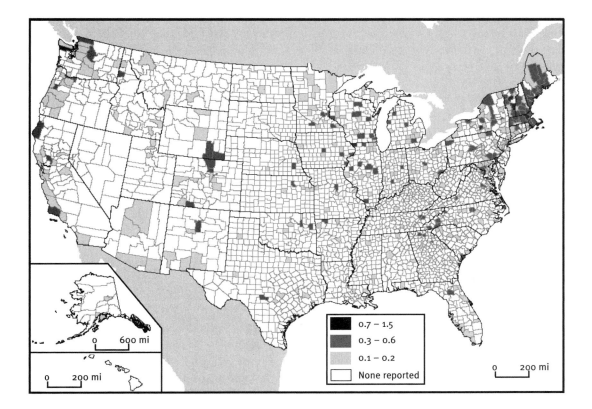

0.7 – 1.5
0.3 – 0.6
0.1 – 0.2
None reported

COUNTY PERCENTAGES BASED ON THE TOTAL NUMBER OF ADHERENTS REPORTED BY THE UNITARIAN UNIVERSALIST ASSOCIATION OF CONGREGATIONS DIVIDED BY THE TOTAL POPULATION IN 2000 REPORTED BY THE U.S. CENSUS BUREAU. SOURCE: RELIGIOUS CONGREGATIONS AND MEMBERSHIP IN THE UNITED STATES, 2000. NASHVILLE, TN: GLENMARY RESEARCH CENTER.

3.18 U.S. Quakers

Friends, or Quakers, as a percentage of all residents is shown in the map below with only two counties holding up to the highest range (reaching 20 percent). These are found in the states of Colorado and Alaska. Idaho, Kansas, Oklahoma, Texas, Indiana, and Ohio hold a mere 6 percent. The remainder of the country holds 0.1 to 2 percent or has none reported. Trailing behind Unitarians as the least represented in the United States are the Quakers.

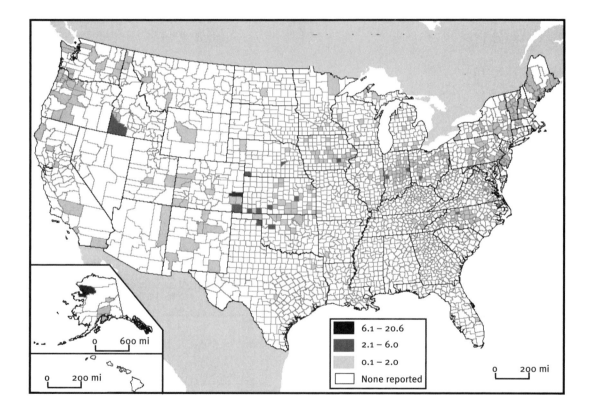

6.1 – 20.6
2.1 – 6.0
0.1 – 2.0
None reported

0 600 mi
0 200 mi
0 200 mi

COUNTY PERCENTAGES BASED ON THE TOTAL NUMBER OF ADHERENTS REPORTED BY THE FRIENDS (OR QUAKERS) DIVIDED BY THE TOTAL POPULATION IN 2000 REPORTED BY THE U.S. CENSUS BUREAU. SOURCE: RELIGIOUS CONGREGATIONS AND MEMBERSHIP IN THE UNITED STATES, 2000. NASHVILLE, TN: GLENMARY RESEARCH CENTER.

3.19 U.S. Black Protestants

The historically black Protestant tradition is the fourth highest for the percentage of U.S. adults who consider themselves affiliated with a major religious tradition. The map below shows the percentage of each state's population that affiliates with a historically black Protestant tradition. Never going above 30 percent, the highest density of black Protestants is in the state of Mississippi with the next highest in the South, in states such as Louisiana, Alabama, Georgia, and North and South Carolina. The majority of the West holds 0 to 2 percent population.

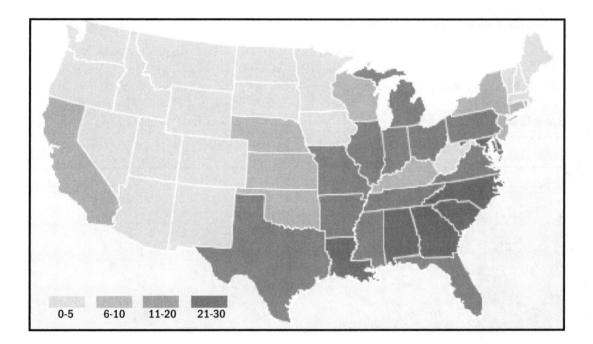

0-5   6-10   11-20   21-30

NOTE: EIGHT TRADITIONS (BUDDHIST, HINDU, JEHOVAH'S WITNESS, MUSLIM, ORTHODOX, OTHER CHRISTIAN, OTHER FAITHS, AND OTHER WORLD RELIGIONS) CONSTITUTE 5% OR LESS OF THE POPULATION IN NEARLY EVERY STATE. IN THESE CASES, THE MAP WILL SHOW LITTLE OR NO VARIATION. SOURCE: THE PEW FORUM ON RELIGION & PUBLIC LIFE: U.S. RELIGIOUS LANDSCAPE SURVEY, 2008.

E. Demographics of Non-Christian Religions

In this section, significant Non-Christian religious groups are considered: Judaism; Islam; Eastern Religions as a group, and Buddhism specifically; and Native American religions. It is also fascinating to put into context all of the religious affiliations, centers, and population percentages we have seen thus far and compare it to this continent's original inhabitants, Native Americans. Of particular interest is the observation that Islam is currently the fastest growing major religion in the U.S.

3.20 U.S. Eastern Religions

The map below of participating eastern religious groups are based on the number of temples per 100,000 in the population of the fifty states. We see a high density of temples per 100,000 in Colorado, South Dakota, and New Mexico (of 20 or more). We see the next highest ranges of temples per 100,000 on either coast. The West making up California, Arizona, Oregon, and Washington, with the east coast having established temples in New York, Vermont, and Florida. The remainder of the states hold from 4 to 0 temples.

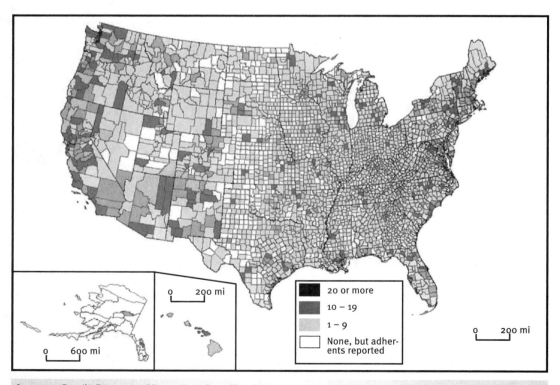

20 or more
10 – 19
1 – 9
None, but adherents reported

INCLUDES: BAHÁ'Í; BUDDHISM; HINDU; JAIN; SIKH; TAO, ZOROASTRIAN. SOURCE: RELIGIOUS CONGREGATIONS AND MEMBERSHIP IN THE UNITED STATES, 2000. NASHVILLE, TN: GLENMARY RESEARCH CENTER.

3.21 U.S. Jewish Distribution

Jews as a percentage of all residents never rise above 32 percent in any county. Southern Utah, the south of Florida, Pennsylvania, and New York all hold the highest percentages, while the middle of the country ranges from four and a half percent to none having been reported. Nevada, California, Michigan, Massachusetts, New Jersey, Maryland, and Virginia all hold within the range of four to 10 percent Jewish. The lowest ranges are in Texas, Idaho, Arizona, Washington, Minnesota, and Ohio. Overall, the Jewish distribution is quite widespread, not having more than 30 percent distribution in any given county.

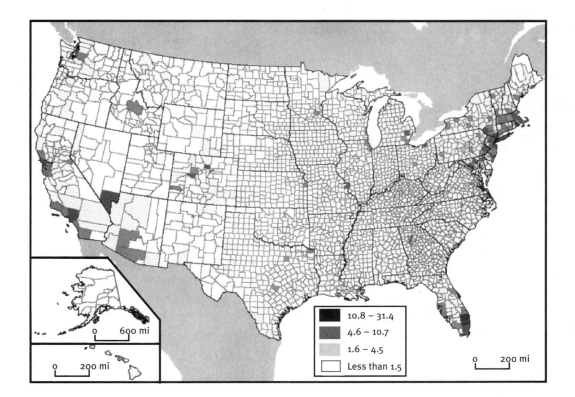

10.8 – 31.4
4.6 – 10.7
1.6 – 4.5
Less than 1.5

600 mi

200 mi

200 mi

County percentages based on the total number of adherents estimated for the Jewish population divided by the total population in 2000 reported by the U.S. Census Bureau. Source: Religious Congregations and Membership in the United States, 2000. Nashville, TN: Glenmary Research Center.

3.22 U.S. Muslim Distribution

Muslims as a percentage of all residents, compared to the distribution of Muslim centers, show only a small amount of consistency. While California and New York hold the highest number of Muslim temples, other counties of different states match the number of Muslims found in the counties of these coastal hubs. New Jersey and Massachusetts both hold a high level of Muslim population, even though their number of temples seems not to convey that scheme. Interestingly, even with New York and California both holding 100 plus temples in their states, none of their counties reach higher than a 10 percent concentration of Muslims.

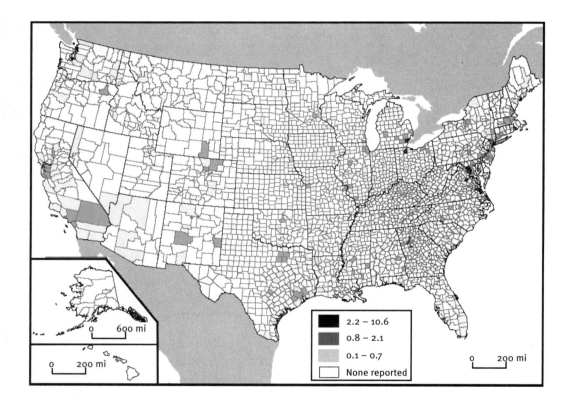

Legend:
- 2.2 – 10.6
- 0.8 – 2.1
- 0.1 – 0.7
- None reported

COUNTY PERCENTAGES BASED ON THE TOTAL NUMBER OF ADHERENTS ESTIMATED FOR THE MUSLIM POPULATION DIVIDED BY THE TOTAL POPULATION IN 2000 REPORTED BY THE U.S. CENSUS BUREAU. SOURCE: RELIGIOUS CONGREGATIONS AND MEMBERSHIP IN THE UNITED STATES, 2000. NASHVILLE, TN: GLENMARY RESEARCH CENTER.

The map below shows the distribution of Buddhist centers in the U.S. with Texas, California, and New York holding the designation for 100 plus centers. Buddhist centers are more evenly distributed across America, as compared to other Jewish, Islamic, and eastern religion centers. The state of Washington is within a range of 50 to 99 centers, while so are South Carolina, Massachusetts, and even Hawaii. Only ten states hold below 10 centers within their borders while the rest have close to 25 to 49 within each. This research is in progress with 2,150 centers having been reported by the Pluralism Project at Harvard University in August 2006.

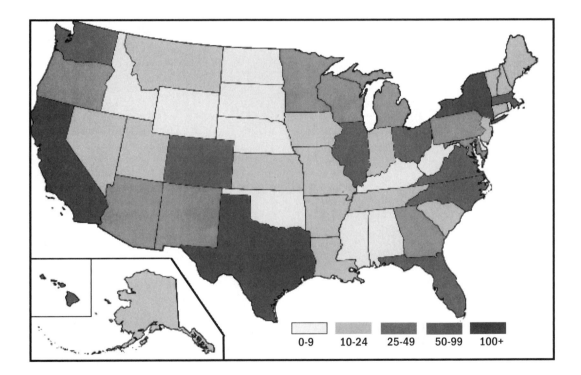

0-9   10-24   25-49   50-99   100+

SOURCE: THE PLURALISM PROJECT AT HARVARD UNIVERSITY: DIRECTOR OF RELIGIOUS CENTERS, 2006.

3.24 U.S. Native American Religions

The map below shows U.S. Native Americans as a percentage of all residents. Arizona, New Mexico, South Dakota, and Alaska are the states that hold more than 60 percent of the total population that have an affiliation with Native American beliefs. The western coast of the 48 territorial states holds 5 to 15 percent of the population of Native Americans, with California, Oregon, and Nevada as part of those western states. The eastern part of the U.S. and the South, excluding the state of Oklahoma, have from 5 to less than 1 percent of the total Native American population of the U.S.

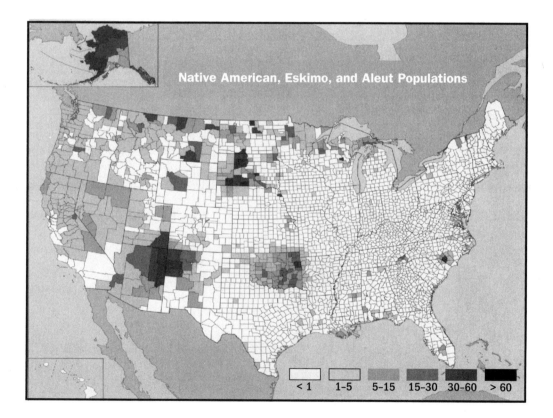

Native American, Eskimo, and Aleut Populations

| < 1 | 1–5 | 5–15 | 15–30 | 30–60 | > 60 |

Source: The Geography Division, U.S. Census Bureau, 1990.

4 Polls and Surveys

THIS SECTION DEALS WITH SUBJECTS THAT are not explored in any other section of this book. These questions of belief, though important to each religious group, are not expressed comparatively in each section. In this section, we consider responses to questions posed by Americans through Gallup, The Pew Research Center, and Harris Interactive in polls ranging from 1952 to 2008. We look at parallels between religion and beliefs on topics such as morality, homosexuality, elections, and the war on Iraq. We have noted differences over the past fifty years in the way in which people think of religion and the world, but many views are also unchanged. For example, the importance of religion to an individual has decreased, while the support for capital punishment has increased greatly in the last half a century. When it comes to gay rights, the majority of the population has become more open to the idea of same sex relations as well as same sex marriage, though among very religious Americans, views have not changed as much. We see the distribution of opinions organized by religious affiliation, gender, political declaration and age group, on national statistics, religion and politics, and social issues such as capital punishment, stem cell research, depth of religious commitment, and election issues. Some results are as expected, such as a little over half of all Americans say religion is "very important" in their lives, while others can be surprising; an overwhelming amount of adults polled believed that God favors the U.S. in the war on terror, a sign of how people in America relate their religious lives to the world around them.

A. Religion in Public Life

How important is religion in America? Well, as we can see from the latest surveys on the subject, extremely. Though we see a significantly large amount of Americans that feel religion is very important in their own lives, there is also a steady decline when compared with the same survey questions from over fifty years ago. A little over half of Americans feel their personal religious beliefs are of great importance in their lives; this number has declined from over three quarters of Americans in 1952. The relationship between morality and religion is examined, with an increase in the percentage of those that think people are not as moral as they used to be when compared to a poll from over half a century ago. A large divide in views on atheism is noticeable, with almost half of America of the opinion that belief in God is necessary in order to be moral. The events of September 11th greatly influenced American views on religion. Declines in the number of members of churches, synagogues, or mosques can be seen since the 9/11 attacks, while the percentage of people that believe religious influence is increasing rose significantly immediately after the attacks. These national percentages are, however, leveling off, especially in the case of religious influence and the importance of religion in each person's own life.

4.01 How important is religion?

Since 1952, Gallup has asked Americans about the importance of religion in their lives. The most recent survey found that 55% say religion is "very important" to them and another 28% call it "fairly important." In 1952, 75% of Americans said that religion was "very important" in their lives, but by 1978, only 52% agreed with that statement. Since 1990, the percentage has ranged from 55% to 59%.

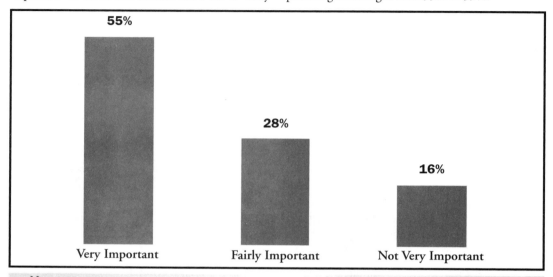

NOTE: DIFFERENCES IN PERCENTAGES ACROSS RELIGIOUS GROUPS ARE SIGNIFICANT FOR ALL DEMOGRAPHIC CHARACTERISTICS RESULTS BASED ON TELEPHONE INTERVIEWS WITH 1,005 NATIONAL ADULTS, AGED 18 AND OLDER, CONDUCTED MAY 2-5, 2005. FOR RESULTS BASED ON THE TOTAL SAMPLE OF NATIONAL ADULTS, ONE CAN SAY WITH 95% CONFIDENCE THAT THE MARGIN OF SAMPLING ERROR IS ±3 PERCENTAGE POINTS.
COPYRIGHT © 2008 GALLUP, INC. ALL RIGHTS RESERVED.

4.02 How important is religion—1952 to 2004?

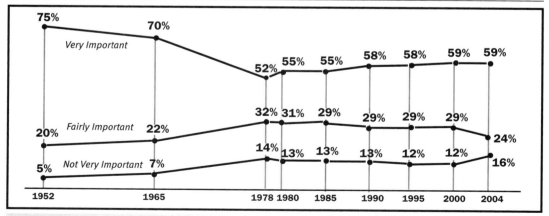

*NUMBERS ARE ROUNDED TO ONE DECIMAL PLACE IN ALL TABLES IN THIS DOCUMENT. NOTE: DIFFERENCES IN PERCENTAGES ACROSS RELIGIOUS GROUPS ARE SIGNIFICANT FOR ALL DEMOGRAPHIC CHARACTERISTICS. PEW RESEARCH CENTER FOR THE PEOPLE & THE PRESS: AMERICANS STRUGGLE WITH RELIGION'S ROLE AT HOME AND ABROAD, 2002

4.03 What is your attitude towards non-belief?

Americans feel mostly positive about people of other faiths, but they tend to look at those without any faith more negatively. Atheists, in particular, are viewed unfavorably by 54% of those surveyed. However, when people are asked for their view of people who are not religious but not atheists, the response is more positive. Roughly half say they have a favorable opinion, with those in the South and Midwest taking an especially negative view toward non-religious individuals. We see a huge regional divide of opinions between the South and Midwest and the East and West.

OPINIONS OF ATHEISTS...	PERCENTAGE			
	EAST	MIDWEST	SOUTH	WEST
Favorable	43	31	26	42
Unfavorable	37	58	66	47
Can't Rate	20	11	8	11
	100	100	100	100

RESULTS BASED ON TELEPHONE INTERVIEWS WITH 1,005 NATIONAL ADULTS, AGED 18 AND OLDER, CONDUCTED MAY 2–5, 2005. FOR RESULTS BASED ON THE TOTAL SAMPLE OF NATIONAL ADULTS, ONE CAN SAY WITH 95% CONFIDENCE THAT THE MARGIN OF SAMPLING ERROR IS ±3% POINTS. PEW RESEARCH CENTER FOR THE PEOPLE & THE PRESS: AMERICANS STRUGGLE WITH RELIGION'S ROLE AT HOME AND ABROAD, 2002

4.04 Are people as moral as they used to be?

Over the past half-century, there has been a growing sense among the older generation that people in this country, especially young people, lack the morals that were once so important to society. In 1952, half of Americans saw no decline in public morals, and 57% said young people had as strong a sense of right and wrong, as did the youth fifty years previously. Today, just 21% think Americans on the whole are as honest and moral as in the past, and an equally small number (19%) think that young people have the same sense of right and wrong as fifty years ago. Young people themselves do not disagree with this characterization. Sixty-nine percent of Americans under age 30 think young people lack the same sense of right and wrong that existed fifty years ago.

PEOPLE AS HONEST AND MORAL AS THEY USED TO BE?	PERCENTAGE		
	YES	NO	DK
March, 2002	21	73	6
1998 (Wash. Post)	26	71	3
1976 (Gallup)	30	66	4
1965 (Gallup)	39	52	9
1952 (Gaffin)	47	46	7
YOUNG PEOPLE HAVE SAME SENSE OF RIGHT AND WRONG AS 50 YEARS AGO?			
March, 2002	19	76	5
1999 (Hart)	15	82	3
1998 (Wash. Post)	20	78	2
1965 (Gallup)	41	46	13
1952 (Gaffin)	57	34	9

RESULTS FOR THE SURVEY ARE BASED ON TELEPHONE INTERVIEWS CONDUCTED UNDER THE DIRECTION OF PRINCETON SURVEY RESEARCH ASSOCIATES OF A NATIONWIDE SAMPLE OF 2,002 ADULTS, 18 YEARS OF AGE OR OLDER, DURING THE PERIOD FEBRUARY 25–MARCH 10, 2002. BASED ON THE TOTAL SAMPLE, ONE CAN SAY WITH 95% CONFIDENCE THAT THE ERROR ATTRIBUTABLE TO SAMPLING AND OTHER RANDOM EFFECTS IS ±2.5 PERCENTAGE POINTS. PEW RESEARCH CENTER FOR THE PEOPLE & THE PRESS: AMERICANS STRUGGLE WITH RELIGION'S ROLE AT HOME AND ABROAD, 2002.

4.05 Is a belief in God necessary in order to be moral?

Although many agree that faith is not a mandatory component of good citizenship, the public is split over whether it is necessary to believe in God in order to be a moral person. Half say it is not necessary to believe in God in order to have good values, while 47% say that it is. There are interesting trends among the different categories of those polled. Those that have attained a higher level of education tended to say that belief in God is not necessary to be a moral individual, while those that were more religiously inclined tended to report that it is. Black Americans have the highest percentage of those that believe God and moral standing go together, in comparison to whites and Hispanics, though white Christians (Evangelical, Mainline, and Catholic) are more likely to agree that good morals do not necessarily result from belief in God. Republicans and Democrats are nearly split on the decision within each party polled. Women are more inclined to say that it is necessary to believe in God in order to be moral than men. In the same poll, southern and non-southern residents were also asked about their beliefs, and residents of the South were more likely to believe that belief in God is directly related to morality.

	YES IT IS	NO, IT IS NOT	DON'T KNOW
	— Percentage —		
Total	47	50	3
Race/Religion			
White	43	54	3
Evangelical	62	36	2
Mainline	39	57	4
Catholic	42	55	3
Black	43	54	3
Hispanic	43	54	3
Religious Commitment			
High	63	33	4
Average	54	43	3
Low	28	70	2
Gender			
Men	40	57	3
Women	53	43	4
Education			
College grad.	33	65	2
Some college	42	56	2
H.S. or less	56	40	4
Political Party			
Republican	49	48	3
Democrat	50	47	3
Independent	41	57	2
Region			
South	56	39	5
Non-South	42	56	2

RESULTS FOR SURVEY BASED ON TELEPHONE INTERVIEWS CONDUCTED UNDER THE DIRECTION OF PRINCETON SURVEY RESEARCH ASSOCIATES AMONG A NATIONWIDE SAMPLE OF 2,002 ADULTS, 18 YEARS OF AGE OR OLDER, DURING THE PERIOD FEBRUARY 25–MARCH 10, 2002. BASED ON THE TOTAL SAMPLE, ONE CAN SAY WITH 95% CONFIDENCE THAT THE ERROR ATTRIBUTABLE TO SAMPLING AND OTHER RANDOM EFFECTS IS ±2.5%. PEW RESEARCH CENTER FOR THE PEOPLE & THE PRESS: AMERICANS STRUGGLE WITH RELIGION'S ROLE AT HOME AND ABROAD, 2002.

4.06 Would you like religion to have more or less influence?

Americans are divided over the influence of organized religion in the U.S. With three choices, they split roughly into thirds—with the highest number saying the influence of religion should stay as it is now, followed by those who said religion should have "less influence," and religion should have "more influence."

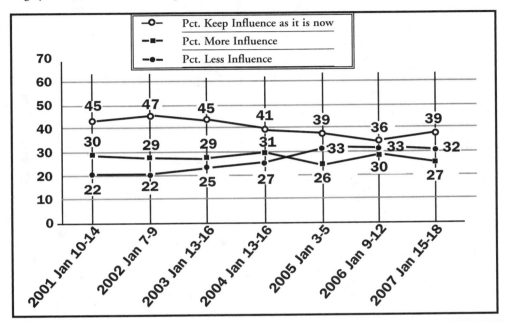

4.07 Would you like religion to have more or less influence (as a function of church attendance)?

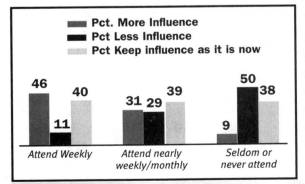

Respondents' church attendance reflects differences in responses on the issue of religion's influence. Weekly churchgoers say that religion should have more influence or stay the same, while those that seldom or never attend church are much more likely to say that religion should have less influence. However, those that attend church nearly weekly or monthly seem to be on an even split over the amount of influence.

4.08 Is the influence of religion growing or waning?

Today, roughly six in ten (59%) say religion is losing influence on American life, while 34% say it is gaining influence. And overwhelmingly, Americans favor more, not less, religion in the United States. Seventy-nine percent of those who say religion's role is declining—representing 50% of the public overall—believe the decline is bad news. Meanwhile, among the minority who feel religion's influence is growing, more say it is good than bad, by a margin of almost two-to-one. While most think religion's influence on American life is in decline, there is a division of opinion over whether religion's influence on government is rising or falling. About as many say religion is losing influence on government leaders and institutions, such as the president, Congress, and Supreme Court (45%), as say religion's political influence is on the rise (42%).

	On American Life	On Government
	Percentage	
Increasing	34	42
Good thing	21	15
Bad thing	11	24
Decreasing	59	45
Good thing	6	8
Bad thing	50	36
No change (vol.)	2	6
Don't know	5	7
	100	100
NET: Want more*	71	51
NET: Want less**	17	32

*Increasing is good or decreasing is bad
**Increasing is bad or decreasing is good

RESULTS FOR THIS SURVEY BASED ON TELEPHONE INTERVIEWS CONDUCTED UNDER THE DIRECTION OF SCHULMAN, RONCA, & BUCUVALAS, INC. AMONG A NATIONWIDE SAMPLE OF 2,003 ADULTS, 18 YEARS OF AGE OR OLDER, FROM JULY 6-19, 2006. FOR RESULTS BASED ON THE TOTAL SAMPLE, ONE CAN SAY WITH 95% CONFIDENCE THAT THE ERROR ATTRIBUTABLE TO SAMPLING IS ±2.5%. COPYRIGHT © 2008 GALLUP, INC. ALL RIGHTS RESERVED.

4.09 Is the influence of religion growing or waning: pre–9/11 compared to just after 9/11 and to 2007?

In the aftermath of 9/11, Americans viewed the country in a new light. In particular, many saw religion play a greater role in life. In a mid-November Pew survey, 78% said the influence of religion on American life was increasing, a figure that decreased only slightly (to 71%) in a December Gallup poll. This perception was relatively short-lived, and six months after the attacks, the public's view of religion's influence returned to pre-9/11 levels. Today, 37% see the influence of religion increasing, while 52% say it is in decline.

* BASED ON TELEPHONE INTERVIEWS CONDUCTED UNDER DIRECTION OF PRINCETON SURVEY RESEARCH ASSOCIATES AMONG NATIONWIDE SAMPLE OF 2,002 ADULTS, 18 YEARS OF AGE OR OLDER, DURING FEBRUARY 25–MARCH 10, 2002. BASED ON TOTAL SAMPLE, ONE CAN SAY WITH 95% CONFIDENCE THE ERROR ATTRIBUTABLE TO SAMPLING AND OTHER RANDOM EFFECTS IS ±2.5%.
PEW RESEARCH CENTER FOR THE PEOPLE & THE PRESS: AMERICANS STRUGGLE WITH RELIGION'S ROLE AT HOME AND ABROAD, 2002.

	March 2001	Nov. 2001	Dec. 2001	*Today
	Percentage			
Increasing	37	78	71	37
Losing	55	12	24	52
Same	4	3	2	3
No opinion	4	7	3	8
(Total)	100	100	100	100

Is this a...	If Increasing	If Losing
	Percentage	
Good thing	85	10
Bad thing	10	84
Other/DK	5	6
(Total)	100	100

4.10 How important is religion in your life?

A steady percentage of Americans were asked how important religion is in their lives—very important, somewhat important or not very important—and most said that religion is "very important" between the years 1992 and 2007.

There are no significant dips or increases, with the highest percentages of those who held religion as "very important" in their lives in 1998 and 2003 at 61%.

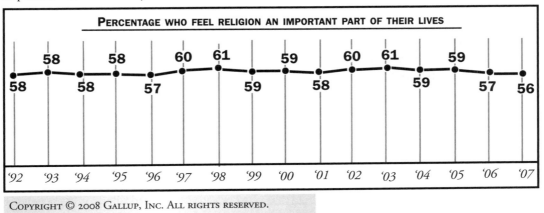

4.11 How religious are you?

One in five Americans identify as "very religious." However, a majority (70%) describe themselves as either very or somewhat religious. The number rises to 93% of born-again Christians, 82% of Catholics, and 84% of Protestant respondents.

	Total	Catholic	Protestant	Agnostic/ Atheist	Born- Again Christian
Very/somewhat religious (NET)	70	82	84	11	93
Very religious	21	16	30	2	46
Somewhat religious	49	66	55	9	46
Not very/at all religious (NET)	30	18	16	89	7
Not very religious	19	16	13	21	6
Not at all religious	12	2	2	68	1

B. Religion and Politics: Economy, Military, Trade

As we will see in the next few pages, religion seems to play a major role in American politics. Almost half of Republicans in the U.S. believe that their religious beliefs are very important in deciding their vote for president. Those willing to vote for a candidate that doesn't believe in God didn't even reach 3%. The country seems split on the influence of organized religion in U.S. politics, though a majority from almost every religious affiliation believe that churches should not endorse political candidates. When Americans in general (including unaffiliated individuals) were asked if God favors the U.S. in the war on terror, an overwhelming amount agreed.

4.12 In which institutions do you have the greatest (and least) confidence?

Only three U.S. institutions out of the fifteen included in this May 23–26 poll command a high degree of confidence from at least half of Americans: the military, the police, and the church (or organized religion). The 74% rating given to the military continues to make it the institution that can claim the most confidence among any of those tested–and by a healthy margin. Roughly one in four have high confidence in television news, newspapers, the criminal justice system, organized labor, Congress, and big business. Health maintenance organizations (HMOs) are rated highly by only 17% of Americans. "None" was allowed as a voluntary response.

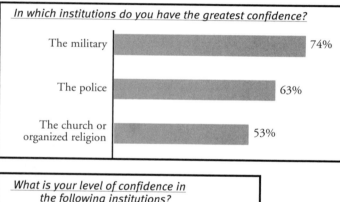

In which institutions do you have the greatest confidence?

The military	74%
The police	63%
The church or organized religion	53%

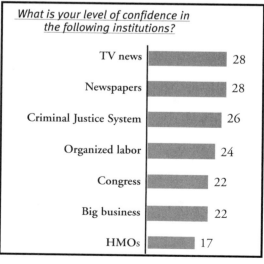

What is your level of confidence in the following institutions?

TV news	28
Newspapers	28
Criminal Justice System	26
Organized labor	24
Congress	22
Big business	22
HMOs	17

4.13 Do you think the U.S. is a Christian nation?

Americans overwhelmingly consider the U.S. a Christian nation: more than two thirds (67%) characterize the country as Christian, down slightly from 71% in March 2005. A decade ago, Americans were somewhat less likely to tie the nation's identity to Christianity. In 1996, 60% considered the U.S. a Christian nation. By 2002, however, the figure had climbed to 67%, and since then views on this question have remained fairly consistent.

	June 1996	Mar 2002	Mar 2005	July 2006
Is the U.S. a Christian nation?	——— PERCENTAGE ———			
Yes	60	67	71	67
No	34	25	26	28
Don't Know	6	8	3	5
	100	100	100	100

4.14 Do you think organized religion has too much or too little influence in U.S. politics (general population/by party)?

Americans are about evenly divided on whether the church or organized religion has too little or too much political influence, with roughly half (48%) who say that it has too much political influence while the other half believes that it has either too little (40%) or the right amount (7%) of political influence. These figures represent a slight shift in favor of saying it is too influential, when compared with data from 1996. At that time, 42% thought the church had too much influence, 44% too little, and 8% the right amount. Democrats and Republicans have different views about how much religion should influence politics. The majority of Democrats (67%) say there is too much religious influence, compared with 28% of Republicans. The majority of Republicans (55%) say there is too little, while only a quarter of Democrats (25%) would agree.

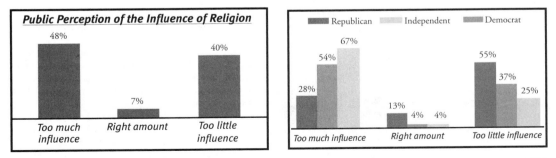

4.15 How ethical do you think society's leaders are (1995 vs 2002)?

In post-Enron and post-9/11 America, the public's estimation of the honesty and ethical standards of government officials and corporate heads are drastically different from that of the mid-1990s. Public officials in Washington are now seen more favorably, heads of major corporations less so. Today, 34% of Americans say Washington public officials have high or very high standards of honesty and ethics, up from just 18% in 1995. Heads of major companies, however, have dropped from a 33% positive rating to only 24%. The shift in opinion on corporate executives occurred fairly consistently across political party lines, while change in attitudes about public officials varies by party affiliation. Military leaders are rated highest in terms of ethics, as they were in 1995. Religious leaders rate second on the current list (55% say they have high standards). Journalists get a relatively strong rating for honesty (44%), higher than either public officials or corporate heads.

HONESTY & ETHICAL STANDARDS	High	Low	DK/Ref
Military Leaders	——	PERCENTAGE	——
2002	70	21	9 =100
1995	63	27	10 =100
Religious Leaders			
2002	55	36	9 =100
1995	55	36	9 =100
Journalists			
2002	44	48	8 =100
Wash. public officials			
2002	34	60	6 =100
1995	18	77	5 =100
Corp. board members			
2002	25	64	11 =100
Business executives			
2002	24	66	10 =100
1995	33	51	6 =100

Results for survey based on telephone interviews conducted under the direction of Princeton Survey Research Associates among a nationwide sample of 2,002 adults, 18 years of age or older, during the period February 25–March 10, 2002. Based on the total sample, one can say with 95% confidence that the error attributable to sampling and other random effects is ±2.5%.. Pew Research Center for the People & the Press: Americans Struggle with Religion's Role at Home and Abroad, 2002.

4.16 How important are your own religious beliefs in deciding your vote for president? (By party–2000; 2003)

In 2000, there was little difference between Republicans and Democrats with regard to the importance of religion, but in a recent survey, 48% of Republicans and "Republican leaners" said religion would be important to their votes in the next election, as do 28% of Democrats and "Democratic leaners."

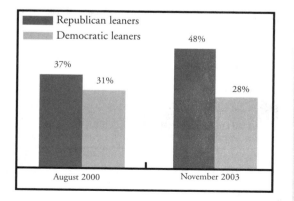

Republican leaners
Democratic leaners

37%   31%   48%   28%

August 2000   November 2003

2000 RESULTS BASED ON TELEPHONE INTERVIEWS WITH RANDOMLY SELECTED NATIONAL SAMPLE OF 1,019 ADULTS, AGED 18 AND OLDER, CONDUCTED AUG. 24–27, 2000. THERE IS 95% CONFIDENCE THAT THE MAXIMUM ERROR ATTRIBUTABLE TO SAMPLING AND OTHER RANDOM EFFECTS IS ±3%. FOR RESULTS BASED ON A SAMPLE OF 832 REGISTERED VOTERS, THERE IS 95% CONFIDENCE THAT THE MAXIMUM ERROR ATTRIBUTABLE TO SAMPLING AND OTHER RANDOM EFFECTS IS ±4%. 2003 RESULTS BASED ON TELEPHONE INTERVIEWS WITH RANDOMLY SELECTED NATIONAL SAMPLE OF 1,004 ADULTS, AGED 18 AND OLDER, CONDUCTED NOV. 10–12, 2003, WITH COMPARABLE RELIABILITY. COPYRIGHT © 2008 GALLUP, INC. ALL RIGHTS RESERVED.

4.17 Do a candidate's religious beliefs affect your willingness to vote for that candidate?

While 25% of Americans say they would be less likely to vote for a Mormon for president, 45% express reluctance about voting for a Muslim and 61% say they would be less likely to support a candidate who does not believe in God. Far fewer express reservations about voting for an evangelical Christian, a Jew, or a Catholic. Moreover, about as many people say they would be more likely to vote for an evangelical Christian or a Jew as say they would be less likely, and about twice as many people see being a Catholic as an asset as see it as a liability (13% vs 7%). By comparison, just 5% say they would be more likely to vote for a Mormon, though two-thirds (66%) say it would make no difference in their vote.

CANDIDATE LIABILITIES: ATHEISM, ISLAM, MORMONISM			
	WILLINGNESS TO SUPPORT		
	LESS LIKELY	MORE LIKELY	NO DIFF. DK
Candidate traits:	PERCENTAGE		
Doesn't believe in God	61	3	34 2
Muslim	45	3	49 3
Mormon	25	5	66 4
Evangelical Christian	16	19	60 5
Jewish	11	9	79 1
Catholic	7	13	79 1

RESULTS FOR SURVEY BASED ON TELEPHONE INTERVIEWS CONDUCTED UNDER THE DIRECTION OF SCHULMAN, RONCA, & BUCUVALAS, INC. AMONG A NATIONWIDE SAMPLE OF 3,002 ADULTS, 18 YEARS OF AGE OR OLDER, FROM AUGUST 1–18, 2007. FOR RESULTS BASED ON THE TOTAL SAMPLE, THERE IS 95% CONFIDENCE THAT THE ERROR ATTRIBUTABLE TO SAMPLING IS ±2%.
SOURCE: PEW RESEARCH CENTER FOR THE PEOPLE & THE PRESS: AMERICANS STRUGGLE WITH RELIGION'S ROLE AT HOME AND ABROAD, 2002.

4.18 Should journalists ask about religion?

Most Americans see nothing improper with journalists asking politicians how their religious beliefs affect their opinions on issues of the day—58% say it is proper for them to do so, while 37% say it is improper.

JOURNALISTS ASKING ABOUT RELIGION IS...	PROPER	IMPROPER	DK
	PERCENTAGE		
Total	58	37	5
18–29	60	35	5
30–49	63	34	3
50–65+	58	38	4
65+	45	45	10
White Protestant	60	35	5
Evangelical	67	28	5
Mainline	52	42	6
Black Protestant	60	32	8
White non-Hisp. Cath.	56	41	3
Unaffiliated	53	45	2

4.19 Should churches endorse political candidates?

While most Americans accept a relationship between religion and politics, a sizable majority (63%) oppose church endorsement of candidates during campaigns. Only 28% say churches should come out in favor of candidates, but that number has grown 6% since 2002.

SHOULD CHURCHES ENDORSE CANDIDATES?	YES	NO	DK
Among...	PERCENTAGE		
Total	28	63	9
White Protestant	32	60	8
Evangelical	38	53	9
Mainline	24	68	6
Black Protestant	29	58	13
White non-Hisp. Cath.	26	68	6
Unaffiliated	21	69	10

RESULTS BASED ON TELEPHONE INTERVIEWS CONDUCTED UNDER DIRECTION OF SCHULMAN, RONCA, & BUCUVALAS, INC. AMONG A NATIONWIDE SAMPLE OF 3,002 ADULTS, 18 YEARS OF AGE OR OLDER, FROM AUGUST 1–18, 2007. THERE IS 95% CONFIDENCE THAT THE ERROR ATTRIBUTABLE TO SAMPLING IS ±2%. PEW RESEARCH CENTER FOR THE PEOPLE & THE PRESS: AMERICANS STRUGGLE WITH RELIGION'S ROLE AT HOME AND ABROAD, 2002

4.20 Does your religion influence your attitude toward the war on terror?

Religious belief seems to have a close relationship with American opinions of the war on terror. Evangelical Protestants, at 60.3%, are the religious group most likely to approve of the Iraq War, followed by Catholics, at a rate of 46.7%. Beliefs about God are strongly related to views on the war on terror and to trust of former president Bush's leadership. The belief that God favors the United States is the single strongest predictor of whether or not an individual trusts Bush, approves of the Patriot Act, thinks Hussein was involved in 9/11, and approves of the Iraq War.

	Agree Iraq War is justified	Believe that Hussein involved in 9/11	Supports expansion of government authority to fight terror	Trust Bush "a lot"
	PERCENTAGE			
Total Sample	45.0	40.7	59.8	20.7
Church Attendance				
Attends Weekly	54.8	48.5	68.6	32.2
Never Attends	30.5	24.4	44.8	8.4
Religious Tradition				
Catholic	46.7	46.2	63.0	23.7
Evangelical Protestant	60.3	51.9	71.9	31.7
Mainline Protestant	44.6	38.4	59.8	17.9
Unaffiliated	25.8	18.0	31.8	6.8
Four God Types				
Type A: Authoritarian	63.1	53.7	76.4	32.0
Type B: Benevolent	46.9	43.5	58.6	22.7
Type C: Critical	37.5	32.4	57.5	12.0
Type D: Distant	29.1	23.5	37.8	9.3
God Favors U.S?				
Those who agree	79.2	64.5	82.3	48.7
Those who disagree	37.3	32.8	52.8	13.7

NOTE: PERCENTAGE DIFFERENCES ARE SIGNIFICANT ACROSS ALL GROUPS. SAMPLE INTERPRETATION: APPROXIMATELY 55% (54.8%) OF THOSE WHO ATTEND CHURCH WEEKLY AGREE THAT THE WAR IN IRAQ WAS JUSTIFIED. STUDY CONDUCTED BY THE GALLUP ORGANIZATION FROM OCTOBER 8, 2005 TO DECEMBER 12, 2005. THE SURVEY HAS 1,721 RESPONDENTS, AND A MARGIN OF ERROR OF ±4%. BAYLOR INSTITUTE FOR STUDIES OF RELIGION: AMERICAN PIETY IN THE 21ST CENTURY, 2006.

4.21 Do the terrorist attacks of 9/11 indicate that religion has too much or too little influence in the world?

| | RELIGION HAS… | | |
	TOO MUCH INFLUENCE	TOO LITTLE INFLUENCE	OTHER/ DK
Total	——— PERCENTAGE ———		
Race/Religion			
White	28	51	50=100
Evangelical	11	71	18=100
Mainline	27	51	22=100
Catholic	26	50	24=100
Black	22	58	20=100
Protestant	16	67	17=100
Secular	57	23	20=100
Religiosity			
High	8	73	19=100
Moderate	23	55	22=100
Low	48	32	20=100

By a nearly 2:1 ratio, more believe that the main lesson of 9/11 is that religion has too little influence in the world (51%) than think the lesson is that religion has too much sway (28%). Perspectives on the role of religion depend largely on the importance of religion in a person's own life. Highly religious Americans, by nearly 10:1, see the terrorist attacks as a sign that religion has too little influence in the world these days, not too much. But among those for whom religion is not particularly important, 48% say the bigger lesson is that religion is too influential, while 32% take the opposing viewpoint. This gap is found within all religious groups.

RESULTS FOR SURVEY BASED ON TELEPHONE INTERVIEWS CONDUCTED UNDER THE DIRECTION OF PRINCETON SURVEY RESEARCH ASSOCIATES AMONG A NATIONWIDE SAMPLE OF 2,002 ADULTS, 18 YEARS OF AGE OR OLDER, DURING THE PERIOD FEBRUARY 25–MARCH 10, 2002. BASED ON THE TOTAL SAMPLE, ONE CAN SAY WITH 95% CONFIDENCE THAT THE ERROR ATTRIBUTABLE TO SAMPLING AND OTHER RANDOM EFFECTS IS ±2.5%. PEW RESEARCH CENTER FOR THE PEOPLE & THE PRESS: AMERICANS STRUGGLE WITH RELIGION'S ROLE AT HOME AND ABROAD, 2002

4.22 Is religion a major cause of war and conflict?

Aside from those who are not deeply religious, men and younger people also express more skepticism about the role of religion in the world. Whereas women predominantly say the lesson of 9/11 is that religion has too little influence in the world, men are more divided. Americans under age 30 are split as to whether the lesson of 9/11 is that there is too much or too little religion in the world, while older respondents strongly believe the latter. Americans also believe that religion's effect is not always positive; 34% say religion plays a major role in causing most wars and conflicts, and nearly as many say it is related to wars and conflicts.

| ROLE OF RELIGION IN CAUSING WARS AND CONFLICTS | | | |
	TOTAL	MEN	WOMEN	SECULAR
	——— PERCENTAGE ———			
A great deal	34	40	28	46
Fair amount	31	31	32	31
Only a little	20	19	21	15
None at all	9	6	12	4
Don't know	6	4	7	4
	100	100	100	100

RESULTS FOR SURVEY BASED ON TELEPHONE INTERVIEWS CONDUCTED UNDER DIRECTION OF PRINCETON SURVEY RESEARCH ASSOCIATES AMONG A NATIONWIDE SAMPLE OF 2,002 ADULTS, 18 YEARS OF AGE OR OLDER, DURING THE PERIOD FEBRUARY 25–MARCH 10, 2002. THERE IS 95% CONFIDENCE THAT THE ERROR ATTRIBUTABLE TO SAMPLING AND OTHER RANDOM EFFECTS IS ±2.5%.

PEW RESEARCH CENTER FOR THE PEOPLE & THE PRESS: AMERICANS STRUGGLE WITH RELIGION'S ROLE AT HOME AND ABROAD, 2002.

4.23 How important is religion in your life?
(By Party/Gender/Race)

A first look at the relationship between party iden- tification and religion underscores the expected (and important) relationship between religion and political orientation. Republicans are significantly more likely to report that religion is very important than independents or Democrats. 66% of Republicans report that religion is very important, the highest of any of the three political groups. 48% of independents say that religion is very important, the lowest of the three groups. Democrats are in the middle; 57% say that religion is very important. 20% of Americans who identify as Democrats are black, compared to only 2% of Republicans, and 8% of independents. Previous research has shown that blacks are the most religious of any racial or ethnic group in America today. This suggests that self-reported importance of religion among Democrats may be different between black Democrats and non-black Democrats.

	AGGREGATE SAMPLE 2004–2007		
	VERY IMPORTANT	FAIRLY IMPORTANT	NOT VERY IMPORTANT
	——————— P E R C E N T A G E ———————		
Republicans	66	24	10
Independents	48	29	22
Democrats	57	26	17
	AGGREGATE SAMPLE 2004–2007 SAYING RELIGION IS VERY IMPORTANT		
Whites, and others who do not identify as black	66		
Republicans	45		
Independents	50		
Democrats	48		
Blacks			
Republicans	#		
Independents	77		
Democrats	83		
	AGGREGATE SAMPLE 2004–2007		
	VERY IMPORTANT	FAIRLY IMPORTANT	NOT VERY IMPORTANT
Male	49	29	21
Female	65	24	11

#= SAMPLE TOO SMALL TO PROVIDE MEANINGFUL DATA. THESE RESULTS ARE BASED ON NINE SURVEYS, WHICH IN TURN ARE BASED ON TELEPHONE INTERVIEWS WITH RANDOMLY SELECTED NATIONAL SAMPLES OF APPROX- IMATELY 1,000 ADULTS EACH, AGED 18 AND OLDER, CONDUCTED BETWEEN MAY 2004 AND MAY 2007. THERE IS 95% CONFIDENCE THAT THE MAXIMUM ERROR ATTRIBUTABLE TO SAMPLING AND OTHER RANDOM EFFECTS IS ±2%. COPYRIGHT © 2008 GALLUP, INC. ALL RIGHTS RESERVED.

C. Social Issues: I. General

The general public takes varying, and at times contradictory, attitudes toward the issues that constitute the so-called "culture of life." Abortion continues to split the country nearly down the middle. More than half prefer that abortion laws be decided at the national level rather than each state deciding for itself. This desire for a national policy prescription extends to other social issues as well. Despite growing antipathy toward Congress and low levels of trust in the federal government generally, a number of Americans also favor a national rather than state-by-state approach to policymaking on stem cell research, gay marriage, and the teaching of creationism and evolution in schools.

4.24 How conservative are you on social issues?

	CONSERVATISM INDEX*		
	HIGH	MEDIUM	LOW
	PERCENTAGE		
Total	28	34	38=100
Gender: Men	31	35	34=100
Women	25	33	42=100
Race: White	26	34	40=100
Black	40	36	24=100
Age: 18–29	23	27	50=100
30–49	29	34	37=100
50–64	23	35	42=100
65+	37	38	25=100
Educ: College grad	18	30	52=100
Some college	29	28	43=100
H.S. or less	33	38	29=100
Region: Northeast	22	28	50=100
Midwest	33	32	35=100
South	32	38	30=100
West	20	34	46=100
Politics: Republican	44	34	22=100
Conservative	53	32	15=100
Mod/Liberal	29	38	33=100
Democrat	23	35	42=100
Mod/Conserv.	29	41	30=100
Liberal	9	22	69=100
Independent	19	32	49=100
Rel: White Protest	32	35	33=100
Evangelical	46	36	18=100
Mainline	12	34	54=100
White Catholic	24	39	37=100
Secular	10	24	66=100

To see how opinions on social issues vary, respondents were sorted into three groups, corresponding to low, medium, and high levels of conservatism; the low group was conservative on zero or one issue (38% of the sample), the medium group on two or three issues (34%), and the high group on four or five issues (28%). By far the most conservative group on these issues is white evangelical Protestants (46% in the high conservative category) and self-described conservative Republicans (53%). Conversely, the least conservative are self-described liberal Democrats (69% in the low conservatism category) and secular individuals (66%). White Catholics fall at about the national average on this scale, and white mainline Protestants are significantly less conservative than the average. Conservatism also varies by education. College graduates are much less conservative on social issues than those with lower levels of education. Interestingly, blacks are more conservative than whites, and men more so than women. Geographically, residents of the South and Midwest are significantly more conservative than those in the West and Northeast. The oldest respondents—those 65 and older—are, perhaps not surprisingly, the most conservative.

*NUMBER OF CONSERVATIVE OPINIONS ON FIVE ISSUES (HIGH=4-5, MEDIUM=2-3, LOW=0-1). ISSUES INCLUDE ABORTION, GAY MARRIAGE, GAY ADOPTION, STEM CELL RESEARCH, AND THE MORNING-AFTER PILL. SURVEY CONDUCTED JULY 6-19 AMONG 2,003 ADULTS. FROM THE LATEST NATIONAL SURVEY BY THE PEW RESEARCH CENTER FOR THE PEOPLE & THE PRESS AND PEW FORUM ON RELIGION & PUBLIC LIFE..

4.25 How does your religion affect your attitude toward health programs, policies, and practices?

A new poll finds that majorities of the adult public support each of twelve different healthcare policies, programs, and practices, including some that are highly controversial. Medicare, health insurance for the elderly and disabled, had 96% support, including 92% or more of all religious categories. Birth control, or contraception, is supported by 93% of all adults, including 90% of Catholics, 88% of born-again Christians, the "very religious," and Evangelicals. 92% of adults, including 93%

Do You Favor...	Total (n=2, 242)	Catholic (n=403)	Episcopalian/ Anglican (n=53)	Lutheran Lutheran (n=115)	Methodist Methodist (n=147)	Non- Denom (n=174)
			PERCENTAGE			
Education and availability of Abortion service	63	56	83	67	75	50
Use of birth control/contraception	93	90	100	95	95	92
Abstinence from sex before marriage	63	66	44	72	65	86
Condom use to prevent HIV and other STDs	92	93	99	96	94	84
Funding of international HIV prevention and treatment	87	86	86	82	90	84
Funding of international birth control programs	70	66	79	75	75	61
Universal health insurance	75	76	65	71	66	68
Sex education in high school	87	89	92	94	91	83
Embryonic stem cell research	70	70	88	70	77	59
Withdrawal of life support for those in vegetative state	68	68	80	75	77	58
Medicare—health insurance for the elderly, disabled	96	98	93	96	97	96
Medicaid—health insurance for peoplewith low incomes	91	92	95	91	91	91

RESULTS OF A NATIONWIDE HARRIS POLL OF 2,242 U.S. ADULTS SURVEYED ONLINE BY HARRIS INTERACTIVE® BETWEEN SEPTEMBER 6 AND 12, 2005. FIGURES FOR AGE, SEX, RACE, EDUCATION, REGION AND INCOME WERE WEIGHTED WHERE NECESSARY TO BRING THEM INTO LINE WITH ACTUAL POPULATION PROPORTION. PROPENSITY SCORE WEIGHTING USED TO ADJUST FOR RESPONDENTS' PROPENSITY TO BE ONLINE.

of Catholics, 82% of born-again Christians, 83% of the (self-defined) "very religious" and 81% of Evangelicals support condom use to prevent HIV and other sexually transmitted diseases. 91% of adults, including 88% of all religions, support Medicaid, health insurance for people with low incomes. 87% of the public supports sex education in high schools, but only 76% of born-again Christians, 77% of the "very religious," and 72% of Evangelicals agree. 63% of the public supports abortion rights, including 56% of Catholics, but only 30% of born-again Christians, 39% of the "very religious" and 28% of Evangelicals support it. 63% of the public, 85% of born-again Christians, 85% of the "very religious," and 91% of Evangelicals support abstinence before marriage.

Presbyterian (n=85)	Baptist (n=221)	Other Christians (n=215)	Jewish (n=75)	Agnostic/ Atheist (n=199)	Born-again Christians (n=413)	Very Religious (n=448)	Evangelical Born-again Christians (n=202)
PERCENTAGE							
72	53	49	83	90	30	39	28
99	94	89	97	99	88	88	88
63	75	76	44	31	85	85	91
99	91	8/4	98	99	82	83	81
89	87	85	92	95	82	86	82
81	62	62	79	87	53	57	48
80	76	68	68	89	63	71	66
90	83	81	94	94	76	77	72
82	62	58	95	96	45	51	38
80	64	61	75	86	47	56	45
97	97	96	92	97	96	96	98
88	92	88	90	91	89	92	90

4.26 What are your views on gay marriage, abortion, stem cell research, etc. (General/By religion and politics)?

A clear majority (56%) continue to oppose allowing gays and lesbians to marry while 35% express support. But nearly as large a majority (54%) supports allowing homosexual couples to enter into legal agreements that would give them many of the same rights as married couples. Abortion continues to split the country nearly down the middle, but there is consensus in one key area: two out of three Americans support finding "a middle ground" when it comes to abortion.

DISPARATE VIEWS ON SOCIAL ISSUES

	GAY MARRIAGE	GAY ADOPTION	CIVIL UNIONS
	PERCENTAGE		
FAVOR	35	42	54
OPPOSE	56	52	42
DON'T KNOW	9	6	4
	100	100	100

PRIORITY ON STEM CELL ISSUE	(PCT.)
CONDUCTING MEDICAL RESEARCH	56
NOT DESTROYING HUMAN EMBRYOS	32
DON'T KNOW	12
	100

ABORTION SHOULD BE…	
GENERALLY AVAILABLE	31
ALLOWED, BUT MORE LIMITED	20
ILLEGAL WITH FEW EXCEPTIONS	35
NEVER PERMITTED	11
DON'T KNOW	3
	100

WHEN IT COMES TO ADOPTION…	
WE NEED TO FIND A MIDDLE GROUND	66
THERE IS NO ROOM FOR COMPROMISE	29
DON'T KNOW	5
	100

DIVIDED VIEWS ON LIFE ISSUES
PRO-LIFE POSITION ON…

	ABORTION	STEM CELLS	DEATH PENALTY	EUTH-ANASIA
	PERCENTAGE			
Total	40	30	24	40
White Prot.	51	36	14	45
Evangelical	68	50	15	58
Mainline	28	18	13	26
White Cath.	43	29	27	42
Secular	16	12	29	22
Conservative Republican	71	55	9	55
Mod/Lib Republican	36	26	16	32
Independent	31	23	26	34
Mod./Cons. Democrat	39	31	36	44
Liberal Dem.	18	15	42	30

Only three-in-ten, by contrast, believe "there's no room for compromise when it comes to abortion laws." This desire to find common ground extends across the political and ideological spectrum. White evangelical Protestants overwhelmingly adopt a pro-life stance on abortion: 68% believe it should not be permitted at all, or should be allowed only in cases of rape, incest, or to save the woman's life. Half of white evangelicals say it is more important to avoid destroying the potential life of human embryos than to conduct stem cell research that may lead to new medical cures. Seculars overwhelmingly dissent from pro-life positions on abortion, stem cell research, and end-of-life questions. More seculars than white evangelicals or mainline Protestants oppose the death penalty for convicted murderers; still, only about three-in-ten (29%) express this view.

BOTH SURVEYS RESULTS OF LATEST NATIONAL SURVEY BY THE PEW RESEARCH CENTER FOR THE PEOPLE & THE PRESS AND PEW FORUM ON RELIGION & PUBLIC LIFE. SURVEY CONDUCTED JULY 6–19 AMONG 2,003 ADULTS.

4.27 Should doctors be permitted to assist suicide, provide means to end life?

Fifty-one percent of Americans think it should be legal for doctors to give the terminally ill means to end their lives. There is less support for physicians actually aiding such patients in suicide. There's still clear differences on how much assistance physicians should be allowed to give terminally ill patients to end their lives.

FAVOR MAKING IT LEGAL FOR DOCTORS TO...		
	GIVE MEANS TO END LIFE	ASSIST IN SUICIDE
	—— PERCENTAGE ——	
Total	**51**	**44**
Men	55	48
Women	47	40
College graduate	62	56
Some college	52	42
H.S. grad or less	44	37
Northeast	54	45
Midwest	51	48
South	43	37
West	62	49
Conserv. Repub	39	29
Mod/Lib Repub	57	52
Independent	60	51
Cons/Mod Dem	46	41
Liberal Democrat	62	55
White Protestant	47	39
Evangelical	34	26
Mainline	65	56
White Catholic	44	46
Secular	73	61

RESULTS FOR REPORT BASED ON 2 SEPARATE TELEPHONE SURVEYS CONDUCTED UNDER THE DIRECTION OF PRINCETON SURVEY RESEARCH ASSOCIATES INTERNATIONAL. FOR RESULTS BASED ON THE TOTAL SAMPLE, ONE CAN SAY WITH 95% CONFIDENCE THAT THE ERROR ATTRIBUTABLE TO SAMPLING IS ± 3 PERCENTAGE POINTS.

4.28 Should social issues be decided by states or the federal government?

This poll asked whether each of four social issues—gay marriage, abortion, stem cells, and teaching creationism—should be decided at the national level or by each state. Only 28% expressed support for a state-level solution on at least three of the four issues. Nearly half (48%) expressed support for a national approach on at least three of these four issues among all major political and demographic groups. The remainder (24%) had mixed views on which level of government should make decisions.

GENERALLY WANT POLICIES SET...*			
	AT NATIONAL LEVEL	BY EACH STATE	MIXED VIEWS
	—— PERCENTAGE ——		
Total	48	28	24=100
18-29	48	28	24=100
30-49	52	25	23=100
50-64	48	33	19=100
65+	39	24	37=100
East	45	32	23=100
Midwest	48	27	25=100
South	51	23	26=100
West	45	33	22=100
Republican	49	27	24=100
Democrat	46	31	23=100
Independent	49	25	26=100
Conservative	50	26	24=100
Moderate	44	31	25=100
Liberal	56	24	20=100
Total Protestant	49	27	24=100
White evangelical	55	25	20=100
White mainline	42	31	27=100
Total Catholic	43	31	26=100
White, non-Hisp	47	30	23=100
Secular	50	25	25=100

*POLLED ON FOUR ISSUES: GAY MARRIAGE, ABORTION, STEM CELLS, AND TEACHING CREATIONISM. THE SURVEY WAS CONDUCTED JULY 6–19, 2,003, AS PART OF A NATIONAL SURVEY BY THE PEW RESEARCH CENTER FOR THE PEOPLE & THE PRESS AND THE PEW FORUM ON RELIGION & PUBLIC LIFE.

II. Homosexuality

As is the case with other social issues, opinions about homosexuality are closely linked with partisanship, ideology, and religion. Despite the overall rise in tolerance toward gays since the 1980s, many Americans remain highly critical of homosexuals, and religious belief is a major factor in these attitudes. The Pew Research Center finds that homosexuality in general—not merely the issue of gay marriage—is a major topic in churches and other houses of worship. In fact, the clergy are nearly as likely to address homosexuality from the pulpit as they are to speak out about abortion or prayer in school, according those who attend church regularly. The surveys also find that people who hear clergy talk about homosexuality are more likely to have highly unfavorable views of gays and lesbians. Recent surveys show that the public has moved decisively in the direction of tolerance on many questions; in particular, discrimination against homosexuals is now widely opposed. Yet despite tolerance in other areas, same sex marriage is still debated.

4.29 What are your feelings about gay marriage and homosexuality?

A 55% majority believes it is a sin to engage in homosexual behavior, and that view is much more prevalent among those who have a high level of religious commitment (76%). About half of all Americans have an unfavorable opinion of gay men (50%) and lesbians (48%), but highly religious people are much more likely to hold negative views. Religiosity is clearly a factor in the recent rise in opposition to gay marriage. Overall, nearly six-in-ten Americans (59%) oppose gay marriage. But those with a high level of religious commitment now oppose gay marriage by more than six-to-one (80%-12%). The public is somewhat more supportive of legal agreements for gays that provide many of the same benefits of marriage; still, a 51% majority also opposes this step.

NATIONAL SURVEY OF 1,515 ADULTS, CONDUCTED OCT. 15–19, 2003 BY THE PEW RESEARCH CENTER FOR THE PEOPLE & THE PRESS AND THE PEW FORUM ON RELIGION AND PUBLIC LIFE.

| | | RELIGIOUS TRADITION* | | |
	TOTAL	EVANG PROT	MAIN PROT	CATH-OLIC
GAY MARRIAGE		— percentage —		
Favor	32	13	37	35
Oppose	59	80	54	55
Don't know	9	7	9	10
	100	100	100	100
HEAR ABOUT GAY ISSUES IN CHURCH*				
Yes, (and was...)	55	68	33	49
Discouraged	39	59	13	28
Accepted	2	1	4	3
No position	10	5	15	13
Other/DK	4	3	1	5
No/DK	45	32	67	51
	100	100	100	100
ACCEPTANCE OF HOMOSEXUALITY WOULD BE...				
Good for country	23	11	25	22
Bad for country	31	52	22	21
No difference	42	32	48	53
Don't know	4	5	5	4
	100	100	100	100
HOMOSEXUALITY...				
Can be changed	42	65	31	29
Can't be changed	42	22	48	57
Don't know	16	13	21	14
	100	100	100	100

* Evangelical Protestant, Mainline Protestant, Catholic
**Based on those who attend at least once a month.

4.30 What are your feelings about gay marriage? (by church attendance)

	Fav.	Opp.	DK
Church attendance		percentage	
Attend weekly or more	21	73	6 =100
Attend less Often	47	43	10 =100
White Evang. Prot.			
Attend weekly or more	9	88	3 =100
Attend less often	23	69	8 =100
White Mainline Prot.			
Attend weekly or more	37	58	5 =100
Attend less often	44	44	12 =100
White non-Hisp. Cath.			
Attend weekly or more	30	59	11 =100
Attend less often	49	42	9 =100

Overall, those who attend church weekly or more are significantly more opposed to gay marriage (73%) than those who attend church less often (43%). These differences extend across a variety of religious groups, including white evangelicals (among whom weekly church attenders are 19 percentage points more opposed to gay marriage compared with less frequent attenders), white mainline Protestants (among whom there is a 14 percentage point gap), and white non-Hispanic Catholics (17-point gap).

RESULTS FOR THIS SURVEY ARE BASED ON TELEPHONE INTERVIEWS CONDUCTED UNDER THE DIRECTION OF SCHULMAN, RONCA, & BUCU-VALAS, INC. AMONG A NATIONWIDE SAMPLE OF 3,002 ADULTS, 18 YEARS OF AGE OR OLDER, FROM AUGUST 1–18, 2007. FOR RESULTS BASED ON THE TOTAL SAMPLE, ONE CAN SAY WITH 95% CONFIDENCE THAT THE ERROR ATTRIBUTABLE TO SAMPLING IS ±2 PERCENTAGE POINTS.

FROM RECENT NATIONAL SURVEY BY THE PEW RESEARCH CENTER FOR THE PEOPLE & THE PRESS AND PEW FORUM ON RELIGION & PUBLIC LIFE.

4.31 Does what you hear in church influence you on issues relating to gay marriage?

People who hear clergy talk about homosexuality are more likely to have highly unfavorable views of gays and lesbians, especially in evangelical churches. Fifty-five percent of Evangelicals who attend services where the issue of homosexuality is addressed have unfavorable views of homosexuals compared with 28 percent of those who regularly attend services in non-Evangelical churches where homosexuality is discussed.

	EVANGELICAL PROTESTANTS		OTHER PROTESTANTS AND CATHOLICS	
	WHO HEAR ABOUT ISSUE	WHO DO NOT	WHO HEAR ABOUT ISSUE	WHO DO NOT
	PERCENTAGE			
Very unfavorable view of gay men	55	32	28	18
Sexual orientation can be changed	76	59	34	32
Acceptance of gays is bad for country	63	44	30	18
Number of cases	(238)	(150)	(140)	(247)

*ANALYSIS COMPARES REGULAR CHURCHGOERS (AT LEAST ONCE-PER-MONTH)
RESULTS FOR THE SURVEY ARE BASED ON TELEPHONE INTERVIEWS CONDUCTED UNDER THE DIRECTION OF PRINCETON SURVEY RESEARCH ASSOCIATES AMONG A NATIONWIDE SAMPLE OF 1,515 ADULTS, 18 YEARS OF AGE OR OLDER, DURING THE PERIOD OCTOBER 15–19, 2003. BASED ON THE TOTAL SAMPLE, ONE CAN SAY WITH 95% CONFIDENCE THAT THE ERROR ATTRIBUTABLE TO SAMPLING AND OTHER RANDOM EFFECTS IS ± 3 PERCENTAGE POINTS. FROM RECENT NATIONAL SURVEY BY THE PEW RESEARCH CENTER FOR THE PEOPLE & THE PRESS AND THE PEW FORUM ON RELIGION & PUBLIC LIFE.

4.32 Should school boards have the right to fire teachers who are known homosexuals?

The decline in anti-homosexual attitudes has occurred at roughly the same rate among traditionally conservative white evangelical Protestants as among more liberal religious groups and seculars.

	1987/88	2002/03	CHANGE
Religious Denomination	——— PERCENTAGE ———		
White Evangelical Prot.	22	40	+18
White Mainline Prot.	44	68	+24
White Catholic	52	68	+16
Black Protestant	39	54	+15
No Religion	59	78	+19
Personal Religiosity**			
Highly religious	34	53	+19
Mixed	56	75	+19
Secular	77	87	+10
Generation (Year of birth)			
Oldest (pre-1913)	22	—	—
Greatest (1913–1927)	27	37	+10
Silent (1928–45)	38	46	+8
Baby Boomers (1946–64)	51	62	+11
Generation X (1965–76)	47	70	+23
Generation Y (1977–later)	—	71	—

* Percent disagreeing with the statement "schools boards ought to have the right to fire teachers who are known homosexuals."
** Agree/disagree with religious items.

As with attitudes about race, views on homosexuality have a strong generational component, with younger generations much less negative toward gays. However, the overall increase in tolerance toward homosexuality is not merely a result of generational replacement. There has also been a significant change of attitude within generations over time, which suggests that people's views on this issue have shifted. We see evidence of this change in the first chart below, which shows changing views on homosexuality from 1987–1988 to 2002–2003. The results show the national percent that disagrees with the proposition that school boards have the right to fire teachers who are known homosexuals. There is a clear increase among all religious sects, age groups, and levels of religiosity, in opposition to teachers losing their jobs because of their sexual preference.

RESULTS FOR THE SURVEY ARE BASED ON TELEPHONE INTERVIEWS CONDUCTED UNDER THE DIRECTION OF PRINCETON SURVEY RESEARCH ASSOCIATES AMONG A NATIONWIDE SAMPLE OF 2,528 ADULTS, 18 YEARS OF AGE OR OLDER, DURING THE PERIOD JULY 14–AUGUST 5, 2003. BASED ON THE TOTAL SAMPLE, THERE IS 95% CONFIDENCE THAT THE ERROR ATTRIBUTABLE TO SAMPLING AND OTHER RANDOM EFFECTS IS ±2 PERCENTAGE POINTS. FROM THE RECENT NATIONAL SURVEY BY THE PEW RESEARCH CENTER FOR THE PEOPLE & THE PRESS AND THE PEW FORUM ON RELIGION & PUBLIC LIFE.

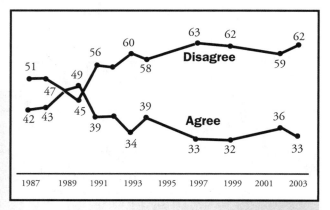

4.33 Do you favor or oppose gay marriage? Civil union for gays?

While only one-in-three Americans (35%) favors gay marriage, majorities express support for civil unions. The poll finds that 54% of Americans favor allowing gay and lesbian couples to enter into legal agreements giving them many of the same rights as married couples. This figure, too, is largely unchanged compared with one year ago – but it is nine percentage points higher than it was in October 2003. Evidence of the continuing red state/blue state divide can be seen on this question. In the East and West, large majorities (62% and 66%, respectively) favor civil unions. In the Midwest and South, by contrast, roughly half (48% and 50%, respectively) oppose even this type of legal recognition of same-sex couples.

| | FAVOR GAY MARRIAGE | | FAVOR CIVIL UNIONS | |
	AUG. 2004	JULY 2005	AUG. 2004	JULY 2005
	PERCENTAGE			
Total	32	36	48	53
White Protestant	22	25	42	46
Evangelical	10	14	26	35
Mainline	34	39	60	60
White Catholic	35	39	60	62
Black Protestant	19	25	28	31
Secular	63	61	76	75
Conservative	15	14	35	31
Moderate	31	40	53	60
Liberal	59	69	70	80
Republican	16	19	38	41
Democrat	38	45	56	59
Independent	36	46	54	61

RESULTS OF RECENT NATIONAL SURVEY BY THE PEW RESEARCH CENTER FOR THE PEOPLE & THE PRESS AND THE PEW FORUM ON RELIGION & PUBLIC LIFE. THE SURVEY WAS CONDUCTED JULY 6–19, 2,003.

As with gay marriage, white evangelicals (66%), black Protestants (62%), and frequent church attenders (60%) stand out for their opposition to civil unions. But sizeable majorities of white mainline Protestants (66%), Catholics (63%), and seculars (78%) support civil unions.

REGARDING GAY MARRIAGE:	FAV.	OPP.	DK	
	PERCENTAGE			
Total	54	42	4	=100
July 2005	53	40	7	=100
August 2004	48	45	7	=100
October 2003	45	47	8	=100
East	62	33	5	=100
Midwest	49	48	3	=100
South	46	50	4	=100
West	66	29	5	=100
Total Protestant	43	53	4	=100
White evangelical	30	66	4	=100
White mainline	66	30	4	=100
Black Protestant	35	62	3	=100
Total Catholic	63	32	5	=100
White, non-Hisp	59	36	5	=100
Secular	78	18	4	=100
Religious Attendance:				
Weekly or more	36	60	4	=100
Less often	67	29	4	=100

REGARDING CIVIL UNIONS	FAV.	OPP.	DK	
	PERCENTAGE			
Conserv Rep.	11	83	6	=100
Mod/Liberal Rep.	33	59	8	=100
Independent	41	49	10	=100
Mod/Cons Dem	40	50	10	=100
Liberal Dem.	71	26	3	=100
White Protestant	27	66	7	=100
Evangelical	14	81	5	=100
Mainline	43	47	10	=100
Black Protestant	25	64	11	=100
Evangelical	15	79	6	=100
Catholic	42	48	10	=100
White non-Hispanic	41	49	10	=100
Unaffiliated	60	30	10	=100

4.34 Do you support or oppose a constitutional ban on gay marriage?

	Total	Among White Evang	Repub-licans	Conser-vatives	Age 65+
		PERCENTAGE			
Oppose gay marriage	56	78	77	78	73
Amend Constitution to ban gay marriage					
Good idea	30	46	45	46	36
Bad idea	24	29	28	29	34
Don't know	2	3	4	3	3
Favor gay marriage	35	14	17	16	16
Don't know	9	8	6	6	11
	100	100	100	100	100

PEW RESEARCH CENTER FOR THE PEOPLE & THE PRESS AND THE PEW FORUM ON RELIGION & PUBLIC LIFE, SURVEY CONDUCTED JULY 6–19, 2,003 ADULTS.

While a majority opposes gay marriage, opponents are divided on whether it would be a good idea to amend the U.S. Constitution to ban it. The result is that just three-in-ten Americans (30%) currently oppose gay marriage and think a constitutional amendment would be a good idea. Even among groups most strongly opposed to gay marriage (white evangelicals, Republicans, conservatives, and senior citizens), less than a majority favor a Constitutional amendment.

4.35 Is homosexuality "curable"?

HOMOSEXUALITY...	Can be changed	Cannot be changed	DK
	PERCENTAGE		
Total	39	49	12 =100
October 2003	42	42	16 =100
Conservative	52	36	12 =100
Moderate	37	49	14 =100
Liberal	21	71	8 =100
Total Protestant	45	42	13 =100
White evangelical	56	29	15 =100
White mainline	22	67	11 =100
Black Protestant	60	30	10 =100
Total Catholic	31	56	13 =100
White, non-Hisp	26	61	13 =100
Secular	27	59	14 =100
Religious Attendance			
Weekly or more	54	34	12 =100
Monthly or less	34	52	14 =100
Seldom or never	22	68	10 =100

Majorities of white evangelicals (51%) and black Protestants (52%) continue to view homosexuality as a choice. White evangelicals, in particular, have changed very little in their views over the past three years. Though most Americans reject the idea that homosexuality is an innate trait, 49% view sexual orientation as a characteristic that cannot be changed (or "cured"), a seven percentage increase since 2003. Views of whether homosexuality can be changed have both political and religious components; 52% of conservatives say homosexuality can be changed, while 71% of liberals disagree. Substantial majorities of white evangelicals and black Protestants say that ho-mosexuality can be changed, while majorities of white mainline Protestants, Catholics, and secular individuals say homosexuality cannot be changed.

RESULTS OF RECENT NATIONAL SURVEY BY THE PEW RESEARCH CENTER FOR THE PEOPLE & THE PRESS AND THE PEW FORUM ON RELIGION & PUBLIC LIFE. SURVEY CONDUCTED JULY 6–19, 2,003. RESULTS HAVE BEEN REPERCENTAGED TO EXCLUDE NONRESPONSE.

III. Capital Punishment

Since the late 1960s, public support for the death penalty has experienced significant dips and rises, but it has never fallen below half. Roughly two-thirds of Americans support the death penalty for people convicted of murder. However, public support for the death penalty was greater in the late 1990s. But most Americans continue to oppose the death penalty for minors. Smaller differences exist among members of different religious traditions, with interesting differences related to frequency of religious attendance. Support for the death penalty is highest among white evangelical Protestants, while white mainline Protestants and white non-Hispanic Catholics favor it at slightly lower rates. Support is lowest among the religiously unaffiliated, but a solid majority of this group still favors capital punishment. Americans who regularly attend religious services are less likely to support the death penalty than those who attend less frequently.

4.36 Do you favor or oppose capital punishment (general public)?

Public support for the death penalty, since the 1960s, has never fallen below 50%. In fact, during the past forty years, support for capital punishment has remained relatively high, reaching a peak of 80% in 1994. Polls show that the share of the public in favor of the death penalty began rising around the time that the Supreme Court temporarily suspended all executions in 1972.

After peaking in the mid-1990s, the percentage of Americans in favor of capital punishment dropped, leveling off after 2000. Pew Research Center surveys show that support for the death penalty for persons convicted of murder has fluctuated within a relatively narrow range (of 62% to 68%) since 2001, while opposition has ranged from 24 to 32% during this time.

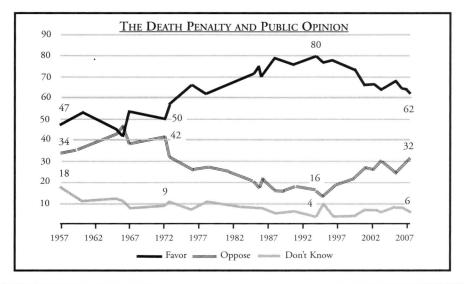

THE DEATH PENALTY AND PUBLIC OPINION

4.37 Do you favor or oppose capital punishment (by politics and by religion)?

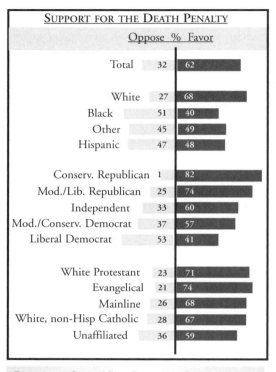

SUPPORT FOR THE DEATH PENALTY		
	Oppose	% Favor
Total	32	62
White	27	68
Black	51	40
Other	45	49
Hispanic	47	48
Conserv. Republican	1	82
Mod./Lib. Republican	25	74
Independent	33	60
Mod./Conserv. Democrat	37	57
Liberal Democrat	53	41
White Protestant	23	71
Evangelical	21	74
Mainline	26	68
White, non-Hisp Catholic	28	67
Unaffiliated	36	59

A survey from August 2007 finds that 62% of Americans favor the death penalty, while 32% oppose it and 6% are unsure. Some of the sharpest differences in public opinion about the death penalty occur along racial lines. More than two-thirds of whites support the death penalty, while only 40% of blacks express the same opinion. Hispanics are evenly split on the issue; 48% support the death penalty, while 47% oppose it. Political conservatives are more likely to support the death penalty, and the politically liberal are more likely to oppose it. Roughly 82% of conservative Republicans support the death penalty; support is lowest among liberal Democrats, with just 41% in favor. Smaller differences exist among members of different religious traditions. Support for the death penalty is highest among white evangelical Protestants, while white mainline Protestants and white non-Hispanic Catholics favor it at slightly lower rates (68% and 67%, respectively). Support is lowest among the religiously unaffiliated, but a solid majority of this group (59%) still favor capital punishment.

4.38 Are you in favor of the death penalty for murderers?

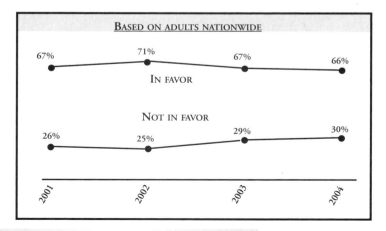

4.39 Do you favor the death penalty (by church attendance and religious affiliation)?

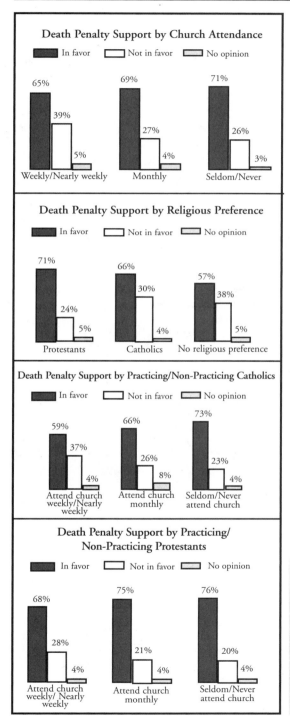

Death Penalty Support by Church Attendance

■ In favor ☐ Not in favor ▨ No opinion

Weekly/Nearly weekly: 65%, 39%, 5%
Monthly: 69%, 27%, 4%
Seldom/Never: 71%, 26%, 3%

Death Penalty Support by Religious Preference

■ In favor ☐ Not in favor ▨ No opinion

Protestants: 71%, 24%, 5%
Catholics: 66%, 30%, 4%
No religious preference: 57%, 38%, 5%

Death Penalty Support by Practicing/Non-Practicing Catholics

■ In favor ☐ Not in favor ▨ No opinion

Attend church weekly/Nearly weekly: 59%, 37%, 4%
Attend church monthly: 66%, 26%, 8%
Seldom/Never attend church: 73%, 23%, 4%

Death Penalty Support by Practicing/ Non-Practicing Protestants

■ In favor ☐ Not in favor ▨ No opinion

Attend church weekly/Nearly weekly: 68%, 28%, 4%
Attend church monthly: 75%, 21%, 4%
Seldom/Never attend church: 76%, 20%, 4%

The combined aggregate results from nine surveys conducted from 2001 through 2004 show some interesting, though subtle, differences in death penalty support by religiosity. Americans who attend religious services on a regular basis are slightly less likely to support the death penalty than those who attend less frequently. Although a majority of frequent and infrequent churchgoers support the death penalty, the data show that 65% of those who attend services weekly or nearly weekly favor capital punishment, compared with 69% of those who attend services monthly and 71% of those who seldom or never attend. Protestants are somewhat more likely to endorse capital punishment than are Catholics and far more likely than those with no religious preference. More than seven-in-ten Protestants support the death penalty, while 66% of Catholics support it. Fifty-seven percent of those with no religious preference favor the death penalty for murder. Practicing Catholics, or those who attend church on a weekly or near weekly basis, are less likely to support capital punishment than are non-practicing Catholics (those who attend services rarely or never). Fewer than six-in-ten practicing Catholics (59%) support the death penalty, compared to 73% of non-practicing Catholics who support it. This result suggests that practicing Catholics are more likely to adhere to the Catholic Church's anti-death penalty position.

4.38, 4.39 Results based on telephone interviews with 6,498 national adults, aged 18 and older, conducted Feb. 19–21, 2001; May 10–14, 2001; Oct. 11–14, 2001; May 6–9, 2002; Oct. 14–17, 2002; May 5–7, 2003; Oct 6–9, 2003; May 2–4, 2004; and Oct. 11–14, 2004. For results based on total sample of national adults, one can say with 95% confidence that the maximum margin of sampling error is ±2 percentage points.

4.40 Do you support the death penalty for murderers who are minors?

SUPPORT FOR DEATH PENALTY		
	OVERALL	FOR MINORS
	percentage	
Total	68	37
Men	70	47
Women	66	27
White	74	38
Black	42	25
Republican	84	46
Independent	69	38
Democrat	52	26
White Protest.	80	38
Evangelical	79	38
Mainline	81	39
White Catholic	66	39
Secular	65	41

Roughly two thirds of Americans support the death penalty for people convicted of murder, but most Americans oppose the death penalty for minors. Earlier this year, the Supreme Court abolished the death penalty in such cases, citing a "national consensus" on the issue. The pattern of opinion on applying the death penalty to minors is quite different than that of the death penalty for adults. There are only small gender differences in support for the death penalty (70% of men, 66% of women). But there is a sizable gender gap in attitudes toward the death penalty for those convicted of murder who are under age 18; 47% of men support the death penalty for minors, compared with only about 27% of women. While there are significant differences among religious groups in views of the overall application of the death penalty, there is striking agreement in opinions on the death penalty for those under age 18. Only about four-in-ten white evangelicals, mainline Protestants, white Catholics and secular individuals favor the death penalty under these circumstances.

RESULTS FOR REPORT BASED ON A NATIONWIDE SAMPLE OF 1,502 ADULTS, 18 YEARS OF AGE OR OLDER, FROM JULY 13–17, 2005. FOR RESULTS BASED ON THE TOTAL SAMPLE, ONE CAN SAY WITH 95% CONFIDENCE THAT THE ERROR ATTRIBUTABLE TO SAMPLING IS ± 3%. COPYRIGHT © 2007 PEW RESEARCH CENTER. ALL RIGHTS RESERVED.

4.41 Do you support the death penalty (1996; 2001; 2007)?

Opinion about the death penalty has remained fairly steady in recent years, though there is less support now than during the 1990s. Support for the death penalty is particularly high among Republicans, and smaller majorities of independents and Democrats also support capital punishment in murder cases. White evangelical Protestants support the death penalty at slightly higher rates than do white mainline Protestants (74% to 68%), while about half of black Protestants oppose it.

RESULTS FOR SURVEY BASED ON TELEPHONE INTERVIEWS CONDUCTED UNDER THE DIRECTION OF SCHULMAN, RONCA, & BUCUVALAS, INC. AMONG A NATIONWIDE SAMPLE OF 3,002 ADULTS, 18 YEARS OF AGE OR OLDER, FROM AUGUST 1–18, 2007. THERE IS 95% CONFIDENCE THAT THE ERROR ATTRIBUTABLE TO SAMPLING IS ± 2%. COPYRIGHT © 2007 PEW RESEARCH CENTER. ALL RIGHTS RESERVED. SOURCE: PEW SURVEY.

CONTINUING SUPPORT FOR DEATH PENALTY	FAV	OPP	DK	
	percentage			
Total	62	32	6	=100
January 2007	64	29	7	=100
July 2005	68	24	8	=100
March 2001	66	27	7	=100
June 1996	78	18	4	=100
White Protestant	71	23	6	=100
Evangelical	74	21	5	=100
Mainline	68	26	6	=100
Black Protestant	38	51	11	=100
Catholic	59	35	6	=100
White non-Hispanic	66	28	6	=100
Attend weekly	55	39	6	=100
Attend less often	73	22	5	=100
Unaffiliated	59	36	5	=100

IV. Abortion

In 1973, the landmark decision of Roe v. Wade, one of the most controversial United States Supreme Court cases, set the standard for legislation regarding abortion. According to the Roe decision, most laws against abortion in the United States violated a constitutional right. The decision overturned all state and federal laws outlawing or restricting abortion that were inconsistent with its holdings. While Roe v. Wade remains controversial, Americans overwhelmingly support keeping abortion legal.

Fewer than three-in-ten favor overturning Roe v. Wade, and a mere 9% say that abortion should not be permitted under any circumstances. Even among evangelicals, the most pro-life of religious groups, fewer than half favor overturning the Roe v. Wade decision, and only 15% say abortion should not be permitted at all. Supreme court rulings on abortions and abortion issues in general necessarily tie in with debates over sex education in schools, personal morality, and distribution of the morning-after pill.

4.42 Should birth control information be provided—even if you favor counselling total abstinence?

Debates over sex education in schools often pit abstinence instruction against providing students with information on birth control methods. But the public sees no conflict in pursuing both of these approaches: 78% favor allowing public schools to provide students with birth control information, and nearly as many (76%) believe schools should teach teenagers to abstain from sex until marriage. Solid majorities in every major religious group say schools should be allowed to provide students with information on birth control methods. But sizable minorities of white evangelical Protestants oppose this action. White evangelicals also are among the most supportive of having public schools teach teenagers to abstain from sex until marriage. Secular individuals express the greatest reservations about abstinence-only education in schools; 62% support that approach, while roughly a third (34%) oppose it. The youngest Americans—those ages 18–24—are highly supportive of schools both promoting abstinence and providing information about birth control. Roughly eight-in-ten (83%) of young Americans favor schools providing birth control information, while 75% think schools should teach teenagers to abstain from sex until marriage.

TEACH ABSTINENCE, BUT ALSO PROVIDE BIRTH CONTROL INFORMATION				
	PROVIDE BIRTH CONTROL INFO?		TEACH ABSTINENCE?	
	FAVOR	OPPOSE	FAVOR	OPPOSE
	——— PERCENTAGE ———			
Total 78	18	76	20	
White Protestant	72	24	85	12
Evangelical	66	30	91	8
Mainline	81	15	77	18
White Catholic	79	18	78	18
Secular	93	5	62	34
Age: 18–24	83	14	75	21
25–29	81	16	73	22
30–49	81	16	78	19
50–64	81	16	79	17
65+	64	29	71	24

THE LATEST NATIONAL SURVEY BY THE PEW RESEARCH CENTER FOR THE PEOPLE & THE PRESS AND THE PEW FORUM ON RELIGION & PUBLIC LIFE. NEW STUDY—BASED ON SEPARATE SURVEYS CONDUCTED JULY 13–17 AMONG 1,502 ADULTS, AND JULY 7–17 AMONG 2,000 ADULTS. COPYRIGHT © 2007 PEW RESEARCH CENTER. ALL RIGHTS RESERVED.

4.43 Do you support abortion (by politics and religion)?

Public opinion about the legality of abortion is largely unchanged from previous polls. While about one-in-three prefer abortion to be generally available to those who want it and one-in-ten take the opposite position that abortion should not be permitted at all, most Americans fall in between, preferring what might be described as a "legal but rare" stance. One-in-five say that abortion should be available, but under stricter limits than it is now, while about one-in-three say that abortion should be illegal except in cases of rape, incest, or to save the woman's life. Just as abortion opinions are largely stable, so too are differences of opinion on the issue across demographic, political, and religious groups. College graduates and people in their 50s and early 60s—the first half of the Baby Boom generation—are more supportive of making abortion generally available than other demographic groups. As in the past, about two-thirds of conservative Republicans say that abortion should only be available in cases of rape, incest, or when the mother's life is threatened (50%), or not permitted at all (18%). Three-quarters of liberal Democrats, in contrast, say abortion should either be generally available (60%) or available, but with stricter limits (14%). White evangelicals and black Protestants stand out for their high levels of opposition to abortion. Among seculars and those who rarely attend church, on the other hand, most say abortion should be generally available.

ABORTION SHOULD BE...	GENERALLY AVAILABLE	ALLOWED, BUT MORE LIMITED	ILLEGAL, WITH FEW EXCEPTIONS	NEVER PERMITTED	DK
	PERCENTAGE				
All	31	20	35	11	3
Men	31	21	35	11	2
Women	31	20	34	12	3
18–29	25	26	35	11	3
30–49	31	20	35	11	3
50–64	40	17	30	10	3
65+	27	17	39	13	4
College graduate	40	27	24	6	3
Some college	29	24	38	6	3
H.S. or less	28	15	39	16	2
Conserv Repub	17	14	50	18	1
Mod/Lib Repub	25	27	39	6	3
Independent	37	23	29	9	2
Mod/Cons Dem	25	20	39	12	4
Liberal Democrat	60	14	13	10	3
Total Protestant	25	21	39	12	3
White evangelical	15	18	51	15	1
White Mainline	37	34	21	4	4
Black Protestant	25	11	40	19	5
Total Catholic	26	18	36	17	3
White, non-Hisp	30	20	32	16	2
Secular	61	21	16	1	1

4.44 Would you favor a complete ban of abortion—or do you support a middle-ground position?

MOST WANT MIDDLE GROUND ON ABORTION, EXCEPT SUPPORTERS OF A COMPLETE BAN			
WHEN IT COMES TO ABORTION POLICY...	MUST FIND A MIDDLE GROUND	NO ROOM FOR COM- PROMISE	DK
PERCENTAGE			
Total	66	29	5
Republican	62	34	4
Democrat	70	24	6
Independent	66	29	5
ABORTION SHOULD BE... (TOTAL POPULATION)			
Generally available	67	26	7
Allowed, but limited	84	13	3
Illegal–few exceptions	64	31	5
Never permitted	34	66	0

Abortion continues to split the country nearly down the middle. But there is a consensus in one key area: two out of three Americans support finding "a middle ground" when it comes to abortion. Only three-in-ten, in contrast, believe "there's no room for compromise when it comes to abortion laws." The desire to find common ground extends broadly across the political and ideological spectrum. Majorities of Republicans (62%), Democrats (70%) and political independents (66%) favor a compromise. So do majorities of liberals, moderates and conservatives. More than six-in-ten white evangelicals also support compromise, as do 62% of white, non-Hispanic Catholics. Only one group expressed unwillingness to find a middle ground; 66% of those who support an outright ban on abortion say there should be no compromise.

4.45 Are Supreme Court decisions on abortion important to you?

RELIGION AND THE SALIENCE OF SUPREME COURT DECISIONS ON ABORTION					
COURT'S ABORTION DECISIONS ARE...	VERY IMPT.	FAIRLY IMPT.	NOT TOO IMPT.	NOT AT ALL IMPT.	DON'T KNOW
percentage					
All	62	20	8	8	2
White Evang. Prot.	69	17	6	6	2
White Mainline Prot.	55	23	13	7	2
White Catholic	59	24	9	7	1
Secular	59	19	5	14	4

More than six-in-ten Americans say Supreme Court decisions on abortion are "very important" to them. Nearly as many view court decisions on the rights of suspected terrorists as important. Fewer people see issues such as religious displays on public property and affirmative action as very important. Nearly seven-in-ten evangelical Christians say that court decisions on abortion are very important to them, more than any other group. But abortion is important across the spectrum, with majorities of mainline Protestants, Catholics, and secular individuals reporting that abortion decisions are very important.

4.46 Do you support legalizing abortion?

Other polling, conducted in July 2005 by the People & the Press and the Pew Forum on Religion & Public Life, reveals that Americans are somewhat ambivalent about abortion, much as they have been for the past two decades. On the one hand, Americans overwhelmingly support keeping abortion legal. Fewer than three-in-ten (29%) favor overturning Roe v. Wade, and a mere 9% say that abortion should not be permitted under any circumstances. Even among evangelicals, the most pro-life of religious groups, fewer than half (48%) favor overturning Roe v. Wade and only 15% say abortion should not be permitted at all. Among Catholics, support for completely outlawing abortion stands at only 11%, while among mainline Protestants and secular individuals, merely one-in-twenty say abortion should never be permitted. At the same time, a majority of Americans say that there should be more restrictions on abortion than currently exist. Approximately one-in-four say that abortion should be available but with stricter limits, while 31% say that abortion should only be legal in cases of rape, incest, or to save the woman's life. Many who favor requiring minors to get parental consent before obtaining an abortion, say that it would be good to reduce the number of abortions performed in the U.S., and express moral concerns about abortion. On each of these questions, evangelical Christians stand out due to their pro-life views; 86% favor parental consent laws, 79% say it would be good to reduce the number of abortions, and 87% say that abortion is sometimes or nearly always morally wrong. Secular individuals, in contrast, stand out for their pro-choice opinions. Half of secular Americans reject the idea that reducing the number of abortions would be positive, and the same number say abortion is not a moral issue.

AMERICAN VIEWS ON LEGALIZED ABORTION...		WHITE			
		EVANG.	MAIN.		
	ALL	PROT	PROT	CATH	SEC
ABORTION SHOULD BE... (—PERCENTAGES—)					
Generally available	35	14	41	31	60
Avail., with more limits	23	17	30	23	23
Illegal except rape/incest/ or to save woman's life	31	53	23	32	13
Not permitted at all	9	15	5	11	3
Don't know	2	1	1	3	1
	100	100	100	100	100
DO YOU SUPPORT OVERTURNING ROE?					
No...	65	48	81	62	82
Yes...	29	48	13	32	14
Don't know	6	4	6	6	4
	(100)	(100)	(100)	(100)	(100)
...BUT WITH RESERVATIONS					
ABORTION IS...					
Not a moral issue	26	12	32	20	50
Sometimes immoral	41	38	44	44	36
Most often immoral	29	49	19	33	10
Don't know	4	1	5	3	4
	(100)	(100)	(100)	(100)	(100)
IT WOULD BE GOOD TO REDUCE ABORTIONS?					
No	33	14	39	30	51
Yes	59	79	49	65	40
Don't know	8	7	12	5	9
	(100)	(100)	(100)	(100)	(100)
PARENTAL CONSENT?					
Oppose	22	11	24	17	25
Favor	73	86	71	80	67
Don't know	5	3	5	3	8
	(100)	(100)	(100)	(100)	(100)

PEW FORUM/RESEARCH CENTER FOR THE PEOPLE & THE PRESS, JULY 2005

4.47 Should legal abortions be hard or difficult to get?

ABORTIONS SHOULD BE...	GENERALLY AVAILABLE	MORE LIMITED	ILLEGAL EXCEPT RAPE/INCEST, SAVE MOTHER	NEVER PERMITTED	DK
All	35	23	31	9	2
Men	34	24	32	8	2
Women	35	21	31	11	2
College grad	46	22	24	7	1
Some College	33	28	29	9	1
H.S. or less	29	22	37	10	2
Conserv. Repub.	13	15	49	22	1
Mod/Lib. Repub.	31	33	35	1	0
Independent	41	27	25	6	1
Mod/Cons. Dem	34	25	31	8	2
Liberal Dem.	64	16	15	3	2
White Prot.	26	22	40	11	1
Evangelical	14	17	53	15	1
Mainline	41	30	23	5	1
White Cath.	31	23	13	3	1
Secular	60	23	13	3	1
Attend church...					
Weekly or more	18	19	43	18	2
Sometimes	39	25	30	5	1
Seldom or never	53	27	16	2	2

Nearly two-thirds of liberal Democrats believe abortion should be available to those who want it, compared with about a third of moderate and conservative Democrats. In contrast, 22% of conservative Republicans believe abortion should not be permitted at all; just 1% of moderate and liberal Republicans agree. Most secular Americans believe abortion should be generally available, and many white mainline Protestants agree. Sixty-eight percent of white Evangelicals believe abortion should not be permitted, or allowed only in cases of rape, incest, or to save the woman's life. 46% of college graduates say abortion should be generally available, and 29% of those with a high school education agree.

SURVEY AMONG A NATIONWIDE SAMPLE OF 1,502 ADULTS, 18 YEARS OF AGE OR OLDER, FROM JULY 13–17, 2005. THERE IS 95% CONFIDENCE THAT THE ERROR ATTRIBUTABLE TO SAMPLING IS ± 3 PERCENTAGE POINTS. COPYRIGHT © 2005 PEW RESEARCH CENTER. ALL RIGHTS RESERVED.

4.48 Do you favor or oppose making the morning-after pill legal?

The public is divided on the question of whether women should be allowed to obtain the morning-after pill without a doctor's prescription; 48% are in favor while 41% are opposed. Slim majorities of Republicans (54%), white evangelicals (53%), and black Protestants (53%) oppose making the morning-after pill available over-the-counter, while majorities of Democrats (55%), white mainline Protestants (57%), and seculars (67%) take the opposite stance. Among those who say abortion should be generally available, nearly eight-in-ten also support allowing women to get the morning-after pill without a prescription.

RESULTS OF RECENT NATIONAL SURVEY BY PEW RESEARCH CENTER FOR THE PEOPLE & THE PRESS AND PEW FORUM ON RELIGION & PUBLIC LIFE, CONDUCTED JULY 6–19, 2003. COPYRIGHT © 2006 PEW RESEARCH CENTER. ALL RIGHTS RESERVED.

ALLOWING MORNING-AFTER PILL W/O PRESCRIPTION (PERCENTAGE)	FAV	OPP	DK
Total	48	41	11
Republican	48	41	11
Democrat	55	36	9
Independent	51	37	12
Total Protestant	43	45	12
White evangelical	35	53	12
White mainline	57	34	9
Black Protestant	35	53	12
Total Catholic	47	45	8
White, non-Hispanic	43	49	8
Secular	67	21	12
Abortion should be...			
Generally available	79	11	10
Allowed, but limited	51	39	10
Illegal–few exceptions	27	59	14
Never permitted	26	66	8

V. Stem Cell Research

As a result of the techniques used in the creation and usage of stem cells, there is a tremendous controversy over human embryonic stem cell research. With current technology, starting a stem cell line requires the destruction of a human embryo. It's not the entire field of stem cell research, but rather, the specific field of human embryonic stem cell research, which is at the center of the ethical debate. The ensuing debate has prompted authorities around the world to seek regulatory frameworks, aware of the social and ethical challenge it presents.

According to a 2001 survey, a third of the population felt that stem cell research should be allowed. As in past years, there continues to be an important link between the public's knowledge about the stem cell debate and support for conducting research. Those who have heard more about the issue are more supportive of stem cell research. More education is also connected to increased support for stem cell research, and every age group except the oldest expressed majority support.

4.49 Should stem cell research be allowed?

In 2001, a Harris Poll reported that a three-to-one majority believed that stem cell research should be allowed. Born-Again Christians are more likely to oppose it than are other Christians (21% vs. 9%); and Catholics are somewhat more likely to oppose it than Protestants (15% vs. 10%). However, majorities of all of the religious groups polled favor stem cell research, which reflects the general trend in support.

STEM CELL RESEARCH...	TOTAL	CATHOLIC	PROTESTANT	OTHER CHRISTIAN	BORN-AGAIN CHRISTIAN	ALL OTHER (NOT BORN-AGAIN)
			PERCENTAGE			
...Should be allowed	73	67	77	66	56	75
...Should not be allowed	11	15	10	13	21	9
Not sure/ Refused	16	18	12	20	21	16

STEM CELL RESEARCH...	TOTAL	I AM... VERY...	SOMEWHAT...	NOT AT ALL/ NOT VERY...	RELIGIOUS
		PERCENTAGE			
...Should be allowed	73	55	76	84	
...Should not be allowed	11	23	9	4	
Not sure/Refused	16	22	16	11	

RESULTS OF NATIONWIDE SURVEY OF 2,242 ADULTS INTERVIEWED ONLINE BY HARRIS INTERACTIVE® BETWEEN JULY 12 AND 18, 2004 AMONG A NATIONWIDE CROSS SECTION OF 2,242 ADULTS (AGED 18 YEARS AND OVER). COPYRIGHT © 2007, HARRIS INTERACTIVE INC. ALL RIGHTS RESERVED.

4.50 Do the possible benefits of stem cell research outweigh your qualms about its ethics?

Roughly one-third of the public opposes stem cell research, saying that protecting the potential life of embryos is more important than conducting the research. The issue of stem cell research continues to divide Americans along political fault lines. Majorities of Democrats (60%) and political independents (55%) say it is more important to conduct stem cell research that might result in new medical cures than it is to avoid destroying the potential life of human embryos, but only 37% of Republicans agree. And nearly twice as many self-identified liberals and moderates as conservatives support stem cell research. There are also differences between religious groups. Solid majorities of the religiously unaffiliated (68%), white mainline Protestants (58%), and white non-Hispanic Catholics (59%) support stem cell research; however, support for stem cell research is much lower (46%) among white non-Hispanic Catholics who attend religious services at least weekly. A majority (57%) of white evangelical Protestants say that it is more important to avoid destroying potential human life than to conduct stem cell research, a view that is particularly pronounced among white evangelicals who attend church at least weekly (68%). Black Protestants remain split over the issue of stem cell research, with 40% favoring it, 40% opposing it, and 20% undecided. As in past years there is an important link between the public's knowledge about the stem cell debate and support for conducting research. Overall, 45% say they have heard a lot about the issue, while 43% have heard a little; just 12% have heard nothing at all about the debate. Public awareness of the debate has not changed much in recent years. Among those who say they have heard a lot about the debate, 62% support conducting research, compared with just 33% of those who have heard nothing at all about the stem-cell debate.

POLITICAL, RELIGIOUS DIVIDES OVER STEM CELL RESEARCH

MORE IMPORTANT TO...	CONDUCT RESEARCH	NOT DESTROY EMBRYOS	DK
	PERCENTAGE		
Total	51	35	14
Republican	37	50	13
Independent	60	26	14
White Protestant	44	44	12
Evangelical	31	57	12
Attend weekly	23	68	9
Less often	47	37	16
Mainline	58	28	14
Black Protestant	40	40	20
White non-Hisp. Cath.	59	32	9
Attend weekly	46	46	8
Less often	67	22	11
Unaffiliated	68	21	11
I have heard about stem cell debate...			
A lot	62	30	8
A little	45	40	15
Nothing at all	33	39	28

4.51 Do you support stem cell research (2002–2006)?

TRENDS IN SUPPORT FOR STEM CELL RESEARCH						
	MAR 2002	AUG 2004	DEC 2004	JULY 2005	JULY 2006	CHANGE '02–'06
PERCENTAGE SUPPORTING STEM CELL RESEARCH						
Total	43	52	56	57	56	+13
18–29	46	54	61	60	57	+11
30–49	46	55	58	56	59	+13
50–64	40	52	55	61	62	+22
65+	34	44	50	49	41	+7
College graduate	55	61	65	69	69	+14
Some College	46	50	56	59	57	+11
High school grad	34	49	54	51	53	+19
Less than HS	36	47	46	43	41	+5
White Protestant	38	48	52	49	57	+19
Evangelical	26	33	33	32	44	+18
Mainline	51	66	69	71	73	+22
White Catholic	43	55	63	61	58	+15
Secular	66	68	70	77	72	+6
Conserv Repub	32	35	40	33	38	+6
Mod/Lib Repub	48	54	55	62	58	+10
Independent	49	57	58	66	65	+16
Cons/Mod Dem	43	58	60	54	59	+16
Liberal Democrat	55	72	85	80	73	+18

A clear majority (56%) say it is more important to continue stem cell research that might produce new medical cures than to avoid destroying the human embryos used in the research. Nearly a third say it is more important to avoid destroying the potential life of human embryos. In the past five years, the proportion favoring stem cell research has increased 13%, with most of those gains occurring before 2004. The number of liberal Democrats who favor stem cell research has dropped 12 points in two years but remains higher than among any other political group. Nearly seven-in-ten college graduates (69%) say it is more important to conduct research than protect human embryos, a view shared by 57% of those who attended some college and 53% of high school graduates, but only 41% of those who did not finish high school.

4.52 Do you approve or disapprove of the President's July 2006 veto of stem cell research?

Sixty percent of Americans, according to a July 21–23 poll, disapprove of President Bush's veto (his first) of a bill that would have expanded federal funding of embryonic stem cell research. Most Americans think Bush made the decision based on his moral principles rather than as an attempt to gain political advantage. Thirty-six percent of Americans approve of Bush's decision to veto a bill that would have expanded funding for embryonic stem cell research, while 58% disapprove. Republicans, self-described conservatives, and those who attend religious services weekly are most likely to support the veto.

	APPROVE OF VETO	DISAPPROVE OF VETO
	percentage	
PARTY AFFILIATION		
Republicans	61	33
Independents	33	61
Democrats	19	75
POLITICAL IDEOLOGY		
Conservatives	59	35
Moderates	28	66
Liberals	12	83
CHURCH ATTENDANCE		
Weekly	53	41
Nearly weekly	34	62
Seldom or never	27	66

4.53 Is stem cell research "morally acceptable" to you (by politics; by religion)?

In a May 2003 survey, 38% in each group said that this research was morally acceptable, while slightly more than half in each group said it was morally wrong. Those who attend church weekly are substantially less likely to feel it is morally acceptable. 71% of those who identify with the pro-choice position said embryonic stem cell research is morally acceptable, versus 38% of pro-life individuals.

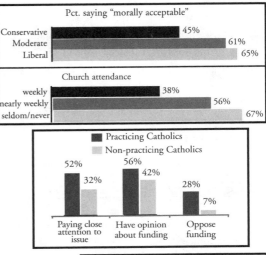

Pct. saying "morally acceptable"

Conservative	45%
Moderate	61%
Liberal	65%

Church attendance

weekly	38%
nearly weekly	56%
seldom/never	67%

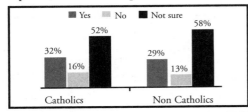

- Yes
- No
- Not sure

Catholics: 32%, 16%, 52%
Non Catholics: 29%, 13%, 58%

- ■ Practicing Catholics
- ▨ Non-practicing Catholics

	Paying close attention to issue	Have opinion about funding	Oppose funding
Practicing Catholics	52%	56%	28%
Non-practicing Catholics	32%	42%	7%

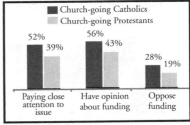

- ■ Church-going Catholics
- ▨ Church-going Protestants

	Paying close attention to issue	Have opinion about funding	Oppose funding
Church-going Catholics	52%	56%	28%
Church-going Protestants	39%	43%	19%

4.54 What influences you most on stem cell research?

Roughly half of opponents say their religious beliefs are the biggest influence on their thinking, while 13% cite what they have seen or read in the media, and 12% mention education on the issue. Conservative Republican opponents are especially likely (70%) to cite religion as their main influence, as are evangelical Protestant opponents (69%). Among supporters, 31% say the biggest influence on their thinking is the media, and 28% mention their education. Just 7% say religion is the most important influence.

	POSITION ON STEM-CELL RESEARCH	
	CONDUCT RESEARCH	NOT DESTROY EMBRYOS
BIGGEST INFLUENCE ON THINKING...	———— PERCENTAGE ————	
Media	31	13
Education	28	12
Religious beliefs	7	52
Personal experience	16	9
Friends and family	5	5
Something else	11	8
Don't know	2	1
	100	100

VI. Depth of Religious Commitment

The fact that very large majorities of the American public believe in God, miracles, the survival of the soul after death, heaven, the resurrection of Jesus Christ, and the Virgin Birth, must come as no great surprise. What may be more surprising is that substantial minorities believe in ghosts, UFOs, witches, astrology, and reincarnation. More than six-in-ten believe in Hell and the Devil. Overall, more people believe in the Devil, Hell, and angels than believe in Darwin's theory of evolution. This section takes a look at Americans' view of God. Is God male or female, spirit or human form? Further questions, such as what, exactly, is the Word of God, and whether different religious groups, such as Muslims, Jews, and Christians, all worship the same God, are asked.

4.55 How religious are you?

Data suggests that most religious Americans believe they can be personally religious without spreading their beliefs, or that they can spread their beliefs by converting others to their religion. A small number of highly religious Americans believe the best way to spread religion is to change society to conform to their religious beliefs. These tables answer questions about religious respondents' beliefs about their roles.

	EXTREMELY RELIGIOUS	VERY RELIG.	SOMEWHAT RELIG.	NOT TOO RELIG.	NOT RELIG. AT ALL	NO OPINION
2006 SEPT.–NOV.	8%	29%	39%	14%	9%	1%

[1]BASED ON 782 ADULTS WHO SAY THEY ARE EXTREMELY OR VERY RELIGIOUS (4 PCT.PTS.)		
	SUFFICIENT TO LIVE BEST POSSIBLE LIFE	NECESSARY TO SPREAD BELIEFS TO OTHERS	NO OPINION
2006 SEPT.–NOV.	48%	49%	2%

[2]BASED ON 358 RELIGIOUS ADULTS WHO SAY IT IS NECESSARY TO SPREAD BELIEFS TO OTHERS (6 PCT. PTS/)		
	BY CONVERTING OTHERS TO YOUR RELIGION	BY CHANGING ASPECTS OF SOCIETY	NO OPINION
2006 SEPT.–NOV.	55%	31%	14%

[1] (Asked of those who say they are extremely or very religious). Do you think it is sufficient to attempt to live the best possible personal life you, personally, can based on your religion's beliefs and principles or do you think it is also necessary to attempt to spread your religion's beliefs and principles to other people?

[2] (Asked of extremely or very religious adults who say it is necessary to spread beliefs to others). Which do you think is the better way to spread your religion's beliefs and principles—[ROTATED: by converting others to your religion, (or) by changing aspects of society to make them consistent with your religion's beliefs and principles]?

QUESTIONS WERE ASKED IN SURVEYS CONDUCTED IN SEPTEMBER AND NOVEMBER, AND THE RESULTS WERE COMBINED TO CREATE AN AGGREGATE OF MORE THAN 2,000 INTERVIEWS. COPYRIGHT © 2008 GALLUP, INC. ALL RIGHTS RESERVED.

4.56 Is it important for America to become more religious?

Thirty-seven percent of Americans classify themselves as extremely or very religious. This group of highly religious Americans is split on the question of whether it's best to live the best possible personally religious life or if it is also necessary to spread their beliefs among the greater American population. 48% believe the former; 49% the latter. More than half of highly religious Americans who believe it is necessary to spread beliefs to others say that it is best accomplished by converting others to one's religion. This type of traditional evangelical view has, within the Christian tradition over the years, been the basis for some leaders' evangelist crusades and for the sponsorship of missionary work in foreign countries. The Mormon religion, as another example, places emphasis on the effort to convert individuals to the Mormon faith, expecting most young men (and in some instances women) of the faith to spend up to two years in missionary work. A little less than a third of the group of highly religious Americans say that spreading one's religious beliefs is best accomplished by changing aspects of society to make them consistent with one's beliefs and practices.

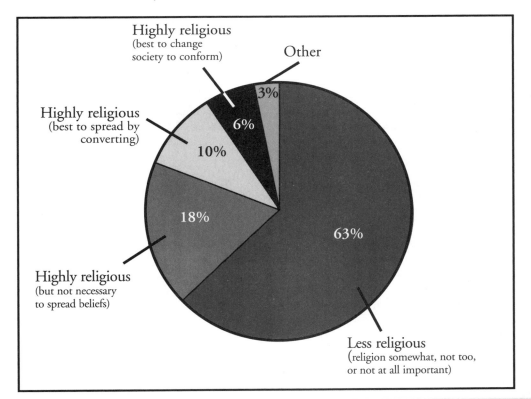

Highly religious (best to change society to conform)

Other

Highly religious (best to spread by converting)

3%

6%

10%

18%

63%

Highly religious (but not necessary to spread beliefs)

Less religious (religion somewhat, not too, or not at all important)

RESULTS FOR STUDY BASED ON TELEPHONE INTERVIEWS WITH 2,013 NATIONAL ADULTS, AGED 18 AND OLDER, CONDUCTED IN SEPTEMBER AND NOVEMBER 2006. RESPONDENTS WERE RANDOMLY DRAWN FROM GALLUP'S NATIONALLY REPRESENTATIVE HOUSEHOLD PANEL, ORIGINALLY RECRUITED THROUGH RANDOM SELECTION METHODS. FOR RESULTS BASED ON TOTAL SAMPLE OF NATIONAL ADULTS, ONE CAN SAY WITH 95% CONFIDENCE THAT THE MARGIN OF SAMPLING ERROR IS ±3%. FOR RESULTS BASED ON 782 ADULTS WHO SAY THEY ARE VERY OR EXTREMELY RELIGIOUS, MAXIMUM MARGIN OF ERROR IS ±4%. FOR RESULTS BASED ON 358 RELIGIOUS ADULTS WHO SAY IT IS NECESSARY TO SPREAD THEIR BELIEFS TO OTHER PEOPLE, MAXIMUM MARGIN OF ERROR IS ±6%. COPYRIGHT © 2008 GALLUP, INC. ALL RIGHTS RESERVED.

4.57 What do you—and don't you—believe in?

According to a recent poll, 82% of Americans believe in God–little has changed since the question was last asked in 2005; Large percentages of the public believe in miracles (79%), heaven (75%), angels (74%), that Jesus is God or the son of God (72%), the resurrection of Jesus (70%), the survival of the soul after death (69%), Hell (62%), the Devil (62%), and the Virgin Birth (Jesus born of Mary) (60%). Roughly equal numbers believe in Darwin's theory of evolution and in creationism. Sizeable minorities believe in ghosts (41%), UFOs (35%), witches (31%), astrology (29%) and reincarnation (21%). While many of these numbers are the same or little changed from 2005, the overall trend is upwards, with slightly more people believing in miracles, angels, and witches than did two years ago. Born-again Christians are more likely to believe in the traditional elements of Christianity than are Catholics or Protestants. 95% believe in miracles, compared to 87% and 89% among Catholics and Protestants. 92% of born-again Christians believe in Hell, compared to 75% of Catholics and 78% of Protestants. Only 16% of born-again Christians, compared to 43% of Catholics and 30% of Protestants, believe in Darwin's theory of evolution. And 60% of born-again Christians, but only 43% of Catholics, believe in creationism.

	Believe in	Don't Believe in	Not Sure	2005 Believe in	Change 2005–2007	Religion Cath.	Prot.	Born-Again Christian
			PERCENTAGE					
God	82	8	10	82	–	92	95	97
Miracles	79	10	12	73	+6	87	89	95
Heaven	75	12	14	70	+5	90	90	97
Angels	74	12	14	68	+6	85	87	95
Jesus is God or the Son of God	72	15	13	70	+2	89	91	96
Resurrection of Jesus Christ	70	16	15	66	+4	87	90	95
Survival of the soul after death	69	12	19	70	–1	79	80	87
Hell	62	22	16	59	+3	75	78	92
The Devil	62	23	15	61	+1	73	79	92
Virgin birth (Jesus born of Mary)	60	22	18	58	+2	72	79	89
Darwin's theory of evolution	42	31	26	N/A	N/A	43	30	16
Ghosts	41	35	24	40	+1	47	41	41
Creationism	39	27	34	N/A	N/A	43	51	60
UFOs	35	36	29	34	+1	36	31	29
Witches	31	51	19	28	+3	32	32	37
Astrology	29	46	25	25	+4	36	25	21
Reincarnation	21	50	29	21	none	24	15	8

This Harris Poll® was conducted online within the United States between November 7 and 13, 2007 among 2,455 adults (aged 18 and over). Copyright © 2007, Harris Interactive Inc. All rights reserved.

4.58 What text do you regard as authentically the Word of God?

Slender majorities believe that all or some of the Old Testament (53%) and the New Testament (52%) are the "Word of God." However, only about a third of all adults (35% and 33%) believe that all of these texts are the word of God. Interestingly, only 23% of all adults believe that the Torah is the word of God, even though it is the same as the first five books of the Old Testament. Born-again Christians are much more likely to think the Old and New Testament are all or mostly the Word of God (88% and 86% respectively) than are Catholics (55% and 54%).

The survey also posed a "yes-no" question, where respondents were asked to choose between two contrasting positions (instead of the being offered only choices of gradations). Offering only a stark choice tended to push respondants to one extreme view or the other.

	ALL	MOST	SOME	NONE	NOT SURE	ALL/MOST	SOME/NONE	CATH.	PROT.	AGN./ ATHEIST	BORN AGAIN CHRISTIAN
PUBLIC ATTITUDES TO SACRED TESTS AND SCRIPTURE						["YES-NO" QUESTION]			RELIGION		
	IS THE WORD OF GOD					IS THE WORD OF GOD					
						PERCENTAGE					
The Old Testament (texts used in the Christian religion)	35	18	16	13	17	53	29	55	74	5	88
The New Testament (texts used in the Christian religion)	33	18	16	14	18	52	30	54	73	6	86
The Torah (the texts used in the Jewish religion)	12	11	18	18	41	23	36	26	28	5	33
The Koran (texts used by Muslims)	3	5	16	34	43	8	50	8	8	4	9
The Book of Mormon (texts used by Mormons)	3	3	17	34	43	6	51	6	6	3	5

4.57, 4.58: HARRIS POLL® CONDUCTED ONLINE WITHIN THE UNITED STATES BETWEEN NOVEMBER 7 AND 13, 2007 AMONG 2,455 ADULTS (AGED 18 AND OVER). FIGURES FOR AGE, SEX, RACE/ETHNICITY, EDUCATION, REGION AND HOUSEHOLD INCOME WERE WEIGHTED WHERE NECESSARY TO BRING THEM INTO LINE WITH THEIR ACTUAL PROPORTIONS IN THE POPULATION. PROPENSITY SCORE WEIGHTING WAS ALSO USED TO ADJUST FOR RESPONDENTS' PROPENSITY TO BE ONLINE. ALL SAMPLE SURVEYS AND POLLS, WHETHER OR NOT THEY USE PROBABILITY SAMPLING, ARE SUBJECT TO MULTIPLE SOURCES OF ERROR WHICH ARE MOST OFTEN NOT POSSIBLE TO QUANTIFY OR ESTIMATE, INCLUDING SAMPLING ERROR, COVERAGE ERROR, ERROR ASSOCIATED WITH NONRESPONSE, ERROR ASSOCIATED WITH QUESTION WORDING AND RESPONSE OPTIONS, AND POST-SURVEY WEIGHTING AND ADJUSTMENTS. THEREFORE, HARRIS INTERACTIVE AVOIDS THE WORDS "MARGIN OF ERROR" AS THEY ARE MISLEADING. ALL THAT CAN BE CALCULATED ARE DIFFERENT POSSIBLE SAMPLING ERRORS WITH DIFFERENT PROBABILITIES FOR PURE, UNWEIGHTED, RANDOM SAMPLES WITH 100% RESPONSE RATES. THESE ARE ONLY THEORETICAL BECAUSE NO PUBLISHED POLLS COME CLOSE TO THIS IDEAL. RESPONDENTS FOR THIS SURVEY WERE SELECTED FROM AMONG THOSE WHO HAVE AGREED TO PARTICIPATE IN HARRIS INTERACTIVE SURVEYS. THE DATA HAVE BEEN WEIGHTED TO REFLECT THE COMPOSITION OF THE ADULT POPULATION. BECAUSE THE SAMPLE IS BASED ON THOSE WHO AGREED TO PARTICIPATE IN THE HARRIS INTERACTIVE PANEL, NO ESTIMATES OF THEORETICAL SAMPLING ERROR CAN BE CALCULATED. COPYRIGHT © 2007, HARRIS INTERACTIVE INC. ALL RIGHTS RESERVED.

4.59 How certain are you that there is a God?

A Harris Poll finds that 42% of all U.S. adults are not "absolutely certain" there is a God, including 15% who are "somewhat certain," 11% who think there is probably no God and 16% who are not sure. Only 76% of Protestants, 64% of Catholics, and 30% of Jews say they are "absolutely certain" there is a God.

	2003	2006	CATH.	PROT.	JEWISH	BORN AGAIN CHRISTIAN
					RELIGIOUS AFFILIATION	
				PERCENTAGE		
Believe in God (NET)	79	73	84	90	64	97
Absolutely certain that there is a God	66	58	64	76	30	93
Somewhat certain that there is a God	12	15	21	14	34	4
Believe there is no God (NET)	9	11	5	3	12	3
Somewhat certain that there is no God	5	6	3	1	8	1
Absolutely certain that there is no God	4	6	2	2	4	2
Not sure whether or not there is a God	12	16	11	7	24	*

Note: Percentages may not add up to exactly 100% due to rounding.

* Less than 0.5

4.60 Do you believe God controls what happens on earth?

W hen asked about God's control over the Earth, each question began with "Do you think God…?" Less than one-third of all adults believe that God "controls what happens on Earth."

	2003	2006	CATH.	PROT.	JEWISH	BORN AGAIN CHRISTIAN
					RELIGIOUS AFFILIATION	
				PERCENTAGE		
Controls what happens on Earth	29	29	27	41	28	57
Observes but does not control what happens on Earth	50	44	58	46	39	37
Neither observes nor controls what happens on Earth	6	8	4	5	11	1
Do not believe in God/Not Sure	15	18	8	8	15	5

4.59 AND 4.60: HARRIS POLL® CONDUCTED ONLINE WITHIN THE UNITED STATES BETWEEN OCTOBER 4 AND 10, 2006 AMONG 2,010 ADULTS (AGED 18 AND OVER). WITH A PURE PROBABILITY SAMPLE OF 2,010, THERE IS A 95% PROBABILITY THAT THE OVERALL RESULTS HAVE A SAMPLING ERROR OF ± 2% POINTS. COPYRIGHT © 2007, HARRIS INTERACTIVE INC. ALL RIGHTS RESERVED.

4.61 How certain are you that there is a God (by region, age, gender, race, party, education, religion)?

Demographic groups likely to say they are absolutely certain there is a God include people aged 40 and up (63% of ages 40–49, 65% of those ages 50–64 and 65% of ages 65 and over) compared to people in age groups under 40 (45% of ages 18 to 24, 43% of ages 25–29 and 54% of ages 30–39); Women (62%) more than men (54%); African Americans (71%) compared to Hispanics (61%) and Whites (57%); people with no college education (62%) or with some college education (57%) compared to college graduates (50%) and those with post-graduate degrees (53%).

"MY BELIEF IN GOD IS...	SOMEWHAT CERTAIN"	ABSOLUTELY CERTAIN"
	——— PERCENTAGE ———	
ALL ADULTS	73	58
REGION		
East	70	56
Midwest	77	59
South	79	63
West	64	51
AGE		
18–24	66	45
25–29	60	43
30–39	70	54
40–49	74	63
50–64	80	65
65 and over	79	65
GENDER		
Male	68	54
Female	78	62
RACE/ETHNICITY		
White	73	57
African American	83	71
Hispanics	75	61
PARTY		
Republican	83	73
Democrat	72	54
Independent	66	51
EDUCATION		
High school or less	76	62
Some college	74	57
College graduate	64	50
Post graduate	73	53
RELIGION		
Catholic	84	64
Protestant	90	76
Jewish	64	30
Born Again Christian	97	93

HARRIS POLL® CONDUCTED ONLINE WITHIN THE UNITED STATES BETWEEN OCTOBER 4 AND 10, 2006, AMONG 2,010 ADULTS (AGED 18 AND OVER). WITH THIS SAMPLE, THERE IS A 95% PROBABILITY THAT THE OVERALL RESULTS HAVE A SAMPLING ERROR OF ± 2% POINTS. COPYRIGHT © 2007, HARRIS INTERACTIVE INC. ALL RIGHTS RESERVED.

4.62 What is your image or conception of God?

A substantial portion (41%) of the public think of God as "a spirit or power that can take on human form but is not inherently human." 27% see God as a "spirit or power that does not take on human form."

	2003	2006	CATH.	PROT.	JEWISH.	BORN AGAIN CHRISTIAN
			RELIGIOUS AFFILIATION.			
Like a human being, with a face, body, arms, legs, eyes, etc.	9	9	9	13	1	9
A spirit or power that can take on human form but is not inherently human	48	41	49	48	25	60
A spirit or power that does not take on human form	27	27	27	26	49	20
Other	5	8	6	6	5	7
Do not believe in God/Not sure	10	15	8	6	20	3

Note: Percentages may not add up to exactly 100% due to rounding.

4.63 Do you see God as having a particular gender?

	2003	2006	MALE	FEMALE	CATH.	PROT.	JEWISH	BORN AGAIN CHRISTIAN
			GENDER		RELIGIOUS AFFILIATION			
					PERCENTAGE			
Male	42	36	34	39	47	46	30	51
Female	1	1	*	2	1	*	7	*
Neither male or female	38	37	39	34	32	35	36	38
Both male and female	11	10	9	10	8	11	11	6
Do not believe in God/Not sure	9	17	18	14	11	8	16	5

Note: Percentages may not add up to exactly 100% due to rounding.   *Less than 0.5%

4.64 Do you believe Jews, Christians, and Muslims all worship the same God?

About half of adults, including a majority of Catholics, believe that Jews, Christians, and Muslims worship the same God. One third believe they do not and 16% are not sure.

	2003	2006	CATH.	PROT.	JEWISH	BORN AGAIN CHRISTIAN
			RELIGIOUS AFFILIATION			
All worship same God	53	51	63	49	48	34
Do not worship same God	32	32	21	36	37	54
Not sure	15	16	16	15	15	11

Note: Percentages may not add up to exactly 100% due to rounding.

4.62, 4.63, 4.64: HARRIS POLL® CONDUCTED ONLINE WITHIN THE U.S. OCTOBER 4–10, 2006 AMONG 2,010 ADULTS (AGED 18 AND OVER). WITH A PURE PROBABILITY SAMPLE OF 2,010 THERE IS A 95% PROBABILITY THAT RESULTS HAVE A SAMPLING ERROR OF ±2% POINTS. COPYRIGHT © 2006, HARRIS INTERACTIVE INC. ALL RIGHTS RESERVED.

VII. Election Issues

Americans continue to be generally comfortable with a role for religion in politics, though these views are not unanimously held. Most want a president who has strong religious beliefs. In general, Republicans are more intense in their view that the president should have strong religious beliefs than are Democrats or independents. Accordingly, a survey finds that the Republican Party continues to hold a substantial advantage over the Democratic Party because it is often viewed as more friendly to religion. The latest national survey by the Pew Research Center finds that social issues such as abortion and gay marriage continue to be greatly overshadowed in the presidential campaign by domestic issues and by the war in Iraq.

4.65 How important is it that a president have strong religious beliefs?

The vast majority (69%) of Americans agree that it is important for a president to have strong religious beliefs. However, there are important political and religious differences in the degree to which Americans agree with this view. Republicans are much more passionate in their view that the president should have strong religious beliefs than are Democrats or independents (44% vs. 265 and 23% completely agree, respectively). Most white evangelical Protestants (54%) and black Protestants (43%) strongly agree that a president should have strong religious beliefs compared to only 21% of white mainline Protestants and 22% of white non-Hispanic Catholics. The religiously unaffiliated are the only group in which the majority (62%) disagrees with the idea that a president should have strong religious convictions.

IMPORTANCE OF CANDIDATE'S RELIGIOUS BELIEFS				
	COMP. AGREE	MOSTLY AGREE	DIS- AGREE	DK
	PERCENTAGE			
Total	30	39	27	4
College grad	22	38	38	2
Some college	29	42	25	4
HS or less	36	38	22	4
Age 18–29	21	37	38	4
Age 65+	36	39	19	6
Northeast	22	41	32	5
Midwest	26	42	27	5
South	40	38	19	3
West	25	35	36	4
Republican	44	39	14	3
Democrat	26	38	33	3
Independent	23	40	33	4
White Protestant	39	41	17	3
Evangelical	54	36	8	2
Mainline	21	45	28	5
Black Protestant	43	41	13	3
Catholic	27	43	27	3
White non-Hispanic	22	47	29	2
Unaffiliated	8	26	62	4

4.66 Do you think a candidate's views on social issues are more important than his views on foreign and domestic issues?

More than three quarters of Americans say domestic issues such as the economy, health care, and the environment will be important in their decisions about whom to support for president; 72% say the same about the war in Iraq. Just 38% say that social issues will be very important in their voting decisions.

IMPORTANCE OF...	IRAQ	DOMESTIC ISSUES	SOCIAL ISSUES
2008 PRIORITIES: DOMESTIC ISSUES AND IRAQ TRUMP SOCIAL ISSUES			
Very important	— PERCENTAGE —		
Total	72	78	38
Republican	63	65	45
Democrat	80	88	36
Independent	70	78	36
White Protestant	67	74	43
Evangelical	66	72	56
Mainline	68	76	28
Black Protestant	78	88	42
Catholic	76	82	31
White non-Hispanic	76	81	28
Unaffiliated*	76	77	33

* Includes self-described atheists, agnostics, and uninvolved in religion.

4.67 Which party do you think is "religion-friendly" (2003–2007)?

The Republican Party is seen as more friendly toward religion than the Democratic Party, though the number who see the Democrats as unfriendly toward religion has decreased since 2006. Currently, 50% of the public says the Republican Party is friendly toward religion, about the same as it has been since 2003. Roughly a quarter say the party is neutral toward religion, and just 9% say it is unfriendly toward religion. In contrast, just three-in-ten say the Democratic Party is friendly toward religion, up slightly from 2006, but still 10% lower than in August 2004 or during the 2004 presidential election. Though most do not see the party as friendly toward religion, they do not see it as particularly unfriendly either. Just 15% say the party is unfriendly; 37% say the party is neutral.

	JULY 2003	AUG 2004	JULY 2005	JULY 2006	AUG 2007
Democratic Party is...	— PERCENTAGE —				
Friendly to religion	42	40	29	26	30
Neutral	36	34	38	42	37
Unfriendly	12	13	20	20	15
Don't know	10	13	13	12	18
	100	100	100	100	100
Republican Party is...					
Friendly to religion	52	52	55	47	50
Neutral	27	24	23	28	23
Unfriendly	10	10	9	13	9
Don't know	11	14	13	12	18
	100	100	100	100	100

4.66, 4.67: RESULTS FOR SURVEYS BASED ON TELEPHONE INTERVIEWS CONDUCTED UNDER DIRECTION OF SCHULMAN, RONCA, & BUCUVALAS, INC. AMONG A NATIONWIDE SAMPLE OF 3,002 ADULTS, 18 YEARS OF AGE OR OLDER, FROM AUGUST 1–18, 2007. FOR RESULTS BASED ON TOTAL SAMPLE, THER IS 95% CONFIDENCE THAT THE ERROR ATTRIBUTABLE TO SAMPLING IS ±2%. COPYRIGHT © 2007 PEW RESEARCH CENTER. ALL RIGHTS RESERVED.

4.68 Which faction has greater influence over the political parties: secular liberals or religious conservatives?

Although the Democratic Party continues to be seen as less friendly to religion than the Republican Party, fewer people today than in 2005 believe that liberals who are not religious have too much control of the Democratic Party. In the current survey, 37% say this is true; in 2005, 44% felt this way. The number of people who say secular liberals have too much control over the party has declined within most of the major religious traditions, though a majority (52%) of white evangelicals continue to feel this way. It also is down nine points among independents and eleven points among Democrats themselves. Currently, about a third of independents and one-quarter of Democrats say secular liberals have too much control over the party.

Notably, though, Republicans today are only slightly less likely than they were two years ago to express this opinion (58% now vs. 60% in 2005). As was the case two years ago, a small plurality (43%) agrees with the statement that "religious conservatives have too much control over the Republican Party," while 41% disagree. About half of white mainline Protestants (49%) think religious conservatives have too much sway over the party, but just 27% of white evangelicals feel this way. Fewer white Catholics today express this view than did so in 2005 (41% now vs. 50% in 2005), but the proportion of people who have no religious affiliation agreeing with this has increased by seven points (63% now vs. 56% in 2005).

WHO HAS TOO MUCH CONTROL?	NON-RELIGIOUS LIBERALS OVER DEM. PARTY		RELIGIOUS CONSERVATIVES OVER GOP	
	JULY 2005	AUG. 2007	JULY 2005	AUG. 2007
	PERCENTAGE			
Total agree	44	37	45	43
Republican	60	58	30	30
Democrat	34	23	58	53
Independent	43	34	54	48
White Protestant	53	42	38	37
Evangelical	60	52	30	27
Mainline	43	32	47	49
White non-Hisp Cath.	48	3	50	41
Unaffiliated	22	29	56	63

RESULTS FOR SURVEY BASED ON TELEPHONE INTERVIEWS CONDUCTED UNDER DIRECTION OF SCHULMAN, RONCA, & BUCUVALAS, INC. AMONG A NATIONWIDE SAMPLE OF 3,002 ADULTS, 18 YEARS OF AGE OR OLDER, FROM AUGUST 1–18, 2007. FOR RESULTS BASED ON TOTAL SAMPLE, THERE IS 95% CONFIDENCE THAT THE ERROR ATTRIBUTABLE TO SAMPLING IS ± 2%. COPYRIGHT © 2007 PEW RESEARCH CENTER. ALL RIGHTS RESERVED.

5 Sources and Methodology

Statistical Sections

THIS SECTION LISTS THE SPECIFIC METHODOLOGY from each of our sources for Part III. It includes sample sizes and other information that may be helpful in interpreting survey results. Each source has its own means and reasons for surveying. In an effort to be faithful to the sources, we provide the information that they include at the end of their reports. For further information about a specific source, please visit the websites given.

HARRIS:

www.harrisinteractive.com

The Harris interactive poll is one of the longest running public opinion polls in the world. Its surveys are nationally representative, and they answer questions about a number of areas.

General note: All sample surveys and polls, whether or not they use probability sampling, are subject to multiple sources of error, which are most often not possible to quantify or to estimate, including sampling error, coverage error, error associated with nonresponse, error associated with question wording and response options, and post-survey weighting and adjustments. Therefore, Harris Interactive avoids the words "margin of error" as they are misleading. All that can be calculated are different possible sampling errors with different probabilities for pure, unweighted, random samples with 100% response rates. These are only theoretical, because no published polls come close to this ideal.

BAYLOR:

www.baylor.edu

After several years devoted to development and pretesting by faculty at Baylor, the Baylor Religion Survey was fielded during the winter of 2005, and the data were made available for analysis in the spring of 2006. The field work was accomplished by the Gallup Organization. It plumbs all facets of American religion and spirituality in depth. Nearly 400 items cover such matters as religious beliefs and practices, including religious consumerism, as well as nonstandard beliefs (astrology, "Bigfoot," alien visitors, etc.) and practices (meditation, New Age therapies, etc).

The Baylor Religion Survey is a nationally representative survey of 1,721 respondents. The survey utilized a mixed-mode sampling design (telephone and self-administered mailed surveys) and demographic measures as well as key religion indicators yield results that look very similar to those produced by other national surveys (e.g., the General Social Survey). The Baylor Religion Survey is merely the first wave of a rich and rewarding new era of religious survey research. Additional waves of the Baylor Religion Survey, with rotating topical modules, take place every other year.

ARIS:

www.gc.cuny.edu

The American Religious Identification Survey (ARIS) 2001 was conducted by the Graduate Center of the City University of new York. It was based on a random digit-dialed telephone survey of 50,281

American residential households in the continental U.S.A. (48 states). The methodology largely replicates the widely reported and pioneering 1990 National Survey of Religious Identification (NSRI) carried out at the Graduate Center of the City University of New York. ARIS 2001 thus provides a unique time series of information concerning the religious identification choices of American adults.

The data was collected over a seventeen-week period, from February to June 2001, at the rate of about 3,000 completed interviews a week by ICR/CENTRIS Survey Research Group of Media, PA, as part of their national telephone omnibus market research (EXCEL/ACCESS) surveys.

The primary question of the interview was: What is your religion, if any? The religion of the spouse/partner was also asked. If the initial answer was 'Protestant' or 'Christian,' further questions were asked to probe which particular denomination. The respondent in this survey was a randomly chosen (based on last birthday) adult 18 years or older. In addition, the survey inquired about twenty other characteristics of persons and households, enabling us to develop a fairly nuanced demographic profile of each religious group.

PEW:

www.pewforum.org

Pew Forum on Religion & Public Life: The Religious Landscape Survey

The Pew Forum on Religion and Public Life was started in 2001 in an effort to promote understanding about the role of religion in public affairs. Its goal is to provide the public with unbiased, relevant information about a variety of public issues. The Pew Forum is a "non-partisan, non-advocacy organization;" it does not take sides in debates over public policy. It provides relevant news through independent research, and serves as a neutral ground for discussion. The Pew Forum also functions as a source for journalists and researchers. It focuses on four main areas of research in its exploration of religion's relationship to politics, law, domestic policy, and foreign affairs.

The U.S. Religious Landscape Survey conducted telephone interviews with a nationally representative sample of 35,556 adults living in continental United States telephone households. The survey was conducted by Princeton Survey Research Associates International (PSRAI). Interviews were done in English and Spanish by Princeton Data Source, LLC (PDS), and Schulman, Ronca and Bucuvalas, Inc. (SRBI), from May 8 to Aug. 13, 2007. Statistical results are weighted to correct known demographic discrepancies.

The vast majority of the interviews (n=35,009) came from standard list-assisted random digit dialing (RDD) sample. This sample was provided by Survey Sampling International, LLC, according to PSRAI specifications. Active blocks of telephone numbers (area code + exchange + two-digit block number) that contained three or more residential directory listings were equally likely to be selected; after selection, two more digits were added randomly to complete the number. This method guaranteed coverage of every assigned phone number regardless of whether that number was directory listed, purposely unlisted or too new to be listed. After selection, the numbers were compared against business directories and matching numbers were purged.

To supplement the RDD interviews, an additional 547 interviews were completed from households that were initially contacted and screened out during data collection for the Pew Research Center's survey of Muslim Americans that was released in May 2007. Specifically, households that were identified as Hindu, Buddhist, or Orthodox Christian were recontacted. This method helped to boost the sample size of low-incidence groups. All of the callback interviewing was conducted at PDS.

Finally, in addition to the RDD and recontact samples, interviews were conducted with 500 "cellphone only" respondents (i.e., individuals who have and use a cellular telephone and do not have a landline telephone in their household). An analysis of the data revealed no significant differences in the religious makeup of the sample that included cell-only respondents and the full sample based solely on respondents from landline households. As a result, cell-only respondents were excluded from the analyses that appear in this report. As many as ten attempts were made to contact every sampled telephone number. Calls were staggered over times of day and days of the week to maximize the chance of making contact with potential respondents. Each household received at least one daytime call in an attempt to find someone at home. Calling procedures and sample management were kept as consistent as possible between two phone rooms.

HARTFORD:

www.facts.hartsem.edu

The Hartford Seminary's Hartford Institute for Religion Research is an organization that gathers information about religious life.

The FACT2005 survey questionnaire was designed by the Research Task Force of The Cooperative Congregational Studies Partnership (CCSP). A copy of the questionnaire on their website (www.fact.hartsem.edu) should be consulted for exact question and response category wordings. The survey was conducted by the Institute for Social Research at Calvin College. A questionnaire was mailed to a random sample of 3,000 congregations, and the accompanying cover letter also included the option of completing the questionnaire online. The sample was originally generated by American Church Lists. Random replacements for non-responding congregations were drawn from an American Church List shadow sample, and from denominational yearbook samples. 884 usable questionnaires were received. To enhance national representation, responses were weighed to the population parameters for region and faith family presented in C. Kirk Hadaway and Penny Long Marler's *How Many Americans Attend Worship Each Week?, An Alternative Approach to Measure, Journal for the*

Scientific Study of Religion, and for size of congregation rural/city/suburban location found in the FACT2000 national survey of 14,301 congregations. Sampling error for such a survey can only be estimated. We estimate it to be ±4% at a 95% confidence level.

In places we present comparisons across faith families; the total of 884 questionnaires includes Jewish, Muslim, and non-Christian congregations, but in a sample of this size they are too few and too diverse to be reliably reported on. They are included in figures that represent the total sample, but we are unable to include them in faith family comparisons.

A survey the size of FACT2005 must use faith families because it does not include sufficient numbers of congregations from any single denomination for analysis. However, several CCSP member denominations conducted over samples of their own congregations to provide the base for their own reporting. These included The Church of the Nazarene, The Episcopal Church, and The Unitarian Universalist Association.

US CENSUS:

www.census.gov

U.S. Census Bureau, Statistical Abstract of the United States: 2003

The Census presents statistics on the growth, distribution, and characteristics of the U.S. population. The principal source of the data is the U.S. Census Bureau, which conducts a decennial census of population, a monthly population survey, a program of population estimates and projections, and a number of other periodic surveys relating to population characteristics.

Decennial censuses—The U.S. Constitution provides for a census of the population every ten years, primarily to establish a basis for apportionment of members of the House of Representatives among the states. Since the 1940 census, in addition to the complete count information, some data have been obtained from representative samples of the population. In the 1990 and 2000 censuses, variable sampling rates were employed. For most of the country, one in every six households (about 17%) received the long form or sample questionnaire; in governmental units estimated to have fewer than 2,500 inhabitants, every other household (50%) received the sample questionnaire to enhance the reliability of sample data for small areas. Exact agreement is not to be expected between sample data and the 100% count. Sample data may be used with confidence where large numbers are involved and assumed to indicate trends and relationships where small numbers are involved.

Current Population Survey (CPS)—This is a monthly nationwide survey of a scientifically selected sample representing the noninstitutional civilian population. The sample is located in 754 areas with coverage in every state and the District of Columbia and is subject to sampling error. At the present time, about 60,000 occupied households are eligible for interview every month; of these, between 6 and 7% are, for various reasons, unavailable for interview. While the primary purpose of the CPS is to obtain monthly statistics on the labor force, it also serves as a vehicle for inquiries on other subjects. Using CPS data, the Bureau issues a series of publications under the general title of Current Population Reports, which cover population characteristics (P20), consumer income (P60), special studies (P23), and other topics. Estimates of population characteristics based on the CPS will not agree with the counts from the census because the CPS and the census use different procedures for collecting and processing the data for racial groups, the Hispanic population, and other topics. Caution should also be used when comparing estimates for various years because of the periodic introduction of changes into the CPS. Beginning in January 1994, a number of changes were introduced into the CPS that effect all data comparisons with prior years. These changes include the results of a major redesign of the survey questionnaire and collection methodology and the introduction of 1990 census population controls, adjusted for the esti-

mated undercount. Beginning with the 2001 CPS Annual Demographic Supplement, the independent estimates used as control totals for the CPS are based on civilian population benchmarks consistent with Census 2000. In March 2002, the sample size of the Annual Demographic Supplement was increased to approximately 78,000 (Population 1 U.S. Census Bureau, Statistical Abstract of the United States: 2003). These changes in population controls had relatively little impact on derived measures such as means, medians, and percent distribution, but did have a significant impact on levels.

ADHERENTS.COM:

www.adherents.com

Adherents.com is an independent website dedicated to collecting and presenting information about religion. Their data comes from primary sources, such as government reports, "statistical sampling surveys and organizational reporting," and from secondary print and web sources. Sixty-five percent of their information comes from print materials such as religion books, general reference works, and periodicals, and the remainder comes from online sources. Adherents.com strives to include information from a variety of sources in order to achieve as high a degree of impartiality as possible.

Beliefs & Opinions

GALLUP:

www.gallup.com

General note—In addition to sampling error, question wording and practical difficulties in conducting surveys can introduce error or bias into the findings of public opinion polls. See footnotes in data section for sample size and information specific to each survey. Copyright © 2008 Gallup, Inc. All rights reserved.

HARRIS:

www.harrisinteractive.com

General note: Sampling error for the various sub-samples shown in the above tables is higher and varies. Unfortunately, there are several other possible sources of error in all polls or surveys that are probably more serious than theoretical calculations of sampling error. They include refusals to be interviewed (nonresponse), question wording and question order, and weighting. It is impossible to quantify the errors that may result from these factors. This online survey is not based on a probability sample and therefore no theoretical sampling error can be calculated.

Figures for age, sex, race/ethnicity, education, region and household income were weighted where necessary to bring them into line with their actual proportions in the population. Propensity score weighting was also used to adjust for respondents' propensity to be online.

All surveys are subject to several sources of error. These include: sampling error (because only a sample of a population is interviewed); measurement error due to question wording and/or question order, deliberately or unintentionally inaccurate responses, nonresponse (including refusals), interviewer effects (when live interviewers are used), and weighting.

With one exception (sampling error), the magnitude of the errors that result cannot be estimated. There is, therefore, no way to calculate a finite "margin of error" for any survey and the use of these words should be avoided. ©2007, Harris Interactive Inc. All rights reserved.

PEW:

www.pewforum.org

General note: In addition to sampling error, one should bear in mind that question wording and practical difficulties in conducting surveys can introduce error or bias into the findings of opinion polls.

The Pew Forum on Religion & Public Life provides opinion leaders with timely, impartial information on issues at the intersection of religion and public affairs. As an independent, nonpartisan and non-advocacy organization, the Forum does not take positions on policy debates. The Forum functions as both a clearinghouse and a town hall. As a clearinghouse, it gathers and disseminates reliable information through polls and reports. As a town hall, it provides a neutral venue for discussion of important issues of religion and public life. Based in Washington, D.C., the Forum is a project of the Pew Research Center and is funded by The Pew Charitable Trusts. Published November 2005.

Contributors and Reviewers

Foreword

Jane Smith returned to Harvard Divinity School in July 2008 as associate dean for faculty and academic affairs and Senior Lecturer in Divinity. She was at Harvard from 1973 to 1986, serving as a professor of comparative religion and, at various times, associate director of the Center for the Study of World Religions and associate dean of HDS. In 1986, Jane left Harvard to become vice president and dean of Iliff School of Theology in Denver. In more recent years, she has been Professor of Islamic Studies at Hartford Seminary and co-director of its Duncan Black Macdonald Center for the Study of Islam and Christian-Muslim Relations. She teaches and writes on women in Islam, Muslim communities in America, and historical and theological relations between Christians and Muslims. A member of the Commission on Interfaith Relations of the National Council of Churches of Christ, she is a frequent participant in Christian-Muslim dialogue. Among her recent publications are *Islam in America* (Columbia UP: revised 2009); *Educating the Muslims of America* (Oxford UP: 2009, co-edited with Farid Senzai and Yvonne Haddad); *Muslims, Christians and the Challenge of Interfaith Dialogue* (Oxford UP: 2007); *Muslim Women in America* (Oxford UP: 2006, co-authored with Yvonne Haddad); and *Muslim Communities in the West: Visible and Invisible* (AltaMira: 2002).

Introduction

Since 1991, **Diana L. Eck** has headed the Pluralism Project, which explores and interprets the religious dimensions of America's new immigration; the growth of Hindu, Buddhist, Sikh, Jain, and Zoroastrian communities in the United States; and the new issues of religious pluralism and American civil society. Her book, *A New Religious America: How A "Christian Country" Has Become the World's Most Religiously Diverse Nation*, was published in 2001 by HarperOne. She received the National Humanities Award from President Clinton and the National Endowment for the Humanities in 1996, the Montana Governor's Humanities Award in 2003, and the Melcher Lifetime Achievement Award from the Unitarian Universalist Association in 2003. In 2005–06 she served as president of the American Academy of Religion. She is currently chair of the Interfaith Relations Commission of the National Council of Churches. In 2009, she delivered the Gifford Lectures at the University of Edinburgh, a series of six lectures entitled The Age of Pluralism.

ESSAYS

"To America's Community of Faith"

Known worldwide as **Pope Benedict XVI**, the head of the Roman Catholic Church, Joseph Alois Ratzinger served as the Bishop of Munich and was an internationally respected theologian and scholar, as well as an accomplished and prolific writer. Before his election as Pope in 2005, he served for twenty-four years as Prefect of the Congregation of the Doctrine of the Faith, the Roman Catholic Church's highest authority on doctrinal and theological issues. Among his books published since becoming Pope are: *The Joy of Knowing Christ: Meditations on the Gospels* (2009); *Light of the World*, in conversation with journalist Peter Seewald (2010); a series on the early history of the Church (*The Fathers; The Apostles; Church Fathers*); and a two-volume spiritual biography of Jesus of Nazareth (2008; 2011). Proceeds from the sale of his many books go toward the Ratzinger Foundation, a charitable organization that funds scholarships for students around the world.

"The American Clergy"

Sue E. S. Crawford serves as associate professor of Political Science and International Relations at Creighton University. She is co-editor of *Christian Clergy in American Politics* (Johns Hopkins UP: 2001) and co-author of *Women with* a Mission: Religion, Gender, and the Politics of Women Clergy (Univ. of Alabama Press: 2005), as well as author of many articles and chapters on clergy and politics.

"The New Convergence"

Gregg Easterbrook is a contributing editor of *The Atlantic Monthly*, *The New Republic*, and *The Washington Monthly*; a visiting fellow at the Brookings Institution; and a columnist for ESPN.com. His recent books include *Sonic Boom: A Guide to Surviving and Thriving in the New Global Economy* (2011) and *The Progress Paradox: How Life Gets Better While People Feel Worse* (2003), both published by Random House.

"Is America a Hospitable Land for Islam?"

John L. Esposito is University Professor, Professor of Religion and International Affairs, Professor of Islamic Studies, and Founding Director of the Prince Alwaleed bin Talal Center for Muslim-Christian Understanding at the Walsh School of Foreign Service, Georgetown University. He has served as a consultant to the U.S. Department of State and to governments, corporations, universities, and the media. In 2003, he received the School of Foreign Service, Georgetown University Award for Outstanding Teaching. A prolific writer and tireless, engaging lecturer, his books include: *What Everyone Needs to Know About Islam* (Oxford UP: 2002) and *Who Speaks for Islam: What a Billion Muslims Really Think* (Gallup: 2008).

"Religion and American Politics"

Jo-Renee Formicola is a widely published author and a professor of political science at Seton Hall University. Her most recent book, *The Politics of Values: Games Political Strategists Play*, was published in paperback in 2008 by Rowan & Littlefield. She was chosen 2008 Ignatian Scholar by the Le Moyne College Alumni Association Board.

"Can 'It' Happen Here?"

Abraham H. Foxman has, since 1987, been the National Director of the Anti-Defamation League. He is the author of *The Deadliest Lies: The Israel Lobby and the Myth of Jewish Control* (Palgrave Macmillan: 2007) and *Never Again?: The Threat of the New Anti-Semitism* (HarperOne: 2004).

"Transforming Tolerance"

Jay Emerson Johnson earned a PhD in philosophical theology from the Graduate Theological Union (GTU) in Berkeley, California, where he is currently a member of the core doctoral faculty. He teaches courses in Christian theology and LGBT/queer studies at Pacific School of Religion and the Church Divinity School of the Pacific, both member schools of the GTU. Dr. Johnson also serves as Senior Director, Academic Research and Resources at PSR's Center for Lesbian and Gay Studies in Religion and Ministry. He has published articles on the intersections of sexuality, spirituality, and Christian theology, and in 2005 his first book was published by Morehouse, *Dancing with God: Anglican Christianity and the Practice of Hope*. Also an Episcopal priest, he serves as associate clergy at the Episcopal Church of the Good Shepherd in Berkeley.

"Look to the Mountains"

Eric Kampmann is among the visionaries of modern publishing, working in sales at major trade houses and directing publishing operations for his pioneering independent book distribution firm, Beaufort Books and Midpoint Trade Books Distribution. He is the author of several books on religious approaches to nature and the outdoors, including *Tree of Life* and *Trail Thoughts*. He has taught publishing methods at Harvard, Columbia, Hofstra, and NYU, and is the author of *The Book Publisher's Handbook*.

"Contemporary American Spiritual Movements"

Don Lattin currently teaches religion writing at the Graduate School of Journalism at the University of California at Berkeley, where he holds a degree in sociology. His work in journalism has appeared in *The San Francisco Chronicle*, where he worked for nearly twenty years. Among his recent books are *The Harvard Psychedelic Club* (2010) and *Jesus Freaks* (2007), both published by HarperOne.

"Can an Atheist be a Good Citizen?"

Rev. Richard John Neuhaus was, until his passing in 2009, the editor-in-chief of *First Things*, the monthly journal of religion, culture, and public life. As a prolific author and advisor to Presidents, Father Neuhaus had, for more than thirty years, greatly influenced the discussion of public issues related to religious concerns. The essay that appears here is excerpted from a longer study in his recent book, *American Babylon: Notes of a Christian Exile* (2009: Basic Books).

"The Spirituality of Despair"

A graduate of Columbia University, **Ames Sweet** is a freelance writer living in New York City, writing on issues related to substance abuse. He has worked as a magazine editor at the AA *Grapevine*, monthly magazine of Alcoholics Anonymous, and as the Director of Communications for a national nonprofit advocacy organization, the National Council on Alcoholism and Drug Dependence. He is currently senior editor of *Together* magazine.

"Intelligent Faith"

Larry Witham is a veteran journalist and author in Washington, D.C. who has written widely on science and religion. The author of ten books, he lives with his wife in Maryland. He is the author of more than ten books, including: *The Measure of God: The Story of the Gifford Lectures* (Harper: 2005); *A City Upon a Hill*, on the impact of sermons in American history (HarperOne: 2007); and *Marketplace of the Gods: How Economics Explains Religion* (Oxford UP: 2010).

"Eastern Religion on American Soil"

Lili Zhang is Assistant Professor of Chinese Religions in the Department of Religious Studies at Nazareth College of Rochester. Her research interests center on comparative religion and Chinese philosophies of Confucianism, Daoism, and Chan Buddhism. She is a contributor to *The Encyclopedia of Postmodern Theology,* and is the author of *On Buddhist Logic,* published in Taiwan.

Naoko Sasaki is a PhD Candidate in the Department of Religion at Syracuse University. She is currently teaching world religions at the Department of Philosophy and Religion of Ohio Northern University in Ada, Ohio. Her research interest is postmodern theology and Zen Buddhist thought, particularly the question of bodily experience and place in postmodern and Buddhist thought.

REVIEWERS

Randall Balmer (Evangelical)

Randall Balmer is professor of American religious history at Barnard College, Columbia University, and a visiting professor at Yale Divinity School. He has also taught in the Columbia University Graduate School of Journalism, and he has been a visiting professor at Dartmouth College and at Princeton, Rutgers, Drew, and Northwestern universities. He is an adjunct professor of church history at Union Theological Seminary. His commentaries on religion in America have appeared in periodicals across the country, including *The New York Times* and *The Nation*. He is the author of a dozen books, including *Mine Eyes Have Seen the Glory: A Journey into the Evangelical Subculture in America* (Oxford UP: 2006), now in its fourth edition, which was made into a three-part documentary for PBS. Mr. Balmer is an Episcopal priest; he lives in rural Connecticut with his wife, Catharine Randall, a professor of French at Fordham University.

Jolene Chu (Jehovah's Witnesses)

Jolene Chu, a researcher for the Watch Tower Society in New York, specializes in the history of Jehovah's Witnesses in the Nazi era. She is also a project coordinator of Holocaust-related education programs and cooperative efforts with groups such as the Survivors of the Shoah Visual History Foundation, Facing History and Ourselves, the Imperial War Museum Holocaust Exhibition, and numerous other research facilities. Chu also serves on the advisory board for the Journal of Genocide Research.

Kathryn S. Eisenbise (Mennonites)

Kathryn S. Eisenbise is a doctoral student at the Graduate Theological Union in Berkeley, California.

Russ Gerber (Christian Science)

Russ Gerber is Media Manager at The First Church of Christ, Scientist in Boston, Massachusetts.

Dr. Thomas D. Hamm (Quaker)

Thomas D. Hamm is archivist and professor of history at Earlham College. He received his PhD in history in 1985 from Indiana University. He was the recipient of the

Thornbrough Prize in 2000 for best article in the *Indiana Magazine of History*. Dr. Hamm's books include: *Quaker Writings: An Anthology* (Penguin: 2011); *The Quakers in America* (Columbia Univ. Press: 2003); and *The Transformation of American Quakerism: Orthodox Friends, 1800–1907* (Indiana Univ. Press: 1988).

Frederick J. Heuser (Presbyterian)

Frederick J. Heuser, PhD is an archivist for and Executive Director of the Presbyterian Historical Society. His book, *A Guide to Foreign Missionary Manuscripts in the Presbyterian Historical Society*, was published in 1988, by Greenwood Press and his most recent book, *Stewards of Our Heritage: A History of the Presbyterian Historical Society*, was published in 2002 by Geneva Press.

Larry Hollon (Methodist)

As General Secretary of United Methodist Communications, Reverend Larry Hollon is the CEO of the communications agency of The United Methodist Church. Before his election as General Secretary, Hollon was an award-winning producer whose primary focus was telling the stories of persons affected by poverty and living under conditions which place them outside the so-called mainstream culture. As director of communications for Church World Service of the National Council of the Churches of Christ in the U.S.A., he has won numerous awards for video and film production including a national Emmy nomination for the "Share the Joy" radio and television campaign. Ordained in the United Methodist Church, Hollon was pastor of Aldersgate United Methodist Church in Omaha, Nebraska, for ten years.

John Hurley (Unitarian Universalists)

John Hurley is Director of Communications with the Unitarian Universalist Association of Congregations. As well as being a historian and archivist, he also oversees and coordinates the Association's communications with constituents and the wider world.

David Jette (Episcopal)

David Jette is Head Verger at Trinity Episcopal Church on Wall Street in New York City.

George Johnson, Jr. (Adventist)

George Johnson Jr., a native of Baltimore, graduated from Columbia Union College, in Takoma Park, Maryland, in May 1997, with a BS degree in communication emphasizing in public relations/journalism and broadcast media. Mr. Johnson has been employed with the Seventh-day Adventist Church since 1997, and began working in the North American Division Office of Communication in October 2002, as the assistant director for media relations for the Seventh-day Adventist Church in North America. In July 2006, he became the associate director in the Office of Communication.

Dr. Louis Komjathy (Taoism)

Louis Komjathy is an Assistant Professor of East Asian Religions at Pacific Lutheran University. His publications include *Title Index to Daoist Collections* (Three Pines Press: 2002), *Cultivating Perfection: Mysticism and Self-transformation in Early Quanzhen Daoism* (Brill: 2007), and *Handbooks for Daoist Practice* (The Yuen Yuen Institute: 2008). On the national and international level, he successfully guided the Daoist Studies Consultation of the American Academy of Religion to Group status. He served as co-chair of the Daoist Studies Group through 2010.

Donald B. Kraybill (Mennonites)

Donald B. Kraybill is a Senior Fellow and Distinguished Professor at the Young Center for Anabaptist and Pietist Studies of Elizabethtown College, Elizabethtown, Pennsylvania. (See www.etown.edu/youngctr.) He has authored and edited more than fifteen books on Anabaptist groups and life, including *The Upside-Down Kingdom* (1990), which received the national Religious Book Award; and the acclaimed *The Amish and the State* (1993).

Andrew Lang (Congregational)

Andrew Lang is minister for Web community in Local Church Ministries, United Church of Christ, in Cleveland, Ohio. He is a member of Liberation United Church of Christ in Lakewood, Ohio.

Richard Liddy (Roman Catholicism)

Fr. Richard Liddy, a priest of the Archdiocese of Newark,

is the director of Seton Hall's Center for Catholic studies and is also Senior Fellow of the Woodstock Theological Center at Georgetown University. In 1993, Liddy published a work on the Canadian philosopher-theologian, Bernard Lonergan, entitled *Transforming Light: Intellectual Conversion in the Early Lonergan* (Liturgical Press). In 2006, he published a second book on Bernard Lonergan's Insight entitled *Startling Strangeness: Reading Lonergan's Insight* (University Press of America).

T. Kenjitsu Nakagaki (Buddhism)

Reverend T. Kenjitsu Nakagaki is head resident minister of the New York Buddhist Church, chair of the Eastern District Buddhist Ministers Association of Buddhist Churches of America, and Buddhist Chaplain at Columbia University. He graduated from Ryukoku University in Kyoto with a BA in Buddhist History in 1983, and graduated from California State University, Fresno with a MA in Linguistics in 1994.

James N. Pellechia (Jehovah's Witnesses)

James N. Pellechia is Associate Editor of *Watch Tower Publications* at the international offices of the Watch Tower Society. He is also the producer of feature and documentary films, including the award-winning film, *Jehovah's Witnesses Stand Firm Against Nazi Assault*, and a lecturer on the modern history of Jehovah's Witnesses. Mr. Pellechia has presented at international academic conferences, university seminars, and research institutions, including the United States Holocaust Memorial Museum. His publications include *The Spirit and the Sword—Jehovah's Witnesses Expose the Third Reich* (Watch Tower Bible and Tract Society of Pennsylvania: 1997). Mr. Pellechia serves as a board member and vice-president of Jehovah's Witness Holocaust-Era Survivors Fund, Inc.

Sarah M. Pike (Nature Religions)

Sarah M. Pike is Professor of Religious Studies at California State University, Chico, where she teaches courses on American religions. Pike is the author of *Earthly Bodies, Magical Selves: Contemporary Pagans and the Search for Community* (Univ. of California Press: 2001) and *New Age and Neopagan Religions in America*

(Columbia UP: 2004) and is currently writing a book about religion and youth culture. She chairs the American Academy of Religion's Committee for the Public Understanding of Religion and is also on the Board of Directors of the AAR.

Lisa J. M. Poirier (Native American)

Lisa J. M. Poirier received her Master's in Philosophy as well as her PhD in Religion both from Syracuse University. She is currently Assistant Professor and Director of Graduate Studies in the Department of Comparative Religion, at Miami University of Ohio.

Ellen Price (Bahá'í)

Ellen Price is Assistant Director of the National Spiritual Assembly's Office of Communications and National Vice President-elect of the Religion Communicators Council (RCC). She also works for the Office of Communications at the U.S. Bahá'í National Center in Evanston, Illinois.

Dilip V. Shah (Jainism)

Dilip V. Shah is the President of The Federation of Jain Associations in North America (JAINA), the umbrella organization of local Jain associations (Sanghs) in the United States and Canada. He also serves as a director at the Jain Sangh of New Jersey in Cherry Hill. He acknowledges valuable contribution from Dr. Yashwant Malaiya, Dr. Tansukh Salgia, Dr. Sulekh Jain, Pravin K. Shah, and Dr. Dilip K Bobra in compiling material presented herein.

Sheetal D. Shah (Hinduism)

Sheetal D. Shah is a member of the Executive council of the Hindu American Foundation.

Suhag A. Shukla (Hinduism)

Suhag A. Shukla, Esq. serves as the legal counsel for the Hindu American Foundation. She graduated from the University of Florida at Gainesville with degrees in both Economics and Religion and received her law degree from the University of Florida College of Law.

Elijah Siegler (Taoism)

Elijah Siegler is originally from Toronto, Canada, and has

been teaching at the College of Charleston since 2004. He has a BA in Comparative Study of Religion from Harvard University (1992) and a PhD in Religious Studies from the University of California at Santa Barbara (2003). Most of his recent research has focused on Taoism in North America and the globalization of Taoist practices. Recently, he has pursued fieldwork at the Healing Tao Center in Chiang Mai Thailand, on Hua Shan, an important Daoist sacred mountain in Shaanxi province China, and in Asheville, N.C. His most recent publication is *New Religious Movements* (Prentice-Hall: 2007).

Harinder Singh (Sikhism)

Harinder Singh serves as the Executive Director of the Sikh Research Institute, a community development organization focused on education through preservation, celebration, and inspiration. An interdisciplinary researcher and global orator, Harinder's expertise is on issues related to the Sikhs and the Panjab. Since 1997, he has developed, taught, and supervised courses and projects in the Sikh Homeland and the Diaspora. He has lectured extensively at forums in the United States, Canada, the United Kingdom, India, and Pakistan. He is active with the Sikh Scholarship Foundation at Oxford and Harvard, the United Communities of San Antonio, the Nanakshahi trust, and the Panjab Virsa Digitization Initiative.

Nikki Stephanopoulos (Eastern Orthodoxy)

Until very recently, Nikki Stephanopoulos was Director of News and Information/Public Relations and Press and Officer of the Greek Orthodox Archdiocese of America. She has been involved with volunteer service in the New York City community since 1982, particularly as a board member of the Neighborhood Coalition Shelter. She has served since 1996 as a member of the Board of Trustees of the National Interfaith Cable Coalition/Hallmark Channel, as vice chairman of the of the Communications Commission of The National Council of Churches, and is a member of the Governing Board of the NCCCUSA. Presvytera Nikki was instrumental in instituting national television broadcasting of the Divine Liturgy from the Cathedral every Sunday, and has served as editor of the Cathedral Newletter since 1983.

Robert Stephanopolous (Eastern Orthodoxy)

Rev. Robert Stephanopoulos, PhD, a priest of the Greek Orthodox Archiocese of America for forty-eight years, retired October 15, 2007, following completion of twenty years as Dean of the Archdiocesan Cathedral of the Holy Trinity, New York City. Author of *Guidelines for Orthodox Christians in Ecumenical Relations* (Standing Conference of Canonical Orthodox Bishops in America: 1973), he is a founding member of Orthodox Dialogues with Catholics, Anglicans, Evangelicals, and Jews. In addition to Guidelines, Father Robert has authored *IAKOVOS: The Making of an Archbishop* (Greek Orthodox Archdiocese of North and South America: 1996) among other titles. He has served as adjunct professor of Eastern Christian Thought at St. John's University in Queens, NY, for twenty-four years. In 2007, St. John's conferred upon him the degree of Doctor of Sacred Theology, honoris causa.

Robert H. Stockman (Bahá'í)

Richard Stockman is the Director of the Wilmette Institute and the Coordinator of its Institute of Bahá'í Studies. He received a PhD in the history of religion from Harvard University in 1990 and teaches comparative religion at DePaul University. He is Senior Researcher at the Bahá'í National Center. His publications include: *Bahá'í Faith in America* (Vols I & II, Bahá'í Trust: 1985, 1994); and *Thornton Chase: First American Bahá'í* (Bahá'í Trust: 2001). He writes and lectures extensively on Bahá'í faith and on issues of comparative religion.

Michael von Rosen (Mormon)

Michael von Rosen works for the Mormon Church's Public Affairs Department, and serves as Publicist for the Mormon Tabernacle Choir.

Rev. Dr. Robert K. Welsh (Disciples of Christ)

Robert K. Welsh, an ordained minister in the Christian Church (Disciples of Christ), has served as president of the Council on Christian Unity since January 1, 1999. In his ministry with the Council on Christian Unity, he offers leadership as the chief ecumenical officer for the Disciples of Christ, representing the Church in a broad spectrum of international, national, and local efforts.

Credits and Acknowledgments

Page 12: Library of Congress (LOC)

Page 24: © Hu Totya / St. Patrick's Cathedral

Page 26: Zenodot Verlag

Page 27: Wolfgang Stuck

Page 28, left: Seperaud

Page 28, right: Omulazimoglu

Page 35: © Joshua Treviño / SCOBA

Page 37: Rembrandt Peale / PaulVIF

Page 41: NYDRIS / © M. Donnelly

Page 43: J. Jones / LOC

Page 45: American Papist (AmP)

Page 47: U.S. Department of Defense / Office of the Chaplaincy

Page 54: White House Archive / Bert Goulait

Page 55: © Emilio Grossi

Page 66: P. Hornig / KF

Page 70: Swastadel

Page 71: © David Shankbone

Page 72: Maryland Historical Trust / LOC

Page 76; 88; 105: SCOBA

Page 109: St. Paul Armenian Church, Fresno, CA

Page 121: © Richard C. Moore / www.ship-paintings.com

Page 115: LOC / Wesleyan Conference

Page 117: Crystal Cathedral Ministries

Page 119: LOC/W.K. Leffler–USNWR

Page 125: Stockton

Page 126: LOC / White House Archive

Page 133: LOC / Smithsonian Institution

Page 138: Abyssinian Baptist Church

Page 139: First Baptist Church, Providence, RI

Page 141: Church of Christian Science

Page 145: LOC

Page 156: LOC / Daderot

Page 159: LOC

Page 161: LOC / National Gallery

Page 164, left: Drake / LOC

Page 164, right: LOC

Page 165: White House Archive / National Archives

Page 167: Ohio History Central Archive

Page 169: © Daniel Case

Page 173: LOC

Page 177: National Gallery / LOC

Page 186: White House Archive / National Archives

Page 187: LOC

Page 188: Smithsonian Institution

Page 190, left: GAFCON

Page 190, right: © Katharine Jefferts Schori

Page 201: Church of St. John the Divine

Page 203: Nicholasink

Page 205; 209: LOC

Page 213: OCRPL.org

Page 229; 235: WTS

Page 231: LOC

Page 240: LOC / Rare Book Division

Page 249; 250; 256: Smithsonian Institution

Page 253: © Time (April 8, 1929)

Page 267: © LDS

Page 268: NYDRIS / NYAF (© Meridian)

Page 283: Zion Lutheran Church (twp-freedom.org)

Page 287; 297: Pennsylvania Office of Tourism & Information / © Alan Walker

Page 313: LOC

Page 314: stmarksumva.org

Page 317: Maryland Historical Society / LOC

Page 320: © highlandsnethodists.org

Page 327: University of Texas Library

Page 333: LOC

Page 342: © John Roemer / PTS

Page 343: Katja / stateuniversity.com

Page 344: © Joe Routon / Casavant

Page 347; 351: LOC

Page 348: A. Chinn / LOC

Page 355: After Benjamin West / LOC

Page 356: Wartegg / LOC

Page 357: Ohio Historical Society

Page 363: Plymouth Township Historical Society

Page 364a: National Archives / U.S. Presidents

Page 364b: LOC / "Challenge of Ideas"

Page 364c: Liberty Film Festival

Page 364d: © Bluesman Blues Historian

Page 379: © SDA

Page 381: Oswald Chambers

Page 382: LOC

Page 391: HDS

Page 392: © Larry Stritof / UUA

Page 393: UUA Archive

Page 396; 399: U.S. Department of State / USIS

The editors gratefully acknowledge the assistance and support rendered by **Mitch Pessin**, and his staff—**John, Jay, Rich**, and **Dan** at **MP Computer Services**.

General Index

The Book of Common Prayer (Episcopal), 188, 191, 193–94
The Book of Concord (Lutheran), 272, 278–79, 286
The Book of Confessions (Presbyterian), 334–35
The Book of Discipline (Methodist), 317–18, 324
Book of Mormon, 250, 256–57, 264
The Book of Order (Presbyterian), 334
Book of Revelation, 51, 86–87, 151, 279, 367–69, 373. See also Apocalypse/ apocalyptic events
"Born-again" Christians. See also Pentecostal movement
    America as a nation of, 805
    Baptists, 133
    Evangelicals, 207, 211, 221
    in the Great Awakening, 380
    Quakers, 361
    Seventh-Day Adventists, 361
    Unitarianism and, 390–91
Bowdoin College, 168
Branch Davidians (Adventist), 367–69, 376, 798
Brandeis University, 524
The Brethren (Mennonite sect), 311–12
A Brief History of the Episcopal Church (Holmes), 204
A Brief History of the Presbyterians (Smylie), 346
Brigham Young University, 268
Brown University (Rhode Island College), 126
Buddhism
    achieving understanding of, 21
    early history and origins, 530–31, 551–52
    history in America, 14–19, 552–54, 821–25
    important dates & landmarks, 554–55
    important figures, 556, 561–63
    organization and infrastructure
        clergy & hierarchy, 574–75
        demographics map by U.S. county, 907
        denominations and demographics, 569–74
        governance & authority, 577–78
        media and resources, 578–79
        seminaries & institutes, 575–77
        social service organizations, 578
    relationship with other religions
        Bahá'í Faith, 540
        Islam, 402
        Judaism, 493
        Quakers, 355
        Unitarianism, 385
    rites and rituals
        life cycle events & family, 567–69
        liturgical calendar, 563–66
        worship and liturgy, 566–67
    scripture and sacred literature, 559–60
    tenets and beliefs
        articles of faith, 557–59
        birth of Buddha, 556
        comparison of branches, 571–73
        schisms and mergers, 570–71

    theologians & thinkers, 560–63
Burial of the dead. See Death and burial
Byzantine Empire, 27–28, 35, 76

C

California, Catholic missions, 40, 42
Caliphate, creation of Islamic, 400–404, 421
Calvinism, 115–16, 123, 159, 206, 272
Campus Crusade for Christ, 212
Canada
    Anglican Church, 192, 198
    Bahá'í Faith in, 535–36
    Christian Science in, 156
    Eastern Orthodoxy in, 79–80, 102
    Jainism in, 630
    Jehovah's Witnesses in, 232, 234
    Lutheran Church, 275, 280
    Mennonite groups, 287, 289, 293, 302
    Mormonism in, 251
    Muslims in, 448
    Native Americans in, 684
    Presbyterian Church, 340–41
Capital punishment. See Death penalty
A Careful and Strict Inquiry into the...Freedom of Will (Edwards), 210
The Case of the Episcopal Churches in the United States (White), 194
Catechism of the Catholic Church, 41, 48–50
The Catholic Hour (radio show), 54–55
Catholic University of America, 40, 54
Catholic Worker Movement, 40, 42
Catholicism. See Christianity; Eastern Orthodoxy; Roman Catholicism
Celebration of the Liturgy (Catholic), 46, 58–61
Celibacy
    Buddhism, 574
    Buddhism and, 567, 572
    Episcopal Church, 200
    Jainism and, 626
    Lutheran Church, 284
    Roman Catholicism, 66
    Sikhism and, 638
Celtic Church of England, 32
Cha'an Buddhism. See Zen Buddhism
Channeling, 798–99
Charismatic Movement (Evangelical), 219, 221
China
    banning of Christian missions, 33
    Buddhism in, 552, 554–55
    Cultural Revolution, 670
    resurgence of religion, viii
    Taoism origins in, 644
The Christian Baptist (Campbell), 174, 177
Christian Church. See Disciples of Christ Church
Christian Coalition, 122, 777
Christian Front, 43
Christian Nurture (Bushnell), 167
Christian Science (Church of Christ, Scientist)

    early history, 141–46
    important dates & landmarks, 146–47
    important figures in, 147–48
    media and resources, 157–58
    organization and infrastructure
        churches and Reading Rooms, 156, 157
        clergy and Lay Readers, 155–56
        denominations and demographics, 155
        governance and authority, 157
        media and resources, 157–58
        schisms within the church, 155
        social service organizations, 157
    rites and rituals
        liturgical calendar, 152
        practitioners, 154
        sacraments and life events, 154–55
        verification of healings, 153–54
        worship and liturgy, 152–53
    scripture and sacred literature, 150
    tenets and beliefs, 148–50
    writers and theologians, 150–52
Christian Science Journal, 144–45, 157–58
Christian Science Monitor, 145–46, 157
Christian Science Parent Church, 155
Christian Science Reading Rooms, 156
Christian Science Sentinel, 145, 158
Christianity
    American politics and, 775–80
    Catholicism. See also Eastern Orthodoxy; Roman Catholicism
        Anglican Church and, 187–89
        Four Marks of the "True Church," 29
        the Great Schism, 27–29, 32, 98–99
        Jesus (the Christ), life of, 24–27
        Peace of Augsburg, 271–72
        timeline in history, 29–34
    Humanism and, 749
    Protestantism. See also Protestant Reformation; specific Protestant denomination
        in American history, 114
        demographics maps. See Maps
        evangelicalism, 115–16
        Great Awakening, 116
        Great Awakening, Second, 118–19
        important dates & landmarks, 120–22
        Landmarkist beliefs, 123
        Luther and the Reformation, 114–15
        mainline/liberal, 119–20
        role of African Americans and women, 117–18
    relationship with other religions
        Bahá'í Faith, 535, 540
        Buddhism, 553–54, 558
        Islam, 402, 428–29
        Native American religions, 677–79
    U.S. immigration policy and, 14–17
Christianity Today International, 228
Church of Christ. See Disciples of Christ Church

Episcopal ritual of, 197
Hinduism, 604
in Islam, 443
Jainism, 628
in Judaism, 512
Lutheran ritual of, 284
in Mennonite groups, 298
Mormonism and, 254–55, 262
Native American religions, 695–96
Nature-based religions, 721–22
Orthodox ritual of, 97
in Quaker religion, 358–59
Seventh-Day Adventists and, 374
Sikhism, 641
Taoism, 670
Unitarianism, 389
On Death and Dying (Kübler-Ross), 722
Death penalty, 44, 352, 577, 738–40, 933–36
Decretum of Canon Law (Burchard of Worms), 32
The Deliverance from Error (al-Ghazali), 433
Demographics, geographic. *See also* Maps
attendance, frequency, 841
belief and practice by religion, 844
children as members, retention, 845
Christian self-description, 840
Christian/Jewish population (2001, 2004), 850
congregation size, 838
congregations, urban vs. rural, 849
household membership, church, 837
measures of vitality, 838
mixed messages, 842
prayer, frequency, 841
religiosity survey (2001), 839
religious affiliation
congregations, 849
national overview, 834–35, 846
preference, 837
self-characterization, 843
self-identification (1900, 2001 surveys), 836
by states, 847–48
transition in/out of religious groups, 839
Demographics, religious. *See also* Maps
about patterns of, 851, 853
age distribution, 796–97, 855–56, 857–58
children per home, 869
clergy, 759–63, 819
by congregation, 852
divorced/separated (1990-2001), 870
Eastern Religions, 823
educational groups, 862–63
ethnic and racial group affiliation, 859–61
gender, 854
immigrant populations, xxx
incarcerated/imprisoned, 883
income groups, 864–65
intermarriage patterns, 872–73
marital status, 866–67, 871

native vs. foreign-born, xxx
politics
1st U.S. Congress (1789) affiliations, 877
109th U.S. Congress (2005) affiliations, 878
faith affiliation of presidents, 874–75
founding fathers' affiliations, 876
party preference (2001), 873
self-identification of religion, 874
signers of Declaration of Independence, 876
U.S governors (2005-2006), 879
Protestant denominations
age, 857
children, 869
education, 863
income, 865
marital status, 867
race, 860
self-description, 854
DePaul University, 543
Destiny of the Mother Church (Knapp), 151
The Dharma Bums (Kerouac), 55, 553
Dianetics, 744
Dianetics: The Modern Science of Mental Health (Hubbard), 750
Dietary restrictions. *See* Fasting and abstinence
Dillard University, 162
Disciples of Christ Church
early history, 173–75
important dates & landmarks, 175–76
important figures, 176–77, 186
organization and infrastructure
clergy and lay ministers, 182–83
denominations and demographics, 15, 183
governance & authority, 185
media and resources, 186
seminaries, 184
shrines & churches, 184–85
social service organizations, 185–86
rites and rituals
life cycle events, 180–81
liturgical calendar, 179–80
worship and liturgy, 180
scripture and sacred literature, 178
tenets and beliefs
articles of faith, 177–78
comparison of branches, 182
theologians & thinkers, 178–79
Discrimination, xenophobia and, 17–19
The Distinguishing Marks of a Work of the Spirit of God, 209
Diversity
American religious freedom and, 14–17
interfaith movement and, 19–20
overcoming xenophobia, 17–19
The Divine Dramatist: George Whitefield (Stout), 228

Divorce
Bahá'í Faith, 546
in Baptist theology, 133
Buddhism, 569
Catholic marriage and, 48, 63–64
in Christian Science theology, 155
Disciples of Christ Church, 181
Eastern Orthodoxy and, 98
Eastern Orthodoxy vs. Roman Catholicism, 100
Episcopal Church and, 197
Hinduism, 605–06
Islam, 444
Islam in America, 458
Jehovah's Witnesses and, 245–46
Lutheran Church and, 284–85
in Mennonite theology, 298
Mormonism and, 263
in Native American religions, 697
in Nature-based religions, 724
in Quaker religion, 359
Seventh-Day Adventists and, 375
Sikhism, 642
Unitarianism, 389
DMT: The Spirit Molecule (Strassman), 717
Doctrine and Covenants (Mormon), 256–57, 264
The Doors of Perception (Huxley), 709–10
Dordrecht Confession, Anabaptist (1632), 288–89, 300
Drug culture. *See* Hallucinogenic drugs; Peyotism
Drug use/abuse, 55, 235, 260–61, 297, 370, 545, 641, 687–88, 694
Druidism, 707

E

"Earth-centered" religions. *See* Native American religions; Nature-based religions
Eastern Orthodoxy. *See also* Catholicism
the Great Schism and, 26–29, 77–78, 98–99
historical roots of, 76–78
history in America, 78–79
important dates & landmarks, 80–82
organization and infrastructure
autocephalous governance, 100–101, 107–08
demographics map by U.S. county, 894
denominations and demographics, 98–99
governance & authority in, 109
hierarchy and religious orders, 101–06
media and resources, 110–12
seminaries, 106–07
shrines & churches, 107–08
social service organizations, 110
U.S. churches, 102
rites and rituals
daily precepts and restrictions, 94–95
family life, 98
life cycle events, 95–97

U.S. Latter-day Saints, 898
U.S. Lutherans, 895
U.S. mainline Protestants, 891
U.S. Mennonites, 897
U.S. Methodists, 896
U.S. Pentacostals, 899
U.S. Presbyterian, 900
U.S. Quakers, 902
U.S. unaffiliated distribution, 888
U.S. Unitarian, 901
March on Washington (1963), 122
Marriage
    Bahá'í Faith, 545–46
    in Baptist theology, 133
    Buddhism, 568, 569
    of Catholic clergy, 66–67
    as Catholic sacrament, 48, 62, 63–64
    in Christian Science theology, 155
    Congregationalist rite of, 167
    Disciples of Christ Church, 181
    Eastern Orthodox, 92, 96–98
    Episcopal Church, 197
    in Evangelical theology, 216–17
    Hinduism, 591, 603–05
    Islam, 441, 443–44
    Islam in America, 458
    Jainism, 627–28
    Jehovah's Witnesses and, 234, 245–46
    Jewish ritual of, 511–12
    Lutheran Church, 284–85
    in Mennonite theology, 298
    Mormonism and, 249, 257, 262–63
    Native American religions, 695–97
    Nature-based religions, 721, 723–24
    in Presbyterian theology, 338–39
    in Quaker religion, 359
    same-sex marriage, 763, 784–86, 931–32
    Seventh-Day Adventist and, 374–75
    Sikhism, 641, 642
    Taoism, 669–70
    Unitarianism, 388–89
The Martyrs Mirror (van Bracht), 288, 290, 308
Mary Baker Eddy (Gill), 151–52, 158
The Mass (Catholic), 46, 58–61
The Mayflower Compact, 159, 163
Megachurches (Evangelical), 225
Mennonite groups. *See also* Anabaptist movement
    early history and origins, 287–89
    history in America, 289
    important dates & landmarks, 289–90
    important figures, 290–92
    important sects of, 299, 303, 310–12
    organization and infrastructure
        clergy & hierarchy, 302–04
        conferences and enclaves, 304–05
        demographics map by U.S. county, 897
        denominations and demographics,
            298–99

governance & authority, 305–06
media and resources, 307–10
seminaries, 304
social service organizations, 306–07
rites and rituals
    life cycle events & family, 297–98
    liturgical calendar, 295–96
    worship and liturgy, 296–97
scripture and sacred literature, 294–95
tenets and beliefs
    articles of faith, 292–94
    comparison of groups, 299–302, 303
    evangelicalism and, 217–18
theologians & thinkers, 295
Mesmerism, 796
Methodist Church
    early history and origins, 313–14
    Great Awakening and, 116
    history in America, 314–15
    important dates & landmarks, 315–16
    important figures, 316
    observing "Puritan Sabbath," 329
    organization and infrastructure
        clergy & hierarchy, 322
        comparison of branches, 319–21
        demographics map by U.S. county, 896
        denominations and demographics, 322
        governance & authority, 324–25
        media and resources, 325–26
        seminaries, colleges & universities, 322–24
        social service organizations, 325
    Protestant "full communion" and, 281
    rites and rituals
        life cycle events, 319
        liturgical calendar, 319
        worship and liturgy, 319–20
    scripture and sacred literature, 317–18
    tenets and beliefs, 317
    unification with Evangelical United Brethren,
        122
Methodist Episcopal Church, 314–15
Middle Ages (476-1499), 26–29, 31–33, 35,
    77–78, 98–99
Middlebury College, 168
Militarism, 293–94
Millennial Dawn (Russell), 231
Millennial Harbinger (Campbell), 174, 177
Millennialism, 116, 118–19
Missionaries
    Baptist Church, 124, 126–28
    Catholics in the New World, 35–37
    Congregationalist, 161–62, 170
    Evangelicals among Native Americans, 210
    Jehovah's Witnesses, 246–47
    Mennonites, 295
    Mormonism and, 250
    Native American religions and, 678–79, 684–85
    Seventh-Day Adventists, 367

The Mists of Avalon (Bradley), 715
Monasticism
    Eastern Orthodoxy, 104–05
    England, Wales & Ireland, 33, 35, 190
    European, 32
    Hindu, 610–11
    Roman Catholicism, 67–68
Moody Bible Institute, 218
"Moonies". *See* Unification Church
The Moorish American (magazine), 465
Moorish Science Temple of America, 450, 464
Moral Majority, 777, 843
Moravian Church, 281, 313–14
Mormon America: The Power and the Promise
    (Ostling), 270
Mormon Tabernacle (Salt Lake City), 267
Mormon War, 250–52
Mormonism
    early history and origins, 249–50
    history in America, 250–52, 263–64
    important dates & landmarks, 252–53
    important figures, 253–54
    organization and infrastructure
        clergy & hierarchy, 266–67
        demographics map by U.S. county, 898
        governance & authority, 268–69
        media and resources, 270
        schisms and mergers, 263–64
        social service organizations, 269
        temples and historical sites, 267–68
    rites and rituals
        daily life & family, 260–63
        liturgical calendar, 259
        worship and liturgy, 259–60
    scripture and sacred literature, 256–58
        secondary sources, 258
    tenets and beliefs
        articles of faith, 254–56
        comparison of factions, 264–65
Mormonism: The Story of a New Religious Tradition
    (Shipps), 270
Mormonism Unvailed [sic] (Howe), 258
Morocco, 447
Mount Holyoke College, 170
Muslim Brotherhood, 405
Muslim Public Affairs Council (MPAC), 16, 453, 462
Muslim Student Association (MSA), 451, 462

N

Nation of Islam (NOI), 451, 465–67
National Association of Evangelicals, 122, 214,
    218, 225–26
National Baptist Convention, 129, 130, 134
National Campmeeting Association, 121
National Catholic Welfare Council, 40
National Council of Churches, 122
National Council of the Congregational Churches
    of the United States, 162

Religious freedom. *See* Separation of church and state

Religious identity/traditions
    finding commonality, x–xi, 19–20
    immigration to America and, 14–17
    overcoming preconceptions, viii–ix
    religious minorities, 17–19

Religious orders, 67–68. *See also Clergy references*; Ordination

Religious Society of Friends. *See* Quakers (Religious Society of Friends)

Religious wars, viii

Renaissance era (1500-1629), 27p, 33, 501, 707, 718, 724

Reorganized Church of Jesus Christ of Latter-day Saints, 263–65

Between Resistance and Martyrdom: Jehovah's Witnesses in the Third Reich (Garbe), 248

Restoration Movement, 174–75, 889

Resurrection of Jesus (33 CE), 26–27, 30

Retrospection and Introspection (Eddy), 141–42, 143

The Revival of the Religious Sciences (al-Ghazali), 433

Revivalism movement, 116–18, 142, 206, 209, 211, 328, 329, 361, 380

Right to life. *See* Abortion

Risáliy-i-Siyásiyyih (`Abdu'l-Baha), 542

Rites and rituals
    Baptist Church, 132–33
    Buddhism, 563–69
    Christian Science, 152–53
    Congregationalism, 166–67
    Disciples of Christ, 179–81
    Eastern Orthodox, 90–92
    Episcopal Church, 195–97
    Evangelical Denominations, 215–17
    of Islam, 435–44
    Methodist Church, 319–20
    Native American religions, 691–97
    Nature-based religions, 718–24
    Presbyterian Church, 337–39
    Roman Catholic, 56–64
    Seventh-Day Adventists, 371–75
    Sikhism, 637–41
    Unitarianism, 387–89

On the Road (Kerouac), 55

Roe vs. Wade (1973), 41, 777, 937, 940

Rolling Away the Stone: Mary Baker Eddy's Challenge to Materialism (Eddy), 151, 158

Roman Catholicism. *See also* Christianity
    historical roots, 35–36
    history in America, 36–39
    important dates & landmarks, 40–42
    important figures, 42–46
    interreligious dialogue, 755–58
    organization and infrastructure
        Charismatic Movement, 219
        demographics map by U.S. county, 907
        denominations and demographics, 64

    hierarchy and religious vocations, 64–68
    media and resources, 74–75
    seminaries, 68–71
    shrines & churches, 71–72
    social service organizations, 73–74
    rites and rituals
        daily life precepts and restrictions, 61
        family life, 63–64
        life cycle events, 62–63
        liturgical calendar of, 56–58
        worship and liturgy, 58–61
    sexual abuse scandal, 34, 36, 41, 736
    tenets and beliefs
        apostolic succession, 26–27
        articles of faith, 46–48
        basic beliefs, 48–51
        canon law, 72–73
        comparison to Eastern Orthodoxy, 99–100
        "full communion" with Protestants, 281
        the life of Jesus, 24–26
        Nicene Creed, 27
        papal infallibility, 26, 28, 34, 46
        scripture and sacred literature, 51–52
        secondary sources & literary figures, 52–56

Roman Curia, 38

Roman Empire (4 BCE-476)
    Catholic timeline during, 30–31
    Christianity in the, 26–27, 76
    division and fall of, 27–28, 31
    Edict of Milan, 26, 30, 76
    during the life of Jesus, 24–26

Romanticism, 382, 704–05

Roots (Haley), 446

Rosicrucians, 704–05, 708, 799

Russia
    Eastern Orthodoxy, 76
    Eastern Orthodoxy in, 78
    resurgence of religion, viii
    Revolution of 1917, 79–80, 101
    sale of Alaska to U.S., 79

Russian Orthodox Church, 78–79, 89, 101, 108

Russian Orthodox Church Outside Russia (ROCOR), 79–80

S

Sabbatarianism, 366, 373

Sacraments
    Baptist Church, 132–33
    Christian Science theology, 154
    Congregationalist practice of, 167
    Eastern Orthodox, 92
    Episcopal Church, 195–97
    Evangelical theology, 215–17
    Jehovah's Witnesses, 245–46
    Lutheran theology, 281–82, 283–84
    Mennonite groups, 296–97

Methodist Church, 319
    Mormon ordinances and, 259–60, 261–62
    Nature-based religion, 711
    Presbyterian Church, 337–39
    Protestant "full communion" and, 275
    Quaker religion, 357
    Roman Catholic, 46–48

Sacred literature. *See* Scripture and sacred literature; The Bible

Saint Peter, Basilica of (Rome), 27

Salvation
    Bahá'í Faith, 540–41
    Calvinist beliefs, 347–48
    Episcopal Church and, 196, 199
    evangelicalism and, 120, 211
    Jehovah's Witnesses theology, 242
    in Methodist theology, 313
    in Mormon theology, 254–55
    Quaker beliefs, 355
    Revivalism movement and, 206
    Taoism, 660
    in Unitarian theology, 385

Salvation Army, 121, 207, 813–15

Salvations (Heim), 386

Same-sex marriage, 763, 784–86, 931–32

Santería, 676, 710–11. *See also* Nature-based religions

Santo Daime, 710–11

The Satanic Verses (Rushdie), 410, 414, 453

Saudia Arabia, 404–05, 409

The Scarlet Letter (Hawthorne), 379

Schleitheim Confession, Anabaptist (1527), 288–89

School prayer, 775–76

Science and Health with Key to the Scriptures (Eddy), 144–46, 150, 158

Science and religion, 745, 765–70, 816–20

Scientology, 676, 750–51, 799

Scopes "Monkey Trial" of 1925, 119, 122, 218, 735–36, 739–40

Scripture and sacred literature. *See also* The Bible; The Qur'án; The Torah
    Bahá'í Faith, 541–44
    Buddhism, 559–63
    Hinduism, 592–94
    Islam, 430–35
    Jainism (Jain Dharma), 621–23
    Judaism, 502–04
    Native American religions, 690
    Nature-based religions, 714–18
    Sikhism, 636–37
    Taoism, 662–63
    Unitarianism, 385–86

The Search for Omm Sety (Cott), 715

Second Coming of Christ. *See also* Apocalypse/apocalyptic events
    in Mormon theology, 255, 263
    in Orthodox theology, 85

Index of Names

A

Abd al-Wahhab, Muhammad ibn, 404, 409
Abdallah, Muhammad ibn. *see* Muhammad
`Abdu'l-Bahá, 535, 537, 539, 546
Abdul-Jabbar, Kareem (aka Lew Alcindor), 452, 457
Abi Talib, Ali ibn, 401
Abraham (biblical patriarch), 398, 428, 471, 481, 532
Abramoff, Jack, 779
Abu Bakr, 401, 422–23
Abu Muslim, 402
Abu Sufyan, Muawiyyak ibn, 402
Abu Talib, 399, 421
Adam (first prophet of Islam), 428
Adams, Abigail, 165
Adams, Don A., 241
Adams, Hannah, 582
Adams, John, 160, 165, 447
Adams, John Quincy, 165, 447, 450
Adams, Samuel, 160, 165
Adb al-Muttalib, Abbas ibn, 402
Addams, Jane, 364
Adler, Cyrus, 517
Aisha bint Abu Bakr, 425
Aisha bint Abu Bakr (wife of Muhammad), 400
al-Affan, Uthman ibn, 401
Alban (Saint), 187, 190
Albanese, Catherine, 784
Al-Basri, Rabi'a al-Adawiyya, 433
Al-Bistami, Abu Yazid (Bayazid), 433
Albright, Jacob, 316, 321
Albright, Madeleine, 17
Al-Farabi, Abu Nasr, 431
Al-Faruqi, Ismail, 453, 455
Alfasi, Isaac, 504
Al-Ghazali, Abu Hamid Muhammad, 432–33
Ali, Dusé Muhammad, 451
Ali, Husayn ibn, 401–2
Al-Khattab, Umar ibn, 423
al-Khattab, Umar ibn (Omar the Great), 401
al-Khattab, Zayd ibn, 405
Allen, Richard, 315
Al-Marayati, Salam, 453
Alnor, William, 155
Alpert, Richard (aka Ram Dass), 709, 797
Al-Sadiq, Ja'far, 435
Al-Shafi'i, Abu Abdullah Muhammad, 435

Altdorfer, Albrect, 26p
Amardas (Sikh guru), 635
Ambrose of Milan (Saint), 83
Ames, William, 164
Ammann, Jakob, 290, 310
Andreae, Jacob, 278
Andrew, James O., 314, 316
Angad (Sikh guru), 635
Angelico, Giovanni (Fra), 25p
Anne (queen of England), 188
Ansari, Anousheh, 457
Ansgar (Saint), 32
Anthony, Susan B., 351, 352
Aquinas, Thomas, 33
Aquinas, Thomas (Saint), 52
Arafat, Yasser, 524
Argue, Donald, 122
Arjun (Sik guru), 635–36
Arminius, Jacobus, 118–19, 125
Asanga (Buddhist monk), 560
Asbury, Francis, 223, 313–14, 315, 321
Ashoka Maurya, 554
Asimov, Isaac, 748
Atatürk, Mustafa Kemal, viii, 405, 409
Athanasius (Saint), 33, 83
Atisa (Buddhist teacher), 555
Atkinson, William Walker, 583
Ätmärämji (Jain monk), 617
Attaturk, Kemal, viii, xi
Attila the Hun, 89
Augustine of Canterbury (Saint), 31, 187, 190
Augustine of Hippo (Saint), 52–53, 67–68, 89

B

Báb (Mizra `Ali-Muhammad), 533, 536, 538–39
Bach, Johann Sebastian, 278, 280
Backus, Isaac, 125–26, 128, 130
Bahá'u'lláh (Mizra Husayn Ali Nuri), 533–34, 536, 537, 539, 546
Bailey, Derrick Sherwin, 786
Bailey, Leonard, 371
Baldwin, James, 14, 21
Bandahur, Banda Singh, 632
Bangs, Lester, 55
Barabbas (Jewish criminal), 26, 83
Barbour, Nelson, 239
Barth, Karl, 335, 815
Bashir, Antony (archibishop), 81

Basil the Great (Saint), 33, 88
Bates, Benjamin E., 165
Baudelaire, Charles, 705
Baurenboim, Daniel, 456
The Beach Boys (singing group), 598
The Beatles (singing group), 55, 598
BeDuhn, Jason, 243
Beecher, Henry Ward, 165
Behe, Michael, 769
Belkin, Samuel, 524
Bellarmine, Robert, 33
Ben Asher, Yaakov, 504
Ben Zakai, Yochanan, 477
Ben Zakkai, Yohanan, 503
Bender, Courtney, 821
Benedict (Saint), 31
Bennett, Dennis, 219
Bennett, John Cook, 258
Berg, David ("Moses"), 798
Berger, Peter, 803
Bering, Vitus, 80
Berrigan, Daniel, 54
Besant, Annie Wood, 582, 799
Bhindranwale, Jarnail Singh, 633
Bhutto, Benazir, 405
Bickerson, William, 263
Biddle, Francis, 233
Biestkens, Nikolaes, 294
Bilal, Charles, 453
Bill, Anne, 155
Bin Laden, Osama, 18, 405, 449, 454
Black Elk (Lakota medicine man), 685
Blacksnake, Owen, 685
Blackwell, Victor, 244
Blatty, William Peter, 56
Blaurock, George, 289, 291
Blavatsky, Helena Petrovna, 552, 582, 705, 798
Blue Bird, James (Sioux minister), 685
Blyden, Edward W., 450
Bodhidarma (Buddhist monk), 555, 560, 571
Bogg, Lilburn W., 251
Boice, James, 219
Boisvert, Donald, 791
Boleyn, Anne, 191
Bolotov, Joasaph, 78, 81
Bonaparte, Napoleon, 801
Bonhoeffer, Dietrich, 802
Boniface (Saint), 32

Edwards, John, 317
Edwards, Jonathan, 116, 120, 160, 163, 167, 206, 209–10, 328, 335, 380, 383
Einhorn, David, 516, 522
Einstein, Albert, 747, 768, 770
Eisendrath, Maurice N., 524
Eisenhower, Dwight D., 15, 122, 451
Eliade, Mircea, 709
Eliot, John, 165, 680, 690
Eliot, T. S., 583
Elizabeth I (queen of England), 188, 191, 193, 327–28
Eller, Cynthia, 715
Ellis, Havelock, 709
Embury, Phillip, 313–14, 315
Emerson, Ralph Waldo, 382, 383–84, 582, 595–96
Engardio, Joel P., 244
England, John (bishop), 39
Epiphanius (Saint), 83
Erasmus, Desiderius, 194
Estavanico of Azamor (Istafan), 446, 450
Estes, Yussuf, 455
Ewing, Finis, 331
Exiguus, Dionysius, 29

F

Fakhry, Majid, 431
Fakir Musafar (Roland Loomis), 710
Falwell, Jerry, 777, 816
Fanning, Tolbert, 178
Farbough, William, 320
Fard, Wallace (aka Ali Fard, W. F. Muhammad), 451, 465–66
Farrakhan, Louis, 452, 466–67
Farrow, Mia, 598
Fatimah bint Muhammad (daughter of Muhammad), 399, 421, 426
Feinstein, Moshe, 520
Fell, Thomas, 352
Fichte, J. G., 278
Finney, Charles Grandison, 118–19, 141, 206–7, 210–11, 329
Fitzgerald, F. Scott, 56
Flavian (Saint), 89
Foley, Mark, 779
Ford, Henry, 514
Ford, Thomas, 250
Fosdick, Harry Emerson, 126, 132, 812
Foucault, Michel, 785
Fox, George, 347–49, 353
Fox, Margaret Fell, 349, 352–53
Fox, Richard W., 809
Francis of Assisi (Saint), 32, 67
Frank, Leo, 514, 523
Franklin, Benjamin, 115
Franks, Bobby, 738–39
Franz, Frederick W., 241

Frederick, John, 272
Frederick William III of Prussia, 280
Freeman, Joseph, 253
Froschauer, Christoph, 294
Frye, Calvin A., 148
Fu Xi (Tao god-king), 663
Fulbright, J. William, 186
Fuller, Andrew, 124, 128
Fuller, Charles E., 208

G

Gabriel (Islamic angel figure), 429
Galileo (Galilei Galileo), 820
Gallagher, Michael (bishop), 43
Gandhi, Mohandas Karamchand, 355, 387, 583, 586, 597, 615
Gandhi, Virchand, 615, 617–18
Gano, John, 130
Gardner, Gerald, 705, 707–8
Gardner, Martin, 743–44
Garfield, James, 186
Garfunkel, Art, 55
Garvey, Marcus, 451, 464–65
Gautama, Siddhartha (the Buddha), 551–54, 556
Gautier, Théophile, 705
Ge Hong (Taoist), 648
Geisler, Norman, 219
Geoghan, John, 34
George, David Lloyd, 186
George, Henry, 38, 40
George III (king of England), 329
Gerhardt, Paul, 280
Gerstner, John, 219
Getsinger, Edward & Louisa, 534
Gibb, Hamilton, 456
Gibbard, Ben, 55
Giles, David, 815
Gill, Gillian, 151–52
Ginsberg, Allen, 55, 562
Ginsburg, Allen, 583
Ginz, Peter, 479
Gladden, Washington, 162, 167
Glover, George, 142
Gobind Rai (Sikh guru), 632
Gobind Singh (Sikh guru), 636
Godse, Nathuram, 596
Going, Jonathan, 127
Goldhizer, Ignaz, 431
Goldwater, Barry, 54
Goodale, Henry, 534
Goodstein, Laurie, 809
Goransen, Stephen, 809
Gottschalk, Stephen, 151
Gould, Stephen Jay, 765, 816
Graham, Billy, 118–20, 122, 132, 206, 209, 218
Grant, Heber J., 261
Grant, Joan, 715
Grant, Ulysses S., 522, 681

Gratz, Rebecca, 521
Grebel, Conrad, 290–91
Greeley, Andrew, 56
Greenleaf, Charles, 534
Greenstein, Micah, 20
Greenwood, Susan, 715
Greer, Allan, 684
Gregory, Louis, 535
Gregory Nazianzus (Saint), 33
Gregory the Theologian (Saint), 88
Griffin, Wendy, 715
Griswold, Alexander Viets, 193
Grof, Stanislov, 710, 717
Guanyin (Taoist), 647–48
Guild, June Purcell, 809
Gurney, Joseph John, 350–51, 352
Guth, Alan, 767

H

Hagar (mother of Ishmael), 398
Haggard, Ted, 779
Halaby, Najeeb, 451
Haley, Alex, 446
Hamblen, J. H., 316
HaNasi, Judah, 482, 503
Handel, George Frideric, 278, 280
Handsome Lake (Indian prophet), 679, 685–86
Hanna, Septimus J., 147
Hargobind (Sikh guru), 636
Harirai (Sikh guru), 636
Harkrishan (Sikh guru), 636
Harnack, Adolf von, 278
Harner, Michael, 715–16
Harris, Barbara, 193
Harris, Elizabeth, 349, 352
Harris, Martin, 253
Harris, Sam, 738
Hatch, Orin, 254
Hawaweeny, Raphael, 81
Hayden, Robert, 543
Hayes, Rutherford B., 317
Hays, Arthur Garfield, 739
Hearst, Phoebe Apperson, 534, 537
Hearst, William Randolph, 209
Hegel, G. W. F., 278
Heim, S. Mark, 386
Heller, Chaim, 520
Helwys, Thomas, 123–24, 128, 130
Hemchandra (Jain philosopher), 617
Henry, Carl F. H., 208, 214, 219, 228
Henry VIII (king of England), 187–88, 190, 192
Henschel, Milton G., 241
Herman (Saint), 80–81
Herzl, Theodor, 522
Heschel, Abraham Joshua, 520
Heschel, Joshua, 524
Heschel, Susannah, 521
Heston, Charlton, 473

Novalis (Georg Philipp Friedrich Freiherr von Hardenberg), 705

O

Obama, Barack, 166, 213, 454
O'Brien, Thomas, 41
Occom, Samuel, 680
Ochs, Adolph S., 201
Ockenga, Harold, 208, 214, 218, 225
O'Connor, Flannery, 53
O'Connor, John, 41
O'Kelly, James, 315
Olcott, Henry Steel, 552, 582, 705
Olevainus, Caspar, 335
Origen Adamantius, 381
Osmond family, 254
Oswald, Lee Harvey, 46
Otterhein, Philip William, 316, 321
Otto, Rudolf, 278
Owen, Robert, 174, 177

P

P. Benedict VIII (1012-1024), 85
P. Benedict XVI (2005-), 29p, 34, 42, 82, 739, 755–58
P. Clement VII (1523-1534), 187
P. Clement XI (1700-1721), 33
P. Clement XIV (1769-1774), 33
P. Damasus I (366-384), 31
P. Fabian (236-250), 30
P. Gregory II (715-731), 32
P. Gregory IX (1227-1241), 32
P. Gregory the Great (590-604), 31
P. Innocent XII (1691-1700), 33
P. John Paul II (1978-2005), 34, 36, 41, 78, 685, 769, 820
P. John XVII (1003-1003), 32
P. Leo I (440-461), 89
P. Leo III (795-816), 32, 99
P. Leo IX (1049-1054), 27–28, 78
P. Leo X (1513-1521), 273
P. Leo XIII (1878-1903), 38, 40
P. Paul III (1534-1549), 33
P. Paul VI (1963-1978), 28, 40–41, 44p, 78
P. Peter of Alexandria (300-311), 83
P. Pius VI (1775-1799), 37, 40
P. Pius X (1903-1914), 40
P. Pius XII (1939-1958), 43, 685
P. Siricius (385-399), 27
P. Stephen II (752-757), 99
P. Symmachus (498-514), 31
P. Victor I (189-198), 30
Pacelli, Eugenio (cardinal), 43
Packer, J. I., 219
Pahnke, Walter, 709
Paine, Thomas, 733
Palmer, Parker, 355
Palmer, Paul, 128

Palmer, Pheobe, 121
Paramahansa Yogananda, 583, 596–97
Pareus, David, 274
Parham, Charles, 219
Parker, Daniel, 130
Parker, Matthew, 191, 194
Parker, Quanah, 679, 681–83
Parr, Jordan, 20
Pärshava, Lord (Jain tirthankara), 613, 617
Pataki, George, 44
Patriarch Athenogoras I (1948-1972), 28, 78, 81
Patriarch Bartholomew (1991-), 29p, 42, 78, 82
Patriarch Cerularius (1043-1059), 27–28
Patriarch Nestorius (428-431), 83
Patriarch Photius I (858-867), 28
Patriarch Shenouda III (Coptic Orthodox, 1971-), 77, 107
Patriarch Theodoros II (Greek Orthodox), 77
Patriarch Tikhon (Russian Orthodox), 79–80, 81
Patterson, Daniel, 142
Paul (Saint), 76
Peck, John Mason, 127, 131
Peck, M. Scott, 796
Peel, Robert, 146, 150–51
Pendleton, W. K., 179
Penn, William, 120, 289, 349, 352
Pepin the Short (king), 32
Pepin the Short (king of the Franks), 99
Percy, Walker, 56
Perry, Troy, 788
Peter (Saint). see Simon Peter
Philip I (of Hesse), 272
Philips, Obbe, 291
Pike, James, 195
Pilate, Pontius, 26, 82–83
Pinchbeck, Daniel, 719
Piper, Lenora, 706
Plato, 50, 52, 89
Plotinus, 52, 89
Polk, James, 317
Polkinghorne, John, 816
Poole, Elijah (aka Elijah Muhammad), 451–52, 465–66
Porter, Katherine Ann, 56
Potter, Charles Francis, 747
Potter, Thomas, 384
Pratt, Parley P., 253
Preus, Robert, 219
Priesand, Sally, 524
Prophet, Elizabeth Claire, 798
Prophet, Mark, 799
Provost, Samuel, 189, 191
Purcell, John B., 174, 177
Pursel, Jach, 799

Q

Qui Chuji (Tao monk), 664
Quimby, Phineas Parhurt, 142

R

Rabbani, Shogi Effendi. see Shogi Effendi
Rabin, Yitzhak, 524
Radmacher, Earl, 219
Rahman, Fazlur, 455–56
Raitt, Bonnie, 364
Raitt, John, 364
Ramanujacharya (Hindu teacher), 595
Ramdas (Sikh guru), 632, 635
Ramon, Ilan, 479
Rand, Ayn, 737–38
Randall, Benjamin, 130
Randi, James, 744
Ranjit Singh (maharaja), 634
Raphall, Morris, 521
Ratzinger, Joseph. see P. Benedict XVI
Raulston, John T., 740
Rauschenbusch, Walter, 128, 132
Ravenscroft, John Stark, 195
Reagan, Ronald, 41, 54, 122, 186, 452, 779
Redgrave, Lynn, 171
Reed, Ralph, 122
Reeves, Keanu, 717
Relly, James, 384
Remey, Charles Mason, 547
Revel, Bernard, 523
Richards, Louisa Greene, 258
Ridgon, Sidney, 253, 263
Rishabha, Lord (Jain tirthankara), 613, 617
Ritschl, Albrecht, 278
Rittenhouse, William, 290
Robbins, Howard, 807
Robbins, Tom, 55
Robert, Benjamin Titus, 320
Roberts, Jane, 798
Roberts, Oral, 219
Robertson, Pat, 122, 777
Robinson, E. Gene, 189, 192, 784, 786, 789–90
Robinson, John, 159, 164
Rogers, Carl, 797
Romney, Mitt, 249, 254
Romulus Augustus (emperor of Rome), 31
Roof, Wade Clark, 797
Roosevelt, Eleanor, 233
Roosevelt, Franklin D., 43–44, 524
Rorty, Richard, 803
Rosenroth, Knorr von, 713
Rosten, Leo, xi, 20
Rousseau, Jean-Jacques, 733
Rove, Karl, 778
Row, John, 334
Rumi, Mawlana Jalal-ad-Din Muhammad, 434
Rushdie, Salman, 409, 414, 453